LEARNING RESOURCES CTR/NEW ENGLAND TECH

3 0147 1001 0916 7

W9-CAO-309

EXCELLENCE

IN BUSINESS COMMUNICATION

HF 5718.2 .U6 T45 1999
Thill, John V.
Excellence in business
communication

DATE DUE

AUG 2 2 2000	
RLL ZTM 35 37 I 7	
2 09 02	
SEP 2 2 2009	

DEMCO INC 38-2971

NEW ENGLAND INSTITUTE
OF TECHNOLOGY
LEARNING RESOURCES CENTER

EXCELLENCE

IN BUSINESS COMMUNICATION

FOURTH EDITION

John V. Thill
Chief Executive Officer
Communication Specialists of America

Courtland L. Bovée
Professor of Business Communication
C. Allen Paul Distinguished Chair
Grossmont College

NEW ENGLAND INSTITUTE
OF TECHNOLOGY
LEARNING RESOURCES CENTER

PRENTICE HALL
Upper Saddle River, New Jersey 07458

5·00   # 38478420

Acquisitions Editor:	Donald J. Hull
Editorial Assistant:	Paula D'Introno
Editor-in-Chief:	Natalie Anderson
Marketing Manager:	Debbie Clare
Production Editor:	John Roberts
Permissions Coordinator:	Monica Stipanov
Managing Editor:	Dee Josephson
Manufacturing Supervisor:	Arnold Vila
Manufacturing Manager:	Vincent Scelta
Senior Designer:	Cheryl Asherman
Design Manager:	Patricia Smythe
Photo Research Supervisor:	Melinda Lee Reo
Image Permission Supervisor:	Kay Dellosa
Photo Researcher:	Melinda Alexander
Cover Design:	Cheryl Asherman
Cover Photos:	*(top)* © Japack Company/Westlight, *(center)* © Digital Art/Westlight, *(bottom)* © Randy Faris/Westlight
Composition:	Carlisle Communications

Credits and acknowledgments for materials borrowed from other sources and reproduced, with permission, in this textbook appear on page A-1.

Copyright © 1999, 1997 by Bovée & Thill LLC.

All rights reserved. No part of this book may be reproduced, in any form or by any means, without written permission from the Publisher.

Library of Congress Cataloging-in-Publication Data
Thill, John V.
   Excellence in business communication / John V. Thill, Courtland L.
Bovée.—4th ed.
     p. cm.
   Includes bibliographical references and index.
   ISBN 0-13-781501-8 (hardcover)
   1. Business communication—United States—Case studies.
I. Bovée, Courtland L.   II. Title.
HF5718.2.U6T45   1998
658.4′5—dc21
                                     98-3072
                                       CIP

Prentice-Hall International (UK) Limited, *London*
Prentice-Hall of Australia Pty. Limited, *Sydney*
Prentice-Hall Canada, Inc., *Toronto*
Prentice-Hall Hispanoamericana, S.A., *Mexico*
Prentice-Hall of India Private Limited, *New Delhi*
Prentice-Hall of Japan, Inc., *Tokyo*
Simon & Schuster Asia Pte. Ltd., *Singapore*
Editora Prentice-Hall do Brasil, Ltda., *Rio de Janeiro*

Printed in the United States of America

10 9 8 7 6 5 4 3 2 1

CONTENTS IN BRIEF

CONTENTS

CHECKLISTS

PREFACE

This fourth edition marks a milestone for *Excellence in Business Communication* and is especially exciting because it has a new publisher, Prentice Hall. Instructors and students will be well served by Prentice Hall's commitment to excellence.

This textbook provides a stimulating and dynamic new way of bringing the real world into the classroom. This is the first textbook that offers business communication experience through real-world simulations featuring actual companies. These simulations provide a unique opportunity for students to apply concepts to real events and to sharpen their business communication problem-solving skills.

Students are introduced to a cross section of real people—men and women who work for some of the world's most fascinating companies and who, on a typical day, encounter a variety of communication problems. In each chapter, students are asked to help these businesspeople find solutions to their communication problems. Moreover, students find it easy to relate to the highly visible companies featured, including such well-respected firms as Hallmark, Club Med, Levi Strauss, American Airlines, and Barnes & Noble, to name just a few.

Excellence in Business Communication is the next step in the evolution of business communication textbooks. Of course, this text covers all the basic principles and presents them in a traditional sequence. But its real-life simulations, involving writing style, and eye-opening graphics all bring the subject to life, capturing the essence of business communication as no other text has done before. We believe this book will instill in students both respect for the field of business communication and confidence that the subject can be understood and mastered.

The textbook itself is the centerpiece of a comprehensive teaching and learning package that targets a single goal: to demonstrate how business communication works in the real world, thus helping students understand the concepts behind effective communication while developing and refining their own abilities.

FEATURES LINK CONCEPTS TO THE REAL WORLD

Excellence in Business Communication, Fourth Edition, paints a vivid picture of the world of business communication. It offers an overview of the wide range of communication skills that are used by businesspeople to present ideas clearly and persuasively. It also gives specific examples of the communication techniques that have led to sound decision making and effective teamwork. In addition, its insights into the way organizations operate help clarify student career interests by identifying the skills needed for a lifetime of career success.

"On-the-Job" Simulations

The opportunity to learn by doing is what sets this textbook apart from others. Students not only learn from other people's successes and failures but also make "on the job" decisions about communication problems. To understand our commitment to this concept, glance at the table of contents. You'll also see that this textbook was written with the cooperation of many well-known businesses, including Federal Express, Campbell Soup, Target, Harley-Davidson, and Hewlett-Packard.

Each chapter opens with an exclusive feature, "On the Job: Facing a Communication Dilemma." This slice-of-life vignette summarizes a communication problem being faced by an actual company. The solution to the dilemma is found in the concepts presented in the chapter, and the dilemma reappears from time to time throughout the chapter to dramatize the connection between the principles discussed and life on the job.

But we don't stop there. Each chapter ends with another exclusive feature, "On the Job: Solving a Communication Dilemma." These simulations are factually based on real companies, and they expand on the chapter-opening dilemma. Students are asked to solve the dilemma by applying the principles discussed in the text, by making decisions about the communication process, and by selecting the best alternatives from the choices offered. Not only do these simulations give students the opportunity to practice real-world decision making, they also tie the textual information to real-life examples, providing a concrete basis for analyzing the chapter principles. This chapter-spanning feature provides a dimension of reality unmatched by other textbooks in the field.

"Behind the Scenes" Special Features

Boxed and carefully placed within each chapter, "Behind the Scenes" sidebars extend the chapter material by focusing on real people, real products, and real companies. We personally interviewed accomplished business communicators at actual companies to provide insights into the business world that cannot be found in other textbooks. Eighteen "Behind the Scenes" special features bring even more of the world of business into the classroom. Examples include

- "Behind the Scenes at Ran Decisions: Earning Points with *Inside Flyer* Magazine"
- "Behind the Scenes at the San Diego Zoo: Even Tapirs Leave a Paper Trail"
- "Behind the Scenes at 3M: The Keys to Masterful Meetings"

The discussion questions at the end of each of these special features give students numerous opportunities to analyze business communication principles and practices.

Up-to-Date Internet Resources

The World Wide Web, a component of the Internet, contains a wealth of valuable resources. To acquaint students with Web sites that relate to the content of *Excellence in Business Communication,* a "Going Online" feature describing an especially useful site is included in each chapter.

Students can access the site by using the URL provided or by going to the Web site for this text <http://www.phlip.marist.edu/> where live links will take students straight to the site of their choice.

Examples of the "Going Online" feature include

- "Create Your Own Web Site"
- "Connect Now with a Virtual Library"
- "Search Thousands of Full-Text Articles Instantly"
- "Link Your Way to a Better Résumé"

To give students practice in exploring the rich resources of the Web, new "Developing Your Internet Skills" exercises are included at the end of each chapter. These exercises are directly tied to the "Going Online" sites showcased within the chapters.

Gallery of Business Communication Professionals

Another unique feature of this text is the inclusion of full-color photographs with incisive captions that focus on 72 highly successful communication professionals from business, industry, government, and the media. Among the individuals featured are Steven Spielberg (DreamWorks SKG), Jeff Bezos (Amazon.com), Howard Schultz (Starbucks), Ann Sakato (Federal Bureau of Investigation), and Jerry Yang (Yahoo).

Strategically placed in the margins throughout each chapter, these captions with accompanying photographs expand the amount of insight to be gained from this book. Each caption relates specifically to the text and gives a communication expert's view about a particular aspect of business communication, adding a new dimension to student learning.

Example After Example of Letters, Memos, and Reports

Throughout *Excellence in Business Communication*, Fourth Edition, you'll find numerous up-to-date sample documents, many collected in our consulting work. These superb business examples provide students with benchmarks for achievement.

The chapters on letters and memos contain outstanding examples from numerous types of organizations and from people working in a variety of functional areas. Many of these documents are fully formatted, and some are presented on the letterheads of such well-known companies as Office Depot, Host Marriott, Chiquita, Duracell, and Mattel Toys. The accompanying analyses help students see precisely how to apply the principles discussed in the text. Poor and improved examples illustrate common errors and effective techniques for correcting them.

The report-writing chapters give numerous examples, too. And the last chapter of the report unit illustrates the step-by-step development of a long report, which appears in its entirety to show how all the parts fit together.

Real-World Issues

The boundaries of business communication are always expanding. So in addition to covering all the traditional subjects, *Excellence in Business Communication*, Fourth Edition, provides material to help students manage a myriad of current issues in business communication:

- *The process approach.* Because both the communication product and the process to achieve it are so important in today's business world, we have strengthened the process approach while maintaining the strong product orientation.
- *Ethics.* Every message, whether verbal or nonverbal, communicates something about our values and ethics. Thus students must be given the means to anticipate and analyze the ethical dilemmas they will face on the job. Moreover, adhering to high ethical standards takes on a new importance in this age of wavering business behavior. Ethical questions addressed in this book include how much to emphasize the positive in business messages (Chapter 6), how to handle negative information in recommendations (Chapter 9), where to draw the line between persuasion and manipulation in sales letters (Chapter 11), and how to use photographs in reports without misleading the audience (Chapter 14). Taking an ethical position in the face of pressures and temptations requires more than courage—it requires strong communication skill.
- *Crisis communication.* Whether it's the bombing of the Murrah Federal Building in Oklahoma City or the deaths from contaminated hamburger served at Jack in the Box fast-food outlets, recent catastrophes emphasize the value of planning for crisis communication (Chapter 1).
- *Communication barriers.* The shift toward a service economy means that more and more careers will depend on interpersonal skills. Whether it's working on an assembly line or the front desk of a hotel, people will be interacting with other people, making it vital for them to overcome communication barriers (Chapter 2).
- *Cultural diversity.* The changing nature of the domestic work force requires strong communication skills to relate to older workers, women, members of various socioeconomic groups, immigrants, and others. Moreover, with such international

agreements as Europe 1992, the North American Free Trade Agreement (NAFTA), and the new General Agreement on Tariffs and Trade (GATT), the continuing globalization of business necessitates strong skills to communicate effectively with people from other cultures (Chapter 3).

- *Business technology.* Advances in communication technology are altering the way people communicate in organizations. Students will be using more computerized interaction and less hard copy. To survive in the business world of today and tomorrow, students will need to master new machines and become comfortable with new communication channels such as the Internet, the global electronic network (Chapter 4).
- *Law.* The increasing tendency of people to sue makes it important to understand the legal implications of written and oral communication, such as the pitfalls of writing recommendation letters (Chapter 9).
- *Employment search.* More and more people are making radical mid-career job changes, whether by choice or because their companies are downsizing and flattening hierarchies. These people need to master new communication skills as well as any information pertaining to their new jobs (Chapter 12).
- *Communication versatility.* Small businesses create most of the new jobs and employ more people than large corporations do. Since these small businesses are unable to support communication specialists for specific jobs, people working for them need to be versatile in their communication skills—writing letters and reports, talking on the phone, giving speeches, making sales presentations, creating presentation slides, and producing professional-looking documents.

Real-World Competencies—SCANS

Like no other business communication text, this edition emphasizes the skills and competencies necessary for students to make the transition from academia to the workplace. As described in the Secretary's Commission on Achieving Necessary Skills (SCANS) report from the Department of Labor, it is essential that students meet national standards of academic and occupational skill. To help accomplish the SCANS goal, this text offers interactive pedagogy (much of which is grounded in real-world situations): Learning Objectives, "On the Job: Facing a Communication Dilemma," "On the Job: Solving a Communication Dilemma," questions in special feature boxes, "In-Depth Critiques," Documents for Analysis, Checklists, end-of-chapter Critical Thinking Questions, boldfaced in-text key terms, photo and illustration programs, Exercises, Cases, and Video Series.

*T*OOLS THAT HELP DEVELOP SKILLS AND ENHANCE COMPREHENSION

Having an accurate picture of how businesspeople communicate is important, but students need more if they are to develop usable skills. That's why in *Excellence in Business Communication,* Fourth Edition, we've included a number of helpful learning tools.

Lively, Conversational Writing Style

Read a few pages of this textbook; then read a few pages of another textbook. We think you'll immediately notice the difference. The lucid writing style in *Excellence in Business Communication* makes the material pleasing to read and easy to comprehend. It stimulates interest and promotes learning. The writing style also exemplifies the principles presented in this book. In addition, we have carefully monitored the reading level of *Excellence in Business Communication* to make sure it's neither too simple nor too difficult.

Checklists

To help students organize their thinking when they begin a communication project, make decisions as they write, and check their own work, we've included 27 checklists throughout the book. Appearing as close as possible to the related discussion, the checklists are reminders, not "recipes." They provide useful guidelines for writing, without limiting creativity. Students will find them handy when they're on the job and need to refresh their memory about effective communication techniques.

Documents for Analysis

In this textbook we have provided a selection of documents that students can critique and revise—22 documents in 9 chapters. Documents include letters, memos, e-mail messages, a letter of application, and a résumé. This hands-on experience in analyzing and improving sample documents will help students revise their own.

Exercises and Cases

A wealth of exercises (117) and cases (81), many of them memo-writing tasks, provide assignments like those that students will most often face at work. The exercises and cases deal with all types and sizes of organizations, domestic and international. Each chapter also includes an exercise or a case that requires access to the World Wide Web, giving students practice with this fast-growing communication technology. We have written these activities for a variety of majors: management, marketing, accounting, finance, information systems, office administration, and many others. With such variety to choose from, students will have ample opportunity to test their problem-solving skills. In *Excellence in Business Communication,* Fourth Edition, most cases feature real companies. Examples include

- "Follow That Lead: E-mail Message Requesting Information on Patagonia"
- "Mercedes Merchandise: Form Letter Announcing a New Upscale Catalog"
- "No, No, Never: Policy Memo to *60 Minutes* Producers"
- "Ketchup Complaint: Sorry, Mom—Heinz Says the Labels Stay"
- "Finding Money Creatively: Fund-Raising Letter at Long Beach Opera"

These cases are yet another tool for demonstrating the role of communication in the real business world.

Learning Objectives

Each chapter begins with a concise list of goals that students are expected to achieve by reading the chapter and completing the simulations, exercises, and cases. These objectives are meant to guide the learning process, to motivate students to master the material, and to aid them in measuring their success.

Margin Notes

Short summary statements that highlight key points and reinforce learning appear in the margins of *Excellence in Business Communication,* Fourth Edition. They are no substitute for reading the chapters but are useful for quickly getting the gist of a section, rapidly reviewing a chapter, and locating areas of greatest concern.

End-of-Chapter Critical Thinking Questions

The 108 Critical Thinking Questions are designed to get students thinking about the concepts introduced in each chapter. The questions may also prompt students to stretch their learning beyond the chapter content. Not only will students find them useful in studying for examinations, but the instructor may also draw on them to promote classroom discussion of issues that have no easy answers.

Appendixes

Excellence in Business Communication, Fourth Edition, contains four appendixes: Appendix A, "Format and Layout of Business Documents," discusses formatting for all types of documents in one convenient place. Appendix B, "Documentation of Report Sources," presents information on conducting secondary research and gives basic guidelines for handling reference citations, bibliographies, and source notes. Appendix C, "Fundamentals of Grammar and Usage," is a primer in brief, presenting the basic tools of language. Appendix D, "Correction Symbols," provides convenient symbols for students to use when revising documents.

Indexes

To assist students and instructors in locating information as conveniently as possible, two types of indexes are included in the book: an Organization/Company/Brand Index and a Subject Index.

Color Art and Strong Visual Program

This text has been attractively printed, and the dramatic use of color gives it exceptional visual appeal. Also, in each chapter, students learn from a rich selection of carefully crafted illustrations—graphs, charts, tables, and photographs—that demonstrate important concepts.

Book Design

The state-of-the-art design is based on extensive research and invites students to delve into the content. It also makes reading easier, reinforces learning, and increases comprehension. For example, the special features do not interfere with the flow of text material, a vital factor in maintaining attention and concentration. The design of this book, like much communication, has the simple objective of gaining interest and making a point.

A THOROUGH REVISION

When preparing the Fourth Edition of *Excellence in Business Communication,* we dedicated ourselves to a thorough revision. For example, we have once again entirely rewritten the technology chapter. Moreover, we emphasize the growing influence of the Internet throughout the text. With an eye to emphasizing and integrating important topics, we have critically evaluated virtually every sentence in the text, making literally hundreds of refinements. Members of the academic and business communities have carefully reviewed it, and we have tested it in the classroom. Instructors, businesspeople, and students have all praised its competent coverage of subject matter, its up-to-date examples, its flexible organization, and its authentic portrayal of business. Here is an overview of the major content changes in the Fourth Edition:

■ *Chapter 1: Communicating Successfully in an Organization* now includes two "In-Depth Critique" sample documents to expose students as early as possible to business letters and memos and maintains emphasis on the six vital themes that recur throughout the book: open communication climate, ethics, intercultural messages, technological tools, audience-centered thinking, and efficient message flow.

■ *Chapter 2: Understanding Business Communication* presents a new transactional model of the communication process to help students clearly envision this basic tenet of business communication and maintains its emphasis on overcoming communication barriers.

■ *Chapter 3: Communicating Interculturally* now clarifies the relationship between growing technology and increasing global opportunities; simulates e-mail on screen (as do many chapters throughout the text); maintains its emphasis on how intercultural differences can block successful communication, both in the U.S. work force and across national boundaries; and increases the emphasis on cultural diversity.

■ *Chapter 4: Communicating Through Technology* updates the discussion emphasizing how technology affects communication; offers guidance about when it is appropriate to use various tools; introduces ways that the Internet is changing business communication; and guides students in selecting the most appropriate messages for e-mail.

■ *Chapter 5: Planning Business Messages* expands the coverage of collaborative writing while emphasizing the composition process: planning (defining your purpose, analyzing your audience, establishing your main idea, and selecting the appropriate channel and medium), composing (organizing and outlining your message, and formulating the message), revising (editing, rewriting, producing, and proofing your message); and strengthens the discussion of electronic channels in relation to oral and written channels.

■ *Chapter 6: Composing Business Messages* now offers guidelines on shaping an e-mail message and advice on e-mail etiquette; it also clarifies the three levels of style—informal, conversational, formal—with most business writing being conversational.

■ *Chapter 7: Revising Business Messages* now includes coverage of critiquing the writing of others so that students can collaborate more smoothly; expands material on active and passive voice, giving more examples; and expands coverage of parallelism and gives more examples.

■ *Chapter 8: Writing Direct Requests* updates discussion of salutations; increases the number of fully formatted sample documents, using the "In-Depth Critique" format; includes a new section on requesting information via the Internet and e-mail; updates all in-text sample messages; and replaces nearly half the end-of-chapter cases.

■ *Chapter 9: Writing Routine, Good-News, and Goodwill Messages* now includes a section on the reading and writing processes involved in summarizing; increases the number of fully formatted sample documents, using the "In-Depth Critique" format; updates all in-text sample messages; replaces nearly half the end-of-chapter cases; and updates chapter material by deemphasizing less used topics such as writing order acknowledgments, providing credit references, and sending out goodwill greetings.

■ *Chapter 10: Writing Bad-News Messages* expands the section on rejecting job applicants; updates chapter material by deemphasizing less used topics such as negative messages about orders; increases the number of fully formatted documents, using the "In-Depth Critique" format; updates all in-text sample messages; strengthens transitions between sections; balances discussion of the direct and indirect approaches to negative messages; and replaces nearly half the end-of-chapter cases.

■ *Chapter 11: Writing Persuasive Messages* completely reorganizes the chapter structure to include a more thorough discussion of persuasion, including avoiding faulty logic and using the Toulmin model to test arguments; expands material on fund-raising letters and selling an idea on the job; shifts emphasis from sales letters to other persuasive messages on the job; increases the number of fully formatted sample documents, using the "In-Depth Critique" format; updates all in-text sample messages; replaces most end-of-chapter cases; introduces coverage of sales letters on the Web; and deemphasizes collections material.

■ *Chapter 12: Writing Short Reports* now incorporates more material on electronic reports; updates and replaces all sample reports and extracts; expands the discussion of business plans while maintaining the clear definition and differentiation of the types of reports used in business applications; strengthens the link to concepts presented in earlier chapters (such as style, tone, "you" attitude, positive language, and concise wording); assembles all material on structural clues under the heading "Helping Readers Find Their Way"; distinguishes between transitions that link ideas within paragraphs and those that link ideas between paragraphs and sections; expands discussion of bullets and numbering; and adds a section on preview and review statements.

■ *Chapter 13: Planning Long Reports* now includes a discussion of two problem-solving methods: relative merit and hypothesis; strengthens transitions between all major sections (especially preview statements); expands discussion of problem statements; clarifies the section on factoring by simplifying the language; emphasizes the reasoning process behind selecting an appropriate organizational plan; and expands the discussion of conclusions.

■ *Chapter 14: Writing Long Reports* now discusses how to introduce sources; uses examples from the sample business report; updates report production material with information on computerized report design; expands coverage of executive summaries; completely revises documentation and citation procedures; and updates the entire sample report, including citation references.

■ *Chapter 15: Writing Résumés and Application Letters* updates and replaces all sample résumés to be more readable, to represent computer-generated documents, to provide a résumé and application written by the same applicant, and to include a two-year graduate; now includes information on e-mail mailing lists, job-oriented Usenet newsgroups, and job banks on the Web; includes a new section on scannable résumés; strengthens all transitions between major sections; adds a brief section on employment portfolios; adds a discussion of how to build job experience through internships, temporary job assignments, and so forth; integrates material on intercultural differences with regard to the employment search; expands the uses for résumés; and emphasizes the importance of continuously updating a résumé.

■ *Chapter 16: Interviewing for Employment and Following Up* strengthens transitions between major sections throughout (especially preview and review statements); expands discussion of the open-ended interview; adds a new section on video résumés/interviews; suggests advantages of videotaping mock interviews for evaluation; improves discussion of thank-you messages; and expands the section on letters of resignation.

■ *Chapter 17: Listening, Interviewing, and Conducting Meetings* reorganizes some material for easier reading; expands coverage of telephone skills; updates and clarifies the entire section on listening; adds examples of each type of listening; strengthens transitions between all major sections; and strengthens the link to intercultural barriers mentioned in Chapters 2 and 3.

■ Chapter 18: *Giving Speeches and Oral Presentations* now includes discussion to help students understand the importance of preview and review statements during a presentation or speech; discusses the benefits of using an outliner from software packages such as PowerPoint; revises writing style to raise the reading level and to delineate the discussions of preparing for and delivering a speech; and expands the discussion of the question-and-answer period after a speech or presentation.

■ *Appendix A: Format and Layout of Business Documents* adds e-mail formatting to the discussion; completely updates specific details of format and layout; and retains the convenience of presenting all formatting material in one well-organized component chapter.

■ *Appendix B: Documentation of Report Sources* simplifies and strengthens discussion by gathering bibliographic entries and source notes into two separate figures; now includes citations for Web sites, e-mail, and newsgroups; emphasizes the reference list (or bibliography) over source notes; emphasizes the author-date method of reference citation (as do most style manuals) while deemphasizing the superscript method that requires separate source notes; and maintains and greatly simplifies the discussion of source notes.

■ *Appendix C: Fundamentals of Grammar and Usage* clarifies the description and discussion of grammatical rules and usage problems.

■ *Appendix D: Correction Symbols* clarifies the use of correction symbols and abbreviations so that students can easily understand teacher evaluations and can readily use proofreading marks when evaluating their own work.

A *TEACHING AND LEARNING PACKAGE THAT MEETS REAL NEEDS*

The instructional package for this textbook is specially designed to simplify the tasks of teaching and learning. The instructor may choose to use the following supplements.

Instructor's Resource Manual

This comprehensive paperback book is an instructor's tool kit. Among the many things it provides are a section about collaborative writing, suggested solutions to exercises, suggested solutions and fully formatted letters for *every* case in the letter-writing chapters, and a grammar pretest and posttest.

Test Bank

This manual is organized by text chapters and includes a mix of multiple-choice, true-false, and fill-in questions for each chapter, approximately 1,500 objective items in all, carefully written and reviewed to provide a fair, structured program of evaluation.

Prentice Hall Custom Test, Windows Version

Based on a state-of-the-art test-generation software program developed by Engineering Software Associates (ESA), *Prentice Hall Custom Test* is suitable for your course and can be customized to your class needs. You can originate tests quickly, easily, and error-free. You can create an exam, administer it traditionally or online, evaluate and track students' results, and analyze the success of the examination—all with a simple click of the mouse.

Acetate Transparency Program

A set of 100 large-type transparency acetates, available to instructors on request, helps bring concepts alive in the classroom and provide a starting point for discussing communication techniques. All transparencies are keyed to the *Instructor's Resource Manual*. Many contrast poor and improved solutions to featured cases from the textbook.

PowerPoint Presentation Software

A set of 100 additional slides is also available on Powerpoint 4.0. Prepared by Randolph T. Barker of Virginia Commonwealth University, they cover the major concepts of the text and allow you to present the material to your class electronically.

Communication Briefings Video Series

Accompanying the text is a series of videos from Communication Briefings, a firm know for its monthly newsletter and its video series. The video set is available without charge to adopters of *Excellence in Business Communication*. Included in the series are the following videos:

- *Everyone's Teamwork Role*
- *Communicating for Results: How to Be Clear, Concise, and Credible*
- *Better Business Grammar*
- *Make the Phone Work for You*
- *Listen and Win: How to Keep Customers Coming Back*
- *How to See Opportunity in a Changing Workplace*
- *Resolving Conflict: Strategies for a Winning Team*
- *Make Presentations Work for You*

In addition, a separate video guide is available. Features include synopses of each video and discussion questions. To order the set, please call 1-800-388-8433 and tell the service representative that you have adopted *Excellence in Business Communication,* Fourth Edition.

College NewsLink

Specific course-related articles from daily newspapers and other major business publications are available to professors and students through Prentice Hall's College Newslink service. Internet links within the articles will also provide access to thousands of corporate, educational, and government World Wide Web sites related to the course. Ask your Prentice Hall sales representative for details.

Web Site

Visit our Web site, PHLIP, at <http://www.phlip.marist.edu>. The site offers a wealth of materials for students and instructors. For students, the site includes the following:

- Live links to all the URLs in the book allow students to go straight to the site of their choice.
- New! The first video segments for business communication on the Web are now available using a technique called character-driven instruction (CDI). Thirteen video segments illustrate the major topics in the text. The videos follow a central character from graduation to the world of work, facing a variety of business communication challenges. These interactive activities involve the students directly in business settings, thus promoting active participation and learning.
- The Prentice Hall Companion Web Site 98 (CW98) offers multiple choice, true or false, and essay questions so that students can quiz themselves chapter-by-chapter on topics covered in the text. Students can take advantage of the online hints feature, receive immediate feedback on their answers, and then e-mail the results to their professor or teaching assistant. This material was prepared by Myles Hassell of the University of New Orleans.
- Links to a wide array of useful resources now supplement each chapter.
- A Study Hall offers four major areas: (1) Ask the Tutor allows students to post questions or comments to a threaded conference message board maintained for their course, (2) the Career Center offers great resources for employment help and includes assistance in preparing a letter of application and a résumé, (3) the Writing Center offers tools and techniques for writing more effectively, (4) the Study Skills Center helps students develop their ability to learn more effectively and to achieve greater success in college.
- The Research Area provides tutorials for developing skills in using the vast resources of Internet.

For instructors, the site includes downloadable resources including the Instructor's Manual and the Lecture Presentation materials (in PowerPoint 4.0). Also included is an archive of teaching materials, faculty Internet resources, and a moderated conference and chat group that provides opportunities for asking questions, making suggestions, and sharing new teaching ideas.

Business Communication Update Newsletter

Delivered exclusively by e-mail every month, the newsletter provides interesting materials that can be used in class, and it offers practical ideas about teaching methodology. To receive a complimentary subscription to the newsletter, simply send a blank message by e-mail to <majordomo@po.databack.com>. In the message area, insert only the following two words: subscribe bcu.

PERSONAL ACKNOWLEDGMENTS

Excellence in Business Communication is the product of the concerted efforts of a number of people. A heartfelt thanks to our many friends, acquaintances, and business associates who agreed to be interviewed so that we could bring the real world into the classroom.

Our thanks to Terry Anderson, whose outstanding communication skills, breadth of knowledge, and organizational ability assured this project's clarity and completeness.

We are grateful to Barbara Schatzman for her remarkable talents and valuable contributions; to George Dovel for his brilliance and wise counsel; to Lianne Downey for her unique insights and perspectives; and to Jackie Estrada for her noteworthy talents and dedication.

We appreciate the remarkable talents and valuable contributions of Deborah Valentine, Emory University; Anne Bliss, University of Colorado, Boulder; Carolyn A. Embree, University of Akron; Carla L. Sloan, Liberty University; Doris A. Van Horn Christopher, California State University, Los Angeles; and Susan S. Rehwaldt, Southern Illinois University.

Recognition and thanks to Don Fitzgerald, Mary Leslie, Donald Anderson, and Quentin Decker at Grossmont College.

We also feel it is important to acknowledge and thank the Association for Business Communication, an organization whose meetings and publications provide a valuable forum for the exchange of ideas and for professional growth.

Thanks to the many individuals whose valuable suggestions and constructive comments contributed to the success of this book. The authors are deeply grateful to Anita S. Bednar, Central State University; Donna Cox, Monroe Community College; Sauny Dills, California Polytechnic State University–San Luis Obispo; Charlene A. Gierkey, Northwestern Michigan College; Sue Granger, Jacksonville State University; Bradley S. Hayden, Western Michigan University; Michael Hignite, Southwest Missouri State; Cynthia Hofacker, University of Wisconsin–Eau Claire; Louise C. Holcomb, Gainesville College; Larry Honl, University of Wisconsin–Eau Claire; Kenneth Hunsaker, Utah State University; Robert O. Joy, Central Michigan University; Paul Killorin, Portland Community College; Al Lucero, East Tennessee State University; Rachel Mather, Adelphi University; Betty Mealor, Abraham Baldwin College; Mary Miller, Ashland University; Richard Profozich, Prince George's Community College; Brian Railsback, Western Carolina University; John Rehfuss, California State University–Sacramento; Joan C. Roderick, Southwest Texas State University; Jean Anna Sellers, Fort Hays State University; Carla L. Sloan, Liberty University; Michael Thompson, Brigham Young University; Betsy Vardaman, Baylor University; Billy Walters, Troy State University; George Walters, Emporia State University; F. Stanford Wayne, Southwest Missouri State; Robert Wheatley, Troy State University; Rosemary B. Wilson, Washtenaw Community College; and Beverly C. Wise, SUNY–Morrisville.

We appreciate the insightful comments and helpful suggestions of the individuals who reviewed the manuscript for this edition: Mary DuBoise, DeVry Institute of Technology; Lindsay English, Ursuline College; and Linda McAdams, Westark Community College.

We want to extend our warmest appreciation to the devoted professionals at Prentice Hall. They include Sandra Steiner, President; James Boyd, Vice President/Editorial Director; Natalie Anderson, Editor-in-Chief; and Donald Hull, Senior Editor; all of Prentice Hall Business Publishing, and the outstanding Prentice Hall sales representatives. Finally, we thank Managing Editor Dee Josephson and Production Editor John Roberts for their dedication, and we are grateful to copyeditor Margo Quinto, photo researcher Melinda Alexander, and senior designer Cheryl Asherman for their superb work.

John V. Thill
Courtland L. Bovée

rnal Communication · External Communication · Characteristics of Effective Communication

FOUNDATIONS

c Forms of Communication · The Process of Communication · How to Improve Communication

OF BUSINESS

ltural Business Communication · Tips for Communicating with People from Other Cultures

COMMUNICATION

n other Cultures · Technology in Oral Communication · How Technology Is Changing Communication

COMMUNICATING SUCCESSFULLY IN AN ORGANIZATION

n the Job

FACING A COMMUNICATION DILEMMA
AT HALLMARK

When You Care Enough to Send the Very Best—Inside or Outside the Company

Have you ever needed to discuss a sensitive topic with someone and been unsure of how to start the conversation? Chances are you can find a Hallmark card to help you. Hallmark is in the communication business, helping people share their thoughts and feelings. The company introduces thousands of new paper cards each year and has recently introduced on-line electronic greeting cards and software for customers to design their own greeting cards. Because Hallmark has more than 12,000 employees and such a diverse range of products, communicating within the company is at least as important as communicating with customers.

As Hallmark's corporate communications director, Dean Rodenbough is responsible for ensuring that employees receive all the information they need to be productive and satisfied and to help the company achieve its goals for growth. Most Hallmark employees are organized into teams, and Hallmark's success depends heavily on strong communication within and between all its teams, as well as between those teams and upper management. Rodenbough is responsible for maintaining the flow of information. For example, information about changes in employee benefits must be distributed to all employees, whereas information about a specific project might be important only for the project team.

Rodenbough also knows that each team has its own responsibilities and special communication needs, so he must determine the right medium and format for each kind of information. For example, creative teams of writers and artists must come up with new ideas for cards. Their responsibilities require a unique combination of individual creativity and team cooperation, and Rodenbough needs to keep that fact in mind when communicating with them. On the other hand, cross-functional teams include people from marketing, sales, customer service, and operations. Because both creative and cross-functional teams make decisions by reaching a consensus rather than by relying on decisions passed down from upper management, Rodenbough pays particular attention to tone when he communicates with them.

Hallmark works hard to attract and keep high-quality employees, viewing them as the company's most important resource. It's up to Rodenbough to make sure that internal communication not only keeps employees motivated and informed about company strategies, progress, and business, but also enables them to understand how they can help move the company forward.

If you were in Rodenbough's position, what would you do to keep communication flowing smoothly and efficiently throughout the organization? What sort of communication climate could you instill to help guarantee that everyone receives necessary information? How would you decide which communication method is best for each of the many messages you need to share with all the people inside Hallmark?[1]

When people browse through Hallmark greeting cards, they are looking for the best way to express a sentiment—whether with joy, sympathy, or humor. In fact, strong communication is the key to success at Hallmark, whether helping people share their thoughts and feelings or conducting operations within the organization.

 COMMUNICATION, BUSINESS, AND YOU

Organizations such as Hallmark bend over backward to see that communication both inside and outside the company is open, honest, and clear. Your ability to communicate increases productivity, both yours and your organization's. It shapes the impressions you make on your colleagues, employees, supervisors, investors, and customers. It allows you to perceive the needs of these **stakeholders** (the various groups you interact with), and it helps you respond to those needs. Whether you run your own business, work for an employer, invest in a company, buy or sell products, design computer chips, run for public office, or raise money for charities, your communication skills determine your success.[2]

> Communication enables organizations to function.

Good communication skills are vital because every member of an organization is a link in the information chain. The flow of information along that chain is a steady stream of messages, whether from inside the organization (staff meetings, progress reports, project proposals, research results, employee surveys, and persuasive interviews) or from outside the organization (loan applications, purchasing agreements, help-wanted ads, distribution contracts, product advertisements, and sales calls). Your ability to receive, evaluate, use, and pass on information affects your company's effectiveness, as well as your own.

> Ask yourself what information your co-workers and supervisors need from you, and then figure out how you can supply it. Also ask yourself what information you need to do your job, and then find ways to get it.

Within the company, you and your co-workers use the information you obtain from one another and from outsiders to guide your activities. The work of the organization is divided into tasks and assigned to various organizational units, each reporting to a manager who directs and coordinates the effort. This division of labor and delegation of responsibility depends on the constant flow of information up, down, and across the organization. So by feeding information to your boss and peers, you help them do their jobs, and vice versa.

> You are a contact point in the external and internal communication networks.

If you are a manager, your day consists of a never-ending series of meetings, casual conversations, speaking engagements, and phone calls, interspersed with occasional periods set aside for reading or writing. From these sources, you cull important points and then pass them on to the right people. In turn, you rely on your employees to provide you with useful data and to interpret, transmit, and act on the messages you send them.

> The manager's role is to make and carry out decisions by collecting facts, analyzing them, and transmitting directions to lower-level employees.

If you are a relatively junior employee, you are likely to find yourself on the perimeter of the communication network. Oddly enough, this situation puts you in an important position in the information chain. Although your span of influence may be limited, you are in a position to observe firsthand things that your supervisors and co-workers cannot see: a customer's immediate reaction to a product display, a supplier's momentary hesitation before agreeing to a delivery date, an odd whirring noise in a piece of equipment, or a slowdown in the flow of customers. These are the little gems of information that managers and co-workers need to do their jobs. If you don't pass that information along, nobody will—because nobody else knows. Such an exchange of information within an organization is called **internal communication.**

> Employees serve as the eyes and ears of an organization, providing direct impressions from the front line.

Robert M. Beavers is senior vice president/zone manager at McDonald's Corporation. Having worked his way up from the bottom, he is now responsible for six regional offices: Phoenix, Denver, San Francisco, Sacramento, Los Angeles, and San Diego. He credits his success to good communication. No matter what the industry, says Beavers, it's communicating with people that makes the difference.

THE INTERNAL COMMUNICATION NETWORK

Communication among the members of an organization is essential for effective functioning, so each organization approaches internal communication in a particular way, depending on its requirements. In a small business with only five or six employees, much information can be exchanged casually and directly. In a large organization such as Hallmark, transmitting the right information to the right people at the right time can be a real challenge, whether communicating by phone, e-mail, fax, or interoffice memo (see Figure 1.1).

As a supplier to vacation spots such as Disney theme parks, Personalized Products, Inc. (PPI) produces souvenirs and toys printed with a wide variety of common names. In this memo, sales manager Tom Beatty reports first-quarter sales to Jacqueline Rogeine, vice president of finance.

INTERNAL MEMORANDUM

The first paragraph gives the reader specific information related to the subject.

TO: Jacqueline Rogeine
FROM: Tom Beatty
DATE: April 10, 1999
SUBJECT: First-Quarter Sales to Disney

Our first-quarter sales to Disney theme parks show a continuing trend toward growth, although margins remain thin. We supplied 38 retail outlets with 52 licensed or personalized items. Gross profits rose 18% from the first quarter last year, so the severe winter evidently had less impact than we originally expected.

The second paragraph presents an easy-to-read chart of data selected from the overall report.

Although you can look over the attached raw data, the items below enjoyed continued popularity:

Product & Number	1998 First Quarter	1999 First Quarter	Percent Increase
Minnie's Tea Set (M30)	$ 102,477	$ 122,460	16.3%
Mickey's Mighty Ball (B44)	204,112	249,425	18.2
"My-Name" Note Cards (P26)	98,934	121,689	18.7
"Needs-a-Name" Doll (D88)	407,332	534,827	23.8
Character T-shirt (P102)	804,231	1,147,638	29.9
TOTAL	**$1,617,086**	**$2,176,039**	**25.7%**

The third and fourth paragraphs provide pertinent information related to other areas in the company.

I'm recommending to Ted in marketing that we supply our field reps with character T-shirts (P102) to present to buyers. We can break two million with this product if we keep promoting it.

Our Asian suppliers assure us that they can keep the products moving our way; however, we need to carefully monitor the spelling of all names. I recommend that we request a fax to proof before signing off on imprinting any item produced overseas.

The final paragraph summarizes the information, asks for follow-up by a certain time, and ends on a positive note.

In general, the figures suggest continued strong growth with no appreciable change in our investment ratio other than adjusting for inflation. After you look over the numbers, let me know whether you have any questions or concerns before the board meets next month. If the trend continues, 1999 may prove to be a record-setting year for PPI.

Figure 1.1
In-Depth Critique: Internal Communication by Memo

Formal Communication Channels

The **formal communication network** is the official structure of an organization, which is typically shown as an organization chart like the one in Figure 1.2. Such charts summarize the lines of authority; each box represents a link in the chain of command, and each line represents a formal channel for the transmission of official messages. Information may travel down, up, and across an organization's formal hierarchy.

Managers who depend on formal channels for communicating risk encountering **distortion,** or misunderstanding. Every link in the communication chain opens up a chance for error. So, by the time a message has made its way all the way up or down the chain, it may bear little resemblance to the original idea. People at lower levels may have only a vague idea of what top management expects of them, and executives may get an imperfect picture of what's happening lower down the chain.

One way to reduce distortion is to reduce the number of levels in the organizational structure. The fewer the links in the communication chain, the less likely it is that misunderstandings will occur.[3] In general, big corporations have more levels than small corporations. But, as Figure 1.3 illustrates, size doesn't necessarily force a company to have a hierarchy with many levels. By increasing the number of people who report to each supervisor, the company can reduce the number of levels in the organization and simplify the communication chain. In other words, a flat structure (having fewer levels) and a wide span of control (having more people reporting to each supervisor) are less likely to introduce distortion than are a tall structure and a narrow span of control. The best way to fight distortion is to make sure communication flows freely down, up, and across the organization chart.

Downward Information Flow

In most organizations, decisions are made at the top and then flow down to the people who will carry them out.[4] Downward messages might take the form of a casual conversation or a formal interview between a supervisor and an individual employee, or they might be communicated orally in a meeting, in a workshop, on videotape, or on voice mail. Messages might also be written for e-mail or for a memo, training manual, newsletter, bulletin board announcement, or policy directive. At Hallmark, Dean Rodenbough oversees the publication of employee newsletters to help get the word out. From top to bottom, each person in the organization must be careful to understand the message, apply it, and pass it along.

Most of what filters downward is geared toward helping employees do their jobs. Typical messages include briefings on the organization's mission and strategies, instructions

The formal flow of information follows the official chain of command.

The communication climate suffers when management distorts or ignores information from below or when management limits the flow of information to employees.

Managers direct and control the activities of lower-level employees by sending messages down through formal channels.

Figure 1.2
Formal Communication Network

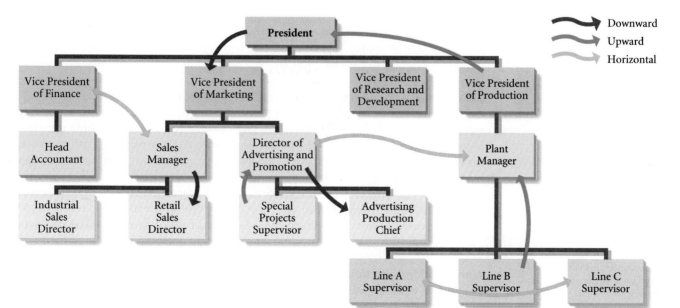

Downward
Upward
Horizontal

President

Vice President of Finance
Vice President of Marketing
Vice President of Research and Development
Vice President of Production

Head Accountant
Sales Manager
Director of Advertising and Promotion
Plant Manager

Industrial Sales Director
Retail Sales Director
Special Projects Supervisor
Advertising Production Chief

Line A Supervisor
Line B Supervisor
Line C Supervisor

Figure 1.3
Organizational Structure and Span of Control

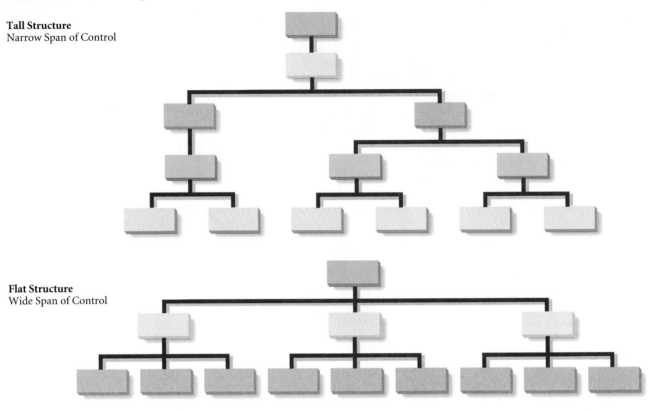

Tall Structure
Narrow Span of Control

Flat Structure
Wide Span of Control

on how to perform various jobs, explanations of policies and procedures, feedback on the employees' performance, and motivational pep talks. Downward communication is especially important in hard times; it lets employees know how the organization is doing, what problems it faces, and what is expected to happen in the future.

Upward Information Flow

Messages directed upward provide managers with the information they need to make intelligent decisions.

Upward communication is just as vital as downward communication. To solve problems and make intelligent decisions, managers must learn what's going on in the organization. Because they can't be everywhere at once, executives depend on lower-level employees to furnish them with accurate, timely reports on problems, emerging trends, opportunities for improvement, grievances, and performance.

The danger, of course, is that employees will report only the good news. People are often afraid to admit their own mistakes or to report data that suggest their boss was wrong. Companies try to guard against the "rose-colored glasses" syndrome by creating reporting systems that require employees to furnish vital information on a routine basis. Many of these reports have a "red flag" feature that calls attention to deviations from planned results. Other formal methods for channeling information upward include e-mail, group meetings, interviews with employees who are leaving the company, and formal procedures for resolving grievances. Hallmark's Rodenbough is directly involved in arranging meetings between various levels of management and employees.

In recent years, many companies have also set up suggestion systems that encourage employees to submit ideas for improving the business. One of the most successful programs is run by Herman Miller, a Michigan manufacturer of office furniture. The company gets 2,000 suggestions a year from its 5,300 employees and accepts 53 percent of them.[5]

Horizontal Information Flow

Official channels also permit messages to flow from department to department.

In addition to the upward and downward flow of communication in the formal communication network, horizontal communication flows from one department to another, either laterally or diagonally. It helps employees coordinate tasks, and it's especially useful for solving complex and difficult problems.[6] For example, in Figure 1.2, the sales manager might send a memo or an e-mail message to the vice president of finance, outlining sales forecasts for the coming period, or the plant manager might phone the director of advertising and promotion to discuss changes in the production schedule.

In many companies, advanced technology provides the physical foundation for inter-departmental communication. Sun Microsystems uses a worldwide computer network to link its 13,000 employees in the United States, England, Scotland, Brazil, Japan, Germany, the Netherlands, France, and Hong Kong. Whether implemented through technology or not, horizontal communication is crucial. Without it, co-workers aren't able to share information, and the results are missed deadlines, duplicated efforts, increased costs (due to rework), decreased product quality, and deteriorating employee relationships.[7]

Informal Communication Channels

Formal organization charts illustrate how information is supposed to flow. In actual practice, however, lines and boxes on a piece of paper cannot prevent people from talking with one another. Every organization has an **informal communication network**—a grapevine—that supplements official channels. As people go about their work, they have casual conversations with their friends in the office. They joke and kid around and discuss many things: their apartments, their families, restaurants, movies, sports, and other people in the company.

Although many of these conversations deal with personal matters, business is often discussed as well. In fact, about 80 percent of the information that travels along the grapevine pertains to business, and 75 to 95 percent of it is accurate.[8] Figure 1.4 illustrates a typical informal communication network, which is often the company's real power structure.

Some top executives are wary of the informal communication network, possibly because it threatens their power to control the flow of information. However, attempts to quash the grapevine generally have the opposite effect. Informal communication increases when official channels are closed or when the organization faces periods of change, excitement, or anxiety. Instead of trying to eliminate the grapevine, sophisticated companies minimize its importance by making certain that the official word gets out.

Some companies try to tap into the grapevine.[9] One service, called In Touch, helps executives keep up with grapevine news by providing an 800 number that employees can call anonymously with any problems or worries. The recorded messages are either summarized

The grapevine is an important source of information in most organizations.

The informal communication network carries information along the organization's unofficial lines of activity and power.

Figure 1.4
Informal Communication Network

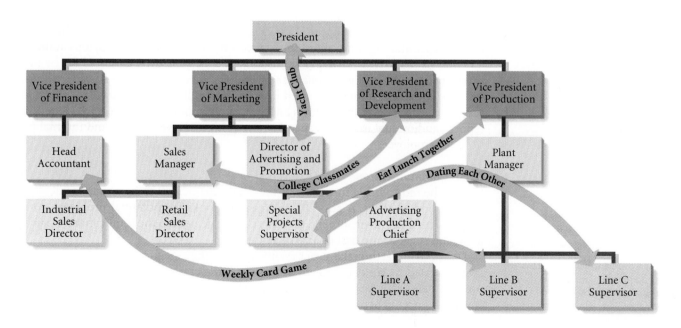

Jack Welch started out in an engineering job in General Electric's plastics business. Now chairman and CEO, Welch believes GE must increase competitiveness and productivity. Thus he has declared war on what he sees as GE's excessive bureaucracy, and he encourages management to bypass formal communication channels and communicate directly with employees.

The external communication network links the organization with the outside world of customers, suppliers, competitors, and investors.

The marketing and public relations departments are responsible for managing much of the organization's formal communication with outsiders.

Marketing focuses on selling goods and services, whereas public relations is more concerned with developing the organization's overall reputation.

The way a company handles a crisis can have a profound impact on the organization's subsequent performance.

or transcribed verbatim for top management.[10] Better yet, successful managers tap into the grapevine themselves to avoid being isolated from what's really happening. Hewlett-Packard trains its managers in **management by walking around (MBWA),** encouraging them to be interested in employees' personal lives as well as their work lives. Disney's Michael Eisner practices MBWA, getting out of his office and making contact with other Disney employees. He often turns up in such "unexecutive" places as the carpentry shop at Disney World, where he chats with the workers.[11]

HE EXTERNAL COMMUNICATION NETWORK

Just as internal communication carries information up, down, and across the organization, **external communication** carries it into and out of the organization. Companies constantly exchange messages with customers, vendors, distributors, competitors, investors, journalists, and government and community representatives. Whether by phone, fax, e-mail, videotape, or letter (see Figure 1.5), much of this communication is carefully orchestrated, and some occurs informally.

Formal Contacts with Outsiders

Even though much of the communication that occurs with outsiders is casual and relatively unplanned, most organizations attempt to control the information they convey to customers, investors, and the general public. Two functional units are particularly important in managing the flow of external messages: the marketing department and the public relations department.

The Role of Marketing and Public Relations

As a consumer, you are often on the receiving end of marketing messages: face-to-face or telephone conversations with salespeople, direct-mail solicitations, TV and radio commercials, newspaper and magazine ads, advertising banners on the Internet, product brochures, and mail-order catalogs. Although these messages are highly visible, they represent only a small part of marketing communication. In addition to advertising and selling products, the typical marketing department is also responsible for product development, physical distribution, market research, and customer service, all of which involve both the transmission and the reception of information.

The public relations (PR) department (also called the corporate communication department) manages the organization's reputation with various groups, including employees, customers, investors, government agencies, and the general public. Professional PR people may have a background in journalism, as opposed to marketing. They view their role as disseminating news about the business to the organization's various audiences.

Whereas marketing messages are usually openly sponsored and paid for by the company, public relations messages are carried by the media if they are considered newsworthy. The communication tools used by PR departments include news releases, lobbying programs, special events, booklets and brochures about the organization, letters, annual reports, audiovisual materials, speeches and position papers, tours, and internal publications for employees.

Crisis Communication

One of the most visible functions of the PR department is to help management plan for and respond to crises. A good PR professional looks for potential problems, constantly scans the business environment, then alerts management to the implications of such problems, and suggests the best course of action.

Disasters of earthquake proportions fall into the category of public relations nightmares created by sudden, violent accidents. Plane crashes, oil spills, chemical leaks, and product defects all belong to this group. The other type of crisis is the sort that builds slowly and occurs because of a company's conscious, but ill-founded, decisions. One ex-

Montana's Save the Wolves Foundation seeks to raise funds for relocating wolves captured from other states into selected wilderness areas of Montana. The foundation communicates externally with representatives of the mass media to try to educate the public and garner support.

Figure 1.5
In-Depth Critique: External Communication by Letter

Save the Wolves Foundation
4542 Audobon Highway • Viper, MT 59274
(406) 266-6223 • Fax (406)723-3229
http://www.wolves.org

March 13, 1999

Mr. Sam Davis, Managing Editor
Montana Times Magazine
468 West Times Drive
Helena, Montana 59601

Dear Mr. Davis:

Thank you for your recent editorial supporting the Montana wolf relocation program. We are as dedicated to preserving domestic livestock herds as are the ranchers who own them. However, killing the wolf predators is both a short-term and a short-sighted solution. We'd like your readers to have some additional information, besides the excellent points you made.

Every one of the 32 wolves we've captured and relocated this year has been examined by a veterinarian. The wolves receive inoculations to prevent rabies, among other diseases. Therefore, the relocated wolves pose little threat of disease to wildlife, their pack, or the occasional domestic animal or human who might encounter them.

In the wilderness areas where they will be relocated, wolves help keep the population of caribou, moose, and deer under control, and they cull injured or sick animals from the herd. However, wolves fear human beings and will avoid people whenever possible. Our North American wolves do not attack humans.

In addition, your readers will be interested to know a little more about wolves in general. Wolves have strong family ties and often mate for life. Female wolves give birth to about four to six pups, and both parents supply food and help train the pups. In fact, the wolf pack is usually a family group. And just as families call to their children, wolves sometimes howl to keep their pack together.

We invite those of your readers who would like to join our efforts to call 1-800-544-8333 to receive more information.

Sincerely,

Carroll Paulding

Carroll Paulding
President

sg

The first paragraph refers to what prompted the communication and ends by clearly stating the purpose of the letter to the editor. The paragraph identifies the two audiences receiving information: the editor of the magazine and magazine readers.

The second and third paragraphs provide specific information on the relocation program and reassure readers of their personal safety.

The fourth paragraph seeks to establish a special connection, or link (sometimes called rapport in oral communication), with the readers.

Finally, the letter ends with a clearly stated invitation placed where readers will notice it.

ample is R. J. Reynolds's attempt to introduce a cigarette aimed at African Americans (who have historically suffered higher rates of smoking-related illness than have other groups). The company badly miscalculated the public's reaction to the new product. Antismoking activists accused the company of sleazy and cynical business practices, and the Department of Health and Human Services blasted the firm for promoting a "culture of cancer." The barrage of bad press prompted RJR to cancel the introduction of Uptown cigarettes.[12]

According to public relations professionals, when disaster strikes, a defensive posture is generally counterproductive. The best course is to be proactive, admit your mistakes, and apologize (see Table 1.1). That's the course that AT&T took when its long-distance service was out of commission for nine hours in January 1990, hanging up 80 million callers.

Most experts recommend handling a crisis with candor and honesty.

Table 1.1	DOS AND DON'TS OF CRISIS COMMUNICATION

When a Crisis Hits:

DOS	DON'TS
Do be prepared for trouble. Identify potential problems. Appoint and train a response team. Prepare and test a crisis management plan.	Don't blame anyone for anything.
	Don't speculate in public.
Do get top management involved as soon as the crisis hits.	Don't refuse to answer questions.
Do set up a news center for company representatives and the media, equipped with phones, computers, and other electronic tools for preparing news releases.	Don't release information that will violate anyone's right to privacy.
	Don't use the crisis to pitch products or services.
■ Issue at least two news updates a day, and have trained personnel on call to respond to questions around the clock.	Don't play favorites with media representatives.
■ Provide complete information packets to the media as soon as possible.	
■ To prevent conflicting statements and provide continuity, appoint a single person, trained in advance, to speak for the company.	
■ Tell receptionists to direct all calls to the news center.	
Do tell the whole story—openly, completely, and honestly. If you are at fault, apologize.	
Do demonstrate the company's concern by your statements and your actions.	

That's also the course followed by Johnson & Johnson in its now classic handling of the Tylenol poisoning scare in 1982.

Don't ignore the impact of a crisis on employees.

When disaster hits, most companies respond, to some degree, through their public relations department, but they often ignore the audience that is likely to be hit hardest—employees. When the *New York Daily News* faced a violent 21-week union strike, morale sank. "Everyone was on edge, and even minor work-related problems were blown out of proportion," said Dawna Fields, manager of public affairs. To minimize the impact of any crisis on employees, be sure to communicate honestly, openly, and often, actively encourage employees to share their concerns, and use caution when sharing personal opinions.[13]

Informal Contacts with Outsiders

Every employee informally accumulates facts and impressions that contribute to the organization's collective understanding of the outside world.

As a member of an organization, you are inherently an informal conduit for communicating with the outside world. In the course of your daily activities, you unconsciously absorb bits of information that add to the collective knowledge pool of your company. During a trip to the shopping mall, you notice how a competitor's products are selling; as you read the paper, you pick up economic and business news related to your work; when you have a problem at the office, you ask your family or friends for advice.

What's more, every time you speak for or about your company, you send a message. In fact, if you have a public-contact job, you don't even have to say anything. All you have to do is smile. Many outsiders may form their impression of your organization on the basis of the subtle, unconscious clues you transmit through your tone of voice, facial expression, and general appearance.

Top managers rely heavily on informal contacts with outsiders to exchange information that might be useful to their companies. Although much of the networking involves interaction with fellow executives, plenty of high-level managers recognize the value of keeping in touch with "the real world." For example, when Stanley Gault was chairman of Rubbermaid, he cornered travelers in airports to ask for ideas on new products. Xerox executives spend one day each month handling customer complaints, and senior executives at Hyatt Hotels serve as bellhops. As Wal-Mart founder Sam Walton used to say when someone asked why he visited Kmart stores: "It's all part of the educational process. I'm just learning."[14]

CHARACTERISTICS OF EFFECTIVE ORGANIZATIONAL COMMUNICATION

Film director Steven Spielberg's talent for using technology to reach a huge and diverse audience is undeniable, even when the subject matter is as difficult as Schindler's List *and* Amistad. *But to successfully direct the creative input of the hundreds of individuals who work together to make a movie, Spielberg first had to master internal, organizational communication. Now, in partnership with Jeffrey Katzenberg and David Geffen, he's using those same communication skills to build the reputation of their new studio, DreamWorks SKG.*

If good management depends on effective communication, it follows that the best-managed companies are those that have built the best internal and external communication networks. What makes their networks the best? What characteristics contribute to effective communication? Six factors are involved:

- Fostering an open communication climate
- Committing to ethical communication
- Understanding the difficulties involved in intercultural communication
- Becoming proficient in communication technology
- Using an audience-centered approach to communication
- Creating and processing messages efficiently

An Open Communication Climate

An organization's communication climate is a reflection of its **corporate culture:** the mixture of values, traditions, and habits that give a place its atmosphere or personality. Some companies tend to choke off the upward flow of communication, believing that it tends to result in time-consuming and unproductive debate. Other companies, such as Hallmark, foster candor and honesty. Their employees feel free to confess their mistakes, to disagree with the boss, and to express their opinions.

The organization's communication climate affects the quantity and quality of the information that passes through the pipeline.

Many factors influence an organization's communication climate, including the nature of the industry, the company's physical setup, the history of the company, and passing events. However, as Hallmark's Dean Rodenbough confirms, one of the most important factors is the style of the top management group.[15]

The management style of the top executives influences the organization's communication climate.

Of all the many ways to categorize management styles, one of the most widely used is Douglas McGregor's Theory X and Theory Y.[16] Theory X managers consider workers to be lazy and irresponsible, motivated to work only by fear of losing their jobs. These managers adopt a directive style. Theory Y managers, on the other hand, assume that people like to work and to take responsibility when they believe in what they are doing. These managers adopt a more supportive management style.

Yet another management approach, called Theory Z, was developed by William Ouchi.[17] Like athletic coaches, Theory Z managers encourage employees to work together as a team. Although the company still looks after employees, it also gives them the opportunity to take responsibility and to participate in decision making. The trend today is toward any style that encourages open communication climates. In such a climate, managers spend more time listening than issuing orders, and workers not only offer suggestions but also help set goals and collaborate on solving problems.[18]

Today more and more companies are recognizing the value of an open communication climate.

A Commitment to Ethical Communication

The second factor contributing to effective communication is the organization's commitment to **ethics,** the principles of conduct that govern a person or a group. Unethical people are essentially selfish and unscrupulous, saying or doing whatever it takes to achieve an end. Ethical people are generally trustworthy, fair, and impartial, respecting the rights of others and concerned about the impact of their actions on society. Former Supreme Court Justice Potter Stewart defined ethics as "knowing the difference between what you have a right to do and what is the right thing to do."[19]

Ethics are the principles of conduct that govern a person or a group.

GOING ONLINE
USE THE POWER OF THE INTERNET TO HELP YOU LEARN ABOUT BUSINESS COMMUNICATION

One of the best ways to find information on the Internet—about business communication or any other topic—is by Navigation Tools in Stockholm, Sweden. The site includes Starting Points, featuring directories and indexes for a stunning array of Internet resources. It guides you to e-mail discussion groups, news groups, search engines, and electronic newsletters. This handy site will add focus to your Web surfing and should be added to your bookmark list.

http://www.it-kompetens.com/navigate.html

Note: To reach the Web sites you find throughout this book, you don't have to type every single URL (universal resources locator) into your browser. Type just one—<http://www.phlip.marist.edu>—the Web site for this book. There, you'll find live links that take you straight to the site of your choice.

Conflicting priorities and the vast gray areas between right and wrong pose ethical problems for an organization's communicators.

Laws provide ethical guidelines for certain types of messages.

Ask yourself how you would feel if you were on the receiving end of the message.

Ethics plays a crucial role in communication. Language itself is made up of words that carry values. So merely by saying things a certain way, you influence how others perceive your message, and you shape expectations and behaviors.[20] Likewise, when an organization expresses itself internally, it influences the values of its employees; when it communicates externally, it shapes the way outsiders perceive it. **Ethical communication** includes all relevant information, is true in every sense, and is not deceptive in any way.

When sending an ethical message, you are accurate and sincere. You avoid language that manipulates, discriminates, or exaggerates. You do not hide negative information behind an optimistic attitude, you don't state opinions as facts, and you portray graphic data fairly. You are honest with employers, co-workers, and clients and never seek personal gain by making others look better or worse than they are. You don't allow personal preferences to influence your perception or the perception of others, and you act in good faith. On the surface, such ethical practices appear fairly easy to recognize. But deciding what is ethical can be quite complex.

Recognizing Ethical Choices
An **ethical dilemma** involves choosing among alternatives that aren't clear-cut (perhaps two conflicting alternatives are both ethical and valid, or perhaps your alternatives lie somewhere in the vast gray area between right and wrong). Suppose you're president of a company that's losing money. You have a duty to your shareholders to try to cut your losses and a duty to your employees to be fair and honest. After looking at various options, you conclude that you'll have to lay off 500 people immediately. You suspect that you may have to lay off another 100 people later on, but right now you need those 100 workers to finish a project. What do you tell them? If you confess to them that their jobs are shaky, many may quit just when you need them most. However, if you tell them that the future is rosy, you'll be stretching the truth.

Unlike a dilemma, an **ethical lapse** is making a clearly unethical or illegal choice. Suppose you have decided to change jobs and have discreetly landed an interview with your boss's largest competitor. You get along great with the interviewer, who is impressed enough with you to offer you a position on the spot. Not only is the new position a step up from your current job, but the pay is double what you're getting now. You accept the job and agree to start next month. Then as you're shaking hands with the interviewer, she asks that when you begin your new job, you bring along profiles of your present company's ten largest customers. Do you comply with her request? How do you decide between what's ethical and what is not?

Making Ethical Choices
One place to look for guidance is the law. If saying or writing something is clearly illegal, you have no dilemma: You obey the law. However, even though legal considerations will resolve some ethical questions, you'll often have to rely on your own judgment and principles. You might apply the Golden Rule: Do unto others as you would have them do unto you. You might examine your motives: If your intent is honest, the statement is ethical, even though it may be factually incorrect; if your intent is to mislead or manipulate the audience, the message is unethical, regardless of whether it is true. You might look at the consequences of your decision and opt for the solution that provides the greatest good to the greatest number of people. You might also ask yourself a set of questions:[21]

- Is this decision legal? (Does it violate civil law or company policy?)
- Is it balanced? (Does it do the most good and the least harm? Is it fair to all concerned in the short term as well as in the long term? Does it promote positive win-win relationships?)
- Is it a decision you can live with? (Does it make you feel good about yourself? Does it make you proud? Would you feel good about your decision if a newspaper published it? If your family knew about it?)
- Is it feasible? (Can it work in the real world? Have you considered your position in the company, your company's competition, its financial and political strength, the likely costs or risks of your decision, and the time available?)

Motivating Ethical Choices

Ethical communication promotes long-term business success and profit. However, improving profits isn't reason enough to be ethical. So how can an organization motivate employees to be ethical? First and foremost, the personal influence of chief executives and managers plays an important role. Top managers can begin encouraging ethical behavior and decision making by being receptive communicators themselves (which requires mastering many of the skills presented in this text). They can also send the right message to employees by rewarding ethical behavior. Managers can lay out an explicit ethical policy, and, in fact, more and more companies are using a written **code of ethics** to help employees determine what is acceptable. In addition, managers can use ethics audits to monitor ethical progress and to point up any weaknesses that need to be addressed.[22]

Organizations can foster ethical behavior

- By helping top managers become more sensitive communicators
- By rewarding ethical actions
- By using ethics audits

An Understanding of Intercultural Communication

The third factor contributing to a positive communication climate is understanding intercultural communication. Not only are more and more businesses crossing national boundaries to compete on a global scale, but the makeup of the global and domestic workforce is changing rapidly. European, Asian, and U.S. firms are establishing offices around the world and are creating international ties through global partnerships, cooperatives, and affiliations.[23] These companies must understand the laws, customs, and business practices of their host countries, and they must deal with business associates and employees who are native to those countries (who perhaps speak another language and who are certainly more familiar with the culture). Domestically, firms are also working with more and more employees whose cultural backgrounds differ. In the United States, women and ethnic minorities are entering the work force in record numbers. By 2005, 47.7 percent of the U.S. workforce will be women, 15 percent will be African Americans, 11 percent will be Hispanics, and 5.5 percent will be Asians or other minorities.[24] So, whether you work abroad or at home, you will be encountering more and more cultural diversity in the workplace. To compete successfully in today's multicultural environment, businesspeople must overcome the communication barriers not only of language but of culture as well (see Chapter 3).

Intercultural communication plays an important role both abroad and at home.

Intercultural communication is discussed in detail in Chapter 3.

A Proficiency in Communication Technology

The fourth factor contributing to effective organizational communication is the ability to use and adapt to technology. The increasing speed of communication and the growing amount of information to be communicated are only two results of the ever-changing technology you will encounter on the job. To succeed, businesspeople today must be able to understand, use, and adapt to the technological tools of communication (see Chapter 4).

Technology's effects on communication are discussed in detail in Chapter 4.

An Audience-Centered Approach to Communication

The fifth factor contributing to effective organizational communication is an **audience-centered approach:** Keep your audience in mind at all times during the process of communication. Empathizing with, being sensitive to, and generally considering your audience's feelings is the best approach for effective communication. The audience-centered approach is more than an approach to business communication; it's actually the modern approach to business in general, behind such concepts as total quality management and total customer satisfaction.

Using an audience-centered approach means keeping your audience in mind at all times when communicating.

Because you care about your audience, you take every step possible to get your message across in a way that is meaningful to your audience. You might actually create lively individual portraits of readers and listeners to predict how they will react. You might simply try to put yourself in your audience's position. You might try adhering strictly to guidelines about courtesy, or you might be able to gather information about the needs and wants of your audience. Whatever your tactic, the point is to write and speak from your audience's point of view.

Communicate from your audience's point of view.

BEHIND THE SCENES AT MOLEX
Staying Connected

John Krehbiel Sr. never imagined that his discovery would turn a small family business into a $1.5 billion global company. It all started when he realized that the black gooey substance his father used to make toys was also an inexpensive electrical insulator. Today, almost 60 years later, his company (named Molex after that gooey substance) is the second largest maker of electronic connectors in the world. The company manufactures more than 50,000 types of electronic-connector products used in just about every electronic gadget imaginable, including cameras, computers, telephones, televisions, pagers, and printers.

IBM is just one of the companies using Molex connectors for a wide range of products. Molex has followed IBM and other important clients, building factories around the world.

Molex builds these products in 44 plants located in 21 countries on 5 continents. Yet, despite the company's size and success, the culture at Molex is as modest and unassuming as the tiny parts it manufactures. "It's a quiet company where the corporate culture dictates that no one calls attention to themselves," says Lou Hecht, the company's corporate secretary and general counsel for the past 23 years. "It started with John Krehbiel Sr. You could walk into his office any time you wanted and talk to him about anything—golf, business—and it didn't make any difference if you were an engineer or a janitor. You wouldn't know that he was one of the 400 richest men in America."

Even today, Molex is unlike other companies of its size, having a relatively flat organizational structure—if not formally, then informally. "Keeping an open-communication environment is very important at Molex," says Hecht. Consider this: No officer at Molex has a private office. Rather, each officer works from a cubicle. And there is no reserved parking. If the president wants a good parking space, he has to arrive early. And it is not unusual to see the company president eating in the employee cafeteria.

Although Molex is now a public company, it's run by third-generation Krehbiels—the brothers Fred and John Jr.—and they try to maintain the same open-door communication pol-

---

Debbie Fields, founder of Mrs. Field's Cookies, uses a chainwide interactive computer and e-mail system to instruct store managers, to plan work schedules, and even to screen job applicants. The computer system makes it easy to maintain the two-way communication between store managers and headquarters that is so necessary.

Organizations save time and money by sending only necessary messages.

An Efficient Flow of Communication Messages

The sixth factor contributing to effective organizational communication is an efficient flow of communication messages. Think for a minute about the number of messages we send and receive, both within the organization and throughout the world:[25]

- Despite computer manufacturers' promises of the paperless office, shipments of office paper have risen 51 percent since 1983.
- In less than ten years, people in the United States added almost 135 million information receivers—e-mail addresses, cellular phones, pagers, fax machines, voice mailboxes, answering machines—up 265 percent from 40.7 million in 1987 to 148.6 million in 1995 (not including their 170 million telephones, up from 143 million).
- In one year, 11.9 billion messages were left on voice mailboxes.
- Even though people are clamoring to get on the Internet, they are sending even more messages through the U.S. Postal Service, and they're talking on their telephones more than ever.

All companies can hold down costs and maximize the benefits of their communication activities if they just follow three simple guidelines:

- *Reduce the number of messages.* Think twice before sending a message. The average cost of dictating, transcribing, and mailing a business letter is between $13.02 and $19.87.[26] So if a message must be put in writing, a letter or memo is a good investment. But if the message merely adds to the information overload, it's probably better left unsent or handled in some other way—say, by a quick telephone call or a face-to-face chat.
- *Speed up the preparation of messages.* First, save time by making sure that written messages are prepared correctly the first time around. Second, save time with standardiza-

icy set by Krehbiel Sr. so long ago. It was by listening to customers that Molex broke into the Japanese market: "We were told that if we made the products in Japan, the Japanese would buy them in large volume," recalls CEO Fred Krehbiel. So Molex did, and the Japanese did. Then in the 1970s, as U.S. manufacturers moved offshore, Molex listened to its customers again and followed their lead by building factories everywhere to provide parts for giants such as Hewlett-Packard, Compaq, and IBM. Currently, 70 percent of the company's revenue is from international sales. To compete in today's global economy, you have to be where your customers are and "you have to make what they want and the way they want it," notes CEO Krehbiel.

Another way that Molex listens to its customers is by turning over decision-making responsibility to its local employees. But having its international units run autonomously by local employees can complicate the communication structure. "The company's systems were local and regional and couldn't communicate back and forth with each other," says Hecht. So, to facilitate a global communication system, the company is installing a single wide-area computer network that can support every aspect of the corporate operation, from forecasting to order management, and can shift orders and production from

continent to continent. Now Hecht sees Molex's biggest task as training all 10,000 employees worldwide on how to use the system. And it has to provide that training in 10 to 12 languages so that Molex units will be able to communicate not only with each other but also with customers worldwide. Notes Hecht, "Our commitment is to be a truly global company in every sense of the word. I think one of the greatest challenges Molex will face is to change people's attitudes from thinking regionally to viewing the profitability of the company as a whole."

Apply Your Knowledge

1. Today's corporations try to open communication channels by managing through teams. Briefly discuss some of the advantages of team decision making. Are there any disadvantages? Please explain.

2. E-mail is rapidly becoming the most efficient way of communicating within organizations. Now organizations are faced with a new challenge: reducing the size and number of e-mail messages sent. What are some of the ways to reduce e-mail overload?

---

tion. Most organizations use form letters to handle repetitive correspondence, and most employ a standard format for memos, reports, and e-mail messages prepared on a recurring basis. In addition, standardization saves your audience's time because the familiar format enables people to absorb the information quickly.

By streamlining the preparation of messages, companies make sure that information is transmitted in a timely manner.

■ *Train the writers and speakers.* When the American Society for Training and Development surveyed major employers, it found that 41 percent provide writing-skills programs for their employees.[27] Many others, including Hallmark, offer seminars and workshops on handling common oral communication situations (such as dealing with customers, managing subordinates, and getting along with co-workers) as well as training in computers and other electronic means of communication.

In-house training benefits even experienced communicators.

Even though you may ultimately receive training on the job, you can start mastering business communication skills right now, in this course. Begin with an honest assessment of where you stand. In the next few days, watch how you handle the communication situations that arise. Then in the months ahead, try to focus on building your competence in areas where you need the most work.

This book has been designed to provide the kind of communication practice that will prepare you for whatever comes along later in your career. The next chapter introduces some concepts of communication in general so that you will be better able to analyze and predict the outcome of various situations. Chapters 3 and 4 discuss the importance of intercultural and technological communication. Chapters 5, 6, and 7 explain how to plan and organize business messages and how to perfect their style and tone. Chapters 8 through 18 deal with specific forms of communication: letters and memos, reports, résumés and application letters, interviews and meetings, and speeches and presentations. As you progress through this book, you will also meet many business communicators like Dean Rodenbough of Hallmark. Their experiences will give you an insight into what it takes to communicate effectively on the job.

Focus on building skills in the areas where you've been weak.

APPLYING WHAT YOU'VE LEARNED

In this chapter, you've met Hallmark's Dean Rodenbough, and throughout the book, you'll meet a cross section of real people—men and women who work for some of the United States' most fascinating organizations. At the beginning of this chapter, you read about the challenge faced by Hallmark as it tried to keep internal communication flowing smoothly and efficiently. Each chapter begins with a similar slice-of-life vignette titled "On the Job: Facing a Communication Dilemma." As you read through the chapter, think about the communication problems faced by the company highlighted in the vignette, and become familiar with the various concepts presented there.

At the end of each chapter is an innovative simulation called "On the Job: Solving a Communication Dilemma." Each simulation starts by explaining how the organization actually solved its communication dilemma. Then you'll play the role of a person at the organization introduced in the vignette, and you'll face a situation you'd encounter on the job in that organization. You will be presented with several communication scenarios, each with several possible courses of action. It's up to you to recommend one course of action from the available choices, even though some of the questions have more than one acceptable answer and some have no truly satisfactory answers. Your instructor may assign the simulations as homework, as teamwork, as material for in-class discussion, or in a host of other ways. These scenarios let you explore various communication ideas and apply the concepts and techniques from the chapter.

Now you're ready for the first simulation. As you tackle each question, think about the material you covered in this chapter and consider your own experience as a communicator. You'll probably be surprised to discover how much you already know about business communication.

On the Job

SOLVING A COMMUNICATION DILEMMA
AT HALLMARK

Hallmark relies on effective communication to keep employees informed of important information such as new products, the company's financial status, and changes in employee benefits. To keep Hallmark's communication climate open and to ensure that all employees receive the information they need, Rodenbough uses many communication channels.

He oversees several company publications. *Noon News* is a daily newsletter for all company employees. Like a small-town newspaper, it fosters a sense of community by including bits of personal information (such as birthdays and anniversaries), want ads, reminders of such things as health plan enrollment deadlines, and information on company products and finances. Another internal publication, *Directions,* is published to distribute information to managers. It has no established publication schedule, because its purpose is to give managers important company information before it becomes public. In addition, computer-monitor signboards in various locations throughout the headquarters building display information that was too late for print deadlines.

Face-to-face communication is also common at Hallmark. Several times a year Rodenbough schedules CEO Forums, at which company president and CEO Irvine Hockaday meets with about 50 employees selected at random from all company divisions. For 90 minutes employees can discuss their concerns directly with the head of the company. With no predetermined agenda, the participants are free to bring up anything they want to discuss. Says Rodenbough, "The forums are

purely for midmanagement and below, so there's no intimidation factor. You can talk to Irv about anything, and you don't have to worry about your VP sitting there taking notes. It's a terrific opportunity for dialogue." Four times a year, Rodenbough arranges a Corporate Town Hall, at which Hockaday holds sessions for 400 employees. Unlike the CEO Forums, these meetings have an agenda and a specific topic. For the first 30 minutes, Hockaday talks about a specific company issue, and then he opens the meeting for an hour of discussion.

Of course, communication also occurs informally when people talk face to face, by telephone, in memos, and by electronic mail. Whatever the channel used, Hallmark cares enough to strive for the very best internal communication, and it's Rodenbough's job to make sure that all necessary information is delivered effectively and efficiently.[28]

Your Mission: You are manager of communications at Hallmark's corporate headquarters. In this position, you're responsible for both internal and external communication. Use your knowledge of communication to choose the best response for each of the following situations. Be prepared to explain why your choice is best.

1. The company's medical insurance plan for the next year contains substantial changes from this year's plan. How should information about these changes first be distributed to employees?
   a. Have the company president present the information at Corporate Town Hall meetings so that employees can give him feedback on their reactions to the changes.

b. Detail the changes in *Noon News.*
c. Publish details in *Directions,* the document distributed to managers, and then outline the changes in *Noon News.*
d. Describe the changes in the annual benefits statement sent to each employee.
2. Suppose the team that handles the shipping of party products is falling behind schedule. The management adviser says that many team members are just going through the motions and are not giving their best to the job. As one way of improving performance, she wants to send a memo to everyone in the department. Which of the following approaches would you recommend that she use?
a. Tell employees that the team's performance is not as good as it could be, and ask for their ideas on how to improve the situation.
b. Explain that you'll have to fire the next person you see giving less than 100 percent (even though you know that company policy prevents you from actually doing so).
c. Ask employees to monitor one another and to report problems to the department manager.
d. Tell all employees that if team performance does not improve, wages will be reduced and evaluations will not be positive.

3. A rumor begins circulating that a major product line will be dropped and the workers in that area will be laid off. The rumor is false. What is the first action you should take?
a. Put a notice on the computer-monitor signboards denying the rumor.
b. Publish a denial in *Directions* asking all managers to tell their employees that the rumor is false.
c. Schedule a meeting with all employees on the affected product line. At the meeting, have the company president explain the facts and publicly state that the rumor is false.
d. Ignore the rumor. Like all false rumors it will eventually die out.
4. In collaboration with a software company, Hallmark has developed PC software with which users can design their own greeting cards. At this time, only the team working on the new cards and upper management know about the product. How will you spread the information to all employees?
a. Announce the product in *Noon News.*
b. Publish an edition of *Directions* explaining the new product.
c. Have the president announce the introduction at a Corporate Town Hall session.
d. Send e-mail to all employees.

Critical Thinking Questions

1. Why do you think good communication in an organization improves employees' attitudes and performance? Explain briefly.
2. Whenever you report negative information to your boss, she never passes it along to her colleagues or supervisors. You believe that the information is important, but who do you talk to? Your boss? Your boss's supervisor? A co-worker who also reports to your boss? A co-worker who reports to a different boss? Briefly explain your answer.
3. You've just been promoted to manager and you've developed a good rapport with most of your employees, but Richardson and Blake keep going to your supervisor with matters that should go through you. Both employees have been at the company for at least 10 years longer than you have, and both know your super-

visor very well. Should you speak with them about this problem? Should you speak with your supervisor? Explain briefly.
4. Because of your excellent communication skills, your boss always asks you to write his reports for him. When you overhear the CEO complimenting him on his logical organization and clear writing style, he responds as if he'd written all those reports himself. You're angry, but he's your boss. What can you do? Briefly explain your answer.
5. To save time and money, your company is considering limiting all memos to one page or less. The CEO asks your opinion. Is it a good idea? Explain briefly.
6. As long as you make sure that everyone involved receives some benefit and that no one gets hurt, is it okay to make a decision that's just a little unethical? Briefly explain your answer.

Exercises

1. For the following tasks, identify the necessary direction of communication (downward, upward, horizontal), suggest an appropriate type of communication (casual conversation, formal interview, meeting, workshop, videotape, newsletter, memo, bulletin board notice, and so on), and briefly explain your suggestion.
a. As personnel manager, you want to announce details about this year's company picnic.
b. As director of internal communication, you want to convince top management of the need for a company newsletter.
c. As production manager, you want to make sure that both

the sales manager and the finance manager receive your scheduling estimates.
d. As marketing manager, you want to help employees understand the company's goals and its attitudes toward workers.
2. Name three ways you might encourage your employees to give you feedback on daily operations. Explain briefly.
3. In your small publishing firm, you have three top-notch editors, and, as the firm grows, you need them to work more and more often as a team. One of the editors, Wilson, is rigid and unforgiving; he is constantly reminding others of his 20 years' experience and unwilling to compromise. Pick an

option and briefly explain why it's the best course of action. Should your first step be to

    a. Fire Wilson and look for a replacement?

    b. Talk privately with Wilson about your need for his cooperation?

    c. Meet with all three of your editors to forge team spirit?

4. An old college chum phoned you out of the blue to say: "I had to call you. You'd better keep this under your hat, but when I heard that my company was buying you guys out, I was dumbfounded. I had no idea that a company as large as yours could sink so fast. Your group must be in pretty bad shape over there!" Your stomach turned suddenly queasy, and you felt a chill go up your spine. You'd heard nothing about any buyout, and before you could even get your college friend off the phone, you were wondering what you should do. Of the following, choose one course of action and briefly explain it.

    a. Contact your CEO directly and relate what you've heard.

    b. Ask co-workers whether they've heard anything about a buyout.

    c. Discuss the phone call confidentially with your immediate supervisor.

    d. Keep quiet about the whole thing (there's nothing you can do about the situation anyway).

5. When Solid State Circuits accidentally released chlorine and endangered the surrounding neighborhoods, local neighbors were up in arms. Two years later, thanks to a companywide community relations campaign, the neighborhood is filled with goodwill and friendship for the company. Solid State's open-door policy ranges from quarterly meetings with the neighborhood's Environmental Concerns Committee to tours of the plant to regularly held softball games between company employees and neighborhood residents—with picnics afterward. Solid State even lends facilities for neighborhood use during holiday socials and rummage sales. One residential neighbor has said, "As the years go by, Solid State will be associated with community interests and involvement." In less than a page, explain why becoming involved in the surrounding community and openly sharing information with local residents should result in such support and goodwill for the company.[29]

6. Briefly explain why you think each of the following is or is not ethical.

    a. Deemphasizing negative test results in a report on your product idea.

    b. Taking a computer home to finish a work-related assignment.

    c. Telling an associate and close friend that she'd better pay more attention to her work responsibilities or risk being fired.

    d. Recommending the purchase of excess equipment to use up your allocated funds before the end of the fiscal year so that your budget won't be cut next year.

7. Your boss wants to send a message welcoming employees recently transferred to your department from your Hong Kong branch. They all speak English, but your boss asks you to review his message for clarity. What would you suggest your boss change in the following paragraph? (Briefly explain your decisions.)

> I wanted to welcome you ASAP to our little family here in the states. It's high time we shook hands in person and not just across the sea. I'm pleased as punch about getting to know you all, and I for one will do my level best to sell you on America.

8. Technological devices such as fax machines, cellular phones, e-mail, and voice mail are making businesspeople more accessible at any time of day or night both at work and at home. What kind of impact might frequent intrusions have on a businessperson's professional and personal life? Please explain your answer in less than a page.

9. As a manufacturer of aerospace, energy, and environmental equipment, Lockheed Martin has developed a code of ethics that it expects employees to follow. Visit Lockheed Martin's Web site at <http://lockheed.com/ethics>, and review the 15 major ethical provisions listed there (such as "Avoid conflicts of interest"). In a brief paragraph, describe three specific things you could do that would violate any of those provisions. Now study Lockheed Martin's Web pages giving the "Warning Signs" of ethics violations and the "Quick Quiz." In another brief paragraph, describe how you could use these pages to avoid ethical problems as you write business letters, memos, and reports. Submit both paragraphs to your instructor.

10. Top management has asked you to speak at an upcoming executive meeting to present your arguments for a more open communication climate. Which of the following would be most important for you to know about your audience before giving your presentation? (Briefly explain your choice.)

    a. How many top managers will be attending.

    b. What management style members of your audience prefer.

    c. How firmly these managers are set in their ways.

11. What would be the most efficient way (phone call, interview, memo, or newsletter) of handling each of the following communication situations? (Briefly explain your answer.)

    a. Informing everyone in the company of your department's new procedure for purchasing equipment.

    b. Leaving final instructions for your secretary to follow while you're out of town.

    c. Disciplining an employee for chronic tardiness.

    d. Announcing the installation of ramps for employees who use wheelchairs.

12. Write a memo introducing yourself to your instructor. Keep it under one page, and use Figure 1.1 as a model for format.

Note: *In references to Web sites (as in exercise 9) and e-mail addresses, angle brackets are used around the material to indicate that no spaces occur between the address parts and to separate the address from the rest of the text. When you type the address into your Web browser or e-mail software, be sure to leave off the angle brackets.*

DEVELOPING YOUR INTERNET SKILLS

GOING ONLINE: USE THE POWER OF THE INTERNET TO HELP
YOU LEARN ABOUT BUSINESS COMMUNICATION, P. 12

What role do you think the Internet might play in your business future? For instance, will you use it as a research tool? As a communications tool? As a marketing tool? Use this mental exercise to train yourself to take advantage of all the Internet has to offer by thinking ahead now, so that in a business crunch, you'll automatically know where to turn. The Navigation Tools site should help spur your thinking.

Chapter 2

After studying this chapter, you will be able to

List the general categories of nonverbal communication

Explain the four channels of verbal communication

Identify the steps in the communication process

Describe what can go wrong when you're formulating messages

Discuss communication barriers and how to overcome them

Summarize what you can do to improve communication

UNDERSTANDING BUSINESS COMMUNICATION

On the Job

FACING A COMMUNICATION DILEMMA AT BEN & JERRY'S HOMEMADE

Serving Up Ice Cream and a Strong Social Message

Every company communicates with customers, employees, and various other groups. But for Ben & Jerry's Homemade, of Waterbury, Vermont, communication has a special importance. The company makes more than premium ice cream; it makes an unusual effort to operate as a force for social change. Co-founders Ben Cohen and Jerry Greenfield intended to start an ice cream parlor and then sell it once the business got going. But something always forced them to keep at it, such as a new competitor or the need to replace or fix equipment. Almost in spite of itself, Ben & Jerry's has grown beyond its founders' expectations. But Cohen and Greenfield don't want to run a conventional business. They want their company to contribute to society and also to help save the rain forests, encourage conservation, help family farmers, and support other causes important to the two founders.

This mission presents Ben & Jerry's with some unusual communication challenges. Perhaps the most important is keeping the founders' vision alive as the company grows. Back when the operation involved only Cohen, Greenfield, and a handful of employees, communicating the company's social goals was fairly easy. But with more employees, more suppliers, shareholders, and customers spread across the nation (and, increasingly, around the globe), communication has become a big challenge indeed. One good example concerns the potential conflict between the founders' social goals and their financial responsibility toward shareholders, who have invested money in the company.

How can Cohen and Greenfield use communication to keep their vision alive in the minds of customers, employees, and investors while meeting their sometimes conflicting goals? What is the process of communication, and how can the managers at Ben & Jerry's use it to keep the company true to the founders' vision? How can misunderstandings arise in business communication, and how can Ben & Jerry's avoid them?[1]

*T*HE BASIC FORMS OF COMMUNICATION

As Cohen and Greenfield are well aware, effective communicators have many tools at their disposal. They know how to put together the words that will convey their meaning. They reinforce their words with gestures and actions. They look you in the eye, listen to what

Actions speak louder than words.

you have to say, and think about your feelings and needs. At the same time, they study your reactions, picking up the nuances of your response by watching your face and body, listening to your tone of voice, and evaluating your words. They absorb information just as efficiently as they transmit it, relying on both nonverbal and verbal cues.

Perhaps a certain amount of inconsistency between words and actions is unavoidable. We don't always say what we really mean; in fact, we don't always *know* what we really mean. Unraveling the mysteries of communication requires perception, concentration, and an appreciation of the communication process.

Nonverbal Communication

The most basic form of communication is **nonverbal communication:** all the cues, gestures, vocal qualities, spatial relationships, and attitudes toward time that allow us to communicate without words. Anthropologists theorize that long before human beings used words to talk things over, our ancestors communicated with one another by using their bodies. They gritted their teeth to show anger; they smiled and touched one another to indicate affection. Although we have come a long way since those primitive times, we still use nonverbal cues to express superiority, dependence, dislike, respect, love, and other feelings.[2]

Nonverbal communication differs from verbal communication in fundamental ways. For one thing, it's less structured, so it's more difficult to study. It also differs in terms of intent and spontaneity. We generally plan our words. When we say, "Please get back to me on that order by Friday," we have a conscious purpose. We think about the message, if only for a moment. However, when we communicate nonverbally, we sometimes do so unconsciously. We don't mean to raise an eyebrow or blush. Those actions come naturally, without our consent.

The Importance of Nonverbal Communication

Although nonverbal communication is often unplanned, it has more impact than verbal communication alone. Nonverbal cues are especially important in conveying feelings; some researchers maintain that they account for 93 percent of the emotional meaning that is exchanged in any interaction.[3] The total impact of any message is probably most affected by the blending of nonverbal and verbal communication.[4]

One reason for the power of nonverbal communication is its reliability. Most people can deceive us much more easily with words than they can with their bodies. Words are relatively easy to control; body language, facial expressions, and vocal characteristics are not. By paying attention to these nonverbal cues, we can detect deception or affirm a speaker's honesty. Not surprisingly, we have more faith in nonverbal cues than we do in verbal messages. If a person says one thing but transmits a conflicting message nonverbally, we almost invariably believe the nonverbal signal.[5] To a great degree, then, an individual's credibility as a communicator depends on nonverbal messages.

Nonverbal communication is important for another reason: It can be efficient from both the sender's and the receiver's standpoints. You can transmit a nonverbal message without even thinking about it, and your audience can register the meaning unconsciously. At the same time, when you have a conscious purpose, you can often achieve it more economically with a gesture than you can with words. A wave of the hand, a pat on the back, a wink—all are streamlined expressions of thought.

The Types of Nonverbal Communication

The meaning of nonverbal communication lies with the observer, who both reads and interprets specific signals in the context of a particular situation and a particular culture. Although there are more than 700,000 specific forms of nonverbal communication,[6] they can be grouped into six general categories:

- *Facial expressions and eye behavior.* Your face is the primary site for expressing your emotions; it reveals both the type and the intensity of your feelings.[7] Your eyes are especially effective for indicating attention and interest, influencing others, regulating interaction, and establishing dominance.

At Ben & Jerry's Homemade, communication is well thought out to further the company's commitment to charity and community service.

Nonverbal communication is the process of communicating without words.

Nonverbal communication has few rules and often occurs unconsciously.

Nonverbal communication is more reliable and more efficient than verbal communication.

People use nonverbal signals to support and clarify verbal communication.

The face and eyes command particular attention as a source of nonverbal messages.

■ *Gestures and postures.* By moving your body, you can express both specific and general messages, some voluntary and some involuntary. Many gestures—a wave of the hand, for example—have a specific and intentional meaning, such as "hello" or "good-bye." Other types of body movement are unintentional and express a more general message. Slouching, leaning forward, fidgeting, and walking briskly are all unconscious signals that reveal whether you feel confident or nervous, friendly or hostile, assertive or passive, powerful or powerless.

■ *Vocal characteristics.* Like body language, your voice carries both intentional and unintentional messages. On a conscious level, you can use your voice to create various impressions. Consider the sentence "What have you been up to?" If you repeat that question four or five times, changing your tone of voice and stressing various words, you can convey quite different messages. However, your vocal characteristics also reveal many things that you are unaware of. The tone and volume of your voice, your accent and speaking pace, and all the little *um*'s and *ah*'s that creep into your speech say a lot about who you are, your relationship with the audience, and the emotions underlying your words.

■ *Personal appearance.* Your appearance helps establish your social identity. People respond to us on the basis of our physical attractiveness. Although an individual's body type and facial features impose limitations, most of us are able to control our attractiveness to some degree. Our grooming, our clothing, our accessories, our "style"—all modify our appearance. If your goal is to make a good impression, adopt the style of the people you want to impress. In most businesses, a professional image is appropriate, but some companies, such as Ben & Jerry's, and even some industries are more casual.

■ *Touching behavior.* Touch is an important vehicle for conveying warmth, comfort, and reassurance. Even the most casual contact can create positive feelings. The accepted norms of touching vary, depending on the gender, age, relative status, and cultural background of the persons involved. In business situations, touching suggests dominance, so a higher-status person is more likely to touch a lower-status person than the other way around. Touching has become controversial, however, because it can sometimes be interpreted as sexual harassment.

■ *Use of time and space.* Like touch, time and space can be used to assert authority. In many cultures, people demonstrate their importance by making other people wait, or they show respect by being on time. People can also assert their status by occupying the best space. In U.S. companies, the chief executive usually has the corner office and the prettiest view. Apart from serving as a symbol of status, space can determine how comfortable people feel talking with each other. When people stand too close or too far away, we feel ill at ease.

Attitudes toward punctuality and comfort zones and all other nonverbal communication vary from culture to culture. In addition, gender has an impact on nonverbal communication. For example, women are generally better than men at decoding nonverbal cues. In social settings with peers and in meetings with colleagues, women have less personal space and are touched more often than men are (both less space and more touching are cues indicating less power for women). Moreover, although sitting at the head of a conference table symbolizes power for a man, if a woman is at the head and at least one man is sitting elsewhere, observers assume that the man is in charge.[8]

To improve nonverbal skills in the United States, pay more attention to nonverbal cues (especially facial expressions), engage in more eye contact, and probe for more information when verbal and nonverbal cues conflict. Most employees are frustrated and distrustful when their supervisors give them conflicting signals. So try to be as honest as possible in communicating your emotions.[9]

Verbal Communication

Although you can express many things nonverbally, there are limits to what you can communicate without the help of language. If you want to discuss past events, ideas, or abstractions, you need symbols that stand for your thoughts. **Verbal communication** con-

---

Margin notes:

Body language and tone of voice reveal a lot about a person's emotions and attitudes.

Physical appearance and personal style contribute to your identity.

Your use of touch, your attitude toward time, and your use of space (all of which are affected by culture) help establish your social relationships.

Nonverbal communication can be different for men and women.

Improve nonverbal skills by paying more attention to cues, both yours and those of others.

Verbal communication is the process of communicating with words.

sists of words arranged in meaningful patterns. In the English language, the pool of words is growing; English currently contains about 750,000 words, although most people in the United States recognize only about 20,000 of them.[10] To create a thought with these words, we arrange them according to the rules of grammar, putting the various parts of speech in the proper sequence. We then transmit the message in spoken or written form, anticipating that someone will hear or read what we have to say.

> Language is composed of words and grammar.

Speaking and Writing

As Figure 2.1 illustrates, businesspeople tend to prefer oral communication channels to written ones. The trade-offs between speaking and writing are discussed in more depth in Chapter 5, but basically, it's generally quicker and more convenient to talk to somebody than to write a memo or letter. Furthermore, when you're speaking or listening, you can pick up added meaning from nonverbal cues and benefit from immediate feedback.

> Businesspeople rely more heavily on oral than on written communication channels for sharing information on a day-to-day basis, but they often put important messages in writing.

On the other hand, relying too heavily on oral communication can cause problems in a company. At Ben & Jerry's Homemade, this reliance has been one of the main sources of the company's growing pains. Both founders are by nature face-to-face communicators. They want their organization to function like a big, happy family in which people share ideas openly and informally, and, for a while, it did. However, as Ben & Jerry's grew and the number of employees increased, keeping everyone adequately informed by word of mouth became difficult. As one employee pointed out, "It's hard to feel you're part of a big family if you don't know the brothers and sisters."[11] For maximum impact, be sure to use both written and spoken channels.

Listening and Reading

Take another look at Figure 2.1. Apart from underscoring the importance of oral communication, it illustrates that people spend more time receiving information than transmitting it. Listening and reading are every bit as important as speaking and writing.

> Effective business communication depends on skill in receiving messages as well as skill in sending them.

Unfortunately, most of us aren't very good listeners. Immediately after hearing a ten-minute speech, we typically remember only half of what was said. A few days later, we've forgotten three-quarters of the message.[12] Worse, we often miss the subtle, underlying meaning entirely. To some extent, our listening problems stem from our education, or lack of it. We spend years learning to express our ideas, but few of us ever take a course in listening. Nevertheless, developing better listening abilities is crucial if we want to foster the understanding and cooperation so necessary for an increasingly diverse workforce.[13]

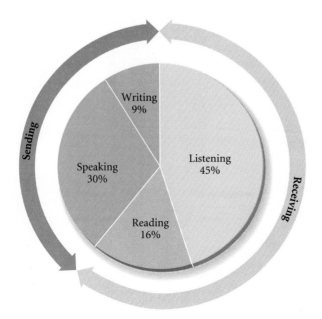

Figure 2.1
The Percentage of Communication Time Businesspeople Spend on Various Communication Channels

If you're listening, as opposed to reading, you have the advantage of being able to ask questions and interact with the speaker. Instead of just gathering information, you can co-operate in solving problems. This interactive process requires additional listening skills, which Chapter 17 discusses.

Likewise, our reading skills often leave a good deal to be desired. Approximately 20 per-cent of the adults in the United States are functionally illiterate; 14 percent cannot fill out a check properly; 38 percent have trouble reading the help-wanted ads in the newspaper; and 26 percent can't figure out the deductions listed on their paychecks.[14] Even those who read adequately don't often know how to read effectively. They have trouble extracting the important points from a document, so they can't make the most of the information con-tained in it.

T HE PROCESS OF COMMUNICATION

> The communication process consists of six phases linking sender and re-ceiver.

Whether you are speaking or writing, listening or reading, communication is more than a single act. Instead, it is a transactional (two-way) process that can be broken into six phases, as Figure 2.2 illustrates:[15]

1. *The sender has an idea.* You conceive an idea and want to share it.
2. *The sender transforms the idea into a message.* When you put your idea into a message that your receiver will understand, you are **encoding**, deciding on the message's form (word, facial expression, gesture), length, organization, tone, and style—all of which depend on your idea, your audience, and your personal style or mood.

Figure 2.2
The Communication Process

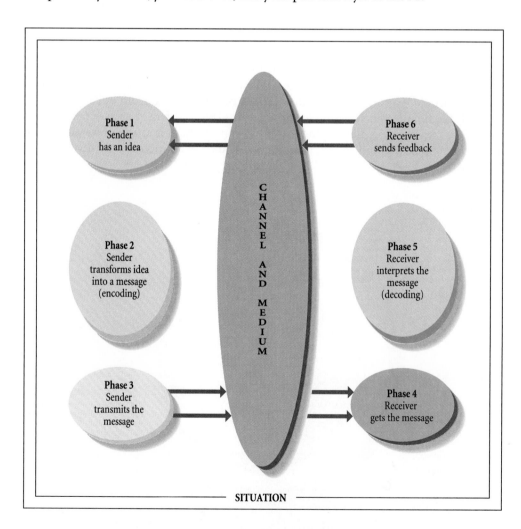

3. *The sender transmits the message.* To physically transmit your message to your receiver, you select a **communication channel** (verbal, nonverbal, spoken, or written) and a **medium** (telephone, computer, letter, memo, report, face-to-face exchange, and so on). The channel and medium you choose depend on your message, the location of your audience, your need for speed, and the formality of the situation.

4. *The receiver gets the message.* For communication to occur, your receiver must first get the message. If you send a letter, your receiver has to read it before understanding it. If you're giving a speech, the people in your audience have to be able to hear you, and they have to be paying attention.

5. *The receiver interprets the message.* Your receiver must cooperate by **decoding** your message, absorbing and understanding it. Then the decoded message has to be stored in the receiver's mind. If all goes well, the message is interpreted correctly; that is, the receiver assigns the same basic meaning to the words as the sender intended and responds in the desired way.

6. *The receiver reacts and sends feedback to the sender.* **Feedback** is your receiver's response, the final link in the communication chain. After getting the message, your receiver responds in some way and signals that response to you. Feedback is a key element in the communication process because it enables you to evaluate the effectiveness of your message. If your audience doesn't understand what you mean, you can tell by the response and refine your message.

The process is repeated until both parties have finished expressing themselves, but communication is effective only when each step is successful.

Estée Lauder credits the success of her skin-care products company, in part, to her communication policy. She keeps herself open to input and feedback from everyone she deals with: customers, retailers, employees, suppliers, and managers.

Feedback is your audience's response; it permits you to evaluate your message's effectiveness.

Formulating a Message

Communication is a dynamic process. Your idea cannot be communicated if you fail to perform any step in that process. Unfortunately, the process can be interrupted before it really begins—while you're trying to put your idea into words. Several things can go wrong when you're formulating a message, including indecision about the content of your message, lack of familiarity with the situation or the receiver, and difficulty in expressing ideas.

Indecision About Content

Deciding what to say is the first hurdle in the communication process. Many people make the mistake of trying to convey everything they know about a subject. Unfortunately, when a message contains too much information, it's difficult to absorb. If you want to get your point across, decide what to include and what to leave out, how much detail to provide, and what order to follow. If you try to explain something without first giving the receiver adequate background, you'll create confusion. Likewise, if you recommend actions without first explaining why they are justified, your message may provoke an emotional response that inhibits understanding.

Include only the information that is useful to your audience, and organize it in a way that encourages its acceptance.

Lack of Familiarity with the Situation or the Receiver

Creating an effective message is difficult if you don't know how it will be used. Unless you know why a report is needed, you are forced to create a very general document, one that covers a little bit of everything.

Lack of familiarity with your audience is an equally serious handicap. You need to know something about the biases, education, age, status, and style of your receiver in order to create an effective message. If you're writing for a specialist in your field, for example, you can use technical terms that might be unfamiliar to a lay person. If you're addressing a lower-level employee, you might approach a subject differently than if you were talking to your boss. Decisions about the content, organization, style, and tone of your message all depend, at least to some extent, on the relationship between you and your audience. If you don't know your audience, you will be forced to make these decisions in the dark, and at least part of your message may miss the mark.

Ask why you are preparing the message and for whom you are preparing it.

An inability to put thoughts into words can be overcome through study and practice.

Difficulty Expressing Ideas

Lack of experience in writing or speaking can also prevent a person from developing effective messages. Some people lack expertise in using language. Such problems can be overcome, but only with some effort. The important thing is to recognize the problem and take action. Taking college courses in communication is a good first step. Many companies offer their own in-house training programs in communication; others have tuition reimbursement programs to help cover the cost of outside courses. Self-help books are another good, inexpensive alternative. You might even join a professional organization or other group (such as Toastmasters or the League of Women Voters) to practice your communication skills in an informal setting.

The fact is that innumerable barriers to communication can block any phase of the communication process. Effective communicators do all they can to remove such barriers. By thinking about some of these barriers, you increase your chances of overcoming them.

Overcoming Communication Barriers

Communication barriers exist between people and within organizations.

Noise is any interference in the communication process that distorts or obscures the sender's meaning. Such communication barriers can exist between people and within organizations.[16]

Communication Barriers Between People

When you send a message, you intend to communicate meaning, but the message itself doesn't contain meaning. The meaning exists in your mind and in the mind of your receiver. To understand one another, you and your receiver must share similar meanings for words, gestures, tone of voice, and other symbols.

Perception is our individual interpretation of the world around us.

Differences in Perception The world constantly bombards us with information: sights, sounds, scents, and so on. Our minds organize this stream of sensation into a mental map that represents our **perception** of reality. In no case is the map in a person's mind the same as the world itself, and no two maps are exactly alike. As you view the world, your mind absorbs your experiences in a unique and personal way. For example, if you go out for pizza with a friend, each of you will notice different things. As you enter the restaurant, one of you may notice the coolness of the air-conditioning; the other may notice the aroma of pizza.

Because your perceptions are unique, the ideas you want to express differ from other people's. Even when two people have experienced the same event, their mental images of that event will not be identical. As senders, we choose the details that seem important and focus our attention on the most relevant and general. As receivers, we try to fit new details into our existing pattern. If a detail doesn't quite fit, we are inclined to distort the information rather than rearrange the pattern.

Overcoming perceptual barriers can be difficult. Try to predict how your message will be received, anticipate your receiver's reactions, and shape the message accordingly—constantly adjusting to correct any misunderstanding. Try not to apply the same solution to every problem, but look for solutions to fit specific problems. Frame your messages in terms that have meaning for your audience, and try to find something useful in every message you receive.[17]

As anchor of NBC's *Evening News, Tom Brokaw* addresses a nationwide audience daily. He must be careful to use words that mean the same thing to everyone, regardless of background or region of the country. Straightforward and simple is best, says Brokaw. Your chances of being misunderstood decrease if you are as accurate and as specific as you can be.

Filtering is screening out or abbreviating information before passing the message on to someone else.

Incorrect Filtering **Filtering** is screening out or abbreviating information before a message is passed on to someone else. In business, the filters between you and your receiver are many: secretaries, assistants, receptionists, and answering machines, to name a few. Just getting through by telephone can take a week if you're calling someone who's protected by layers of gatekeepers (operators, secretaries, assistants). Worse yet, your message may be digested, distilled, and probably distorted before it's passed on to your intended receiver. Those same gatekeepers may also translate, embellish, and augment your receiver's ideas and responses before passing them on to you. To overcome filtering barriers, try to establish more than one communication channel (so that information can be verified through multiple sources), eliminate as many intermediaries as possible, and decrease distortion by condensing message information to the bare essentials.

Language Problems   When you choose the words for your message, you signal that you are a member of a particular culture or subculture and that you know the code. The nature of your code—your language and vocabulary—imposes its own barriers on your message. For example, the language of a lawyer differs from that of an accountant or a doctor, and the difference in their vocabularies affects their ability to recognize and express ideas.

Barriers also exist because words can be interpreted in more than one way. Language uses words as symbols to represent reality: Nothing in the word *cookie* automatically ties it to the physical thing that is a cookie. We might just as well call a cookie a zebra. Language is an arbitrary code that depends on shared definitions, but there's a limit to how completely any of us can share the same meaning for a given word.

Even on the literal (denotative) level, words are imprecise. People in the United States generally agree on what a cookie is. However, your idea of a cookie is a composite of all the cookies you have ever tasted or seen: oatmeal cookies, chocolate chip cookies, sugar cookies, and vanilla wafers. Someone from another culture may have a different range of cookie experiences: meringues, florentines, and spritz. You both agree on the general concept of cookie, but the precise image in your minds differs.

On the subjective (connotative) level, the differences are even greater. Your interpretation of the word *cookie* depends partly on how you feel about cookies. You may have very pleasant feelings about them: You may remember baking them with your mother or coming home from school on winter afternoons to cookies and milk. Or you may be on a diet, in which case cookies will be an unpleasant reminder that you think you're too fat and must say no to all your favorite foods.

To overcome language barriers, use the most specific and accurate words possible. Always try to use words your audience will understand. Increase the accuracy of your messages by using language that describes rather than evaluates and by presenting observable facts, events, and circumstances.

Poor Listening   Perhaps the most common barrier to reception is simply a lack of attention on the receiver's part. We all let our minds wander now and then, regardless of how hard we try to concentrate. People are especially likely to drift off when they are forced to listen to information that is difficult to understand or that has little direct bearing on their own lives. If they are tired or concerned about other matters, they are even more likely to lose interest. As already mentioned, too few of us listen well.

To overcome listening barriers, verify your interpretation of what's been said (by paraphrasing what you've understood). Empathize with speakers (by trying to view the situation through their eyes), and resist jumping to conclusions. Clarify meaning by asking nonthreatening questions, and listen without interrupting.

Differing Emotional States   Every message contains both a content meaning, which deals with the subject of the message, and a relationship meaning, which suggests the nature of the interaction between sender and receiver. Communication can break down when the receiver reacts negatively to either of these meanings. You may have to deal with people when they are upset—or when you are. You may also have conflicting emotions about the subject of your message or the audience for it.

To overcome emotional barriers, be aware of the feelings that arise in yourself and in others as you communicate, and attempt to control them. For example, choose neutral words to avoid arousing strong feelings unduly. Avoid attitudes, blame, and other subjective concepts. Most important, be alert to the greater potential for misunderstanding that accompanies emotional messages.

Differing Backgrounds   Differences in background can be one of the hardest communication barriers to overcome. When your receiver's life experience differs substantially from yours, communication becomes difficult. Age, education, gender, social status,

GOING ONLINE
BEEF UP YOUR INTER-NET LANGUAGE SKILLS
Your success in Internet communication depends on how well you understand the language. That's where Netlingo can help. Keep the site's "pocket dictionary" floating toolbar on your desktop while you surf, and you'll have instant access to definitions of common Net terms, which don't always mean what you'd expect. For instance, you know from this chapter that *cookie* means different things in different cultures—but do you know what *cookie* means to a Netizen? Better look it up.

http://www.netlingo.com

Your denotative (literal) and connotative (subjective) definitions of words may differ dramatically from those of other people.

Listening ability decreases when information is difficult to understand and when it has little meaning for your audience.

Your audience may react either to the content of a message or to the relationship between sender and receiver that it implies.

In business communication, try to maintain your objectivity.

Try to understand the other person's point of view, and respect the inevitable differences in background and culture.

As corporate vice president of human resources at Avon Products, Marcia Worthing long ago recognized the impact of differing cultural backgrounds. Her solution was to institute cultural sensitivity courses to help employees deal with the growing changes both in the customer base and in the work-force.

Some information isn't necessary.

The complexity of messages is related to

- Your conflicts about the content
- The dry or difficult nature of the subject

Business messages rarely have the benefit of the audience's full and undivided attention.

economic position, cultural background, temperament, health, beauty, popularity, religion, political belief, even a passing mood can all separate one person from another and make understanding difficult. Communicating with someone from another country is probably the most extreme example of how background may impede communication, and culture clashes frequently arise in the workplace (see Chapter 3). But you don't have to seek out a person from an exotic locale to run into cultural gaps. You can misunderstand even your best friends and closest relatives, as you no doubt know from personal experience.

To overcome the barriers associated with differing backgrounds, avoid projecting your own background or culture onto others. Clarify your own and understand others' backgrounds, spheres of knowledge, personalities, and perceptions. And don't assume that certain behaviors mean the same thing to everyone.

Communication Barriers Within Organizations

Although all communication is subject to misunderstandings, business communication is particularly difficult. The material is often complex and controversial. Moreover, both the sender and the receiver may face distractions that divert their attention. Further, because the opportunities for feedback are often limited, it is difficult to correct misunderstandings.

Information Overload   Too much information is as bad as too little because it reduces the audience's ability to concentrate effectively on the most important messages. People facing information overload sometimes try to cope by ignoring some of the messages, by delaying responses to messages they deem unimportant, by answering only parts of some messages, by responding inaccurately to certain messages, by responding hastily to each message, or by reacting only superficially to all messages.

To overcome information overload, realize that some information is not necessary, and make necessary information easily available. Give information meaning, rather than just passing it on, and set priorities for dealing with the information flow.

Message Complexity   When formulating business messages, you communicate both as an individual and as a representative of an organization. Thus you must adjust your own ideas and style so that they are acceptable to your employer. In fact, you may occasionally be asked to write or say something that you disagree with personally.

Business messages may also deal with subject matter that can be technical or difficult to express. Imagine trying to write an interesting insurance policy, a set of instructions on how to operate a scraped-surface heat exchanger, the guidelines for checking credit references, an explanation of why profits have dropped by 12 percent in the last six months, or a description of your solid-waste-management program. These topics are dry, and making them clear and interesting is a real challenge.

To overcome the barriers of complex messages, keep them clear and easy to understand. Use strong organization, guide readers by telling them what to expect, use concrete and specific language, and stick to the point. Be sure to ask for feedback so that you can clarify and improve your message.

Message Competition   Communicators are often faced with messages that compete for attention. If you're talking on the phone while scanning a report, both messages are apt to get short shrift. Even your own messages may have to compete with a variety of interruptions: The phone rings every five minutes, people intrude, meetings are called, and crises arise. In short, your messages rarely have the benefit of the receiver's undivided attention.

To overcome competition barriers, avoid making demands on a receiver who doesn't have the time to pay careful attention to your message. Make written messages visually appealing and easy to understand, and try to deliver them when your receiver has time to read them. Oral messages are most effective when you can speak directly to your receiver (rather than to intermediaries or answering machines). Also, be sure to set aside enough time for important messages that you receive.

Differing Status　Employees of low status may be overly cautious when sending messages to a manager and may talk only about subjects they think the manager is interested in. Similarly, higher-status people may distort messages by refusing to discuss anything that would tend to undermine their authority in the organization. Moreover, belonging to a particular department or being responsible for a particular task can narrow your point of view so that it differs from the attitudes, values, and expectations of people who belong to other departments or who are responsible for other tasks.

To overcome status barriers, keep managers and colleagues well informed. Encourage lower-status employees to keep you informed by being fair-minded and respectful of their opinions. When you have information that you're afraid your boss might not like, be brave and convey it anyway.

Status barriers can be overcome by a willingness to give and receive bad news.

Lack of Trust　Building trust is a difficult problem. Other organization members don't know whether you'll respond in a supportive or responsible way, so trusting can be risky. As Ben & Jerry's Cohen and Greenfield know well, without trust, free and open communication is effectively blocked, threatening the organization's stability. However, just being clear in your communication isn't enough.

To overcome trust barriers, be visible and accessible. Don't insulate yourself behind assistants or secretaries. Share key information with colleagues and employees, communicate honestly, and include employees in decision making.

For communication to be successful, organizations must create an atmosphere of fairness and trust.

Structural barriers block upward, downward, and horizontal communication.

Inadequate Communication Structures　Organizational communication is affected by formal restrictions on who may communicate with whom and who is authorized to make decisions. Designing too few formal channels blocks effective communication. Strongly centralized organizations, especially those with a high degree of formalization, reduce communication capacity, and they decrease the tendency to communicate horizontally—thereby limiting the ability to coordinate activities and decisions. Tall organizations tend to provide too many vertical communication links, so messages become distorted as they move through the organization's levels. To overcome structural barriers, offer opportunities for communicating upward, downward, and horizontally (using such techniques as employee surveys, open-door policies, newsletters, memos, e-mail, and task groups). Try to reduce hierarchical levels, increase coordination between departments, and encourage two-way communication.

Your choice of a communication channel and medium depends on the

- Message
- Audience
- Need for speed
- Situation

Incorrect Choice of Medium　If you choose an inappropriate communication medium, your message can be distorted so that the intended meaning is blocked. You can select the most appropriate medium by matching your choice with the nature of the message and of the group or the individual who will receive it. **Media richness** is the value of a medium in a given communication situation. It's determined by a medium's ability (1) to convey a message using more than one informational cue (visual, verbal, vocal), (2) to facilitate feedback, and (3) to establish personal focus (Figure 2.3).

Face-to-face communication is the richest medium because it is personal, it provides immediate feedback, it transmits information from both verbal and nonverbal cues, and it conveys the emotion behind the message. Telephones and some other interactive electronic media aren't as rich; although they allow immediate feedback, they don't provide visual nonverbal cues such as facial expressions, eye contact, and body movements.[18] Written media can be personalized through addressed memos, letters, and reports, but they lack the immediate feedback and the visual and vocal nonverbal cues that contribute to the meaning of the message. The leanest media are generally impersonal written messages such as bulletins, fliers, and standard reports. Not only do they lack the ability to transmit nonverbal cues and to give feedback, they also eliminate any personal focus.

To overcome media barriers, choose the richest media for nonroutine, complex messages. Use rich media to extend and to humanize your presence throughout the organization, to communicate caring and personal interest to employees, and to gain employee commitment to organizational goals. Use leaner media to communicate simple, routine messages. You can send information such as statistics, facts, figures, and conclusions through a note, memo, or written report.[19]

Figure 2.3
A Continuum of Media Richness

To ensure effective communication, use richer media for messages that are complex, ambiguous, and nonroutine.

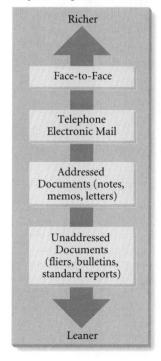

Richer

Face-to-Face

Telephone
Electronic Mail

Addressed
Documents (notes,
memos, letters)

Unaddressed
Documents
(fliers, bulletins,
standard reports)

Leaner

Behind the Scenes at J•A•M•S/Endispute
Resolving Your Communication Problems Without Going to Court

According to Jack Unroe, communication breakdown is one of the biggest contributors to conflict. Unroe is president and CEO of J•A•M•S/Endispute, a company that provides third-party mediators to help people communicate effectively and to settle their disputes without going to court. "Roughly 95 percent of all civil lawsuits never go to trial," notes Unroe. "Most people resolve their disputes. The question is when—the sooner they do it, the less money they spend and the better chance they have of repairing their relationship."

To help people settle their differences, J•A•M•S/Endispute mediators focus on helping them communicate more effectively.

J•A•M•S/Endispute repairs relationships by bringing parties back together, getting them to communicate, finding innovative ways to resolve conflict, and settling disputes in private—just some of the advantages of using one of the 350 experienced professional mediators, attorneys, and retired judges affiliated with the company. These professionals help their clients settle disputes by meeting with the parties involved to clarify the issues on all sides. Then they steer all parties toward settlement by acting as facilitators. They interpret and reframe the issues, brainstorm possible solutions, identify the pros and cons of each suggestion, and provide an opportunity for the parties involved to really listen to each other—possibly for the first time.

"People don't listen well, and they often don't show it when they are listening," notes senior mediator Dwight Golann, who helps train the company's mediators and teaches mediation techniques to law students at Suffolk University Law School. Because most conflicts don't get resolved until both parties feel that they have been heard and reach a point at which they can listen to each other, Golann teaches his students a mixture of techniques that show they are listening well: taking notes, maintaining direct eye contact, nodding, rephrasing what they hear, and listening for the feelings behind the words. Golann notes that "most people are busy pulling their own arguments together while they are

Charley Shin is CEO of Gosh Enterprises, franchiser for the Charley's Steakery restaurants. Shin first began while he was a student at Ohio State. He's often found on "youngest millionaire" lists, giving credit to just about everyone but himself. Shin learned early that his business thrives on good communication—with employees, with customers, and now with new franchise owners who receive his special newsletters and attend extensive training sessions.

Closed Communication Climate   As discussed in Chapter 1, communication climate is influenced by management style, and a directive, authoritarian style blocks the free and open exchange of information that characterizes good communication. At Ben & Jerry's, everyone works hard to maintain an open communication climate. To overcome climate barriers, spend more time listening than issuing orders. Make sure you respond constructively to employees, and of course, encourage employees and colleagues to offer suggestions, help set goals, participate in solving problems, and help make decisions.

Unethical Communication   An organization cannot create illegal or unethical messages and still be credible or successful in the long run. Relationships within and outside the organization depend on trust and fairness. To overcome ethics barriers, make sure your messages contain all information that ought to be there. Make sure that information applies to the situation. And make sure your message is completely truthful.

Inefficient Communication   Producing worthless messages wastes time and resources, and it contributes to the information overload already mentioned. Reduce the number of messages by thinking twice before sending one. Then speed up the process, first, by preparing messages correctly the first time around and, second, by standardizing format and material when appropriate. Be clear about the writing assignments you accept as well as the ones you assign.

Physical Distractions   Communication barriers are often physical: bad connections, poor acoustics, illegible copy. Although noise of this sort seems trivial, it can completely block an otherwise effective message. Your receiver might also be distracted by an uncomfortable chair, poor lighting, or some other irritating condition. In some cases, the barrier may be related to the receiver's health. Hearing or visual impairment or even a headache can interfere with reception of a message. These annoyances don't generally block communication entirely, but they may reduce the receiver's concentration.

listening, but it's difficult to listen and frame your argument at the same time."

That's why Golann and Unroe advise clients to "listen and be audience centered. Spend time figuring out what the other party is thinking. Don't spend time trying to overwhelm them with what you know." Unroe explains that most people want "to overwhelm you with their side of the story—their issue and how they have been wronged. But they don't pause long enough to internalize what's on the other party's mind." He adds that "if you understand the other party's thinking better, the chances of resolving a dispute increase significantly."

One way to understand the other party better is to allow that party to openly express his or her thoughts and feelings. Both Unroe and Golann see emotion as the biggest potential barrier to communication. "People are angry. They feel someone else is at fault, and they may have years of emotion bottled up inside of them—resulting from issues that no longer exist." Because most people associate being emotional with being weak, the more emotional party is at a disadvantage. Golann trains mediators to look for emotional hot spots by observing the body language of the parties involved—including gestures, nervousness, and looking away. Once the emotional hot spots have been identified, mediators can "discuss the issue, trace it back to its source, and help people distinguish the past problem

from the present situation—so they can move on and focus on resolving it."

Of course, resolving conflict is the biggest benefit of mediation. However, by participating in the mediation process, people also learn how to recognize the early symptoms of conflict, manage it, compromise, communicate more effectively, and continue good business relationships (even while they are involved in a dispute). By mastering these essential skills, they can get back to the business of running their business.

Apply Your Knowledge

1. As a junior mediator for J•A•M•S/Endispute, you have been asked to speak to the owners of a company that has experienced an unusually high rate of employee turnover in the past year. The owners are concerned that their communication practices are ineffective. What general advice can you offer regarding employer-employee communications?

2. You have been invited to observe the initial mediation session of two partners in a software venture who have been embroiled in a conflict for two years. During the initial session, the mediator allows both parties to explain their side of the story. One of them is plainly very angry and at one point seems near tears. Can this approach be productive? Please give your reasons.

To overcome physical barriers, exercise as much control as possible over the physical transmission link: If you're preparing a written document, make sure its appearance doesn't detract from your message. If you're delivering an oral presentation, choose a setting that permits the audience to see and hear you without straining. When you are the audience, learn to concentrate on the message rather than the distractions.

 # HOW TO IMPROVE COMMUNICATION

As you learn how to overcome more and more communication barriers, you become more and more successful as a business communicator. Think about the people you know. Which of them would you call successful communicators? What do these people have in common? Chances are, the individuals on your list share five traits:

- *Perception.* They are able to predict how you will receive their message. They anticipate your reaction and shape the message accordingly. They read your response correctly and constantly adjust to correct any misunderstanding.
- *Precision.* They create a "meeting of the minds." When they finish expressing themselves, you share the same mental picture.
- *Credibility.* They are believable. You have faith in the substance of their message. You trust their information and their intentions.
- *Control.* They shape your response. Depending on their purpose, they can make you laugh or cry, calm down, change your mind, or take action.
- *Congeniality.* They maintain friendly, pleasant relations with you. Regardless of whether you agree with them, good communicators command your respect and goodwill. You are willing to work with them again, despite your differences.

Effective communication requires perception, precision, credibility, control, and congeniality.

Effective communicators overcome the main barriers to communication by creating their messages carefully, minimizing noise in the transmission process, and facilitating feedback.

Create the Message Carefully

In general terms, your purpose is to bring your audience closer to your views.

The best way to create messages carefully is to focus on your audience so that you can help them understand and accept your message. You want to create a bridge of words that leads audience members from their current position to your point, so you have to know something about your audience's current position. If you're addressing strangers, try to find out more about them; if that's impossible, try to project yourself into their position by using your common sense and imagination. Then you'll be ready to create your message:

Give your audience a framework for understanding the ideas you communicate.

To make your message memorable
- Use words that evoke a physical, sensory impression
- Use telling statistics

The key to brevity is to limit the number of ideas, not to shortchange their development.

Tie the message to your audience's frame of reference.

By highlighting and summarizing key points, you help your audience understand and remember the message.

- Tell your audience at the outset what to expect from your message. Let them know the purpose of your message, and tell them what main points they will encounter. Even if you don't want to reveal controversial ideas at the beginning of a message, you can still give your audience a preview of the topics you plan to cover.
- Balance general concepts with specific illustrations. Once you've stated your overall idea at the beginning of your message, develop that idea by using vivid, concrete examples. The most memorable words are the ones that create a picture in your audience's mind by describing colors, objects, scents, sounds, and tastes. Specific details such as numbers, figures, and percentages can also be vivid.
- Keep your messages as brief and as clear as possible. With few exceptions, one page is easier to absorb than two, especially in a business environment, where so many messages compete for attention. However, you have to be careful to develop each main idea adequately. You're better off covering three points thoroughly than eight points superficially.
- Show how new ideas are related to ideas that already exist in the minds of your audience. The meaning of the new concept is clarified by its relationship to the old. Such connections also help make the new concepts acceptable.
- When you come to an important idea, say so. By explicitly stating that an idea is especially significant, you wake people up; you also make it easier for them to file the thought in the proper place. You can call attention to an idea visually, using headlines, bold type, and indented lists and by using charts, graphs, maps, diagrams, and illustrations. If you're delivering your message orally, use your body and voice to highlight the important concepts.
- Before concluding your message or even a major section of a long message, take a moment or two to review the points you've just covered. Restate the purpose, and show how the main ideas relate to it. This simple step will help your audience remember your message and will help simplify the overall meaning of complex material.

Minimize Noise

Even the most carefully constructed message will fail to achieve results if it does not reach your audience. As far as possible, try to eliminate potential sources of interference. Then make sure your choice of communication channel and medium doesn't interfere with your message. Choose the method that will be most likely to attract your audience's attention and enable them to concentrate on the message. If a written document seems the best choice, try to make it physically appealing and easy to comprehend. Use an attractive, convenient format, and pay attention to such details as the choice of paper and the quality of type. If possible, deliver the document when you know the reader will have time to study it.

The careful choice of channel and medium helps focus your audience's attention on your message.

If the message calls for an oral delivery channel, try to eliminate physical barriers. The location should be comfortable and quiet, with adequate lighting, good acoustics, and few visual distractions. In addition, think about how your own appearance will affect the audience. An outfit that screams for attention creates as much noise as a squeaky air-conditioning system. Another way to reduce interference, particularly in oral communication, is to deliver your message directly to the intended audience. The more people who filter your message, the greater the potential for message distortion.

Facilitate Feedback

In addition to minimizing noise, giving your audience a chance to provide feedback is crucial. But one thing that makes business communication difficult is the complexity of the feedback loop. If you're talking face to face with another person, feedback is immediate and clear. However, if you're writing a letter, memo, or report that will be read by several people, feedback will be delayed and mixed. Some of the readers will be enthusiastic or will respond promptly; others will be critical or reluctant to respond, and revising your message to take into account their feedback will be difficult.

When you plan a message, think about the amount of feedback you want to encourage. Although feedback is generally useful, it reduces your control over the communication situation. You need to know whether your message is being understood and accepted, but you may not want to respond to comments until you have completed your argument. If you are communicating with a group, you may not have the time to react to every impression or question.

So think about how you want to obtain feedback, and choose a form of communication that suits your needs. Some channels and media are more compatible with feedback than others. If you want to adjust your message quickly, talk to the receiver face to face or by phone. If feedback is less important to you, use a written document or give a prepared speech.

As Cohen and Greenfield know from their experience at Ben & Jerry's, feedback isn't always easy to get, even when you encourage it. In some cases, you may have to draw out the other person by asking questions. If you want to know specific things, ask specific questions, but also encourage your audience to express general reactions; you can often learn something very interesting that way.

Regardless of whether the response to your message is written or oral, encourage people to be open and to tell you what they really think and feel. Of course, you have to listen to their comments, and you must do so objectively. You can't say "Please tell me what you think" and then get mad at the first critical comment. So try not to react defensively. Your goal is to find out whether the people in your audience have understood and accepted your message. If you find that they haven't, don't lose your temper. After all, the fault is at least partially yours. Instead of saying the same thing all over again, only louder this time, try to find the source of the misunderstanding. Then revise your message. Sooner or later, if you keep trying, you'll succeed. You may not win the audience to your point of view, but at least you'll make your meaning clear, and you'll part with a feeling of mutual respect.

> Make feedback more useful by
> - Planning how and when to accept it
> - Being receptive to your audience's responses
> - Encouraging frankness
> - Using it to improve communication

O n the Job

SOLVING A COMMUNICATION DILEMMA AT BEN & JERRY'S HOMEMADE

Communication—with customers, the public, investors, and government officials—plays a key role in Ben & Jerry's success. To begin with, this company's communicators use every opportunity to get their messages across to customers and the general public. The labels on most food products discuss ingredients and flavor, but Ben & Jerry's labels also show information about world peace, the environment, and other issues. Some products are even designed to convey messages. For example, a percentage of sales from Peace Pops goes to promoting world peace, and Rainforest Crunch is made with nuts from the South American rain forest (which supports the native people directly and gives them a financial incentive to nurture the forest instead of cutting it down). Both labels and products act as transmission channels for Ben & Jerry's messages.

Annual reports, which communicate with shareholders, are usually slick and glossy. However, an annual report from Ben & Jerry's is likely to be illustrated with whimsical drawings of cows, ice cream cones, and endangered species. Investors, employees, government officials, and other readers can have no doubt about the company's orientation after reading one of its reports.

In addition to communicating with customers and shareholders, communicating with employees is crucial. At Ben & Jerry's, internal communication ranges from meetings in which all employees are encouraged to speak their minds about company policies and practices to the following formal mission statement (which is published in the annual report and posted on the company's Web site):

- *Product mission.* To make, distribute, and sell the finest quality all-natural ice cream and related products in a wide variety of innovative flavors made from Vermont dairy products.

- *Economic mission.* To operate the company on a sound financial basis of profitable growth, increasing value for our shareholders and creating career opportunities and financial rewards for our employees.
- *Social mission.* To operate the company in a way that actively recognizes the central role that business plays in the structure of society by initiating innovative ways to improve the quality of life in a broad community: local, national, and international.

Communicating what the company is about and what it wants to accomplish is a vital part of Cohen and Greenfield's efforts to keep their unusual business effort alive and well.[20]

Your Mission: You've recently been hired as Ben & Jerry's director of communications. You have three responsibilities: (1) developing guidelines and practices to help the company communicate more effectively, (2) helping individual employees and managers with specific communication problems, and (3) acting as the company's official voice by talking to reporters, welcoming tour groups, and so on. Use good judgment and common sense to help identify the best answer in each of the following hypothetical situations. Be prepared to explain why your choice is best.

1. A reporter from the *New York Times* is writing an article on fat and cholesterol in the U.S. diet. She wants to know how Ben & Jerry's can claim to be so socially responsible when the company sells products that aren't exactly healthful. The article is running in tomorrow's editions, so the reporter doesn't have time to let you think about it and call back with an answer. Which is the best response?
   a. You know that anything you say might provoke a negative re-action, so you simply say, "I'm sorry; we don't comment on health-related issues."
   b. You know that you have to establish some credibility, and pretending that a steady diet of ice cream is acceptable is not the way to do that, so you say, "We don't encourage anyone to eat excessive amounts of ice cream. We do believe, how-ever, that modest amounts of ice cream can be compatible with a generally healthful lifestyle that includes a balanced diet and regular exercise. Consumers should also consider our new low-fat and nonfat products."
   c. You want to take control of the conversation, so you tell her that "until we conduct our own research, we're not willing to accept without question the negative image that the medical profession has created for ice cream."
   d. Simply say, "We can't be held responsible for our customers' health. After all, we make only ice cream, and people could have unhealthy eating habits that extend beyond dessert."
2. The manager of one of the production plants realizes that his communication skills are important for several reasons: He holds primary responsibility for successful communication in-side the plant; he needs to communicate with the managers who report to him; and his style sets an example for other managers. He asks you to sit in on face-to-face meetings for several days to observe his nonverbal messages. You witness the following four habits; which do you think is the most negative?
   a. He rarely comes out from behind his massive desk when meeting people; at one point he gave an employee a congrat-ulatory handshake, and the employee had to lean way over his desk just to reach him.
   b. When an employee hands him a report and then sits down to discuss it, he alternates between making eye contact and making notes on the report.
   c. He is consistently pleasant, even if the person he is meeting is delivering bad news.
   d. He interrupts meetings to answer the phone, rather than let-ting an assistant get the phone; then he apologizes to visitors for the interruption.
3. At a recent companywide meeting, employees were told that shareholders have been pressuring company management to pay them a higher dividend and that the board of directors has agreed to do it. (Dividends are a portion of the company's prof-its set aside for shareholders; higher dividends mean less money for other purposes.) Then, when the employees returned to work, they found the latest issue of the company newsletter, in which an article by Jerry Greenfield asked employees to volun-tarily shorten their lunch periods to increase ice cream produc-tion so that more money could be given to charities. Which of the following best describes the effect of the two messages?
   a. The two messages are compatible; shareholders will get more money from the existing profit margin, and charities will get more from the employees' working longer hours. You don't foresee any problems.
   b. Employees will actually work less because they'll resent the shareholders' request for higher dividends.
   c. Employees will begin to question the wisdom of the com-pany's charitable contributions.
   d. Confusion is the most likely result because the two messages conflict. Some employees are likely to think that their sacri-fice of working longer for the same pay is going to benefit the shareholders, not the charities.
4. As one of the most talked-about companies in the country, Ben & Jerry's is the subject of many school reports and case studies. Many of the people working on these projects contact the com-pany directly for information. In fact, nearly 40,000 students, researchers, and other people asked for help from 1992 through 1997. Many of these requests ask for the same information, such as quarterly financial reports. How should the company re-spond to this huge task?
   a. Use the Internet and World Wide Web to make standard-ized information available to all researchers. Most students now have Internet access at home or at school, so this op-tion will meet their needs while saving the company time and money.
   b. Write and publish a book that answers the most frequently asked questions. When people phone or e-mail for help, sug-gest that they visit the library or purchase the book.
   c. The people asking for help are likely to be customers or po-tential customers, so it's vital to give them all the help they need. Hire sufficient staff to address every inquiry.
   d. The buying potential of an individual student is not likely to compensate for all the work of helping him or her find infor-mation for a school report. Set up a phone line with a recorded message thanking people for calling but explaining that you just don't have the staff time available to help researchers.

ritical Thinking Questions

1. How can nonverbal communication help you run a meeting? How can it help you call the meeting to order, emphasize important topics, show approval, express reservations, regulate the flow of conversation, and invite a colleague to continue with a comment?
2. Which communication channels are more susceptible to noise, written or spoken? Why?
3. How can you as the receiver help a sender successfully communicate a message? Briefly explain.
4. Do you think it is easier to communicate with members of your own sex? Why or why not?
5. How can you impress on your employees the importance of including negative information in messages?
6. Under what circumstances might you want to limit the feedback you receive from an audience of readers or listeners? Briefly explain.

ocument for Analysis

Read the following document; then (1) analyze the strengths and weaknesses of each sentence and (2) revise the document so that it follows this chapter's guidelines.

It has come to my attention that many of you are lying on your time cards. If you come in late, you should not put 8:00 on your card. If you take a long lunch, you should not put 1:00 on your time card. I will not stand for this type of cheating. I simply have no choice but to institute a time-clock system. Beginning next Monday, all employees will have to punch in and punch out whenever they come and go from the work area.

The time clock will be right by the entrance to each work area, so you have no excuse for not punching in. Anyone who is late for work or late coming back from lunch more than three times will have to answer to me. I don't care if you had to take a nap or if you girls had to shop. This is a place of business, and we do not want to be taken advantage of by slackers who are cheaters to boot.

It is too bad that a few bad apples always have to spoil things for everyone.

xercises

1. Write a short description of your classroom's communication potential. What furniture is in the room? How is the room arranged? Are students seated in rows? In a circle? Where is the instructor's space? At the front of the room? In the middle? What are the acoustics like? Are there any windows in the room? Do they offer pleasing views? Could they be distracting? Are there any chalkboards or other visual aids that might affect communication? Is the temperature comfortable? Are heaters or air conditioners noisy? Explain how these and other factors influence the communication that goes on in your classroom. Conclude your description with a statement about the kind of communication your classroom encourages. (An inflexible atmosphere for one-way lectures? An open forum of give and take? An intimate setting for private conversations between members of small groups?)
2. On the World Wide Web, visit the home pages for United Airlines at <http://www.UAL.com> and for Singapore Airlines at <http://www.singaporair.com>. Identify the verbal and nonverbal cues that help you understand each company as well as the products and services that each company offers. Examine the presentation of both text and visual elements, including photographs and graphics. Consider the layout of the page, background "noise," and repetition. Think about the needs of the audience. Is each page informative and easy to use? Do the links take the user to appropriate and clearly presented data? In 500 words, explain which site is more effective and why.
3. Your boss has asked you to research and report on corporate child-care facilities. Of course, you'll want to know who (besides your boss) will be reading your report. List four or five other things you'll want to know about the situation and about your audience before starting your research. Briefly explain why the items on your list are important.
4. Briefly describe a miscommunication you've had with a coworker, fellow student, friend, or family member. Can you identify what barriers prevented your successful communication? Please explain.
5. Basing your decisions on the relative richness of communication media, such as face-to-face interviews, telephone conversations, written messages (such as memos, letters, and reports), and bulletins or newsletters, advise your employees how best to send the following messages, and explain your rationale.
   a. A technical report on the durability of your production equipment
   b. A reminder to employees about safety rules

c. A performance evaluation of an employee who has been consistently missing deadlines

d. A confirmation of tomorrow's luncheon meeting with an important client

e. The quarterly statistics on inventory control

f. Your resignation before joining another company

6. You've accepted an invitation from the chamber of commerce to speak about controlled growth in the community. You know that your audience will consist mostly of local businesspeople, but how can you find out more? Is it possible to determine where they stand on the issue of growth, how much they know about the topic, and what information they need to have before they'll accept your message? You have one month before the speech. List any methods you can think of that will help you learn as much as you can about the audience you'll be addressing.

7. You've agreed to help a colleague by reviewing his report. His language needs to be more specific and more memorable, so you've compiled a list of words and phrases that should be replaced. Please suggest one or two appropriate alternatives for the underlined sections in the following:

a. A <u>pale, grayish yellow</u> cover

b. <u>Soft</u> leather

c. The <u>people buying this product</u>

d. During this <u>period of business prosperity</u>

e. Concern for <u>seriously declining</u> profits

8. You are writing a report on the U.S. sales of your newest product. Of the following topics, identify those that should and should not be included in your report (please explain your choices):

a. Regional breakdowns of sales across the country

b. Sales figures of competitors who are selling similar products worldwide

c. Predictions of how the struggling U.S. economy will affect sales over the next six months

d. The impact of Japanese competitors' selling similar products in the United States

e. An evaluation of your company's selling this product internationally

9. Describe the kinds of vocal signals and body movements you can use to highlight the key points of your speech.

10. You're stuck. Your boss has asked you to make your presentation to the board at lunch. You dread the prospect. It's bad enough that you have to convince such a stuffy group to spend more money on employee training and education, but to have to do it over lunch at a formally set table for nine in the middle of a busy restaurant is too much. What can you do to get the board members' attention, keep it, and overcome the interruptions and noise of the restaurant's waiters and lunch crowd?

11. In order to obtain just the right amount of feedback, choose the appropriate form of communication for the following (briefly explain your choices).

a. Disclosing your idea for a new product to your five-member team

b. Obtaining comments from your boss on your approach to completing the annual stockholders' report

c. Convincing top management and co-workers that your plan for improving companywide communication is the best plan

d. Getting opinions from your co-workers about remodeling the local office

12. Whenever your boss asks for feedback on an idea, she blasts anyone offering criticism no matter how gently the news is broken to her. This defensive reaction has caused people to start agreeing with everything she says. You think that the situation is unhealthy for the company and for your boss. So, despite the likelihood of her reacting defensively, you want to talk to her about it. List some of the things you'll say when you meet with her tomorrow.

DEVELOPING YOUR INTERNET SKILLS
GOING ONLINE: BEEF UP YOUR INTERNET LANGUAGE SKILLS, P. 27

Do you think the Internet is creating a new language recognized and understood worldwide? How might this benefit the business world? Can you think of any terms coined by Net users that have spilled over into everyday usage? Does this kind of lingo exclude certain groups, or does it broaden everyone's knowledge?

COMMUNICATING INTERCULTURALLY

After studying this chapter, you will be able to

Outline the two trends that have made intercultural business communication so important

Define culture and intercultural communication

Discuss nine ways people can differ culturally

Summarize how to learn about a particular culture

Discuss some general skills to help communicate in any culture

Identify some of the common sources of misunderstanding that occur in written and oral intercultural communication

Explain the importance of speaking and listening effectively when communicating face to face with people from other cultures

O n the Job

FACING A COMMUNICATION DILEMMA AT TARGET STORES

Taking Aim at Cultural Diversity

Rafael Rodriguez is a stock clerk supervisor at the Target store in Pasadena, California. Rodriguez is Hispanic, his manager is African American, and the employees he supervises have cultural backgrounds as diverse as the communities served by the nearly 700 Target retail outlets across the United States. Moreover, as in most other Target stores, some of Rodriguez's employees have grown up in the United States, whereas others have recently immigrated and speak English as a second language.

Supervising people in the fast-paced world of retailing is demanding under any circumstances, and his team's rich cultural mix makes Rodriquez's job even more of a challenge. The unique combination of influences present in one culture can condition people to think, feel, and behave quite differently from people in another culture. Some differences are dramatic, such as in the importance of social status. Other differences, such as personal values and decision-making approaches, can be more subtle and more difficult to perceive. Rodriguez finds that basic language barriers often prevent employees from understanding each other, but the potential for problems goes beyond language differences. In one case, a recently immigrated employee was inadvertently making some female coworkers uncomfortable by asking personal questions about hair styles and nose piercing. His questions were innocent, but, because of his cultural background, he couldn't see the invisible boundary that his colleagues had built around their personal lives.

Such cultural differences—and the misunderstandings that result from them—can affect teamwork, productivity, and job satisfaction. If you were Rafael Rodriguez, what steps would you take to foster a productive and satisfying work environment? How would you make sure employees overcome cultural barriers so that they can communicate effectively and work together efficiently?[1]

Like so many large companies in the United States and abroad, Target employs people with broad ethnic and cultural diversity. One key to Target's success is its commitment to training employees in the subtleties of intercultural exchanges. Training sessions may stress differences in social as well as business customs to encourage understanding, communication, and cooperation.

Technology has made global communication both quick and easy.

The globalization of business is accelerating as more companies cross national borders to find customers, materials, and money.

T HE IMPORTANCE OF INTERCULTURAL BUSINESS COMMUNICATION

Target is by no means alone in dealing with a multicultural workforce. Regardless of the organization you join, you are likely to be dealing with people who come from various national, religious, and ethnic backgrounds. Like Target's Rafael Rodriguez, you may find yourself trying to bridge differences in both language and culture as you exchange business messages with co-workers, customers, suppliers, investors, and competitors from other cultures.

Of course, communicating across language and cultural barriers at home is only one way your communication skills will be challenged. Communicating across national borders will also challenge your skills. More and more companies around the world are hopping national borders to conduct business.

Communicating with Cultures Abroad

Thanks to technological advances in communication and transportation, companies can quickly and easily span the globe in search of new customers and new sources of materials and money. Even firms that once thought they were too tiny to expand into a neighboring city have discovered that they can tap the sales potential of overseas markets with the help of fax machines, the Internet, overnight delivery services, and e-mail (Figure 3.1). This rise of international business has expanded international business communication by increasing exports, relaxing trade barriers, and increasing foreign competition in domestic markets.

More and more businesses report that a large part of their overall sales now come from *exports* (products sold to customers in other countries). Nestlé, which is based in Switzerland, sells over 95 percent of its products in other countries. Likewise, some U.S. companies are seeing export sales dwarf sales at home: Boston-based Gillette makes 70 percent of its sales through exports.[2]

Relaxing trade barriers has also quickened the pace of international trade. Mexico, Canada, and the United States have agreed to lower trade barriers throughout the continent, creating a single market of 360 million people. Moreover, discussions are under way to extend that agreement throughout the Americas.[3] The goal is to increase *imports* (products purchased from businesses in other countries) by reducing the hassles of bringing goods across the borders. Similarly, the nations of the European Economic Community have been eliminating trade barriers. Since 1993, capital, products, and employees have been flowing freely across European borders, creating a unified market of 320 million people.[4]

As companies move into the global marketplace, they increase the competition in domestic markets for employees, customers, and materials. At the same time, 30 percent of U.S. manufacturers recently reported that three of their top five competitors *in the U.S. market* are non-U.S. firms. In this fast-paced global marketplace, companies are finding that good communication skills are essential for meeting customers, making sales, and working effectively with colleagues in other countries.

Communicating with a Culturally Diverse Workforce

In addition to communicating with people in other countries, you'll be communicating with people in your own country whose culture and language differ from yours. First, if you work in the local branch of a foreign firm or if your company does business with local branches of foreign firms, you may find that differences in language and culture interfere with your message exchange.

Cultural diversity is the degree to which the population is made up of people from varied national, ethnic, racial, and religious backgrounds.

Second, no matter where you work, you'll face language and cultural barriers as you communicate with members of an increasingly diverse domestic workforce. A country's workforce reflects its **cultural diversity,** the degree to which the population is made up of people from various national, ethnic, racial, and religious backgrounds.

Wickman Hospital Products, Inc., a large U.S. company, is interested in developing a client base in Mexico. Wickman's marketing department suggested a direct-mail campaign supplemented with personalized e-mail communications. Each Mexican hospital was initially sent a letter of introduction, detailed product information, and a carton of sample products. A week later, the following e-mail message was sent.

Figure 3.1
In-Depth Critique: E-Mail Is One of the Technologies Shrinking the World

```
╔═══════════════════════ E-Mail ═══════════════════════╗
```

Comments: authenticated sender is <jacksont@wickman.com>
From: "Timothy A. Jackson" <jacksont@wickman.com>
To: jHerrera@stlukeshosp.org
Date: Thurs, 19 June 1997, 10:30:23, CDT
Subject: Wickman Hospital Products, Inc.
Return-Receipt-To: jackson@wickman.com
Priority: normal

Dear Sr. Herrera:

Wickman Hospital Products is eager to serve you. Did you have time to look over the materials we sent you recently? You may be especially interested in our fine line of disposable pads and bedding.

For your convenience, Charles Garrison can give you detailed information about any of our products. You can contact him by e-mail, phone or post:

E-mail	garrison@wickman.com
Phone	(800) 773-4558
Post	Charles Garrison Customer Representative Wickman Hospital Products P.O. Box 511 Columbus, Ohio, 43216-0508 USA

You can also place an order right away, browse through our entire line of products, and review product specifications. Just visit our Internet home page: <http://www.wickman.com>. You can count on delivery within 48 hours of the the time we receive your e-mail, Internet order form, or phone call.

Please let us help you supply St. Luke's Hospital with the finest products available.

Timothy A. Jackson, International Sales
Wickman Hospital Products

The header containing routing information, subject, and so forth is a common feature of most e-mail programs.

The message begins politely and with a reminder of previous communication.

This paragraph gives helpful information, suggests actions, and provides an e-mail address for each action.

The letter closes by urging use of the Internet. When this message is sent, the angle brackets placed around the Uniform Resource Locator, or URL, convert the Web address to a live link (also called a hot link). The URL appears in a distinctive color, and the angle brackets are no longer visible. To visit the linked Web page, the recipient merely clicks on the URL.

In the United States, for example, the high degree of cultural diversity in the domestic workforce has been partially shaped by immigration trends, with new arrivals from Europe, Canada, Latin America, and Asia.[5] As these immigrants join the domestic workforce, they bring their own language and culture. Out of every seven people in the United States, one person speaks a language other than English when at home.[6]

Members of the U.S. workforce also come from differing ethnic backgrounds. African Americans represent 12 percent of the U.S. population, and, by the year 2000 they will represent nearly 14 percent. Hispanic Americans (including people with backgrounds from Mexico, Cuba, Puerto Rico, and Central and South America) currently account for 9 percent of the population; Asian Americans (including people with backgrounds from Vietnam, Cambodia, and other Asian nations) account for nearly 3 percent.[7]

Of course, people also differ in terms of their gender, age, physical abilities, family status, and educational background. Like language and culture, these elements contribute to the diversity of the workforce. They shape how people view the world. And they also affect how business messages are conceived, planned, sent, received, and interpreted.

THE BASICS OF INTERCULTURAL BUSINESS COMMUNICATION

As discussed in Chapter 2, differences in background can be a difficult communication barrier to overcome. When you plan to communicate with people of another culture—whether in another country or in your own country—it's important to be aware of cultural differences. Consider the communication challenge that Mazda's managers faced when the Japanese auto manufacturer opened a plant in the United States. Mazda officials passed out company baseball caps and told their U.S. employees that they could wear the caps at work, along with their mandatory company uniform (blue pants and khaki shirts). The employees assumed that the caps were a *voluntary* accessory, and many decided not to wear them. The Japanese managers, who regarded failure to wear the caps as a sign of disrespect, were upset. Managers acknowledged that the caps were voluntary but believed that employees who really cared about the company would *want* to wear the caps. However, the U.S. employees had a different view: They resented being told what they should want to do, and they began cynically referring to all Mazda's directives as "mandatory-voluntary."[8]

Understanding Culture

You belong to several cultures. The most obvious is the culture you share with all the people who live in your own country. You also belong to other cultural groups, including an ethnic group, a religious group, and perhaps a profession that has its own special language and customs. **Culture** is a shared system of symbols, beliefs, attitudes, values, expectations, and norms for behavior. All members of a culture have similar assumptions about how people should think, behave, and communicate, and they all tend to act on those assumptions in much the same way.

Distinct groups that exist within a major culture are referred to as **subcultures.** Groups that might be considered subcultures in the United States are Mexican Americans, Mormons, wrestling fans, Russian immigrants, and Harvard graduates.

By bridging cultural differences, you can successfully achieve **intercultural communication,** the process of sending and receiving messages between people of different cultures. When communicating with a person from another culture, you will be most effective if you can identify the differences between your cultures and accommodate those differences without expecting either the other party or yourself to give up your identity.[9]

Recognizing Cultural Differences

Y. A. Cho, chief operating officer of Korean Airlines, says, "In dealing with American business people, I'm amazed at how naive most are about other cultures and the way that oth-

Culture is a shared system of symbols, beliefs, attitudes, values, expectations, and norms for behavior.

Subcultures are distinct groups that exist within a major culture.

Intercultural communication is the process of sending and receiving messages between people of different cultures.

ers do business."[10] When you write to or speak with someone in another culture, you encode your message using the assumptions of your own culture. However, the receiver decodes it according to the assumptions of the other culture, so your meaning may be misunderstood. The greater the difference between the sender's culture and the receiver's culture, the greater the chance for misunderstanding.[11]

Cultural misunderstandings often arise when companies with entirely different ways of doing business join forces. Look at Daimler-Benz and Chrysler. When these two companies announced their engagement, employees and investors alike were stunned.[12] Except for the fact that both companies make cars, they couldn't be more different in culture and product. Pegged as a middle-class company that is willing to take chances, Chrysler sells over 2.3 million Jeeps, vans, rugged pickup trucks, and cars annually—mostly to U.S. customers. Daimler-Benz, by contrast, is slow-moving and intensely conservative. Each year it sells about 726,000 cars that ooze quality and luxury and appeal to an elite group of mostly European buyers.[13]

Operational differences such as these are just the tip of the problem iceberg. Cultural differences will also show up in employees' social values, ideas of status, decision-making habits, attitudes toward time, use of space, cultural context, body language, manners, and legal and ethical behavior. Acknowledging and exploring these differences is an important step toward understanding how meshed cultures affect the way we do business and communicate. Without an understanding of these differences, businesspeople can unknowingly act improperly and unacceptable, hurting their own reputations and those of their organizations.[14]

Social Values

Although the United States is home to millions of people having different religions and values, the major influence is the Puritan work ethic. The predominant U.S. view is that money solves many problems, that material comfort (earned by individual effort) is a sign of superiority, and that people who work hard are better than those who don't. By and large, people in the United States assume that people from other cultures also dislike poverty and value hard work. In fact, many societies condemn materialism, and some prize a more carefree lifestyle.

As a culture, people in the United States are goal oriented. They want to get their work done efficiently, and they assume that everyone else does too. They think they're improving things if they can figure out a way for two people using modern methods to do the same work as four people using the "old way." In countries such as India and Pakistan, where unemployment is high, creating jobs is more important than working efficiently. Executives in those countries would rather employ four workers than two, and their values influence their actions as well as the way they encode and decode messages.

Roles and Status

Culture dictates the roles people play, including who communicates with whom, what they communicate, and in what way. For example, in many countries women still don't play a prominent role in business, so female executives who visit these countries may find that they're not taken seriously as businesspeople. When in modern Western Europe, women can usually behave as they would in the United States, but they should be more cautious in Latin American and Eastern European countries, and they should be extremely cautious in the Middle East and the Far East.[15]

Concepts of status also differ. Most U.S. executives send status signals that reflect materialistic values. The big boss has a large corner office, deep carpets, an expensive desk, and handsome accessories. In other cultures, status is communicated in other ways. The highest-ranking executives in France sit in the middle of an open area, surrounded by lower-level employees. In the Middle East, fine possessions are reserved for the home, and business is conducted in cramped and modest quarters. An executive from another culture who assumes that such office arrangements indicate a lack of status would be making a big mistake.

During Nelson Mandela's decades of struggling for human rights and democracy, he has been the victim of, and the victor over, cultural differences. Now president of South Africa, Mandela is working to reassure the members of all cultures that he and his government value all minorities for their contributions.

GOING ONLINE
MASTER THE ART OF INTERCULTURAL COMMUNICATION
"Building bridges between people" is the motto of the International/Intercultural Development Education Connection. On the home page, click "Communication" and then click "General Communication" to visit dozens of interesting electronic sources that will help you communicate more effectively with intercultural audiences.

http://www.escotet.com/index1.html

People from the United States emphasize hard work, material success, and efficiency more than many other people do.

People from other cultures demonstrate their status differently than do people in the United States.

Decision-Making Customs

In the United States and Canada, businesspeople try to reach decisions as quickly and efficiently as possible. The top people are concerned with reaching an agreement on the main points, and they leave the details to be worked out later by others. In Greece, that approach would backfire. A Greek executive assumes that anyone who ignores the details is being evasive and untrustworthy. Spending time on each little point is considered a mark of good faith. Similarly, Latin Americans prefer to make their deals slowly, after much discussion.

Many cultural groups take longer than U.S. and Canadian businesspeople to reach decisions, and many rely more heavily on group consensus.

Cultures also differ in terms of who makes the decisions. In the United States, many organizations are dominated by a single figure who says yes or no to the major deals. It is the same in Pakistan, where you can get a decision quickly if you reach the highest-ranking executive.[16] In other cultures, decision making is shared. In Japan, the negotiating team arrives at a consensus through an elaborate, time-consuming process. Agreement must be complete—there is no majority rule. And, as do businesses everywhere, Japanese firms expect their managers to follow the same decision-making process regardless of whether they're in Tokyo or in Toledo, Ohio.

Concepts of Time

Differing perceptions of time are another factor that can lead to misunderstandings. German and U.S. executives see time as a way to plan the business day efficiently, focusing on only one task during each scheduled period. Because time is so limited, German and U.S. executives try to get to the point quickly when communicating.

Although businesspeople in the United States, Germany, and some other nations see time as a way to organize the business day efficiently, people in other cultures see time as more flexible.

However, executives from Latin America and Asia see time as more flexible. In those cultures, building a foundation for the business relationship is more important than meeting a deadline for completing a task. Seen in this light, it's not surprising that people in such cultures do not observe strict schedules. Instead, they take whatever time is needed to get to know each other and to explore the background issues.[17]

A salesperson from Chicago who calls on a client in Mexico City and is kept waiting 30 minutes in the outer office might infer that the client attaches a low priority to the visit and might feel angry and insulted. In fact, the Mexican client doesn't mean to imply anything at all by the delay. In Mexico, a wait of 30 minutes is a matter of course; the workday isn't expected to follow a rigid, preset schedule.[18]

Concepts of Personal Space

People from various cultures have different "comfort zones."

Like time, space means different things in different cultures. The classic story of a conversation between a U.S. executive and a Latin American executive is that the interaction may begin at one end of a hallway and end up at the other, with neither party aware of having moved. During the conversation the Latin American executive instinctively moves closer to the U.S. executive, who unconsciously steps back, resulting in an intercultural dance across the floor.

People in Canada and the United States usually stand about five feet apart during a business conversation. Five feet is uncomfortably close for people from Germany or Japan, but for Arabs or Latin Americans it is uncomfortably far. Because of these differing concepts of personal space, a Canadian manager may react negatively (without knowing exactly why) when a Latin American colleague moves closer during their conversation. And the Latin American colleague may react negatively (again, without knowing why) when the Canadian manager backs away.

Cultural Context

Whereas U.S. businesspeople rely mostly on words to convey meaning, people in other cultures rely heavily on situational cues and implicit understanding.

One of the ways we assign meaning to a message is according to its **cultural context,** the pattern of physical cues and implicit understanding that conveys meaning between two members of the same culture. However, people convey contextual meaning differently from culture to culture. In the **high-context culture** of South Korea or Taiwan, people rely less on verbal communication and more on the context of nonverbal actions and environmental setting to convey meaning. The rules of everyday life are rarely explicit in high-context cultures; as they grow up, people learn how to recognize situational cues (such as gestures and tone of voice) and how to respond as expected.[19]

In the **low-context culture** of the United States or Germany, people rely more on verbal communication and less on circumstances and implied meaning. Expectations are usually spelled out in a low-context culture through explicit statements, such as "Please wait until I'm finished" or "You're welcome to browse." In this way, a businessperson in a low-context culture not only explains his or her own actions but also cues the other person about what to do or what to expect next.[20]

Imagine the confusion and frustration of someone from a low-context culture trying to sell products to a client from a high-context culture. If the client says nothing after the salesperson names a price, the salesperson may assume that the silence means rejection and may try to save the sale by naming a lower figure. However, in the high-context culture, silence means only that the client is considering the first offer. By misinterpreting this silence and lowering the price, the salesperson loses needed profits.

Body Language

Gestures help members of a culture clarify confusing messages, but differences in body language are a major source of misunderstanding during intercultural communication. Furthermore, don't make the mistake of assuming that someone from another country who speaks your language has mastered the body language of your culture. Instead, learn some of the basic differences in the way people supplement their words with body movement. Take the signal for *no*. People in the United States and Canada shake their heads back and forth; people in Bulgaria nod up and down; people in Japan move their right hands; people in Sicily raise their chins. Or take eye contact. Businesspeople in the United States assume that a person who won't meet their gaze is evasive and dishonest. However, in many parts of Latin America and Asia, keeping your eyes lowered is a sign of respect, and among many Native American groups, a child's maintaining eye contact with an adult is a sign of disrespect.[21]

Sometimes people from different cultures misread an intentional signal sent by body language; sometimes they overlook the signal entirely or assume that a meaningless gesture is significant. An Arab man indicates a romantic interest in a woman by running a hand backward across his hair; most Westerners would not understand the significance of this gesture.[22] An Egyptian might mistakenly assume that a Westerner who exposes the sole of his or her shoe is offering a grave insult. The more open you are to nonverbal messages, the better you will communicate in your own and other cultures.[23]

Social Behavior and Manners

What is polite in one culture may be considered rude in another. In Arab countries, it's impolite to take gifts to a man's wife but acceptable to take gifts to his children. In Germany, giving a woman a red rose is considered a romantic invitation, inappropriate if you are trying to establish a business relationship with her. In India you might be invited to visit someone's home "any time." If you're not familiar with the culture, you may be reluctant to make an unexpected visit, and you might therefore wait for a definite invitation. But your failure to take the invitation literally is an insult, a sign that you do not care to develop the friendship.

In any culture, rules of etiquette may be formal or informal. Formal rules are the specifically taught "rights" and "wrongs" of how to behave in common social situations, such as table manners at meals. When formal rules are violated, members of a culture can explain why they feel upset. In contrast, informal social rules are more difficult to identify and are usually learned by watching how people behave and then imitating that behavior. Informal rules govern how males and females are supposed to behave, when it is appropriate to use a person's first name, and so on. When informal rules are violated, members of a culture are likely to feel uncomfortable, although they may not be able to say exactly why.[24]

Legal and Ethical Behavior

From culture to culture, what is considered legal and ethical behavior varies widely. In some countries, companies are expected to pay government officials extra fees for approving government contracts. These payments aren't illegal or unethical, merely routine. However, the same payments are seen as bribes in the United States, Sweden, and many other countries,

Deepak Chopra, M.D., is one of the most prolific (and profitable) authors on the planet, with best-sellers, clinics, audiotapes, and other communication products featuring his name and smiling face. What brought him fame and fortune? A sincere objective of helping people—and a keen talent for translating Eastern concepts to a Western audience. His speaking and writing skills are top-drawer, and his intercultural communication talents are unsurpassed.

Variations in the meaning of body language can cause problems because people are unaware of the messages they are transmitting.

The rules of polite behavior vary from country to country.

People often encounter differing standards of legal and ethical behavior in the course of doing business in other countries.

BEHIND THE SCENES AT PARKER PEN
Do as the Natives Do—But Should You Eat the Roast Gorilla Hand?

If offered, you should eat the roast gorilla hand—so says Roger E. Axtel, vice president of the Parker Pen Company. In his 18 years living and traveling in the 154 countries where Parker sells pens, Axtel learned that communicating with foreign nationals demands more than merely learning their language. The gorilla hand (served rising from mashed yams) was prepared for a meal in honor of a U.S. family-planning expert who was visiting a newly emerged African nation, and the guest of honor was expected to eat it, so he did. Learning the behavior expected of you as you conduct business internationally can be daunting if not overwhelming. Axtel recommends the following basic rules to help you get off to a good start.

1. *What's in a name?* The first transaction between even ordinary citizens—and the first chance to make an impression for better or worse—is an exchange of names. In the United States, there is little to get wrong. Not so elsewhere. In the Eastern Hemisphere, where name frequently denotes social rank or family status, a mistake can be an outright insult, and so can using someone's given name without permission. One overseas deputy director for an international telecommunications corporation always asks, "What would you like me to call you?" He advises that it's "better to ask several times than to get it wrong." Even then, "I err on the side of formality." An-

other frequent traveler insists that his company provide him with a list of key people he will meet—country by country, surnames underlined—to be memorized on the flight over.

2. *Eat, drink, and be wary.* Away from home, eating is a language all its own. No words can match it for saying "glad to meet you . . . glad to be doing business with you . . . glad to have you here." Mealtime is no time for a thanks-but-no-thanks response. Accepting what is on your plate is tantamount to accepting host, country, and company. So no matter how tough things may be to swallow, swallow. Often what's offered constitutes your host country's proudest culinary achievements. Squeamishness comes not so much from the thing itself as from your unfamiliarity with it. After all, a sheep's eye (a delicacy in Saudi Arabia) has remarkably the same look and consistency as an oyster. Most business travelers say there's no alternative to taking at least a few bites. It helps to slice unfamiliar food very thin so that you minimize the texture and the reminder of where it came from. Another useful dodge is not knowing what you're eating. What's for dinner? Don't ask.

3. *Clothes can make you or break you.* Wherever you are, try not to look out of place. Wear something you look natural in, something you know how to wear, and something that fits in with your surroundings. For ex-

where they are both illegal and unethical. In fact, U.S.-based companies are generally not allowed to bribe officials anywhere in the world. (The U.S. Foreign Corrupt Practices Act, which governs company payments to foreign officials, allows a few exceptions, such as small payments that speed but don't actually influence government actions.)[25]

When you conduct business around the world, you may also find that other legal systems differ from what you're accustomed to. In the United Kingdom and the United States, someone is innocent until proven guilty, a principle that is rooted in English common law. In Mexico and Turkey, someone is presumed guilty until proven innocent, a principle that is rooted in the Napoleonic code.[26] These distinctions can be particularly important if your firm must communicate about a legal dispute in another country.

Dealing with Language Barriers

Language shapes our world view, dictating our perception of the universe, so the potential for misunderstanding cross-cultural interaction is great.[27] Even the way information is approached and processed can differ greatly among cultures. For example, an English speaker feels responsible for transmitting the meaning of a message, but a Chinese speaker is more likely to expect the receiver to discover the meaning in a message that uses indirectness and metaphor. Further, an English speaker often places sentences in a chronological sequence to establish a cause-and-effect pattern. However, a Chinese speaker often begins by creating a context with generalizations that form a web (or frame) to receive and support a given topic.[28]

Language differences can trip you up even if you're a U.S. executive doing business in an English-speaking country. A U.S. paper products manufacturer learned this the hard

ample, a woman dressed in a tailored suit, even with high heels and flowery blouse, looks startlingly masculine in a country full of diaphanous saris. More appropriate attire might be a silky, loose-fitting dress in a bright color. With few exceptions, the general rule everywhere, whether for business, for eating out, or even for visiting people at home, is that you should be very conservative.

4. *English spoken here—you hope.* Many people outside the United States speak English. Even where people from the

When trying to communicate with people in a culture different from your own, eating unfamiliar foods may be a challenge. Even so, experts such as Parker Pen's Roger Axtel advise you to eat at least a little, even if your choice is between mealworms and crickets.

United States aren't understood, their language often is. Of course, some languages are incomprehensible as pronounced by outsiders, but no matter how you twist most native tongues, some meaning gets through—or at least you get an A for effort. Memorizing a toast or greeting nearly always serves to break the ice, if not the communication barrier.

Apply Your Knowledge

1. Select a non-English-speaking nation that trades with the United States. With the help of either a foreign language instructor or a translation dictionary, type or print the accepted translation for the following business terms: (a) contract, (b) sale, (c) delivery date, (d) duplicate copies, and (e) negligence. Separately, show three friends the list of translated terms only. Ask each to pronounce the terms. In your notebook, spell phonetically the pronunciations you hear. When finished, compare the pronunciations. How different are they? Which terms produced the greatest variety?

2. Should colleges and universities that offer a business major require a separate degree or certification program for international business? What courses from the curriculum at your school would you require for such a degree or certificate? What new courses can you suggest?

---

way while trying to crack the English market for paper napkins by using its usual advertising slogan: "There is no finer paper napkin for the dinner table." Unfortunately for the U.S. company, *napkin* is the British term for *diaper*.[29]

Also likely are misunderstandings involving vocabulary, pronunciation, or usage when U.S. businesspeople deal with people who use English as a second language—and some 650 million people fall into this category. Some of these millions are extremely fluent; others have only an elementary command of English. Although you may miss a few subtleties when dealing with those less fluent in your own language, you'll still be able to communicate. However, don't assume that the other person understands everything you say. Your message can be mangled by slang, idioms, and local accents. One group of English-speaking Japanese employees who transferred to Toyota's U.S. office had to enroll in a special course to learn that "Jeat yet?" means "Did you eat yet?" and that "Cannahepya?" means "Can I help you?"

When you deal with people who don't speak your language at all, you have three options: You can learn their language, use an intermediary or a translator, or teach them your language. Becoming fluent in a new language requires a major commitment. At the U.S. State Department, foreign service officers take six months of language training and then continue their studies at their foreign posts. Even the Berlitz method, famous for the speed of its results, requires a month of intensive effort. Language courses can be quite expensive as well. So unless you're planning to spend several years abroad or to make frequent trips over an extended period, learning another language may take more time and more money than you can afford.

A more practical approach is to use an intermediary or a translator. An experienced translator can analyze a message, understand its meaning in the cultural context, consider

English is the most prevalent language in international business, but it's a mistake to assume that everyone understands it.

Watch for clues to be sure that your message is getting through to people who don't speak your language.

If you have a long-term business relationship with people of another culture, it is helpful to learn their language.

how to convey the meaning in another language, and then use verbal and nonverbal signals to encode or decode the message for someone from another culture. If your company has an overseas subsidiary, you may want to seek help from local employees who are bilingual. You can also hire bilingual professionals such as advertising consultants and lawyers.

The option of teaching other people to speak your language doesn't appear to be very practical at first glance. However, many companies do, in fact, offer language-training programs for employees. Tenneco is a U.S.-based company that instituted an English-language training program for its Spanish-speaking employees in a New Jersey plant. The training concentrated on practical English for use on the job, and, thanks to the classes, accidents and grievances both declined and productivity improved.[30] Nevertheless, requiring employees to use a specific language when they're on the job can create communication problems. In general, the magnitude of the language barrier depends on whether you are writing or speaking. Written communication is generally easier to handle.

Barriers to Written Communication

Because so many international business letters are written in English, U.S. firms don't always worry about translating their correspondence. Moreover, regardless of where they're located, some multinational companies ask all their employees to use English when writing to employees in other lands. For example, Nissan employees use English for internal memos to colleagues in other countries, even though the corporation is based in Japan. Similarly, English is the official business language of Philips, the global electronics giant based in the Netherlands.[31]

Most routine business correspondence is written in English, but marketing messages are generally translated into the language of the country where the product is to be sold.

However, many other forms of written communication must be translated. Advertisements are almost always translated into the language of the culture in which the products are being sold. Warranties, repair and maintenance manuals, and product labels require translation, as well. In addition, many multinational companies translate policy and procedure manuals for use in overseas offices. Reports from foreign branches to the home office may be written in one language and then translated into another. One multinational company, E. I. Du Pont de Nemours & Company, translates roughly 70,000 pages of documents a year.[32]

When documents are translated literally, communication can break down. For example, the advertising slogan "Come alive with Pepsi" was once mistranslated for German audiences as "Come out of the grave" and for Thai audiences as "Bring your ancestors back from the dead."[33] To overcome barriers to written communication, follow these recommendations:[34]

- Use the skills of bilingual employees or professional translators.
- Write short messages.
- Keep your wording clear and simple.
- Avoid slang.
- Use your fax machine to transmit the information (with speed and clarity).

Barriers to Oral Communication

Oral communication usually presents more problems than written communication. If you've ever studied another language, you know it's easier to write in that language than to conduct a conversation. Even if the other person speaks your language, you may have a hard time understanding the pronunciation if the person isn't proficient. For example, many nonnative English speakers can't distinguish between the English sounds *v* and *w*, so they say "wery" for "very." At the same time, many people from the United States cannot pronounce the French *r* or the German *ch*.

Differences in pronunciation, vocal inflections, and vocabulary can pose problems when you're speaking to people from other cultures.

Also, because people use their voices in different ways, listeners might misunderstand their intentions. Russian speakers, for instance, speak in flat, level tones in their native tongue. When they speak English, they maintain this pattern, and non-Russian listeners may assume that the speakers are bored or rude. Middle Easterners tend to speak more loudly than Westerners and may therefore mistakenly be considered more emotional. On the other hand, the Japanese are soft-spoken, a characteristic that implies politeness or humility to Western listeners.

Idiomatic expressions are another source of confusion. If a U.S. executive tells an Egyptian executive that a certain product "doesn't cut the mustard," chances are communication will fail. Even when the words make sense, their meanings may differ according to the situation. For example, suppose you are dining with a German woman who speaks English quite well. You inquire, "More bread?" She says, "Thank you," so you pass the breadbasket. She looks confused; then she takes the breadbasket and sets it down without taking any bread. In German, *thank you (danke)* can be used as a polite refusal as well as a signal of acceptance. If the woman had wanted more bread, she would have used the word *please* (*bitte* in German).

When speaking in English to people who speak English as a second language, you may find these guidelines helpful:

- *Try to eliminate noise.* Pronounce words clearly, stop at distinct punctuation points, and make one point at a time.
- *Look for feedback.* Be alert to signs of confusion in your listener. Realize that nods and smiles don't necessarily mean understanding.
- *Rephrase your sentence when necessary.* If someone doesn't seem to understand you, choose simpler words; don't just repeat the sentence in a louder voice.
- *Don't talk down to the other person.* Try not to overenunciate, and don't "blame" the listener for not understanding. Use phrases such as "Am I going too fast?" rather than "Is this too difficult for you?"
- *Use objective, accurate language.* Avoid throwing around adjectives such as *fantastic* and *fabulous,* which people from other cultures might consider unreal and overly dramatic.
- *Let other people finish what they have to say.* If you interrupt, you may miss something important. You'll also show a lack of respect.

Dealing with Ethnocentric Reactions

Although language and cultural differences are significant barriers to communication, they can be overcome by maintaining an open mind. Unfortunately, many of us lapse into **ethnocentrism,** the tendency to judge all other groups according to our own group's standards, behaviors, and customs. When we make such comparisons, we too often decide that our group is superior.[35]

By reacting ethnocentrically, you ignore the distinctions between your own culture and another person's culture. You assume that others will act the same way you do, that they will operate from the same assumptions, and that they will use language and symbols in the same way you do. If they do not, you may mistakenly believe that they are in error or that their way is invalid or inferior to your own. An ethnocentric reaction makes you lose sight of the possibility that your words and actions will be misunderstood. It also makes you likely to misinterpret or belittle the behavior of others.

Ethnocentric people are often prone to **stereotyping,** attempting to predict individuals' behavior or character on the basis of their membership in a particular group or class. When someone first starts to investigate the culture of another group, he or she may stereotype characteristics as a way of understanding the common tendencies of that group's members, but the next step is to move beyond the stereotypes to relationships with real people. Unfortunately, when ethnocentric people stereotype an entire group of people, they do so on the basis of limited, general, or inaccurate evidence, and they frequently develop biased attitudes toward the group.[36] They fail to communicate with individuals as they really are. Instead of talking with Abdul Karhum, unique human being, ethnocentric people think only about talking to an Arab. Although they've never met an Arab, they may already believe that all Arabs are, say, hagglers. Abdul Karhum's personal qualities become insignificant in the face of such preconceptions. Everything he says and does will be forced to fit the preconceived image, even if it's wrong.

Often, both parties in an intercultural exchange are guilty of ethnocentrism, stereotyping, and prejudice. It is little wonder, then, that misunderstandings arise. Fortunately, a healthy dose of open-mindedness can prevent a lot of problems. At Target, Rafael

Colin Powell is a former Chairman of the Joint Chiefs of Staff, a well-paid autobiographer, and a popular man to watch for a future presidential campaign. He serves as general chairman of the Presidents' Summit for America's Future, a program that encourages corporate philanthropy. Born in Harlem and raised in the South Bronx, Powell has always made a special effort to serve as a role model for young African Americans. He advises students that racism is the other person's problem and to reach down inside themselves: Rely on yourself, says Powell, just like I did.

Ethnocentrism is the tendency to judge all other groups according to your own group's standards, behaviors, and customs and to see other groups as inferior by comparison.

Stereotyping is the attempt to categorize individuals by trying to predict their behavior or character on the basis of their membership in a particular group.

Rodriguez works hard to move his people away from ethnocentrism and toward understanding and tolerance.

TIPS FOR COMMUNICATING WITH PEOPLE FROM OTHER CULTURES

You may never completely overcome linguistic and cultural barriers or ethnocentric tendencies, but you can communicate more effectively with people from other cultures if you work at it. Once you've acknowledged that cultural differences exist, the next step is to learn as much as possible about those cultures in which you plan to do business. You can also develop general skills for dealing with cultural diversity in your own and in other countries. If you'll be negotiating across cultures, it's important to learn how to conduct yourself and what to expect. Finally, you'll want to consider how to handle both written and oral communication with people from other cultures.

CHECKLIST FOR DOING BUSINESS ABROAD

A. Social Customs

1. How do people react to strangers? Are they friendly? Hostile? Reserved?
2. What words and gestures do people use to greet each other?
3. What are the appropriate manners when you enter and leave a room? Should you bow? Nod? Shake hands?
4. How are names used for introductions? How are introductions handled (by age, gender, authority)?
5. What are the attitudes toward touching people?
6. How do you express appreciation for an invitation to lunch or dinner or to someone's home? Should you bring a gift? Send flowers? Write a thank-you note?
7. Does custom dictate how, when, or where people are expected to sit in social or business situations?
8. Are any phrases, facial expressions, or hand gestures considered rude?
9. How close do people stand when talking?
10. How do you attract the attention of a waiter in a restaurant? Do you tip the waiter?
11. When is it rude to refuse an invitation? How do you politely refuse?
12. What are the acceptable eye contact patterns?
13. What gestures indicate agreement? Disagreement? Respect?
14. What topics may be discussed in a social setting? In a business setting? What topics are unacceptable?

B. Concepts of Time

1. How is time expressed?
2. What are the generally accepted working hours?
3. How do businesspeople view scheduled appointments?
4. How do people react to time in social situations?

C. Clothing and Food

1. What occasions require special clothing? What colors are associated with mourning? With love? With joy?
2. Are some types of clothing considered taboo for one sex or the other?
   - a. What is appropriate business attire for men?
   - b. What is appropriate business attire for women?
3. What are the attitudes toward human body odors? Are deodorants/perfumes used?
4. How many times a day do people eat? How are hands or utensils used when eating?
5. What types of places, food, and drink are appropriate for business entertainment? Where is the seat of honor at a table?

D. Political Patterns

1. How stable is the political situation? How does its stability (or instability) affect business inside and outside the country?
2. How is political power manifested? Military power? Economic strength?
3. What are the traditional institutions of government?
4. What channels are used for expressing political opinion?
   - a. What channels are used to express official government positions?
   - b. What channels are used to express unofficial government positions?
5. What media of information are important? Who controls them?

Learning About a Culture

When you're preparing to do business with people from a particular culture, you'll find that you can communicate more effectively if you study that culture in advance. Before Procter & Gamble advertises a new product outside the United States, company researchers thoroughly investigate what people want and need. That way, P&G marketers can shape the advertising message to the language and customs of the particular culture.

If you're planning to live in another country or to do business there repeatedly, you might want to learn the language. The same holds true if you'll be working closely with a subculture that has its own language, such as Vietnamese Americans. Even if you're doing business in your own language, you show respect by making the effort to learn the subculture's language. In addition, you'll learn something about the culture and the customs of its people. If you don't have the time or the opportunity to learn a new language, at least learn a few words.

Read books and articles about the culture and talk to people who have done business with that culture's members. Concentrate on learning something about the culture's his-

Learning as much as possible about another culture will enhance your ability to communicate with its members.

---

6. In social or business situations, is it appropriate to talk politics?

E. Workforce Diversity
1. Is the society homogeneous?
2. What ethnic groups are represented?
3. What languages are spoken?
4. How diverse is the workforce?
5. What are the current and projected immigration patterns? How do these trends influence the composition of the workforce?

F. Religion and Folk Beliefs
1. To which religious groups do people belong? Is one predominant?
2. How do religious beliefs influence daily activities?
3. Which places have sacred value? Which objects? Which events?
4. Is there a tolerance for minority religions?
5. How do religious holidays affect business and government activities?
6. Does religion affect attitudes toward smoking? Drinking? Gambling?
7. Does religion require or prohibit eating specific foods? At specific times?
8. What objects or actions portend good luck? Bad luck?

G. Economic and Business Institutions
1. What are the primary resources and principal products?
2. What kinds of vocational and technological training are offered?
3. What are the attitudes toward education?
   ■ a. Do most businesspersons have a college degree?
   ■ b. Are women educated as well as men?

4. Are businesses generally of one type?
   ■ a. Are they large public corporations?
   ■ b. Are they government owned or controlled?
   ■ c. Are they family businesses?
5. Is it appropriate to do business by telephone?
6. Do managers make business decisions unilaterally, or do they involve employees?
7. Are there any customs related to exchanging business cards?
8. How are status and seniority shown in an organization? In a business meeting?
9. Are businesspeople expected to socialize before conducting business?

H. Ethics, Values, and Laws
1. Is money or a gift expected in exchange for arranging business transactions? What are the legal, ethical, and business consequences of giving what's expected? Of not giving?
2. What ethical issues might affect business transactions?
3. What legal issues might affect business transactions?
4. Is competitiveness or cooperation of greater importance?
5. What are the attitudes toward work? Toward money?
6. Is politeness more important than factual honesty?
7. How is a *friend* defined? What are the responsibilities of a friend?
8. What virtues are admired in a business associate? In a friend?

tory, religion, politics, values, and customs. Find out about a country's subcultures, especially its business subculture, and any special rules or protocol. Here is a brief sampling of intercultural communication tips from seasoned business travelers:

- In Spain let a handshake last five to seven strokes; pulling away too soon may be interpreted as rejection. In France, however, the preferred handshake is a single stroke.
- Don't give a gift of liquor in Arab countries.
- In Pakistan don't be surprised when businesspeople excuse themselves in the middle of a meeting to conduct prayers. Muslims pray five times a day.
- Allow plenty of time to get to know the people you're dealing with in Africa; they're suspicious of people who are in a hurry.
- You'll insult your hosts if you turn down food, drink, or hospitality of any kind in Arab countries. But don't accept too quickly, either. A polite refusal (such as "I don't want to put you to any trouble") is expected before you finally accept.
- Stress the longevity of your company when dealing with German, Dutch, and Swiss firms.

> Learning general intercultural communication skills will help you adapt in any culture, which is important if you interact with people from a variety of cultures or subcultures.

These are just a few examples of the variations in customs that make intercultural business so interesting. This chapter's Checklist for Doing Business Abroad (pages 48–49) can help you start your investigation of another culture by examining its social customs, concepts of time, clothing and food, political patterns, workforce diversity, religion and folk beliefs, economic and business institutions, ethics, values, and laws.

Developing Intercultural Communication Skills

Learning all you can about a particular culture is a good way to figure out how to send and receive intercultural messages effectively, but remember two important points: First, don't expect ever to understand another culture completely. No matter how much you study Italian culture, for example, you'll never be an Italian or share the experiences of having grown up in Italy. Second, don't fall into the overgeneralization trap; don't look at people as stereotypical "Italians" or "African Americans" and then never move beyond that view. The trick is to learn useful general information and, at the same time, to be aware of and open to variations and individual differences.

These two points are especially important if you interact with people from a variety of cultures or subcultures, as Target's Rodriguez does. You may not have the time or interest to learn a lot about every culture, but you can communicate more effectively if you develop general skills that help you adapt in any culture:[37]

When Wilma Mankiller became the first woman chief of the Cherokee Nation, she learned that even within a culture, biases can exist. But she stuck it out, overcoming death threats and less frightening resistance to win her people's hearts and a second term in office, meanwhile setting a positive example for women and minorities. She's now "retired" to a steady job of writing and speaking to promote intercultural understanding. She recently received the Medal of Freedom at the White House.

- *Take responsibility for communication.* Don't assume that it's the other person's job to make the communication succeed.
- *Withhold judgment.* Learn to listen to the whole story and accept differences in others without judging them.
- *Show respect.* Learn how respect is communicated—through gestures, eye contact, and so on—in various cultures.
- *Empathize.* Imagine the other person's feelings and point of view; consider what he or she is trying to communicate and why.
- *Tolerate ambiguity.* Learn to control your frustration when placed in an unfamiliar or confusing situation.
- *Look beyond the superficial.* Don't be distracted by such things as dress, appearance, or environmental discomforts.
- *Be patient and persistent.* If you want to communicate with someone from another culture, don't give up easily.
- *Recognize your own cultural biases.* Learn to identify when your assumptions are different from the other person's.
- *Be flexible.* Be prepared to change your habits and attitudes when communicating with someone from another culture.
- *Emphasize common ground.* Look for similarities from which to work.

- *Send clear messages.* Make both your verbal and nonverbal signals clear and consistent.
- *Increase your cultural sensitivity.* Learn about variations in customs and practices so that you'll be more aware of potential areas for miscommunication.
- *Deal with the individual.* Communicate with each person as an individual, not as a stereotypical representative of another group.
- *Learn when to be direct.* Investigate each culture so that you know when to send your message in a straightforward manner and when to be indirect.

These skills will help you communicate with anybody, regardless of culture. For more ideas on how to improve communication in the workplace, see this chapter's Checklist for Communicating with a Culturally Diverse Workforce.

CHECKLIST FOR COMMUNICATING WITH A CULTURALLY DIVERSE WORKFORCE

A. Accepting Cultural Differences
1. Adjust the level of communication to the education level of your employees.
2. Encourage employees to openly discuss their culture's customs so that differences won't seem strange or inexplicable.
3. Create a formal forum in which all employees can become familiar with the specific beliefs and practices of the cultures represented in the company workforce.
4. Provide training to help employees recognize and overcome ethnocentric reactions and stereotyping.
5. Make available books, articles, and videotapes about various cultures so that interested employees can learn more.
6. Help stamp out negative or stereotyped labels by paying attention to how people identify their own groups.

B. Handling Oral and Written Communications
1. Define and explain key terms that people will need to know on the job.
2. Repeat and summarize information frequently to emphasize important points.
3. Use familiar words whenever possible.
4. Don't cover too much information at one time.
5. Be specific and explicit, using descriptive words, exact measurements, and examples when possible.
6. Give the reason for asking employees to follow a certain procedure and explain what will happen if the procedure is not followed.
7. Use written summaries and visual aids (when appropriate) to clarify your points.
   - a. Give employees written information they can take away to go over later.
   - b. Use pictures that show actions (especially when explaining safety procedures).
   - c. Use international symbols (such as ∅), which are understood cross-culturally.
   - d. Augment written material with video presentations to make the material come alive.

8. Demonstrate and encourage the right way to complete a task, use a tool, and so on.
9. Reduce barriers caused by language differences.
   - a. Offer managers training in the language of the employees they supervise.
   - b. Offer employees training in the language that most people in the company (and customers) use.
   - c. Ask bilingual employees and managers to serve as translators when needed, but rotate this assignment to avoid resentment.
   - d. Recruit bilingual employees and managers or have trained translators available to give the organization greater flexibility in dealing with linguistic differences.
   - e. Print important health and safety instructions in as many languages as needed to enable all employees to understand.

C. Assessing How Well You've Been Understood
1. Be alert to facial expressions and other nonverbal signs that indicate confusion or embarrassment.
2. Encourage employees to ask questions in private and in writing.
3. Observe how employees use the information you've provided to do their jobs, and review any points that may have been misunderstood.
4. Research the nonverbal reactions of other cultures so that you're prepared to spot subtle signs of misunderstanding.

D. Offering Feedback to Improve Communication
1. Focus on the positive by explaining what *should* be done rather than on the negative by discussing what *shouldn't* be done.
2. Offer feedback in terms of the person's behaviors and the situation, rather than a judgment about the person.
3. Be supportive as you offer feedback, and reassure individuals that their skills and contributions are important.

Negotiating Across Cultures

People from other cultures often have different approaches to negotiation and may vary in their tolerance for open disagreement.

Whether you're trying to make a sale, buy a business, or rent an office, negotiating with people from other cultures can test your communication skills. More U.S. companies than ever are trying to form alliances with foreign companies, and more than half of these partnerships fail.[38] First, you may find that your approach to negotiation differs from the approach of the people with whom you're negotiating. For example, negotiators from the United States tend to take a relatively impersonal view of negotiations. They see their goals in economic terms and usually presume, at least at the outset, that the other party is trustworthy. In contrast, Chinese and Japanese negotiators prefer a more sociable negotiating atmosphere. They try to forge personal ties as the basis for building trust throughout the negotiating process. In their view, any immediate economic gains are less important than establishing and maintaining a long-term relationship. French negotiators are likely to be even less personal than U.S., Chinese, and Japanese negotiators. They may favor an atmosphere of formal hospitality and start by distrusting the other party.[39]

Second, cultures differ in their tolerance for open disagreement. Although U.S. negotiators typically enjoy confrontational, debate-oriented negotiation, Japanese negotiators shun such tactics. To avoid the unpleasant feelings that might result from open conflict, Japanese companies use a go-between, or a third person, to assist in the negotiation. Chinese negotiators also try to prevent public conflict. They make concessions slowly and stay away from proposal-counterproposal methods. If you try to get a Chinese negotiating team to back down from a position they have taken, you will cause them to lose face—and you will very likely lose the deal.

In addition, negotiators from other cultures may use different problem-solving techniques, protocol, schedules, and decision-making methods. If you learn about your counterparts' culture before you start to negotiate, you'll be better equipped to understand their viewpoints. Moreover, showing flexibility, courtesy, patience, and a friendly attitude will go a long way toward finding a solution that works for both sides.

Handling Written Communication

Unless you are fluent in the language of your intended audience, you will ordinarily write in your own language and, if needed, have your letters or other written materials translated by a professional translator. Be especially concerned with clarity:

- Use short, precise words that say exactly what you mean.
- Rely on specific terms and concrete examples to explain your points.
- Stay away from slang, idioms, jargon, and buzz words. Abbreviations, acronyms (such as CAD/CAM), and unfamiliar product names may also lead to confusion.
- Construct sentences that are shorter and simpler than those you might use when writing to someone fluent in your own language.
- Use short paragraphs. Each paragraph should stick to one topic and should be no more than eight to ten lines.
- Help readers follow your train of thought by using transitional phrases. Precede related points with expressions such as *in addition* and *first, second, third.*

International business letters generally have a formal tone and a relatively elaborate style.

Your word choice should also reflect the relationship between you and your audience. In general, U.S. businesspeople will want to be somewhat more formal than they would be when writing to people in their own country. In many cultures, people use a more elaborate style, so your audience will expect more formal language in your letter. Consider the letter in Figure 3.2. It might sound stilted to a U.S. reader, but it is typical of business letters in many other countries. In Germany, business letters usually open with a reference to the business relationship and close with a compliment to the recipient. Of course, be careful not to carry formality to extremes, or you'll sound unnatural.

Letter writers in other countries also use various techniques to organize their thoughts. If you are aware of some of their practices, you'll be able to concentrate on the message without passing judgment on the writers. Letters from Japanese businesspeople, for ex-

This letter was written by a supplier in Germany to a nearby retailer. The tone is more formal than would be used in the United States, but the writer clearly focuses on his audience.

Figure 3.2
In-Depth Critique: German Business Letter, with Translation

Furtwangen Handcrafts
Kussenhofstrasse 150
Furtwangen, Germany

Herrn
Karl Wieland
Geschäftsführer
Schwarzwald-Geschenke
Friedrichstraße 98

70174 Stuttgart
GERMANY

15. Mai 1999

Sehr geehrter Herr Wieland,

Da die Touristensaison bald beginnt, möchten wir die Gelegenheit ergreifen, Ihnen unsere neue Reihe handgeschnitzter Kuckucksuhren vorzustellen. Im letzten Jahr waren Sie so freundlich, zwei Dutzend unserer Uhren zu kaufen. In Anerkennung unserer guten Geschäftsbeziehugen bieten wir Ihnen nunmehr die Möglichkeit, die neuen Modelle auszuwählen, bevor wir diese Reihe anderen Geschäften zum Kauf anbieten.

Wie Sie wissen, verwenden unsere Kunsthandwerker nur das beste Holz. Nach alt-bewährten Mustern, die von Generation zu Generation weitergereicht werden, schnitzen sie sorgfältig jedes Detail von Hand. Unsere Uhrwerke sind von hervorra-gender Qualität, und wir testen jede Uhr, bevor sie bemalt und versandt wird. Auf alle Furtwangener Kunsthandwerk-Uhren geben wir eine Garantie von 5 Jahren.

Beiliegend erhalten Sie eine Ausgabe unserer neuesten Broschüre und ein Bestellformular. Um unserer Wertschätzung Ausdruck zu verleihen, übernehmen wir die Versandkosten, wenn Sie vor dem 15, Juni bestellen.

Wir wünschen Ihnen weiterhin viel Erfolg in Ihrer neuen Stuttgarter Niederlassung. Wir sind davon überzeugt, daß Sie mit Ihrer größeren Ausstellungsfläche und er-weitertem Angebot Ihre Stammkunden zufriedenstellen werden und viele neue Besucher gewinnen werden.

Mit freundlichen Grüßen

Frederick Semper

Frederick Semper

ample, are slow to come to the point. They typically begin with a remark about the season or weather. This is followed by an inquiry about your health or congratulations on your success. A note of thanks for your patronage might come next. After these preliminaries, the main idea is introduced.

Handling Oral Communication

Some transactions simply cannot be handled without face-to-face contact. In many countries, business relationships are based on personal relationships, and until you establish rapport nothing happens. In addition, personal contact gives you the benefit of immediate feedback so that you can clarify your own message as well as the other person's. As a consequence,

Face-to-face communication lets you establish a personal relationship with people from other cultures and gives you the benefit of immediate feedback.

Figure 3.2
(Continued)

Furtwangen Handcrafts
Kussenhofstrasse 150
Furtwangen, Germany

The addressee's title, Geschäftsführer, literally means "business leader": A common English translation would be "managing director."

Mister
Karl Wieland
Business Leader
Black Forest Gifts
Friedrichstrasse 98

70174 Stuttgart
GERMANY

May 15, 1999

Very honorable Mister Wieland,

Because the tourist season will begin soon, we would like to seize the opportunity to introduce our new line of hand-carved cuckoo clocks to you. Last year you were so friendly as to buy two dozen of our clocks. In recognition of our good business relationship, we now offer you the opportunity to select the new models before we offer this line to other businesses for purchase.

By offering the retailer an early selection of products, a five-year guarantee, and free shipping costs for an early order, Herr Semper shows his concern for his audience.

As you know, our artisans use only the best wood. According to time-honored patterns that are passed on from generation to generation, they carefully carve every detail by hand. Our clockworks are of superior quality, and we test every clock before it is painted and shipped. We give you a guarantee of five years on all Furtwangen Handcrafts clocks.

Enclosed you will find a copy of our newest brochure and an order form. To express our appreciation, we take over the shipping costs if you order before June 15.

We continue to wish you a lot of success in your new Stuttgart location. We are convinced that you will satisfy your regular clientele with your larger exhibition area and expanded stock and will gain many new visitors.

With friendly greetings

Frederick Semper

Frederick Semper

The closing compliment is typical of German business letters.

Also note that, in German business letters, the sender's title is not included under the typed name on the closing block.

executives in charge of international operations often have a hectic travel schedule. When Procter & Gamble's current CEO was head of the international division, he spent nearly 70 percent of his time meeting with managers and high-level contacts in other countries.[40]

When using oral communication, be alert to the possibilities for misunderstanding. Recognize that you may inadvertently be sending conflicting signals or that you may be misreading the other person's cues. To help overcome language and cultural barriers, follow these suggestions:

- Try to be aware of unintentional meanings that may be read into your message. Clarify your true intent with repetition and examples.
- Listen carefully and patiently. If you do not understand a comment, ask the person to repeat it.
- Recognize that gestures and expressions mean different things in different cultures. If the other person's body language seems at odds with the message, take time to clarify the meaning.

- Adapt your conversation style to the other person's. Whether the other person appears to be direct and straightforward or indirect and oblique, adjust your style to match.
- At the end of a conversation, be sure that you and the other person agree on what has been said and decided. Clarify what will happen next.
- If appropriate, follow up by writing a letter or memo summarizing the conversation and thanking the person for meeting with you.

In short, take advantage of the other person's presence to make sure that your message is getting across and that you understand his or her message too.

On the Job

SOLVING A COMMUNICATION DILEMMA AT TARGET STORES

Besides making sure his team members stock shelves efficiently, Rafael Rodriguez makes sure they work and communicate well with each other and with him. Because English is a second language for some team members, Rodriguez makes sure that each employee understands his instructions by using easily understood vocabulary, avoiding idioms, and encouraging questions. He's patient when resolving problems and misunderstandings based on cultural differences, and he follows company policy about providing plenty of opportunity for team members to learn about the cultures of their co-workers.

When Patrick Navarez immigrated to the United States from the Philippines, he was the only Asian on Rodriguez's team. Navarez quickly ran into problems when he tried to start conversations with some of his female co-workers by asking questions about their hair, nose rings, and other fashion choices. When other co-workers realized he was invading personal territory without knowing it, they explained that his questions were too personal. The whole team was eventually able to laugh with him about his cultural blunder, and not long after, Navarez had a chance to educate his co-workers. When a Vietnamese employee joined the team, other team members expected Navarez and the new employee to feel a sense of camaraderie based on their shared culture. But Navarez explained that even though they were both Asian, their languages and cultures were very different.

All levels of management at Target are ethnically diverse, and the company offers diversity training to help employees understand and work better with their co-workers. When Rodriguez visited corporate headquarters in Minneapolis, he met many executives who were Hispanic, Asian, and African American, confirming his belief that his ethnicity would not prevent his being promoted if he performed well on the job.

For many of Rodriguez's team members, the stock clerk job is their first real exposure to cultural differences. At Target, they're motivated to communicate across cultures and to cooperate in order to get the job done. They all realize that they can move up in the company, and they each have an evaluation twice a year, receiving constructive feedback on job performance. Team members who communicate well are likely to receive good evaluations, and with Rodriguez's help, the stock clerks on his team are learning early how to succeed in a diverse workforce.[41]

Your Mission: Like Rodriguez, you supervise a culturally diverse team of Target stock clerks. You want to foster cooperation among the team members and encourage them to perform well. Use your skill in intercultural communication to choose the best response in each of the following situations. Be prepared to explain why your choice is best.

1. One of your Hispanic American team members, Miguel Gomez, has started making derogatory remarks about team members who are African American. Gomez is refusing to work with them and tells you that he would rather work with other team members who are Hispanic American. How do you resolve the problem?
   a. To avoid conflict, let him work with the co-workers who make him most comfortable.
   b. Tell him he has to work with whomever you assign him to. If he refuses, fire him.
   c. Schedule a time for him to sit down with you and the African American team members so that all of you can discuss cultural differences.
   d. Speak with him privately about the company's goals regarding a diverse work force, and then sign him up for the company diversity training program.

2. Amy Tam is not stocking shelves correctly: She's stacking cans too high and mixing brands in the displays. You think language may be a problem; perhaps she does not comprehend all your instructions. How do you make sure that she understands you?
   a. Write everything down in a list so that Tam can refer to it if she has questions.
   b. Have Tam repeat what you have said. If she can repeat it, she must understand it.
   c. Speak slowly and clearly, using simple terms. Pause often, repeating or writing down phrases or instructions that Tam does not seem to understand.
   d. To get and keep Tam's attention and to clarify your meaning, speak a bit more loudly and exaggerate your hand motions.

3. You have hired a new stock clerk. Vasily Pevsner has recently immigrated from Russia. He works well alone, but he resists working together with other team members. How do you handle the situation?
   a. Stay uninvolved and let the situation resolve itself. Pevsner has to learn how to get along with the other team members.
   b. Tell the rest of the team to work harder at getting along with Pevsner.
   c. Tell Pevsner he must work with others or he will not progress in the company.
   d. Talk privately with Pevsner to find out why he doesn't want to work with others. Then help him understand the importance of working together as a team.

4. Your employees are breaking into ethnically based cliques. Members of ethnic groups eat together, socialize together, and chat in their native language while they work. Some other team members feel left out and alienated. How do you encourage a stronger team attitude?

a. Ban the use of languages other than English at work.
b. Do nothing. This is normal behavior.
c. Have regular team meetings and encourage people to mingle and get to know each other better.
d. Send all of your employees to diversity training classes.

Critical Thinking Questions

1. Your office in Turkey desperately needs the supplies that have been sitting in Turkish customs for a month. Should you bribe a customs official to speed up delivery? Explain.
2. What actions might you take to minimize the potential problems of differing concepts of time between your office in New York and your office in Venezuela?
3. A Canadian retail chain is opening a new store in Tijuana, Mexico (a border city south of San Diego, California). What cultural differences might this retailer's managers encounter when they start to hire and train local employees?
4. Your company has relocated to a U.S. city where a Vietnamese subculture is strongly established. Many of your employees will be from this subculture. What can you do to ensure effective communication between your management and the Vietnamese Americans you are currently hiring?
5. What are some of the intercultural communication issues to consider when deciding whether to accept an overseas job with a firm that's based in your own country? A job in your own country with a local branch of a foreign-owned firm? Explain.
6. How do you think company managers from a country that has a relatively homogeneous culture might react when they have to do business with the culturally diverse staff of a company in a less homogeneous country? Explain your answer.

Exercises

1. A U.S. manager wants to export T-shirts to a West African country, but a West African official expects a special payment before allowing the shipment into his country. How can the two sides resolve their different approaches without violating U.S. rules against bribing foreign officials? Team up with a classmate to role-play a meeting in which the U.S. manager tries to convince the West African official to authorize the shipment without being paid. Then discuss how the two parties handled their cultural differences.
2. You've been assigned to host a group of Swedish college students who are visiting your college for the next two weeks. They've all studied English and speak the language well. What can you tell them that will help them fit into the culture on your campus? Make a brief list of the important formal and informal behavioral rules they should understand to communicate effectively with students on your campus. Next to each item, note one problem that might occur if the Swedish visitors don't consider that rule when communicating.
3. Choose a specific country, such as India, Portugal, Bolivia, Thailand, or Nigeria—the less familiar you are with it, the better. Research the culture and write a brief summary of what a U.S. manager would need to know about concepts of personal space and rules of social behavior to conduct business successfully in that country.
4. As the director of marketing for a telecommunications firm based in Germany, you're negotiating with an official in Guangzhou, China, who's in charge of selecting a new telephone system for the city. You insist that the specifications be spelled out in detail in the contract. However, your Chinese counterpart argues that in developing a long-term business relationship, such minor details are unimportant. What can you do or say to break this intercultural deadlock and obtain the contract without causing the official to lose face?
5. Although English is the international language of business, the English spoken in the United States differs from that spoken in Great Britain. By going to the library or interviewing someone who's lived in Great Britain, research five specific phrases that have different meanings in these two cultures. What problems would you have if you were unaware of the different meanings and misinterpreted these phrases during a business conversation?
6. Germany is a low-context culture; by comparison, France and England are more high-context. These three translations of the same message were posted on a lawn in Switzerland: the German sign read, "Walking on the grass is forbidden"; the English sign read, "Please do not walk on the grass"; and the French sign read, "Those who respect their environment will avoid walking on the grass."[42] How does the language of each sign reflect the way information is conveyed in the cultural context of each nation? Write a brief (two- to three-paragraph) explanation.
7. Team up with two other students and list ten examples of slang or idiom (in your own language) that would probably be misinterpreted or misunderstood during a business conversation with someone from another culture. Next to each example, suggest other words you might use to convey the same message. Do the alternatives mean *exactly* the same as the original slang or idiom?
8. Differences in gender, age, and physical abilities contribute to the diversity of today's workforce. Working with a classmate, role-play a conversation in which:

a. A woman is being interviewed for a job by a male human resources manager
b. An older person is being interviewed for a job by a younger human resources manager
c. A person using a wheelchair is being interviewed for a job by a person who can walk

How did differences between the applicant and the interviewer shape the communication? What can you do to improve communication in such situations?

9. Imagine that you're the lead negotiator for a company that's trying to buy a factory in Prague. Your parents grew up near Prague and speak Czech at home, so you understand and speak the language fairly well. However, you wonder about the advantages and disadvantages of using a translator anyway. For example, you may have more time to think if you wait for an intermediary to translate the other side's position. Decide whether to hire a translator, and then write a brief (two- or three-paragraph) explanation of your decision.

10. What communication problems would you face if you had to defend yourself in court in another country but didn't understand the language or the legal traditions? If you were assigned a translator, how might this additional person affect the communication process? Explain.

11. Suppose you transferred to a college in another country. How would you learn appropriate classroom behavior? Make a list of what you would need to know. For example, you might want to find out how to approach your instructors when you have questions. To get the answers to these questions, draft a letter to a college student in another nation.

12. Choose two countries from the following list: Argentina, Belgium, Canada, Egypt, Japan, Korea, Indonesia, Malaysia, Vietnam, Zaire. On the World Wide Web, read about three cultural or business aspects of each country, and then (in not more than 500 words) explain (a) why it's important to understand those aspects when communicating in your chosen country, (b) how computers and other electronic technology can help such intercultural communication, and (c) how computers and other electronic technology can hinder such intercultural communication. To locate information on the World Wide Web, use Insane Search, a Web site that enables you to use 16 search engines simultaneously to locate Web sites that are related to your selections. You can find Insane Search at the following address: <http://www. cosmix.com/motherload/insane/>.

DEVELOPING YOUR INTERNET SKILLS
GOING ONLINE: MASTER THE ART OF INTERCULTURAL COMMUNICATION, P. 41

From General Communication, investigate the New Media for a New World option and read David Carlson's "Moscow Diary." How do you think the Internet can contribute to improvements in intercultural communication? (Quiz: What does the Russian word *mir* mean?) After you've finished perusing this behind-the-scenes, informative, and highly entertaining view of Moscow, send your comments to the author, using the link provided.

After studying this chapter, you will be able to

Describe the technological tools now available for creating and distributing printed documents

Discuss the internal and external databases used in business research

Judge the benefits and limitations of spell checkers and grammar checkers

Explore the communication role of electronic mail and Internet technologies in today's business organizations

Describe the technologies available for group communication

Assess the ways technology is changing business communication

COMMUNICATING THROUGH TECHNOLOGY

 n the Job

FACING A COMMUNICATION DILEMMA AT HEWLETT-PACKARD

From Trauma to Triumph, One Step at a Time

Hewlett-Packard (HP) relies on communication to keep the company operating smoothly. With more than 120,000 employees in 73 divisions and hundreds of sales and support facilities around the globe, Hewlett-Packard needs to keep in touch. New communication technology makes it possible for people on opposite sides of the world to work together nearly as easily as people sitting in adjoining cubicles. Technology like this is changing the workplace, requiring a new way of thinking about work.

As a systems technology specialist at Hewlett-Packard in Colorado Springs, Colorado, Mike Stevens spends a lot of his time looking at business processes to decide how they can be redesigned (or reengineered) for greater efficiency and effectiveness. That often means helping the company "reinvent the way it does business," explains Stevens. It also means using good communication skills to coordinate interaction with co-workers.

Even though it's relatively easy for Stevens to use technology in his own job, he must also help others adapt to changes in the communication processes and technology they use. It's a delicate situation: Some people enjoy change (particularly at a fast-moving company such as HP); others are reluctant to let go of methods that have been successful in the past. In order to communicate clearly and effectively with co-workers outside the team, Stevens and his team members must first communicate well with each other.

If you were Mike Stevens, what steps would you take to help other employees understand and adapt to changing processes? How would you use technology to improve communication with your team members and the other HP employees who rely on you for help?[1]

*T*ECHNOLOGY IN CONTEMPORARY BUSINESS COMMUNICATION

As Hewlett-Packard and other companies try to compete in the global economy, they are always looking for better ways to communicate. Businesspeople such as HP's Mike Stevens must choose from an ever-expanding list of communication tools to remain competitive. You'll probably use most or all of the technologies discussed in this chapter, as well as some future innovations that we can only dream about right now. The better you understand the technological issues involved, the more effective you'll be as a communicator.

In business communication today, you not only have to think about what you're going to say and how you're going to say it; you also have to decide which technological tools you'll use to do so. No hard rules dictate which tool to use in each case (partly because the technology keeps changing), but here are some factors to consider:

- *Audience expectations.* What would you think if your college tried to deliver your diploma by fax machine? It would seem a little strange, wouldn't it? You expect the college to use a certain set of technologies (such as mail delivery or a phone-in system). Business audiences have similar expectations for various kinds of messages. Knowing what people expect is part of getting to know your audience.

- *Time and cost.* Time is often the biggest factor in your technology choice. You'd probably choose the phone to send an urgent message, for instance. Many of the technologies discussed in this chapter were designed specifically to help people communicate faster, but cost can be an issue as well, both how much you have to spend and how much is appropriate for the situation. Spending $500 to create a presentation for customers might be appropriate, but spending that much to tell your colleagues when you'll be on vacation would be wasteful.

- *Nature of the message.* What you need to say in a document also affects your choice of technologies. For instance, business messages often require some sort of visual support (diagrams, photographs, or tables). A telephone call wouldn't be a good choice in such cases, but a printed report would be. If you need to convey emotion and excitement, delivering your message in person might be best. However, if you can't visit every member of your audience, sending your message on videotape might be a good substitute.

- *Presentation needs.* Sometimes the way you need to present your document will dictate which tools you use. If you're sending a report to an important client, you might want to stretch your budget to use typeset printing, color graphics, and professional binding. For short internal messages, however, you probably wouldn't want to spend the time or the money to present things so nicely.

- *Work environment.* One of the most significant communication advances in recent years is the dramatically improved quality and availability of portable tools for creating, sending, and receiving messages. Millions of businesspeople spend some or all of their time outside traditional office settings, working from their cars, their homes, hotel rooms, and other locations. Well-equipped "road warriors" can now communicate with as much convenience and impact as their desk-bound colleagues.

Some tools can create more than one type of message or document. Likewise, you may have two or three technological options when it comes to one particular message or document. The trick is to pick the tool that does the best overall job in each situation.

*T*ECHNOLOGY IN WRITTEN COMMUNICATION

When preparing written documents, you can take advantage of technological developments at every step. You're probably familiar with some of them, but others are just now starting to appear. In business communication, a variety of tools can help you create both printed and electronic documents.

Creating Printed Documents

Whether you're writing a one-paragraph memo or a 500-page report, technology can help you create an effective document with less time and effort. Some of these tools apply only

Technology helps Hewlett-Packard employees communicate with speed and convenience. At the Colorado Springs division, HP employees understand that they need to adapt to evolving electronics and also that good writing and speaking skills are now more important than ever.

General guidelines for choosing communication technology include considering

- Audience expectations
- Time and cost
- Nature of the message
- Presentation needs
- Work environment

Ted Turner increased his wealth as a pioneer in cable TV, founding CNN and the Turner Broadcasting System, then broke new ground by taking his company global. Now that he's sold off a major interest in his media empire to Time Warner, he's making waves as a philanthropist: His $1 billion gift to the United Nations is considered the largest donation ever made by a private individual. Turner's well-seasoned advice is to manage technology to create our world instead of merely being dragged along by it.

The most common means for creating printed documents is word-processing software.

to printed documents, but others can help you with electronic documents as well. **Word-processing software** is the dominant tool for creating printed documents, and it can do far more than you could ever attempt on a typewriter. If two or more people are developing a single document, they can use a category of software known as *groupware.* These systems keep track of revisions, let people attach electronic notes to each other's sections, enforce a common format for all sections, and take care of other issues that come up in any collaborative writing project. Groupware can include a variety of computing and communication tools to help people work together.[2]

The tool most appropriate for assembling finished pages with graphics elements is desktop publishing (DTP) software.

In the same way that word-processing software was created to computerize typewriters, **desktop publishing (DTP)** software was created to computerize the process of assembling finished pages. If you wanted a first-class report with photos and drawings, the old way of doing things involved cutting strips of printed text and pasting them onto a blank page along with the photos and drawings. Desktop publishing software does the same thing, only it all happens on your computer screen. Word processing and DTP are the core technologies for creating printed documents, and you can take advantage of a growing selection of specialized tools as well. The following sections present a brief overview of document creation to give you a better idea of how the various pieces of hardware and software can help you with planning, composing, revising, producing, distributing, and storing documents.

Planning Documents

Some of the writing you'll do on the job requires very little planning. For a memo to your staff regarding the company picnic or a letter requesting information from a supplier, you can often collect a few facts and get right down to writing. In other cases, however, you won't be able to start writing until you've done extensive research. This research often covers both the audience you'll be writing to and the subject matter you'll be writing about. Technology can help you with planning tasks, with research tasks, and with outlining your thoughts once you've done your research.

Technology helps you manage communication with

- Contact managers
- Personal information managers
- Project management software

Managing Communication Projects   Some computer software can actually help you plan and manage communication projects. These tools fall into three general (sometimes overlapping) categories. First, *contact managers* help you maintain communication with a large number of people. They store information about the people you need to contact (names, addresses, product preferences, and so on) and help automate many tasks, such as generating follow-up letters after you've spoken with someone on the phone. Second, *personal information managers (PIMs)* help you manage all kinds of information, from to-do lists to document outlines to e-mail messages. Personal information managers are similar in some ways to contact managers, but they are generally much more powerful when it comes to managing, sorting, and storing information. Third, *project management software* helps you plan and coordinate the activities needed to complete projects, and it helps you communicate with others regarding project status.

Researching Audience and Content   Sometimes the information you need for a document can be found inside your company, in its sales records, existing research reports, and other *internal sources.* At other times, the information you need will be found outside the company, in books, magazines, and other *external sources.* Technology can help in both cases.

Research is often one of the most important steps in business communication, and technology provides several helpful tools, including

- Online databases, both private and public
- Statistical analysis software
- Text retrieval software
- Web sites
- CD-ROM information sources

Much of your company's internal information may be stored in one or more **databases,** which are collections of facts ranging from financial figures to the text of reports. For information on sales trends, you might use a computer to search through your company's sales records. You can use *spreadsheets* or *statistical analysis* software to sort through numerical data and *text retrieval* software to sort through reports and other textual material (Figure 4.3).

The list of external sources of business information is long and is getting longer all the time. If you need some recent forecasts on household income, you can tap into Econbase, a database of economic forecasts and projects. If you need to see whether Congress passed any tax laws in the last week that might affect your company, you can try accessing Tax Notes Today, which explains all recent government actions regarding federal and state taxes.[3] These and thousands of other databases, on topics ranging from accounting to zoology, are available to anyone with a properly equipped computer—although usually for a fee. By using commercial online services or the Internet, you can access a huge number of databases and even the catalogs in many academic libraries around the world.

Another useful research tool is the **CD-ROM** (compact disk–read only memory), a type of compact disk that can be read by special computer equipment. An individual CD-ROM can contain either a single volume of information or collections of documents ranging from back files of newspapers to sets of books on a particular subject. For example, Microsoft *Encarta* is a multimedia encyclopedia that contains not only textual information but also animated drawings, short video clips, and audio tracks.[4]

Outlining Content   Once you've collected the necessary information for your report, the next step is to outline how you want to present your ideas. You've probably outlined reports, possibly using note cards to arrange and sort the various sections. Computer-based outliners perform the same function, only without the need to fill out all those cards. Once you type in the titles of your sections, you can quickly move sections around, experimenting with order and organization. Computer outliners further boost your productivity by saving you from retyping the section titles once you've finished outlining. Most word-processing packages contain built-in outliners, although you might want to consider specialized outlining tools such as Inspiration. This tool lets you outline and organize ideas visually by moving and connecting blocks and arrows that represent a flow of ideas.[5]

Composing Documents

When you're ready to start writing, the computer once again demonstrates how it can enhance the communication process. Composing a document on your computer involves keyboarding, of course, but that's just the beginning. Technology offers a number of ways to get text into your document, and you're no longer limited to just text, either. The right software makes it relatively easy to add a wide variety of graphic elements to your document, and even audio notes if you have the right equipment.

Entering Text   Composing means sitting at the keyboard and typing. Word processors help make this task as painless as possible, by enabling you to erase and move text easily. The fact that you're on a computer, however, opens up some interesting possibilities for text entry.

To start with, if you don't know how to keyboard or don't like to, your worries may be over sooner than you think. *Pen-based computers* let you write with an electronic stylus on a special pad that converts your handwriting to text the computer can recognize. The most common applications of pen-based computers involve portable applications such as recording information in various parts of a large factory.

With some computers, you don't have to write or type at all. *Voice recognition systems,* which convert your voice to text, free you from keyboard or pen input. Such breakthroughs are particularly important for people with physical impairments, giving them the means to become more active communicators.

Some of the text that business communicators use in their documents is "prewritten"; it already appears in other documents. Say that you want to announce to the media that you've developed a new product or hired an executive. Such announcements are called press releases, and they usually end with a standard paragraph about the company and its line of business. Any standard block of text used in various documents without being changed is called a *boilerplate*. With a good word processor, you don't have to retype the boilerplate each time you write a press release. You simply store the paragraph the first time you write it and then pop it into a document whenever you need it. Not only does this save time, it also reduces mistakes, because you're not retyping the paragraph every time you use it. A related concept applies to manipulating existing text. If you're a national sales

Technology provides several options for entering text into a document:

- Keyboarding (typing)
- Pen-based computers
- Voice recognition systems
- Scanning and OCR

A boilerplate is any standard block of text used in various documents without being changed.

manager compiling a report that includes summaries from your four regional managers, you can use your word processor's *file merge* capability to combine the four documents into one, saving yourself the trouble of retyping all four.

Using a boilerplate or file merge capability assumes that the text you want to include is in electronic format, saved on a computer disk. But sometimes you have only printed versions of the document. In such cases you can use a *scanner,* a device that essentially takes a picture of a printed document and converts it to an electronic format that your computer can handle. Scanners produce just a visual image of the document, though, and the process requires an additional step if you want to use the words from the document as normal input to your word processor. A technology called *optical character recognition (OCR)* lets your computer "read" the scanned image, picking out the letters and words that make up the text.

Scanning and OCR technologies raise the legal and ethical issues of plagiarism and image manipulation. Of course, people have had the ability to copy words and images for quite some time, but the new computer tools make copying even easier. Now you can scan a photo you have on file, retouch it as you see fit, and then include it in your own document. It's also possible to make products and people look better than they really are and to depict situations or events that never actually happened. As technology continues to expand these options, business communicators will continue to face new and challenging ethical issues.

Adding Graphics and Sound to Documents   Computers can do some amazing things with text entry, but that's only part of the story. With the right equipment, you can add full-color pictures and even sound recordings to your documents. The software for creating business visuals falls into two basic groups: presentation software and graphics software. *Presentation software* helps you create overhead transparencies and other visuals for meetings, discussed later in the chapter. *Graphics software* ranges from products that can create simple diagrams and flowcharts to comprehensive tools designed for artists and graphic designers. You can create your pictures from scratch, use *clip art* (collections of uncopyrighted images), or scan in drawings or photos. Much of the graphic design and artwork that you see in business publications was created with software packages such as CorelDRAW! and Freehand.

Graphics software can add a visual element to your message.

Inserting your visuals into a document used to be a chore, but increasing standardization of computer file formats has made the task somewhat easier. Say you want to distribute some ideas you have for a new corporate logo, and you want to include your sketches in a memo. You've already created several logos in CorelDRAW!, but your memo is in Microsoft Word. No problem—you simply save the CorelDRAW! file in a special transfer format, then switch to your memo in Microsoft Word and activate a command to insert the picture. The logos pop into your memo, and you can shrink or enlarge them to fit.

Adding sound bites to your documents is an exciting new way to get your message across. Several systems now allow you to record a brief message or other sound and attach it to particular places in a document. Of course, to actually hear the sound, the person receiving the memo has to load the memo into his or her multimedia computer.

Revising Documents

When it's time to revise and polish your message, your word processor can help in a variety of ways, starting with the basics of adding, deleting, and moving text. *Cut and paste* is a term used in both word processing and desktop publishing to indicate cutting a block of text out of one section of a document and pasting it in somewhere else. The *search and replace function* helps you track down words or phrases and change them if you need to. This can be a great time saver in long documents if you need to change a word or phrase that appears in several places.

Spell checkers, grammar checkers, and computerized thesauruses can all help with the revision process, but they can't take the place of good writing and editing skills.

Beyond the basic revision tools, three advanced software functions can help bring out the best in your documents. A *spell checker* compares your document with an electronic dictionary stored on your disk drive, highlights words that it doesn't recognize, and suggests correct spelling. Spell checkers are a wonderful way to weed major typos out of your documents, but it's best not to use them as replacements for good spelling skills. If you use *their* when you mean to use *there,* your spell checker will fly right past the error, because *their* is in fact spelled correctly. If you're in a hurry and accidentally omit the *p* at the end of *top,* your spell checker will read *to* as correct. Or if you mistakenly type the semicolon instead of the *p,* your spell checker will read *to;* as a correctly spelled word.

A computer *thesaurus* gives you alternative words, just as your printed thesaurus does, but you can get them faster and more easily. It may also be able to do something that you would need a second type of reference book—called a reverse dictionary—to do. The electronic version of the American Heritage dictionary provides a thesaurus and a special WordHunter function that, like a reverse dictionary, gives you the term when all you know is part of the definition. If you're racking your brain to remember the word that means a certain quantity of paper, you simply type *quantity AND paper* and then WordHunter searches for every definition in the dictionary that includes those two terms. In a few seconds, the word *ream* pops into view, and you say, "Aha! That's the word I was looking for."

The third major revision tool is the *grammar checker,* which tries to do for your grammar what a spell checker does for your spelling. The catch here is that checking your spelling is much easier than checking your grammar. A spell checker simply compares each word in your document with a list of correctly spelled words. A grammar checker has to determine whether you're using words correctly and constructing sentences according to the complex rules of composition. The computer doesn't have a clue about what you're trying to say, so determining whether you've said it correctly is monstrously difficult. Moreover, even if you've used all the rules correctly, a grammar checker still can't tell whether your document communicates clearly. However, grammar checkers can perform some helpful review tasks and point out things you should consider changing, such as passive voice, long sentences, and words that tend to be misused or overused.[6]

Producing Finished Documents

Consider the memo shown in Figure 4.1. Many simple hardware and software packages are capable of producing documents like this one, combining text and graphics so that the appearance is both professional and inviting. It's important that you balance graphics and text. The bar chart in this memo is centered to give a formal impression, and the colors used in the graphic are balanced by the letterhead logo. The manner in which you package your ideas has a lot to do with how successful your communication will be. A document that looks tired and out of date will make even your innovative ideas seem dull. Today's computer software makes it easy for anyone to produce great-looking documents in a hurry. Word processors and desktop publishing software can help you by:

- *Adding a first-class finish.* From selecting attractive typefaces to adding color graphics, you can use your computer tools to turn a plain piece of text into a dazzling and persuasive document. Used improperly, however, these same tools can turn your text into garish, high-tech rubbish. Knowing how to use the tools of technology is a key issue for today's business communicators.

    Computer software can help you add a first-class look to your most important business documents.

- *Managing document style.* With so many design and formatting choices at your fingertips, it's often difficult to maintain consistency throughout your document. *Style sheets* are collections of formatting rules available in high-end word processors and DTP packages that can save a lot of formatting effort. Every time you need to add a section to your report, for instance, your style sheet can ensure that all the sections are formatted consistently (with the same typeface, margins, word spacing, etc.). You can also use style sheets to make sure that all the documents created by everyone in a department or even an entire company have a consistent look.

- *Generating supporting elements.* If you've ever written a report with footnotes or endnotes, an index, and a table of contents, you know how much work these supporting elements can be. Fortunately, a computer can help keep track of your footnotes; it will renumber them all every time you add or delete a reference. For indexes and tables of contents, you simply flag the terms you want to include, and the software assembles the lists for you.

Figure 4.1
In-Depth Critique: The Importance of Appearance

A colorful letterhead can add to a professional appearance.

A contemporary typeface can help your document appear lively, not tired.

Colorful graphics are great for drawing attention to important points.

Balancing graphics, text, and color creates a polished appearance that lends credibility to your message.

Laser and inkjet printers are popular ways of producing documents in business today.

CalPlus

9408 Sepulveda Way • Los Angeles, California 90064 • (213) 556-4103

MEMO

DATE: April 14, 1999
TO: Alden Maxwell, Vice President, Marketing
FROM: Louise Ellison, Manager, Promotions
SUBJECT: Using sports as a selling tool for promoting our new calcium-plus soft drink

After doing a little research, I'm more convinced than ever that sponsoring a sporting event would be an excellent way to build awareness of our new calcium-plus soft drink.

The experiences of other companies show that sports sponsorship is an extremely cost-effective approach to promotion. For example, Volvo found that it can reach as many people by spending $3 million on tennis tournaments as it can by spending $25 million on media advertising.

If we decide to go forward with a sponsorship, our first priority should be to identify a sport that is popular with our target customers. As the chart below indicates, auto racing is currently the number-one sport among corporate sponsors, possibly because it appeals to both men and women:

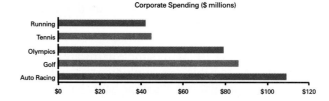

Corporate Spending ($ millions)

Although the "mainstream" sports currently receive the lion's share of corporate dollars, we might achieve more impact with a lesser-known event. Timberline Company has really scored with its sponsorship of the Iditarod dog-sled race across Alaska, a contest that appeals to customers for rugged footwear.

Over the next few days, I plan to do some more research to identify sporting events that would give us the most exposure among the health-conscious women who represent our primary market. I hope to pinpoint three or four possibilities and prepare some preliminary cost estimates for discussion at the Tuesday staff meeting.

High-end word-processing software can handle most aspects of final document production, but many communicators prefer to finish off their documents with desktop publishing instead. In addition to giving you more control over spacing, graphics, color, and other elements, DTP makes many layout and design tasks easier than word processing can. When moving a column of text, for instance, with DTP you can grab it, move it wherever you want, and resize it along the way if you like.

Printing and Distributing Documents

With a thoroughly revised document, you're ready to print and distribute copies to your audience. *Printers* come in a variety of shapes, sizes, and capabilities, from low-cost portables that fit in your briefcase to inkjet to high-resolution color units that can print photographs. Many offices today are equipped with laser printers, which produce a printed image by drawing with a low-power laser beam. For results that look the very best, pages can be printed using a *typesetter* or an *imagesetter,* both of which are similar in concept to laser printers but which produce sharper images.

Technology does some of its most amazing feats when it's time to distribute your documents. For multiple copies of your document, you can print as many as you like on your office printer or print a single copy and reproduce it with a *photocopier.* For high-volume and complex reproduction (involving colors or photographs, for instance), you'll want to take your document to a *print shop,* a company that has the special equipment needed for such jobs.

When you need to send the same document (sales letter, invoice, or other customer communication) to a large number of people, *mail merge* automatically combines a standard version of the document with a list of names and addresses. It will produce one copy for each person on your mailing list, saving you the trouble of inserting the name and address each time. The names and addresses can come from your own customer databases or from mailing lists you can rent from firms that specialize in collecting names and addresses.

Fax machines have had a major impact on the distribution of printed documents. Using regular telephone lines, you can transmit (fax) an exact reproduction (a facsimile) of a document from one machine to another. Fax machines are indispensable for international business, particularly since they overcome the delay problems of regular mail and the time-zone problems of trying to contact someone by telephone.[7] Personal computers (PCs) can be equipped with *fax modems,* which combine data transmission with fax capabilities.

Many companies now distribute information on CD-ROM rather than on paper. For instance, several of HP's product catalogs are available either on CD-ROM or in printed form. The cost of producing CD-ROMs is rapidly decreasing, and most personal computers now include CD-ROM drives. CD-ROMs hold a large amount of information, and their small size saves money in postage and shipping.

Creating Electronic Documents

A growing number of business documents are never put on paper; they're written on a computer and sent to other computers on the same network. A **network** is a group of computers that are connected so that they can share information. Networks vary greatly in size and nature. Small, private-office setups, sometimes called **local area networks (LANs),** connect computers in a single building or local area. **Wide area networks (WANs),** a group of LANs, connect computers in separate locations. Some internal networks also include software such as e-mail programs and search tools. Many LANs, WANs, or intranets (discussed later in this chapter) also connect to larger outside networks. A **gateway** controls the passage of information between internal and external networks.

The world's largest network is the **Internet,** which is actually a network of networks.[8] It is the fastest-growing means of communication in the business world today. Microsoft CEO Bill Gates says, "The Internet is the most important single development to come along since the IBM PC was introduced in 1981."[9]

You can access the Internet through a commercial online service, such as CompuServe, Prodigy, or America Online, or directly through a service provider. Once you are connected, you need additional software to actually do anything:

- Electronic mail lets you send and receive mail via the Internet. There is more information on e-mail later in this chapter.
- **Telnet** lets you connect to a remote computer and run programs on that computer. (You must be authorized and have an account on the remote computer.)
- **File transfer protocol (FTP)** lets you copy files from a remote computer to your computer.
- Search engines (Yahoo!, Lycos, and Excite are among the most popular) help you locate information on other computers. Because the Internet is growing so fast, new search tools appear and existing ones become obsolete very quickly. You can find an annotated list of most of the currently available Internet search tools at <http://www.search.com> on the Web.
- The **World Wide Web,** or the **Web,** is a graphical approach to storing and accessing information on the Internet. There is more information on the Web later in this chapter.

Susan Mersereau is vice president and general manager of Weyerhauser Information Systems. As such, Mersereau heads the group responsible for the company's worldwide telecommunications program, linking voice and data communications, e-mail, fax, and videoconferencing facilities. To manage change, says Mersereau, you must control vast amounts of information, which is something technology can help you do.

Fax machines (and computers equipped with fax modems) are an integral part of the business communication process, providing fast transmission of printed documents all over the world.

The Internet is actually a network of networks.

Some of the software available on the Internet includes

- Electronic mail
- Telnet
- File transfer protocol
- Search engines
- World Wide Web

Figure 4.2
In-Depth Critique: Electronic Mail

Gretchen Plaxton, a budget analyst at Robson Brothers Manufacturing, encountered some unexpected problems in setting up her computer for an important budget briefing. Her e-mail message was waiting for Li Chau when she returned to her office, and the two women were able to solve Plaxton's problem by closing time.

This computer screen shows how a timely message can be sent to anyone connected to the system—whether across the globe or in the same building.

Plaxton has the space to explain the situation so that Chau can respond without needing any more information.

At the end of the second paragraph, Chau has included a type of e-mail symbol known as an emoticon—in this case a sideways "sad face" that clues the reader in to how the writer is feeling (see "Make Your E-Mail Interesting" in Chapter 6).

Chau can let Plaxton know whether she will be available and what time would be convenient—again by e-mail—simply by clicking on the reply button and typing in her response.

E-Mail

Date: Tues, 16 June 1998, 11:45:23, CDT
To: lichau@robson.com
From: gplaxton@robson.com (Gretchen R. Plaxton)
Subject: Help!

Li,

You're not answering your phone, so I guess you're not back from your software demonstration. I really need your expertise! I've spent the better part of this morning trying to get my computer set up for tomorrow's budget briefing, but nothing seems to help. Everything was working fine in my office, but now that I've moved my machine to the conference room, I keep getting application errors in the graphics software!

I have to meet Roland from production for lunch at noon, but I'll be back in the office by 1:00. Can you come look at my machine after that? The budget meeting is set for tomorrow at 9 a.m. sharp! So I can't really wait for the consultant we started on retainer last month (she's tied up until after 4:00). If I can't get things running by end of business today, I'm in deep trouble. I'll be up all night hand drawing flip charts--and with my artistic talent, they won't be pretty!(:<)

If you get back before I do, leave a message on my voice mail, or e-mail me. I'm desperate, Li. Please say you'll come rescue me.

Hope to hear from you very soon.

Gretchen

Electronic mail (e-mail) helps businesses communicate quickly and informally.

E-Mail

Electronic mail, generally called e-mail, is one of the most useful Internet features for business. **E-mail** refers to documents created, transmitted, and read entirely on computer (Figure 4.2). If you can save a file on your computer, you can probably send it via e-mail. For the people who use it, e-mail has changed the style of business communication in dramatic ways. The advantages of e-mail include the following:[10]

- *Speed.* An e-mail message often arrives at its destination anywhere in the world in a matter of seconds. With e-mail, you can correspond back and forth repeatedly in the time it used to take for one message to be delivered.
- *Cost.* The cost of sending an e-mail message is usually less than the cost of a first-class stamp. It is definitely less than the cost of overnight delivery services ($6 to $20 or more).

- *Portability.* You can receive and send e-mail anywhere you can connect your computer to a phone line.
- *Convenience.* The person you want to contact need not be sitting at the computer or even have the computer turned on when your message arrives. This feature solves the problems of phone tag (two people calling back and forth leaving messages without ever connecting) and of coordinating phone calls across time zones. For instance, HP has employees in almost every time zone around the world, and many of them need to communicate with far-flung colleagues. With e-mail, a sales representative in Germany can easily communicate with a technical specialist in California, even though the two are separated by nine time zones.
- *Record keeping.* You can save and organize messages you send and receive, so e-mail can provide a good record of the communication on a specific project.
- *News services.* Several electronic news services are available. You specify the topic or the key words of interest to you, and the service gathers articles on those topics from newspapers, magazines, and wire services, and sends you the results via e-mail. Some of the services are free; others cost up to $400 a year or more.[11]
- *Egalitarianism.* With most e-mail systems, anybody can send messages to just about anybody else. Lower-level employees (who may otherwise have no contact with upper management) can send e-mail messages to top managers as easily as to their colleagues—the electronic equivalent of an open-door policy.[12]
- *Open communication.* People sometimes write things in e-mail that they wouldn't dream of saying in person or typing in a printed document.[13] This new openness can help companies communicate better and circulate useful opinions from more people. As you can imagine, however, such openness can also create tension and interpersonal conflict.
- *Distribution lists.* Within an e-mail program, you can create distribution lists—groups of people to whom you routinely send information. Then when you want to send a message you specify the name of the list rather than typing all the names again.
- *Automated mail.* Some companies use software that automatically retrieves or distributes information. For example, say you want to get information about the services and prices of Netcom On-Line Communication Services, an Internet service provider. You simply send e-mail (without an actual message) to <info@netcom.com>, and the computer automatically responds.

Some of the main benefits of e-mail also create its worst problems. Because it's so easy and cheap to send e-mail, people tend to overuse it, distributing messages more widely than necessary. Also, some company executives receive hundreds of messages a day, many of which are the electronic equivalent of junk mail. Besides wasting time, overuse can overload e-mail systems, resulting in lost messages or even system crashes.

Privacy is another problem with e-mail. E-mail messages may seem more private than phone calls, but it is surprisingly easy for e-mail to end up in places you did not intend it to go. People do not always screen the distribution list carefully and send information to people who should not have it or do not need it. Even if your message originally goes only where you intended it to go, a recipient can easily forward it on to someone else. Like paper mail, e-mail can be used as evidence in court cases.[14] Moreover, employers have the legal right to monitor your e-mail on the job.[15] A good rule of thumb is not to put anything in e-mail that you would not write in any other business correspondence.[16]

Internet Discussion Groups

Two forms of discussion groups are common on the Internet: discussion mailing lists and Usenet newsgroups. A **discussion mailing list** (of which there are more than 100,000) consists of people with a common interest. You can subscribe by sending a message to the list's e-mail address. From then on, you will automatically receive via e-mail a copy of any message posted to that list by any other subscriber of that list. It's like subscribing to an electronic newsletter to which everyone can contribute.[17]

GOING ONLINE
*CREATE YOUR
OWN WEB SITE*
You'll learn how to create your own Web site using valuable Web development links, utilities, and online tutorials. Through this massive, user-friendly resource library, you'll learn about document and Web-page design, navigation, structure, and more. You'll even learn how to have your Web site translated into a foreign language.

http://www.stars.com

The World Wide Web is the part of the Internet that can accommodate graphics.

Usenet newsgroups are similar to mailing lists, but they are accessed differently. Mailing lists are accessed by e-mail. Newsgroups are accessed by a newsgroup reader program in Netscape, Internet Explorer, or some other browser. Once you subscribe, you can read messages posted by other subscribers and leave messages for the other subscribers to read. You can get and submit information on more than 10,000 subjects. For example, the newsgroup <alt.business.misc> is a forum for small-business owners.[18]

World Wide Web

The **World Wide Web, WWW,** or **Web,** is a very powerful system of interconnections on the Internet. Being familiar with terms helps you use the Web:

- *Multimedia.* When using the Web, you can access not only text files but also graphic, photographic, audio, and video files. Figure 4.3 shows a Web page with text and graphics.
- *Browser.* To find your way around the Web, you need a piece of software called a **browser.** Three popular browsers are Netscape Navigator, Microsoft's Internet Explorer, and NCSA Mosaic.
- *Home page.* Every site on the Web has its own **home page,** or starting place. This site might be a very complex document containing graphics and hyperlinks (as in Figure 4.3), or it might be quite simple.
- *URL.* Each resource or site on the Web has a unique address called a uniform resource locator (**URL**). The URL for Hewlett-Packard's Web site is <http://www.hp.com>.
- *Hyperlinks.* Hyperlinks, or **links,** are interactive connections among sites on the web.
- *Hypertext.* Hypertext is a method of cross-referencing between files by using links. When you click on a link, hypertext uses the URL to find the file or site. This is a con-

Figure 4.3
Web Pages Help Businesses Communicate Internally and Externally

This site on the World Wide Web shows a typical home page with graphics and hyperlinks.

venient way of finding related information. For example, look at HP's site in Figure 4.3. If you want more information on HP products, click on the button labeled "Products."

■ *Web site.* Thousands of companies and individuals now have their own Web sites. At HP's site, for instance, clicking on buttons or links provides information about new products, the company's annual report, a current press release, any job openings, or a variety of other topics. A Web site provides an interactive means of advertising.

Intranets

Not all Web sites are available to anyone cruising the Net. Some are reserved for the private use of a single company's employees and stakeholders. An **intranet** uses the same technologies as the Internet and the World Wide Web, but the information provided and the access allowed are restricted to the boundaries of a companywide LAN or WAN. In some cases, suppliers, distribution partners, and key customers may also have access, but intranets are protected from unauthorized access through the Internet by a *firewall*, a special type of gateway that controls access to the local network. People on an intranet can get out to the Internet, but unauthorized people on the Internet cannot get in.[19] As a leading computer company, Hewlett-Packard, not surprisingly, owns one of the largest intranets in the world.[20]

Possibly the biggest advantage of an intranet is that it eliminates the problem of employees' using different types of computers within a company. On an intranet, all information is available in a format compatible with Macintosh, PC, or UNIX-based computers. The need to publish internal documents on paper is virtually eliminated because everyone can access the information electronically.

Besides saving paper, an intranet can save a company money in the form of employee hours. Employees can find information much faster and more easily by using a well-designed database on an intranet than by digging through a filing cabinet or card catalog. Some of the communication uses companies have for intranets include updating policy manuals, posting job openings and submitting job applications, accessing marketing and sales presentations from anywhere in the world, updating and managing employee benefits, accessing company records and databases, collaborating from anywhere in the world to develop new products, scheduling meetings, setting up company phone directories, and publishing company newsletters.[21] In fact, just about any information that can help employees communicate is a good candidate for an intranet. As video and audio technologies progress, you can expect to see more multimedia applications on intranets as well.

John L. Sims is vice president of strategic resources for Digital Equipment, which leads the world in computer network technology. At Digital, employees stay online with the company's own VAX stations, a family of computerized workstations. Machines can't do it alone, says Sims. It takes good people to use them.

An intranet is an Internet-type network whose information and access are restricted to a single organization.

ECHNOLOGY IN ORAL COMMUNICATION

Written documents are only part of the business communication picture. Oral communication is just as important, whether it's face to face or on the phone, whether it's with one other person or with a group. Here's a quick look at the technologies used to improve communication between individuals and groups.

Technologies for one-on-one oral communication include the basic telephone and advanced options such as voice mail.

Individual Communication

Telephones are still an organization's lifeline. Phones link businesses with their customers, suppliers, news media, investors, and all the other parties that affect their success. Phones keep employees in touch with each other and give them quick access to the people and the information they need to do their jobs.

As it has every other aspect of communication, technology has transformed the way businesspeople use their phones. Many business phone systems act as computers. *Call-management systems* give companies better control over calls both coming in and going out. For inbound calls, a *PBX (private branch exchange)* system can screen and route calls. Some are run by a human operator; others are nearly or completely computerized. To reach employees who are out of the office, a company can equip them with cellular phones

Katherine M. Hudson is vice president and director of corporate information systems at Eastman Kodak Company. Hudson and her worldwide team lead the corporate information systems division, which is responsible for Kodak's global computing and telecommunications. Such networks allow us to exchange ideas more readily, says Hudson, but people still have to dream up the ideas to communicate.

Technologies for group presentations include teleconferencing, videoconferencing, presentation tools, and group decision-making systems.

The development and evolution of technology is changing business communication, and its effects are both positive and negative.

or *pagers,* small radio receivers that signal employees to call the office. For outbound calls, computers can track who called whom, automatically dial numbers from a list of potential customers, and perform other time- and money-saving tasks.

The combination of phones and computers has also created an entirely new method of communication. *Voice mail* is similar to e-mail in concept, except that it doesn't require each user to have a computer (messages are stored on a central computer) and it lets you send, store, and retrieve spoken, rather than written, messages. Much more than a glorified answering machine, voice mail sends verbal messages to any number of "mailboxes" on the system. Messages can be several minutes long, and you can review your recordings before releasing them. When people need to get their messages, they enter a confidential code; then they can listen to, delete, and forward messages to other people on the system. Voice mail solves the time-zone difficulties of communicating across the country or internationally. It can also reduce a substantial amount of interoffice paperwork.[22]

Voice mail can make employees more productive, but it's not universally loved. The biggest complaint comes from customers who call a company and reach a computerized voice-mail system instead of a person. In a recent survey, 95 percent of the people questioned said they prefer reaching a person on their first call to a business.[23] Businesses that use voice mail need to balance the productivity gains with the potential effects on customer satisfaction.

Group Communication

Technology can also lend a hand when people need to communicate in groups. Group communication used to take place in person (in the same room), but technology has given people a new degree of freedom. Through *teleconferencing* (which encompasses audioconferencing and videoconferencing via phone lines and satellite), it's now possible to conduct meetings with people who are scattered across the country or around the globe.[24] New technology also allows videoconferencing over the Internet.

In more traditional gatherings, when all participants can meet in one location, technology provides an array of presentation tools to make meetings more productive and more interesting. You're no doubt familiar with *overhead transparencies.* You might also use *35-mm slides* (just like the slides you can produce with a camera), or you could make use of a *computer-based presentation,* in which the computer's display is transferred to either a large-screen television or an LCD (liquid crystal display) panel or LCD projector. Presentation software can help you create these visual materials. But beyond visuals, technology can even help groups make decisions and formulate plans. You can connect everyone through computers using *group decision support systems,* which range from simple vote-counting systems to advanced tools that help people consider a decision from various points of view.[25]

H OW TECHNOLOGY IS CHANGING COMMUNICATION

Communication technology is changing the way we do business. Some of the effects are unquestionably positive; others are not. New technology is increasing the flow of information. Businesspeople can now get more information on more subjects faster than ever before. At the same time, technology is producing information overload, burdening people with unwanted messages. Although much of this additional information is useful, you have to be careful not to bury yourself and your company in information you don't need. By pressing just a few keys or buttons, anyone can send e-mail, voice mail, and faxes to hundreds or even thousands of people—whether the information is actually needed or not. Of course, technology can also help you sort through all that information to find just the bits you need.

By compressing time and distance, technology promotes teamwork and improves profits. Doing business with someone in another country is no longer the slow, complicated, even exotic adventure it once was. Electronic communication makes it easier to work with colleagues, suppliers, and customers, no matter where they are. E-mail, voice mail, and faxes facilitate communication within a company and around the world. All three technologies overcome time zones and working hours. E-mail and faxes are even being accepted as legally binding contracts.[26] So, because it costs less for people to produce and distribute messages, communication technology can directly boost profits. It can also improve profits indirectly by making a company more competitive, say, by searching databases to uncover a new market opportunity.

However, the same technology can isolate some people from business and employment opportunities. Anyone who doesn't have access to e-mail, fax machines, or other technological tools tends to be left out of the communication flow. This isolation presents a challenge to businesses that are trying to compete and to people who lack experience with communication technology but who are applying for jobs that require some knowledge of it. By keeping up with the newest technological developments, you will be able to compete in business and for jobs.

Today's technology is also changing organizational structures, flattening the hierarchy, and allowing more people to work away from the office. Although corporate structure used to define communication flow, e-mail in particular frees communication from the confines of the organization chart. Using today's technology, anyone can send messages to anyone else with equal access, a big change from the old days when messages just moved up and down the chain of command.[27] Moreover, communication technology has loosened the strings that bind the traditional company together. In many firms, co-workers and even entire departments are no longer in a single location. **Telecommuting** lets people work (linked through computers, phones, and faxes) where it is most convenient for them—whether at home, in a suburban satellite office (where people can work close to home but away from the company's main office), or on the road (traveling to sell products or to service customer accounts). Telecommuting can cover a lot more territory than the area around town, too. Technology allows many professionals to work with people across the country and around the world.

Of course, this same technology is blurring the line between work life and home life. E-mail, faxes, and other technologies that speed up and extend the reach of business communication can increase the pressure on those people who use them. From home computers to car phones to portable fax machines, technology can make it easy to feel that you're always "plugged in" and that you're expected to respond instantly to every message you receive, whether you're at home, on a business trip, or on vacation.

Mike Stevens's experience at Hewlett-Packard emphasizes some important lessons about technology: First, even though it helps him communicate with more people more efficiently, it doesn't solve *all* his problems. Second, it adds to the complexity of his job. Third, technology doesn't come cheap; Hewlett-Packard spends millions of dollars on all the communication equipment and software that Stevens and his co-workers use. Fourth, and most important, whether in the form of handwritten notes, electronic newsletters, or global videoconferences, communication efforts are only as good as the people involved. Technology cannot do the thinking, planning, or communicating. Humans must do that. Only those who learn to balance the complexity and expense of technology with good communication skills will succeed in business and in the future.

BEHIND THE SCENES AT BEST DOMESTIC SERVICES AGENCY
Using Technology to Find the Best Match

Maurice Wingate knows how to please his customers. As president and owner of Best Domestic Services Agency, he makes sure his customers are satisfied by matching their needs with the qualifications and experiences of his domestic staffers, including housekeepers, chefs, nannies, and chauffeurs. Wingate knows that his customers want to do business with an agency they can depend on—one that provides quality, reliable domestic-care providers and fast (sometimes emergency) service. As a parent of an infant, Wingate understands his clients' concerns for security. That is why his company performs an intense pre-screening of all applicants and requires at least three references before recommending a child-care provider.

Few agencies are as thorough or accommodating as Best Domestic. In fact, that's one reason the company was nominated Emerging Corporation of the Year by *Black Enterprise* magazine. Headquartered in New York City and with offices in California, Florida, and Connecticut, Best Domestic is one of the few agencies that provides emergency caregiver services 24 hours a day 7 days a week. The company can offer this emergency service because the agency's custom computer database program matches zip codes and other key criteria between the company's 6,000 clients and 7,000 service providers. "It's similar to the software programs used by computer dating services—except we provide the babysitters so our clients can keep their appointments or go to work when their child is sick."

Using technology to match client profiles with service providers from its computerized database, Best Domestic can provide quality chefs, chauffeurs, nannies, housekeepers, and adult caregivers in record-breaking time.

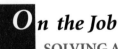n the Job
SOLVING A COMMUNICATION DILEMMA AT HEWLETT-PACKARD

Changing technology has changed the nature of many jobs at Hewlett-Packard, and part of Mike Stevens's job is to keep up with the latest developments in communication technology. But new technology alone doesn't make a business operate smoothly. Many procedures and processes must be redefined to operate efficiently with the new technology. People who use the processes must be informed and retrained.

Before reengineering an HP process, the team's first task is to define it. How do you do that? "You write a document describing it," says Stevens. "Then once you've got your document, you want the rest of the team to review it, to add to it, to modify it, to get it right. So you mail it—you e-mail it." Using the latest e-mail and groupware programs, team members can work together on a document before it ever leaves their computers.

Stevens says that technology of this type is having a major impact in the workplace. Many of the processes he reengineers require a new way of thinking about work: Jobs that were once regarded as solitary endeavors are being "reinvented" as team efforts.

Stevens and his team work together closely, and the communication technology they use makes such teamwork possible.

When the team has finalized the document, Stevens has several options for distributing it. He can, of course, deliver or mail printed copies to the people affected by the new process, but he is more likely to distribute the document by e-mail. Or he might put the document on a company-private Web site (or *intranet*). Other company employees then have immediate access to the information.

However, Stevens cautions that these rapid exchanges of information carry their own risks. Today's technology can foster a carelessness that business communicators can't afford. "The impression that you make on people is extremely important," he explains, and you can't depend on technology to supply what impresses them most: your courtesy, intelligence, and common sense. Stevens says that good writing and speaking skills are in demand more than ever as new technology continues to help us do our jobs and communicate with each other.[28]

Wingate admits that "without technology we could not run the company the way we do today." The company uses a wide area network to share data among all four offices. This information includes job requirements, salary, location, age of children, and types of living arrangements for clients and matching data for service providers. When a client contacts Best Domestic (by phone, e-mail, fax, or the company's Web site), a placement counselor enters specific information into the computer, creating a client profile. Then the computer searches the database of service providers, matches key criteria, and generates a list of approximately 20 candidates—all of whom fall within the client's specifications. "We plan on using scanners in the future to scan our forms and applications (including photos) directly into the database, saving the company time by eliminating the keyboarding." With a weekly average of 200 applications, that's a lot of time saved.

Another way the company saves time is by using standardized forms and word-processing templates for normal business correspondence. "We use boilerplates for our standard invoices, collection letters, reference check letters, bad check notices, thank-you letters, corporate solicitations, job placement forms, and job applications." The company also uses templates for its company letterhead and fax cover sheets. This standardization of routine documents allows the company to focus on the most important aspect of the business—customer service and personal attention. "Our customers require lots of personal attention, especially since we're finding someone to care for their loved ones."

Of course, Wingate knows that personal attention is also important to effectively manage his four distant locations. "I visit each office every four months, but I'm in contact with them almost daily." Wingate uses his laptop with fax capabilities, pager, car phone, cell phone, e-mail, and voice mail to communicate with his offices. The company plans to open offices in Atlanta and Philadelphia in the near future and would like to have a presence in most major service-care markets by the year 2000. By selectively incorporating future technological developments into his operation, Wingate knows he is one step closer to reaching his goal.

Apply Your Knowledge

1. As manager of the Best Domestic Florida office, you are having a terrible technology day. You forgot to turn on the answering machine last evening, so the phones have been ringing off the hook since 8:00 A.M. Then Maurice Wingate phoned you from his car phone to discuss the plans for his upcoming visit, but you were cut off. The fax machine jammed, and you lost three customer applications. Then the company network went down, so you can't access the company database. As manager, what can you do to lessen the impact of future technology failures? Please explain.

2. Faxing employee profiles to clients is an important step in your search-and-match process at Best Domestic Agency. Please list some of the rules your employees should obey to ensure effective fax communications.

Your Mission: You are an HP systems technology specialist, part of a team responsible for investigating, modifying, and implementing the latest business technology for all employees at your division. Most of your job consists of defining and redefining business processes and then communicating the information to the people who use those processes. Choose the best solutions for the following situations, and be prepared to explain why your choice is best.

1. Your boss asks you to document the process for handling new orders. You write a document describing the process as you understand it; then you want feedback from the rest of your team members. How should you allow your team to collaborate on the document?
   a. Distribute a paper copy of the document to each team member and then schedule a meeting so that all of you can go through the document, make changes, and agree on the final version.
   b. Distribute a paper copy of your document to each team member, asking each member to write comments on the copy and return it to you.
   c. Send a copy of the document to the whole team via e-mail. Have each member use a different color for comments, and when the team has reached a consensus incorporate everything into the finished report.
   d. Use a groupware program that allows individual team members to access the document directly to make any changes they wish.

2. The manager of HP's documentation department asks you to redesign the process for writing product manuals. Currently each writer is responsible for an entire project. You are being asked for a process that makes it easier for the writers to share projects and incorporate suggested changes. What is the first step to take?
   a. Talk to the writers involved. Find out how they work together now, what kinds of information they need to share, and how they think the new process should be set up.
   b. Contact documentation departments at other HP divisions or other companies to see what kind of programs they are using.
   c. Search the World Wide Web for information on available groupware packages.
   d. Attend a trade show that features electronic publishing products so that you can see the alternatives firsthand.

3. With management's approval, you have decided on a new groupware program for the documentation department. You have purchased the necessary software and hardware. Now it is time to implement the new process. Some of the writers are eager to make the change. Others are happy with the old process and reluctant to try something new. You expect that all of the writers will have some concerns about the installation procedure and the new process. Which of the following is the best approach to take? Why?
   a. Notify the writers by e-mail that you will be installing the new software, and ask them to send you their questions and

concerns. Compile a list of the issues the writers raise and your answers to their questions. Send the list to the writers by e-mail.

b. Telephone each writer individually, and schedule a time for the installation. Address each writer's concerns over the phone.

c. Schedule a meeting with the manager and all the writers to explain the installation procedure. At the meeting you will also address writers' concerns about the new process.

d. Send all the writers to an off-site training session on the new software, and install the program on their machines while they are gone. Let the class instructors answer questions and address concerns about the new process.

4. The marketing manager wants to make monthly sales figures available to employees at your division. He asks you to recommend a process for sharing this information. Which of the following solutions do you recommend? Why?

a. Use divisionwide e-mail.

b. Use voice mail to broadcast the information.

c. Create a private Web site to be updated with monthly figures.

d. Send a paper copy to be posted in each department.

Critical Thinking Questions

1. Is it important for everyone in a company to know how to use the latest technological tools for document preparation? Why or why not?

2. Would you choose word-processing or desktop publishing software as a tool for writing memos to your staff? Why?

3. Considering how fast and easy it is, should e-mail replace meetings and other face-to-face communication in your company? Why or why not?

4. Why are companies interested in group technologies such as teleconferencing, groupware, and intranets?

5. How could a global corporation such as Coca-Cola take advantage of Internet technology to keep its people around the world in touch with each other?

6. What are the implications for companies that are slow to adopt new communication technologies and for employment candidates who have limited experience with such technologies?

Exercises

1. You are responsible for recommending word-processing software to the headquarters staff at Federal Express. Using computer magazines available in the library, read reviews of leading word-processing products. On the basis of your research, select the one product you think is best, and write a brief recommendation.

2. You're a consultant hired by Chrysler to investigate how the company and its dealers can use technology to communicate with potential customers. Interview several people who've bought a car, and ask them what types of communication technology the manufacturers and car dealers used. Ask them what types of technology they expected manufacturers and dealers to use. Did one technology seem to work better than another? Write a couple of paragraphs explaining to Chrysler what you've learned.

3. For each of the following tasks, decide which communication technology, if any, would be the best to use, and be prepared to explain your choices in class.

a. The CEO of a major corporation wants to explain the company's performance to 27,000 employees, who are located in 14 sites across North America and Europe.

b. A small-business owner wants to convince her bank that the normal loan qualification shouldn't apply in her case and that the bank should approve her request for a $2 million business-expansion loan.

c. A manager needs to warn three employees that their job performance is below company standards.

4. Computer viruses are software programs designed to wreak havoc in computer systems. They can cause millions of dollars of damage in lost time and destroyed data, so they are understandably an important concern for businesses. By interviewing a computer expert or researching library articles, learn the extent of the virus problem. Then draft a brief (less than one page) explanation, listing the things that companies can do to protect themselves.

5. List the technological skills you already have and could discuss in a job interview. Can you type? Have you used e-mail or on-line services? Have you surfed the Web? Have you used photocopiers, calculators, answering machines, voice-mail systems? What experience do you have with video cameras, video players, videoconferencing equipment? Which brands, models, or systems are you familiar with? Which software do you have experience using?

6. Interview several local businesspeople or college administrators to find out the following (write a one-page summary of your findings):

a. What communication technology they use

b. What tasks they use the technology for

c. The advantages of using the technology

d. The disadvantages of using the technology

e. How technology has affected their ability to communicate on the job

7. The year 2000 presents a surprisingly difficult challenge for many business computer systems. In the early days of the computer industry, memory was so expensive and so limited that programmers assigned only two digits to record the year in customer records and other computer files. So, instead of recording 1959 or 1979, these systems recorded simply 59 or

79, and the 19 part of the date was assumed. Over the years, companies amassed huge databases with these abbreviated dates. Trouble is, when the date clicks over at 12:00 A.M. on January 1, 2000, all these systems are going to assume that the year is 1900. The potential database disaster is so big that a small industry of consultants and software developers started appearing around 1995 to help companies address the issue. Assume that your company is facing this challenge and write a one-page memo to the CEO explaining why you need to hire a consultant to help solve the problem. (Do any research necessary to understand the extent of the problem.)

8. You will be out of town for the next week, attending an important meeting that was called at the last minute. While you're away, you want your clients to be able to get the personal attention they deserve, so you've made arrangements with an associate to cover for you. Of course, not every client will need help before your return on May 16; most of them should be able to leave a message on your voice mail so that you can get back to them when you return. Compose a message to record on your voice-mail system letting your clients know that you haven't abandoned them and that they can either leave a message or contact your associate (Bill Comden at 578-3737). Make sure the message is brief while still containing all the necessary information.

9. Your boss refuses to adopt computers for communication purposes—choosing to rely on dictation, typewriters, and simple face-to-face contact. What arguments might you use to persuade your boss to give communication technology a try? Be prepared to discuss your arguments in class.

10. Many magazines have established Web pages in addition to using print. For example, *Backpacker* mag-azine's BaseCamp page (at <http://www.bpbasecamp.com>) aims to give the magazine a wider audience through the Web. Consider whether the information provided on the home page and linked pages effectively addresses the needs of the intended audience. Send an e-mail message to BaseCamp, *Backpacker* magazine, or to one of the linked information pages (including the companies that designed and maintain the home page) asking for additional information. Print both your query and your response for submission.

DEVELOPING YOUR INTERNET SKILLS

GOING ONLINE: CREATE YOUR OWN WEB SITE, P. 68

Think of a Web site you might like to create, either now or in some imaginary future. Picture the kind of graphics and text you'd use, the overall style and tone (irreverent? funny? serious? all business?) that would be appropriate to your purpose (which you will need to define). After looking over the Web Developers' Virtual Library—or WDVL (stars.com)—how do you think these tools might help you accomplish your imaginary Web site?

II

P a r t

THE WRITING

PROCESS

After studying this chapter, you will be able to

Describe the basic tasks in the composition process

Define both the general and the specific purposes of your business messages

Test the purpose of your business messages

Develop an audience profile

Analyze the needs of your audience

Establish the main idea of your messages

Select an appropriate channel and medium for transmitting a particular message to a particular audience

PLANNING BUSINESS MESSAGES

O n the Job
FACING A COMMUNICATION DILEMMA AT MATTEL
The Bimbo with a Brain

Dressed in a zebra-striped bathing suit, she made her grand entrance in 1959, a curvaceous blonde with a mane of platinum hair. Though decades have passed, she's still one of America's hottest items. You know her. Her name is Barbie, and she's some doll.

Since Barbie's debut, the Mattel toy company has sold more than a billion copies of the 11-inch-tall dolls. In fact, 90 percent of all U.S. girls between the ages of 4 and 10 own at least one Barbie; many also own her boyfriend Ken and a group of her girlfriends, not to mention her $200 dream house, her red Ferrari, her vacation hideaway, her horse, her cats, and her incredible, ever-expanding wardrobe. Mattel has even extended into Barbie software. Barbie's appeal is practically universal. She appears in 67 countries around the world, modified in facial characteristics and clothing to suit local tastes: Asian Barbie, Greek Barbie, Icelandic Barbie, Peruvian Barbie . . .

Still, not everybody loves her. Feminists complain that Barbie is a materialistic bubble-head concerned only with possessions, popularity, and appearances. Susan Reverby, director of the women's studies program at Wellesley College, sums it up by saying that Barbie is a bimbo. Reverby won't allow her own little girl to play with Barbie. "I don't want my daughter to think that being a woman means she has to look like Barbie and date someone like Ken," Reverby says.

The people at Mattel are sensitive to the criticism. Jill Barad, president and chief executive officer, has set out to redeem Barbie's reputation by giving her a career. Hailed as one of the most powerful women in corporate America, Barad herself is a role model for many women. She has tried to add a new dimension to Barbie's appeal by giving her not just one job, but many. After plunging into the workforce in 1983 as an employee of McDonald's, Barbie has gone on to bigger and better things. She's been an astronaut, a surgeon, a veterinarian, an Olympic athlete, and the leader of a rock band—and she has the clothes to prove it.

Barad faces the communication challenge of sending a message that will satisfy both Barbie's critics and her faithful fans. The critics want Barbie to be a strong, serious woman with a social conscience—the type of person who volunteers at a settlement house for homeless people after putting in a ten-hour day on Wall Street. The fans want Barbie to be what she has always been—a popular, pretty girl who wears glamorous clothes and has fun all the time.

How can Jill Barad plan messages that will appease one group without upsetting the other? What consideration should she give her purpose? Her audience? What is the best communication channel for her messages? What is the best medium?[1]

Careful planning helps Mattel's employees compose effective messages that are meaningful to the consumers, business contacts, and other employees who receive them. When people at Mattel plan business messages, they clarify their purpose for communicating, try to understand their audience, focus on the main idea of the message, and decide on the best way to send it.

NDERSTANDING THE COMPOSITION PROCESS

Jill Barad's dilemma is not unique. In your own career, some of your tasks will be routine, needing little more than jotting down a few sentences on paper or in an e-mail message; others will be more complex, requiring reflection, research, and careful document preparation. Regardless of the job you hold, the amount of time you actually spend composing messages, or the complexity of your task, effective communication will be the key.[2] Even if you have trouble thinking of what you'll say, you can gain control over your messages by separating the various composition activities into a process.

The composition process helps you gain control over your messages.

A Ten-Stage Process

Although some communicators reject any structured composition process as artificial, the fact is that your final message (the product) and the way you achieve it (the process) are irrevocably linked, so successful communicators like Jill Barad concentrate on both.[3] The process presented here will be most valuable if you view it not as a recipe, not as a list of how-to directives, not as a fixed sequence of steps but as a way to understand the various tasks involved in composition.[4] The composition process varies with the situation, the communicator, and the organization. So the stages do not necessarily occur in 1-2-3 order. Communicators often jump back and forth from one stage to another.

The composition process is flexible; it's not a fixed prescription of sequenced steps.

The **composition process** may be viewed as ten separate stages that fall into three simple categories: planning, composing, and revising (see Figure 5.1):

- *Planning.* During the planning phase, you think about the fundamentals of your message: your reason for communicating, your audience, the main idea of your message, and the channel and medium that will best convey your thoughts. The stages of planning include (1) defining your purpose, (2) analyzing your audience, (3) establishing your main idea, and (4) selecting the appropriate channel and medium.
- *Composing.* Having collected all the information you'll need, you decide on the organization of ideas and the tone you'll adopt. Then you formulate the message, committing your thoughts to words, creating sentences and paragraphs, and selecting illustrations and details to support your main idea. The stages of composing include (5) organizing your message and (6) formulating your message.
- *Revising.* Having formulated your thoughts, you step back to see whether you have expressed them adequately. You review the content and organization of your message, its overall style and readability, and your word choice. You revise and rewrite until your message comes across as clearly and effectively as possible. Then, once you have produced the message, you proofread it for details such as grammar, punctuation, and format. The stages of revision include (7) editing your message, (8) rewriting your message, (9) producing your message, and (10) proofing your message.

Figure 5.1
The Composition Process
Good communicators realize that the composition process often occurs out of order as they jump back and forth from one stage to another.

PLANNING	1. Define purpose 2. Analyze audience 3. Establish main idea 4. Select channel and medium
COMPOSING	5. Organize message 6. Formulate message
REVISING	7. Edit message 8. Rewrite message 9. Produce message 10. Proof message

Good composition includes such important considerations as spelling and usage, but the central part of any composition process is thinking.[5] This ten-stage process helps you assess the possibilities for achieving a specific objective. It gives you control over your composition by helping you focus on the specific tasks that make up successful composition.

Collaboration

Collaboration affects the composition process.

In many organizations, the process of preparing a message is a team effort. **Collaborative writing,** in which more than one writer works on a document, can result in a better product than one person could produce alone. Collaboration brings multiple perspectives and various skills to a project. It combines the strengths of all the team members to increase productivity, enrich knowledge, and enhance interpersonal relationships.[6]

Today's computers make collaborative writing more feasible than it once was. They allow you the freedom to experiment and explore various approaches to the writing process and the subject matter. Electronic tools such as groupware, e-mail, and computer conferencing help you communicate quickly and effectively as you maintain an ongoing dialogue with other team members.[7]

Collaborative writing isn't without problems. Of course, as a member of a collaborative team, you need writing skills such as researching, drafting, editing, and proofreading. However, team members coming from different backgrounds will have different concerns (a technical expert may focus on accuracy and meeting scientific standards; an editor may focus on organization and coherence; a manager may focus on schedules, cost, and corporate goals). So, in addition to being able to write, you must also be able to attend meetings regularly, plan and organize efficiently, accept responsibility, volunteer willingly, contribute ideas freely, elicit and listen to ideas, cooperate, and resolve conflicts.[8] You must be able and willing to overcome differences in writing styles, working styles, and personality traits. You must be open to the opinions of others and focus on your team's objectives instead of your own.

Collaborative writing is used in any number of business situations, ranging from one writer asking a co-worker's opinion to many writers cooperating in an all-out team effort. You might sit down with your boss to plan a memo, work independently during the writing phase, and then ask your boss to review the message and suggest revisions. Or your message may be particularly long and important so that the process involves more people: a project manager, researchers, writers, typists, graphic artists, and editors.[9] For efforts of this type, the review and revision stages might be repeated several times to respond to input not only from various team members but also from various departments.

To get organized, your team will select a leader, clarify goals, and resolve conflicts.[10] To be effective, your team will agree on purpose, audience awareness, and writing style.

Schedules

Scheduling affects the composition process.

When composing a message, whether alone or in collaboration with co-workers, allotting your time properly is an important consideration. Any realistic schedule would give you the time you need for thoroughly planning, composing, and revising your message. But business messages are often composed under pressure and on a schedule that is anything but realistic. Especially when time is short, carefully schedule yourself, and stick to your schedule. Of the time you're given, try using roughly half for planning, gathering material, and immersing yourself in the subject matter. Try using less than a quarter of your time for composing, and use more than a quarter of the time for revising (so that you don't shortchange important final steps such as polishing and proofing).[11]

EXAMINING THE COMPOSITION PROCESS

This textbook breaks the composition process into three chapters. Chapter 6 discusses composing business messages, and Chapter 7 covers revising business messages. The rest of Chapter 5 focuses on planning business messages. The result of planning can be as simple as a handwritten checklist of topics to cover in a phone conversation, or it can be a detailed strategy that spells out scheduling and collaborative responsibilities, objectives, audience needs, and media choices. By defining your purpose, you set clear objectives for measuring your efforts. By analyzing your audience, you focus on their needs and point of

Pulitzer Prize–winning columnist William Safire writes political columns for the New York Times. *When planning how to organize your thoughts in writing, says Safire, use a combination of your experience, intuition, and common sense.*

view. By establishing your main idea, you shape and control your message. By selecting a channel and medium, you present your message in the best light possible.[12]

S TAGE 1: DEFINING YOUR PURPOSE

When planning a business message, think about your purpose. Of course you want to maintain the goodwill of the audience and create a favorable impression for your organization, but you also have a particular goal you want to achieve. That purpose may be straightforward and obvious (placing an order), or it may be more difficult to define (Barad's purpose of satisfying both critics and fans of Barbie). When the purpose is unclear, it pays to spend a few minutes thinking about what you hope to accomplish.

The purpose of the message helps you decide whether to proceed, how to respond to your audience, which information to focus on, and which channel and medium to use.

Common Purposes of Business Messages

All business messages have a **general purpose:** to inform, to persuade, or to collaborate with your audience. The purpose determines both the amount of audience participation you need and the amount of control you have over your message. If your message is intended strictly to inform, you require little interaction with your audience. Your readers or listeners absorb information, accept it, or reject it, but they don't contribute to message content; you control the message. If your message is persuasive, you require a moderate amount of audience participation, so you'll retain a moderate amount of message control. Finally, if you seek collaboration from your audience, you require maximum audience participation, so your control of the message is low. You can't adhere to a rigid plan because you need to adjust to new input and unexpected reactions.

In addition to having a general purpose, your messages also have a **specific purpose.** Ask yourself, "What should my audience do or think after reviewing this message?" Then state your purpose as precisely as possible, identifying the members of the audience who should respond.

Your general purpose may be to inform, to persuade, or to collaborate.

To determine the specific purpose, think of how the audience's ideas or behavior should be affected by the message.

Defer a message or do not send it at all if

- *The purpose is not realistic*
- *The timing is not right*
- *You are not the right person to deliver the message*
- *The purpose is not acceptable to the organization*

How to Test Your Purpose

Once you've established your purpose, pause for a moment to consider whether it's worth pursuing at this time. There's no point in creating a message that is unlikely to accomplish its purpose. Before you decide to send the message, ask yourself these questions:

- *Is the purpose realistic?* Most people resist change. So if your purpose involves a radical shift in action or attitude, you'll do better to go slowly. Instead of suggesting your whole program at once, consider proposing the first step and viewing your message as the beginning of a learning process.
- *Is this the right time?* An idea that is unacceptable when profits are down, for example, may easily win approval when business improves. If an organization is undergoing changes of some sort, you may want to defer your message until things stabilize and people can concentrate on your ideas.
- *Am I the right person to deliver the message?* Even though you may have done all the work yourself, your boss may have a better chance of accomplishing results because of her or his higher status. Achieving your objective is more important than taking the credit. In the long run, people will recognize the quality of your work. Also bear in mind that some people are simply better writers or speakers than others. If the stakes are high and you lack experience or confidence, you might want to play a supporting role rather than take the lead.
- *Is the purpose acceptable to the organization?* As the representative of your company, you are obligated to work toward the organization's goals. Say you're a customer service representative who answers letters from customers. If you receive an abusive letter that unfairly attacks your company, your initial reaction might be to fire back an angry reply. Would top managers want you to counterattack, or would they want you to regain the customer's goodwill? Your response should reflect the organization's priorities.

As vice president of consumer market development for General Motors, Shirley Young is responsible for recommending ways to improve customer satisfaction as well as ways to enhance marketing effectiveness. Given such broad involvement, Young's business messages include all three common purposes: informing, persuading, collaborating.

STAGE 2: ANALYZING YOUR AUDIENCE

Once you are satisfied that you have a legitimate purpose in communicating, take a good look at your intended audience. Who are the members, what are their attitudes, and what do they need to know? The answers to these questions will indicate something about the material you'll cover and the way you'll cover it.

Develop Your Audience's Profile

If you're communicating with someone you know well, perhaps your boss or a co-worker, audience analysis is relatively easy. You can predict their reactions pretty well without a lot of research. On the other hand, if your audience is made up of strangers, you have to do some investigating to learn about them before you can use common sense to anticipate their reactions.

- *Determine audience size and composition.* Audience size affects the amount of audience participation in oral presentations and the degree of formality in written documents. Audience size also affects the diversity of backgrounds and interests you'll encounter, so you need to look for the common denominators that tie the members of an audience together. At the same time, you want to respond to the particular concerns of individuals. Because a marketing manager and a production or finance manager need different information, be sure to include a variety of evidence that touches on everyone's area of interest.
- *Identify the primary audience.* When several people will be receiving your message, try to identify those who are most important to your purpose. If you can reach these decision makers or opinion molders, the other members of the audience will follow their lead. Although higher-status people usually make the decisions, occasionally a person in a relatively low position will have influence in one or two particular areas.
- *Estimate the audience's probable reaction.* Your approach to organizing your message depends on your audience's probable reaction. If you expect a favorable response with very little criticism or debate, you can be straightforward about stating your conclusions and recommendations. You can also use a minimal amount of evidence to support your points. On the other hand, when you face a skeptical audience, you may have to introduce your conclusions and recommendations more gradually and provide more proof.
- *Gauge the audience's level of understanding.* If you and your audience share the same general background, you can assume that audience members will understand your material without any difficulty. Otherwise, you'll have to decide how much you need to educate them. The trick is to provide the information they need without being stodgy or obvious.
- *Define your relationship with the audience.* If you're unknown to your audience, you'll have to earn their confidence before you can win them to your point of view. If you're communicating with a familiar group, your credibility has already been established, so you can get down to business immediately. You can build credibility or overcome people's preconceptions of you by providing ample evidence for any material outside your usual area of expertise. Your status relative to your audience also affects the style and tone of your presentation, depending on whether you're addressing your boss, your peers, employees of lower status, customers, or suppliers.

Satisfy Your Audience's Informational Needs

As Jill Barad points out, the key to effective communication is determining your reader's needs and then responding to them. You do that by telling people what they need to know in terms that are meaningful to them. A good message answers all the audience's questions.

Ask yourself some key questions about your audience:

- Who are they?
- What is their probable reaction to your message?
- How much do they already know about the subject?
- What is their relationship to you?

Focus on the common interests of the audience, but be alert to their individual concerns.

A gradual approach and plenty of evidence are required to win over a skeptical audience.

Vary the tone and structure of the message to reflect your relationship with the audience.

GOING ONLINE
LEARN MORE ABOUT ANALYZING AN AUDIENCE
Find out more about audience analysis with a table that's based on developing information for the Web. A carefully constructed audience cluster diagram graphically illustrates the discussion and reinforces the points made in this textbook.

http://www.december.com/web/develop/wdaudience.html

- *Find out what the audience wants to know.* In many cases, the audience's information needs are readily apparent. When Jill Barad answers letters requesting information about Barbie, all she normally has to do is respond to the consumers' questions. In other cases, an audience may not be particularly good at telling you what is needed. Your boss might say, "Find out everything you can about the Polaroid Corporation, and write a memo on it." That's a pretty big assignment. Ten days later, you submit your 25-page report, and, instead of heaping you with praise, your boss says: "I don't need all this. All I want is Polaroid's five-year financial record." So when you get a vague request, pin it down. One good approach is to restate the request in more specific terms. Another approach is to get a fix on its priority. You might ask, "Should I drop everything else and devote myself to this for the next week?"

- *Anticipate unstated questions.* Try to think of information needs that your audience may not even be aware of. Suppose your company has just hired a new employee from out of town, and you've been assigned to coordinate this person's relocation. At a minimum, you would write a welcoming letter describing your company's procedures for relocating employees. With a little extra thought, however, you might decide to include some information about the city: perhaps a guide to residential areas, a map or two, brochures about cultural activities, or information on schools and transportation facilities.

- *Provide all the required information.* Once you've defined your audience's needs, be certain to satisfy those needs completely. One good way to test the thoroughness of your message is to use the journalistic approach: Check to see whether your messages answer *who, what, when, where, why,* and *how.* Whenever you request any action, take particular care to explain exactly what you are expecting. Until readers get a clear picture of what they're supposed to do, they can't possibly do it. If you want them to send you a check for $5, tell them; if you want them to turn in their time cards on Friday by 3:00 P.M., say so.

- *Be sure the information is accurate.* There's no point in answering all your audience's questions if the answers are wrong. In business, you have a special duty to check things before making a written commitment, especially if you're writing to someone who is outside the company. Your organization is legally bound by any promises you make, so make sure that your company will be able to follow through. You may sincerely believe that you have answered someone's questions correctly and then later realize that your information was incorrect. If that happens, the most ethical thing for you to do is to contact the person immediately and correct the error. Most people will respect you for your honesty.

- *Emphasize ideas of greatest interest to the audience.* When deciding how to respond to your audience's information needs, remember that some points will be of greater interest and importance than others. The head of engineering and someone from the shipping department might be interested in different things. If you don't know the audience, or if you're communicating with a large group of people, you'll have to use your common sense to identify points of particular interest. Such factors as age, job, location, income, or education can give you a clue. Remember that your main goal as a business communicator is to tell your audience what they need to know.

Satisfy Your Audience's Motivational Needs

Some types of messages, particularly persuasive and bad news messages, are intended to motivate audience members to change their beliefs or behavior. The problem is that people resist ideas that conflict with their existing beliefs and practices. They may selectively screen out threatening ideas or distort your message to fit their preconceived map of reality. To overcome resistance, arrange your message so that the information will be as acceptable as possible (see Chapter 1).

Five questions to ask yourself that will help you satisfy the audience's information needs:

- What does the audience want to know?
- What does the audience need to know?
- Have I provided all desired and necessary information?
- Is the information accurate?
- Have I emphasized the information of greatest interest to the audience?

In the race against Nike for market share, Reebok International's founder and chairman, Paul Fireman, plans his advertising messages for specific audiences rather than trying to appeal to the entire shoe market at one time. He uses sniper shots, not shotgun blasts.

The Greek-born, internationally popular composer Yanni broke global revenue records with his televised concerts at the Acropolis, in front of the Taj Majal, and in Beijing's Forbidden City. But each concert took years of meticulous planning. "My least favorite word to hear in a location like this is 'whoops,' " the musician told reporters while in China. A careless stage worker could create an international incident by bashing a carved pillar—and a business writer could just as easily lose an overseas customer with a carelessly worded letter.

Remember that your audience
- May have little time
- May be distracted
- May give your message low priority

The main idea is the "hook" that sums why a particular audience should do or think as you suggest.

Satisfy Your Audience's Practical Needs

Many business messages are directed toward people who are themselves in business: your customers, suppliers, co-workers. So, regardless of where these people work or precisely what they do, their days are filled with distractions:

- First-level supervisors are involved in at least 200 separate activities or incidents in an eight-hour day.
- Most activities are very brief. One study of supervisors shows one activity every 48 seconds.
- A study of chief executives reports that periods of desk work average 10 to 15 minutes each.
- Responding to mail takes less than 5 percent of a manager's time, and most executives react to only about 30 percent of the mail they receive.[13]

In other words, many in your audience will review your message under difficult circumstances with many interruptions, and they are likely to give it a low priority. So make your message as convenient as possible for your audience. Try to be brief. In general, a 5-minute talk is easier to follow than a 30-minute presentation; a two-paragraph letter is more manageable than one that's two pages long, and a two-page memo is more likely to be read than a ten-page report.

If your written message has to be long, make it easy for readers to follow so that they can pick it up and put it down several times without losing the thread of what you're saying. Begin with a summary of key points, use plenty of headings, and put important points in list format so that they'll stand out. Put less important information in separate enclosures or appendixes, and use charts and graphs to dramatize important ideas.

If you're delivering a long message orally, be sure to give listeners an overview of the message's structure, and then express your thoughts clearly and logically. You might also use flip charts, slides, or handouts to help listeners understand and remember key points. You're the guide; lead audience members through your message by telling them where they've been and where they're going.

 TAGE 3: ESTABLISHING THE MAIN IDEA

Every business message can be boiled down to one main idea. Regardless of the issue's complexity, one central point sums up everything. This point is your theme, your main idea. Everything else in the message either supports this point or demonstrates its implications.

A topic and a main idea are different. The **topic** is the broad subject of the message. The **main idea** makes a statement—one of many possible statements—about the topic. It provides a rationale, explaining your purpose in terms that the audience can accept. Barad might give a presentation on the topic of Barbie's image, with the aim of persuading management critics that Barbie has become an acceptable role model for young girls. Her main idea might be that Barbie's careers and culturally diverse friends have made the character a better person.

The main idea has to strike a response in the intended audience. It has to motivate people to do what you want by linking your purpose with their own. When you're preparing a brief letter, memo, or meeting agenda, the main idea may be pretty obvious, especially if you're dealing with simple facts that have little or no emotional content for the audience. In such cases, the main idea may be nothing more than "Here is what you wanted." If you're responding to a request for information about the price and availability of your company's products, your main idea would be something like "We have these items at competitive prices."

Finding the "angle" or "hook" is more complicated when you're trying to persuade someone or when you have disappointing information to convey. In those situations, look for a main idea that will establish a good relationship between you and your audience. Focus on some point of agreement or common interest.

In longer documents and presentations, in which a mass of material needs to be unified, the problem of establishing a main idea becomes still more challenging. You need to identify a generalization that encompasses all the individual points you want to make. For these tough assignments, you may need to take special measures to pinpoint your main idea.

Use Prewriting Techniques

Identifying the main idea often requires creativity and experimentation. The best approach is to **brainstorm,** letting your mind wander over the possibilities, testing various alternatives against your purpose, your audience, and the facts at your disposal. How do you generate those possibilities? Successful communicators use various approaches. You have to experiment until you find a prewriting method that fits your mental style. Here are a few approaches that might work for you:

- *Storyteller's tour.* Turn on your tape recorder and pretend that you've just run into an old friend on the street. She says, "So, what are you working on these days?" Give her an overview of your message, focusing on your reasons for communicating, your major points, your rationale, and the implications for your intended audience. Listen critically to the tape; then repeat the exercise until you are able to give a smooth, two-minute summary that conveys the gist of your message. The summary should reveal your main idea.
- *Random list.* On a computer screen or a clean sheet of paper, list everything that pops into your head pertaining to your message. When you've exhausted the possibilities, study the list for relationships. Sort the items into groups, as you would sort a deck of cards into suits. Look for common denominators; the connection might be geographical, sequential, spatial, chronological, or topical. Part of the list might break down into problems, causes, and solutions; another part, into pros and cons. Regardless of what categories finally emerge, the sorting process will help you sift through your thoughts and decide what's important and what isn't.
- *FCR worksheet.* If your subject involves the solution to a problem, you might try using an FCR worksheet to help you visualize the relationships among your findings (F), your conclusions (C), and your recommendations (R). For example, you might find that you're losing sales to a competitor who offers lower prices than you do (F). From that finding, you might conclude that your loss of sales is due to your pricing policy (C). This conclusion would lead you to recommend a price cut (R). To make an FCR worksheet, divide a computer screen or a sheet of paper into three columns. List the major findings in the first column, then extrapolate conclusions and write them in the second column. These conclusions form the basis for the recommendations, which are listed in the third column. An analysis of the three columns should help you focus on the main idea.
- *Journalistic approach.* For informational messages, the journalistic approach may provide a good point of departure. The answers to six questions—who, what, when, where, why, and how—should clarify the main idea.
- *Question-and-answer chain.* Perhaps the best approach is to look at the subject from your audience's perspective. Ask yourself: "What is the audience's main question? What do they need to know?" Examine your answers to those questions. What additional questions emerge? Follow the chain of questions and answers until you have replied to every conceivable question that might occur to the audience. By thinking about your material from their point of view, you are more likely to pinpoint the main idea.

Some techniques for establishing the main idea:
- Storyteller's tour
- Random list
- FCR worksheet
- Journalistic approach
- Question-and-answer chain

Limit the Scope

There's a limit to how much you can communicate in a given number of words. What can be accomplished depends on the nature of the subject, the audience members' familiarity with the topic, their receptivity to your conclusions, and your credibility. In general, presenting routine information to a knowledgeable audience that already knows and respects

The main idea should be geared to the length of the message.

BEHIND THE SCENES AT ALLSTATE INSURANCE
Editing for Action: Fine Print That Insures Success

"My job is to help management create the future," says Patrick Williams. To carry out that heady challenge for his employer, Allstate Insurance Company, Williams edits one of the nation's top all-employee publications, *Allstate Now.* Part of the 85-member corporate relations department at the company's headquarters in Northbrook, Illinois, Williams plans his maga-paper (a magazine that's put out in an eight-page newspaper-size format) so that it plays a key role in helping employees participate in the Allstate story.

For Allstate's management, communicating with employees is critical to the future of the company. All employees must know where the company is going, what it is trying to achieve, and whether they are going to help it get there. Throughout the corporate relations department, therefore, the attitude is proactive—not telling people what has happened but helping people make things happen. For Williams, that means careful planning.

The planning actually begins at the highest level of the company. The board of directors meets annually with corporate relations management to formulate a communications policy for the coming year. They address such issues as where Allstate is going, how communications can help the company get there, what issues the employees must understand to get the company there, and how management can help employees understand those issues. Working within the framework established at that meeting, Williams plans the articles that will appear in each monthly issue of *Allstate Now.*

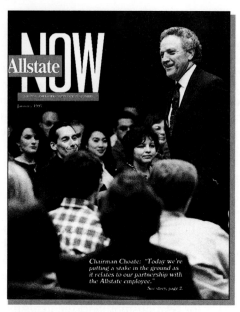

Allstate's Patrick Williams carefully plans his company's in-house magazine to keep employees informed about what's going on and to help them participate in making things happen.

you can be done quickly. Building consensus about a complex and controversial subject takes longer, especially if the audience is composed of skeptical or hostile strangers.

Although you adjust your message to fit the time or space available, don't change the number of major points. Regardless of how long the message will be, stick with three or four major points—five at the very most. According to communication researchers, that's all your audience will remember.[14] If you're delivering a long message, say, a 60-minute presentation or a 20-page report, the major points can be developed in considerable detail. You can spend about ten minutes or ten paragraphs (or over three pages of double-spaced, printed text) on each of your key points and still have room for the introduction and conclusion. If your message is brief, four minutes or one page, you'll have only a minute or a paragraph each for the introduction, conclusion, and major points.

STAGE 4: SELECTING THE APPROPRIATE CHANNEL AND MEDIUM

Various types of messages require various communication channels.

The communication media available to businesspeople have mushroomed in the past two decades: audiotapes, videotapes, faxes, e-mail, Web sites, voice mail, teleconferences—to name a few. You can now select not only from the traditional oral and written channels but also from the newer electronic channel, which includes some features of the other two.

Eight weeks before publication, Williams meets with his editorial board, which is made up of ten managers of Allstate's various departments, including law, planning, sales, underwriting, advertising, and human resources—the people who plan the future of the company and give it direction. Listening closely to learn what they think is ahead, Williams decides what Allstate employees will need to hear about. "On the other hand," he quickly points out, "it is equally important to listen to employees, my readers in the company, to learn their information needs. My job as editor is to bring these two groups together."

Every issue must include four articles, each demonstrating one of Allstate's "Four Commitments"—to customers, to community and society, to employees, and to being the best. Williams then has to consider whether the content is appropriate to the publication or whether it could be better communicated by others in a memo or at a meeting. He also asks himself whether the article is what his readers want: "Is the subject technical or financial? Is the article full of data to be digested? Is it new, important, complex, or controversial?" Finally, with all those factors in mind, Williams selects articles and plans their organization and approach by asking himself, "How will this story, its picture and headline, help the company and employees?" He does not ask whether the story is amusing or entertaining but, "Will it help the company and employees?"

The next step is to create and design the articles. Photographs are decided on first because they have to be set up and shot. Meanwhile Williams and his staff interview the appropriate people. The format of each article is determined by its purpose. For example, the purpose of one article, which had to convey both good news and bad news, was to inform, reestablish trust, and allay fears. To accomplish that, Williams believed that readers needed to hear "the sound of another person's voice." In this case, the voice was to be that of a top manager. He invited several Allstate employees to join the interview session, and they posed questions for the top manager to answer. This lively question-and-answer session provided the basis for the article.

The result of all that careful planning? Eight weeks after an editorial board discussion, nearly 50,000 employees arrived on a Friday morning to find the latest issue of *Allstate Now* on their desks. When they finished reading it, they had been unobtrusively assured, through words and pictures, of their important place in creating Allstate's future.

Apply Your Knowledge

1. As editor of *Allstate Now,* how would you plan to communicate the following changes at Allstate as being in the best interests of the employees: (a) dropping the slogan "The Good Hands People," (b) moving corporate headquarters from Illinois to Texas, (c) acquiring the home and auto insurance divisions of a major competitor?
2. Imagine you're planning articles for *Allstate Now.* List the advantages and disadvantages of the following changes: (a) expanding the publication from 8 to 16 pages per issue, (b) publishing every two weeks instead of monthly, (c) receiving permission to use color photographs and a second color in the design.

Your selection of channel and medium can make the difference between effective and ineffective communication.[15] So, when choosing a channel (oral, written, or electronic) and a medium (face-to-face conversation, telephone conversation, e-mail, voice mail, videotape, written report, and so on), do your best to match your selections to your message and your intentions.[16]

Every medium has limitations that filter out parts of the message. For example, flyers or bulletin boards are nondynamic and ineffective for communicating extremely complex messages, but they're perfect for simple ones. Moreover, every medium influences your audience's perception of your intentions. If you want to emphasize the formality of your message, use a formal medium, such as a written memo or letter. If you want to emphasize the confidentiality of your message, use voice mail rather than a fax, send a letter rather than a memo, or address the matter in an interview rather than during a meeting. If you want to instill an emotional commitment to corporate values, consider a visual medium, such as a videotape or videoconference.[17]

Various cultures tend to favor one channel over another. For example, the United States, Canada, and Germany emphasize written media, whereas Japan emphasizes oral media—perhaps because its high-context culture carries so much of the message in nonverbal cues and "between the lines" interpretation.[18] Within the United States, the basic choice of oral, written, or electronic channels depends on the purpose, the audience, and the characteristics of the three communication channels (see Table 5.1).

Table 5.1		
An Oral Message Is Best When	*A Written Message Is Best When*	*An Electronic Message Is Best When*
You want immediate feedback from the audience	You don't need immediate feedback	You don't need immediate feedback, but you do need speed
Your message is relatively simple and easy to accept	Your message is detailed, complex, and requires careful planning	Your message is emotional, you may or may not need immediate feedback, but you're physically separated (videotape, teleconference)
You don't need a permanent record	You need a permanent, verifiable record	You don't need a permanent record, but you want to overcome time-zone barriers (voice mail, fax)
You can assemble the audience conveniently and economically	You are trying to reach an audience that is large and geographically dispersed	You are trying to reach an audience that is large and geographically dispersed, and you want to reach them personally (teleconference, videotape)
You want to encourage interaction to solve a problem or to reach a decision	You want to minimize the chances for distortion that occur when a message is passed orally from person to person	You want to minimize oral distortion, but you're in a hurry and in a distant location (e-mail)

Oral Communication

In general, use oral communication if your purpose is to collaborate with the audience.

The chief advantage of oral communication is the opportunity it provides for immediate feedback. This is the channel to use when you want the audience to ask questions and make comments or when you're trying to reach a group decision. Face-to-face communication is useful when you're presenting controversial information, because you can read the audience's body language and adjust your message accordingly.[19]

Your choice between a face-to-face conversation and a telephone or conference call would depend on audience location, message importance, and your need for the sort of nonverbal feedback that only body language can reveal. In fact, oral communication takes many forms, including conversations, telephone calls, interviews, small group meetings, seminars, workshops, training programs, formal speeches, and major presentations. Chapters 19 and 20 explore these media in more detail.

In general, the smaller the audience, the more interaction among the members. If your purpose involves reaching a decision or solving a problem, select an oral medium geared toward a small audience. Be sure the program is relatively informal and unstructured so that ideas can flow freely. Gatherings of this sort can be arranged quickly and economically.

At the opposite extreme are formal presentations to large audiences, which are common at events such as sales conventions, shareholder meetings, and ceremonial functions. Often these major presentations take place in a big facility, where the audience can be seated auditorium-style. Their formality makes them unsuitable for collaborative purposes requiring audience interaction.

Written Communication

Written communication increases the sender's control but eliminates the possibility of immediate feedback.

Written messages also take many forms. At one extreme are the scribbled notes people use to jog their own memories; at the other are elaborate, formal reports that rival magazines in graphic quality. Regardless of the form, written messages have one big advantage: They let you plan and control the message. A written format is appropriate when the information is complex, when a permanent record is needed for future reference, when the audience is large and geographically dispersed, and when immediate interaction with the audience is either unimportant or undesirable.

For extensive coverage of letters and memos, see Chapters 8 through 11. Reports are thoroughly discussed in Chapters 14 through 18. In addition, Appendix A presents a detailed discussion of the accepted formats for business documents. Although many types of written communication are specialized, the most common are letters, memos, and reports.

Letters and Memos

With a few exceptions, most letters and memos are relatively brief documents, generally one or two pages. Memos are the "workhorses" of business communication; they are used for the routine, day-to-day exchange of information within an organization. Letters go to outsiders, and they perform an important public relations function in addition to conveying a particular message. Memos are usually brief, lacking a salutation and emphasizing the needs of readers who have time only to skim messages. They can also be sent to any number of receivers, whereas letters are sent to only one. Because of their open construction and method of delivery, memos are less private than letters. You often use memos to designate responsibility, communicate the same material to many people, communicate policy and procedure, confirm oral agreements or decisions, and place specific information on record.

Letters (see Figure 5.2), memos, and e-mail messages (see Figure 5.3) can be classified by function into four categories: direct requests; routine, good-news, and goodwill messages; bad-news messages; and persuasive messages. Their function determines their organization, but style and tone are governed by your relationship with your audience.

Letters and memos are organized according to their purpose; the relationship between writer and reader dictates their style and tone.

Many organizations rely on form letters (and sometimes form memos) to save time and money on routine communication. Form letters are particularly handy for such one-time mass mailings as sales messages about products, explanations of policies and procedures, information about organizational activities, goodwill messages such as seasonal greetings, and acknowledgments of job applications. A variation of the form letter is the boilerplate, or standard paragraph, that can be selected to suit an occasion or an audience. Letters containing boilerplates are used for messages that need to be slightly more individualized than a form letter, such as Jill Barad's replies to inquiries about Mattel's products and activities.

Reports and Proposals

Factual, objective documents such as reports and proposals may be distributed to either insiders or outsiders, depending on their purpose and subject. They come in many formats—including preprinted forms, letters, memos, and manuscripts—and range in length from a few pages to several hundred. In general, reports and proposals are longer than letters and memos and have a larger number of distinct elements.

Reports are generally longer and more formal than letters and memos, and they have more components.

Reports and proposals also tend to be more formal than letters and memos. As in all forms of business communication, the organization, style, and tone of reports and proposals depend on the message's purpose, on the relationship between writer and reader, and on the traditions of the organization. Thus the basic composition process is much the same for all.

Electronic Communication

Although oral messages can be in person and face to face, they can also be transmitted electronically using voice mail, teleconferencing, audiotape, videotape, closed-circuit television, and so on. Similarly, although written messages can be handwritten, typed, or printed, they can also be transmitted electronically using faxes, e-mail, computer conferencing, and so on. Electronic media are useful when you need speed, when you're physically separated from your audience, when you need to overcome time-zone barriers, and when you need to reach a dispersed audience personally. Chapter 4 introduced the technological features of electronic media; following are a few pointers on when to select electronic media over traditional oral or written media:[20]

In general, use electronic communication for speed, to overcome time-zone barriers, and to reach a widely dispersed audience personally.

■ *Voice mail* is usually used to replace short memos and phone calls that need no response. It is most effective for short, unambiguous messages.

Figure 5.2
In-Depth Critique: A Typical Letter

When Jeff Hagen responds to a consumer, he is careful to show respect, make the message as personal as possible, and match the customer's tone, in this case by keeping the approach light and cheerful.

Jeff Hagen uses letterhead stationery but doesn't let that make his message too formal or unfriendly.

The formal salutation indicates Hagen's respect for a customer he doesn't know.

The body of the letter is brief but still includes friendly remarks designed to maintain goodwill.

The close is an optimistic look at the future.

 General Mills Consumer Services

P.O. Box 1113, Minneapolis, MN 55440

March 13, 1999

Mr. Julius Croghan
231 Ruffin Avenue
Cedar Spring, South Carolina 29302

Dear Mr. Croghan:

Thank you very much for your delightful comments. It was kind of you to share your thoughts, and you've brightened our day here at General Mills.

Many of our products have long attracted loyal fans. I'm happy to see that you are among that group.

At General Mills, customer feedback is critical to our success. It's through communications like yours that we become aware of consumer concerns and preferences.

I have enclosed gift coupons and hope you will continue to use and enjoy our products.

Sincerely,

Jeffrey N Hagen

Jeffrey N. Hagen
Director, Consumer Services

- *Teleconferencing* is best for informational meetings, but it's ineffective for negotiation. It's an efficient alternative to a face-to-face meeting, but it can't totally simulate it. For example, because it discourages the "secondary" conversations that usually occur during a meeting of more than four or five people, it could prevent participants from sharing valuable information. On the other hand, its discouraging of secondary conversations might help participants focus on the topic.
- *Videotape* is often effective for sending a motivational message to a large number of people. By communicating nonverbal cues, it can strengthen your image of sincerity and trustworthiness; however, it offers no opportunity for immediate feedback.

The president of a chain of Texas-based pet stores, Pet Paradise, has asked his administrative assistant, Maria Hernandez, to notify all 47 store managers that their September 5 meeting in San Antonio has been rescheduled for September 26. Hernandez could phone or fax the message, but either of these methods would take considerable time. By choosing e-mail, Hernandez minimizes her own efforts and allows each manager to receive the important news almost immediately.

Figure 5.3
In-Depth Critique: A Typical E-Mail Message

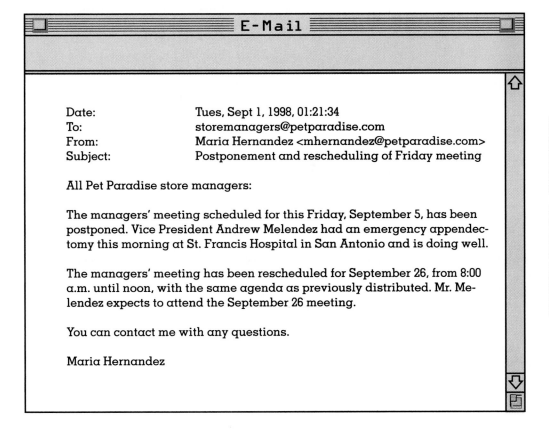

Date:	Tues, Sept 1, 1998, 01:21:34
To:	storemanagers@petparadise.com
From:	Maria Hernandez <mhernandez@petparadise.com>
Subject:	Postponement and rescheduling of Friday meeting

All Pet Paradise store managers:

The managers' meeting scheduled for this Friday, September 5, has been postponed. Vice President Andrew Melendez had an emergency appendectomy this morning at St. Francis Hospital in San Antonio and is doing well.

The managers' meeting has been rescheduled for September 26, from 8:00 a.m. until noon, with the same agenda as previously distributed. Mr. Melendez expects to attend the September 26 meeting.

You can contact me with any questions.

Maria Hernandez

Because Hernandez has all managers' e-mail addresses in one file, she needs to key in only the name of that file to reach each manager.

Hernandez first states the critical message and then gives the reason for the postponement.

She then gives information on the rescheduled meeting and tries to anticipate the managers' questions.

- *Fax* messages are usually used to overcome time-zone barriers when a hard copy is required. A fax has all the characteristics of a written message, except that it may lack the privacy of a letter, and depending on the quality of your audience's machine (thermal versus plain-paper, for example), your message may appear less crisp, perhaps even less professional, than other written messages.
- *E-mail* offers advantages of speed, lower cost, and increased access to other employees. This medium is best at communicating brief, noncomplex information that's time sensitive, but its effectiveness depends on the skills of the people using it.
- *Computer conferencing* offers the advantage of democracy; that is, more attention is focused on an idea than on who communicates it. However, too much emphasis on the message (to the neglect of the person communicating it) can threaten corporate culture, which needs a more dynamic medium of communication.

Message planning encompasses valuable tasks that help you gain more control over the composition process. Use this chapter's Checklist for Planning Business Messages not as a recipe for well-planned messages but as a reminder of what tasks and choices to address as you develop your business messages. Also remember that the planning stages discussed here may be useful at any time during the composition process, depending on your purpose, your audience, and your message.

CHECKLIST FOR PLANNING BUSINESS MESSAGES

A. Purpose
1. Determine whether the purpose of your message is to inform, to persuade, or to collaborate.
2. Identify the specific behavior you hope to induce in the audience.
3. Make sure that your purpose is worthwhile and realistic.

B. Audience
1. Identify the primary audience.
2. Determine the size and composition of the group.
3. Analyze the audience's probable reaction to your message.
4. Determine the audience's level of understanding.
5. Evaluate your relationship with the audience.
6. Analyze the audience's informational, motivational, and practical needs.

C. Main Idea
1. Stimulate your creativity with brainstorming techniques.
2. Identify a "hook" that will motivate the audience to respond to your message in the way you intend.
3. Evaluate whether the main idea is realistic given the length limitations imposed on the message.
4. Collect any necessary information.

D. Channel and Medium
1. If your purpose is to collaborate, give an informal, relatively unstructured oral presentation to a small group.

2. If you are celebrating an important public occasion, give a prepared speech to a large audience.
3. If you need a permanent record, if the message is complex, or if immediate feedback is unimportant, prepare a written message.
   - a. Send a letter if your message is relatively simple and the audience is outside the company.
   - b. Send a memo if your message is relatively simple and the audience is inside the company.
   - c. Write a report if your message is objective and complex.
4. If you need to communicate quickly, overcome time-zone differences, or personally reach a widely dispersed audience, choose electronic communication.
   - a. Use voice mail if your message is short and clear.
   - b. Use teleconferencing for informational meetings.
   - c. Use videotape for sending motivational messages to a large number of people.
   - d. Use fax machines to overcome time-zone barriers.
   - e. Use e-mail for speed, lower cost, and increased access to other employees.
   - f. Use computer conferencing to focus attention on ideas instead of status.

On the Job

SOLVING A COMMUNICATION DILEMMA AT MATTEL

Convincing the world that Barbie is more than just a bimbo is not an easy task, but Jill Barad is doing her best with careful planning and a thorough understanding of her audience. Part of Barad's problem is that Mattel's purposes are mixed. On the one hand, the company wants Barbie to be a worthy role model for little girls. On the other hand, Mattel wants to sell dolls and accessories—and that means that Barbie must retain her traditional appeal. After all, hundreds of millions of people have voted with their pocketbooks for the Barbie doll whose number one priority is what to wear. Nearly $2 billion in yearly sales—40 percent of Mattel's total revenue—is at stake. Barad knows that completely changing Barbie's image could jeopardize the doll's mystique and hurt sales.

To a great extent, that mystique depends on Barbie's lack of a strong identity. Mattel intentionally says very little about Barbie's character because they want little girls to decide what Barbie is like. Her bland personality and her wide assortment of clothes and accessories allow for endless possibilities. Barbie can be whatever a child wants her to be.

Still, an image of Barbie emerges from a variety of messages—advertising, public relations events, the official Barbie Web site, and *Barbie* magazine, a glossy publication sent to 650,000 members of Barbie's fan club. The magazine describes Barbie's clothes and activities. In a recent issue, for example, Ken took Barbie out to dinner at a "sumptuous restaurant." For the occasion, Barbie chose her "ravishing new pink ruffled evening dress." Perhaps the strongest statement about Barbie's personality was a two-hour cartoon special, featuring her experiences with her all-girl rock band. But even there, Barbie's character remained a mystery. All she did on the show was sing and play music.

Although in many ways Mattel has reinforced the popular image of Barbie, the company has raised her consciousness. In the mid-1970s, the company surveyed mothers and asked their opinion of Barbie. Many responded that she lacked ambition and should get a job. According to Jill Barad, the public was delighted when Mattel reacted by launching Barbie's career. Now Barbie is a better person, says Barad, who comments that Barbie "does have talent and skills, and goes to work and makes money, and that's how she affords her car!" She has also embraced cultural diversity. Barbie's pals are African American, Asian, and Hispanic, and there are African American and Hispanic versions of Barbie herself.

Mattel is also winning points for Barbie by emphasizing the doll's therapeutic value. Children's Hospital in Los Angeles uses Barbie to help youngsters who are going through an amputation. The hospital staff removes Barbie's arm or leg, fits her with an artificial limb, and gives her to the child as a gift. Ellen Zaman, director of patient family services, notes, "It helps the children understand what will happen to them."

As a symbol of popular culture, Barbie has also gained a measure of respectability. Scholars write learned articles analyzing her significance. The Toy Manufacturers of America have acknowledged her unique place in the history of toys. The Smithsonian Institution sponsored a special Barbie exhibit. For her thirtieth birthday, a crowd of toy manufacturers, collectors, and fans assembled at Lincoln Center to pay tribute to America's number one doll. Needless to say, Barbie wowed them in her rose gown, her pink feather boa, and her lavish earrings.[21]

Your Mission: You have recently joined Mattel's marketing department. One of your responsibilities is to respond to letters about Barbie. Your goals are to emphasize Barbie's positive qualities, to reinforce her popularity with youngsters, and to handle her critics as diplomatically as possible. Choose the best alternatives for handling the following correspondence, and be prepared to explain why your choice is best:

1. You have received a letter from Alice Brown, a reporter for *Ms.* magazine, who is writing an article tentatively entitled "Barbie: Reflection or Molder of Contemporary Values?" Brown has asked you for information about the marketing campaign that Mattel has employed to mold Barbie's image over the years. When responding to Brown's request, what should your purpose be?
   a. The general purpose is to inform. The specific purpose is to provide Brown with a brief summary of the evolution of Mattel's marketing campaign for Barbie over the past 30 years.
   b. The general purpose is to persuade. The specific purpose is to convince Brown that Barbie is a worthy role model for young girls and that the marketing campaign portrays Barbie as a socially aware, successful career woman.
   c. The general purpose is to collaborate. The specific purpose is to work with Brown to develop an article that examines the evolution of Mattel's marketing campaign for Barbie.

   d. The general purpose is to respond. The specific purpose is to convey details requested by a journalist.
2. Assume that your purpose is to convince Brown of Barbie's worthiness as a role model who is a socially aware, successful career woman. Does this purpose meet the tests suggested in the chapter?
   a. Yes. The purpose is realistic. The timing is right. You are the right person to send the message. And the purpose is acceptable to the organization.
   b. Not completely. Realistically, Brown may not accept Barbie as an admirable role model for young girls. Even though Barbie now has a career and some friends from other cultural backgrounds, her basic image has not changed a great deal.
   c. The purpose is fine, but you are not the right person to send the message. Mattel's president should respond.
   d. The timing is right for this message. Stress Barbie's involvement in social causes and in career activities. Show how unimportant fashion is to Barbie's new lifestyle.
3. When planning your reply, what assumptions can you safely make about your audience?
   a. The audience includes not only Alice Brown but also the readers of *Ms.* magazine. Given their feminist bias, the readers will probably be hostile to business in general and to Barbie in particular. They probably know virtually nothing about the toy business. Furthermore, they probably mistrust you because you are a Mattel employee.
   b. Alice Brown will probably be the only person who reads the letter directly. She is the primary audience; the readers of her article are the secondary audience. Brown will be happy to hear from Mattel and will read the information with an open mind. As a journalist, Brown is probably intelligent and objective. However, she may not know a great deal about Mattel or about marketing. Although she is a stranger to you, she trusts your credibility as a Mattel spokesperson.
   c. Alice Brown is probably the sole and primary audience for the letter. The fact that she is writing an article about Barbie suggests that she enjoyed playing with the doll as a child and that she knows a great deal about Barbie already. In all likelihood, she will respond positively to your reply and will trust your credibility as a Mattel representative.
   d. Alice Brown may be an industrial spy working for a rival toy company. She will show your reply to people who work for your competitor; they will analyze the information and use it to improve their own marketing program at your expense.
4. Which channel and medium of communication should you use in replying to Alice Brown?
   a. Call her on the phone to ask for clarification of her needs; then follow up with a letter report (4 to 20 pages, written in letter format).
   b. Call her on the phone, ask for clarification of her needs, and answer her while you have her on the line.
   c. Write a letter asking for clarification of her needs, and follow up with a letter report.
   d. Send a form letter used for replying to all inquiries about Barbie.

Critical Thinking Questions

1. Some writers argue that it's a waste of time for them to plan messages because they inevitably change their plans as they go along. How would you respond to this argument? Briefly explain.
2. Your supervisor has asked you to prepare a message that, in your opinion, serves no worthwhile purpose. What will you do? Explain.
3. As editor of your company's newsletter, how would you go about discovering the needs of your fellow employees? Write a one-page explanation.
4. List several main ideas you might use if you were trying to persuade top management to invest in word-processing equipment and software.
5. What would be the best medium for a personnel manager to use for explaining employee benefits to new employees? Explain your answer.
6. If you were a member of the public relations department, what medium would you recommend using to inform the local community that your toxic-waste cleanup program has been successful? Why?

Exercises

1. For each of the following communication tasks, state a specific purpose (if you have trouble, try beginning with "I want to ...").
   a. A report to your boss, the store manager, about the outdated items in the warehouse
   b. A memo to clients about your booth at the upcoming trade show
   c. A letter to a customer who hasn't made a payment for three months
   d. A memo to employees about the office's high water bills
   e. A phone call to a supplier checking on an overdue parts shipment
   f. A report to future users of the computer program you have chosen to handle the company's mailing list
2. Make a list of communication tasks you'll need to accomplish in the next week or so (a job application, a letter of complaint, a speech to a class, an order for some merchandise, etc.). For each, determine a general and a specific purpose.
3. List five messages you have received lately, such as direct-mail promotions, letters, e-mail messages, phone solicitations, and lectures. For each, determine the general and the specific purpose; then answer the following questions: Was the message well timed? Did the sender choose an appropriate channel and medium for the message? Did the appropriate person deliver the message? Was the sender's purpose realistic?
4. Barbara Marquardt is in charge of public relations for a cruise line that operates out of Miami. She is shocked to read a letter in a local newspaper from a disgruntled passenger, complaining about the service and entertainment on a recent cruise. Marquardt will have to respond to these publicized criticisms in some way. What audiences will she need to consider in her response? What channels and media should she choose? If the letter had been published in a travel publication widely read by travel agents and cruise travelers, how might her course of action differ?
5. For each of the following communication tasks, write brief answers to three questions: Who is my audience? What is my audience's general attitude toward my subject? What does my audience need to know?
   a. A final-notice collection letter from an appliance manufacturer to an appliance dealer, sent ten days before legal collection procedures will be initiated
   b. An unsolicited sales letter asking readers to purchase computer disks at near-wholesale prices
   c. An advertisement for peanut butter
   d. Fliers, to be attached to doorknobs in the neighborhood, announcing reduced rates for chimney lining or repairs
   e. A cover letter sent along with your résumé to a potential employer
   f. A request (to the seller) for a price adjustment on a piano that incurred $150 in damage during delivery to a banquet room in the hotel you manage
6. Rewrite the following message so that it includes all the information that the reader needs. (Make up any necessary details.)

   I am pleased to offer you the position of assistant buyer at Fontaine and Sons at an annual salary of $15,500. I hope to receive notice of your acceptance soon.

7. Frank Kroll has been studying a new method for testing the durability of the electric hand tools his company manufactures. Now he needs to prepare three separate reports on his findings: first, a report for the administrator who will decide whether to purchase the new equipment needed for using this method; second, a report for the company's engineers who design and develop the hand tools; and third, a report for the trainers who will be showing workers how to use the new equipment. To determine the audience's needs for each of these reports, Frank has made a list of the following questions: (1) Who are the readers? (2) Why will they read my report? (3) Do they need introductory or background material? (4) Do they need definitions of terms? (5) What level and type of language is needed? (6) What level of detail is needed? (7) What result does my report aim for? Put yourself in Frank's shoes, and answer these questions for each of the three audiences:
   a. The administrator
   b. The engineers
   c. The trainers

8. Choose an electronic device that you know how to operate well (videocassette recorder, personal computer, telephone answering machine, etc.). Write two sets of instructions for operating the device: one set for a reader who has never used that type of machine and one set for someone familiar with that type of machine in general but who has never operated the specific model.

9. Work with a classmate to complete this task. Each partner must independently visit the site at <http:// www.hrblock. com/tax.> Working together only by e-mail (not in person and not using any other electronic technology), plan, compose, and revise your joint explanation of the Web site. Summarize *what* is on the Web page and linked pages, and then critique the site. Explain why it does or does not communicate efficiently and effectively, and whether it provides complete and accessible information for the intended audience. When you and your collaborator are satisfied with your explanation, print it out for submission to your instructor.

10. You're looking for a job as a salesperson, so you'd better be able to sell yourself first. What special qualities do you have that make you a desirable sales employee? Use the techniques described in the chapter to come up with a main idea you can use in your efforts to market yourself. In no more than a paragraph, draft a statement of your main idea that tells your audience (potential employers) what to do or think about you and why.

DEVELOPING YOUR INTERNET SKILLS

GOING ONLINE: LEARN MORE ABOUT
ANALYZING AN AUDIENCE, P. 82

Recalling the imaginary Web site you conjured for the Going Online exercise in Chapter 4, draw a similar cluster diagram for your primary and secondary audiences. If time permits, go ahead and use the categories in the audience analysis table to compile more information about your own imagined audience. What new ideas does this give you about content?

After studying this chapter, you will be able to

Identify the characteristics of a well-organized message

Explain why organization is important to both the audience and the communicator

Break a main idea into subdivisions grouped under logical categories

Arrange ideas in direct or indirect order, depending on the audience's probable reaction

Compose a message using a style and tone that are appropriate to your subject, purpose, audience, and format

Use the "you" attitude to interest the audience in your message

Compose an appropriate e-mail message

COMPOSING BUSINESS MESSAGES

**n the Job**
FACING A COMMUNICATION
DILEMMA AT CLUB MED
Fun in the Sun—For Everyone This Time

When you think about Club Med, what comes to mind? You probably envision sunny skies, blue water, and carefree single adults relaxing and mingling on the beach in some tropical paradise. That was the image the French company cultivated for many years, from its humble "camping club" beginnings in the 1950s to its emergence as a worldwide resort operator in the 1970s and 1980s. In fact, one business reference even uses the phrase "sun, sea, and sex" to describe the company's philosophy during those decades of growth.

That philosophy was certainly profitable—until the 1990s, when people began to shift away from freewheeling lifestyles. Then a series of unfortunate events put an end to society's enchantment with traveling to exotic locations. These events were not like anything that business executives normally have to face: French tourists were kidnapped in Turkey; political tension and sporadic violence broke out in Israel; civil war erupted in the former Yugoslavia—those were just a few of the locations where Club Med has resorts. Also, Japanese and Australian tourists boycotted Club Med resorts to protest French nuclear tests in the South Pacific, and a hurricane destroyed a Club Med village in the Caribbean. The result of all this upheaval was a dramatic decline in business, leading to losses that bottomed out at $50 million in 1993.

So in 1993, when Serge Trigano took the company's reins from his father, one of the fundamental appeals of Club Med—its exotic locations—was no longer all that appealing; many of its resorts seemed to be in hot spots whose very names had become more frightening than enchanting. Trigano knew he couldn't control the world, but he could control Club Med's strategy and, to a large extent, its reputation. Recognizing society's shifting concerns, he set about expanding the company's market by adding vacation programs that were aimed not only at singles but also at married couples, families with children, and senior citizens.

Once these new programs were in place, Trigano needed to inform travel agents of the new programs and encourage the agents to recommend Club Med vacations for everyone, not just young singles. Travel agents account for 85 percent of Club Med business, so their support is crucial if the new programs are to succeed.

If you were Serge Trigano, what sort of letter could you write to stimulate a travel agent's interest in your resorts and new vacation programs? How important will organization be to your letter? Will an outline help? What style will work best?[1]

*S*TAGE 5: ORGANIZING YOUR MESSAGE

Like Serge Trigano, all business communicators face the problem of conveying a complicated web of ideas in an understandable fashion. People simply don't remember dissociated facts and figures, so successful communicators rely on organization to make their messages meaningful.[2] Before thinking about how to achieve good organization, however, think about what it means and why it's important.

What Good Organization Means

The definition of a well-organized message varies from country to country, but in the United States and Canada, it generally refers to a linear message that proceeds point by point. If you've ever received an unorganized message, you're familiar with the frustration of trying to sort through a muddle of ideas. Consider this letter from Jill Saunders, the office manager at Boswell & Sons, mapmakers:

Our president, Mr. Boswell, was in an accident last year, and he hasn't been able to work full-time. His absence has affected our business, so we don't have the budget we used to. His two sons are working hard, so we aren't bankrupt by any means, and soon Mr. Boswell will be coming back full-time.

Boswell & Sons has been doing business with ComputerTime since I was hired six years ago. Your building was smaller then, and it was located on the corner of Federal Avenue and 2nd N.W. Mr. Boswell bought our first laser printer there. I still remember the day. It was the biggest check I'd ever written. Of course, over the years, I've gotten used to larger purchases.

We have seven employees. Although all of them aren't directly involved in producing the maps we sell, they all need to have their computers working so that they can do their jobs. The CD-ROM drive we bought for my assistant, Suzanne, has been a problem. We've taken it in for repairs three times to the authorized service center, and Suzanne is very careful with the machine and hasn't abused it. She likes playing interactive adventure games on lunch breaks. It still doesn't work right, and she's tired of hauling it back and forth. We're all putting in longer hours to make up for Mr. Boswell's not being here, and none of us has a lot of spare time.

This is the first time we've returned anything to your store, and I hope you'll agree that we deserve a better deal.

This letter displays the sort of disorganization that U.S. and Canadian readers find frustrating. By taking a closer look at the letter, you can identify the four most common faults responsible for organization problems:

- Taking too long to get to the point. Saunders wrote two paragraphs before introducing the topic: the faulty drive. Then she waited until the final paragraph to state her purpose: requesting an adjustment.
- Including irrelevant material. Saunders introduced information that has no bearing on her purpose or her topic. Does it matter that the computer store used to be smaller or

Employees at Club Med use their strong communication skills not only to communicate with travel agents but also to attract guests of all ages, including families with children, singles, and retired folks. Serge Trigano motivates his marketing staff to work hard to support Club Med's new image.

Most unorganized communication suffers from problems with content, grouping, or sequence.

As general manager of Ford's plastic products division, Ronald E. Goldsberry exemplifies the busy executive whose day is fragmented by such diverse activities as merger coordination, budget decisions, personnel problems, products decisions, and on and on. Goldsberry appreciates business messages that do not waste his time. He advises that you make your message efficient, clear, and logical in organization.

A message is well organized when all the pieces fit together in a coherent pattern.

that it was in a different location? What difference does it make whether Saunders's boss is working only part-time or whether her assistant likes playing computerized games during lunch?

■ Getting ideas mixed up. Saunders seems to be making six points: (1) her company has money to spend, (2) it's an old customer, (3) it pays by check, (4) it has purchased numerous items at the store, (5) the CD-ROM drive doesn't work, and (6) Saunders wants an adjustment. However, the ideas are in the wrong places. It would be more logical to begin with the fact that the drive doesn't work, and some of these ideas should be combined under the general idea that the company is a valuable customer.

■ Leaving out necessary information. The customer service representative may want to know the make, model, and price of the drive; the date on which it was purchased; the specific problems it has had; and whether the repairs were covered by the warranty. Saunders also failed to specify what she wants the store to do. Does she want a new CD-ROM drive of the same type? A different model? Or simply her money back?

Achieving good organization can be a challenge. Nevertheless, by working with these four common faults, you can establish what good organization means. Four guidelines can help you recognize a well-organized message:

■ Make the subject and purpose clear.
■ Include only information that is related to the subject and purpose.
■ Group the ideas and present them in a logical way.
■ Include all the necessary information.

Each guideline not only helps you communicate clearly and logically but also helps you communicate ethically—by making sure you state all information as truthfully, honestly, and fairly as possible. Observing these four rules changes the original letter so that the message can be effectively and ethically communicated (see Figure 6.1).

Why Good Organization Is Important

The main reason for being well organized is to improve the chances that people will understand exactly what you mean.

You might be asking yourself whether it matters that the message is well organized, as long as the point is eventually made. Why not just let the ideas flow naturally and trust that the audience will grasp the meaning? But when you consider the cost of misinterpreted messages (such as wasted time reading and rereading unclear messages, poor decision making, and shattered business relationships), you begin to realize the value of clear writing and good organization.[3] By arranging your ideas logically and diplomatically, you increase the chances of satisfying your audience's needs for information, motivation, and practicality. Plus you simplify your communication task.

Good organization also helps you get your ideas across without upsetting the audience.

■ Helping your audience understand your message. The less work required of your audience to figure out your message, the better they understand what you're trying to say. As Club Med's Serge Trigano points out, you want your information to be "user-friendly and understandable." If you're interested in getting your message across, good organization is one of the handiest tools because it makes your message easier to understand. A well-organized message satisfies the audience's need for information.

■ Helping your audience accept your message. Good organization helps motivate your audience to accept your message. As the letter in Figure 6.2 shows, you can soften refusals, leave a good impression, and be more convincing by organizing messages diplomatically. You can also use good organization to enhance your credibility and add authority to your messages.

Well-organized messages are efficient because they contain only relevant information.

■ Saving your audience's time. Well-organized messages are efficient. They contain only relevant ideas, so your audience doesn't waste time on superfluous information. Moreover, all the information in a well-organized message is in a logical place. The audience can follow the thought pattern without a struggle, and they can save even more time by looking for just the information they need instead of reading everything.

This letter from Boswell & Sons asking about ComputerTime's exchange policy is organized to give all needed information in a sequence that helps the reader understand the message.

Figure 6.1
In-Depth Critique: Letter with Improved Organization

 Boswell & Sons

Route 7, Hancock Highway, Clear Lake, Iowa 50401
Voice: (515) 788-4343 E-mail: boswell@aol.com Fax: (515) 788-4344

September 13, 1999

Customer Service
ComputerTime
556 Seventh Avenue
Mason City, Iowa 50401

Dear Customer Service Representative:

Boswell & Sons bought an Olympic Systems, Model PRS-2, CD-ROM drive from your store on November 15, 1998, during your pre-Christmas sale, when it was marked down to $199.95. We didn't use the unit until January, because it was bought for my assistant, who unexpectedly took six weeks' leave from mid-November through December. You can imagine her frustration when she first tried using it and it didn't work.

In January, we took the drive to the authorized service center and were assured that the problem was merely a loose connection. The service representative fixed the drive, but in April we had to have it fixed again—another loose connection. For the next three months, the drive worked reasonably well, although the response time was occasionally slow. Two months ago, the drive stopped working again. Once more, the service representative blamed a loose connection and made the repair. Although the drive is working now, it isn't working very well. The response time is still slow, and the motor seems to drag sometimes.

What is your policy on exchanging unsatisfactory merchandise? Although all the repairs have been relatively minor and have been covered by the one-year warranty, we are not satisfied with the drive. We would like to exchange it for a similar model from another manufacturer. If the new drive costs more than the old one, we will pay the difference, even though we generally look for equipment with heavy business discounts.

Boswell & Sons has done business with your store for six years and until now has always been satisfied with your merchandise. We are counting on you to live up to your reputation for standing behind your products. Please let us hear from you soon.

Sincerely,

Jill Saunders

Jill Saunders

lv

The first paragraph clearly states the purpose of this letter.

The second paragraph explains the situation so that the reader will understand the problem. The writer includes no irrelevant information, and the ideas are presented logically.

The third paragraph states precisely what adjustment is being requested.

The letter includes all the necessary information.

■ Simplifying your communication task. Finally, being well organized helps you compose your message more quickly and efficiently. By thinking about what you're going to say and how you're going to say it before you begin to write, you can proceed more confidently. You can use your organization plan to get some input from your boss to be sure you're on the right track before you spend hours working on a draft. If you're working on a large and complex project, you can use the plan to divide the writing job among co-workers to finish the assignment as quickly as possible.

Organizing what you're going to say before you start to write makes the job much easier.

Figure 6.2
In-Depth Critique: Letter Demonstrating a Diplomatic Organizational Plan

This letter from ComputerTime responds to the inquiry from Boswell & Sons about the unsatisfactory CD-ROM drive. Although the information is effectively negative, the letter diplomatically achieves a positive feeling.

COMPUTERTIME
556 Seventh Avenue, Mason City, IA 50401
(515) 979-8870 / Comptime@netins.net

September 17, 1999

Ms. Jill Saunders
Boswell & Sons
Route 7, Hancock Highway
Clear Lake, IA 50401

Dear Ms. Saunders:

Thank you for letting us know about your experience with the Olympic CD-ROM drive that you bought last November. It's important that we learn of unusual problems with the equipment we stock.

As you know, regularly priced equipment returned to ComputerTime within 30 days is covered by the unconditional refund that has been our tradition for 22 years. Your drive, however, is still covered by the manufacturer's warranty. Your needs will receive immediate attention if you write to

Mr. George Bender
Olympic Systems
P.O. Box 7761, Terminal Annex
Los Angeles, CA 90010

From experience, I know that the people at Olympic truly care about having satisfied customers.

We, too, value your business, Ms. Saunders. Please don't miss our Tax Days sale in April, which will feature more of the low prices and high-quality equipment that you've come to rely on.

Sincerely,

Linda Davis

Linda Davis
Customer Service

hg

The letter begins with a neutral statement that the reader should not find objectionable.

The refusal is stated indirectly and is linked with a solution to the reader's problem.

The letter closes on an appreciative note and confidently assumes normal dealings in the future.

How Good Organization Is Achieved

To organize a message, first group the ideas, then put them in sequence.

Understanding the need for good organization is half the battle. Knowing how to organize your messages well is the other half. Serge Trigano of Club Med achieves good organization by following this two-step process: First define and group the ideas; then establish their sequence with a carefully selected organizational pattern.

Define and Group Ideas

In business, deciding what to say is more important than deciding how to say it.

The prewriting techniques described in Chapter 5 will help you generate your main idea, but they won't necessarily tell you how to develop it or how to group the supporting details in the most logical and effective way. To decide on the final structure of your message, you need to visualize how all the points fit together. One way to do this is to construct an outline. Whether you use the outlining features provided with word-processing software or simply jot down three or four points on the back of an envelope, making a plan and sticking to it will help you cover the important details.

When you're preparing a long and complex message, an outline is indispensable because it helps you visualize the relationship among the various parts. Without an outline, you may be inclined to ramble. As you're describing one point, another point may occur to you—so you describe it. One detour leads to another, and, before you know it, you've forgotten the original point. With an outline to guide you, however, you can communicate in a more systematic way, covering all the necessary ideas in an effective order and with proper emphasis. Following an outline also helps you express the transitions between points so that your message is coherent and the audience will understand the relationship among your ideas.

You're no doubt familiar with the basic alphanumeric outline, which uses numbers and letters to identify each point and indents them to show which ideas are of equal status. (Chapter 15 tells more about the various formats that can be used in this type of outlining.) A more schematic approach illustrates the structure of your message in an "organization chart" like one that depicts a company's management structure (Figure 6.3). The main idea is shown in the highest-level box, and, like a top executive, it establishes the big picture. The lower-level ideas, like lower-level employees, provide the details. All the ideas are logically organized into divisions of thought, just as a company is organized into divisions and departments.[4]

> An outline or a schematic diagram will help you visualize the relationship among parts of a message.

Start with the Main Idea The main idea, placed at the top of an organization chart, helps you establish the goals and general strategy of the message. This main idea summarizes two things: (1) what you want your audience to do or think and (2) why they should do so. Everything in the message should either support this idea or explain its implications.

> The main idea is the starting point for constructing an outline.

State the Major Points In an organization chart, the boxes directly below the top box represent the major supporting points, corresponding to the main headings in a conventional outline. These are the "vice presidential" ideas that clarify the message by expressing it in more concrete terms. To fill in these boxes, break the main idea into smaller units. In general, try to identify three to five major points. If you come up with more than seven main divisions of thought, go back and look for opportunities to combine some of the ideas. The big question then is deciding what to put in each box. Sometimes the choices are fairly obvious. At other times you may have hundreds of ideas to sort through and group together. In either case, be sure to consider both your purpose and the nature of the material.

> The main idea should be supported by three to five major points, regardless of the message's length.

If your purpose is to inform and the material is factual, the groupings are generally suggested by the subject itself. They are usually based on something physical that you can visualize or measure: activities to be performed, functional units, spatial or chronological relationships, parts of a whole. When you're describing a process, the major support points

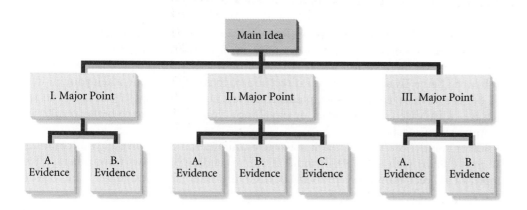

Figure 6.3
"Organization Chart" for Organizing a Message

As principal co-anchor for Date-line NBC, *and after a long career with some of the most successful news programs on television, Jane Pauley's writing skills are top drawer. She understands the importance of good organization if you want to convey information effectively: first defining the main idea and then breaking it down into logical pieces by considering your purpose and subject matter.*

Each major point should be supported with enough specific evidence to be convincing, but not so much that it's boring.

Use direct order if the audience's reaction is likely to be positive and indirect order if it is likely to be negative.

are almost inevitably steps in the process. When you're describing a physical object, the vice presidential boxes correspond to the components of the object. When you're giving a historical account, each box represents an event in the chronological chain.

When your purpose is to persuade or collaborate, the major support points may be more difficult to identify. Instead of relying on a natural order imposed by the subject, develop a line of reasoning that proves your central message and motivates your audience to act. The boxes on the organization chart then correspond to the major elements in a logical argument. Basically, the supporting points are the main reasons your audience should accept your message.

Illustrate with Evidence   The third level on the organization chart shows the specific evidence you'll use to illustrate your major points. This evidence is the flesh and blood that helps your audience understand and remember the more abstract concepts. Say you're advocating that the company increase its advertising budget. To support this point, you could provide statistical evidence that your most successful competitors spend more on advertising than you do. You could also describe a specific case in which a particular competitor increased its ad budget and achieved an impressive sales gain. As a final bit of evidence, you could show that, over the past five years, your firm's sales have gone up and down in unison with the amount spent on advertising.

If you're developing a long, complex message, you may need to carry the organization chart (or outline) down several levels. Remember that every level is a step along the chain from the abstract to the concrete, from the general to the specific. The lowest level contains the individual facts and figures that tie the generalizations to the observable, measurable world. The higher levels are the concepts that reveal why those facts are significant.

The more evidence you provide, the more conclusive your case will be. If your subject is complex and unfamiliar to your audience or if they are skeptical, you'll need a lot of facts and figures to demonstrate your points. On the other hand, if your subject is routine and the audience is positively inclined, you can be more sparing with the evidence. You want to provide enough support to be convincing, but not so much that your message becomes boring or inefficient. Of course you'll need to document your sources of information, and you may sometimes need to obtain permission to use copyrighted material.

Another way to keep the audience interested is to vary the type of detail. As you plan your message, try to incorporate the methods described in Table 6.1. Switch from facts and figures to narration; add a dash of description; throw in some examples or a reference to authority. Reinforce it all with visual aids. Think of your message as a stew, a mix of ingredients, seasoned with a blend of spices. Each separate flavor adds to the richness of the whole.

Establish Sequence with Organizational Patterns

Once you've defined and grouped your ideas, you're ready to decide on their sequence. When you're addressing a U.S. or Canadian audience with minimal cultural differences, you have two basic options:

- Direct approach (deductive). Putting the main idea first, followed by the evidence
- Indirect approach (inductive). Putting the evidence first and the main idea later

These two basic approaches may be applied either to short messages (memos and letters) or to long ones (reports, proposals, presentations). To choose between the two alternatives, you must first analyze your audience's likely reaction to your purpose and message. As Club Med's Serge Trigano knows, the direct approach is generally fine when your audience will be receptive: eager, interested, pleased, or even neutral. If they'll be resistant to your message—displeased, uninterested, or unwilling—you'll usually have better results with the indirect approach.

Bear in mind, however, that each message is unique. You can't solve all your communication problems with a simple formula. If you're sending bad news to outsiders, for example, an indirect approach is probably best. On the other hand, you might want to get di-

Table 6.1		
Type of Detail	*Example*	*Comment*
Facts and figures	Sales are strong this month. We have received two new contracts worth $5 million and have a good chance of winning another with an annual value of $2.5 million.	Most common form of detail in business messages. Adds more credibility than any other form of development. May become boring if used in excess.
Example or illustration	We've spent the past four months trying to hire recent accounting graduates for our internal audit staff, and, so far, only one person has agreed to join our firm. One woman told me that she would love to work for us, but she can get $5,000 more a year elsewhere.	Adds life to a message, but one example does not prove a point. Idea must be supported by other evidence as well.
Description	Upscale hamburger restaurants are designed for McDonald's graduates who still love the taste of a Big Mac but who want more than convenience and low prices. The adult hamburger establishments feature attractive waitresses, wine and beer, half-pound burgers, and substantial side dishes, such as nachos and potato skins. "Atmosphere" is a key ingredient in the formula for success.	Useful when you need to explain how something looks or functions. Helps audience visualize the subject by creating a sensory impression. Does not prove a point, but clarifies points and makes them memorable. Begins with overview of object's function; defines its purpose, lists major parts, and explains how it operates; relies on words that appeal to senses.
Narration	Under former management, the company operated in a casual style. Executives came to work in blue jeans, meetings rarely started on time, and lunch rarely ended on time. When Mr. Wilson took over as CEO, however, the company got religion—financial religion. A Harvard MBA who favors Brooks Brothers suits, Mr. Wilson has embarked on a complete overhaul of the operation. He has cut the product line from 6,000 items to 1,200 and has chopped $12 million of expenses.	Good for attracting attention and explaining ideas, but lacks statistical validity.
Reference to authority	I talked with Jackie Lohman in the Cleveland plant about this idea, and she was very supportive. As you know, Jackie has been in charge of that plant for the past six years. She is confident that we can speed up the number 2 line by 150 units per hour if we add another worker.	Bolsters a case and adds variety and credibility. Works only if "authority" is recognized and respected by audience, although he or she may be an ordinary person.
Visual aids	Graphs, charts, tables	Essential when presenting specific information. Used more often in memos and reports than in letters.

rectly to the point in a memo to an associate, even if your message is unpleasant. The direct approach might also be the best choice for long messages, regardless of the audience's attitude, because delaying the main point could cause confusion and frustration. Just remember that the first priority is to make the message clear.

Patterns for Short Messages   Once you've analyzed your audience's probable reaction and chosen a general approach, you can choose the most appropriate organizational pattern: direct request; routine, good-news, or goodwill message; bad-news message; or persuasive message. Table 6.2 summarizes how each type of message is structured. In each organizational plan, the opening, the body, and the close all play an important part

Short messages follow one of four organizational plans, depending on the audience's probable reaction.

Table 6.2				
Audience Reaction	*Organizational Plan*	*Opening*	*Body*	*Close*
Eager or interested	Direct requests	Begin with the request or main idea.	Provide necessary details.	Close cordially and state the specific action desired.
Pleased or neutral	Routine, good-news, or goodwill messages	Begin with the main idea or the good news.	Provide necessary details.	Close with a cordial comment, a reference to the good news, or a look toward the future.
Displeased	Bad-news messages	Begin with a neutral statement that acts as a transition to the reasons for the bad news.	Give reasons to justify a negative answer. State or imply the bad news, and make a positive suggestion.	Close cordially.
Uninterested or unwilling	Persuasive messages	Begin with a statement or question that captures attention.	Arouse the audience's interest in the subject. Build the audience's desire to comply.	Request action.

in getting your message across. When used with good judgment, these basic types of business messages can be powerful tools of communication.[5]

Direct requests get straight to the point because the audience usually wants to respond.

■ **Direct requests.** The most straightforward business message is the direct request. This type of message lets you get to the point in the first paragraph or, if you're talking with someone face to face or on the phone, allows you to get right down to business. Use this organizational pattern when your audience will be interested in complying or eager to respond. The direct approach is the most natural approach, perhaps the most useful and businesslike. This type of message is discussed in greater detail in Chapter 8.

The direct approach is effective for messages that will please the reader or will cause no particular reaction.

■ **Routine, good-news, and goodwill messages.** Other messages that call for the direct approach are also easy to organize. Use this organizational pattern when the audience will feel neutral about your message or will be pleased to hear from you. If you're providing routine information as part of your regular business, the audience will probably be neutral, neither pleased nor displeased. If you're announcing a price cut, granting an adjustment, accepting an invitation, or congratulating a colleague, the audience will be pleased to hear from you. Using the direct approach for routine, good-news, and goodwill messages has many advantages. You put your audience in a good frame of mind, you encourage readers to be receptive to whatever else you have to say, and you emphasize the pleasing aspect of your message by putting it right up front. This type of message is discussed in more detail in Chapter 9.

If you have bad news, try to put it somewhere in the middle, cushioned by other, more positive ideas.

■ **Bad-news messages.** This organizational pattern uses the indirect approach and is appropriate when the audience will be displeased about what you have to say. If you're turning down a job applicant, refusing credit, or denying a request for an adjustment, the audience will be disappointed. Astute businesspeople know that every person encountered has the potential to be a customer, a supplier, or a contributor or to influence someone who is a customer, a supplier, or a contributor. So they take a little extra care with their bad-news messages (Figure 6.4). The first and last sections of any letter make the biggest impression. In Figure 6.4, if Levasseur had refused in the first sentence, the reader might never have bothered to go on to the reasons or might have been in the wrong frame of mind to consider them. By putting the explanation before the refusal, Levasseur focused attention on the reasons. Of course, you have to be sincere about your reasons. A reader can spot a phony excuse right away. The indirect approach is neither manipulative nor unethical. As long as you can be honest and rea-

The following letter shows how Jamie Levasseur, advertising manager at Ballinger & Crown, responded when asked to act as industry chairperson for a dinner sponsored by the National Conference of Christians and Jews. Note how she cushions the bad news.

Figure 6.4
In-Depth Critique: Letter Delivering Bad News

$\mathcal{B}$ALLINGER & $\mathcal{C}$ROWN

676 Fifth Avenue, Ninth Floor, New York, New York 10103
Voice: (212) 397-8888 Fax: (212)397-8877

March 6, 1999

Ms. Joanne Lippman
Public Relations Officer
National Conference of Christians and Jews
2237 Welch Avenue
Houston, Texas 77219

Dear Ms. Lippman:

Your invitation to act as industry chairperson for NCCJ's upcoming Anniversary Citation Dinner is a great honor. I thoroughly enjoyed serving in the role last year. Your members are a fine group with high ideals, and working with them was a privilege.

This year I'm involved with a construction project here at B&C that is consuming all my time—and then some. Therefore, although I would enjoy repeating the experience of working with NCCJ, I believe that someone else would be better able to give the assignment the attention it deserves.

Perhaps one of my colleagues would have the time to do the job the way it ought to be done. Enclosed is a brief list of colleagues (with address and phone information) who have voiced some interest in working with NCCJ. We want the advertising industry to be well represented.

I wish you and the rest of your committee the greatest success in achieving the goals set this year by NCCJ.

Sincerely,

Jamie Levasseur

Jamie Levasseur
Advertising Manager

sw

Enclosure

The letter begins with a neutral statement that provides a transition to the refusal.

The midsection explains the reason for the refusal and then states the bad news.

The writer takes care to introduce a positive thought.

The letter closes on a cordial note.

sonably brief, you're better off opening a bad-news message with a neutral point and putting the negative information after the explanation. This type of message is discussed further in Chapter 10.

■ **Persuasive messages.** The indirect approach is also useful when you know that your audience will resist your message (will be uninterested in your request or unwilling to comply without extra coaxing). Resistance might be the likely reaction to a sales or collection letter, an unsolicited job application, or a request for a favor of some kind. Although you might argue that people are likely to feel manipulated by the indirect approach, the fact remains that you have to capture people's attention before you can

Using the indirect approach gives you an opportunity to get your message across to a skeptical or hostile audience.

persuade them to do something. If you don't, you really have no way to get the message across. You also have to get your audience to consider with an open mind what you have to say; to do that, you have to make an interesting point and provide supporting facts that encourage the audience to continue paying attention. Once you have them thinking, you can introduce your real purpose. This type of message is discussed at greater length in Chapter 11.

Patterns for Longer Messages   Most short messages can use one of the four basic organizational patterns. Longer messages (namely, reports and presentations) require a more complex pattern to handle the greater mass of information. These patterns can be broken into two general categories: informational and analytical.

In general, the direct approach is used to organize informational reports and presentations. Operating instructions, status reports, technical descriptions, and descriptions of company procedures all fall into this category. Long informational messages have an obvious main idea, often with a descriptive or "how to" overtone. The development of subordinate ideas follows the natural breakdown of the material to be explained; subtopics can be arranged in order of importance, sequentially, chronologically, spatially, geographically, or categorically.

Analytical reports and presentations are designed to lead the audience to a specific conclusion. When your purpose is to collaborate with your audience to solve a problem or to persuade them to take a definite action, your organizational pattern must highlight logical arguments or focus the audience's attention on what needs to be done. Your audience may respond in one of two ways to your material, and your choice of organizational plan should depend on the reaction you anticipate:

- If you expect your audience to agree with you, use a structure that focuses attention on conclusions and recommendations.
- If you expect your audience to be skeptical about your conclusions and recommendations or hostile toward them, use a structure that focuses attention on the rationale that supports your point of view.

You'll learn more about organizing longer messages in Chapter 12. For now, the important thing is to master the basic steps in structuring a message.

TAGE 6: FORMULATING YOUR MESSAGE

Once you've completed the planning process, you're ready to begin composing the message. If your schedule permits, put your outline or organization chart aside for a day or two; then review it with a fresh eye, looking for opportunities to improve the flow of ideas. When you feel confident that your structure will achieve your purpose with the intended audience, you can begin to write.

Composing Your First Draft

As you compose the first draft, don't worry about getting everything perfect. Just put down your ideas as quickly as you can. You'll have time to revise and refine the material later. Composition is easier if you've already figured out what to say and in what order, although you may need to pause now and then to find the right word. You may also discover as you go along that you can improve on your outline. Feel free to rearrange, delete, and add ideas, as long as you don't lose sight of your purpose.

If you're writing the draft in longhand, leave space between lines so that you'll have plenty of room for making revisions. If you're using a typewriter, leave wide margins and double-space the text. Probably the best equipment for drafting the message is a computer with word-processing software, which allows you to make changes easily. You might try dictating the message, particularly if you're practicing for an oral delivery or if you're trying to create a conversational tone.

The organization of a longer message should reflect both the purpose of the message and the audience's probable reaction.

When your purpose is to inform, the major points are organized in a natural order implied by the subject's characteristics.

When your purpose is to persuade or collaborate, the approach is analytical, with major points corresponding to logical arguments or to conclusions and recommendations.

Composition is the process of drafting your message; polishing it is a later step.

Controlling Your Style and Tone

Style is the way you use words to achieve a certain tone, or overall impression. You can vary your style—your sentence structure and vocabulary—to sound forceful or passive, personal or impersonal, colorful or colorless. The right choice depends on the nature of your message and your relationship with the reader.

Your use of language is one of your credentials, a badge that identifies you as being a member of a particular group. Try to make your style clear, concise, and grammatically correct, and try also to make it conform to the norms of your group. Every organization has its own stylistic conventions, and many occupational groups share a particular vocabulary.

Although style can be refined during the revision phase (see Chapter 7), you'll save time and a lot of rewriting if you compose your message in an appropriate style. Your tone is affected by planning-stage elements such as your purpose and your audience's probable reaction to your message. Other elements affecting the tone of your message include thinking about the relationship you want to establish with your audience, using the "you" attitude, emphasizing the positive, establishing credibility, being polite, and projecting your company's image.

Think About the Relationship You Want to Establish

The first step toward getting the right tone is to think about your relationship with the audience. Who are you, and who are they? Are you friends of long standing with common interests, or are you total strangers? Are you equal in status, experience, and education, or are you clearly unequal? Your answers to these questions will help you define your relationship with the audience so that you can give the right impression in your message.

The tone of your business messages may span a continuum from informal to conversational to formal. Club Med's Trigano writes in a somewhat informal style, appropriate for his company's size and atmosphere. Most business messages fall around the conversational level of formality, using plain language that is neither stiff nor full of slang. Your conversational tone may become less or more formal, depending on the situation.

If you're addressing an old friend, your conversational tone might tend toward an informal level. Of course, in business messages, your tone would never be as informal as it would with family members or school chums. On the other hand, if you're in the lower echelon of a large organization, your conversational tone would tend to be more formal and respectful when communicating with the people above you. Some people in high positions are extremely proud of their status and resent any gesture from a lower-level employee that is remotely presumptuous. They may not like you to offer your own opinions, and they may resent any implied criticism of their actions or decisions. If you're writing to someone of this type, your message may be ineffective unless you show a deep appreciation of rank. Also remember that businesspeople in the United States are generally less formal than their counterparts in most other cultures.[6] So to avoid embarrassment or misunderstanding when communicating across cultures, increase your level of formality.

Although various situations require various tones, most business communication sounds businesslike without being stuffy. The tone suggests that you and your audience are sensible, logical, unemotional people—objective, interested in the facts, rational, competent, and efficient. You are civilized people who share a mutual respect for each other.

To achieve this tone, avoid being too familiar. Don't mention things about anyone's personal life unless you know the individual very well. Such references are indiscreet and presumptuous. Avoid phrases that imply intimacy, such as "just between you and me," "as you and I are well aware," and "I'm sure we both agree." Also, be careful about sounding too folksy or chatty; the audience may interpret this tone as an attempt on your part to seem like an old friend when, in fact, you're not.

Humor is another type of intimacy that may backfire. It's fine to be witty in person with old friends. It's difficult, however, to hit just the right note of humor in business messages, particularly if you don't know the readers very well, because what seems humorous to you may be deadly serious to others. When you are communicating across cultures, the chances are slim that your audience will appreciate your humor or even realize that you're trying to be funny.[7]

When composing the message, vary the style to create a tone that suits the occasion.

GOING ONLINE
CONNECT NOW WITH A VIRTUAL LIBRARY
You can have more than 200 essential sources of information right at your fingertips with the Virtual Reference Desk. The site includes an almanac, encyclopedia, dictionary, thesaurus, atlas, Zip Code directory, virtual newspaper, weather site, e-mail address locater, 260 search engines in 19 categories, and more.

http://www.refdesk.com/outline.html

To achieve a warm but businesslike tone

- Don't be too familiar
- Use humor only with great care
- Don't flatter the other person
- Don't preach
- Don't brag
- Be yourself

BEHIND THE SCENES AT RAN DECISIONS
Earning Points with InsideFlyer

Communicating your expertise can become a big business—especially if you're in the right place at the right time. That's what happened to Randy Petersen, founder of Ran Decisions, publisher of Inside-Flyer magazine. "I was one of those goofy people in the 1980s who honestly believed the airlines when they said you can fly for free. So I read the rules, accumulated some frequent flyer miles, and flew to Hawaii for free. That's when I realized that these promotions really worked."

It wasn't long before Petersen was hooked on free airline travel award programs. "People were constantly asking me to interpret the rules." An entrepreneur at heart, Petersen immediately recognized an opportunity, became the world's leading authority on frequent flyer miles, quit his job, and packaged his knowledge in a newsletter. "I found a niche, got in early, and earned my credibility"—something Petersen sees as the cornerstone of his success.

The first copy of InsideFlyer (February 1986) was quite different from the 48-page glossy magazine of today. "I didn't use a desktop publishing program. I collected a few articles and clip-outs, and literally pasted together a mock-up newsletter. Then I handed it out to business travelers at JFK and La Guardia airports asking them if they would be willing to pay a nominal amount of money to learn how to get free upgrades and frequent flyer stuff. They said yes, and I was in business."

Initially, Petersen's business was a one-person operation. Today he employs a staff of 35 at the magazine's Colorado

To explain frequent flyer award programs effectively, Randy Petersen focuses on his audience, organizing his magazine in a way that's logical and easy to read.

Also avoid obvious flattery. Although most of us respond well to honest praise and proper respect, we're suspicious of anyone who seems too impressed. When someone says, "Only a person of your outstanding intellect and refined tastes can fully appreciate this point," little warning lights flash in our minds. We suspect that we're about to be conned.

Avoid preaching to your audience. Few things are more irritating than people who assume that they know it all and that we know nothing. People who feel compelled to give lessons in business are particularly offensive. If, for some reason, you have to tell your audience something obvious, try to make the information unobtrusive. Place it in the middle of a paragraph, where it will sound like a casual comment as opposed to a major revelation. Alternatively, you might preface an obvious remark with "as you know" or some similar phrase.

Bragging is closely related to preaching and is equally offensive. When you praise your own accomplishments or those of your organization, you imply that you're better than your audience. References to the size, profitability, or eminence of your organization may be especially annoying (unless, of course, those in your audience work for the same organization). You're likely to evoke a negative reaction with comments such as "We at McMann's, which is the oldest and most respected firm in the city, have a reputation for integrity that is beyond question."

Perhaps the most important thing you can do to establish a good relationship with your audience is to be yourself. People can spot falseness very quickly, and they generally don't like it. If you don't try to be someone you're not, you'll sound sincere.

Springs headquarters, where Petersen serves as the company's editor/publisher. "It takes a lot of work to publish our magazine. We do a tremendous amount of research, and our facts must be current. We are not just a newsletter. We are in the customer service and information-processing business."

Because explaining frequent flyer awards and rules is not easy, the magazine's writers try to organize the details in a logical, easy-to-read, and informative manner by including lots of sub-headings, using short paragraphs, and listing program information alphabetically. The writers also use an audience-centered approach by keeping the tone of the magazine friendly and personal. "This is a challenge. We're not a business journal."

But publishing InsideFlyer has become a big business: More than 40 million people participate in the frequent flyer award programs, and they have 2 trillion miles earned (of which approximately 77 percent will be redeemed). The magazine currently boasts a circulation of 85,000 copies for its domestic edition and 40,000 copies for its international edition. Add that to sales of the company's 520-page Official Frequent Flyer Guidebook, its 487-page quarterly publication The Miles Guide, and numerous related products, and you'll understand why Petersen says, "We've really become a small publishing company. We have always made money from our words from day one—just by communicating information."

The more than 93 international frequent flyer, hotel, and credit-card award programs, give Petersen a lot of information to communicate—including letters like the one he wrote to United Airlines recommending changes to the carrier's award program. Petersen earns extra miles with the airlines by adopting a "you" attitude when making these types of requests: "Your recent (award) changes run the risk of alienating some of your member base. Your competition probably hopes that I can't change your mind on this one." Petersen generally begins these letters with a neutral point or compliment "simply because it is good manners and shows respect. We have developed a terrific rapport with the airlines and hotels, and I don't want to jeopardize a relationship that is mutually beneficial—it's just common sense."

Apply Your Knowledge

1. As assistant editor of InsideFlyer, you are responsible for verifying the factual information included in each monthly publication. You are quite frustrated because the airlines keep changing the rules for their award programs—sometimes while the monthly issue is at press. Randy Petersen has asked you to outline the draft of a letter to the airlines expressing the company's frustration and displeasure with the frequently changing rules. How would you begin this letter? What key points would you emphasize in the body of the letter? Would you use the direct or the indirect approach? Why?

2. Your company wants to publish a quarterly company newsletter for its employees. What are some of the main issues that should be resolved before a company newsletter is published? Please explain.

Use the "You" Attitude

By using an audience-centered approach, you try to see the subject through your audience's eyes. Then you can project this approach in your messages by adopting a "you" attitude, that is, by speaking and writing in terms of your audience's wishes, interests, hopes, and preferences. Talk about the other person, and you're talking about the thing that most interests him or her. Too many business messages have an "I" or "we" attitude, which causes the sender to sound selfish and uninterested in the receiver. The message tells what the sender wants; the recipient is expected to go along with it.

On the simplest level, you can adopt the "you" attitude by replacing terms that refer to yourself and your company with terms that refer to your audience. In other words, use you and yours instead of I, me, and mine or we, us, and ours:

The "you" attitude is best implemented by expressing your message in terms of the audience's interests and needs.

Instead of This	Use This
To help us process this order, we must ask for another copy of the requisition.	So that your order can be filled promptly, please send another copy of the requisition.
We are pleased to announce our new flight schedule from Atlanta to New York, which is any hour on the hour.	Now you can take a plane from Atlanta to New York any hour on the hour.
We offer the printer cartridges in three colors: black, blue, and green.	Select your printer cartridge from three colors: black, blue, and green.

Using *you* and *yours* requires finesse.[8] If you overdo it, you're likely to create some rather awkward sentences. You also run the risk of sounding like a high-pressure carnival barker at the county fair.[9] The "you" attitude is not intended to be manipulative or insincere. It is an extension of the audience-centered approach. In fact, the best way to implement the "you" attitude is to be sincere in thinking about your audience. It isn't just a matter of using one pronoun as opposed to another; it's a matter of genuine empathy. You can use *you* 25 times in a single page and still ignore your audience's true concerns. Look back at the letter in Figure 6.4. The first paragraph uses the pronoun *your* quite correctly and effectively. The third paragraph also displays effective use of the "you" attitude, even though no form of the word *you* ever appears in that paragraph. In the final analysis, it's the thought that counts, not the pronoun. If you're talking to a retailer, try to think like a retailer; if you're dealing with a production supervisor, put yourself in his or her position; if you're writing to a dissatisfied customer, imagine how you would feel at the other end of the transaction. The important thing is your attitude toward the members of your audience and your appreciation of their position.

On some occasions, you'll do better to avoid using *you*. For instance, when someone makes a mistake and you want to point it out impersonally to minimize the possibility of ill will, you might say, "We have a problem," instead of "You caused a problem." Using *you* in a way that might sound dictatorial is also impolite:

Avoid using *you* and *yours*

- To excess
- When assigning blame
- If your organization prefers a more formal style

The word *you* does not always indicate a "you" attitude, and the "you" attitude can be displayed without using the word *you*.

INSTEAD OF THIS	USE THIS
You should never use that kind of paper in the copy machine.	That type of paper doesn't work very well in the copy machine.
You must correct all five copies before noon.	All five copies must be corrected by noon.
You need to make sure the staff follows instructions.	The staff may need guidance in following instructions.

In addition, remember that the use of personal pronouns may not be acceptable in other cultures. In Japan, for example, people are uncomfortable with the personal touch of the "you" attitude. Japanese writers refer to their audience's company rather than to their receiver: "Your company [not you] will be pleased with the survey results."[10] You're always better off using the style and tone preferred by the culture you're dealing with.

Keep in mind the attitudes and policies of your organization as well. Some companies have a tradition of avoiding references to *you* and *I* in their memos and formal reports. If you work for a company that expects a formal, impersonal style, confine your use of personal pronouns to informal letters and memos.

Emphasize the Positive

Another way of showing sensitivity to your audience is to emphasize the positive side of your message.[11] Focus on the silver lining, not on the cloud. Stress what is or will be instead of what isn't or won't be. Most information, even bad news, has at least some redeeming feature. If you can make your audience aware of that feature, you will make your message more acceptable.

Explain what you have done, what you can do, and what you will do—not what you haven't done, can't do, or won't do.

INSTEAD OF THIS	USE THIS
It is impossible to repair this vacuum cleaner today.	Your vacuum cleaner will be ready by Tuesday.
We apologize for inconveniencing you during our remodeling.	The renovations now under way will help us serve you better.
We never exchange damaged goods.	We are happy to exchange merchandise that is returned to us in good condition.

In addition, when you're criticizing or correcting, don't hammer on the other person's mistakes. Avoid referring to failures, problems, or shortcomings. Focus instead on what the person can do to improve:

INSTEAD OF THIS	USE THIS
The problem with this department is a failure to control costs.	The performance of this department can be improved by tightening up cost controls.
You filled out the order form wrong. We can't send you the paint until you tell us what color you want.	So that your order can be processed properly, please check your color preferences on the enclosed card.
You broke the dish by running cold water on it right after you took it from the oven.	These dishes are sensitive to temperature shock and should be allowed to cool gradually after they are removed from the oven.

If you're trying to persuade the audience to buy a product, pay a bill, or perform a service for you, emphasize what's in it for them. Don't focus on why you want them to do something. Instead of saying, "Please buy this book so that I can make my sales quota," say, "The plot of this novel will keep you in suspense to the last page." Instead of saying, "We need your contribution to the Boys and Girls Club," say, "You can help a child make friends and build self-confidence through your donation to the Boys and Girls Club." An individual who sees the possibility for personal benefit is more likely to respond positively to your appeal.

Show your audience how they will benefit from complying with your message.

In general, try to state your message without using words that might hurt or offend your audience. Substitute mild terms (euphemisms) for those that have unpleasant connotations. Instead of advertising "cheap" merchandise, announce your bargain prices. Don't talk about "pimples and zits"; refer more delicately to complexion problems. You can be honest without being harsh. Gentle terms won't change the facts, but they will make those facts more acceptable:

Avoid words with negative connotations; use meaningful euphemisms instead.

INSTEAD OF THIS	USE THIS
toilet paper	bathroom tissue
used cars	resale cars
high-calorie food	high-energy food

On the other hand, don't carry euphemisms to extremes. If you're too subtle, people won't know what you're talking about. "Derecruiting" workers to the "mobility pool" instead of telling them they have six weeks to find another job isn't really very helpful. When using euphemisms, you walk a fine line between softening the blow and hiding the facts. It would not be ethical to speak to your community about relocating refuse when you're really talking about your plans for disposing of toxic waste. Such an attempt to hide the facts would very likely backfire, damaging your business image and reputation. In the final analysis, people respond better to an honest message delivered with integrity than they do to sugar-coated double-talk.

Establish Credibility

Because the success of your message may depend on the audience's perception of you, their belief in your competence and integrity is important. You want people to believe that you know what you're doing and that your word is dependable. Club Med's Trigano believes in building credibility over time by carefully building one's reputation. The first step is to promise only what you can do and then to do what you promise. After that, you can enhance credibility through your writing and speaking style.

Don't make false promises.

To enhance your credibility

- Show that you understand the other person's situation
- Establish your own credentials or ally yourself with a credible source
- Back up your claims with evidence, not exaggerations
- Use words that express confidence
- Believe in yourself and your message

If you're communicating with someone you know well, your previous interactions influence your credibility. The other person knows from experience whether you're trustworthy and capable. If the person is familiar with your company, the firm's reputation may be ample proof of your credibility.

But what if you are complete strangers? Even worse, what if the other person starts off with doubts about you? First and foremost, show an understanding of the other person's situation by calling attention to the things you have in common. If you're communicating with someone who shares your professional background, you might say, "As a fellow engineer (lawyer, doctor, teacher, or whatever), I'm sure you can appreciate this situation." Another approach is to use technical or professional terms that identify you as a peer.

You can also gain the audience's confidence by explaining your credentials, but you need to be careful that you don't sound pompous. Generally, one or two aspects of your background are all you need to mention. Possibly your title or the name of your organization will be enough to impress the audience with your abilities. If not, perhaps you can mention the name of someone who carries some weight with your audience. You might begin a letter with "Professor Goldberg suggested that I contact you," or you could quote a recognized authority on a subject, even if you don't know the authority personally. The fact that your ideas are shared by a credible source adds prestige to your message.

Your credibility is also enhanced by the quality of the information you provide. If you support your points with evidence that can be confirmed through observation, research, experimentation, or measurement, your audience will recognize that you have the facts, and they will respect you. Exaggerated claims, on the other hand, are unethical and do more harm than good.

You also risk losing credibility if you seem to be currying favor with insincere compliments. So support compliments with specific points:

INSTEAD OF THIS

My deepest heartfelt thanks for the excellent job you did. It's hard these days to find workers like you. You are just fantastic! I can't stress enough how happy you have made us with your outstanding performance.

USE THIS

Thanks for the fantastic job you did filling in for Gladys at the convention with just an hour's notice. Despite the difficult circumstances, you managed to attract several new orders with your demonstration of the new line of coffeemakers. Your dedication and sales ability are truly appreciated.

The other side of the credibility coin is too much modesty and not enough confidence. Many writing authorities suggest that you avoid such words as if, hope, and trust, which express a lack of confidence on your part:

INSTEAD OF THIS

We hope this recommendation will be helpful.

If you'd like to order, mail us the reply card.

We trust that you'll extend your service contract.

USE THIS

We're glad to make this recommendation.

To order, mail the reply card.

By extending your service contract, you can continue to enjoy top-notch performance from your equipment.

When Body Shop founder Anita Roddick decided to use her business as a vehicle for social and environmental change, she focused worldwide attention on her credibility with customers. Indeed, as Roddick and her business have become symbols of social responsibility, they have drawn criticism and investigation. Any mistakes and errors will be magnified, says Roddick, "but by emphasizing social issues in addition to profits, we are trying to change the focus of business."

The ultimate key to being believable is to believe in yourself. If you are convinced that your message is sound, you can state your case with authority so that the audience has no doubts. When you have confidence in your own success, you automatically suggest that your audience will respond in the desired way. If you lack faith in yourself, however, you're likely to communicate an unsteady attitude that undermines your credibility.

Be Polite

The best tone for business messages is almost always a polite one. By being courteous to your audience, you show consideration for their needs and feelings. You express yourself with kindness and tact.

Undoubtedly, you'll be frustrated and exasperated by other people many times in your career. When that happens, you'll be tempted to say what you think in blunt terms. To be sure, it's your job to convey the facts, precisely and accurately. Nevertheless, venting your emotions will rarely improve the situation and may jeopardize the goodwill of your audience. Instead, be gentle when expressing yourself:

Although you may be tempted now and then to be brutally frank, try to express the facts in a kind and thoughtful manner.

INSTEAD OF THIS	USE THIS
You really fouled things up with that last computer run.	Let me tell you what went wrong with that last computer run so that we can make sure things run smoothly next time.
You've been sitting on my order for two weeks now. When can I expect delivery?	As I mentioned in my letter of October 12, we are eager to receive our order as soon as possible. Could you please let us know when to expect delivery.

Of course, some situations require more diplomacy than others. If you know your audience well, you can get away with being less formal. However, when corresponding with people who outrank you or with those outside your organization, you usually include an added measure of courtesy. In general, written communication requires more tact than oral communication. When you're speaking, your words are softened by your tone of voice and facial expression. You can adjust your approach depending on the feedback you get. Written communication, on the other hand, is stark and self-contained. If you hurt a person's feelings in writing, you can't soothe them right away. In fact, you may not even know that you have hurt the other person, because the lack of feedback prevents you from seeing his or her reaction.

Use extra tact when writing and when communicating with higher-ups and outsiders.

In addition to avoiding things that give offense, try to find things that might bring pleasure. Remember a co-worker's birthday, send a special note of thanks to a supplier who has done a good job, acknowledge someone's help, send a clipping to a customer who has expressed interest in a subject. People remember the extra little things that indicate you care about them as individuals. In this impersonal age, the human touch is particularly effective.

Another simple but effective courtesy is to be prompt in your correspondence. If possible, answer your mail within two or three days. If you need more time to prepare a reply, write a brief note or call to say that you're working on an answer. Most people are willing to wait if they know how long the wait will be. What annoys them is the suspense.

Project the Company's Image

Even though establishing the right tone for your audience is your main goal, give some thought to projecting the right image for your company. When you communicate with outsiders, on even the most routine matter, you serve as the spokesperson for your organization. The impression that you make can enhance or damage the reputation of the entire company. Thus your own views and personality must be subordinated, at least to some extent, to the interests and style of the company.

CEO William Gates wants Microsoft to maintain its image of competitiveness well into the future, when he predicts that his company's software "will be used in business, in the home, in the pocket, and in the car." But a company's image is also projected through its employees, so when you're speaking for your company, it's important to align your personal values with those of your organization.

You can save yourself a great deal of time and frustration if you master the company style early in your career. In a typical corporation, 85 percent of the letters, memos, and reports are written by someone other than the higher-level managers who sign them. Most of the time, managers reject first drafts of these documents for stylistic reasons. In fact, the average draft goes through five revisions before it is finally approved.[12]

You might wonder whether all this effort to fine-tune the style of a message is worthwhile. The fact is, people in business care very much about saying precisely the right thing

---

CHECKLIST FOR COMPOSING BUSINESS MESSAGES

A. Organization
1. Recognize good organization.
   - ☐ a. Subject and purpose are clear.
   - ☐ b. Information is directly related to subject and purpose.
   - ☐ c. Ideas are grouped and presented logically.
   - ☐ d. All necessary information is included.
2. Achieve good organization through outlining.
   - ☐ a. Decide what to say.
     - i. Main idea
     - ii. Major points
     - iii. Evidence
   - ☐ b. Organize the message to respond to the audience's probable reaction.
     - i. Use the direct approach when your audience will be neutral, pleased, interested, or eager.
     - ii. Use the indirect approach when your audience will be displeased, uninterested, or unwilling.
3. Choose the appropriate organizational plan.
   - ☐ a. Short messages
     - i. Direct request
     - ii. Routine, good-news, or goodwill message
     - iii. Bad-news message
     - iv. Persuasive message
   - ☐ b. Long messages
     - i. Informational pattern
     - ii. Analytical pattern

B. Formulation
1. Compose your first draft.
   - ☐ a. Get ideas down as quickly as you can.
   - ☐ b. Rearrange, delete, and add ideas without losing sight of your purpose.
2. Vary the style to create a tone that suits the occasion.
   - ☐ a. Establish your relationship with your audience.
     - i. Use the appropriate level of formality.
     - ii. Avoid being overly familiar, using inappropriate humor, including obvious flattery, sounding preachy, bragging, and trying to be something you're not.
   - ☐ b. Extend your audience-centered approach by using the "you" attitude.
   - ☐ c. Emphasize the positive aspects of your message.
   - ☐ d. Establish your credibility to gain the audience's confidence.
   - ☐ e. Use a polite tone.
   - ☐ f. Use the style that your company prefers.

---

in precisely the right way. Their willingness to go over the same document five times demonstrates just how important style really is. For a reminder of the tasks involved in composition, see this chapter's Checklist for Composing Business Messages.

Shaping Your E-Mail Message

An e-mail message is more than an electronic memo or a one-way telephone call.[13] You can send e-mail to co-workers, supervisors, and staff, but you can also send e-mail outside the company to customers, suppliers, and competitors. Moreover, you can send it across the globe as easily as across the hall.[14] Organization and style are just as important for e-mail messages as for any other type of message. So communicate your points quickly and efficiently by making your e-mail message audience centered, easy to follow, and interesting.

Make Your E-Mail Audience Centered

Even though e-mail may have an image of speed and informality, take enough time to compose your e-mail messages carefully. Think about your audience. Consider your reader's interests, needs, and feelings.

How formal you make your message depends on your audience, as well as on your purpose. Although e-mail may at times seem transitory, it can emulate "snail mail" by having conventional business language, a respectful style, and a more formal format (including a traditional greeting, formalized headings, and a formal closing and signature).[15] Of course e-mail can be as informal and casual as a conversation between old friends—just be sure that such a style is appropriate for the situation. Regardless of the level of formality required, do your best to use correct spelling and proper grammar. Some e-mail users insist that spelling and grammar take a back seat to your readiness to communicate.[16] But in business communication, e-mail needs to be as clear and as easy to understand as possible.

Margin notes:

Make your e-mail messages
- Audience-centered
- Easy to follow
- Interesting

The formality of your e-mail depends on your audience.

Because e-mail is so effortlessly sent abroad, focusing on your audience also means being culturally aware. When communicating with someone in another culture, take into account cultural differences. For example, be sure to give metric measurements (followed by English-system equivalents); spell out what format or system you're using for dates, times, numbers, and money; and use more formal greetings for people in those parts of the world that expect them.[17]

You need to be culturally aware when writing e-mail.

Because e-mail is read on-screen, keep your audience's terminal in mind (Figure 6.5). Computers and e-mail systems vary, so you want to ensure that your readers won't be confused by message lines that run off the screen or that wrap incorrectly. Press the Enter key at the end of each line, making sure that your line length is fewer than 80 characters (or fewer than 60 characters if your message is likely to be forwarded, because forwarding often indents messages a tab length). And, of course, don't use font features such as boldface and italics unless you're certain your reader's computer and e-mail software can reproduce such features.[18]

Consider how your message will appear on your audience's screen.

Remember to make responding easy. State clearly the type of response you need. Give enough information in your e-mail message for your audience to be able to respond. Word your message so that your audience can respond as briefly as possible, perhaps with a yes or a no. Also, ask for your audience's response early in your message, perhaps even in your subject line.[19]

Make responding easy.

The following message is typical of those sent using the Eudora Pro software package.

Figure 6.5
In-Depth Critique: On-Screen E-Mail Message

```
╔═══════════════════ E-Mail ═══════════════════╗

    X-Sender: joand@mail.signa.com
    Date: Mon, 04 May 1998 04:43:33-0600
    To: signa-users@signa.com
    From: "Howard F. Jones" <Howie@signa.com>
    Subject: Now Track Your Time Online
    X-Info: SIGNA
    X-ListMember: tandy@signa.com [signa-users@signa.com]

    Dear Customer,

    An exciting change has been made at SIGNA in the past two weeks.

    You now have access to an online time-checking mechanism that allows
    you to track your online time usage. If you are on a metered service plan
    that is billed in an hourly format, this will give you the tool needed to
    maximize your connection. This tool is currently located on our home page.

    If you would like us to send out more reviews of our interesting customer
    sites, please drop me a line and let me know. I can be reached seven days
    a week at Howie@signa.com.

    Thank you,

    Howard F. Jones
    President
    SIGNA, Inc.
```

The subject line captures customer interest.

Line length is well under 80 characters.

Jones has a friendly tone in this message to his customers.

The "you" attitude is apparent in the focus of the message as well as in the request for feedback.

Make Your E-Mail Easy to Follow

Some readers receive more e-mail than they can read, so your best chance of getting your message across is to make your e-mail easy to follow. Use short, focused paragraphs that are organized in a logical fashion. Consider using the method newspaper reporters use writing from the top down. That way you'll be sure to get your point across as early as possible, in case your reader doesn't have the time or interest to finish reading your message.[20]

In fact, try to keep your message short and concise. Many e-mail messages are less than three paragraphs long and fit into one screen. Whenever possible, try to limit your message to one screen or window. Of course, some e-mail messages will be longer than one screen; a few may even be longer than several screens. When it's necessary to send a long e-mail message, consider including a brief table of contents in the first screen, perhaps with a short paragraph that summarizes and highlights the key points. Also, use headings to break up long passages of text. Not only do they help your reader understand you, but they can serve as shortcuts, highlighting the material your reader may want to read or skip. And remember that lists are an efficient way to present information. You can use bullets (asterisks) to emphasize key points and numbered lists for sequential points. Embedding a list within text can also save you some space.[21]

Make Your E-Mail Interesting

When your readers are deciding which messages to spend time on, they look at whom each is from, they check the subject line, and they may scan the first screen. If your message can't attract your reader's attention by that time, your e-mail will probably go unread and will perhaps be deleted.[22] You can make your e-mail more interesting—from start to finish.

An interesting subject line does more than just describe or classify the content of your message. By applying key words, humor, quotations, or questions, you can grab your reader's attention. You have 25 to 30 characters to build interest for you message (longer lines are often truncated). Try wording your subject line so that it tells your reader what to do. For example: Send figures for July sales is much more informative than July sales figures. Of course, you don't want to use wild statements just to attract your reader's attention. Using urgent in your subject lines too often will soon have an effect quite different from the one intended.

Your e-mail header displays who your message is to and from. Even so, adding a greeting makes your e-mail message more personal.[23] Naturally, whether you use a formal greeting (Dear Professor Ingersoll) or a more casual one (Hi Marty!) depends on your audience and your purpose.

Even though you can't usually use underlining, fonts, or graphics to emphasize various parts of your message, you can use keyboard characters such as asterisks, dashes, carets, hyphens, colons, slashes, pipes, and capital letters. For example, you can surround a word with asterisks to *make* it stand out. Or you can indicate underlining like _this_. You can open up your message by using white space

```
--------------------------------------------------------------------------------------
|                                                                                    |
| and by inserting lines or boxes made of asterisks or hyphens and pipes. |
|                                                                                    |
--------------------------------------------------------------------------------------
```

You can make a headline with all capital letters, but don't overdo it. TOO MANY CAPITAL LETTERS LOOKS LIKE SHOUTING! You can even use extra character spaces to emphasize your most i m p o r t a n t points.[24] Of course you must guard against overusing any of these techniques, or else your message will look jumbled and confusing.

To emphasize or clarify the meaning of a comment in a less formal message, you can also use your keyboard to create little sideways pictures (emoticons). For example, you can make a sideways happy face with a colon, a hyphen, and a closing parenthesis: :-) (variations might look like (:->) or d:-) or <(:->) and so on). Other emotions can also be expressed, such as boo hoo (:-<) and uh oh (:-o) and my lips are sealed (:-x) and so on. As with other enhancement techniques, emoticons can be overdone. When used sparingly, they can add power, but when overused, they can make your message look more like graffiti.[25]

Consider writing e-mail from the top down.

E-mail's subject line offers you an opportunity to gain your reader's interest.

Use a greeting to make your e-mail more personal.

Create interesting typographical effects with keyboard characters.

Be careful not to overdo emoticons.

Your closing and signature also personalize your e-mail message. In most cases, use simple closings, such as Thanks or Regards, rather than more traditional business closings such as Sincerely yours. Of course, you may want to use a more formal closing for international e-mail.

For your signature, you can simply type your name or initials on a separate line. You might put one or two hyphens before your name to set it off from the body of your e-mail. Or you may want to use a signature file, a short identifier that may include your name, company name, postal address, fax number, other e-mail addresses, and sometimes even a short quotation or thought. Some users think you should include only the information needed to contact you. Once you create a signature file, you can save it in your mail program and add it to e-mail messages without retyping. You can also use a digital copy of your handwritten signature, which is becoming acceptable as legal proof of business transactions, especially when accompanied by a date stamp that is automatically inserted by your mail program.[26]

After a simple closing, you can include a signature in several ways.

On the Job

SOLVING A COMMUNICATION DILEMMA AT CLUB MED

For many years Club Med targeted single adults, promising them a relaxing yet socially active vacation. To combat disasters in and around many of its locations in the early 1990s and to respond to the shifts in society's view of freewheeling lifestyles, the company began targeting senior citizens and families with children. Families spend billions of dollars on vacations every year, and the 50-plus age group is growing at a rate triple that of the general population, making both groups attractive to the Club Med marketing staff.

Many Club Med resorts added facilities and entertainment aimed at children and older people. The company introduced the "Forever Young" program tailored for older customers, sending them to resorts featuring accessibility, interesting day trips, and sports such as tennis and golf. The headline for the ad campaign was: "With age comes wisdom and patience, not to mention a great deal at Club Med." The company significantly increased its advertising budget to promote the new programs.

But advertising alone was not enough to make the programs successful. Up to 85 percent of Club Med's business comes through travel agents, so success depended heavily on agents' recommendations. Club Med reorganized its marketing staff to optimize relationships with travel agents. And in the fall of 1996, Club Med published a sales manual that describes its vacation programs and includes demographic profiles of guests (to help travel agents match potential clients with appropriate resorts).

The new programs have been very successful, and travel agents have responded well to Club Med's efforts. According to a recent study, half of the company's clients were married couples and another 15 percent were children. Plus, 15 percent of the company's revenues came from clients over the age of 50. The changes also improved Club Med's financial picture. After substantial losses in 1993, company profits increased significantly for three years, including an 87 percent increase from 1995 to 1996.

Your Mission: You are on the sales staff at Club Med. The company recently introduced new vacation programs geared toward senior citizens, a market quite different from the typical Club Med visitor. You know that travel agents are your best source of business, and you want the agents you work with to support the new programs.

You plan to send them brochures describing the program, and you have also written a draft of a letter to introduce yourself and encourage the agents to recommend Club Med vacations for a wider range of customers.

Here is a copy of your draft. Read it and then select the best responses to the questions that follow. Be prepared to explain why your choice is best.[27]

Dear travel partner:

Do you think of Club Med as a vacation destination for swinging singles? Our resorts are popular with young adults, but that is not all that Club Med has to offer.

I'm sure it isn't news to you that the 55-and-older age group is the fastest growing vacation market today. People in this older group are looking for new and different places to vacation, and we think they would enjoy Club Med resorts. Our new "Forever Young" program is geared to people 55 and older. The enclosed brochure describes the program, and I'm sure you will find the program to be a great way to satisfy your clients.

I am excited about working with you to help a wider range of customers enjoy Club Med vacations. Please feel free to call me if I can be of any assistance to you.

1. Does the letter conform to the guidelines for good organization?
   a. No. The opening sentence is unprofessional, and it might be offensive to some people. The letter does not get to the point until the end of the second paragraph, and even then it is vague. There is not enough information to support the main purpose, and the information is poorly organized. The first paragraph should introduce the new program, then subsequent paragraphs should contain supporting information, describing how the Forever Young program meets the needs of senior citizen vacationers.

b. The letter includes unnecessary information. You are including a brochure, so you just need to refer the reader to the brochure.

c. The letter is basically well organized, but there is not enough information to support the main point. It says that senior citizens would enjoy Club Med, but it does not have enough detail to convince a travel agent to risk sending customers there.

d. The letter is well organized. The subject and purpose are clear. All necessary information is included, and the information is directly related to subject and purpose. Information is grouped and presented logically.

2. You decide to rewrite the draft. Your first step is to develop an outline. What should you use as your main idea?
   a. The 55-and-older age group is a rapidly growing source of vacation business.
   b. Club Med is not just for singles anymore.
   c. Club Med's sales staff has been reorganized to better support travel agents.
   d. New programs at Club Med can help agents arrange successful vacations for a broader range of clients.

3. What basic points will you use to develop and support the main idea?
   a. People go on vacation to have fun. Senior citizens will be attracted to Club Med because of its reputation for providing fun vacations.
   b. Senior citizens have more money and time for vacations than ever before. They like to feel younger, so they would enjoy being around the younger clients at Club Med resorts. Because business has been declining, Club Med is putting a lot of effort into attracting the older crowd. The program's success depends on the travel agents' support.
   c. As baby boomers mature, the senior citizen vacation market will grow quickly. Today's senior citizens are more active than the seniors of previous generations, so they are looking for a different kind of vacation. Club Med provides a good balance of activities and relaxation. Senior citizens

will like the all-inclusive price because they know up front how much their vacation will cost. Return business is important at Club Med as well as for travel agents, and 40 percent of Club Med clients return within two years for another vacation.

d. Senior citizens as a group are fussy about how they spend their money; they want top value for their dollar. They will be attracted to Club Med because of its reputation for quality and service.

4. Which organizational plan should the letter follow?
   a. Indirect. You are targeting a totally different customer than the agents are used to sending to your resorts, so agents may be skeptical. By reminding the agents of your past success and describing how the new program was developed, you will pique interest in the program. Include information on how the senior citizen vacation market is changing, and describe how Club Med is responding to those changes. Close by asking the agents to send you a broader range of clients, and offer your assistance.
   b. Indirect. Open by saying Club Med wants to expand its customer base and explain why. Refer the agents to the brochure for information on the program. Close by asking the agents to recommend your resorts to their senior citizen clients.
   c. Indirect. Start by mentioning the rapid growth in the senior citizen vacation market. Describe what kind of vacation typical senior citizens are looking for. Refer the agents to the brochure for information on Club Med's program for senior citizens. Close by asking the agents to recommend your resorts to their senior citizen clients.
   d. Direct. The new programs will benefit the agents as well as Club Med, so they will be eager to recommend the resorts for their senior clients. State in the first paragraph that you want the agents to recommend Club Med vacations to a broader range of clients, then explain why doing so is a good idea. Finish by providing your phone number so that they can contact you for assistance or more information.

Documents for Analysis

DOCUMENT 6.A: DEFINING AND GROUPING IDEAS

The writer of the following list is having trouble grouping the ideas logically for an insurance information brochure. Revise the list and develop a logical outline, paying attention to appropriate subordination of ideas. Rewrite where necessary to give phrases a more consistent sound.

ACCIDENT PROTECTION INSURANCE PLAN

- Coverage is only pennies a day
- Benefit is $100,000 for accidental death on common carrier
- Benefit is $100 a day for hospitalization as result of motor vehicle or common carrier accident
- Benefit is $20,000 for accidental death in motor vehicle accident

- Individual coverage is only $17.85 per quarter; family coverage is just $26.85 per quarter
- No physical exam or health questions
- Convenient payment—billed quarterly
- Guaranteed acceptance for all applicants
- No individual rate increases
- Free, no-obligation examination period
- Cash paid in addition to any other insurance carried
- Covers accidental death when riding as fare-paying passenger on public transportation, including buses, trains, jets, ships, trolleys, subways, or any other common carrier
- Covers accidental death in motor vehicle accidents occurring while driving or riding in or on automobile, truck, camper, motor home, or nonmotorized bicycle

DOCUMENT 6.B: CONTROLLING YOUR STYLE AND TONE
Read the following document; then (1) analyze the strengths and weaknesses of each sentence and (2) revise the document so that it follows this chapter's guidelines.

I am a new publisher with some really great books to sell. I saw your announcement in Publishers Weekly about the bookseller's show you're having this summer, and I think it's a great idea. Count me in, folks! I would like to get some space to show my books. I thought it would be a neat thing if I could do some airbrushing on T-shirts live to help promote my hot new title, T-Shirt Art. Before I got into publishing, I was an airbrush artist, and I could demonstrate my techniques. I've done hundreds of advertis-ing illustrations and have been a sign painter all my life, so I'll also be promoting my other book, hot off the presses, How to Make Money in the Sign Painting Business.

I will be starting my PR campaign about May 1999 with ads in PW and some art trade papers, so my books should be well known by the time the show comes around in August. In case you would like to use my appearance there as part of your publicity, I have enclosed a biography and photo of myself.

P.S. Please let me know what it costs for booth space as soon as possible so that I can figure out whether I can afford to attend. Being a new publisher is mighty expensive!

Critical Thinking Questions

1. When organizing the ideas for your business message, how can you be sure that what seems logical to you will also seem logical to your audience?
2. Do you think that cushioning bad news is manipulative?
3. Which organizational plan would you use to ask employees to work overtime to meet an important deadline: a direct request or a persuasive message? Why?
4. Which organizational plan would you use to let your boss know that you'll be out half a day next week to attend your father's funeral: a routine message or a bad-news message? Why?
5. When composing business messages, how can you be yourself and project your company's image at the same time?
6. Is it ever okay to use an indirect approach when writing e-mail? How can you use a buffer when you have to state your purpose in the subject line? Explain.

Exercises

1. Suppose you are preparing to recommend to top management the installation of a new heating system (called cogeneration). The following information is in your files. Eliminate from the list topics that aren't essential; then arrange the other topics so that your report will give management a clear understanding of the heating system and a balanced, concise justification for installing it.

    History of the development of the cogeneration heating process
    Scientific credentials of the developers of the process
    Risks assumed in using this process
    Your plan for installing the equipment in your building
    Stories about its successful use in comparable facilities
    Specifications of the equipment that would be installed
    Plans for disposing of the old heating equipment
    Costs of installing and running the new equipment
    Advantages and disadvantages of using the new process
    Detailed ten-year cost projections
    Estimates of the time needed to phase in the new system
    Alternative systems that management might wish to consider

2. Indicate whether the direct or indirect approach would be best in each of the following situations, then briefly explain why. Would any of these messages be inappropriate for e-mail? Explain.
    a. A letter from a consumer asking when next year's automobiles will be put on sale locally
    b. A letter from a recent college graduate requesting a letter of recommendation from a former instructor
    c. A letter turning down a job applicant
    d. An announcement that because of high air-conditioning costs, the plant temperature will be held at 78 degrees during the summer months
    e. A final request to settle a delinquent debt
3. If you were trying to persuade people to take the following actions, how would you organize your argument?
    a. You want your boss to approve your plan for hiring two new people.
    b. You want to be hired for a job.
    c. You want to be granted a business loan.
    d. You want to collect a small amount from a regular customer whose account is slightly past due.
    e. You want to collect a large amount from a customer whose account is seriously past due.
4. Suppose that end-of-term frustrations have produced this e-mail message to Professor Anne Brewer from a student who feels that he should have received a B in his accounting class. If this message were recast into three or four clear sentences, the teacher might be more receptive to the student's argument. Rewrite the message to show how you would improve it.

    I think that I was unfairly awarded a C in your accounting class this term, and I am asking you to change the grade to a B. It was a difficult term. I don't get any money from home, and I have to work mornings at the Pancake House (as a cook), so I had to rush to make your class, and those two times that I missed class were because they wouldn't let me off work because of special events at the Pancake House (unlike some other students who just take off when they choose). On the midterm examination, I originally got a 75 percent, but you said in class that there were two different ways to answer the third question and that you would change the grades of students who used the "optimal cost" method and had been counted off 6 points for doing this. I don't think that you took this into account, because I got 80 percent on the final, which is clearly a B. Anyway, whatever you decide, I just want to tell you that I really enjoyed this class, and I thank you for making accounting so interesting.

5. Substitute inoffensive phrases for the following:
   a. you claim that
   b. it is not our policy to
   c. you neglected to
   d. in which you assert
   e. we are sorry you are dissatisfied
   f. you failed to enclose
   g. we request that you send us
   h. apparently you overlooked our terms
   i. we have been very patient
   j. we are at a loss to understand

6. Rewrite the following letter to Mrs. Bruce Crandall (1597 Church Street, Grants Pass, Oregon 97526) so that it conveys a helpful, personal, and interested tone:

   We have your letter of recent date to our Ms. Dobson. Owing to the fact that you neglected to include the size of the dress you ordered, please be advised that no shipment of your order was made, but the aforementioned shipment will occur at such time as we are in receipt of the aforementioned information.

7. Rewrite these sentences to reflect your audience's viewpoint.
   a. We request that you use the order form supplied in the back of our catalog.
   b. We insist that you always bring your credit card to the store.

c. We want to get rid of all our 14-inch monitors in order to make room in our warehouse for the new 20-inch models. Thus we are offering a 25 percent discount on all sales this week.
   d. I am applying for the position of bookkeeper in your office. I feel that my grades prove that I am bright and capable, and I think I can do a good job for you.
   e. As requested, we are sending the refund for $25.

8. Revise these sentences to be positive rather than negative.
   a. To avoid the loss of your credit rating, please remit payment within ten days.
   b. We don't make refunds on returned merchandise that is soiled.
   c. Because we are temporarily out of Baby Cry dolls, we won't be able to ship your order for ten days.
   d. You failed to specify the color of the blouse that you ordered.
   e. You should have realized that waterbeds will freeze in unheated houses during winter months. Therefore, our guarantee does not cover the valve damage, and you must pay the $9.50 valve-replacement fee (plus postage).

9. Provide euphemisms for the following words and phrases.
   a. stubborn
   b. wrong
   c. stupid
   d. incompetent
   e. loudmouth

10. Ben Cohen and Jerry Greenfield sell millions of gallons of Ben & Jerry's Homemade ice cream each year. They are also strong advocates for global issues, peace, and charity. Visit their Web site at <http://www.benjerry.com>, and consult their index. Click on various topics, and consider how Cohen and Greenfield project the company's image and their personal advocacy. Write an e-mail message to a fellow student explaining why the Web page enables Cohen and Greenfield to be themselves, advocate their causes, and advertise their business. Print your e-mail message for submission to your instructor.

DEVELOPING YOUR INTERNET SKILLS
GOING ONLINE: CONNECT NOW WITH A VIRTUAL LIBRARY, P. 107

After exploring the virtual reference desk at this site, list as many ways as you can think of to use this extensive site effectively in a business setting.

REVISING BUSINESS MESSAGES

After studying this chapter, you will be able to

Edit your messages for content and organization, style and readability, and word choice

Choose the most correct and most effective words to make your point

Rewrite sentences to clarify the relationships among ideas and to make your writing interesting

Identify elements of paragraphs

Rewrite paragraphs using the appropriate development technique

Choose the best design for written documents

Proofread your messages for mechanics and format

On the Job
FACING A COMMUNICATION DILEMMA AT McDONALD'S
A Little More Polish on the Golden Arches, Please

If you hanker for a Big Mac, a Coke, and some fries, here's a job for you: being a quality control representative for McDonald's. David Giarla has been one for ten years, and he still loves the smell of Egg McMuffins in the morning. On a typical day, he visits seven or eight McDonald's, samples the food, inspects the kitchen, surveys the storeroom, and chats with the manager and employees. If he likes what he eats and sees, everybody breathes a sigh of relief and goes back to flipping burgers and wiping tables. But if the food, service, or facilities are not up to snuff, watch out. Giarla might file a negative report with headquarters. If enough negative reports pile up, McDonald's might cancel the franchisee's license.

Giarla's aim, however, is not to get people into trouble. On the contrary, he wants the store managers to succeed. He believes that by holding them to McDonald's high standards, he can help them build their businesses. When he spots a problem, he always points it out and gives the manager a chance to fix it before he files a negative report. His aim is to offer criticism in a diplomatic and constructive manner, and he usually succeeds.

Next time you're in a McDonald's, put yourself in Giarla's position. What would you tell the manager and employees to help them improve their operation? How would you phrase your suggestions? What words would you choose, and how would you arrange them in sentences and paragraphs?[1]

STAGE 7: EDITING YOUR MESSAGE

Whether offering criticism or praise, David Giarla understands that once you've completed the first draft of your message, you owe it to yourself and to your audience to review and refine it. Plan to go over a document at least three times: once for content and organization, once for style and readability, and once for mechanics and format. The letter in Figure 7.1 has been edited using the proofreading marks shown in Appendix D. The letter in Figure 7.2 shows how the thoroughly revised letter looked when completed.

Figure 7.1
In-Depth Critique: Sample Edited Letter

This letter responds to Louise Wilson's request for information about the Commerce Hotel's frequent-guest program.

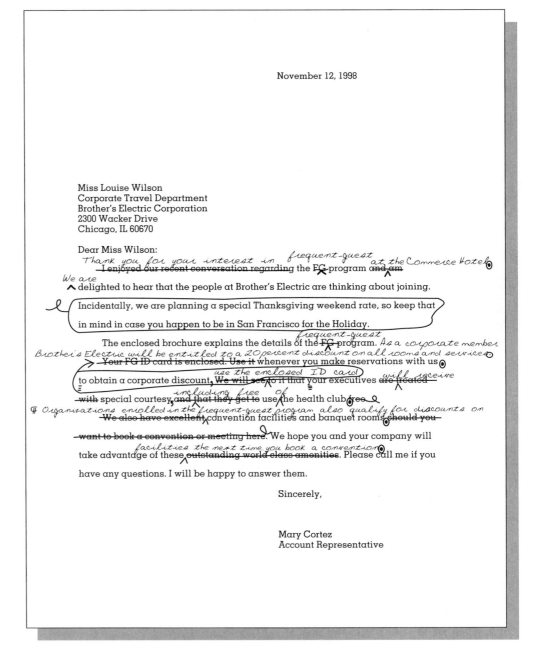

Content and organization: In the first paragraph, stick to the point (the main idea). In the middle, highlight the key advantage of the frequent-guest program, and, in subsequent paragraphs, discuss details. Eliminate redundancies.

Style and readability: Reword to stress the "you" viewpoint. Clarify the relationships among ideas through placement and combination of phrases. Moderate the excessive enthusiasm, and eliminate words (such as amenities) that might be unfamiliar to your reader.

Mechanics and format: To prevent confusion, spell out the abbreviated phrase FG.

Professionals such as David Giarla at McDonald's understand the importance of careful revision. The most successful communicators make sure their messages are the best they can be.

The tendency is to separate revision from composition, but editing is an ongoing activity that occurs throughout the composition process. You edit and revise as you go along; then you edit and revise again after you've completed the first draft. Although the basic editing principles discussed here apply to both written and oral communication, the steps involved in revising a speech or an oral presentation are slightly different, as Chapter 18 explains.

Evaluating Your Content and Organization

Ideally, let your draft age a day or two before you begin the editing process so that you can approach the material with a fresh eye. Then read through the document quickly to evaluate its overall effectiveness. You're mainly concerned with content, organization, and

The revised letter gives the requested information in a more organized fashion and has a friendlier style and clearer mechanics.

Figure 7.2
In-Depth Critique: Final
Revised Letter

333 Sansome Street ➤ San Francisco, CA 94104

(800) 323-7347 ➤ (415) 854-2447 ➤ Fax (415) 854-7669

www.CommerceHotel.com

November 12, 1998

Miss Louise Wilson
Corporate Travel Department
Brother's Electric Corporation
2300 Wacker Drive
Chicago, IL 60670

Dear Miss Wilson:

Thank you for your interest in the frequent-guest program at the Commerce Hotel. We are delighted to hear that the people at Brother's Electric are thinking about joining.

The enclosed brochure explains the details of the frequent-guest program. As a corporate member, Brother's Electric will be entitled to a 20 percent discount on all rooms and services. To obtain your corporate discount, use the enclosed ID card whenever you make reservations with us. Your executives will receive special courtesy, including free use of the health club.

Organizations enrolled in the frequent-guest program also qualify for discounts on convention facilities and banquet rooms. We hope you and your company will take advantage of these facilities the next time you book a convention. Please call me if you have any questions. I will be happy to answer them.

Sincerely,

Mary Cortez

Mary Cortez
Account Representative

The first paragraph now provides a "you" attitude, spells out what was previously abbreviated, and contains no irrelevant material.

The second paragraph now clarifies the benefits of the frequent-guest program and personalizes those benefits by using the "you" attitude.

The last paragraph now combines a final benefit with more information about services available. It also concludes with a friendly tone.

flow. Compare the draft with your original plan. Have you covered all points in the most logical order? Is there a good balance between the general and the specific? Do the most important ideas receive the most space, and are they placed in the most prominent positions? Have you provided enough support and double-checked the facts? Would the message be more convincing if it were arranged in another sequence? Do you need to add anything? On the other hand, what can you eliminate? In business, it's particularly important to weed out unnecessary material.

In the first phase of editing, spend a few extra moments on the beginning and ending of the message. As Dave Giarla knows, these are the sections that have the greatest impact on the audience. Be sure that the opening of a letter or memo is relevant, interesting, and geared to the reader's probable reaction. In longer messages, check to see that the first few

After a day or two, review your message for content and organization.

Michael D. Eisner, chairman and CEO of the Walt Disney Company, has kept Walt Disney's legacy alive and fiscally healthy through recent years of dramatic change and growth. His detail-oriented business sense is apparent in every branch of Disney's multi-faceted operations, including the renewed stature of Disney's animation studios as the best in the industry. For Eisner, careful review and revision of budgets, reports, and long-term strategic growth proposals are critical to running a company.

Readability depends on word choice, sentence length, sentence structure, organization, and the message's physical appearance.

The two key aspects of word choice are

- Correctness
- Effectiveness

If in doubt, check it out.

Plain English is close to spoken English and can be easily understood.

paragraphs establish the subject, purpose, and organization of the material. Review the conclusion to be sure that it summarizes the main idea and leaves the audience with a positive impression.

Reviewing Your Style and Readability

When editing a message's style and readability, ask yourself whether you've achieved the right tone for your audience. Look for opportunities to make the material more interesting through the use of lively words and phrases. At the same time, be particularly conscious of whether your message is clear and readable. Check your vocabulary and sentence structure to be sure you're relying mainly on familiar terms and simple, direct statements. You might even apply a readability formula to gauge the difficulty of your writing.

The most common readability formulas measure the length of words and sentences to give you a rough idea of how well educated your audience must be to understand your message. Figure 7.3 shows how one readability formula, the Fog Index, has been applied to an excerpt from a memo. (The "long words" in the passage have been underlined.) As the calculation shows, anyone who reads at a ninth-grade level should be able to read this passage with ease.

Of course, readability indexes can't be applied to languages other than English. Counting syllables makes no sense in other languages. For example, compare the English *forklift driver* with the German *Gabelstaplerfahrer.* Chinese and Japanese characters don't lend themselves to syllable counting at all.[2]

Although readability formulas can easily be applied, they ignore some important variables that contribute to reading ease, such as sentence structure, the organization of ideas, and the appearance of the message on the page.[3] To fully evaluate the readability of your message, ask yourself whether you have effectively emphasized the important information. Are your sentences easy to decipher? Do your paragraphs have clear topic sentences? Are the transitions between ideas obvious?

Assessing Your Word Choice

When choosing and revising words,[4] business communicator Dave Giarla pays attention to two things: correctness and effectiveness. Even though the rules of grammar are constantly changing to reflect changes in the way people speak, grammatical errors decrease your credibility with your audience. So if you have doubts about what is correct, don't be lazy. Look up the answer, and use the proper form of expression. Check the grammar and usage guide in this book (Appendix C), or consult any number of special reference books available in libraries and bookstores. Most authorities agree on the basic conventions.

Just as important as using the correct words is choosing the best words for the job at hand. Word effectiveness is generally more difficult to achieve than correctness, particularly in written communication. Following are some of the techniques professional writers use to improve the effectiveness of their style.

Plain English

Plain English is a way of writing and arranging language so that your audience can understand your meaning. If you've ever tried to make sense of an obtusely worded legal document or credit agreement, you can understand the movement toward requiring contracts and other such documents to be written in plain English. Because it's close to the way we speak, plain English is easily understood by anyone with an eighth- or ninth-grade education.[5]

The growing focus on plain-English laws has already led to plain-English loan and credit-card application forms, insurance policies, and real estate contracts. Even so, plain English has some limitations. It lacks the precision necessary for scientific research, intense feeling, and personal insight. Moreover, it fails to embrace every culture and dialect equally.[6] Needless to say, it's intended for areas where English is the primary language; however, the lessons of plain English can also help you simplify messages intended for audiences who may speak English only as a second or even third language.

Figure 7.3
The Fog Index

1. **Select writing Sample.**
   Keep the sample between 100 and 125 words long.

   I called Global Corporation to ask when we will re-ceive copies of its <u>insurance policies</u> and <u>engineering</u> reports. Cindy Turner of Global said that they are putting the <u>documents together</u> and will send them by Express Mail next week. She told me that they are late because most of the <u>information</u> is in the hands of Global's <u>attorneys</u> in Boston. I asked why it was in Boston; we had <u>understood</u> that the account is ser-viced by the <u>client's</u> Dallas branch. Turner explained that the account <u>originally</u> was sold to Global's Boston <u>division,</u> so all paperwork stays there. She promised to <u>telephone</u> us when the package is ready to ship.

2. **Determine average sentence length.**
   Count the number of words in each sentence. Treat inde-pendent clauses (stand-alone word groups containing subject and predicate) as separate sentences. For exam-ple, "In school we studied; we learned; we improved" counts as three sentences. Then add the word counts for all the sentences to get the total word count, and divide that by the number of sentences. This excerpt has an av-erage sentence length of 14 words:

   $$18 + 21 + 21 + 7 + 13 + 12 + 5 + 12 =$$
   $$109 \text{ words} \div 8 \text{ sentences} = 14$$

3. **Determine percentage of long words.**
   Count the number of long words—that is, all words that have three or more syllables (underlined in excerpt). Do not count proper nouns, combinations of short words (such as *paperwork* and *anyway*), and verbs that gain a third syllable by adding -*es* or -*ed* (as in *trespasses* and *created*). Divide the number of long words by the total number of words in the sample and multiply the answer by 100. The percentage of long words in this excerpt is 10 percent:

   $$11 \text{ long words} \div 109 \text{ total words} = 10 \text{ percent}$$

4. **Determine the grade level required to read the passage.**
   Add the numbers of average sentence length and per-centage of long words. Multiply the sum by 0.4, and drop the number following the decimal point (if there is one). The grade level required to easily read this excerpt is 9:

   $$14 \text{ words per sentence} + 10 \text{ percent long words} =$$
   $$24 \times 0.4 = 9.6 - 0.6 = 9 \text{ (Fog Index)}$$

GOING ONLINE
IMPROVE YOUR WRITING STYLE WITH PROVEN TECHNIQUES

You can improve your work quickly and easily with the *Elements of Style,* by William Strunk Jr., a classic in its field. The contents include rules of usage, principles of composition, commonly misused words and expressions, words commonly misspelled, and dozens of before-and-after examples.

http://www.columbia.edu/acis/bartleby/strunk

Functional words (conjunctions, prepositions, articles, and pronouns) express relationships among content words (nouns, verbs, adjectives, and adverbs).

Content words have both a denotative (dictionary) meaning and a connotative (associative) meaning.

The more abstract a word, the more it is removed from the tangible, objective world of things that can be perceived with the senses.

In business communication, use concrete, specific terms whenever possible; use abstractions only when necessary.

Dan Rather is managing editor and anchor of CBS Evening News. *Along with three others, he writes and heavily revises each evening's newscast right up to airtime. Rather is noted for his concern over each word he uses.*

Functional Words and Content Words

Words can be divided into two categories. Functional words express relationships and have only one unchanging meaning regardless of the context. They include conjunctions, prepositions, articles, and pronouns. Your main concern with functional words is to use them correctly. Content words—nouns, verbs, adjectives, and adverbs —are multidimensional and therefore are subject to various interpretations. These words carry the meaning of a sentence. Content words are the building blocks; functional words are the mortar. In the following sentence, all the content words are in italics:

Some objective observers of the *cookie market give Nabisco* the *edge* in *quality,* but *Frito-Lay is lauded* for *superior distribution.*

Both functional words and content words are necessary, but your effectiveness as a communicator depends largely on your ability to choose the right content words for your message. So take a closer look at two important dimensions for classifying content words.

Connotation and Denotation   As you know from reading Chapter 2, content words have both a denotative and a connotative meaning. The **denotative meaning** is the literal, or dictionary, meaning; the **connotative meaning** includes all the associations and feelings evoked by the word. Some words have more connotations than others. If you say that a person has failed to pass the test, you're making a strong statement; your're suggesting that the person is inferior, incompetent, second rate. On the other hand, if you say that the person has achieved a score of 65 percent, you suggest something else. By replacing the word *failed,* you avoid a heavy load of negative connotations.

In business communication, generally use terms that are low in connotative meaning. Words that have relatively few possible interpretations are less likely to be misunderstood. Furthermore, because you are usually trying to deal with things in an objective, rational manner, you want to avoid emotion-laden comments.

Abstraction and Concreteness   Content words also vary in their level of abstraction. An abstract word expresses a concept, quality, or characteristic instead of standing for a thing you can touch or see. Abstractions are usually broad concepts that encompass a category of ideas. They are often intellectual, academic, or philosophical. *Love, honor, progress, tradition,* and *beauty* are abstractions. Concrete terms are anchored in the tangible, material world. They stand for something particular: *chair, table, horse, rose, kick, kiss, red, green, two.* These words are direct and vivid, clear and exact.

You might suppose that concrete words are better than abstract words, because they are more precise. However, imagine trying to talk about business without referring to such concepts as *morale, productivity, profits, quality, motivation,* and *guarantees.* Nevertheless, abstractions can be troublesome. They tend to be fuzzy and subject to many interpretations. They also tend to be boring. It isn't always easy to get excited about ideas, especially if they're unrelated to concrete experience. The best way to minimize such problems is to blend abstract terms with concrete ones, the general with the specific. State the concept, and then pin it down with details expressed in more concrete terms. Save the abstractions for ideas that cannot be expressed any other way. For example, instead of referring to McDonald's principles of operation, Dave Giarla talks about specifics such as fast service, good food, and clean facilities.

Words That Communicate

Wordsmiths are journalists, public relations specialists, editors, letter and report writers—anyone who earns a living by crafting words. Unlike poets, novelists, or dramatists, wordsmiths don't try for dramatic effects. They are mainly concerned with being clear, concise, and accurate in their use of language. To reach this goal, they emphasize words that are strong, familiar, and short, and they avoid hiding them under unnecessary syllables. When you edit your message, do your best to think like a wordsmith.

Strong Words   Nouns and verbs are the most concrete words in any message, so use them as much as you can. Although adjectives and adverbs obviously have parts to play, use them sparingly. They often call for subjective judgments, and business communication strives to be objective. Verbs are especially powerful because they carry the action; they tell what's happening in the sentence. The more dynamic and specific the verb, the better. Instead of settling for *rise* or *fall*, look for something more meaningful and descriptive, like *soar* or *plummet*.

Verbs and nouns are more concrete than adverbs and adjectives.

AVOID WEAK PHRASES	USE STRONG TERMS
wealthy businessperson	tycoon
business prosperity	boom
hard times	slump

Familiar Words   You'll communicate best with words that are familiar to your readers. At the same time, bear in mind that words familiar to one reader might be unfamiliar to another:

Familiar words are preferable to unfamiliar ones, but try to avoid overworked terms (clichés).

AVOID UNFAMILIAR WORDS	USE FAMILIAR WORDS
ascertain	find out, learn
consummate	close, bring about
peruse	read, study

Although familiar words are generally the best choice, beware of terms so common that they have become virtually meaningless. Readers tend to gloss over such clichés and go directly to whatever is coming next:

interface	time frame	strategic decisions
track record	frame of reference	dialogue
viable	prioritize	scenario

Also handle technical or professional terms with care. Used in moderation, they add precision and authority to a message. However, many people simply don't understand them, and even a technically sophisticated audience will be lulled to sleep by too many. Let your audience's vocabulary be your guide. If they share a particular jargon, you may enhance your credibility by speaking their language.

Short Words   Although certainly not true in every case, short words are generally more vivid and easier to read than are long words. Thus they often communicate better than long words:

Short words are generally more vivid than long ones and improve the readability of a document.

AVOID LONG WORDS	USE SHORT WORDS
During the preceding year, the company accelerated productive operations.	Last year the company sped up operations.
The action was predicated on the assumption that the company was operating at a financial deficit.	The action was based on the belief that the company was losing money.

Camouflaged Verbs   In the words you use, watch for endings such as *-ion, -tion, -ing, -ment, -ant, -ent, -ence, -ance,* and *-ency*. Most of them change verbs into nouns and adjectives. In effect, the words that result are camouflaged verbs. Getting rid of these camouflaged verbs will strengthen your writing:

Turning verbs into nouns or adjectives weakens your writing style.

AVOID CAMOUFLAGED VERBS	USE VERBS
The manager undertook implementation of the rules.	The manager implemented the rules.
Verification of the shipments occurs weekly.	Shipments are verified weekly.

Bias-Free Language

Most of us think of ourselves as being sensitive, unbiased, ethical, and fair. Being fair and objective isn't enough, however; you must also *appear* to be fair.[7] **Bias-free language** avoids unethical, embarrassing blunders in language related to culture, gender, race, ethnicity, age, and disability.

Avoid biased language that might offend the audience.

Cultural Bias   Whether working with employees from diverse cultures or dealing with businesses and customers in other countries, be careful to avoid cultural bias in your business messages. Avoid using slang ("give me the skinny on sales"), abbreviations and acronyms ("FYI, the MIS is back on line"), and idioms ("You need to go with what you have").[8] Avoid using a restrictive viewpoint; for example, change *domestic sales* to *U.S.-based sales* in a letter to European readers. Also, if you're having your message translated into another language, the best way to avoid undetected cultural bias is to have it back-translated. Perhaps most important of all, avoid judging international associates and intercultural workers by their use of English. Employees and associates may misuse English grammar or structure, but that fact alone indicates nothing about their creativity or talent.

Don't use slang, idioms, or restrictive viewpoints when communicating interculturally, and don't judge associates by their grammar or language structure.

Gender Bias   For many years, the word *man* was used to denote humanity, describing a human being of either gender and any age. Today, however, *man* is associated more with an adult male human being. Some of the most commonly used words contain the word *man,* but some gender-free alternatives exist:

Replace words that inaccurately exclude women or men.

UNACCEPTABLE	PREFERABLE
mankind	humanity, human beings, human race, people
if a man drove 50 miles at 60 miles per hour	if a person (or someone or a driver) drove 50 miles at 60 miles per hour
man-made	artifical, synthethic, manufactured, constructed, of human origin
manpower	human power, human energy, workers, workforce, personnel

Here are some simple ways to replace occupational terms that contain the word *man* with words that can represent people of either gender:

UNACCEPTABLE	PREFERABLE
businessman	business executive, business manager, businessperson
salesman	sales representative, salesperson, salesclerk
insurance man	insurance agent
foreman	supervisor

Avoid using female-gender words such as *authoress* and *actress; author* and *actor* denote both women and men. Similarly, avoid special designations, such as *woman doctor* or *male nurse.* Use the same label for everyone in a particular group. Don't refer to a woman as a *chairperson* and then call the man a *chairman.*

The pronoun *he* has also traditionally been used to refer to both males and females. Here are some simple ways to avoid this outdated usage:

UNACCEPTABLE	PREFERABLE
The average worker . . . he	The average worker . . . he or she
The typical business executive spends four hours of his day in meetings.	Most business executives spend four hours a day in meetings.

Avoid identifying certain roles with a specific gender:

UNACCEPTABLE	PREFERABLE
the consumer . . . she	consumers . . . they
the nurse/teacher . . . she	nurses/teachers . . . they

If you're discussing categories of people, such as bosses and office workers, avoid referring to a boss as *he* and an office worker as *she*. Instead, reword sentences so that you can use *they,* or reword them so that you don't have to use any pronoun. It's also appropriate sometimes to use *she* when referring to a boss and *he* when referring to an office worker. Another way to avoid bias is to make sure you don't always mention men first. Vary the traditional pattern with *women and men, gentlemen and ladies, she and he, her and his.* Finally, identify women by their own names, not by their role or marital status—unless it is appropriate to the context:

UNACCEPTABLE	PREFERABLE
Phil Donahue and Marlo	Phil Donahue and Marlo Thomas
Phil Donahue and Ms. Thomas	Mr. Donahue and Ms. Thomas

The preferred title for women in business is Ms., unless the individual asks to be addressed as Miss or Mrs. or has some other title, such as Dr.

Racial and Ethnic Bias   The guidelines for avoiding racial and ethnic bias are much the same as those for avoiding gender bias. The central principle is to avoid language suggesting that members of a racial or ethnic group have the same stereotypical characteristics:

Eliminate references that reinforce racial or ethnic stereotypes.

UNACCEPTABLE	PREFERABLE
our new black CEO	our new CEO
Jim Wong is an unusually tall Asian.	Jim Wong is tall.

The best solution is to avoid identifying people by race or ethnic origin unless such a label is relevant:

UNACCEPTABLE	PREFERABLE
Mario M. Cuomo, Italian American politician and ex-governor of New York	Mario M. Cuomo, politician and ex-governor of New York

Age Bias   As with gender, race, and ethnic background, mention the age of a person only when it is relevant:

Avoid references to an individual's age or physical limitations.

UNACCEPTABLE	PREFERABLE
Mary Kirazy, 58, has just joined our trust department.	Mary Kirazy has just joined our trust department.

When referring to older people, avoid such stereotyped adjectives as *spry* and *frail.*

Always refer to people first and their disabilities second.

Disability Bias   There is really no painless label for people with a physical, mental, sensory, or emotional impairment. However, if you must refer to such individuals in terms of their limitations, avoid using terms such as *handicapped, crippled,* or *retarded,* and be sure to put the person first and the disability second:[9]

UNACCEPTABLE	PREFERABLE
Crippled workers face many barriers on the job.	Workers who have physical disabilities face many barriers on the job.

Most of all, avoid mentioning a disability unless it is pertinent. When it is pertinent, present the whole person, not just the disability, by showing the limitation in an unobtrusive manner:

UNACCEPTABLE	PREFERABLE
An epileptic, Tracy has no trouble doing her job.	Tracy's epilepsy has no effect on her job performance.

The 1990 Americans with Disabilities Act guarantees equal opportunities for people who have or have had a condition that might handicap them. The goal of bias-free communication is to abandon stereotyped assumptions about what a person can do or will do and to focus on an individual's unique characteristics. So describe people without disabilities as *typical* rather than *normal.* People having disabilities are certainly *atypical,* but they are not necessarily *abnormal.*[10]

Critiquing the Writing of Another

In business, many documents are written for someone else's signature.[11] When you need to critique the work of another, you want to help that person communicate effectively, and to do that you must provide specific, constructive comments. To help the writer make meaningful changes, concentrate on three elements:[12]

When critiquing someone else's writing, focus on

- Purpose
- Accuracy
- Clear language

■ *Does the document accomplish the intended purpose?* Is the purpose clearly stated? Does the body support the stated purpose? You might outline the key points to see whether they support the main idea. Is the conclusion supported by the data? Are the arguments presented logically? Be sure to determine whether the directions given with the initial assignment were clear and complete. If the document fails to accomplish its purpose, it must be rewritten.

■ *Is the factual material correct?* A proposal to provide nationwide computer-training services for $15 million would be disastrous if your intention was to provide those services for $150 million. Be sure you pay strict attention to detail. All factual errors must be corrected.

■ *Does the document use ambiguous language?* Readers must not be allowed to interpret the meaning in any way other than intended. If you interpret a message differently from what an author intended, the author is at fault, and the document must be revised to clarify problem areas.

If any one of these elements needs attention, the document must be rewritten, revised, or corrected. However, once these elements are deemed satisfactory, the question is whether to request other changes. If the three elements are in fact acceptable, consider three points before requesting a major revision.[13]

■ *Can the document truly be improved?* If the changes you want are purely subjective and cosmetic, they will not actually improve the document.

■ *Can you justify the time needed for a rewrite?* If time is short, you may need to use what you have (as long as the elements of purpose, accuracy, and specificity are fulfilled).

■ *Will your request have a negative impact on morale?* If unexplained or inconsistent changes are regularly made to a person's writing efforts, that writer can become demoralized.

Requesting other changes depends on whether they are

■ Cosmetic
■ Time consuming
■ Bad for morale

 # STAGE 8: REWRITING YOUR MESSAGE

As you edit your business message, you'll find yourself rewriting passages, sentences, and even whole sections to improve its effectiveness. David Giarla would caution you to remember that in your search for perfection, you're probably also facing a deadline, so try to stick to the schedule you set during the planning stage. Do your best to revise and rewrite thoroughly but economically. Also, you'll probably want to keep copies of your revised versions. As you rewrite, concentrate on how each word contributes to an effective sentence and how that sentence develops a coherent paragraph.

Create Effective Sentences

In English, words don't make much sense until they're combined in a sentence to express a complete thought. Thus, *Jill, receptionist, the, smiles,* and *at* can be organized into "Jill smiles at the receptionist." Now you can begin exploring the possibilities for improvement, looking at how well each word performs its particular function. Nouns and noun equivalents are the topics (or subjects) you're communicating about, and verbs and related words (or predicates) make statements about those subjects. In a more complicated sentence, adjectives and adverbs modify the subject and the statement, and various connectors hold the words together.

Every sentence contains a subject (noun or noun equivalent) and a predicate (verb and related word).

The Three Types of Sentences

Sentences come in three basic varieties: simple, compound, and complex. A **simple sentence** has a single subject and a single predicate, although it may be expanded by nouns and pronouns serving as objects of the action and by modifying phrases. In the following examples, the subject is underlined once, and the predicate verb is underlined twice:

Profits have increased in the past year.

A **compound sentence** expresses two or more independent but related thoughts of equal importance, joined by *and, but,* or *or.* In effect, a compound sentence is a merger of two or more simple sentences (independent clauses) that deal with the same basic idea:

Wage rates have declined by 5 percent, and employee turnover has been high.

The independent clauses in a compound sentence are always separated by a comma or by a semicolon (in which case the conjunction—*and, but, or*—is dropped).

A **complex sentence** expresses one main thought (the independent clause) and one or more subordinate thoughts (dependent clauses) related to it, often separated by a comma. The subordinate thought, which comes first in the following sentence, could not stand alone:

Although you may question Gerald's conclusions, you must admit that his research is thorough.

When constructing a sentence, use the form that best fits the thought you want to express. The structure of the sentence should match the relationship of the ideas. If you have

To give your writing variety, use the three types of sentences:

■ Simple
■ Compound
■ Complex

Vaughn Beals, CEO of Harley-Davidson, turned his company around by revising design, work flow, quality, and services. His close attention to detail improved his product's image, and so it is with communication. When you're striving for high-quality, error-free messages, you do a lot of revising.

two ideas of equal importance, express them as two simple sentences or as one compound sentence. However, if one idea is less important than the other, place it in a dependent clause to form a complex sentence. This compound sentence uses a conjunction to join two ideas that aren't truly equal:

> The chemical products division is the strongest in the company, and its management techniques should be adopted by the other divisions.

In the following complex sentence, the first thought has been made subordinate to the second. Note how much more effective the second idea is when the cause-and-effect relationship has been established:

> Because the chemical products division is the strongest in the company, its management techniques should be adopted by the other divisions.

In complex sentences, the placement of the dependent clause should be geared to the relationship between the ideas expressed. If you want to emphasize the idea, put the dependent clause at the end of the sentence (the most emphatic position) or at the beginning (the second most emphatic position). If you want to downplay the idea, bury the dependent clause within the sentence.

MOST EMPHATIC:	The handbags are manufactured in Mexico, *which has lower wage rates than the United States.*
EMPHATIC:	*Because wage rates are lower there,* the handbags are manufactured in Mexico.
LEAST EMPHATIC:	Mexico, *which has lower wage rates,* was selected as the production point for the handbags.

To make your writing as effective as possible, balance all three sentence types. If you use too many simple sentences, you can't properly express the relationship among ideas. If you use too many long, compound sentences, your writing will sound monotonous. On the other hand, an uninterrupted series of complex sentences is hard to follow.

Sentence Style
Of course, sentence style varies from culture to culture. German sentences are extremely complex with a lot of modifiers and appositives; Japanese and Chinese languages don't even have sentences in the same sense that Western languages do.[14] Basically, whether a sentence in English is simple, compound, or complex, it should be grammatically correct, efficient, readable, interesting, and appropriate for your audience. In general, strive for simplicity.

Keep Sentences Short   Long sentences are usually harder to understand than short sentences because they are packed with information that must all be absorbed at once. Most good business writing therefore has an average sentence length of 20 words or fewer. That figure is the average, not a ceiling. To be interesting, your writing should contain both longer and shorter sentences.

Long sentences are especially well suited for grouping or combining ideas, listing points, and summarizing or previewing information. Medium-length sentences (those with about 20 words) are useful for showing the relationships among ideas. Short sentences are tailor-made for emphasizing important information.

Rely on the Active Voice   Active sentences are generally preferable to passive sentences because they are easier to understand.[15] You're using **active voice** when the subject (the "actor") comes before the verb, and the object of the sentence (the "acted upon") follows

Break long sentences into shorter ones to improve readability.

Active sentences are stronger than passive ones.

the verb: "John rented the office." You're using **passive voice** when the subject follows the verb and the object precedes it: "The office was rented by John." As you can see, the passive verb combines the helping verb *to be* with a form of the verb that is usually similar to the past tense. Using passive verbs makes sentences longer and de-emphasizes the subject. Active verbs produce shorter, stronger sentences:

AVOID PASSIVE SENTENCES	USE ACTIVE SENTENCES
Sales were increased by 32 percent last month.	Sales increased by 32 percent last month.
The new procedure is thought by the president to be superior.	The president thinks the new procedure is superior.

Of course, in some situations, using the passive voice makes sense. You may want to be diplomatic when pointing out a problem or error of some kind, so you might say, "The shipment was lost" rather than "You lost the shipment." The passive version seems less like an accusation because the emphasis is on the lost shipment rather than on the person responsible. Similarly, you may want to point out what's being done without taking or attributing either the credit or the blame, so you might say something like "The production line is being analyzed to determine the source of problems." You may want to avoid personal pronouns in order to create an objective tone, so in a formal report, you might say, "Criteria have been established for evaluating capital expenditures."

> Use passive sentences to soften bad news, to put yourself in the background, or to create an impersonal tone.

Eliminate Unnecessary Words and Phrases Some words and combinations of words have more efficient, one-word equivalents. So you would avoid saying "This is to inform you that we have begun production" when "We have begun production" is enough.

> Be on the lookout for
> - Inefficient phrases
> - Redundancies
> - Unneeded relative pronouns and articles

COMBINATIONS TO AVOID	EFFICIENT EQUIVALENTS
for the sum of	for
in the event that	if
on the occasion of	on
prior to the start of	before

Other word combinations are redundant: Avoid saying "Visible to the eye" because *visible* is enough—nothing can be visible to the ear. Avoid saying "surrounded on all sides" because *surrounded* implies on all sides. Also take a close look at double modifiers. Do you really need to say "modern, up-to-date equipment," or would "modern equipment" do the job?

Relative pronouns such as *who, that,* and *which* frequently cause clutter, and sometimes even articles are excessive (mostly too many *the*s). However, well-placed relative pronouns and articles serve an important function by preventing confusion. For example, without *that,* the following sentence is ambiguous:

CONFUSING:	The project manager told the engineers last week the specifications were changed.
CLEAR:	The project manager told the engineers last week *that* the specifications were changed.
CLEAR:	The project manager told the engineers *that* last week the specifications were changed.

Here are some other ways to prune your prose:

POOR	IMPROVED
consensus of opinion	consensus
at this point in time	at this time, now
irregardless	(no such word; use *regardless*)
each and every	(either word, but not both)
due to the fact that	because
at an early date	soon (or a specific date)
at the present time	now
in view of the fact that	because
until such time as	when
we are of the opinion	we believe, we think
with reference to	about
as a result of	because
for the month of December	for December

Avoid needless repetition.

Use infinitives to replace some phrases.

In general, be on the lookout for the needless repetition of words or ideas. Try not to string together a series of sentences that all start with the same word or words, and avoid repeating the same word too often within a given sentence. Another way to save words is to use infinitives in place of some phrases. This technique not only shortens your sentences but makes them clearer as well:

POOR	IMPROVED
In order to be a successful writer, you must work hard.	To be a successful writer, you must work hard.
He went to the library for the purpose of studying.	He went to the library to study.
The employer increased salaries so that she could improve morale.	The employer increased salaries to improve morale.

Obsolete formal phrases can obscure meaning.

Avoid Obsolete and Pompous Language   The language of business used to be much more formal than it is today, and a few out-of-date phrases remain from the old days. Perhaps the best way to eliminate them is to ask yourself, "Would I say this if I were talking with someone face to face?"

OBSOLETE	UP-TO-DATE
as per your letter	as in your letter (do not mix Latin and English)
hoping to hear from you soon, I remain	(omit)
yours of the 15th	your letter of June 15
awaiting your reply, we are	(omit)
in due course	today, tomorrow (or a specific time)
permit me to say that	(permission is not necessary; just say what you wish)

we are in receipt of	we have received
pursuant to	(omit)
in closing, I'd like to say	(omit)
attached herewith is	here is
the undersigned	I, me
kindly advise	please let us know
under separate cover	in another envelope, by parcel post
we wish to inform you	(just say it)
attached please find	enclosed is
it has come to my attention	I have just learned; Ms. Garza has just told me
our Mr. Lydell	Mr. Lydell, our credit manager
please be advised that	(omit)

Being a good communicator, McDonald's Dave Giarla understands that pompous language is similar to out-of-date phrases. It also sounds stiff, puffed up, and roundabout. People are likely to use pompous language when they are trying to impress somebody. In hopes of sounding imposing, they use big words, trite expressions, and overly complicated sentences.

The use of pompous language suggests that you are a pompous person.

POOR	IMPROVED
Upon procurement of additional supplies, I will initiate fulfillment of your order.	I will fill your order when I receive more supplies.

Moderate Your Enthusiasm   An occasional adjective or adverb intensifies and emphasizes your meaning, but too many ruin your writing:

Business writing shouldn't be gushy.

POOR	IMPROVED
We are extremely pleased to offer you a position on our staff of exceptionally skilled and highly educated employees. The work offers extraordinary challenges and a very large salary.	We are pleased to offer you a position on our staff of skilled and well-educated employees. The work offers challenges and an attractive salary.

Break Up Strung-Out Sentences   A strung-out sentence is a series of two or more sentences unwisely connected by *and*—in other words, a compound sentence taken too far. You can often improve your writing style by separating the string into individual sentences:

In many cases, the parts of a compound sentence should be separated into two sentences.

POOR	IMPROVED
The magazine will be published January 1, and I'd better meet the deadline if I want my article included.	The magazine will be published January 1. I'd better meet the deadline if I want my article included.

Avoid Hedging Sentences   Sometimes you have to write *may* or *seems* to avoid stating a judgment as a fact. Nevertheless, when you have too many such hedges, you aren't really saying anything:

Don't be afraid to present your opinions without qualification.

POOR	IMPROVED
I believe that Mr. Johnson's employment record seems to show that he may be capable of handling the position.	Mr. Johnson's employment record shows that he is capable of handling the position.

Avoid starting sentences with it *and* there.

Watch for Indefinite Pronoun Starters   If you start a sentence with an indefinite pronoun (an expletive) such as *it* or *there*, odds are that the sentence could be shorter:

POOR	IMPROVED
It would be appreciated if you would sign the lease today.	Please sign the lease today.
There are five employees in this division who were late to work today.	Five employees in this division were late to work today.

When you use the same grammatical pattern to express two or more ideas, you show that they are comparable thoughts.

Express Parallel Ideas in Parallel Form   When you have two or more similar (parallel) ideas to express, try to use a **parallel construction**; that is, use the same grammatical pattern. The repetition of the pattern tells readers that the ideas are comparable and adds a nice rhythm to your message. In the following examples, parallel construction makes the sentences more readable:

POOR	IMPROVED
Miss Simms had been drenched with rain, bombarded with telephone calls, and her boss shouted at her.	Miss Simms had been drenched with rain, bombarded with telephone calls, and shouted at by her boss.

Parallelism can be achieved through a repetition of words, phrases, clauses, or entire sentences:

PARALLEL WORDS:	The letter was approved by Clausen, Whittaker, Merlin, and Carlucci.
PARALLEL PHRASES:	We have beaten the competition in supermarkets, in department stores, and in specialty stores.
PARALLEL CLAUSES:	I'd like to discuss the issue after Vicki gives her presentation but before Marvin shows his slides.
PARALLEL SENTENCES:	In 1997 we exported 30 percent of our production. In 1998 we exported 50 percent.

If there's anyone who understands the concept of "work on it until it's right," that would be Tiger Woods, whose youth and swing have been credited for his electrification of the staid world of professional golf. Of Asian, African, and American Indian descent, he's become an icon, a winner, and a well-paid product endorser. But Woods also finds time to conduct golf clinics for inner-city kids, encouraging them all to go that extra step that makes the difference between ordinary and excellent.

Eliminate Awkward Pointers   To save words, business writers sometimes direct their readers' attention elsewhere with such expressions as *the above-mentioned, as mentioned above, the aforementioned, the former, the latter, respectively.* These words cause the reader to jump from one point in the message to another, a process that hinders effective communication. A better approach is to be specific in your references, even if you must add a few more words:

POOR	IMPROVED
Computer supplies for legal secretaries and beginning clerks are distributed by the Law Office and Stenographic Office, respectively.	Computer supplies for legal secretaries are distributed by the Law Office; those for beginning clerks are distributed by the Stenographic Office.

Correct Dangling Modifiers   Sometimes a modifier is not just an adjective or adverb but an entire phrase defining a noun or verb. Be careful to construct your sentences so that this type of modifier refers to something in the main part of the sentence in a way that makes sense. Consider this sentence:

Make sure that modifier phrases are really related to the subject of the sentence.

Walking to the office, a red sports car passed her.

The construction implies that the red sports car has the office and the legs to walk there. The modifier is said to be dangling because it has no real connection to the subject of the sentence—in this case, the sports car. This is what the writer is trying to say:

A red sports car passed her while she was walking to the office.

Flipping the clauses produces another correct sentence:

While she was walking to the office, a red sports car passed her.

Dangling modifiers make sentences confusing and sometimes ridiculous:

POOR	IMPROVED
Working as fast as possible, the budget was soon ready.	Working as fast as possible, the committee soon had the budget ready.
After a three-week slump, we increased sales.	After a three-week slump, sales increased.

The first example shows one frequent cause of dangling modifiers: passive construction in the independent clause. When the clause is made active instead of passive, the connection with the dangling modifier becomes more obvious.

Passive construction is often the cause of dangling modifiers.

Avoid Long Sequences of Nouns   When nouns are strung together as modifiers, the resulting sentence is hard to read. You can clarify the sentence by putting some of the nouns in a modifying phrase. Although you add a few more words, your audience won't have to work as hard to understand the sentence.

Stringing together a series of nouns may save a little space, but it causes confusion.

POOR	IMPROVED
The window sash installation company will give us an estimate on Friday.	The company that installs window sashes will give us an estimate on Friday.

Keep Words Together That Work Together   To avoid confusing readers, keep the subject and predicate of a sentence as close together as possible. Otherwise, readers will have to read your sentence twice to figure out who did what.

Subject and predicate should be placed as close together as possible, as should modifiers and the words they modify.

POOR	IMPROVED
A 10 percent decline in market share, which resulted from quality problems and an aggressive sales campaign by Armitage, the market leader in the Northeast, was the major problem in 1994.	The major problem in 1994 was a 10 percent loss of market share, which resulted from both quality problems and an aggressive sales campaign by Armitage, the market leader in the Northeast.

The same rule applies to other parts of speech. Adjectives, adverbs, and prepositional phrases usually make the most sense when they're placed as close as possible to the words they modify:

POOR	IMPROVED
We will deliver the pipe soon that you ordered last Tuesday.	We will soon deliver the pipe that you ordered last Tuesday.

Emphasize parts of a sentence by

- Giving them more space
- Putting them at the beginning or the end of the sentence
- Making them the subject of the sentence

Emphasize Key Thoughts   In every message, some ideas are more important than others. You can emphasize these key ideas through your sentence style. One obvious technique is to give important points the most space. When you want to call attention to a thought, use extra words to describe it. Consider this sentence:

The chairperson of the board called for a vote of the shareholders.

To emphasize the importance of the chairperson, you might describe her more fully:

The chairperson of the board, who has considerable experience in corporate takeover battles, called for a vote of the shareholders.

You can increase the emphasis even more by adding a separate, short sentence to augment the first:

The chairperson of the board called for a vote of the shareholders. She has considerable experience in corporate takeover battles.

Another way to emphasize an idea is to place it at either the beginning or the end of a sentence:

LESS EMPHATIC	MORE EMPHATIC
We are cutting the *price* to stimulate demand.	To stimulate demand, we are cutting the *price*.

You can also call attention to a thought by making it the subject of the sentence. In the following example, the emphasis is on the person:

I can write letters much more quickly using a computer.

In this version, the computer takes center stage:

The *computer* enables me to write letters much more quickly.

Techniques like this give you a great deal of control over the way your audience interprets what you have to say.

Develop Coherent Paragraphs

Paragraphs are functional units that revolve around a single thought.

A paragraph is a cluster of sentences that are all related to the same general topic. It is a unit of thought. A series of paragraphs makes up an entire composition. Each paragraph is an important part of the whole, a key link in the train of thought. As you edit a message, think about the paragraphs and their relationship to one another.

Elements of the Paragraph

Most paragraphs consist of a topic sentence, related sentences, and transitional elements.

Paragraphs vary widely in length and form. You can communicate effectively in one short paragraph or in pages of lengthy paragraphs, depending on your purpose, your audience, and your message. The typical paragraph contains three basic elements: a topic sentence, related sentences that develop the topic, and transitional words and phrases.

The topic sentence

- Reveals the subject of the paragraph
- Indicates how it will be developed

Topic Sentence   Every properly constructed paragraph is **unified**; it deals with a single topic. The sentence that introduces that topic is called the **topic sentence.** In informal and creative writing, the topic sentence may be implied rather than stated. In business writing, the topic sentence is generally explicit and often is the first sentence in the paragraph. The topic sentence gives readers a summary of the general idea that will be covered in the rest of the paragraph. The following examples show how a topic sentence can both introduce the subject and suggest the way that subject will be developed:

The medical products division has been troubled for many years by public relations problems. [In the rest of the paragraph, readers will learn the details of the problems.]

To get a refund, you must supply us with some additional information. [The details will be described.]

Related Sentences   The sentences that explain the topic sentence complete the unified thought of the paragraph. These related sentences must all have a bearing on the general subject, and they must provide enough specific details to make the topic clear:

The medical products division has been troubled for many years by public relations problems. Since 1991 the local newspaper has published 15 articles that portray the division in a negative light. We have been accused of everything from mistreating laboratory animals to polluting the local groundwater. Our facility has been described as a health hazard. Our scientists are referred to as "Frankensteins," and our profits are considered "obscene."

The developmental sentences are all more specific than the topic sentence. Each one provides another piece of evidence to demonstrate the general truth of the main thought. Also, the clear relation of each sentence to the general idea being developed gives the paragraph its unity. A paragraph is well developed when it contains enough information to make the topic sentence convincing and interesting.

> Paragraphs are developed through a series of related sentences that provide details about the topic sentence.

Transitional Elements   Some ideas are simply too big to be handled conveniently in one paragraph. Unless you break up the thoughts somehow, you'll end up with a three-page paragraph that's guaranteed to intimidate even the most dedicated reader. So what do you do when you want to package a big idea in short paragraphs? Break the idea into subtopics, treat each subtopic in a separate paragraph, and be careful to provide plenty of transitional elements.

It's a fact that short paragraphs (of 100 words or fewer) are easier to read than long ones. So, in addition to being unified and well developed, effective paragraphs are **coherent;** that is, they are arranged in a logical order so that the audience can understand the train of thought. In Figure 7.4, coherence is achieved through the use of transitions that show how one thought is related to another. You can establish transitions in various ways:

> Transitional words and phrases show readers how paragraphs and the ideas within them are related.

- Use connecting words: *and, but, or, nevertheless, however, in addition,* and so on.
- Echo a word or phrase from a previous paragraph or sentence: "A *system* should be established for monitoring inventory levels. This *system* will provide . . . "
- Use a pronoun: "Ms. Arthur is the leading candidate for the president's position. *She* has excellent qualifications."
- Use words that are frequently paired: "The machine has a *minimum* output of . . . Its *maximum* output is . . . "

> Some transitional devices:
>
> - Connecting words (conjunctions)
> - Repeated words or phrases
> - Pronouns
> - Words that are frequently paired

Five Ways to Develop a Paragraph

Paragraphs can be developed in many ways. Your choice of technique depends on your subject, your intended audience, and your purpose. Remember also that in actual practice you'll often combine two or more methods of development in a single paragraph.

Before settling for the first approach that comes to mind, think about the alternatives. Think through various methods before committing yourself. If you fall into the easy habit of repeating the same old paragraph pattern time after time, your writing will be boring.

Figure 7.4
In-Depth Critique: E-Mail Excerpt with Short, Focused Paragraphs

The following excerpt is from a report put together by Holland & Moore, a corporate research company.

```
┌─────────────────────────────────────────────────────────┐
│ ▣ ▤▤▤▤▤▤▤▤▤▤▤▤▤▤ E-Mail ▤▤▤▤▤▤▤▤▤▤▤▤▤ ▣ │
├─────────────────────────────────────────────────────────┤
│                                                      ⇧  │
│                                                         │
│   Date: Thursday, 24 September 1998, 11:14:09, EST       │
│   To: "Lee Gifford" <lgifford@research.marketpix.com>    │
│   From: "Jeffrey Coombs" <jeffc@hmr.com>                 │
│   Subject: Donner Profile                                │
│   Cc: "Donna Holland" <Holland@hmr.com>                  │
│   Bcc:                                                   │
│   Attachments:                                          │
│                                                         │
│   Mr. Gifford, here is the information you requested on  │
│   the Donner Corporation:                               │
│                                                         │
│   Donner Corporation faced a major transformation,      │
│   growing from a small, single-product company to a     │
│   large, multiproduct corporation in just three years.  │
│   This changeover involved much more than simply adding │
│   on to the plant and hiring more people because the    │
│   staff and facilities were not good enough for a       │
│   first-rate operation. The task therefore required     │
│   both physical expansion and quality improvement.      │
│                                                         │
│   The physical expansion alone was a major undertaking. │
│   The investment in facilities required $18 million.    │
│   Over a three-year period, the organization spent more │
│   on the new plant and equipment than it had spent in   │
│   the past seventeen years of its operation.            │
│                                                         │
│   To raise its competitive capability, the company had  │
│   to develop new programs and organizational units and, │
│   at the same time, expand and upgrade its existing     │
│   operations. It also needed to double the size of its  │
│   staff by recruiting high-caliber people from many     │
│   fields. This staffing had to be accomplished in an    │
│   increasingly competitive labor market and without     │
│   benefit of an experienced human resources department. │
│                                                      ⇩  │
│                                                      ▣  │
└─────────────────────────────────────────────────────────┘
```

Short paragraphs increase the message clarity and effectiveness.

Each paragraph is organized around a topic sentence.

The separate paragraphs are linked by transitional elements.

Five ways to develop paragraphs:

- Illustration
- Comparison or contrast
- Cause and effect
- Classification
- Problem and solution

Illustration When you develop a paragraph by illustration, you give examples that demonstrate the general idea:

Some of our most popular products are available through local distributors. For example, Everett & Lemmings carries our frozen soups and entrees. The J. B. Green Company carries our complete line of seasonings, as well as the frozen soups. Wilmont Foods, also a major distributor, now carries our new line of frozen desserts.

Comparison or Contrast Similarities or differences among thoughts often provide a strong basis for paragraph development:

In previous years, when the company was small, the recruiting function could be handled informally. The need for new employees was limited, and each manager could comfortably screen and hire her or his own staff. Today, however, Gambit Products must undertake a major recruiting effort. Our successful bid on the Owens contract means that we will be doubling our labor force over the next six months. To hire that many people without disrupting our ongoing activities, we will create a separate recruiting group within the human resources department.

Cause and Effect   When you develop a paragraph using the cause-and-effect technique, you focus on the reasons for something:

The heavy-duty fabric of your Wanderer tent probably broke down for one of two reasons: (1) a sharp object punctured the fabric, and, without reinforcement, the hole was enlarged by the stress of erecting the tent daily for a week, or (2) folding and storing the tent while it was still wet gradually rotted the fibers.

Classification   Paragraphs developed by classification show how a general idea is broken into specific categories:

Successful candidates for our supervisor trainee program generally come from one of several groups. The largest group, by far, consists of recent graduates of accredited data-processing programs. The next largest group comes from within our own company, as we try to promote promising clerical workers to positions of greater responsibility. Finally, we do occasionally accept candidates with outstanding supervisory experience in related industries.

Problem and Solution   Another way to develop a paragraph is to present a problem and then discuss the solution:

Selling handmade toys by mail is a challenge because consumers are accustomed to buying heavily advertised toys from major chains. However, if we develop an appealing catalog, we can compete on the basis of product novelty and quality. In addition, we can provide craftsmanship at a competitive price: a rocking horse made from birch wood, with a hand-knit tail and mane; a music box with the child's name painted on the top; a real Indian teepee, made by Native American artisans.

STAGE 9: PRODUCING YOUR MESSAGE

Once you've planned, composed, edited, and rewritten your message, give some thought to its presentation. Oral presentations are discussed in Chapter 18, and visual aids are discussed in Chapter 14. In the following sections, you'll get an idea of basic decisions about the design of written documents. To help people comprehend long, uninterrupted pages of text, you can use design elements such as white space, headings, and boldface type (just as this textbook does) to provide visual clues to the importance of various ideas and their relationships.[16]

Written documents require decisions about design elements.

- *White space.* The blank space free of text or artwork is known as **white space.** It provides contrast, and, perhaps even more important, it gives readers a resting point. White space includes the open area surrounding headings, the margin space, the vertical space between columns, the space created by ragged line endings, the paragraph indents or extra space between unindented paragraphs, and the horizontal space between lines of type. You'll decide how much white space to allow for each of these areas.

  White space is free of text and artwork.

- *Margins and line justification.* Margins define the space around your text and between text columns. They're influenced by the way you place lines of type, which can be set (1) justified (flush on the left and flush on the right), (2) flush left with a ragged-right

BEHIND THE SCENES AT THE LA JOLLA PLAYHOUSE
Greasepaint, Bright Lights, and Rewrites

On a typical midseason day at the La Jolla Playhouse, while the actors are rehearsing and the directors, composers, and designers are discussing endless set, score, and costume details, Constance Harvey is likely to be holed up in her office at a computer terminal, writing. No, she's not a playwright, but her job is almost as important to the internationally acclaimed regional theater. Harvey is the theater's publicist, and, without the material she writes, the Playhouse could easily slip from public view. Harvey writes nearly every word the theater sends to reviewers, reporters, entertainment editors, television journalists, potential donors, and season subscribers. Her challenge is to attract local and national media attention to reach audiences, critics, and theater artists.

Every season La Jolla Playhouse offers an eclectic mix of plays that might include anything from a period comedy performed by clown Bill Irwin to a musical by British rockers Ray Davies (*80 Days*) or Pete Townshend (*Tommy*)—and Harvey must capture the mood of each production. For example, the press release she wrote for Tennessee Williams's *The Glass Menagerie* demanded a quiet feeling, whereas her announcements about the performances of the wacky Flying Karamazov Brothers required a kind of verbal free-fall. Harvey's messages must be full of information for calendar event editors—names, dates, times, locations, and so forth—and her copy must have appealing, pithy phrases that magazine editors can easily lift and use as two- or three-line descriptions of a play. When successful, her writing stirs interest and has a direct effect on ticket sales, donations, and future productions.

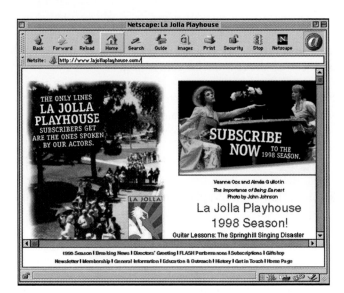

As publicist for the La Jolla Playhouse, Constance Harvey routinely revises and proofs the material she writes, whether it's intended for reviewers, season subscribers, reporters, or the theater's Web page.

margin, (3) flush right with a ragged-left margin, or (4) centered. Justified type will "darken" your message's appearance and will make it look like a form letter. Justified type is often considered more difficult to read because large gaps can appear between words and because more words are hyphenated; excessive hyphenation is distracting and hard to read. Even so, many magazines and newspapers use justified type because it yields greater word density. Flush-left–ragged-right type "lightens" your message's appearance, giving it an informal, contemporary feeling of openness. Centered type lends a formal tone to your message but slows reading because your audience has to search for the beginning of each line. The same problem is also true of flush-right–ragged-left type.

Flush-left–ragged-right type gives your message an open feeling.

■ *Headings and captions.* Headings and subheadings are usually set larger than the type used for text and are often set in a different typeface. They invite readers to become involved in your message, but you should avoid centering heads that contain more than two lines because, like centered text, they slow your readers as they search for the beginning of each line. You can link headings as closely as possible with the text they introduce by providing more space above the heading than below it. Next to headings, captions are the most widely read part of a message, tying photographs and illustrations into the rest of your message. Although usually placed below the exhibits they describe, captions can also be placed beside or above their exhibits.

Headings help your readers quickly identify the content and organization of your message.

■ *Typefaces.* **Typeface** refers to the physical design of letters, numbers, and other characters, which makes your message look authoritative, friendly, expensive, classy, casual, and so on. **Serif typefaces** have small crosslines (called serifs) at the ends of each letter

To accomplish all this, Harvey begins with an inflated first draft, which includes everything. Her ultimate objective is simplicity and completeness, but she's not afraid to be abstract and colorful—like her subject matter. The first draft goes to her assistant, who reads it for content. "I have two questions for that person," says Harvey, "Does it make sense, and what have I left out?" As she revises that first draft, Harvey keeps her assistant's comments in mind, but she also tries to anticipate the questions that might be asked by some of the theater critics who make up her primary audience. They are very important to the Playhouse, and over the years Harvey has learned their needs and preferences. If her releases don't supply enough background about a play or an artist, or if her facts aren't straight, these critics call and let her know. Harvey also solicits input from the theater's associate artistic director, who gives her feedback on whether the press release falls in line with a production's artistic concept.

When she is finally satisfied with her second draft, she is ready to "proof it to death." She looks for errors in grammar and punctuation and reads the words aloud to test the rhythm. "To me, that's a dead giveaway," Harvey explains. "If the rhythm is off, then I don't know what I'm talking about, or I've missed the point. And if I've missed the point, then I'm not going to be able to convey it." She also makes sure she hasn't repeated a word too often. "There are only so many ways you can say *production*, and if I've said it already four or five times in the three preceding lines, it has to go." At the same time, she watches for passive voice. She has a bad habit of burying verbs in sentences, covering up more active and more interesting phrases.

"One of my rules of proofing is that three people have to see it, because I don't trust myself. I'm too familiar with the copy and the content." Nevertheless, embarrassing mistakes do slip by. Early in Harvey's career, no one noticed that the names of the producer and the artistic director were missing from a program's title page—until hours before the presses were scheduled to run. In the ensuing uproar, Harvey phoned the printer, who said it was too late for changes. She insisted, threatening to throw herself on the printing press if he didn't acquiesce. Eventually, he did add the missing names, albeit in the wrong places. Now Harvey keeps a special watch for mistakes in the boilerplate copy that everyone takes for granted.

Apply Your Knowledge

1. To demonstrate that writing can almost always be improved, select an article on any subject from a newspaper or magazine. (1) Make a list of the words you would exchange for more colorful, more precise, or less biased words. (2) List your revisions on a separate sheet. (3) Rewrite any sentences that could be enlivened by a more active voice. (4) Look for paragraphs that could be shortened or simplified without losing meaning.

2. One of the most frustrating problems business writers face is having their words and work misunderstood. List the steps you can take to avoid uttering, "But that's not what I meant!"

---

stroke.[17] (Figure 7.5). Serif faces such as Times Roman (which is built into most laser printers) are commonly used for text. Typefaces with rounded serifs can look friendly; those with squared serifs can look official. **Sans serif typefaces** have no serifs. Faces such as Helvetica are ideal for display treatments that use larger type. Many great-looking documents are based on a single sans serif typeface for heads and subheads with a second serif typeface for text and captions. Using too many typefaces clutters the document.

Although serif typefaces are considered easier to read than sans serif, both have their place in document design.

Serif typefaces are commonly used for text.

Sans serif typefaces are commonly used for headings.

Figure 7.5
Common Typefaces

Serif Typeface	Sans Serif Typeface
Times Roman is often used for text.	Helvetica is often used for headings.
TIMES ROMAN IS HARDER TO READ IN ALL CAPS.	HELVETICA IS A CLEANER FACE EVEN IN ALL CAPS.

Avoid using type styles that slow your readers down.

- *Type styles.* Type style is any modification that lends contrast or emphasis to type. Using boldfaced type for subheads breaks up long expanses of text, but too much will darken your document's appearance. Use italic type for emphasis, to indicate a quote, or in captions. Be careful to avoid any style that slows your audience's reading. Underlining can interfere with your reader's ability to recognize the shapes of words, and using all capitals slows reading.[18] Shadowed or outlined type can seriously hinder legibility, so use these styles carefully.

You decide on each design element according to its function. Effective design guides your readers through your message, so be sure to be consistent, balanced, restrained, and detail oriented:

For effective design, pay attention to

- Consistency
- Balance
- Restraint
- Detail

- *Consistency.* Be consistent in your use of design elements within a message (and sometimes even from message to message). Margins, typeface, type size, and spacing (in paragraph indents, between columns, and around photographs) should be consistent throughout a message. Also be sure that all recurring elements, such as vertical lines, columns, and borders, are handled consistently.
- *Balance.* To create a pleasing design, balance the space devoted to text, artwork, and white space.
- *Restraint.* Strive for simplicity in design. Don't clutter your message with too many design elements, too much highlighting, or too many decorative touches.
- *Detail.* Track all details that affect your design and thus your message. Headings and subheads that appear at the bottom of a column or a page (widows) can offend readers when the promised information doesn't appear until the next column or page. A layout that appears off balance can be really distracting, and any typographical errors can sabotage an otherwise good-looking design.

CHECKLIST FOR REVISING BUSINESS MESSAGES

A. Editing Your Message
1. Content and organization
   - a. Review your draft against the message plan.
   - b. Cover all necessary points in logical order.
   - c. Organize the message to respond to the audience's probable reaction.
   - d. Provide enough support to make the main idea convincing and interesting.
   - e. Eliminate unnecessary material; add useful material.
   - f. Be sure the beginning and ending are effective.
2. Style and readability
   - a. Be sure you've achieved the right tone.
   - b. Increase interest with lively words and phrases.
   - c. Make sure your message is readable.
       - i. Check vocabulary.
       - ii. Check sentence structure.
       - iii. Consider using a readability index.
3. Word choice
   - a. Use plain English.
   - b. Use concrete words that avoid negative connotations.
   - c. Rely on nouns, verbs, and specific adjectives and adverbs.
   - d. Select words that are strong, familiar, and short; avoid clichés, camouflaged verbs, and hedging words.
   - e. Use bias-free language.

B. Rewriting Your Message
1. Sentence style
   - a. Fit the sentence structure to the thought.
   - b. Tailor the sentence style to the audience.
   - c. Aim for an average sentence length of 20 words.
   - d. Write mainly in the active voice, but use the passive voice to achieve specific effects.
   - e. Eliminate unnecessary words and phrases.
   - f. Avoid obsolete and pompous language.
   - g. Moderate your enthusiasm.
   - h. Break up strung-out sentences.
   - i. Avoid hedging sentences.
   - j. Watch for indefinite pronoun starters.
   - k. Express parallel ideas in parallel form.
   - l. Eliminate awkward pointers.
   - m. Correct dangling modifiers.
   - n. Avoid long sequences of nouns.
   - o. Keep subject and verb close together, and keep adverbs, adjectives, and prepositional phrases close to the words they modify.
   - p. Emphasize key points through sentence style.

Avoid last-minute compromises. Don't reduce type size or white space to squeeze in text. On the other hand, avoid increasing type size or white space to fill space. If you've planned your message so that your purpose, your audience, and your message are clear, you can design your document to be effective.[19]

S TAGE 10: PROOFREADING YOUR MESSAGE

When you proofread your message, you ensure that it's letter perfect. Although grammar, spelling, punctuation, and typographical errors may seem trivial to some people, most readers will view your attention to detail as a sign of your professionalism. If a writer lets mechanical errors slip through, the reader automatically wonders whether the writer is unreliable in more important ways.

Credibility is affected by your attention to the details of mechanics and format.

Also, give some attention to the finer points of format. Have you followed accepted conventions and company guidelines for laying out the document on the page? Have you included all the traditional elements that belong in documents of the type you are creating? Have you been consistent in handling margins, page numbers, headings, exhibits, source notes, and other details? To resolve questions about format and layout, see Appendix A.

Finally, if you compose your business messages on a computer, many of the mechanical and grammatical problems discussed in this chapter can be checked electronically. Spell checkers and grammar checkers were discussed in Chapter 4. They're available either as part of word-processing programs such as Microsoft Word, Corel WordPerfect, Word Pro, and Claris Works or as special stand-alone programs for medical, technical, and foreign-language applications. Although both types of programs can flag problem areas, they can't actually fix any of those errors for you. For a reminder of the tasks involved in revision, see this chapter's Checklist for Revising Business Messages.

Electronic grammar and spell checkers can be helpful if you don't rely too heavily on them.

2. Effective paragraphs
   - ☐ a. Be sure each paragraph contains a topic sentence, related sentences, and transitional elements.
   - ☐ b. Edit for unity, effective development, and coherence.
   - ☐ c. Choose a method of development that suits the subject: illustration, comparison or contrast, cause and effect, classification, problem and solution.
   - ☐ d. Vary the length and structure of sentences within paragraphs.
   - ☐ e. Mix paragraphs of different lengths, but aim for an average of 100 words.

C. Producing Your Message
1. Design elements
   - ☐ a. Use appropriate white space around headings, in margins, between columns, at line endings, in paragraph indents or between unindented paragraphs, and between lines of type.
   - ☐ b. Choose margins and line justification that won't darken your document.
   - ☐ c. Use headings to break up long passages of text and to guide your readers through your message.

   - ☐ d. Select typefaces that complement the tone of your message.
   - ☐ e. Use only as many type styles as you actually need, avoiding any style that slows the reader's progress.
2. Design decisions
   - ☐ a. Be consistent, balanced, restrained, and detail oriented.
   - ☐ b. Avoid last-minute compromises.

D. Proofing Your Message
1. Mechanics and format
   - ☐ a. Review sentences to be sure they are grammatically correct.
   - ☐ b. Correct punctuation and capitalization errors.
   - ☐ c. Look for spelling and typographical errors.
   - ☐ d. Review the format to be sure it follows accepted conventions.
   - ☐ e. Use the format consistently throughout the message.
2. Electronic grammar and spell checkers
   - ☐ a. Use electronic checkers to point out errors you might overlook.
   - ☐ b. Be aware of program limitations so that you don't rely too heavily on electronic checkers.

On the Job

SOLVING A COMMUNICATION DILEMMA AT McDONALD'S

Over the past ten years, David Giarla has learned a great deal about the art of communication. By nature, he is a positive individual, and his communication style reflects that fact. Although his job is to spot problems, you're more likely to hear him use words such as *outstanding, terrific,* and *delicious* rather than *bad, dreadful,* or *unacceptable.* Perhaps that's why the managers and employees on his regular route always greet him with a smile.

Giarla calls on seven or eight McDonald's every day. If you work in one of his restaurants, you have a good chance of serving Giarla breakfast, lunch, a snack, or dinner on any given day. You know he's coming, but you don't know when—and that keeps you on your toes.

On a typical visit, Giarla pulls into the parking lot and checks for rubbish. The ideal McDonald's is blindingly clean from the street to the storeroom. He enters the restaurant. Are the lines moving quickly? They'd better be. Are the order takers smiling? You bet. A perky teenager behind the counter recognizes Giarla and asks, "Big Breakfast and a regular Diet Coke?" "Correctomundo," he replies.

He carries his tray to a table. Is it spotless? Yup. He inspects his food. Hmm. The biscuit looks a little small. He nibbles a hash brown, then heads for the kitchen. "Great hash browns," he says to the person at the deep fryer. "You should get a raise." He pauses a minute to inspect the dates stamped on the hamburger wrappers. Good. They're fresh. So are the cucumbers, cheese, and milk shake mix.

Business is picking up, so Giarla pitches in to help make Egg McMuffins. "These are going to be terrific," he announces. He finds that helping out builds rapport. He tries hard to cultivate goodwill between McDonald's headquarters and the restaurant managers and employees. He does not view himself as "the enemy spy." On the contrary, McDonald's is a team effort, and he is a coach—one of 300 field consultants who spend their days happily checking out the Golden Arches from coast to coast.

When Giarla spots the restaurant manager, he mentions the small-biscuit problem. Could someone be overkneading the dough, he wonders. He recommends that the biscuit maker review the McDonald's videotape that provides instructions for preparing biscuits and other items.

On to the next stop, where a helper crams too much food into a bag. More stops reveal more opportunities for improvement: a ceiling tile is stained and needs to be replaced; a cheeseburger bun is dented—probably because someone wrapped it too tightly; a storeroom is messy; a soft-serve cone is six inches high instead of the recommended three inches. Giarla calls attention to all these problems. You might expect the restaurant managers and employees to resent the criticism, but by and large they welcome his suggestions. Why? Because Giarla knows how to communicate.[20]

Your Mission: You have recently joined McDonald's as a quality control representative. Like David Giarla, you cover seven or eight restaurants a day. Most of the managers are cooperative, and most of the restaurants maintain high standards. But there is one exception. Over the past few months, you have pointed out a variety of problems to a particular McDonald's manager. You have been friendly, polite, and constructive in your suggestions, but nothing has been done to correct most of the problems. On your last visit, you warned the manager that you would have to file a negative report with headquarters if you didn't see some improvement imme-

diately. You have decided to put your suggestions in writing and to give the manager one week to take action. Here is the first draft of your letter. Using the questions that follow, analyze it according to the material in this chapter. Be prepared to explain your analysis.

Please correct the problems listed below. I will visit your facility within the next few days to monitor your progress. If nothing has been done toward rectifying these infractions of McDonald's principles of operation, you will be reported to headquarters for noncooperation and unsatisfactory levels of performance. As you know, I have mentioned these deviations from acceptable practice on previous visits. You have been given ample opportunity to comply with my suggestions. Your failure to comply suggests that you lack the necessary commitment to quality that has long been the hallmark of McDonald's restaurants.

On two occasions, I have ascertained that you are using expired ingredients in preparing hamburgers. On February 14, a package of buns with a freshness date of January 31 was used in your facility. Also, on March 2, you were using cheese that had expired by at least ten days. McDonald's is committed to freshness. All our ingredients are freshness dated. Expired ingredients should be disposed of, not used in the preparation of products for sale to the public. For example, you might contact local charities and offer the expired items to them free of charge, provided, of course, that the ingredients do not pose a health hazard (e.g., sour milk should be thrown out). The Community Resource Center in your area can be reached by calling 555-0909. Although I have warned you before about using old ingredients, the last time I visited your facility I found expired ingredients in the storeroom.

Your bathrooms should be refurbished and cleaned more frequently. The paper towel dispenser in the men's room was out of towels the last time I was there, and the faucet on the sink dripped. This not only runs up your water bill but also creates a bad impression for the customer. Additionally, your windows need washing. On all my visits, I have noticed fingerprints on the front door. I have never, in fact, seen your door anything but dirty. This, too, creates a negative impression. Similarly, the windows are not as clean as they might be. Also, please mop the floors more often. Nobody wants to eat in a dirty restaurant.

The most serious infraction pertains to the appearance of store personnel. Dirty uniforms are unforgivable. Also, employees, particularly those serving the public, must have clean fingernails and hands. Hair should be neatly combed, and uniforms should be carefully pressed. I realize that your restaurant is located in an economically depressed area, and I am aware that many of your employees are ethnic minorities from impoverished backgrounds and single-parent families. Perhaps you should hold a class in basic cleanliness for these people. It is likely that they have not been taught proper hygiene in their homes.

In addition, please instruct store personnel to empty the trash more frequently. The bins are constantly overflowing, making it difficult for customers to dispose of leftover food and rubbish. This is a problem both indoors and outdoors.

Also bear in mind that all patrons should be served within a few minutes of their arrival at your place of business. Waiting in line is annoying, particularly during the busy lunch hour when people are on tight schedules. Open new lines when you must in order to accommodate the flow of traffic. In addition, instruct the order takers and order fillers to work more rapidly during busy times. Employees should not be standing around chatting with each other while customers wait in line.

As I mentioned above, I will visit your facility within a few days to check on your progress toward meeting McDonald's criteria of operation. If no visible progress has been made, I will have no alternative other than to report you to top management at headquarters. If you have any questions or require clarification on any of these items, please feel free to contact me. I can be reached by calling 555-3549.

1. How would you rate this draft in terms of its content and organization?
   a. Although the style of the letter needs work, the content and organization are basically okay.
   b. The draft is seriously flawed in both content and organization. Extensive editing is required.
   c. The content is fine, but the organization is poor.
   d. The organization is fine, but the content is poor.
2. What should be done to eliminate the biased tone of the fourth paragraph?
   a. Omit the last three sentences of the paragraph.

b. Omit the last three sentences and add something like the following: "Please have your employees review the videotape that deals with McDonald's standards of personal appearance."
   c. Revise the last three sentences along the following lines: "Given the composition of your labor force, you may need to stress the basics of personal hygiene."
3. Which of the following is the best alternative to this sentence: "If nothing has been done toward rectifying these infractions of McDonald's principles of operation, you will be reported to headquarters for noncooperation and unsatisfactory levels of performance."
   a. "If nothing has been done to correct these infractions, you will be reported to headquarters for noncompliance."
   b. "If you don't shape up immediately, headquarters will hear about it."
   c. "By correcting these problems promptly, you can avoid being reported to headquarters."
   d. "You can preserve your unblemished reputation by acting immediately to bring your facility into compliance with McDonald's principles of operation."
4. Take a look at the third paragraph of the letter. What is its chief flaw?
   a. There is no topic sentence.
   b. The topic sentence is too narrow for the ideas encompassed in the paragraph.
   c. The transition from the previous paragraph is poor.
   d. The paragraph deals with more than one subject.
   e. The topic sentence is not adequately developed with specific details in subsequent sentences.

Critical Thinking Questions

1. You have so little time for your current project that you have to skip a few of the tasks in the composition process. You've already cut down everything you can in the planning and composing categories. Which tasks in the revision category would be best to cut: editing, rewriting, producing, or proofreading? Explain.
2. In what business situations might you want to use words of high connotative value?

3. How could cultural bias differ from racial and ethnic bias? What examples can you think of?
4. What specific techniques of style could you use to create a formal, objective tone? An informal, personal tone?
5. Which design elements are necessary to consider when designing your formal business letter? Which are not necessary?
6. Given the choice of only one, would you prefer to use a grammar checker or a spell checker? Why?

Documents for Analysis

Read the following documents; then (1) analyze the strengths and weaknesses of each sentence and (2) revise each document so that it follows this chapter's guidelines.

DOCUMENT 7.A: CREATING EFFECTIVE SENTENCES
The move to our new offices will take place over this coming weekend. For everything to run smooth, everyone will have to clean out their own desk and pack up the contents in boxes that will be provided. You will need to take everything off the walls too, and please pack it along with the boxes.

If you have a lot of personal belongings, you should bring them home with you. Likewise with anything valuable. I do not mean to infer that items will be stolen, irregardless it is better to be safe than sorry.

On Monday, we will be unpacking, putting things away, and then get back to work. The least amount of disruption is anticipated by us, if everyone does their part. Hopefully, there will be no negative affects on production schedules, and current deadlines will be met.

DOCUMENT 7.B: ASSESSING YOUR WORD CHOICE

Dear Ms. Giraud:

Enclosed herewith please find the manuscript for your book, *Careers in Woolgathering*. After perusing the first two chapters of your 1,500-page manuscript, I was forced to conclude that the subject matter, handicrafts and artwork using wool fibers, is not coincident with the publishing program of Framingham Press, which to this date has issued only works on business endeavors, avoiding all other topics completely.

Although our firm is unable to consider your impressive work at the present time, I have taken the liberty of recording some comments on some of the pages. I am of the opinion that any feedback that a writer can obtain from those well versed in the publishing realm can only serve to improve the writer's authorial skills.

In view of the fact that your residence is in the Boston area, might I suggest that you secure an appointment with someone of high editorial stature at the Cambridge Heritage Press, which I believe might have something of an interest in works of the nature you have produced.

Wishing you the best of luck in your literary endeavors, I remain

Arthur J. Cogswell
Editor

DOCUMENT 7.C: DEVELOPING COHERENT PARAGRAPHS

For delicious, air-popped popcorn, please read the following instructions: The popper is designed to pop 1/2 cup of popcorn kernels at one time. Never add more than 1/2 cup. A half cup of corn will produce three to four quarts of popcorn. More batches may be made separately after completion of the first batch. Popcorn is popped by hot air. Oil or shortening is not needed for popping corn. Add only popcorn kernels to the popping chamber. Standard grades of popcorn are recommended for use. Premium or gourmet type popping corns may be used. Ingredients such as oil, shortening, butter, margarine, or salt should never be added to the popping chamber. The popper, with popping chute in position, may be preheated for two minutes before adding the corn. Turn the popper off before adding the corn. Use electricity safely and wisely. Observe safety precautions when using the popper. Do not touch the popper when it is hot. The popper should not be left unattended when it is plugged into an outlet. Do not use the popper if it or its cord has been damaged. Do not use the popper if it is not working properly. Before using the first time, wash the chute and butter/measuring cup in hot soapy water. Use a dishcloth or sponge. Wipe the outside of the popper base. Use a damp cloth. Dry the base. Do not immerse the popper base in water or other liquid. Replace the chute and butter/measuring cup. The popper is ready to use.

 Exercises

1. Write a concrete phrase for each of these vague phrases.
   a. sometime this spring
   b. a substantial saving
   c. a large number attended
   d. increased efficiency
   e. expanded the work area
2. List words that are stronger than the following:
   a. ran after
   b. seasonal ups and downs
   c. bright
   d. suddenly rises
   e. moves forward
3. As you rewrite these sentences, replace the clichés with fresh, personal expressions.
   a. Being a jack-of-all-trades, Dave worked well in his new selling job.
   b. Moving Leslie into the accounting department, where she was literally a fish out of water, was like putting a square peg into a round hole, if you get my drift.
   c. I knew she was at death's door, but I thought the doctor would pull her through.
   d. Movies aren't really my cup of tea; as far as I am concerned, they can't hold a candle to a good book.
   e. It's a dog-eat-dog world out there in the rat race of the asphalt jungle.

4. Revise the following sentences, using shorter, simpler words.
   a. The antiquated calculator is ineffectual for solving sophisticated problems.
   b. It is imperative that the pay increments be terminated before an inordinate deficit is accumulated.
   c. There was unanimity among the executives that Ms. Jackson's idiosyncrasies were cause for a mandatory meeting with the company's personnel director.
   d. The impending liquidation of the company's assets was cause for jubilation among the company's competitors.
   e. The expectations of the president for a stock dividend were accentuated by the preponderance of evidence that the company was in good financial condition.
5. Rewrite each of the following to eliminate bias.
   a. For an Indian, Maggie certainly is outgoing.
   b. He needs a wheelchair, but he doesn't let his handicap affect his job performance.
   c. A pilot must have the ability to stay calm under pressure, and then he must be trained to cope with any problem that arises.
   d. Candidate Renata Parsons, married and the mother of a teenager, will attend the debate.
   e. Senior citizen Sam Nugent is still an active salesman.
6. Rewrite each sentence so that it is active rather than passive.
   a. The raw data are submitted to the data-processing division by the sales representative each Friday.

    b. High profits are publicized by management.

    c. The policies announced in the directive were implemented by the staff.

    d. Our computers are serviced by the Santee Company.

    e. The employees were represented by Janet Hogan.

7. Condense these sentences to as few words as possible.

    a. We are of the conviction that writing is important.

    b. In all probability, we're likely to have a price increase.

    c. Our goals include making a determination about that in the near future.

    d. When all is said and done at the conclusion of this experiment, I'd like to summarize the final windup.

    e. After a trial period of 3 weeks, during which time she worked for a total of 15 full working days, we found her work was sufficiently satisfactory so that we offered her full-time work.

8. Write up-to-date versions of these phrases; write *none* if you believe there is no appropriate substitute.

    a. as per your instructions

    b. attached herewith

    c. in lieu of

    d. in reply I wish to state

    e. please be advised that

9. Remove all the unnecessary modifiers from these sentences.

    a. Tremendously high pay increases were given to the extraordinarily skilled and extremely conscientious employees.

    b. The union's proposals were highly inflationary, extremely demanding, and exceptionally bold.

10. Rewrite these sentences so that they no longer contain any hedging.

    a. It would appear that someone apparently entered illegally.

    b. It may be possible that sometime in the near future the situation is likely to improve.

    c. Your report seems to suggest that we might be losing money.

    d. I believe Nancy apparently has somewhat greater influence over employees in the typing pool.

    e. It seems as if this letter of resignation means you might be leaving us.

11. Rewrite these sentences to eliminate the indefinite starters.

    a. There are several examples here to show that Elaine can't hold a position very long.

    b. It would be greatly appreciated if every employee would make a generous contribution to Mildred Cook's retirement party.

    c. It has been learned in Washington today from generally reliable sources that an important announcement will be made shortly by the White House.

    d. There is a rule that states that we cannot work overtime without permission.

    e. It would be great if you could work late for the next three Saturdays.

12. Present the ideas in these sentences in parallel form.

    a. Mr. Hill is expected to lecture three days a week, to counsel two days a week, and must write for publication in his spare time.

    b. She knows not only accounting, but she also reads Latin.

    c. Both applicants had families, college degrees, and were in their thirties, with considerable accounting experience but few social connections.

    d. This book was exciting, well written, and held my interest.

    e. Don is both a hard worker and he knows bookkeeping.

13. Rewrite these sentences to clarify the dangling modifiers.

    a. Running down the railroad tracks in a cloud of smoke, we watched the countryside glide by.

    b. Lying on the shelf, Ruby saw the seashell.

    c. Based on the information, I think we should buy the property.

    d. Being cluttered and filthy, Sandy took the whole afternoon to clean up her desk.

    e. After proofreading every word, the memo was ready to be signed.

14. Rewrite the following sentences to eliminate the long strings of nouns.

    a. The focus of the meeting was a discussion of the bank interest rate deregulation issue.

    b. Following the government task force report recommendations, we are revising our job applicant evaluation procedures.

    c. The production department quality assurance program components include employee training, supplier cooperation, and computerized detection equipment.

    d. The supermarket warehouse inventory reduction plan will be implemented next month.

    e. The State University business school graduate placement program is one of the best in the country.

15. Rearrange the following sentences to bring the subjects closer to their verbs.

    a. Trudy, when she first saw the bull pawing the ground, ran.

    b. It was Terri who, according to Ted, who is probably the worst gossip in the office (Tom excepted), mailed the wrong order.

    c. William Oberstreet, in his book *Investment Capital Reconsidered*, writes of the mistakes that bankers through the decades have made.

    d. Judy Schimmel, after passing up several sensible investment opportunities, despite the warnings of her friends and family, invested her inheritance in a jojoba plantation.

    e. The president of U-Stor-It, which was on the brink of bankruptcy after the warehouse fire, the worst tragedy in the history of the company, prepared an announcement for the press.

16. Explore the Web site at <http://owl.trc.purdue. edu/writing. labs.html>, and briefly explain (a) the services of each lab listed at this site and (b) the benefits each lab offers writers.

17. Write a paragraph on each of the following topics—one by illustration, one by comparison or contrast, one by discussion of cause and effect, one by classification, and one by discussion of problem and solution.

    a. Types of cameras (or dogs or automobiles) available for sale

    b. Advantages and disadvantages of eating at fast-food restaurants

    c. Finding that first job

    d. Good qualities of my car (or house, apartment, or neighborhood)

    e. How to make a dessert recipe (or barbecue a steak or make coffee)

DEVELOPING YOUR INTERNET SKILLS
GOING ONLINE: IMPROVE YOUR WRITING STYLE
WITH PROVEN TECHNIQUES, P. 126

While you're doing one of the exercises in this chapter—revising your writing—make it a point to log on and check *Elements of Style* to see what tips you can glean for improving your prose. When you're working on a document, which do you think you're more likely to use—a print version of a writing stylebook that might be on a bookshelf across the room (or in a library) or an online version just a few moments and clicks away? Why? Will your answer be different when you're working in a business office?

culturalRequests · *Organizing Direct Requests* · *Placing Orders* · *Requesting Routine Formats*

LETTERS, MEMOS,

nizing Positive Messages · *Replying to Requests for Information and Action* · *News Messages* ·

AND OTHER BRIEF

eying Bad News About Orders · *Communicating Negative Planning Persuasive Messages* ·

MESSAGES

nizing Persuasive Messages · *Preparing Persuasive Messages on the job* · *News Messages*

8

Chapter

After studying this chapter, you will be able to

Clearly state the main idea of each direct request you write

Indicate your confidence that the request will be filled

Provide sufficient detail for the reader to be able to comply with your request

Clarify complicated requests by using lists and tables

Close with a courteous request for specific action

At Barnes & Noble, direct requests are common, both inside and outside the organization. Whether employees are dealing with customers face to face, composing memos to co-workers, or writing letters to suppliers, they make an effort to consider and understand their audience's needs and problems when making a request.

WRITING DIRECT REQUESTS

O n the Job

FACING A COMMUNICATION DILEMMA AT BARNES & NOBLE

May the Best Seller Win!

Lots of gloomy news has been written about the sad state of reading in the United States, but the book business has actually boomed in recent years. Consumers buy in the neighborhood of $10 billion worth of books each year; they spend more on books than they do on going to the movies, buying or renting videotaped movies, and buying prerecorded music. At the forefront of the continuing expansion of the U.S. book market is Leonard Riggio. As chairman and CEO of Barnes & Noble, Riggio is considered by many to be the most powerful person in publishing.

Riggio got his start as a clerk in a college bookstore and eventually opened six college bookstores of his own. His next move was to become the principal owner of Barnes & Noble, whose Fifth Avenue store in New York City competes for the title of world's largest bookstore (the other contender is Foyles, in London). After that he purchased B. Dalton Bookseller, Bookstop, and Doubleday book chains. Today Barnes & Noble is the largest book retailer in the United States, with annual sales of nearly $2.5 billion and an aggressive expansion plan. Of course, despite its achievements, Riggio's chain is hardly alone in the book market.

Bookstores fall into three categories: (1) independent bookstores, which are individually owned outlets ranging from tiny specialty shops to warehouse-sized giants; (2) chains such as Crown Books; and (3) online booksellers such as Amazon.com, which let customers search for and order books by visiting a Web site on the Internet. Riggio competes to one degree or another with every category, but in terms of sheer size, a handful of other large, national chains—including Borders, Crown, and Book-A-Million—are his primary rivals.

As you read this chapter, put yourself in Leonard Riggio's shoes. To stay ahead of your competitors, you must send messages to customers and store managers, requesting both information and action. How can you obtain the information you need to make intelligent decisions? How will you phrase your requests so that store managers will respond with positive action in the race against competitors, both the bookstores that occupy physical building space and those that occupy the new virtual space of the Internet?[1]

NTERCULTURAL REQUESTS

Like so many U.S. executives, Leonard Riggio knows that making requests across cultural boundaries can be frustrating. He has to cut through red tape, overcome language barriers, and become familiar with the cultural differences involved; even the mail system in a particular region or country can cause problems. Depending on where you're doing business, just deciding whether to make your request in writing can be tricky. On the one hand, paper-oriented countries such as France, Germany, and England use a steady stream of correspondence to lead up to meetings and negotiations.[2] On the other hand, some Arabic, Asian, and Latin American countries consider paperwork a poor second choice for conducting business.

Whether written or oral, your request will be most effective if you follow the customs of your audience. Not all requests are organized directly. For example, an Arab letter would probably begin with a generalized blessing upon the reader and the reader's family.[3] Other cultures begin with an explanation and work up to the request at the end of the message. So, whenever you can, learn about the customs of your audience and follow them to the degree possible.

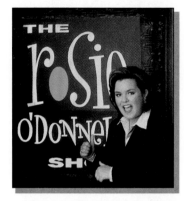

While the competition presumably quails, Rosie O'Donnell's popular television talk show continues to rise in the TV ratings. Her successful formula? Genuine respect, care, and enthusiasm for her guests. These qualities invariably ensure a good response to any request—she even got the First Lady to warble a tune (and has raised nearly half a million dollars for her children's foundation).

ORGANIZING DIRECT REQUESTS

When you're addressing a U.S. or Canadian audience, when cultural differences are minimal, and when you can assume that your audience will be interested in what you have to say (or at least willing to cooperate with you), make a **direct request** by following the direct, or deductive, plan to organize your message. Present the request or the main idea first, follow up with necessary details, and close with a cordial statement of the action you want. This approach works well when your request requires no special tact or persuasion.

People making direct requests (such as Barnes & Noble's Leonard Riggio) may be tempted to begin with personal introductions ("I am CEO of a large bookstore chain, and I'm interested in expanding our selection of reference books"). However, this type of beginning is usually a mistake. The essence of the message, the specific request, is buried and may get lost. A better way to organize a direct request is to state what you want in the first sentence or two and let the explanation follow.

Even though you expect a favorable response, the tone of your initial request is important. Instead of demanding immediate action ("Send me your catalog no. 33A"), soften your request with such words as *please* and *I would appreciate.* An impatient demand for rapid service isn't necessary, because you can generally assume that your audience will comply once the reason for your request is understood.

The middle part of a direct request usually explains the original request ("I would like to order a sample of several of your reference works to determine whether they would appeal to our customers"). Such amplifying details help your audience fulfill your request correctly.

In the last section, clearly state the action you're requesting. You may wish to tell the audience where to send the sought-after information or product, indicate any time limits, or list details of the request that were too complex or numerous to cover in the introductory section. Then close with a brief, cordial note reminding the audience of the importance of the request ("If the sample books sell well, you can expect to receive additional orders from Barnes & Noble on a monthly basis").

Now let's take a closer look at the three main sections of a direct request. Although this discussion focuses on letters and memos, remember that this organizational plan may be appropriate for brief oral and electronic messages as well.

For direct requests
- State the request or main idea
- Give necessary details
- Close with a cordial request for specific action

Assume that your reader will comply once he or she understands your purpose.

Word the request itself carefully so that it says exactly what you want.

Edward Lewis, publisher and CEO, and Clarence O. Smith, president of Essence Communications Inc. (ECI), together launched Essence *magazine in 1970. It quickly became a leading source of information for African-American women. During ECI's growth into its present status as a large and diverse media company, the pair's success has depended on a unique relationship with readers and strong alliances with leading corporations and financial institutions. Building these relationships meant writing thousands of direct requests, skillfully presented to ensure positive replies.*

In the middle section
■ Call attention to how the reader will benefit from granting your request
■ Give details of your request

Ask the most important question first; then ask related, more specific questions.

Use numbered lists when you're requesting several items or answers.

Direct Statement of the Request or Main Idea

The general rule for the first part of a direct request is to write not only to be understood but also to avoid being misunderstood. If you request "1990 census figures" from a government agency, the person who handles your request won't know whether you want a page or two of summary figures or a detailed report running to several thousand pages. So be as specific as possible in the sentence or two that begins your message.

Also, be aware of the difference between a polite request in question form (which requires no question mark) and a question that is part of a request:

POLITE REQUEST IN QUESTION FORM	QUESTION THAT IS PART OF A REQUEST
Would you please help us determine whether Kate Kingsley is a suitable applicant for a position as landscape designer.	Did Kate Kingsley demonstrate an ability to work smoothly with clients?

Many direct requests include both types of statements, so be sure to distinguish between the polite request that is your overall reason for writing and the specific questions that belong in the middle section of your letter or memo.

Finally, if you have more than one request, consider the following ways of writing them:

■ When you have several requests, use headings to express categories of requests, with each category containing several requests. Categorizing your needs makes the reader's job easier.
■ When you have an unusual or complex request, state the request and then provide supporting details right underneath it. In other words, make each request a short paragraph.
■ When you have a list of requests, include space beneath each request so that the reader can write on your letter or memo. This method saves everyone's time and effort. It also controls the length of the reader's response.

Justification, Explanation, and Details

To make the explanation a smooth and logical outgrowth of your opening remarks, you might make the first sentence of your message's middle section audience centered by stating a service-to-the-reader benefit. For instance, a Barnes & Noble manager might write, "By keeping Barnes & Noble informed about your products, you can expand your distribution channel. For example, if a unique readership exists for one of your new references, I can help you reach those customers."

Another possible approach for the middle section is to ask a series of questions, particularly if your inquiry concerns machinery or complex equipment. You might ask about technical specifications, exact dimensions, and the precise use of the product. The most important question is asked first. If cost is your main concern, you might begin with a question such as "What is the price of your least expensive laser printer?" Then you may want to ask more specific but related questions about, say, the cost of toner cartridges and maintenance service.

If you're requesting several items or answers, number the items and list them in logical order or in descending order of importance. Furthermore, so that your request can be handled quickly, ask only the questions that are central to your main request. Also, avoid asking for information that you can find on your own, even if your effort takes considerable time.

If you're asking many people to reply to the same questions, consider wording them so that they can be answered yes or no or with some other easily counted response. You may even want to provide respondents with a form or with boxes they can check to indicate their answers. If you need more than a simple yes-or-no answer, pose an open-ended question. For example, a question such as "How fast can you repair computer monitors?" is more likely to elicit the information you want than "Can you repair computer monitors?" Keep in mind also that phrasing questions in a way that hints at the response you want is not likely to get you accurate information. So try to phrase your questions objectively. Finally, deal with only one topic in each question. If the questions need amplification, keep each question in a separate paragraph.

Other types of information that belong in this section include data about a product (model number, date and place of purchase, condition), your reason for being concerned about a particular matter, and other details about your request. Upon finishing this middle section, your audience should understand why the request is important and should be willing to satisfy it.

When you prepare questions
- Ask only questions that relate to your main request
- Don't ask for information you can find yourself
- Make your questions open-ended and objective
- Deal with only one topic in each question

Courteous Close with Request for Specific Action

Close your letter with two important elements: (1) a request for some specific response (complete with any time limits that apply) and (2) an expression of appreciation or goodwill. Help your reader respond easily by including your phone number, office hours, and other helpful information.

However, don't thank the reader "in advance" for cooperating. If the reader's reply warrants a word of thanks, send it after you've received the reply. If you're requesting information for a research project, you might offer to forward a copy of your report in gratitude for the reader's assistance. If you plan to reprint or publish materials that you ask for, indicate that you'll get any necessary permission. When asking for information about an individual, be sure to indicate that you'll keep all responses confidential.

Close with
- A request for some specific response
- An expression of appreciation
- Information about how you can be reached

PLACING ORDERS

Because they're usually processed without objection, and because they refer to a product that the reader knows about, orders are considered one of the simplest types of direct request. When placing an order, you need not excite your reader's interest; just state your needs clearly and directly.

To see what to include in a good order letter, examine any mail-order form supplied by a large firm: It offers complete and concise directions for providing all the information needed to fill an order. After the date, the order form probably starts with "Please send the following" or "Please ship." If you complete the rest of the form and mail it, these statements constitute a legal and binding offer to purchase the goods ordered; the supplier's shipment of those goods constitutes an acceptance of the offer and thus completes a legal contract.

Order blanks are arranged to document precisely the goods you want, describing them by catalog number, quantity, name or trade name, color, size, unit price, and total amount due. This complete identification helps prevent errors in filling the order. When drafting an order letter, follow the same format, presenting information about the items you want in column form, double-spacing between the items, and totaling the price at the end.

Order blanks provide space for delivery information, such as how and where to send the shipment. In your letter be sure to specify the delivery address, especially if it is not the address from which you send your letter. (Sometimes the billing and delivery addresses are different.) Also indicate how the merchandise is to be shipped: by truck, air freight, parcel post, air express, or delivery service. Unless you specify the mode of transportation, the seller chooses.

In any letter sent with money, mention the amount of payment, explain how the amount was calculated, and if necessary, explain to what account the amount should be charged. Again, the order form provides an excellent model. Here's an example:

CEO and founder Jeffrey Bezos's Amazon.com bookstore, selling 2.5 million titles available over the Internet, has astonished everyone with its huge overnight success. Providing books faster, cheaper, more conveniently, and in greater abundance isn't Bezos's only secret. He's using Web technology to make constant direct requests— asking customers not only to buy, but to add Amazon.com links to their own web sites, to write book reviews, to explore new Web pages and read features, to subscribe to e-mail reviews, and to send comments and requests. Once they're interacting—they're hooked.

Please send the following items to the above address by air freight. I am ordering from your current spring–summer catalog:

The general request is stated first.

Count	Stock I.D.	Description	Price Per Item	Price Total
10	342	Navajo bracelets (turquoise and silver tubular beads)	$8.95	$ 89.50
10	343	Navajo necklaces (turquoise and silver tubular beads)	11.95	119.50
10	344	Navajo loop earrings (turquoise and silver)	9.95	99.50
10	574	Navajo hand-woven rugs (Windsong pattern, 20" × 38")	16.99	169.90
5	575	Navajo hand-woven rugs (Windsong pattern, 42" × 65")	49.95	249.75
3	595	Navajo hand-woven rugs (Sundance pattern, 5'5" × 8'2")	99.99	299.97

All necessary details are provided (in a format similar to an order form).

TOTAL SALES	$1,028.12
SHIPPING	46.00
AMOUNT DUE	$1,074.12

Information about tax and shipping was provided in the catalog, so the writer calculated the amount due.

When ordering nonstandard items, include a complete description.

Not every item ordered through the mail, via e-mail, or by fax is neatly displayed in a catalog, Web site, or newspaper advertisement. If the goods are somewhat unusual, the problem of identifying them becomes more complex. For instance, a general contractor ordering supplies for several ongoing jobs at various sites mailed this order to Jefferson's Wood Windows:

Our customers have selected the following windows to replace existing construction:

- 3647 John Street
  - 2 Pozzi CW2836-4 (Casement bow window, wood, true divided lite)
  - 1 Pozzi CW2836-5 (Casement bow window, wood, true divided lite)
- 815 Silverton Avenue
  - 4 Kolbe FN 236 (French casement, wood, true divided lite)
  - 2 Pozzi D2830 (Double-hung, wood, true divided lite)
- 7700 Main Street
  - 3 Andersen G436 (Gliding window, Perma-Shield, mullion fillers)

Once you have confirmed the item numbers and availability with each manufacturer, please call me at (816) 997-6040 to verify the pricing. We need these delivered by September 17, so please inform me of any possible delay.

CHECKLIST FOR ORDERS

A. Direct Statement of the Request
1. Use wording that indicates an order rather than a request: "Please send me" or "please ship" instead of "I want" or "I need," which are neither polite nor legally appropriate for a business order.
2. Open with a general description of your order that encompasses all the details.

B. Justification, Explanation, and Details
1. For complex orders, provide a general explanation of how the requested materials will be used.
2. Provide all specifications: quantity, price (including discounts), size, catalog number, product description, shipping instructions (date and place), arrangements for payment (method, time, deposits), and cost totals.
3. Use a format that presents information clearly and makes it easy to total amounts.
4. Double-check the completeness of your order and the cost totals.

C. Courteous Close with Request for Specific Action
1. Include a clear summary of the desired action.
2. Whenever possible, suggest a future reader benefit of complying with the order.
3. Close on a cordial note.
4. Clearly state any time limits that apply to your order, and explain why they are important.

Note the specific details included in the letter and the clarity about what is needed at each location. In any order for nonstandard items, the additional description helps the reader identify your needs accurately. In special cases, such as ordering machine parts, you may even make drawings of the parts you need and add an explanation of their particular use.

A final suggestion about placing orders: Be thorough and clear. If you supply unclear or insufficient information, your reader must make an extra effort to get the missing details. The delays and cross-communications that result will hold up delivery of your order and may lead to mistakes in filling it. To make sure your order is filled correctly, retain a copy of your letter, fax, or e-mail message. If you haven't received a response in a reasonable time (two weeks, in most cases), write or call to see whether your order has arrived and is being processed. (To remind yourself of the tasks involved in placing orders, see this chapter's Checklist for Orders.)

REQUESTING ROUTINE INFORMATION AND ACTION

When you need to know about something, elicit an opinion from someone, or suggest a simple action, you usually need only ask. In essence, simple requests say, "This is what I want to know [or what I want you to do], why I want to know it, and how you might benefit from helping me." If your reader is able and willing to do what you want, such a straightforward request will get the job done with a minimum of fuss.

> When making a routine request, say
> - What you want to know
> - Why you want to know
> - Why it is in the reader's interest to help you

Despite their simple organization, routine requests deserve a tactful touch. In many organizations, e-mail, memos, and letters like these are sent to hundreds or even thousands of employees, customers, clients, and shareholders. So the potential for creating a positive impression is second only to the risk of causing ill will through ambiguous wording or a discourteous tone. When writing even a routine request, keep the purpose of your message in mind. That is, ask yourself what you want recipients to understand or do as a result of reading the message. As you prepare the request, remember that even the briefest note can create confusion and hard feelings.

> Exactly what do you want the reader to understand or do as a result of reading your request for action?

Requests to Company Insiders

Although requests to fellow employees are often oral and casual, some messages are better sent by e-mail or put in permanent, written form. A clear, thoughtfully written memo or e-mail message can save time and questions by helping readers understand precisely what is required.

> A request in memo form
> - Provides a permanent record
> - Saves time and questions
> - Tells precisely what is needed

Figure 8.1
In-Depth Critique: Memo
Requesting Routine Action
from Company Insiders

Hydel Interior Alternatives (HIA) provides interior office designs for businesses. HIA recently decided to upgrade its wellness and benefits program, but it will have to charge employees a nominal fee to pay for use of a sports complex. The following memo seeks employee input about the new program and the possible fee.

Hydel Interior Alternatives

INTERNAL MEMORANDUM

To: All Employees
From: Mike Ortega, Human Resources
Date: October 10, 1998
Subj: New Wellness Program Opportunity

The readers are busy, so the purpose of the communication is stated in the first paragraph.

The benefits package committee has asked me to contact everyone about an opportunity to save money and stay healthier in the bargain. As you know, we've been meeting to decide on changes in our benefits package. Last week, we sent you a memo detailing the Synergy Wellness Program.

In addition to the package as described in the memo (life, major medical, dental, hospitalization), Synergy has sweetened the pot by offering HIA a 10 percent discount. To meet the requirements for the discount, we have to show proof that at least 25 percent of our employees participate in aerobic exercise at least three times a week for at least 20 minutes. (Their actuarial tables show a resulting 10 percent reduction in claims.)

The second and third paragraphs present the situation that makes the inquiry necessary.

During warm weather, many of us walk the nature trail on our lunch break. Those walks will satisfy Synergy's requirements, but we have those nasty winters when no one can venture outside. After looking around, we discovered a gymnasium with an indoor track just a few blocks south on Haley Boulevard. Sports Midwest will give our employees unlimited daytime access to their indoor track, gym, and pool for a group fee that comes to approximately $4.50 per month per employee if at least half of us sign up. Payroll says you can have the amount automatically deducted, if you wish.

In addition to walking, we can swim, play volleyball, jazzercise, form our own intramural basketball teams, and much more. Our spouses and children can also participate at a deeply discounted monthly fee. If you have questions, please e-mail or call me or any member of the committee. Let us know your wishes on the following form.

Sign and return the following no later than **Friday, October 30.**

The final paragraph lists reader benefits, requests action, and provides an easy-to-use response form.

===

_____ Yes, I will participate in the Synergy Wellness program and pay $4.50 a month.
_____ Yes, I am interested in a discounted family membership.
_____ No, I prefer not to participate.

Signature _____

Employee ID Number _____

A routine request follows the standard direct plan. Start with a clear statement of your reason for writing; then provide whatever explanation is needed to justify the request. Close with a specific account of what you expect, and include a deadline if appropriate. The memo in Figure 8.1 was sent to all employees of an interior design company.

In the following memo, the writer refers to a previous memo on the same topic and then requests a response from employees:

Are you interested in having a day-care center on site?

Several suggestions in the cafeteria suggestion box indicate that parents at Timken want convenient, affordable child care. Therefore, your answers to the following questions will help us determine your needs.

1. How many children would you enroll in the new center?

2. How much do you currently pay each week for each child in day care?

3. Do you think the cost is too high? In your opinion, what would be a reasonable weekly charge for each child?

4. What qualities do you look for in a day-care center?

5. What qualifications do you expect of the caregivers?

You may respond on this form and return it to Human Resources by Friday. We appreciate your prompt response so that we may begin analyzing the possibilities.

The memo begins with the central question.

A little background information orients the reader.

The numbered questions focus responses so that they will be easier to tally.

Specific instructions for replying close the memo. The courteous tone helps ensure a prompt response.

As chief of the Small Business Administration (and the first Puerto Rican–born ever appointed by the President to a major government agency), Aida Alvarez depends on information and cooperation from her staff and others. She turns to principles learned as a Harvard English major and print journalist to write requests that get prompt results: using clear, courteous, and direct statements.

This matter-of-fact memo assumes some shared background. Such a style is appropriate when you're communicating about a routine matter to someone in the same company.

When used well, memos and e-mail messages can communicate efficiently, concisely, and powerfully. When misused, they can waste time and effort, can swell the ocean of information that offices must deal with, and can even tarnish your business reputation. So avoid writing frequent, long, and unneeded messages. Also, don't put anything in a memo or e-mail message that you wouldn't want to share with absolutely everyone (including the press and any Senate committee you can think of).[4]

Adjust the writing style to take shared reference points into account.

Requests to Other Businesses

Many letters and e-mail messages to other businesses are requests for information about products, such as a Barnes & Noble letter requesting a catalog from a reference book distributor. They are among the simplest of all letters to write because businesses welcome the opportunity to tell you about their goods and services. In fact, you can often fill out a coupon, a response card, or an online form and then mail or e-mail it to the correct address. In other cases, you might write a brief note requesting further information about something you saw or heard about in an advertisement. One or two sentences will most likely do the job. Companies commonly check on the effectiveness of their advertisements, so mention where you saw the advertisement or heard about the product.

Of course, many inquiries are prompted by something other than an advertisement, and they demand a more detailed letter or e-mail message. If the message will be welcome, or if the reader won't mind answering it, the direct approach is still appropriate. The following is such a letter:

When writing a letter in response to an advertisement
- *Say where you saw the ad*
- *Specify what you want*
- *Provide a clear and complete return address on the letter*

If the reader is not expecting your letter, supply more detail.

BEHIND THE SCENES AT NUMA FINANCIAL SYSTEMS
Promoting a Business on the Internet

Stephen Eckett is founder and managing director of Numa Financial Systems, a virtual consulting company—that is, his company's only existence is a Web site on the Internet. Although Eckett's company is registered in the United Kingdom, he works mainly from France, and his clients live all over the world.

Like many consultants, Eckett is a one-man operation. He markets his knowledge through Numa's Web site and offers advice on how to connect to the Internet to research financial markets and manage investment portfolios. Eckett knows that responding to direct requests is one way to promote his business. Of course, Eckett doesn't charge you for his online advice; rather, he hopes that if you interact with Numa's Web site you will eventually hire him as a consultant or purchase his book *Investing Online* (a practical guide to using the Internet for investing in the global stock market and trading currencies). In fact, Eckett sells his book directly through his Web site to customers all over the world. He also plans to offer investment software, conference registrations, and journal subscriptions in the near future.

Eckett believes that the key to building his consulting business is effective customer interaction. That's why he takes online information requests very seriously. He gets more than 50 requests for information each day, including requests for investment advice, job applications, book orders, and information on advertising services via the Numa Web site. Because

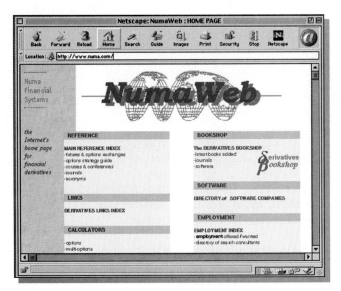

Through his Web site, Stephen Eckett of Numa Financial Systems receives more than 50 requests a day for information.

he's received so many of these online requests, Eckett has some practical advice on how to compose direct requests for e-mail so that people will respond by taking positive action.

Would you please supply me with information about the lawn services you provide.

Pralle Realty owns approximately 27 pieces of rental property in College Station, and we're looking for a lawn service to handle all of them. We are making a commitment to provide quality housing in this college town, and we are looking for an outstanding firm to work with us.

1. **Lawn care:** What is your annual charge for each location for lawn maintenance, including mowing, fertilizing, and weed control?

2. **Shrubbery:** What is your annual charge for each location for the care of deciduous and evergreen bushes, including pruning, fertilizing, and replacing as necessary?

3. **Contract:** How does Agri-Lawn Service structure large contracts? What kind of additional information do you need from us?

We hope to hear from you by February 15. We want to have a lawn-care firm in place by March 15.

The overall request is stated at the beginning. Phrased politely in question form, it requires no question mark.

The explanation for the request keeps the reader's attention by hinting at the possibility of future business.

To avoid burdening the reader with an impossibly broad request, the writer asks a series of specific questions, itemized in a logical sequence.

To avoid receiving useless yes-or-no answers, the writer asks some open-ended questions.

The courteous close specifies a time limit.

"Be concise," says Eckett. "Get straight to the point. Include the reason for the request in the first few lines, and don't write long paragraphs of text; it's awkward and tiring to read on a computer screen. Break your messages up into smaller units, and make each paragraph only a few lines long. Don't try to get too clever with the layout of the message because the recipient may be using a different e-mail program that alters the text presentation entirely. Be sure to keep the subject heading as precise and detailed as space allows. If the editor of a newsletter on gold investment receives 50 e-mail information requests a day, the subject heading "Gold" will not be very useful.

Eckett notes that informality is a big advantage of e-mail. He adds, however, that it is fine to be informal if you are writing to your brother, an old school friend, or an established work colleague—but not when making contact with someone for the first time or when it is still early in a business relationship. He emphasizes the importance of perfect grammar and spelling—especially if you want to get positive action. For example, if he receives a message littered with spelling errors, or even just phrased inelegantly, chances are strong that he will respond with a prewritten auto-reply message.

According to Eckett, e-mail information requests have a tremendous advantage over the fax and phone. Not only is e-mail faster and cheaper, but the recipient can immediately file the requests by topic and wait until later to perform an automatic search by date, sender, subject heading, or key words.

So, if you need to find or follow up on an information request, it's a matter of five seconds to filter, search, or sort though 5,000 messages. Eckett personally sorts his e-mail into some 60 categories. "It's far better than wading though a filing cabinet of curled fax paper."

Eckett does note a situation in which e-mail might not be a good choice. He believes that, even though e-mail is a great tool for simple information requests, it may not be effective for initiating contact with a more senior person (such as a corporate manager). Eckett says that it is best to contact that person by phone. He adds that e-mail requests from unknown parties will seldom reach the senior person, even if they are sent to that person's direct e-mail address.

Apply Your Knowledge

1. Eckett has hired you to help him respond to his Web site inquiries. Knowing that he is a stickler for good grammar and spelling, you are concerned because your e-mail software does not have a grammar or spelling checker. You are not the best typist. What easy steps can you take to prevent errors in your e-mail communications?

2. Aside from good grammar, spelling, and short paragraphs, please list some (perhaps creative) ways that you can make sure that your e-mail request will evoke a positive response.

This letter should bring a prompt and enthusiastic reply because the situation is clearly described, the possibility of current and future business is suggested, and the questions are specific and easy to answer. Also, the letter implies confidence in the opinion and assistance of the reader. Because the letter will be sent to a business and pertains to a possible sale, the writer did not enclose a stamped, preaddressed envelope.

If you aren't using letterhead stationery, be sure to write your address on the letter clearly and completely. Many inquiries are not answered because the address was illegibly handwritten or was written only on the return envelope, which the recipient discarded.

Requests to Customers and Other Outsiders

Businesses often ask individuals outside the organization to provide information or to take some simple action: attend a meeting, return an information card, sign a document, confirm an address, supplement information on an order. These messages are often short and simple, but some situations require a more detailed explanation. Readers might be unwilling to respond unless they understand how the request benefits them. So more complex letters, with several paragraphs of explanation, are sometimes necessary.

Businesses sometimes need to reestablish a relationship with former customers. In many cases, customers who are unhappy about some purchase or about the way they were treated make no complaint: They simply stay away from the offending business. A letter of inquiry encouraging customers to use idle credit accounts offers them an opportunity to register their displeasure and then move on to a good relationship. In addition, a customer's response to an inquiry may provide the company with insights into ways to improve its products and customer service. Even if they have no complaint,

Requests to customers often spell out in detail
- *What exactly is needed*
- *How filling the request will benefit them*

Routine requests to customers can be used to reestablish communication.

CHECKLIST FOR ROUTINE REQUESTS

A. Direct Statement of the Request
1. Phrase the opening to reflect the assumption that the reader will respond favorably to your request.
2. Phrase the opening so clearly and simply that the main idea cannot be misunderstood.
3. Write in a polite, undemanding, personal tone.
4. Preface complex requests with a sentence or two of explanation, possibly a statement of the problem that the response will solve.

B. Justification, Explanation, and Details
1. Justify the request, or explain its importance.
2. Explain to the reader the benefit of responding.
3. State desired actions in a positive and supportive, not negative or dictatorial, manner.
4. Itemize parts of a complex request in a numbered series.
5. List specific questions.
   - a. Don't ask questions that you could answer through your own efforts.
   - b. Arrange questions logically.
   - c. Number questions.
   - d. Word questions carefully to get the types of answers you need: numbers or yes's and no's if you need to tally many replies; lengthier, more-detailed answers if you want to elicit more information.
   - e. Word questions to avoid clues about the answer you prefer so as not to bias the reader's answers.
   - f. Limit each question to one topic.

C. Courteous Close with Request for Specific Action
1. Courteously request a specific action and make it easy to comply, perhaps by enclosing a return, postage-paid envelope or by explaining how you can be reached.
2. Indicate gratitude, possibly by promising to follow up in a way that will benefit the reader.
3. Clearly state any important deadline or time frame for the request.

---

customers still welcome the personal attention. Such an inquiry to the customer might begin this way:

> When a good charge customer like you has not bought anything from us in six months, we wonder why. Is there something we can do to serve you better?

When sending routine requests to individuals rather than to other businesses, consider enclosing a stamped, preaddressed envelope.

Letters of inquiry sent to someone's home frequently include a stamped, preaddressed envelope to make it easy for the customer to reply.

Inquiry letters similar to the one above are sent from one business to another. For example, a sales representative of a housewares distributor might send this type of letter to a retailer. To review material discussed here, see this chapter's Checklist for Routine Requests.

WRITING DIRECT REQUESTS FOR CLAIMS AND ADJUSTMENTS

You are entitled to request an adjustment whenever you receive a product or service that doesn't live up to the supplier's standards.

Satisfied customers bring additional business to the firm; dissatisfied customers do not. In addition, dissatisfied customers complain to anyone who'll listen, creating poor public relations. So, even though **claims** (or formal complaints) and **adjustments** (or claim settlements) may seem like unpleasant concepts, progressive organizations such as Barnes & Noble want to know when their clients or customers are dissatisfied with their services or merchandise. So if you have a complaint, it's in your best interests, and the company's, to bring your claim or request for an adjustment to the organization's attention. Communicate at once with someone in the company who can make the correction. A phone call or visit may solve the problem, but a written claim letter is better because it documents your dissatisfaction.

Tone is of primary importance; keep your claim businesslike and unemotional.

Your first reaction to a clumsy mistake or a defective product is likely to be anger or frustration, but the person reading your letter probably had nothing to do with the problem. Making a courteous, clear, concise explanation will impress the reader much more favorably than an abusive, angry letter. Asking for a fair and reasonable solution will increase your chances of receiving a satisfactory adjustment.

In most cases, and especially in your first letter, assume that a fair adjustment will be made, and follow the plan for direct requests. Begin with a straightforward statement of the problem, and give a complete, specific explanation of the details. In the middle section of your claim letter, provide any information the adjuster will need to verify your complaint about faulty merchandise or unsatisfactory service. Politely request specific action in your closing, and suggest that the business relationship will continue if the problem is solved satisfactorily.

Companies usually accept the customer's explanation of what's wrong, so ethically speaking, it's important to be entirely honest when filing claims for adjustment or refund. Also, be prepared to back up your claim with invoices, sales receipts, canceled checks, dated correspondence, catalog descriptions, and any other relevant documents. Send copies and keep the originals for your files.

If the remedy is obvious, tell your reader exactly what will return the company to your good graces—for example, an exchange of merchandise for the right item or a refund if the item is out of stock. If you're uncertain about the precise nature of the trouble, you could ask the company to make an assessment. When you're dissatisfied with an expensive item, you might request that an unbiased third person either estimate the cost of repair or suggest another solution. Be sure to supply your telephone number and the best time to call (as well as your address) so that the company can discuss the situation with you if necessary.

The following letter was written to a gas and electric company. As you read it, compare the tone with that in Figure 8.2. If you were the person receiving the complaint, which version would you respond to more favorably?

We have been at our present location only three months, and we don't understand why our December utility bill is $115.00 and our January bill is $117.50. Businesses on both sides of us, in offices just like ours, are paying only $43.50 and $45.67 for the same months. We all have similar computer and office equipment, so something must be wrong.

Small businesses are helpless against big utility companies. How can we prove that you read the meter wrong or that the November bill from before we even moved in here got added to our December bill? We want someone to check this meter right away. We can't afford to pay these big bills.

In general, it's a good idea to suggest specific and fair compensation when asking for an adjustment. However, in some cases you wouldn't request a specific adjustment but ask the reader to resolve the problem. In a letter like this, define the problem and express your dissatisfaction in as much detail as possible, while conveying a sincere desire to find a fair solution. A courteous tone will allow the reader to save face and still make up for the mistake.(This chapter's Checklist for Claims and Requests for Adjustment will remind you of the tasks involved in such messages.)

MAKING ROUTINE CREDIT REQUESTS

If your credit rating is sound, your application for business credit may be as direct as any other type of simple request. Whether the application is directed to a local bank, to a supply company, wholesaler, or manufacturer, or to a national credit-card company, the information needed is the same. You might phone the company for a credit application or write a letter as simple as this:

We would like to open a credit account with your company. Please send an application blank, and let us know what references you will need.

In your claim letter

- Explain the problem and give details
- Provide backup information
- Request specific action

Be prepared to document your claim. Send copies and keep the original documents.

GOING ONLINE
EXPAND YOUR KNOWLEDGE ABOUT CREDIT
Visit Experian Expo to understand what consumer credit is all about, from the basics of credit reports to the effects of bankruptcy. Expo attractions include a Consumer Service Center (for getting your questions answered), Small Business Credit Café (for details about small business credit), and Skyway to Loans (for making a personal, home, or business loan). You can even order a copy of your consumer credit report.

http://www.experian.com/index.html

Figure 8.2
In-Depth Critique: The Importance of Appearance

Most people would react much more favorably to this version of the complaint letter about high utility bills. As this rational and clear approach demonstrates, a courteous approach is best for any routine request. If you must write a letter that gives vent to your anger, go ahead; but then tear that one up and write a letter that will actually help solve the problem.

The European Connection
Specialist Purveyors of European Antiques
— for over 30 years —
P.O. Box 804 • Cayucos, California 93430
Telephone: (805) 979-7727 Fax: (805) 979-2828
EuroConnect@nemesis.net

February 24, 1999

Customer Service Representative
City of San Luis Obispo Utilities
955 Morro Street
San Luis Obispo, CA 93401

Dear Customer Service Representative:

The utility meter in our store may not be accurate. Please send someone to check it.

We have been at our present location since December 1, almost three months. Our monthly bill is nearly triple those of neighboring businesses in this building, yet we all have similar storefronts, furnished with similar merchandise and equipment. In December we paid $115.00, and our January bill was $117.50; the highest bills that neighboring businesses have paid were $43.50 and $45.67.

If your representative could visit our store, he or she could do an analysis of how much energy we are using. We understand that you regularly provide this helpful service to customers.

We would appreciate hearing from you this week. You can reach me by calling 979-7727 during business hours.

Sincerely,

Laura Covington

Laura Covington
Proprietor

The problem is stated clearly and calmly in the first paragraph.

The second paragraph explains the particulars of the situation so that the person reading the letter will understand why the writer thinks a problem exists.

The last paragraph requests specific action and makes responding easy by providing a phone number.

The second step is to supply the necessary information.

Before you get a credit account, you'll have to supply such information as the name of your company, the length of time you've been in business, the name of your bank, and the addresses of businesses where you have existing accounts. Businesses trying to establish credit are also expected to furnish a financial statement and possibly a balance sheet. In general, the lender wants proof that your income is stable and that you can repay the loan. You might put this information in your original letter, but it will probably be requested again on the standard credit application form.

CHECKLIST FOR CLAIMS AND REQUESTS FOR ADJUSTMENT

A. Direct Statement of the Request
1. Write a claim letter as soon as possible after the problem has been identified.
2. State the need for reimbursement or correction of the problem.
3. Maintain a confident, factual, fair, unemotional tone.

B. Justification, Explanation, and Details
1. To gain the reader's understanding, praise some aspect of the good or service, or at least explain why the product was originally purchased.
2. Present facts honestly, clearly, and politely.
3. Eliminate threats, sarcasm, exaggeration, and hostility.
4. Specify the problem: product failed to live up to advertised standards; product failed to live up to sales representative's claims; product fell short of company policy; product was defective; customer service was deficient.
5. Make no accusation against any person or company, unless you can back it up with facts.
6. Use a nonargumentative tone to show your confidence in the reader's fairness.
7. If necessary, refer to documentation (invoices, canceled checks, confirmation letters, and the like), but mail only photocopies.
8. Ask the reader to propose fair adjustment, if appropriate.
9. If appropriate, clearly state what you expect as a fair settlement, such as credit against the next order you place, full or partial refund of the purchase price of the product, replacement or repair of the defective merchandise, or performance of services as originally contracted.
10. Do not return the defective merchandise until you have been asked to do so.
11. Avoid uncertainty or vagueness that might permit the adjusters to prolong the issue by additional correspondence or to propose a less-than-fair settlement.

C. Courteous Close with Request for Specific Action
1. Summarize desired action briefly.
2. Simplify compliance with your request by including your name, address, phone number (with area code), and hours of availability.
3. Note how complying with your request will benefit the reader.

A request to buy on credit is sometimes included with a company's first-time order for goods. In such cases, the customer often sends copies of the latest financial statement along with the order letter. If the order is made by e-mail or on the Internet, indicate that financial statements are available. A company whose credit standing is good can confidently ask that the order be accepted on a credit basis. Because the main idea in this situation is to get permission to buy on credit, the letter should open with that request. Figure 8.3 is an example of the way an order may be combined with a request for credit. Note how the request for credit is supported by documentation of financial stability. In addition, the writer has encouraged a favorable response by adopting a confident tone and mentioning the probability of future business.

Order letters are often combined with a request for credit.

A request for credit
- *Is supported by documentation*
- *Adopts a confident tone*
- *Hints at future business*

INQUIRING ABOUT PEOPLE

The need to inquire about people arises often in business. For example, some companies ask applicants to supply references before awarding credit, contracts, jobs, promotions, scholarships, and so on. If you're applying for a job and your potential employer asks for references, you may want to ask a close personal or professional associate to write a letter of recommendation. Or, if you're an employer considering whether to hire an applicant, you may want to write directly to the person the applicant named as a reference. Whatever the situation, just remember that the approach to writing letters of inquiry about people is similar to the approach for requests already discussed; that is, such inquiries include a direct statement of the request (or main idea), a justification of the request (explanation of the situation with details), and a courteous close that includes a request for specific action.

Figure 8.3
In-Depth Critique: E-Mail
Message Combining an Order
with a Routine Credit Request

CrossTerrain, Inc., sells hybrid bikes (suitable on all road surfaces). This
message combines an order with a request for credit.

```
┌─────────────────────────────────────────────────────────────┐
│▒▒▒▒▒▒▒▒▒▒▒▒▒▒▒▒▒▒▒▒▒▒ E-Mail ▒▒▒▒▒▒▒▒▒▒▒▒▒▒▒▒▒▒▒▒▒▒│
├─────────────────────────────────────────────────────────────┤
```

Date: Thursday, 26 November 1998, 15:10:27, PDT
X-Sender: fapatov@CrossT.com
To: Willa Deerwalk <deerwalk@cai.com>
From: "Frank Apatov" <fapataov@ctbikes.com>
Subject: New Order
X-Info: Wolf.com

To: Ms. Willa Deerwalk
          Cycle Accessories, Inc.
          468 Montmartre Road
          Helena, Washington 45410
From: CrossTerrain, Inc.
          11549 Helena Parkway
          Helena, Washington 45442
          (918) 367-3423 Fax (918) 323-3824
Re: New Order

Dear Ms. Deerwalk:

Cycling season will soon be here, and we are planning a spring
promotion for May 1. We expect to move a large quantity of
accessories and hope you can help us by shipping the following
order by April 15:

No.	Item	Description	Price Per	Extension
25	RA335	Auto Rack Mount/Hybrid Bike	$35.00	$ 875.00
25	LT890	Headlight Assembly Kit	15.00	375.00
25	MR223	Rearview Mirror Kit	10.00	250.00
20	RF977	Reflector Set	8.00	160.00
40	WB232	Water Bottle Kit	5.00	200.00
32	RP447	Rain Poncho in Seat Pouch	12.00	384.00
		TOTAL		$2,244.00

I've attached our standard financial statement, including references.
We ask for terms of 2/10, net 30, FOB your dock. Please let me know
if you need any additional information.

Pete Weinstein at Sports West recommended you because of the
quality of your products and your record of on-time shipping.
He provided me with your catalog and price sheet. We are trying
to keep more of our orders in-state and are looking forward to
doing continued business with Cycle Accessories.

Sincerely,

Frank Apatov
Buyer

Attachment

The message starts strong with a positive statement and a possible reader benefit.

The order is clearly stated in an easy-to-read table.

Financial information necessary for granting credit accompanies the order. The message also states the terms of credit that are being requested.

Terms of 2/10 refers to a request for a 2 percent discount if the bill is paid within 10 days of receipt rather than the standard 30 days. Net 30 means that the bill is due in full within 30 days of receipt. "FOB (freight on board) your dock" means that shipping will be paid by the purchaser from the point of loading indicated, in this case, Cycle Accessories' dock.

The message ends on a positive note with a compliment to the receiver and an additional reader benefit.

On the Job

SOLVING A COMMUNICATION DILEMMA AT BARNES & NOBLE

Leonard Riggio has reached the top of the U.S. bookselling market through a combination of building huge bookstores, stocking books that interest each community, and using effective communication to reach employees and customers. Of course, top managers in any retail business must request information from store managers and other employees. Riggio is using the information he receives to help his company grow, evolve, and win the battle with competitors.

More and more book battles are being fought in "superstores," gigantic stores with up to 175,000 titles on the shelf (compared with 15,000 to 25,000 in the typical mall store). Barnes & Noble is by far the leader in superstores, with more than 430 giant outlets across the country. In addition to offering discount prices and a comprehensive selection of hardcover and paperback books, Barnes & Noble superstores regularly offer special events such as children's story hours and book signings by both locally and nationally known authors.

Riggio also maintains a strong presence in shopping malls with the B. Dalton chain, although the company is closing smaller mall stores as quickly as it adds the large superstores. The newest competitive arena is the Internet, which Riggio entered energetically in 1997 with a site called BarnesandNoble.com. The early leader in online book sales was Amazon.com, a Seattle company that offers more than a million titles through its popular Web site. Barnes & Noble, racing to catch up, eventually opened a site about the same size as Amazon.com's. "We have to be a player," says Stephen Riggio (Leonard's younger brother and the company's chief operating officer). "Online book selling is going to be a very big thing."

As a lifelong lover of books, Leonard Riggio believes that a bookstore should be a "marketplace of ideas." He wants to expose customers to a wide variety of literary works. B. Dalton's Discovery program, for example, showcases books by both new and unknown writers. The program can boost a book's sales tenfold by bringing it to the attention of customers in B. Dalton stores.

Of course, rival bookstores are also working hard to improve their communication with customers. For instance, managers at Waldenbooks know what members of their Preferred Reader Program like, so they notify the fans of mystery novels when new mysteries are available, they alert computer users about new computer books, and so on. As the book chains expand, the independents are fighting back by offering specialized books and individualized customer service. Competition is fierce, but Riggio's talent for communicating with customers and employees should keep his chain on top for a long time to come.[5]

Your Mission: You have recently taken a job as Leonard Riggio's administrative assistant. He relies on you to draft letters to Barnes & Noble store managers and outside contacts. Using the principles outlined in this chapter for writing direct requests, handle each of the following letters to the best of your ability. Be prepared to explain your choices.

1. Riggio asks you to contact the store managers to find out whether the company's new Web site is affecting sales in retail stores. Which of the following is the best opening for this letter?

   a. I have recently joined Mr. Riggio's staff as his administrative assistant. He has asked me to write to you to obtain your input on the impact of the company's new Web site on store sales. Please reply to the following questions within five working days. [List of questions follows.]

   b. Please tell us what you think of BarnesandNoble.com. Mr. Riggio is trying to evaluate its impact on our business. Within the next few days, can you take a few moments to jot down your thoughts on its impact. Specifically, Mr. Riggio would like to know . . . [List of questions follows.]

   c. By April 15, please submit written answers to the following questions on the new Barnes & Noble Web site. [List of questions follows.]

   d. Is the new Web site affecting sales in your store? We're polling all store managers for their reaction to online retailing. Is it thumbs up or thumbs down on the Web?

2. Which of the following is the best choice for the middle section of the letter?

   a. Specifically, has store business decreased since the Web site went online? If so, what is the percentage decrease in sales over the previous six months? Over the comparable period last year? Have customers mentioned the Web site? If so, have their comments been positive or negative? Has employee morale been affected by the site? How?

   b. By replying to the following questions, you will help us decide whether to continue with the Web site as is, revise it, or drop it entirely:
      1. Has business decreased in your store since the Web site went live? If it has, what is the percentage decrease in sales over the previous six months? Over the comparable period last year?
      2. Have customers mentioned the site? If so, have their comments been positive or negative? Give some typical examples.
      3. Has employee morale been affected by the Web site initiative? How?

   c. By circling the response that most accurately reflects your store's experience, please answer the following questions regarding the company's new Web site:
      1. Since the Web site went live, sales have
         a. increased
         b. decreased
         c. remained about the same
      2. Customers (have/have not) mentioned the Web site. Their comments have been primarily (positive/negative).
      3. Employee morale (has/has not) been affected by the Web site.

   d. Mr. Riggio needs to know the following: (1) How have overall store sales changed since the company's new Web site went live? (2) What do customers think of the site? Attach complimentary customer comments. (3) What do employees think of the site? Attach complimentary employee comments.

3. For a courteous close with a request for specific action, which of the following paragraphs is the best?

   a. Thank you for your cooperation. Please submit your reply in writing by April 15.

b. Mr. Riggio is meeting with his senior staff on April 17 to discuss the Web site. He would like to have your reaction in writing by April 15 so that he can present your views during that meeting. If you have any questions, please contact me at 697-2886.

c. You may contact me at 697-2886 if you have any questions or need additional information about this survey. Mr. Riggio requires your written response by April 15 so that he can discuss your views with his senior staff on April 17.

d. Thank you for your input. As the frontline troops in the battle for sales, you are in a good position to evaluate the impact of the new Web site. We here at corporate headquarters want to increase overall company sales, but we need your feedback. Please submit your written evaluation by April 15 so that Mr. Riggio can use the results as ammunition in his meeting with senior staff on April 17.

4. To promote a new line of children's books featuring Walt Disney's Mickey Mouse, Riggio has ordered 795 large cutout cardboard displays of the famous cartoon character. The Barnes & Noble warehouse has received the shipment; however, 50 of the displays are bent and cannot be used in promoting the new line of children's books. You have been asked to prepare a fax letter requesting an adjustment. Select the best version.

a. On March 25, we ordered 795 cardboard cutouts of Mickey Mouse (item #90067-C in your April catalog). When the shipment arrived last week, we discovered that 50 of the cutouts were bent. Whether the damage occurred during shipping or at your place of business, I do not know. However, I do know that we cannot use the cutouts in their present form. If you can replace them before April 25, please do so. We are withholding payment until the matter is straightened out.

b. Please call me immediately at 697-2886 to discuss a problem with the Mickey Mouse cutouts that we ordered from you. Fifty of them are bent and cannot be used in our nationwide book promotion scheduled for May 1.

Time is running short, I know, but we would really like you to replace the 50 damaged cutouts if you can do so in time for our promotion. If that is not possible, we will adjust our payment to reflect a sale of 745 cutouts as opposed to 795.

Thanks for your cooperation. The good cutouts are really cute, and we expect they will boost our book sales.

c. Of the 795 Mickey Mouse cardboard cutouts received last week, 50 are not in good condition. I inspected them myself, and several of us tried to fix the cutouts, but they don't look very good. Therefore, please replace these 50 before April 25.

d. Fifty of the Mickey Mouse cardboard cutouts that we ordered from your firm on March 25 arrived in poor condition. Can you replace them before April 25? If so, we would still like to use them in our May 1 book promotion.

I am enclosing a copy of the invoice for your convenience. As you can see, our original order was for 795 cutouts (catalog item #90067-C), priced at $5.00 each. Our bill for the total order is $4,397.50. We will send payment in full when we receive the 50 undamaged cutouts. If replacements are not available by April 25, we will send you a check for the 745 good cutouts, which we plan to use in any case. Including tax and handling costs, the adjusted total would be $4,139.50.

Would you like us to return the damaged items? Perhaps they can be salvaged for another purpose.

Please call me at 697-2886 any time this week to discuss the situation. We are eager to receive the replacement cutouts so that our bookstores can benefit from the Mickey Mouse display during our nationwide book promotion scheduled for May 1.

Critical Thinking Questions

1. Why is it important to know about any cultural differences between you and your audience when you're organizing a request?
2. For U.S. and Canadian requests, why is it inappropriate to begin your request with a brief personal introduction?
3. What precautions should be taken when writing secondary questions in a direct request? Explain what harm could be done by overlooking such precautions.
4. Which is the most important element of an order letter: the legality of the offer, the clarity of the order, or the explanation of how items will be used? Briefly explain.

5. Every time you send a direct-request memo to Ted Jackson, he's slow to answer or refuses to comply. You're beginning to get impatient. Should you send Jackson a memo to ask what's wrong? Complain to your supervisor about Jackson's uncooperative attitude? Arrange a face-to-face meeting with Jackson? Bring up the problem at the next staff meeting? Explain.
6. You have a complaint against one of your suppliers, but you have no documentation to back it up. Should you request an adjustment anyway? Why or why not?

Documents for Analysis

Read the following documents; then (1) analyze the strengths and weaknesses of each sentence and (2) revise each document so that it follows this chapter's guidelines.

DOCUMENT 8.A: REQUESTING ROUTINE INFORMATION FROM A BUSINESS

Our college is closing its dining hall for financial reasons, so we want to do something to help the students prepare their own food in their dorm rooms if they so choose. Your colorful ad in *Collegiate Magazine* caught our eye. We need the following information before we make our decision.

1. Would you be able to ship the microwaves by August 15? I realize this is short notice, but our board of trustees just made the decision to close the dining hall last week and we're scrambling around trying to figure out what to do.

2. Do they have any kind of a warranty? College students can be pretty hard on things, as you know, so we will need a good warranty.
3. How much does it cost? Do you give a discount for a big order?
4. Do we have to provide a special outlet?
5. Will students know how to use them, or will we need to provide instructions?

As I said before, we're on a tight time frame and need good information from you as soon as possible to help us make our decision about ordering. You never know what the board might come up with next. I'm looking at several other companies, also, so please let us know ASAP.

DOCUMENT 8.B: REQUESTING ROUTINE INFORMATION FROM A CUSTOMER

I'm writing to inquire about your recent order for a High Country backpack. You didn't tell us which backpack you wanted, and you know they make a lot of different ones. They have the canvas models with the plastic frames and vinyl trim and they have the canvas models with leather trim and they have the ones that have more pockets than the other ones. Plus they come in lots of different colors.

Also they make the ones that are large for a big-boned person and the smaller versions for little women or kids. So you can see why I didn't know which one to send you. Also, we have to have payment when you place your order and you didn't include a check or credit card number (we need your signature if you order by credit card).

Actually, if you could drive to our store in Eureka it would help a lot because then you could see all of them and try them on. Plus we have a lot of other neat equipment you could look at. I realize you live kind of far from here, but it would be worth the trip. If you really can't come, then you just need to do the things I mentioned and we'll get it right out to you.

Cases

PLACING ORDERS

1. Paper shortage: Memo faxed to Reliable Office Supplies Your environmental consulting company, Environmental Services, is a "microbusiness"—a small business with only one or two employees. Because most of your business is conducted by phone, fax, or modem, last year you moved out of San Diego and into the surrounding foothills.

Serene as the woods may be, your company still demands lots of your time. You are everything from CEO to janitor and cafeteria chef. That's why Reliable Office Supplies, a mail-order distributor, attracted your attention.

Reliable's catalog offered you credit, free same-day shipping, 24-hour operators, and a gift of coffee mugs and cookies with your first order. How many times had you wasted half a day trekking into the city for a ream of paper? You gave Reliable a chance. You called the 800 number on Saturday, and by Tuesday the paper was on your doorstep (along with the goodies, which you devoured at your desk). Then, a few weeks later, you received a promotional catalog bearing a special imprint on the cover:

PRIVATE SALE!!! On 8/02/98 you ordered Cascade Laser Paper. Only during the *Environmental Services Private Sale* will you see Cascade Laser Paper for $4.49 per ream. That's a great discount off the already low price on page 21. Call or fax us today! Use private sale item #735BC15161.

How could you resist? Moreover, the time you've been losing shopping for "bargains" at the discount store is costing you hundreds of dollars, whereas Reliable's pricing is sometimes only a few dimes higher.

Your Task: You plan to fax an order to Reliable. You need six reams of the Cascade Laser Paper; one carton of PM brand standard one-ply, 2¼-inch calculator rolls (stock no. 02PF8677; $46.00); one AT&T brand QS2000 high-yield laser printer toner cartridge (stock no. 02QS02000; $125.99); and one dozen 8½-by-11-inch Tops Prism brand perforated legal pads in orchid (stock no. Q2TP631, color code 40; $18.29).

You want to save the catalog's order blank, so type the information in memo form and fax it to Reliable at 1-800-326-3233. Your account number is BB5554432-999, and your address is 4888 Oak Road, Jamul, CA 91917. You don't have information on shipping charges, so request that the amount be included on your bill.[6]

2. Wakeboard mania: Letter from Performance Ski & Surf ordering more equipment Your boss is amazed. Bill Porter, owner of Performance Ski & Surf, hasn't seen sporting equipment sell this rapidly in Orlando, Florida, since in-line skating became popular. Since May, you haven't been able to keep wakeboards in stock. It doesn't seem to matter much which brand—Wake Tech, Neptune, or Full Tilt—your customers are snapping them up and heading out to the water, locals and tourists alike. Wakeboards are outselling traditional trick water skis by 20 to 1.

"Maybe it's because they don't require big, fast boats," you suggest. "I heard they're using fishing trawlers out in Seattle, and they're still catching wind because the slower boats make bigger wakes to launch from."

Porter nods thoughtfully as he gazes at a photograph of professional wakeboarder Dean Lavelle at nearby Lake Butler. He's holding the same kind of rope any water skier holds, but he's 15 feet in the air. His short, stubby, fiberglass wakeboard (which is strapped to his feet) is higher than his head and from the grimace on his face, it looks as if he's mid-flip.

"I just hope none of these kids get hurt trying to imitate the pros," Butler says.

"Nah," you say. "Extreme sports—it's the way of the 1990s. Look at what happened to snowboarding. You'll see wakeboarders at the Olympics soon."

Your Task: Butler has asked you to order another 12 Wake Techs, 8 Neptunes, and 10 Full Tilts. "Don't worry about colors or models; we'll be lucky to get this order filled at all from what I hear." He suggests that you draft a form letter for the three orders, and he'll supply the addresses and account numbers when you're finished.[7]

3. Vacation dreams: E-mail message ordering tourist information from Trinidad and Tobago

For two years, you've been slaving away at your first management job as an assistant branch manager for Bank of America. The promotion has kept you more than busy (you never realized how much overtime salaried managers are expected to put in). You're really looking forward to that two-week paid vacation you've worked so hard to earn.

"So what's it going to be?" the branch manager asked you this morning. "Hawaii or Disneyworld?"

"Huh?" you mumbled—after all, it was only 7 A.M. You caught yourself, cleared your throat, and politely answered that you hadn't decided yet. (Your vacation isn't until December, and this is a cold day in February.)

"I know your vacation is 10 months away," your manager said, "but I need to know your plans today for a report I'm filing with the head office. Just drop your first and second choices for vacation dates on my desk by 3 P.M. I'll let you know by next week how that fits into everyone else's schedule." Then she turned on her heel and strode off toward the vault.

By 3 P.M.? First and second choices? You don't even know where you're going! In the heat of desperation, an idea strikes. You hurry over to the customer waiting area, pick up a glossy copy of *Saveur* magazine, and begin flipping through the ads. You already know you don't want any ordinary vacation; you want to go somewhere exotic, somewhere tropical, like the spot where those two people are lounging in front of that plummeting waterfall. (How they got that beach umbrella to balance on the rocks, you'll never understand.) "In Tobago, Nature is in balance, as well as in abundance," reads the caption. Yes, that's it!

Your Task: Striding confidently back to your computer, you spread the ad out on your desk, call up your e-mail program, and tap in the address for ordering the *Trinidad & Tobago: Come to Life* tourist information booklet: <tourism-info@tidco.co.tt>. You can almost feel those tropical breezes warming your snow-weary bones as you type the order. Create this e-mail message and print it out for your instructor.[8]

REQUESTING ROUTINE INFORMATION AND ACTION

4. Please tell me: Request for information about a product

You're a consumer, and you've probably seen hundreds of products that you'd like to buy (if not, look at the advertisements in your favorite magazine for ideas). Choose a big-ticket item that is rather complicated, such as a stereo system or a vacation in the Caribbean.

Your Task: You surely have some questions about the features of your chosen product or about its price, guarantees, local availability, and so on. Write to the company or organization offering it, and ask four questions that are important to you. Be sure to include enough background information so that the reader can answer your questions satisfactorily.

If requested to do so by your instructor, mail a copy of your letter (after your instructor has had an opportunity to review it) to the company or organization. After a few weeks, you and your classmates may wish to compare responses and to answer this question: How well do companies or organizations respond to unsolicited inquiries?

5. Web site: E-mail message at Morning Star Enterprises requesting additional information

In southeastern Montana they call her the "contrary warrior," a tribute to her obstinate spirit and Northern Cheyenne heritage. But Suzanne Small Trusler is the best boss you've ever had. With her husband Tom, she owns the only construction company in Lame Deer, Montana, that employs strictly Northern Cheyenne workers. As new project liaison, you've been with the company for a few months, helping develop bids for new business.

It seems as if reporters are always calling for interviews. They've heard of Trusler's long fight to keep Morning Star Enterprises alive. It was tougher during the 1970s. First, she's a woman, and second, she's Native American—already two strikes against her, despite her experience and education. Then she insisted on hiring workers from the local reservation, and that really stirred up trouble.

Today the controversy and politicking are behind her, and Trusler's company is thriving. Annual revenues have topped $5 million. During peak season, Morning Star hires nearly a hundred workers. Now Trusler receives business awards and participates in high-profile conferences. Her success has encouraged other Native Americans to open their own businesses.

Last week one of your summer interns, Bob Beartracker, suggested that it was time to present Trusler with a new territory to conquer: the World Wide Web. He thinks Morning Star Enterprises should build a Web site, not only to reach potential customers but also to spread Trusler's inspiration across a wider field.

You agree. Beartracker found an advertisement for a company that creates Web sites (Webs Are Us), but the classified ad gives little information beyond a phone number and an e-mail address.

Your Task: You'll be in a strategy meeting with Trusler next week, and you need enough information to convince her of the benefits of Beartracker's idea. (You might even invite him to sit in on the meeting.) Write an e-mail message requesting more information from Webs Are Us about what the company can do for Morning Star. The e-mail address is <webs@websrus.com>.[9]

6. Shrinking vacation: E-mail to a *Los Angeles Times* advice column

"Hey," you exclaim to no one in particular after ripping open your paycheck and glancing at the stub. "They cheated me!"

LaDonna sticks her head up from the next cubicle. "What are you screaming about?"

"They ripped me off for vacation time!" you fume, waving the slip under LaDonna's nose. "Look right there, in the little square. It says I've only got 45.36 accrued hours for vacation and sick time. What happened to the 71 hours I had two weeks ago?"

Your colleague just smiles sweetly at you. "You didn't read the memo they sent around, did you?"

"What memo?" You're really not interested in memos right now. You're just wondering how soon you can get in to see the boss—or maybe you should go straight to personnel.

"The memo that explained a new company policy wherein every time we're late"—she looks at you pointedly— "and that includes late coming back from lunch, they're going to deduct the time from our sick leave and vacation time. Looks like you've been busted," she adds with a less-than-sympathetic grin.

"They can't do this to me! It's not fair!" you sputter. "I'll take it to the labor commissioner!"

"Hey, if you really think it's not fair, why don't you write in to that column in the *L.A. Times*," your colleague suggests. LaDonna always did enjoy office controversies.

"What column," you mumble morosely, resigning yourself to your fate. You've been counting in your head, and they're probably accurate with their figures. You never could get anywhere on time and you estimate you've been late about 10 times in the last 14 working days—that is, if you count the extra 15 minutes you took for lunch a few times. And you thought no one noticed!

"It's called 'Shop Talk.' Here, I have a copy. Check it out."

You look over the column and it's all about work-related problems, in a question-and-answer format. But the answers are supplied by real attorneys, working for a variety of law firms in and around southern California and specializing in employment law, employee benefits, employee rights, and so on. What harm could it do? You just might have a point of contention, because no one discussed the "tardies" with you before deducting the vacation time and you received no detailed listing of the dates and exact amounts of time you were late. Is this a legal action for an employer to take?

Your Task: Write an e-mail message to the *Los Angeles Times,* and send it to <shoptalk@latimes.com>, include your initials and home town as requested. Keep in mind the column's published request: The paper wants questions that raise issues of general interest. And don't forget its disclaimer that answers provided do not constitute legal advice. But if the attorney answering your query says your employer's action was illegal, you might have a pretty good argument for talking your way back into your vacation time.[10]

7. Resolute rodent: E-mail request about Rattie the trained electrician As a teaching assistant working at a South Dakota high school, you've heard about the NetDay2000 project, a nationwide volunteer effort to wire schools for Internet access. But today was the first time you heard about Rattie (also known as Judy's Rat), a real live rodent who's been trained to scuttle through small spaces, pulling a string that's attached to computer wire. She could be the answer to your local volunteers' worst nightmare—rooms 323 and 324 of Black Hills High School in Sioux Falls. Those are the two rooms that need the wiring most desperately if your students are going to surf the Net.

The wiring team has tried and tried again, but they haven't been able to push or pull the necessary category 5 cable through the ceiling connecting the rooms. Even if your team members could squeeze into the tight crawl space, one of them could easily slip and fall through the flimsy drop-ceiling panels. But a rat . . . that could be your answer.

Intrigued, you decide to find out whether Rattie is available for work projects outside her native California. If Rattie isn't available, maybe you can train another rat to do what she does. Perhaps you can learn how she was trained by Dr. Judy Reavis, a radiation oncologist and vice president of Hermes Systems Management in Benicia, California. Reavis apparently rescued the little rodent from a laboratory experiment. Then, as a NetDay volunteer, she learned of the problems volunteers were having stringing wire through difficult quarters. So she trained her pet rat to move through all sorts of insulation and tubing while heading toward a tapping sound that marks her destination. Traveling quickly through her task, the ro-

dent emerges to her reward, a plate of catfood, while NetDay volunteers retrieve her string and pull the attached cable along her path.

Your Task: The friend who told you about Rattie says there's a column called "Judy's Rat" that's linked to NetDay's Web site at <www.schoolwire.org>. He says it features an animated caricature of the furry celebrity and includes a section in which the techno-rodent answers kids' questions about the technology appearing in their schools (thanks to Judy Reavis and other volunteers). Check the site for an address, then compose an e-mail message phrasing your questions for the famous rat's owner. Include your telephone number and snail mail address to provide maximum reply options.[11]

8. Blockbuster shake-up: Memo from top brass requesting info from retail managers Everyone knew there was trouble at Blockbuster's new headquarters in Dallas when CEO Bill Fields, a former Wal-Mart whiz, suddenly resigned. Then Sumner Redstone and Tom Dooley (chairman and deputy chairman of Blockbuster's parent company, Viacom) flew in to assess the damage wrought by Fields's departure. They started by giving orders, particularly to you, Fields's former executive assistant.

Before he resigned to take a position with Hudson's Bay Company in Canada, Fields's strategy had been to boost Blockbuster's revenues and profits by establishing a new niche as a "neighborhood entertainment center." Using tricks he'd learned at Wal-Mart, he ordered the reconfiguration of more than 1,000 Blockbuster outlets, surrounding the cash registers with flashy displays of candy, potato chips, new and used videotapes for sale, magazines, and tie-in toys. His stated goal was to add $1 in retail purchases to every video rental transaction. Meanwhile, he also moved Blockbuster's headquarters from Florida to Dallas, losing some of the company's top staff when they declined to make the move. Then Fields started construction on an 818,000-square-foot warehouse 25 miles outside Dallas to centralize a new, sophisticated distribution operation for Blockbuster's North American outlets. But revenues were still falling.

Redstone and Dooley's new plan is to get Blockbuster back into its core business—video rentals—ignoring gloomy analysts who say satellite dishes and cheap tape sales are slowly sinking the rental industry. "This is still a healthy, growing business," Dooley insists. He believes that consumers coming in to rent videos were confused by the array of retail products in front of them. "We want people to think of Blockbuster as the place to go to rent tapes," he says.

Dooley and Redstone have brought in new management and are making changes in everything from store format to marketing and advertising to inventory control and overhead reduction. Now they've turned to you. "We've got a job you'll love," Dooley smiles. "We know you can handle it."

Your Task: "Draft a memo that will pick the brains of retail managers in the stores that Fields reconfigured," Dooley orders. "I want to know whether customers walk out when current hits aren't available, whether the emphasis on retail products affected cash flow, and whether sales and rental figures have changed now that we've ordered all that clutter out of the limelight. Ask them where the cash is coming from: tape rentals, tape sales, or candy bars? More importantly, what about profit margins? I want a full report from every manager by the end of next week!" To get that kind of cooperation, you'd better organize your questions effectively.[12]

REQUESTING CLAIMS AND ADJUSTMENTS

9. Bolga boo-boo: E-mail to Getrade (Ghana) Ltd. from Pier 1 Imports The way you heard it, in 1993 your employer, Pier 1 Imports, sent a buyer to Accra, Ghana, to find local handicrafts to slake your customers' insatiable thirst for African art. Free-market reforms in Ghana during the 1980s helped ease export procedures, but so far the Ghanaian entrepreneurs who sprang forward to take advantage of the change are having trouble meeting demand from large-quantity buyers like Pier 1 (and your rival, Cost Plus). The shipment that just arrived from Getrade (Ghana) Ltd., one of your best Ghanaian suppliers, is a good example of what's been going wrong.

Your customers love the bowl-shaped Bolga baskets woven by the Fra-fra people of northern Ghana. You can't keep them in stock. So this was to be a huge shipment—3,000 Bolga baskets. You requested baskets in the traditional Bolga shape but woven in solid colors, since your customers prefer solid to mixed colors. Getrade was to ship 1,000 green, 1,000 yellow, and 1,000 magenta. Your overseas buyer heard that the Body Shop ordered similar baskets with traditional mixed-color patterns and a flatter shape. You sympathize with Ladi Nylander, chairman and managing director of Getrade, who is trying hard to adapt to the specific tastes of his U.S. buyers. He's hiring local artisans to carve, shape, and weave all sorts of items—often from designs provided by Pier 1. Personally, you can understand how Getrade got confused. But you know Pier 1 can't sell the 3,000 mixed-color, flat Bolga baskets that you've been shipped.

Your Task: As assistant buyer, it's your job to compose the e-mail message alerting Getrade to the mix-up. You decide that if you want the mistake corrected, you'd better direct your message to Nylander at <Nylander@Getrade.co.za>. If you're lucky, it may be simply that the Body Shop's order got mixed up with yours.[13]

10. Unmannered manor: Letter requesting reimbursement from Property Vision in London As executive assistant to Barry Lansdon, CEO of Lansdon Holdings, you often handle routine letter-writing tasks. But this situation is stretching your abilities.

Last May, Lansdon decided to invest in some property in Great Britain. He'd heard that some of the most historically significant manor houses were on the market, and the notion of joining the landed British gentry—even part-time—fired his imagination. He contacted the people at Property Vision of London (with your help), and they replied with a dozen suggestions, including Testcombe Manor in Chilbolton, Hampshire (US$2.8 million), where Edward VII once halted his private train to go fishing. You liked the seventeenth-century farmhouse in Kent (US$625,000), but it was Huns-

don House that caught your employer's fancy: The 87-acre estate (US$2.8 million) had supposedly been Henry VIII's hunting lodge.

When Lansdon and his wife flew over to inspect this genuine Tudor mansion, they suffered quite a shock. The kingly aura conferred by wall-mounted rhinoceros trophies and wallpaper flecked with real gold was impressive. But only one-quarter of the building could ever have heard Henry VIII's footsteps. It turned out that Hunsdon House had been demolished, then rebuilt in the 1700s—nearly two centuries after Henry's death. Moreover, the Lansdons discovered that "medieval" also applied to the plumbing system. They learned that insurers would require them to hire a full-time caretaker (at US$40,000 a year), and the sheer size of the estate demanded a butler (US$55,000), a housekeeper (US$35,000), and a gardener (US$35,000) to keep the spectacular gardens in bloom. And, if the Lansdons stayed for more than 90 days a year, they'd have to pay British taxes to boot.

"We never would have made the trip if they'd told us even half of this," Mr. Lansdon sighed as he handed you a folder. "I think we have every right to ask for a reimbursement. You'll find an itemized expense list inside."

Your Task: Write the claim letter to Mr. William Gething of Property Vision, 36 Brock Street, London, England W1Y 1AD, UK (Voice: 0171-493-4944, Fax: 0171-491-2548).[14]

11. Follow that lead: E-mail message requesting information on Patagonia Your editor has asked you to gather information for a business profile about a unique company that would interest the local businesses. One such company, Patagonia, has created quite a stir in the business community, and you want to find out more about it.

Your Task: Explore Patagonia's Web site, <http://www.patagonia.com/menu/htm>. While you're online, get any information you can for the profile: Where is the company headquarters located? What is the company best known for? What types of stores carry Patagonia's products? What products does Patagonia offer? Where are Patagonia dealers? Finally, request product information by linking to the online guide service, sign the guest registry, order a Patagonia catalog, and send an e-mail message requesting further information.

MAKING ROUTINE CREDIT REQUESTS

12. Beanie Babies: Letter requesting credit from Ty, Inc. Bubbles (the fish), Inch (the worm), Ziggy (the zebra)—if you hear another parent ask for them, you're going to walk out the door of Sandy's Gifts and never return. No, not really. You love the brightly colored, fuzzy little bean-bag toys as much as anyone, but you hate seeing adults look as disappointed as their kids when you tell them you don't carry them.

"You mean you don't even have Bongo the monkey or Pinky the flamingo?"

"Sorry, not yet," you apologize. "But we've had so many requests, we're hoping to have them in stock soon. If you leave your name and phone number . . ."

Sandy Applegate, the store's owner, is sympathetic when you tell her what's been happening, but she doesn't know what to do. Her cash flow situation just doesn't allow for any new stock purchases until after Christmas. Who would have thought the $5 bean-bag animals (called "Beanie Babies" by manufacturer Ty, Inc.) would be so popular?

"But think of the sales we're missing," you interject. "Won't they give you credit?"

"Well, we've never done business with them before," Sandy says thoughtfully, "but you might have a point. After all, Sandy's Gifts

rected by Kenneth Branagh. You have to get authentic-looking food for 150 actors ready by shooting time—tomorrow at 1 P.M.

McComb is a pro, and you have full confidence in her as she races about the office, handing out assignments to a cluster of nervous assistants. You know that she knows what to do with a banquet for 150 if the shooting is canceled at the last moment (feed it to friends), and how to handle temperamental ingredients (avoid them) and star-quality special requests (indulge them if the budget's right). She previously created a circa-1948 wedding banquet for Branagh's *Dead Again.* After four days of shooting, her fancy tower of cheeses melted into what McComb called a "*quesadilla muerte.*" Then Branagh cut the scene from the movie anyway. For *Apollo 13,* McComb spent a full week recreating a 1969 picnic complete with hams and Jello-molds, and for *Star Trek: The Next Generation,* she found puffy green cakes at an Oriental market that earned her fame as the inventor of "algae puff hors d'oevres."

Zipping by your desk, McComb tosses you a catalog of food retailers, blurting only one word, "Asparagus." Thank goodness the set is in Hollywood, not London. She means asparagus for 150, and luckily most of your produce suppliers are in California. Flipping through the pages, you come across Mr. Spear, a grower/shipper in the San Joaquin Valley who specializes in overnight retail shipments of jumbo spears, picked in the morning, shipped in the afternoon, on your table the next day—three pounds for $16.95, plus shipping. Quick work with your calculator tells you that you need about 75 pounds, or $424 worth, if you have to pay retail. It's already noon.

You've never worked with Mr. Spear before, but you need the grower to ship the asparagus without prepayment in order to get it to McComb's kitchens by 10 A.M. tomorrow. Standard office practice is to ask for a wholesale price and free shipping when ordering such large amounts. But if those terms aren't available, you'll pay full retail price as long as Mr. Spear can meet the deadline. You'll have to pass on the extra cost to Branagh's ever-growing production budget.

Your Task: Mr. Spear's people will want to review Meg McComb's credentials before they'll ship on credit, so you'd better fax your request immediately and include a copy of McComb's highly impressive client list. Call the number they list in the catalog, 1-800-677-7327, to get the fax number.[16]

has been in business for almost ten years, at the same location. How many retail shops can say that today? And our credit with other vendors is excellent. Why don't you give it a try? You've been wanting to learn more about managing the store, haven't you?"

She's right. This is a great opportunity!

Your Task: Write a letter for Sandy's signature to New Account Sales, Ty, Inc., P.O. Box 5377, Oakbrook, Illinois 60522, requesting credit to purchase two dozen Beanie Babies. Introduce the store, its reputation, and the reasons Ty might like to comply.[15]

13. Please, Mr. Spear: Fax requesting credit for movie-scene banquet ingredients A few months ago you landed the most exciting job you could imagine, as a production assistant for Meg McComb, one of the best known movie food stylists in Hollywood. But some days it's just a little too exciting. Like today, your boss has been hired to concoct a twelfth-century feast for a period costume drama di-

DEVELOPING YOUR INTERNET SKILLS
GOING ONLINE: EXPAND YOUR KNOWLEDGE ABOUT CREDIT, P. 163

Explore the links on this site to learn about business credit. What does a business credit "snapshot" include? Reviewing the "Business 101" page and the sample business credit snapshot report probably made you more aware of credit-foolish mistakes a business can make. How might this information help you in future evaluations of the risk involved in offering credit to a potential client or customer? How will you incorporate this knowledge in any credit refusal letters you might need to write?

9

Chapter

After studying this chapter, you will be able to

Decide when to write a routine, good-news, or goodwill message

Adjust the basic organizational pattern to fit the type of message you are writing

Add resale and sales promotion material when appropriate

Encourage your reader to take any desired action

Write credit approvals and recommendation letters

Use the correct form for such specialized messages as instructions and news releases

Establish the proper tone when writing goodwill letters

WRITING ROUTINE, GOOD-NEWS, AND GOODWILL MESSAGES

On the Job

FACING A COMMUNICATION DILEMMA AT CAMPBELL SOUP COMPANY

Keeping Millions of People Happy, One Spoonful at a Time

You might say that Karen Donohue is in the problem business. As supervisor of consumer response at Campbell Soup Company, she's in charge of answering consumer questions and responding to consumer complaints, both of which require strong communication skills and a special talent for working with people.

Working with customers can be a challenge in any business, but consider the size of Campbell's customer base. Every second of every hour, consumers around the world buy 100 packages of Campbell's soups and other products—that's more than 8.6 million purchases every single day. In addition to the well-known soup brands, Campbell's markets Pace picante sauce, Pepperidge Farm cookies, Prego pasta sauces, V8 vegetable juice, Franco-American pasta, and Spaghetti-Os, among others. Walk into just about any kitchen in the country, and you'll find a Campbell's brand on the shelf.

Campbell has a history of high-quality products stretching back nearly to the Civil War. Soup sales took off after 1897, when an executive in the company, who was also a chemist, figured out how to remove most of the water from soup, making it easier and cheaper to ship long distances. This distribution advantage helped Campbell become one of the first U.S. companies to market products nationwide.

Campbell stumbled a bit during the 1980s, thanks in part to changing consumer tastes and some diversification efforts away from the core business lines. However, with new products tailored to local markets, new management, and a narrower focus on key products, Campbell has been back on track through the late 1990s.

Now the challenge is to maintain that healthy growth as the company continues to hold its own in the United States and to grow overseas. As one of Campbell's leading in-house consumer advocates, Donohue is an important link between the public and the research kitchens. As the company's eyes and ears, she's in a key position to relay information back to the company while at the same time making sure consumers are satisfied with Campbell's products. If you were Karen Donohue, how would you communicate with the public to answer their inquiries and complaints? How would you plan and write positive business messages?[1]

ORGANIZING POSITIVE MESSAGES

As Campbell Soup's Karen Donohue understands, most business communication consists of messages that present neutral information, answer requests positively, and establish positive relationships, so you'll probably get a lot of practice composing these **routine, good-news,** and **goodwill messages.** Whether you use letters, memos, e-mail, or phone, understanding how positive messages are organized will allow you to compose excellent examples quickly. Of course, as Campbell's Karen Donohue knows, intercultural positive messages are best when organized according to the audience's expectations, but when you're communicating with a U.S. or Canadian audience, whose cultural differences are minimal, use the direct plan. Whether written or oral, positive messages begin with a clear statement of the main idea, followed by any necessary details, and they end with a courteous close.

In an effort to promote company products as wholesome food that tastes good, the people at Campbell Soup Company do their very best to communicate positive messages to consumers. They also strive to maintain good relationships with fellow employees and outside contacts. All these messages focus on clearly stating the main idea while showing a genuine understanding of the audience.

Clear Statement of the Main Idea

Almost all business communication has two basic purposes: (1) to convey information and (2) to produce in the audience a favorable (or at least accepting) attitude or response. When you begin a message with a statement of your purpose, you're preparing your audience for the explanation that follows. Make your opening clear and concise. The following introductory statements make the same point; however, one is cluttered with unnecessary information that buries the purpose, whereas the other is brief and to the point:

INSTEAD OF THIS	WRITE THIS
I am pleased to inform you that after deliberating the matter carefully, our human resources committee has recommended you for appointment as a staff accountant.	You've been selected to join our firm as a staff accountant, beginning March 20.

The best way to write a clear opening is to have a clear idea of what you want to say. Before you put one word on paper, ask yourself this: What is the single most important message I have for this audience?

Necessary Details

The middle part of a positive message is typically the longest section of a routine, good-news, or goodwill message. Your reason for communicating can usually be expressed in a sentence or two, but you'll need more space or time to explain your point completely so that your audience will have no confusion or lingering doubt. The task of providing necessary details is easiest when you're responding to a series of questions. You can simply answer them in order, possibly in a numbered sequence.

In addition to providing details in the middle section, maintain the supportive tone established at the beginning. This tone is easy to continue when your message is purely good news, as in this example:

Your educational background and internship have impressed us, and we believe you would be a valuable addition to Green Valley Properties. As discussed during your interview, your salary will be $3,300 per month, plus benefits. In that regard, you will meet with our benefits manager, Paula Sanchez, at 8:00 A.M. on Monday, March 20. She will assist you with all the paperwork necessary to tailor our benefit package to your family situation. She will also arrange for various orientation activities to help you acclimate to our company.

Organizational plan for routine, good-news, and goodwill messages:

- Main point
- Details
- Close

Before you begin, have a clear idea of what you want to say.

Answer questions in the order they were asked.

BEHIND THE SCENES AT CITIBANK
Solving Problems, Saving Business

Jane Wolchonok is the director of service quality for the Northeast division of Citibank's Consumer Banking Group. She and her nine-member executive communications department handle the most serious and complicated service problems arising in the 230 regional branches in the New York metropolitan area. Here's what usually happens: A Citibank customer has a problem and is dissatisfied with the resolution or the lack of a resolution. The customer complains to a Citibank senior manager, and the complaint winds up in Wolchonok's department. Wolchonok not only oversees the handling of such problems but also sets service quality priorities for the division. In addition, she's responsible for monitoring the execution of various service programs.

"I wouldn't call our correspondence routine," Wolchonok quickly points out. "Anytime you deal with a person's money, tensions are heightened. Our responses to customer complaints must be prompt and correct, and they must address each customer's specific problem, which means our letters are anything but routine."

The events causing the problems aren't routine, either. And they're not usually the customer's fault. For example, "One of our customers made a $20,000 payment to reduce a credit line, but his account was credited with only $200. We investigated his complaint, found he was correct, and restored the missing $19,800—with interest. We not only wrote a letter telling the customer we had corrected the problem, but we also sent along a small gift. Because of the size of the error, we wanted to emphasize the fact that we really regretted what had happened." On another occasion, a man's deposits were unaccounted for on three occasions over a six-month period. "First," says Wolchonok, "mislaying a deposit is a rare occurrence. Second, each lost deposit was in the same amount. It turned out that when the customer deposited his paycheck, he was writing his branch number in the space intended for his account number. Some processors caught it, but others didn't. When we didn't, the funds were misallocated."

Although some situations may be similar, Wolchonok doesn't use form letters. "Of course, we've developed some paragraphs we've come to rely on from time to time. But we customize every response to the spirit in which the customer has contacted us. We begin with a welcoming and orienting comment. In the case of the missing credit line payment, we might begin, 'Thank you for your letter to our chairman letting us know about our error with your line of credit.' That reminds our readers what we're writing about. In addition, I feel

In addition to being a gifted co-median, television superstar, and creator of highly successful TV series, Bill Cosby is also a popular Hollywood spokesperson, a respected author, and a top stage performer. He's dealt with difficult public scrutiny, being forced to handle personal traumas in the spotlight, but his passion to change the images of African Americans in the media has not diminished. Such positive messages, says Cosby, must be based on fact and performance if they are to create a lasting impact.

When a routine message must convey mildly disappointing information, put the negative answer into as favorable a context as possible. Look at the following example:

INSTEAD OF THIS	WRITE THIS
No, we no longer carry the Sportsgirl line of sweaters.	The new Olympic line has replaced the Sportsgirl sweaters that you asked about. Olympic features a wider range of colors and sizes and more contemporary styling.

A bluntly negative explanation was replaced with a more complete description that emphasized how the audience could benefit from the change. Be careful, though: You can use negative information in this type of message only if you're reasonably sure the audience will respond positively to your message. (Otherwise, use the indirect approach, which is described more thoroughly in Chapter 10.)

Courteous Close

Your message is most likely to succeed if your audience is left with the feeling that you have their personal welfare in mind. In addition, if follow-up action is required, clearly state who will do what next. By highlighting a benefit to the audience, this closing statement clearly summarizes the desired procedure: "Mail us your order this week so that you can be wearing your Shetland coat by the first of October."

REPLYING TO REQUESTS FOR INFORMATION AND ACTION

Whether sent by snail mail, fax, or e-mail, many memos and letters are written in response to an inquiry or a request. If the answer is yes or is straightforward information,

In response to customer inquiries and complaints, the Northeast Division of Citibank's Consumer Banking Group creates some 6,000 letters a year.

that taking responsibility for the error in the opening statement builds a bond between the customer and the bank. We go on to spell out the action we've taken, explaining why we've done things that way." Wolchonok also insists on a courteous close to point out that Citibank does not consider the customer's recent experience an acceptable level of service: "We made it clear to the fellow with the missing deposits, for example, that we held our own people accountable for catching his error."

Wolchonok's department creates approximately 6,000 letters a year, 90 percent of which deal with problem situations.

"Of those," Wolchonok estimates, "90 percent are favorably disposed of. That is, we resolve the situation to the customer's satisfaction. Our goal is nothing less than to restore the confidence of the customer in the bank." So Wolchonok and her people make the unusual routine. "We know we've done our job right when a customer writes to thank us and to say that, based on his experience, he'd recommend Citibank to anyone." That's as good as goodwill gets in business today.

Apply Your Knowledge

1. Wolchonok has asked you to respond to an inquiry from a large depositor demanding to know why you closed a branch in her neighborhood. Outline the key points of your letter, and write the opening paragraph in the Citibank model.

2. The editor of a foreign-language newspaper (which serves a close-knit community where there are two busy branches) has written to Citibank's board members, pressing them to advertise in his publication. He states that he has a great deal of influence in the community, and he implies that he will use it against the bank if his request is not honored. How would you respond? Outline the key points of your letter, and write the opening paragraph.

---

then the direct plan is appropriate. Any request is important to the person making it, whether inside or outside the organization. That person's opinion of your company and its products, your department, and you yourself will be influenced by how promptly, graciously, and thoroughly you handle the request. Readers' perceptions are the reason Campbell's Karen Donohue is so sensitive to the tone of her memos, letters, and other messages.

Admittedly, complying with a request isn't always easy. The information may not be immediately at hand, and decisions to take some action must often be made at a higher level. Furthermore, because a letter written on letterhead stationery is legally binding, plan your response carefully.

> When written on letterhead stationery, a reply legally commits the company to any promised action.

Fortunately, however, many requests are similar. For example, a human resources department gets a lot of inquiries about job openings. Companies usually develop form responses to handle repetitive queries like these. Although form responses are often criticized as being cold and impersonal, you can put a great deal of thought into wording them, and you can use computers to personalize and mix paragraphs. Thus a computerized form letter prepared with care may actually be more personal and sincere than a quickly dictated, hastily typed "personal" reply.

When a Potential Sale Is Involved

Prospective customers often request an annual report, a catalog, a brochure, a swatch of material, or some other type of sample or information to help them make a decision about a product learned about through advertising. A polite and helpful response may prompt them to buy. When the customer has not requested the information and is not looking forward to a response, you must use persuasive techniques like those described in Chapter 11. But in a "solicited" letter that the customer is anticipating, you may use the direct plan.

When you're answering requests and a potential sale is involved, you have three main goals: (1) to respond to the inquiry and answer all questions, (2) to encourage the future

Three main goals when a potential sale is involved:

- Respond to the immediate request
- Encourage a sale
- Convey a good impression of you and your firm

sale, and (3) to leave your reader with a good impression of you and your firm. The following letter succeeds in meeting those three objectives:

You requested a copy of our brochure "Entertainment Unlimited," and Blue Ocean Communications is pleased to send it to you. This booklet describes the vast array of entertainment options available to you with an Ocean Satellite Device (OSD).

A clear, conversational statement of the main point is all that's required to start.

On page 12 of "Entertainment Unlimited," you'll find a list of the 138 channels that the OSD brings into your home. You'll have access to movie, sport, and music channels; 24-hour news channels; local channels; and all the major television networks. OSD gives you a clearer picture and more precise sound than those old-fashioned dishes that took up most of your yard—and OSD uses only a small dish that mounts easily on your roof.

Key information is presented immediately, along with resale and sales promotion.

More music, more cartoons, more experts, more news, and more sports are available to you with OSD than with any other cable or satellite connection in this region. Yes, it's all there, right at your fingertips.

Referencing this product's superior benefits encourages readers to take one more step toward purchase.

Just call us at 1-800-786-4331, and an OSD representative will come to your home to answer your questions. You'll love the programming and the low monthly cost. Call us today!

The personal close confidently points toward the sale.

When No Potential Sale Is Involved

Two goals when no sale is involved:

- Respond to the request
- Leave a favorable impression of your company or foster good working relationships

Some requests from outsiders and most requests from fellow employees are not opportunities to sell a product. In replies to those requests, you have two goals: (1) to answer all the questions honestly and completely and (2) to leave a favorable impression that prepares the way for future business or smoothes working relationships. Figure 9.1 is an e-mail message responding to requests from fellow employees. See the Checklist for Positive Replies to review the primary tasks involved in this type of business message.

RESPONDING FAVORABLY TO CLAIMS AND ADJUSTMENT REQUESTS

In general, it pays to give customers the benefit of the doubt.

As anyone in business knows, customers sometimes return merchandise to a company, complain about its services, ask to be compensated, and the like. Such complaints are golden opportunities for companies to build customer loyalty.[2] The most sensible reaction is to assume that the customer's account of the transaction is an honest statement of what happened—unless the same customer repeatedly submits dubious claims, a customer is patently dishonest (returning a dress that has obviously been worn, claiming it's the wrong size), or the dollar amount in dispute is very large. Few people go to the trouble of requesting an adjustment unless they actually have a problem. Once the complaint is made,

This message is a reply that the advertising director wrote to a house-wares manager whose merchandise wasn't being featured correctly in regional newspaper ads. The tone of the memo, although respectful, is less formal than the tone would be in a message in which a potential sale is involved.

Figure 9.1
In-Depth Critique: E-Mail Replying to a Routine Request

```
================= E-Mail =================

Date: Tuesday, 5 January 1999, 10:15:32
X-Sender: wsimmons@west.woolworth.com
To: "Avery Mendoza, Housewares Manager"
<amendoza@lvn.woolworth.com>
From: "Wilimina Simmons" <wsimmons@west.woolworth.com>
Subject: Sale ads for 12-ounce glass tumblers
```

Dear Avery Mendoza:

At last we've traced the problem and have corrected the newspaper ads you alerted us to in your last message:

1. Incorrect stock numbers have been corrected and cross-checked on all paperwork, both at the main warehouse and in advertising.

2. The ads that mistakenly featured 20-ounce glass tumblers have been revised to feature the 12-ounce glass tumblers you intended.

3. Ad layout people have been alerted to prevent future discrepancies by getting department managers' approval before printing.

Apparently, the housewares vendor transposed the item numbers for these glasses on the packing slips, and the error made its way all the way through inventory at our main warehouse and onto our stock-number sheets here in the advertising department. So every time you sent us your weekly features for 12-ounce glass tumblers (stock number HW779-898), our layout people traced the number on our stock sheets and mistakenly came up with 20-ounce tumblers.

I know you had to sell the more expensive 20-ounce tumblers for the 12-ounce sale price until we could get the ads corrected. I'm sending a message to your store manager, explaining the mix-up and taking full responsibility for it. If there is any way I can help you with ad features in the future, please contact me.

Thanks,

Wilimina Simmons
Regional Advertising Director

The good news is announced without any fanfare, and the specific actions are enumerated for easy reference.

The problem's cause and eventual solution are explained to demonstrate awareness and goodwill.

An appreciative, personal, cooperative close confirms the desire to foster good working relationships.

CHECKLIST FOR POSITIVE REPLIES

A. Initial Statement of the Good News or Main Idea
1. Respond promptly to the request.
2. Indicate in your first sentence that you are shipping the customer's order or fulfilling the reader's request.
3. Avoid such trite and obvious statements as "I am pleased to," "We have received," "This is in response to," or "Enclosed please find."
4. If you are acknowledging an order, summarize the transaction.
   - a. Describe the merchandise in general terms.
   - b. Express appreciation for the order and the payment, if they have arrived.
   - c. Welcome a new customer aboard.
5. Convey an upbeat, courteous, you-oriented tone.

B. Middle, Informational Section
1. Imply or express interest in the request.
2. If possible, answer all questions and requests, preferably in the order posed.
   - a. Adapt replies to the reader's needs.
   - b. Indicate what you have done and will do.
   - c. Include any details or interpretations that the reader may need in order to understand your answers.
3. Provide all the important details about orders.
   - a. Provide any necessary educational information about the product.
   - b. Provide details of the shipment, including the approximate arrival time.
   - c. Clear up any questions of charges (shipping costs, insurance, credit charges, or discounts for quick payment).
4. Use sales opportunities when appropriate.
   - a. Enclose a brochure that provides routine information and specifications, if possible, pointing out its main value and the specific pages of potential interest to the reader.
   - b. Call the customer's attention to related products with sales promotion material.
   - c. Introduce price only after mentioning benefits, but make price and the method of payment clear.
   - d. Send a credit application to new customers and cash customers, if desirable.
5. If you cannot comply with part of the request, perhaps because the information is unavailable or confidential, tell the reader why and offer other assistance.
6. Embed negative statements in positive contexts, or balance them with positive alternatives.

C. Warm, Courteous Close
1. Avoid clichés ("Please feel free to").
2. Direct a request to the reader (such as "Please let us know if this procedure does not have the effect you're seeking") or specify the action you want the reader to take, if appropriate.
   - a. Make the reader's action easy.
   - b. Refer to the reader benefit of fulfilling your request.
   - c. Encourage the reader to act promptly.
3. Use resale material when acknowledging orders to remind the reader of benefits to be derived from this order.
4. Offer additional service, but avoid suggestions of your answer's being inadequate, such as "I trust that," "I hope," or other doubtful statements.
5. Express goodwill or take an optimistic look into the future, if appropriate.

however, customers may come to view the original transaction as less important than the events that come after the complaint.[3]

The usual human response to a bad situation is to say, "It wasn't my fault!" However, businesspeople like Karen Donohue who receive requests for claims or adjustments can't take that stance. Even when the company's terms of adjustment are generous, a grudging tone can actually increase the customer's dissatisfaction.

An ungracious adjustment may increase customer dissatisfaction.

To protect your company's image and to regain the customer's goodwill, refer to your company's errors carefully. Don't blame an individual or a specific department, and avoid such lame excuses as "Nobody's perfect" or "Mistakes will happen." Don't promise that problems will never happen again; such guarantees are unrealistic and often beyond your control. Instead, explain your company's efforts to do a good job; in so doing, you imply that the error was an unusual incident.

Imagine that a large mail-order clothing company has decided to create a form letter to respond to the hundreds of claims it receives each year. The most common customer complaint is not receiving exactly what was ordered. The form letter can be customized through word processing and is individually signed:

Your letter concerning your recent Klondike order has arrived and has been forwarded to our director of order fulfillment. Your complete satisfaction is our goal; when you are satisfied, then we are satisfied. Our customer service representative will contact you soon to assist with the issues raised in your letter.

Whether you are skiing or driving a snowmobile, Klondike Gear offers you the best protection from wind, snow, and cold—and Klondike has been taking care of your outdoor needs for over 27 years! Because you're a loyal customer, enclosed is a $5 gift certificate. You may wish to consider our new line of quality snow goggles.

Thank you for taking the time to write to us. Your input helps us better serve you and all our customers.

This letter exemplifies the following points:

- Because a form letter like this is sent to people with various types of requests or complaints, it cannot start with a clear good-news statement.
- The letter starts instead with what might be called a "good attitude" statement; it is you-oriented to put the customer at ease.
- At no time does this letter suggest that the customer was mistaken in writing to Klondike about the order in question.
- The letter includes some resale and sales promotion, made more personal by the use of *you*.
- The letter closes with a statement of the company's concern for all its customers.

You may send form letters in response to claims, but word them carefully so that they are appropriate in a variety of circumstances.

A claim letter written as a personal answer to a unique situation would start with a clear statement of the good news: the settling of the claim according to the customer's request. Here is a more personal response from Klondike Gear:

Here is your heather-blue wool-and-mohair sweater (size large) to replace the one returned to us with a defect in the knitting on the left sleeve. Thanks for giving us the opportunity to correct this situation. Customers' needs have come first at Klondike Gear for 27 years. Our sweaters are handmade by the finest knitters in this area, and Klondike inspects all our sweaters before sending them on to our customers.

Our newest catalog is enclosed. Browse through it, and see what wonderful new colors and patterns we have for you. Whether you are skiing or driving a snowmobile, Klondike Gear offers you the best protection available from wind, snow, and cold. Let us know how we may continue to serve you and your sporting needs.

Say that a customer is technically wrong (he washed a permanent-press shirt in hot water) but feels he's right ("The washing instructions were impossible to find!"). Remember that refusing to make an adjustment may mean losing that customer as well as many of the customer's friends, who will hear only one side of the dispute. It makes sense, therefore, to weigh the cost of making the adjustment against the cost of losing future business from one or more customers.

✓✓✓✓
✓✓✓
✓✓
✓✓✓
✓✓✓
✓✓✓✓
✓✓✓
✓✓✓
✓✓✓✓
✓✓✓
✓✓✓✓
✓✓✓
✓✓
✓✓✓
✓✓✓
✓✓✓✓
✓✓✓
✓✓✓✓
✓✓✓
✓✓✓✓
✓✓✓
✓✓✓✓

CHECKLIST FOR FAVORABLE RESPONSES TO CLAIMS AND ADJUSTMENT REQUESTS

A. Initial Statement of the Good News or Main Idea
1. State immediately your willingness to honor the reader's claim.
2. Accept your reader's account as entirely accurate unless good business reasons demand a different interpretation of some points.
3. Adopt a tone of consideration and courtesy; avoid being defensive, recriminatory, or condescending.
4. Thank the reader for taking the time to write.

B. Middle, Informational Section
1. Minimize or, if possible, omit any disagreements with your reader's interpretation of events.
2. Maintain a supportive tone through such phrases as "Thank you for," "May we ask," "Please let us know," and "We are glad to work with you."
3. Apologize only under extreme circumstances; then do so crisply and without an overly apologetic tone.
4. Admit your firm's faults carefully.
   ◼ a. Avoid blaming any particular person or office.
   ◼ b. Avoid implying general company inefficiency.
   ◼ c. Avoid blaming probability ("Mistakes will happen").
   ◼ d. Avoid making unrealistic promises about the future.
   ◼ e. Remind the reader of your firm's quality controls.
5. Be careful when handling the customer's role in producing the problem.
   ◼ a. If appropriate, honor the claim in full but without negative comment.
   ◼ b. If appropriate, provide an objective, non-vindictive, impersonal explanation.

C. Warm, Courteous Close
1. Clarify any necessary actions that your reader must take.
2. Remind the reader of how you have honored the claim.
3. Avoid negative information.
4. Encourage the customer to look favorably on your company and/or the product in question (resale information).
5. Encourage the customer to continue buying other goods from you (sales promotion), but avoid seeming greedy.

When complying with an unjustified claim, let the customer know that the merchandise was mistreated, but maintain a respectful and positive tone.

Three options when a third party is at fault:

- Honor the claim
- Honor the claim with an explanation of what went wrong
- Refer the customer to the third party for satisfaction of the claim

If you choose not to contest the claim, start off with a statement of the good news: You're replacing the merchandise or refunding the purchase price. The explanatory section needs more attention, however. Your job is to make the customer realize that the merchandise was mistreated without falling into a tone that is condescending ("Perhaps you failed to read the instructions carefully") or preachy ("Next time, please allow the machine to warm up before using it at full power"). Keep in mind that a courteous tone is especially important to the success of your message, regardless of the solution you propose.

At times a customer will submit a legitimate claim for a defect or damage that was not caused by either of you. If the merchandise was damaged while in transit, the carrier is responsible. If the defect was caused by the manufacturer, you have a claim for replacement from that firm.

When a third party is at fault, you have three options: (1) Honor the customer's claim with the standard good-news letter and no additional explanation; (2) honor the claim but explain that you were not really at fault; or (3) take no action on the claim and suggest that your customer file against the firm that caused the defect or damage. Common business sense tells you, however, that the third option is almost always a bad choice. (The exception is when you're trying to dissociate yourself from any legal responsibility for the damaged merchandise, especially if it has caused a personal injury, in which case you would send a bad-news message.)

Of the other two options, the first is more attractive. By honoring the claim without explanation, you are maintaining your reputation for fair dealing at no cost to yourself; the carrier or manufacturer that caused the damage in the first place will reimburse you. (To review the tasks involved in this type of message, see this chapter's Checklist for Favorable Responses to Claims and Adjustment Requests.)

APPROVING ROUTINE CREDIT REQUESTS

These days much of our economy runs on credit. Consumers often carry a wallet full of plastic credit cards, and businesses of all sizes operate more smoothly because they can pay for their purchases over time. Because credit is so common, most credit requests are routine.

Letters approving credit are good-news messages and the first step in what may be a decades-long business relationship. So open your letter with the main idea.

In the middle section, include a reasonably full statement of the credit arrangements: the upper limit of the account, dates that bills are sent, possible arrangements for partial monthly payments, discounts for prompt payments, interest charges for unpaid balances, and due dates. State the terms positively and objectively, not negatively or in an authoritarian manner:

State credit terms factually and in terms of the benefits of having credit.

INSTEAD OF THIS	WRITE THIS
Your credit balance cannot exceed $5,000.	With our standard credit account, you can order up to $5,000 worth of fine merchandise.
We expect your payment within 30 days of receipt of our statement.	Payment is due 30 days after you receive our statement.

Because the letter approving credit is considered a legal document, check the wording for accuracy, completeness, and clarity.

The final section of the letter provides resale information and sales promotion highlighting the benefits of buying from you. The following letter was written both to approve credit and to bring in customers:

Include resale and sales promotion information in a credit letter.

Congratulations! Your credit application to Jake's Building Center has been approved, with $3,000 in credit available to you. Just use the enclosed card when you shop at any of our three Jake's Building Centers. With this card, you can purchase tools, appliances, paint, plumbing and electrical supplies, lawn products, and much more.

The good-news opening gets right to the point.

Our statements are sent out on the twentieth of each month and will list each credit purchase, the total amount due, and the monthly payment due. If you pay the total amount by the fifteenth of the following month, no interest is charged. If you elect to pay the smaller monthly amount, interest will be calculated at the rate of 1 1/2 percent on the amount still owed and added to your next statement.

An objective statement of the terms constitutes a legal contract. Positive, you-oriented wording avoids an authoritarian tone.

Jake's Building Centers are located in Murphysboro, Pinkneyville, and Carbondale, Illinois, with free delivery within 50 miles of each store. Come to us for everything you need to build, repair, or remodel your home or business. Count on our high quality and low prices whenever you purchase one of our top-of-the-line products. Come see us for your next building project!

The courteous close provides resale for the store and sales promotion noting a range of customer benefits.

CHECKLIST FOR CREDIT APPROVALS

A. Initial Statement of the Good News or Main Idea

1. Cheerfully tell the reader that he or she now has approved credit with your firm.
2. Tell the reader, with brief resale, that he or she will soon be enjoying the use of any goods that were ordered with the request; specify the date and method of shipment and other purchase details.
3. Establish a tone of mutual warmth and trust.

B. Middle, Informational Section

1. Explain the conditions under which credit was granted.
2. Include or attach a full explanation of your firm's credit policies and expectations of payment.
3. Stress the advantages of prompt payment in a way that assumes your reader will take advantage of them ("When you pay your account in full within ten days . . .").
4. Include legally required disclosure statements.
5. Inform or remind the reader of the general benefits of doing business with your firm (resale).
   - a. Tell the consumer about free parking, mail and phone shopping, personalized shopping services, your home-decorating bureau, bridal consultants, restaurants, child care, gift wrapping, free deliveries, special discounts or purchase privileges, and other benefits, if your firm offers them.
   - b. If the customer is a retailer or wholesaler, tell about nearby warehouses, factory representatives, quantity discounts, free window or counter displays, national advertising support, ads for local newspapers and other media, repair services, manuals, factory guarantees, prompt and speedy deliveries, toll-free phone number, research department, and other benefits, if your firm offers them.
6. Inform or remind the reader of a special sale, discount, or promotion (sales promotion).
7. Avoid exaggerations or flamboyant language that might make this section of your letter read like an advertisement.

C. Warm, Courteous Close

1. Summarize the reasons the reader will enjoy doing business with your firm.
2. Use the "you" attitude, and avoid clichés.
3. Invite the reader to a special sale or the like or provide resale information to motivate him or her to use the new account.

See this chapter's Checklist for Credit Approvals to quickly review the tasks involved in this type of message.

CONVEYING POSITIVE INFORMATION ABOUT PEOPLE

Professors, supervisors, and managers are often asked to write letters recommending students or employees for jobs, and nearly anyone may be asked to recommend acquaintances for awards, membership in organizations, and other honors. Such letters may take the direct approach when the recommendation is generally positive. Employers use the same type of organizational plan when telling job applicants the good news—that they got the job.

Recommendation Letters

Letters of recommendation have an important goal: to convince readers that the person being recommended has the characteristics required for the job or other benefit. It is important, therefore, that they contain all the relevant details:

- The full name of the candidate
- The job or benefit that the candidate is seeking
- Whether the writer is answering a request or taking the initiative

■ The nature of the relationship between the writer and the candidate
■ Facts relevant to the position or benefit sought
■ The writer's overall evaluation of the candidate's suitability for the job or benefit sought

Recommendation letters are usually confidential; that is, they're sent directly to the person or committee who requested them and are not shown to the candidate. However, recent litigation has made it advisable in some situations to prepare a carefully worded letter that satisfies both parties.

Oddly enough, the most difficult recommendation letters to write are those for truly outstanding candidates. Your audience will have trouble believing uninterrupted praise for someone's talents and accomplishments. So illustrate your general points with a specific example or two that point out the candidate's abilities, and discuss the candidate's abilities in relation to the "competition."

Most candidates aren't perfect, however. Omitting reference to a candidate's shortcomings may be tempting, especially if the shortcomings are irrelevant to the demands of the job in question. Even so, you have an obligation to your audience, to your own conscience, and even to the better-qualified candidate who's relying on honest references to refer to any shortcoming that is serious and related to job performance. Moreover, you may be held liable for omitting negative information, especially if doing so poses a foreseeable and substantial risk of physical harm to others.[4]

Of course, the danger in writing a critical letter is that you might engage in libel—that is, make a false and malicious written statement that injures the candidate's reputation. On the other hand, if that negative information is truthful and relevant, it may be unethical and illegal to omit it from a recommendation. So if you must refer to a possible shortcoming, you can best protect yourself by sticking to the facts and placing your criticism in the context of a generally favorable recommendation.

You can also avoid trouble by asking yourself the following questions before mailing a recommendation letter:

■ Does the person receiving this frank, personal information have a legitimate right to the information?
■ Is all the information I have presented related directly to the job or other benefit being sought?
■ Have I put the candidate's case as strongly and as honestly as I can?
■ Have I avoided overstating the candidate's abilities or otherwise misleading the reader?
■ Have I based all my statements on firsthand knowledge and provable facts?

Good News About Employment

Finding suitable job applicants and then selecting the right person is a task fraught with hard choices and considerable anxiety. In contrast, writing a letter to the successful applicant is a pleasure. Most of the time, such a letter is eagerly awaited, so the direct approach is appropriate:

Welcome to Lake Valley Rehabilitation Center. A number of excellent candidates were interviewed, but your educational background and recent experience at Memorial Hospital make you the best person for the position of medical records coordinator.

As we discussed, your salary is $26,200 a year. We would like you to begin on Monday, February 1. Please come to my office at 8:00 A.M. I will give you an in-depth orientation to Lake Valley and discuss the various company benefits available to you. You can also sign all the necessary employment documents.

Two devices for convincing the reader when the candidate is outstanding:

■ Use examples
■ Use comparisons with the "competition"

A recommendation letter presenting negatives may be carefully worded to satisfy both the candidate and the person or company requesting information.

A serious shortcoming cannot be ignored, but beware of being libelous:

■ Include only relevant, factual information
■ Avoid value judgments
■ Balance criticisms with favorable points

To compete successfully in today's fast-pace business environment, "The goal is to get as many smart people in the world as possible to work with you," says Thornton May, vice president of research and education at Cambridge Technology Partners. "The real source of competitive advantage in any organization is how it deals with the fact that the people inside it don't know everything they need to know." Routine communications that work can help make those smart employees smarter.

After lunch, Vanessa Jackson will take you to the Medical Records department and help you settle in to your new responsibilities at Lake Valley Home. I look forward to seeing you first thing on February 1.

This letter takes a friendly, welcoming tone, and it explains the necessary details: job title, starting date, salary, and benefits. The explanation of the first day's routine helps allay the bewilderment and uncertainty that might afflict the new employee.

Although letters like these are pleasant to write, they constitute a legal job offer. You and your company may be held to any promises you make. So attorneys sometimes recommend stating salary as a monthly amount and keeping the timing of performance evaluations and raises vague; you want to avoid implying that the newly hired employee will be kept on, no matter what, for a whole year or until the next scheduled evaluation.[5]

> ## **W**RITING DIRECTIVES AND INSTRUCTIONS

Directives are memos that tell employees *what* to do. Instructions tell people inside and outside the company *how* to do something and may take the form of e-mail messages, memos, letters, or even booklets. Directives and instructions are both considered routine messages because readers are assumed to be willing to comply.

The goal in writing directives and instructions is to make the point so obvious and the steps so self-explanatory that readers won't have to ask for additional help. Directives and instructions are especially important within companies: Faulty internal directives and bungled instructions are expensive and inefficient. The following directive does a good job of explaining what employees are expected to do:

New security badges will be issued to all employees between January 20 and January 24. Each employee must report in person to the human resources office (Building B, Room 106) to exchange the old (red) security badges for the new (yellow) security badges. The electronic security system will not recognize the old badges on February 1 and thereafter.

If you are unable to make this exchange between January 20 and January 24, contact Theresa Gomez before January 15 either by phone at 4-6721 or by e-mail at <tgomez@biotech.com>.

This directive is brief and to the point. Drawn-out explanations are unnecessary because readers are expected simply to follow through on a well-established procedure. Yet it also covers all the bases, answering these questions: Who? What? When? Where? Why? How?

Instructions answer the same questions, but they differ from directives in the amount of explanation they provide. Karen Donohue of Campbell might write a simple three-sentence directive to employees to tell them of a change in the policies regarding employee scholarships; however, a detailed set of instructions would be more appropriate to explain the procedure for applying for a scholarship.

When writing instructions, take nothing for granted. Assuming that readers know nothing about the process you're describing is better than risking confusion and possible damage or harm by overlooking some basic information. Figure 9.2 is a set of instructions for writing instructions.

> ## **W**RITING BUSINESS SUMMARIES

Businesspeople are bombarded with masses of information, and at one time or another, everyone in business relies on someone else's summary of a situation, publication, or document. To write a summary, gather the information (whether by reading, talking

---

A letter telling someone that she or he got the job is a legal document, so make sure all statements are accurate.

Directives tell employees what to do; instructions tell readers how to do something.

Madeleine Albright, Secretary of State in the Clinton administration, didn't reach the high position by mincing words. Known for her forthrightness, the former United Nations ambassador also recognizes that goodwill comes from ample preparation to avoid making ignorant gaffes—and that means learning everything you can about your intended audience.

Writing summaries involves

- Gathering information
- Organizing information
- Presenting information in your own words

How to Write Useful Instructions

When you need to explain in writing how to do something, a set of step-by-step instructions is your best choice. By enumerating the steps, you make it easy for readers to perform the process in the correct sequence. Your goal is to provide a clear, self-sufficient explanation so that readers can perform the task independently.

Gather Equipment
1. Writing materials (pen and paper, typewriter, computer)
2. Background materials (previous memos, policy manuals, manufacturer's booklets, etc.)
3. When necessary, the apparatus being explained (machine, software package, or other equipment)

Prepare
1. Perform the task yourself, or ask experts to demonstrate it or describe it to you in detail.
2. Analyze prospective readers' familiarity with the process so that you can write instructions at their level of understanding.

Make Your Instructions Clear
1. Include four elements: an introduction, a list of equipment and materials, a description of the steps involved in the process, and a conclusion.
2. Explain in the opening why the process is important and how it is related to a larger purpose.
3. Divide the process into short, simple steps presented in order of occurrence.
4. Present the steps in a numbered list, or if presenting them in paragraph format, use words indicating time or sequence, such as *first* and *then*.
5. If the process involves more than ten steps, divide them into groups or stages identified with headings.
6. Phrase each step as a command ("Do this" instead of "You should do this"); use active verbs ("Look for these signs" instead of "Be alert for these signs"); use precise, specific terms ("three weeks" instead of "several weeks").
7. When appropriate, describe how to tell whether a step has been performed correctly and how one step may influence another. Warn readers of possible damage or injury from a mistake in a step, but limit the number of warnings so that readers do not underestimate their importance.
8. Include diagrams of complicated devices, and refer to them in appropriate steps.
9. Summarize the importance of the process and the expected results.

Test Your Instructions
1. Review the instructions to be sure they are clear and complete. Also judge whether you have provided too much detail.
2. Ask someone else to read the instructions and tell you whether they make sense and are easy to follow.

Figure 9.2
Instructions for Writing Instructions

with others, or observing circumstances), organize that information, and then present it in your own words. Although many people assume that summarizing is a simple skill, it's actually more complex than it appears. A well-written summary has at least three characteristics.

First, as in writing any business document, be sure the content is accurate. If you're summarizing a report or a group of reports, make sure you present the information without error. Check your references, and then check for typos.

Second, make your summary comprehensive and balanced. The purpose of writing your summary is usually to help colleagues or supervisors make a decision, so include all the information necessary for your readers to understand the situation, problem, or proposal. If the issue you're summarizing has more than one side, present all sides fairly and equitably. Make sure you include all the information necessary. Even though summaries are intended to be as brief as possible, your readers need a minimum amount of information to grasp the issue being presented.

Three characteristics of a well-written summary:

- Accuracy
- Comprehensiveness and balance
- Clear sentence structure and good transitions

Third, make your sentence structure clear, and include good transitions.[6] The only way your summary will save anyone's time is if your sentences are uncluttered, use well-chosen words, and proceed logically. Then, to help your readers move from one point to the next, your transitions must be just as clear and logical. Basically, when writing your summary, be sure to cut through the clutter. Identify those ideas that belong together, and organize them in a way that's easy to understand.[7]

ONVEYING GOOD NEWS ABOUT PRODUCTS AND OPERATIONS

It's good business to spread the word about positive developments such as the opening of new facilities, the appointment of a new executive, the introduction of new products or new customer services, or the sponsorship of community events. Imagine that So-Good Foods has successfully introduced a new line of vegetable chips to the stores it serves (carrot, turnip, and yam chips—not the same old potato chips). To maintain its position on supermarket shelves, So-Good decides to offer a new discount program to stores that buy large quantities of its vegetable chips. It supplements the personal visits of its sales force with a good-news message describing the new program to existing customers. The letter begins by trumpeting the news, fills in the details of the discount program in the middle, and closes with a bit of resale information and a confident prediction of a profitable business relationship.

When the audience for a good-news message is large and scattered, however, it's usually easier to communicate through the mass media. When McDonald's opened its first restaurant in Moscow, it sent announcements to newspapers, magazines, radio stations, and TV networks. The specialized documents used to convey such information to the media are called **news releases.** Written to match the style of the medium for which they are intended, news releases are typed on plain 8½-by-11-inch paper or on special letterhead—not on regular letterhead. Figure 9.3 illustrates the correct format. The content of this news release follows the customary pattern for a good-news message: good news, followed by details and a positive close. Although it avoids explicit references to any reader, it still displays the "you" attitude by presenting information presumed to be of interest to all readers. To write a successful news release, keep the following points in mind:[8]

Specially formatted news releases convey good news to the media, which in turn disseminate it to the public.

- Include no marketing or sales material in your news release.
- Put your most important idea first. (Don't say "Calco's president, James Grall, announced today that the company will move its headquarters to the Main Street office." Instead, start with the news: "Calco will move its headquarters to the Main Street office, President James Grall announced today.")
- Be brief (break up long sentences and keep paragraphs short).
- Eliminate clutter such as redundancy and extraneous facts.
- Be as specific as possible.
- Avoid adjectives and adverbs (understatement goes a long way with the media).

In addition to issuing written news releases, many large companies hold news conferences or create their own videotapes, which are sent to TV networks.

WRITING GOODWILL MESSAGES

Goodwill is the positive feeling that encourages people to maintain a business relationship.

Business isn't all business. To a great extent, it's an opportunity to forge personal relationships. You can enhance your relationships with customers and with other businesspeople by sending friendly, unexpected notes with no direct business purpose. Goodwill messages like these have a positive effect on business because people prefer to deal with organizations that are warm and human and interested in more than just money.

This news release demonstrates the proper format for the targeted medium (in this case, print).

Figure 9.3
In-Depth Critique: News Release Format

NEWS RELEASE

FOR IMMEDIATE RELEASE
February 9, 1998

CONTACT: Liz Greene

JUST IN TIME FOR VALENTINE'S DAY, RECENT SURVEY REVEALS VIDEO RENTERS' FAVORITE ROMANTIC MOVIE TITLES

DALLAS – Searching for the perfect movie for a romantic Valentine's Day rendezvous? A recent survey of active video renters showed that "Gone With The Wind" topped the list of favorite all-time romantic movies. Following the epic 1939 film on the survey results were, respectively, "Sleepless in Seattle," "Pretty Woman," "Casablanca," "Ghost," "When Harry Met Sally," "Titanic," "An Affair to Remember," "Somewhere in Time," and "My Best Friend's Wedding."

"The results of the survey showed an interesting mix of classic and contemporary films," said Karen Raskopf, vice president of corporate communications at Blockbuster, the nation's leading video rental chain and the company that commissioned the survey. "And I'm glad to say that you can rent just about all of them at Blockbuster, with the exception of 'Titanic,' which will be released on video later this year. But right now we do carry the 'Titanic' soundtrack, which has been the best-selling CD in the history of our video stores."

To help consumers in their search for the perfect Valentine gift or movie rental, Blockbuster commissioned the survey to help develop ideas for a special section of

- more -

Blockbuster Entertainment Group •1201 Elm Street • Dallas, TX 75270
Tel: (214) 854-3000 • Fax: (214) 854-4332

Most news is released immediately.

Provide your own suggestion for a title, or leave two inches so that the editor can insert a headline.

This release for a newspaper starts with a dateline and a summary.

Put a release on one page if you can, but indicate carryover to a second page like this.

Such goodwill messages might be considered manipulative and thus unethical unless you make every attempt to be sincere, honest, and truthful. Without sincerity, skillful writing is nothing more than clever, revealing the writer as interested only in personal gain and not in benefiting customers or fellow workers. One way to come across as sincere is to avoid exaggeration. What do you think a reader's reaction would be to these two sentences?

We were overjoyed to learn of your promotion.

Congratulations on your promotion.

Make sure your messages are grounded in reality.

Figure 9.3
(*continued*)

Head the second page like this, with a short title and a page number.

The "plug" is in the last paragraph.

Indicate the end of the release like this.

SURVEY REVEALS FAVORITE ROMANTIC MOVIE TITLES
Page two

romance movies many of their stores will be offering this week. Some of the romance

titles featured include:

- Bridges of Madison County (1995)
- Romeo and Juliet (1968)
- Far and Away (1992)
- Sense and Sensibility (1995)
- Ghost (1990)
- Somewhere in Time (1980)
- Love Story (1970)
- Up Close and Personal (1996)
- Officer and A Gentleman (1982)
- A Walk in the Clouds (1995)
- The American President (1995)
- Only You (1994)
- Breakfast at Tiffany's (1961)
- Romancing the Stone (1984)
- Don Juan Demarco (1995)
- Sixteen Candles (1984)
- Four Weddings and A Funeral (1994)
- Sleepless in Seattle (1993)
- French Kiss (1995)
- The Truth About Cats and Dogs (1996)

For a great Valentine's Day gift idea, Blockbuster stores will also be offering

white, stuffed toy bears, called "Bear Hugs." The white bear is available at participating

Blockbuster stores while supplies last, and retails for $9.99, or for just $4.99 with two

movie rentals.

Blockbuster operates nearly 6,000 video and music neighborhood entertainment

stores in the United States, its territories and 25 other countries and may be accessed

internationally at www.blockbuster.com. Blockbuster is a unit of Viacom Inc., one of the

world's largest entertainment and publishing companies and a leading force in nearly

every segment of the international media marketplace.

###

Most likely, your audience wouldn't quite believe that anyone (except perhaps a relative or very close friend) would be "overjoyed." On the other hand, readers will accept your simple congratulations—a human, understandable intention.

To demonstrate your sincerity, back up any compliments with specific points:

INSTEAD OF THIS	WRITE THIS
Words cannot express my appreciation for the great job you did. Thanks. No one could have done it better. You're terrific! You've made the whole firm sit up and take notice, and we are ecstatic to have you working here.	Thanks for taking charge of the meeting in my absence. You did an excellent job. With just an hour's notice, you managed to pull the legal and public relations departments together so that we could present a united front in the negotiations. Your dedication and communication abilities have been noted and are truly appreciated.

Note also the difference in the words used in these two examples. Your reader would probably believe the more restrained praise to be more sincere. Offering help in a goodwill message is fine, but promise only what you can and will provide. Avoid giving even the impression of an offer of help when none is intended.

Although goodwill messages have little to do with business transactions, they might include some sales information if you have the opportunity to be of particular service or want to remind the reader of your company's product. However, any sales message should be subdued and secondary to the helpful, thoughtful message. In the following example, the owner of a children's clothing shop succeeds in establishing a relationship with the new mother at a very special time in her life:

Congratulations on the birth of your son at Springfield Memorial Hospital. Nothing matches the joy of a new mother welcoming her tiny baby into the world. To commemorate this joyful occasion, Bundles from Heaven is sending you this special gift—a beautifully illustrated book for you to keep track of all the important events in your son's life.

Our shop serves Springfield, meeting the clothing and equipment needs of babies like yours. That's our only business. Stop in sometime and introduce us to your little son!

The mothers receiving this letter won't feel a great deal of pressure to buy but will feel that the owner took notice of this very special event in their lives. If you include a sales pitch in this type of letter, make sure that it takes a back seat to your goodwill message. Honesty and sincerity must come across above all else.

Congratulations

One prime opportunity for sending congratulations is news of a significant business achievement: for example, being promoted or attaining an important civic position (Figure 9.4). Highlights in people's personal lives—weddings and births, graduations, success in nonbusiness competitions—are another reason for sending congratulations. You may congratulate business acquaintances on their achievements or on their spouse's or children's achievements. You may also take note of personal events, even if you don't know the reader well. Of course, if you're already friendly with the reader, you can get away with a personal tone.

Some alert companies develop a mailing list of potential customers by assigning an employee to clip newspaper announcements of births, engagements, weddings, and graduations or by obtaining information on real estate transactions in the local community. Then they introduce themselves by sending out a form letter that might read like this:

Congratulations on your new home! Our wish is that it brings you much happiness.

To help you commemorate the occasion, we've enclosed a key chain with your new address engraved on the leather tab. Please accept this with our best wishes.

In this case, the company's letterhead is enough of a sales pitch. This simple message has a natural, friendly tone, even though the sender has never met the recipient.

Messages of Appreciation

An important managerial quality is the ability to see employees (and other business associates) as individuals and to recognize their contributions. People often value praise more

---

Offer help only when you are able and willing to provide it.

If a sales pitch ever appears in a goodwill message, make it only the slightest hint.

GOING ONLINE
SEND AN ELECTRONIC GOODWILL MESSAGE
Send a free electronic greeting card from the My Sentiments Fine Art Greeting Cards collection. You can choose from a variety of backgrounds and even add music. Many languages are available. Recipients will receive an e-mail notice that a greeting is waiting for them. Great for holidays, birthdays, or announcing a new product or service.

http://www.art-cards.com

Taking note of significant events in someone's personal life helps cement the business relationship.

A message of appreciation documents a person's contributions.

Figure 9.4
In-Depth Critique: Letter Congratulating a Business Acquaintance

This sample congratulatory note moves swiftly to the subject: the good news. It gives reasons for expecting success and avoids such extravagances as "Only you can do the job!"

Office DEPOT, Inc.
2200 Old Germantown Road, Delray Beach, FL 33445   407/278-4800

March 3, 1999

Mr. Ralph Lambert, President
Lambert, Cutchen & Browt, Inc.
14355 Pasadena Parkway
Pasadena, TX 74229

Dear Mr. Lambert:

Congratulations on your firm's recent selection to design and print media advertisements for the National Association of Business Suppliers (ABS). We learned of your success at our convention in Atlanta last month.

We have long believed that the success of individual franchises is directly linked to the healthy growth of the industry at large. We can think of no better firm to help our industry achieve wide recognition than Lambert, Cutchen & Browt.

We have admired your success in promoting associations of other industries such as soft drinks, snack foods, and recycling. Your "Dream Vision 2000" ads for the bottling industry were both inspirational and effective in raising consumer awareness, and we look for similar positive responses to your ABS campaign.

Again, accept our warm congratulations. We look forward to seeing the results of the survey you conducted during our convention. And we will follow your media campaign with great interest.

Sincerely,

Janice McCarthy

Janice McCarthy
Director, Media Relations

tw

The reason for congratulating the reader is expressed early and concisely.

The compliment becomes more effective when coupled with statements that show your knowledge of the recipient's work.

The letter ends with a personal note of congratulations. It expresses interest in following the future success of the individual or business.

---

highly than monetary rewards. A message of appreciation may also become an important part of an employee's personnel file:

Thanks for creating computerized spreadsheets to track our marketing efforts and sales by both region and product. Your personal understanding of the scope of this division's responsibilities is evident in the detail and thoroughness of the spreadsheets. I particularly appreciate the historical data you included and the fine documentation and training you provided so that the data included in the spreadsheets can be consistent over time—regardless of who is working on them.

Your talents in conceptualizing the scope of the project, executing it on time, and following through with the final details are a great asset to our division.

cc: Employee file, Human Resources

With its references to specific qualities and deeds, this note may provide support for future pay increases and promotions.

Suppliers also like to know that you value some exceptional product or the service you received. Long-term support deserves recognition too. Your praise doesn't just make the supplier feel good; it also encourages further excellence. The brief message that follows expresses gratitude and reveals the happy result:

Thank you for sending the air-conditioning components via overnight delivery. You allowed us to satisfy the needs of two customers who were getting very impatient with the heat.

Special thanks to Susan Brown who took our initial call and never said "it can't be done." Her initiative on our behalf is greatly appreciated.

When you write a message of appreciation to a supplier, try to mention specifically the person or people you want to praise. Your expression of goodwill might net the employee some future benefit. In any case, your message honors the company that the individual represents.

Be sure to thank guest speakers at meetings, even if they've been paid an honorarium or their travel expenses—and surely if they have not. They may have spent hours gathering and organizing material for an informative and interesting presentation, so reward their hard work. Messages of appreciation are also appropriate for acknowledging money donations to campaigns or causes. They usually include a few details about the success of the campaign or how the funds are being used so that the donors will feel good about having contributed.

Condolences

In times of serious trouble and deep sadness, written condolences and expressions of sympathy leave their mark. Granted, this type of message is difficult to write, but don't let the difficulty of the task keep you from responding promptly. Those who have experienced a health problem, the death of a loved one, or a business misfortune like to know that they're not alone.

Begin condolences with a brief statement of sympathy, such as "I was deeply sorry to hear of your loss." In the middle, mention the good qualities or the positive contributions made by the deceased. State what the person or business meant to you. In closing, you can offer your condolences and your best wishes. One considerate way to end this type of message is to say something that will give the reader a little lift, such as a reference to a brighter future.

You're not obligated to offer help to the reader; a good condolence message is often help enough. However, if you want to and can offer assistance, do so. Remember, the bereaved and grieving often suffer financially as well as emotionally, and reestablishing a business or a life often takes a great deal of time and effort. A simple gesture on your part may mean much to the reader.

Here are a few general suggestions for writing condolence messages:

- *Keep reminiscences brief.* Recount a memory or an anecdote (even a humorous one), but don't dwell on the details of the loss, lest you add to the reader's anguish.
- *Write in your own words.* Write as if you were speaking privately to the person. Don't quote "poetic" passages or use stilted or formal phrases. If the loss is a death, refer to it as such rather than as "passing away" or "departing."

Anyone who does you or your organization a special favor should receive written thanks.

Steinway & Sons manufactures pianos and wants them to be played by such special artists as Elton John and Vladimir Ashkenazy. As vice president of the worldwide concert and artist department, Peter Goodrich uses goodwill messages to let these artists know that "we are thinking about them and that we appreciate the fact that they play our pianos."

In condolence messages, try to find a middle path between being superficial and causing additional distress.

- *Be tactful.* Mention your shock and dismay, but keep in mind that the bereaved and distressed loved ones take little comfort in such lines as, "Richard was too young to die" or "Starting all over again will be so difficult." Try to strike a balance between superficial expressions of sympathy and heartrending references to a happier past and a possibly bleak future.
- *Take special care.* Be sure to spell names correctly and to be accurate in your review of facts.
- *Write about special qualities of the deceased.* You may have to rely on reputation to do this, but let the grieving person know the value of his or her loved one.
- *Write about special qualities of the bereaved person.* A pat on the back helps a bereaved family member feel more confident about handling things during such a traumatic time.[9]

Above all, don't let the fear of saying something wrong keep you from saying anything at all. A supervisor, George Bigalow, sent the following condolence letter to his administrative assistant, Janice Case, after learning of the death of Janice's husband:

My sympathy to you and your children. All your friends at Carter Electric were so very sorry to learn of John's death. Although I never had the opportunity to meet him, I do know how very special he was to you. Your tales of your family's camping trips and his rafting expeditions were always memorable.

Here's a longer condolence letter sent by a friendly competitor on the occasion of a serious business disruption:

We just heard of the terrible fire at your furniture store and your decision to close the store temporarily. Please accept our sympathy for your loss. However, the strength of Frankfort Furniture was not the building, but rather your family's managerial skills and team spirit. And those haven't changed.

Promptness is especially important in condolence messages.

You know that Frankfort Furniture is more than just our neighbor on Main Street. Together, our stores offer this community a wide variety of furniture styles. We look forward to your store reopening in the near future.

These specifics reassure the reader that the store owner has friends as well as competitors.

Jack, we'd like to help. What can we do to assist? Do you need warehouse space? I have a couple of ideas. Please call me when you're ready to consider some facility options.

The offer of help is not too specific, so it doesn't intrude on the message of sympathy.

Your many friends in Springfield wish you well and know that you and Ann have the strength and ability to rise above this setback.

The closing ties together a reminder of friendship and a look toward the future.

As a reminder of the tasks involved with this type of message, see the Checklist for Goodwill Messages.

CHECKLIST FOR GOODWILL MESSAGES

A. Planning Goodwill Messages

1. Choose the appropriate type of goodwill message for your purpose.
   - a. Offer congratulations to make the reader feel noticed.
   - b. Express praise or thanks to show your appreciation for good performance.
   - c. Offer condolences to show appreciation for the deceased or the person suffering a loss.
2. Be prompt when sending out goodwill messages so that they lose none of their impact.
3. Send a written goodwill message rather than a telephone message, because a written message can be savored more than once; but keep in mind that a telephone message is better than none at all.

B. Format

1. Use the format most appropriate to the occasion.
   - a. Use letter format for condolences and for any other goodwill message sent to outsiders or mailed to an employee's home.
   - b. Use memo format for any goodwill messages sent through interoffice mail, except for condolences.
   - c. Use a preprinted greeting card for condolences (with a brief handwritten message added).

2. Handwrite condolences (and replies to handwritten invitations); otherwise, type the goodwill message.
3. Use special stationery, if available.
4. For added impact, present congratulations in a folder with a clipping or photo commemorating the special event.

C. Opening

1. State the most important idea first to focus the reader's attention.
2. Incorporate a friendly statement that builds goodwill right at the beginning.
3. Focus on the good qualities of the person or situation.

D. Middle

1. Provide sufficient details, even in a short message, to justify the opening statement.
2. Express personalized details in sincere, not gushy, language.
3. Be warm but concise.
4. Make the reader, not the writer, the focus of all comments.

E. Close

1. Use a positive or forward-looking statement.
2. Restate the important idea, when appropriate.

On the Job

SOLVING A COMMUNICATION DILEMMA AT CAMPBELL SOUP COMPANY

Campbell Soup has been steadily climbing away from its past business troubles with solid performance throughout the 1990s. Products matched to local and regional tastes and carefully chosen acquisitions continue to help the company grow. For example, Germany and France are two of the largest soup-consuming markets in the world (the French consume four times as much soup per capita as people in the United States do), and Campbell has made major acquisitions in both countries lately. The company barely turned a profit in 1990, but it earned more than $800 million in 1996 (on sales of $7.7 billion).

With growth comes more customers, of course, and more customers means more questions for consumer response supervisor Karen Donohue. Whenever people write, phone, or send e-mail, she's in charge of making sure their questions and complaints are answered satisfactorily. Many of these questions are routine and repetitive ("What are the most popular flavors of Campbell's Soup?"), but many others require special, personalized communication skills.

Like many companies these days, Campbell uses the World Wide Web as a two-way communication vehicle between the company and its customers. The company's home page provides links to recipes, financial and investment news, educational support programs, and an online store, as well as Donohue's domain, the consumer response center. Here, Donohue answers some of the most frequently asked questions (for example: How many Os are in a 15-ounce can of Spaghetti-Os? Answer: 1,750), and she invites consumers to e-mail other questions and comments. Consumers who wish to speak with a Campbell's representative instead of sending e-mail can call a toll-free number listed on-screen.

Not surprisingly, Karen Donohue plays a major role in Campbell's efforts to better meet the needs of its millions of customers worldwide. Whether she's responding to dissatisfied customers or answering simple requests for information, Donohue is in a position to help satisfy consumers while gaining important insights into their needs and purchase behaviors. As Campbell moves into the next century, she will be communicating with consumers and employees to make sure the giant food producer keeps sales and profits cooking.[10]

Your Mission: You have joined Campbell's consumer marketing staff. As an assistant to Karen Donohue, you are responsible for handling correspondence with both consumers and Campbell employees. Your objective is to improve the flow of communication between the public and the company so that Campbell can respond quickly and knowledgeably to changing consumer needs. Choose the best alternatives for responding to the situations described below, and be prepared to explain why your choice is best.

1. Donohue has received a letter from a Mrs. Felton who is pleased that Campbell offers a line of Healthy Request reduced-sodium soups but would like to see more flavors added. Which of the following is the best opening paragraph for your reply?

    a. The Campbell Soup Company was founded in 1869 in Camden, New Jersey. The Dorrance family took control from the founders in 1894. At the turn of the century, John Dorrance invented the soup condensation process, which enabled the company to sell a 10-ounce can for a dime. He was a conservative man and a stickler for quality. His only son, the late Jack Dorrance, followed his father into the business and had a similar management philosophy. As chairperson of the company, he used to pinch the tomatoes and taste the carrots occasionally to be sure that the folks in the factory were maintaining high standards. Mr. Dorrance took personal interest in the development of the low-salt line and would be pleased to know that it appeals to you.

    b. Thank you for your enthusiastic letter about Campbell's Healthy Request soups. We are delighted that you enjoy the flavors currently available, and we are working hard to add new varieties to the line.

    c. Good news! Our world-renowned staff of food technologists is busy in the test kitchen at this very moment, experimenting with additional low-sodium recipes for Healthy Request soups. Hang on to your bowl, Mrs. Felton, more flavors are on the way!

2. Which of the following versions is preferable for the middle section of the letter to Mrs. Felton?

    a. You can expect to see several exciting new Healthy Request soups on your supermarket shelf within the next year. Before the new flavors make their debut, however, they must undergo further testing in our kitchens and in selected markets across the country. We want to be sure our soups satisfy consumer expectations.

        While you're waiting for the new flavors of Healthy Request, you might like to try some of Campbell's other products designed especially for people like you who are concerned about health and nutrition. I'm enclosing coupons that entitle you to sample both Pepperidge Farm Five-Star Fibre bread and Pace picante sauce "on the house." We hope you enjoy them.

    b. We are sorry that the number of Healthy Request flavors is limited at this time. Because of the complexities of testing flavors both in the Campbell kitchens and in test markets around the country, we are a bit behind schedule in releasing new varieties. But several new flavors should be available by the end of the year, if all goes according to plan. In the meantime, please accept these coupons; they can be redeemed for two other fine Campbell products designed for the health-conscious consumer.

    c. Additional flavors of Healthy Request reduced-sodium soups are currently in formulation. They will arrive on supermarket shelves soon. In the meantime, why not enjoy some of Campbell's other fine products designed for the health-conscious consumer? The enclosed coupons will allow you to sample Pace picante sauce and Pepperidge Farm Five-Star Fibre bread at our expense.

3. Campbell has received a letter from the American Heart Association asking for information on the fat and sodium content of Campbell's products. Your department has developed a brochure that provides the necessary data, and you plan to send it to the association. Which of the following cover letters should you send along with the brochure?

    a. Please consult the enclosed brochure for the answers to your questions regarding the composition of Campbell's products. The brochure provides detailed information on the sodium and fat content of all Campbell's products, which include such well-known brands as V-8, Pepperidge Farm, and Franco-American, as well as Campbell's Soups.

    b. Thanks for your interest in Campbell's products. We are concerned about nutrition and health issues and are trying to reduce the salts and fats in our products. At the same time, we are striving to retain the taste that consumers have come to expect from Campbell. In general, we feel very good about the nutritional value of our products and think that after you read the enclosed brochure you will too.

    c. Thank you for your interest in Campbell's Soup. The enclosed brochure provides the information you requested about the fat and sodium content of our products. Over the past ten years, we have introduced a number of reduced-sodium and low-fat products designed specifically for consumers on restricted diets. In addition, we have reformulated many of our regular products to reduce the salt and fat content. We have also revised our product labels so that information on sodium and fat content is readily apparent to health-conscious consumers. If you have any questions about any of our products, please contact our consumer information specialists at 1-800-227-9876.

4. Campbell has received a letter from a disgruntled consumer, Mr. Max Edwards, who was disappointed with his last can of Golden Classic beef soup with potatoes and mushrooms. It appears that the can contained an abundance of potatoes, little beef, and few mushrooms. You have been asked to reply to Mr. Edwards. Which of the following drafts is best?

    a. We are extremely sorry that you did not like your last can of Golden Classic beef soup with potatoes and mushrooms. Although we do our very best to ensure that all our products are of the highest quality, occasionally our quality-control department slips up and a can of soup comes out a bit short on one ingredient or another. Apparently you happened to buy just such a can—one with relatively few mushrooms, not much beef, and too many potatoes. The odds against that ever happening to you again are probably a million to one. And to prove it, here's a coupon that entitles you to a free can of Golden Classic soup. You may pick any flavor you like, but why not give the beef with potatoes and mushrooms another try? We bet it will meet your standards this time around.

    b. You are right, Mr. Edwards, to expect the highest quality from Campbell's Golden Classic soups. And you are right to complain when your expectations are not met. Our goal is to provide the best, and when we fall short of that goal, we want to know about it so that we can correct the problem.

And that is exactly what we have done. In response to your complaint, our quality-control department is reexamining its testing procedures to ensure that all future cans of Golden Classic soup have an even blend of ingredients. Why not see for yourself by taking the enclosed coupon to your supermarket and redeeming it for a free can of Golden Classic soup? If you choose beef with potatoes and mushrooms, you can count on getting plenty of beef and mushrooms this time.

c. Campbell's Golden Classic soups are a premium product at a premium price. Our quality-control procedures for this line have been carefully devised to ensure that every can of soup has a uniform distribution of ingredients. As you can imagine, your complaint came as quite a surprise to us, given the care that we take with our products. We suspect that the uneven distribution of ingredients was just a fluke, but our quality-control department is looking into the matter to ensure that the alleged problem does not recur.

We would like you to give our Golden Classic soup another try. We are confident that you will be satisfied, so we are enclosing a coupon that entitles you to a free can. If you are not completely happy with it, please call me at 1-800-227-9876.

Critical Thinking Questions

1. As a local retailer, would you take the time to reply to requests for information and action when no potential sale is involved? Why or why not?
2. Your company's error cost an important business customer a new client—you know it and your customer knows it. Do you apologize, or do you refer to the incident in a positive light without admitting any responsibility? Briefly explain.
3. Your customer is clearly at fault and lying. Will you disallow her claim? Why or why not?
4. You've been asked to write a letter of recommendation for an employee who is disabled and uses a wheelchair. The disability has no effect on the employee's ability to do the job, and you feel confident about writing the best recommendation possible. Nevertheless, you know the prospective company, and its facilities aren't well suited to wheelchair access. Do you mention the employee's disability in your letter? Explain.
5. Since press releases are published as news items, is it okay to mention the benefits of your company's products, or would that be unethical? Explain your answer.
6. Should resale and sales promotion be subdued (if included at all) in goodwill messages? Explain.

Documents for Analysis

Read the following documents; then (1) analyze the strengths and weaknesses of each sentence and (2) revise each document so that it follows this chapter's guidelines.

DOCUMENT 9.A: RESPONDING TO CLAIMS AND ADJUSTMENT REQUESTS WHEN BUYER'S AT FAULT

We read your letter requesting your deposit refund. We couldn't figure out why you hadn't received it, so we talked to our maintenance engineer as you suggested. He said you had left one of the doors off the hinges in your apartment in order to get a large sofa through the door. He also confirmed that you had paid him $5.00 to replace the door since you had to turn in the U-Haul trailer and were in a big hurry.

This entire situation really was caused by a lack of communication between our housekeeping inspector and the maintenance engineer. All we knew was that the door was off the hinges when it was inspected by Sally Tarnley. You know that our policy states that if anything is wrong with the apartment, we keep the deposit. We had no way of knowing that George just hadn't gotten around to replacing the door.

But we have good news. We approved the deposit refund, which will be mailed to you from our home office in Teaneck, New Jersey. I'm not sure how long that will take, however. If you don't receive the check by the end of next month, give me a call.

Next time, it's really a good idea to stay with your apartment until it's inspected as stipulated in your lease agreement. That way, you'll be sure to receive your refund when you expect it. Hope you have a good summer.

DOCUMENT 9.B: RESPONDING TO CLAIMS AND ADJUSTMENT REQUESTS WHEN COMPANY'S AT FAULT

Thank you for contacting us about your purchase of the "Knights of Balthazar" game for your MacIntosh. We apologize for the problem and want you to know how it happened.

We outsource our packaging to a firm called TriTech, which does the design work and prints the boxes. Unfortunately, the box that contained your CD for Balthazar was mistakenly labeled. It will work only on an IBM (or compatible) platform.

We are taking care of our customers even though this problem was caused by TriTech. If you will send the entire CD, the box, the warranty card, and your receipt, we will gladly replace it with a CD that will work in your computer. We also need to know how much memory you have and the system you are running. (Balthazar won't work on anything less than a System 7.)

Thanks for your patience. Again, we apologize for this even though it was beyond our control. We always want to do the right thing for our customers. Incidentally, I am enclosing our latest catalog of interactive CD games. We hope to do business with you in the future.

DOCUMENT 9.C: LETTER OF RECOMMENDATION

Your letter to Tanaka Asata, President of SONY, was forwarded to me because I am the human resources director. In my job as head

of HR, I have access to performance reviews for all of the SONY employees in the United States. This means, of course, that I would be the person best qualified to answer your request for information on Nick Oshinski.

In your letter of the 15th, you asked about Nick Oshinski's employment record with us because he has applied to work for your company. Mr. Oshinski was employed with us from January 5, 1992, until March 1, 1997. During that time, Mr. Oshinski received ratings ranging from 2.5 up to 9.6 with 10 being the top score. As you can see, he must have done better reporting to some managers than to others. In addition, he took all vacation days, which is a bit unusual. Although I did not know Mr. Oshinski personally, I know that our best workers seldom use all the vacation time they earn. I do not know if that applies in this case.

In summary, Nick Oshinski performed his tasks well depending on who managed him.

C ases

REPLYING TO REQUESTS FOR INFORMATION AND ACTION

1. Window shopping at Wal-Mart: Writing a positive reply via e-mail The Wal-Mart chain of discount stores is one of the most successful in the world, designing, importing, and marketing across national borders. In particular, Wal-Mart rarely fails to capitalize on a marketing scheme, and its online shopping page is no exception. To make sure the Web site remains effective and relevant, the Web master asks various people to peruse the site and give their feedback. As administrative assistant to Wal-Mart's director of marketing, you have just received a request from the Web master to visit Wal-Mart's Web site and give feedback on the shopping page.

Your Task: Visit Wal-Mart at <http://www.wal-mart.com> and do some online "window shopping." As you browse through the shopping page, consider the language, layout, graphics, ease of use, and background noise. Then compose a positive reply to the Web master, and send your feedback to <cserve@wal-mart.com>. Print a copy of your e-mail message for submission to your instructor.

RESPONDING FAVORABLY TO CLAIMS AND ADJUSTMENT REQUESTS

2. Mercedes merchandise: Form letter announcing a new, upscale catalog Mercedes-Benz owners take their accessories seriously, so many of them are upset when they purchase "rip-off" Mercedes baseball caps that fall apart. Such merchandise is produced by "sweatshop entrepreneurs," your boss's polite term for merchandisers who pirate the Mercedes logo, paste it onto cheap

baseball caps, and then sell their wares at swap meets and in flea markets. When the logo falls off, you get the irate letters.

You're working for Steve Beaty, vice president of accessories marketing for Mercedes-Benz. This is big business; today nearly every brand of automobile has its accompanying goods for proud owners: ties, T-shirts, watches, shoes, hats, jackets, sweaters. Most are sold right in the showrooms, and they're extremely popular, whether it's Saturn sneakers or Land Rover tweeds. Some of the upscale manufacturers have been striving to provide logo-bearing clothing and gadgets that meet their customers' high-class budgets as well as their tastes. But simply raising prices has backfired. The second most common customer complaint you've been receiving is, "Why should I pay twice the price for an ordinary shirt just because it carries the Mercedes triangle?"

Beaty agrees with these customers, so he went to work with other company executives to produce a brand new, 55-page, glossy, full-color "Mercedes-Benz Personal & Automotive Accessories" catalog loaded with expensive loot. Mercedes-Benz has recruited world-class, top-of-the-line manufacturers and designers to produce merchandise worthy of the company's highly refined clientele. The new catalog presents Wittnauer watches, Caran D'Ache ballpoints, Bally bomber jackets, and silk boxers designed by artist Nicole Miller—all emblazoned with the triangle logo or images of Mercedes-Benz models, past and present. The catalog even features a $3,300 collapsible aluminum mountain bike for slipping into the trunk of your 500SL.

Your Task: Beaty wants you to develop a form letter—a very classy one, of course—to send with a copy of the new catalog to all the customers who have sent complaints about shoddy or overpriced merchandise during the last year or so. He thinks they'll be quite happy with this reply.[11]

3. Red Dirt to go: E-mail to a mainland customer from Paradise Sportswear Whoever said you can turn a failure into a success was right. Robert Hedin would agree, but he'd probably add with a chuckle that it could take several failures before you finally hit "pay dirt." As the owner of Paradise Sportswear in Hawaii, Hedin was nearly done in by Hurricane Iniki in 1992, which wiped out his first silk-screened and airbrushed T-shirt business. He tried again, but then Hawaii's red dirt started seeping into his warehouse and ruining his inventory. Finally, a friend suggested that he stop trying to fight Mother Nature. Hedin took the hint: He mortgaged his condo and began producing Red Dirt Shirts, all made with dye created from the troublesome local dirt. Bingo: Projected sales for Paradise Sportswear in 1997 were $3.5 million.

So popular are Hedin's Red Dirt Sportswear designs, they're being snapped up by locals and tourists alike in Hedin's eight Paradise Sportswear retail outlets—and now in every Kmart on the islands. Last year Hedin added a new line: Lava Blues, made with real Hawaiian lava rock.

"You can make 500 shirts with a bucket of dirt," grins Hedin as he shows you around the operation on your first day. He's just a few years away from the usual retirement age, but to you he looks like a kid who's finally found the right playground.

Recently Hedin decided to capitulate to all the requests he's received from retail outlets on the mainland. Buyers kept coming to the islands on vacation, discovering Hedin's "natural" sportswear, and plaguing him with personal visits, letters, and e-mail, trying to set up a deal. For a long time, the answer was no; he simply couldn't handle the extra work. But now he's hired you.

As special sales representative, you'll help Hedin expand slowly into this new territory, starting with one store. Wholesaling to the local Kmarts was easy enough, but handling all the arrangements for shipping to the mainland was too much for the current staff. So you'll start with the company Hedin has chosen to become the first mainland retailer to sell Red Dirt and Lava Blues sportswear: Surf's Up in Chicago, Illinois—of all places. The boss figures that with less competition than he'd find on either coast, his island-influenced sportswear will be a big hit in Chicago, especially in the dead of winter.

Your Task: You'll be sending a positive response to the e-mail received from Surf's Up buyer Ronald Draeger, who said he fell in love with the Paradise clothing concept while on a surfing trip to Maui. Let him know he'll have a temporary exclusive, and that you'll be sending a credit application and other materials by snail mail. His e-mail address is <surfsup@insnet.com>.[12]

4. Try us again: Letter and coupons from M&M/Mars You took a lot of teasing from friends when you went to work for M&M/Mars candy manufacturers. If they only knew: After a few weeks, you finally got tired of sampling the wares, and now the only desserts you want to see are the kind Mom bakes from scratch. Still, working in consumer relations is fun. Especially when you answer letters like this one:

I bought a box of frozen Dove Bars at the local Ralph's supermarket and when I got them home and opened them, the chocolate coating was crushed on every single bar! I live twenty miles from the market. Returning them was just too inconvenient. And at $4 for only 4 bars, one expects perfection! Imagine my disappointment!

The letter didn't include the proof-of-purchase panel from the end of the box, but company policy is to respond favorably to anyone who takes the time to write a letter.

Your Task: You're going to send the consumer, Tom Doppler (5335 West Reno #11, Mesquite, Nevada 89024) two coupons: one for a free box of Dove Bars and one for $1 off any M&M/Mars frozen dessert product.

APPROVING ROUTINE CREDIT REQUESTS

5. Satellite farming: Letter granting credit from Deere & Company This is the best part of your job with Deere & Co. in Moline, Illinois: saying yes to a farmer. In this case, it's Arlen Ruestman in Toluca, Illinois.

Ruestman wants to take advantage of new farming technology. Your company's new GreenStar system uses satellite technology originally developed by the defense department: the Global Positioning System (GPS). By using a series of satellites orbiting Earth, the system can pinpoint (to the meter) exactly where a farmer is positioned at any given moment as he drives his GreenStar-equipped combine over a field. For farmers like Ruestman, that means a new ability to micromanage even 10,000 acres of corn or soybeans.

For instance, using the GreenStar system, farmers can map crop yields from a given area and then examine potential causes of yield variations. After careful analysis, they can determine exactly how much herbicide or fertilizer to spread over precisely which spot—eliminating waste and achieving better results. With cross-referencing and accumulated data, farmers can analyze why crops are performing well in some areas and not so well in others. Then they can program farm equipment to treat only the problem area—for example, spraying an insect infestation two meters wide, 300 yards down the row.

Some farms have already saved as much as $10 an acre on fertilizers alone. For 10,000 acres, that's $100,000 a year. Once Ruestman retrofits your GreenStar precision package on his combine and learns all its applications, he should have no problem saving enough to pay off the $7,350 credit account you're about to grant him.

Your Task: Write a letter to Mr. Ruestman (P.O. Box 4067, Toluca, IL 61369), informing him of the good news.[13]

CONVEYING POSITIVE INFORMATION ABOUT PEOPLE

6. On a course for Harvard: Reply to a request for a recommendation letter After working for several years for Karen Donohue in Campbell Soup Company's consumer response department, one of your co-workers, Angela Cavanaugh, has decided to apply for admission to the Harvard Business School's MBA program. She has asked Donohue to write a letter of recommendation for her. Here are the facts about Angela Cavanaugh:

1. She has an undergraduate degree in journalism from the University of Iowa, where she was an honors student.
2. She joined Campbell directly after graduating and has worked for the firm for the past five years.
3. Her primary responsibility has been to answer letters from consumers; she has done an outstanding job.
4. Her most noteworthy achievement has been to analyze a year's worth of incoming mail, categorize the letters by type and frequency, and create a series of standardized replies. The department now uses Cavanaugh's form letters to handle approximately 75 percent of its mail.
5. Although Cavanaugh has outstanding work habits and is an excellent writer, she lacks confidence as a speaker. Her reluctance to present her ideas orally has prevented her from advancing more rapidly at Campbell. This could be a problem for her at Harvard Business School, where skill in classroom discussion influences a student's chances of success.

Your Task: Because you have worked closely with Cavanaugh, Karen Donohue has asked you to draft the letter, which Donohue will sign.[14]

7. Cold comfort: E-mail offering a regional sales position with Golight Winter in Nebraska ranch country is something to sneeze at—and to shiver over. That's why rancher Jerry Gohl invented the Golight, a portable spotlight that can be mounted on a car or truck roof and rotated 360 degrees horizontally and 70 degrees vertically *by remote control.* No more getting out of the truck in freezing, predawn temperatures to adjust a manual spotlight in order to check on his livestock in the dark. In fact, Gohl hardly has any time left to check the livestock at all these days: His invention

has become so popular that three-year-old Golight, Inc., expects to sell more than $2 million worth of the remote-controlled lights next year.

The company expanded fast, with Golights becoming popular all over the world among hunters, boaters, commuters who fear dark-of-night roadside tire changes, and early morning fishing enthusiasts who can scope out the best shoreline sites by controlling the spotlight from inside their warm and cozy vehicles. Sales reps have been hired for every part of the country and overseas, but Gohl has been holding out for just the right person to replace him in the Nebraska territory. After all, the company president knows better than anyone what the local ranchers need and how they think—that's why his invention was such a success there. He didn't want to jinx his good fortune by choosing the wrong replacement.

Finally, last week he met a young man named Robert Victor who seems to fit the bill. Robert grew up on a Nebraska ranch, helping his dad with those 4 A.M. chores. He's young, but he's felt the bite of Nebraska's cold, he knows the rancher mind, and best of all, he's been bringing in top dollar selling agricultural equipment in Montana for the past few years. Now he wants to return to his home state. Jerry liked him from the first moment they shook hands. "He's got the job if he wants it," the boss tells you. "Better send him some e-mail before someone else grabs him. He can start as soon as he's settled."

Your Task: Compose the message communicating Gohl's offer to Robert Victor: salary plus commission as discussed, full benefits (paid vacation, health and dental insurance) if he's still around in six months. His e-mail address is <rvictor@ism.net>. Sign with your name, as Gohl's personnel manager.[15]

WRITING DIRECTIVES AND INSTRUCTIONS

8. No, no, never: Policy memo to *60 Minutes* producers *Hard Copy* does it; *A Current Affair* does it; and the number of syndicated TV news tabloids willing to pay sources for information seems to be multiplying exponentially. As ratings soar and tabloid TV shows proliferate, so does competition for information from people plugged into a hot topic (such as a disgruntled Michael Jackson employee, a Tonya Harding relative, or an O. J. Simpson pal). In some circles, money might buy the lead story of the week.

You've been a *60 Minutes* assistant producer on Hewitt's team for one week—a dream job you earned after years of work, starting as an audience seater for Oprah, moving up to production assistant, and then getting a job as assistant producer for Paramount's *Hard Copy.* Now you're learning that things are done differently here at *60 Minutes* (and at other network-produced news magazine shows). You just spoke with an informant who phoned to offer *60 Minutes* the inside scoop of the decade—for a price. You took the offer straight to Don Hewitt, long-time executive producer of *60 Minutes.* You were expecting praise, but Hewitt was not pleased.

Fuming, he stressed that *60 Minutes* didn't gain its reputation by throwing money around to win ratings. It goes against journalistic ethics. He pointed out that hard investigative work goes into every story and that team effort brings out the facts, exposes the truth—not some cooked-up story concocted by a greedy, money-hungry, disgruntled ex-employee! After a glaring silence, Hewitt relaxed a bit. "Okay, you're new. You've been working for someone else. But now you know where we stand. The answer is no, no, no."

Your Task: You're not the first producer wanting to buy into a breaking story, and Hewitt decides it's time to put his policy in writing. Hewitt also decides that you should write the memo for him. (Penance, you wonder?) Translate Hewitt's message into an appropriate memo for issuing a company directive.[16]

WRITING BUSINESS SUMMARIES

9. Gardening by computer: Summary of CD-ROM releases for Rodale executives Rodale Press has been publishing gardening magazines and books since 1942. First came J. I. Rodale's demonstration farm in Emmaus, Pennsylvania, and his resulting *Organic Gardening* magazine—which is still the most widely read gardening publication in the world, according to the company history you read when you came on board. Now the company has its own Web site, selling its popular books and magazines about gardening, health, fitness, backpacking, running, bicycling, and woodworking to a new generation of computer-literates. That's why Rodale executives are thinking hard about releasing the company's first CD-ROM, and gardening is the subject of choice. After all, it's the foundation on which the entire company was built.

"Microsoft is doing well with its *Complete Gardening* CD-ROM," says your boss, who is vice president of sales and marketing for Rodale. "And I've heard about one called *3-D Landscape* from a company named Books That Work. But has anyone duplicated what Rodale does so well?"

You know she means a CD-ROM that matches the company's mission statement (a framed version of which hangs over your desk): "Our mission is to show people how they can use the power of their bodies and minds to make their lives better. 'You can do it,' we say on every page of our magazines and books.'" Any CD-ROM would also have to emphasize organic gardening techniques to pass muster among Rodale family members, who still own the company.

Your Task: You've volunteered to research other gardening CD-ROMs presently in the marketplace, writing a brief summary for Rodale's top management that will indicate what's out there for consumers already, who's published them, and how Rodale's special expertise might fit into the mix.[17]

10. How did Nike do it? Summary of a PR disaster Jill Montaine has been the proud owner of Jill's Jackets in Los Angeles for seven years, ever since her designs started showing up on celebrities at the best parties in Beverly Hills. Word of mouth spread so fast

that it wasn't long before she moved out of her converted garage studio and into her own showcase shop on Rodeo Drive. Now she's worried.

"I don't know what I'm going to do. This could ruin me," she confesses to you (her store manager). She showed up early this morning shortly before you opened the shop for business. You sympathize. Montaine started out sewing all her own designs and selling them on consignment at local boutiques. When her popularity grew, she hired subcontractors outside the United States, most recently in Southeast Asia, to keep up with the order demands. Yesterday she learned that one of her overseas subcontractors has imposed new, harsh rules on his workers. Long hours, no breaks, unsanitary and hazardous working conditions—in common lingo, he's turned the operation into the worst kind of overseas sweatshop. And Jill's Jackets is his only client.

Montaine is worried about how much of her money has gone into his pockets instead of workers' paychecks, and she has already taken steps to replace him with another subcontractor. Now she's worried over how quickly this news might spread and destroy her reputation in the United States. Word of mouth is everything in the upscale fashion business, and similar stories have nearly ruined others—including some more famous than Jill's Jackets.

"Why don't you find out how other companies have handled this kind of situation?" you suggest gently.

"Oh, you're right! That's a great idea." Relief spreads quickly over Montaine's face. "What did Nike do? Can you find out? How did they handle this kind of PR disaster?"

Your Task: Grateful for your suggestion, Montaine has left the shop in haste, heading off to a luncheon fashion show that she hopes will take the sting out of the bad publicity. Meanwhile, she's asked you to leave the clerks in charge of the store and zip over to the library. She wants you to read up on Nike's response to the accusations of overseas labor abuse that arose during the spring of 1997. Then you are to type up a summary of your findings and fax it to her home machine.[18]

CONVEYING GOOD NEWS ABOUT PRODUCTS AND OPERATIONS

11. China calling: Announcement from AT&T about transpacific cable As head of public relations for AT&T's international operations, you've handled some pretty impressive announcements. But this one has everyone in the company excited. It's a historic event, you muse, as you head back to your office from a top-level meeting that was electronically linked with AT&T executives still on location in China. This will be the first time the United States and China are connected by an undersea fiberoptic communication cable. What can it mean for the global future? Better political relations? Or just bigger phone bills for U.S. citizens who have relatives in China?

Ah, but there's so much work to be done before you'll know all the implications of this shared venture. After all, it was just today that the group of ten telecommunications firms from several countries signed a "memorandum of understanding" in Beijing. They'll be spending an estimated $1.4 billion and working together to put the undersea cable in place. The projected completion date is December 1999 for the cable, which will stretch more than 16,770 miles. The technology, of course, will be state of the art. The cable will carry voice, data, and images at least eight times as fast as any existing communication links with China can—so say your engineers. You heard them with your own ears: a million calls simultaneously. Imagine. In a short while, you'll be able to pick up a phone in the U.S. and make a direct-dial call to China. That is, if the intervening seas don't provide any unexpected hazards—and if it's all smooth sailing with the intercompany, intercultural cooperation the project is going to demand. Yes, it will be quite a communications coup, all the way around.

Your Task: The top brass have charged you with drafting the contents of an announcement about the transpacific cable to be released to the U.S. news media. AT&T's CEO Robert E. Allen wants you to make up a quote for him—but he's going to review your draft before it's released in final form on your corporate news release letterhead. Be sure to mention the other nine companies involved—and better double-check the English spelling of their names: Sprint, MCI Communications, SBC Communications, Hong Kong Telecommunications, Korea Telecom, Singapore Telecommunications, Nippon Telegraph & Telephone Corp., Kokusai Denshin Denwa, and China Telecom.[19]

12. Daily Blast: Disney and Microsoft target the Internet kids
They're known as the Internet Generation—kids between the ages of 3 and 15 who are growing up in an era when the Information Superhighway leads right into the family den. And two of the most ubiquitous companies in the world—Microsoft and Disney—have their corporate eyes on this lucrative market-in-the-making.

The two companies first teamed up with Disney's Daily Blast, a multimedia, interactive Web site designed to attract and hold the interest of the grade school set (kids 3 to 12 years old). After a month-long free trial, Disney offered its "smorgasbord" of games, stories, news items and quizzes, comic books, and other colorful and noisy activities to subscribers for $4.95 a month. Your boss, Disney Online President Jake Winebaum, told the news media at the time that, although nearly everything on the Web is free and that's what consumers expect, he was confident families would be willing to subscribe to bring "quality family programming" into their homes via the tool kids are most eager to explore: the Internet.

But just in case subscriptions were slow to pour into Disney's offices, the company signed an agreement with Microsoft to provide the Daily Blast for Channel 6 on the Microsoft Network (MSN). That guaranteed Disney at least 2 million customers, for which Microsoft is paying the equivalent subscription fees. Moreover, Microsoft agreed to share the marketing costs to promote the Daily Blast. The arrangement was to be exclusive for 10 months, after which other networks could sign similar agreements with Disney.

Those ten months are nearly up, and now Disney and the Microsoft Network are cooking up a new scheme. They've unveiled plans this week to produce a kind of Daily Blast for kids 12 to 15 years old. Holding their interest won't be easy, but Winebaum and Bill Gates are confident they can use what they've learned from the Daily Blast experience to avoid pitfalls. After all, some of their early subscribers are growing up, and the companies would love to keep their attention—as would advertisers on the site. As yet unnamed, the new site will again be offered on a subscription basis and as a 10-month exclusive on MSN. It will feature more sophisticated games and comics, news items and other information features that will help kids with their homework, plus plenty of graphics, sounds, and interactive quizzes—all geared to appeal to their audience's "aging" tastes and trend consciousness. The executives figure parents who pay for the subscriptions will love and support the site as a "safe" and educational Internet experience for their offspring.

"These kids have grown up with PCs, and for them computers are completely second nature," Winebaum tells you confidently. He should know—he has two kids in this age group. "They will own this medium—and you can quote me on that," he adds.

Your Task: Winebaum has asked you to help him draft the news release announcing the new Disney-Microsoft venture. It will have to pass through both companies for approval, of course, and before it's released they will need to agree on a name for the new site. But he wants to be ready. Where the Internet, Disney, and Microsoft are concerned, timing is crucial and sooner is always better than later. Leave space for the site name to be added later if you must. And remember: At this stage, the plans are top secret; this draft is CONFIDENTIAL—FOR YOUR EYES ONLY.[20]

WRITING GOODWILL MESSAGES

13. Now they've "Got Milk!": E-mail thanking agency for cultural crisis counseling You thought everybody loved the "Got Milk?" advertising campaign you've been overseeing as executive director of the California Milk Processor Board. From billboards to TV commercials, these clever ads are getting your message across so well they've increased product recognition levels (the key indicator of advertising success) to around 90 percent. But now you've discovered how miserably the ads are failing with the Hispanic demographic group, which makes up no less than one-third of California's population. Your job is on the line here.

Your expensive San Francisco ad agency, which developed the campaign and produced the ads in both English and Spanish, can't explain it. Frustrated, you pace the office. "Why, why, why?" you ask your bewildered staff, not really expecting an answer. "What's not to love about these crazy commercials? What about the guy who dies and thinks he's gone to heaven when he spots a huge plate of chocolate chip cookies? He takes a giant bite, and with his mouth full of cookie, he opens the refrigerator. No milk! He panics, suddenly realizing he's definitely *not* in heaven! 'Got milk?' the voice-over asks. People love it! Or what about the guy who's volunteered for a lab experiment. Just as the white coats seal him into a closed room he discovers he's got cereal, but no milk! The look on his face as he pounds on the glass . . . "

"Calm down," an assistant urges, "you're starting to look just like him! Here," she hands you a business card. "Call Anita Santiago—she runs Santiago Advertising, which specializes in capturing the Hispanic market. I'll bet she can answer your questions."

She sure does. Santiago is the first person to explain that, first of all, the "got milk" slogan so clever in English translates into Spanish as "Are you lactating?" Second, to this Hispanic group, running out of milk is no laughing matter but indicates that one has failed one's family. With your eager approval, Santiago's agency produces a new campaign for the Hispanic market, called "Generations." It's aimed at new mothers and poses the question, "Have you given them enough milk today?" And instead of focusing on deprivation, the new ads show milk as an almost sacred ingredient in cherished recipes handed down from grandmother to mother to daughter in traditional Hispanic families.

Now, four months later, you're staring at the figures and you can't believe it. Milk recognition has gone up to 91 percent among Hispanic consumers! Santiago has conquered the cultural and communication gap—and has saved the Milk Processor Board from a very embarrassing gaffe (not to mention saving your job).

She deserves high praise, not only for her expertise but for her creative genius as well.

Your Task: Write an e-mail message to Anita Santiago at <anita@santiago.com> congratulating her on the new figures and thanking her for all she's done.[21]

14. Phenix fuss: Letter thanking volunteers When Joann and Faron Roberts opened a 400-square-foot bookstore in San Bernardino, California, they dreamed of going places—but they never imagined their eight boxes of books and $7,000 in savings would take them so far so fast. The Phenix Information Center has outgrown three locations since that 1992 opening, becoming "one of the top ten African American bookstores in the nation," according to one New York publisher. Never mind that it's nearly 75 miles east of Los Angeles; Phenix has built a reputation for extravagant book-signing events that bring out the local community in droves—people of all colors from as far away as San Diego and Palm Springs. What Joann and Faron do with these events "borders on pageantry," says the publishing expert.

When they started out, the Robertses simply loved books and their own cultural heritage, and they wanted to make a difference. They didn't know they'd be hosting authors of such diverse and popular appeal as Colin Powell, Johnnie Cochran, Christopher Darden, George Foreman, Kareem Abdul-Jabbar, and Walter Mosley, not to mention the local poets and writers whose careers have been unmistakably boosted by the "Phenix treatment."

Now that you're working with Joann and Faron, you, too, have come under their dynamic influence. You love the store, selling not only books, tapes, and CDs, but also children's games, Afrocentric gift wrap, cards with African American themes, and customized wedding invitations. You love Joann's enthusiasm—and Faron's commitment. He wrote the store's mission statement, which begins, "We are a community-sensitive enterprise . . . " Phenix (the spelling was Faron's idea) hosts community service workshops, writers' groups, author readings, genealogical research groups—you name it, if it will help the community, they've probably thought of it.

But most amazing is the group of 60 volunteers who help stage the book-signings. Joann's written proposal convinced Random House to send Colin Powell so far off the beaten track. But the event made local history—and Phenix's reputation. The volunteers rehearsed every detail for two full months, coordinating with police and Secret Service to manage the thousands who showed up at 3:00 A.M. for a 10:00 A.M. signing. They lined up sponsors, arranged to use a nearby theater, and won support from the mayor's office. Volunteer poets wrote and recited works in Powell's honor; volunteer jazz musicians serenaded the crowd. Volunteers even helped arrange a color guard from March Air Force base, a borrowed baby grand piano, and a borrowed antique desk for Powell to sit at.

Since then, these devoted volunteers have helped make Phenix the number one choice among publishers booking author tours. George Foreman was impressed when he pulled up in a limo to sign his cookbook and discovered that the huge community barbecue on the town square was being staged in his honor. He stayed three hours overtime. Johnnie Cochran was so moved by the choir that sang for him, he sent flowers the next day.

Your Task: "It's past time we do something for these people," Joann says to you one morning. "First, you write them a glowing thank-you letter—but make it sincere. Then I'm going to think up an event just for our volunteers . . . something they'll never forget . . . " She gets a distant gleam in her eye and you start writing the letter that says thanks and that hints of a party to remember.[22]

DEVELOPING YOUR INTERNET SKILLS

GOING ONLINE: SEND AN ELECTRONIC GOODWILL MESSAGE, P. 191

Send a message to someone you think needs some encouragement. Now send another of your own choice. Was the digital postcard as easy to complete as you expected? Run into any snags? How could you make this process simpler, and how might this service improve business relations?

After studying this chapter, you will be able to

Choose correctly between indirect and direct approaches to a bad-news message

Establish the proper tone from the beginning of your message

Present bad news in a reasonable and understandable way

Write messages that motivate your audience to take constructive action

Close messages so that your audience is willing to continue a business relationship with your firm

WRITING BAD-NEWS MESSAGES

On the Job

FACING A COMMUNICATION DILEMMA AT AMERICAN AIRLINES

When Saying No Is Part of Your Job

Few businesspeople enjoy saying no to well-meaning potential partners, but for Donna Burnley of American Airlines, saying no is a necessary part of ensuring top-quality customer service. As a senior commodity manager, she spends $23 million a year on in-flight food service supplies such as glasses, china, silverware, and napkins. In addition, Burnley manages two warehouses and oversees the maintenance and repair of the in-flight food preparation and serving equipment.

Naturally, many companies would like a part of that business, but few can meet Burnley's strict criteria. Perhaps the biggest challenge these suppliers face is meeting the complicated demands of an airline that flies to more than 170 locations across the Americas, Europe, Asia, Africa, and Australia. As Burnley puts it, "There are relatively few suppliers capable of manufacturing the volume of custom catering equipment required." She can't choose suppliers solely on the basis of their price or quality; she needs partners who can also manufacture and distribute reliably on a global scale.

If you were in Donna Burnley's shoes, how would you respond to requests from well-meaning companies who offer good products but can't meet all of American's requirements? How would you handle a supplier whose quality or customer service had slipped below acceptable levels? What steps could you take to deliver these bad-news messages in a professional manner that doesn't offend the recipients, while still getting your point across?[1]

ORGANIZING BAD-NEWS MESSAGES

As Donna Burnley realizes, some people interpret being rejected for a job or for credit as a personal failure; even rejections in less sensitive areas usually complicate people's lives. Admittedly, business decisions should not be made solely to avoid hurting someone's feelings, but mixing bad news with consideration for your reader's needs helps your audience understand that the unfavorable decision is based on a business judgment, not on any personal judgment.

As are direct requests and routine, good-news, and goodwill messages, bad-news messages are best communicated across cultures by using the tone, organization, and other cultural conventions that your audience expects. Only then can you avoid the inappropriate or even offensive approaches that could jeopardize your business relationship.[2] For example, in Latin countries, people consider it discourteous and impolite to bring negative messages to the boss, so they attempt to avoid such messages altogether. People in Germany tend to be more direct with bad news, but in Japan, bad news can be presented so positively that a U.S. businessperson might not detect it at all.[3]

When you need to communicate bad news to a U.S. or Canadian audience that has minimal cultural differences, consider tone and arrangement. Your tone contributes to your message's effectiveness by supporting three specific goals:

- Helping your audience understand that your bad-news message represents a firm decision
- Helping your audience understand that, under the circumstances, your decision was fair and reasonable
- Helping your audience remain well disposed toward your business and possibly toward you

With the right tone, you can make an unwelcome point while preserving your audience's ego.

To accomplish the right tone, make liberal use of the "you" attitude—for example, by pointing out how your decision might actually further your audience's goals. In addition, convey concern by looking for the best in your audience; assume that your audience is interested in being fair, even when they are at fault. Finally, you can ease disappointment by using positive words rather than negative ones. Just be sure that your positive tone doesn't hide the bad news behind difficult language.[4] You want to convey the bad news, not cover it up.

How you arrange the main idea and supporting data can also ease your audience's disappointment. The two basic strategies described in Chapter 6 are (1) the indirect plan, which presents supporting data before the main idea, and (2) the direct plan, which presents the main idea before the supporting data.

Indirect Plan

The indirect plan is actually a familiar approach. You've probably used it many times to say something that might upset another person. Instead of beginning a business message with a blunt no, which could keep your audience from reading or listening to your reasons, use the indirect plan to ease your audience into the part of your message that demonstrates that you're fair-minded and eager to do business on some other terms.

The indirect plan consists of four parts: (1) a buffer; (2) reasons supporting the negative decision; (3) a clear, diplomatic statement of the negative decision; and (4) a helpful, friendly, and positive close. By presenting the reasons for your decision before the bad news itself, you gradually prepare the audience for disappointment. In most cases, this approach is more appropriate than an abrupt statement of the bad news.

Buffer

The first step in using the indirect plan is to put the audience in an accepting mood by making a neutral, noncontroversial statement closely related to the point of the message; this statement is called a **buffer**. In a memo telling another supervisor that you can't spare anyone from your customer service staff for a temporary assignment to the order fulfillment department, you might begin with a sentence like this: "Customer service is one of our major concerns at National Investments. In addition, this department shares your goal of processing orders quickly and efficiently."

If possible, base the buffer on statements made by the person you're responding to. If you use an unrelated buffer, you seem to be "beating around the bush"; that is, you appear unethical, so you lose your audience's respect. Another goal when composing your buffer is to avoid giving the impression that good news will follow. Building up the audience at the beginning only makes the subsequent letdown even more painful. Imagine your reaction to the following openings:

American Airlines must maintain strong relationships with customers, employees, and investors. One way it builds and retains these relationships is by focusing on audience feelings. By explaining the reasons for any bad news and by focusing on the positive aspects of a negative situation, people at American Airlines communicate their understanding and demonstrate their goodwill.

In a bad-news message, the "you" attitude translates into

- Emphasizing the audience's goals instead of your own
- Looking for the best in your audience
- Using positive rather than negative phrasing

A buffer is a neutral lead-in to bad news.

Your résumé indicates that you would be well suited for a management trainee position with our company.

Your résumé shows very clearly why you are interested in becoming a management trainee with our company.

The second opening emphasizes the applicant's favorable interpretation of her qualifications rather than the company's evaluation, so it's less misleading but still positive. Here are some other things to avoid when writing a buffer:

Use a buffer that is

- Neutral
- Relevant
- Not misleading
- Assertive
- Succinct

- *Avoid saying no.* An audience encountering the unpleasant news right at the beginning usually reacts negatively to the rest of the message, no matter how reasonable and well phrased it is.
- *Avoid using a know-it-all tone.* When you use phrases such as "you should be aware that," the audience expects your lecture to lead to a negative response and therefore resists the rest of your message.
- *Avoid wordy and irrelevant phrases and sentences.* Sentences such as "We have received your letter," "This letter is in reply to your request," and "We are writing in response to your request" are irrelevant. You make better use of the space by referring directly to the subject of the letter.
- *Avoid apologizing.* An apology weakens your explanation of the unfavorable decision.
- *Avoid writing a buffer that is too long.* The point is to briefly identify something that both you and your audience are interested in and agree on before proceeding in a businesslike way.

Not only is Mae C. Jemison an astronaut (the first African American woman to travel in space), she's also a physician, a chemical engineer, and founder of the Jemison Group (a company that researches, develops, and markets advanced technologies). When communicating bad news, says Jemison, show that you understand your audience's needs, but don't undermine your message with apologies.

Table 10.1 shows types of buffers you could use to open a bad-news message tactfully.

Some critics believe that using a buffer is manipulative, dishonest, and thus unethical. In fact, buffers are unethical only if they're insincere. Breaking bad news with kindness and courtesy is the human way. Consideration for the feelings of others is never dishonest, and that consideration helps your audience accept your message.

After you've composed a buffer, evaluate it by asking yourself four questions: Is it pleasant? Is it relevant? Is it neutral, saying neither yes nor no? Does it provide for a smooth transition to the reasons that follow? If you can answer yes to every question, you may proceed confidently to the next section of your message.

Reasons

Present reasons to show that your decision is reasonable and fair.

If you've done a good job of composing the buffer, the reasons will follow naturally. Cover the positive points first; then move to the less positive ones. Provide enough detail for the audience to understand your reasons, but be concise; a long, roundabout explanation may make the audience impatient.

The goal is to explain *why* you have reached your decision before you explain *what* that decision is. If you present your reasons effectively, they will help convince the audience that your decision is justified, fair, and logical. However, someone who realizes you're saying no before he or she understands why may either quit paying attention altogether or be set to rebut the reasons when they're finally given.

Focus on how the audience might benefit from your negative message.

When giving your reasons, be tactful by highlighting just how the decision benefits your audience instead of focusing on why the decision is good for you or your company. For example, when saying no to a credit request, show how your decision will keep the person from becoming overextended financially. Facts and figures are often helpful in convincing members of your audience that you're acting in their best interests.

As you explain your reasons, avoid hiding behind company policy to cushion the bad news. If you say, "Company policy forbids our hiring anyone who does not have two years' management experience," you seem to imply that you haven't considered the person on her or his own merits. Although skilled and sympathetic communicators may sometimes quote company policy, they also briefly explain it so that the audience can try to meet the requirements at a later time.

Table 10.1	TYPES OF BUFFERS	

Buffer	Strategy	Example
Agreement	Find a point on which you and the reader share similar views.	We both know how hard it is to make a profit in this industry.
Appreciation	Express sincere thanks for receiving something.	Your check for $127.17 arrived yesterday. Thank you.
Cooperation	Convey your willingness to help in any way you realistically can.	Employee Services is here to smooth the way for all of you who work to achieve company goals.
Fairness	Assure the reader that you've closely examined and carefully considered the problem, or mention an appropriate action that has already been taken.	For the past week, we have carefully monitored those using the photocopying machine to see whether we can detect any pattern of use that might explain its frequent breakdowns.
Good news	Start with the part of your message that is favorable.	A replacement knob for your range is on its way, shipped February 10 via UPS.
Praise	Find an attribute or an achievement to compliment.	Your résumé shows an admirable breadth of experience, which should serve you well as you progress in your career.
Resale	Favorably discuss the product or company related to the subject of the letter.	With their heavy-duty, full-suspension hardware and fine veneers, the desks and file cabinets in our Montclair line have become a hit with value-conscious professionals.
Understanding	Demonstrate that you understand the reader's goals and needs.	So that you can more easily find the printer with the features you need, we are enclosing a brochure that describes all the Panasonic printers currently available.

Avoid apologizing when giving your reasons. Apologies are appropriate only when someone in your company has made a severe mistake or has done something terribly wrong. If no one in the company is at fault, an apology gives the wrong impression.

The tone of the language you use to explain your reasons greatly influences your audience's reception of the bad news that follows. So avoid negative, counterproductive words like these:

INSTEAD OF THIS	SAY THIS
We have received your *broken* clock.	We have received the clock you sent us.
I *cannot understand* what you mean.	Please clarify your request.
The *damage* won't be fixed for a week.	The item will be repaired next week.
There will be a *delay* in your order.	We will ship your order as soon as possible.
You are clearly *dissatisfied*.	We are doing what we can to make things right.
Your account is in *error*.	Corrections have been made to your account.
The breakage was not our *fault*.	The merchandise was broken during shipping.
Sorry for your *inconvenience*.	The enclosed coupon will save you $5 next time.
We *regret* the misunderstanding.	I'll try my best to be clearer from now on.
I was *shocked* to hear the news.	The news reached me yesterday.
Unfortunately, we haven't received it.	It hasn't arrived yet.
The enclosed statement is *wrong*.	Please recheck the enclosed statement.

BEHIND THE SCENES AT ADLAI STEVENSON HIGH SCHOOL
Keeping Doors Open While Delivering Bad News

Richard DuFour is committed to developing the potential of all the people in his organization. As superintendent of Adlai Stevenson High School, DuFour tries to encourage innovation by recognizing the efforts and achievements of the school's 3,150 students and its 352 teachers, administrators, and support staff. Yet DuFour must sometimes deliver bad news to individuals associated with the school—including parents. To keep his readers well disposed toward the school, he communicates these messages carefully by considering his readers' needs and helping them understand the circumstances that led up to his decision.

When the Board of Education allocated additional funds to expedite the school's technology plan, DuFour knew that keeping the teachers excited about adopting new technology and integrating technology into classroom instruction were important school goals. So he decided to offer grants to teachers who developed technology proposals that furthered those goals. Eighty-four teachers submitted applications valued at $450,000. But with only $130,000 in grant money available, DuFour had to send 69 teachers bad-news letters. "My biggest concern in writing these letters was that the teachers might interpret the rejection as a lack of appreciation for their initiative."

To make the rejection as painless as possible, DuFour begins his letter with a buffer thanking the teacher for spend-

Whenever Superintendent Richard DuFour must send someone a negative message, he tries to nurture his school's innovative spirit by using a buffer and keeping doors open to staff, teachers, parents, and students.

ing the time, energy, and creativity to develop a technology grant proposal. Only then does he explain that "demand exceeded capacity by almost four to one, making our task very difficult." DuFour typically uses the direct approach when communicating with school personnel, so now he moves right to the point: "Although your proposal has merit, it is not among those rated highest by our committee and thus will not be funded by the Board this year." He explains how the winners were selected and softens the bad news by leaving the door open—encouraging teachers to participate in

---

Sometimes the "you" attitude is best observed by avoiding the word you.

Furthermore, protect the audience's pride by using language that conveys respect, and avoid an accusing tone. Use third-person, impersonal, passive language to explain your audience's mistakes in an inoffensive way. Say, "The appliance won't work after being immersed in water" instead of "You shouldn't have immersed the appliance in water." In this case, the "you" attitude is better observed by avoiding the word *you*.

When refusing the application of a management trainee, a tactfully worded letter might give these reasons for the decision not to hire:

> Because these management trainee positions are quite challenging, our human relations department has researched the qualifications needed to succeed in them. The findings show that the two most important qualifications are a bachelor's degree in business administration and two years' supervisory experience.

Well-written reasons are

- Detailed
- Tactful
- Individualized
- Unapologetic
- Positive

This paragraph does a good job of stating the reasons for the refusal:

- It provides enough detail to make the reason for the refusal logically acceptable.
- It implies that the applicant is better off avoiding a program in which she would probably fail, given the background of others who would be working alongside her.
- It doesn't rest solely on company policy. A relevant policy exists but is presented as logical rather than rigid.

the future: "Should the program be continued, we hope you will consider revising your application and resubmitting it for consideration."

By keeping doors open, DuFour can fuel the school's innovative spirit. Another way to nurture that spirit is to recognize student achievement. That's why each year the school awards scholarships to its outstanding seniors. However, when the Adlai Stevenson's parent association decided to sponsor a separate scholarship program in addition to the one already sponsored by the school, DuFour worried "that the selection criteria used by the parents might not be objective." He knew that their "hearts were in the right place," but he had to let them know that the school "could not support this plan." Of course, if the communication was mishandled, the message could be misinterpreted, and these parent volunteers "might feel that their efforts were unappreciated, which could sever our long-standing good relationship."

DuFour begins his letter by restating the association's request: "As I understand it, the proposal calls for the parent's association to select the criteria and then award scholarships independent of the school." He knows that "restating the issue is important because it shows people that they have been heard." He also tries to accomplish this same objective by adopting an audience-centered approach. He shows the group how their proposal would conflict with their own by-laws, and then he turns the bad news into a win-win situation by identifying 11 alternative funding projects "which are more consistent with the association's mission and will benefit all parties." He even offers to assist the parents in exploring other options.

As a result of DuFour's letter-writing efforts, the parents are satisfied despite the bad news, the teachers continue to develop technology initiatives even after being rejected, and the students continue to benefit from innovative programs. Perhaps that's one reason why Adlai Stevenson High School is consistently recognized by *Redbook* magazine as one of the best high schools in the United States.

Apply Your Knowledge

1. Each year Adlai Stevenson High School receives more than 3,000 applications for the 25 teaching positions to be filled. Only candidates who advance to the final stages of the selection process are interviewed. Once a position has been filled, the school notifies the other finalists that they have not been chosen. How should the school handle this bad-news letter? Should they use the direct or the indirect approach? How can they de-emphasize the bad news? Please explain.

2. When you are explaining the reasons for bad news, is it beneficial to discuss the process involved in reaching the decision? Why?

- It offers no apology for the decision.
- It avoids negative personal expressions ("You do not meet our requirements").

Although specific reasons help the audience accept bad news, reasons cannot always be given. When reasons involve confidential, excessively complicated, or purely negative information, or when the reasons benefit only you or your firm (such as enhancing the company's profits), don't include them. Move directly to the next section.

Sometimes detailed reasons should not be provided.

The Bad News

When the bad news is a logical outcome of the reasons that come before it, the audience is psychologically prepared to receive it. However, the audience may still react emotionally if the bad news is handled carelessly. Three techniques are especially useful for saying no as clearly and as painlessly as possible. First, de-emphasize the bad news:

- Minimize the space or time devoted to it.
- Subordinate it in a complex or compound sentence ("My department is already short-handed, so I'll need all my staff for at least the next two months").
- Embed it in the middle of a paragraph.

To make bad news less painful

- Deemphasize the bad news visually and by sentence structure
- Use a conditional statement
- Tell what you did do, not what you didn't do

Second, use a conditional (*if* or *when*) statement to imply that the audience could possibly have received, or might someday receive, a favorable answer: "When you have more

Jane Bryant Quinn is a financial columnist for Newsweek. *She points out that companies can paint an overall positive picture and then use phrases such as "subject to," "except for," and "despite the" to moderate the impact of bad news.*

When writing a bad-news message, avoid negative wording and personal language.

managerial experience, you are welcome to reapply." Such a statement could motivate applicants to improve their qualifications.

Third, tell the audience what you did do, can do, or will do rather than what you did not do, cannot do, or won't do. Say "We sell exclusively through retailers, and the one nearest you that carries our merchandise is . . ." rather than "We are unable to serve you, so please call your nearest dealer." Here's the same principle applied to the letter rejecting the job applicant: "The five positions currently open have been staffed with people whose qualifications match those uncovered in our research." A statement like this need not be followed by the explicit news that you won't be hiring the reader. By focusing on the positive and only implying the bad news, you soften the blow.

Of course, when implying bad news, be sure your audience understands the entire message—including the bad news. It would not be ethical to overemphasize the positive. So if an implied message might leave doubt, state your decision in direct terms. Just be sure to avoid blunt statements that are likely to cause pain and anger. The following phrases are particularly likely to offend:

INSTEAD OF THIS	USE THIS
I must refuse your request.	I won't be in town on the day you need me.
We must deny your application.	The position has been filled.
I am unable to grant your request.	Contact us again when you have established . . .
We cannot afford to continue the program.	The program will conclude on May 1.
Much as I would like to attend . . .	Our budget meeting ends too late for me to attend . . .
We must reject your proposal.	We've accepted the proposal from AAA Builders.
We must turn down your extension request.	Please send in your payment by June 14.

Positive Close

An upbeat, positive close

- Builds goodwill
- Offers a suggestion for action
- Provides a look toward the future

As American's Donna Burnley will attest, after giving your audience the bad news, your job is to end your message on an upbeat note. You might propose an attainable solution to the audience's problem: "The human resources department has offered to bring in temporary workers when I need them, and they would probably consider doing the same for you." In a message to a customer or potential customer, an off-the-subject ending that includes resale information or sales promotion is also appropriate. If you've asked someone to decide between alternatives or to take some action, make sure she or he knows what to do, when to do it, and how to do it with ease. Whatever type of close you choose, follow these guidelines:

- Keep your close as positive as possible. Don't refer to, repeat, or apologize for the bad news, and refrain from expressing any doubt that your reasons will be accepted (avoid statements such as "I trust our decision is satisfactory").
- Encourage additional communication *only* if you're willing to discuss your decision further (avoid phrases such as "If you have further questions, please write").
- Keep a positive outlook on the future. Anticipate no problems (avoid statements such as "Should you have further problems, please let us know").
- Be sincere. Steer clear of clichés that are insincere in view of the bad news (avoid saying, "If we can be of any help, please contact us").
- Be confident about keeping the person as a customer (avoid phrases such as "We hope you will continue to do business with us").

If you are the one who has to reject the applicant for the management trainee position, you could observe these guidelines by writing a close like this:

Many companies seek other qualifications in management trainees, so I urge you to continue your job search. You'll certainly find an opening in which your skills and aspirations match the job requirements exactly.

Keep in mind that the close is the last thing the audience has to remember you by. Try to make the memory a positive one.

Direct Plan

A bad-news message organized on the direct plan would start with a clear statement of the bad news, proceed to the reasons for the decision, and end with a courteous close. Stating the bad news at the beginning can have two advantages: (1) It makes a shorter message possible, and (2) the audience needs less time to reach the main idea of the message, the bad news itself.

Although the indirect approach is preferable for most bad-news messages, you may sometimes want to move right to the point. Memos are often organized so that the bad news comes before the reasons. In fact, some managers expect all internal correspondence to be brief and direct, regardless of whether the message is positive or negative. Routine bad-news messages to other companies often follow the direct plan, especially if they relay decisions that have little or no personal impact. Using a buffer can actually cause ill will in people who see them frequently (such as people searching for employment).[5] In addition, you'll sometimes know from experience that your audience simply prefers reading the bad news first in any message. Of course, the direct plan is also appropriate when you want to present an image of firmness and strength; for example, the last message in a collection series, just before the matter is turned over to an attorney, usually gets right to the point.

So, in any number of circumstances, you may want to use the direct plan and save your positive comments for the close. Whichever approach you choose, remember that a tactful tone and a focus on reasons will help make any bad-news message easier to accept.

CONVEYING BAD NEWS ABOUT ORDERS

Businesses must sometimes convey bad news concerning orders. When Donna Burnley must relate bad news to suppliers, she is careful to focus her audience's attention on what can be done rather than on what cannot. When writing to a would-be customer, you have three basic goals:

- To work toward an eventual sale along the lines of the original order
- To keep instructions or additional information as clear as possible
- To maintain an optimistic, confident tone so that your reader won't lose interest

For example, when you must back order for a customer, you have one of two types of bad news to convey: (1) You're able to send only part of the order, or (2) you're able to send none of the order. When sending only part of the order, you actually have both good news and bad news. In such situations, the indirect plan works very well. The buffer contains the good news (that part of the order is en route) along with a resale reminder of the product's attractiveness. After the buffer come the reasons for the delay of the remainder of the shipment. A strong close encourages a favorable attitude toward the entire transaction (Figure 10.1).

Even when you're unable to send the customer any portion of an order, you still use the indirect approach. However, because you have no good news to give, your buffer only confirms

As senior vice president of human resources for Metropolitan Life Insurance, Catherine Rein supports the direct method for bad news when you want to maintain a position of strength. Cutting a program can bother those responsible for it, explains Rein, but well-made decisions must prevail.

Use the direct plan when

- Your boss prefers that internal messages come right to the point
- The message has little personal impact
- You want to make your point emphatically

The basic goal of a bad-news letter about orders is to protect or make a sale.

Use the indirect plan when telling a customer that you cannot immediately ship the entire order.

Figure 10.1
In-Depth Critique: Letter Advising of a Back Order

For a customer whose order for a recliner and ottoman will be partly filled, your letter might read like this one.

1284 North Telegraph Road
Monroe, MI 48161-5138

September 9, 1998

Dr. Elizabeth Fawnworth
2524 St. Georgen Common
Boston, MA 22290-2827

Dear Dr. Fawnworth:

Thank you for your order of the special edition recliner and matching ottoman. The recliner with custom features will be shipped today. The leather trim you designated turned out beautifully, and we're sure the recliner will make a handsome addition to your study.

The roll-around ottoman has proved to be one of our most popular items. Our plant manager reports that, even though he has almost doubled production this year, we are still experiencing some delays. We estimate that your ottoman will be shipped no later than November 15 to arrive by Thanksgiving.

Remember that all La-Z-Boy products carry a lifetime guarantee. We know you will enjoy your recliner and ottoman for many years. I've enclosed a catalog that includes our latest designs. Please call me at (616) 358-2899 if you'd like to talk about any of our special fabrics or custom designs. We look forward to serving you again in the future.

Cordially,

Suzanne Godfrey

Suzanne Godfrey
Manager, Custom Designs

Enclosure

In the indirect plan, the buffer conveys the good news and confirms the wisdom of the customer's choice.

The reasons for the shipping delay are stated in a way that indicates that the ottoman is a popular choice. The bad news is cushioned by the pledge to take care of the problem by a definite time.

The bad news itself is implied by telling the reader what is being done, not what cannot be done.

The positive close also opens the door to future business.

---

the sale, and the explanation section states your reason for not filling the order promptly. For a brief outline of back-order tasks, see this chapter's Checklist for Bad News About Orders.

COMMUNICATING NEGATIVE ANSWERS AND INFORMATION

The businessperson who tries to say yes to everyone probably won't win many promotions or stay in business for long. Occasionally, your response to inquiries must simply be no. It's a mark of your skill as a communicator to be able to say no clearly yet not cut yourself off from future dealings with the other person.

✓✓✓✓
✓✓✓
✓✓✓
✓✓✓
✓✓✓
✓✓✓
✓✓✓
✓✓✓
✓✓✓
✓✓✓
✓✓✓
✓✓✓
✓✓✓
✓✓✓
✓✓✓
✓✓✓
✓✓✓
✓✓✓
✓✓✓
✓✓✓
✓✓✓

CHECKLIST FOR BAD NEWS ABOUT ORDERS

A. Overall Strategy
1. Use the indirect plan in most cases.
2. Use the direct plan when the situation is routine (between employees of the same company), when the reader is not emotionally involved in the message, or when you know that the reader would prefer the bad news first.

B. Buffer
1. Express appreciation for the specific order.
2. Extend a welcome to a new customer.
3. Avoid negative words *(won't, can't, unable to)*.
4. Use resale information on the ordered merchandise to build the customer's confidence in the original choice (except for unfillable orders).

C. Reasons
1. Emphasize what the firm is doing rather than what it isn't doing, what it does have rather than what it lacks.
2. Avoid apologies and expressions of sorrow or regret.
3. Handle back orders carefully.
   ▪ a. Specify shipping dates.
   ▪ b. Give reasons why the item is out of stock, such as high popularity or exceptional demand, that may stimulate the customer's desire for the item.
   ▪ c. Reinforce the customer's confidence with resale (for consumers, emphasize personal attention, credit, repair services, free delivery, special discounts, telephone shopping, and other services; for dealers, emphasize free counter and window displays, advertising materials, sales manuals, factory guarantees, and nearby warehousing).
   ▪ d. Refer to sales promotion material, if desirable.

D. The Bad News
1. State the bad news as positively as possible.
2. State the bad news clearly.
3. Stress the reader benefit of the decision to buy.

E. Positive, Friendly, Helpful Close
1. Remind the reader of how his or her needs are being met, if appropriate.
2. Use resale information to clinch the sale, especially for back orders.
3. Adopt a tone that shows you remain in control of the situation and will continue to give customers' orders personal attention.

Depending on your relationship with the reader, you could use either the direct plan or the indirect plan when writing negative messages. If the reader is unlikely to be deeply disappointed, use the direct plan. Otherwise, use a buffer that expresses your appreciation for being thought of, assures the reader of your attention to the request, compliments the reader, or indicates your understanding of the reader's needs. Continue with the reasons for the bad news and the bad news itself, couched in terms that show how the reader's problem can be solved and what you can do to help. Then close with a statement of interest, encouragement, or goodwill. You can demonstrate your sincerity (and minimize the reader's hostility or disappointment) by promptly fulfilling any promises you make.

> Use the direct plan when your negative answer or information will have little personal impact; use the indirect plan in more sensitive situations.

Providing Bad News About Products

When you must provide bad news about a product, the situation and the reader will dictate whether to use the direct or the indirect plan. If you were writing to tell your company's bookkeeping department about increasing product prices, you'd use the direct plan. The reader would have to make some arithmetical adjustments when the increases were put into effect but presumably wouldn't be emotionally involved in the matter. However, you would probably use the indirect plan to convey the same information to customers or even to your own sales department (because a change that weakens your products' competitive edge threatens sales representatives' incomes and possibly their jobs).

The e-mail message in Figure 10.2 was written to tell one company's sales managers that their request for a licensing agreement had been rejected. The middle section of the memo presents an honest statement of the bad news. The effect of the bad news is diminished by the problem-solving tone, by the avoidance of any overt statement that such a setback may affect commissions, and by the upbeat close.

> Consider the direct or indirect plan for telling the reader bad news about a product.

Figure 10.2
In-Depth Critique: E-Mail
Message Providing Bad News
About Products

When Sybervantage pursued licensing agreements with Warner, the company expected to be entering into a lucrative arrangement in which both companies would profit. Now that Warner has rejected the request, Sybervantage must adjust its strategic planning and must keep its sales force both motivated and involved.

E-Mail

Return-Path: <leslie@Sybervant.com>
Date: Thu, 27 Aug 1998 08:09:19
From: Frank Leslie <leslie@Sybervant.com.>
To: All Sales Managers
Subject: August 29 Meeting

The memo begins on a complimentary note to buffer the bad news.

Thank you for your continuing efforts to make Sybervantage a leader in video-game development. Recent reports indicate that we captured a 10% increase in market share over the second quarter of last year. That increase is directly attributable to your energy and enthusiasm. Now we're facing a situation that will put us to the test.

The bad news is presented along with possible explanations.

As you know, many of us in R&D have been working to develop concept games based on Looney Tunes characters. Presently we have eight games in various stages of development. However, Warner has turned down our requests for licensing agreements. It wasn't a matter of money; we offered them top dollar. I believe that Warner saw the tremendous potential and simply decided to develop its own character-based games.

The third paragraph indicates the action that will be taken to lessen the impact of the bad news and actively involves the readers in the possibility of a solution.

On August 29, we will hold day-long meetings here in Orlando to discuss our options. We'd like all of you to be present. Our purpose will be to decide whether we want to pursue another licensing agreement, or continue as we started, by developing our own character-based games. Meetings will take place at the Ramada Renaissance by the airport. Lunch will be provided. Call or e-mail Shirley in my office for reservations.

We have an opportunity to reshape Sybervantage for the 21st century. Our company has a great future, and I'm looking forward to the synergy we can create.

See you there,

Frank Leslie
President

Denying Cooperation with Routine Requests

Consider the direct or indirect plan to tell someone you cannot do what has been requested.

When people ask you for information or want you to do something and you can't honor the request, you may answer with either the direct plan or the indirect plan. Say that you have asked a company to participate in your research project concerning sales promotion. However, that company has a policy against disseminating any information about projected sales figures. How would you react to the following letter?

Our company policy prohibits us from participating in research projects in which disclosure of discretionary information might be necessary. Therefore, we decline your invitation to our sales staff to fill out questionnaires for your study.

Thank you for trying to include Qualcomm Corporation in your research. If we can be of further assistance, please let us know.

This letter would offend most readers, for several reasons:

■ The direct plan is used, even though the reader is outside the company and may be emotionally involved in the response.
■ The tone of the first paragraph is unnecessarily negative and abrupt.
■ The writer hides behind company policy, a policy that the reader may find questionable.
■ The offer to help is an unpleasant irony, given the writer's unwillingness to help in this instance.

Wording, tone, and format conspire to make a letter either offensive or acceptable. The letter that follows conveys the same negative message as the preceding letter without sounding offensive:

He was never considered a smooth public communicator, but in the midst of what had to be the worst news in decades—the death of his former wife, Princess Diana— England's Prince Charles (left), shown here with French President Jacques Chirac, suddenly demonstrated a new awareness of the needs of his audience. After some initial gaffes by the Royal Family, Prince Charles interceded to arrange ample public mourning opportunities. In the following weeks, he displayed an uncharacteristic warmth and compassion toward the public. As a result, the media responded with high praise for the prince's handling of a tragic bad-news situation.

We at Qualcomm Corporation appreciate and benefit from the research of companies such as yours. Your present study sounds interesting, and we certainly wish we could participate.

The buffer is supportive and appreciative.

Unfortunately, our board requires strict confidentiality of all sales information until quarterly reports are mailed to stockholders. As you know, we release news reports at the same time the quarterly reports go out and will include you in all our future mailings.

Without falling back on references to "company policy," the writer fully explains the reason for the policy. The bad news is implied, not stated explicitly.

Although we cannot release projected figures, we are more than willing to share data that are part of the public record. I've enclosed several of our past earnings reports for your inspection. We look forward to seeing the results of your study. Please let us know if there is any additional way we can help.

The close is friendly, positive, and helpful.

As you think about the different impact these two letters might have on you, you can see why effective business writers like Donna Burnley take the time and the trouble to give negative messages the attention they deserve.

Declining Invitations and Requests for Favors

When you must say no to an invitation or a requested favor, your use of the direct or the indirect plan depends on your relationship with the reader. For example, say the president of your community college asks you to host graduation on your corporate grounds, but your companywide sales meetings will take place at the same time. If you don't know the president well, you'll probably use the indirect plan.

However, if you are friends with the president and work frequently on projects for the college, you might use the direct approach.

Consider the direct or indirect plan to turn down an invitation or a request for a favor.

Sandra, thanks for asking us to host your '99 graduation. You know we've always supported the college and would love to do this for you. Unfortunately, our company sales meetings will be going on during the same time. We'll have so many folks tied up with logistics, we wouldn't have the personnel to adequately take care of graduation.

Have you called Jerry Kane over at the Botanical Gardens? I can't think of a prettier site for graduation. Roberta in my office volunteers over there and knows Jerry. She can fill you in on the details, if you'd like to talk to her first.

Thanks again for considering us. Let's have lunch in mid-June to plan our involvement with the college for the next school year. You can think of all kinds of ways to make me sorry I had to say no! I'll look forward to seeing you and catching up on family news.

This letter gets right to the point but still uses some blow-softening techniques: It compliments the person and organization making the request and looks toward future opportunities for cooperation.

REFUSING ADJUSTMENT OF CLAIMS AND COMPLAINTS

Use the indirect plan in most cases of refusing to make an adjustment.

Almost every customer who requests an adjustment is emotionally involved; therefore the indirect plan is generally used for a refusal. Your job as a writer is to avoid accepting responsibility for the unfortunate situation and yet avoid blaming or accusing the customer. To steer clear of these pitfalls, pay special attention to the tone of your letter. Keep in mind that a tactful and courteous letter can build goodwill while denying the claim (Figure 10.3).

When refusing to make an adjustment

- *Demonstrate understanding of the complaint*
- *Explain your refusal*
- *Suggest alternative action*

When refusing to adjust a claim, avoid language that might have a negative impact on the reader. Instead, demonstrate that you understand and have considered the complaint. Then, even if the claim is unreasonable, rationally explain why you are refusing the request (but don't apologize or rely on company policy). End the letter on a respectful and action-oriented note. This chapter's Checklist for Refusals to Make Adjustments reminds you of the tasks involved in such messages.

You may be tempted to respond to something particularly outrageous by calling the person a crook, a swindler, or an incompetent. Resist! If you don't, you could be sued for **defamation,** a false statement that tends to damage someone's character or reputation. (Written defamation is called *libel;* spoken defamation is called *slander.*) By this definition, someone suing for defamation would have to prove (1) that the statement is false, (2) that the language is injurious to the person's reputation, and (3) that the statement has been "published."

If you can prove that your accusations are true, then you haven't defamed the person. The courts are likely to give you the benefit of the doubt because our society believes that ordinary business communication should not be hampered by fear of lawsuits. However, beware of writing an irate letter just to let off steam: If the message has no necessary business purpose and is expressed in abusive language that hints of malice, you'll lose the case. To avoid being accused of defamation, follow these guidelines:

- Avoid using any kind of abusive language or terms that could be considered defamatory.
- If you wish to express your own personal opinions about a sensitive matter, use your own stationery (not company letterhead), and don't include your job title or position. Take responsibility for your own actions without involving your company.

Brodie's Stereo/Video has received a letter from George Pulkinen, who purchased a portable CD player a year ago. Pulkinen says that the unit doesn't work correctly and inquires about the warranty. Pulkinen believes that the warranty covers one year, but it actually covers only three months. This is Brodie's response.

Figure 10.3
In-Depth Critique: Letter Refusing a Claim

NUMBER ONE IN ENTERTAINMENT

BRODIE'S

S/V

STEREO
VIDEO

68 Lake Itasca Boulevard • Hannover, MN 55341
Voice: (612) 878-1312 • Fax: (612) 878-1316

May 3, 1999

Mr. George Pulkinen
237 Lake Street
Lake Elmo, MN 55042

Dear Mr. Pulkinen:

Thank you for your letter describing the problem with your portable Sony CD Walkman. We believe, as you do, that electronic equipment should be built to last. That's why we stand behind our products with a 90-day warranty.

The buffer covers a point that reader and writer agree on.

Even though your Walkman is a year old and therefore out of warranty, we can still help. Please package your CD player carefully and ship it to our store in Hannover. Include your complete name, address, phone number, and a brief description of the problem along with a check for $35. After examining the unit, we will give you a written estimate of the needed parts and labor. Then just let us know—either by phone or by filling out the prepaid card we will provide—whether you want us to make the repairs.

The reason puts the company's policy in a favorable light.

The bad news, stated indirectly, tactfully leaves the repair decision to the customer.

If you choose to repair the unit, the $35 will be applied toward your bill, payable by check or major credit card. If you decide not to repair the unit, the $35 will pay for the technician's time in examining the unit. Sony also has service centers available in your area. If you would prefer to take the unit to one of them, please see the enclosed list.

A positive alternative action should help soothe the customer.

Thanks again for inquiring about our service. I've also enclosed a catalog of our latest high-tech electronic gear. For the month of June, Sony is offering a "Trade-Up Special," at which time you can receive trade-in credit for your Walkman when you purchase a newer model. Please visit Brodie's very soon.

The close blends sales promotion with acknowledgment of the customer's interests.

Sincerely,

Walter Brodie

Walter Brodie
Proprietor

mk

Enclosure

- Provide accurate information and stick to the facts.
- Never let anger or malice motivate your messages.
- Consult your company's legal department or an attorney whenever you think a message might have legal consequences.
- Communicate honestly, and make sure what you're saying is what you believe to be true.

CHECKLIST FOR REFUSALS TO MAKE ADJUSTMENTS

A. Buffer
1. Use a topic of mutual agreement or a neutral topic to start, but keep to the subject of the letter.
2. Indicate your full understanding of the nature of the complaint.
3. Avoid all areas of disagreement.
4. Avoid any hint of your final decision.
5. Keep the buffer brief and to the point.
6. Maintain a confident, positive, supportive tone.

B. Reasons
1. Provide an accurate, factual account of the transaction.
2. Offer enough detail to show the logic of your position.
3. Emphasize ways that the product should have been handled or the contract followed, rather than the reader's negligence.
4. Word the explanation so that the reader can anticipate the refusal.
5. Avoid relying on unexplained company policy.
6. Avoid accusing or preaching (*you should have*).
7. Do not blame or scold the reader.
8. Do not make the reader appear or feel stupid.
9. Inject a brief resale note after the explanation, if desirable.

C. The Bad News
1. Make the refusal clear using tactful wording.
2. Avoid any hint that your decision is less than final.
3. Avoid words such as *reject* and *claim.*
4. Make a counterproposal for a compromise settlement or partial adjustment (if desirable) in a willing not begrudging tone, in a spirit of honest cooperation, and without making it sound like a penalty.
5. Include a resale note for the company or product.
6. Emphasize a desire for a good relationship in the future.
7. Extend an offer to replace the product or provide a replacement part at the regular price.

D. Positive, Friendly, Helpful Close
1. Eliminate any reference to your refusal.
2. Avoid any apology.
3. Eliminate words suggesting uncertainty.
4. Refer to enclosed sales material.
5. Make it easy for readers to comply with any suggested action.

REFUSING TO EXTEND CREDIT

Use the indirect plan when turning down a credit applicant.

Credit is refused for a variety of reasons, all involving sensitive personal or legal considerations. When denying credit to the applicant with a proven record of delinquent payments and to the applicant with an unstable background, you would probably be justified in offering little hope for future credit approval. You could be more encouraging to other types of applicants. You most certainly would like their current cash business, and you may want their future credit business.

In a letter denying credit to a business

- **Be more factual and less personal than in a letter to an individual**
- **Suggest ways to continue doing business**

Denials of business credit, as opposed to denials of individual credit, are less personally sensitive but more financially significant. Businesses have failed because major suppliers have suspended credit at inconvenient times. When refusing to extend credit to a business, explain your reasons as factually and as impersonally as possible (perhaps the firm's latest financial statements don't meet your criteria, or its credit rating has fallen below an acceptable minimum). Also, explain the steps that must be taken to restore credit. Emphasize the benefits of continued dealings on a cash basis until the firm's creditworthiness has been established or restored. You might offer discounts for cash purchases or assistance in cooperative merchandising to reduce the firm's inventory and increase its cash flow. Third-party loans are another possibility you might suggest.

Be aware that credit is a legally sensitive subject.

Whether dealing with business customers or consumers, companies that deny credit exercise good judgment to avoid legal action. A faulty decision may unfairly do damage to a person's reputation, which in turn may provoke a lawsuit and other bad publicity for the company. Handling credit denials over the phone instead of in writing is no guarantee of avoiding trouble; companies that orally refuse credit still proceed with caution. For a reminder of the tasks involved in this type of message, see this chapter's Checklist for Credit Refusals.

CHECKLIST FOR CREDIT REFUSALS

A. Buffer
1. Introduce a topic that is relevant and that both you and the reader can agree on.
2. Eliminate apologies and negative-sounding words.
3. Phrase the buffer to avoid misleading the reader.
4. Limit the length of the buffer.
5. Express appreciation for the credit request.
6. Introduce resale information.

B. Reasons
1. Check the lead-in from the buffer for smoothness.
2. Make a transition from the favorable to the unfavorable message.
3. Make a transition from the general to the specific.
4. Avoid a condescending lecture about how credit is earned.
5. Avoid relying on unexplained company policy.
6. Stress the benefits of not being overextended.
7. Encourage a later credit application, if future approval is realistic.
8. Phrase reasons in terms of experience with others.
9. Carefully present reasons for the refusal.
   - ■ a. Clearly state the reasons if the reader will accept them.
   - ■ b. Explain your general credit criteria.
   - ■ c. Refer to a credit-reporting agency you have used.
   - ■ d. Use *insufficient information* as a reason only if this is the case.
   - ■ e. To avoid the risk of legal action, omit reasons entirely for extraordinarily sensitive or combative readers or when evidence is unusually negative or involves behavioral flaws.
10. Remind the reader of the benefits of cash purchases.

C. The Bad News
1. Make the refusal clear to the reader.
2. Offer only honest encouragement about considering the credit application at a later date.
3. Avoid negative words, such as *must decline*.
4. Suggest positive alternatives, such as cash and layaway purchases.
5. Handle refusals of business credit differently.
   - ■ a. Recommend cash purchases for small, frequent orders.
   - ■ b. Describe cash discounts (include figures).
   - ■ c. Suggest reducing inventory so that the business can strengthen its credit rating.
   - ■ d. Offer promotional and marketing aid.
   - ■ e. Suggest a later review of the credit application, if future approval is realistic.

D. Positive, Friendly, Helpful Close
1. Avoid business clichés, apologies, and words of regret.
2. Suggest actions the reader might take.
3. Encourage the reader to look to the future, when the application may be approved.
4. Include sales promotion material only if the customer would not be offended.

CONVEYING UNFAVORABLE NEWS ABOUT PEOPLE

From time to time, most managers must convey bad news about people. Letters to prospective employers may be written in direct order. On the other hand, letters to job applicants and employees are often written in indirect order, because the reader will most certainly be emotionally involved.

> Use the indirect plan when giving someone bad news about his or her own job; use the direct plan when giving bad news about someone else's job.

Refusing to Write Recommendation Letters

Even though many states have passed new laws to protect employers who provide open and honest job references for former employees, legal hazards persist.[6] That's why many former employers still refuse to write recommendation letters—especially for people whose job performance has been, on balance, unsatisfactory. Prospective employers don't usually have a personal stake in the response, so letters refusing to provide a recommendation may be brief and direct:

> In letters informing prospective employers that you will not provide a recommendation, be direct, brief, and factual (to avoid legal pitfalls).

We received your request for a recommendation for Yolanda Johnson. According to guidelines from our human resources department, we are authorized to confirm only that Ms. Johnson worked for Tandy, Inc., for three years from June 1995 to July 1998. Best of luck as you interview the administrative applicants.

In letters telling job applicants that you will not write a recommendation, use the utmost tact.

GOING ONLINE
PROTECT YOURSELF WHEN YOU WRITE A JOB REFERENCE

Reduce your legal liability: Learn about state job reference requirements (several states have laws that may require you to write a reference). Learn about the types of statements that may form the basis of a lawsuit against you. Find out how to avoid lawsuits for invasion of privacy and violation of state blacklisting laws. Discover what employee information you can usually provide safely. Learn about when you have an absolute legal obligation to provide information about a former employee.

http://www.toolkit.cch.com/text/p05_8610.htm

In a letter turning down a job applicant, treat the reader with respect; by applying for a job, he or she has complimented your company.

In performance reviews, say what's right as well as what's wrong, and explain how the employee can improve performance.

Letters to the applicants themselves are another matter. Any refusal to cooperate may seem a personal slight and a threat to the applicant's future. The only way to avoid ill feelings is to handle the applicant gently:

Thank you for letting me know about your job opportunity with Coca-Cola. Your internship there and the MBA you've worked so hard to earn should place you in an excellent position to land the marketing job.

Although we can't write formal recommendations here at PepsiCo, I can certainly send Coke a confirmation of your employment dates. For more in-depth recommendations, be sure to ask the people you worked with during your internship to write evaluations of your work performance, and don't forget to ask several of your major professors to write evaluations of your marketing skills. Best of luck to you in your career.

This letter deftly and tactfully avoids hurting the reader's feelings because it makes positive comments about the reader's recent activities, implies the refusal, suggests an alternative, and uses a polite close.

Rejecting Job Applications

It's also difficult to tell job applicants tactfully that you aren't going to offer them employment. But don't let that stop you from communicating the bad news. Rejecting an applicant with silence is unacceptable. At the same time, poorly written rejection letters do have negative consequences, ranging from the loss of qualified candidates for future openings to the loss of customers (not only the rejected applicants but also their friends and family).[7] When delivering bad news to job applicants, remember three principles:[8]

- *Open with the direct plan.* Job applicants know that good news will most probably come by phone and that bad news will most likely come by letter. So if you try to buffer the bad news that your reader is expecting, you will seem manipulative and insincere.
- *Clearly state why the applicant was not selected.* Make your rejection less personal by stating that you hired someone with more experience or whose qualifications match the position requirements more closely.
- *Close by suggesting alternatives.* If you believe the applicant is qualified, mention other openings within your company. You might suggest professional organizations that could help the applicant find employment. Or you might simply mention that the applicant's resumé will be considered for future openings. Any of these positive suggestions may help the applicant be less disappointed and view your company more positively.

A rejection letter need not be long. After all, the applicant wants to know only one thing: Did I land the job? Your brief message conveys the information clearly and with some consideration for the applicant's feelings.

Giving Negative Performance Reviews

A performance review is a manager's formal or informal evaluation of an employee. Few other communication tasks require such a broad range of skill and strategy as that needed for performance reviews, whether positive or negative. The main purpose of these reviews is to improve employee performance by (1) emphasizing and clarifying job requirements, (2) giving employees feedback on their efforts toward fulfilling those requirements, and (3) guiding continued efforts by developing a plan of action, along with its rewards and opportunities. In addition to improving employee performance, performance reviews help companies set organizational standards and communicate organizational values.[9]

Positive and negative performance reviews share several characteristics: The tone is objective and unbiased, the language is nonjudgmental, and the focus is problem solution.[10]

Also, to increase objectivity, more organizations are giving their employees feedback from multiple sources. [11]

Be aware that employee performance reviews can play an important role in lawsuits. It's difficult to criticize employees face to face, and it's just as hard to include criticism in written performance evaluations. Nevertheless, if you fire an employee for incompetence and the performance evaluations are all positive, the employee can sue your company, maintaining you had no cause to terminate employment. [12] Also, your company could be sued for negligence if an injury is caused by an employee who received a negative evaluation but received no corrective action (such as retraining). [13] So, as difficult as it may be, make sure your performance evaluations are well balanced and honest.

When you need to give a negative performance review, remember the following guidelines: [14]

- *Confront the problem right away.* Avoiding performance problems only makes them worse. The one acceptable reason to wait is if you need time to calm down and regain your objectivity.
- *Plan your message.* Be clear about your concerns, and include examples of the employee's specific actions. Think about any possible biases you may have, and get feedback from others. Collect all relevant facts (both strengths and weaknesses).
- *Deliver the message in private.* Whether in writing or in person, make sure you address the performance problem privately. Don't send performance reviews by e-mail or fax. If you're reviewing an employee's performance face to face, conduct the review in a meeting arranged expressly for that purpose, and consider holding the meeting in a conference room, the employee's office, or some other neutral area.
- *Focus on the problem.* Discuss the problems caused by the employee's behavior (without attacking the employee). Compare the employee's performance with what's expected, with company goals, or with job requirements (not with other employees' performance). Identify the consequences of continuing poor performance, and show you're committed to helping solve the problem.
- *Ask for a commitment from the employee.* Help the employee understand that planning for and making improvements are the employee's responsibility. However, finalize decisions jointly so that you can be sure any action to be taken is achievable. In fact, set a schedule for improvement and for following up with evaluations of that improvement.

Donna Burnley would recommend that even if your employee's performance has been disappointing, you would do well to mention some good points in your performance review. Then you must clearly and tactfully state how the employee can better meet the responsibilities of the job. If the performance review is to be effective, be sure to suggest ways that the employee can improve. [15] For example, instead of telling an employee only that he damaged some expensive machinery, suggest that he take a refresher course in the correct operation of that machinery. The goal is to help the employee succeed.

Terminating Employment

When writing a termination letter, you have three goals: (1) to present the reasons for this difficult action, (2) to avoid statements that might involve the company in legal action, and (3) to leave the relationship between the terminated employee and the firm as favorable as possible. For both legal and personal reasons, present specific reasons for asking the employee to leave. [16] Make sure that all your reasons are accurate and verifiable. Avoid words that are open to interpretation, such as *untidy* and *difficult*. Make sure the employee leaves with feelings that are as positive as the circumstances allow. You can do this by telling the truth about the termination and by helping as much as you can to make the employee's transition as smooth as possible. [17] To review the tasks involved in this type of message, see this chapter's Checklist for Unfavorable News About People.

Carefully word a termination letter to avoid creating undue ill will and grounds for legal action.

CHECKLIST FOR UNFAVORABLE NEWS ABOUT PEOPLE

A. Buffer
1. Identify the applicant or employee clearly when writing to a third party.
2. Express the reasons for writing—clearly, completely, and objectively.
3. Avoid insincere expressions of regret.
4. Avoid impersonal business clichés.

B. Reasons
1. Include only factual information.
2. Avoid negative personal judgments.
3. Word negative job-related messages carefully to avoid legal difficulties.
   - a. Avoid terms with legal definitions (*slanderous, criminal*).
   - b. Avoid negative terms with imprecise definitions (*lazy, sloppy*).
   - c. Whenever possible, embed negative comments in favorable or semifavorable passages.
   - d. Avoid generalities, and explain the limits of your observations about the applicant's or employee's shortcomings.
   - e. Eliminate secondhand information.
   - f. Stress the confidentiality of your letter.
4. For letters refusing to supply a recommendation to job seekers, suggest another avenue for getting a recommendation.
5. For rejection letters, emphasize the positive qualities of the person hired rather than the shortcomings of the rejected applicant.
6. For performance reviews, describe the employee's limitations and suggest methods for improving performance.

C. The Bad News
1. Understate negative decisions.
2. Imply negative decisions whenever possible.

D. Positive, Friendly, Helpful Close
1. For refusals to supply recommendations and for rejection letters, extend good wishes.
2. For performance reviews, express a willingness to help further.
3. For termination letters, make suggestions for finding another job, if appropriate.

On the Job

SOLVING A COMMUNICATION DILEMMA AT AMERICAN AIRLINES

Donna Burnley knows that saying no is never pleasant, but her professional responsibilities require her to be very selective. Even though she is responsible for getting supplies and equipment to more than 170 locations worldwide, she relies on only a couple of dozen suppliers. Narrowing the field necessarily means saying no, even to nice, ethical people who come to her with nothing but good intentions.

However, Burnley does have a choice about how she manages these unpleasant situations. First, she can follow a thorough, objective decision process to ensure that she makes the right decisions. She says that American's purchasing process "is designed to maximize total value by having me identify product specifications, assess supplier capabilities, research industry and raw material trends, understand the production process, and monitor the quality of end products and services." In other words, when she makes a decision, she knows what she's talking about.

Second, she can use her communication skills to convey negative messages in a professional and courteous manner. In fact, Burnley says that effective communication is one of her primary responsibilities when working with outside suppliers.

Because her decision process is so methodical and thorough, Burnley does have the advantage of having clear, objective reasons when she has to say no. For example, she and her team hire independent testing laboratories to evaluate the quality of the supplies and equipment they buy, so it's relatively easy to explain to rejected suppliers why they were rejected. This evaluation not only helps ease the disappointment of not being selected, but it gives those suppliers the concrete, factual information they need to improve and perhaps be reconsidered in the future.[18]

Your Mission: You're on the purchasing staff at American Airlines, working as an assistant to Donna Burnley. Your job includes responding to requests and proposals from the airline's current suppliers and companies that would like to become suppliers. These requests cover a variety of topics, from meetings to making sales presentations.

1. Your glassware supplier has announced a dramatic price increase that affects all of the products that American buys from them. The increase averages 12 percent, which is a lot of money in a tight-margin business such as air travel. In all other respects, this company has been a stellar performer, offering great products with superb customer service. However, this price increase is both unexpected and unacceptable. As much as everyone likes working with this company, either they'll have to cancel the price increase, or American will be forced to find a new glassware supplier. You do have some room for compromise, however. An increase of only 3 or 4 percent would be acceptable. Which of the following paragraphs does the best job of presenting the bad news and the reasons?

   a. It's too bad that this is such a penny-pinching business, but that's the way things are. We can live with your current prices, but not the proposed increase. We'd love to go along with you, but I'm afraid we just can't.

   b. As you are probably aware, the airline industry competes primarily on price, so managing our costs carefully is about the only option we have for maintaining a minimal level of profitability. Your current prices fit our cost structure well.

Unfortunately, the proposed 12 percent increase does not, leaving us no choice but to find another supplier.

c. As you are probably aware, the airline industry competes primarily on price, so managing our costs carefully is about the only option we have for maintaining a minimal level of profitability. Your current prices fit our cost structure well, but the proposed 12 percent increase is more than we can afford. If the increase goes into effect, we will have to find another supplier.

2. Continuing with the case of the glassware price increase, which of the following closing paragraphs would you choose and why?

a. We do appreciate quality and service, but we are not going to pay ridiculous prices to get them. I am confident that we can use American's vast buying power to find a more reasonable supplier somewhere in the world.

b. We do respect your need to be profitable in a tough business environment. Consequently, we are open to some negotiation about a smaller price increase, if you would consider that. I will be contacting you by phone in the next few days to discuss this option.

c. We are saddened by our decision, let me assure you. We'll miss not only the quality of your products but the quality of the people we've dealt with at your firm as well. We've come to know many of them almost as personal friends. Please give my best wishes to everyone in your office.

3. Personal contacts are an important source of new business opportunities in many industries. In some cases, businesspeople develop these contacts through active participation in industry or professional groups, visits to trade shows, alumni societies, and other groups. You've recently received a request from a former college classmate (Marcia DeLancey) who is now a sales manager for a plastics manufacturer. She wants to visit your office to present her company's plastic containers. However, you are already familiar with the company and know that it is too small to meet your needs for on-time global deliveries. You didn't know DeLancey all that well; in fact, you had to think for a minute to remember who she was (this is the first contact you've had with her since you both graduated five years ago). Which of the following openings would be most appropriate, keeping in mind that you know her company can't make the grade?

a. Congratulations on reaching such an impressive position at your new company. I hope you enjoy your work as much as I enjoy mine. Thank you for your recent inquiry—evaluating such requests is one of my key responsibilities.

b. Great to hear from you; I'd love to catch up on old times with you and find out how you're doing in your new job. I bounced around a bit after college, but I really feel that I've found my niche here at American.

c. I'm sorry to say that American has already evaluated your company and found its resources were not a good match for our international delivery needs. However, I do appreciate your getting in touch, and I hope all is well with you.

4. American, like many corporate buyers, wants to establish stable, dependable relationships with suppliers. Having a supplier falter on the job or even go out of business without warning would be a huge disruption for you. As a result, your department is concerned about every supplier's financial health. The company that provides American with napkins and paper towels has done a good job for years, but recent events have left the company in precarious financial shape. Your office has already told the company that American would be forced to find another paper source if the company's finances didn't improve. Unfortunately, they've gotten even worse, and it's time to act. You've already written the buffer, reasons, and bad news, and now you need a positive close. Which of these would you choose?

a. Thank you very much for the service you've provided in the past. All of us here at American Airlines wish you the best in resolving your current situation. If you are able to meet these financial criteria in the future, by all means please get back in touch with us.

b. I understand that you're bound to be disappointed by our decisions. If you don't think our decision was valid or if there is more information that you believe we need to evaluate, please feel free to call me or my immediate supervisor to discuss the situation. We have to deal with quite a few suppliers, as you know, and I suppose there is a chance that we missed something in our initial evaluation.

c. I'm very sorry that we have to terminate our purchasing agreement with you. We relied on your company's products for many years, and it's a shame that we won't be able to in the future. I hope this decision doesn't affect your work force too negatively. If there's anything we can do to help, please don't hesitate to call.

Critical Thinking Questions

1. You have to tell a local restaurant owner that your plans have changed and you have to cancel the 90-person banquet scheduled for next month. Do you need to use a buffer? Why or why not?

2. Why is it important to end your bad-news message on a positive note?

3. If company policy changes, should you explain those changes to employees and customers at about the same time, or should you explain to employees first? Why?

4. If the purpose of your letter is to convey bad news, should you take the time to suggest alternatives to your reader? Why or why not?

5. The policy at your company is to refuse refunds on merchandise after 30 days. An important customer has written to request a refund on a purchase made 31 days ago, or he'll take his business elsewhere. How do you respond? Explain your answer.

6. When giving a negative performance review, should the impact be softened by addressing the problem a little at a time? Why or why not?

Documents for Analysis

Read the following documents; then (1) analyze the strengths and weaknesses of each sentence and (2) revise each document so that it follows this chapter's guidelines.

DOCUMENT 10.A: CONVEYING BAD NEWS ABOUT ORDERS

We want to take this opportunity to thank you for your past orders. We have included our new catalog of books, videos, films, and slides to let you know about our great new products. We included our price list also. Please use this list rather than the old one as we've had a slight increase in prices.

Per your request, we are sorry we can't send you the free examination copies of the textbooks you requested. The books, *Communication for Business* and *Winning the Presentation Game*, are two of our new titles that are enjoying brisk sales. It seems everyone is interested in communication skills these days.

We do apologize for not sending the exam copies for free. Our prices continue to rise along with everyone else's, and it's just not feasible to send everyone free copies. If you'd still like to have a look, please notice the prices in the list I've included and don't forget shipping and handling. You can also fax your order to the number shown on the sheet or e-mail your order over the Internet.

I'm sure these books would make a great addition to your collection. Again, we are sorry we couldn't grant your request, but we hope you order anyway.

DOCUMENT 10.B: COMMUNICATING NEGATIVE ANSWERS AND INFORMATION

Your spring fraternity party sounds like fun. We're glad you've again chosen us as your caterer. Unfortunately, we have changed a few of our policies, and I wanted you to know about these changes in advance so that we won't have any misunderstandings on the day of the party.

We will arrange the delivery of tables and chairs as usual the evening before the party. However, if you want us to set up, there is now a $100.00 charge for that service. Of course, you might want to get some of the brothers and pledges to do it, which would save you money. We've also added a small charge for cleanup. This is only $3.00 per person (you can estimate because I know a lot of people come and go later in the evening).

Other than that, all the arrangements will be the same. We'll provide the skirt for the band stage, tablecloths, bar setup, and of course, the barbecue. Will you have the tubs of ice with soft drinks again? We can do that for you as well, but there will be a fee.

Please let me know if you have any problems with these changes and we'll try to work them out. I know it's going to be a great party.

DOCUMENT 10.C: REFUSING ADJUSTMENT OF CLAIMS AND COMPLAINTS

I am responding to your letter of about six weeks ago asking for an adjustment on your fax/modem, model FM39Z. We test all our products before they leave the factory; therefore, it could not have been our fault that your fax/modem didn't work.

If you or someone in your office dropped the unit, it might have caused the damage. Or the damage could have been caused by the shipper if he dropped it. If so, you should file a claim with the shipper. At any rate, it wasn't our fault. The parts are already covered by warranty. However, we will provide labor for the repairs for $50.00, which is less than our cost since you are a valued customer.

We will have a booth at the upcoming trade fair there and hope to see you or someone from your office. We have many new models of office machines that we're sure you'll want to see. I've enclosed our latest catalog. Hope to see you there.

ases

CONVEYING BAD NEWS ABOUT ORDERS

1. More to come: Letter explaining delay of Tesla videotapes
Membership is expanding so rapidly at the nonprofit International Tesla Society that volunteers at the organization's headquarters and museum in Colorado Springs can hardly keep up with the daily mail. Many of the letters are orders for the rare books, diaries, patents, videotapes, audiotapes, and T-shirts advertised in the Society's Museum Bookstore Catalog.

Inventor Nikola Tesla, who emigrated from Yugoslavia to the United States in 1884, was responsible for the alternating current electrical system now used worldwide (which replaced Edison's direct current system). Called a "genius," a "mental giant," and "a man ahead of his time," Tesla also holds the patent for radio technology (although Guglielmo Marconi got the credit), and he invented a host of other devices that dazzled turn-of-the-century society: remote-controlled submarines, magnetic resonators, and lightning-generating "Tesla coils." For a time, Tesla was so well known he even appeared on the cover of *Time* magazine. Then, for reasons biographers still debate, the world forgot about Nikola Tesla.

Now people are catching up with many of Tesla's ideas—and the thousands of unexploited patents he left behind. Industrial and amateur inventors alike are developing working models from his drawings and notes for new concepts that may, like AC power, revolutionize today's technology. That's why the International Tesla Society hosts an annual symposium at which inventors can demonstrate what they've built and attend lectures on the most esoteric aspects of Tesla research. People from many countries attend; others order videotapes of the lectures and workshops.

Last year's symposium was so popular that you've depleted your supply of videotape copies for 17 of the 29 master tapes (no one in the all-volunteer operation rushed out to duplicate the missing tapes). Now you've received a letter from a German engineer ordering the complete set. He included $495 in U.S. funds, plus $12.50 for overseas shipping, and, as a Tesla Society member, he's expecting the usual "same-day shipping." It's going to take about two weeks to get copies of the 17 missing tapes.

Your Task: Write to Josef Mandelheim, Sonnenstrasse 4, 86669 Erlingshofen, Germany, explaining the back-order situation. With your letter, send the 12 lecture videotapes you have on hand.[19]

2. Seattle blend: Letter explaining delays for Cedar Grove compost Ever since word got out about your company's "gourmet compost" (with a little help from your marketing department), Pacific Northwest gardeners can't seem to get enough of Cedar Grove Composting's $20 a cubic yard blend of rotting plant materials, vegetables, and of course, coffee grounds. The fact that your company picks up its composting materials as part of a mandatory recycling program in Seattle and surrounding King County is probably part of the appeal. But some pundits think it has something to do with a nationwide mania for anything rich, aromatic, brown, and expensive coming from Seattle.

"It has a good, rich smell," Mary Heide, manager of Sky Nursery in Shoreline, Washington, told the press, while one of her employees raved about its "rich, brown coffee color—kind of a mocha color from a Seattle point of view." That was it. The orders from gardening retailers started pouring in as their customers heard of the stuff and demanded it for their gardens, despite the fact that your prices are 30 percent higher than everyone else's. It didn't help matters that your general manager, Jan Allen, publicized your $3 million, high-speed fans, cooling chambers, and other devices that "air out" the compost as it cures by telling the media that competing brands just "sit around in static piles. Ours has a higher degree of intelligence."

Your Task: As manager of Cedar Grove's wholesale division, you have a backlog of requests from retailers who are eager to fulfill their customers' demands, and you have to let them know that it's going to be about four weeks before you can fill their orders. Better write this bad-news form letter with as much care and concern as Cedar Grove puts into its compost.[20]

COMMUNICATING NEGATIVE ANSWERS AND INFORMATION

3. No time for talking: Memo from Trident Aquaculture Farming the ocean? You thought it was a crazy idea when you first heard of Trident Aquaculture, but you went for an interview anyway, offering your skills as an office manager. You changed your mind after winding up as administrative assistant for Michael D. Willinsky, president of the company and a skilled biologist and fish farmer who helped create the most innovative and promising sea-farming cage ever tested in the open ocean.

After trials in the blustery, icy seas off Nova Scotia and in New York's frozen St. Lawrence River, Willinsky's research team proved that their unique cage design—measuring about 41 feet in diameter and based on Buckminster Fuller's geodesic dome—could survive 80–110 mph winds, 6- to 12-foot waves, strong currents, and fast-moving ice floes. Thanks to regular hand-feeding and protection from predators, the Arctic charr salmon raised inside the Nova Scotia dome matured in a record 18 months (wild Arctic charr mature in 6 to 8 years).

Seaside communities are desperate for economic alternatives to the traditional fishing industry, now that overfishing, pollution, and coastal development have depleted the world's natural fish supply. About 70,000 U.S. and Canadian fishermen lost their livelihood in 1993, when several major Atlantic fishing areas were closed to commercial fishing because of severe depletion. Yet the demand for fish products has increased. Willinsky's prototype sea dome promises to provide a sustainable supply of fresh- or saltwater fish, renew economic activity in coastal areas, and provide new jobs in the fishing industry.

One result is that Willinsky has become a popular speaker among government and industry leaders. But your boss has to divide his time between pursuing research and development, promoting aquaculture, and managing his company. Next month he travels to Hawaii to speak at an international conference on ocean farming, sponsored by the United Nations Food and Agriculture Organization. Willinsky's U.S. research partner, Michael A. Champ, wants Willinsky to appear at a joint speaking engagement for the New Bedford, Massachusetts, chamber of commerce. Unfortunately, the date falls during Willinsky's week in Hawaii.

Your Task: Willinsky has asked you to fax Champ. Write the informal memo to Michael A. Champ, President, Environmental Systems Development Company (at 1-703-899-7326 in Falls Church, Virginia) and suggest an alternative date.[21]

4. Feeling at home in Denmark: Letter to Web House critiquing its home page Web House is an award-winning Danish company that designs home pages and other Internet materials for international clients. Christian Broberg has hired you as an independent consultant to critique the company's home page from a U.S. point of view. You'll need to visit the Web House home page, <http://www.webhouse.dk>, and study it from the perspective of a U.S. business manager. Consider all aspects of clear intercultural communication.

Your Task: Write a letter to Christian Broberg, Assistant Director (Web House, Hasserisgade 30, 9000 Aalborg, Denmark), and explain why the design of the Web House home page may cause problems for English-speaking clients. Your message is not entirely good news, so take extra care in the way you explain your viewpoints to someone from another country.

5. Navajo Joe's: Letter rejecting interior design proposal Atmosphere is everything at Navajo Joe's coffeehouse in Window Rock, Arizona, in the middle of a Navajo reservation the size of West Virginia. "We've got Starbucks and Hank Williams," brags owner Manny Wheeler, a 26-year-old art history graduate of Arizona State University who grew up on the "big rez." While a student, Wheeler hung out in coffeehouses all over Phoenix. When he came home, he took odd jobs but kept fine-tuning his business plan all the while. He knew Navajos loved their coffee as much as their fry bread, but as far as he knew, nothing resembling an urban-style coffeehouse existed on any reservation. Finally, with a loan from his aunt, furniture from second-hand stores, and decor consisting of Wheeler's original art and cast-offs from his grandmother's yard (an old saddle, rotting wagon harness, and so on), Navajo Joe's was born.

Wheeler has just hired you for your summer break from business school, and he's showing you around the place.

"I like the colors," says the 29-year-old musician whose band, Burn in Effigy, plays weekends here. You look up at the black ceiling and yellow walls, then at the arrow holes in the back wall—no, not a sign of Navajo history, but left over from the archery store that once filled the space. One of Wheeler's paintings catches your eye—a black and gray abstract of a bronc rider done on a slab of cardboard. "That's my Cubist phase," Wheeler explained on your first day. "Dude from Chicago offered me $500 for it. I said it's not for sale." Another wall features Johnny Cash album covers and weird tabloid headlines: "Nude Sunbathers Attacked by Crazed Sea Gulls!" You marvel at the lack of a telephone and the fact that Wheeler drives 250 miles round-trip to Albuquerque three times a month to buy coffee beans. And you note the music—sometimes country and western, sometimes surf music, sometimes the tribal radio station.

"I look at this coffeehouse as an art piece," Wheeler explains proudly. "You keep adding to it until you have a sense of what works."

Well, you can't argue with success. Somehow Wheeler is appealing to Navajos of all generations. For the younger crowd, it's double lattes with a splash of hazelnut and late night chess games. For the old timers, Wheeler had to work a little harder. They couldn't figure out that wall menu, with its mochas and Konas and no regular coffee. They walked out scratching their heads. Wheeler considered brewing up some sheepherder's coffee for them—then settled for keeping a warm pot of Farmer's Bros. on hand. It worked like a charm.

At the end of your first week, the coffeehouse played host to a pair of business partners from Albuquerque who had heard of Wheeler's success. Luther and Marilyn Busby own Native Design, a big-city interior decorating firm that specializes in Southwestern decor for businesses. They loved Wheeler's operation and insisted on presenting him with a "cost-effective" proposal for sprucing up Navajo Joe's decor. "You'll triple your business," they assured him enthusiastically. You held your breath, but Wheeler was polite. He drawled, "Sure . . . send me a proposal."

Your Task: The written proposal finally arrived and Wheeler's reaction was exactly as you had expected. But what you didn't plan for was his insistence that you write the rejection letter. "You're a business student, aren't you?" he winks. "Tell 'em they don't know a thing about business on the rez . . . or whatever you think is an appropriate way to say not in my lifetime!"[22]

REFUSING ADJUSTMENT OF CLAIMS AND COMPLAINTS

6. Your monkey, your choice: Letter from Duncan's Exotic Pets refusing a damage claim As a well-known exotic animal dealer in the Cincinnati area, your boss, Roger Duncan, has dealt with his share of customers experiencing buyer's regret. Despite his warnings, many of them still buy their exotic pets for the wrong reasons. When Melissa Carpenter bought Binky, a red-tailed guenon monkey, she begged Mr. Duncan to reduce his price to $10,000 because she had "fallen in love with Binky's soulful eyes and adorable button nose." Now she wants to return poor Binky, and you have never seen your boss so angry.

"Listen to this!" fumes Mr. Duncan as he reads Carpenter's letter:

While I was at work, I locked your monkey in his own room—which I equipped with his own color TV (with cable) and which I spent days wallpapering with animal pictures. Then last night your monkey somehow unlocked the door, ripped out my telephone, opened the refrigerator, smashed eggs all over my kitchen and my new Persian carpet, broke 14 of the china dishes my mother gave me when I got married, and squeezed toothpaste all over my Louis XIV settee I inherited from my grandmother!

"Not only does she demand that I take poor Binky back after she's abused him through her ignorance and neglect," snapped Mr. Duncan, "but she wants me to pay $150,000 in damages for her car, her apartment, and her state of mind."

Your boss is so upset that you decide to write Ms. Carpenter yourself.

Your Task: Write to Melissa Carpenter (876 Newton Ave., Cincinnati, OH 45202) and include a copy of her contract. It clearly states Roger Duncan's policy: refunds only if animals are returned in good health, and absolutely no warranty against damages. Each pet comes with specific care instructions, including warnings about certain idiosyncrasies that could cause problems in the wrong environment.

Despite the fact that Binky is probably traumatized by his experiences, Mr. Duncan has generously agreed to accept his return, refunding Ms. Carpenter's $10,000. However, he will not accept liability for any loss of property or for any claims of mental duress on the part of Ms. Carpenter. [23]

7. Ketchup complaint: Sorry, Mom—Heinz says the labels stay
As a mother, a children's media consultant, and the founder of Action for Children's Television, Peggy Charen has written a letter to H.J. Heinz of Pittsburgh ketchup fame, complaining about a recent move by the company to involve kids in its new label designs. "I don't think children are the proper target for marketing efforts," the letter complains.

Working in Heinz consumer relations, you've been hearing some ripples of concern among parents ever since Heinz began its campaign by sending art posters and label-design contest rules to classrooms around the nation. Heinz also promoted the design contest with magazine ads asking, "Hey kids, wanna be famous?" At the same time, the company donated $450,000 to the National Endowment for the Arts to be used for children's art programs.

In the company's 120 years, this is only the second time the famous ketchup labels have been changed, and Heinz wanted to be sure they would appeal to "families"—meaning the kids who are now influencing family buying decisions more than ever, according to marketing experts. Among single-parent and working-parent families, screaming, demanding, tantrum-throwing, or simply TV-influenced kids are determining which brands Mom and Dad choose in the supermarket aisles. (Mom and Dad are too tired to fight or care.) Some experts estimate that kids' influence directly affects over $172 billion in annual consumer spending. So the kids' label-design contest was a great way to remind families that ketchup is still as important as salsa, according to Al Banisch, senior product manager for Heinz.

"Heinz took great care to minimize the commerciality, so to speak, of this program," Banisch told a recent meeting of staff from your department. "The materials sent to schools were packed with art facts and art history and art learning. This was really very much an educational exercise."

More than 2,000 classrooms took part, with over 60,000 entries pouring in to be judged by a Heinz panel that included children's horror writer R. L. Stine. The three winners each received $5,000 and the satisfaction of seeing their designs on new bottles: the 17-year-old's oil painting of a tomato, the 12-year-old's American flag with dribbled ketchup stripes, and the 6-year-old's grinning face constructed of two tomatoes, a pickle, and smiling hot dog mouth.

But Peggy Charen isn't impressed. She praises Heinz's NEA grant, but adds that she's worried that kids in the classroom will be "thinking much too long about ketchup. I don't want my grandchildren thinking ketchup is an important part of their lives." She wants Heinz to stop the commercial use of the children's artwork.

Your Task: As a consumer relations representative for H.J. Heinz, write a letter explaining to Ms. Charen that the three new labels are here to stay.[24]

8. It's legal: Memo to Salem State College employee defending video surveillance Maybe it was bad employee relations, but it was legal. That's what your school's lawyers told you, human resources director for Salem State College, after you passed on an angry memo from an employee in the college's Small Business Development Center (SBDC).

In her memo, Nancy Kim expressed her horror and outrage at discovering—too late—that when she slipped behind a divider after hours to change from her office attire into her jogging outfit for the trek home, she was recorded on videotape by cameras installed in the department for security reasons. The SBDC houses a lot of expensive computer equipment, and your security department felt that the video surveillance was warranted; they had suspicions about a night intruder. However, no one informed the employees who work in the department that the cameras had been installed and were operating 24 hours a day. Your security department may have thought that was a good strategy for catching any dishonest employees red-handed, so to speak. But in light of what happened to Kim, it just seems like a rude and embarrassing misjudgment.

Kim has demanded an apology and $5,000 in damages for the indignity she has suffered. Although she hasn't yet contacted her union representatives or a lawyer, she does hint that those will be her next steps. Your legal department insists she has no claim; employees relinquish their privacy rights the minute they step into the workplace. The only federal law limiting employer surveillance is the 1986 Electronic Communications Privacy Act, which prohibits employers from listening in on spoken personal conversations. Otherwise, they can tally phone numbers and call duration; videotape employees; and review e-mail, Internet access, and computer files. Only the state of Connecticut has passed a law also limiting employer surveillance in bathrooms and other areas designated for "health and personal comfort."

The college's attorneys have provided you with a copy of an article quoting Robert Ellis Smith, publisher of *Privacy Journal*. He says, "Employees are at the mercy of employers.... There is no protection in the workplace." According to the article, 63 percent of employers in an American Management Association survey of 900 midsize and large companies use some kind of employee surveillance—and 23 percent of them don't tell workers. Moreover, 16 percent use video cameras for their employee monitoring.

Legally, it sounds as if the college is in the right. But personally, you can't help but agree that Kim was wronged. Nevertheless, the legal department wants to discourage Kim from any form of litigation or pursuit of the case with her union representatives or the Massachusetts Labor Relations Committee. They want you (instead of the legal department) to handle the response in hopes of downplaying the college's concern about the incident. Go ahead and apologize, they say, but don't invite further action. This is not going to be easy, you think with a sigh.

Your Task: Write an answering memo to Nancy Kim, denying her request for monetary compensation.[25]

REFUSING TO EXTEND CREDIT

9. Grand finale: No credit for burials in space by Celestis "I know you'll understand my request," the letter began, "and I'm sure your company has enough money from its wealthy customers to cover my needs temporarily." Now, for many businesses, such a letter might well mean a new customer, but for Celestis, Inc., of Houston, Texas, those words won't start a profitable relationship.

In the first place, this company's business is space burials, or rather, "space memorials." Celestis offers "grand finale" space voyages for a symbolic portion of a person's cremated remains—about a quarter of an ounce, or approximately 1 percent of the total.

By special arrangement with Orbital Sciences Corporation in Virginia, you are able to promise your customers a blastoff aboard a high-flying L-1011 jet, which releases a Pegasus rocket into the atmosphere. The rocket then lifts and releases a small satellite into orbit, containing 30 lipstick-sized ash capsules

secured in a honeycomb arrangement. No, you won't scatter customers' ashes in space, nor do you release the 1½-inch capsules (cluttering space with debris). They remain on the satellite until it reenters and burns up in Earth's atmosphere, some 18 months to 10 years later.

The cost for this service is less than $5,000 per person—a bargain, when you think of the technology involved. So far, your most famous customers have been Gene Roddenberry (creator of the *Star Trek* TV series), Timothy Leary (1960s LSD philosopher), and Gerald O'Neill (space colony advocate).

As a member of the Celestis marketing team, you think the concept is terrific and should be accessible to many people. But there's no way the company is going to offer credit for something like this. In fact, all arrangements for the Celestis space memorial must be paid for in advance.

Your Task: Write a letter responding to Gerald C. Hertsbacher's request for credit, tactfully explaining why you cannot grant it. He lives at 9760 Sepulveda Blvd., Apt. R, Sherman Oaks, CA 91403.[26]

10. Cash for celebrities: Credit refusal from Stylefile "Of all the nerve!" exclaims Elizabeth Harrison, co-owner of Stylefile, a New York PR agency. "We can put celebrities into the front row of any fashion show in the world—but not on credit!" She tosses the credit request from a relatively obscure designer on your secretarial desk, shaking her head in disgust. "Tell him to find an L.A. agency—or maybe one from Peoria. We don't need his business."

We might not need his business now, you think, but today's unknown fashion designer can rise to great heights in no time. After all, even Donna Karan, Todd Oldham, and Jean-Paul Gautier were nobodies once upon a time. And their current fame could as easily evaporate if they don't play the game right. In the fashion world, that means famous faces at every show, which is how the 32-year-old Harrison and her 25-year-old partner, Lara Shriftman, earn their huge fees. Stylefile specializes in "celebrity hunting," luring stars to fashion shows to lend glitz, glamour, and media buzz. The tactic never fails.

For instance, when Harrison snagged rock star/actress Courtney Love to fly to New York for a big-name designer's show the same year Love was nominated for an Oscar, the lead story in *Women's Wear Daily* the following Monday made more fuss over Love's appearance than over the clothes in question. And when Boy George and six friends arrived 30 minutes late for a Todd Oldham show, everyone flew into an uproar trying to reclaim his front-row seats. He sat, but his friends wound up standing—Harrison was relieved that a rival agency was handling that particular fiasco. But armed with their database of 10,000 publicists, managers, agents, and celebrities, Harrison and Shriftman have seen plenty of action.

The fee for landing an A-list celebrity like Love, Nicole Kidman, Leonardo DiCaprio, or the artist formerly known as Prince (or whoever is on top this month) could easily be as high as $3,000 per star—payable in advance, of course (about $750 for B-list names). Some fashion designers simply keep Stylefile on retainer. That helps Harrison and Shriftman cover expenses for their coast-to-coast airline flights, or those late-night dinners at expensive restaurants, the designer clothing, parties in Southhampton, stretch limos, and gifts that keep celebrities and their publicists happy and willing to cooperate when Stylefile calls with a request. In return for attending a show, celebrities usually receive free transportation, accommodations, clothing, and, infrequently, some spending money or a trip to the designer's private boutique.

You gaze at the letterhead. Franklin Desuaro. Could be famous someday. Too bad Stylefile can't give him a break—it's his first show and he's only asking for B-list names (Shannon Doherty, Jamie Gertz, etc.). He'll be competing with all the other fall shows and probably won't attract much attention unless Hollywood looks interested. But you know Harrison's rules. Once the lights go down and the reviews come out, it's too easy to forget about paying Stylefile for those glamorous faces in the crowd. So—no celebrities on credit.

Your Task: As Harrison's executive assistant, write a letter for her signature to Mr. Desuaro (836 W. 37th Street, New York, NY 10018) explaining Stylefile's policy.[27]

CONVEYING UNFAVORABLE NEWS ABOUT PEOPLE

11. Geek Squad fake: He never worked for us Ever since *Newsweek, People,* and the *Wall Street Journal* made a big fuss over the Geek Squad—Minneapolis's 24-hour, "on-site, rapid response

Computer Task Force" support consultants—you've been dealing with some very strange correspondence. But the letter on your desk right now looks like downright fraud. It's a request for a job reference regarding an individual claiming he was once a member of the Geek Squad. But no one on the team has ever heard of him; this "Sammy Stanton" has obviously lied to his potential employer, Computer Savvy.

Well, you can almost understand why. You've been working on the Squad yourself for only a few months, and it was quite a coup to land the job as "Special Agent" for the colorful company. Although the computer support firm is only four years old and your boss ("Chief Inspector" Robert Stephens) is only 28, the flair with which he does business has not escaped notice, to say the least. Now pulling in over half a mil a year, the company has more than 2,500 clients, including 3M, General Mills, IBM, Cargill, Twentieth Century Fox, and Warner Brothers. You suspect they fell in love with the whole concept: a team of ten computer geeks in signature black suits, white socks, and fedoras, carrying official "Geek Squad" badges and pulling up for a corporate house call, "Ghostbusters" style, in one of the company's black retrofitted ice cream trucks, or the 1958 Simca that Stephens is so proud of. Even the company's Web site (<www.geeksquad.com>) is a cool configuration of dossiers for every Special Agent, stamped "Top Secret" and complete with front and side view mug shots.

Naturally, Hollywood and the New York publishing houses have come calling. A two-book deal with Simon & Schuster is in the works, a CBS radio program is in development, and both Disney and Paramount have courted Stephens over movie rights to the offbeat company's story. Not bad for a guy who (according to Stephens's dossier) dropped a scholarship from the Art Institute of Chicago to study computer science. He wound up researching virtual reality flight simulators for the Navy and the FAA before starting his consulting company with $200 and lots of imagination.

Now that you think about it, glancing at black-and-white photos of the team and their "Geekmobiles" plastered on the office walls, this whole "Dragnet" meets "Ghostbusters" thing may have been a form of artistic expression for Stephens, and the fact that team members are incredibly computer savvy may have been a mere bonus . . . Computer Savvy—Got to finish that letter about Sammy Stanton right away, because out there in the mean city is a computer about to break down, and you know who they're gonna call . . .

Your Task: Dash off a quick response to Rosalie Sherman, Personnel Manager at Computer Savvy (6501 Cathy Avenue N.E., Albuquerque, New Mexico, 87109-3643), explaining that "Sammy Stanton" is no friend to the Geek Squad. Then flip your two-way back on and let 'em know you're ready for the next assignment.[28]

12. Try Lady Bugs: Letter rejecting an application at Fluker Farms cricket ranch It seemed almost like a joke to Richard Fluker back in 1953 when a co-worker invited him to buy into a cricket ranch in Port Allen, Louisiana. Back then, $300 was nothing to sneeze at. But Fluker thought it over and finally agreed to give it a go; after all, crickets were good fishing bait, and fishing was a long-entrenched Louisiana pastime.

Surely the elder Fluker didn't know then that the company he passed on to his son, David Fluker, would one day be looking at a balance sheet showing upwards of $6 million in annual sales. That's not only from crickets, mind you. Fluker Farms has grown along with a general interest in pets (particularly reptiles). The company now ships live crickets, mealworms, and iguanas to pet stores, zoos, and universities around the world, and it has also moved into "dry goods"—as in freeze-dried crickets, as well as reptile leashes and other accessories. Fluker Farms even markets chocolate-covered crickets for brave humans—a big hit at trade shows, especially when the samplers get an "I Ate a Bug Club" button.

But Fluker Farms is no joke, and the number of applicants who want to work for you has increased as the business has grown. As human resources manager for the company, it's your job to screen them.

Last week you interviewed about a dozen candidates for a job in research and development. The company is looking for other insects it can profit from, testing them as pet food and evaluating their "shelf-life" potential in both live and freeze-dried forms. With pet stores expanding into superstores, the demand for new food varieties is also growing. So the researcher you hire has to understand the feeding habits of reptiles and birds, must be acquainted with the life cycles of insects, and must possess the kind of imagination that can come up with a new idea and figure out how to make it profitable. That's not an easy spot to fill.

Your Task: The candidates you saw all carried excellent credentials, every one of them with multiple degrees and a research background, but only one had the right personality for Fluker Farms—the combination of imagination, knowledge, and resourcefulness you're looking for, plus five years of reptile research. Now you have the onerous task of writing rejection letters to the other candidates. As they say when you're facing a difficult job, pick a small step and begin—so start with a letter to Werner Speker, whom you liked personally, but whose post-graduate work has been mostly with felines, not reptiles. He's at 4265 Broadview Road, Baton Rouge, LA 70815.[29]

DEVELOPING YOUR INTERNET SKILLS

GOING ONLINE: PROTECT YOURSELF WHEN YOU

WRITE A JOB REFERENCE, P. 220

As you explore this section of the online *SOHO Guidebook,* you'll see how complicated the ins and outs of reference writing have become. Do you think these constraints are good for employees? For employers? Why or why not?

WRITING PERSUASIVE MESSAGES

After studying this chapter, you will be able to

Strengthen your persuasive messages with an appropriate appeal

Use attention, interest, desire, and action (the AIDA plan) to organize persuasive messages

Write a message persuading your audience to take action or to grant you an adjustment

Compose a persuasive message on the job

Design a persuasive letter around selling points and benefits

Apply the techniques of persuasion to prompt your audience to pay an overdue bill

O n the Job

FACING A COMMUNICATION DILEMMA AT UNITED NEGRO COLLEGE FUND

Raising Dollars for Diplomas

William H. Gray III was facing the challenge of a lifetime. He left a 13-year career in the U.S. Congress (including a stint as House Majority Whip) to join the nonprofit United Negro College Fund (UNCF). As president and CEO, he now held the reins of his organization's most ambitious fund-raising effort ever, dubbed Campaign 2000. The program's goal was to raise $250 million in three years. Philanthropist Walter Annenberg started things off by pledging a gift of $50 million, but it was up to Gray and his team to raise the remaining $200 million.

The money raised during this drive would serve as an endowment base for UNCF's members, 40 private colleges and universities that have historically been dedicated to higher education for African Americans. The United Negro College Fund had already been raising more than $50 million every year (through contributions, grants, scholarships, and other donations), so Campaign 2000 was quite an additional challenge. If successful, however, the campaign would enable UNCF's members to educate twice as many African American students as before.

The percentage of African American students enrolled in college was dropping, a trend that was expected to continue as tuition costs climbed. At the same time, battles over both minority scholarships and public funding for private institutions that serve minorities were raising concerns about future funding from these sources. The combination of higher tuition and uncertain funding was clouding the future of African American higher education.

William Gray knows that persuading individuals, charitable foundations, and companies to open their wallets takes careful planning. If you were in his place, how would you convince your audience to donate money to UNCF's Campaign 2000? What sort of persuasive messages would you send? How would you organize these messages? What would you do to get your audience's attention?[1]

To persuade potential donors to consider giving to United Negro College Fund, William Gray finds out who his readers are and what they're interested in. Then he crafts his fundraising letter to get attention, create interest, encourage desire, and motivate action. Whether persuading individuals, charities, or profit-making companies, Gray possesses strong communication skills and uses them constantly.

Questions to ask before you begin to write a persuasive message:

- What legal and ethical issues apply here?
- Who is my audience?
- How will my credibility affect my message?
- What tools can help me persuade my audience?
- Would emotional or logical appeals be best?

To motivate members of your audience, offer to satisfy their needs.

Demographics include characteristics such as age, gender, occupation, income, and education.

Psychographics include characteristics such as personality, attitudes, and lifestyle.

PLANNING PERSUASIVE MESSAGES

Much more than simply asking somebody to do something, **persuasion** is the attempt to change an audience's attitudes, beliefs, or actions.[2] Persuasive messages aim to influence audiences who are inclined to resist. So they depend heavily on strategic planning—like that carried out by William H. Gray III of the United Negro College Fund. Before you begin to write a persuasive message, consider some important questions: What legal and ethical issues apply here? Who is my audience? How will my credibility affect my message? What tools can help me persuade my audience? Would emotional or logical appeals be best?

Ethical Persuasion

The word *persuasion* is used negatively when associated with dishonest and unethical practices, such as coaxing, urging, and sometimes even tricking people into accepting an idea, buying a product, or taking an action they neither want nor need. However, the positive meaning of *persuasion* is influencing your audience members by informing them and by aiding their understanding, thereby allowing them the freedom to choose.[3] Ethical businesspeople inform customers of the benefits of an idea, an organization, a product, a donation, or an action so that customers can recognize how well that idea, organization, product, donation, or action will fill a need they truly have.

When you are trying to influence people's actions, knowledge of the law is crucial. However, merely avoiding what is illegal may not always be enough. To maintain the highest standards of business ethics, make every attempt to persuade without manipulating. Choose words that won't be misinterpreted when deemphasizing negatives, and be sure you don't distort the truth. Show consideration for your audience by adopting the "you" attitude with honest concern for their needs and interests. Your consideration of audience needs is more than ethical; it's the proper use of persuasion. Moreover, it's more likely to achieve the response you intended and to satisfy your audience's needs.

Audience Needs

The best persuasive messages are closely connected to your audience's existing desires and interests.[4] One of the most effective ways to motivate members of your audience is offering to satisfy their needs. Of course, people have many needs, but some researchers believe that certain needs have priority and that the most basic needs (such as security and safety) must be met before a person will seek to fulfill higher-level needs (such as esteem and status).[5] For example, say that you supervise someone who consistently arrives late for work. Once you've analyzed the need that motivates him to arrive late, you can craft an appeal (a "hook") that will interest him in your message about changing his behavior.

Because people's needs differ, people respond differently to any given message. Not everyone is interested in economy, for instance, or fair play; as a matter of fact, some people's innermost needs make appeals to status and greed much more effective. To accommodate these individual differences, analyze your audience and then construct a message that appeals to their needs. A letter requesting an adjustment for defective merchandise could focus on issues of fairness or on legal issues, depending on the reader. A sales letter for sheepskin seat covers might emphasize prestige to Porsche drivers and comfort to Chevrolet drivers.

To assess various individual needs, you can refer to specific information such as **demographics** (the age, gender, occupation, income, education, and other quantifiable characteristics of the people you're trying to persuade) and **psychographics** (the psychological characteristics of a person, such as personality, attitudes, and lifestyle). In addition, both types of information are strongly influenced by culture.

When analyzing your audience, take into account their cultural expectations and practices so that you don't undermine your persuasive message by using an inappropriate appeal or by organizing your message in a way that seems unfamiliar or uncomfortable. Persuasion is different in different cultures. For example, in France using an aggressive, hard-sell technique is no way to win respect from your audience. In fact, such an approach would probably antagonize your audience. In Germany, where people tend to focus on technical matters, plan on verifying any figures you use for support, and make sure they are exact. In Sweden, audiences tend to focus on theoretical questions and strategic implications, whereas in the United States audiences are usually concerned with more practical matters.[6] Your understanding and respect for cultural differences will not only help you satisfy the needs of audience members but also help them respect you.

Mary Kay Ash, founder of Mary Kay Cosmetics, uses every imaginable form of communication (from hand-written memos to training manuals, videocassettes, and gala award shows) to motivate and manage the 100,000 salespeople in her company.

Writer Credibility

For you to persuade a skeptical or hostile audience, they must believe that you know what you're talking about and that you're not trying to mislead them. Your **credibility** is your capability of being believed because you're reliable and worthy of confidence. Without credibility, your efforts to persuade will seem manipulative.

One of the best ways to gain credibility is to support your message with facts. Testimonials, documents, guarantees, statistics, research results, and the like all provide seemingly objective evidence for what you have to say, so they add to your credibility. The more specific and relevant your proof, the better. Another good way to improve your credibility is to name your sources, especially if they're respected by your audience. Still other ways of gaining credibility include:

- *Being enthusiastic.* Your excitement about the subject of your message can infect your audience.
- *Being objective.* Your understanding of and willingness to acknowledge all sides of an issue help you present fair and logical arguments in your persuasive message.
- *Being sincere.* Your honesty, genuineness, good faith, and truthfulness help you focus on your audience's needs.
- *Being an expert.* Your knowledge of your message's subject area (or even of some other area) helps you give your audience the quality information they need to make a decision.
- *Having good intentions.* Your willingness to keep your audience's best interests at heart helps you create persuasive messages that are ethical.
- *Being trustworthy.* Your honesty and dependability help you earn your audience's respect.
- *Establishing common ground.* Those beliefs, attitudes, and background experiences that you have in common with members of your audience will help them identify with you.

Gain credibility by supporting your argument with facts such as testimonials, documents, guarantees, statistics, and research results.

Your credibility is improved if you are enthusiastic, objective, sincere, expert, and trustworthy and if your intentions are good and you establish common ground.

Once you are committed to ethical persuasion, to satisfying the needs of your audience, and to building your credibility, you can concentrate on strengthening your message with some important persuasive tools.

Semantics and Other Persuasive Tools

When you're trying to build your credibility, how do you let your audience know that you're enthusiastic and trustworthy? Simply claiming outright that you have these traits is sure to raise suspicion. However, **semantics** (the meaning of words and other symbols) can do much of the job for you. The words you choose say much more than their dictionary definition. For instance, *useful, beneficial,* and *advantageous* may be considered synonyms, yet they are not interchangeable:

Semantics is the meaning of words and other symbols.

Two ways of using semantics are choosing your words carefully and using abstractions to enhance emotional content.

She suggested a useful compromise. (The compromise allowed the parties to get to work.)

She suggested a beneficial compromise. (The compromise not only resolved the conflict but also had a positive effect, perhaps for both parties.)

She suggested an advantageous compromise. (The compromise benefited her or her company more than it benefited the other party.)

Another way semantics can affect persuasive messages is in the variety of meanings that people attribute to certain words. Abstractions are subject to interpretation because they refer to things that people cannot experience with their senses. So use abstractions to enhance the emotional content of a persuasive message. For example, you may be able to sell more flags by appealing to your audience's patriotism (which may be interpreted in many ways) than by describing the color and size of the flags. You may have better luck collecting an overdue bill by mentioning honesty and fair play than by repeating the sum owed and the date it was due. However, be sure to include the details along with the abstractions; the very fact that you're using abstract words leaves room for misinterpretation.

Of course, even using semantics skillfully isn't the whole story. Persuading audience members to change their attitudes or to take action can be difficult. Here are some other tools to use in persuasive messages:[7]

> Other persuasive tools include focusing on your goals, using simple language, anticipating opposition, being specific, being moderate, providing sufficient support, and creating a win-win situation.

- *Focus on your goal.* Your message will be clearest if you shift your focus away from changing minds and emphasize the action you want your audience to take.
- *Use simple language.* In most persuasive situations, your audience will be cautious, watching for fantastic claims, unsupportable descriptions, and emotional manipulation. So speak plainly and simply.
- *Anticipate opposition.* Think of every possible objection in advance. In your message, you might raise and answer some of these counterarguments, to prove you're fair-minded.

BEHIND THE SCENES AT NORTON'S FLORIST AND GIFTS
Running a Small Business Can Be Taxing

Dennis Norton has his hands in a lot of pots these days—including flower pots. As president of Norton's Florist and Gifts in Ann Arbor, Norton writes a lot of letters to solicit new business for the company's four flower shops—letters trying to persuade credit-card customers to adopt preferred in-house charge accounts, offering them special discounts "so they will keep buying from us."

But letters to potential customers are only part of the persuasive messages Norton writes. As chair of the Ann Arbor Chamber of Commerce and head of the Small Business Tax Committee, he writes many letters to state and local authorities, outlining the position of local small businesses on various legislative issues. "There is a tremendous amount of written communication at this level. We've had a fair amount of success convincing them to introduce legislation—some of which has successfully passed."

Of course, sometimes Norton doesn't want legislation to pass. When the University of Michigan School of Public Policy studied the merits of an Ann Arbor city income tax and concluded that businesses within the city would benefit from the tax, Norton wrote a persuasive memo to change the beliefs of the people who supported the tax. Throughout the memo, Norton argued against the income tax and tried to convince the readers that the tax would

As president of Norton's Florist and Gifts, Dennis Norton sends persuasive messages to employees and customers. In addition, as chairman of the Ann Arbor Chamber of Commerce and head of the Small Business Tax Committee, he sends many persuasive messages to local authorities and state offices.

- *Be specific.* Back up your claims with evidence, and when necessary cite facts and figures. Let your audience know that you've done your homework.
- *Be moderate.* Asking your audience to make major changes in attitude or beliefs will most likely evoke a negative response. Asking audience members to take one step toward that change may be a more reasonable goal.
- *Provide sufficient support.* It is up to you to prove that the change you seek is necessary.
- *Create a win-win situation.* Make it possible for both you and your audience to gain something. Audience members will find it easier to deal with change if they stand to benefit.

All of these tools will help your persuasive message be accepted, but none of them will actually convince your audience to take the action you want. To persuade people, you'll need a strong argument, whether based on emotion or on logic.

Emotion and Logic

You can diffuse negative emotions by planning carefully. For example, when people's needs are not being met, they're likely to respond emotionally. A person who lacks a feeling of self-worth is likely to be sensitive to the tone of respect in a message. So in a collection letter to such a person, you can carefully avoid any hint that the person might be considered dishonorable. Otherwise, the person might become upset and pay no attention to your message. Not even the best-crafted, most reasonable message will persuade someone who is emotionally unable to accept it.

But aside from simply avoiding negative emotions, how do you actually convince an audience that your position is the right one, that your plan will work best, that your company

> You can diffuse negative emotions in order to help people accept your message.

---

seriously damage city businesses. He appealed to his readers' logic, supporting his position with facts, and even appealed to his readers' emotions through careful word choice.

Norton's memo grabbed the reader's attention by immediately pointing out a serious conflict between the income tax proposal and the city's plans to attract businesses to the Ann Arbor area: "Ann Arbor has been promoting itself as the next Silicon Valley, actively trying to attract high-tech businesses to the area. . . . The attractiveness of Ann Arbor as a place to relocate will be seriously eroded with the imposition of a city income tax." He further appealed to his readers' logic by asking them to "imagine the difficulty a prospective employee will have choosing a job inside the city limits and paying income tax when there is an equally attractive job offer outside the city limits which would not require payment of city income taxes."

Norton added to the credibility of his argument by pointing out that employees wouldn't be the only ones leaving the city: "A serious flight out of the city by small businesses is a very real probability" threatening the survival of Ann Arbor's business district. He supported his position by citing the pattern of deterioration experienced by other cities once businesses moved out, and he enhanced his argument by appealing to the readers' emotions with terms such as *seriously erode* and *vicious spiral* to describe this pattern

of deterioration. Finally, Norton closed by requesting that the university's study be disregarded because it "did not go far enough to understand the impact (of a city income tax) on businesses."

As a result of Norton's hard work, the Ann Arbor Chamber of Commerce and several local organizations announced their opposition to the city income tax. "It seems that everyone was waiting for the Chamber to state its position before they jumped on the bandwagon." Norton's memo played an integral role in organizing the opposition by convincing the Chamber that "the city income tax would be bad for Ann Arbor businesses."

Apply Your Knowledge

1. As the owner of a small business and a member of your local chamber of commerce, briefly discuss the benefits of writing persuasive messages as a collaborative group of individual businesses.

2. List some of the reasons why it is important to know your audience when writing persuasive messages.

Both emotional and logical appeals are needed to write successful persuasive messages.

will do the most with a reader's donations? Is it better to appeal to your readers' emotions? Perhaps you're better off appealing strictly to their logic? For the best results when writing persuasive messages, appeal to both.

To persuade your audience, you can call on human emotion by basing your argument on the needs or sympathies of audience members, as long as your **emotional appeal** is subtle.[8] You can make use of the emotion surrounding certain words. *Freedom*, for instance, brings forth strong feelings, as do words such as *success, prestige, credit record, savings, free, value,* and *comfort*. Using words like these puts the audience in a certain frame of mind and helps them accept your message. Also, emotion works with logic in a unique way: People need to find rational support for an attitude they've already embraced emotionally.

Emotional appeals are best if subtle.

A **logical appeal** calls on human reason. In any argument you might use to persuade an audience, you make a claim and then support your claim with reasons or evidence. When appealing to your audience's logic, you might use several types of reasoning:

Logical appeals use more than one type of reasoning:

- Analogy
- Induction
- Deduction

- **Analogy** is reasoning from specific evidence to specific evidence. To persuade employees to attend a planning session, you might use a town meeting analogy, comparing your company to a small community and your employees to valued members of that community.
- **Induction** is reasoning from specific evidence to a general conclusion. To convince potential customers that your product is best, you might report the results of test marketing in which individuals preferred your product over others.
- **Deduction** is reasoning from a generalization to a specific conclusion. To persuade your boss to hire additional employees, you might point out industrywide projections that industry activity (and thus your company's business) will be increasing rapidly over the next three months.

Of course, regardless of the reasoning used, an argument or statement can easily appear to be true when it's actually false. Whenever you appeal to your audience's reason, do everything you can to ensure that your arguments are logically sound.

Avoiding Faulty Logic

In any rational appeal, your high ethical standards dictate that you provide information, facts, and knowledge that can be used in decision making. To make this information persuasive, you must make your arguments relevant, well-grounded, and systematic. You make your points lucid and your arguments sound by steering clear of faulty logic:[9]

Avoid faulty logic such as hasty generalizations, begging the question, attacking your opponent, oversimplifying, assuming a false cause, using faulty analogies, and using illogical support.

- *Avoid hasty generalizations.* Make sure you have plenty of evidence before drawing conclusions.
- *Avoid begging the question.* Make sure you can support your claim without simply restating it in different words.
- *Avoid attacking your opponent.* Be careful to address the real question. Attack the argument your opponent is making, not your opponent's character.
- *Avoid oversimplifying a complex issue.* Make sure you present all the facts rather than relying on an "either/or" statement that makes it appear as though only two choices are possible.
- *Avoid assuming a false cause.* Make sure to use cause-and-effect reasoning correctly so that you do not assume one event caused another just because it happened first.
- *Avoid faulty analogies.* Be careful that the two objects or situations being compared are similar enough for the analogy to hold. Even if *A* resembles *B* in one respect, it may not in all respects.
- *Avoid illogical support.* Make sure the connection between your claim and your support is truly logical and not based on a leap of faith, a missing premise, or irrelevant evidence.

The Toulmin model of logic helps you uncover hidden assumptions that your audience may not accept.

When organizing and shaping your persuasive message, always think carefully about the argument you're using. You can test your argument to see whether it's logical. For example, the Toulmin model of logic can help you discover whether you've made hidden assumptions that your audience may not accept.

Using the Toulmin Model

As you shape your argument, you'll make it stronger (1) by finding common ground (basing your major argument on points that your audience already accepts) and (2) by stating the points in your case clearly.[10]

1. State your claim clearly.
2. Support your claim with a clear reason.
3. If your audience already accepts your reason (already holds the same belief, value, or principle presented in your reason), you may proceed to your conclusion.
4. If your audience does not already accept your reason, you must support it with another clearly stated claim, and support that claim with another clear reason, and so forth until you achieve common ground (find a reason based on beliefs, values, or principles that your audience already agrees with). Only then may you return to step 3.

As you can see, you are basically supporting your claim with evidence that is itself backed by a chain of reasons (all of which your audience must accept before you can move forward). This approach may remind you of the question-and-answer chain discussed briefly in Chapter 5 and at more length in Chapter 12.

ORGANIZING PERSUASIVE MESSAGES

Once you have carefully and thoroughly planned your persuasive message, you're ready to organize it. One way to organize persuasive messages is the **AIDA** plan, which has four phases: (1) attention, (2) interest, (3) desire, and (4) action. In the attention phase, you convince your audience right at the beginning that you have something useful or interesting to say. The audience wants to know "What's in this message for me?" So try to tell them in the attention phase, without making extravagant claims or threats and without bringing up irrelevant points (Figure 11.1).

In the interest phase, you explain how your message is related to the audience. Continuing the theme that you started with, you paint a more detailed picture with words. Your goal is to get the audience thinking, "This is an interesting idea; could it possibly solve my problems?" In Figure 11.1, the interest section ties together a factual description and the benefits of instituting the new recycling plan. Also, the benefits relate specifically to the attention phase that precedes this section.

In the desire phase of a persuasive message, you back up claims and thereby increase your audience's willingness to take the action that you'll suggest in the next section. Whatever evidence you use to prove your claim, make sure it's directly relevant to your point.

In the action phase, you suggest the action you want your audience to take. All persuasive messages end with a section that urges specific action, but the ending is more than a statement such as "Institute this program as soon as possible" or "Send me a refund." In fact, this section offers a good opportunity for one last reminder of the main benefit the audience will realize from taking the action you want. The secret of the action phase is to make the action easy. In sales letters, you might ask readers to call a toll-free number for more information. You might ask your audience to fill out an enclosed order form, and UNCF's William Gray might use a preaddressed, prepaid envelope for donations.

The Indirect Approach

The AIDA plan is tailor-made for using the indirect approach, allowing you to save your main idea for the action phase. Be sure to use the indirect approach when

- Your audience is negative (has strong resistance to your message)
- Your message is relatively short and clear (so that readers don't have to wait long for your main idea)
- You know your readers won't object to the indirect plan

Organize persuasive messages using the AIDA plan:

- Attention
- Interest
- Desire
- Action

Begin every persuasive message with an attention-getting statement that is

- Personalized
- You-oriented
- Straightforward
- Relevant

In the interest section

- Continue the opening theme in greater detail
- Relate benefits specifically to the attention-getter

In the desire section

- Provide relevant evidence to prove your claim
- Draw attention to any enclosures

Close a persuasive message with an action ending that suggests a specific step the audience may take.

Using AIDA with the indirect approach allows you to save your idea for the action phase.

Figure 11.1
In-Depth Critique: Persuasive Letter Using the AIDA Plan

Randy Thumwolt uses the AIDA plan in this persuasive memo about a program that could solve two problems at once: (1) the high annual cost of plastics and (2) the rising number of consumer complaints about the company's failure to recycle plastics.

HOST MARRIOTT SERVICES

INTERNAL MEMORANDUM

To: Eleanor Tran, Comptroller
From: Randy Thumwolt, Purchasing Director
Date: August 22, 1998
Subject: Cost Cutting in Plastics

In the attention phase, background information and specific numbers grab the reader's attention.

As you know, we purchase five tons of plastic product containers each year. The price of the polyethylene terephthalate (PET) tends to rise and fall as petroleum costs fluctuate. You asked me earlier to find some ways to cut our annual costs for plastics. In my memo of January 5, I suggested that we bulk-purchase plastics during winter months, when petroleum prices tend to be lower. Thanks for approving that suggestion. So far, I estimate that we will realize a 10 percent savings this year.

In the interest phase, the writer clearly describes the problems the company is still facing.

Even so, our costs for plastic containers are exorbitant ($2 million annually). In addition, we have received an increasing number of consumer letters complaining about our lack of a recycling program for the PET plastic containers both on the airplanes and in the airport restaurants. I've done some preliminary research and have come up with the following ideas:

The desire phase makes suggestions in an easy-to-read list and provides detailed support in an attachment.

1. Provide recycling containers at all Host Marriott airport restaurants.
2. Offer financial incentives for the airlines to collect and separate PET containers.
3. Set up a specially designated dumpster at each airport for recycling plastics.
4. Contract with A-Batt Waste Management for collection.

I've attached a detailed report of the costs involved. As you can see, our net savings the first year should run about $500,000. I've spoken to Ted Macy in marketing. If we adopt the recycling plan, he wants to build a PR campaign around it.

In the action phase, the writer provides another reader benefit and urges action within a specific time frame.

The PET recycling plan will help build our public image while improving our bottom line. If you agree, let's meet with Ted next week to get things started.

When you use the indirect approach in persuasive messages, your goal is to explain your reasons and build interest before revealing your purpose. So the attention phase takes on increased importance. Getting your readers' attention is thoroughly covered in the discussion of sales letters later in this chapter.

The Direct Approach

Using AIDA with the direct approach allows you to use your main idea as your attention-getter.

The AIDA plan can also be adapted for the direct approach, allowing you to use your main idea as the attention-getter. You build interest with your argument, build desire with your evidence, and emphasize your main idea in the action phase with the specific action you want your audience to take. The direct approach is often shorter than the indirect approach, so it is appreciated by readers who are busy and pressed for time. Use the direct approach when

- Your audience is objective (and has no real resistance to your message)
- Your message is long and complex (so that you satisfy your reader's curiosity)
- You know that your reader prefers the direct plan (for example, most supervisors appreciate messages that save them time and communicate the subject matter quickly)

However, even though you're presenting your main idea first, make sure you include a brief justification or explanation so that your reader doesn't have to accept your idea on blind faith.

POOR	IMPROVED
I recommend building our new retail outlet on the West Main Street site.	After comparing the four possible sites for our new retail outlet, I recommend West Main Street as the only site that fulfills our criteria for visibility, proximity to mass transportation, and square footage.

In his attempts to regain market share from the Japanese, Black & Decker's CEO, Nolan Archibald, used persuasive messages to transform an entire corporate culture, recapture customers with his vision, and recruit the talent he needed. To persuade others to adopt your point of view, says Archibald, present your case as though you were on the other side and needed to be convinced yourself.

Remember that your persuasive messages take careful planning and organization. Your success depends on your commitment to being ethical, analyzing your audience's needs, maintaining your own credibility, using semantics carefully, balancing emotion and logic, and choosing the most appropriate organizational plan. Following these guidelines will help you craft strong persuasive messages, no matter what the situation.

REPARING PERSUASIVE MESSAGES ON THE JOB

Within an organization, you may write persuasive messages for any number of reasons, including to implement top management's decisions, to sell a supervisor on your idea for cutting costs, to suggest more-efficient operating procedures, to elicit cooperation from competing departments, and to win employee support for a new benefits package. When writing a persuasive message to someone within your organization, consider three special aspects affecting your approach: corporate culture, corporate subcultures, and position or power.[11]

An organization's culture heavily influences the types of messages considered effective. All the previous messages in the organization establish a tradition and practice that define persuasive writing within that culture. If you accept and use that tradition, you are essentially establishing one type of common ground with your audience, and you will be rewarded by being accepted into the corporate culture. If you never learn the tradition or reject it, you'll have difficulty achieving common ground, and your persuasion attempts will suffer.

Organizations are made up of various functional areas such as accounting, finance, manufacturing, marketing, research, human resources, and so on. Each of these areas (or subcultures) tends to create its own approaches and traditions for helping the corporation succeed, valuing other functional areas, communicating, using language, and persuading. Moreover, each subculture tends to mistrust the language and customs of other subcultures. When writing a persuasive message within your subculture, you can use the accepted communication and language traditions with confidence. When writing a persuasive message outside your subculture, however, anticipate problems from readers whose general mind-set and specific business traditions may differ from yours.

Holding a position in an organization affords businesspeople a commensurate amount of authority, expertise, and power. Therefore, the position you hold influences how you organize and write persuasive messages. Say you are a first-line manager. When writing a per-

When writing persuasive messages within an organization consider three influences:

- Corporate culture
- Subcultures
- Position

Every message written for a corporation adds to the corporate tradition.

Each functional area within a corporation develops its own subculture.

Your position relative to your audience's position within an organization influences how you approach your persuasive message.

A former teacher, Lane Nemeth founded Discovery Toys, a company that markets educational toys, books, and software through home demonstration parties. Whether you're wooing investors, negotiating a loan, or ordering inventory, advises Nemeth, let your readers know you can understand their concerns.

Three problems with external requests for action:

- They reach people who are already busy and reluctant to comply.
- They frequently offer nothing tangible in return.
- They must compete with so many other requests.

Highlight the direct and indirect benefits of complying with your request.

Make only reasonable requests.

suasive message to top management, you may try to be diplomatic and to persuade by using an indirect approach. But some managers may perceive your indirect persuasion as manipulative and time wasting. On the other hand, you may consciously try to save your supervisors time by using a direct approach. But some supervisors might perceive your direct persuasion as brash and presumptuous. Similarly, when writing a persuasive message to employees, you may try to ease into a major change by persuading with an indirect approach, but your employees might perceive your indirect approach as weak or even wishy-washy. Or you may decide to persuade them with a direct approach to reinforce your image of authority, in which case your employees might perceive your direct approach as rude and unfeeling.

The way you word and organize persuasive messages that will be read within the organization depends on organizational culture, your position, and your audience's position, not to mention the particular situation. So be sure to analyze your company's traditions, your department's practices, and your audience before deciding on an approach. In Figure 11.2, Bette McGiboney has chosen the direct plan to persuade her boss to accept her idea.

RITING PERSUASIVE REQUESTS FOR ACTION

Many persuasive messages are written to solicit funds, favors, information, or cooperation. Within an organization, persuasive techniques are often required to get someone to change policies or procedures, to spend money on new equipment and services, to promote a person, or to protect turf.[12] Persuasive letters to outsiders might solicit donations, request an adjustment, or ask for some other type of help.

As UNCF's William Gray knows well, creating an external persuasive message is one of the most difficult persuasive tasks you could undertake. First, people are busy, so they're reluctant to do something new. Second, the request offers no guarantee of any tangible reward in return. Third, competing requests are plentiful. In fact, the public relations departments of many large corporations receive so many requests for donations to worthy causes that they must sometimes resort to lotteries to decide which to support.

Why do people respond to requests for action on an issue that is more important to you than to them? If you're lucky, they may believe in the project or cause that you're writing about. Even so, you must convince them that your request will give them some benefit, perhaps an intangible benefit down the road or a chance to make a meaningful contribution. Also, especially in the case of requests for professional favors or information, people may think that they are obliged to "pay their dues" by helping others.

When making a persuasive request, therefore, take special care to highlight both direct and indirect benefits. Direct benefits might include a reduced work load for the supervisor who institutes flextime or a premium for someone who responds to a survey. Indirect benefits might include better employee morale or the prestige of giving free workshops to small businesses.

The attention-getting device at the beginning of persuasive requests for action usually serves to show readers that you know something about their concerns and that you have some reason for making such requests. In this type of persuasive message, more than in most others, a flattering comment about your reader is acceptable, especially if it's sincere. The body of the letter or memo covers what you know about the problem you're trying to solve with the reader's help: the facts and figures, the benefits of helping, your experience in attacking the problem. The goal is to give you and your request credibility, to make the reader believe that helping you will indeed help solve a significant problem. Once you've demonstrated that your message is relevant to your reader, you can request some specific action. Be aware, however, that a persuasive memo is somewhat more subdued than a letter to an outsider might be.

The most important thing to remember when preparing a persuasive request for action is to keep your request within bounds. Nothing is so distressing as a request so general, all-encompassing, or inconsiderate that it seems impossible to grant, no matter how worthy the cause. Also be careful not to doom your request to failure by asking your reader to do

Bette McGiboney is administrative assistant to the athletic director of Auburn University. Each year, after season tickets have been mailed out, the cost of the athletic department's toll-free number skyrockets as fans call to complain about their seats, or about receiving the wrong number of tickets, or to order last-minute tickets. The August phone bill is usually over $3,000, in part because each customer is put on hold while operators serve others. McGiboney has an idea that may solve the problem.

Figure 11.2
In-Depth Critique: E-Mail Selling an Idea to a Boss

```
┌──────────────────────── E-Mail ────────────────────────┐
```

Date: Wednesday, 22 July 1999, 3:44:05
X-Sender: mcgibon@ath.auburn.edu
To: housel@ath.auburn.edu
From: "Bette McGiboney" ,mcgibon@ath.auburn.edu.
Subject: Savings on toll-free number

Dear David:

As you know, our billing for the toll-free number coming into the ticket office usually runs at least $3,000 for the month of August, compared with an average of $493 for the other eleven months. Tiger fans who call in August usually have at least a five-minute wait on hold. Here's an idea that will not only save us money but also help us manage our time and better serve our fans.

Under this plan, callers will hear the same messages and be offered the same options as before. However, if an operator isn't available when a caller presses "0" for ticket information, a new message will request a name and phone number so that we can return the call within the next two business days.

I estimate that reducing the on-hold time could eliminate at least $2,000 from our August bill (based on a conversation with Tandy Robertson, our AT&T representative). The good news is that the idea costs nothing and can be implemented immediately. We can use quiet times of the day to return phone calls, thus spreading our work more evenly.

I've discussed the idea informally with our operators, and they would like to try it. After football season, we can use our fall interns to call a random selection of customers to see how they liked the new message system. The plan will help us in the following ways:

- Provide better customer service
- Help us manage our time and stress levels
- Save us money on our toll-free line

I've attached a sheet with possible wording for the new message. Please let me know by the end of the month whether you'd like to give this a try.

Thanks,

Bette

This message follows the AIDA plan. The attention paragraph convinces the reader that Bette has something useful to say by presenting the main idea (a new plan for handling phone calls from fans).

The interest paragraph explains how the new plan will work, creating more interest in the idea.

The third and fourth paragraphs create desire by presenting supporting evidence such as cost savings, and the bulleted benefits draw the reader to the meat of the message.

The action paragraph is simple and direct with a specific time frame. It also takes care of a chore that might have caused the reader to delay.

GOING ONLINE
*LOBBY MOVERS AND
SHAKERS IN THE
U.S. GOVERNMENT*

The Thomas site is sponsored by
the Library of Congress and named
in honor of Thomas Jefferson. It offers a smorgasbord of information
about Congress, its members and
committees, and issues under consideration, with links to just about
any governmental matter you can
conceive. For anyone who wants to
lobby government leaders, a visit
here could prove most useful; you'll
discover information and access
links that could take days to accomplish without a computer (if at all).
For instance, see whether you can
find a link here that will lead you to
a current tally of the public debt, all
$X-trillion of it, tracked up to the
moment and down to the penny.
(Hint: We found this link by clicking on "House Members" and visiting a representative's home page,
but there are other ways.)

http://thomas.loc.gov/

Know the laws governing sales letters, and avoid both legal and ethical
pitfalls by being genuinely concerned
about your audience's needs.

all your work for you: to provide information that you were too lazy to seek, to spend time saving you from embarrassment or inconvenience, or to provide total financial support for a cause that nobody else is supporting. To review the tasks involved in such messages, see this chapter's Checklist for Persuasive Requests for Action.

WRITING SALES AND FUND-RAISING MESSAGES

Two distinctive types of persuasive messages are sales letters and fund-raising letters. These messages often come in special direct-mail packages that can include brochures, reply forms, or other special inserts. Both types of messages are often written by specialized and highly skilled professionals like William Gray of UNCF.

How do sales messages differ from fund-raising messages? Sales messages are usually sent by for-profit organizations seeking to solve readers' problems by persuading them to spend money on products. On the other hand, fund-raising messages are usually sent by nonprofit organizations seeking to solve other people's problems by persuading readers to donate their money or time. Nevertheless, the fact is that sales and fund-raising messages are competing for business and public attention, time, and dollars.[13] Both types of messages attempt to persuade readers to spend their time or money on the value being offered—whether that value is the convenience of a more efficient vacuum cleaner or the satisfaction of helping save children's lives. Sales and fund-raising messages require a few more steps than other types of persuasive messages.

Sales Letters

Whether you're selling a good, service, or company image, remember that the focus of your message is your audience. As with any message, persuasive or not, knowing the law can help you avoid serious legal problems. The laws governing sales letters are specific:

- Sales letters are considered binding contracts in many states, so avoid even implying offers or promises that you can't deliver.
- Making a false statement in a sales letter is fraud if the recipient can prove that (1) you intended to deceive, (2) you made the statement regarding a fact rather than an opinion or a speculation, (3) the recipient was justified in relying on the statement, and (4) the recipient was damaged by it (in a legal sense). Misrepresenting the price, quality, or performance of a product in a sales letter is fraud. So is a testimonial by a person misrepresented to be an expert.
- Using a person's name, photograph, or other identity in a sales letter without permission constitutes invasion of privacy—with some exceptions. Using a photo of the members of a local softball team in a chamber of commerce mailer may be perfectly legal if team members are public figures in the community and if using the photo doesn't falsely imply their endorsement. On the other hand, using a photo of your governor, without consent, on a letter about the profits to be made in worm farming could be deemed an invasion of privacy.
- Publicizing a person's private life in a sales letter can also result in legal problems. Stating that the president of a local bank (mentioned by name) served six months in prison for income tax evasion is a potentially damaging fact that may be considered an invasion of privacy. You would also risk a lawsuit by publicizing another person's past-due debts or by publishing without consent another person's medical records, x-rays, or photograph.

As with other persuasive messages, following the letter of the law isn't always enough. To write sales letters of the highest ethical character, focus on solving your readers' problem rather than on selling your product. If you're genuinely concerned about your audience's needs and interests, you'll find it easier to avoid legal or ethical pitfalls. Once you're firmly committed to focusing on your audience, you can begin planning your sales letter by figuring out what features would most interest your readers.

CHECKLIST FOR PERSUASIVE REQUESTS FOR ACTION

A. Attention

1. Demonstrate that you understand the audience's concerns.
2. Introduce a direct or indirect benefit that can be developed as a central selling point.
3. Construct statements so that they don't sound like high-pressure sales tactics or bribes.
4. Use an effective opening: a comment or assertion the audience will agree with, a compliment (if sincere), a frank admission that you need the audience's help, a problem that is the basis of your request, one or two rhetorical questions, a statement of what is being done or has been done to solve a problem.

B. Interest and Desire

1. Early in the body of the message, introduce the reason you are writing.
   - a. Mention the main audience benefit before the actual request.
   - b. Thoroughly explain your reason for asking the favor.
2. Include all necessary description: physical characteristics and value of the project.
3. Include all facts and figures necessary to convince members of your audience that their contribution will be enjoyable, easy, important, and of personal benefit (as much as is true and possible).
   - a. In a request for cooperation, explain the problem, facts, suggestions, other participants' roles, and the audience's part.
   - b. In a request for a donation, explain the problem, past and current attempts to remedy it, future plans, your organization's involvement, and projected costs, along with suggestions about how the audience can help.
   - c. Describe the possible direct benefits.
   - d. Describe the possible indirect benefits.

4. Anticipate and answer possible objections.
   - a. Ignore objections if they are unimportant or might not occur to the audience or if you can focus on positive facts instead.
   - b. Discuss objections (usually) about half or two-thirds of the way through the body of the letter or memo.
   - c. Acknowledge objections calmly; then overcome them by focusing on more important and more positive factors.
   - d. Turn objections into an advantage by looking at them from another viewpoint or by explaining the facts of the situation more clearly.
   - e. Overcome objections to providing restricted material by giving assurance that you will handle it in whatever limited way is specified.
5. Introduce any enclosures after you have finished the key message, with an emphasis on what to do with them or what information they offer.

C. Action

1. Confidently ask for the audience's cooperation.
2. Make the desired action clear and easy.
3. Stress the positive results of action.
4. Include the due date for a response (if necessary), and tie it in with audience benefits (if possible): adequate time for ordering supplies, prominent billing on the program, and so forth.
5. Replace negative or tentative statements, such as "If you can donate anything," with positive, confident statements, such as "To make your contribution, just return . . ."
6. Tie in the last sentence with an appeal or a statement featured in the opening paragraph (if appropriate), as a last audience-benefit plug.

Determining Selling Points and Benefits

Selling points are the most attractive features of an idea or product; benefits are the particular advantages that readers will realize from those features. One selling point of a security system for students' dorm rooms is its portability. The benefit to students is the ability to protect their possessions from theft without investing in a full-blown permanently installed alarm system (Figure 11.3).

Obviously, you can't write about selling points or benefits without a thorough understanding of your subject as well as of your audience. So take a good look at your product. Ask yourself (or someone else, if necessary) everything that you think a potential buyer might want to know about it. If you were writing the sales letter in Figure 11.3, you would need to have a full description of what the portable security system looks like, what it does, and how it works. Some selling points of the SecureAbel Alarms are that they can be installed with a screwdriver, have an activator that hooks to your key chain or belt loop, and

Know your products' selling points, but talk about their benefits to consumers.

Start with a thorough knowledge of the product.

Figure 11.3
**In-Depth Critique: Letter
Selling a Product**

The following sales letter for SecureAbel Alarms uses the AIDA plan to persuade students to buy its dorm-room alarm systems.

SecureAbel Alarms, Inc.

5654 Lakemont Drive • Altoona, PA 16602 • Voice: (814) 983-4424 • Fax: (814) 983-4422 • http://www.secure.com

October 14, 1998

Mr. Samuel Zolezzi
Penn State University, North Halls
104 Warnock Commons
State College, PA 16802

Dear Mr. Zolezzi:

Did you know that one out of four college students becomes a victim of theft? How would you feel if you returned to your dorm and discovered that your hard-earned stereo, computer, or microwave had been stolen? Remember, locked doors won't stop a determined thief.

It happened to me when I was in college. That's why I've developed a portable security system for your dormitory room. It works like an auto alarm and can be installed with an ordinary screwdriver. The small activator hooks to your key chain or belt loop. Just press the "lock" key. A "beep" tells you your room is secure, and a blinking red light warns intruders to stay away.

If a thief tries to break in, a loud alarm sounds. Your possessions will be safe. And, even more important, you can activate the system from your bedside, so you're safe while you sleep.

You'd expect this peace of mind to cost a fortune—something most college students don't have. But we're offering the SecureAbel Dorm Alarm System for only $75. Here's what you'll receive by return mail:

- The patented alarm unit
- Two battery-operated programmable remote units
- A one-year warranty on all parts
- Complete and easy-to-follow installation instructions

Order additional alarm boxes to install on your window or bathroom door for only $50. Act now. Fill out the response card, and mail it along with your choice of payment method in the enclosed envelope. Don't give thieves and criminals a chance. Protect yourself and your belongings. Send in your card today.

Sincerely,

Dan Abel

Dan Abel, President

Enclosures

Beginning with a provocative question draws the reader into the letter and raises the awareness of a need. Benefits have both a logical appeal (protecting possessions) and an emotional appeal (personal safety).

In the second paragraph, the writer seeks to establish a common bond with the reader and explains how the product works by comparing it with something the reader is familiar with, a car alarm.

The third paragraph mentions an additional threat to safety and hence another benefit of the security system.

The bulleted list creates the sense of added value to the offer.

The final paragraph urges quick action.

Form a mental picture of the product's typical buyer; then relate selling points and benefits to that picture.

Think about how the product's features can help potential buyers; then concentrate on how your product's selling points can actually satisfy your audience's needs.

have a blinking red light to warn intruders to stay away. You would also investigate prices and discounts, delivery schedules, and packaging.

Once you have a complete file on your product, collect data about your audience and try to form a mental image of the typical buyer for the product. This mental image will help you focus on the central concerns of potential buyers in your audience. Then you can check the selling points you've already come up with against your audience's actual needs.

Now think about how your product can benefit your audience. Some benefits of the SecureAbel Alarms are their ease of installation, their ease of activation, and their giving you a feeling of safety and security. Be sure to focus on relatively few product benefits, and determine which benefits are most appealing to your audience. Ultimately, you'll single out one benefit that will become the hallmark of your campaign. Safety seems to be the key benefit emphasized by SecureAbel Alarms.

Choosing the Format and Approach

Once you know what you need to say and who you want to say it to, decide how you're going to say it. Will you send just a letter, or will you include brochures, samples, response cards, and the like? Will the letter be printed with an additional color or special symbols or logos? How many pages will it run? You'll also need to decide whether to conduct a multistage campaign, with several mailings and some sort of telephone or in-person follow-up, or to rely on a single hard-hitting mailing.

All these decisions depend on the audience you're trying to reach—their characteristics, their likely acceptance of or resistance to your message—and what you're trying to get them to do. In general, expensive items and hard-to-accept propositions call for a more elaborate campaign than low-cost products and simple actions.

Getting Attention

Sales letters are prepared according to the AIDA plan used for any persuasive message, so they start with an attention-getting device. Professionals use some common techniques to attract audience attention. When you're preparing a sales letter, consider emphasizing:

- *A piece of genuine news.* "In the past 60 days, auto manufacturers' inventories have shrunk by 12 percent."
- *A personal appeal to the reader's emotions and values.* "The only thing worse than paying taxes is paying taxes when you don't have to."
- *The most attractive feature plus the associated benefit.* "New control device ends problems with employee pilferage!"
- *An intriguing number.* "Here are three great secrets of the world's most loved entertainers."
- *A sample of the product.* "Here's your free sample of the new Romalite packing sheet."
- *A concrete illustration with story appeal.* "In 1985 Earl Colbert set out to find a better way to process credit applications. After ten years of trial and error, he finally developed a procedure so simple but thorough that he was cited for service to the industry by the American Creditors Association."
- *A specific trait shared by the audience.* "Busy executives need another complicated 'time-saving' device like they need a hole in the head!"
- *A provocative question.* "Are you tired of watching inflation eat away at your hard-earned profits?"
- *A challenge.* "Don't waste another day wondering how you're going to become the success you've always wanted to be!"
- *A solution to a problem.* "Tired of arctic air rushing through the cracks around your windows? Stay warm and save energy with StormSeal Weather-stripping."

A look at your own mail will show you the prevalence of these few techniques in sales letters. Using these proven attention-getting devices will give your sales letters added impact. Look again at Figure 11.3 and see how many of them it uses.

Of course, not all attention-getting devices are equally effective. The best is the one that makes your audience read the rest of the letter. Look closely at the following three examples. Which seems most interesting to you?

How would you like straight A's this semester?

Get straight A's this semester!

Now you can get straight A's this semester, with . . .

If you're like most people, you'll find the first option the most enticing. The question invites your response—a positive response designed to encourage you to read on. The

Sandra Gordon is vice president of communications for the National Easter Seal Society, a nonprofit agency. Each year more than a million people receive Easter Seal services, which requires both money and volunteers. Gordon advises that letters soliciting donations, whether of time or of funds, must give donors reasons to respond—benefits besides helping those who receives services.

Several tried-and-true attention-getting devices are used in sales letters for a wide variety of products.

Choose an attention-getter that encourages the reader to read more.

second option is fairly interesting too, but its commanding tone may make you wary of the claim. The third option is acceptable, but it certainly conveys no sense of excitement, and its quick introduction of the product may lead you to a snap decision against reading further.

Sales letters prepared by professionals also use a variety of formatting devices to get your attention, including personalized salutations, special sizes or styles of type, underlining, color, indentions, and so on. Whatever special techniques are used, the best attention-getter for a sales letter is a hook that gets the reader thinking about the needs your product might be able to help fill.

Emphasizing the Central Selling Point

To determine your product's central selling point, ask

- What does the competition offer?
- What is special about my product?
- What are potential buyers really looking for?

Say that your company's alarm device is relatively inexpensive, durable, and tamperproof. Although these are all attractive features, you want to focus on only one. Ask what the competition has to offer, what most distinguishes your product, and what most concerns potential buyers. The answers to these questions will help you select the **central selling point,** the single point around which to build your sales message. Highlight this point in your heading or first paragraph, and make it stand out through typography, design, or high-impact writing.[14]

Highlighting Benefits

Determining the central selling point will help you define the benefits to potential buyers. Perhaps your company's alarm device has been built mainly to overcome the inability of your competitors' products to resist tampering by would-be burglars. Tamper resistance is your central selling point; its benefits are that burglars won't be able to break in easily and therefore the likelihood of a burglary will be reduced. You'll want to mention this benefit repeatedly, in words and pictures (if possible), near the beginning and the end of your letter. You might get attention by using a news item to stress this benefit: "Burglaries of businesses in our county have increased 7.7 percent over the past year; police department officials cite burglars' increasing sophistication and familiarity with conventional alarm devices." You might pose a provocative question: "Worried about the reliability of your current alarm system in repelling today's sophisticated burglars?"

Selling points + "you" attitude = benefits.

In the rest of the letter, continue to stress the central selling point but weave in references to other benefits: "You can get this worry-free protection for much less than you might think." Also, "The same technology that makes it difficult for burglars to crack your alarm system makes it durable, even when it must be exposed to the elements." Remember, sales letters reflect the "you" attitude through references to benefits, so always phrase the selling points in terms of what such features will do for potential customers.

Using Action Terms

To give force to a message

- Use action terms
- Use colorful verbs and adjectives

Active words give force to any business message, but they are especially important in sales letters. Compare the following:

INSTEAD OF THIS	WRITE THIS
The NuForm desk chair is designed to support your lower back and relieve pressure on your legs.	The NuForm desk chair supports your lower back and relieves pressure on your legs.

The second version says the same thing in fewer words and puts more emphasis on what the chair does for the user ("supports") than on the intentions of the design team ("is designed to support").

In general, use colorful verbs and adjectives that convey a dynamic image. Be careful, however, not to overdo it: "Your factory floors will sparkle like diamonds" is hard to believe and may prevent your audience from believing the rest of your message.

Talking About Price

The price people will pay for a product depends on the prices of similar products, the general state of the economy, and the psychology of the buyer. Price is therefore a complicated issue and often a sensitive one.

Whether the price of your product is highlighted or downplayed, prepare your readers for it. Such words as *luxurious* and *economical* provide unmistakable clues about how your price compares with competitors' prices, and they help your readers accept the price when you finally state it. If your price is relatively high, definitely stress features and benefits that justify it. If the price is low, you may wish to compare the features of your product with those of the competition's products, either directly or indirectly. In either case, if the price you eventually mention is a surprise to the reader, you've made a mistake that will be hard to overcome.

Here's an example from a sales letter offering a product at a bargain price:

All the Features of Name-Brand Pantyhose at Half the Price!

Why pay for fancy packaging or that little tag with a famous name on it when you can enjoy cotton lining, reinforced toes, and matchless durability for only $1.99?

In this excerpt, the price falls right at the end of the paragraph, where it stands out. In addition, the price issue is featured in a bold headline. This technique may even be used as the opening of a letter if the price is the most important feature and the audience for the letter is value conscious.

If price is not a major selling point, you can handle it in several ways. You could leave out the price altogether or mention it only in an accompanying brochure. You could deemphasize the price by putting the actual figures in the middle of a paragraph close to the end of your sales letter, well after you've presented the benefits and selling points. The same paragraph might include a discussion of related topics, such as credit terms, special offers, and volume discounts. Mentioning favorable money matters before the actual price also reduces its impact.

Only 100 prints of this exclusive, limited-edition lithograph will be created. On June 1, they will be made available to the general public, but you can reserve one now for only $350, the special advance reservation price. Simply rush the enclosed reservation card back today so that your order is in before the June 1 publication date.

Emphasis on the rarity of the edition signals value and thus prepares the reader for the big-ticket price that follows. The actual price, buried in the middle of a sentence, is tied in with another reminder of the exclusivity of the offer.

The pros use two other techniques for minimizing price. One is to break a quantity price into units. Instead of saying that a case of wine costs $144, you might say that each bottle costs $12. The other is to compare your product's price with the cost of some other product or activity: "The cost of owning your own spa is less than you'd pay for a health-club membership." Your aim is to make the cost seem as small and affordable as possible, thereby eliminating price as a possible objection.

Supporting Your Claims

You can't assume that people will believe what you say about your product just because you said it in writing. You'll have to prove your claims, especially if your product is complicated, expensive, or representative of some unusual approach.

Support for your claims may take several forms. Samples and brochures, often with photographs, are enclosed in the sales package and are referred to in the letter. The letter also describes or typographically highlights examples of how the product has benefited

---

Margin notes:

You can prepare readers for your product's price by subtle choice and arrangement of words.

If the price is an attractive feature, emphasize it by displaying it prominently.

To deemphasize price

- Bury actual figures in the middle of a paragraph near the end
- Mention benefits and favorable money matters before the actual price
- Break a quantity price into units
- Compare the price with the cost of some other product or activity

Types of support for product claims:

- Samples
- Brochures
- Examples
- Testimonials
- Statistics
- Guarantees

others, includes testimonials (actual quotations) from satisfied customers, or cites statistics from scientific studies of the product's performance. Guarantees of exchange or return privileges, which may also be woven into the letter or set off in a special way, indicate that you have faith in the product and are willing to back it up.

It's almost impossible to provide too much support. Try to anticipate every question your audience may ask. Put yourself in your audience's place so that you can ask, and answer, all the what-ifs.[15]

Motivating Action

The overriding purpose of a sales letter is to get your reader to do something. Many consumer products sold through the mail simply ask for a check—in other words, an immediate decision to buy. On the other hand, organizations such as UNCF and companies selling big-ticket and more complex items frequently ask for just a small step toward the final decision to buy or to donate, such as sending for more information or authorizing a call by a fund-raiser sales representative.

Aim to get the reader to act as soon as possible.

Try to persuade readers to take action, whatever it is, right away. Convince them that they must act now, perhaps to guarantee a specific delivery date. If there's no particular reason to act quickly, many sales letters offer discounts for orders placed by a certain date or prizes or special offers to, say, the first 500 people who respond. Others suggest that you charge purchases to a credit card or pay them off over time. Still others offer a free trial, an unconditional guarantee, or a no-strings request card for information, all in an effort to overcome readers' natural inertia. Motivating action can be a challenge in sales letters and even more of a challenge when you're trying to raise funds.

Fund-Raising Letters

Fund-raising letters use many of the same techniques used in sales letters.

Most of the techniques used to write sales letters can be used to write fund-raising letters, as long as your techniques match your audience, your goals, and the cause or organization you're representing (Figure 11.4). Be careful to establish value in the minds of your donors. Above all, don't forget to include the "what's in it for me?" information—for example, telling your readers how good they'll feel after making a donation.[16]

Planning Fund-Raising Messages

By reading your mail from donors, you can learn about the tone, language, and concerns your donors prefer.

To make sure that your fund-raising letters outshine the competition's letters, take some time to get ready before you actually begin writing.[17] You can begin by reading the mail you receive from donors. Learn as much as you can about your audience by noting the tone of their letters, the language they use, and the concerns they raise. This exercise will help you write letters that donors will both understand and relate to.

By keeping a file of competing fund-raising letters, you can find out what works and what doesn't.

You might also keep a file of competing fund-raising letters. Study these samples to find out what other fund-raisers are doing and what new approaches they're taking. Most important, find out what works and what doesn't. Then you can continue with your other research efforts such as performing interviews, holding focus groups, and reading trade journals to find out what people are concerned about, what they're interested in, and what gets their attention.

Be sure to focus on the concerns of your readers, not the concerns of your organization.

Finally, before you start writing, know whose benefits to emphasize. Make a two-column list, and, on one side, list what your organization does; on the other side, list what your donors want. You'll discover that the two columns are quite different. Make sure that the benefits you emphasize relate to what your donors want (not to what your organization does). Then you can work on stating those donor benefits in specific detail. For example: "Your donation of $100 will provide 15 people with a Christmas dinner."

Personalizing Fund-Raising Messages

Because fund-raising letters depend so heavily on emotional appeals, keep your message personal. A natural, real-life lead-in is usually the best. People seem to respond best to slice-of-life stories. In fact, storytelling is perfect when your narrative is unforced and goes

As president of the nonprofit Decatur High School Band Parents Association, Monty Nichols is faced with the daunting task of raising a million dollars to help send the band to Osaka, Japan, for an international band festival. Nichols and his board have decided to contact local businesses for help. The following letter makes a compelling case for donations.

Figure 11.4
In-Depth Critique: Letter Raising Funds

Decatur High School Band
27 Linwood Lane • Decatur, Illinois 62525
(217) 864-7768

Dear Corporate Friend:

You have been a loyal supporter of our award-winning Decatur High School Band, and we appreciate what you've helped us accomplish. Because of you, we were able to participate in three festival competitions this year, and we brought home three "Grand Champion" trophies. Now we have the unprecedented opportunity to represent Decatur in the Osaka International Band Festival in 1999. Only 25 top bands from the United States have been invited, and, thanks to your sponsorship, Decatur High School Band is one of them.

Your continued support will help the Decatur High School Band accept Osaka's exciting invitation. The Decatur City Council, the Decatur School Board, and our own Parents Association Board believe that the trip will be an opportunity for our 130 band members to learn about another culture. Even more important, our Decatur ambassadors will bring their experiences back to our community and their classmates in speeches, photographs, and interviews with the local media.

Let us paint your logo on our band trailer as one of our Golden Sponsors. We'll also include your name in all our programs and mailings between now and the time of the trip. You'll be helping band members

1. Learn about other cultures
2. Share information abroad about our way of life in the United States
3. Teach others in Decatur what they learn
4. Help Decatur become recognized as a good home for international businesses

We estimate total costs at $500,000. The city of Osaka has pledged $25,000 toward financing the trip, and we have already received pledges from Akworth Nissan and the city for $25,000 each. Our band members will be holding fundraising events such as car washes, bake sales, a spring fair, and many others over the next two years. But your support will make our dream a reality.

Please help our young ambassadors make this trip. Mark your pledge card and return it today. You'll receive personal letters from the kids expressing their appreciation. And you'll be proof of our city's motto, "Dreams come true in Decatur."

Cordially,

Monty Nichols

Monty Nichols
President
Decatur High School Band Parents Association

Enclosure

The "you"-oriented opening focuses on the reader's generosity and grabs attention.

The next three paragraphs create interest by emphasizing benefits to the reader and by providing details of the trip and costs.

The easy-to-read list of benefits creates desire to participate in a worthwhile project.

The last paragraph urges action by naming additional reader benefits and enclosing a response card.

straight to the heart of the matter.[18] Professional fund-raiser Conrad Squires advises you to "find and use relevant human-interest stories," to "show donors the faces of the people they are helping," and to "make the act of sending a contribution as real and memorable and personal" as you can.[19] Those devices make people feel the warmth of other lives.[20]

So that your letters remain personal, immediate, and effective, steer clear of three common mistakes:[21]

Human-interest stories are the best way to interest your readers in fund-raising letters.

■ Avoid letting your letter sound like a business communication of any kind.
■ Avoid wasting space on warm-up (the things you write while you're working up to your real argument).
■ Avoid assuming that the goals of your organization are more important than your readers' concerns (a deadly mistake).

To personalize fund-raising letters

■ Avoid sounding businesslike
■ Avoid warming up to your real argument
■ Avoid assuming that your organization's goals are more important than your reader's concerns

The last item is crucial when writing fund-raising letters. Squires says: "The more space you spend writing about the reader, the better response you're likely to get."[22]

"You've proven you are somebody who really cares what happens to children, Mr. Jones."

"Ms. Smith, your company's kindness can change the world for Meta Singh and his family."

"You are cordially invited to join . . ."

Also, it's up to you to help your donors identify with recipients. A busy company executive may not be able to identify with the homeless man she passes on the street every day. But every human being understands pain. So do your best to portray that homeless man's pain in words the busy executive can understand.[23]

Strengthening Fund-Raising Messages
The best fund-raising letters do four things: (1) thoroughly explain a specific need, (2) show how important it is for readers to help, (3) spell out exactly what amount of help

---

CHECKLIST FOR SALES AND FUND-RAISING LETTERS

A. Attention
1. Design a positive opening that awakens in the reader a favorable association with the product, need, or cause.
2. Write the opening so that it's appropriate, fresh, honest, interesting, specific, and relevant.
3. Promise a benefit to the reader.
4. Keep the first paragraph short, preferably two to five lines, sometimes only one.
5. Design an attention-getter that uses a human-interest story for fund-raising letters or any of the following techniques for sales letters: significant fact about the product, solution to a problem, special offer or gift, testimonial, stimulation of the senses or emotions, reference to current events, action picture, startling fact, agreeable assertion, comparison, event or fact in the reader's life, problem the reader may face, quotation.

B. Interest
1. State information clearly, vividly, and persuasively, and relate it to the reader's concerns.
2. Develop the central selling point, or explain the urgency of the fund-raising need.
3. Feature the product or need in two ways: physical description and reader benefits.

■ a. Interweave benefits with a physical description, or place benefits first.
■ b. Describe the objective details of the need or of the product (size, shape, color, scent, sound, texture, and so on).
■ c. Through psychological appeals, present the sensation, satisfaction, or pleasure your reader will gain, translating the product, service, or donation into the fulfillment of needs and desires.
■ d. Blend cold facts with warm feelings.

C. Desire
1. Enlist one or more appeals to support the central idea (selling point or fund-raising goal).
■ a. Provide one paragraph of desire-creating material in a one-page letter with a descriptive brochure; provide several paragraphs if the letter itself is two or more pages long, with or without an enclosed brochure.
■ b. Emphasize reader benefits.
■ c. If the product is valued mainly because of its appearance, describe its physical details.
■ d. If the product is machinery or technical equipment, describe its sturdiness of construction, fine crafting, and other technical

is being requested, and (4) describe in detail the benefits of helping.[24] Here are some fund-raising guidelines that will help you accomplish these four major tasks:[25]

- Do whatever you can to interest your readers at the absolute beginning of your letter. If you can't catch your readers' interest then, you never will.
- Tell your story with simple, warm, and personal language.
- Be sure to give readers an opportunity to accomplish something important.
- Make the need so urgent and strong that your readers find it hard to say no. "Won't you send a gift now, knowing children's lives are on the line?" Donors want to feel needed. They want the excitement of coming to your rescue.
- Make it extremely easy to respond by asking for a small gift.
- Make the amount of money you want absolutely clear and appropriate to your audience.
- Explain why the money is needed as soon as possible.
- Write no longer than you have to. For example, people expect telegram-type messages to be short. For fund-raising letters, however, longer messages are usually the most effective, as long as you keep your sentences and paragraphs short, maximize content, and minimize wordiness. If you're writing a long message, just make sure it's interesting and no longer than necessary.
- Include all the basics in your reply form—your name, address, telephone number; a restatement of your request and the gift amount; your donor's name, address, and code number (or space enough for a label); information on how to make out the check; and information on tax deductibility.
- Use interesting enclosures. Enclosures that simply give more information about a project or the purpose of your organization don't inspire readers to respond. To increase returns, use enclosures that are fun or that give the donor something to do, sign, send, or keep.

Strong fund-raising letters

- Explain a specific need thoroughly
- Show how important it is for readers to help
- Spell out exactly what amount of help is being requested
- Describe in detail the benefits of helping

---

    details in terms that help readers visualize themselves using it.
- e. Include technical sketches and meaningful pictures, charts, and graphs, if necessary.
- f. If the main point is to elicit a donation, use strong visual details, good narrative, active verbs, and limited adjectives to strengthen the desire to help.
2. Anticipate and answer the reader's questions.
3. Use an appropriate form of proof.
- a. Include facts about users' experience with the charitable organization or product, including verifiable reports and statistics from donation recipients or product users.
- b. Provide names (with permission only) of other satisfied buyers, users, or donors.
- c. Present unexaggerated testimonials from persons or firms who have used the product or donated funds and whose judgment the reader respects.
- d. For sales letters, provide the results of performance tests by recognized experts, testing laboratories, or authoritative agencies.
- e. For fund-raising letters, provide the details of how donations are spent, using recognized accounting or auditing firms.

- f. In sales letters, offer a free trial or a guarantee, and refer to samples if they are included.
4. Note any enclosures in conjunction with a selling point or reader benefit.

D. Action
1. Clearly state the action you desire.
2. Provide specific details on how to order the product, donate money, or reach your organization.
3. Make action easy through the use of a mail-back reply card, preaddressed envelope, phone number, or promise of a follow-up call or visit.
4. Offer a special inducement to act: time limit or situation urgency, special price for a limited time, premium for acting before a certain date, free gift for buying or donating, free trial, no obligation to buy but more information or a suggested demonstration, easy payments with no money down, credit-card payments.
5. Supply a final reader benefit.
6. Include a postscript conveying important donation information or an important sales point (if desired for emphasis).

These guidelines should help you reach the humanity and compassion of your readers by focusing on specific reader benefits, detailing the unique need, emphasizing the urgency of the situation, and spelling out the exact help needed.

Like sales letters, fund-raising letters are simply particular types of persuasive messages. Each category has its unique requirements, some of which only professional writers can master. (See this chapter's Checklist for Sales and Fund-Raising Letters as a reminder of the tasks involved in these messages.)

 ## WRITING COLLECTION MESSAGES

The purpose of the collection process is to maintain goodwill while collecting what is owed. Collection is a sensitive issue; it's also closely governed by federal and state laws. The Fair Debt Collection Practices Act of 1978 outlines restrictions on collection procedures. The following practices are prohibited:

- Falsely implying that a lawsuit has been filed
- Contacting the debtor's employer or relatives about the debt
- Communicating to other persons that the person is in debt
- Harassing the debtor (although definitions of harassment may vary)
- Using abusive or obscene language
- Using defamatory language (such as calling the person a *deadbeat* or a *crook*)
- Intentionally causing mental distress
- Threatening violence
- Communicating by postcard (not confidential enough)
- Sending anonymous C.O.D. communications
- Misrepresenting the legal status of the debt
- Communicating in such a way as to make the receiver physically ill
- Giving false impressions, such as labeling the envelope "Tax Information"
- Misrepresenting the message as a government or court document

To protect people from unreasonable persecution and harassment by debt collectors, the law also delineates when you may contact a debtor, how many times you may call, and what information you must provide to the debtor (timely responses, accurate records, and understandable documents). However, that doesn't mean you can't be tough in collection letters. As long as what you state is true and lawful, it can't be construed as harassment or misrepresentation.

> A debtor's response is likely to be emotional, especially when the debtor is conscientious, so use tact.

Conscientious customers are embarrassed about past-due accounts. In such an emotional state, they may consciously or unconsciously blame you for the problem, procrastinate, avoid the situation altogether, or react aggressively. Your job is to neutralize those feelings by using **positive appeals,** by accentuating the benefits of complying with your request for payment. If positive appeals fail, you may have to consider a **negative appeal,** which stresses the unpleasant consequences of not acting rather than the benefits of acting. Of course, using abusive or threatening language and harassing your customer are ineffective and illegal. Persuasion is the opposite of force, so continue to use a polite and businesslike tone as you point out some of the actions legally available to you.

> Positive appeals are usually more effective than negative ones.

> If positive appeals fail, you may need to point out the actions legally available to you.

Don't forget that your real aim is to persuade the customer to make the payment. So your best approach is to try to maintain the customer's goodwill. One key to success in collecting is remembering that collection is a process, not just a single demand.[26] As the past-due period lengthens, a series of collection letters reflecting the increasing seriousness of the problem is sent to the customer at predetermined intervals: notification, reminder, inquiry, urgent notice, and ultimatum. At the later stages, the customer's credit and buying

> Steps in the collection series:
> - Notification
> - Reminder
> - Inquiry
> - Urgent notice
> - Ultimatum

history, the amount of money owed, and the customer's overall credit rating determine the content and style of collection messages.

Notification

Most creditors send bills to customers on a regular schedule, depending on the terms of the credit agreement. Typically, this standard notification is a form letter or statement, often computerized, stating clearly the amount due, the date due, the penalties for late payment, and the total amount remaining to be paid. The standardized form, far from being an insult to the recipient, indicates the creditor's trust that all will go according to plan.

The standardized notification is a sign of trust.

Reminder

If the payment has not been received within a few days after the due date, most creditors send out a gentle reminder. Again, the tone of the standardized letter is reassuring, conveying the company's assumption that some minor problem has delayed payment. In other words, the firm still believes that the customer has every intention of paying what is due and needs only to be reminded. Thus the tone is not too serious:

The reminder notice, which still assumes only a minor problem, may be a standardized form or an informal message.

Our records show that your September payment is more than a week overdue. If you have recently mailed your check for $154.87, we thank you. If not, please send it in quickly.

Using a different strategy, some companies send out a copy of the unpaid bill at this stage, with a handwritten note or preprinted stamp or sticker indicating that payment has not yet been received.

Inquiry

As frustrating as it may be to send out a reminder and still get no response, don't assume that your customer plans to ignore the debt, especially if the customer has paid bills promptly in the past. So avoid accusations in your inquiry message. However, the time has passed for assuming that the delay is merely an oversight, so you may assume that some unusual circumstance is preventing payment:

The inquiry
- *Assumes that something unusual is preventing payment*
- *Is personalized*
- *Avoids any suggestion of customer dissatisfaction*

According to our records, we have not received your September payment of $154.87. Because this payment is four weeks overdue, we are quite concerned. You have a history of paying your bills on time, so we must conclude that there is a problem. Please contact us at (800) 536-4995 to discuss this payment, or send us your check for $154.87 right away. We want to help you correct this situation as quickly as possible.

Personalization at this stage is appropriate because you're asking your customer to work out an individualized solution. The letter also avoids any suggestion that the customer might be dissatisfied with the purchase. Instead, it emphasizes the reader's obligation to communicate about the problem and the creditor's willingness to discuss it. Including the writer's name and a phone number helps motivate a response at this stage.

Urgent Notice

The urgent notice stage represents a significant escalation. Convey your desire to collect the overdue payment immediately and your willingness to get serious, but avoid any overt threats. To communicate a sense of urgency, you might have a top official in the company

An urgent notice
- *Might be signed by a top company official*
- *Might indicate the negative consequences of noncompliance*
- *Should leave an opening for payment without loss of face*

sign the letter or resort to a negative appeal. Whatever the strategy, an urgent notice still leaves an opening for the debtor to make a payment without losing face:

I was very surprised this morning when your file reached my desk with a big tag marked OVERDUE. Usually, I receive customer files only when a serious problem has cropped up.

An attention-getter focuses on the unusual circumstances leading to this letter.

Opening your file, I found the following facts: Your order for five cases of Panza serving trays was shipped six months ago. Yet we still haven't received the $232.70 due. You're in business too, Mr. Rosen, so you must realize that this debt needs to be paid at once. If you had a customer this far behind, you'd be equally concerned.

The recipient is reminded of the order. Personalization and an attempt to emphasize common ground may motivate the reader to respond.

Please see that a check for $232.70 is mailed to us at once. If you need to work out an alternate plan for payment, call me now at (712) 693-7300.

The preferred action is spelled out; an option is also suggested in case of serious trouble.

Sincerely,

Artis Knight
Vice President

The name of a ranking official lends weight to the message.

Ultimatum

An ultimatum

- Should state the exact consequences of nonpayment
- Must avoid any hint of defamation or harassment
- Need not take a personal, helpful tone

Some people's finances are in such disorder that you won't get their attention until the ultimatum stage. But, don't send an ultimatum unless you intend to back it up and are well supported by company policy. Even then, maintain a polite, businesslike manner and avoid defaming or harassing the debtor.

By itemizing the precise consequences of not paying the bill, you can encourage debtors to reevaluate their priorities. You're no longer interested in hearing why it has taken them so long to respond; you're interested in putting your claim at the top of their list. The tone of the ultimatum need not be as personal or individualized as the inquiry or urgent notice. At this stage, you're in a position of justified authority and should no longer be willing to return to an earlier stage of communication and negotiation:

On December 12, 1998, you placed a catalog order with Karting Klothes for our extra-large wheeled duffel bag, and you applied for a credit account with us. We approved your application, and on December 17 mailed the duffel bag to you with an invoice for $92.87. According to our credit application, which you signed, payment is due within 20 days of the date of the invoice. As of February 7, your payment was significantly overdue.

Karting Klothes sent you reminders on January 7 and again on February 7. In both these letters, we asked you to contact us to discuss your payment. We also asked you to make a partial payment as a show of your good faith. You did neither.

Karting Klothes has already canceled your credit privileges and will turn your account over to a collection agency if we do not receive your payment for $92.87 by March 10. To reinstate your account and to avoid the problems associated with a bad credit rating, mail your check immediately.

This letter outlines the steps that have already been taken, implying that the drastic action to come is the logical next step. Although earlier collection messages were based on persuasion, this one is essentially a bad-news letter.

If a letter like this doesn't yield results, the only remaining remedy is to begin legal collection procedures. As a final courtesy, you might want to send the debtor a notice of the action you're about to take. By maintaining until the bitter end your respect for the customer, you may still salvage some goodwill.

On the Job

SOLVING A COMMUNICATION DILEMMA AT UNITED NEGRO COLLEGE FUND

In more than 50 years of operation, the United Negro College Fund (UNCF) has raised more than $1 billion and has sent 300,000 students through college. With Campaign 2000, William H. Gray and his team at UNCF wanted to raise enough money to double the number of students that member colleges could afford to educate. The goal of this fund-raising program was to raise $250 million in three years.

The son of a man who had served as president of two African American colleges in the 1940s, Gray could envision the generations of students who would graduate from college because contributors to the United Negro College Fund had provided the support needed to build a better future. He knew that the key to success would be persuasive communication. "An organization must have a strong message to communicate," Gray pointed out. "You must be able to explain your cause and what makes it different from other philanthropic causes. You should also have a history of doing good work."

Five decades of good work gave UNCF the credibility that is so important in persuasive messages. Through a compelling combination of emotional and logical appeals, UNCF requested donations to Campaign 2000. Communicators reached out to potential donors through direct mail, telephone solicitations, advertising, and special events.

As the weeks and months passed, donations and pledges for future contributions started to arrive. More than half the money came from foundations and major corporations such as Nations-Bank, EDS (Electronic Data Services), American Airlines, Frito-Lay, Texas Instruments, Wal-Mart, Coca-Cola, Dow Jones, J. C. Penney, and Exxon. Individual donors also gave generously. For example, Michael Bolton donated his time to give a concert that raised $135,000 for the campaign.

The program was a success and then some. Gray and his staff beat the initial goal by $30 million, raising a total of $280 million. The United Negro College Fund now funds more than 450 programs, including scholarships, faculty development, and college preparation for high school students.

Your Mission: As William Gray's executive assistant, you are responsible for drafting correspondence to businesses about their involvement with the United Negro College Fund. Use your knowledge of persuasive messages to choose the *best* alternative in each of the following situations. Be prepared to explain why your choice is best.[27]

1. Gray wants to reduce the amount of money spent renting office space for UNCF personnel who work with colleges around the country. He would like companies to donate a small section of their facilities for use as UNCF local offices. You have been asked to draft a form letter that will be signed by Gray and sent to large companies in ten cities' where UNCF currently maintains offices. These companies have made contributions to UNCF in the past, so they're familiar with your work. Which of the following versions is the best attention-getter for this letter?

   a. No, this is not another letter asking for a cash contribution. We know that you've been generous with your donations in the past, and we appreciate your help. Instead of asking for money, we're looking for a valuable resource you may be able share with us: a few hundred square feet of unused office space.

   b. Don't let that unused office space go to waste month after month! Space that sits idle doesn't help you. Let the United Negro College Fund take idle space off your hands. We're looking for office space in (city). If you let us have any office space you're not using, you'll be giving us a chance to continue our work with member colleges and students in your area.

   c. Did you know that the United Negro College Fund is seeking donated office space in your area? Even a few hundred square feet of empty space will help. We don't care whether the offices have purple walls, torn carpeting, or windows overlooking the local recycling plant. Our workers will be so busy helping hundreds of African American college students in (city) get a good education that they'll never notice.

   d. If you could put your empty office space to productive use—and earn a charitable contribution at the same time—wouldn't you be interested? Donate some of your unused space to the United Negro College Fund, and you'll gain a tax break as well as the satisfaction of providing additional help to the hundreds of African American students who attend member colleges in your area.

2. Which of the following versions is the most compelling interest and desire section for your letter?

   a. Let's face it, everyone is looking for ways to reduce costs these days. We can cut our costs if you help. We need donated office space. We're not looking for a palace; our field representatives can work productively in as little as 400 square feet of office space. Please take a moment right now to look over your facilities and decide how much empty space you want to donate to our worthy cause.

b. You may know of one large office, two smaller offices, or even a portion of an open work area that you no longer use. Just 400 square feet would allow our field representatives to work more closely with local member colleges and students. We will adapt any empty office space, regardless of its location, at no cost to (name of company). Of course, we will pay for all insurance and moving costs as well as for utilities and other expenses connected with using the donated space.

Donating space you no longer need or use will cost you nothing. We'll even prepare all the paperwork you need to support a charitable tax deduction. But you'll get more than just a tax break. You'll also get the satisfaction of helping African American students get a good college education.

c. The United Negro College Fund's local representatives can work productively in as little as 400 square feet of empty office space. So please look around. Check every nook and cranny in your facility. See whether you have a large, empty office or two smaller, empty offices. Even a portion of an open work area that you no longer use may be suitable.

Your donation of empty office space—regardless of the location in (city)—will help the United Negro College Fund. You can be proud of this donation, which will help us serve member colleges and universities in your area. Help us educate the next generation of leaders by donating your unused office space today.

d. The United Negro College Fund needs your help. Any office space—as little as 400 square feet—will help us put local representatives near member colleges and the students they serve. Please take a moment to see whether you have one large office, two smaller offices, or a portion of an open work area that you no longer use.

If you donate this empty space, we'll take care of all the other details. So you get a tax break, and we get free office space. We both benefit. But the people who will benefit most from this arrangement are the African American students who attend our member colleges in your area.

3. Which of the following versions would be the best action section for your letter?

a. Your donation of unused office space will make a real difference to the United Negro College Fund and to the colleges and students we serve. If you have any questions about donating office space or about the tax consequences,

please call me toll-free at (800) 555-0334. I'd be happy to discuss the details with you. Because the leases for all current facilities expire at the end of this year, we are interested in arranging for new office space no later than October 15.

b. Your donation of free office space for our local representatives would be much appreciated. If you have space that you are willing to donate, call me immediately toll-free at (800) 555-0334. I will be ready to answer any questions about donating space or the tax consequences. Please respond by October 15 if possible.

c. If you can donate unused office space, you will help the United Negro College Fund as well as your company. If you are willing to donate space, please take a moment to call me toll-free at (800) 555-0334. I will try to answer any questions you may have about donating space or the tax consequences. Please do your best to call before October 15, because the leases for all current facilities expire at the end of the year.

d. If you have any questions about donating office space or the tax consequences, please call me toll-free at (800) 555-0334. I would be happy to discuss the details with you. The first company in (city) that offers appropriate space will be entitled to the tax break that this donation can provide, so be sure to call as soon as possible.

4. Like many charitable organizations, the UNCF prepares television commercials about its work and asks stations to air them without charge, as a public service. The advertising agency is putting the finishing touches on a new commercial to spotlight the organization's latest fund-raising campaign. Gray has asked you to compose a letter requesting television station managers around the United States to air the new UNCF commercial for free at least once a week during the next two months. Which of the following appeals to the audience would be the most effective in such a letter?

a. An entirely emotional appeal stressing the need of the students and the satisfaction of helping a worthy cause.

b. An entirely logical appeal stressing that the commercials can be aired whenever the station has commercial time that hasn't been sold to another advertiser, which means the station won't lose money.

c. A combination of emotional and logical appeals, stressing both the satisfaction of helping a worthy cause and the rational reasoning behind airing the commercial whenever the station has unsold commercial time.

d. A combination of emotional and logical appeals, stressing the need for giving commercial air time generously so that UNCF receives the support it needs to send African American students to college and stressing the importance of donating commercial time at the best hours of the day so that this worthy cause can be brought to the attention of all viewers.

Critical Thinking Questions

1. If you must persuade your audience to take some action, aren't you being manipulative and unethical? Explain.
2. How many of a manager's daily tasks require persuasion? List as many as you can think of.
3. Are emotional appeals ethical? Why or why not?
4. Is it honest to use a hook before presenting your request? Explain.

5. Why is it important to maintain goodwill in your collection letter? Briefly explain.
6. For over a year, you've tried repeatedly to collect $6,000 from a client who is able to pay but simply refuses. You're writing one last letter before turning the matter over to your attorney. What sort of things can you say in your letter? What things should you avoid saying? Explain your answers.

Documents for Analysis

Read the following documents; then (1) analyze the strengths and weaknesses of each sentence and (2) revise each document so that it follows this chapter's guidelines.

DOCUMENT 11.A: WRITING PERSUASIVE REQUESTS FOR ACTION

At Tolson Auto Repair, we have been in business for over 25 years. We stay in business by always taking into account what the customer wants. That's why we are writing. We want to know your opinions to be able to better conduct our business.

Take a moment right now and fill out the enclosed questionnaire. We know everyone is busy, but this is just one way we have of making sure our people do their job correctly. Use the enclosed envelope to return the questionnaire.

And again, we're happy you chose Tolson Auto Repair. We want to take care of all your auto needs.

DOCUMENT 11.B: WRITING SALES AND FUND-RAISING LETTERS

We know how awful dining hall food can be, and that's why we've developed the "Mealaweek Club." Once a week, we'll deliver food to your dormitory or apartment. Our meals taste great. We have pizza, buffalo wings, hamburgers and curly fries, veggie roll-ups, and more!

When you sign up for just six months, we will ask what day you want your delivery. We'll ask you to fill out your selection of meals. And the rest is up to us. At "Mealaweek," we deliver! And payment is easy. We accept MasterCard and VISA or a personal check. It will save money especially when compared with eating out.

Just fill out the enclosed card and indicate your method of payment. As soon as we approve your credit or check, we'll begin delivery. Tell all your friends about Mealaweek. We're the best idea since sliced bread!

Cases

WRITING PERSUASIVE REQUESTS FOR ACTION

 **1. Selling sales letters: E-mail message promoting a new idea at Sears, Roebuck** As marketing manager for Sears, Roebuck, you know that sales messages can make or break a business. One of your company's most difficult tasks is getting customers to read a sales letter. During a recent seminar, you heard a reference made to the "PSALM" method, and you decide to learn more about it. Explore the Web site at <http://www.socal.com/writingbiz/page1.htm> and find out what is meant by the PSALM approach. What does the author of this approach identify as the most common mistakes in sales letters? You are enthusiastic about how this new approach has changed your thinking about sales letters, and you would like everyone in your department to seriously consider it.

Your Task: Write an e-mail message to everyone in your department, selling the idea of the PSALM method to your colleagues.

2. Avoiding depression: Letter requesting severance package at Intermed You've heard the old saying that when your next door neighbor loses her job, it's a recession; when you lose yours, it's a depression. After 15 years as a loyal manager at Intermed, a surgical equipment manufacturer, you might be about to experience your own "depression." In a companywide meeting this morning, your CEO informed everyone that Intermed has just been bought out by Urohealth Systems and that a substantial number of layoffs are anticipated.

As manager of Intermed's technical support department, you're glad to know that Urohealth is unlikely to let most of your hourly (or nonexempt) staff go. But you've also heard that after Urohealth's last acquisition, middle managers like you were, to put it politely, "downsized" in wholesale numbers. You're fairly certain your job will disappear within weeks.

Not one to go down without a fight—and preferring to keep a positive perspective—you decide to take a proactive approach. Before they have a chance to fire you, you're going to negotiate a reasonable, friendly, and equitable parting of company. And better to negotiate the terms of your voluntary termination now, with your Intermed superiors, before Urohealth brings in new upper management staff.

So you buckle down to study the inevitable. First, you look at your current compensation and decide to ask for four weeks' severance pay for each of your 15 years of service. (You want to start high, but you're prepared to settle for three week's severance pay, or even two, if you have to.) Second, you consider your stock purchases over the years (part of your benefits program). You've heard that some managers lost their recent stock purchases when they were terminated, and since the company's stock is likely to increase in value after Urohealth's acquisition, you'd like to keep all of yours. You're willing to trade some of your severance pay to keep all of your stock, you decide.

Also, your 401(K) (personal retirement savings plan) may be in jeopardy. The company's agreement has been to match your savings to the plan each year, so long as you are still employed by them. Since you won't be on the payroll through December 31, they're likely to balk at this year's matching amount. Better make this part of your severance request, for the company to make its matching contribution despite your early departure.

Finally, conventional wisdom says it can take up to a year for someone with your skills and experience to find another job. You'd like Intermed to provide outplacement counseling and the use of an office, telephone, and office equipment, plus payment of your job-hunting expenses, for at least 90 days. Considering all you've done for them over the years—and your current managers are quite happy with your work—your requests aren't going to be extravagant.

Your Task: Write a persuasive letter to Shirley Barnett, Intermed's Director of Human Resources, 500 Livingston Street, Northvale, NJ 07647, outlining your proposed voluntary termination and suggested severance package.[28]

3. Helping out: Persuasive memo to Bread & Circus store managers Bread & Circus is a chain of organic food stores with locations in the Washington, D.C., area. The stores are big and well lit, like their more traditional grocery store counterparts. They are also teeming with a wide variety of attractively displayed foods and related products.

However, Bread & Circus is different from the average supermarket. Its products include everything from granola sold in bulk to environmentally sensitive household products. The meats sold come from animals that were never fed antibiotics, and the cheese is from cows said to be raised on small farms and treated humanely.

Along with selling these products to upscale shoppers, the company has been giving food to homeless shelters. Every third weekend, Bread & Circus donates goods and supplies to three soup kitchens downtown. Company executives believe they are in a unique position to help others.

You are the chief operating officer (COO) of Bread & Circus. You've been asked to find ways to expand the program and involve the company's eight branches, most of which are in the suburbs. Ideally, the company would be able to increase the number of people it helps and to get more of its employees involved.

You don't have a great deal of extra money for the program, so the emphasis has to be on using resources already available to the stores. One idea is to use trucks from suburban branches to make the program "mobile." Another idea is to join forces with a retailing chain to give food and clothing to individuals. The key is to be original and not exclude any ideas, no matter how absurd they might seem. The only stipulation is to keep ideas politically neutral. Bread & Circus executives want to make it clear that they do not want to be seen as supporting any party or candidate. They just want to be good corporate citizens.

Your Task: Send persuasive memos to all managers at Bread & Circus, requesting ideas to expand the program. Invite employees to contribute ideas, for this or any other charitable project for the company.[29]

4. The glass bicycle: Persuasive letter from Owens-Corning requesting bids for manufacturing rights A student design group from Brazil's University of São Paulo has come up with the winning bicycle design in the Global Design Challenge. Sponsored by Owens-Corning, the competition called on teams from eight top design and engineering schools in the United States, Canada, Europe, Asia, and South America to design a bicycle that would cost less than $100 and would incorporate mainly glass-fiber composites in the construction. The winning entry is called the Kangaroo. Its framework is made of polyester reinforced with glass fiber, and its estimated manufacturing cost is $82. Moreover, some unique features make it a product of truly worldwide potential. An adjustable wheelbase can be shortened to allow easy maneuvering in city traffic, and the seat and handlebars can be adjusted within a range to suit 95 percent of the world's population. Since more than half of the people on the globe depend on bicycles as their primary means of transportation, and since bicycles require no fossil fuel for operation, this product has tremendous potential in countries from Abu Dhabi to Zimbabwe.

As Owens-Corning's North American licensing manager, your job is to sign up companies to produce and market the Kangaroo bicycle for the U.S., Mexican, and Canadian markets. A manufacturing deal has been arranged with a Chinese producer who can deliver the bicycles to any West Coast NAFTA port for $86, including shipping, taxes, and tariffs. Your problem is that you have no distribution system to handle bicycles, so you must find a marketing partner who will license the rights to distribute and market the Kangaroo in North America. Your preference is to find a single marketer to serve the entire region, and priority will be given to companies such as Schwinn, Nishiki, and Cannondale Bicycles who are currently using Owens-Corning materials in their products. You are planning to license the marketing rights for a five-year term for an initial payment of $350,000 plus 8 percent of the gross sales.

Your Task: Write a persuasive letter to Mr. Gregg Bagni, Marketing Director, Schwinn Bicycle & Fitness (1690 38th Street, Boulder, CO 80301-2602), requesting a bid on the North American marketing rights and offering him first refusal. Point out the features you think will make the Kangaroo a widespread success, and be sure to spell out the financial terms. He can then determine whether the deal makes sense from his perspective. But don't give him too much time—ask for a response within ten days.[30]

5. Nap Time: Memo requesting space for "day sleepers" at Phidias & Associates It's been one of those days . . . you were dragging by 10 A.M., ready to slump over onto your drafting table at Phidias & Associates architectural firm in San Francisco. Even that incredibly bright bay view outside the office windows hasn't helped perk you up, and the coffee is just giving you stomach pains. Now how are you supposed to be creatively inspired when you can barely get your eyes to focus and your head feels like it's full of cotton? No, you weren't out partying last night—you've just been working long, late hours on a rush job for one of the firm's biggest clients. San Francisco is the workaholic city, but this is too much. If only you could stretch out for a little catnap, you'd be good as new in 15 minutes . . .

Groggily, your mind brings up the memory of an item you spotted in the *Wall Street Journal* a year ago and tore out. You seem to remember stuffing it into a desk drawer with the vague notion of presenting it during one of those officewide, corporate-spirit "pep rallies" your employers are so fond of. You rummage around in the drawer—ah, there it is. A paragraph or two in the "Work Week" column, all about a minitrend toward "nap rooms" in the workplace. At first, your work ethic was shocked at the concept, but then your creative self started to glow at the thought. After all, didn't they teach you in school that Thomas Edison kept a cot in his office and got his best ideas when he was napping? And the article quotes an expert, William A. Anthony, author of *The Art of Napping* and professor of rehabilitation counseling at Boston University. He says that most people aren't sleep deprived, they're "nap ready."

It's not as if there haven't been precedent or pioneers out there in the business world. Shelly Ginenthal, the human resources director of *Macworld Magazine,* says their two-person nap room was installed in 1986 and usually has a waiting line. Must not be interfering with productivity if they're still using it more than ten years later, you muse. And here's another firm, Yarde Metals in Bristol, Connecticut, whose president, Bruce Yarde, says, "A quick little nap can rejuvenate you." So he's fighting employee stress with a 25-person nap room. Wow. That's almost like your old kindergarten. And yet another—you like this one best—an architectural firm in Kansas City, Missouri, Gould Evans Goodman Associates, has plans on its drawing boards to add a nap space to its offices. If they can do it in Kansas City, why not here?

Your Task: After you've had a good night's sleep, write a memo to Jonas T. Phidias, the senior partner, persuading him that the distinguished offices of Phidias & Associates could benefit from the addition of a corporate nap room. Be sure you've used your best persuasive skills, though, or you might send the wrong message to your employer.[31]

6. Korean recognition: E-mail to Garden Grove city council The request seems reasonable enough: members of the Korean Chamber of Commerce of Orange County asked the city council of Garden Grove, California, to erect two signs designating a portion of Garden Grove Boulevard as the Korean Business District. Essentially, that's what the neighborhood is, and it has been home to your Korea House restaurant for many years.

But some members of the community complained when the issue was brought up during a city council session. "We should be focusing on the unification of the community as a whole and its general diversity," they proclaimed, "not dividing the city up into little ethnic districts." Some council members had been intrigued, however, by the prospect of creating a new tourist destination by marking the Korean Business District officially (that's what it actually is and has been for as long as you remember). However, the issue was tabled for later consideration.

As owner of Korea House, you agree with those council members who think the designation would attract visitors. Moreover, the Korean Chamber of Commerce has returned to the city council with an offer to pay for the two cement structures itself. It is willing to spend up to $30,000 for the design and installation of the signs—one west of Brookhurst Street and another east of Beach Boulevard—to mark the highly concentrated Korean business area.

Your Task: As a member of the Korean Chamber, you've been asked to support the request with an e-mail message to Cathy Standiford, Garden Grove's Deputy City Manager, at <cstandiford@ch.ci.garden-grove.ca.us>.[32]

7. Too good to be true: E-mail to Page South requesting adjustment Page South offered its pager services for a mere $5 a month. Two weeks ago, you bought an inexpensive pager and signed a two-year contract. You had expected your pager to be up and running as soon as you bought it, but your co-workers and clients have been getting a busy signal when they dial your pager number. You've called Page South to get the problem resolved, but it's going to take them a week to fix it. Obviously, you don't want to be charged for any time the pager isn't in service, so you discuss the situation with the local manager. She tells you to contact Judy Hinkley at the company's regional business office.

Your Task: Send an e-mail message to Hinkley at <Judy@pg-south.com> and request an adjustment to your account. Request credit or partial credit for one month of service. Remember to write a summary of events in chronological order, supplying exact dates for maximum effectiveness.

8. Phone frustration: Persuasive letter to Pacific Bell requesting resolution of telephone service overcharges You are a freelance business researcher, and your time is valuable, especially when you're using online research facilities. These valuable resources are becoming more and more important in your work, so you can't afford to sit around waiting for your Internet searches to download files at 14,400 bits per second (14.4 Kbps) or even 28.8 Kbps. You often deal with massive files that can take forever to transfer at these rates. You determined that an ISDN (Integrated Services Digital Network) connection would be a faster alternative for your online work. You contacted Pacific Bell Telephone in November and requested residential ISDN service (you work from home).

When the confirming work order arrived, you discovered that PacBell had your account set up as business service, so you called the service representative to change it to the lower residential rate. As a result, your business service was disconnected, and it took PacBell two weeks to reconnect you. On top of that, when the initial bill arrived, there was a $125 charge for disconnecting the business service, and another $75 charge for reinstallation, but no credit for the two weeks of downtime. You have made at least 13 calls to the customer service department, both locally and at Pacific Telephone headquarters in Sacramento. You even left a message on the customer feedback section of PacBell's Internet home page. But none of these actions have resolved the situation.

Your Task: Compose a persuasive letter to Ms. Claire Abell (PacBell's director of consumer affairs at 6640 Rosecrans Road, Sacramento, CA 99054), explaining your frustration with this billing problem and asking for immediate adjustment.[33]

WRITING SALES AND FUND-RAISING MESSAGES

9. All natural: Letter promoting crystal Deodorant Stones of America When Larry Morris first walked into your advertising office and placed what looked like a large piece of rock salt in your hand, proclaiming that this product could make Arid, Dial, Ban, and all the

others obsolete, all you could do was stare at the thing. You couldn't imagine how this clear, hard rock could keep anyone's underarms sweet smelling. In the first place, what were you supposed to do with it? Wear it around your neck? You looked at Morris with a skeptical squint—was this some new "crystal healing" device?

But Morris, owner of Deodorant Stones of America (DSA), smiled patiently and sat down to explain his new product. The only ingredients are mineral salts, used for centuries in Thailand to get rid of body odors by destroying the skin bacteria that cause the unpleasant smells. The stones contain no perfumes, preservatives, oils, emulsifiers, alcohol, propellants, or harsh chemicals. The naturally occurring minerals (potassium alum, ammonium, barium, calcium, iron, magnesium, manganese, phosphorus, silicon, sodium, strontium, and titanium) are crystallized over a period of several months, then hand-shaped and smoothed for rubbing over the skin. When either the skin or the stone is wet, an invisible layer of the mineral salts sticks to the skin, but it won't stain clothing or clog pores. Morris says the minerals kill odor-causing bacteria so thoroughly that the stones are 300 percent as effective as conventional chemical deodorants.

Deodorant Stones of America now sells about 7 million stones annually, in 50 states and seven countries, under several brand names: Fresh Foot (Foot Deodorant Stone), The Jock's Rock (World Class Deodorant), Nature's Crystal (Body Deodorant), Thai Deodorant Stone, and Pure & Natural (push-up sticks and spray). Morris wants to expand, and he's hired you to write an all-purpose sales letter directed to both consumers and retailers.

Your Task: You've tried the stone and signed the contract. You especially liked the fact that it gave off absolutely no odor at all and worked for a full 24 hours. Write the sales letter for one or all of the product names listed above.[34]

10. Power pioneers: Sales letter touting ONSI's fuel cells If you can turn water (H_2O) into hydrogen and oxygen by running an electrical current through it (electrolysis), can you produce an electrical current by combining hydrogen and oxygen? A British lawyer, Sir William Robert Grove, proved in 1839 that you could. He produced the world's first electricity-generating "fuel cell." But until now, no one could produce a commercially viable version of Grove's invention.

The simple device is somewhat like a battery; it produces an electrical current by means of an electrochemical reaction. It's also like a combustion or turbine engine; it continues to operate as long as it's supplied with fuel (some form of hydrogen and oxygen). Best of all, the fuel cell's only by-products are water, heat, and, if certain fuels are used, carbon dioxide.

Analysts predict that two decades from now fuel cells will account for 15 percent of growth in the global power-producing industry. So far, ONSI Corporation is the only company to reach the marketplace with fuel cells that can be used for large-scale power generation. Since you signed on several months ago as a marketing representative, ONSI has sold 57 of its 200-kilowatt fuel cells to hospitals, hotels, office buildings, and research centers in the United States, Europe, and Asia. Southern California Gas Company, which is using ten of them, is saving energy costs of 5 to 40 percent a year.

ONSI's phosphoric-acid cells are rated 85 percent efficient if, in addition to the electrical current, the heat they generate is captured to produce hot water. The unit is about 12 feet tall by 24 feet long and costs $600,000—twice the price of a gas turbine generator of comparable power output. But it's highly reliable, producing enough electricity to power a 30-unit apartment building. Moreover, it emits less than one-hundredth of the nitrogen oxide pollutants and only 75 percent of the carbon dioxide produced by a fossil-fuel power plant. Such emissions more than meet pollution-control standards mandated by many governments—a bonus that makes the cells attractive despite the high price tag.

Your Task: Write a brief introductory sales letter touting the benefits of fuel cells for large institutions. Plan to enclose a separate brochure with detailed technical information about ONSI's phosphoric-acid fuel cells.[35]

11. The bride wore hiking boots: Persuasive letter to "We Do" bridal superstore When Shari and Randy Almsburg of Dublin, Ohio, decided to tie the knot, they knew just what they wanted. "We always enjoyed hiking. In fact, we met each other on a hike. That's why we wanted to wrap our wedding plans around our favorite hobby." Enter "Tie the Knot," a one-owner company specializing in bizarre wedding plans.

"Actually, the bride wearing a white dress and a pair of hiking boots was *not* our most unusual wedding," says owner and wedding consultant, Todd Dansing (whose own wedding took place a mile high just before the happy couple plunged to Earth by parachute). "We recently helped plan an underwater wedding in a shark tank at the aquarium in Chicago for two marine biologists whose work involved feeding the fish. Our main problem there was this huge turtle that kept bumping into the preacher." Dansing tells you of other unusual weddings that took place in airplanes, on boats, under water, and in exotic locations such as Arizona's Painted Desert. Whatever your wedding plans, Todd believes he can find the necessary resources and save you time and money in the process.

Todd's marketing efforts to date have involved mostly word of mouth and free press coverage of his unusual weddings (although reporters kept their distance when two snake handlers from the zoo tied the knot). But his brother-in-law has invested capital in the business, so Todd hires you to help him tell the world about his services. You suggest that he consider affiliating with an established wedding service or store.

You and Todd visit "We Do," a bridal superstore located in Dublin, Ohio, and you help Todd see the potential for marketing his unusual, offbeat wedding service to this large company. We Do is a 26,000-square-foot matrimonial Mecca that sells 600 styles of bridal gowns and everything else traditional couples need for a wedding. The franchise hopes to open 40 stores eventually, so if Todd can strike a deal with We Do, his future profit potential will be high.

Your Task: Write a letter for Todd's signature to Carol Feinberg, CEO of We Do. Suggest that Tie the Knot would make a great consultant for couples with offbeat wedding tastes. Emphasize Todd's experience, and point out the ways this venture will provide additional market share for We Do. Think of possible objections, such as Todd's lack of capital and small company size, and try to assure Feinberg that Tie the Knot is the right business to help capitalize on a unique opportunity.[36]

12. Finding money creatively: Fund-raising letter from Long Beach Opera Long Beach Opera is a small, creative opera company, renowned for its daring, sometimes offbeat, performances. Located in a major metropolitan area, it has been hampered by having to compete with larger, more affluent opera companies that have large followings and budgets to match.

Despite the competition, Long Beach Opera has benefited from critical acclaim, and it has built a small but loyal following since its premier performance more than 18 years ago. Now the company is at a crossroads. Most recently it mounted a production of *Elegy for Young Lovers*. However, the show had to close after only a week because of poor attendance. Bills continue to come in, and the bank account is bare. The creative director won't even discuss continuing the season unless a solution can be found.

Out of the darkness comes an angel. A local university with a brand-new performing arts center would like to form an alliance with Long Beach Opera. Although the university isn't offering large sums of cash, its board members are willing to let the company use the performing arts center and other campus facilities at no cost. They would also consider some joint ventures in money-making educational events such as lectures and exhibitions. These events would be fairly easy and inexpensive to produce, and they could generate some immediate cash flow.

But the *coup de théâtre* for Long Beach Opera would be access to the university's key donors, alumni, and supporters of the arts.

The company's management team believes that, properly cultivated, this group could provide the sound financial base the company needs for future operations. Everyone on the team is excited.

The chairperson of the opera's board, the creative director, the development director, and the head of the university's fine arts department recently held a strategy session. After agreeing in principle to finalize the alliance between Long Beach Opera and the university, all agreed that the first order of business is to raise funds. It was generally agreed that business and community leaders should be informed and invited to lend their financial support to the new venture.

A symposium is planned, at which the new venture will be introduced. The symposium will include musical previews of Long Beach's upcoming season, a presentation by the creative director, and messages from key university staff. The goal of the symposium is to raise $500,000 in pledges.

Your Task: As development director of Long Beach Opera, you have been asked to draft a letter to community and business leaders. Your goals are to convince them of the opera's viability, get them to attend the symposium, and convince them to pledge their financial support.[37]

WRITING COLLECTION MESSAGES

13. A Firm but gentle nudge: Urgent notice collection letter at Coast Federal Bank You are the director of marketing at Coast Federal Bank (CFB), a consumer-oriented bank with branches mainly in southern California. Because your bank is surrounded by some of the top educational institutions in the country, you have long considered student loans to be an important product.

You've just finished reviewing this month's collection reports and you realize that, for the sixth straight month, your bad debt ratio (loans over 90 days past due) has increased. In addition, your average collection time has increased more than 20 days in the same period. This trend disturbs you, and you know your loan committee (which meets in three days) will be even more disturbed.

When CFB began an aggressive marketing campaign for student loans a little over ten years ago, tuition costs at local public and private universities were less than half what they are today. As the cost of education has skyrocketed (creating a growing demand for financing), your interest rates on these loans have remained virtually unchanged. And with your collection ratio going downhill, you can see profits eroding rapidly.

You're also concerned because many of your student loans were made to parents of college students as part of the PLUS (Parent Loans to Undergraduate Students) program. These parents are some of the bank's best customers, local executives and community leaders with whom you have other important business dealings. You are anxious to maintain your good image and relationship with these customers, so you're hesitant to implement a get-tough collection policy.

You have begun developing a strategy to improve collection of student loans. You plan to stress loyalty to your customers, commitment to supporting local educational institutions, and your desire to work with people who will demonstrate good-faith efforts. You think that refinancing and extended payment options might encourage some people to improve their payment records.

Your loan committee will meet in three days. You're aware that some more conservative committee members may want to recommend selling the entire delinquent student loan business to a collection firm. You feel this action would be extremely detrimental to your bank's reputation and long-term growth.

Your Task: Develop a customer relations collection letter designed to encourage your student loan borrowers to improve their payment records. Assume that your bank's computer program will personalize each letter with the customer's name and address. Make your communication personal and directed to the individual customer.[38]

14. One last try: Ultimatum collection letter from Arciero Brothers Phil Arciero was ecstatic when his concrete company, Arciero Brothers, was selected as one of the construction subcontractors for a huge entertainment complex being built by Moorfield Construction. Located near one of the country's leading vacation destinations, the complex was designed to include restaurants, theaters, a video arcade, and a kiddyland play park.

With a venture of this magnitude it wasn't surprising that more than 200 subcontractors were needed to handle the building and infrastructure work. Arciero Brothers specializes in building foundations, sidewalks, and parking lots. Although Arciero has been in business for more than 20 years, the entertainment complex is the largest contract he's ever been awarded.

The project took nearly 24 months to complete. Arciero Brothers was on site throughout the first 21 months of the job. Phil Arciero hired new employees, including laborers and skilled tradespeople, and bought extra equipment to handle the new work and continue to meet the needs of his existing customers.

Moorfield Construction paid Arciero 10 percent of his estimate at the beginning of the job. Interim payments were made monthly, until the total payments reached 85 percent of the contract bid. Moorfield was to withhold the final 15 percent until the entire project was approved by the city building inspectors, a common practice in the construction industry. It has been nearly five months since the entertainment complex passed final inspection and opened for business.

Your Task: As the controller at Arciero Brothers, you've already paid your workers, drawing against your credit line at the bank to do it. You've called Moorfield Construction once a week, requesting payment of the more than $100,000 that is still outstanding on your contract. Moorfield officials say "paperwork foul-ups" are the reason for the slow payment. You're aware that none of the other subcontractors have received their final payments and that some of them are hiring attorneys to file mechanic's liens (legal collection proceedings) directly against the owner of the complex. You've talked to Phil Arciero about the dilemma. Neither of you wants to jeopardize potential future business from Moorfield Construction or from the entertainment complex owners. But to preserve your rights, and to increase your chances of being paid (liens are paid in the order filed), you and Arciero decide to have your attorney file a mechanic's lien. You recommend to Arciero that you write a polite but firm letter to Moorfield, with a copy to the owners of the entertainment center, demanding immediate payment of the full amount owed you and informing Moorfield of the lien. Address your letter to Moorfield Construction (9 Corporate Park #600, Irvine, CA 92714), and address the copy to James Penny, Vice President of Finance, Edwards Theaters Inc. (12100 Wilshire Boulevard, Los Angeles, CA 90025).[39]

DEVELOPING YOUR INTERNET SKILLS

*GOING ONLINE: LOBBY MOVERS AND SHAKERS
IN THE U.S. GOVERNMENT, P. 242*

Follow the links to the home page of one of your congressional representatives, or any representative you choose. Draft and send a persuasive but short e-mail message about an issue that concerns you. If you can't think of one, go back to the Thomas home page and review some of the items now under consideration by Congress. You can go as far as your time and interest permit.

REPORTS AND

PROPOSALS

WRITING SHORT REPORTS

On the Job
FACING A COMMUNICATION DILEMMA AT FEDERAL EXPRESS
Delivering On Time, Every Time

Imagine collecting, transporting, and delivering more than 3 million letters and packages every day. Now imagine that every one of these parcels absolutely, positively has to arrive at its destination when expected. That's the standard against which Federal Express managers—and customers—measure performance. Living up to this exacting standard day in and day out presents founder and CEO Frederick W. Smith and his entire management team with a variety of communication challenges.

When Federal Express began operation in 1973, its services covered 22 U.S. cities. Today it delivers throughout the United States and to 212 countries around the world. To make those deliveries on time, every time, Federal Express employs more than 137,000 people, operates nearly 600 airplanes, and maintains a fleet of 38,500 trucks and vans.

But keeping packages in motion is only part of the challenge. Federal Express must also battle a host of rivals, including United Parcel Service (UPS), the U.S. Postal Service, Airborne Express, DHL, and other delivery companies. Competition is fierce, so Federal Express is constantly on the lookout for innovative ways to serve customers better. One important way Federal Express helps commercial and industrial customers is by taking over their warehouse and inventory chores. Instead of just acting as a shipping service, Federal Express operates like part of the customer's organization.

Smith's newest service innovations involve electronic commerce in general and the Internet in particular. To get around the tedious work of filling out shipping forms and telephoning a pickup request, Federal Express now lets customers place orders online with a new service called FedEx interNetShip. Also, to help customers capitalize on the selling power of the World Wide Web, the FedEx VirtualOrder service can handle everything from setting up a product catalog on a Web site to the more traditional service of delivering the goods. Carson's Ribs, a Chicago company, now ships fully cooked, flash-frozen orders of ribs overnight via Federal Express. Customers just visit Carson's Web site, then the Federal Express driver delivers tomorrow's dinner.

With competitors offering more and customers expecting more, Smith and his management team have their work cut out for them. Monitoring and controlling the Federal Express operation, training new employees, making a host of decisions—all these activities require the communication of timely, accurate information. To keep the business running smoothly, maintain satisfied customers, and hold competitors at bay, Federal Express managers receive and prepare reports of all kinds. How can Smith and his managers use reports for internal communication? How can writers make their reports readable? What makes one report better than another?[1]

At Federal Express, reports of all kinds are used to track both system and employee performance, as well as to assemble information needed for making managerial decisions. Not only does Frederick Smith read innumerable reports, he wrote a very famous one, which detailed the idea of his air express delivery service and persuaded investors to fund him.

 # WHAT MAKES A GOOD BUSINESS REPORT

Business reports are like bridges spanning time and space. Organizations such as Federal Express use them to provide a formal, verifiable link among people, places, and times. Some reports are needed for internal communication; others are vehicles for corresponding with outsiders. Some are required as a permanent record; others are needed to solve an immediate problem or to answer a passing question. Many move upward through the chain of command to help managers monitor the various units in the organization; some move downward to explain management decisions to lower-level employees responsible for day-to-day operations.

You may be surprised at the variety of messages that qualify as reports. The term covers everything from a fleeting image on a computer screen to preprinted forms to informal letters and memos to formal three-volume manuscripts. Many reports are delivered orally, as discussed in Chapter 18. In general, however, most businesspeople think of **reports** as written, factual accounts that objectively communicate information about some aspect of the business. Reports can be printed on paper or distributed electronically. Although business reports serve hundreds of purposes, six basic uses are common (Table 12.1).

In large part, reports are a managerial tool. Even the most capable managers must rely on other people to observe events or collect information for them. Like Frederick Smith, managers are often too far away to oversee everything themselves, and they don't have enough time. In addition, they often lack the specialized background required to research and evaluate certain subjects. Thus reports are usually prepared for managers or on their behalf.

The goal in developing a report is to make the information as clear and convenient as possible. If Frederick Smith received information that was inaccurate, incomplete, or difficult to decipher, any decisions he based on it would be bad ones, so Federal Express would suffer along with Smith's reputation. Because time is precious, you tell your readers what they need to know—no more, no less—and you present the information in a way that is geared to their needs. Some managers like to use a computer to compare information from the reports they receive. Some managers like to get their reports orally, face to face; but many managers prefer the convenience and permanence of paper reports and, increasingly, of electronic reports distributed over the Internet or corporate intranets.

Regardless of the medium you use for your message, try to keep the likes and dislikes of your readers in mind. As you make decisions about the content, format, style, and organization of the report, your readers' needs are your main concern. Before you write, decide whether to use letter, memo, or manuscript format (see Appendix A for details), whether to employ a formal or an informal style; and how to group your ideas.

When thinking about these issues, ask yourself the following questions and tailor the report accordingly:

- *Who initiated the report?* **Voluntary reports,** which are prepared on your own initiative, usually require more detail and support than **authorized reports,** which are prepared at the request of someone else. When writing a voluntary report, you give more background on the subject, and you explain your purpose more carefully. An authorized report is organized to respond to the reader's request.
- *What subject does the report cover?* A report's vocabulary and format are dictated by its subject matter. For example, audit reports (that verify an accountant's inspection of a firm's financial records) contain a lot of numbers, often in the form of tables. Reports from the legal department (perhaps on the company's patents) contain many legal

A business report is any factual, objective document that serves a business purpose.

GOING ONLINE
SPOTLIGHT ON SAMPLE BUSINESS REPORTS
You can better understand report organization, style, and format if you look at a wide variety of actual business reports. To do this, enter the phrase "business reports" in the search window of Cyber411, a parallel search engine that contracts 13 other search engines to do the actual work and then collates the results from all the engines and presents them to you.

Note: In the option windows, choose "phrase" and "fast" for the most effective search.

http://www.cyber411.com

When making decisions about the format, style, and organization of a report, consider its

- Origin
- Subject
- Timing
- Distribution
- Purpose
- Probable reception

Table 12.1		THE SIX MOST COMMON USES OF REPORTS		
Purpose of Report	*Common Examples*	*Preparation and Distribution*	*Features*	
To monitor and control operations	Plans, operating reports, personal activity reports	Internal reports move upward on a recurring basis; external reports go to selected audiences	**Format:** Standard memo or preprinted form **Style:** Telegraphic **Organization:** Topical **Order:** Direct	
To implement policies and procedures	Lasting guidelines, position papers	Internal reports move downward on a nonrecurring basis	**Format:** Matches policies and procedures manual **Style:** Fully developed text **Organization:** Topical **Order:** Direct	
To comply with regulatory requirements	Reports for IRS, SEC, EEOC, Revenue Canada, Canadian Human Rights Commission, and other industry regulators	External reports are sent on a recurring basis	**Format:** Standardized; perhaps preprinted or electronic form **Style:** Skeletal **Organization:** To follow reader's instructions **Order:** Direct	
To obtain new business or funding	Sales proposals	External reports are sent on a nonrecurring basis	**Format:** Letter or manuscript **Style:** Fully developed text **Organization:** Problem-solution **Order:** Commonly direct	
To document client work	Interim progress reports, final reports	External reports are sent on a nonrecurring basis	**Format:** Letter or manuscript **Style:** Fully developed text **Organization:** Around sequential steps or key findings **Order:** Usually direct	
To guide decisions	Research reports, justification reports, troubleshooting reports	Internal reports move upward on a nonrecurring basis	**Format:** Memo or manuscript **Style:** Fully developed text **Organization:** Around conclusions or logical arguments	

terms. When you and your reader are familiar with the subject and share the same background, you don't need to define terms or explain basic concepts. The presentation format, style, and organization are dictated by the characteristics of the subject.

■ *When is the report prepared?* **Routine reports** are submitted on a recurring basis (daily, weekly, monthly, quarterly, annually) and require less introductory and transitional material than do **special reports,** nonrecurring reports that deal with unique situations. Routine reports are often prepared on preprinted or computerized forms (either of which the writer simply fills in), or they're simply organized in a standard way.

■ *Where is the report being sent?* **Internal reports** (used within the organization) are generally less formal than **external reports** (sent to people outside the organization). Many internal reports, especially those under ten pages, are written in memo format. On the other hand, external reports may be in letter format (if they are no longer than five pages) or in manuscript format (if they exceed five pages).

- *Why is the report being prepared?* **Informational reports** focus on facts; **analytical reports** include analysis, interpretation, conclusions, and recommendations. Informational reports are usually organized around subtopics; analytical reports are generally organized around logical arguments and conclusions. (Chapter 13 explains this difference in greater detail.)
- *How receptive is the reader?* When the reader is likely to agree with the content of the report, the material is presented in direct order, starting with the main idea (key findings, conclusions, recommendations). If the reader may have reservations about the report, the material is presented in indirect order, starting with the details and leading up to the main idea.

As you can see, the origin, subject, timing, distribution, purpose, and probable reception of a report have quite an impact on its format, style, and organization.

*H*OW ELECTRONIC TECHNOLOGY AFFECTS *BUSINESS REPORTS*

Reports aren't necessarily confined to paper in today's business environment. Virtually all of the reports discussed in this chapter can be and are being adapted to computerized formats. You can now file your taxes electronically; the SEC actually requires corporations to file reports electronically; and thousands of companies have set up electronic reporting procedures to communicate with employees, customers, and suppliers.[2]

Electronic reports fall into two basic categories: First are those that essentially replace paper reports. You can draft a report using your word processor, but rather than printing it and making copies, you can distribute the file electronically. Most e-mail systems now have the ability to attach files to support electronic document distribution. The other category of electronic reports includes those that are unique to the electronic format. For example, an intranet site can offer text, video, and sound in a single integrated "report."

If you explore software for electronic reports, you'll discover a class of software known as *report writers* or *reporting tools*. Unfortunately, these tools don't magically write business reports for you. They are designed to extract and format data from computerized databases. For instance, you can use a personnel database to generate a report that ranks employees by income or a customer database to generate mailing labels for all your customers. Once the report is generated, you can print it or distribute it electronically. Also, some report writers allow you to work interactively with the database, in effect creating a "live" report that responds to your queries and inputs.[3]

Electronic reports offer both advantages and disadvantages, compared with their paper counterparts. Potential advantages include the following:

- *Cost savings.* Assuming you have the necessary hardware and software in place, electronic reports can save a significant amount of money in terms of paper, printing or photocopying, and distribution.
- *Space savings.* A basic CD-ROM can hold the equivalent of hundreds of pages of text (and higher-capacity CD-ROMs and other massive storage devices are on the way), so electronic reports can be stored in far less space than paper reports. This can be a significant advantage for large businesses, businesses with heavy government reporting requirements, and businesses that must keep historical records for many years.
- *Faster distribution.* Electronic documents can reach their audiences in a few seconds, compared with the few hours or days it can take to send paper documents to other locations.
- *Multimedia communication.* You can integrate sound and video with some electronic reports, bringing text to life.
- *Easier maintenance.* Documents on intranet and Internet Web sites are great examples of how much easier it is to correct and update electronic documents. If a single figure changes in a sales report after you've distributed it, your options with a paper report are to reprint and redistribute the entire thing, send out a corrected page, or send a memo to all the recipients asking them to pencil in the correction by hand. With an electronic

Margin notes:

Electronic reports are becoming more popular.

Report writing software can pull information out of computerized databases and organize it in any format you want.

Electronic reports have distinct advantages.

BEHIND THE SCENES AT THE SAN DIEGO ZOO
Even Tapirs Leave a Paper Trail

When zoo curator Rick Barongi flew to Panama to rescue six wild Barid's tapirs, he probably wasn't thinking about the report he'd have to write at the end of his adventure. Left to starve at the ranch of deposed dictator Manuel Noriega, the long-nosed mammals (distant relatives of horses and rhinos) were in the care of people who regard these endangered animals as creatures to be hunted for food in the tropical forests of Panama.

Barongi made four trips to Noriega's government-seized estate, and for the last one, he organized an international team of zoo experts to accompany him. They saved five of the tapirs, and they helped educate local officials about the special care needed by such endangered animals in captivity.

After braving touchy politics, hair-raising traffic, and tropical heat (not to mention the razor-sharp canine teeth of unhappy, 300-pound tapirs), Barongi returned home to his regular job as children's zoo director at the San Diego Zoo, and he promptly turned out an eight-page activity report on "The Panama Tapir Project." Writing reports is as much a part of Barongi's working life as making sure the baby mon-

keys that live in the nursery beneath his office are diapered and fed properly by their keepers. As director of the children's zoo, he's responsible for a million-dollar budget, a staff of 20 keepers, and a collection of domestic and exotic animals larger than many entire zoos. To manage both people and animals successfully, Barongi writes a lot of memo and letter reports.

Barongi explains that when obtaining new animals for the children's zoo, he usually sends a memo report to all departments affected by the animals' arrival. For example, when he acquired a colony of naked mole rats, "a bizarre rodent from Africa," Barongi's superiors were concerned about the cost of building the rodents' new exhibit/home. So Barongi's first memo report about these animals was written to justify that cost. Later, he organized information about the rats in a direct format for subsequent short reports to the zoo's veterinary hospital (reserving space for the mole rats' month-long quarantine) and to the public relations and photography departments (initiating publicity about the new residents). Barongi says he strives to keep such reports "really short—I don't want to be redundant."

report, you simply make the change and let everyone know via e-mail. When you offer your readers access to an electronic report on an intranet site, you have an added bonus: Because the only existing copy of the report is always current, you don't have to worry that people will hang on to obsolete or incorrect information.

Electronic reports have some disadvantages.

For all their advantages, however, electronic reports are not a cure-all for business communication problems, nor are they without some risks and disadvantages:

- *Hardware and software costs.* Naturally, you need some kind of computer equipment to distribute electronic documents. If those systems aren't already in place, their purchase, installation, and maintenance involve an extra expense.
- *System compatibility.* As discussed in Chapter 4, corporate intranets are helping businesspeople get around the computer compatibility problem, but companies that lack intranets may find themselves with incompatible computer systems that inhibit the use of electronic documents.
- *Training.* Beyond the ability to read, there is little training involved in reading most paper business reports. However, reading electronic reports can require training in using Web browsers, accessing databases, or other skills.
- *Data security and integrity.* Because information in electronic reports is not fixed on paper, it's vulnerable to tampering and inadvertent corruption. The growth of electronic commerce on the Internet will be determined to a large degree by how much confidence the public has in the security and privacy of credit-card transactions and other purchase details. And even innocent computer errors can affect electronic reports. Sending word-processor files over the Internet is still a shaky proposition: Because the files are handled by various systems that don't always work in harmony, your carefully crafted document can end up as electronic rubbish.[4]

Many businesses see electronic documents as a way to cut costs while improving worker productivity and customer service, so you'll probably write and read many electronic reports on the job.

From elephants to naked mole rats, and from rescue missions abroad to new exhibits at home, San Diego Zoo's Rick Barongi writes more than a few short reports as children's zoo director.

If people are interested, they'll call him for more background information.

But some of Barongi's reports require more thoroughness. His dream is to revamp and expand the children's section of San Diego's huge zoo, making it an interactive, state-of-the-art conservation learning experience that will be set in a simulated rain forest. Barongi is currently preparing a justification report to persuade the zoo's board of directors to raise funds for the project. He wants this preliminary report to be "short, colorful, and eye-catching," but he also wants to include enough supporting data to make the project seem feasible, exciting, and essential to the zoo's future.

The short report will draw on months of brainstorming by a zoo task force, set up by Barongi to plan a "children's zoo for the twenty-first century." It will be about ten pages, with watercolor illustrations to convey a feeling of the lush, tropical setting that Barongi and his colleagues envision. To save everyone's time, he will use the direct approach, opening with a plan for the zoo that will transform it into an interactive learning center "not just for children, but for all age groups."

Apply Your Knowledge

1. If you were proposing a major renovation of a museum or a zoo exhibit area, would you use a direct approach or an indirect approach? Why?

2. How would Barongi's proposal for the new children's zoo differ if the idea had actually originated with the board of directors?

*P*LANNING SHORT REPORTS

When planning your report, be sure to follow the customs your audience expects. The guidelines discussed here are for addressing U.S. and Canadian audiences having minimal cultural differences. In addition to your audience, also consider your purpose and subject matter. Both elements influence the format and length of your report, as well as its basic structure.

Deciding on Format and Length

Decisions about format and length may be made for you by the person who requests the document. Such guidance is often the case with monitor/control reports, justification reports, proposals, progress reports, and compliance reports. Generally speaking, the more routine the report, the less flexibility you have in deciding format and length.

When you do have some leeway in length and format, your decisions are based on your readers' needs. As Frederick Smith can attest, your goal is to tell your audience what they need to know in a format that is easy for them to use. Whether you deliver your report on paper or electronically, when you select a format, you have four options:

Before writing complicated decisions, Supreme Court Justice Sandra Day O'Connor devotes considerable time to organizing her thoughts and developing a logical order for her arguments and opinions. She maintains that time spent in planning is never wasted.

You may present a report in one of four formats: preprinted form, letter, memo, or manuscript.

- *Preprinted form.* Basically for "fill in the blank" reports. Most are relatively short (five or fewer pages) and deal with routine information, often mainly numerical. Use this format when it's requested by the person authorizing the report.
- *Letter.* Common for reports of five or fewer pages that are directed to outsiders. These reports include all the normal parts of a letter, but they may also have headings, footnotes, tables, and figures.
- *Memo.* Common for short (fewer than ten pages) informal reports distributed within an organization. Memos have headings at the top: *To, From, Date,* and *Subject.* In addition, like longer reports, they often have internal headings and sometimes have visual

aids. Memos exceeding ten pages are sometimes referred to as memo reports to distinguish them from their shorter cousins. They also begin with the standard memo headings. The Checklist for Short Informal Reports at the end of this chapter provides guidelines for preparing memo reports and other short informal reports.

■ *Manuscript.* Common for reports from a few pages to several hundred pages that require a formal approach. As their length increases, reports in manuscript format require more elements before the text of the report (prefatory parts) and after the text (supplementary parts). Chapter 14 explains these elements and includes additional instructions as well as a checklist for preparing formal reports.

Appendix A, "Format and Layout of Business Documents," contains more specific guidelines for physically preparing these four kinds of reports.

> **Length depends on**
> ■ Your subject
> ■ Your purpose
> ■ Your relationship with your audience

The length of your report obviously depends on your subject and purpose, but it's also affected by your relationship with your audience. If they are relative strangers, if they are skeptical or hostile, if the material is nonroutine or controversial, you usually have to explain your points in greater detail. You can afford to be brief if you are on familiar terms with your readers, if they are likely to agree with you, and if the information is routine or uncomplicated. In general, short reports are more common in business than long ones, and you'll probably write many more 5-page memos than 250-page formal reports.

Selecting the Information to Include

Should you cover all the material obtained during your research, or should you eliminate some of the data? When deciding on the content of your report, first put yourself in the audience's position. What major questions do you think your audience has about the subject? By developing a **question-and-answer chain,** you can think ahead to the questions your readers may have and anticipate their sequence. Your objective is to answer all those questions in the order that makes the most sense.

> **Reports answer the audience's key questions.**

Your audience usually has one main question of greatest importance: "Why are we losing money?" or "What's the progress on this project?" No matter what the main question is, be sure to define it as precisely as you can before you begin formulating your answer. The main question is simply the reason you've been asked to write the report, and, once you've defined it, you can sketch a general answer, based on the information available. Your answer, like the question, should be broad.

Now you're ready to determine, on the basis of your answer to the main question, what additional questions your audience is likely to ask. A typical question-and-answer chain might look like the following:

Main question: Why are we losing money?

General answer: We're losing money because our production costs are higher than our prices.

Question 1:   Why are our production costs high?

Question 2:   Why are our prices low?

Your next step is to answer these questions, and your answers again raise additional questions. As you forge the chain of questions and answers, the points multiply and become increasingly specific (Figure 12.1). When you've identified and answered all of your audience's probable questions, you will have defined the content of your report or presentation. The process is similar to outlining.

> **Pursue the chain of questions and answers from the general to the specific.**

The question-and-answer chain clarifies the main idea of the report (your answer to the main question) and establishes the flow of ideas from the general to the specific. Effective reports and presentations use a mix of broad concepts and specific details. When the mix is right, the message works: Members of the audience grasp both the general meaning of the ideas and the practical implications of those ideas. The general ideas sum up and give direction to the message, and the specific ideas clarify and illustrate their meaning. For

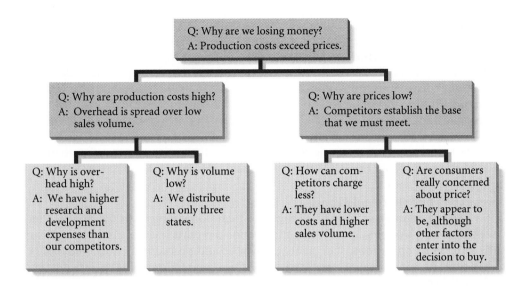

Figure 12.1
A Typical Question-and-Answer Chain

every piece of information you are tempted to include, ask why the audience needs it and how it relates to the main question.

Choosing Direct or Indirect Order

As Chapter 6 explained, audience attitude is the basis for decisions about organization. When the audience is considered either receptive or open minded, use the direct approach: Lead off with a summary of your key findings, conclusions, and recommendations. This "up-front" approach is by far the most popular and convenient order for business reports because it saves time and makes the rest of the report easy to follow. For those who have questions or want more information, later parts of the report provide complete findings and supporting details. In addition to being more convenient for readers, the direct approach also produces a more forceful report. You sound sure of yourself when you state your conclusions confidently at the outset.

> The direct approach saves time and makes the report easy to understand by giving readers the main idea first.

However, confidence may sometimes be misconstrued as arrogance. If you're a junior member of a status-conscious organization or if your audience is skeptical or hostile, you may want to use indirect order—introducing the complete findings and supporting details before the conclusions and recommendations, which come last. The indirect approach gives you a chance to prove your points and gradually overcome your audience's reservations. By deferring the conclusions and recommendations, you imply that you've weighed the evidence objectively without prejudging the facts. You also imply that you're subordinating your judgment to that of the audience, whose members are capable of drawing their own conclusions when they have access to all the facts.

> The indirect approach helps overcome resistance by withholding the main idea until later in the report.

Although the indirect approach has its advantages, some report readers will always be in a hurry to get to "the answer," flipping to the recommendations immediately and defeating your purpose. For this reason, consider length when deciding on direct or indirect order. In general, the longer the message, the less effective an indirect approach is likely to be. Furthermore, an indirect argument is harder to follow than a direct argument. Because both the direct and indirect approaches have merit, businesspeople often combine them. They reveal their conclusions and recommendations as they go along, rather than putting them either first or last.

Structuring Ideas

What method of subdivision will make your material both clear and convincing? Should you use a **topical organization,** based on order of importance, sequence, chronology, location, spatial relationships, or categories? Should you use **logical organization** to arrange your ideas around logical arguments that reflect the reasoning behind the report's conclusions and

> *Topical organization* is based on order of importance, sequence, chronology, location, spatial relationships, or categories. *Logical organization* is based on logical arguments that reflect the reasoning process behind the conclusions and recommendations.

recommendations? Regardless of whether you use the direct or the indirect approach, you must still deal with the question of how your ideas will be subdivided and developed. The key is first to decide whether the purpose of the report is to provide information or analysis. From there, you can choose an organizational plan that suits your topic and goals.

Informational reports differ from analytical reports in their purpose and thus in their organization. Informational reports are intended mainly to educate readers, but analytical reports are designed to persuade readers to accept certain conclusions or recommendations. In informational reports the information alone is the focus of attention. In analytical reports the information plays a supporting role. The facts are a means to an end rather than an end in themselves. Typically, the end is either a decision or an action.

Organizing Informational Reports

Informational reports are usually written to explain something in straightforward terms. Having hundreds of uses in business, informational reports include those for monitoring and controlling operations, statements of policies and procedures, most compliance reports, most personal activity reports, some justification reports, some reports documenting client work, and some proposals.

When writing informational reports, you don't usually have to be too concerned about reader reaction. Because readers will presumably respond unemotionally to your material, you can present it in the most direct fashion possible. What you do need to be concerned about with informational reports is reader comprehension. As Frederick Smith knows, the information in any report must be presented logically and accurately so that readers will understand exactly what you mean and will be able to use the information in a practical way.

When structuring an informational report, you can let the nature of whatever you're describing serve as the point of departure. If you're describing a machine, each component can correspond to a part of your report. If you're describing an event, you can approach the discussion chronologically, and if you're explaining how to do something, you can describe the steps in the process.

Some informational reports, especially compliance reports and internal reports prepared on preprinted forms, are organized according to instructions supplied by the person requesting the information. In addition, many proposals conform to an outline specified in the request for a proposal issued by the client, which might include a statement of the problem, background, scope of work, restrictions, sources and methods, work schedule, qualifications of personnel, facilities, anticipated costs, and expected results.

Informational reports take many forms. The two examples that follow, a brief periodic report and a personal activity report on a seminar, will give you an idea of the typical organization and tone.

A Periodic Report   A periodic report is a monitor/control report that describes what has happened in a department or division during a particular period. Corporate annual reports are periodic reports that are more formal and polished. The purpose of these recurring documents is to provide a picture of how things are going so that corporate managers will be up to date and can take corrective action if necessary. Periodic reports are usually written in memo format and don't need much of an introduction; a subject line on the memo is adequate. They should follow the same general format and organization from period to period. Most are organized in this sequence:

- *Overview of routine responsibilities.* Briefly describe activities related to each of the writer's normal responsibilities. In some cases the overview focuses on statistical or financial results; in other cases it's written in paragraph form.
- *Discussion of special projects.* Briefly describe any new or special projects that have been undertaken during the reporting period.
- *Plans for the coming period.* Give a schedule of activities planned for the next reporting period.
- *Analysis of problems.* Discuss the possible causes of and solutions for any problems. Although often included in the overview of routine responsibilities or in the discussion of

Informational and analytical reports differ in their purpose, organization, and focus.

The purpose of informational reports is to explain, whereas analytical reports are meant to convince the audience that the conclusions and recommendations developed in the text are valid.

Make clarity your main objective in informational reports.

Periodic reports are recurring monitor/control reports that keep managers informed about departments reporting to them.

Periodic reports expose any problems that exist.

Most periodic reports are organized similarly:
- *Overview*
- *Project discussion*
- *Coming plans*
- *Problem analysis*

special projects, this analysis is sometimes set off in a separate section to call attention to areas that may require high-level intervention.

The important thing to remember when writing periodic reports is to be honest about problems as well as accomplishments. In fact, Frederick Smith will tell you that, at Federal Express, the bad news is probably more important than the good news because problems require action, whereas good news often does not.

The periodic report in Figure 12.2 was prepared by Roger Watson, real estate director for a San Francisco coffee retailer. According to Watson, "Real estate scouting is a crucial activity for our company as we expand eastward from our California base. My manager needs to know that my department is making good decisions when we select new store locations."

A Personal Activity Report   A personal activity report is a form of monitor/control report that calls for a person's description of what occurred during a conference, convention, trip, or other activity. It's intended to inform management of any important information or decisions that emerged during the activity.

Personal activity reports are ordinarily written in memo format. Because they're nonrecurring documents, they require more of an introduction than periodic reports. They're often organized chronologically, but some are organized around topics that reflect the audience's interests. Figure 12.3 on page 275 is an example of a personal activity report organized by topic. This seminar attendance report was prepared by Carrie Andrews, the human resources manager of a small insurance firm based in Indianapolis.

> Personal activity reports describe the facts and decisions that emerge during conventions, trips, and business meetings.

Organizing Analytical Reports

Analytical reports are usually written to respond to special circumstances. Most of the decision-oriented reports mentioned in this chapter are analytical, such as justification reports, research reports, and troubleshooting reports. So are many proposals and final reports to clients.

Regardless of which type of analytical report you're writing, organize your ideas so that they will convince readers of the soundness of your thinking. Your choice of a specific approach is based on your estimate of the readers' probable reactions: direct if you think they are likely to agree with you, indirect if you think they will resist your message. If you use the direct approach, you can base the structure of the report on your conclusions and recommendations, using them as the main points of your outline. If you use an indirect approach, your organization can reflect the thinking process that will lead readers to your conclusions.

> Analytical reports may be organized around conclusions and recommendations (direct approach) when the audience is receptive.

> Analytical reports may be organized around logical arguments (indirect approach) when the audience is unreceptive.

A Justification Report   Justification reports are internal proposals used to persuade top management to approve an investment in a project. When your readers want to know what they ought to do as opposed to what they ought to conclude, the things you want your readers to do become the main subdivisions of your report. When organizing a report around recommendations, you usually take five steps:

1. Establish the need for action in the introduction, generally by briefly describing the problem or opportunity.
2. Introduce the benefit that can be achieved, without providing any details.
3. List the steps (recommendations) required to achieve the benefit, using action verbs for emphasis.
4. Explain each step more fully, giving details on procedures, costs, and benefits.
5. Summarize the recommendations.

The company's board of directors asked Alycia Jenn, the business development manager at a Chicago-based retail chain, to suggest whether the company should set up a retailing site on the World Wide Web, and, if so, how to implement the site. As Jenn noted, "Setting up shop on the Internet is a big decision for our company. We don't have the big computer staffs that our larger competitors have, and our business development

In order to make profitable the hundreds of Burger King restaurants he's opened in African American neighborhoods, La Van Hawkins of UrbanCityFoods relies on the kind of information a short report can convey: profit figures, market statistics, sales strategy recommendations, promotional plans, and so on. It's a quick way to gain a clear perspective—and make the right decisions.

Figure 12.2
**In-Depth Critique: Sample
Periodic Report**

Roger Watson doesn't want to burden his boss with a lot of details about every one of the company's more than 500 sites. His monthly reports are concise and presented in a summary format. "If Joan has questions about a specific location and needs more information," says Watson, "we usually just talk by phone after she's read my report."

MEMO

TO:	Joan Chen, V.P. New Business Development	DATE:	August 1, 1999
FROM:	Roger Watson, Real Estate Director	SUBJECT:	July location scouting

The brief introduction orients the reader but doesn't waste time with unnecessary explanations.

During the last two weeks of July, I scouted four Denver locations for our coffee outlets. George Spindle recommended these sites in his business development report (which is on the intranet under "Regional reports" if you'd like to review it). All four sites are in existing office buildings.

HOW THE DENVER SITES COMPARE

Headings stand out to make report review easier for the reader.

Here's a quick look at the basic aspects of each site. Lease rates are comparable at all four locations, ranging from $34 to $38 a square foot.

The table organizes summary information in the most time-saving format.

Site	Space	Availability	Competition	Visibility
Lakewood	260 square feet	Now	Starbucks has begun construction 4 blocks north; no other stores within a 16-block radius	None; on the second of two retail floors in this building
Glendale	525 square feet; with additional 150 square feet in one year	January	2 Starbucks (2 blocks south and 8 blocks west); Chicago Blues (across street, but poor visibility)	Superb corner location; windows on both streets
McNichols Arena	420 square feet	December	JavaLand 3 blocks east; Starbucks 4 blocks south	Good visibility but little evening/weekend traffic
University of Denver	Two options: 340 square feet, 655 square feet	Now for the smaller site; March for the larger	Five independents in the immediate area; Starbucks on campus (2 blocks west)	Good visibility, and street is a major retail location

SCOUTING PLANS FOR SEPTEMBER

Our schedule has been pretty tight for the last six months. Following are the plans for our efforts in September:

Details of upcoming efforts help the reader maintain a timely overview of the progress.

Denver: I'll contract Shure Research to conduct foot traffic counts at all four sites (we should have those numbers in 10 days). I've asked George's team to do a permits search to study future building plans in each location. I'll be talking with Melissa Hines next week about construction restrictions. (She's the Smith, Allen broker who helped us with the Grand Junction sites last year.)

Minneapolis: Jean-Luc Goddard wants us to review several sites he's had his eye on. I'll send Margie or visit them myself if my schedule permits.

---

team is stretched rather thin already. On the other hand, I know that more and more people are shopping online, and we don't want to be left out if this mode of retailing really takes off. After studying the issue for several weeks, I concluded that we should go ahead with a site, but we have to be careful about how we implement it." Her memo appears in Figure 12.4 on pages 276–77.

A Business Plan Proposal

Focusing on conclusions or recommendations is the most forceful and efficient way to organize an analytical report, but it isn't the best solution for every situation. Sometimes you

Carrie Andrews attended a seminar on legal issues in employee recruiting and interviewing. Says Andrews, "I prepared this report for my boss, the company president, and the four people who work for me. We can't afford to send everyone in the department to seminars such as this, so it's important that I share the information I received with the people who couldn't attend."

Figure 12.3
In-Depth Critique: Sample Personal Activity Report

MEMO

TO: Jeff Balou;   DATE: March 14, 1999
        all members of HR staff
FROM: Carrie Andrews   SUBJECT: Recruiting and
                                                hiring seminar

As you all know, the process of recruiting, screening, and hiring new employees can be a legal minefield. Because we don't have an in-house lawyer to help us make every decision, it's important for all of us to be aware of what is legally acceptable and what isn't.

Last week I attended an American Management Association seminar on this subject. I got enough useful information to warrant updating our online personnel handbook and perhaps developing a quick training session for all interviewing teams. First, here's a quick look at the things I learned.

AVOIDING LEGAL MISTAKES
- How to write recruiting ads that accurately portray job openings and that don't discriminate
- How best to comply with the Americans with Disabilities Act
- How to use an employment agency effectively and safely (without risk of legal entanglements)

SCREENING AND INTERVIEWING MORE EFFECTIVELY
- How to sort through résumés more efficiently (including looking for telltale signs of false information)
- How to avoid interview questions that could get us into legal trouble
- When and how to check criminal records

MEASURING APPLICANTS
- Which types of preemployment tests have proven most effective
- Which drug-testing issues and recommendations affect us

As you can see, the seminar addressed a lot of important information. We cover the basic guidelines for much of this already, but a number of specific recommendations and legal concepts should be emphasized.

One eye-opening part of the seminar was learning about the mistakes other companies have made. Some companies have lost millions of dollars in employment-discrimination lawsuits. The risks are huge, so we have to protect ourselves and avoid discriminating against any applicants.

It will take me a couple of weeks to get the personnel handbook updated, but we don't have any immediate hiring plans anyway. I'll keep the seminar handouts and my notes on my desk, in case you want to peruse them. After I've updated the handbook, we can get together and decide whether we need to train the interviewing team members. Although we have a lot of new information, I think we can highlight what people need to be aware of and let them read the new sections as their schedules allow.

If you have any questions in the meantime, don't hesitate to e-mail me or drop by for a chat.

The introduction states Andrews's reason for attending the seminar.

The organization of this report around the three areas of knowledge gained by Andrews helps readers focus on what is important.

Bullets make the new knowledge stand out for easy reader reference.

Although reporting on personal activity, this report wastes no time on unimportant activities such as how many sessions were offered during the seminar or what was served for lunch. Rather, the report is full of the information needed by department members and the plans for how to disseminate it.

---

can achieve better results by encouraging readers to weigh all the facts before you present your conclusions or recommendations.

A **business plan** documents an organization's overall goals and the operational methods it will use to reach those goals.[5] Small businesses, divisions of larger businesses, and nonprofit organizations write business plans for internal use to guide operations and to provide benchmarks for measuring progress toward goals.[6] In addition, top managers and entrepreneurs frequently send their business plans to external audiences (such as bankers or consultants) when they need financing or are contracting for managerial support services.

A business plan explains overall goals and the ways they will be accomplished.

Business plans can be used as proposals to raise support and funding for an idea, a project, or a business.

Figure 12.4
In-Depth Critique: Sample Justification Report Focusing on Recommendations

In her justification report, Alycia Jenn uses her recommendations to organize her thoughts. Because the board of directors wouldn't be interested in a lot of technical detail, she keeps her discussion at a fairly high level. She also maintains a formal and respectful tone for this audience.

Jenn clarifies the purpose and origin of the report in the introduction.

For clarity, her recommendations are simple and to the point.

Her reasons for recommending that the firm establish a Web site are logically and clearly presented.

Her recommendations include not only establishing a Web site but also hiring a consultant to implement it and making sure to integrate it with existing systems.

MEMO

TO: Board of Directors, Executive Committee members
FROM: Alycia Jenn, Business Development Manager
DATE: July 6, 1999
SUBJECT: World Wide Web retailing site

In response to your request, my staff and I investigated the potential for establishing a retailing site on the World Wide Web. After analyzing the behavior of our customers and major competitors and studying the overall development of electronic retailing, we have three recommendations:

1. Yes, we should establish an online presence within the next six months.
2. We should engage a firm that specializes in online retailing to design and develop the Web site.
3. We must take care to integrate online retailing with our store-based and mail-order operations.

WE SHOULD SET UP A WEB SITE

First, does a Web site make financial sense today? Studies suggest that our competitors are not currently generating significant revenue from their Web sites. Stallini's is the leader so far, but its sales haven't broken the $1 million mark. Moreover, at least half of our competitors' online sales are from current customers who would have purchased the same items in-store or by mail order. The cost of setting up a retailing site is around $120,000, so it isn't possible to justify a site based solely on current financial return.

Second, do we need to establish a presence now in order to remain competitive in the future? The online situation is too fluid and unpredictable to answer this question in a quantitative profit-and-loss way, but a qualitative view of strategy indicates that we should set up a site:

- As younger consumers (more comfortable with online shopping) reach their peak earning years (ages 35–54), they'll be more likely to buy online than today's peak spenders.
- The Web is erasing geographical shopping limits, presenting both a threat and an opportunity. Even though our customers can now shop Web sites anywhere in the world (so that we have thousands of competitors instead of a dozen), we can now target customers anywhere in the world.
- If the growth in online retailing continues, this will eventually be a viable market. Establishing a site now and working out any problems will prepare us for high-volume online business in the years ahead.

WE SHOULD ENGAGE A CONSULTANT TO IMPLEMENT THE SITE

Implementing a competitive retailing site can take anywhere from 1,000 to 2,500 hours of design and programming time. We have some of the expertise needed in-house, but the marketing and information systems departments have only 300 person-hours in the next six months. I recommend that we engage a Web-design consultant to help us with the design and to do all of the programming.

Bruce Rogow was a junior engineering major at San Diego State University (SDSU) when he was first struck by the idea of leading a team of students to design, build, and race a solar car at the World Solar Challenge race across the Australian outback. The race itself would be the least of Rogow's challenges: First he had to convince students and faculty of the project's benefits; then he had to keep them motivated (and working long, hard hours) while he tackled administrative and engineering roadblocks that even he couldn't predict.

Ultimately, the SDSU Solar Car Project succeeded, and it drew involvement from various academic departments, dozens of student volunteers, several corporate benefactors, and many news organizations. Rogow challenged the science, engineering, and computer

2

WE MUST INTEGRATE THE WEB INTO EXISTING OPERATIONS

The studies we reviewed showed that the most successful Web retailers are careful to integrate their online retailing with their store- and mail-based retailing. Companies that don't integrate carefully find themselves with higher costs, confused customers, and Web sites that don't generate much business. Before we begin designing our Web site, we should develop a plan for integrating the Web into our existing marketing, accounting, and production systems. The online site could affect every department in the company, so it's vital that everyone has a chance to review the plans before we proceed.

SUMMARY

1. Yes, establish a Web site now even though it doesn't make immediate financial sense, because we might lose business if we don't have a site in the near future.
2. Use the services of a Web designer, because we don't have enough person hours available in-house.
3. Integrate the Web site with existing operations, particularly in marketing, accounting, and production.

Figure 12.4
(continued)

Her close briefly summarizes her recommendations and the reasons behind them.

students on his team to design and test *Suntrakker* (as the car was named). But he also challenged SDSU's business students to come up with a proposal that would help him raise the support *Suntrakker* needed.

"We needed to raise $145,000," Rogow recalls. "And since we had no faculty support in the beginning, we had to have something that would give us credibility. The business plan gave us much more than that."

Three students from an entrepreneurship class agreed to work with Rogow on a plan that eventually filled more than 70 pages. "The business plan mapped out every detail of our project, from start to finish, and made us look at things we had not considered. It also earned us respect from the faculty and was responsible for a $5,000 donation from our local power company." Rogow now believes that the business plan made the difference between "thriving and just surviving" (Figure 12.5).

A Troubleshooting Report   Whenever a problem exists, someone must investigate it and propose a solution. A troubleshooting report is a decision-oriented document prepared for submission to top management. When you want your readers to concentrate on *why* your ideas make sense, your best bet is to let your logical arguments provide the structure for your report. The main points in your outline correspond to the reasons that underlie your conclusions and recommendations. You support each reason with the evidence you collected during your analysis.

Binh Phan, the national sales manager of a New Hampshire sporting goods company, was concerned about his company's ability to sell to its largest customers. His boss, the vice president of marketing, shared these concerns and asked Phan to analyze the situation and recommend a solution. As Phan says, "We sell sporting goods to retail chains across the country. Large nationwide chains with superstores modeled after Toys 'R' Us have been revolutionizing the industry, but we haven't had as much success with these big customers as we've had with smaller companies that operate on only a local or a regional basis. With more and more of the industry in the hands of the large chains, we knew we had to fix the situation." The main idea of Phan's report is that the company should establish separate sales teams for its major accounts rather than continuing to service them through the company's four regional divisions. However, Phan knew that his plan would be controversial because it required a big change in the company's organization.

Liz Claiborne attributes the success of her clothing designs to the reports prepared by her marketing department: reports that analyze sales figures, define women's roles and issues, identify trends, and communicate recommendations that can be translated into fashions. When writing such analytical reports, it is important to use the facts in a convincing way.

Figure 12.5
In-Depth Critique: Bruce
Rogow's Proposal (Business
Plan Excerpt)

Bruce Rogow's business plan is a type of unsolicited proposal, with the benefits up front and the financial information at the close. Detailed and thorough, it includes sections describing the vehicle, the management team, and even "Critical Risks." Appendixes include an organization chart, résumé, design schematics, letters of support, lists of volunteers and contributors, and a telemarketing script. Here is an excerpt from the executive summary (a miniversion of the report that gives busy executives a detailed overview).

Remember to answer questions about who (voluntary), what (business plan), when (special, nonrecurring), where (external), why (analytical), and how (receptive readers).

For a business plan intended to raise funds, use the indirect approach to introduce your objectives, justification, and benefits. Include ample details supported by facts, figures, personnel qualifications, endorsements, and so forth.

Convey a confident tone by writing thoughtful, well-developed paragraphs. Provide good introductions and transitions, headings, and lists.

Business plans may be prepared for external and internal readers. Not usually compared with competing plans (as are solicited proposals or bids), business plans must still motivate readers to invest or contribute. Many businesses periodically update their plans as their objectives change and as they seek funding from new sources.

THE EXECUTIVE SUMMARY

Purpose of the Plan

This document will acquaint the reader with three principal topics by

- Showing what the San Diego State University (SDSU) SUNTRAKKER project is
- Showing that the team-oriented, interdepartmental disciplines at SDSU possess the tenacity and know-how to build and race a solar-powered vehicle in the World Solar Challenge Race in Australia in 1993
- Defining and articulating how this business team expects to promote and generate the necessary support, funds, and materials from the student body, alumni, community, and local businesses to seize and execute this opportunity

Project Profile

The SUNTRAKKER Solar Car Project was conceived in July 1990 when a small group of San Diego State University engineering students, motivated by the successes of the General Motors Sunrayce, committed themselves to designing and building a superior solar-powered vehicle to compete in the World Solar Challenge.

From modest beginnings, the SUNTRAKKER project quickly evolved into a cross-disciplinary educational effort encompassing students from many colleges of San Diego State University. The Project has provided student participants and volunteers with valuable real-life experiences, and brought them together in an effort that benefits not only the students and the university but also the environment.

Sponsors of this project are not only contributing to the success of the overall SUNTRAKKER project but will enhance their goodwill, advertising, and name promotion by association with the project. In addition, the SUNTRAKKER offers a unique opportunity for companies that can donate parts and accessories to showcase their name and field test their products in this highly publicized international contest.

The Nature and Value of the Project

The explicit purpose of the project is to design, build, test, and race a world-class solar-powered car with the express purpose of spurring the technological development of energy-efficient vehicles. Although winning the World Solar Challenge is the explicit focus of the project, the implicit goal is to promote ongoing technological research in the field of alternative energy sources, with a view toward conserving the earth's precious nonrenewable natural resources and encouraging international cooperation.

Competitions such as the World Solar Challenge are catalysts for innovation; they provide focus and expand our perspectives beyond the present technology horizon in many different disciplines. The competition stimulates development of seemingly impractical vehicles, yet actually promotes interest and involvement in real-life educational and practical experiences culminating in tangible benefits to the global community. Futuristic and evolutionary projects such as the SUNTRAKKER provide a stimulus to researchers and forward-thinkers to strive toward the common goal of making alternative energy sources a viable reality.

When Phan wrote the actual report, he used descriptive rather than informative headings to give his report an objective feel:

   I. Introduction
  II. Organizational Issues
 III. Commission Issues
 IV. Recommendation
  V. Summary

Figure 12.5
(continued)

2

Form of Organization

The SDSU SUNTRAKKER project has been founded as a tax-exempt, nonprofit student organization. The orgaization's primary purposes are to build the SUNTRAKKER and to represent SDSU in the World Solar Challenge Race in 1993.

The SUNTRAKKER project is organized by function, with directors of marketing, design, production, logistics, public relations, and finance. Together, the departments constitute the management review committee in charge of all activities. Each department director reports to the project manager, Bruce Rogow. In turn, Mr. Rogow, who is responsible for coordinating the whole team effort, reports to a board of advisers. The advisory board, headed by Dr. William Guentzler, oversees the project and acts as a resource think thank to assist in critical problem solving. (See Appendix AS for an organizational chart fo the SUNTRAKKER project.)

Growth Trend of Market

Technology developed from the SUNTRAKKER project has direct applicability to the coming hybrid electric and solar-powered vehicle markets throughout the world, especially here in southern California. Because of massive pollution problems and rising population growth rates, trasportation needs mandate that we find alternatives to the fossil-fueled vehicles now in popular use.

In many areas of California, pollution has become the driving factor in the search for alternative vehicle power sources. The South Coast Air Quality Management District, encompassing the greater southern California area, has enacted a plan to replace 40 percent of gasoline-powered vehicles now operating in metropolitan areas with nonemissions vehicles. The plan directs that government and commercial fleets greater than 15 vehicles be required to buy alternative-powered vehicles if they want to increase their fleet size.

Subheads make it easy for readers to locate particular points.

Sections in the executive summary correspond to major sections in the report and summarize the information provided later.

By phrasing his headings in an objective manner, he reassured his readers and prevented them from reacting negatively to ideas that had not yet been fully explained. Figure 12.6 is a copy of Phan's report.

Organizing an analytical report around a list of reasons that collectively support your main conclusions or recommendations is a natural approach to take. Many problems are solved this way, and readers tend to accept the gradual accumulation of evidence, even though they may question one or two points. However, not every problem or reporting situation can be handled with this organizational plan. Some analytical reports are organized to highlight the pros and cons of a decision; others might be structured to compare two or more alternatives against a set of criteria. The best organizational approach in any given situation depends on the nature of the facts at your disposal. Essentially, you choose a structure that matches the reasoning process you used to solve the problem. The objective is to focus your reader's attention on the rationale for your conclusions and recommendations.

MAKING REPORTS AND PROPOSALS READABLE

Choosing format, length, and a basic organizational plan for your report is an important set of decisions. When you're ready to write your report, you must find the most effective way to communicate your message to your audience. Three decisions affect the way your report will be received and understood by readers: the degree of formality, a consistent time perspective, and appropriate structural clues.

Choosing the Proper Degree of Formality

The issue of formality is closely related to considerations of format, length, and organization. If you know your readers reasonably well and if your report is likely to meet with their approval, you can generally adopt a less formal tone. In other words, you can speak to readers

Figure 12.6
In-Depth Critique: Sample
Troubleshooting Report

Binh Phan's troubleshooting report would definitely stir emotions, so he had to make sure the logic was solid. Moreover, he was careful that his introduction didn't reveal his position.

Instead of summarizing his recommendations, Phan begins by discussing the report's purpose and scope, the background of the study, and his methods of research.

MEMO

TO: Robert Mendoza, Vice President of Marketing
FROM: Binh Phan, National Sales Manager
DATE: September 12, 1998
SUBJECT: Major accounts sales problems

INTRODUCTION

This report outlines the results of my investigation into the recent slowdown in sales to major accounts and the accompanying rise in sales- and service-related complaints from some of our largest customers.

As we discussed at last quarter's management retreat, major account sales dropped 12 percent over the last four quarters, whereas overall sales were up 7 percent. During the same time, we've all noticed an increase in both formal and informal complaints from larger customers regarding how confusing and complicated it has become to do business with us.

My investigation started with in-depth discussions with the four regional sales managers, first as a group and then individually. The tension I felt in the initial meeting eventually bubbled to the surface during my meetings with each manager. Staff members in each region are convinced that other regions are booking orders they don't deserve, with one region doing all the legwork only to see another region get credited with the sale and, naturally, the commission and quota credit.

I followed up the sales manager discussions with informal talks and e-mail exchanges with several sales reps from each region. Virtually everyone who is involved with our major national accounts has a story to share. No one is happy with the situation, and I sense that some reps are walking away from major customers because the process is so frustrating.

ORGANIZATIONAL ISSUES

In the body, Phan presents the facts and his observations in an objective tone, without revealing his own point of view.

When we divided the national sales force into four geographical regions last year, the idea was to focus our sales efforts and clarify responsibilities for each prospective and current customer. The regional managers have gotten to know their market territories very well, and sales have increased beyond even our most optimistic projections.

Unfortunately, while solving one problem, we seem to have created another. In the past 12 to 18 months, several regional customers have grown to national status. In addition, a few national retailers have taken on (or expressed interest in) our products. As a result, a significant portion of both our current sales and our future opportunities lie with these large national accounts.

I uncovered more than a dozen cases in which sales reps from two or more regions found themselves competing with each other by pursuing the same customer from different locations.

Moreover, the complaints from our major accounts about overlapping or nonexistent account coverage are a direct result of the regional organization. In some

---

Write informal reports in a personal style, using the pronouns I and you.

Being formal means putting your readers at a distance and establishing an objective, businesslike relationship.

Intercultural communication often calls for more formal language.

in the first person, referring to yourself as *I* and to your readers as *you.* This personal approach is often used in brief memo or letter reports, although there are many exceptions.

Longer reports, especially those dealing with controversial or complex information, are traditionally handled in a more formal vein. You'll also tend to use a more formal approach when writing a report to be sent beyond your own work area to other parts of the organization, customers, and suppliers. Communicating with people in other cultures often calls for more formality, for two reasons. First, the business environment outside the United States tends to be more formal in general, and that formality must be reflected in your communication style. Second, the things you do to make a document informal, such as using humor and idiomatic language, are the hardest things to transfer from culture to culture. Less formality in these cases increases the risk of offending people and of miscommunicating.

Figure 12.6
(continued)

2

cases, customers aren't sure which of our reps they're supposed to call with problems and orders. In others, no one has been in contact with them for several months.

An example should help illustrate the problem. AmeriSport, with retail outlets across the lower tier of the country, was being pitched by reps from our West, South, and East regions. Because we give our regional offices a lot of negotiating freedom, the three reps were offering the client different prices. But all of AmeriSport's buying decisions are made at their headquarters in Tampa, so all we did was confuse the customer.

The irony of this situation is that we're often giving our weakest selling and support efforts to the largest customers in the country.

COMMISSION ISSUES

The regional organization issues are compounded because of the way we assign commissions and quota credit. Salespeople in one region can invest a lot of time in pursuing a sale, only to have the customer place the order in another region. So some sales rep in the second region ends up with the commission on a sale that was partly or even entirely earned by someone in the first region.

Also, sales reps sometimes don't pursue leads in their regions if they think that a rep in another region will get the commission. For example, Athletic Express, with outlets in 35 states spread across all four regions, finally got so frustrated with us that the company president called our headquarters. Athletic Express has been trying to place a large order for tennis and golf accessories, but none of our local reps seem interested in paying attention. I spoke with the rep responsible for Nashville, where the company is headquartered, and asked her why she wasn't working the account more actively. Her explanation was that last time she got involved with Athletic Express, the order was actually placed from their L.A. regional office, and she didn't get any commission after more than two weeks of selling time.

RECOMMENDATION

Our sales organization should reflect the nature of our customer base. To accomplish that goal, we need a group of reps who are free to pursue accounts across regional borders—and who are compensated fairly for their work. The most sensible answer is to establish a national accounts group. Any customers whose operations place them in more than one region would automatically be assigned to the national group.

Further, we need to modify our commission policy to reward people for team selling. I'll talk with the sales managers to work out the details, but in general, we'll need to split commissions whenever two or more reps help close a sale. This policy will also involve a "finder's fee" for a rep who pulls in leads at the regional level that are passed on to the national account team.

He saves his recommendations for the fourth section, where he adds up the reasons.

You achieve a formal tone by using the impersonal style, eliminating all references to *I* (including *we, us,* and *our*) and *you*. The style is borrowed from journalism, which stresses the reporter's objectivity. However, be careful that avoiding personal pronouns doesn't lead to overuse of such phrases as *there is* and *it is,* which are both dull and wordy. Also, avoiding personal pronouns makes it easy to slip into passive voice, which can also be dull and wordy.

When you write in a formal style, you impose a certain distance between you and your readers. You remain businesslike, unemotional, and objective. You use no jokes, no similes or metaphors, and very few colorful adjectives or adverbs. You eliminate your own subjective opinions and perceptions and retain only the objective facts.

The formal style does not guarantee objectivity of content, however. The fairness of a report is determined far more by the selection of facts than by the way they're phrased. If you omit crucial evidence, you're not being objective, even though you're using an impersonal style. In addition, you can easily destroy objectivity by exaggerating and using overblown language: "The catastrophic collapse in sales, precipitated by cutthroat pricing on the part of predatory and unscrupulous rivals, has jeopardized the very survival of the

You are not being objective if you

- Omit crucial evidence
- Use exaggerated language

Figure 12.6
(continued)

3

SUMMARY

The regional sales organization is working at the regional and local levels but not at the national level. We should establish a national accounts group to handle sales that cross regional boundaries.

To make sure that the sales reps (at both the regional and national levels) are adequately motivated and fairly compensated, we need to devise a system of commission splitting and finders' fees. We'll then have one set of reps who are focused on the local and regional levels and another set who are pursuing national accounts. The two groups will have incentives to work together rather than against each other, as is now the case.

once-soaring hot-air balloon division." This sentence has no personal references, but its objectivity is highly questionable.

Despite such drawbacks, the impersonal style is a well-entrenched tradition. You can often tell what tone is appropriate for your readers by looking at other reports of a similar type in your company. If all the other reports on file are impersonal, you should probably adopt the same tone yourself, unless you're confident that your readers prefer a more personal style. Most organizations, for whatever reasons, expect an unobtrusive, impersonal writing style for business reports.

Establishing a Time Perspective

In what time frame will your report exist? Will you write in the past or present tense? The person who wrote this paragraph never decided:

> Twenty-five percent of those interviewed *report* that they *are* dissatisfied with their present brand. The wealthiest participants *complained* most frequently, but all income categories *are* interested in trying a new brand. Only 5 percent of the interviewees *say* they *had* no interest in alternative products.

By flipping from tense to tense when describing the same research results, you only confuse your readers. Is the shift significant, they wonder, or are you just being sloppy? Such confusion can be eliminated by using tense consistently.

Also be careful to observe the chronological sequence of events in your report. If you're describing the history or development of something, start at the beginning and cover each event in the order of its occurrence. If you're explaining the steps in a process, take each step in proper sequence.

Helping Readers Find Their Way

As you begin to write, remember that readers have no concept of how the various pieces of your report are related to one another. Because you have done the work and outlined the report, you have a sense of its wholeness and can see how each page fits into the overall structure; but readers see the report one page at a time. Your job is to give readers a preview or road map of the report's structure so that they can see how the parts of your argument are related. These directions are particularly important for people from other cultures and countries, whose language skills and business expectations may differ from yours—as Frederick Smith knows from his worldwide business dealings through Federal Express.

In a short report, readers are in little danger of getting lost. As the length of a report increases, however, so do readers' opportunities for becoming confused and losing track of the relationship among ideas. If you want readers to understand and accept your message, help them avoid this confusion. Five tools are particularly useful for giving readers a sense

Be consistent in the verb tense you use.

Follow a proper chronological sequence in your report.

Your job is to guide readers through the structure of your report.

of the overall structure of your document and for keeping them on track as they read along: the opening, headings and lists, smooth transitions, previews and reviews, and the ending.

The Opening

As the name suggests, the **opening** is the first section in any report. A good opening accomplishes at least three things:

- Introduces the subject of the report
- Indicates why the subject is important
- Previews the main ideas and the order in which they will be covered

In the opening tell readers what to expect, tell them why your subject is important, and orient them toward your organizational plan.

If you fail to provide readers with these clues to the structure of your report, they'll read aimlessly and miss important points, much like drivers trying to find their way through a strange city without a map.

If your audience is skeptical, the opening downplays the controversial aspects of your message while providing the necessary framework for understanding your report. Here's a good example of an indirect opening, taken from the introduction of a controversial memo on why a new line of luggage has failed to sell well. The writer's ultimate goal is to recommend a shift in marketing strategy.

The performance of the Venturer line can be improved. In the two years since its introduction, this product line has achieved a sales volume lower than we expected, resulting in a drain on the company's overall earnings. The purpose of this report is to review the luggage-buying habits of consumers in all markets where the Venturer line is sold so that we can determine where to put our marketing emphasis.

The paragraph quickly introduces the subject (disappointing sales), tells why the problem is important (drain on earnings), and indicates the main points to be addressed in the body of the report (review of markets where the Venturer line is sold), without revealing what the conclusions and recommendations will be.

Headings and Lists

A **heading** is a brief title at the start of a subdivision within a report that cues readers about the content of the section that follows. Headings are useful markers for clarifying the framework of a report. They visually indicate shifts from one idea to the next, and, when *subheadings* (lower-level headings) and headings are both used, they help readers see the relationship between subordinate and main ideas. In addition, busy readers can quickly understand the gist of a document simply by scanning the headings.

Use headings to give readers the gist of your report.

Headings within a given section that are of the same level of importance should be phrased in parallel form. In other words, if one heading begins with a verb, all same-level headings in that section should begin with verbs. If one is a noun phrase, all should be noun phrases. Putting comparable ideas in similar terms tells readers that the ideas are related. The only exception might be such descriptive headings as "Introduction" at the beginning of a report and "Conclusions" and "Recommendations" at the end. Many companies specify a format for headings. If yours does, use that format. Otherwise, try the scheme shown in Figure 12.7.

Phrase all same-level headings within a section in parallel terms.

A **list** is a series of words, names, or items arranged in a specific order. Setting off important ideas in a list provides an additional structural clue. Lists can show the sequence of ideas or visually heighten their impact. In addition, they facilitate the skimming process for busy readers. Like headings, list items should be phrased in parallel form. You might also consider multilevel lists, with subentries below each major item (much like an outline).[7]

Use lists to set off important ideas and to show sequence.

When you're creating a list, you can separate items with numbers, letters, or bullets (a general term for any kind of graphical element that precedes each item). Numbers are the best choice when you want to indicate sequence or priority, as in this example:

1. Find out how many employees would like on-site day-care facilities

2. Determine how much space the day-care center would require

3. Estimate the cost of converting a conference room for the on-site facility

Figure 12.7
Heading Format for Reports

TITLE

The title is centered at the top of the page in all capital letters, usually boldfaced (or underlined if typewritten), often in a large font (type size), and often using a sans serif typeface. When the title runs to more than one line, the lines are usually double-spaced and arranged as an inverted pyramid (longer line on the top).

FIRST-LEVEL HEADING

A first-level heading indicates what the following section is about, perhaps by describing the subdivisions. All first-level headings are grammatically parallel, with the possible exception of such headings as "Introduction," "Conclusions," and "Recommendations." Some text appears between every two headings, regardless of their levels. Still boldfaced and sans serif, the font may be smaller than that used in the title but still larger than the typeface used in the text and still in all capital letters.

Section-Level Heading

Like first-level headings, second-level headings indicate what the following material is about. All second-level headings within a section are grammatically parallel. Still boldfaced and sans serif, the font may either remain the same or shrink to the size used in the text, and the style is now initial capitals with lower case. Never use only one second-level heading under a first-level heading. (The same is true for every other level of heading.)

Third-Level Heading

A third-level heading is worded to reflect the content of the material that follows. All third-level headings beneath a second-level heading should be grammatically parallel.

Fourth-Level Heading. Like all the other levels of heading, fourth-level headings reflect the subject that will be developed. All fourth-level headings within a subsection are parallel.

Fifth-level headings are generally the lowest level of heading used. However, you can indicate further breakdowns in your ideas by using a list:

1. *The first item in a list.* You may indent the entire item in block format to set it off visually. Numbers are optional.
2. *The second item in a list.* All lists have at least two items. An introductory phrase or sentence may be italicized for emphasis, as shown here.

These three steps need to be taken in the order indicated, and the numbers make that clear. Letters and bullets help you indicate choices without implying order or hierarchy:

A. Convert an existing conference room

B. Build an add-on room

C. Lease space in an existing day-care center

Bullets can add a decorative touch while helping readers distinguish the items in a list. Most word processors make it easy to add a variety of bullet styles, some more appropriate than others. The first list here is fine in this context; the second is too frivolous:

- Cut everyone's salary by 10 percent
- Close the employee cafeteria
- Reduce travel expenses

☞ Cut everyone's salary by 10 percent
☞ Close the employee cafeteria
☞ Reduce travel expenses

When you use lists, make sure to introduce them clearly so that people know what they're about to read. If necessary, add further discussion after the lists (such as this paragraph is doing). Moving your readers smoothly into and out of lists requires careful use of transitions—the subject of the next section.

Smooth Transitions

Such phrases as *to continue the analysis, on the other hand,* and *an additional concept* are another type of structural clue. These are examples of **transitions,** words or phrases that tie ideas together within a report and keep readers moving along the right track. Here is a list of transitions frequently used to move readers smoothly between sentences and paragraphs:

Additional detail:	moreover, furthermore, in addition, besides, first, second, third, finally
Causal relationship:	therefore, because, accordingly, thus, consequently, hence, as a result, so
Comparison:	similarly, here again, likewise, in comparison, still
Contrast:	yet, conversely, whereas, nevertheless, on the other hand, however, but, nonetheless
Condition:	although, if
Illustration:	for example, in particular, in this case, for instance
Time sequence:	formerly, after, when, meanwhile, sometimes
Intensification:	indeed, in fact, in any event
Summary:	in brief, in short, to sum up
Repetition:	that is, in other words, as I mentioned earlier

Although transitional words and phrases are useful, they're not sufficient in themselves to overcome poor organization. Your goal is to put your ideas in a strong framework and then to use transitions to link them together even more strongly.

In longer reports transitions that link major sections or chapters are often complete paragraphs that serve as mini-introductions to the next section or as summaries of the ideas presented in the section just ending. Here's an example:

Given the nature of this problem, the alternatives are limited. As the previous section indicates, we can stop making the product, improve it, or continue with the current model. Each of these alternatives has advantages and disadvantages. The following section discusses pros and cons of each of the three alternatives.

Previews and Reviews

You may have heard the old saying "tell 'em what you're going to tell 'em, tell 'em, then tell 'em what you just told 'em." The more formal way of giving this advice is to tell you to use *preview sections* before and *review sections* after important material in your report. Using a preview section to introduce a topic helps readers get ready for new information. Previews are particularly helpful when the information is complex or unexpected. You don't want the reader to get halfway into a section before figuring out what it's all about.

Review sections, obviously enough, come after a body of material and summarize the information for your readers. Summaries that come at the end of chapters in some textbooks

Use transitions consisting of a single word, a few words, or a whole paragraph to provide additional structural clues.

Howard Schultz, chairman and CEO of Starbucks Coffee Company and author of Pour Your Heart Into It, *believes that "a company can provide long-term value for shareholders without sacrificing its core belief in treating its employees with respect and dignity." Every month Schultz carefully reviews reports that convey employee comments and criticisms along with the usual sales and profit analysis.*

Previews tell readers where they're going.

Reviews tell readers where they've been.

are review sections. Long reports and reports dealing with complex subjects can often benefit from multiple review sections, and not just a single review at the very end.

The Ending

Re-emphasize your main ideas in the ending.

Research shows that the **ending,** the final section of a report, leaves a strong and lasting impression. That's why it's important to use the ending to emphasize the main points of your message. In a report written in direct order, you may want to remind readers of your key points or your conclusions and recommendations. If your report is written in indirect order, end with a summary of key points (except in short memos). In analytical reports, end with conclusions and recommendations as well as key points. Be sure to summarize the benefits to the reader in any report that suggests a change of course or some other action. In general, the ending ties up all the pieces and reminds readers how those pieces fit together. It provides a final opportunity to emphasize the wholeness of your message. Furthermore, it gives you one last chance to check that the report says what you really wanted to say.[8]

CHECKLIST FOR SHORT INFORMAL REPORTS

A. Format

1. For brief external reports, use letter format, including a title or a subject line after the reader's address that clearly states the subject of the document.
2. For brief internal reports, use memo or manuscript format.
3. Present all short informal reports properly.
   - ■ a. Single-space the text.
   - ■ b. Double-space between paragraphs.
   - ■ c. Use headings where helpful, but try not to use more than three levels of headings.
   - ■ d. Call attention to significant information by setting it off visually with lists or indention.
   - ■ e. Include visual aids to emphasize and clarify the text.

B. Opening

1. For short, routine memos, use the subject line of the memo form and the first sentence or two of the text as the introduction.
2. For all other short reports, cover these topics in the introduction: purpose, scope, background, restrictions (in conducting the study), sources of information and methods of research, and organization of the report.
3. If using direct order, place conclusions and recommendations in the opening.

C. Body (Findings and Supporting Details)

1. Use direct order for informational reports to receptive readers, developing ideas around subtopics (chronologically, geographically, categorically).
2. Use direct order for analytical reports to receptive readers, developing points around conclusions or recommendations.
3. Use indirect order for analytical reports to skeptical or hostile readers, developing points around logical arguments.

4. Use an appropriate writing style.
   - ■ a. Use an informal style (*I* and *you*) for letter and memo reports, unless company custom calls for the impersonal third person.
   - ■ b. Use an impersonal style for more formal short reports in manuscript format.
5. Maintain a consistent time frame by writing in either the present or the past tense, using other tenses only to indicate prior or future events.
6. Give each paragraph a topic sentence.
7. Link paragraphs by using transitional words and phrases.
8. Strive for readability by using short sentences, concrete words, and terminology that is appropriate for your readers.
9. Be accurate, thorough, and impartial in presenting the material.
10. Avoid including irrelevant and unnecessary details.
11. Include documentation for all material quoted or paraphrased from secondary sources, using a consistent format.

D. Ending

1. In informational reports summarize major findings at the end, if you wish.
2. Summarize points in the same order in which they appear in the text.
3. In analytical reports using indirect order, list conclusions and recommendations at the end.
4. Be certain that conclusions and recommendations follow logically from facts presented in the text.
5. Consider using a list format for emphasis.
6. Avoid introducing new material in the summary, conclusions, or recommendations.

On the Job

SOLVING A COMMUNICATION DILEMMA AT FEDERAL EXPRESS

Entrepreneur Frederick Smith was sure that his new transportation network would increase Federal Express's efficiency and decrease the cost of moving packages from state to state. He wanted to fly packages from around the country to a central hub in Memphis, where they would be sorted and flown to their final destinations. To raise money for this venture, Smith used business reports, and they have remained important through the years as he and his managers have built Federal Express into a global business with $12 billion in annual revenues.

For example, because of Federal Express's heavy orientation toward customer satisfaction, the company has a strong emphasis on training. Training costs money, and reports are used to justify training expenditures. One of those expenditures might be for computer networking equipment to support the company's interactive training program. Of course, before managers buy equipment, these items are thoroughly and objectively investigated and analyzed. Then managers can read through special, nonrecurring reports, study the justification for each major purchase, and weigh the pros and cons.

Reports are also important to the company's internal auditors, who are charged with studying how the company controls its finances, operations, and legal compliance. Internal auditors visit the departments they are assigned to examine, conduct their investigations, and then write reports to communicate their findings and any ideas for improvement. The analytical reports that Federal Express's auditors prepare contain recommendations as well as conclusions.

The human resources and internal audit departments are only two of the many Federal Express departments that prepare and receive reports. As Frederick Smith and his managers strive against competitors, work toward customer satisfaction, and keep the business running smoothly, business reports are sure to continue to play a key role at Federal Express.[9]

Your Mission: You have recently joined Federal Express as Frederick Smith's administrative assistant. Your job is to help him with a variety of special projects. During an average week, he might ask you to handle three or four assignments and then report back to him in writing. In each of the following situations, choose the best communication alternative from among those listed, and be prepared to explain why your choice is best.

1. To keep tabs on the industry, Smith has asked you to research two services offered by FedEx's top three competitors: the online pickup request (scheduling a pickup online rather than over the telephone) and package tracking (entering a tracking number on a Web site to see where a package is during transit). How should you introduce your report? Choose the best introduction from the four shown below.

   a. Recognizing that Federal Express no longer has the overnight delivery business to itself, management has decided to examine the effect of online pickup-request and package-tracking services offered by other companies. Specifically, management wants to review two issues:

      1. What online pickup-request and package-tracking services are offered by the top three competitors?

   2. How can Federal Express use its own online services to compete more effectively?

   The following pages present the results of a two-week study of these questions.

   b. Major changes are occurring in the overnight delivery business. Our online pickup-request and package-tracking services have attracted a great deal of customer use since we introduced them. Not surprisingly, however, we are not the only express shipping company offering such services. With more and more shippers and receivers conducting more and more business online, the demand for such services will only increase. Federal Express can capitalize on this market demand and compete more effectively if we (1) publicize our fast, easy online services more heavily and (2) introduce additional online services for time-pressured customers. These conclusions are examined in detail in the following pages.

   c. I am happy to report that Federal Express is still ahead of all competitors. However, I have to point out that rivals are doing everything they can to keep up the pressure. The two-week study of competitors' online services that I recently conducted shows that UPS and others offer a variety of services similar to our own offerings.

   Let me stress that customers have already tracked millions of packages and placed millions of pickup requests using these online services. Although this is obviously an important service, I want to emphasize that customers are going to continue expecting more and more of these online conveniences. Because of this trend, I want to present two recommendations that Federal Express might pursue.

   d. Since Federal Express was founded nearly 35 years ago, the company has looked for ways to turn customer convenience into both a competitive advantage and a way to operate more efficiently (and therefore, more profitably). In the past few years, the Internet has proven to be a very effective way to expand our customer service options while decreasing the amount of time our customer service representatives need to spend on the phone.

   At the request of senior management, an examination of the online pickup-request and package-tracking services offered by competitors was conducted. The following pages present the findings of this study, which addressed the following questions:

      1. What online pickup-request and package-tracking services do competitors offer?
      2. How do Federal Express's services compare?
      3. What challenges and opportunities do such services represent?

2. Smith has asked you to provide a brief overview of UPS, Airborne Express, and DHL Worldwide Express, all of which are important Federal Express competitors. This overview will be handed out at a stockholder's meeting in Memphis. Because some stockholders may not be fully informed about the competition, Smith has

asked you to write a brief informational memo on the subject. He wants you to cover the following points for each competitor: (1) annual sales, (2) number of employees, (3) names of top executives, and (4) main services. You have to write this immediately, so you'll just have to use whatever facts you can find. Which of the following versions is preferable?

a. The three companies in question, UPS, Airborne Express, and DHL Worldwide Express, are a mixed bag in terms of size. Their sales range from $22 billion (UPS) to $4 billion (DHL) to $2 billion (Airborne Express).

Similarly, the number of employees varies from competitor to competitor. Airborne employs about 21,000 people, DHL employs about 50,000, and UPS employs more than 336,000. James P. Kelly is the CEO of UPS. Patrick Foley was chairman of Hyatt Hotels and Braniff Airlines before joining DHL as CEO of DHL Airways (the U.S. segment of the company) in 1988. Rob Kuijpers serves as CEO of DHL International (the international segment of the company, based in Brussels). Airborne is headed by CEO Robert Cline.

All four competitors offer domestic and international delivery. Although DHL offers delivery throughout the United States, it is better known for international delivery. In fact, DHL's market share outside the United States is larger than Federal Express's and UPS's combined. In contrast, only 2 percent of Airborne's deliveries are international. UPS went worldwide in 1985 and now serves more than 200 countries.

b. Federal Express's $12 billion in annual sales puts the company about halfway between the sales figures of UPS on the high side and DHL and Airborne Express on the low side. Similarly, Federal Express's 137,000 employees puts it roughly halfway between UPS and the two smaller rivals.

Federal Express's founder, Frederick Smith, has been CEO since he began the company more than 20 years ago. James P. Kelly is CEO of UPS, Patrick Foley is CEO of DHL Airways, and Robert Cline is CEO of Airborne. All three competitors serve customers around the world as well as around the United States.

c. Here's the lowdown on the poor hapless souls that Federal Express will mow down in the next year:

- UPS is the top dog of delivery services. It has annual sales of $22 billion and employs something like 300,000 people. James P. Kelly is the top banana here. We know that UPS delivers around the world, but we don't know how many countries it serves or how many packages it sends around the globe every year.
- Airborne Express is teeny compared with UPS and with Federal Express. Its sales are puny—just a little over $2 billion or so—and only 21,000 people work for the company. A lot less than half of Airborne's deliveries go to international destinations. Robert Cline is the head honcho.
- DHL's Patrick Foley has the arduous task of being CEO and competing with Federal Express's vastly superior services. Like Airborne, DHL's annual sales of $4 billion are anemic when compared with UPS and Federal Express. But it does have 50,000 workers toiling away at domestic and international deliveries.

d. Here are the annual sales, number of employees, names of top executives, and international presence of three of our competitors:

- UPS is our largest competitor, with $22 billion in annual sales (compared with our own $12 billion in annual sales). UPS employs more than 330,000. The CEO is James P. Kelly. Since 1985, UPS has offered both domestic and international delivery service, but we don't have data on the number of global deliveries or the number of countries served.
- DHL has annual sales of $4 billion, and the number of employees is 50,000. CEO Patrick Foley was chairman of Hyatt Hotels and Braniff Airlines before joining DHL Airways (the domestic segment of the company) in 1988. Although DHL offers delivery throughout the United States, it is better known for international delivery, where it holds 41 market share. The company handles more than 50 million international shipments every year.
- Airborne Express has annual sales of just over $2 billion, and the company employs 21,000 people. Robert Cline is Airborne's CEO. Like the other three competitors, Airborne offers both domestic and international delivery, but only 2 percent of its deliveries are to overseas destinations.

3. Smith wants to celebrate Federal Express's thirty-fifth anniversary by creating a special advertising insert on the company's history. He wants to distribute this insert inside the April issue of a national business magazine. The magazine's publisher is excited about the concept and has asked Smith to send her "something in writing." Smith asks you to draft the proposal, which should be no more than ten pages long. Which of the following outlines should you use?

a. Version One
 I. An overview of Federal Express's history
  A. How company was founded
  B. Overview of company services
  C. Overview of markets served
  D. Overview of transportation operations
 II. The Federal Express magazine insert
  A. Historic events to be included
  B. Employees to be interviewed
  C. Customers to be discussed
  D. Production schedule
 III. Pros and cons of Federal Express magazine insert
  A. Pros: Make money for magazine, draw new customers for Federal Express
  B. Cons: Costs, questionable audience interest

b. Version Two
 I. Introduction: Overview of the Federal Express special insert
  A. Purpose
  B. Content
  C. Timing
 II. Description of the insert
  A. Text
   1. Message from CEO
   2. History of Federal Express
   3. Interviews with employees
   4. Customer testimonials
  B. Advertising
   1. Inside front and back covers

  2. Color spreads

  3. Congratulatory ads placed by customers

 III. Next steps

 IV. Summary

c. Version Three

Who: Federal Express

What: Special magazine insert

When: Inserted in April issue

Where: Coordinated by magazine's editors

Why: To celebrate Federal Express's anniversary

How: Overview of content, production responsibilities, and schedule

d. Version Four

 I. Introduction: The rationale for producing a magazine insert promoting Federal Express

  A. Insert would make money for magazine

  B. Insert would boost morale of Federal Express employees

  C. Insert would attract new customers

 II. Insert description

  A. Interview with founder Frederick Smith

  B. Interviews with employees

  C. Description of historic moments

  D. Interviews with customers

  E. Advertisements

 III. Production plan

  A. Project organization

  B. Timing and sequence of steps

  C. Federal Express's responsibilities

  D. Magazine's responsibilities

 IV. Detailed schedule

 V. Summary of benefits and responsibilities

4. Smith has asked you to think about ways of attracting new customers that need Federal Express's expertise in managing international parts and parcel distribution. You have talked with executives at Laura Ashley and National Semiconductor, two current customers, and discovered that they are most concerned about the time needed to process orders and deliver parts to stores or factories. Federal Express can cut the delivery time from as much as 21 days to as little as 4 days after ordering. You believe that an advertising campaign featuring testimonials from these two satisfied customers will give Federal Express a tremendous advantage over other competitors, who haven't yet developed a track record with large global companies. As a relatively junior person at Federal Express, you are a little apprehensive about suggesting your idea. You don't want to seem presumptuous, but on the other hand, you think your idea is good. You have decided to raise the issue with Smith. Which of the following approaches is preferable?

a. Instead of writing a report, arrange a meeting to discuss your ideas with Smith, the advertising manager, and an executive from the company's advertising agency. This allows you to address the issues and ideas firsthand in an informal setting.

b. You write the following short report:

> You recently asked me to give some thought to how Federal Express might attract new customers for its international parts distribution business. I decided to sound out two of our largest customers to get a feel for why they hired us to handle this operation. Interestingly, they didn't choose Federal Express because they wanted to reduce their shipping

costs. Rather, they were interested in reducing the time needed to process and ship orders to stores and factories.

> Many companies are in the same situation as Laura Ashley and National Semiconductor. They're not just looking for the carrier with the lowest prices, they're looking for the carrier with the proven ability to process orders and get shipments to their destinations as quickly as possible. Instead of waiting as long as 21 days for shipments to reach their destination, these companies can promise delivery in 4 days.

> Clearly, our track record with Laura Ashley and National Semiconductor is the key to capturing the attention of other global companies. After all, how many competitors can show they have the ability to cut as much as 17 days off the time needed to process and deliver an order? Of course, companies might be skeptical if we made this claim on our own, but they would be more likely to accept it if our customers told their own stories. That's why Federal Express should ask executives from Laura Ashley and National Semiconductor to offer testimonials in an advertising campaign.

c. You write the following short report:

> In response to your request, I have investigated ways in which Federal Express might attract new customers for its international parts distribution business. In conducting this investigation, I have talked with executives at two of our largest customers, Laura Ashley and National Semiconductor, and discussed the situation with our advertising manager and our advertising agency. All agreed that companies are interested in more than merely saving money on international shipments. Typically, a global company has to keep a lot of parts or materials on hand and be ready to ship these whenever a store or factory places an order. As soon as an order arrives, the company packages the parts and ships it out. The store or factory doesn't want to wait a long time because it, in turn, has to keep a lot of money tied up in parts to be sure it doesn't run out before the new shipment arrives. Thus, if the company can cut the time between ordering and delivery, it will save its stores or factories a lot of money and, at the same time, build a lot of customer loyalty.

> As a result, shipping costs are less important than the need to process orders and get shipments to their destinations as quickly as possible. Instead of delivery in 21 days, these companies can promise deliveries in 4 days. If we can show global companies how to do this, we will attract many more customers.

d. You write the following short report:

> This report was authorized by Frederick W. Smith on May 7. Its purpose is to analyze ways of attracting more customers to Federal Express's international parts distribution business. Laura Ashley and National Semiconductor are two large, global companies that use our international parts distribution service. Both companies are pleased with our ability to cut the time between ordering and parts delivery. Both are willing to give testimonials to that effect.

> These testimonials will help attract new customers if they are used in newspaper, magazine, and television advertising. A

company is more likely to believe a satisfied customer than someone who works for Federal Express. If the advertising de-

partment and the advertising agency start working on this idea today, it could be implemented within two months.

Critical Thinking Questions

1. How do you explain the fact that so many kinds of documents qualify as reports? What makes them all reports? Please explain.
2. Have you ever written any reports that led to a decision or action? Did your report achieve the desired results? Did you use direct or indirect order? Why? How did you subdivide the ideas, and why did you use that structure? How might you have applied some of the ideas presented in this chapter to make the report more effective? Briefly explain.
3. Could the increased speed of electronic reporting create any problems with the quality of the information people see or the decisions they make? Explain your answer.
4. What are the advantages and disadvantages of the direct and the indirect approaches? Briefly explain.
5. Why do you think some organizations prefer a formal tone for internal reports? What are the advantages and disadvantages of such a tone? Explain briefly.
6. How can a writer help readers understand the structure of a report? Please explain.

Exercises

1. Team up with a classmate to research one of the following topics. Working together, plan an analytical report focusing on your conclusions. Write out the main idea, and draft an informative outline with first- and second-level headings.
   a. Trends in the U.S. trade deficit with China and Japan, and the implications for business in the next century
   b. The impact on small businesses of recent increases in the minimum wage
   c. The impact of drug abuse in the workplace
2. Select one of the following topics and plan an analytical report focusing on your recommendations. Develop the main idea, and draft an informative outline with first- and second-level headings.
   a. How to reduce the amount of electricity consumed by your college
   b. How to prepare your home to withstand a severe weather problem, such as a strong hurricane or a major snowstorm
   c. How to reduce the cost of car insurance
3. Team up with a classmate to practice writing informative openings. For the analytical report you outlined in either exercise 1 or exercise 2, draft an opening that tells what the report covers, explains why the subject is important, and previews the main ideas and the order in which ideas will be presented. Swap with your teammate and critique each other's opening section. Does each opening give sufficient clues to the structure of the report? How can these openings be improved?
4. Team up with a classmate to practice writing emphatic and informative endings. For the analytical report you outlined in exercise 1 or 2, draft an ending that includes conclusions, recommendations, and key points. Swap with your teammate and compare each ending with the Checklist for Short Informal Reports. How well does each ending communicate the main points and the overall message? How can these endings be improved?
5. Attend the next meeting of the college's student government and take notes on what occurs. Then write a brief (two-page) personal activity report on that meeting, using the memo format. Think about what your audience, the other students in your business communication class, will want to know about the issues discussed and conclusions reached during that meeting. What key question should you answer in this report?
6. American Management Systems (AMS) has, for more than a quarter century, developed and implemented management plans and has placed management personnel in positions around the globe. The company's Web site, <http://www.amsinc.com>, provides perspective on the company as well as information about positions in management. Following suggestions in the Checklist for Short Informal Reports, prepare a brief internal report analyzing the clarity of presentation and the persuasive aspects of the AMS Web page.

Cases

1. My progress to date: Periodic report on your academic career As you know, the bureaucratic process involved in getting a degree or certificate is nearly as challenging as any course you could take.

Your Task: Prepare a periodic report detailing the steps you've taken toward completing your graduation or certification require-

ments. After examining the requirements listed in your college catalog, indicate a realistic schedule for completing those that remain. In addition to course requirements, include such steps as completing the residency requirement, filing necessary papers, and paying necessary fees. Use memo format for your report, and address it to anyone who is helping or encouraging you through school.

2. Gavel to gavel: Personal report of a meeting Meetings, conferences, and conventions abound in the academic world, and you have probably attended your share.

Your Task: Prepare a report on a meeting, convention, or conference that you have recently attended. Use memo format, and direct the report to other students in your field who were not able to attend.

3. The importance of a good breakfast: Justification report for longer business hours Imagine that you work for a restaurant that's near campus and that's open only for lunch and dinner. You think there is significant demand for a good place to eat breakfast, and you believe the restaurant could more than make up for the additional cost of opening at 6:00 A.M. instead of 11:30 A.M.

Your Task: Develop a budget for the expanded hours of operation, including personnel costs, management time, utilities, and changes to the food inventory. Next write a report explaining your concept, describing the major budget items, and briefly predicting the benefits that this expansion will bring. (Feel free to make up any details you need, but keep it realistic.) Write your report in memo format to the owner or manager of the business.

4. Selling something special: Proposal to a business Pick a company or business that you know something about. Now think of a customized item or service that you believe the business needs. Examples might be a specially designed piece of equipment, a workshop for employees on improving their communication skills, a program for curtailing shoplifting, a catering service to a company's construction site, or a customized word-processing system, to name just a few possibilities.

Your Task: Write a proposal to the owners or managers of this business. Convince them that they need the product you're selling. Include a statement of the problem, purpose (benefits), scope (areas in which your product will help the business), methods and procedures, work plan and schedule, your qualifications, projected costs, and any other pertinent information. Use letter format.

5. Restaurant review: Report on a restaurant's food and operations Visit any restaurant, possibly your school cafeteria. The

workers and fellow customers will assume that you are an ordinary customer, but you are really a spy for the owner.

Your Task: After your visit write a short memo to the owner, explaining (a) what you did and what you observed, (b) any violations of policy that you observed, and (c) your recommendations for improvement. The first part of your report (what you did and what you observed) will be the longest. Include a description of the premises, inside and out. Tell how long the various steps of ordering and receiving your meal took. Describe the service and food thoroughly. You are interested in both the good and bad aspects of the establishment's decor, service, and food. For the second section (violations of policy), use some common sense. If all the servers but one have their hair covered, you may assume that policy requires hair to be covered; a dirty window or restroom obviously violates policy. The last section (recommendations for improvement) involves professional judgment. What management actions will improve the restaurant?

6. Pumping up gasoline sales: Report on suggested advertising approaches Gasoline advertising is heating up in Brazil, where Esso, Shell, Atlantic-Arco, Texaco, and Ipiranga compete with Petrobras, the state-owned monopoly. All are in a race to increase their share of Brazil's 5-billion-liter gasoline-products market. However, Brazilian drivers know that Petrobras actually produces and refines the gasoline that every one of its competitors sells. What differentiates one brand from another are the additives that the oil companies put into their individual formulations. Esso's advertising in Brazil is handled by the ad agency McCann-Erickson. Knowing that rivals put a variety of ingredients into their formulations, the agency recommends that Esso use a new advertising approach: Alert drivers to the differences among brands and warn them to look closely at the quality of the gasoline they use.

Your Task: As the McCann-Erickson manager assigned to the Esso account, draft a one-page memo to Esso's managers in which you justify your agency's recommendation. Use your contact's first name, Don, and your own first name in the memo heading. Explain why you believe Esso should adopt this new advertising approach, discuss the main benefit you see in using this approach, and summarize your position.[10]

7. Preparing for the worst: Report on crisis management When the anonymous call came in, Campbell Soup officials refused to take any chances. The caller claimed to have put poison in Campbell's tomato juice cans at a New England supermarket. The company quickly decided to yank the product from 84 area stores. Even though the call turned out to be a hoax, Campbell Soup believes it's best to be prepared for the worst. Moreover, an important part of any crisis-management plan is the way company officials tell the public about the situation.

Your Task: You're a public relations consultant with special expertise in crisis management. You've been asked to recommend how and when Campbell Soup should reveal any threats and the steps that have been taken in response. In addition, you want to suggest ways of reassuring consumers that Campbell Soup products are pure and completely safe. Draft the outline for an impersonal but informal analytical report to CEO David W. Johnson that includes your recommendations and the justifications for those recommendations. Be sure the headings you choose show what your report will cover, including the need for action, the benefits to be achieved, the list of recommendations (without details), and a summary.[11]

8. Fishing for more revenue: Report for a nonprofit organization The Historic Fishing Village of Puget Sound has asked you to determine why revenues have been lower than expected and to suggest how to improve revenues. You've found two probable causes for the low revenue: (a) unusually bad weather during prime tourism periods and (b) shoddy, inexpensive merchandise in the gift shop.

Your Task: Draft a two-page troubleshooting report to present to the nonprofit's trustees. Be sure to support your conclusions, and address the report to the trustees as a group. Make up whatever details you need about the merchandise and about ways to improve revenues. Bear in mind that the trustees originally approved the purchase of merchandise for the gift shop, so you'll want to use objective language to avoid offending them.

DEVELOPING YOUR INTERNET SKILLS

GOING ONLINE: SPOTLIGHT ON SAMPLE BUSINESS REPORTS, P. 265

Conduct the "business reports" search as suggested. Now follow a Webcrawler listing of the "Library of Business Reports," a site sponsored by Alvest. If you click "business," you'll be able to read a list of business reports available for purchase—note the way titles are used to encourage your interest. Now go back to the Alvest page and click on the "free report of the week." Read the report. (If you are unable to find this report, read any legitimate business report on any site your search uncovers.) Compare the report you've read with the types of reports described in this chapter. What category does it fall under (what is its purpose)? Look at the format, style, organization, and order of the report and identify each in the terms you've learned (direct versus indirect, and so on).

PLANNING LONG REPORTS

After studying this chapter, you will be able to

Develop a statement defining the problem to be solved and a statement defining the purpose of the report

Identify and outline the issues that have to be analyzed during your study

Prepare a work plan for conducting the investigation

Organize the research phase of the investigation, including the identification of secondary and primary sources of data

Draw sound conclusions and develop practical recommendations

Develop a final outline and visual aid plan for your report

O*n the Job*

FACING A COMMUNICATION DILEMMA AT HARLEY-DAVIDSON
Driven to Success, But Now What?

Success certainly is popular. Employees like it; business partners like it; investors, executives, and the local communities usually like it. Unfortunately, so do competitors.

The story of Milwaukee-based Harley-Davidson is a story of remarkable highs and equally remarkable lows. In the early 1970s, the company controlled 99.7 percent of the high-end U.S. motorcycle market and saw no reason to panic when Japanese manufacturers began to push from low-cost bikes into the heavyweight segment. After all, if your customers love your product so much that they tattoo your logo on their chests, can't you count on their loyalty?

Unfortunately, Honda and the other Japanese manufacturers attacked Harley's two major weaknesses: cost and quality. Before long, Harley's market share had tumbled to 23 percent, and the company was staring at bankruptcy.

Harley responded in truly inspiring fashion, virtually reinventing itself in the late 1980s and early 1990s. In doing so, it also became a symbol of reinvigorated U.S. business. In fact, business schools across the country now study the company's turnaround to learn more about contemporary product design and manufacturing. Market share climbed back into the 70 percent range, as CEO Richard F. Teerlink and the rest of the Harley team capitalized on the one thing other manufacturers could never have: the Harley-Davidson mystique. A product that was once associated with biker gangs became a status symbol for successful professionals who wanted to feel like temporary outlaws.

Once again, though, Harley faces a challenge that will test its ingenuity and resourcefulness. Demand has outpaced production by such a degree that customers have had to wait as long as two years for a new Harley. Meanwhile, the Japanese makers, along with Germany's BMW, have studied Harley's reborn success and are hungry for a bigger piece of the pie. They're getting it, too, pushing Harley's market share back below 50 percent by 1997.

Teerlink realizes that to stay in the fast lane, he needs careful research and analysis of issues ranging from product design to inventory control to customer needs. If you were in charge of writing reports on these issues, how would you go about planning them? What steps would you take to define each problem, conduct the research, and analyze the data necessary for such reports?[1]

When Harley-Davidson saw its market share tumble to record lows, CEO Richard F. Teerlink realized that every facet of the operation needed careful analysis, which required equally careful research. Teerlink and all of Harley's managers received staggering amounts of information in the form of reports.

When planning most business reports, you define the problem and the purpose, outline the issues for investigation, prepare a work plan, conduct research, and then analyze and interpret data.

Narrow the focus of your investigation by defining your problem.

 IVE STEPS IN PLANNING REPORTS

Whether you're employed by Harley-Davidson or by another business, you usually have some work to do before you begin to write a report. As Richard Teerlink knows, it's easy to let "happy and fuzzy" thinking interfere with your effectiveness—especially when preparing reports. Writing a report involves careful planning. Even if you're preparing a strictly informational report that does nothing more than transmit facts, you must still gather those facts and arrange them in a convenient format. Before putting a single word on the page, follow the series of steps that form the foundation of any report:

1. Define the problem and the purpose.
2. Outline the issues for investigation.
3. Prepare a work plan.
4. Conduct research.
5. Analyze and interpret data, drawing conclusions and developing recommendations.

The relative importance of these five steps depends on the type of assignment. **Informational reports,** which contain facts alone, may require very little in the way of conclusions and recommendations. Monitor/control reports, statements of policies and procedures, interim progress reports, and many compliance reports are examples. On the other hand, **analytical reports** include conclusions and recommendations and require all five steps. Examples include decision-oriented reports, business plans, proposals, and final reports to clients.

S TEP 1: DEFINING THE PROBLEM AND THE PURPOSE

Your first step is to write a **problem statement,** a statement that defines the problem your report will cover. This problem may be negative or positive; it may deal with the problem of shrinking sales or the need for more child-care facilities. The problem you cover is merely the matter you intend to deal with, whether you're gathering information, supporting a decision, or actually solving a problem. Be careful not to confuse a simple topic (campus parking) with a problem (the lack of enough campus parking). A clear problem statement helps you decide what information you'll need in order to complete your report. Also, be sure to consider the company's perspective and the individual perspectives of the people who will read your report.[2] If you're the only person who thinks this issue is a problem, the audience won't be very interested in your solution. You may have to spend some time convincing people that a problem exists.

Linda Moreno is a cost accounting analyst for Electrovision, a high-technology company based in San Francisco. She was recently asked to find ways of reducing employee travel costs (her complete report appears in Chapter 14). Because she was supposed to suggest specific cost reductions, she phrased her problem statement carefully: "Electrovision needs to find ways to reduce travel costs while still enabling employees to work effectively." If her assignment had been restricted to simply reporting on spending patterns, her problem statement would have been phrased differently: "We need to understand how our travel budget is being spent." You can see from these two statements how much influence the problem statement has on your investigation. If Moreno's manager expected her to suggest cost reductions, but all she did was collect cost data, her report would have failed to meet expectations. Because she was assigned an analytical report rather than an informational report, Moreno had to go beyond mere data collection to draw conclusions and make recommendations. No matter what kind of report you're doing, however, defining the problem and the purpose requires asking questions to clarify the assignment.

Asking the Right Questions

As in Moreno's case, the problem is often defined for you by the person who authorizes the report. When this is the case, talk over the objectives of the report before you begin your investigation—to ensure that you understand exactly what is required. Specifically, try to answer the following questions:

- What needs to be determined?
- Why is this issue important?
- Who is involved in the situation?
- Where is the trouble located?
- When did it start?
- How did the situation originate?

Not all these questions apply in every situation, but asking them helps you clarify the boundaries of your investigation. You can then draft a written statement of the problem being investigated, which will serve as a guide to whatever problem you're trying to solve or whatever question you're trying to answer in the report.[3]

Developing the Statement of Purpose

Once you've asked some preliminary questions and determined the problem, you're ready to write a clear **statement of purpose,** which defines the objective of the report. In contrast to the problem statement, which defines only what you're going to investigate, the statement of purpose defines what the report should accomplish.[4]

The most useful way to phrase your purpose is to begin with an infinitive phrase. If Linda Moreno had been given an informational assignment, she might've stated her purpose this way:

Purpose: To summarize Electrovision's spending on travel and entertainment

However, her analytical report had to go beyond information:

Purpose: To analyze Electrovision's travel costs and suggest practical ways to reduce these costs while still enabling employees to work effectively

Using an infinitive phrase (*to* plus a verb) encourages you to take control and decide where you're going before you begin. When you choose such a phrase—*to inform, to confirm, to analyze, to persuade, to recommend*—you pin down your general goal in preparing the report. At the same time, be sure to define the benefit (the information or the recommended action) that your reader will gain from reading your report. The more specific your purpose, the more useful it will be as a guide to planning and writing the report.

Your audience's reaction dictates all the decisions you'll make about content, structure, outline, and so forth. So it's important to anticipate that reaction. Double-check your statement of purpose with the person who authorized the report. When the authorizer sees the purpose written down in black and white, he or she may decide to point the study in another direction.

Ted Koppel is anchor of ABC's Nightline. He points out that you don't have to become an expert on every subject you undertake, but he urges you to learn enough about the subject you are investigating to pose intelligent questions.

Prepare a written statement of your purpose; then review it with the person who authorized the study.

S TEP 2: OUTLINING ISSUES FOR INVESTIGATION

Once you've defined the problem and established the purpose of your report, you're ready to begin your investigation. To organize the research effort, you can break the problem into a series of logical, connected questions that try to identify causes and effects. This process is sometimes called **problem factoring.** You probably subconsciously approach most problems in this way. When your car's engine won't start, what do you do? You use the available evidence to organize your investigation, to start a search for cause-and-effect relationships. If the engine doesn't turn over at all, for instance, you might suspect a dead battery. In contrast, if the engine does turn over but won't fire, you can conclude that the battery is okay but perhaps you're out of gas. When you speculate on the cause of a problem, you're forming a **hypothesis,** a potential explanation that needs to be tested. By subdividing a problem and forming hypotheses based on available evidence, you can tackle even the most complex situations.

Linda Moreno used the factoring process to structure her investigation into cost reduction at Electrovision (Figure 13.1). "I began with a two-part question," says Moreno. "Why have our travel costs grown so dramatically, and how can we reduce them? Then I factored the first part into two subquestions: Do we have adequate procedures for tracking and controlling costs? Are these procedures being followed?

"Looking into cost-control procedures, I speculated that the right kind of information was not reaching the executives who were responsible for these costs. From there, the questioning naturally led to the systems and procedures for collecting this information. If we didn't have the right procedures in place or if people weren't following procedures, the information wouldn't reach the people in charge."

Once Moreno had determined what was wrong with Electrovision's cost-control system, she could address the second part of the main question: the problem of recommending improvements. The process of outlining the issues enabled Moreno and her colleagues to solve a problem methodically, just as outlining a report enables you to write in a systematic way. It's worth noting, however, that the way you outline an investigation may be different from the way you outline the resulting report. Solving the problem is one thing; "selling" the solution is another. During your investigation, you might analyze five possible causes of a problem and discover that only two are relevant. In your report, you might not even introduce the three unrelated possibilities that you investigated.

Developing a Logical Structure

Because any subject can be factored in many ways, your job is to choose the most logical method, the one that makes the most sense. Start by looking carefully at the purpose of your report. Informational assignments are structured differently from analytical ones.

Many assignments require both information and analysis, so it's up to you to discern the overall purpose of the report. Is your general goal to provide background information that someone else will use or interpret? Then an informational outline is appropriate over-

Outline the issues you plan to study.

The outline of issues for analysis is often different from the outline of the final report.

Informational and analytical studies are factored differently.

Figure 13.1
Factoring the Travel-Cost Problem at Electrovision

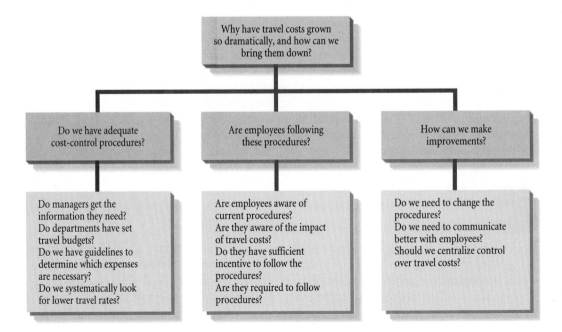

all, even though subsections of the study may require some analysis to discover and emphasize important facts. Is the purpose of your report to scrutinize the data and generate your own conclusions and recommendations? Then use an analytical outline overall, even though your opinions will obviously be based on facts. For problem solving you may use a variety of structural schemes, as long as you take care to avoid errors in logic.

Informational Assignments

Investigations that lead to factual reports, offering little analysis or interpretation of the data, are generally organized on the basis of subtopics dealing with specific subjects. These subtopics can be arranged in various ways:

- *According to importance.* If you're reviewing five product lines, you might organize your study in order of the sales for each product line, beginning with the line that produces the most revenue and proceeding to the one that produces the least revenue.
- *According to sequence.* If you're studying a process, proceed step by step—1, 2, 3, and so on.
- *According to chronology.* When investigating a chain of events, organize the study according to what happened in January, what happened in February, and so on.
- *According to spatial orientation.* If you're studying a physical object, study it left to right (or right to left in some cultures), top to bottom, or outside to inside.
- *According to geography.* If location is important, factor your study geographically.
- *According to category.* If you're asked to review several distinct aspects of a subject, look at one category at a time, such as sales, profit, cost, or investment.

These methods of subdivision are commonly used when preparing monitor/control reports, policies and procedures, compliance reports, and interim progress reports.

> Studies that emphasize discovering and reporting facts may be factored by subtopic.

Analytical Assignments

Analytical studies result in decision-oriented reports, final reports for clients, and some compliance reports. Such reports usually contain analyses, conclusions, and recommendations, and they're generally categorized by a problem-solving method. The two most common structural approaches for this method are (1) relative merit and (2) hypothesis.

When the problem is to evaluate how well various alternatives meet your criteria, the natural way to subdivide your analysis is to focus on the criteria. For example, if the problem is to decide where to build a new plant, you might factor the investigation along the following lines:

> Studies that focus on problem solving may be structured around hypotheses that the report writer plans to prove or disprove during the investigation.

Where should we build a new plant?

I.   Construction costs
     A. Location A
     B. Location B
     C. Location C

II. Labor availability
     A. Location A
     B. Location B
     C. Location C

III. Transportation facilities
     A. Location A
     B. Location B
     C. Location C

Another way of using relative merits is to identify the alternatives first and then analyze how well each alternative meets your criteria.

When the report's purpose is to discover causes, predict results, or suggest a solution to a problem, one natural way to proceed is to formulate hypothetical explanations. If your problem were to determine why your company was having trouble hiring secretaries, you'd begin factoring the problem by speculating on the causes. Then you'd collect information to confirm or disprove each reason. Your outline of the major issues might look something like this:

Why are we having trouble hiring secretaries?
I.   We don't pay them enough.
     A. What do we pay our secretaries?
     B. What do comparable companies pay their secretaries?
     C. How important is pay in influencing secretaries' job choices?
II. Our location is poor.
     A. Are we accessible by public transportation and major roads?
     B. Is the area physically attractive?
     C. Are housing costs affordable?
     D. Is crime a problem?
III. The supply of secretaries is diminishing.
     A. How many secretaries were available five years ago as opposed to now?
     B. What was the demand for secretaries five years ago as opposed to now?

In many cases, however, identifying and clarifying problems is only part of the challenge. You'll often be called on to suggest and implement solutions. Developing solid problem-solving skills will help not only your business reports but many other aspects of your career as well. You will be able to solve problems efficiently and effectively if you follow a clear problem-solving process:[5]

1. Define and limit the problem so that you know exactly what you're trying to solve—and what you're not trying to solve.
2. Analyze the problem and gather data about it.
3. Establish criteria for possible solutions.
4. Brainstorm possible solutions.
5. Choose the best possible solution, based on the criteria you set in step 3.
6. Implement the chosen solution.

You won't cover all six of these steps in every report you write, of course, but knowing how to solve problems will help you make better decisions and recommendations in your reports.

Preparing a Preliminary Outline

Organize your study by preparing a detailed preliminary outline.

As you go through the factoring process, you may want to use an outline format to represent your ideas. Of course, if a few notes are enough to guide you through a short, informal report in memo form, perhaps an outline isn't necessary. However, a preliminary outline gives you a convenient frame of reference for your formal investigation. Furthermore, a detailed outline can definitely be worthwhile under certain circumstances:

- When you're one of several people working on an assignment
- When your investigation will be extensive and will involve many sources and types of data
- When you know from experience that the person who requested the study will revise the assignment during the course of your investigation and you want to keep track of the changes

Two widely used systems of outlining, the alphanumeric system and the decimal system, are illustrated in Figure 13.2. Both are perfectly acceptable, but some companies favor one method over the other. Many outlining programs for personal computers give you a choice and then help you switch from outline format to report format as you write.

Figure 13.2
Two Common Outline Formats

```
ALPHANUMERIC                        DECIMAL
I. _____           1.0 _____
   A. _____               1.1 _____
   B. _____               1.2 _____
      1. _____                  1.2.1 _____
      2. _____                  1.2.2 _____
         a. _____                     1.2.2.1 _____
         b. _____                     1.2.2.2 _____
      3. _____                  1.2.3 _____
   C. _____               1.3 _____
II. _____           2.0 _____
   A. _____               2.1 _____
      1. _____                  2.1.1 _____
         a. _____                     2.1.1.1 _____
         b. _____                     2.1.1.2 _____
      2. _____                  2.1.2 _____
      3. _____                  2.1.3 _____
   B. _____               2.2 _____
```

You usually write the headings at each level of your outline in the same grammatical form. In other words, if item I uses a verb, items II, III, and IV also use verbs. This parallel construction enables readers to see that the ideas are related, of similar importance, and on the same level of generality. It makes the outline a useful tool for establishing the table of contents and headings in your final report, and it is considered the correct format by most of the people who might review your outline. When wording the outline, you must also choose between descriptive (topical) and informative (talking) headings. As Table 13.1 indicates, descriptive headings label the subject that will be discussed, whereas informative headings (in either question or summary form) suggest more about the meaning of the issues.

Use the same grammatical form for each group of items in your outline.

Although outlines with informative headings take a little longer to write, they're generally more useful in guiding your work, especially if written in terms of the questions you plan to answer during your investigation. In addition, they're easier for others to review. If other people are going to comment on your outline, they may not have a very clear idea of what you mean by the descriptive heading "Advertising." However, they will get the main idea if you use the informative heading "Cuts in ad budget may explain sales decline."

Informative outlines are generally more helpful than descriptive outlines.

Remember that at this point you're only developing a preliminary outline to guide your investigation. Later on, when you've completed your research and are preparing a final outline or a table of contents for the report, you may want to switch from an outline of your questions to an outline that summarizes your findings.

Following the Rules of Division

Once you've prepared your outline, sit back for a minute and check it over. Ask yourself whether the structure is significant, consistent, exclusive, and complete:

Follow the rules of division to ensure that your study will be organized in a logical, systematic way.

- *Divide a topic into at least two parts.* A topic cannot be divided into only one part. For example, if you wanted to divide a topic such as "Alternatives for Improving Division Profits," you wouldn't look only at increasing sales. You would need at least one other subtopic, such as reducing production costs or decreasing employee absenteeism. If you were interested only in increasing sales, then that would be your topic, which you would probably divide into at least two subtopics.
- *Choose a significant, useful basis or guiding principle for the division.* You could subdivide production problems into two groups: problems that arise when the machines are turned off and problems that occur when the machines are turned on. However, this

Table 13.1	TYPES OF OUTLINE HEADINGS	

| | *Informative (Talking) Outline* | |
Descriptive (Topical) Outline	*Question Form*	*Summary Form*
I. Industry Characteristics	I. What is the nature of the industry?	I. Flour milling is a mature industry.
A. Annual sales	A. What are the annual sales?	A. Market is large.
B. Profitability	B. Is the industry profitable?	B. Profit margins are narrow.
C. Growth rate	C. What is the pattern of growth?	C. Growth is modest.
1. Sales	1. Sales growth?	1. Sales growth averages less than 3 percent a year.
2. Profit	2. Profit growth?	2. Growth in profits is flat.

basis for breaking down the subject would not be of much use to anyone. A better choice might be dividing the subject into problems caused by human error versus problems caused by machine failure.

- *When subdividing a whole into its parts, restrict yourself to one category at a time.* If you switch from one category to another, you get a mixed classification, which can confuse your analysis. Say you're subdividing your study of the market for toothpaste according to sales of fluoride versus nonfluoride brands. You would upset the investigation by adding another category to your analysis (such as sales broken down by geographical region). If you are dealing with a long, complex subject, you'll no doubt have to use several categories of division before you complete your work, but the shift from one category to another must be made at a logical point, after you've completed your study of a particular issue. For example, after you've looked at sales of fluoride versus nonfluoride toothpaste, you might then want to look at toothpaste sales by geographical location or socioeconomic group.
- *Make certain that each group is separate and distinct.* As you divide a topic into groups, those groups must be mutually exclusive, or you'll end up talking about the same item twice, under two separate headings. Subdividing a population into males, females, and teenagers wouldn't make any sense because the categories overlap.
- *Be thorough when listing all the components of a whole.* It would be misleading to subdivide an engine into parts without mentioning the pistons. An important part of the whole would be missing, and the resulting picture of the engine would be wrong.

Most important, of course, is whether your outline follows a logical flow when compared with your investigation and its results. For instance, if you're searching for cause-and-effect relationships, you might want to start with the observed effects and work backward to the causes in a logical manner.

TEP 3: PREPARING THE WORK PLAN

Once you've defined the problem and outlined the issues for analysis, you are ready to establish a work plan based on your preliminary outline. In business, most report writing situations involve a firm deadline with finite time and resources to get the job done. In other words, you not only have to produce quality reports, you have to do so quickly and efficiently. A carefully thought-out work plan is the best way to make sure you produce quality work on schedule.

If you are preparing this work plan for yourself, it can be relatively informal: a simple list of the steps you plan to take, an estimate of their sequence and timing, and a list of the sources of information you plan to use. If you're conducting a lengthy, formal study, however, you'll want to develop a detailed work plan that can guide the performance of many tasks over a span of time. Most proposals require a detailed work plan, which becomes the basis for a contract if the proposal is accepted. A formal work plan might include these elements (especially the first two):

Prepare a work plan that identifies the tasks you will perform.

- *Statement of the problem.* Include the problem statement so that anyone working with you is clear about the nature of the challenge you face. Including the problem statement can also help you stay focused on the core problem and avoid distractions that are likely to arise during your investigation and writing.
- *Statement of the purpose and scope of your investigation.* As you saw earlier in the chapter, your statement of purpose describes what you plan to accomplish with this report. The scope defines the boundaries of your work, explicitly stating which issues you will cover and which issues you won't cover. If you've ever misunderstood a homework assignment and delivered something that didn't meet expectations, you know how frustrating misunderstandings about expectations can be for both the writer and the reader. Particularly with complex, lengthy investigations, make sure that the task is clearly defined before you start. If it's possible and appropriate, verify your purpose and scope with your intended audience before starting. As with homework, you usually won't have time to rework business reports if you discover at the last minute that you're on the wrong track.
- *Discussion of the sequence of tasks to be accomplished.* Indicate sources of information, required research, and any constraints (on time, money, personnel, or data). For simple reports, the list of necessary tasks will be short and probably rather obvious. Longer reports and complex investigations, however, require thorough planning. You may need to reserve time with customers or executives or schedule outside services such as telephone researchers or print shops.
- *Description of the end products that will result from the investigation.* In many cases, the output of your efforts will be the report itself. In other cases, though, you'll need to produce something above and beyond a report, such as a new marketing plan, some improvements to a business process, or even a tangible product. As with the rest of your work plan, make sure these expectations are clear up front, and make sure you've scheduled enough time and resources to complete the job.
- *Review of project assignments, schedules, and resource requirements.* Indicate who will be responsible for what, when tasks will be completed, and how much the investigation will cost. You may also want to include a brief section on coordinating the writing and production of the report if more than one person will be involved. Collaborative writing has some important advantages over writing a report by yourself, of course, but making sure everyone works together productively can also be a challenge.
- *Plans for following up after the report is delivered.* Follow-up can range from something as simple as making sure people received the information they needed to something as complex as conducting additional research to evaluate the results of proposals contained in the report. Even if follow-up isn't required or expected, doing some informal follow-up can help you find ways to improve your future reports. Following up is also a good way to communicate to your audience that you care about the effectiveness of your work and the impact you can have on the organization.

Some work plans also include a tentative outline of the report (Figure 13.3). With a plan in place, you're ready to get to work, which usually means starting with research.

Over the years, Connie Chung has worked long hours on NBC, CBS, and now ABC. Her days are always full: meeting with network executives and affiliates, holding briefing sessions with researchers, interviewing subjects, planning story lineups for upcoming programs, taping broadcasts, and more. To coordinate the efforts of everyone involved in producing a program, says Chung, a detailed work plan is essential.

S TEP 4: CONDUCTING THE RESEARCH

The value of your report depends on the quality of the data it's based on. So when the time comes to gather facts and figures, your first concern is to get organized. If you're working alone on a project, getting organized may mean nothing more than setting up a file and checking out a few books and periodicals from the nearest library. If you're part of a team, you will work out your assignments and coordinate activities. Your work plan will be a big help during this research effort.

Figure 13.3
In-Depth Critique: Sample
Work Plan for a Formal Study

This work plan was developed for a report on whether to launch a company newsletter.

Problem statement is clear enough for anyone to understand without background research.

Statement of purpose is specific, delineating exactly what will be covered in the report.

Tasks to be accomplished are clearly laid out.

Although no description of the end product is included here, a preliminary outline is presented for guidance.

This plan includes no plans for following up, but it clearly states the assignments and the schedules for completing them.

STATEMENT OF THE PROBLEM

The rapid growth of our company over the past five years has reduced the sense of community among our staff. People no longer feel like part of an intimate organization where they matter as individuals.

PURPOSE AND SCOPE OF WORK

The purpose of this study is to determine whether a company newsletter would help rebuild employee identification with the organization. The study will evaluate the impact of newsletters in other companies and will attempt to identify features that might be desirable in our own newsletter. Such variables as length, frequency of distribution, types of articles, and graphic design will be considered. Costs will be estimated for several approaches. In addition, the study will analyze the personnel and the procedures required to produce a newsletter.

SOURCES AND METHODS OF DATA COLLECTION

Sample newsletters will be collected from 50 companies similar to ours in size, growth rate, and types of employees. The editors will be asked to comment on the impact of their publications on employee morale. Our own employees will be surveyed to determine their interest in a newsletter and their preferences for specific features. Production procedures and costs will be analyzed through conversations with newsletter editors and printers.

PRELIMINARY OUTLINE

I. Do newsletters affect morale?
   A. Do people read them?
   B. How do employees benefit?
   C. How does the company benefit?
II. What are the features of good newsletters?
   A. How long are they?
   B. What do they contain?
   C. How often are they published?
   D. How are they designed?
III. How should a newsletter be produced?
   A. Should it be written, edited, and printed internally?
   B. Should it be written internally and printed outside?
   C. Should it be totally produced outside?
IV. What would a newsletter cost?
   A. What would the personnel costs be?
   B. What would the materials costs be?
   C. What would outside services cost?
V. Should we publish a company newsletter?
VI. If so, what approach should we take?

WORK PLAN

Collect/analyze newsletters	09/01-09/14
Interview editors by phone	09/16-09/20
Survey employees	09/14-09/28
Develop sample	09/28-10/05
Develop cost estimates	10/07-10/10
Prepare report	10/10-10/24
Submit final report	10/25

Work plans contain a list of the sources you'll consult. *Primary sources* of information provide, as the name implies, firsthand information that is collected for your report's specific purpose. In contrast, *secondary sources* of information have been previously collected for other purposes.[6] Most business reports call for a mix of both secondary and primary sources. However, you're likely to find that much of what you need to know has never been collected, so you'll have to conduct your own research. For example, you probably wouldn't locate much existing information on what Harley-Davidson dealerships should look like. Reliance on primary sources is one of the main differences between business reports and school reports. Even so, business report writers begin by researching secondary sources.

Consult primary and secondary sources of information.

Reviewing Secondary Sources

Even though you may plan to rely heavily on primary sources, it's a good idea to begin your study with a thorough review of the information that has already been collected. By searching the literature, you avoid the embarrassment of failing to report something that's common knowledge. You also save yourself the trouble of studying something that has already been done. Once you gain a feel for the structure of the subject, you can decide what additional research will be required.

Conduct secondary research by locating information that has already been collected, usually in the form of books, periodicals, and reports.

Finding Sources

Depending on your subject, you may find useful information in general reference works, popular publications, or government documents. CD-ROM products now offer a wide variety of research materials, from product databases to nationwide phone directories. You can also search online databases via the Internet or using services such as Dialog (a gateway to more than 450 databases). As you learned in Chapter 4, the Internet offers a variety of search and retrieval tools to help you find articles, research reports, Web sites, and other sources of information (Figure 13.4).

In addition, each field of business has a handful of specialized references that are considered indispensable. You'll quickly come to know these sources once you've joined a particular industry. In addition, don't overlook internal sources. Often the most useful references are company reports, memos, and information stored in the company's databases. Also check company brochures, newsletters, and annual reports to shareholders.

If you're working for a large organization with a company library, you may have the help of a professional librarian in identifying and obtaining other useful materials for your investigation. If not, look for the nearest public library or university library, and ask the librarians there for help. Reference librarians are trained to know where to find just about everything, and many of them are pleased to help people pursue obscure information.

GOING ONLINE
SEARCH THOUSANDS OF FULL-TEXT ARTICLES INSTANTLY
The Electronic Library's easily searchable database contains more than 150 full-text newspapers; 900 full-text magazines; national and international newswires; 2,000 literary works; over 18,000 photos, images, and maps; television and radio transcripts; and movie and software reviews. Use it free for a month. All materials can be downloaded and printed for your immediate use.

http://www.elibrary.com

Choosing and Using Sources

When it comes to choosing your references, be selective. Avoid dated or biased material. If possible, check on who collected the data, the methods they used, their qualifications, and their professional reputations.[7] Common sense will help you judge the credibility of the sources you plan to use. Ask yourself the following questions about each piece of material:

- *Does the source have a reputation for honesty and reliability?* Naturally, you'll feel most comfortable using information from a source that has established a reputation for accuracy. But even a good reputation doesn't mean you should let your guard down completely; even the finest reporters and editors make mistakes.
- *Is the source potentially biased?* Some of the information you'll find in your research will have been produced and distributed by people or organizations with a particular point of view. Bias isn't necessarily bad; in fact, getting people to believe one thing and not another is the purpose of much of the world's communication efforts. If you gather some facts from the Tobacco Institute or the American Association of Retired Persons, you have a fairly clear idea of what these organizations stand for and what biases their

Ask questions about the reference works you use:
- Are they up-to-date?
- Are they objective?
- Who collected the data? How?
- What are the authors' qualifications and reputations?

Figure 13.4
Using Search Engines on the Internet

If you can think of a research topic, chances are good that there's information about it on the Internet. However, searching for that information can be frustrating if you don't know where or how to look. *Search engines* are Internet research tools that can help you identify and screen resources.

A search engine travels the Web, indexes documents it finds on Web sites, and places those documents in a database. When you enter key words or phrases to be searched, the engine scans its database and returns all documents or "hits" that contain a match. Effective searches often require linking key words together. *Boolean search operators*, such as *AND, WITH, NEAR, OR*, and *NOT*, can help you limit or expand your search. For example, if you searched for "Ford AND automobiles," you would receive documents that contain both words. Entering "Ford WITH automobiles" would retrieve documents in which the words appear beside each other. Entering "Ford NEAR automobiles" would return hits where the two words appear close to each other. Searching for "Ford OR automobiles," would return documents containing at least one, but not necessarily both words. And if you entered "Ford NOT automobiles" you would see all documents that refer to Ford but do not mention automobiles. The NOT operator can be especially effective for limiting unwanted hits. Most search engines recognize Boolean search operators, although some substitute symbols, such as plus and minus signs, to achieve the same results.

Each engine has qualities that distinguish it from the others. Some engines index all the pages they find. Others index only the most popular pages. Many will also search Usenet newsgroups instead of Web sites, depending on which one you specify when you enter your query. And each search engine updates it database on its own schedule. Scheduling differences create great variation in search results. It is always best, therefore, to try your search on several engines. Yahoo!, Infoseek, Alta Vista, Excite, Open Text, and Cyber411 are a few of the more popular search engines available. There are many others, however, some of which are designed for locating specific types of information.

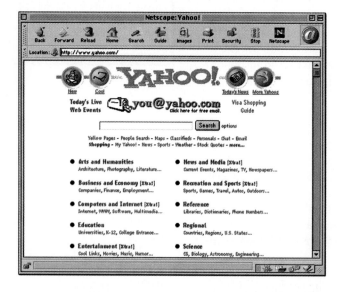

Yahoo! <http://www.yahoo.com/> is actually called a *Web directory* because it files all of its documents in categories. It works best when you want to locate many similar sites under a particular subject or title. Yahoo! supports case-sensitive matching, which can be very helpful when you are searching for documents containing proper names. For example, by entering "China," you are assured of receiving only documents that refer to the country, and not to porcelain dishes. The documents that Yahoo! returns are given priority when key words appear either in the title or multiple times in the text. Also, general categories are ranked higher than narrowly focused categories.

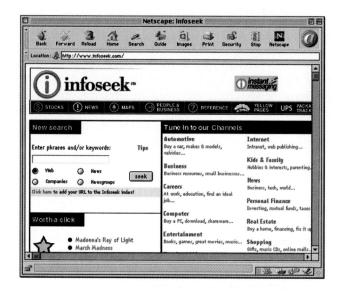

Infoseek <http://www.infoseek.com> has a reputation for consistently finding the most relevant Web sites. It ranks sites by the proximity of the search terms to each other within the document. With Infoseek, you can search for documents by their title, Internet address (URL), or text. The engine also supports case-sensitive searches and searching by phrases. In addition to its search engine capabilities, Infoseek maintains a web directory similar to Yahoo!'s. Infoseek excels at bringing you specific information without making you wade through a lot of irrelevant documents.

Alta Vista <http://www.altavista.com/> is commonly known as having the largest search engine database on the Web. It claims to contain well over 20 million pages. This distinction makes it the engine of choice when you want the most comprehensive results or when you are searching for obscure information. Alta Vista allows you to limit your returns by date or by instructing the engine to prioritize documents that contain particular words.

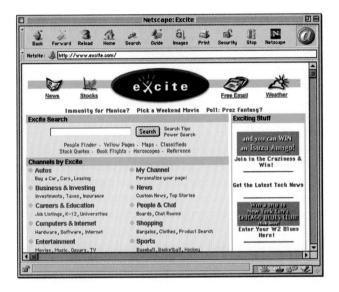

Excite <http://www.excite.com> is known for having the broadest search capabilities and one of the most up-to-date databases of any search engine. Excite maintains a Web directory and is capable of searching by phrases. In addition, it allows you to sort the hits by the number of pages they contain so that you may identify the documents that hold the most information. However, Excite ranks its hits by popularity, as determined by the number of links that point to each site. Consequently, the most relevant hits might not be retrieved first. Excite performs best with mainstream topics that are widely discussed.

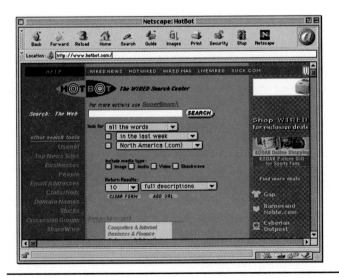

HotBot <http:/www.hotbot.com> recently earned *PC Magazine's* Editor's Choice award for search indexes. That's not surprising, as HotBot offers more search options than any other search engine on the Net. HotBot allows you to limit your searches to exact matches or near matches by specifying parameters using convenient dropdown menus. You can also direct the engine to search by domain, such as com, org, and edu, or by specific geographical locations such as Europe, Asia, and Africa. HotBot has the other search engines beat on currency, too, claiming to re-index about 110 million pages every two weeks. You can even direct HotBot to search only the most recently published pages. And HotBot's new NewsBot feature gives you one-stop access to all the latest stories from the Web's top news sites.

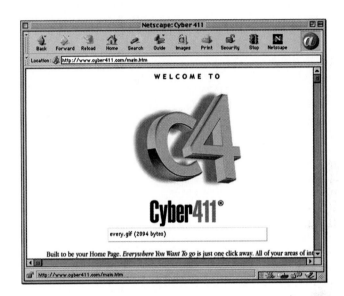

Cyber411 <http://www.cyber411.com> is a *metasearch engine*, searching 15 major search engines at once, including all of those described here. This broad approach can make your search much more efficient when you are looking for large amounts of information. However, Cyber411's search parameters are not very complex. Consequently, you may also want to search individual engines if you are looking for a very focused topic.

Regardless of which search engine you choose, your results will be best if you spend a few minutes becoming acquainted with it before initiating your search. Each engine has a "tips" or "help" page that explains which operators it uses, whether it recognizes misspellings, whether case-sensitivity is supported, how it ranks pages for relevancy, and whether it is capable of searching phrases. You should also become acquainted with each engine's advanced search capabilities, because they will usually bring the best hits. Getting to know each engine's strengths and weaknesses at the start of your search can save you a lot of time and frustration down the road.

You can obtain more information about search engines by going to Search Engine Watch <http://www.searchenginewatch.com>. This site discusses how search engines work and provides live links to dozens of different types of search engines, including news and specialty search engines. You'll also find search engine reviews and resources, as well as techniques for conducting advanced searches.

messages may have. However, organizations with neutral names, such as the Heritage Foundation, People for the American Way, or the U.S. Committee for Energy Awareness, aren't as easy to categorize. Without knowing what these organizations stand for, you're at their mercy when it comes to interpreting the information they produce. Also, an organization's source of funding may influence its information output. Again, there is nothing inherently unethical about this type of reporting; you just need to be aware of it when you interpret the information.

- *Where did the source get its information?* Many secondary sources are themselves derived from other sources, making you even further removed from the original information. If a newspaper article says that pollutants in a local river dropped by 50 percent in the last year, chances are the reporter who wrote the article didn't make those measurements directly. He or she got the number from someone else.
- *Can you verify the material independently?* A good way to uncover mistakes or biases is to search for the same information from another source. Verifying material can be particularly important when the information goes beyond simple facts to include projections, interpretations, and estimates.
- *Will the source's claims stand up to thoughtful scrutiny?* Finally, step back and ask yourself whether the things you read or hear make sense. If a researcher claims that the market for a particular product will triple in the next five years, ask yourself what will have to happen for that prediction to come true. Will three times as many customers buy the product? Will existing customers buy three times as much as they currently buy? Why?

Stop when you reach the point at which additional effort provides little new information.

You probably won't have time to conduct a thorough background check on all your sources, so focus your efforts on the most important or most suspicious pieces of information.

The amount of library research you do depends on the subject you're studying and the purpose of your investigation. Linda Moreno conducted fairly extensive research, both to analyze Electrovision's expense problems and to find potential solutions. Because travel costs are a concern to so many companies, business newspapers and magazines publish quite a few articles on the subject.

Regardless of the amount of research you do, retain complete and accurate notes on the sources of all the material you collect, using one of the systems explained in Appendix B, "Documentation of Report Sources." Documenting your sources through footnotes, endnotes, or some similar system lends credibility to your report. It also helps you steer clear of plagiarism.

Collecting Primary Data

Conduct primary research by collecting information yourself.

When the information you need is not available from secondary sources, you collect and interpret the data yourself by doing primary research, going out into the real world to gather information through your own efforts. The four main ways of collecting primary data are examining documents, making observations, surveying people, and conducting experiments.

Documents

Documentary evidence and historical records are sources of primary data.

In business a great deal of information is filed away for future reference. By scouring a company's files, you can often piece together an accurate, factual, historical record from the tidbits of evidence revealed in various letters, memos, and reports. Philadelphia National Bank has cataloged five generations of correspondence so that its senior managers can understand past events and operations. By researching the bank's previous positions on certain issues or by studying the roots of company trends, managers can gain valuable insight into current problems and situations.[8]

Business documents that qualify as primary data include sales reports prepared by field representatives, balance sheets and income statements, policy statements, correspondence with customers and suppliers, contracts, and log books. Many government and legal documents are also primary sources because they represent a decision made by the people who were present at some official proceeding.

A single document may be both a secondary source and a primary source. When citing summaries of financial and operations data from an annual report, you're using it as a secondary source. That same report, however, would be considered a primary source if you were analyzing its design features or comparing it with annual reports from other years or other companies.

Observations

Informal observations are a rather common source of primary data in business. You simply use your five senses (especially your eyes and ears) to gather information. For instance, many reports are based on the writer's visiting a facility and observing operations. More objective information can be gathered through formal observations, which give observers a structure for noting what they see, thereby minimizing opportunities for interpretation.

In general, observation is a useful technique when you're studying objects, physical activities, processes, the environment, or human behavior. However, it can be expensive and time consuming, and the value of the observation depends on the reliability of the observer. Many people have a tendency to see what they want to see or to interpret events in light of their own experience. However, if the observer is trustworthy and has proper instructions, observation can provide valuable insights.[9]

Surveys

Often the best way to obtain answers to your questions is to ask people with relevant experience and opinions. Such surveys include everything from conducting a single interview to distributing thousands of questionnaires.

When you need specialized information that hasn't been recorded anywhere, you may want to conduct a personal interview with an expert, which is the simplest form of survey. Many experts come from the ranks of your own organization: people from other departments who have specialized knowledge, your predecessor in the job, long-time employees who have seen it all. On occasion you may also want to talk with outsiders who have some special expertise.

Doing an interview may seem an easy way to get information, but it requires careful preparation. You don't want to waste anyone's time, and you want your efforts to be productive. Chapter 17 presents some helpful pointers on conducting effective interviews.

Although they have the same purpose, interviews are quite different from formal, large-scale surveys in which a sample population answers a series of carefully tested questions. In Linda Moreno's work at Electrovision, she needed to know why people were traveling and whether there were suitable alternatives to frequent travel.

A formal survey requires a number of important decisions:

- Will face-to-face interviews, phone calls, printed questionnaires, or computer-based surveys be most useful?
- How many individuals will you contact to get results that are *reliable* (that is, reproducible if the same study were repeated)? Who will those people be? What sample is an accurate reflection of the population?
- What specific questions will you ask to get a *valid* picture (a true reflection of the group's feelings on the subject)?[10]

Your answers to these questions have a profound effect on the results of your survey.

Having seen rival preelection polls that come up with conflicting projections of who's going to win, you may wonder whether it makes sense to rely on survey results at all. The answer is it does, as long as you understand the nature of surveys. For one thing, surveys reveal only what people think about something at a specific time. For another, pollsters ask various people different questions in various ways and, not surprisingly, get differing answers. Just because surveys produce differing results doesn't mean that surveys are a poor form of research. Conducting a reliable, valid survey is not easy. Generally speaking, it helps to have the advice of a specialist.

Observation applies your five sense and your judgment to the investigation.

Steve Jobs co-founded and still serves Apple Computer, although he's also involved with NeXT, a software development company. Jobs sees an added dimension to researching what customers want: technology. He cautions that customers are unable to foresee what technology can do, so in addition to asking customers what they want, it's important to acquaint them with what's possible.

A formal survey is a way of finding out what a cross section of people thinks about something.

Two important research criteria are
- Reliability—when the same results would be obtained if the research were repeated
- Validity—when research measures what it is intended to measure

One of the most crucial elements of a survey is the questionnaire. To develop one, begin by listing the points you're trying to determine. Then break these points into specific questions, choosing an appropriate type of question for each point (Figure 13.5 shows some variations). The following guidelines will help you produce valid results:

Developing an effective questionnaire requires care and skill.

- *Provide clear instructions.* Respondents need to know exactly how to fill out the questionnaire.
- *Keep the questionnaire short and easy to answer.* People are most likely to respond if they can complete the questionnaire within 10 or 15 minutes. So ask only questions that are relevant to your research. In addition, don't ask questions that require too much work on the respondent's part. People aren't willing to dig up the answers to questions like "What was your monthly rate of water consumption in 1996?"
- *Formulate questions that provide easily tabulated or analyzed answers.* Numbers and facts are easier to deal with than opinions are. Nevertheless, you may be able to elicit countable opinions with multiple-choice questions or to group open-ended opinions into a limited number of categories.
- *Avoid questions that lead to a particular answer, because they bias your survey.* Harley-Davidson would gain little useful information by asking customers, "Do you prefer that our dealerships stay open on Sundays for your convenience?" The question obviously calls for a yes answer. A less biased question would be: "What day of the week are you most likely to visit one of our dealerships?"
- *Ask only one thing at a time.* A compound question like "Do you read books and magazines regularly?" doesn't allow for the respondent who reads one but not the other.
- *Avoid questions with vague or abstract words.* Instead of asking "Are you frequently troubled by colds?" ask, "How many colds did you have in the past 12 months?"
- *Include a few questions that rephrase earlier questions.* Such questions will help you cross-check the validity of respondents' answers.
- *Pretest the questionnaire.* Have a sample group identify questions that are subject to misinterpretation.[11]

If you're mailing your questionnaire, rather than administering it in person, include a persuasive cover letter that explains why you're conducting the research. Try to convince the person that her or his response is important to you. If possible, offer to share the results with the respondent. Mention that you won't disclose information that can identify individual respondents. Include a preaddressed envelope with prepaid postage so that the respondent won't have to find an envelope or postage to return the questionnaire to you. Remember, however, that even under the best of circumstances you may not get more than a 10 to 20 percent response.

Computer-based interviewing (CBI) can be an excellent way to gather and analyze data. Two big advantages of CBI are real-time customization (the computer can change the flow and content of the interview on the basis of each person's answers) and the ability to automatically sort and compile data during the interview. Computer-based interviewing can be conducted in several ways, including mailing survey disks or inviting people to respond at an Internet Web site. TK Associates International is a consulting firm in Portland, Oregon, that helps U.S. companies market to Japanese consumers and businesses, and it has used its Web site to conduct a survey of more than 2,000 Japanese computer users.[12] This application of CBI was particularly helpful because the company was researching Web-based marketing opportunities.

Experiments

Experiments are far more common in technical fields than in general business. That's because an experiment requires extensive manipulation of the factors involved, which is often very expensive (and may even be unethical when people are one of the factors). Nevertheless, experiments do have their place. Say you want to find out whether a change in lighting levels increases the productivity of the pattern cutters in your dress-

Question Type	Example
OPEN-ENDED	How would you describe the flavor of this ice cream?
EITHER-OR	Do you think this ice cream is too rich? _____ Yes _____ No
MULTIPLE-CHOICE	Which description best fits the taste of this ice cream? (Choose only one.) a. Delicious b. Too fruity c. Too sweet d. Too intensely flavored e. Bland f. Stale
SCALE	Please make an X on the scale to indicate how you perceive the texture of this ice cream. $\longleftarrow\longrightarrow$ Too light Light Creamy Too creamy
CHECKLIST	Which flavors of ice cream have you had in the past 12 months? (Check all that apply.) _____ Vanilla _____ Chocolate _____ Strawberry _____ Chocolate chip _____ Coffee
RANKING	Rank these flavors in order of your preference, from 1 (most preferred) to 5 (least preferred): _____ Vanilla _____ Cherry _____ Maple nut _____ Chocolate ripple _____ Coconut
SHORT-ANSWER	In the past month, how many times did you buy ice cream in the supermarket? _____ In the past month, how many times did you buy ice cream in ice cream shops? _____

Figure 13.5
Types of Survey Questions

making business. The most objective approach is to conduct an experiment using two groups of cutters: one working under existing conditions and the other working under the new lighting.

When conducting an experiment, it's important to carefully control the factors (called variables) you're not testing. Thus, in the lighting experiment, for the results to be valid, the only difference between the two groups and their environments should be the lighting. Otherwise, differences in productivity could be attributed to such factors as age differences between the two groups or experience on the job. It's even possible that introducing any change in the pattern cutters' environment, whether it be lighting or something else entirely, is enough to increase their productivity.

The aim when conducting an experiment is to keep all variables the same except for the one you're testing.

 STEP 5: ANALYZING AND INTERPRETING DATA

After you've completed your research, you're ready to analyze your data and interpret the findings. The analytical process is essentially a search for relationships among the facts and

Analyze your results by calculating statistics, drawing reasonable and logical conclusions, and, if appropriate, developing a set of recommendations.

bits of evidence you've compiled. By themselves, the data you've collected won't offer much meaning or insight. It's the *analysis* of these facts and the *interpretation of the findings* that give you the information you need in order to understand or solve a problem.

Looking at the data from various angles, you attempt to detect patterns that will enable you to answer the questions outlined in your work plan. Your mind begins to fit pieces together and to form tentative conclusions. As your analysis proceeds, you either verify or reject each conclusion. Your mind constantly filters, sorts, and combines ideas, so this is where your critical thinking skills will be put to the test.

Calculating Statistics

Much of the information you compile during the research phase will be in numerical form. If data have been collected carefully, this information is precise, measurable, and objective—and therefore credible. However, raw statistics are of little practical value. The numbers must be manipulated so that you and your readers can interpret their significance.

Averages

Figure 13.6
Three Types of Averages: Mean, Median, and Mode

Sales-person	Sales	
Wilson	$ 3,000	
Green	5,000	
Carrick	6,000	
Wimper	7,000	Mean
Keeble	7,500	Median
Kemble	8,500	
O'Toole	8,500	Mode
Mannix	8,500	
Caruso	9,000	
Total	$63,000	

The same set of data can be used to produce three kinds of averages: mean, median, and mode.

One useful way of looking at data is to find the **average,** which is a number that represents a group of numbers. Consider the data presented in Figure 13.6, for example, showing the sales booked by a group of nine salespeople over one week. To analyze this information, you could calculate the average—but which average? Depending on how you planned to use the data, you could choose the mean, the median, or the mode.

The most commonly used average is the *mean,* or the sum of all the items in the group divided by the number of items in the group. The mean is useful when you want to compare one item or individual with the group. In the example, the mean is $7,000. If you were the sales manager, you might well be interested in knowing that Wimper's sales were average; that Wilson, Green, and Carrick had below-average sales; and that Keeble, Kemble, O'Toole, Mannix, and Caruso's sales were above average. One problem with using the mean, however, is that it can give you a false picture if one of the numbers is extreme. Say that Caruso's sales for the week were $27,000. The mean would then be $9,000, and eight of the nine salespeople would be performing "below average."

The *median* is the "middle of the road" average: It's found in the midpoint of a series.[13] Above and below the median are an equal number of items. In a numerical ranking like the one shown in Figure 13.6, the median is the number right in the middle of the list: $7,500. The median is useful when one (or a few) of the numbers is extreme. For example, even if Caruso's sales were $27,000, the median would still be $7,500.

The *mode* is the number that occurs more often than any other in your sample.[14] It's the best average for answering a question such as "What is the usual amount?" If you wanted to know what level of sales was most common, you would answer with the mode, which is $8,500. Like the median, the mode is not affected by extreme values. It's much easier to find than the median, however, when you have a large number of items or individuals.

While you're analyzing averages, you should also consider the *range,* or the spread of a series of numbers. In the example, the fact that sales per person ranged from $3,000 to $9,000 may raise the question of why there is such a wide gap between Wilson's performance and Caruso's. A range tells you the context in which the averages were calculated and demonstrates what values are possible.

Trends

If you were overseeing the work of Wilson, Caruso, and the other salespeople, you might be tempted to make some important personnel decisions on the basis of the week's sales figures. You would be a lot smarter, however, to compare them with sales figures from other weeks, looking for a **trend,** a steady upward or downward movement in a pattern of events taking place over time. By examining the pattern over a number of weeks, you could begin to see which salespeople were consistently above average and which were consistently below. You could also see whether sales for the group as a whole were increasing, declining, or remaining steady and whether there were any seasonal fluctuations in the sales pattern.

This type of trend analysis is very common in business. By looking at data over a period of time, you can detect patterns and relationships that will help you answer important questions.

Trend analysis involves an examination of data over time so that patterns and relationships can be detected.

Correlations

Once you have identified a trend, look for the cause. Say that Caruso consistently produces the most sales. You would undoubtedly be curious about the secret of her success. Does she call on her customers more often? Is she a more persuasive person? Does she have larger accounts or a bigger sales territory? Is she simply more experienced than the others?

To answer these questions, you could look for a **correlation,** a statistical relationship between two or more variables. For example, if salespeople with the largest accounts consistently produced the highest sales, you might assume that these two factors were correlated, or related in a predictable way. You might conclude that Caruso's success was due, at least in part, to the average size of her accounts.

A correlation is a statistical relationship between two or more variables.

However, your conclusion might be wrong. Correlations are useful evidence, but they do not necessarily prove a cause-and-effect relationship. Caruso's success might well be the result of several other factors. To know for sure, you would have to collect more evidence.

Drawing Conclusions

Regardless of how much evidence you amass, at some point in every analysis you move beyond hard facts that can be objectively measured and verified. When you reach that point, you begin to formulate a **conclusion,** which is a logical interpretation of what the facts in your report mean. Reaching good conclusions based on the evidence at hand is one of the most important skills you can develop for your business career. A sound conclusion meets the following criteria:

Conclusions are interpretations about what the facts mean.

- *It fulfills the original statement of purpose.* After all, this is why you took on the project in the first place.
- *It is based strictly on the information included in the rest of the report.* In other words, the conclusion must consider all the information in the report and no information not included in the report. While drawing a conclusion, you can introduce no new information. (If it's important, it should be in the body of the report.) Nor can you ignore any information in your report that doesn't support your conclusion.
- *It is logical.* People sometimes toss the word *logical* into a conversation without thinking much about its true meaning. For the purposes of writing a business report, a logical conclusion is one that follows accepted patterns of reasoning.

As education manager for the San Diego Wild Animal Park, Deirdre Ballou was part of the enthusiastic group developing a proposal for the Heart of Africa project that just couldn't be refused. Ballou and her colleagues thoroughly researched statistics published by zoo and museum professional organizations. "Committees and board members respect (and will listen to) people who have done their homework," says Ballou.

Reasoning falls into two distinct categories. With **inductive reasoning,** you arrive at a general conclusion after analyzing many specific pieces of evidence. If every one of your stores experienced a sales decline during a recent blizzard (specific evidence), you could reasonably conclude that harsh weather can have a negative effect on sales (general conclusion).

Deductive reasoning, in contrast, works from general principles to specific conclusions. This includes the classic form of argumentation called a syllogism, in which you state a general principle (the major premise), then a specific case (the minor premise), and then draw a conclusion based on the relationship of the two premises. Say that you study employee productivity problems and discover that radios distract some employees from their work. If you were to conclude that radios are affecting productivity, you could construct a syllogism such as this:

BEHIND THE SCENES AT GANNETT COMPANY
Getting the Scoop on a Media Giant

Sheila J. Gibbons is director of public affairs for Gannett Company, the nation's largest newspaper publisher. Gannett owns 118 newspapers, including *USA Today*, as well as 10 television stations and 16 radio stations. In the course of a year, Gibbons's department compiles and publishes a half dozen in-depth reports for higher management.

"We're working on one right now," says Gibbons, "a 'white paper' analyzing media coverage of Gannett. Management wants a 'big-picture' assessment of how the outside world looks at us. The various newspapers, electronic media, and magazines are all being reviewed—everything that has appeared about us in the last 12 months."

When planning the report, Gibbons considers issues such as (1) how Gannett is perceived by the public and (2) how those perceptions are affected by Gannett's being both a large corporation and a media company. Says Gibbons: "First, we don't know a lot about the public perception of Gannett. Many see us as *USA Today*, so if you mention *USA Today* and Gannett, people connect them. But if you mention Gannett alone, they don't necessarily connect it with *USA Today*. We want to know what implications this has for Gannett. Second, attitudes about large corporations tend to shift back and forth between positive and negative, and people tend to vary how much or how little they trust the media. Because our company

is both large and media-concerned, we are curious about how all these factors affect public perceptions of Gannett."

"So far, we're only in the information-gathering stage," points out Gibbons, who has taken an unusual approach to the research for this report. "I've given part of that assignment to our college intern. She is reviewing data, looking for themes and a consistency of views. She is not 'of Gannett,' so she won't be biased by our philosophy and corporate culture. Another staff member is looking into the impact of image campaigns that have been launched by other large corporations."

Whenever she works with college interns or with new staff members, Gibbons asks them first to review files and old reports and to take note of the various forms such communication has taken in the past. "That's the best way to learn how the company communicates," says Gibbons. In other words, get to know your audience through background reading.

The shape of the final report is beginning to emerge. Gibbons says she'll "use a cover to make it stand out from routine paperwork, followed by a title page and an executive summary written as an inverted pyramid. In all, there will be about ten pages of text, normal for our long reports. Any illustrations will go in the appendix. I'll probably not do a bibliography for this particular report. First, we're looking at everything that's been written or said about us in a one-year period, so any bibliography will be extensive. Second, the intended audience will be looking for a short assessment of an important issue. My

---

Major premise: Things that distract employees reduce productivity (general principle).

Minor premise: Radios are distracting employees (specific case).

Conclusion: Therefore, radios reduce productivity.

To support your conclusion, you have to be able to demonstrate that both premises are true. In addition, you need to consider cause-and-effect relationships. Maybe it's not radios themselves that are distracting people but the fact that employees argue constantly about which stations to listen to. The music may in fact help relieve stress or boredom, if only you could get people to agree.

Conclusions need to be logical, but this doesn't mean they automatically flow from the evidence. Most business decisions require assumptions and judgment; relatively few are based strictly on the facts. Your personal values or the organization's values may also influence your conclusions; just be sure that you are conscious of how these biases may be affecting your judgment. Nor can you expect members of a team to examine the evidence and all arrive at the same conclusion. One of the key reasons for bringing additional people into a decision is to gain the value of their unique perspectives and experiences.

Developing Recommendations

Drawing a conclusion is one thing; deciding what to do about it and then recommending action is another. Recommendations are inappropriate in a report when you're not expected to supply them, so be sure you know the difference between conclusions and recommendations. Recall that a conclusion is an opinion or interpretation of what the facts

USA Today *is just one of the dozens of newspapers, television stations, and radio stations owned by Gannett Company, and as Gannet's director of public affairs, Sheila Gibbons plans, prepares, and publishes numerous reports every year.*

job is to simplify the complexities. The language will be kept simple to encourage readership, and the report will be concise and tightly written to benefit the time-pressured executives who will receive it. One other thing: There will be no typos."

This report, like others Gibbons prepares, will go to her boss, the vice president of public affairs and government relations, and from there to selected Gannett executives. Although this particular report will be unusual, Gibbons expects all members of the management committee to read it and give her a response.

"All our reports are analytical reports. Each has a portion that leads to recommendations for further action." Small-group conferences (usually four or five people) meet to hash over the findings and recommendations, and Gibbons gets feedback from them. "In this case, there will no doubt be a lot of discussion," Gibbons speculates. "The conference will address whether there is anything we should do to improve the way others see us, report on us, and so forth." The result may well be additional projects for Gibbons's department during the coming year.

Apply Your Knowledge

1. Sheila Gibbons points out that one of the biggest worries for anyone doing long reports is that the report may not see the "light of day." List the circumstances that might lead to a long report's being tabled before it can be read. If you're responsible for the preparation of such a report, what could you do to prevent the circumstances you've listed?

2. If you were the intern Sheila Gibbons assigned to research how other media report on Gannett, how would you define the scope of your task? How many examples of each of the media—press, electronic media, magazines—would you include? For instance, among television stations, would you cover only the major networks? All nationally available cable channels? Or some combination of these? How would you decide the combination? Answer similar questions for the press and magazines. Would you recommend that Gibbons report the findings by media group? By broad theme? By issues uncovered? Why?

---

mean; a **recommendation** suggests what ought to be done about the facts. Here's an example of the difference:

> Recommendations are suggestions for action.

CONCLUSION	RECOMMENDATION
I conclude that on the basis of its track record and current price, this company is an attractive buy.	I recommend that we write a letter to the president offering to buy the company at a 10 percent premium over the market value of its stock.

When you've been asked to take the final step and translate your conclusions into recommendations, be sure to make the relationship between them clear. Keep in mind that your assumptions and personal values may enter into your recommendations, but to be credible they must be based on logical analysis and sound conclusions.

When you develop recommendations of your own, consider whether your suggestions are practical and acceptable to your readers; they're the people who have to make the recommendations work. Be certain that you have adequately described the steps that come next. Don't leave your readers scratching their heads and saying, "This all sounds good, but what do I do on Monday morning?"

> Good recommendations are
> - Practical
> - Acceptable to readers
> - Explained in enough detail for readers to take action

Preparing the Final Outline

Once you've completed your research and analysis, you can prepare the final outline of the report. Sometimes you can use the preliminary outline that guided your research as a fi-

> The final outline of the report should be geared to your purpose and the audience's probable reaction.

nal blueprint for the report. More often, however, you have to rework it to take into account your purpose, your audience's probable reactions, and the things you learned during your study. As already mentioned, informational reports are generally organized around topics suggested by the information itself, such as steps in a process, divisions of a company, or results in various geographical areas. Analytical reports, on the other hand, are organized around conclusions or recommendations if the audience is receptive, and around problem-solving approaches if the audience is skeptical or hostile. The placement of conclusions and recommendations depends on the audience's probable response. Put them up front if you expect a positive reaction, toward the end if you anticipate resistance.

The final outline is phrased so that the points on the outline can serve as the headings that appear in the report. Bear in mind that the phrasing of the headings will affect the tone of the report. If you want a hard-hitting, direct tone, use informative phrasing. If you prefer an objective, indirect tone, use descriptive phrasing. Be sure to use parallel construction when wording the points on the outline.

Visual aid: Illustration in tabular, graphic, schematic, or pictorial form.

Once you have an outline in mind, you can begin to identify which points can be, and should be, illustrated with visual aids—tables, graphs, schematic drawings, or photographs. (See Chapter 14 for more details on visual aids.) Ask yourself whether there is some way to visually dramatize the key elements of your message. You might approach the problem as though you were writing a picture book or making a movie. Think of each main point on your outline as a separate scene. Your job is to think of a "picture," a chart or graph, that will communicate that point to the audience.

Then take your analysis a step further. Undoubtedly, some of the supporting items on your outline involve the presentation of detailed facts and figures. This sort of information may be confusing and tedious when presented in paragraph form. Often the best approach is to display it in a table, which arrays the data in a convenient format. You might want to use flowcharts, drawings, or photographs to clarify physical relationships or procedures.

Use visual aids to simplify, clarify, and emphasize important information.

When planning the illustrations for your report or presentation, aim to achieve a reasonable balance between the verbal and the visual. The ideal blend depends on the nature of the subject. Some topics are more graphic than others and require more visual aids. But remember that illustrating every point dilutes the effectiveness of all your visual aids. In a written report, particularly, too many visuals can be a problem. If readers are told in every paragraph or two to consult a table or chart, they are likely to lose the thread of the argument you are trying to make. Furthermore, readers tend to assume that the amount of space allocated to a topic indicates its relative importance. If you use visual aids to illustrate a minor point, you may be sending a misleading message about its significance.

O n the Job

SOLVING A COMMUNICATION DILEMMA AT HARLEY-DAVIDSON

Harley-Davidson had regained its reputation for building dependable motorcycles, but higher demand had created two new problems for CEO Richard Teerlink: how to increase production and boost sales without sacrificing quality and how to stay on top in a world where mammoth motorcycles have become status items. The crux of Harley's new problem was that many customers simply aren't willing to wait two years for a motorcycle. Teerlink refused to risk disappointing Harley customers by compromising quality for quantity. To keep Harley on track toward higher sales, he and his management team needed to collect and analyze mountains of information, much of it in the form of reports.

One key to Harley's stunning turnaround in the late 1980s and early 1990s was its revamped manufacturing process. After analyzing information on Honda's manufacturing processes, the Harley staff had installed a system of inventory management known as just-in-time (JIT). Similar systems have propelled some of the world's leading manufacturers to success. By lowering the number of parts and supplies held in waiting, JIT enabled Harley to funnel more money into research to improve product quality and to speed up the manufacturing process.

But more research and faster processes weren't the only changes wrought by JIT. It forced Harley to change everything—from its purchasing practices to the layout of its factories. Harley forged cooperative relationships with a select group of suppliers who could deliver high-quality parts on time. In turn, these relationships enabled the company to cut costs and increase quality. Because Harley now uses fewer suppliers, it can place larger orders that qualify for bulk discounts. Also, Harley's design and production teams can work more closely with a smaller number of suppliers to ensure the quality of parts and supplies.

By redesigning its production machinery and creating more-standardized parts for multiple bike models, Harley can now build individual models in smaller batches that allow product upgrades more frequently and that boost quality by limiting defects to fewer parts. Reports help Harley management stay informed about the details they need to keep this lean-and-mean manufacturing process running smoothly.

Thanks to the emphasis on quality rather than quantity, Harley's share of the U.S. heavyweight motorcycle market is up to 64 percent, well ahead of second-place Honda. As it continues to expand its production capacity, Harley is eager to gain additional market share in Europe and Japan.

Teerlink's strategy is built on three related initiatives: double production levels to more than 200,000 bikes a year by 2003, improve customer satisfaction to keep brand loyalty high, and improve and expand the worldwide dealer network. To double its manufacturing capacity, Harley expanded its three factories in Wisconsin and Pennsylvania, and it's adding a new factory in Kansas City, Missouri. Building and modifying large, complex factories requires numerous reports, ranging from site selection analyses and environmental impact statements to staffing and training plans.

Reports also play a key role in Harley's efforts to improve customer satisfaction. For example, performance reports can help managers track customer satisfaction and complaint resolution. Research reports help product planners gauge customer expectations and competitive strengths. For instance, knowing that European customers balk at the prices that Harley gets in other markets, the company retooled its European product offerings with an eye toward less expensive models.

Last, Teerlink and other Harley managers rely on reports to help them make decisions and monitor progress in the effort to improve the dealer network. Among the improvements planned in this area is an Internet-based system that provides fast two-way communication between individual dealers and Harley factory personnel.[15]

Your Mission: Richard Teerlink realizes that to stay on top, Harley can't afford to grow complacent and forget how intense the competition is today. He is particularly interested in continuing to improve customer service at Harley dealerships around the world. As his executive assistant, you've been asked to plan a report that will outline ways to increase customer satisfaction by improving customer service. You'll need to conduct the necessary research, analyze the findings, and present your recommendations. From the following, choose the best responses, and be prepared to explain why your choices are best.

1. Which of the following represents the most appropriate statement of purpose for this study?

   a. **The purpose of this study is to identify any customer service problems in Harley-Davidson's worldwide dealer network.**
   b. **This study answers the following question: "What improvements in customer service can our dealers make in order to increase overall customer satisfaction?"**
   c. **This study identifies those dealers in the worldwide network who are most responsible for poor customer satisfaction.**
   d. **This study identifies steps that dealers should take to change customer service practices.**

2. You have tentatively identified the following factors for analysis:

   I. To improve customer service, we need to hire more salespeople
      A. Compute competitors' employee-to-sales ratio
      B. Compute our employee-to-sales ratio

   II. To improve customer service, we need to hire better salespeople
      A. Assess skill level of competitors' salespeople
      B. Assess skill level of our salespeople
   III. To improve customer service, we need to retrain our salespeople
      A. Review competitors' training programs
      B. Review our training programs
   IV. To improve customer service, we need to compensate and motivate our people differently
      A. Assess competitors' compensation levels and motivational techniques
      B. Assess our compensation levels and motivational techniques

   Should you proceed with the investigation on the basis of this preliminary outline, or should you consider other approaches to factoring the problem?
   a. Proceed with this outline.
   b. Do not proceed. Factor the problem by asking customers how they perceive Harley's current customer service efforts. In addition, ask dealers what they think they should be doing differently.
   c. Do not proceed. Factor the problem by considering what successful car dealers do in terms of customer service.
   d. Do not proceed. Factor the problem by considering what the rest of the company, aside from the dealers, could be doing to improve customer service.

3. Which of the following work plans is the best option for guiding your study of ways to improve customer service?
   a. Version One

   Statement of Problem: As part of Harley-Davidson's continuing efforts to offer the most attractive heavyweight motorcycles in the world, Richard Teerlink wants to improve customer service at the dealer level. The challenge here is to identify service improvements that are meaningful and valuable to the customer without being too expensive or time consuming.

   Purpose and Scope of Work: The purpose of this study is to identify ways to increase customer satisfaction by improving customer service at our dealerships worldwide. A four-member study team, composed of the vice president of marketing and three dealers, has been appointed to prepare a written service-improvement plan. To accomplish this objective, this study will survey customers to learn what changes they'd like to see in terms of customer service. The team will analyze these potential improvements in terms of cost and time requirements and then will design new service procedures that dealers can use to better satisfy customers.

   Sources and Methods of Data Collection and Analysis: The study team will assess current dealer efforts by (1) querying dealership employees regarding their customer service, (2) observing employees in action dealing with customers, (3) surveying current Harley owners regarding their purchase experiences, and (4) surveying visitors to dealerships who decide not to purchase Harleys (by intercepting a sample of these people as they leave the dealerships). The team will also visit competitive dealerships to determine firsthand how they treat customers, and the team will mail questionnaires to a sample of registered motorcycle owners and classify the results by brand name. Once all these data have been collected, the team will analyze them to determine where buyers and potential buyers consider customer service to be lacking. Finally, the team will design procedures to meet their expectations.

Schedule:

Query dealer employees	Jan 10–Jan 20
Observe employees in action	Jan 21–Jan 30
Survey current Harley owners	Jan 15–Feb 15
Survey nonbuyers at dealerships	Jan 20–Jan 30
Visit competitive dealerships	Jan 31–Feb 15
Conduct mail survey of registered owners	Jan 15–Feb 15
Analyze data	Feb 15–Mar 1
Draft new procedures	Mar 2–Mar 15
Prepare final report	Mar 16–Mar 25
Present to management/dealer committee	Mar 28

b. Version Two

Statement of Problem: Harley's dealerships need to get on the ball in terms of customer service, and we need to tell them what to do in order to fix their customer service shortcomings.

Purpose and Scope of Work: This report will address how we plan to solve the problem. We'll design new customer service procedures and prepare a written report that dealers can learn from.

Sources and Methods of Data Collection: We plan to employ the usual methods of collecting data, including direct observation and surveys.

Schedule:

Collect data	Jan 10–Feb 15
Analyze data	Feb 15–Mar 1
Draft new procedures	Mar 2–Mar 15
Prepare final report	Mar 16–Mar 25
Present to management/dealer committee	Mar 28

c. Version Three

Task 1—Query dealer employees: We will interview a sampling of dealership employees to find out what steps they take to ensure customer satisfaction. Dates: Jan 10–Jan 20

Task 2—Observe employees in action: We will observe a sampling of dealership employees as they work with potential buyers and current owners, in order to learn firsthand what steps employees typically take. Dates: Jan 21–Jan 30

Task 3—Survey current Harley owners: Using a sample of names from Harley's database of current owners, we'll ask owners how they felt about the purchase process when they bought their bikes and how they feel they've been treated since then. We'll also ask them to suggest steps we could take to improve service. Dates: Jan 15–Feb 15

Task 4—Survey nonbuyers at dealerships: While we are observing dealership employees, we will also approach people who visit dealerships but leave without making a purchase. In the parking lot, we'll go through a quick survey, asking

them what they think about Harley's customer service policies and practices and whether these had any bearing on their decisions not to buy a Harley. Dates: Jan 21–Jan 30

Task 5—Visit competitive dealerships: Under the guise of shoppers looking for new motorcycles, we will visit a selection of competitive dealerships to discover how they treat customers and whether they offer any special services that Harley doesn't. Dates: Jan 31–Feb 15

Task 6—Conduct mail survey of registered owners: Using vehicle registration files from several states, we will survey a sampling of motorcycle owners (of all brands). We will then sort the answers by brand of bike owned to see which dealers are offering which services. Dates: Jan 15–Feb 15

Task 7—Analyze data: Once we've collected all these data, we'll analyze them to identify (1) services that customers would like to see Harley dealers offer, (2) services offered by competitors that aren't offered by Harley dealers, and (3) services currently offered by Harley dealers that may not be all that important to customers. Dates: Feb 15–Mar 1

Task 8—Draft new procedures: From the data we've analyzed, we'll select new services that should be considered by Harley dealers. We'll also assess the time and money burdens that these services are likely to present, so that dealers can see whether each new service will yield a positive return on investment. Dates: Mar 2–Mar 15

Task 9—Prepare final report: This is essentially a documentation task, during which we'll describe our work, make our recommendations, and prepare a formal report. Dates: Mar 16–Mar 25

Task 10—Present to management/dealer committee: We'll summarize our findings and recommendations and will make the full report available to dealers at the quarterly meeting. Date: Mar 28

d. Version Four

Problem: To identify meaningful customer service improvements that can be implemented by Harley dealers.

Data Collection: Use direct observation and surveys to gather details about customer service at Harley dealers and at competing dealers. Have the study team survey current Harley owners, talk with people who visited Harley dealerships but did not buy, and send a questionnaire to registered motorcycle owners.

Schedule:

Step 1:	Data collection. Work will begin on January 10 and end on February 15.
Step 2:	Data analysis. Work will start on February 15 and end on March 1.
Step 3:	Drafting new procedures. Work will start on March 2 and end on March 15.
Step 4:	Preparation of the final report. Work will start on March 16 and end on March 25.
Step 5:	Presentation of the final report. The report will be presented to management and the dealer committee on March 28.

4. Assume that your survey results indicate that BMW motorcycle dealers rank highest in terms of customers' satisfaction with the treatment they received while buying motorcycles. Which of the following conclusions can you safely draw from this result?
   a. Harley needs to improve its customer service.
   b. BMW sells the most motorcycles in the regions of the country covered by the survey.
   c. Because BMW is not one of the world's leading motorcycle manufacturers, customer service is not very important.
   d. None of the above.

Critical Thinking Questions

1. What are the advantages and disadvantages of knowing a lot about the problem you are researching? Explain.
2. Analyze any recent school or work assignment that required you to conduct research. Was the assignment informational, analytical, or a mix? How did you approach your investigation? Did you rely mostly on primary or on secondary sources? Now that you've studied this chapter, can you identify two ways to improve the research techniques you used during that assignment? Briefly explain.
3. Imagine you've detected a correlation in the trend data collected for an analytical report. What kind of research might help you determine whether a cause-and-effect relationship exists between the two variables? Why?
4. Put yourself in the position of a manager who is supervising an investigation but doing very little of the research personally. Why would a work plan be especially useful to the manager? To the researcher? Explain.
5. If you have a clear and detailed statement of purpose, why do you need a problem statement as well? Would it be a good idea to combine the two? Why or why not?
6. After an exhaustive study of an important problem, you have reached a conclusion that you know your company's management will reject. What do you do? Explain your answer.

Exercises

1. You're getting ready to launch a new lawn-care business offering mowing, fertilizing, weeding, and other services. The lawn surrounding a nearby shopping center looks like it could use better care, so you target that business for your first sales proposal. To help prepare this proposal, write your answers to these questions:
   a. What problem statement and statement of purpose would be most appropriate? (Think about the reader's viewpoint.)
   b. What questions will you need answered before you can write a proposal to solve the reader's problem? Be as specific as possible.
   c. Will you conduct primary or secondary research? Why? What sources will you use?
   d. What conclusions and recommendations might be practical, acceptable to the reader, and specific enough for the shopping center to take action? (Think about the purpose of the report.)
2. Now turn the situation around and assume that you're the shopping center's facilities manager. You report to the general manager, who must approve any new contracts for lawn service. Before you contract for lawn care, you want to prepare a formal study of the current state of your lawn's health. The report will include conclusions and recommendations for your boss's consideration. Draft a work plan, including the problem statement, the statement of purpose and scope, a description of what will result from your investigation, the sources and methods of data collection, and a preliminary outline.
3. Assume that your college president has received many student complaints about campus parking problems. You are appointed to chair a student committee organized to investigate the problems and recommend solutions. The president turns over to you the file labeled "Parking: Complaints from Students," and you jot down the essence of the complaints as you inspect the contents. Your notes look like this:
   - Inadequate student spaces at critical hours
   - Poor night lighting near the computer center
   - Inadequate attempts to keep resident neighbors from occupying spaces
   - Dim marking lines
   - Motorcycles taking up full spaces
   - Discourteous security officers
   - Spaces (usually empty) reserved for college officials
   - Relatively high parking fees
   - Full fees charged to night students even though they use the lots only during low-demand periods
   - Vandalism to cars and a sense of personal danger
   - Inadequate total space
   - Resident harassment of students parking on the street in front of neighboring houses

   Your first job is to organize for committee discussion four or five areas that include all (or most) of these specific complaints. Choose the main headings for your outline, and group these specific complaints under them.
4. As the new manager at The Gap clothing store, located in your local mall, you've been assigned to research and write a factual report about the day-to-day variations in store sales throughout a typical week. What's the most logical way to factor this problem and structure your informational report? Why? Indicate the subtopics you might use in your report.

5. After years of work, you've almost completed your first motion picture, the story of a group of unknown musicians finding work and making a reputation in a difficult world. Unfortunately, some of your friends leave the first complete screening saying that the 132-minute movie is simply too long. Others can't imagine any more editing cuts. You decide to test the movie on a regular audience, members of which will be asked to complete a questionnaire that may or may not lead to additional editing. You obtain permission from a local theater manager to show your film at 4:30 and 8:30, after the regularly scheduled matinee and after the evening show. Design a questionnaire that can solicit valid answers.

6. Visit the Xerox Web site at <http://www.xerox.com> and carefully review the products and services discussed on the home page and linked pages. Prepare a survey instrument that Xerox could use for customer feedback on these products. Remember to avoid questions that are leading, and pretest your questionnaire on family and friends before submitting it to your instructor.

7. Some students on your campus have complained about the high cost of college textbooks. Team up with three other students to study the average cost of the textbooks purchased by students in this class. Start by designing a survey; then conduct the research, tabulate your results, and report the findings.
   a. List the survey questions you'll ask and decide whether you'll interview the students or ask them to write down their own answers.
   b. Pretest the questionnaire on several students to see whether the questions make sense.
   c. Conduct the research.
   d. Analyze the survey answers by determining the mean, the median, and the mode of the amounts spent on textbooks.
   e. Write a one- or two-page summary of your findings, including an interpretation of the data you've gathered.

8. Because of the success of your pizza delivery service, you're considering whether to expand. You'll need at least one additional delivery van if you expand, but you know that buying a van will lead to other expenses, such as maintenance, insurance, and so on. Before you can make a decision, you want to factor the problem and develop an outline to guide your investigation. As you do so, include a list of at least six questions to research and answer.

9. You're the advertising manager at a regional ice cream company. Your boss, the director of marketing, has asked you to report on how the company should use advertising to support new-product introductions, using this statement of purpose:

   Statement of purpose: To analyze various methods of advertising new products when they are introduced and to recommend the most effective and cost-efficient program

   a. How should you factor this problem? Will you use descriptive or informative headings for your preliminary outline?
   b. Develop an outline, following the rules of division.
   c. Exchange outlines with a student in your class and critique each other's work. Comment on the organization, the logic, the consistency, and the completeness of the other student's outline. On the basis of the suggestions you receive, revise your own outline.

10. Now put yourself on the other side of the desk: You're the regional ice cream company's director of marketing. Your advertising manager has submitted a full report, and you're reviewing the conclusions. Identify and discuss the errors of logic underlying the following conclusions and recommendations in the report:
    a. As soon as we started advertising the new Apricot Swirl on television, sales increased, so we need to advertise every new fruit-flavored product on television.
    b. Coupons really work, and if we don't use them to promote every new product we introduce, they will all fail.
    c. Newspaper advertising didn't help Apricot Swirl, so let's not use it on any other new-product launch.
    d. Peanut Swirl isn't as good a flavor as the other new products, so it shouldn't receive the same extensive advertising support.

DEVELOPING YOUR INTERNET SKILLS

GOING ONLINE: SEARCH THOUSANDS OF FULL-TEXT ARTICLES INSTANTLY, P. 303

You can test the search results of the Electronic Library without signing up even as a trial subscriber. Pick a topic you're required to research for a sample report and enter your key words or phrase. Choose the sources you want to search—newspapers and newswires, books, magazines, photo archives, and so forth. Now review the resulting list. (If you want to sign on as a trial subscriber, you will then be able to read the articles and view any photos. Otherwise, you should be able to make a comparative evaluation by reviewing the list.) How did your search results differ from results obtained from an ordinary search engine? Do you think this kind of information would be useful to you? How could you narrow or qualify your search to reap the kind of results that would be helpful?

COMPLETING FORMAL REPORTS AND PROPOSALS

After studying this chapter, you will be able to

Describe how organizations produce formal reports and proposals

Prepare all the necessary parts of a formal report

Assemble all the parts of a formal report in the proper order, using an appropriate format

Prepare and assemble all the parts of a formal proposal

Critique formal reports prepared by someone else

O *n the Job*

FACING A COMMUNICATION DILEMMA AT LEVI STRAUSS
Placing a High Value on Reports

Robert Haas takes both business ethics and business communication seriously. As chairman and CEO of Levi Strauss and Company, and as great-great-grandnephew of founder Levi Strauss, Haas defines Levi's goal as "responsible commercial success." In other words, he envisions his company as being run according to principles such as teamwork, trust, ethical management, environment care, diversity, and individual respect.

Haas recognizes the importance of communicating his vision throughout the company, to customers, and in the community. In fact, effective communication is one of his company's fundamental values, affecting everything from personal interactions to community relations. One way to communicate such a complex vision is through reports, so Haas makes sure he knows everything he can about developing reports that are clear, that are well organized, and that contain all the elements necessary to promote easy understanding.

Haas not only helps create reports but he relies on them to make decisions and to set company policy. If you were Robert Haas, how would you approach the challenge of communicating complex ideas and issues? What steps would you take to make sure an audience gets what it needs from long reports? What features would you include to help readers find and understand the information in your reports? And how would you use reports in your own decision making?[1]

R *EPORT PRODUCTION*

Experienced business communicators such as Robert Haas realize that planning a report or proposal, conducting the necessary research, developing visual aids, organizing the ideas, and drafting the text are demanding and time-consuming tasks. They also know that the process of writing a report or proposal doesn't end with these steps. After careful editing and rewriting, you still need to produce a polished final version.

How the final version is actually produced depends on the nature of your organization. The traditional approach was usually a team effort, with secretaries or other support

Robert Haas isn't the only one in his company who places value on reports. Employees at Levi Strauss and Company know how important it is to produce reports that are easily understood, logical, attractive, persuasive, and thorough. So they include all the necessary components to accomplish these goals.

In organizations that produce many reports and proposals, the preparation process involves teamwork.

personnel handling the typing, formatting, and other tasks. For important, high-visibility reports, a graphics department could sometimes help with charts, drawings, covers, and other visual elements.

However, as personal computers have become commonplace in the business office, more and more employees are expected to handle most or even all of the formatting and production of their own reports. In fact, many of the advances in computer hardware and software in recent years have been designed specifically to give all businesspeople the ability to produce great-looking reports by themselves. The good news is that these computer tools are now generally easy enough for the average businessperson to use productively. A software "suite" such as Microsoft Office makes it easy to produce reports with graphics, tables, spreadsheet data, and even database records. Even advanced report features such as photography are relatively simple these days, with the advent of low-cost, color desktop scanners. And inexpensive color printers with near photo-quality output have put color reports within just about everybody's reach. Used effectively, color helps improve both the reader's interest in your material and the effectiveness of your message.

Personal computers can automatically handle many of the mechanical aspects of report preparation.

The bad news is that continually improving computer tools increase your audience's expectations. People are influenced by packaging, so a handsomely bound report with full-color graphics may influence many readers more than a plain, typewriter-style report containing the exact same information. To make matters even more challenging, paper reports are starting to compete with various multimedia electronic reports, such as Web sites and CD-ROMs. Instead of producing a lengthy report full of tables and other information, you can now provide the information electronically and let readers pick and choose what they want to read.

Be sure to schedule enough time to turn out a document that looks professional.

No matter which tools you use, make sure you leave enough time for formatting and production. Murphy's law (which says that if something can go wrong, it will) applies to just about every aspect of using computers. Data communication problems, incompatible or corrupted disk files, printing problems, and other glitches can consume hours. You don't want computer trouble to sabotage all your thinking, planning, and writing, so make sure you can create and produce the report before the deadline.

Once you've completed a major report and sent it off to your audience, you'll naturally expect a positive response, and quite often you'll get one—but not always. You may get halfhearted praise or no action on your conclusions and recommendations. Even worse, you may get some serious criticism. Try to learn from these experiences. Sometimes you won't get any response at all. If you don't hear from your readers within a week or two, you might want to ask politely whether the report arrived. In hopes of stimulating a response, you might also offer to answer any questions or provide additional information.

Ask for feedback, and learn from your mistakes.

Regardless of how the final product is produced, it will be up to you to make sure that all necessary components are included. Depending on the length and formality of your report, various prefatory and supplementary parts may be necessary. The more formal your report, the more components you'll include.

COMPONENTS OF A FORMAL REPORT

A formal report's manuscript format and impersonal tone convey an impression of professionalism. A formal report can be either short (fewer than ten pages) or long (ten pages or more). It can be informational or analytical, direct or indirect. It may be directed to readers inside or outside the organization. Robert Haas knows that what sets a formal report apart from other reports is its polish.

A formal report conveys the impression that the subject is important.

The three basic divisions of a formal report:

- Prefatory parts
- Text
- Supplementary parts

The parts included in a report depend on the type of report you're writing, the requirements of your audience, the organization you're working for, and the length of your report. The components listed in Figure 14.1 fall into three categories, depending on where they are found in a report: prefatory parts, text of the report, and supplementary parts. For an illustration of how the various parts fit together, see Linda Moreno's Electrovision report in "In-Depth Critique: Analyzing a Formal Report," starting on page 338.

PREFATORY PARTS	TEXT OF THE REPORT	SUPPLEMENTARY PARTS
Cover	Introduction	Appendixes
Title fly	Body	Bibliography
Title Page	Summary	Index
Request for proposal	Conclusions	
Letter of transmittal	Recommendations	
Table of contents	Notes	
List of Illustrations	Visual aids	
Synopsis or executive summary		

Figure 14.1
Parts of a Formal Report

A business plan's mission statement doesn't have to be boring, believes Debi Coleman, chair and CEO of Merix, a high-tech supplier based in Oregon. So Coleman commissioned a cutting-edge "visual statement" for the company, a collage of symbolic images featuring the "M" logo as a mother ship, with smaller ships representing suppliers, partners, and customers zooming in and out of its docking bays.

When a particular section is designed to stand apart, it generally starts on a new page, and the material after it starts on a new page as well. Most prefatory parts (such as the table of contents, for example) should be placed on their own pages. Often, however, the parts in the text of the report need not stand alone. If your introduction is only a paragraph long, don't bother with a page break before moving into the body of your report. If the introduction runs longer than a page, however, a page break can signal the reader that a major shift is about to occur in the flow of the report.

Prefatory Parts

Although the prefatory parts are placed before the text of the report, you may not want to write them until after you've written the text. Many of these parts—such as the table of contents, list of illustrations, and executive summary—are easier to prepare after the text is complete because they directly reflect the contents. Other parts can be prepared at almost any time.

Cover

Many companies have standard covers for reports, made of heavy paper and imprinted with the company's name and logo. Report titles are either printed on these covers or attached with gummed labels. If your company has no standard covers, you can usually find something suitable in a good stationery store. Look for a cover that is appropriate to the subject matter, attractive, and convenient. Also, make sure it can be labeled with the report title, the writer's name (optional), and the submission date (also optional).

Think carefully about the title you put on the cover. A business report is not a mystery novel, so give your readers all the information they need: the who, what, when, where, why, and how of the subject. At the same time, try to be reasonably concise. You don't want to intimidate your audience with a title that's too long, awkward, or unwieldy. One approach is to use a subtitle. You can reduce the length of your title by eliminating phrases such as *A report of, A study of,* and *A survey of.*

Put a title on the cover that is informative but not too long.

Title Fly and Title Page

The **title fly** is a plain sheet of paper with only the title of the report on it. You don't really need one, but it adds a touch of formality to a report.

The **title page** includes four blocks of information, as shown in Moreno's Electrovision report: (1) the title of the report; (2) the name, title, and address of the person, group, or organization that authorized the report (usually the intended audience); (3) the name, title, and address of the person, group, or organization that prepared the report;

The title page usually includes four blocks of information.

and (4) the date on which the report was submitted. On some title pages the second block of information is preceded by the words *Prepared for* or *Submitted to,* and the third block of information is preceded by *Prepared by* or *Submitted by.* In some cases the title page serves as the cover of the report, especially if the report is relatively short and intended solely for internal use.

Letter of Authorization and Letter of Acceptance

If you were authorized in writing to prepare the report, you may want to include in your report the letter or memo of authorization (and sometimes even the letter or memo of acceptance). The **letter of authorization** (or *memo of authorization*) is a document requesting that a report be prepared. It normally follows the direct-request plan described in Chapter 8, and it typically specifies the problem, scope, time and money restrictions, special instructions, and due date.

The **letter of acceptance** (or *memo of acceptance*) acknowledges the assignment to conduct the study and to prepare the report. Following the good-news plan, the acceptance confirms time and money restrictions and other pertinent details. This document is rarely included in reports.

Letter of Transmittal

The **letter of transmittal** (or *memo of transmittal*) conveys your report to your audience. (In a book, this section is called the preface.) The letter of transmittal says what you'd say if you were handing the report directly to the person who authorized it, so the style is less formal than the rest of the report. For example, the letter would use personal pronouns (*you, I, we*) and conversational language. Moreno's Electrovision report includes a one-page transmittal memo from Moreno to her boss (the person who requested the report).

In general, the transmittal letter appears right before the table of contents. However, if your report will be widely distributed, you may decide to include the letter of transmittal only in selected copies, in order to make certain comments to a specific audience. If your report discusses layoffs or other issues that affect people in the organization, you might want to discuss your recommendations privately in a letter of transmittal to top management. If your audience is likely to be skeptical of or even hostile to something in your report, the transmittal letter is a good opportunity to acknowledge their concerns and explain how the report addresses the issues they care about.

The letter of transmittal follows the routine and good-news plans described in Chapter 9. Begin with the main idea, officially conveying the report to the readers and summarizing its purpose. Such a letter typically begins with a statement like "Here is the report you asked me to prepare on . . . " The rest includes information about the scope of the report, the methods used to complete the study, and the limitations that became apparent. In the middle section of the letter you may also highlight important points or sections of the report, make comments on side issues, give suggestions for follow-up studies, and offer any details that will help readers better understand and use the report. You may also wish to acknowledge help given by others. The concluding paragraph is a note of thanks for having been given the report assignment, an expression of willingness to discuss the report, and an offer to assist with future projects.

If the report does not have a synopsis, the letter of transmittal may summarize the major findings, conclusions, and recommendations. This material would be placed after the opening of the letter.

Table of Contents

The table of contents indicates in outline form the coverage, sequence, and relative importance of the information in the report. In fact, the headings used in the text of the report are the basis for the table of contents. Levi's Aspirations Statement lists headings and subheadings in the table of contents to serve as a quick outline of the report. Depending on the length and complexity of the report, your contents page may show only the top two or three levels of headings, sometimes only first-level headings. Of course, excluding some levels of headings may frustrate readers who want to know where to find every subject you

---

Marginal notes (left column):

A letter of authorization usually follows the direct-request plan.

Use the good-news plan for a letter of acceptance.

Use a less formal style for the letter of transmittal than for the report itself.

Use the good-news plan for a letter of transmittal.

The synopsis of short reports is often included in the letter of transmittal.

The table of contents outlines the text and lists prefatory and supplementary parts.

cover. On the other hand, a simpler table of contents helps readers focus on the major points. No matter how many levels you include, make sure readers can easily distinguish between them (see Table 13.1 for examples of various levels of headings).

The table of contents is prepared after the other parts of the report have been typed so that the beginning page numbers for each heading can be shown. The headings should be worded exactly as they are in the text of the report. Also listed on the contents page are the prefatory parts (only those that follow the contents page) and the supplementary parts. If you have fewer than four visual aids, you may wish to list them in the table of contents too; but if you have four or more visual aids, show them separately in a list of illustrations.

Be sure the headings in the table of contents match up perfectly with the headings in the text.

List of Illustrations

For simplicity's sake, some reports refer to all visual aids as illustrations or exhibits. In other reports, as in Moreno's Electrovision report, tables are labeled separately from other types of visual aids, which are called figures. Regardless of the system used to label visual aids, the list of illustrations gives their titles and page numbers.

If you have enough space on a single page, include the list of illustrations directly beneath the table of contents. Otherwise, include the list on a separate page following the contents page. When tables and figures are numbered separately, they should also be listed separately. The two lists can appear on the same page if they fit; otherwise, start each list on a separate page.

Put the list of illustrations on a separate page if it won't all fit on one page with the table of contents; start the list of figures and the list of tables on separate pages if they won't both fit on one page.

Synopsis or Executive Summary

A **synopsis** is a brief overview (one page or less) of a report's most important points, designed to give readers a quick preview of the contents. It's often included in long informational reports dealing with technical, professional, or academic subjects and can also be called an *abstract*. Because it's a concise representation of the whole report, it may be distributed separately to a wide audience; interested readers can then order a copy of the entire report.

Provide an overview of the report in a synopsis or an executive summary.

The phrasing of a synopsis can be either informative or descriptive, depending on whether the report is in direct or indirect order. In an informative synopsis, you present the main points of the report in the order in which they appear in the text. A descriptive synopsis, on the other hand, simply tells what the report is about, in only moderately greater detail than the table of contents; the actual findings of the report are omitted. Here are examples of statements from each type:

An informative synopsis summarizes the main ideas; a descriptive synopsis states what the report is about.

Informative synopsis: Sales of super-premium ice cream make up 11 percent of the total ice cream market.

Descriptive synopsis: This report contains information about super-premium ice cream and its share of the market.

The way you handle a synopsis reflects the approach you use in the text. If you're using an indirect approach in your report, you're better off with a descriptive synopsis. An informative synopsis, with its focus on conclusions and key points, may be too confrontational if you have a skeptical audience. You don't want to spoil the effect by providing a controversial beginning. No matter which type of synopsis you use, however, be sure to present an accurate picture of the report's contents.[2]

Use a descriptive synopsis for a skeptical or hostile audience, an informative synopsis for most other situations.

Many business report writers prefer to include an **executive summary** instead of a synopsis or an abstract. A synopsis is essentially a prose table of contents that outlines the main points of the report; an executive summary is a fully developed "mini" version of the report itself, intended for readers who lack the time or motivation to study the complete text. So an executive summary is more comprehensive than a synopsis, often as much as 10 percent as long as the report itself.

Put enough information in an executive summary so that an executive can make a decision without reading the entire report.

Unlike a synopsis, an executive summary may contain headings, well-developed transitions, and even visual aids. It is often organized in the same way as the report, using a direct or an indirect approach, depending on the audience's receptivity. However, executive summaries can also deviate from the sequence of material in the remainder of the report.

After reading the summary, audience members know the essentials of the report and are in a position to make a decision. Later, when time permits, they may read certain parts of the report to obtain additional detail. Linda Moreno's Electrovision report provides one example of an executive summary.

Many reports require neither a synopsis nor an executive summary. Length is usually the determining factor. Most reports of fewer than 10 pages either omit such a preview or combine it with the letter of transmittal. However, if your report is over 30 pages long, you'll probably include either a synopsis or an executive summary as a convenience for readers. Which one you'll provide depends on the traditions of your organization.

Text of the Report

Apart from deciding on the fundamental issues of content and organization, you must also make decisions about the design and layout of the report. You can use a variety of techniques to present your material effectively. Many organizations have format guidelines that make your decisions easier, but the goal is always to focus readers' attention on major points and on the flow of ideas. Headings, typographical devices (such as capital letters, italics, and boldface type), white space, and so on are useful tools, as are visual aids. Also, as discussed in Chapter 13, use preview and review statements to frame sections of your text. This strategy keeps your audience informed and reinforces the substance of your message. For example, Levi's Aspirations Statement includes an overview at the beginning of each major section to explain what the section covers.

Introduction

The introduction of a report serves a number of important functions:

- Putting the report in a broader context by tying it to a problem or an assignment
- Telling readers the report's purpose
- Previewing the report's contents and organization
- Establishing the tone of the report and the writer's relationship with the audience

The length of the introduction depends on the length of the report. In a relatively brief report, the introduction may be only a paragraph or two and may not be labeled with a heading of any kind. On the other hand, the introduction to a major formal report may extend to several pages and can be identified as a separate section by the first-level heading "Introduction." (See Linda Moreno's Electrovision report.)

Here's a list of topics to consider covering in an introduction, depending on your material and your audience:

- *Authorization.* When, how, and by whom the report was authorized; who wrote it; and when it was submitted. This material is especially important when no letter of transmittal is included.
- *Problem/purpose.* The reason for the report's existence and what is to be accomplished as a result of the report's having been written.
- *Scope.* What is and what isn't going to be covered in the report. The scope indicates the report's size and complexity.
- *Background.* The historical conditions or factors that have led up to the report. This section enables readers to understand how the problem developed and what has been done about it so far.
- *Sources and methods.* The secondary sources of information used and the surveys, experiments, and observations carried out. This section tells readers what sources were used, how the sample was selected, how the questionnaire was constructed (a sample questionnaire and cover letter should be included in the appendix), what follow-up procedures were employed, and the like. It provides enough detail to give

Aids to understanding the text of a report:

- Headings
- Typographical devices
- Visual aids
- Preview and review statements

An introduction has a number of functions and covers a wide variety of topics.

When grad student Jerry Yang partnered with David Filo to found Yahoo!, the popular Internet search engine, they wound up developing more than software. It took a business plan with convincing arguments for their "diversified media company," backed by solid facts and figures, to land their first $1 million financial stake.

readers confidence in the work and to convince them that the sources and methods were satisfactory.

- *Definitions.* A brief introductory statement leading into a list of terms used in the report and their definitions. Naturally, if your audience is familiar with the terms you've used throughout the report, a list of definitions isn't necessary. Moreno's Electrovision report doesn't include a list of definitions because the topic doesn't involve any unfamiliar terminology. However, if you have any question about your readers' knowledge, be sure to include definitions of any terms that might lead to misinterpretation. In addition, if you've used familiar or general terms in a specific way, be sure to explain exactly what you mean. For example, the term *market* could be used in a number of different ways, from a physical location to a collection of potential customers. Note that terms may be defined in other places as well: in the body (as the terms are used), in explanatory footnotes, or in a glossary (an alphabetical listing of terms placed in the supplementary section).

- *Limitations.* Factors affecting the quality of the report, such as a budget too small to do all the work that should have been done, an inadequate amount of time to do all the necessary research, unreliability or unavailability of data, or other conditions beyond your control. This is the place to mention doubts about any aspect of the report. Although candor may lead readers to question the results, it will also enable them to assess the results more accurately and help you maintain the integrity of your report. However, limitations are no excuse for conducting a poor study or writing a bad report.

- *Report organization.* The organization of the report (what topics are covered and in what order), along with a rationale for following this plan. This section is a road map that helps readers understand what's approaching at each turn of the report and why.

Some of these items may be combined in the introduction; some may not be included at all. You can decide what to include by figuring out what kind of information will help your readers understand and accept the report. Also give some thought to how the introduction relates to the prefatory parts of the report. In longer reports you may have a letter of transmittal, a synopsis or an executive summary, and an introduction, all of which cover essentially the same ground.

To avoid redundancy, balance the various sections. If the letter of transmittal and synopsis are fairly detailed, for example, you might want the introduction to be relatively brief. However, remember that some people may barely glance at the prefatory parts, so be sure your introduction is detailed enough to provide an adequate preview of your report. If you feel that your introduction must repeat information that has already been covered in one of the prefatory parts, simply use different wording.

Body

The body of the report follows the introduction. It consists of the major sections or chapters (with various levels of headings) that present, analyze, and interpret the findings gathered as part of your investigation. These chapters contain the "proof," the detailed information necessary to support your conclusions and recommendations. (See the body of Linda Moreno's Electrovision report.)

One of the decisions to make when writing the body of your report is how much detail to include. Your decision depends on the nature of your information, the purpose of your report, and the preferences of your audience. Some situations call for detailed coverage; others lend themselves to shorter treatment. In general, provide only enough detail in the body to support your conclusions and recommendations, and put additional details in tables, charts, and appendixes.

> Restrict the body to those details necessary to prove your conclusions and recommendations.

You can also decide whether to put your conclusions in the body or in a separate section or both. If the conclusions seem to flow naturally from the evidence, you'll almost inevitably cover them in the body. However, if you want to give your conclusions added emphasis, you may include a separate section to summarize them. Having a separate section

BEHIND THE SCENES AT THE ROCKY MOUNTAIN INSTITUTE
Energy Efficiency—Getting the Word to the World

The Rocky Mountain Institute (RMI) has plans to save the world's resources. Its primary tool? Words. The nonprofit environmental think tank expends most of its own energy convincing governments, corporations, utilities, architects, and anyone else who will listen that "it's cheaper to save energy than to waste it." To get this message to the world, RMI's 40 researchers produce thousands of pages of written reports each year for some 200 clients in over 32 countries. Many of these reports are highly technical, but the institute's founders, Amory and Hunter Lovins, like to present them in witty, straightforward language that anyone can understand. They've even invented words when necessary—like *negawatt,* a measure of electricity *saved.*

Amory, a child prodigy who became a Harvard and Oxford scholar, built his reputation as an energy wizard in the mid-1970s, when his book *Soft Energy Paths* correctly predicted that economic growth could be accompanied by lowered energy consumption. Hunter, RMI's president and executive director, is an attorney-turned-activist who rides rodeo and dirt bikes in her spare time. For years the married couple traveled the world as energy-efficiency consultants, but in 1982 they settled in Snowmass, Colorado, in a state-of-the-art, environmentally sound building that serves as home and office for RMI's research team.

The institute's programs are in five areas: energy efficiency, water usage, economic renewal of rural areas, sustainable agriculture, and global security through more efficient resource use

and distribution. "What we do concerns policy," Hunter explains. "We do very little hardware testing, invention, or fiddling around." Instead, staffers may use the telephone to contact officials who have successfully implemented efficiency programs. The researchers ask what worked and what didn't, how much it cost, what roadblocks were overcome, and where to obtain any equipment that was used. This information may be combined with hardware evaluations, supply sources, and implementation recommendations in reports as long as 600 pages; Hunter calls them "tomes as big as a Manhattan phone book."

Other reports are smaller and friendlier and wind up in the hands of consumers (such as the popular soft-cover *Practical Home Energy Savings*). However, most begin as commissions from such company clients as Pacific Gas & Electric, General Motors, and the World Bank.

Hunter admits that organizing such lengthy reports can be challenging. She must often rewrite early drafts to make sure readers can follow the flow of what she calls "the argument." When the U.S. Environmental Protection Agency (EPA) commissioned a 100-page report from RMI to serve as a manual for local water utilities, "they were interested in what water-efficiency measures existed and how to implement them," says Hunter. The first draft, written by a junior staff member, wandered a bit, so Hunter reshaped it. "I try in the introduction to set up a structure of argument that is sign-posted along the way. For example, I'll say, 'In almost every instance it will be more cost-effective for you to save water than to try to bring in new supplies, and this is true because of the following six reasons.' Then I have six subheads or chapters, depending on

---

is particularly appropriate in longer reports; the reader may lose track of the conclusions if they're given only in the body.

Summary, Conclusions, and Recommendations

Summaries, conclusions, and recommendations serve different purposes.

The final section of the text of a report tells readers "what you told them." In a short report this final wrap-up may be only a paragraph or two. A long report generally has separate sections labeled "Summary," "Conclusions," and "Recommendations." Here's how the three differ:

- *Summary.* The key findings of your report, paraphrased from the body and stated or listed in the order in which they appear in the body.
- *Conclusions.* Your analysis of what the findings mean. These are the answers to the questions that led to the report.
- *Recommendations.* Opinions, based on reason and logic, about the course of action that should be taken. The author of the Electrovision report listed four specific steps the company should take to reduce travel costs.

If the report is organized in direct order, the summary, conclusions, and recommendations are presented before the body and are reviewed only briefly at the end. If the report is organized in indirect order, these sections are presented for the first time at the end and are covered in detail. Many report writers combine the conclusions and recom-

the amount of material. I try to prove the argument at each step along the way, and then I sum it all up." For the EPA report, Hunter stressed RMI's recommendations throughout the body, then briefly reinforced them in a "Final Note."

Of course, organization wasn't the only problem. Hunter also had to revise the document six times in response to comments from various EPA officials. Some of their comments were helpful, Hunter remembers, "but one guy scrawled in big red letters all the way across the page, 'Where's the beef?' That wasn't very useful. On the other hand, he was a senior guy at EPA, so we had to figure out what he meant by that. That took a lot of phone calls."

More than a year and plenty of headaches later, the "Water Efficiency" report was accepted and printed. It's rich with case studies, and it includes a table of contents, a formal introduction, brief overviews introducing each section, 172 footnotes, 7 appendixes, 9 figures, and 5 tables. There's no bibliography or index, but an appendix lists over a hundred names and addresses of water-efficiency contacts. Because the institute retained the right to distribute the booklet, "Water Efficiency" has now become part of RMI's save-the-world toolbox.

Rocky Mountain Institute in Snowmass, Colorado, is both home and office to the Lovinses and their staff of 40. The institute's goal is to save the world's resources, and it pursues this objective by preparing written reports for such clients as governments, corporations, utility companies, and architects. Employees at RMI understand how important it is to produce reports that are easily understood, logical, attractive, persuasive, and thorough.

Apply Your Knowledge

1. Hunter Lovins says that executive summaries often omit important information that executives need. What steps would you take to avoid this problem?

2. Amory Lovins has written a groundbreaking treatise proving that plutonium waste from nuclear power reactors can be used to develop nuclear weapons. How would you arrange this material for a report to be distributed among government policy makers in countries that might fund nuclear power programs in developing nations?

---

mendations under one heading because it seems like the natural thing to do. It is often difficult to present a conclusion without implying a recommendation. (See Moreno's Electrovision report.)

Whether you combine them or not, if you have several conclusions and recommendations, you may want to number and list them. An appropriate lead-in to such a list might be, "The findings of this study lead to the following conclusions." A statement that could be used for a list of recommendations might be, "Based on the conclusions of this study, the following recommendations are made." Present no new findings either in the conclusions or in the recommendations section.

In reports that are intended to lead to action, the recommendations section is particularly important; it spells out exactly what should happen next. It brings all the action items together in one place and gives the details about who should do what, when, where, and how. Readers may agree with everything you say in your report but still fail to take any action if you're vague about what should happen next. Your readers must understand what's expected of them and must have some appreciation of the difficulties that are likely to arise. So providing a schedule and specific task assignments is helpful because concrete plans have a way of commanding action.

In action-oriented reports, put all the recommendations in a separate section and spell out precisely what should happen next.

Source Documentation

When writing the text of the report, you need to decide how to acknowledge your sources. You have an ethical and a legal obligation to give other people credit for their work.

Give credit where credit is due.

Linda J. Wachner is CEO of lingerie maker Warnaco and is often called on to make decisions based on reports. But if a report makes a recommendation and lacks the detail to support it, the recommendation is useless. Likewise, a recommendation buried in too much detail may be too difficult to uncover. Wachner advises balancing the amount of detail to complement the subject and its complexity.

Visual aids help communicators get through to an audience.

Beginning with your visual aids offers several advantages.

In general, use visual aids only to supplement the story you are telling in words.

Refer to every visual aid by number.

Acknowledging your sources also enhances the credibility of your report. By citing references in the text, you demonstrate that you have thoroughly researched the topic. Mentioning the names of well-known or important authorities on the subject also helps build credibility for your message. In fact, it's often a good idea to mention a credible source's name several times if you need to persuade the audience.

On the other hand, you don't want to make your report read like an academic treatise, dragging along from citation to citation. The source references should be handled as conveniently and inconspicuously as possible. One approach, especially for internal reports, is simply to mention a source in the text:

According to Dr. Lewis Morgan of Northwestern Hospital, hip replacement operations account for 7 percent of all surgery performed on women ages 65 and over.

However, if your report will be distributed to outsiders, include additional information on where you obtained the data. Most college students are familiar with citation schemes suggested by the Modern Language Association (MLA) or American Psychological Association (APA). The *Chicago Manual of Style* is a reference often used by typesetters and publishers. All of these encourage the use of *in-text citations,* in which you insert the author's last name and a year of publication or a page number directly in the text. An alternative is to use numbered footnotes (bottom of the page) or endnotes (end of the report). (Linda Moreno's Electrovision report uses the author–page number system, whereas this textbook uses endnotes.) For more information on citing sources, see Appendix B, "Documentation of Report Sources."

Visual Aids

Conveying an important idea is the main reason businesspeople like Robert Haas include visual aids in their reports and proposals, but which comes first: visual aid or text? Say you've just completed the research for an important report or oral presentation. You're about to begin the composition phase. Your first impulse might be to start with the introduction and proceed page by page until you've completed the text or script. Almost as an afterthought you might throw in a few visual aids—tables, charts, graphs, schematic drawings, illustrations, photographs—to illustrate the words.

Although this approach makes some sense, many experienced businesspeople prefer to begin with the visual aids, which has three advantages. First, if much of the fact-finding and analytical work is already in tabular or graphic form, you already have a visual point of departure. Sorting through and refining your visuals will help you decide exactly what you're going to say. Second, many important business projects involve both a written report and an oral presentation of results. Similar visual aids, modified for different media, can be used for both communication situations. By starting with the visual aids, you develop a graphic story line that serves two purposes. Finally, the text or script explains and refers to the tables, charts, and graphs, so you save time by having them ready before you start to compose, particularly if you plan to use quite a few visuals. However, the illustrative material in a report or presentation should supplement the written or spoken word, not replace it, so restrict your use of visual aids to situations in which they do the most good. Table 14.1 helps you identify those situations.

Every visual aid you use should be clearly referred to by number in the text of your report. Some report writers refer to all visual aids as exhibits and number them consecutively throughout the report; many others number tables and figures separately (everything that isn't a table is regarded as a figure). In a very long report with numbered chapters (as in this book), visual aids may have a double number (separated by a period or a hyphen) representing the chapter number and the individual illustration number within that chapter.

Table 14.1	WHEN TO USE VISUALS

Purpose	Application
To clarify	Support text descriptions of "graphic" topics: quantitative or numerical information; explanations of trends; descriptions of procedures, relationships, locations, or composition of an item.
To simplify	Break complicated descriptions into components that can be depicted with conceptual models, flowcharts, organization charts, or diagrams.
To emphasize	Call attention to particularly important points by illustrating them with line, bar, and pie charts.
To summarize	Review major points in the narrative by providing a chart or table that sums up the data.
To reinforce	Present information in visual and written form to increase readers' retention.
To attract	Make material seem more interesting by decorating the cover or title page and by breaking up the text with visual aids.
To impress	Build credibility by putting ideas in visual form to convey the impression of authenticity and precision.
To unify	Depict the relationship among points—for example, with a flowchart.

Help your readers understand the significance of any visual aids by referring to them before they appear in the text. The reference helps readers understand why the table or chart is important. The following examples show how you can make this connection in the text:

Figure 1 summarizes the financial history of the motorcycle division over the past five years, with sales broken into four categories.

Total sales were steady over this period, but the mix of sales by category changed dramatically (see Figure 2).

The underlying reason for the remarkable growth in our sales of low-end fax machines is suggested by Table 4, which provides data on fax machine sales in the United States by region and model.

Ideally, it is best to place each visual aid right beside or right after the paragraph it illustrates so that readers can consult the explanation and the visual aid at the same time. Many word-processing programs and desktop publishing systems let you create layouts with artwork and text on the same page. If you don't have these programs, the most practical approach is to put visual aids on separate pages and mesh them with the text after the report has been typed.

Knowing what points you want to present visually and knowing exactly what format to use are separate things. The construction of visual aids requires a good deal of both imagination and attention to detail. Your main concern is always your audience. What format is most meaningful and convenient for them? When illustrating the text of any report, you face the problem of choosing the specific form that best suits your message. Moreover, good business ethics demands you choose a form of visual aid that will not mislead your audience.

Tables When you have to present detailed, specific information, choose a **table,** a systematic arrangement of data in columns and rows. Tables are ideal when the audience needs the facts, all the facts, and when the information would be either difficult or tedious to handle in the main text.

Most tables contain the standard parts illustrated in Figure 14.2. What makes a table a table is the grid that allows you to find the point at which two factors intersect. So every

Introduce each visual in your text before the visual appears.

Place each visual aid as close to its introduction as possible.

Use tables to help your audience understand detailed information.

Figure 14.2
Parts of a Table

	TABLE 1	Title			
	Multicolumn Head			**Single Column Head**	**Single Column Head**
Stub head	**Subhead**	**Subhead**			
Line head	XXX	XXX	XX	XX	
Line head					
Subhead	XX	XXX	XX	XX	
Subhead	XX	XXX	XX	XX	
Total	XXX	XXX	XX	XX	

Source: (In the same format as a text footnote; see Appendix B).
*Footnote (for explanation of elements in the table; a superscript number or small letter may be used instead of an asterisk or other symbol).

table includes vertical columns and horizontal rows, with useful headings along the top and side. Tables projected onto a screen during an oral presentation should be limited to three column heads and six row heads; tables presented on paper may include from one or two heads to a dozen or more. If the table has too many columns to fit comfortably between the margins of the page, turn the paper horizontally and insert it in the report with the top toward the binding.

Although formal tables set apart from the text are necessary for complex information, you can present some data more simply within the text. You make the table, in essence, a part of the paragraph, typed in tabular format. These text tables are usually introduced with a sentence that leads directly into the tabulated information. Here's an example:

Half the people surveyed are very concerned about artificial coloring in the prepackaged foods they eat. Women and older people are most concerned:

	Percentage Who Are Very Concerned	Percentage Who Are Slightly Concerned
Men	44	40
Women	53	39
Adults 18–49	49	40
Adults 50–65	55	32

Source: "Artificial Coloring in Prepackaged Food," *Food Processing News*, January 1995, 113.

Tabular information can be included in text without a formal title.

When preparing a numerical table, be sure to identify the units you're using: dollars, percentages, price per ton, or whatever. All items in a column are expressed in the same unit. Although many tables are numerical, word tables can be just as useful. They are particularly appropriate for presenting survey findings or for comparing various items against a specific standard.

Use line charts to
- Indicate changes over time
- Plot the interaction of two variables

Line and Surface Charts A **line chart** illustrates trends over time or plots the relationship of two variables. In line charts that show trends, the vertical axis shows the amount, and the horizontal axis shows the time or the quantity being measured. Ordinarily, the two scales begin at zero and proceed in equal increments; however, the

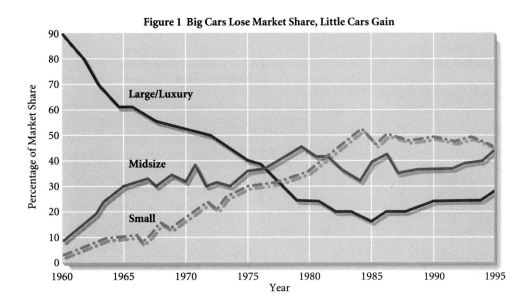

Figure 14.3
Line Chart Plotting Three Lines

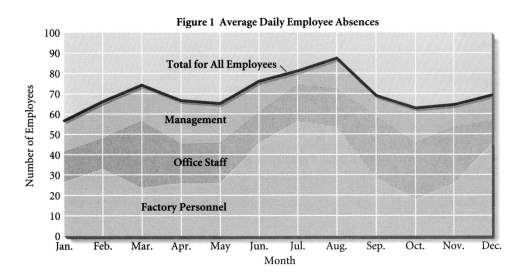

Figure 14.4
Surface Chart

vertical axis can be broken to show that some of the increments have been left out. A broken axis is appropriate when the data are plotted far above zero, but be sure to clearly indicate the omission of data points.

A simple line chart may be arranged in many ways. One of the most common is to plot several lines on the same chart for comparative purposes, as shown in Figure 14.3. Try to use no more than three lines on any given chart, particularly if the lines cross. Another variation of the simple line chart has a vertical axis with both positive and negative numbers. This arrangement is handy when you have to illustrate losses.

A **surface chart** is a form of line chart with a cumulative effect; all the lines add up to the top line, which represents the total (Figure 14.4). This form of chart helps you illustrate changes in the composition of something over time. When preparing a surface chart, put the most important segment against the baseline, and restrict the number of strata to four or five.

A surface chart is a kind of line chart showing cumulative effect.

Bar Charts A **bar chart** is a chart in which amounts are visually portrayed by the height or length of rectangular bars. Bar charts are almost as common in business reports as line charts, and in some ways they're more versatile. As Figure 14.5 illustrates, bar charts are particularly valuable when you want to

Bar charts, in which numbers are visually portrayed by rectangular bars, can take a variety of forms.

Figure 14.5
The Versatile Bar Chart

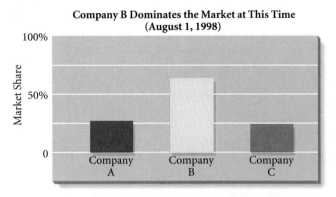

- Compare the size of several items at one time
- Show changes in one item over time
- Indicate the composition of several items over time
- Show the relative size of components of a whole

You can be creative with bar charts in many ways. You might align the bars either vertically or horizontally and double the bars for comparisons. You might even use bar charts to show both positive and negative quantities.

Pie Charts   Another type of chart you see frequently in business reports is the **pie chart,** in which numbers are represented as slices of a complete circle, or *pie.* As you can see from the pie chart in Figure 14.6, this type of chart helps you show exactly how each part is related to the whole. You can combine pie charts with tables to expand the usefulness of such visuals.

When composing pie charts, try to restrict the number of slices in the pie to a maximum of seven. Otherwise, the chart looks cluttered and is difficult to label. If necessary, lump the smallest pieces together in a "miscellaneous" category. Ideally, the largest or most important slice of the pie, the segment you want to emphasize, is placed at the twelve o'clock position; the rest are arranged clockwise either in order of size or in some other logical progression. You might want to shade the segment that is of the greatest interest to your readers or use color to distinguish the various pieces. In any case, label all the segments and indicate their value in either percentages or units of measure so that your readers will be able to judge the value of the wedges. The segments must add up to 100 percent.

Flowcharts and Organization Charts   If you need to show physical or conceptual relationships rather than numerical ones, you might want to use a flowchart or an

GOING ONLINE
DESIGN EFFECTIVE COMPUTER GRAPHICS
Mambo is a jump station to more than 65 Web sites containing the latest information about the imaginative world of computer graphics. The site provides links to company, university, and government labs displaying colorful portfolios; Usenet groups; and software companies. It also includes frequently asked questions (FAQs), bibliographies, conferences, and utilities.

http://www.mambo.ucsc.edu/psl/cg.html

Figure 1 Percentage of Sales Among the Six Leading Restaurant Chains

Figure 14.6
Pie Chart

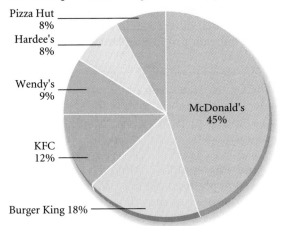

organization chart. A **flowchart** illustrates a sequence of events from start to finish. Flowcharts are indispensable for illustrating processes, procedures, and relationships. The various elements in the process you want to portray may be represented by pictorial symbols or geometric shapes, as shown in Figure 14.7.

An **organization chart,** as the name implies, illustrates the positions, units, or functions of an organization and how they are related. An organization's normal communication channels are almost impossible to describe without the benefit of a chart like the one in Figure 14.8.

Use flowcharts to
- Show a series of steps from beginning to end
- Show relationships

Use organization charts to depict the interrelationships among the parts of an organization.

Figure 1 Flow of Clients Through Health Center

Figure 14.7
Flowchart

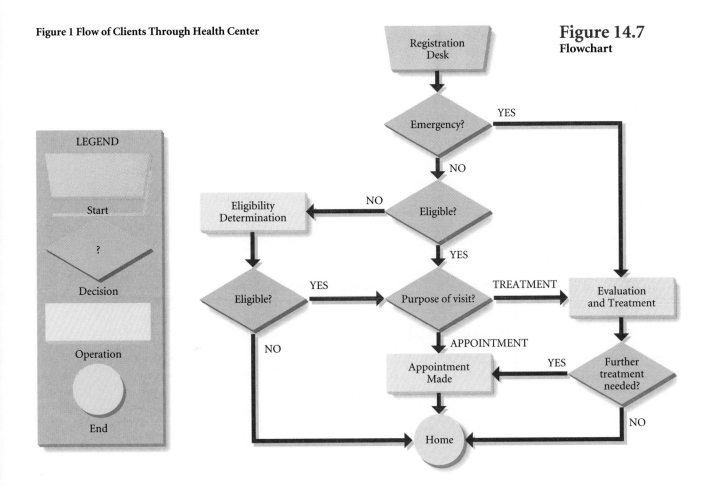

Use maps to
- Represent statistics by geographical area
- Show location relationships

Maps   For certain applications, maps are ideal. One of the most common uses is to show concentrations of something by geographical area. In your own reports, you might use maps to show regional differences in such variables as your company's sales of a product. You might indicate proposed plant sites and their relationship to key markets.

Most U.S. office-supply stores carry blank maps of various regions of the world, including all or part of the United States. You can illustrate these maps to suit your needs, using dots, shading, color, labels, numbers, and symbols. In addition, you can use specialized computer programs to select maps of various regions and insert just the portions you need into your business documents.

Use drawings and diagrams to show
- How something looks or works
- How something is made or used

Drawings, Diagrams, and Photographs   Although less common than other visual aids, drawings, diagrams, and photographs are also used in business reports. Drawings and diagrams are most often used to show how something looks or operates. Figure 14.9 is from an article explaining how a new satellite network will let people place calls to any one point on the earth from any other point on the earth. This diagram was professionally prepared, but even a hand-drawn sketch can be much clearer than words alone when it comes to giving your audience an idea of how an item looks or how it can be used. In industries such as engineering and architecture, computer-aided design systems produce detailed diagrams and drawings. A variety of widely available software programs for microcomputers provide a file of symbols and pictures of various types, which can be used (sparingly) to add a decorative touch to reports and presentations.

Use photographs
- For visual appeal
- To show exact appearance

Photographs have always been popular in certain types of business documents, such as annual reports, where their visual appeal is used to capture the interest of readers. As the technology for reproducing photographs improves and becomes less expensive, even analytical business reports for internal use are beginning to include more photographs. Digital cameras now make it easy to drop photographic images directly into a report or presentation. Nothing can demonstrate the exact appearance of a new

Figure 14.8
Organization Chart

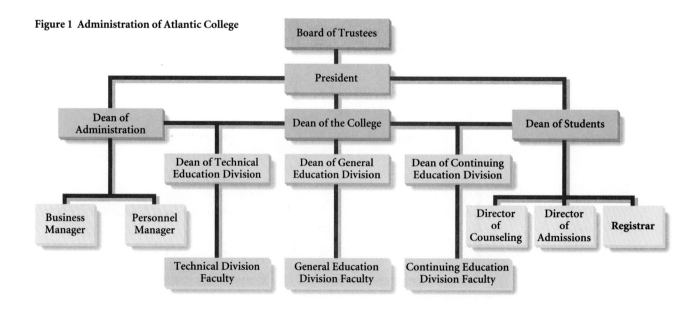

Figure 1 Administration of Atlantic College

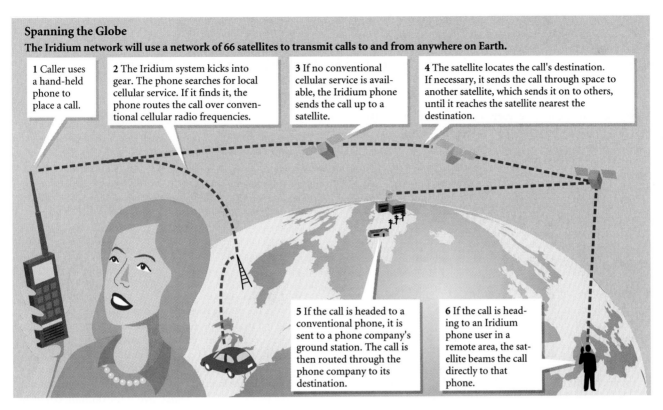

Figure 14.9
Diagram

facility, a piece of property or equipment, or a new product the way a photograph can. In some situations, however, a photograph shows too much detail. This is one of the reasons repair manuals, for instance, frequently use drawings instead of photos. With a drawing, you can select how much detail to show and focus the reader's attention on particular parts or places.

Technology has created new opportunities and an important new ethical concern for people who use photography in reports and other materials. Software tools such as Photoshop now make it easy for computer users to make dramatic changes to photos—without leaving a clue. Small changes to photos have been possible for a long time, of course (more than a few people have blemishes airbrushed out of their yearbook photos), but computers make drastic changes easy and undetectable. You can remove people from photographs, put Person A's head on Person B's body, and make products look more attractive than they really are. As with other technological tools, stop and ask yourself where the truth lies before you start making changes.[3]

> Computer-graphics systems cut the time and cost involved in producing visual aids.

Supplementary Parts

Supplementary parts follow the text of the report and include any appendixes, the bibliography, and the index. They are more common in long reports than in short ones.

An **appendix** contains materials related to the report but not included in the text because they're too lengthy or bulky or because they lack direct relevance. Frequently included in appendixes are sample questionnaires and cover letters, sample forms, computer printouts, and statistical formulas; a glossary of terms may be put in an appendix or may stand as a separate supplementary part. The best place to include visual aids is in the text body nearest the point of discussion. If any graphics are too large to fit on one page or are

> Put into an appendix materials that are
> - Bulky or lengthy
> - Not directly relevant to the text

REPORT WRITER'S NOTEBOOK
Creating Colorful Visual Aids with Computers for Maximum Clarity and Impact

More and more people are learning to use graphics software to create striking and attractive visual aids. No matter which type of software you use, your design is likely to look more professional than a graphic drawn by hand. Once you've designed your visual, you can also use your computer and software to plan the colors.

You know from your own experience that color helps make a point more effectively than black and white. However, there's more to using color than simply picking hues that appeal to you. To choose an effective color scheme, ask yourself these questions:

- *What colors will best convey the effect I want?* As a general rule, bright, solid colors are more pleasing to the eye and easier to distinguish than pastel or patterned colors. Yellow, blue, and green are usually good choices, but the possibilities are numerous. Just keep in mind that too many colors may overwhelm the message. Use color as an accent, bright color for emphasis and darker or lighter colors for background information. Color can also visually connect related points or set apart points that represent significant change.
- *Are these colors appropriate for my message, purpose, and audience?* Liking red is not a good reason for using it in all

your graphic designs. It's too "hot" for some people and conveys the wrong message in some instances; for example, using red to show profits in an annual report might confuse readers because they're likely to associate your graphic with "red ink," or losses. Also remember that people in other cultures will make color associations that differ from yours.

- *Is my audience familiar with these colors?* Unless your aim is to shake up your audience, avoid uncommon colors or unusual combinations. In general, conventional colors are best for conventional audiences. However, young or trendy audiences probably won't be jarred by unfamiliar colors.

---

only indirectly relevant to your report, they too may be put in an appendix. Some organizations specify that all visual aids be placed in an appendix.

Each type of material deserves a separate appendix. Identify the appendixes by labeling them, for example, "Appendix A: Questionnaire," "Appendix B: Computer Printout of Raw Data," and the like. All appendixes should be mentioned in the text and listed in the table of contents.

List your secondary sources in the bibliography.

A **bibliography** is a list of sources consulted when preparing the report. Linda Moreno labeled her bibliography as "Sources" in her Electrovision report. You might also call this section "Works Cited" or "References." The construction of a bibliography is shown in Appendix B.

An **index** is an alphabetical list of names, places, and subjects mentioned in the report and the pages on which they occur, as in the index for this book. An index is rarely included in unpublished reports.

COMPONENTS OF A FORMAL PROPOSAL

Certain analytical reports are called proposals, including bids to perform work under a contract and pleas for financial support from outsiders. As Levi's Robert Haas can tell you, such bids and pleas are nearly always formal. The goal is to impress the potential client or supporter with your professionalism, and that goal is best achieved through a structured and deliberate approach.

Formal proposals contain most of the same prefatory parts as other formal reports.

Formal proposals contain many of the same components as other formal reports (Figure 14.10). The difference lies mostly in the text, although a few of the prefatory parts are also different. With the exception of an occasional appendix, most proposals have few supplementary parts.

■ *Can I improve the effect by changing any of the colors?* When you have the opportunity to use more than one color, choose those that contrast. Colors without contrast blend together and obscure the message. At the same time, be careful to use vivid or highly saturated colors sparingly.

Of course, your color choices may be limited or dictated in certain situations. Some organizations specify the exact color or combination to be used on company logos and other official symbols or illustrations. At other times you'll be free to decide on any combination of colors that works best for the visual aid you're preparing. That's when you'll find graphics software especially useful.

Depending on the capabilities of your software and your computer monitor, you can try out various colors and combinations and see the results immediately. Even the most basic program offers three colors. More sophisticated programs can give you thousands or even millions of color and shading choices.

To start, select a background color from the program's "palette" of available colors. Then choose a dominant color to set the tone for the overall color scheme.

Continue adding colors as necessary, until you find the combination that works best. Because you can test many colors and combinations with a quick click of the mouse, you can come to a final decision more quickly (and with less effort) than if you had to do it without the software.

Once you've decided on colors, you can print out a hard copy or an acetate transparency using a color printer or color plotter. You can also create full-color slides using a film recorder, or you can simply project the colorful image from your computer screen through an overhead projector to a large viewing screen.

Apply Your Knowledge

1. Would you use green or red to shade a visual aid showing the geographic areas where your firm does business? Would you use green or red to shade the areas where your firm does not do business? Why?
2. How can you use color in a line chart to help your audience differentiate between current and projected sales? Between expected and actual sales? Explain your answers.

PREFATORY PARTS	TEXT OF THE PROPOSAL	SUPPLEMENTARY PARTS
Cover	Introduction	Appendixes
Title fly	Body	
Title Page	Summary	
Request for proposal		
Letter of transmittal		
Table of contents		
List of Illustrations		
Synopsis or executive summary		

Figure 14.10
Parts of a Formal Proposal

Prefatory Parts

The cover, title fly, title page, table of contents, and list of illustrations are handled the same as in other formal reports. However, other prefatory parts are quite different:

■ *Copy of the RFP.* Instead of having a letter of authorization, a formal proposal may have a copy of the **request for proposal (RFP),** which is a letter or memo soliciting a proposal or bid for a particular project. The RFP is issued by the client to whom the proposal is being submitted and outlines what the proposal should cover. If the RFP includes detailed specifications, it may be too long to bind into the proposal; in that case, you may want to include only the introductory portion of the RFP. Another option is to omit the RFP and simply refer to it in your letter of transmittal.

Use a copy of the request for proposal in place of the letter of authorization.

REPORT WRITER'S NOTEBOOK
In-Depth Critique: Analyzing a Formal Report

The report presented in the following pages was prepared by Linda Moreno, manager of the cost accounting department at Electrovision, a high-tech company based in Los Gatos, California. Electrovision's main product is optical character recognition equipment, which is used by the U.S. Postal Service for sorting mail. Moreno's job is to help analyze the company's costs. She has this to say about the background of this report:

"For the past three or four years, Electrovision has been on a roll. Our A-12 optical character reader was a real breakthrough, and the post office grabbed up as many as we could make. Our sales and profits kept climbing, and morale was fantastic. Everybody seemed to think that the good times would last forever. Unfortunately, everybody was wrong. When the Postal Service announced that it was postponing all new-equipment purchases because of cuts in its budget, we woke up to the fact that we are essentially a one-product company with one customer. At that point management started scrambling around looking for ways to cut costs until we could diversify our business a bit.

"The vice president of operations, Dennis McWilliams, asked me to help identify cost-cutting opportunities in the travel and entertainment area. On the basis of his personal observations, he felt that Electrovision was overly generous in its travel policies and that we might be able to save a significant amount by controlling these costs more carefully. My investigation confirmed his suspicion.

"I was reasonably confident that my report would be well received. I've worked with Dennis for several years and know what he likes: plenty of facts, clearly stated conclusions, and specific recommendations for what should be done next. I also knew that my report would be passed on to other Electrovision executives, so I wanted to create a good impression. I wanted the report to be accurate and thorough, visually appealing, readable, and appropriate in tone."

When writing the analytical report that follows, Moreno used an organization based on conclusions and recommendations, presented in direct order. The first two sections of the report correspond to Moreno's two main conclusions: that Electrovision's travel and entertainment costs are too high and that cuts are essential. The third section presents recommendations for achieving better control over travel and entertainment expenses. As you review the report, analyze both the mechanical aspects and the way Moreno presents her ideas. Be prepared to discuss the way the various components convey and reinforce the main message.

REDUCING ELECTROVISION'S TRAVEL
AND ENTERTAINMENT COSTS

Prepared for
Dennis McWilliams,
Vice President of Operations
Electrovision, Inc.

Prepared by
Linda Moreno, Manager
Cost Accounting Services
Electrovision, Inc.

February 15, 1999

Capitalize the title; use uppercase and lowercase letters for all other lines.

Follow the title with the name, title, and organization of the recipient.

Balance the white space between the items on the page.

When centering the lines horizontally on the title page, allow an extra 1/2-inch margin on the left side if it's a left-bound report.

For future reference, include the report's publication date.

The "how to" tone of Moreno's title is appropriate for an action-oriented report that emphasizes recommendations. A more neutral title, such as "An Analysis of Electrovision's Travel and Entertainment Costs," would be more suitable for an informational report.

Use memo format for transmitting internal reports, letter format for transmitting external reports.

Present the main conclusion or recommendation right away if you expect a positive response.

Use an informal, conversational style for the letter or memo of transmittal.

Acknowledge any help that you have received.

Close with thanks, an offer to discuss results, and an offer to assist with future projects, if appropriate.

MEMORANDUM

TO: Dennis McWilliams, Vice President of Operations

FROM: Linda Moreno, Manager of Cost Accounting Services

DATE: February 15, 1999

SUBJECT: Reducing Electrovision's Travel and Entertainment Costs

Here is the report you requested January 30 on Electrovision's travel and entertainment costs.

Your suspicion was right. We are spending far too much on business travel. Our unwritten policy has been "anything goes," leaving us with no real control over T&E expenses. Although this hands-off approach may have been understandable when Electrovision's profits were high, we can no longer afford the luxury of going first class.

The solutions to the problem seem rather clear. We need to have someone with centralized responsibility for travel and entertainment costs, a clear statement of policy, an effective control system, and a business-oriented travel service that can optimize our travel arrangements. We should also investigate alternatives to travel, such as videoconferencing. Perhaps more important, we need to change our attitude. Instead of viewing travel funds as a bottomless supply of money, all traveling employees need to act as though they were paying the bills themselves.

Getting people to economize is not going to be easy. In the course of researching this issue, I've found that our employees are deeply attached to their first-class travel privileges. I think they would almost prefer a cut in pay to a loss in travel status. We'll need a lot of top management involvement to sell people on the need for moderation. One thing is clear: People will be very bitter if we create a two-class system in which top executives get special privileges while the rest of the employees make the sacrifices.

I'm grateful to Mary Lehman and Connie McIlvain for their help in rounding up and sorting through five years' worth of expense reports. Their efforts were truly herculean.

Thanks for giving me the opportunity to work on this assignment. It's been a real education. If you have any questions about the report, please give me a call.

In this report Moreno decided to write a brief memo of transmittal and include a separate executive summary. Short reports (fewer than ten pages) often combine the synopsis or executive summary with the memo or letter of transmittal.

CONTENTS

iii

Include no element that appears before the "Contents" page.

Word the headings exactly as they appear in the text.

Include only the page numbers where sections begin.

Moreno included only first- and second-level headings in her table of contents, even though the report contains third-level headings. She prefers a shorter table of contents that focuses attention on the main divisions of thought. She used informative titles, which are appropriate for a report to a receptive audience.

LIST OF ILLUSTRATIONS

iv

Number the contents pages with lowercase roman numerals centered at the bottom margin.

Because figures and tables were numbered separately in the text, Moreno listed them separately here. If all had been labeled as exhibits, a single list of illustrations would have been appropriate.

EXECUTIVE SUMMARY

This report analyzes Electrovision's travel and entertainment (T&E) costs and presents recommendations for reducing those costs.

Travel and Entertainment Costs Are Too High

Travel and entertainment is a large and growing expense category for Electrovision. The company spends over $16 million per year on business travel, and these costs have been increasing by 12 percent annually. Company employees make roughly 3,390 trips each year at an average cost per trip of $4,720. Airfares are the biggest expense, followed by hotels, meals, and rental cars.

The nature of Electrovision's business does require extensive travel, but the company's costs appear to be excessive. Every year Electrovision employees spend more than twice as much on T&E as the average business traveler. Although the location of the company's facilities may partly explain this discrepancy, the main reason for Electrovision's high costs is the firm's philosophy and managerial style. Electrovision's tradition and its hands-off style almost invite employees to go first class and pay relatively little attention to travel costs.

Cuts Are Essential

Although Electrovision has traditionally been casual about travel and entertainment expenses, management now recognizes the need to gain more control over this element of costs. The company is currently entering a period of declining profits, prompting management to look for every opportunity to reduce spending. At the same time, rising airfares and hotel rates are making travel and entertainment expenses more important to the bottom line.

Electrovision Can Save $6 Million per Year

Fortunately, Electrovision has a number of excellent opportunities for reducing its travel and entertainment costs. Savings of up to $6 million per year should be achievable, judging by the experience of other companies. American Express suggests that a sensible travel-management program can save companies as much as 35 percent a year (Gilligan 39–40). Given that we purchase many more first-class tickets than the average company, we should be able to achieve even greater savings. The first priority should be to hire a director of travel and entertainment to assume overall responsibility for T&E spending. This individual should establish a written travel and entertainment policy and create a budget and a cost-control system. The director should also retain a nationwide travel agency to handle our reservations and should lead an investigation into electronic alternatives to travel.

v

Begin by stating the purpose of the report.

Present the points in the executive summary in the same order as they appear in the report; use subheadings that summarize the content of the main sections of the report without repeating those that appear in the text.

Type the synopsis or executive summary in the same manner as the text of the report. Use single spacing if the report is single spaced, and use the same format as used in the text for margins, paragraph indentions, and headings.

Moreno decided to include an executive summary because her report was aimed at a mixed audience. She knew that some readers would be interested in the details of her report and some would prefer to focus on the big picture. The executive summary was aimed at the big-picture group. Moreno wanted to give these readers enough information to make a decision without burdening them with the task of reading the entire report.

The hard-hitting tone of this executive summary is appropriate for a receptive audience. A more neutral approach would be better for hostile or skeptical readers.

At the same time, Electrovision should make employees aware of the need for moderation in travel and entertainment spending. People should be encouraged to forgo any unnecessary travel and to economize on airline tickets, hotels, meals, rental cars, and other expenses.

In addition to economizing on an individual basis, Electrovision should look for ways to reduce costs by negotiating preferential rates with travel providers. Once retained, a travel agency should be able to accomplish this.

Finally, we should look into alternatives to travel. Although we may have to invest money in videoconferencing systems or other equipment, we may be able to recover these costs through decreased travel expenses. I recommend that the new travel director undertake this investigation to make sure it is well integrated with the rest of the travel program.

These changes, although necessary, are likely to hurt morale, at least in the short term. Management will need to make a determined effort to explain the rationale for reduced spending. By exercising moderation in their own travel arrangements, Electrovision executives can set a good example and help other employees accept the changes. On the plus side, cutting back on travel with videoconferencing or other alternatives will reduce the travel burden on many employees and help them balance their business and personal lives much better.

vi

Number the pages of the executive summary with lowercase roman numerals centered about 1 inch from the bottom of the page.

This executive summary is written in an impersonal style, which adds to the formality of the report. Some writers prefer a more personal approach. Generally speaking, you should gear your choice of style to your relationship with the readers. Moreno chose the formal approach because several members of her audience were considerably higher up in the organization. She did not want to sound too familiar. In addition, she wanted the executive summary and the text to be compatible, and her company prefers the impersonal style for formal reports.

REDUCING ELECTROVISION'S TRAVEL AND ENTERTAINMENT COSTS

INTRODUCTION

Electrovision has always encouraged a significant amount of business travel, believing that it is an effective way of operating. To compensate employees for the inconvenience and stress of frequent trips, management has authorized generous travel and entertainment (T&E) allowances. This philosophy has been good for morale, but the company has paid a price. Last year Electrovision spent $16 million on T&E—$7 million more than it spent on research and development.

This year the cost of travel and entertainment will have a bigger impact on profits, owing to changes in airfares and hotel rates. The timing of these changes is unfortunate because the company anticipates that profits will be relatively weak for a variety of other reasons. In light of these profit pressures, Dennis McWilliams, Vice President of Operations, has asked the accounting department to take a closer look at the T&E budget.

Purpose, Scope, and Limitations

The purpose of this report is to analyze the T&E budget, evaluate the impact of recent changes in airfares and hotel costs, and suggest ways to tighten management's control over T&E expenses. Although the report outlines a number of steps that could reduce Electrovision's expenses, the precise financial impact of these measures is difficult to project. The estimates presented in the report provide a "best guess" view of what Electrovision can expect to save. Until the company actually implements these steps, however, we won't know exactly how much the travel and entertainment budget can be reduced.

Sources and Methods

In preparing this report, the accounting department analyzed internal expense reports for the past five years to determine how much Electrovision spends on travel and entertainment. These figures were then compared with average statistics compiled by Dow Jones (publisher of *The Wall Street Journal*) and presented as the Dow Jones Travel Index. We also analyzed trends and suggestions published in a variety of business journal articles to see how other companies are coping with the high cost of business travel.

Center the title of the report on the first page of the text, 2 inches (2½ inches if top-bound) from the top of the page.

Begin the introduction by establishing the need for action.

Mentioning sources and methods increases the credibility of a report and gives readers a complete picture of the study's background.

Use the arabic numeral 1 for the first page of the report; center the number about 1 inch from the bottom of the page.

In a brief introduction like this one, some writers would omit the subheadings within the introduction and rely on topic sentences and on transitional words and phrases to indicate that they are discussing such subjects as the purpose, scope, and limitations of the study. Moreno decided to use headings because they help readers scan the document. Also, to conserve space, Moreno used single spacing and 1-inch side margins.

Using arabic numerals, number the second and succeeding pages of the text in the upper right-hand corner where the top and right-hand margins meet.

2

Report Organization

This report reviews the size and composition of Electrovision's travel and entertainment expenses, analyzes trends in travel costs, and recommends steps for reducing the T&E budget.

THE HIGH COST OF TRAVEL AND ENTERTAINMENT

Although many companies view travel and entertainment as an "incidental" cost of doing business, the dollars add up. At Electrovision the bill for airfares, hotels, rental cars, meals, and entertainment totaled $16 million last year. Our T&E budget has increased by 12 percent per year for the past five years. Compared to the average U.S. business traveler, Electrovision's expenditures are high, largely because of management's generous policy on travel benefits.

$16 Million per Year Spent on Travel and Entertainment

Electrovision's annual budget for travel and entertainment is only 8 percent of sales. Because this is a relatively small expense category compared with such things as salaries and commissions, it is tempting to dismiss T&E costs as insignificant. However, T&E is Electrovision's third-largest controllable expense, directly behind salaries and information systems.

Last year Electrovision personnel made about 3,390 trips at an average cost per trip of $4,720. The typical trip involved a round-trip flight of 3,000 miles, meals and hotel accommodations for two or three days, and a rental car. Roughly 80 percent of the trips were made by 20 percent of the staff—top management and sales personnel traveled most, averaging 18 trips per year.

Figure 1 illustrates how the travel and entertainment budget is spent. The largest categories are airfares and lodging, which together account for $7 out of every $10

Place the visual aid as close as possible to the point it illustrates.

Placement of visual aids titles should be consistent throughout a report. Options for placement include above, below, or beside the visual aid.

Give each visual aid a title that clearly indicates what it's about.

Figure 1
Airfares and Lodging Account for Over Two-Thirds of Electrovision's Travel and Entertainment Budget

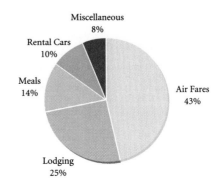

Moreno opened the first main section of the body with a topic sentence that introduces an important fact about the subject of the section. Then she oriented the reader to the three major points developed in the section.

3

that employees spend on travel and entertainment. This spending breakdown has been relatively steady for the past five years and is consistent with the distribution of expenses experienced by other companies.

Although the composition of the T&E budget has been consistent, its size has not. As mentioned earlier, these expenditures have increased by about 12 percent per year for the past five years, roughly twice the rate of the company's growth in sales (see Figure 2). This rate of growth makes T&E Electrovision's fastest-growing expense item.

Introduce visual aids before they appear, and indicate what readers should notice about the data.

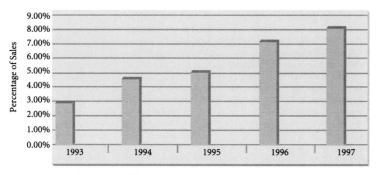

Figure 2
Travel and Entertainment Expenses Have Increased as a Percentage of Sales

Number the visual aids consecutively, and refer to them in the text by their numbers. If your report is a book-length document, you may number the visual aids by chapter: Figure 4-2, for example, would be the second figure in the fourth chapter.

Electrovision's Travel Expenses Exceed National Averages

Much of our travel budget is justified. Two major factors contribute to Electrovision's high travel and entertainment budget:

- With our headquarters on the West Coast and our major customer on the East Coast, we naturally spend a lot on cross-country flights.
- A great deal of travel takes place between our headquarters here on the West Coast and the manufacturing operations in Detroit, Boston, and Dallas. Corporate managers and division personnel make frequent trips to coordinate these disparate operations.

However, even though a good portion of Electrovision's travel budget is justifiable, the company spends considerably more on travel and entertainment than the average business traveler (see Figure 3).

Moreno originally drew the bar chart in Figure 2 as a line chart, showing both sales and T&E expenses in absolute dollars. However, the comparison was difficult to interpret because sales were so much greater than T&E expenses. Switching to a bar chart expressed in percentage terms made the main idea much easier to grasp. The chart in Figure 3 is very simple, but it creates an effective visual comparison. Moreno included just enough data to make her point.

4

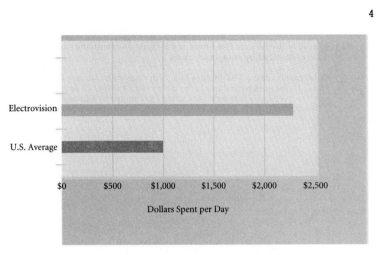

Figure 3
Electrovision People Spend Over Twice as Much as the Average Business Traveler
Source: *The Wall Street Journal* and company records

The Dow Jones Travel Index calculates the average cost per day of business travel in the United States, based on average airfare, hotel rates, and rental car rates. The average fluctuates weekly as travel companies change their rates, but it has been running at about $1,000 per day for the last year or so. In contrast, Electrovision's average daily expense over the past year has been $2,250—125 percent higher than average. This figure is based on the average trip cost of $4,720 listed earlier and an average trip length of 2.1 days.

Spending Has Been Encouraged

Leaving a bit more white space above a heading than below it helps readers associate that heading with the text it describes.

Although a variety of factors may contribute to this differential, Electrovision's relatively high T&E costs are at least partially attributable to the company's philosophy and management style. Because many employees do not enjoy business travel, management has tried to make the trips more pleasant by authorizing first-class airfare, luxury hotel accommodations, and full-size rental cars. The sales staff is encouraged to entertain clients at top restaurants and to invite them to cultural and sporting events.

The cost of these privileges is easy to overlook, given the weakness of Electrovision's system for keeping track of T&E expenses:

Moreno was as careful about the appearance of her report as she was about its content.

5

- The monthly financial records provided to management do not contain a separate category for travel and entertainment; the information is buried under Cost of Goods Sold and under Selling, General, and Administrative Expenses.
- Each department head is given authority to approve any expense report, regardless of how large it may be.
- Receipts are not required for expenditures of less than $100.
- Individuals are allowed to make their own travel arrangements.
- No one is charged with the responsibility for controlling the company's total spending on travel and entertainment.

GROWING IMPACT ON THE BOTTOM LINE

During the past three years, the company's healthy profits have resulted in relatively little pressure to push for tighter controls over all aspects of the business. However, as we all know, the situation is changing. We're projecting flat to declining profits for the next two years, a situation that has prompted all of us to search for ways to cut costs. At the same time, rising airfares and hotel rates have increased the impact of T&E expenses on the company's financial results.

Lower Profits Underscore the Need for Change

The next two years promise to be difficult for Electrovision. After several years of steady increases in spending, the Postal Service is tightening procurement policies for automated mail-handling equipment. Funding for the A-12 optical character reader has been canceled. As a consequence, the marketing department expects sales to drop by 15 percent. Although Electrovision is negotiating several promising R&D contracts with nongovernment clients, the marketing department does not foresee any major procurements for the next two to three years.

At the same time, Electrovision is facing cost increases on several fronts. As we've known for several months, the new production facility now under construction in Salt Lake City, Utah, is behind schedule and over budget. Labor contracts in Boston and Dallas expire within the next six months, and plant managers there anticipate that significant salary and benefits concessions may be necessary to avoid strikes. Moreover, marketing and advertising costs are expected to increase as we attempt to strengthen these activities to better cope with competitive pressures. Given the expected decline in revenues and increase in costs, the Executive Committee's prediction that profits will fall by 12 percent in the coming fiscal year does not seem overly pessimistic.

Airfares and Hotel Rates Are Rising

Business travelers have grown accustomed to frequent fare wars and discounting in the travel industry in recent years. Excess capacity and aggressive price competition, particularly in the airline business, made travel a relative bargain.

Bulleted lists make it easy for readers to identify and distinguish related points.

Informative headings focus readers' attention on the main points of the report. Thus they are most appropriate when the report is in direct order and is aimed at a receptive audience. Descriptive headings are more effective when a report is in indirect order and the readers are less receptive.

Because airfares represent Electrovision's biggest T&E expense, Moreno included a subsection that deals with the possible impact of trends in the airline industry. Airfares are rising, so it is especially important to gain more control over employees' air travel arrangements.

6

Documenting the facts adds weight to Moreno's argument.

However, that situation has changed, as weaker competitors have been forced out and the remaining players have grown stronger and smarter. Airlines and hotels are better at managing inventory and keeping occupancy rates high, and high occupancy translates into higher prices because suppliers have less reason to compete on price. Last year saw some of the steepest rate hikes in years. Business airfares (tickets most likely to be purchased by business travelers) jumped over 40 percent in many markets. The trend is expected to continue, with rates increasing another 5 to 10 percent overall (Phillips 331; "Travel Costs Under Pressure" 30; Dahl B6).

Given the fact that air and hotel costs account for 70 percent of Electrovision's T&E budget, the trend toward higher prices in these two categories will have serious consequences on the company's expenses unless management takes action to control these costs.

METHODS FOR REDUCING TRAVEL AND ENTERTAINMENT COSTS

Pointing out both the benefits and risks of taking action gives recommendations an objective flavor.

By implementing a number of reforms, management can expect to reduce Electrovision's T&E budget by as much as 40 percent. This estimate is based on the general assessment made by American Express (Gilligan 39–40) and the fact that we have an opportunity to significantly reduce air travel costs by reducing or eliminating first-class travel. However, these measures are likely to be unpopular with employees. To gain acceptance for such changes, management will need to sell employees on the need for moderation in travel and entertainment allowances.

Four Ways to Trim Expenses

By researching what other companies are doing to curb travel and entertainment expenses, the accounting department has identified four prominent opportunities that should enable Electrovision to save about $6 million annually in travel-related costs.

Institute Tighter Spending Controls

A single individual should be appointed director of travel and entertainment to spearhead the effort to gain control of the T&E budget. More than a third of all U.S. companies now employ travel managers in an effort to keep costs in line ("Businesses Use Savvy Managers" 4). The director should be familiar with the travel industry and should be well versed in both accounting and information technology. The director should also report to the vice president of operations. The director's first priorities should be to establish a written travel and entertainment policy and to implement a system for controlling travel and entertainment costs.

Electrovision currently has no written policy on travel and entertainment, a step widely recommended by air travel experts (Smith D4). Creating a policy would

Moreno created a forceful tone by using action verbs in the third-level subheadings of this section. This approach is appropriate to the nature of the study and the attitude of the audience. However, in a status-conscious organization, the imperative verbs might sound a bit too presumptuous coming from a junior member of the staff.

7

clarify management's position and serve as a vehicle for communicating the need for moderation. At a minimum, the policy should include the following provisions:

- All travel and entertainment should be strictly related to business and should be approved in advance.
- Except under special circumstances to be approved on a case by case basis, employees should travel by coach and stay in mid-range business hotels.
- The travel and entertainment policy should apply equally to employees at all levels in the organization. No special benefits should be allowed for top executives.

To implement the new policy, Electrovision will need to create a system for controlling travel and entertainment expenses. Each department should prepare an annual T&E budget as part of its operating plan. These budgets should be presented in detail so that management can evaluate how travel and entertainment dollars will be spent and recommend appropriate cuts.

To help management monitor performance relative to these budgets, the director of travel should prepare monthly financial statements showing actual travel and entertainment expenditures by department. The system for capturing this information should be computerized and should be capable of identifying individuals who consistently exceed approved spending levels. The recommended average should range between $2,000 and $2,500 per month for each professional employee, depending on the individual's role in the company. Because they make frequent trips, sales and top management personnel can be expected to have relatively high travel expenses.

The director of travel should also be responsible for retaining a business-oriented travel service that will schedule all employee business trips and look for the best travel deals, particularly in airfares. In addition to centralizing Electrovision's reservation and ticketing activities, the agency will negotiate reduced group rates with hotels and rental car agencies. The agency selected should have offices nationwide so that all Electrovision facilities can channel their reservations through the same company. By consolidating its travel planning in this way, Electrovision can increase its control over costs and achieve economies of scale. This is particularly important in light of the dizzying array of often wildly different airfares available between some cities. It's not uncommon to find dozens of fares along commonly traveled routes (Rowe 30).

The director should also work with the agency to explore low-cost alternatives, such as buying tickets from airfare consolidators (the air travel equivalent of factory outlet malls). In addition, the director can help coordinate travel across the company to secure group discounts whenever possible (Barker 31; Miller B6).

The bulleted list format not only calls attention to important points but adds visual interest. You can also use visual aids, headings, and direct quotations to break up large, solid blocks of print.

When including recommendations in a report, specify the steps required to implement them.

Moreno decided to single space her report to save space; however, double spacing can make the text of a long report somewhat easier to read, and it provides more space for readers to write comments.

8

Reduce Unnecessary Travel and Entertainment

One of the easiest ways to reduce expenses is to reduce the amount of traveling and entertaining that occurs. An analysis of last year's expenditures suggests that as much as 30 percent of Electrovision's travel and entertainment is discretionary. The professional staff spent $2.8 million attending seminars and conferences last year. Although some of these gatherings are undoubtedly beneficial, the company could save money by sending fewer representatives to each function and by eliminating some of the less valuable seminars.

Similarly, Electrovision could economize on trips between headquarters and divisions by reducing the frequency of such visits and by sending fewer people on each trip. Although there is often no substitute for face-to-face meetings, management could try to resolve more internal issues through telephone, electronic, and written communication.

Electrovision can also reduce spending by urging employees to economize. Instead of flying first class, employees can fly tourist class or take advantage of discount fares. Instead of taking clients to dinner, Electrovision personnel can hold breakfast meetings, which tend to be less costly. Rather than ordering a $50 bottle of wine, employees can select a less expensive bottle or dispense with alcohol entirely. People can book rooms at moderately priced hotels and drive smaller rental cars. In general, employees should be urged to spend the company's money as though it were their own.

Obtain Lowest Rates from Travel Providers

Apart from urging individual employees to economize, Electrovision can also save money by searching for the lowest available airfares, hotel rates, and rental car fees. Currently, few Electrovision employees have the time or specialized knowledge to seek out travel bargains. When they need to travel, they make the most convenient and most comfortable arrangements. However, if Electrovision contracts with a professional travel service, the company will have access to professionals who can more efficiently obtain the lower rates from travel providers.

Judging by the experience of other companies, Electrovision may be able to trim as much as 30 to 40 percent from the travel budget by looking for bargains in airfares and negotiating group rates with hotels and rental car companies. Electrovision should be able to achieve these economies by analyzing its travel patterns, identifying frequently visited locations, and selecting a few hotels that are willing to reduce rates in exchange for guaranteed business. At the same time, the company should be able to save up to 40 percent on rental car charges by negotiating a corporate rate.

Note how Moreno made the transition from section to section. The first sentence under the second heading on this page refers to the subject of the previous paragraph and signals a shift in thought.

9

The possibilities for economizing are promising, but it's worth noting that making the best arrangements is a complicated undertaking, requiring many trade-offs such as the following:

- The best fares might not always be the lowest. Indirect flights are often less expensive than direct flights, but they take longer and may end up costing more in lost work time.
- The cheapest tickets may have to be booked 30 days in advance, often impossible for us.
- Discount tickets may be nonrefundable, which is a real drawback if the trip has to be canceled at the last minute.

Electrovision is currently ill-equipped to make these and other trade-offs. However, by employing a business-oriented travel service, the company will have access to computerized systems that can optimize its choices.

Replace Travel with Technological Alternatives

We might be able to replace a significant portion of our interdivisional travel with electronic meetings that utilize videoconferencing, real-time document sharing on PC screens, and other alternatives. Naturally, we don't want to reduce employee or team effectiveness, but many companies are using these new tools to cut costs and reduce wear and tear on employees.

Rather than make specific recommendations in this report, I suggest that the new travel director conduct an in-depth study of the company's travel patterns as part of an overall cost-containment effort. A thorough analysis of why employees travel and what they accomplish will highlight any opportunities for replacing face-to-face meetings. Part of this study should include limited-scope tests of various communication systems as a way of measuring their impact on both workplace effectiveness and overall costs.

The Impact of Reforms

By implementing tighter controls, reducing unnecessary expenses, negotiating more favorable rates, and exploring "electronic travel," Electrovision should be able to reduce its travel and entertainment budget significantly. As Table 1 illustrates, the combined savings should be in the neighborhood of $6 million, although the precise figures are somewhat difficult to project.

Pointing out possible difficulties demonstrates that you have considered all the angles and builds readers' confidence in your judgment.

The use of informative titles for exhibits is consistent with the way headings are handled and is appropriate for a report to a receptive audience. The use of complete sentences helps readers focus immediately on the point of the illustrations.

TABLE 1

Electrovision Can Trim Travel and Entertainment Costs by an Estimated $6 Million per Year

Source of Savings	Amount Saved
Switching from first-class to coach airfare	$2,300,000
Negotiating preferred hotel rates	940,000
Negotiating preferred rental car rates	460,000
Systematically searching for lower airfares	375,000
Reducing interdivisional travel	675,000
Reducing seminar and conference attendance	1,250,000
TOTAL POTENTIAL SAVINGS	**$6,000,000**

To achieve the economies outlined in the table, Electrovision will incur expenses for hiring a director of travel and for implementing a T&E cost-control system. These costs are projected at $95,000: $85,000 per year in salary and benefits for the new employee and a one-time expense of $10,000 for the cost-control system. The cost of retaining a full-service travel agency is negligible because agencies normally receive a commission from travel providers rather than a fee from clients.

Even though estimated savings may be difficult to project, including dollar figures helps management envision the impact of your suggestions.

The measures required to achieve these savings are likely to be unpopular with employees. Electrovision personnel are accustomed to generous travel and entertainment allowances, and they are likely to resent having these privileges curtailed. To alleviate their disappointment

- Management should make a determined effort to explain why the changes are necessary.
- The director of corporate communication should be asked to develop a multi-faceted campaign that will communicate the importance of curtailing travel and entertainment costs.
- Management should set a positive example by adhering strictly to the new policies.
- The limitations should apply equally to employees at all levels in the organization.

The table on this page puts Moreno's recommendations in perspective. Note how she called attention in the text to the most important sources of savings and also spelled out the costs required to achieve these results.

11

CONCLUSIONS AND RECOMMENDATIONS

Electrovision is currently spending $16 million per year on travel and entertainment. Although much of this spending is justified, the company's costs appear to be high relative to competitors', mainly because Electrovision has been generous with its travel benefits.

Electrovision's liberal approach to travel and entertainment was understandable during years of high profitability; however, the company is facing the prospect of declining profits for the next several years. Management is therefore motivated to cut costs in all areas of the business. Reducing T&E spending is particularly important because the impact of these costs on the bottom line will increase as a result of fare increases in the airline industry.

Electrovision should be able to reduce travel and entertainment costs by as much as 40 percent by taking four important steps:

1. *Institute tighter spending controls.* Management should hire a director of travel and entertainment who will assume overall responsibility for T&E activities. Within the next six months, this director should develop a written travel policy, institute a T&E budget and a cost-control system, and retain a professional, business-oriented travel agency that will optimize arrangements with travel providers.

2. *Reduce unnecessary travel and entertainment.* Electrovision should encourage employees to economize on travel and entertainment spending. Management can accomplish this by authorizing fewer trips and by urging employees to be more conservative in their spending.

3. *Obtain lowest rates from travel providers.* Electrovision should also focus on obtaining the best rates on airline tickets, hotel rooms, and rental cars. By channeling all arrangements through a professional travel agency, the company can optimize its choices and gain clout in negotiating preferred rates.

4. *Replace travel with technological alternatives.* With the number of computers already installed in our facilities, it seems likely that we could take advantage of desktop videoconferencing and other distance-meeting tools. This won't be quite as feasible with customer sites, since these systems require compatible equipment at both ends of a connection, but it is certainly a possibility for communication with Electrovision's own sites.

Because these measures may be unpopular with employees, management should make a concerted effort to explain the importance of reducing travel costs. The director of corporate communication should be given responsibility for developing a plan to communicate the need for employee cooperation.

Use a descriptive heading for the last section of the text. In informational reports, this section is generally called "Summary"; in analytical reports, it is called "Conclusions" or "Conclusions and Recommendations."

Emphasize the recommendations by presenting them in list format, if possible.

Do not introduce new facts in this section of the text.

Because Moreno organized her report around conclusions and recommendations, readers have already been introduced to them. Thus she summarizes her conclusions in the first two paragraphs. A simple list is enough to remind readers of the four main recommendations. In a longer report she might have divided the section into subsections, labeled "Conclusions" and "Recommendations," to distinguish between the two. If the report had been organized around logical arguments, this would have been the readers' first exposure to the conclusions and recommendations, and Moreno would have needed to develop them more fully.

12

WORKS CITED

Barker, Julie. "How to Rein in Group Travel Costs." *Successful Meetings* Feb. 1998: 31.

"Businesses Use Savvy Managers to Keep Travel Costs Down." *Christian Science Monitor* 17 July 1996: 4.

Dahl, Jonathan. "1997: The Year Travel Costs Took Off." *Wall Street Journal* 29 Dec. 1997: B6.

Gilligan, Edward P. "Trimming Your T&E Is Easier Than You Think." *Managing Office Technology* Nov. 1995: 39–40.

Miller, Lisa. "Attention, Airline Ticket Shoppers." *Wall Street Journal* 7 July 1997: B6.

Phillips, Edward H. "Airlines Post Record Traffic." *Aviation Week & Space Technology* 8 Jan. 1998: 331.

Rowe, Irene Vlitos. "Global Solution for Cutting Travel Costs." *European* 12 Oct. 1997: 30.

Smith, Carol. "Rising, Erratic Air Fares Make Company Policy Vital." *Los Angeles Times* 2 Nov. 1996: D4.

"Travel Costs Under Pressure." *Purchasing* 15 Feb. 1998: 30.

List references alphabetically by the author's last name or, when the author is unknown, by the title of the reference. See Appendix B for additional details on preparing reference lists.

Moreno's list of references follows the style recommended in the MLA Style Manual.

■ *Letter of transmittal.* The way you handle the letter of transmittal depends on whether the proposal is solicited or unsolicited. If the proposal is solicited, the transmittal letter follows the pattern for good-news messages, highlighting those aspects of your proposal that may give you a competitive advantage. If the proposal is unsolicited, the transmittal letter takes on added importance; in fact, it may be all the client reads. The letter must persuade the reader that you have something worthwhile to offer, something that justifies the time required to read the entire proposal. The transmittal letter for an unsolicited proposal follows the pattern for persuasive messages (see Chapter 11).

Use the good-news pattern for the letter of transmittal if the proposal is solicited; use the persuasive plan if the proposal is unsolicited.

■ *Synopsis or executive summary.* Although you may include a synopsis or an executive summary for your reader's convenience if your proposal is quite long, these components are somewhat less useful in a formal proposal than they are in a formal report. If your proposal is unsolicited, your transmittal letter will already have caught the reader's interest, making a synopsis or an executive summary pointless. It may also be pointless if your proposal is solicited, because the reader is already committed to studying the text to find out how you propose to satisfy the terms of a contract. The introduction to a solicited proposal would provide an adequate preview of the contents.

Most proposals do not require a synopsis or an executive summary.

Text of the Proposal

The text of a proposal performs two essential functions: It persuades the client to award you a contract, and it spells out the terms of that contract. The trick is to sell the client on your ideas without making promises that will haunt you later.

A proposal is both a selling tool and a contractual commitment.

If the proposal is unsolicited, you have some latitude in arranging the text. However, the organization of a solicited proposal is governed by the request for proposal. Most RFPs spell out precisely what you should cover, and in what order, so that all bids will be similar in form. This uniformity enables the client to evaluate the competing proposals in a systematic way. In fact, in many organizations a team of evaluators splits up the proposals and looks at various sections. An engineer might review the technical portions of all the proposals submitted, and an accountant might review the cost estimates.

Follow the instructions presented in the RFP.

Introduction

The introduction orients readers to the rest of the proposal. It identifies your organization and your purpose and outlines the remainder of the text. If the proposal is solicited, the introduction should refer to the RFP; if not, it should mention any factors that led you to submit the bid. You might refer to previous conversations you've had with the client, or you might mention mutual acquaintances. Subheadings often include the following:

■ *Background or statement of the problem.* Briefly reviews the client's situation, worded to establish the need for action. In business selling situations, the reader may not have the same perception of the problem as the writer has. With unsolicited proposals, potential clients and other readers may not even think they have a problem. You have to convince them a problem exists before you can convince them to accept your solution. You can do this by discussing the reader's current situation and explaining how things could be better—in a way that is meaningful to your reader.

■ *Overview of approach.* Highlights your key selling points and their benefits, showing how your proposal will solve the client's problem. The heading for this section might also be "Preliminary Analysis" or some other wording that will identify this section as a summary of your solution to the problem.

■ *Scope.* States the boundaries of the study, what you will and will not do. This brief section may also be labeled "Delimitations."

■ *Report organization.* Orients the reader to the remainder of the proposal and calls attention to the major divisions of thought.

As chairman of the board of Computer Associates International, Charles B. Wang must often make fast decisions on proposals. A clear purpose stated concisely saves time and promotes understanding, advises Wang, and that allows your reader to make the right decision.

CHECKLIST FOR FORMAL REPORTS AND PROPOSALS

A. Quality of the Research
1. Define the problem clearly.
2. State the purpose of the document.
3. Identify all relevant issues.
4. Accumulate evidence pertaining to each issue.
5. Check evidence for accuracy, currency, and reliability.
6. Justify your conclusions by the evidence.
   - a. Do not omit or distort evidence in order to support your point of view.
   - b. Identify and justify all assumptions.

B. Preparation of Reports and Proposals
1. Choose a format and length that are appropriate to your audience and the subject.
2. Prepare a sturdy, attractive cover.
   - a. Label the cover clearly with the title of the document.
   - b. Use a title that tells the audience exactly what the document is about.
3. Provide all necessary information on the title page.
   - a. Include the full title of the document.
   - b. Include the name, title, and affiliation of the recipient.
   - c. Give the name, title, and affiliation of the author.
   - d. Provide the date of submission.
   - e. Balance the information in blocks on the page.
4. Include a copy of the letter of authorization or request for proposal, if appropriate.
5. Prepare a letter or memo of transmittal.
   - a. Use memo format for internal documents.
   - b. Use letter format for external documents.
   - c. Include the transmittal letter in only some copies if it contains sensitive or personal information suitable for some but not all readers.
   - d. Place the transmittal letter right before the table of contents.
   - e. Use the good-news plan for solicited proposals and other reports; use the persuasive plan for unsolicited proposals.
   - f. Word the letter to "convey" the document officially to the readers; refer to the authorization; and discuss the purpose, scope, background, sources and methods, and limitations.
   - g. Mention any special points that warrant readers' attention.
   - h. If you use direct order, summarize conclusions and recommendations (unless they are included in a synopsis).
   - i. Acknowledge all who were especially helpful in preparing the document.
   - j. Close with thanks, offer to be of further assistance, and suggest future projects, if appropriate.
6. Prepare the table of contents.
   - a. Include all first-level headings (and all second-level headings or perhaps all second- and third-level headings).
   - b. Give the page number of each heading.
   - c. Word all headings exactly as they appear in the text.
   - d. Include the synopsis (if there is one) and supplementary parts in the table of contents.
   - e. Number the table of contents and all prefatory pages with lowercase roman numerals centered at the bottom of the page.
7. Prepare a list of illustrations if you have four visual aids or more.
   - a. Put the list in the same format as the table of contents.
   - b. Identify visual aids either directly beneath the table of contents or on a separate page under the heading "List of Illustrations."
8. Develop a synopsis or an executive summary if the document is long and formal.
   - a. Tailor the synopsis or executive summary to the document's length and tone.
   - b. Condense the main points of the document, using either the informative approach or the descriptive approach, according to the guidelines in this chapter.
   - c. Present the points in the synopsis in the same order as they appear in the document. Remember that an executive summary can deviate from the order of points made in the report.
9. Prepare the introduction to the text.
   - a. Leave a 2-inch margin at the top of the page, and center the title of the document.
   - b. In a long document (ten pages or more), type the first-level heading "Introduction" three lines below the title.
   - c. In a short document (fewer than ten pages), begin typing three lines below the title of the report or proposal without the heading "Introduction."
   - d. Discuss the authorization (unless it's covered in the letter of transmittal), purpose, scope, background, sources and methods, definitions, limitations, and text organization.

10. Prepare the body of the document.
    - a. Carefully select the organizational plan (see Chapter 13).
    - b. Use either a personal or an impersonal tone consistently.
    - c. Use either a past or a present time perspective consistently.
    - d. Follow a consistent format in typing headings of different levels, using a company format guide, a sample proposal or report, or the format in this textbook as a model (see Appendix A).
    - e. Express comparable (same-level) headings in any given section in parallel grammatical form.
    - f. Group ideas into logical categories.
    - g. Tie sections together with transitional words, sentences, and paragraphs.
    - h. Give ideas of equal importance roughly equal space.
    - i. Avoid overly technical, pretentious, or vague language.
    - j. Develop each paragraph around a topic sentence.
    - k. Make sure all ideas in each paragraph are related.
    - l. Double-space if longer than ten pages.
    - m. For documents bound on the left, number all pages with arabic numerals in the upper right-hand corner (except for the first page, where the number is centered 1 inch from the bottom); for top-bound documents, number all pages with arabic numerals centered 1 inch from the bottom.

11. Incorporate visual aids into the text.
    - a. Number visual aids consecutively throughout the text, numbering tables and figures (other visual aids) separately if that style is preferred.
    - b. Develop explicit titles for all visual aids except in-text tables.
    - c. Refer to each visual aid in the text, and emphasize the significance of the data.

- d. Place visual aids as soon after their textual explanations as possible, or group them at the ends of chapters or at the end of the document for easy reference.

12. Conclude the text of reports and proposals with a summary and, if appropriate, conclusions and recommendations.
    - a. In a summary, recap the findings and explanations already presented.
    - b. Place conclusions and recommendations in their order of logic or importance, preferably in list format.
    - c. To induce action, explain in the recommendations section who should do what, when, where, and how.
    - d. If appropriate, point out the benefits of action, to leave readers with the motivation to follow recommendations.

13. Document all material quoted or paraphrased from secondary sources, using a consistent format (see Appendix B).

14. Include appendixes at the end of the document to provide useful and detailed information that is of interest to some but not all readers.
    - a. Give each appendix a title, such as "Questionnaire" or "Names and Addresses of Survey Participants."
    - b. If there is more than one appendix, number or letter them consecutively in the order they're referred to in the text.
    - c. Type appendixes in a format consistent with the text of the report or proposal.

15. Include a bibliography if it seems that readers would benefit or the document would gain credibility.
    - a. Type the bibliography on a separate page headed "Bibliography" or "Sources."
    - b. Alphabetize bibliography entries.
    - c. Use a consistent format for the bibliography (see Appendix B).

Body

The core of the proposal is the body, which has the same purpose as the body of other reports. In a proposal, however, the body must cover some specific information:

■ *Proposed approach.* May also be titled "Technical Proposal," "Research Design," "Issues for Analysis," or "Work Statement." Regardless of the heading, this section is a description of what you have to offer: your concept, product, or service. If you're proposing to develop a new airplane, you might describe your preliminary design by using drawings or calculations to demonstrate the soundness of your solution. To convince the client that your proposal has merit, focus on the strengths of your product in relation to the client's needs. Point out any advantages that you have over your competitors. In this example, you might describe how your plane's unique wing design provides superior fuel economy, a particularly important feature specified in the client's request for proposal.

■ *Work plan.* Describes how you will accomplish the work that must be done (necessary unless you're proposing to provide a standard, off-the-shelf item). For each phase of the work plan, describe the steps you'll take, their timing, the methods or resources you'll use, and the person or persons who will be responsible. Indicate any critical dates when portions of the work will be completed. If your proposal is accepted, the work plan will become contractually binding. Any slippage in the proposed schedule may jeopardize the contract or cost your organization a considerable amount of money. Therefore don't promise to deliver more than you can realistically achieve within a given period.

■ *Statement of qualifications.* Describes your organization's experience, personnel, and facilities in relation to the client's needs. If you work for a large organization that frequently submits proposals, you can usually borrow much of this section intact from previous proposals. Be sure, however, to tailor any of this boilerplate material to suit the situation. The qualifications section can be an important selling point, and it deserves to be handled carefully.

■ *Costs.* Typically has few words and many numbers but can make or break the proposal. If your price is out of line, the client will probably reject your bid. However, before you deliver a low bid, remember that you'll have to live with the price you quote in the proposal. It's rarely worthwhile to win a contract if you're doomed to lose money on the job. Because it's often difficult to estimate costs on experimental projects, the client will be looking for evidence that your costs are realistic. Break down the costs in detail so that the client can see how you got your numbers: so much for labor, so much for materials, so much for overhead.

In a formal proposal it pays to be as thorough and accurate as possible. Carefully selected detail enhances your credibility. So does successful completion of any task you promise to perform.

Summary

You may want to include a summary or conclusion section because it's your last opportunity to persuade the reader to accept your proposal. Summarize the merits of your approach, reemphasize why you and your firm are the ones to do the work, and stress the benefits. Make this section relatively brief, assertive, and confident. To review the ideas and procedures presented in this chapter, consult the Checklist for Formal Reports and Proposals.

In the approach section, demonstrate the superiority of your ideas, products, or services.

Use the work plan to describe the tasks to be completed under the terms of the contract.

In the qualifications section, demonstrate that you have the personnel, facilities, and experience to do a competent job.

The more detailed your cost proposal is, the more credibility your estimates will have.

O n the Job

SOLVING A COMMUNICATION DILEMMA AT LEVI STRAUSS

Levi Strauss CEO Robert Haas uses reports to communicate to employees, customers, and the community. He also uses them to make decisions. He believes strongly in good communication, even to the point of editing his staff's memos for grammar.

Haas relied on a report for the California Public Employees' Retirement System (CalPERS) to support his claim that empowered employees lead to greater business success. That is, he concluded from the report that stock prices actually rise when people on the front lines are given greater authority to act and make decisions that are in the best interest of both the customer and the company.

A key report at Levi Strauss is based on Haas's vision of an ethically driven business. Called the Aspirations Statement, this report helps guide the decisions and actions of all 37,500 of Levi's employees. It clearly outlines the type of values and behaviors that the company expects from its employees. It covers issues ranging from trust to empowerment and even to good business communication skills—all of which help the company become the organization that it aspires to be. By laying out these complex issues clearly and presenting them in a way that all employees can understand, Haas's report helps ensure that everyone is "reading off the same page." It helps him lead the company forward.

Although most business reports are not accessible to the general public, anyone visiting Levi's corporate Web site, <www.levistrauss.com>, can see how much the company values the written word. The site makes a number of reports available to the public, from the Aspirations Statement to a complete history of the company. All of these reports are clear and concise, and all have the components necessary for making the material easily understandable.[4]

Your Mission: As manager of internal communication, you are responsible for maintaining the communication channels up, down, and across the organization. One of your most important tasks is keeping Levi's 37,500 employees updated on the company's progress toward reaching the goals of the Aspirations Statement. Each year, you prepare a long report that is distributed both in printed form and online. Study the following questions, select the best answer in each case, and be prepared to support your choices.

1. From the boardroom to the warehouse, just about every employee in today's business world is overwhelmed with data and information. Because people have too much information to digest and too little time to read, the executive summary has become a particularly important part of corporate reports. Which of the following approaches would you take with the executive summary in your report this year?

   a. Use the executive summary to provide a quick score card for the company's performance in each of the areas addressed by the Aspirations Statement. Readers may be tempted to skip the detail contained in the body of the report, but at least they'll get the highlights in the executive summary.

   b. Use the executive summary to highlight changes in the report from previous years. You believe that the report is widely read within the company every year, so people will need guidance to understand how this new report differs in content and organization from the ones they've read in the past.

   c. Do not use an executive summary at all. This report is made available to everyone in the company, not just a handful of executives, so an executive summary is not appropriate.

2. One of your responsibilities in preparing this report is to recommend specific steps the company can take to improve on any of the areas of concern that you've uncovered in your investigation. One of those areas involves one of the company's customer service centers. Several customer service reps complained to your staff that the center's manager places so much emphasis on community service that the quality of the work is slipping. For example, employees who want to help out at AIDS awareness rallies or environmental clean-up projects are allowed to do so on company time, as often as they want. This frequently leaves the center short-handed, and employees who choose not to participate in these outside events are overloaded and increasingly resent both the volunteering program in general and particular employees who seem to be taking advantage of it. Remember, this report is distributed worldwide, so even though it's intended only for internal use, you must assume that people outside the company (including competitors and the news media) may gain access to it. How should you word your recommendation on this issue?

   a. Another concern we uncovered at a customer service center was a conflict between the company's desire to support the local community and the need to maintain a productive work environment. The specific problem involved too many employees taking too much volunteer time off work, leaving their co-workers overloaded. We've already discussed our concerns with the center manager involved, who is working with the next level of management to resolve the situation in a way that better balances these sometimes-conflicting needs. However, it seems possible that similar situations might be developing at other locations. We recommend that all regional managers discuss the issue with their employees to see whether specific situations need to be resolved or whether the company's overall stance on volunteerism needs to be reviewed.

   b. Our investigation raised some concerns about the management style of Sarah Blackstone, manager of the Denver customer service center. Her commendable interest in supporting the local community through employee volunteerism is unfortunately in conflict with her responsibilities as a business manager. Too many employees are taking too much time off work to participate in community activities, leaving other employees behind to take up the slack. The result is both a decline in customer service and a growing resentment among the employees who stay in the office and have to work harder and longer to cover for their absent co-workers.

   c. Our investigation raised some concerns about the management style of Sarah Blackstone, manager of the Denver customer service center. Her commendable interest in supporting the local community through employee volunteerism is unfortunately in conflict with her responsibilities as a business manager. Too many employees are taking too much time off work to participate in community activities, leaving other employees behind to take up the slack. The result is both a decline in customer service and a growing resentment among the employees who stay in the office and have to work harder and longer to cover for their absent co-workers. We strongly recommend that Ms. Blackstone retake the standard LS&Co management-training program to help re-align her priorities with the company's business priorities.

3. Much of the information you've collected from your interviews around the world is difficult or impossible to represent numerically. However, you believe that readers would appreciate a brief summary of the interview results. For one of the issues you would like to summarize, you posed the following open-ended question to 153 employees and managers: "How would you describe our progress toward empowering front-line employees with the authority to make decisions and take actions that satisfy our customers quickly and completely?" The answers range from simple, one-sentence responses to long, involved answers complete with examples. All together, the responses fill 13 pages. What's the best way of summarizing your findings?

a. Pick a half dozen responses that in your opinion represent the range of responses. For example, you might include one that says "we've made no progress at all," one that says "I believe we've been very successful at our empowerment efforts," and four more that fall between these two extremes.

b. Create a five-step measurement scale that ranges from "little or no progress" to "completely successful." Together with a few experienced members of your staff, review each response and decide in which of the five categories it belongs. Then create a chart that shows how the 153 responses are distributed among the five categories. Explain how you developed the chart, and offer to provide a complete listing of the responses to any reader who requests one.

c. Because the information is not quantitative, it's impossible to summarize and boil down to a few facts and figures. It would therefore be inappropriate to summarize the information at all. Simply include all 13 pages of responses as an appendix in your report.

4. Assume that you chose answer (b) in question 3, and now you need to create the chart. Given the kind of information you're trying to communicate, which of the following chart types would be most effective? Explain your answer.

a. A line chart, with a point for each of five categories and a line connecting the five points.

b. A bar chart with five bars that indicate the number of responses in each category.

c. A pie chart with five slices that indicate the number of responses in each category.

Critical Thinking Questions

1. What are the advantages and disadvantages of managers' and professional staffers' (e.g., lawyers, accountants, engineers, and consultants) using such computer tools as page layout programs, graphic design software, and scanners? Explain your answer.

2. Would you include a letter of authorization with a periodic personal activity report? Would you include a letter of transmittal? Why or why not?

3. Under what circumstances would you include more than one index in a lengthy report? Explain your answer.

4. In what ways might visual aids help people overcome some of the barriers to communication discussed in Chapter 2? Please explain.

5. You're writing a report to the director of human resources on implementing participative management throughout your company. You want to emphasize that since the new approaches were implemented six months ago, absenteeism and turnovers have been sharply reduced in all but two departments. How do you visually present your data in the most favorable light? Explain.

6. If you were submitting a solicited proposal to build an indoor pool, would you include as references the names and addresses of other clients for whom you recently built similar pools? Would you include these references in an unsolicited proposal? Where in either proposal would you put these references? Why?

Exercises

1. As the head of the career center at a Midwestern journalism school, you want to show students that they have many options after graduation. Create a pie chart based on the following information, which shows career areas pursued by journalism school graduates during a recent year. Summarize these findings (in two or three sentences) for publication in the student newspaper.

Media jobs		11,276
Newspapers/wire services	3,162	
Broadcast/radio/TV	1,653	
Public relations	2,407	
Advertising	2,142	
Magazines	286	
Other media	1,626	
Graduate study		1,346
Nonmedia jobs		5,324
Unemployed		2,454
Total graduates		20,400

2. The pet-food manufacturer you work for is interested in the results of a recent poll of U.S. pet-owning households. Look at the statistics that follow and decide on the most appropriate scale for this chart; then create a line chart of the trends in cat ownership. What conclusions do you draw from the trend you've charted? Draft a paragraph or two discussing the results of this poll and the potential consequences for the pet-food business. Support your conclusions by referring readers to your chart.

In 1980, 22 million U.S. households owned a cat. In 1985, 24 million households owned a cat. In 1990, 28 million households owned a cat. In 1995, 32 million households owned a cat.

3. Team up with a classmate to design graphics based on a comparison of the total tax burden of the U.S. taxpayer with that of people in other nations. One teammate should sketch a horizontal or vertical bar chart and the other should sketch pie charts from the estimates that follow. Then exchange visual aids and analyze how well each conveys the situation of the U.S. taxpayer. Would the bar chart look best with vertical or horizontal bars? Why? What scale is best? How does using pie

charts enhance or obscure the meaning or impact of the data? What suggestions can each student make for improving the other's visual aid?

Estimates show that Swedish taxpayers spend 51 percent of their incomes on taxes, British taxpayers spend 48 percent, French taxpayers spend 37 percent, Japanese taxpayers spend 28 percent, and U.S. taxpayers spend 27 percent.

4. Last year's sales figures are in for the department store where you work (Table 14.2). Construct visual aids based on these figures that will help you explain seasonal sales variations among the departments to the store's general manager.
5. With a team of three or four other students, brainstorm and then sketch at least three ways to visually compare the populations of all 50 states in the United States. You can use any of the graphic ideas presented in this chapter, as well as any ideas or examples you find from other sources.
6. Because of your experience with creating and designing presentation materials, your company asks you to design its Web page. No one else in your company has the technical expertise to help you, so you begin by searching the Internet. You discover the Web sites at <http://www.kudonet.com/%7Erhondamo/create.html> and <http://www.pstbbs.com/tammyb/web/html>. Explore the following links:

Table 14.2	STORE SALES IN 1997, IN THOUSANDS		
Month	*Lingerie*	*Sporting Goods*	*Housewares*
January	$39	$55	$83
February	37	50	81
March	37	51	78
April	25	55	77
May	26	60	79
June	30	65	85
July	30	65	79
August	27	60	77
September	27	51	77
October	27	53	78
November	31	60	82
December	40	65	85

"Search Engines"; "Shareware & Freeware"; "Icons, graphics, color, and styles"; and "General Help." Now try your hand at Web page design, and print a copy of your sample home page for submission.

C ases

SHORT FORMAL REPORTS

1. Keeping an eye on the kids: Report that summarizes survey data for an on-site day-care facility You're the human resources manager at a 200-employee manufacturing firm. Employees at your company have expressed a strong desire for some kind of on-site child-care facility. You're in charge of investigating the situation and developing the company's response. You know that any facility will require a balance between what the company can afford to pay and what employees are willing to pay, relative to other day-care alternatives.

Table 14.3 indicates trends in on-site day care among local employers. Because you have to compete with other organizations for employees, offering comparable employee benefits such as on-site day care is an important business decision. Tables 14.4, 14.5, and 14.6 show the data collected in an internal employee survey.

Your Task: Write a report to your boss summarizing the survey results and suggesting the next step in the planning process.

2. Sailing past the sunsets: Report using statistical data to suggest a new advertising strategy As manager of Distant Dreams, a travel agency in Waco, Texas, you are interested in the information in Table 14.7. Dollar income seems to be shifting toward the 35–44 age group. Tables 14.8 and 14.9 are also broken down by age group. Your agency has traditionally concentrated its advertising on people nearing retirement—people who are closing out successful careers and now have the time and money to vacation abroad. Having examined the three sets of data, however, you realize that it's time for a major shift in emphasis.

Table 14.3	DAY-CARE FACILITIES OFFERED BY LOCAL EMPLOYERS	
	Percentage with On-Site Day-Care	
Organization Type	*1990*	*1995*
By Industry		
Retailing	6%	14%
Consumer services	8	11
Business services	11	25
Government and nonprofit	15	17
Manufacturing	27	30
By Size		
Up to 50 employees	2	2
51–100 employees	5	6
101–250 employees	12	14
251–500 employees	28	32
More than 500 employees	35	45

Your Task: Write a report to Mary Henderson, who writes your advertisements, explaining why future ads should still be directed to people who want to explore far reaches of the world but to people in other age groups as well as those in their fifties and sixties. Justify your explanation by referring to the data you have examined.

Table 14.4 — AGES OF EMPLOYEE DEPENDENTS

Age Range	Number of Children
Under 1	14
2–3	32
4–5	25
6–7	22
8–9	13
10–11	28
Over 12	112

Table 14.5 — SERVICES AND FEATURES DESIRED IN AN ON-SITE DAY-CARE FACILITY

Service or Feature	Must Have	Nice to Have	Not Important
Nurse	3%	77%	0%
Arts and crafts	54	41	5
Outdoor play area	36	52	12
Educational activities	25	59	16
Organized games and contests	12	62	26
Sleeping arrangements	34	34	32
Evening hours (after 6 P.M.)	33	52	15
Early morning hours (before 8 A.M.)	7	48	45
Snacks	74	21	5
Lunch	88	12	0

Table 14.6 — AMOUNT EMPLOYEES ARE WILLING TO PAY

Per Child per Month	Percentage of Employees Willing to Pay
Less than $100	100%
$101–$200	95
$201–$300	89
$301–$400	64
$401–$500	50
$501–$600	28
More than $600	12

Table 14.7 — PERCENTAGE OF TOTAL U.S. HOUSEHOLD INCOME EARNED BY VARIOUS AGE GROUPS

Age Group	1985	1990	1995
25–34	23%	24%	26%
35–44	22	25	28
45–54	22	21	19
55–64	19	17	15
Over 65	14	13	12

Table 14.8 — PREFERENCES IN TRAVEL AMONG VARIOUS AGE GROUPS

Travel Interests	Age Group		
	18–34	35–54	55+
I am more interested in excitement and stimulation than rest and relaxation.	67%	42%	38%
I prefer to go where I haven't been before.	62	58	48
I like adventurous travel.	62	45	32
I love foreign and exotic things.	41	25	21
Vacation is a time for self-indulgence, regardless of the cost.	31	16	14
I don't see the need for a travel agent.	67	63	52

Table 14.9 — BASIC DESIRE FOR TRAVEL AMONG VARIOUS AGE GROUPS

Attitude Toward Travel	Age Group		
	18–34	35–54	55+
Travel is one of the most rewarding and enjoyable things one can do.	71%	69%	66%
I love the idea of traveling and do so at every opportunity.	66	59	48
I often feel the need to get away from everything.	56	55	33

3. Picking the better path: Report helping a client choose a career You are employed by Open Options, a career-counseling firm, and your main function is to help clients make career choices. Today a client with the same name as yours (a truly curious coincidence!) came to your office and asked for help deciding between two careers, careers that you yourself had been interested in (an even greater coincidence!).

Your Task: Do some research on the two careers and then prepare a short report that your client can study. Your report should compare at least five major areas, such as salary, working conditions, and education required. Interview the client to understand her or his personal preferences regarding each of the five areas. For example, what is the minimum salary the client will accept? By comparing the client's preferences with the research material you collect, such as salary data, you will have a basis for concluding which of the two careers is better. The report should end with a career recommendation.

4. Selling overseas: Report on the prospects for marketing a product in another country Select (a) a product and (b) a country. The product might be a novelty item that you own (an inexpensive but accurate watch or clock, a desk organizer, or a coin bank). The country should be one that you are not now familiar with. Imagine that you are with the international sales department of the company that manufactures and sells the novelty item and that you are proposing to make it available in the country you have selected.

The first step is to learn as much as possible about the country where you plan to market the product. Check almanacs and encyclopedias for the most recent information, paying particular attention to descriptions of the social life of the inhabitants and their economic conditions. If your library carries resources such as *Yearbook of International Trade Statistics, Monthly Bulletin of Statistics,* or *Trade Statistics* (all put out by the United Nations), you may want to consult them. In addition, check the card catalog and recent periodical indexes for sources of additional information; look for (among other matters) cultural traditions that would encourage or discourage use of the product. If you have online access, check both Web sites and any relevant databases you can find.

Your Task: Write a short report that describes the product you plan to market abroad, briefly describes the country you have selected, indicates the types of people in this country who would find the product attractive, explains how the product would be transported into the country (or possibly manufactured there if materials and labor are available), recommends a location for a regional sales center, and suggests how the product should be sold. Your report is to be submitted to the chief operating officer of the company, whose name you can either make up or find in a corporate directory. The report should include your conclusions (how the product will do in this new environment) and your recommendations for marketing (steps the company should take immediately and those it should develop later).

5. Who uses coupons? Report summarizing important demographics You are employed by Supermarket Coupons Incorporated. Your company is interested in distributing its manufacturing client's coupons to supermarket customers in the most cost-conscious manner. Your boss is advocating using the Internet exclusively to deliver client's coupons. She believes that a major shift from the print media to computer media would result in substantial savings for all concerned (your company, your manufacturing clients, customers, and supermarkets). Your responsibilities are (a) to determine which demographic groups (by age, sex, economic class, profession) use coupons received through the mail, clipped from newspapers and magazines, and picked up from in-store displays and (b) to determine whether these groups would be interested in downloading coupons from the Internet.

Here are a few Internet sources to get you started on your search. (Most sites provide an e-mail link that might help you find additional sources of information for your report.)

- <http://www.interstate.net/gscable/demograp.html>
- <http://www.marketingtools.com/publications/AD/95-AD/9501af02.html>
- <http://www.xenon.chem.vidaho.edu/hypermail/demograph/0011.html>
- <http://www.marketingtools.com/ad_current/AD752.html>

Your Task: Write a short formal report that summarizes your findings on which demographic groups use manufacturer's coupons and which of those groups would be interested in downloading coupons.

LONG FORMAL REPORT REQUIRING NO ADDITIONAL RESEARCH

6. Customer service crisis: Report summarizing and explaining customer service problems You are the operations manager for Continental Security Systems (CSS), a mail-order supplier of home-security systems and components. Your customers are do-it-yourself homeowners who buy a wide range of motion sensors, automatic telephone dialers, glass breakage detectors, video cameras, and other devices.

The company's aggressive pricing has yielded spectacular growth in the last year, and everyone is scrambling to keep up with the orders that arrive every day. Unfortunately, customer service has often taken a back seat to filling those orders. Your boss, the company's founder and president, knows that service is slipping, and she wants you to solve the problem. You started with some internal and external surveys to assess the situation. Some of the most

Table 14.10	**CUSTOMER COMPLAINTS OVER THE LAST 12 MONTHS**	

Type of Complaint	Number of Occurrences	Percentage of Total
Delays in responding	67	30%
Product malfunction	56	25
Missing parts	45	20
No answer when calling for help	32	14
Rude treatment	18	8
Overcharge	5	2

Note: Percentages don't add to 100 because of rounding.

Table 14.11	**HOW COMPLAINTS WERE RESOLVED**

Resolution	Percentage
Employee receiving the phone call solved the problem	20%
Employee referred customer to manager	30
Customer eventually solved the problem by himself/herself	12
Unable to solve problem	23
Resolution unknown	15

Table 14.12	**CUSTOMER PERCEPTIONS AND OPINIONS**

Statement	Agree	Disagree
CSS offers a competitive level of customer service	12%	88%
I recommended CSS to friends and colleagues	4	96
I plan to continue buying from CSS	15	85
I enjoy doing business with CSS	9	91

significant findings from the research are presented in Tables 14.10, 14.11, and 14.12.

Your Task: Prepare a report that explains the data you collected in your research. Keep the report factual and objective; everyone knows that growth has strained the company's resources, so you have no need to place blame. (For the purposes of this exercise, feel free to make up any facts you need regarding the company.)

LONG FORMAL REPORTS REQUIRING ADDITIONAL RESEARCH

7. Equipment purchase: Report on competitive product features Say that your office or home needs some new equipment. Choose one of the following, and figure out which brand and model would be the best buy.

a. Cellular phone	e. Photocopier
b. Calculator	f. Personal computer
c. Telephone answering machine	g. Word-processing software
d. Home-security system	h. Desktop scanner

Your Task: Write a long formal report describing the features of the available alternatives, listing the benefits and drawbacks of each, and making a clear recommendation. Be sure to include a discussion of the factors on which you've based your decision (including cost, reliability, and so on).

8. Group effort: Report on a large-scale topic The following topics may be too big for any one person, yet they need to be investigated:

   a. A demographic profile (age, gender, socioeconomic status, residence, employment, educational background, and the like) of the students at your college or university
   b. The best part-time employment opportunities in your community
   c. The best of two or three health clubs or gyms in your community
   d. Actions that can be taken in your community or state to combat alcohol (or other drug) abuse
   e. Improvements that could be made in the food service at your college or university
   f. Your college's or university's image in the community and ways to improve it
   g. Your community's strengths and weaknesses in attracting new businesses

Your Task: Because these topics require considerable research, your instructor may wish to form groups to work on each. If your group writes a report on the first topic, summarize your findings at the end of the report. For all the other topics, reach conclusions and make recommendations in the report.

9. Secondary sources: Report based on library research Perhaps one of the following questions has been keeping you awake at night:

a. What's the best way for someone in your financial situation to invest a $5,000 inheritance?

b. What can be done about parking problems on campus?

c. Of three careers that appeal to you, which best suits you?

d. How do other consumers regard a product that you use frequently?

e. Which of three cities that you might like to live in seems most attractive?

f. What's the surest and easiest route to becoming a millionaire?

Your Task: Answer one of these questions, using secondary sources for information. Be sure to document your sources in the correct form. Give conclusions and recommendations in your report.

FORMAL PROPOSALS

10. Top dogs: Proposal to furnish puppies to Docktor Pet Centers You are the business manager for Sandy's Kennels of Alma, Kansas, one of the country's largest dog-breeding operations. Every year you sell 7,500 puppies to pet shops around the country, at an average price of $130 a dog. The pet stores then sell the dogs for $225 to $300, depending on the breed.

Your business involves both breeding and reselling animals. In your own kennels, you raise 52 breeds of dogs; in addition, you buy dogs from other breeders at approximately $60 a dog and resell them to pet stores. Your dogs are all pedigreed animals with American Kennel Club (AKC) papers. In addition, they come with all the required puppy vaccinations and are guaranteed to be healthy.

For several years you've been trying to win a long-term contract to supply puppies to Docktor Pet Centers, the country's largest petstore chain. Finally, you've been invited to submit a proposal to provide 2,000 dogs a year to Docktor Pet's 220 retail outlets. The specifications stipulate that you will ship approximately 150 dogs a month from January through October and 250 dogs in November and in December. The puppies should be eight to ten weeks old at the time of shipment and should have all the necessary shots and AKC papers. Docktor is willing to accept a variety of breeds but has requested that each shipment contain a mix of large and small dogs and males and females. The chain is willing to pay from $115 to $130 a dog, depending on the breed.

Your Task: Using your imagination to supply the details, write a proposal describing your plan to provide the dogs.[5]

11. When is a program not a program? Proposal to produce a television infomercial. If you have cable television, you already know something about "infomercials." As you flip through the channels, you can't help noticing these half-hour "programs" that extol the benefits of products ranging from baldness cures to exercise equipment to car wax. Many of the ads are in a talk-show format and feature celebrities talking with people who have used the product and want to share their success stories. Other infomercials focus primarily on product demonstrations.

This form of "direct-response television" has proliferated because the ads are relatively inexpensive to produce and because cable air time often comes cheap. Whereas producing a 30-second network commercial might cost $200,000, a marketer can get by with as little as $150,000 to produce a 30-minute infomercial. In addition, placing an infomercial can cost only hundreds or thousands of dollars instead of tens of thousands or hundreds of thousands.

You've recently joined the staff of American Telecast, one of the three major producers of infomercials, with annual revenues of $150 million. American Telecast's claims to fame include the highly successful Richard Simmons weight-loss-plan "long-form marketing program." Your boss has handed you a magazine ad for Audio-Forum, a company that sells audiocassettes that teach people how to speak foreign languages, how to play the piano or read music, how to improve their vocabulary or their speech, and even how to touch-type. "This looks like the kind of product we could really run with in an infomercial—especially the foreign language stuff," says your boss. She wants you to come up with an unsolicited proposal that will entice Audio-Forum into entering the infomercial game.

You look through the company's highly detailed ad, which you remember having seen in several magazines. The portion of the ad devoted to language-learning tapes says, "Learn to speak a foreign language fluently on your own and at your own pace" and goes on to give the course's credentials (developed for the U.S. State Department for diplomatic personnel who need to learn a language quickly), to describe what each course consists of, and to list the languages available. Both an order form and a toll-free number are provided. You remember reading somewhere that Audio-Forum has been quite successful with its magazine direct-marketing approach.

Your Task: Write a proposal to Audio-Forum, 96 Broad St., Guilford, CT 06437, indicating American Telecast's desire to produce an infomercial for Audio-Forum's language-learning tapes. Use your imagination to fill in any additional details.[6]

DEVELOPING YOUR INTERNET SKILLS
GOING ONLINE: DESIGN EFFECTIVE COMPUTER GRAPHICS, P. 332

Find some information here that might help you visually enhance a business report. Write down a brief description of what you've found. What did you discover about computer graphics that you didn't know before? What resources did you find that might help future writing projects? Did you see anything visually arresting that gave you ideas for illustrating your own work? If so, what was it? Did you find anything that offended or confused you? If so, why do you think it failed (unless that was its purpose)?

EMPLOYMENT

MESSAGES

After studying this chapter, you will be able to

Analyze your work skills and qualifications

Identify what type of job and employer you want

List your best prospects for employment

Develop a strategy for "selling" yourself to these prospects

Prepare an effective résumé

Write an application letter that gets you an interview

Like most companies today, Pinkerton is looking for applicants who are well educated, well trained, and well spoken. The process usually begins with a résumé and culminates with an interview.

WRITING RÉSUMÉS AND APPLICATION LETTERS

On the Job

FACING A COMMUNICATION DILEMMA AT PINKERTON

Keeping a Private Eye on Hiring

When you screen more than a million job applicants a year, you're sure to gain an in-depth knowledge of employment messages. That's the kind of expertise that Pinkerton has developed. Just one of the many security and protection services Pinkerton performs around the world is screening job applicants for clients (as well as for its own operations), but the company takes great pride in matching the right person to the right job.

Pinkerton clients range from General Motors, which spends roughly $100 million with Pinkerton every year, to the Academy of Motion Picture Arts and Sciences, which relies on Pinkerton to protect the rich and famous during the Academy Awards presentation in Los Angeles. Uniformed security services make up the bulk of Pinkerton's business, but the company is working to become a one-stop shop for asset-protection services. These include electronic surveillance systems, undercover investigations, access control, insurance investigations, crisis management, ethics-monitoring programs, and a wide variety of related services.

In charge of all this is CEO Denis Brown, whose background is even more diverse than Pinkerton's—his jobs have ranged from helping develop the Global Positioning System to turning around a troubled supercomputer maker. Throughout his career, Brown has reviewed plenty of job applications for all kinds of positions.

If you were Brown, what qualities would you look for in a job applicant? How would you want Pinkerton to evaluate the résumés and application letters it receives? What would you think constitutes a good résumé? A good application letter? What steps would you take to screen job candidates?[1]

THINKING ABOUT YOUR CAREER

As Pinkerton's Brown will tell you, getting the job that's right for you takes more than sending out a few letters and signing up with the college placement office. Planning and research are important if you want to find a company that suits you. So before you limit your employment search to a particular industry or job, analyze what you have to offer and what you hope to get from your work. Then you can identify employers who are likely to want you and vice versa.

What Do You Have to Offer?

What are your marketable skills? First, jot down ten achievements you're proud of—learning to ski, taking a prizewinning photo, tutoring a child, editing the school paper. Analyze each achievement, and you'll begin to recognize a pattern of skills that are valuable to potential employers.

What you have to offer:
- Functional skills
- Education and experience
- Personality traits

Second, look at your educational preparation, work experience, and extracurricular activities. What kinds of jobs have your knowledge and experience qualified you for? What have you learned from participating in volunteer work or class projects that could benefit you on the job? Have you held any offices, won any awards or scholarships, or mastered a second language?

Third, take stock of your personal characteristics to determine the type of job you'll do best. Are you aggressive, a born leader? Or would you rather follow? Are you outgoing, articulate, great with people? Or do you prefer working alone? Make a list of what you believe are your four or five most important traits. Ask a relative or friend to rate your traits as well. If you're having trouble figuring out your interests and capabilities, consult your college placement office or career guidance center for advice.

What Do You Want to Do?

Knowing what you *can* do is one thing. Knowing what you *want* to do is another. Don't lose sight of your own values. Discover the things that will bring you satisfaction and happiness on the job.

- *Decide what you'd like to do every day.* Talk to people in various occupations. You might contact relatives, local businesses, or former graduates (through your school's alumni relations office). Read about various occupations. Start with your college library or placement office. One of the liveliest books aimed at college students is Lisa Birnbach's *Going to Work.* Another useful source is the 13-volume *Career Information Center* encyclopedia of jobs and careers. Also consider how much independence you want on the job, how much variety you like, and whether you prefer to work with products, machines, people, ideas, numbers, or some combination thereof. Do you like physical work, mental work, or a mix? Constant change or a predictable role?

  Envision the ideal "day at the office." What would you enjoy doing every day?

- *Establish some specific compensation targets.* What do you hope to earn in your first year on the job? What kind of pay increase do you expect each year? What's your ultimate earnings goal? Would you be comfortable with a job that paid on commission, or do you prefer a steady paycheck? What occupations offer the kind of money you're looking for? Are these occupations realistic for someone with your qualifications? Are you willing to settle for less money in order to do something you really love? Consider where you'd like to start, where you'd like to go from there, and the ultimate position you'd like to attain. How soon after joining the company would you like to receive your first promotion? Your next one? What additional training or preparation will you need to achieve them?

  How much do you want to earn, and how high do you hope to climb?

- *Consider the type of environment you prefer.* Think in broad terms about the size and type of operation that appeals to you, the location you prefer, the facilities you envision, and especially the corporate culture you're most comfortable with. Would you rather work for a small, entrepreneurial operation or a large company? A profit-making company or a nonprofit organization? Are you attracted to service businesses or manufacturing operations? Do you want regular, predictable hours, or do you thrive on flexible, varied hours? Would you enjoy a seasonally varied job (say, in education, which may give you summers off, or in retailing, with its selling cycles)? Or would you prefer a steady pace year-round? Would you like to work in a city, a suburb, a small town, or an industrial area? Do you favor a particular part of the country? A country abroad? Do

  What type of industry and organization do you want to work for?

you like working indoors or outdoors? Is it important to you to work in an attractive place, or will simple, functional quarters suffice? Do you need a quiet office to work effectively, or can you concentrate in a noisy, open setting? Is access to public transportation or freeways important? Perhaps the most important environmental factor is the corporate culture. Would you be happy in a well-defined hierarchy, where roles and reporting relationships are clear, or would you prefer a less structured situation? What qualities do you want in a boss? Are you looking for a paternalistic organization or one that fosters individualism? Do you like a competitive environment or one that rewards teamwork?

What type of corporate culture best suits you?

Where Do You Find Employment Information?

Find out where the job opportunities are.

Once you know what you have to offer and what you want, you can start finding an employer to match. If you haven't already committed yourself to any particular career field, first find out where the job opportunities are. Which industries are strong? Which parts of the country are booming, and which specific job categories offer the best prospects for the future?

Whether your major is business, biology, or political science, start your search for information by keeping abreast of business and financial news. Subscribe to a major newspaper and scan the business pages every day. Watch TV programs that focus on business, such as *Wall Street Week,* and read the business articles in popular magazines such as *Time* and *Newsweek.* You might even want to subscribe to a business magazine such as *Fortune, Business Week,* or *Forbes.*

You can obtain information about the future for specific jobs in the *Dictionary of Occupational Titles* (U.S. Employment Service), *Occupational Outlook Handbook* (U.S. Bureau of Labor Statistics), and the employment publications of Science Research Associates. For an analysis of major industries, see the annual Market Data and Directory issue of *Industrial Marketing* and Standard & Poor's industry surveys.

Study professional and trade journals in the career fields that interest you. Also, talk to people in those fields; for names of the most prominent, consult *Standard & Poor's Register of Corporations, Directors and Executives.* You can find recent books about the fields you're considering by checking *Books in Print* at your library. It's often possible for students to network with executives in their field of interest by joining or participating in student business organizations, especially those with ties to organizations such as the American Marketing Association or the American Management Association.

Once you've identified a promising industry and a career field, list specific organizations that appeal to you by consulting directories of employers, such as the *College Placement Annual* and *Career: The Annual Guide to Business Opportunities.* (Other directories are listed in Chapter 16.) Write to the organizations on your list and ask for their most recent annual report and any descriptive brochures or newsletters they've published. If possible, visit some of the organizations on your list, contact their human resources departments, or talk with key employees.

You can find ads for specific job openings by looking in local and major newspapers. (However, newspaper ads that don't list the company's name may be misleading and may not even represent a real job opening, so be careful.) In addition, check the trade and professional journals in career fields that interest you; *Ulrich's International Periodicals Directory* (available at the library) lists these publications. Job listings can also be obtained from your college placement office and from state employment bureaus. A source of growing importance to your job search is the Internet, or more specifically the World Wide Web.

For helpful hints and useful Web addresses, you can turn to innumerable books, such as *What Color Is Your Parachute?* by Richard Nelson Bolles (which is even available in an electronic edition on the Web). The World Wide Web offers information not only from employers seeking applicants but also from people seeking work. You can use the World Wide Web for a variety of job-seeking tasks:

Martina L. Bradford is vice president of external affairs at AT&T, overseeing one of the largest and most profitable regions of the United States. Bradford targeted the high-growth company as a potential employer only after studying the industry thoroughly. She advises that you analyze where your skills fit in best and target your efforts toward that company.

- *Finding career counseling.* When analyzing your skills and work expectations, you can begin your self-assessment with the *Keirsey Temperament Sorter,* an online personality test. You'll find job-seeking pointers and counseling from online career centers. Some are run by colleges and universities that put a lot of effort into creating interesting and helpful sites. Others are commercial and can run the gamut from award-winning to depressing. So make sure the advice you get is both useful and sensible. One good commercial site is Mary-Ellen Mort's *Job-Smart.* You can also obtain online résumé assistance from sites such as Job Smart Resume Guide, the Riley Guide, Job Bank USA Resume Resources, Career Mosaic's Resume Writing Guide, and Intellimatch Power Resume Builder.

- *Making contacts.* You can use the Web to locate and communicate with potential employers. Usenet newsgroups are dedicated to your field of interest, and members leave messages for one another on an electronic bulletin board. Listservs (or Internet mailing lists) are similar to Usenet newsgroups, except they mail each message to every member's e-mail address. Commercial systems such as Prodigy, America Online, and CompuServe have their own discussion groups (called Special Interest Groups, RoundTables, Clubs, or Bulletin Boards) that are also devoted to a particular interest, but they make a profit from the time users spend using their services. Once you locate a potential contact, you can communicate quickly and nonintrusively by using e-mail to request information or to let an employer know you're interested in working for that company.

- *Researching employers' companies.* By visiting a company's Web site, you can find out about its mission, products, annual reports, employee benefits, and job openings. You can locate company Web sites by knowing the URL (or Web address), by using links from other sites, or by using a search engine such as Alta Vista, Lycos, or Excite.

- *Searching for job vacancies.* Online indexes list openings from multiple companies and include College Grad Job Hunter (offering links to organizations with entry-level jobs), Online Career Center (offering searchable information), Career Mosaic, America's Job Bank, CareerPath, Help Wanted USA, The Main Quad, Monster Board, CareerCity, and many others. To locate any of these organizations, simply use a search engine such as Alta Vista or Excite. Of course, even the Web offers no central, unified marketplace, so plan on visiting hundreds of sites to learn what jobs are available. Also remember that only a small percentage of jobs are currently listed on the Web. Employers generally prefer to fill job vacancies through the "hidden job market," finding people without advertising, whether on the Internet or in newspapers (Figure 15.1).

- *Posting your résumé online.* You can post your résumé online either through an index service or on your own home page. To post your résumé on an index service, simply prepare the information to be input into the database and transmit it by mail, fax, modem, or e-mail. Then employers contact your index service, specifying all the key words to be found in qualifying résumés, and your index service sends the employer a list of names along with résumés or background profile sheets. By posting your résumé on your own home page, you can retain a nicer looking format, and you can even include color photographs of yourself, links to papers you've written or recommendations you've received, and sound or video clips. Most campus placement offices are retooling to help you take advantage of Web opportunities. But keep in mind that many job openings are not listed on the Internet. The World Wide Web cannot replace other techniques for finding employment; it's just one more tool in your overall strategy.[2]

Employers find job candidates through

- Employee referrals
- On-campus interviews
- Unsolicited résumés
- Placement agencies
- Advertisements

Sorting out the best 3,000 from more than 85,000 applicants makes FBI Special Agent recruiter Jo Ann Sakato a hiring expert. Top candidates possess a college degree and professional work experience, giving them "skills from various backgrounds and almost every occupation," says Sakato. "One of our strengths is the diversity of our Special Agent workforce."

How Do You Build Toward a Career?

Employers are seeking people who are able and willing to adapt to diverse situations, who thrive in an ever-changing workplace, and who continue to learn throughout their careers. Companies want leaders who are versatile, and they are encouraging their managers to get varied job experience.[3] Employers want team players with strong work records, so try to gain skills you can market in various industries.

Figure 15.1
How Organizations Prefer to
Find New Employees

Employers prefer filling positions from within their organization or from an employee's recommendation. Placing want ads is often viewed as a last resort. In contrast, typical job hunters begin pursuing work from the opposite direction (starting with want ads).

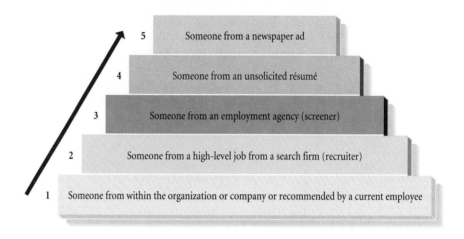

5 — Someone from a newspaper ad

4 — Someone from an unsolicited résumé

3 — Someone from an employment agency (screener)

2 — Someone from a high-level job from a search firm (recruiter)

1 — Someone from within the organization or company or recommended by a current employee

Your chances of getting a job are increased by career-building efforts:

- Developing an employment portfolio
- Gaining intercultural experience
- Participating in an internship program
- Networking with others in your field
- Taking interim jobs and classes
- Expanding your life experience

Consider keeping an employment portfolio. Get a three-ring notebook and a package of plastic sleeves that open at the top. Collect anything that shows your ability to perform, such as classroom or work evaluations, certificates, awards, and papers you've written. This employment portfolio accomplishes two things: Employers are impressed that you're not just talking about what you've done but have tangible evidence of your professionalism. Also, you can be relaxed because you can discuss your skills and accomplishments calmly and enthusiastically.

Your chances of being hired are better if you've studied abroad and learned another language. At the least, employers expect graduates to have a sound understanding of international affairs. Companies are looking for employees with intercultural sensitivity and an ability to adapt in other cultures.[4]

Gain a competitive edge by participating in an internship program. Not only will an internship help you gain valuable experience and relevant contacts, but it will provide you with important references and with items for your portfolio.[5]

Join networks of professional colleagues and friends who can help you stay abreast of where your occupation, industry, and company are going. As you search for a permanent job that fulfills your career goals, take interim job assignments, consider temporary work or freelance jobs. Employers will be more willing to find (or even create) a position for someone they've learned to respect, and your temporary or freelance work gives them a chance to see what you can do. You might even consider starting your own business.

If you're unable to find actual job experience, work on polishing and updating your skills. While you're waiting for responses to your résumé or to hear about your last interview, take a computer course, or use the time to gain some other educational or life experience that would be difficult to get while working full time. Become familiar with the services offered by your campus career center (or placement office). These centers offer a variety of services, including individual placement counseling, credential services, job-fairs, on-campus interviews, job listings, advice on computerized résumé-writing software, workshops in job-search techniques, résumé preparation, interview techniques, and more.[6]

Once an employer hires you and you're on the job, don't think you've reached the end of the process. The best thing you can do for your long-term career is to continue learning. Listen to and learn from those around you who have experience. Be ready and willing to take on new responsibilities, and actively pursue new or better skills. Employers appreciate applicants and employees who demonstrate a willingness and enthusiasm to learn, to listen, and to gain experience.

Of course, to get hired, you usually need an interview, and to get that interview, you usually need a résumé. A good résumé can distinguish you from all the other people looking for work. So make sure your résumé is well written.

W *RITING YOUR RÉSUMÉ*

A **résumé** is a structured, written summary of a person's education, employment background, and job qualifications. A résumé is a form of advertising, designed to help you get an interview. This interview may serve any number of purposes—to get a job, get a promotion, obtain membership in a professional organization, become a member of a nonprofit board. As in all forms of advertising, your objectives are to call attention to your best features and to downplay your disadvantages, without distorting or misrepresenting the facts.[7] You arrange these facts according to your purpose.

Executives like Pinkerton's Denis Brown believe a good résumé shows that a candidate (1) thinks in terms of results, (2) knows how to get things done, (3) is well rounded, (4) shows signs of progress, (5) has personal standards of excellence, (6) is flexible and willing to try new things, and (7) possesses strong communication skills. As you put your résumé together, think about how the format and style, content, and organization help you convey these seven qualities.

The purpose of the résumé is to get you an interview.

Your résumé is a structured, written summary of your educational and employment background, and it shows your qualifications for a job.

Controlling the Format and Style

Quick—you have less than 45 seconds to make a good impression. That's the amount of time a typical recruiter devotes to each résumé before tossing it into either the "maybe" or the "reject" pile.[8] If your résumé doesn't *look* sharp, chances are nobody will read it carefully enough to judge your qualifications.

It's important to use a clean typeface on high-grade, letter-size bond paper (in white, off-white, light ivory, or other light earth tone). Be sure your application letter and envelope are on matching-colored stationery. Leave ample margins all around, and be sure any corrections are unnoticeable. Avoid italic typefaces, which can be difficult to read. If you have reservations about the quality of your printer (dot-matrix printing is not suitable for most résumés) or typewriter, you might want to turn your résumé over to a professional service. To make duplicate copies, use offset printing or photocopying.

In terms of layout, your objective is to make the information easy to grasp.[9] Break up the text by using headings that call attention to various aspects of your background, such as your work experience and education. Underline or capitalize key points, or set them off in the left margin. Use indented lists to itemize your most important qualifications. Leave plenty of white space, even if doing so forces you to use two pages rather than one.

Pay attention to mechanics. Check the headings and itemized lists to make sure they're grammatically parallel. Be sure your grammar, spelling, and punctuation are correct. Because your résumé has only seconds to make an impression, the "you" attitude and audience focus are crucial. Keep your writing style simple and direct. Instead of whole sentences, use short, crisp phrases starting with action verbs. You might say, "Coached a Little League team to the regional playoffs" or "Supervised a fast-food restaurant and four employees."

As a rule of thumb, try to write a one-page résumé. If you have a great deal of experience and are applying for a higher-level position, you may wish to prepare a somewhat longer résumé. The important thing is to give yourself enough space to present a persuasive but accurate portrait of your skills and accomplishments.

The key characteristics of a good résumé are
- Neatness
- Simplicity
- Accuracy
- Honesty

Tailoring the Contents

Most potential employers expect to see certain items in any résumé. The bare essentials are name and address, academic credentials, and employment history. Otherwise, make sure your résumé emphasizes your strongest, most impressive qualifications. Think in terms of an image or a theme you'd like to project. Are you academically gifted? Are you a campus leader? A well-rounded person? A creative genius? A technical wizard? If you know what you have to sell, you can shape the elements of your résumé accordingly. Don't exaggerate, and don't alter the past or claim skills you don't have, but don't dwell on negatives, either. By focusing on your strengths, you can convey the desired impression without distorting the facts.

Name and Address

The first thing an employer needs to know is who you are and where you can be reached: your name, address, and phone number (as well as your e-mail address or URL, if you have it). If you have an address and phone number at school and another at home, you may include both. At the same time, if you have a work phone and a home phone, list both and indicate which is which. Many résumé headings are nothing more than the name and address centered at the top of the page. You really have little need to include the word *Résumé,* but if you have a specific job in mind, you could use a heading that indicates that fact:

Qualifications of Craig R. Crisp for Insurance Sales Representative

Résumé Sheet of Mary Menendez, an Experienced Retail Fashion Buyer

Public Relations Background of Bradley R. (Brad) Howard

Susan Lee Selwyn's Qualifications for the Position of Teaching Assistant in the Dade County School District

Profile of Michael de Vito for Entertainment Management

Whatever heading you use, make sure the reader can tell in an instant who you are and how to communicate with you.

Career Objective or Summary of Qualifications

Experts disagree about stating a career objective on your résumé. Some argue that your objective will be obvious from your qualifications. They also point out that such a statement is counterproductive (especially if you would like to be considered for a variety of openings) because it labels you as being interested in only one thing. Other experts point out that employers will undoubtedly try to categorize you anyway, so you might as well be sure they attach the right label. If you decide to state your objective, be as specific as possible about what you want to do:

Human Resources Management, requiring international experience

Advertising assistant, with print media emphasis

If you have two types of qualifications (such as a certificate in secretarial science and two years' experience in retail sales), prepare two separate résumés, each with a different objective. If your immediate objective differs from your ultimate one, combine the two in a single statement:

A marketing position with an opportunity for eventual managerial status

Proposal writer, with the ultimate goal of becoming a contracts administrator

As an alternative to stating your objective, you might want to summarize your qualifications in a brief statement that highlights your strongest points, particularly if you have had a good deal of varied experience. Use a short, simple phrase:

Summary of qualifications: Ten years of experience in commission selling

Hospital administrator responsible for 350-bed facility

The opening section shows at a glance
- Who you are
- How to reach you

Stating your objective or summarizing your qualifications helps the recruiter categorize you.

Education

If you're still in school, education is probably your strongest selling point. So present your educational background in depth, choosing facts that support your "theme." Give this section a heading, such as "Education," "Professional College Training," or "Academic Preparation." Then, starting with the school you most recently attended, list for each school the name and location, the term of your enrollment (in months and years), your major and minor fields of study, significant skills and abilities you've developed in your course work, and the degrees or certificates you've earned. Showcase your qualifications by listing courses that have directly equipped you for the job sought, and indicate any scholarships, awards, or academic honors you've received.

The education section also includes off-campus training sponsored by business, industry, or government. Include any relevant seminars or workshops you've attended, as well as the certificates or other documents you've received. Mention high school or military training only if your achievements are pertinent to your career goals. Whether you list your grades depends on the job you want and the quality of your grades. If you choose to show grade-point averages for your total program or your major, be sure to mention the scale if a 5-point scale is used instead of a 4-point scale.

Education is usually given less emphasis in a résumé after you've worked in your chosen field for a year or more. If work experience is your strongest qualification, save the section on education for later in the résumé and provide less detail.

> If education is your strongest selling point, discuss it thoroughly and highlight it visually.

Work Experience

Like the education section, the discussion of your work experience focuses on your overall theme. Tailor your description to highlight the relationship between your previous responsibilities and your target field. Call attention to the skills you've developed and the progression from jobs of lesser to greater responsibility.

When describing your work experience, you'll usually list your jobs in chronological order, with the current or last one first. Include any part-time, summer, or intern positions even if the jobs have no relation to your present career objective. Employers will see that you have the ability to get and hold a job, which is an important qualification in itself. If you have worked your way through school, say so. Employers interpret this as a sign of character.

Each listing includes the name and location of the employer. Then, if the reader is unlikely to recognize the organization, briefly describe what it does. When you want to keep the name of your current employer confidential, identify the firm by industry only ("a large film-processing laboratory"), or use the name but request confidentiality in the application letter or in an underlined note ("Résumé submitted in confidence") at the top or bottom of the résumé. If an organization's name or location has since changed, state the current name or location and then "formerly . . ."

Before or after each job listing, state your functional title, such as "clerk typist" or "salesperson." If you were a dishwasher, say so. Don't try to make your role seem more important by glamorizing your job title, functions, or achievements. You also state how long you worked on each job, from month/year to month/year. Use the phrase "to present" to denote current employment. If a job was part-time, say so.

Be honest about the positions you've held, the companies you've worked for, and your dates of employment. You'll be courting trouble if you list jobs you never held, claim to have worked for a firm when you didn't, or change dates to cover up a gap in employment. These days, more employers are checking candidates' backgrounds, so inaccuracies are likely to be exposed sooner or later.

Devote the most space to the jobs that relate to your target position. If you were personally responsible for something significant, be sure to mention it ("Devised a new collection system that accelerated payment of overdue receivables"). Facts about your accomplishments are the most important information you can give a prospective employer, so quantify your accomplishments whenever possible ("Designed a new ad that increased sales by 9 percent").

> The work experience section lists all the related jobs you've had:
> - Name and location of employer
> - What the organization does (if not clear from its name)
> - Your functional title
> - How long you worked there
> - Your duties and responsibilities
> - Your significant achievements or contributions

> Quantify your accomplishments whenever possible.

Relevant Skills

Include miscellaneous facts that relate to your career objective:

- Command of other languages
- Computer expertise
- Date you can start working
- Availability of references

You may also want to include a section that describes other aspects of your background that pertain to your career objective. If you were applying for a position with a multinational organization, you would mention your command of another language or your travel experience. Other skills you might mention include the ability to operate a computer, word processor, or other equipment. In fact, you might title a special section "Computer Skills" or "Language Skills" and place it near your "Education" or "Work Experience" section.

If your academic transcripts, samples of your work, or letters of recommendation might increase your chances of getting the job, insert a line at the end of your résumé offering to supply them on request. If your college placement office keeps these items on file for you, you can say "References and supporting documents available from . . ."; be sure to include the exact address of the placement office. Many potential employers prefer that you list your references on the résumé. As a convenience for the prospective employer, you may also list the month and, if you know it, the day you will be available to start work.

Activities and Achievements

Nonpaid activities may provide evidence of work-related skills.

Your résumé also describes any volunteer activities that demonstrate your abilities. List projects that require leadership, organization, teamwork, and cooperation. Emphasize career-related activities such as "member of the Student Marketing Association." List skills you learned in these activities, and explain how these skills relate to the job you're applying for. Include speaking, writing, or tutoring experience; participation in athletics or creative projects; fund-raising or community service activities; and offices held in academic or professional organizations. (However, mention of political or religious organizations may be a red flag to someone with different views, so use your judgment.) Note any awards you've received. Again, quantify your achievements with numbers whenever possible. Instead of saying that you addressed various student groups, state how many and the approximate audience sizes. If your activities have been extensive, you may want to group them into divisions: "College Activities," "Community Service," "Professional Associations," "Seminars and Workshops," and "Speaking Activities." An alternative is to divide them into two categories: "Service Activities" and "Achievements, Awards, and Honors."

Personal Data

Provide only the personal data that will help you get the job.

To differentiate your résumé, you might want to mention your hobbies, travel experiences, or personal characteristics, particularly if they suggest qualities that relate to your career goals. This section helps present you as a well-rounded person, and it can be used to spark conversation during an interview.[10] However, civil rights laws prohibit employers from discriminating on the basis of gender, marital or family status, age (although only those 40 to 70 are protected), race, color, religion, national origin, and physical or mental disability. Thus be sure to exclude any items that could encourage discrimination.

If military service is relevant to the position you are seeking, you may list it in this section (or under "Education" or "Work Experience"). List the date of induction, the branch of service, where you served, the highest rank you achieved, any accomplishments related to your career goals, and the date you were discharged.

Choosing the Best Organizational Plan

Select an organizational pattern that focuses attention on your strengths.

Although you may want to include a little information in all categories, emphasize the information that has a bearing on your career objective and minimize or exclude any that is irrelevant or counterproductive. You do this by adopting an organizational plan—chronological, functional, or targeted—that focuses attention on your strongest points. The "right" choice depends on your background and goals.

The Chronological Résumé

Most recruiters prefer the chronological plan—a historical summary of your education and work experience.

The most traditional type of résumé is the **chronological résumé,** in which a person's employment history is listed sequentially in reverse order, starting with the most recent experience. When you organize your résumé chronologically, the "Work Experience" section dominates the résumé and is placed in the most prominent slot, immediately after the name and address and the objective. You develop this section by listing your jobs in reverse order, beginning with the most recent position and working backward toward earlier jobs. Under each listing you describe your responsibilities and accomplishments, giving the most space to the most recent positions. If you are just graduating from college, you can vary the chronological plan by putting your educational qualifications before your experience, thereby focusing attention on your academic credentials.

The chronological approach is the most common way to organize a résumé, and many employers prefer it. Robert Nesbit, a vice president with Korn/Ferry International, speaks for many recruiters: "Unless you have a really compelling reason, don't use any but the standard chronological format. Your résumé should not read like a treasure map, full of minute clues to the whereabouts of your jobs and experience. I want to be able to grasp quickly where a candidate has worked, how long, and in what capacities."[11]

The chronological approach is especially appropriate if you have a strong employment history and are aiming for a job that builds on your current career path. This is the case for Roberto Cortez, whose résumé appears in Figure 15.2.

The Functional Résumé

In a **functional résumé,** you organize your résumé around a list of skills and accomplishments and then identify your employers and academic experience in subordinate sections. This pattern stresses individual areas of competence, and it's useful for people who are just entering the job market, people who want to redirect their careers, and people who have little continuous career-related experience. Figure 15.3 illustrates how a recent graduate used the functional approach to showcase her qualifications for a career in retail.

> A functional résumé focuses attention on your areas of competence.

The Targeted Résumé

A **targeted résumé** is a résumé organized to focus attention on what you can do for a particular employer in a particular position. Immediately after stating your career objective, you list any related capabilities. This list is followed by a list of your achievements, which provide evidence of your capabilities. Schools and employers are listed in subordinate sections.

> A targeted résumé shows how you qualify for a specific job.

Targeted résumés are a good choice for people who have a clear idea of what they want to do and who can demonstrate their ability in the targeted area. This approach was effective for Erica Vorkamp, whose résumé appears in Figure 15.4 on page 382.

Adapting Your Résumé to an Electronic Format

Although it was once considered unacceptable to fax a résumé to a potential employer, many executives now say they would indeed accept a résumé by fax if they've given no other specific guidelines.[12] Moreover, if employers advertise job openings online and provide an e-mail address for responses, sending your résumé by e-mail and responding via the Internet isn't only acceptable, it is preferable.

> An electronic résumé is helpful if your résumé will be scanned or if you post it on the Internet or submit it via e-mail.

Large companies have been storing résumés in centralized databases for some time. Now, when employers look for potential employees, more and more of them are searching online databases as well as their own in-house files.[13] Depending on where you wish to apply and how you wish to be perceived, you may want to consider the unique characteristics of electronic résumés—whether they are printed out and end up being scanned into a database, sent to employers by e-mail, or posted on the Internet. You can convert your traditional paper résumé into a scannable résumé in three steps (Figure 15.5 on page 383):[14]

1. *Save your résumé as a plain ASCII text file.* ASCII is a common text language that allows your résumé to be read by any scanner and accessed by any computer. All word-processing programs allow you to save files as ASCII. However, this language does have its limitations. ASCII will not handle decorative or uncommon typefaces, underlining, italics, graphics, or shading. Stick to a popular Times Roman or Helvetica typeface, and use blank spaces to align text (rather than tabs). To help your résumé

> To make your résumé scannable
> - Save it as an ASCII file
> - Provide a list of key words
> - Balance clear language with up-to-date jargon

Figure 15.2
In-Depth Critique:
Chronological Résumé

Cortez calls attention to his achievements by setting them off in a bulleted list. Because they come first, his most recent achievements will get the most attention. The section titled "Intercultural Qualifications" emphasizes his international background and fluency in Spanish, which are important qualifications for his target position.

ROBERTO CORTEZ
5687 Crosswoods Drive
Falls Church, Virginia 22046
Home: (703) 987-0086   Office: (703) 549-6624

OBJECTIVE

Accounting management position requiring a knowledge of international finance

EXPERIENCE

March 1995 to present	Staff Accountant/Financial Analyst, Inter-American Imports (Alexandria, Virginia)

- Prepare accounting reports for wholesale giftware importer with annual sales of $15 million
- Audit financial transactions with suppliers in 12 Latin American countries
- Create computerized models to adjust accounts for fluctuations in currency exchange rates
- Negotiate joint-venture agreements with major suppliers in Mexico and Colombia

October 1991 to March 1995	Staff Accountant, Monsanto Agricultural Chemicals (Mexico City, Mexico)

- Handled budgeting, billing, and credit-processing functions for the Mexico City branch
- Audited travel/entertainment expenses for Monsanto's 30-member Latin American sales force
- Assisted in launching an online computer system (IBM)

EDUCATION

1989 to 1991	MBA with emphasis on international business George Mason University (Fairfax, Virginia)
1985 to 1989	BBA, Accounting Universidad Nacional Autónoma de Mexico (Mexico City, Mexico)

INTERCULTURAL QUALIFICATIONS

- Born and raised in Mexico City
- Fluent in Spanish and German
- Traveled extensively in Latin America

References Available on Request
Résumé Submitted in Confidence

Cortez emphasizes his achievements by using an indented list.

The chronological organization highlights Cortez's impressive career progress.

Cortez's language and cultural skills are highlighted by presenting them in a special qualifications section.

---

appear more readable, you might sparingly use an asterisk or a lowercase letter *o* to indicate a bullet. Be sure to use a lot of white space to allow scanners and computers to recognize when one topic ends and another begins.

2. *Provide a list of key words.* Emphasizing certain words will help potential employers select your résumé from the thousands they scan. Because computers scan for nouns (rather than the active verbs you've included in your traditional paper résumé), you can provide those key nouns in a separate list and place it right after your name and address. These key words may or may not actually appear in your résumé, but they accomplish two things: They give potential employers a quick picture of you, and

Although Glenda Johns has not held any paid, full-time positions in retail sales, she has participated in work-experience programs, and she knows a good deal about the profession from doing research and talking with people in the industry. As a result, she was able to organize her résumé in a way that demonstrates her ability to handle such a position.

Figure 15.3
In-Depth Critique:
Functional Résumé

Glenda S. Johns

Home:	457 Mountain View Road	School:	1254 Main Street
	Clear Lake, IA 50428		Council Bluffs, IA 51505
	(515) 633-5971		(712) 438-5254

OBJECTIVE

Retailing position that utilizes my experience

RELEVANT SKILLS

- Personal Selling/Retailing
  - Led housewares department in fewest mistakes while cashiering and balancing register receipts
  - Created end-cap and shelf displays for special housewares promotions
  - Sold the most benefit tickets during college fund-raising drive for local community center
- Public Interaction
  - Commended by housewares manager for resolving customer complaints amicably
  - Performed in summer theater productions in Clear Lake, Iowa
- Managing
  - Trained part-time housewares employees in cash register operation and customer service
  - Reworked housewares employee schedules as assistant manager
  - Organized summer activities for children 6–12 years old for city of Clear Lake, Iowa—including reading programs, sports activities, and field trips

EDUCATION

- AA, Retailing Mid-Management (3.81 GPA / 4.0 scale), Iowa Western Community College, June 1998
- In addition to required retailing, buying, marketing, and merchandising courses, completed electives in visual merchandising, business information systems, principles of management, and business math

WORK EXPERIENCE

- Assistant manager, housewares, at Jefferson's Department Store during off-campus work experience program, Council Bluffs, Iowa (winter 1997–spring 1998)
- Sales clerk, housewares, at Jefferson's Department Store during off-campus work experience program, Council Bluffs, Iowa (winter 1996–spring 1997)
- Assistant director, Summer Recreation Program, Clear Lake, Iowa (summer 1996)
- Actress, Cobblestone Players, Clear Lake, Iowa (summer 1995)

REFERENCES AND SUPPORTING DOCUMENTS

Available from Placement Office, Iowa Western Community College, Council Bluffs, Iowa 51505

Because she is a recent graduate, the applicant describes her experience first.

The use of action verbs and specific facts enhances this résumé's effectiveness.

The applicant's sketchy work history is described but not emphasized.

GOING ONLINE
LINK YOUR WAY TO A BETTER RÉSUMÉ
Learn how to stand out in a crowded job market. Find a helpful list of dos and don'ts, some suggested résumé headings, a sample chronological résumé, a chart of action words to create an accomplishment-oriented impression, and a checklist for preparing scannable résumés.

http://www.bridgew.edu/depts/carplan/resume.htm

---

they show that you're sensitive to the requirements of today's electronic business world. When choosing your key words, consider the following categories: job titles (staff accountant), job-related tasks (instead of "created a computerized accounting model" simply list "computerized accounting model"), skills or knowledge (Excel, fluent Spanish), degrees (MBA or master of business administration), major (accounting major), certifications (CPA), school (George Mason University), class ranking (top 20 percent), interpersonal traits or skills (intercultural experience, organized, proven leader, willing to travel, written and oral communication skills).

Figure 15.4
In-Depth Critique:
Targeted Résumé

When Erica Vorkamp developed her résumé, she chose not to use a chronological pattern, which would focus attention on her lack of recent work experience. Instead, she used a targeted approach that emphasizes her ability to organize special events.

The capabilities and achievements are all related to the specific job target, giving a very selective picture of the candidate's abilities.

Erica Vorkamp

993 Church Street, Barrington, IL 60010
(312) 884-2153

Qualifications for Special Events Coordinator
for the City of Barrington

CAPABILITIES

- Plan and coordinate large-scale public events
- Develop community support for concerts, festivals, and entertainment
- Manage publicity for major events
- Coordinate activities of diverse community groups
- Establish and maintain financial controls for public events
- Negotiate contracts with performers, carpenters, electricians, and suppliers

ACHIEVEMENTS

- Arranged 1998's week-long Arts and Entertainment Festival for the Barrington Public Library, involving performances by 25 musicians, dancers, actors, magicians, and artists
- Supervised the 1997 PTA Halloween Carnival, an all-day festival with game booths, live bands, contests, and food service that raised $7,600 for the PTA
- Organized the 1995 Midwestern convention for 800 members of the League of Women Voters, which extended over a three-day period and required arrangements for hotels, meals, speakers, and special tours
- Served as chairperson for the 1996 Children's Home Society Fashion Show, a luncheon for 400 that raised $5,000 for orphans and abused children

EDUCATION

- BA, Psychology, Northwestern University (Evanston, Illinois), September 1979 to June 1984, Phi Beta Kappa

WORK HISTORY

- First National Bank of Chicago, June 1984 to October 1986, personnel counselor/campus recruiter; scheduled and conducted interviews with graduating MBA students on 18 Midwestern campuses; managed orientation program for recruits hired for bank's management trainee staff
- Northwestern University, November 1981 to June 1984, part-time research assistant; helped Professor Paul Harris conduct behavioral experiments using rats trained to go through mazes

---

This work history has little bearing on the candidate's job target, but she felt that recruiters would want to see evidence that she has held a paying position.

3. *Balance common language with current jargon.* To maximize matches (or *hits*) between your résumé and an employer's search, use words that potential employers will understand. For example, don't call a keyboard an input device. Also, use abbreviations sparingly, except for common ones such as BA or MBA. At the same time, learn the important buzz words used in your field, and use them. Places to look for the most current trends include want ads in major newspapers such as the *Wall Street Journal* and the résumés in your field that are posted online. Be careful to check and recheck the spelling, capitalization, and punctuation of any jargon you include, and use only those words you see most often.

If Roberto Cortez (see Figure 15.2) knows that the employers he's targeting will be scanning his résumé into a database, or if he wants to submit his résumé via e-mail or to post it on the Internet, he will change his formatting and add a key word list. The information he provides can remain essentially the same and appear in the same order.

Figure 15.5
In-Depth Critique:
Electronic Résumé

Roberto Cortez
5687 Crosswoods Drive
Falls Church, Virginia 22046

Home: (703) 987-0086   Office: (703) 549-6624
RCortez@silvernet.com

KEY WORDS

Financial executive, accounting management, international finance, financial analyst, accounting reports, financial audit, computerized accounting model, exchange rates, joint-venture agreements, budgets, billing, credit processing, online systems, MBA, fluent Spanish, fluent German

OBJECTIVE

Accounting management position requiring a knowledge of international finance

EXPERIENCE

Staff Accountant/Financial Analyst, Inter-American Imports (Alexandria, Virginia)
March 1995 to present
  o Prepare accounting reports for wholesale importer, annual sales of
    $15 million
  o Audit financial transactions with suppliers in 12 Latin American countries
  o Create computerized models to adjust for fluctuations in currency exchange
    rates
  o Negotiate joint-venture agreements with suppliers in Mexico and Colombia

Staff Accountant, Monsanto Agricultural Chemicals (Mexico City, Mexico)
October 1991 to March 1995
  o Handled budgeting, billing, credit-processing functions for the Mexico City
    branch
  o Audited travel/entertainment expenses for Monsanto's 30-member Latin
    American sales force
  o Assisted in launching an online computer system (IBM)

EDUCATION

MBA with emphasis on international business, George Mason University (Fairfax,
Virginia) 1989 to 1991

BBA, Accounting, Universidad Nacional Autónoma de Mexico (Mexico City, Mexico)
1985 to 1989

INTERCULTURAL QUALIFICATIONS

Born and raised in Mexico City
Fluent in Spanish and German
Traveled extensively in Latin America

References and formatted résumé available on request

Cortez has removed all boldfacing, rules, tabs, bullets, and two-column formatting.

Cortez uses a lowercase letter o in his indented lists.

If Cortez truly wanted to submit his résumé in confidence, he would not submit it to an online index or post it on a home page, where his current employer might run across it, so stating the need for confidentiality is no longer necessary.

The final note informs the reader of the availability not only of references but also of a fully formatted version of this electronic résumé.

Make sure your name and address are the first lines on your résumé (with no text appearing above or alongside your name). Also, particular sections are sometimes omitted from electronic résumés—special interests and references, for example.[15] To find out what employers expect to see, check online résumés in your field. If most of them list a career objective, then perhaps you should too. If you're mailing your résumé, you may want to send both a well-designed traditional one and a scannable one.

BEHIND THE SCENES AT MOBIL CORPORATION
How to Write a Résumé with the Winning Edge

Henry Halaiko is manager of recruiting operations for Mobil Corporation, and he's a busy person: Year-round, he coordinates Mobil's college relations and recruiting. During a recruiting cycle, he provides a strategic framework for the company's interaction with campuses. "I work with the office of Career Planning and Placement," says Halaiko. "In December I reserve space at next fall's on-campus recruiting. In September, we post our openings, list our requirements, and describe the work locations. Interested students submit résumés to the placement office, which forwards them to Mobil for consideration. At Mobil, the line managers who posted the openings screen the résumés. Then we write to those students who match our needs, and we set up an on-campus interview for October or November. The placement office notifies those students we decide not to schedule for an interview. The managers who screened the résumés conduct the on-campus interviews. Finally, when mutual interest extends beyond the initial interview, an on-site day of

Large companies such as Mobil are involved in multiple industries, and even though they may actively recruit at only a small number of campuses and in only specialized fields, these firms are always interested in hiring people with good communication skills, regardless of academic field or college.

from four to six interviews is scheduled. These fall interviews result in hiring people who will report to work after their graduation. The whole process, from initial campus interview to an accepted job offer, shouldn't take more than 60 days."

Mobil typically gets (from all sources) around 30,000 résumés a year to review. One large university, for example, forwarded 1,651 résumés in response to Mobil's posting. Of them, 253 students were interviewed. On average, 1 in 12 of those interviewed is offered a position, a total each year of between 700 and 800 students hired. "Seventy-five percent of our new hires are from the campus program," says Halaiko. "We promote largely from within, so there's little room for outside hiring beyond entry-level positions. But because everyone who submits a résumé is a potential employee—not to mention a customer, a stockholder, and an influence on others—the company is sensitive even to unsolicited résumés. Each one is reviewed, answered, and filed for future consideration."

The obvious question is, How do I make myself stand out in such a crowd? "This is not a science," Halaiko says. "We're looking for whole people. I go through a résumé looking for personal standards of excellence in the classroom, at work, and in extracurricular activities; for flexibility, a willingness to try new things; and for strong oral and written communication skills, regardless of major. It's to your advantage not only to list your job responsibilities but also to list your accomplishments and achievements as well. Give some indication of your level of success. Most candidates will say something like, 'I worked in the toy department, replenishing inventory, closing the books.' What I'm looking for is someone who adds, 'I was responsible for increasing sales by 12 percent during such-and-such a promotion.' This conveys to me that he or she is interested in performance and takes pride in accomplishment. People who describe themselves in this way want to do things better, more effectively. The same is true of

Two other quick points. First, when sending your résumé to a public access area (such as a résumé database) or when posting it on your own home page, leave out Social Security numbers and other identification codes. You might also leave out the names of references and previous employers. Simply say that references are available on request, and refer to "a large accounting firm" or "a wholesale giftware importer" rather than naming companies.

Second, avoid attaching fully designed résumés to e-mail messages. Your audience will have to spend extra effort to open your résumé, and chances are that your résumé will be in a format that your audience can't read.

Writing the Perfect Résumé

The "perfect" résumé responds to the reader's needs and preferences and avoids some common faults.

Regardless of whether your résumé is electronic or paper, and regardless of what organizational plan you follow, the key to writing the "perfect" résumé is to put yourself in the

extracurricular activities. Don't just say, 'I was on the team or in the fraternity.' Add that you accomplished certain objectives in those roles."

Should you stress your grade-point average? "We aren't one of those companies who take the posture that we won't consider anyone below, say, a 3.5 GPA. We certainly look for academic excellence, and 2.8 is more or less a threshold because so many students fall above that level. But we look beyond that to roundedness. Did you carry a 3.0 but work full-time to pay for your education? Was your 2.9 earned in a tough course schedule? Have your grades progressed?"

What role do letters have in this process? Usually, submitting a résumé to the placement office is the appropriate response to a posting. "But even this early," Halaiko adds, "we welcome a cover letter in several situations. If you have a low GPA but feel it does not adequately reflect who you are, if you took courses outside your major (which is a real plus), if your résumé doesn't show how you used your time (that you were going from a part-time job to class, then to an extracurricular activity, then home to care for a family), write to tell me. It shows you have a high capacity for work and learning. We're interested in people who have enthusiasm for work." Once the interview process has begun, several letters are called for. First, acknowledge the letter inviting you to the first interview and confirm your interest. After the interview, write the interviewer a personalized follow-up letter, focusing on something that was specifically discussed in the interview.

As a package, your letters and résumé should convey a sincere interest in the work described in the posting. Tailor your résumé to that particular position. "You'd probably not be considered if we posted an opening for a job in technical marketing or sales and your résumé said you were seeking a career in design engineering. Don't misrepresent what your real interests are just to get an interview," Halaiko points out. "That wastes your time and mine."

Are there any other no-no's? "If there's a classic error on a résumé, it's the one-page résumé with a half or a third of the page devoted to references. What that shows me is, you haven't done much."

In the end, says Halaiko, "There's no better feeling than having successfully recruited the candidate everyone was after but for whom the Mobil opportunity offered the best match of interests and needs." As an applicant, you can have the same feeling about completing a job search.

Apply Your Knowledge

1. After the deadline for responding to posted job opportunities, you learn that Mobil Corporation will be recruiting at your school to fill a vacancy for which you'd be perfect. On-campus interviews are to be held in three weeks. What strategies will you use to bring your interest and qualifications to the attention of Halaiko and the Mobil managers who will be conducting the initial interviews? How will you address the fact that you "missed the posting deadline"?

2. Take a copy of your résumé. (If you don't yet have a résumé, this can be your first step toward creating one.) Highlight each duty or responsibility you've listed for each job you've held. On a separate sheet of paper, list those duties down the right-hand side. To the left of each one, write out the kind of performance statement Halaiko referred to in his toy department example. For each duty/responsibility, select your performance/result that best illustrates your ability. When you're finished, review the list. Does it reveal anything new about your career interests? Does it change your "feeling" for what you are really good at? In what situations will your résumé stand out from the pack? Incorporate the achievement statements into your résumé.

reader's position. Think about what the prospective employer needs, and then tailor your résumé accordingly.

People like Pinkerton's Denis Brown read thousands of résumés every year and complain about the following common résumé problems:

- *Too long.* The résumé is not concise, relevant, and to the point.
- *Too short or sketchy.* The résumé does not give enough information for a proper evaluation of the applicant.
- *Hard to read.* A lack of "white space" and of such devices as indentions and boldfacing makes the reader's job more difficult.
- *Wordy.* Descriptions are verbose, with numerous words used for what could be said more simply.

CHECKLIST FOR RÉSUMÉS

A. Content and Style

1. Prepare the résumé before the application letter to summarize the facts the letter will be based on.
2. Present the strongest qualifications first.
3. Use short noun phrases and action verbs, not whole sentences.
4. Use facts, not opinions.
5. Avoid using too many personal pronouns.
6. Omit the date of preparation.
7. Omit mention of your desired salary, work schedule, or vacation schedule.

B. Contact Information

1. Use a title or your name and address as a heading.
2. List your name, address, area code, and telephone number—for both school or work and home, if appropriate.

C. Career Objective and Skills Summary (optional)

1. Be as specific as possible about what you want to do.
   - a. State a broad and flexible goal to increase the scope of your job prospects.
   - b. Prepare two different résumés if you can do two unrelated types of work.
2. Summarize your key qualifications.
3. State the month and, if you know it, the day on which you will be available to start work.

D. Education

1. List all relevant schooling and training since high school, with the most recent first.
   - a. List the name and location of every post-secondary school you have attended, with the dates you entered and left and the degrees or certificates you obtained.
   - b. Indicate your major (and minor) fields in college work.
   - c. State the numerical base for your grade-point average, overall or in your major, if your average is impressive enough to list. Note the numerical scale (4.0 or 5.0).
2. List relevant required or elective courses in descending order of importance.
3. List any other related educational or training experiences, such as job-related seminars or workshops attended and certificates obtained. (Give dates.)

E. Work Experience

1. List all relevant work experience, including paid employment, volunteer work, and internships.
2. List full-time and part-time jobs, with the most recent one first.
   - a. State the month/year when you started and left each job.

- *Too slick.* A résumé that appears to have been written by someone other than the applicant raises the question of whether the qualifications have been exaggerated.
- *Amateurish.* The applicant appears to have little understanding of the business world or of the particular industry, as revealed by including the wrong information or presenting it awkwardly.
- *Poorly reproduced.* The print is faint and difficult to read.
- *Misspelled and ungrammatical throughout.* Recruiters conclude that candidates who make these kinds of mistakes don't have good verbal skills, which are important on the job.
- *Boastful.* The overconfident tone makes the reader wonder whether the applicant's self-evaluation is realistic.
- *Dishonest.* The applicant claims to have expertise or work experience that he or she does not possess.
- *Gimmicky.* The words, structure, decoration, or material used in the résumé depart so far from the usual as to make the résumé ineffective.

Guard against making these mistakes in your own résumé, and compare your final version with the suggestions in this chapter's Checklist for Résumés.

Also, update your résumé continuously. You'll need it whether you're applying for membership in a professional organization, working toward a promotion, or changing employers. People used to spend most of their career with one company, but today the

  b. Provide the name and location of the firm that employed you.
  c. List your job title and briefly describe your responsibilities.
  d. Note on-the-job accomplishments, such as an award or a suggestion that saved the organization time or money.
F. **Activities, Honors, and Achievements**
  1. List all relevant unpaid activities, including offices and leadership positions; significant awards or scholarships not listed elsewhere; projects you have undertaken that show an ability to work with others; and writing or speaking activities, publications, and roles in academic or professional organizations.
  2. In most circumstances, exclude mention of religious or political affiliations.
G. **Other Relevant Facts**
  1. List other information, such as your typing speed or your proficiency in languages other than English.
  2. Mention your ability to operate any machines, equipment, or computer software used in the job.
H. **Personal Data**
  1. Omit personal details that could be regarded negatively or be used to discriminate against you.

  2. Omit or downplay references to age if it could suggest inexperience or approaching retirement.
  3. Describe military service (branch of service, where you served, rank attained, and the dates of induction and discharge) here or, if relevant, under "Education" or "Work Experience."
  4. List job-related interests and hobbies, especially those indicating stamina, strength, sociability, or other qualities that are desirable in the position you seek.
I. **References**
  1. Offer to supply the names of references on request.
    a. Supply names of academic, employment, and professional associates—but no relatives (unless you worked for them in a family-owned or operated business).
    b. Provide a name, a title, an address, and a telephone number (with area code) for each reference.
    c. List no name as a reference until you have that person's permission to do so.
  2. Exclude your present employer if you do not want the firm to know you are seeking another position, or add "Résumé Submitted in Confidence" at the top or bottom of the résumé.

average person beginning a job in the United States will probably work in ten or more jobs for five or more employers before retiring.[16] So keeping your résumé updated is a good idea.

Whenever you submit your résumé, you accompany it with a cover or application letter. This document lets your reader know what you're sending, why you're sending it, and how your reader can benefit from reading it. Because your application letter is in your own style (rather than the choppy, shorthand style of your résumé), it gives you a chance to make a good personal impression.

RITING APPLICATION MESSAGES

Like your résumé, your application letter is a form of advertising, so organize it like a sales letter: Use the AIDA plan, focus on the "you" attitude, and emphasize reader benefits (as discussed in Chapter 11). You need to stimulate your reader's interest before showing how you can satisfy the organization's needs. Make sure your style projects confidence; you can't hope to sell a potential employer on your merits unless you truly believe in them yourself and sound as though you do.

Of course, this approach isn't appropriate for job seekers in every culture. If you're applying for a job abroad or want to work with a subsidiary of an organization based in

Follow the AIDA plan when writing your application letter: attention, interest, desire, action.

another country, you may need to adjust your tone. For instance, blatant self-promotion is considered bad form in some cultures. Other cultures stress group performance over individual contributions. And as for format, in some countries (including France), recruiters prefer handwritten letters to printed or typed ones. So research your company carefully before drafting your application letter.

For U.S. and Canadian companies, let your letter reflect your personal style. Be yourself, but be businesslike too; avoid sounding cute. Don't use slang or a gimmicky layout. The only time to be unusually creative in content or format is when the job you're seeking requires imagination, such as a position in advertising. In most cases you'll use a printer or typewriter to produce your application letter.

Finally, showing that you know something about the organization can pay off. Imagine yourself in the recruiter's situation: How can you demonstrate that your background and talents will solve a particular problem or fill a need? By using a "you" attitude and showing you've done some homework, you'll capture the reader's attention and convey your desire to join the organization. The more you can learn about the organization, the better you'll be able to write about how your qualifications fit its needs.[17]

Also, during your research, find out the name, title, and department of the person you're writing to. Reaching and addressing the right person is the most effective way to gain attention. So be sure to avoid phrases such as "To Whom It May Concern" and "Dear Sir."

Writing the Opening Paragraph

A **solicited application letter** is one sent in response to an announced job opening. An **unsolicited letter,** also known as a *prospecting letter,* is one sent to an organization that has not announced an opening. When you send a solicited letter, you usually know in advance what qualifications the organization is seeking. However, you also have more competition because hundreds of other job seekers will have seen the listing and may be sending applications. In some respects, therefore, an unsolicited application letter stands a better chance of being read and of receiving individualized attention.

Whether your application letter is solicited or unsolicited, your qualifications are presented similarly. The main difference is in the opening paragraph. In a solicited letter, no special attention-getting effort is needed because you have been invited to apply. However, the unsolicited letter starts by capturing the reader's attention and interest.

Getting Attention

One way to spark attention in the opening paragraph is to show how your strongest work skills could benefit the organization. A 20-year-old secretary with 1½ years of college might begin like this:

> When you need a secretary in your export division who can take shorthand at 125 words a minute and transcribe notes at 70—in English, Spanish, or Portuguese—call me.

Here's another attention-getter. It describes your understanding of the job's requirements and then shows how well your qualifications fit the job:

> Your annual report states that Mobil Corporation runs training programs about workforce diversity for managers and employees. The difficulties involved in running such programs can be significant, as I learned while tutoring inner-city high school students last summer. My 12 pupils were enrolled in vocational training programs and came from an eclectic mix of ethnic and racial backgrounds. The one thing they had in common was the lack of familiarity with the typical employer's expectations. To help them learn the "rules of the game," I developed exercises that cast them in various roles: boss, customer, new recruit, and co-worker. Of the 12 students, 10 have subsequently found full-time jobs and have called or written to tell me how much they gained from the workshop.

You write a solicited application letter in response to an announced job opening.

You write an unsolicited application letter to an organization that has not announced a job opening.

Within a year of becoming president of Godfather's Pizza, Herman Cain returned the floundering chain to profitability. Now principal owner (following a leveraged buyout), Cain says his success springs from his love of the restaurant business. Simple ambition isn't enough to succeed in any business, he advises, so send résumés to companies whose business you have a real passion for.

Mentioning the name of a person known to and highly regarded by the reader is bound to capture some attention:

When Janice McHugh of your franchise sales division spoke to our business communication class last week, she said you often need promising new marketing graduates at this time of year.

References to publicized company activities, achievements, changes, or new procedures can also be used to gain attention:

Today's issue of the *Detroit News* reports that you may need the expertise of computer programmers versed in robotics when your Lansing tire plant automates this spring.

Another type of attention-getting opening uses a question to demonstrate an understanding of the organization's needs:

Can your fast-growing market research division use an interviewer with 1 1/2 years of field survey experience, a BA in public relations, and a real desire to succeed? If so, please consider me for the position.

A catch-phrase opening can also capture attention, especially if the job sought requires ingenuity and imagination:

Haut monde—whether said in French, Italian, or Arabic, it still means "high society." As an interior designer for your Beverly Hills showroom, not only could I serve and sell to your distinguished clientele, but I could do it in all these languages. I speak, read, and write them fluently.

In contrast, a solicited letter written in response to a job advertisement usually opens by identifying the publication in which the ad ran and then describes what the applicant has to offer:

Your ad in the April issue of *Travel & Leisure* for a cruise-line social director caught my eye. My eight years of experience as a social director in the travel industry would allow me to serve your new Caribbean cruise division well.

Note that all these openings demonstrate the "you" attitude and many indicate how the applicant can serve the employer.

Clarifying Your Reason for Writing

The opening paragraph of your application letter also states your reason for writing: You are applying for a job, so the opening paragraph identifies the desired job or job area:

Please consider my application for an entry-level position in technical writing.

Your firm advertised a fleet sales position (on March 23, 1997, in the *Baltimore Sun*). Won't you consider me, with my 16 months of new-car sales experience, for that position?

Another way to state your reason for writing is to use a title at the opening of your letter:

Subject: Application for bookkeeper position

After this clear signal, your first paragraph can focus on getting attention and indicating how hiring you may benefit the organization.

Oprah Winfrey has a humanistic approach to running her company, Harpo Productions. She's known to be demanding of her 135 employees, but she's also generous. Winfrey reminds applicants to get attention by emphasizing how they can help the employer. And don't be afraid to be yourself, she says.

Start a solicited application letter by mentioning how you found out about the open position.

State in the opening paragraph that you are applying for a job.

Summarizing Your Key Selling Points

The middle section of an application letter

- Summarizes your relevant qualifications
- Emphasizes your accomplishments
- Suggests desirable personal qualities
- Justifies salary requirements
- Refers to your résumé

The middle section of your application letter presents your strongest selling points in terms of their potential benefit to the organization, thereby creating interest in you and a desire to interview you. If your selling points have already been mentioned in the opening, don't repeat them. Simply give supporting evidence. Otherwise, spell out your key qualifications, together with some convincing evidence of your ability to perform.

To avoid a cluttered application letter, mention only the qualifications that indicate you can do the job. Show how your studies and your work experience have prepared you for that job, or tell the reader about how you grew up in the business. Be careful not to repeat the facts presented in your résumé; simply interpret those facts for the reader:

Experience in customer relations and college courses in public relations have taught me how to handle the problem-solving tasks that arise in a leading retail clothing firm like yours. Such important tasks include identifying and resolving customer complaints, writing letters that build good customer relations, and above all, promoting the organization's positive image.

When writing a solicited letter responding to a help-wanted advertisement, discuss each requirement specified in the ad. If you are deficient in any of the requirements, stress other solid selling points to help strengthen your overall presentation.

Stating that you have all the necessary requirements for the job is rarely enough to convince the reader, so back up assertions of your ability by presenting evidence of it. Cite one or two of your key qualifications; then show how you have effectively put them to use.

INSTEAD OF THIS

I completed three college courses in business communication, earning an A in each course, and have worked for the past year at Imperial Construction.

WRITE THIS

Using the skills gained from three semesters of college training in business communication, I developed a collection system for Imperial Construction that reduced its 1998 bad-debt losses by 3.7 percent, or $9,902, from those of 1997. The new system included collection letters that offered discount incentives for speedy payment rather than timeworn terminology.

This section of the letter also presents evidence of a few significant job-related qualities. The following paragraph demonstrates that the applicant is diligent and hard working:

While attending college full-time, I trained 3 hours a day with the varsity track team. In addition, I worked part-time during the school year and up to 60 hours a week each summer in order to be totally self-supporting while in college. I can offer your organization the same level of effort and perseverance.

Other relevant qualities worth noting include the abilities to learn quickly, to handle responsibility, and to get along with people.

Another matter to bring up in this section is your salary requirements—but only if the organization has asked you to state them. The best strategy, unless you know approximately what the job pays, is to suggest a salary range or to indicate that the salary is negotiable or open. You might also consult the latest government "Area Wage Survey" at the library; this document presents salary ranges for various job classifications and geographical areas. If you do state a target salary, tie your request to the benefits you would provide the organization, much as you would handle price in a sales letter:

For the past two years, I have been helping a company similar to yours organize its database. I would therefore like to receive a salary in the same range (the mid-20s) for helping your company set up a more efficient customer database.

Toward the end of this section, refer the reader to your résumé. You may do so by citing a specific fact or general point covered in the résumé.

You will find my people skills an asset. As you can see in the attached résumé, I've been working part-time with a local publisher since my sophomore year, and during that time, I have successfully resolved more than a few "client crises."

Writing the Closing Paragraph

The final paragraph of your application letter has two important functions: to ask the reader for a specific action and to make a reply easy. In almost all cases, the action you ask for is an interview. Don't demand it, however; try to sound natural and appreciative. Offer to come to the employer's office at a convenient time or, if the firm is some distance away, to meet with its nearest representative. Make the request easy to fulfill by stating your phone number and the best time to reach you. Refer again to your strongest selling point and, if desired, your date of availability:

> Close by asking for an interview and making the interview easy to arrange.

After you have reviewed my qualifications, could we discuss the possibility of putting my marketing skills to work for your company? Because I will be on spring break the week of March 8, I would like to arrange a time to talk then. You can reach me by calling (901) 235-6311 during the day or (901) 529-2873 any evening after 5:00.

An alternative approach is to ask for an interview and then offer to get in touch with the reader to arrange a time for it, rather than requesting a reply. Whichever approach you use, mail your application letter and résumé promptly, especially if they have been solicited.

Writing the Perfect Application Letter

The "perfect" application letter, like the "perfect" résumé, accomplishes one thing: It gets you an interview. It conforms to no particular model because it's a reflection of your special strengths. Nevertheless, an application letter contains the basic components. In Figure 15.6, an unsolicited letter for a retail position, the applicant gains attention by focusing on the needs of the employer. The letter in Figure 15.7, written in response to a help-wanted ad, highlights the applicant's chief qualifications. Compare your own letters with the tasks in this chapter's Checklist for Application Letters.

RITING OTHER TYPES OF EMPLOYMENT MESSAGES

In your search for a job, you may prepare three other types of written messages: job-inquiry letters, application forms, and application follow-up letters.

Writing Job-Inquiry Letters

Some organizations will not consider you for a position until you have filled out and submitted an **application form,** a standardized data sheet that simplifies comparison of applicants' qualifications. The inquiry letter is sent to request such a form. To increase your chances of getting the form, include enough information about yourself in the letter to show that you have at least some of the requirements for the position you are seeking:

> Use a job-inquiry letter to request an application form, which is a standardized data sheet that simplifies comparison of applicants' credentials.

Figure 15.6
In-Depth Critique: Sample
Unsolicited Application Letter

In her unsolicited application letter, Glenda Johns manages to give a snapshot of her qualifications and skills without repeating what is said in her résumé (which appears in Figure 15.3).

Glenda S. Johns

Home: 457 Mountain View Road, Clear Lake, IA 50428 (515) 633-5971
School: 1254 Main Street, Council Bluffs, IA 51505 (712) 438-5254

June 16, 1999

Ms. Patricia Downings, Store Manager
Wal-Mart
840 South Oak
Iowa Falls, Iowa 50126

Dear Ms. Downings:

You want retail clerks and managers who are accurate, enthusiastic, and experienced. You want someone who cares about customer service, who understands merchandising, and who can work with others to get the job done. When you're ready to hire a manager trainee or a clerk who is willing to work toward promotion, please consider me for the job.

Working as clerk and then as assistant department manager in a large department store has taught me how challenging a career in retailing can be. Moreover, my AA degree in retailing (including work in such courses as retailing, marketing, and business information systems) will provide your store with a well-rounded associate. Most important, I can offer Wal-Mart's Iowa Falls store more than my two years' of study and field experience. You'll find that I'm interested in every facet of retailing, eager to take on responsibility, and willing to continue learning throughout my career. Please look over my résumé to see how my skills can benefit your store.

I understand that Wal-Mart prefers to promote its managers from within the company, and I would be pleased to start out with an entry-level position until I gain the necessary experience. Do you have any associate positions opening up soon? Could we discuss my qualifications? I will phone you early next Wednesday to arrange a meeting at your convenience.

Sincerely,

Glenda Johns

Glenda Johns

Enclosure

The applicant gains attention in the first paragraph.

The applicant points out personal qualities that aren't specifically stated in her résumé.

Knowledge of the company's policy toward promotions is sure to interest the reader.

Even though the last paragraph uses the word I, *the concern and the focus of the letter are clearly centered on the audience and convey a "you" attitude.*

Please send me an application form for work as an interior designer in your home furnishings department. For my certificate in design, I took courses in retail merchandising and customer relations. I have also had part-time sales experience at Capwell's department store.

Instead of writing a letter of this kind, you may want to drop in at the office you're applying to. You probably won't get a chance to talk to anyone other than the receptionist or a human resources assistant, but you can pick up the form, get an impression of the organization, and demonstrate your initiative and energy.

Kenneth Sawyer grabs attention by focusing on a phrase the employer used in a want ad: "proven skills." Sawyer elaborates on his own proven skills throughout the letter, and he even uses the term in the closing paragraph.

Figure 15.7
In-Depth Critique: Sample Solicited Application Letter

Kenneth Sawyer
2893 Jack Pine Road, Chapel Hill, NC 27514

February 2, 1999

Ms. Angela Clair
Director of Administration
Cummings and Welbane, Inc.
770 Campus Point Drive
Chapel Hill, NC 27514

Dear Ms. Clair:

In the January 31 issue of the *Chapel Hill Post,* your ad mentioned "proven skills." I believe I have what you are looking for in an administrative assistant. In addition to experience in a variety of office settings, I am familiar with the computer software that you use in your office.

I recently completed a three-course sequence at Hamilton College on Microsoft Word and PowerPoint. I learned how to apply those programs to speed up letter- and report-writing tasks. A workshop on "Writing and Editing with the Unix Processor" gave me experience with other valuable applications such as composing and formatting sales letters, financial reports, and presentation slides.

These skills have been invaluable to me as assistant to the chief nutritionist at our campus cafeteria (please refer to my résumé). I'm particularly proud of the order-confirmation system I designed, which has sharply reduced the problems of late shipments and depleted inventories.

Because "proven skills" are best explained in person, I would appreciate an interview with you. Please phone me any afternoon between 3 and 5 p.m. at (919) 220-6139 to let me know the day and time most convenient for you.

Sincerely,

Kenneth Sawyer

Kenneth Sawyer

Enclosure: Résumé

The opening states the reason for writing and links the writer's experience to stated qualifications.

By discussing how his specific skills apply to the job sought, the applicant shows that he understands the job's responsibilities.

In closing, the writer asks for an interview and facilitates action.

Filling Out Application Forms

Some organizations require an application form instead of a résumé, and many require both an application form and a résumé. When filling out an application form, try to be thorough and accurate, because the organization will use this as a convenient one-page source for information about your qualifications. Be sure to have your résumé with you to remind you of important information. If you can't remember something and have no record of it, provide the closest estimate possible. If the form calls for information that you cannot provide because you have no background in it, such as military experience, write "Not applicable." When filling out applications on the premises, use a pen (unless specifically requested to use a pencil). If you're allowed to take the application form with you, use a typewriter to fill it out.

Your care in filling out application forms suggests to the employer that you will be thorough and careful in your work.

CHECKLIST FOR APPLICATION LETTERS

A. Attention (Opening Paragraph)

1. Open the letter by capturing the reader's attention in a businesslike way.
   - a. Summary opening. Present your strongest, most relevant qualifications, with an explanation of how they can benefit the organization.
   - b. Name opening. Mention the name of a person who is well known to the reader and who has suggested that you apply for the job.
   - c. Source opening. When responding to a job ad, identify the publication in which the ad appeared, and briefly describe how you meet each requirement stated in the ad.
   - d. Question opening. Pose an attention-getting question that shows you understand an organization's problem, need, or goal and have a genuine desire to help solve or meet it.
   - e. News opening. Cite a publicized organizational achievement, contemplated change, or new procedure or product; then link it to your desire to work for the organization.
   - f. Personalized opening. Present one of your relevant interests, mention previous experience with the organization, or cite your present position or status as a means of leading into a discussion of why you want to work for the organization.
   - g. Creative opening. Demonstrate your flair and imagination with colorful phrasing, especially if the job requires these qualities.
2. State that you are applying for a job, and identify the position or the type of work you seek.

B. Interest and Desire, or Evidence of Qualifications (Next Several Paragraphs)

1. Present your key qualifications for the job, highlighting what is on your résumé: job-related education and training; relevant work experience; and related activities, interests, and qualities.
2. Adopt a mature and businesslike tone.
   - a. Eliminate boasting and exaggeration.
   - b. Back up your claims of ability by citing specific achievements in educational and work settings or in outside activities.
   - c. Demonstrate a knowledge of the organization and a desire to join it by citing its operations or trends in the industry.
3. Link your education, experience, and personal qualities to the job requirements.
   - a. Relate aspects of your training or work experience to those of the target position.
   - b. Outline your educational preparation for the job.
   - c. Provide proof that you learn quickly, are a hard worker, can handle responsibility, and/or get along well with others.
   - d. Present ample evidence of the personal qualities and the work attitudes that are desirable for job performance.
   - e. If asked to state salary requirements, provide current salary or a desired salary range, and link it to the benefits of hiring you.
4. Refer the reader to the enclosed résumé.

C. Action (Closing Paragraph)

1. Request an interview at the reader's convenience.
2. Request a screening interview with the nearest regional representative if company headquarters is some distance away.
3. State your phone number (with area code) and the best time to reach you, to make the interview request easy to comply with, or mention a time when you will be calling to set up an interview.
4. Express appreciation for an opportunity to have an interview.
5. Repeat your strongest qualification, to help reinforce the claim that you have something to offer the organization.

Application forms rarely seem to provide the right amount of space or to ask the right kinds of questions to reflect one's skills and abilities accurately. Swallow your frustration, however, and show your cooperation by doing your best to fill out the form completely. If you get an interview, you'll have an opportunity to fill in the gaps. You might also ask the person who gives you the form if you may submit a résumé and an application letter as well.

Writing Application Follow-Ups

If your application letter and résumé fail to bring a response within a month or so, follow up with a second letter to keep your file active. This follow-up letter also gives you a chance to update your original application with any recent job-related information:

Use a follow-up letter to let the employer know you're still interested in the job.

Since applying to you on May 3 for an executive secretary position, I have completed a course in office management at South River Community College. I received straight A's in the course. My typing speed has also increased to 75 words per minute.

Please keep my application in your active file, and let me know when you need a skilled executive secretary.

Even if you have received a letter acknowledging your application and saying that it will be kept on file, don't hesitate to send a follow-up letter three months later to show that you are still interested:

Three months have elapsed since I applied to you for an underwriting position, but I want to let you know that I am still very interested in joining your company.

I recently completed a four-week temporary work assignment at a large local insurance agency. I learned several new verification techniques and gained experience in using the online computer system. This experience could increase my value to your underwriting department.

Please keep my application in your active file, and let me know when a position opens for a capable underwriter.

Unless you state otherwise, the human resources office is likely to assume that you've already found a job and are no longer interested in the organization. In addition, organizations' requirements change. Sending a letter like this demonstrates that you are sincerely interested in working for the organization, that you are persistent in pursuing your goals, and that you continue upgrading your skills to make yourself a better employee—and it might just get you an interview.

O n the Job

SOLVING A COMMUNICATION DILEMMA AT PINKERTON

Whether it's safeguarding movie stars or making sure a multinational corporation hires the right people, it's all in a day's work for Pinkerton. The security company founded by Allan Pinkerton in 1850 made its name with such exploits as tracking Butch Cassidy and the Sundance Kid and protecting Abraham Lincoln before his inauguration. Thomas Wathen bought Pinkerton in 1987 and began expanding it into a worldwide network that now encompasses more than 200 offices, 47,000 employees, and nearly $1 billion in annual revenue. Denis Brown took the reins in 1994 with the goal of continuing that growth while improving the company's profit margins.

With the company's services so dependent on the quality of people it hires, Brown must screen job seekers and pick only those individuals who have the experience, attitude, and talent to perform well in whatever unique and demanding situation the company assigns them to. These security officers also need excellent communication skills to interact with the public and handle troubles that might range from petty theft to terrorism.

Pinkerton follows the same five-step approach to screening, evaluating, and selecting employees, regardless of whether it's filling internal openings or helping clients evaluate job candidates. In the first step, each candidate fills out a job application and sits through an initial interview with Pinkerton personnel. Only candidates whose qualifications meet Pinkerton's job requirements move to the second step. Next, prospective employees fill out questionnaires measuring attitudes toward honesty and willingness to follow company rules.

Again, only people who meet Pinkerton's standards advance. In the third step, candidates participate in a ten-minute interview session conducted over the telephone by a computerized voice system. They answer roughly 100 questions about job stability, career goals, work ethic, enthusiasm, and other aspects of their work history by pushing buttons on the telephone keypad—one button for *yes*, another for *no*, and a third for *uncertain*.

Just a few minutes after each candidate hangs up the phone, Pinkerton personnel can call the computer center and get the results. This information helps the staff members pinpoint topics to be addressed in the fourth step of the process, an in-depth personal interview.

At least 30 percent of the applicants are weeded out by this point. In the fifth step, Pinkerton investigators check the backgrounds of those candidates who have completed the personal interview successfully. Once they have the results of the investigation, Pinkerton personnel are then able to decide which candidates to hire.[18]

Your Mission: As a member of Pinkerton's human resources department, you regularly review résumés that arrive uninvited. You're particularly on the lookout for recent college graduates who might be good candidates for management training positions in Pinkerton's comprehensive security operations for General Motors, which span the United States, Canada, and Mexico. General Motors accounts for roughly 10 percent of Pinkerton's annual revenue, so keeping this customer satisfied is extremely important. Give Denis Brown your best advice regarding the following applicants, and be prepared to explain your recommendations.

1. You have received résumés from four people. On the basis of only the career objectives listed, which one of the candidates will you consider hiring as a management trainee?

   a. Career Objective: An entry-level management position in a large company
   b. Career Objective: To invest my management talent and business savvy and shepherd a business toward explosive growth
   c. Career Objective: A management position in which a degree in business administration and experience in managing personnel will be useful
   d. Career Objective: To learn all I can about personnel management in an exciting environment with a company whose reputation is outstanding

2. On the basis of only the education sections of another four résumés, which of the following candidates would you recommend?

   a. **EDUCATION**
      Morehouse College, Atlanta, GA, 1994–1998.
      Received B.A. degree with a major in Business Administration and a minor in Finance. Graduated with a 3.65 grade-point average. Played varsity football and basketball. Worked 15 hours per week in the library. Coordinated the local student chapter of the American Management Association. Member of Alpha Phi Alpha social fraternity.
   b. **Education:** I attended Wayne State University in Detroit, Michigan, for two years and then transferred to the University of Michigan at Ann Arbor, where I completed my studies. My major was economics, but I also took many business management courses, including employee motivation, leadership, history of management theory, and organizational behavior. I selected courses based on the professors' reputations for excellence, and I received mostly A's and B's. Unlike many college students, I viewed the acquisition of knowledge—rather than career preparation—as my primary goal. I believe I have received a well-rounded education that has prepared me to approach management situations as problem-solving exercises.
   c. ACADEMIC PREPARATION
      University of Connecticut, Storrs, Connecticut. Graduated with a B.A. degree in 1997. Majored in Physical Education. Minored in Business Administration. Graduated with a 2.85 average.
   d. **Education: North Texas State University and University of Texas at Tyler.** Received B.A. and M.B.A. degrees. I majored

in business as an undergraduate and concentrated in manufacturing management during my M.B.A. program. Received a special $2,500 scholarship offered by Rotary International recognizing academic achievement in business courses. I also won the MEGA award in 1995. Dean's list.

3. Which of the following four candidates would you recommend, strictly on the basis of the experience sections?

   a. **RELATED WORK EXPERIENCE**
      McDonald's, Peoria, IL, 1994–1995. Part-time cook. Worked 15 hours per week while attending high school. Prepared hamburgers, chicken bits, and french fries. Received employee-of-the-month award for outstanding work habits.
      University Grill, Ames, IA, 1995–1998. Part-time cook. Worked 20 hours per week while attending college. Prepared hot and cold sandwiches. Helped manager purchase ingredients. Trained new kitchen workers. Prepared work schedules for kitchen staff.
   b. **RELATED EXPERIENCE**
      Although I have never held a full-time job, I have worked part-time and during summer vacations throughout my high school and college years. During my freshman and sophomore years in high school, I bagged groceries at the A&P store three afternoons a week. The work was not terribly challenging, but I liked the customers and the other employees. During my junior and senior years, I worked at the YMCA as an after-school counselor for elementary school children. The kids were really sweet, and I still get letters from some of them. During summer vacations while I was in college, I did construction work for a local home builder. The job paid well, and I also learned a lot about carpentry. The guys I worked with were a mixed bag who expanded my vocabulary and knowledge of the world. I also worked part-time in college in the student cafeteria, where I scooped food onto plates. This did not require much talent, but it taught me a lot about how people behave when standing in line. I also learned quite a bit about life from my boss, Sam "The Man" Benson, who has been managing the student cafeteria for 25 years.
   c. **PREVIOUS WORK EXPERIENCE**
      The Broadway Department Store, Sherman Oaks, CA, Summers, 1995–1998. Sales Consultant, Furniture Department. I interacted with a diverse group of customers, including suburban matrons, teenagers, career women, and professional couples. I endeavored to satisfy their individual needs and make their shopping experience memorable, efficient, and enjoyable. Under the direction of the sales manager, I helped prepare employee schedules and fill out departmental reports. I also helped manage the inventory, worked the cash register, and handled a variety of special orders and customer complaints with courtesy and aplomb. During the 1998 annual storewide sale, I sold more merchandise than any other salesperson in the entire furniture department.
   d. **EXPERIENCE RELATED TO MANAGEMENT**
      Belle Fleure, GA, Civilian Member of Public Safety Committee, January–December 1998.
      ■ Organized and promoted a lecture series on vacation safety and home security for the residents of Belle Fleure, GA; recruited and trained 7 committee members to help plan and produce the lectures; persuaded local businesses

to finance the program; designed, printed, and distributed fliers; wrote and distributed press releases; attracted an average of 120 people to each of three lectures

■ Developed a questionnaire to determine local residents' home-security needs; directed the efforts of 10 volunteers working on the survey; prepared written report for city council and delivered oral summary of findings at town meeting; helped persuade city to fund new home-security program

■ Initiated the Business Security Forum as an annual meeting at which local business leaders could meet to discuss safety and security issues; created promotional flyers for the first forum; convinced 19 business owners to fund a business security survey; arranged press coverage of the first forum

4. You've received the following résumé. What action will you take?

Maria Martin
1124 2nd S.W.
Rhinelander, WI 54501
(715) 369-0098

Career Objective: To build a management career in a growing U.S. company

Summary of Qualifications: As a student at the University of Wisconsin in Madison, carried out various assignments that have required skills related to a career in management. For example:

Planning Skills. As president of the university's foreign affairs forum, organized six lectures and workshops featuring 36 speakers from 16 foreign countries within a nine-month period. Identified and recruited the speakers, handled their travel arrangements, and scheduled the facilities.

Interpersonal Skills. As chairman of the parade committee for Homecoming Weekend, worked with the city of Madison to obtain approval, permits, and traffic control for the parade. Also encouraged local organizations such as the Lion's Club, the Kiwanis Club, and the Boy Scouts to participate in the parade. Coordinated the efforts of the 15 fraternities and 18 sororities that entered floats in the parade. Recruited 12 marching bands from surrounding communities and coordinated their efforts with the university's marching band. Also arranged for local auto dealers to provide cars for the ten homecoming queen candidates.

Communication Skills. Wrote over 25 essays and term papers dealing with academic topics. Received an A on all but two of these papers. As a senior, wrote a 20-page analysis of the paper products industry, interviewing the five top executives at the Rhinelander paper company. Received an A1 on this paper.

a. Definitely recommend that Pinkerton take a look at this outstanding candidate.
b. Turn down the candidate. She doesn't give enough information about when she attended college, what she majored in, or where she has worked.
c. Call the candidate on the phone and ask for more information. If she sounds promising, send her an application form that requests more specific information about her academic background and employment history.
d. Consider the candidate's qualifications relative to those of other applicants. Recommend her if you do not have three or four other applicants with more directly relevant qualifications.

ritical Thinking Questions

1. According to experts in the job-placement field, the average job seeker places too much importance on the résumé and not enough on other elements of the job search. Which elements do you think are most important? Explain.
2. How would you locate information about overseas employment opportunities in general? About job requirements at specific overseas companies? Briefly explain.
3. As an employer, what would you do to detect résumé inflation such as misrepresented job qualifications, salaries, and academic credentials? Please explain.

4. Stating your career objective might limit your opportunities by labeling you too narrowly. Not stating your career objective, however, might lead an employer to categorize you incorrectly. Which outcome is riskier? Do summaries of qualifications overcome such drawbacks? If so, how? Briefly explain.
5. When writing a solicited application letter and describing the skills requested in the employer's ad, how can you avoid using *I* too often? Explain and give examples.
6. How can you make your letter of application unique without being cute or gimmicky? Explain and give examples.

Documents for Analysis

Read the following documents; then (1) analyze the strengths or weaknesses of each sentence and (2) revise each document so that it follows the guidelines presented in this chapter.

DOCUMENT 15.A: WRITING AN APPLICATION MESSAGE
I'm writing to let you know about my availability for the brand manager job you advertised. As you can see from my enclosed résumé, my background is perfect for the position. Even though I don't have any real job experience, my grades have been outstanding considering that I went to a top-ranked business school.

I did many things during my undergraduate years to prepare me for this job:

■ Earned a 3.4 out of a 4.0 with a 3.8 in my business courses
■ Elected representative to the student governing association

- Selected to receive the Lamar Franklin Award
- Worked to earn a portion of my tuition

I am sending my résumé to all the top firms, but I like yours better than any of the rest. Your reputation is tops in the industry, and I want to be associated with a business that can pridefully say it's the best.

If you wish for me to come in for an interview, I can come on a Friday afternoon or anytime on weekends when I don't have classes. Again, thanks for considering me for your brand manager position.

DOCUMENT 15.B: WRITING AN APPLICATION MESSAGE

I saw your ad for a finance major in our paper last week. I hope the position isn't already filled because I'd like to interview for it. I've enclosed my résumé, which includes the work I've done since graduation.

Your ad said you were looking for a motivated person who wouldn't mind traveling. That would be me! I've also done the type of work you mentioned: budgeting, forecasting, and working with information systems. I know quite a bit about computers.

I know you get many résumés and mine is probably not all that special, but there's one thing that sets me apart: I'm friendly and eager to work. My present position is with a Silicon Valley company, which is in financial trouble. I'm afraid my whole division is going to be downsized, so I want to have something lined up in advance.

Could you send me some information about the financial stability of your company and its history of layoffs. I certainly wouldn't want to jump from the frying pan into the fire, so to speak. (Ha.) At any rate, thank you for considering my application and résumé. I hope you call me very soon.

DOCUMENT 15.C: WRITING APPLICATION FOLLOW-UP MESSAGES

Did you receive my résumé? I sent it to you at least two months ago and haven't heard anything. I know you keep résumés on file, but I just want to be sure that you keep me in mind. I heard you are hiring health-care managers and certainly would like to be considered for one of those positions.

Since I last wrote you, I've worked in a variety of positions that have helped prepare me for management. To wit, I've become lunch manager at the restaurant where I work, which involved a raise in pay. I now manage a wait-staff of 12 girls and take the lunch receipts to the bank every day.

Of course, I'd much rather be working at a real job, and that's why I'm writing again. Is there anything else you would like to know about me or my background? I would really like to know more about your company. Is there any literature you could send me? If so, I would really appreciate it.

I think one reason I haven't been hired yet is that I don't want to leave Atlanta. So I hope when you think of me, it's for a position that wouldn't require moving. Thanks again for considering my application.

 ases

THINKING ABOUT YOUR CAREER

1. Taking stock and taking aim: Application package for the right job Think about yourself. What are some things that come easily to you? What do you enjoy doing? In what part of the country would you like to live? Do you like to work indoors? Outdoors? A combination of the two? How much do you like to travel? Would you like to spend considerable time on the road? Do you like to work closely with others or more independently? What conditions make a job unpleasant? Do you delegate responsibility easily, or do you like to take charge? Are you better with words or numbers? Better at speaking or writing? Do you like to be motivated by fixed deadlines? How important is job security to you? Do you want your supervisor to state clearly what is expected of you, or do you like the freedom to make many of your own decisions?

Your Task: After answering these questions, consult reference materials (from your college library or placement center) and choose a location, a company, and a job that suits the profile you have just developed. With guidance from your instructor, decide whether to apply for a job you're qualified for now or one you'll be qualified for with additional education. Then, as directed by your instructor, write one or more of the following: (a) a job-inquiry letter, (b) a résumé, (c) a letter of application, or (d) a follow-up letter to your application letter.

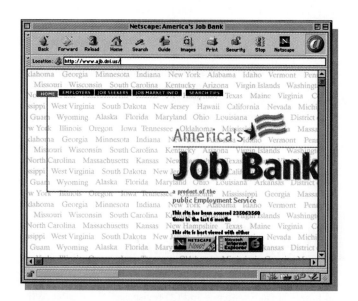

2. Scanning the possibilities: Résumé for the Internet In your search for a position, you discover that America's Job Bank is a Web site that lists hundreds of companies advertising on the Internet. Your chances of getting an interview with a leading company will be enhanced if you submit your résumé and cover letter electronically. On the Web, explore <http://www.ajb.dni.us> and <http://www.careersite.com>.

Your Task: Prepare a scannable résumé that could be submitted to the site that best fits your qualifications, experience, and education. Print out the résumé for your instructor.

3. Online application: Electronic cover letter introducing a résumé *Motley Fool* is a "Generation X" online magazine accessed via the World Wide Web. Although its founders and writers are extremely creative and motivated, they lack business experience and need a fellow "X'er" to help them manage the business. Articles in a recent edition included "The Soul of the Dead," about the influence of the Grateful Dead on more than one generation of concertgoers. Other articles deal with lifestyle issues, pop movies, music, and "trends for an old-young generation."

Your Task: Write an e-mail message that will serve as your cover letter, and attach your résumé as a file to be downloaded. Address your message to Louis Corrigan, Managing Editor. Try to limit your message to one screen (about 23 lines). You'll need a creative "hook" and reassurance that you are the right person to help *Motley Fool* become financially viable.

WRITING A RÉSUMÉ AND AN APPLICATION LETTER

4. "Help wanted": Application for a job listed in the classified section Among the jobs listed in today's *New Orleans Sentinel* (500 Canal Street, New Orleans, LA 70130) are the following:

ACCOUNTANT/MANAGER

Supervisor needed for 3-person bookkeeping department. Degree in accounting plus collection experience helpful. L. Cichy, Reynolds Clothiers, 1572 Abundance Dr., New Orleans 70119.

ACTIVIST—MAKE DEMOCRACY WORK

The state's largest consumer lobbying organization has permanent positions (full- or part-time) for energetic individuals with excellent communication skills who are interested in working for social change. Reply Sentinel Drawer 973.

ATTENDANT

For video game room, 4647 Almonaster Ave., New Orleans 70216.

CONVENIENCE FOOD STORE MANAGER

Vacancies for managers and trainees in New Orleans area. We are seeking energetic and knowledgeable individuals who will be responsible for profitable operation of convenience food stores and petroleum product sales. Applicants should possess retail sales or managerial training. Interested candidates mail résumés and salary requirements to Prestige Products, Inc., 444 Sherwood Forest Blvd., Baton Rouge, LA 70815. Equal opportunity employer M/F.

Your Task: Send a résumé and an application letter to one of these potential employers.

WRITING OTHER TYPES OF EMPLOYMENT MESSAGES

5. Crashing the last frontier: Letter of inquiry about jobs in Alaska Your friend can't understand why you would want to move to Alaska. So you explain: "What really decided it for me was that I've never seen the Northern Lights."

"But what about the bears? The 60-below winters? The permafrost?" asks your friend.

"No problem. Anchorage doesn't get much colder than Buffalo does. It is just windier and wetter. Anyhow, I want to live near Fairbanks, which is near the gold-mining area—and the university is there. Fairbanks has lots of small businesses, like a frontier town in the West about 50 years ago. I think it still has homesteading tracts for people who want to do their own building and are willing to stay for a certain number of years."

"Your plans seem a little hasty," your friend warns. "Maybe you should write for information before you just take off. How do you know you could get a job?"

Your Task: Take your friend's advice and write to the Chamber of Commerce, Fairbanks, AK 99701. Ask what types of employment are available to someone with your education and experience, and ask who specifically is hiring year-round employees.

DEVELOPING YOUR INTERNET SKILLS

GOING ONLINE: LINK YOUR WAY TO A BETTER RÉSUMÉ, P. 381

Read over the section on using action words in your résumé, paying particular attention to the charts that give examples of "Action Statements with Accomplishment-Oriented Results" and "Positive Action Verbs." Then move on to read about something you may not have considered: the computer-scannable résumé. Now choose one or both of these tasks: (1) If you don't have a current résumé, look over the charts and examples and let them inspire you while you develop a new résumé that incorporates action verbs and accomplishment statements. (2) Turn your readable résumé into a computer-scannable résumé by following the guidelines on this site. Look over your new résumé(s) and think of ways to improve your presentation. Can you choose better words to describe your accomplishments? Can you eliminate any wordy job descriptions and then add more detail about your most important accomplishments? What words can you replace with action verbs? For the scannable résumé, have you missed any key words that could catch an employer's eye during a database search?

INTERVIEWING FOR EMPLOYMENT AND FOLLOWING UP

After studying this chapter, you will be able to

Describe the dual purpose of the job interview

Explain the steps in the interview process

Identify and adapt to various types of interviews

List the types of questions you are likely to encounter during a job interview

Discuss how to perform well during the three phases of a typical job interview

Write the six most common types of messages required to follow up after an interview

O n the Job

FACING A COMMUNICATION DILEMMA
AT HERMAN MILLER, INC.

How to Tell a Good Dancer Before the Waltz Begins

Looking for a company that cares about people? You might try Herman Miller, a highly successful establishment that manufactures office furniture in Zeeland, Michigan. Founded in 1923 by D. J. DePree, Herman Miller is justifiably famous for its corporate culture. It may be the only company on the Fortune 500 list that actually has a "vice president for people." Participation is the name of the game in this organization. Employees at all levels are consulted about important decisions and reap the rewards if the business does well.

When Herman Miller's recruiters interview a job candidate, they look at the person's education and experience, of course, but they also look for something else: the ability to get along with others. If the candidate's personality is outstanding, the company may be willing to overlook a lack of relevant experience. A senior vice president of research was once a high school football coach. The senior vice president of marketing and sales used to be the dean of agriculture at Michigan State. And the vice president for people had been planning to become a prison warden but joined Herman Miller instead.

On the surface, these people didn't seem like good candidates for management jobs in the office furniture business, but Herman Miller looked beyond the superficial to see their true potential. The most important quality in a Herman Miller employee is the capacity for teamwork. "To be successful here," says one Herman Miller executive, "you have to know how to dance."

How do you know whether someone is a good dancer before you actually begin the waltz? That's the challenge facing Herman Miller's recruiters when they interview job candidates. The challenge facing candidates is how to prepare for a job interview. What would you do? What can you do during an interview? Is there anything you could do after the interview?[1]

INTERVIEWING WITH POTENTIAL EMPLOYERS

As Herman Miller's recruiters can tell you, the best way to prepare for a job interview is to think carefully about the job itself. With the right job, you stand to be happy in your work. Thus it pays to approach job interviews with a sound appreciation of their dual purpose.

Herman Miller's recruiters look at a candidate's education and experience, but even more important is the candidate's personality. It's a challenge to find people who can operate in the company's participative environment without regarding the culture as permissive.

The organization's main objective is to find the best person available for the job; the applicant's main objective is to find the job best suited to his or her goals and capabilities.

An interview helps both the interviewer and the applicant achieve their goals.

By focusing on your audience, your potential employer, you will learn about the organization you want to work for and the people who will make the hiring decision. Be sure to consider any cultural differences when preparing for interviews, and base your approach on what your audience expects. The advice in this chapter is most appropriate for companies and employers in the United States and Canada.

The Interview Process

Various types of organizations approach the recruiting process in various ways, so adjust your job search accordingly. In any case, once you get your foot in the door, you move to the next stage and prepare to meet with a recruiter during an **employment interview,** a formal meeting during which an employer and an applicant ask questions and exchange information to see whether the applicant and the organization are a good match. Applicants often face a series of interviews.

An employment interview is a formal meeting in which employers and applicants ask questions and exchange information to learn more about each other.

The Typical Sequence of Interviews

Most employers conduct two or three interviews before deciding whether to offer a person a job. The first interview, generally held on campus, is the **preliminary screening interview,** which helps employers eliminate (screen out) unqualified applicants from the hiring process. Those candidates who best meet the organization's requirements are invited to visit company offices for further evaluation. Some organizations make a decision at that point, but many schedule a third interview to complete the evaluation process before extending a job offer.

Most organizations interview an applicant several times before extending a job offer.

Screening interviews are fairly structured, so applicants are often asked roughly the same questions. Many companies use standardized evaluation sheets to "grade" each applicant so that all the candidates are measured against the same criteria. Your best approach to a screening interview is to follow the interviewer's lead. Keep your responses short and to the point. However, if an opportunity presents itself, emphasize the "theme" you used in developing your résumé. You want to give the interviewer a way to differentiate you from other candidates, and, at the same time, you want to demonstrate your strengths and qualifications.

The next round of interviews is designed to help the organization narrow the field a little further. Typically, if you're invited to visit a company, you will talk with several people: a member of the human resources department, one or two potential colleagues, and your potential supervisor. You might face a **panel interview,** meeting with several interviewers who ask you questions during a single session. Your best approach during this round of interviews is to show interest in the job, relate your skills and experience to the organization's needs, listen attentively, ask insightful questions, and display enthusiasm.

Types of Interviews

Interviews take various forms, depending on what the recruiter is attempting to discover about the applicant. In the **directed interview,** generally used in screening, the employer controls the interview by preparing a series of questions to be asked in a set order. Working from a checklist, the interviewer asks you each question in order, staying within a specific time period. Your answers are noted. Although useful in gathering facts, the directed interview is generally regarded as too structured to measure an applicant's personal qualities.

Companies use a variety of interviewing techniques to evaluate various attributes.

In contrast, the **open-ended interview** is a less formal, unstructured interview with an open, relaxed format. By posing broad, open-ended questions, the interviewer encourages you to talk freely, perhaps even to divulge more than you should. This type of interview is good for bringing out an applicant's personality. Interviewers also ask behavioral or situational questions to determine how candidates would handle real-life work problems. Some companies interview several candidates simultaneously to see how they interact—whether they smile, support one another's comments, or try to score points at one another's expense.[2] Other companies ask the candidate to participate in a series of simulated exercises, either individually or in a group. Trained observers evaluate the candidates' performance using predetermined criteria and then advise management on how well each person is likely to handle the challenges normally faced on the job.[3]

Perhaps the most unnerving type of interview is the **stress interview,** designed to see how well a candidate handles stressful situations (an important qualification for certain jobs). During a stress interview you might be asked pointed questions designed to irk or unsettle you. You might be subjected to long periods of silence, criticisms of your appearance, deliberate interruptions, and abrupt or even hostile reactions by the interviewer. Many corporate managers believe that stress interviews are inappropriate and unethical.[4]

Interviewing by video is an option that has worked for some job seekers. The University of Tennessee uses a videoconferencing system that allows recruiters to interview students from the Tullahoma campus (some 3½ hours away from the main campus in Knoxville).[5] Some applicants use video "résumés" on CD-ROMs that can be played on office computers. These videos are more like interviews than résumés, and they require the same strategies as interviews. Such video interviews can save you time, showcase your strong personality, and facilitate long-distance job searches. But video interviews entail a risk: Your appearance may jog a negative memory or a dislike that the recruiter is unaware of, or you may encounter discrimination that you'll never know about.[6] Whatever types of interviews you face, if you are successful, you may be asked to take one or more preemployment tests before starting your new job.

Preemployment Testing

Given the high cost of hiring unsuitable employees, more and more companies are turning to preemployment testing to determine whether applicants have the necessary skills and psychological characteristics to handle a particular job. Even though many of the tests are related to specific job skills such as typing ability, the real growth is occurring in tests designed to weed out dishonest candidates and substance abusers. Many employers now require newly hired employees to undergo drug and alcohol testing. Many also administer "honesty" tests, which ask applicants questions designed to bring out their attitudes toward stealing and work habits.

> Preemployment tests attempt to provide objective, quantitative information about candidates' skills, attitudes, and habits.

Some employers prefer not to go to the extra expense of administering them or feel that educated judgment works just as well. Some applicants question the validity of honesty and drug tests or consider them an invasion of privacy. However, used in conjunction with other evidence, the tests attempt to provide an objective, quantitative measure of applicants' qualifications, which may work to the advantage of both employer and applicant. To protect candidates' interests, employment tests must meet strict criteria of fairness set forth by the Equal Employment Opportunity Commission.

What Employers Look For

In general, employers are looking for two things: proof that a candidate can handle a specific job and evidence that the person will fit in with the organization. Employers are most concerned with attitude, communication skill, and work experience.[7] They also care about intelligence, enthusiasm, creativity, and motivation.

> Interviewers try to determine what you can do and what kind of person you are.

Qualifications for the Job

Every position requires specific qualifications. To become an auditor, for example, you must know accounting; to become a sales manager, you must have several years of sales experience. When you're invited to interview for a position, the interviewer may already have some idea of whether you have the right qualifications, based on a review of your résumé. During the interview, you'll be asked to describe your education and previous jobs in more depth so that the interviewer can determine how well your skills match the requirements. In many cases, the interviewer will be seeking someone with the flexibility to apply diverse skills in several areas.[8]

> Suitability for the specific job is judged on the basis of
> - Academic preparation
> - Work experience
> - Job-related personality traits

Another consideration is whether a candidate has the right personality traits for the job. A personal interview is vital because a résumé can't show whether a person is lively and outgoing, subdued and low key, able to take direction, or able to take charge. Each job requires a different mix of personality traits. The task of the interviewer is to find out whether a candidate will be effective in the job.

A Good Fit with the Organization

Interviewers try to determine more than whether the applicant has the right professional qualifications and personality for a particular job. They also try to decide whether the candidate will be compatible with the other people in the organization. Every interviewer approaches this issue a little differently.

Compatibility with the organization is judged on the basis of
- *Appearance*
- *Age*
- *Personal background*
- *Attitudes and style*

- *Physical appearance.* Includes clothing, grooming, posture, eye contact, handshake, facial expressions, and tone of voice.
- *Age.* Job discrimination against middle-aged people is prohibited by law, but if you feel that your youth could count against you, counteract its influence by emphasizing your experience, dependability, and mature attitudes.
- *Personal background.* To broaden your interests, hobbies, awareness of world events, and so forth, you can read widely, make an effort to meet new people, and participate in discussion groups, seminars, and workshops.
- *Attitudes and personal style.* Interviewers are likely to be impressed by openness, enthusiasm, interest, courtesy, sincerity, willingness to learn, and self-confidence.

What Applicants Need to Find Out

Candidates are responsible for deciding whether the work and the organization are compatible with their goals and values.

What things should you find out about the prospective job and employer? By doing a little advance research and asking the right questions during the interview, you can probably find answers to all the following questions and more:

- Are these my kind of people?
- Can I do this work?
- Will I enjoy the work?
- Is the job what I want?
- Does the job pay what I'm worth?
- What kind of person would I be working for?
- What sort of future can I expect with this organization?

In order to find out the answers to these questions, you'll need to keep your wits about you. The best way to do that is to be prepared for the interview.

How to Prepare for a Job Interview

It's perfectly normal to feel a little anxious before an interview. So much depends on it, and you don't know quite what to expect. But don't worry too much; preparation will help you perform well. Before the interview, do some basic research, think about questions, bolster your confidence, polish your interview style, and plan to look good. If you do these things, you'll be ready when you arrive.

Do Some Basic Research

Be prepared to relate your qualifications to the organization's needs.

Learning about the organization and the job is important because it enables you to review your résumé from the employer's point of view (Figure 16.1). Consider Microsoft, for example. With a little research, you would discover that Microsoft is moving aggressively into international markets and now operates in 48 countries around the world. You'd also learn that the company is making the largest commitment it's ever made to research and development, with the goal of enhancing its entire range of products to encompass the Internet.[9] Knowing these facts might help you pinpoint aspects of your background (such as language capabilities and communication skills) that would appeal to Microsoft's recruiters. The fastest way to learn about a company is by visiting its Web site.

GOING ONLINE
BE PREPARED FOR CHALLENGING INTERVIEW QUESTIONS
Career Magazine presents excellent articles about job interviews: "Behavioral Interviews: A Job Candidate's Toughest Obstacle," "Face-to-Face Interview Preparation," "How to Handle a Panel Interview," "How to Answer Some of Those Awkward—and All Too Common—Interview Questions." The site also provides a career forum, job fair listings, and career links.

http://www.careermag.com/newsarts/interviewing.html

WHERE
TO LOOK

- *Annual report:* Summarizes year's operations; mentions products, significant events, names of key personnel
- *In-house magazine or newspaper:* Reveals information about company operations, events, personnel
- *Product brochures and publicity releases:* Provide insight into organization's operations and values (obtain from public relations office)
- *Stock research reports:* Help you assess stability and prospects for growth (obtain from local stockbroker)
- *Business and financial pages of local newspapers:* Contain news items about organizations, current performance figures
- *Periodicals indexes:* Contain descriptive listings of magazine and newspaper articles about organizations (obtain from library)
- *Better Business Bureau and chamber of commerce:* Distribute information about some local organizations
- *Former and current employees:* Have insight into job and work environment
- *College placement office:* Collects information on organizations that recruit and on job qualifications and salaries

WHAT TO
FIND OUT

About the Organization

- *Full name:* What the organization is officially known as (for example, 3M is Minnesota Mining & Manufacturing Company)
- *Location:* Where the organization's headquarters, branch offices, and plants are
- *Age:* How long the organization has been in business
- *Products:* What goods and services the organization produces and sells
- *Industry position:* What the organization's current market share, financial position, and profit picture are
- *Earnings:* What the trends in the organization's stock prices and dividends are (if the firm is publicly held)
- *Growth:* What changes in earnings and holdings the organization has experienced in recent years and its prospects for expansion
- *Organization:* What subsidiaries, divisions, and departments make up the whole

About the Job

- *Job title:* What you will be called
- *Job functions:* What the main tasks of the job are
- *Job qualifications:* What knowledge and skills the job requires
- *Career path:* What chances for ready advancement exist
- *Salary range:* What the organization typically offers and what pay is reasonable in this industry and geographic area
- *Travel opportunities:* How often, long, and far you'll be allowed (or required) to travel
- *Relocation opportunities:* Where you might be allowed (or required) to move and how often you might be moved

Figure 16.1
Finding Out About the Organization and the Job

Think Ahead About Questions

Most job interviews are essentially question-and-answer sessions: You answer the interviewer's questions about your background, and you ask questions of your own to determine whether the job and the organization are right for you. By planning for your interviews, you can handle these exchanges intelligently.

Employers usually gear their interview questions to specific organizational needs, and many change their questions over time. In general, you can expect to be asked about your skills, achievements, and goals; your attitude toward work and school; your relationships with work supervisors, colleagues, and fellow students; and, occasionally, your hobbies and interests. For a look at the types of questions that are often asked, see Figure 16.2. Jot down a brief answer to each one. Then read the answers over until you feel comfortable with each one. You may want to tape record them and then listen to make sure they sound clear and convincing. Although practicing your answers will help you feel prepared and confident, you don't want to memorize responses or sound overrehearsed. Another suggestion is to give a list of interview questions to a friend or relative and have that person ask you various questions at random. Through practice you'll learn to articulate answers and to look at the person as you answer.

Practice answering interview questions.

Questions About College
1. What courses in college did you like most? Why?
2. Do you think your extracurricular activities in college were worth the time you devoted to them? Why or why not?
3. When did you choose your college major? Did you ever change your major? If so, why?
4. Do you feel you did the best scholastic work you are capable of?
5. Which of your college years was the toughest? Why?

Questions About Employers and Jobs
6. What jobs have you held? Why did you leave?
7. What percentage of your college expenses did you earn? How?
8. Why did you choose your particular field of work?
9. What are the disadvantages of your chosen field?
10. Have you served in the military? What rank did you achieve? What jobs did you perform?
11. What do you think about how this industry operates today?
12. Why do you think you would like this particular type of job?

Questions About Personal Attitudes and Preferences
13. Do you prefer to work in any specific geographical location? If so, why?
14. How much money do you hope to be earning in five years? In ten years?
15. What do you think determines a person's progress in a good organization?
16. What personal characteristics do you feel are necessary for success in your chosen field?
17. Tell me a story.
18. Do you like to travel?
19. Do you think grades should be considered by employers? Why or why not?

Questions About Work Habits
20. Do you prefer working with others or by yourself?
21. What type of boss do you prefer?
22. Have you ever had any difficulty getting along with colleagues or supervisors? With other students? With instructors?
23. Would you prefer to work in a large or a small organization? Why?
24. How do you feel about overtime work?
25. What have you done that shows initiative and willingness to work?

Figure 16.2
Twenty-Five Common Interview Questions

The questions you ask in an interview are just as important as the answers you provide. By asking intelligent questions, you can demonstrate your understanding of the organization and steer the discussion into those areas that allow you to present your qualifications to peak advantage. More important, you can get the information you need to evaluate the organization and the job. While recruiters like those at Herman Miller are trying to decide whether you are right for them, you must decide whether Herman Miller or any other company is right for you.

Before the interview, prepare a list of about a dozen questions, using a mix of formats to elicit various types of information. Start with a warm-up question to help break the ice. You might ask a Herman Miller recruiter, "What departments usually hire new graduates?" After that, you might build rapport by asking an open-ended question that draws out her opinion: for example, "How do you think the current economic environment will affect Herman Miller's ability to expand?" Indirect questions are another approach. You can get useful information and show that you've prepared for the interview with comments such as "I'd really like to know more about Herman Miller's plans for increasing product distribution" or "That recent *Business Week* article about the company was very interesting." Of course, any questions you ask should be put into your own words so that you don't sound like every other candidate. For a list of other good questions you might use as a starting point, see Figure 16.3.

Types of questions to ask during an interview:
- Warm-up
- Open-ended
- Indirect

Figure 16.3
Fifteen Questions to Ask the Interviewer

1. What are this job's major responsibilities?
2. What qualities do you want in the person who fills this position?
3. Do you want to know more about my related training?
4. What is the first problem that needs the attention of the person you hire?
5. What are the organization's major strengths? Weaknesses?
6. Who are your organization's major competitors, and what are their strengths and weaknesses?
7. What makes your organization different from others in the industry?
8. What are your organization's major markets?
9. Does the organization have any plans for new products? Acquisitions?
10. What can you tell me about the person I would report to?
11. How would you define your organization's managerial philosophy?
12. What additional training does your organization provide?
13. Do employees have an opportunity to continue their education with help from the organization?
14. Would relocation be required, now or in the future?
15. Why is this job now vacant?

Take your list of questions to the interview on a notepad or clipboard. If you need to, jot down the briefest notes during the meeting, and be sure to record them in more detail afterward. Having a list of questions should impress the interviewer with your organization and thoroughness. It will also show that you're there to evaluate the organization and the job as well as to sell yourself.

Bolster Your Confidence

By overcoming your tendencies to feel self-conscious or nervous during an interview, you can build your confidence and make a good impression. The best way to counteract apprehension is to try to remove its source. You may be shy because you think you have some flaw that will prompt other people to reject you. Bear in mind, however, that you're much more conscious of your limitations than other people are. If some aspect of your appearance or background makes you uneasy, correct it or exercise positive traits to offset it, such as warmth, wit, intelligence, or charm. Instead of dwelling on your weaknesses, focus on your strengths so that you can emphasize them to an interviewer. Make a list of your good points and compare them with what you see as your shortcomings. Remember, too, that all the other candidates for the job are probably just as nervous as you are. In fact, even the interviewer may be nervous.

Polish Your Interview Style

Confidence helps you walk into an interview, but the only way you'll walk out with a job is if you give the interviewer an impression of poise, good manners, and good judgment as well as self-confidence. One way to develop an adept style is to stage mock interviews with a friend. After each practice session, have your friend critique your performance, using the list of interview faults shown in Figure 16.4 to identify opportunities for improvement. You can even videotape these mock interviews and then evaluate them yourself. The taping process can be intimidating, but it helps you work out any problems before you begin actual job interviews.

As you stage your mock interviews, pay particular attention to your nonverbal behavior. In the United States, you are more likely to be invited back for a second interview or offered a job if you maintain eye contact, smile frequently, sit in an attentive position, and use frequent hand gestures. These nonverbal signals convince the interviewer that you are alert, assertive, dependable, confident, responsible, and energetic.[10] Of course some companies based in the United States are owned and managed by people from other cultures. So during your basic research, find out about the company's cultural background and preferences.

Barbara Walters has conducted countless political and celebrity interviews, and she has the reputation of going for emotional revelations. But an employment interview is simply an exchange of information to see whether company and candidate are a good match. According to Walters, a nervous interview that sounds rehearsed is a disaster. You can be focused and still be yourself. Just being asked to an interview should give you more confidence.

Figure 16.4
Marks Against Applicants (in General Order of Importance)

1. Has a poor personal appearance
2. Is overbearing, overaggressive, conceited; has a "superiority complex"; seems to "know it all"
3. Is unable to express self clearly; has poor voice, diction, grammar
4. Lacks knowledge or experience
5. Is not prepared for interview
6. Has no real interest in job
7. Lacks planning for career; has no purpose or goals
8. Lacks enthusiasm; is passive and indifferent
9. Lacks confidence and poise; is nervous and ill at ease
10. Shows insufficient evidence of achievement
11. Has failed to participate in extracurricular activities
12. Overemphasizes money; is interested only in the best dollar offer
13. Has poor scholastic record; just got by
14. Is unwilling to start at the bottom; expects too much too soon
15. Makes excuses
16. Is evasive; hedges on unfavorable factors in record
17. Lacks tact
18. Lacks maturity
19. Lacks courtesy; is ill-mannered
20. Condemns past employers
21. Lacks social skills
22. Shows marked dislike for schoolwork
23. Lacks vitality
24. Fails to look interviewer in the eye
25. Has limp, weak handshake

The way you speak is almost as important as what you say.

Like other forms of nonverbal behavior, the sound of your voice can have a major impact on your success in a job interview.[11] You can work with a tape recorder to overcome voice problems. If you tend to speak too rapidly, practice speaking more slowly. If your voice sounds too loud or too soft, practice adjusting it. Work on eliminating speech mannerisms such as *you know, like,* and *um,* which might make you sound inarticulate. Speak in your natural tone, and try to vary the pitch, rate, and volume of your voice to express enthusiasm and energy. If you speak in a flat, emotionless tone, you convey the impression that you are passive or bored.

When nonverbal behavior is less of a concern, you can use live chat rooms on the Internet to simulate interviews. For example, by using the chat rooms on America Online, CompuServe, or Prodigy, you can create a private room and invite other Internet users to meet you there for a one-on-one mock interview.[12] You'll be able to practice answering questions, but you'll have no way of evaluating gestures, voice, or appearance over the Internet.

Plan to Look Good

To look like a winner
- Dress conservatively
- Be well groomed
- Smile when appropriate

When your parents nagged at you to stand up straight, comb your hair, and get rid of your gum, they were right. You can impress an interviewer just by the way you look. The best policy is to dress conservatively. Wear the best-quality businesslike clothing you can, preferably in a dark, solid color. Avoid flamboyant styles, colors, and prints.

Good grooming makes any style of clothing look better. Make sure your clothes are clean and unwrinkled, your shoes unscuffed and well shined, your hair neatly styled and combed, your fingernails clean, and your breath fresh. If possible, check your appearance in a mirror before entering the room for the interview. Don't spoil the effect by smoking cigarettes during the interview. Finally, remember that one of the best ways to look good is to smile at appropriate moments.

Be Ready When You Arrive

For the interview, plan to take a small notebook, a pen, a list of the questions you want to ask, two copies of your résumé protected in a folder, an outline of what you have learned about the organization, and any past correspondence about the position. You may also want to take a small calendar, a transcript of your college grades, a list of references, and your portfolio containing samples of your work, performance reviews, and certificates of achievement. Recruiters are impressed by such tangible evidence of your job-related accomplishments. In an era when many people exaggerate their qualifications, visible proof of your abilities carries a lot of weight.[13]

Be sure you know when and where the interview will be held. The worst way to start any interview is to be late. Check the route you will take, even if it means phoning the interviewer's secretary to ask. Find out how much time it takes to get there; then plan to arrive early. Allow a little extra time just in case you run into a problem on the way.

Once you arrive, relax. You may have to wait a little while, so bring along something to read or occupy your time (the less frivolous or controversial, the better). If company literature is available, read it while you wait. In any case, be polite to the interviewer's assistant. If the opportunity presents itself, ask a few questions about the organization or express enthusiasm for the job. Refrain from smoking before the interview (nonsmokers can smell smoke on the clothing of interviewees), and avoid chewing gum in the waiting room. Anything you do or say while you wait may well get back to the interviewer, so make sure your best qualities show from the moment you enter the premises.

How to Be Interviewed

The way to handle the actual interview depends on where you stand in the interview process. If you are being interviewed for the first time, your main objective is often to differentiate yourself from the many other candidates who are also being screened. Say you've signed up to talk with a recruiter on campus, who may talk with 10 or 15 applicants during the course of the day. Without resorting to gimmicks, you need to call attention to one key aspect of your background so that the recruiter can say, "Oh yes, I remember Jones—the one who sold used Toyotas in Detroit." Just be sure the trait you accentuate is relevant to the job in question. In addition, you'll want to be prepared in case an employer such as Herman Miller expects you to demonstrate a particular skill (such as problem solving) during the screening interview.

If you have progressed to the initial selection interview, you should broaden your sales pitch. Instead of telegraphing the "headline," give the interviewer the whole story. Touch at least briefly on all your strengths, but explain three or four of your best qualifications in depth. At the same time, probe for information that will help you evaluate the position objectively. As important as it is to get an offer, it's also important to learn whether the job is right for you.

If you're asked back for a final visit, your chances of being offered a position are quite good. At this point, you'll talk to a person who has the authority to make the offer and negotiate terms. This individual may already have concluded that you have the right background for the job, so she or he will be concerned with sizing up your personality. In fact, both you and the employer need to find out whether there is a good psychological fit. Be honest about your motivations and values. If the interview goes well, your objective should be to clinch the deal on the best possible terms.

Regardless of where you are in the interview process, every interview will proceed through three stages: the warm-up, the question-and-answer session, and the close.

The Warm-up

Of the three stages, the warm-up is most important, even though it may account for only a small fraction of the time you spend in the interview. Psychologists say that 50 percent of the interviewer's decision is made within the first 30 to 60 seconds, and another 25 percent is made within 15 minutes. If you get off to a bad start, it's extremely difficult to turn the interview around.[14]

Body language is important at this point. Because you won't have time to say much in the first minute or two, you must sell yourself nonverbally. Begin by using the interviewer's name if you're sure you can pronounce it correctly. If the interviewer extends a hand, respond with a firm but gentle handshake. Then wait until you are asked to be seated. Let the

Be prepared for the interview:
- Take proof of your accomplishments
- Arrive on time
- Wait graciously

Present a memorable "headline" during a screening interview.

As director of admissions for Cornell's Johnson Graduate School of Management, Daphne Atkinson oversees thousands of written applications and personal interviews. She offers this advice: first do the introspective work required to understand your personal goals and objectives, then apply common sense and self-knowledge to answer interview questions.

BEHIND THE SCENES AT IBM
Secrets to Winning an Interview

Jim Greenwood is area manager at IBM's National College Recruiting, South, in Atlanta, Georgia. Greenwood, his staff, and IBM managers nationwide work year-round arranging career fairs, booking speaking engagements, and responding to inquiries—all to attract the best students for the company. Greenwood also coordinates recruiting activity at 40 campuses. Of the more than 8,000 entry-level people hired by IBM in a recent year, 2,800 were college graduates—75 percent of them from targeted campuses.

Whether at the IBM Information Day or any other career fair, be aware that the interview process begins when you step up to a company representative. "On that first day," says Greenwood, "the managers who want to recruit at a given school are there, so bring a résumé. Seek out managers in the skill group that is of interest to you. Talk with them about your background and interests. Our managers know their requirements, and if there's a match, they will sign you up to be interviewed the next day." That will be your second interview, the 30-minute job interview people mistakenly think of as the first interview.

"We do a total assessment," Greenwood says. At the site interview, managers explore technical background and breadth, interests, likes, and dislikes. "We're looking for people who can communicate. When you get into an environment, say a lab or a marketing department, you have to relate to people, sell your ideas, explain how things are to be done."

Greenwood listens for your level of interest. "If you did an internship at Hewlett-Packard, I might say, 'Tell me about your job.' Then I'll ask, 'What did you do? What did you like about it? What didn't you like? What kind of programming did you do? What languages? How proficient are you in those languages? Which do you like the best? Why? Do you like to program? Do you like to write code?'"

IBM's Jim Greenwood encourages the members of his college recruiting staff to listen to the questions applicants ask. That way, they can judge how much applicants know about their field and the company.

interviewer start the discussion, and listen for cues that tell you what he or she is interested in knowing about you as a potential employee.

The Question-and-Answer Stage

Questions and answers will consume the greatest part of the interview. During this phase, the interviewer will ask you about your qualifications and discuss many of the points mentioned in your résumé. You'll also be asked whether you have any questions of your own.

As questions are asked, tailor your answers to make a favorable impression. Don't limit yourself to yes or no answers. Be sure you pause to think before responding if you're asked a difficult question. Consider the direction of the discussion, and guide it where you wish with your responses.

Another way you can reach your goal is to ask the right questions. If you periodically ask a question or two from the list you've prepared, you'll not only learn something but demonstrate your interest as well. It's especially useful to probe for what the company is looking for in its new employees. Once you know that, you can show how you meet the firm's needs. Also try to zero in on any reservations the interviewer might have about you so that you can dispel them.

Paying attention when the interviewer speaks can be as important as giving good answers or asking good questions. Listening should make up about half the time you spend in an interview. For tips on becoming a better listener, read Chapter 17. Be alert to nonverbal communication. The interviewer's facial expressions, eye movements, gestures, and posture may tell you the real meaning of what is being said. If the interviewer says one thing but sends a different message nonverbally, you may want to discount the verbal message. Be especially aware of how your comments are received. Does the interviewer nod in

Paying attention to both verbal and nonverbal messages can help you turn the question-and-answer stage to your advantage.

Greenwood also listens to the types of questions you ask. "They tell me how well informed you are, what you have done to prepare yourself for the interview, whether you researched us, and whether you know about our products and our corporate culture. But don't try to bluff or tell us what you think we want to hear. Ask questions that matter and that make the right impression. Don't ask the interviewer, 'What do you do?' That shows a lack of preparation and interest. Instead ask about the future: 'What technology are you developing? Where's it going?' You should also raise legitimate concerns—the size of a company like IBM, for example. Ask, 'How are you structured? How do I get my ideas across? How do I interact with other departments?'"

Greenwood's goal is for you to leave the interview feeling positive about IBM and knowing when you will learn the outcome. He wants you to feel "that you were given a good, courteous interview." So, what about follow-up? "Don't write for the sake of writing," says Greenwood. "But if you want to stress special interests or reinforce skills, or if you feel you blew the interview and want to be reconsidered, write to the department manager."

Regarding that much-discussed situation of needing experience to get a job but needing a job to get experience, Greenwood offers this advice: "Getting experience is important, whether it's work-study, a cooperative education program, or work you did over the summers, maybe a preprofessional internship. Experience helps you focus your academic choices,

prepares you for your job search, and lets you sift and sort out what you do and don't want. That shows in the interview—you have a sharper focus on your wants and needs." To come across well in an interview, you have to stress what experience you have and relate it to what you can do once you're employed.

Apply Your Knowledge

1. You're scheduled for a job interview in your chosen profession. You anticipate that the interviewer will ask you to describe your job-related experience. Although you have no full-time experience, you've held positions in a preprofessional organization and have completed an internship in a job similar to the one for which you're applying. To prepare for your interview, write a description of your job-related experience, specifying what experience you have and relating it to what you can do for the employer once you get the job.

2. How would you handle this situation? A company—your first choice both as a career and as a place to work—has offered you a position, but the starting salary you've been offered is below your expectation and below what you've already been offered by another firm (your third choice as a career and as a workplace). Lay out a strategy that you think will get you both the position you most desire and the salary you expect.

---

agreement or smile to show approval? If so, you're making progress. If not, you might want to introduce another topic or modify your approach.

Bear in mind that employers cannot legally discriminate against a job candidate on the basis of race, color, gender, age (from 40 to 70), marital status, religion, national origin, or disability. Although questions that touch on these areas are not prohibited by federal law, the Equal Employment Opportunity Commission looks upon such questions with "extreme disfavor."[15] In the course of your interviews, you may be asked questions that are directly or indirectly related to

- Your religious affiliation or organizations and lodges you belong to
- Your marital status or former name
- The names or relationships of people you live with
- Your spouse, spouse's employment or salary, dependents, children, or child-care arrangements
- Your height, weight, gender, pregnancy, or any health conditions or disabilities that are not reasonably related to job performance
- Arrests or criminal convictions that are not related to job performance or that occurred more than seven years ago

How you respond depends on how badly you want the job, how you feel about revealing the information asked for, what you think the interviewer will do with the information, and whether you want to work for a company that asks such questions. If you don't want the job, you can tell the interviewer that you think a particular question is unethical and mention that you plan to contact the proper government agency. You can also simply refuse to answer, but, in many cases, doing so will leave an unfavorable impression on the interviewer.[16]

Think about how you might respond if you are asked to answer unlawful interview questions.

CHECKLIST FOR INTERVIEWS

A. Preparation

1. Determine the requirements and general salary range of the job.
2. Research the organization's products, structure, financial standing, and prospects for growth.
3. Determine the interviewer's name, title, and status in the firm.
4. Prepare (but don't overrehearse) answers for the questions you are likely to be asked about your qualifications and achievements, your feelings about work and school, your interests and hobbies.
5. Develop relevant questions to ask, such as what training the organization might offer after employment, what type of management system the firm has, whether its executives are promoted from within, and why the position is vacant.
6. Plan your appearance.
   - a. Dress in a businesslike manner, regardless of the mode of dress preferred within the organization.
   - b. Select conservative, good-quality clothing to wear to the interview.
   - c. Check your clothing to make sure it's clean and wrinkle free.
   - d. Choose traditional footwear, unscuffed and well shined.
   - e. Wear a minimum of jewelry, but wear a wristwatch to keep track of the time.
   - f. Use fragrances sparingly, and avoid excessive makeup.
   - g. Choose a neat, well-groomed, conventional hairstyle.
   - h. Clean and manicure your fingernails.
   - i. Check your appearance just before going into the interview, if possible.
7. In a briefcase or portfolio, take a pen and paper, a list of questions, two copies of your résumé, and samples of your work (if appropriate).
8. Double-check the location and time of the interview.
   - a. Map out the route beforehand, and estimate the time you'll need to get there.
   - b. Plan your arrival for 10 to 15 minutes before the interview.
   - c. Add 10 or 15 more minutes to cover problems that may arise en route.

B. Initial Stages of the Interview

1. Greet the interviewer by name, with a smile and direct eye contact.

Van Carlisle is CEO of FireKing International, maker of fireproof filing cabinets. As such, he tries to perform each task at the optimum level, and he likes working with people who do their homework and who are honest, energetic, and thorough. Carlisle advises applicants to show their own commitment to performance by being well prepared for interviews.

If you want the job (and you don't want to leave an unfavorable impression), you can choose a more tactful approach than simply refusing. You might (1) ask how the question is related to your qualifications for the job, (2) explain that the information is personal, (3) respond to what you think is the interviewer's real concern, or (4) answer both the question and the concern. Of course, if you answer an unethical question, you still run the risk that your answer may hurt your chances, so think carefully before answering.[17]

When a business can show that the safety of its employees or customers is at stake, it may be allowed to ask questions that would seem discriminatory in another context. Despite this exception, if you believe that an interviewer's questions are unreasonable, unrelated to the job, or designed to elicit information in an attempt to discriminate, you may complain to the Equal Employment Opportunity Commission or to the state agency that regulates fair employment practices. To report discrimination on the basis of age or physical disability, contact the employer's equal opportunity officer or the U.S. Department of Labor. Be prepared to spend a lot of time and effort if you decide to go to court—and remember that you may not win.[18]

The Close

Like the opening, the end of the interview is more important than its duration would indicate. In the last few minutes, you need to evaluate how well you've done and correct any misconceptions the interviewer might have.

You can generally tell when the interviewer is trying to conclude the session by watching for verbal and nonverbal cues. The interviewer may ask whether you have any more questions, sum up the discussion, change position, or indicate with a gesture that the interview is over. When you get the signal, respond promptly, but don't rush. Be sure to thank the interviewer for the opportunity and express an interest in the organization. If you can do so comfortably, try to pin down what will happen next, but don't press for an immediate decision.

2. Offer a firm but not crushing handshake if the interviewer extends a hand.
3. Take a seat only after the interviewer invites you to be seated or has taken his or her own seat.
4. Sit with an erect posture, facing the interviewer.
5. Listen for cues about what the interviewer's questions are trying to reveal about you and your qualifications.
6. Assume a calm and poised attitude.
7. Avoid gum chewing, smoking, and other displays of nervousness.

C. Body of the Interview
1. Display a genuine, not artificial, smile when appropriate.
2. Convey interest and enthusiasm.
3. Listen attentively so that you can give intelligent responses.
4. Take few notes, and expand on key points later.
5. Sell the interviewer on hiring you.
   - a. Relate your knowledge and skills to the position you are seeking.
   - b. Stress your positive qualities and characteristics.
6. Answer questions wisely.
   - a. Keep responses brief, clear, and to the point.

   - b. Avoid exaggeration, and convey honesty and sincerity.
   - c. Avoid slighting references to former employers.
7. Avoid alcoholic drinks if you are interviewed over lunch or dinner.

D. Salary Discussions
1. Put off a discussion of salary until late in the interview, if possible.
2. Let the interviewer initiate the discussion of salary.
3. If asked, state that you would like to receive the standard salary for the position. (Know the standard salary for the position in your region of the country.)

E. Closing Stages of the Interview
1. Watch for signs that the interview is about to end.
2. Tactfully ask when you will be advised of the decision on your application.
3. If you're offered the job, either accept or ask for time to consider the offer.
4. Thank the interviewer for meeting with you, with a warm smile and a handshake.

If this is your second or third visit to the organization, the interview may culminate with an offer of employment. You have two options: Accept it or request time to think it over. The best course is usually to wait. If no job offer is made, the interviewer may not have reached a decision yet, but you may tactfully ask when you can expect to know the decision.

If you do receive an offer during the interview, you'll naturally want to discuss salary. However, let the interviewer raise the subject. If asked your salary requirements, say that you would expect to receive the standard salary for the job in question. If you have additional qualifications, point them out: "With my 18 months of experience in the field, I would expect to start in the middle of the normal salary range."

If you don't like the offer, you might try to negotiate, provided you're in a good bargaining position and the organization has the flexibility to accommodate you. You'll be in a fairly strong position if your skills are in short supply and you have several other offers. It also helps if you're the favorite candidate and the organization is booming. However, many organizations are relatively rigid in their salary practices, particularly at the entry level. Still, in the United States and some European countries, it is acceptable to ask, "Is there any room for negotiation?"

Even if you can't bargain for more money, you may be able to win some concessions on benefits and perquisites. The value of negotiating can be significant because benefits often cost the employer 25 to 45 percent of your salary. In other words, if you're offered an annual salary of $20,000, you'll ordinarily get an additional $5,000 to $9,000 in benefits: life, health, and disability insurance; pension and savings plans; vacation time; or even tuition reimbursement.[19] If you can trade one benefit for another, you may be able to enhance the value of the total package. For example, life insurance may be relatively unimportant to you if you're single, whereas extra vacation time might be very valuable indeed. Don't inquire about benefits, however, until you know you have a job offer.

Be realistic in your salary expectations and diplomatic in your negotiations.

Keep a written record of your job interviews.

Interview Notes

If yours is a typical job search, you'll have many interviews before you accept a final offer. For that reason, keeping a notebook or binder of interview notes can be helpful. To refresh your memory of each conversation, as soon as the interview ends, jot down the names and titles of the people you met. Next write down in capsule form the interviewer's answers to your questions. Then briefly evaluate your performance during the interview, listing what you handled well and what you didn't. Going over these notes can help you improve your performance in the future.[20] Whenever you need to review important tips, try consulting this chapter's Checklist for Interviews. In addition to improving your performance during interviews, interview notes will help you keep track of any follow-up messages you'll need to send.

*F*OLLOWING UP AFTER THE INTERVIEW

Touching base with the prospective employer after the interview, either by phone or in writing, shows that you really want the job and are determined to get it. It also brings your name to the interviewer's attention once again and reminds him or her that you're waiting to know the decision. As Herman Miller's recruiters will advise you, following up shows your continued interest in the job.

The two most common forms of follow-up are the thank-you message and the inquiry. These are generally handled by letter, but a phone call is often just as effective, particularly if the employer seems to favor a casual, personal style. The other four types of follow-up messages—request for a time extension, letter of acceptance, letter declining a job offer, and letter of resignation—are sent only in certain cases. These messages are better in writing, because it's important to document any official actions relating to your employment. Regardless of which type of follow-up message you're sending, the principles outlined here will help you write it well.

Six types of follow-up messages:
- Thank-you message
- Inquiry
- Request for a time extension
- Letter of acceptance
- Letter declining a job offer
- Letter of resignation

Thank-You Letter

A note or phone call thanking the interviewer
- Is organized like a routine message
- Closes with a request for a decision or future consideration

Express your thanks within two days after the interview, even if you feel you have little chance for the job. Acknowledge the interviewer's time and courtesy, and be sure to restate the specific job you're applying for. Convey the idea that you're still interested, and ask politely for a decision.

Keep your thank-you message brief (less than five minutes for a phone call or only one page for a letter), and organize it like a routine message. As do all good business messages, it demonstrates the "you" attitude, and it sounds positive without sounding overconfident. You don't want to sound doubtful about your chances of getting the job, but you don't want to sound arrogant or too sure of yourself either.

The following thank-you letter shows how to achieve all that in three brief paragraphs:

As senior vice president of human resources at Levi Strauss and Company, Donna J. Goya believes that developing people is vital to successful business management. You want to be in a company that cares about people, says Goya. You can show that you care about people by expressing your thanks to the interviewer either by phone or in a letter.

After talking with you yesterday, touring your sets, and watching the television commercials being filmed, I remain very enthusiastic about the possibility of joining your staff as a television/film production assistant. Thanks for taking so much time to show me around.

The opening reminds the interviewer of the reasons for meeting and graciously acknowledges the consideration shown to the applicant.

During our meeting, I said that I would prefer not to relocate, but I've reconsidered the matter. I would be pleased to relocate wherever you need my skills in set decoration and prop design.

This paragraph indicates the writer's flexibility and commitment to the job if hired. It also reminds the recruiter of special qualifications.

Now that you've explained the details of your operation, I feel quite strongly that I can make a contri-

After Michael Espinosa's interview with Gloria Reynolds, he sent the following thank-you message.

Figure 16.5
In-Depth Critique:
Thank-You Note

MICHAEL ESPINOSA
585 Montoya Road
Las Cruces, New Mexico 88005

January 5, 1999

Ms. Gloria Reynolds, Editor
Las Cruces News
317 N. Almendra Street
Las Cruces, NM 88001

Dear Ms. Reynolds:

Our conversation on Tuesday about your newspaper's opening for a food-feature writer was enlightening. Thank you for taking time to talk with me about it.

Your description of the profession makes me feel more certain than ever that I want to be a newspaper writer. Following your advice, I am going to enroll in an evening journalism course.

After I achieve the level of writing skills you suggested, I would deeply appreciate the chance to talk with you again.

Sincerely,

Michael Espinosa

Michael Espinosa

The main idea is the expression of thanks for the interviewer's time and information.

The writer specifically refers to points discussed in the interview. Enthusiasm and eagerness to improve skills are qualities that will impress the interviewer.

The letter closes with a specific and cordial request.

---

bution to the sorts of productions you're lining up. You can also count on me to be an energetic employee and a positive addition to your crew. Please let me know your decision as soon as possible.

The letter closes on a confident and you-oriented note, ending with the request for a decision.

Even if the interviewer has said that you are unqualified for the job, a thank-you message like that shown in Figure 16.5 may keep the door open. A letter of this type will probably go into the file for future openings because it demonstrates courtesy and interest.

Letter of Inquiry

An inquiry about a hiring decision follows the plan for a direct request.

If you're not advised of the interviewer's decision by the promised date or within two weeks, you might make an inquiry. An inquiry is particularly appropriate if you have received a job offer from a second firm and don't want to accept it before you have an answer from the first. The following inquiry letter follows the general plan for a direct request; the writer assumes that a simple oversight, and not outright rejection, is the reason for the delay.

When we talked on April 7 about the fashion coordinator position in your Park Avenue showroom, you said you would let me know your decision before May 1. I would still like the position very much, so I'm eager to know what conclusion you've reached.	*The opening paragraph identifies the position and introduces the main idea.*
To complicate matters, another firm has now offered me a position and has asked that I reply within the next two weeks.	*The reason for the request comes second. The writer tactfully avoids naming the other firm.*
Because your company seems to offer a greater challenge, I would appreciate knowing about your decision before Thursday, May 12. If you need more information before then, please let me know.	*The courteous request for a specific action comes last, in the context of a clearly stated preference for this organization.*

Request for a Time Extension

A request for a time extension follows the plan for a direct request but pays extra attention to easing the reader's disappointment.

If you receive a job offer while other interviews are still pending and you want more time to decide, write to the offering organization and ask for a time extension. Employers understand that candidates often interview with several companies. They want you to be sure you are making the right decision, and most of them are happy to accommodate you with a reasonable extension. Just be sure to preface your request with a friendly opening like the one shown in the following sample letter. Ask for more time, stressing your enthusiasm for the organization. Conclude by allowing for a quick decision if your request for additional time is denied. Ask for a prompt reply confirming the time extension if the organization grants it.

The customer relations position in your snack foods division seems like an exciting challenge and a great opportunity. I'm very pleased that you offered it to me.	*The letter begins with a strong statement of interest in the job.*
Because of another commitment, I would appreciate your giving me until August 29 to make a decision. Before our interview, I scheduled a follow-up interview with another company. I'm interested in your organization because of its impressive quality-control procedures and friendly, attractive work environment. But I do feel obligated to keep my appointment.	*The writer stresses professional obligations, not her desire to learn what the other company may offer. Specific reasons for preferring the first job offer help reassure the reader of her sincerity.*
If you need my decision immediately, I'll gladly let you know. However, if you can allow me the added time to fulfill the earlier commitment, I'd be grateful. Please let me know right away.	*The expression of willingness to yield or compromise conveys continued interest in the position.*

This type of letter is, in essence, a direct request. However, because the recipient may be disappointed, be sure to temper your request for an extension with statements indicating your continued interest.

Letter of Acceptance

When you receive a job offer that you want to accept, reply within five days. Begin by accepting the position and expressing thanks. Identify the job that you're accepting. In the next paragraph, cover any necessary details. Conclude by saying that you look forward to reporting for work.

> I'm delighted to accept the graphic design position in your advertising department at the salary of $1,575 a month.
>
> Enclosed are the health insurance forms you asked me to complete and sign. I've already given notice to my current employer and will be able to start work on Monday, January 18.
>
> The prospect of joining your firm is very exciting. Thank you for giving me this opportunity for what I'm sure will be a challenging future.

The good-news statement at the beginning confirms the specific terms of the offer.

Miscellaneous details are covered in the middle.

The letter closes with another reference to the good news and a look toward the future.

As always, a good-news letter should convey your enthusiasm and eagerness to cooperate.

Be aware that a job offer and a written acceptance of that offer constitute a legally binding contract, for both you and the employer. So before you write an acceptance letter, be sure you want the job.

A letter of acceptance follows the good-news plan.

Written acceptance of a job offer is legally binding.

Letter Declining a Job Offer

After all your interviews, you may find that you need to write a letter declining a job offer. The best approach is to open warmly, state the reasons for refusing the offer, decline the offer explicitly, and close on a pleasant note, expressing gratitude. By taking the time to write a sincere, tactful letter like the one shown here, you leave the door open for future contact.

> One of the most interesting interviews I have ever had was the one last month at your Durham textile plant. I'm flattered that you would offer me the computer analyst position that we talked about.
>
> During my job search, I applied to five highly rated firms like your own, each one a leader in its field. Both your company and another offered me a position. Because my desire to work abroad can more readily be satisfied by the other company, I have accepted that job offer.
>
> I deeply appreciate the hour you spent talking with me. Thank you again for your consideration and kindness.

The opening paragraph is a buffer.

Tactfully phrased reasons for the applicant's unfavorable decision precede the bad news and leave the door open.

A sincere and cordial ending lets the reader down gently.

The bad-news plan is ideally suited to this type of letter.

A letter declining a job offer follows the bad-news plan.

Letter of Resignation

If you get a job offer and are currently employed, you can maintain good relations with your employer by writing a letter of resignation to your immediate supervisor. Make the letter sound positive, regardless of how you feel. Say something favorable about the organization, the people you work with, or what you've learned on the job. Then state your intention to leave and give the date of your last day on the job. Be sure you give your current employer at least two weeks' notice.

A letter of resignation also follows the bad-news plan.

My sincere thanks to you and to all the other Emblem Corporation employees for helping me learn so much about serving the public these past 11 months. You have given me untold help and encouragement.

An appreciative opening serves as a buffer.

You may recall that when you first interviewed me, my goal was to become a customer relations supervisor. Because that opportunity has been offered to me by another organization, I am submitting my resignation. I regret leaving all of you, but I can't pass up this opportunity.

Reasons stated before the bad news itself and tactful phrasing help keep the relationship friendly, should the writer later want letters of recommendation.

I would like to terminate my work here two weeks from today but can arrange to work an additional week if you want me to train a replacement.

An extra paragraph discusses necessary details.

My sincere thanks and best wishes to all of you.

A cordial close tempers any disappointment.

CHECKLIST FOR FOLLOW-UP MESSAGES

A. Thank-You Messages

1. Thank the interviewer in writing within two days after the interview, and keep your letter to one page.
2. If you have no alternative, thank the interviewer by phone, keeping the message under five minutes.
3. In the opening express thanks and identify the job and the time and place of the interview.
4. Use the middle section for supporting details.
   - a. Express your enthusiasm about the organization and the job.
   - b. Add any new facts that may help your chances.
   - c. Try to undo any negative impressions you may have left during the interview.
5. Use an action ending.
   - a. Offer to submit more data.
   - b. Express confidence that your qualifications will meet the organization's requirements.
   - c. Look forward to a favorable decision.
   - d. Request an opportunity to prove that you can aid the organization's growth or success.

B. Inquiries

1. Phone or write an inquiry if you are not informed of the decision by the promised date, especially if another organization is awaiting your reply to a job offer.
2. Follow the plan for direct requests: main idea, necessary details, specific request.

C. Requests for a Time Extension

1. Send this type of letter if you receive a job offer while other interviews are pending and you want more time before making your decision.
2. Open with an expression of warmth.
3. In the middle section explain why you need more time and express your continuing interest in the organization.
4. Conclude by allowing for a quick decision if your request for more time is denied and by asking the interviewer to confirm the time extension if it is granted.

D. Letters Accepting a Job Offer

1. Send this message within five days of receiving the offer. State clearly that you accept the offer with pleasure, and identify the job you're accepting.
2. Fill out the letter with vital details.
3. Conclude with a statement that you look forward to reporting for work.

E. Letters Declining a Job Offer

1. Open a letter of rejection warmly.
2. Fill out the letter with an explanation of why you are refusing the offer and an expression of appreciation.
3. End on a sincere, positive note.

F. Letters of Resignation

1. Send a letter of resignation to your current employer as soon as possible.
2. Begin with an appreciative buffer.
3. Fill out the middle section with your reasons for looking for another job and the actual statement that you are leaving.
4. Close cordially.

This letter follows the bad-news plan. By sending one like it, you show that you are considerate and mature, and you also help ensure the good feeling that may help you get another job in the future. Compare your messages with the suggestions in this chapter's Checklist for Follow-Up Messages.

On the Job

SOLVING A COMMUNICATION DILEMMA AT HERMAN MILLER, INC.

Herman Miller's corporate culture reflects the philosophy of Max DePree, son of the firm's founder and, until recently, chairman of the board. DePree based his management style on his assumptions about human nature. In his view, the idea of motivating people is nonsense. "Employees bring their own motivation," he said. "What people need from work is to be liberated, to be involved, to be accountable, and to reach their potential."

DePree believed that good management consists of establishing an environment in which people can unleash their creativity. "My goal for Herman Miller is that when people both inside and outside the company look at all of us, they'll say, 'Those folks have a gift of the spirit.'" He wanted the organization, like its products, to be a work of art. To carry out his philosophy, DePree created an employee bill of rights, which includes "The right to be needed, the right to understand, the right to be involved, the right to affect one's own destiny, the right to be accountable, and the right to appeal."

The company's organizational structure, now in the hands of president and CEO Michael Volkema, reinforces DePree's philosophy. All employees are assigned to work teams. The team leader evaluates the workers every six months, and the workers evaluate the leader as well. Teams elect representatives to caucuses that meet periodically to discuss operations and problems. Through the team structure, employees have a say in decisions that affect them. They also have a vehicle for dealing with grievances. If a problem isn't resolved by the team supervisor, employees can go directly to the next executive level—all the way to Volkema, if needed.

But like all good things, Herman Miller's corporate culture has its downside. Teamwork takes time, and an egalitarian approach to decision making can be frustrating if you value efficiency. Although today's business environment requires decisive action, it takes a special kind of talent to draw the line between participation and permissiveness. Finding people who appreciate the distinction—and who can operate effectively in this climate—is a real challenge.

To identify people who have the right mix of attitudes, Herman Miller uses what it calls "value-based" interviewing. During an initial job interview, the staffing department probes the candidate's work style, likes, and dislikes by posing "what if" questions. By evaluating how the candidate would handle a variety of scenarios, the recruiter gets a good idea of how well the individual would fit into the company. If the fit seems good, the candidate is invited back for follow-up interviews with members of the department where he or she would be working. During these follow-up interviews, the candidate's functional expertise is evaluated along with his or her psychological makeup. By the end of the interview process, Herman Miller has a good idea of whether the candidate "knows how to dance."[21]

Your Mission: As a member of Herman Miller's staffing department, you are responsible for screening job candidates and arranging for candidates to interview with members of Herman Miller's professional staff. Your responsibilities include the development of interview questions and evaluation forms for use by company employees involved in the interview process. You also handle all routine correspondence with job candidates. In each of the following situations, choose the best alternative, and be prepared to explain why your choice is best.

1. Herman Miller has decided to establish a management training program for recent college graduates. The training program is designed to groom people for careers in finance, strategic planning, marketing, administration, and general management. To recruit people for the program, the firm will conduct on-campus interviews at several colleges—something it has not generally done. You and the other Herman Miller interviewers will be talking with 30 or 40 applicants on campus. You will have 20 minutes for each interview. Your goal is to identify the candidates who will be invited to come to the office for evaluation interviews. You want the preliminary screening process to be as fair and objective as possible, so how will you approach the task?

   a. Meet with all the Herman Miller interviewers to discuss the characteristics that successful candidates will exhibit. Allow each interviewer to use his or her own approach to identify these characteristics in applicants. Encourage the interviewers to ask whatever questions seem most useful in light of the individual characteristics of each candidate.

   b. Develop a list of 10 to 15 questions that will be posed to all candidates. Instruct the Herman Miller interviewers to stick strictly to the list so that all applicants will respond to the same questions and be evaluated on the same basis.

   c. Develop a written evaluation form for measuring all candidates against criteria such as academic performance, relevant experience, capacity for teamwork, and communication skills. For each criterion, suggest four or five questions that interviewers might use to evaluate the candidate. Instruct the interviewers to cover all the criteria and to fill out the written evaluation form for each applicant immediately after the interview.

   d. Design a questionnaire for candidates to complete before their interviews. Then ask the interviewers to outline the ideal answers they would like to see a candidate offer for each item on this questionnaire. These ideal answers give you a standard against which to measure actual candidate answers.

2. During the on-campus screening interviews, you ask several candidates, "Why do you want to work for this organization?" Of the following responses, which would you rank the highest?

   a. "I'd like to work here because I'm interested in the office furniture business. I've always been fascinated by industrial design and the interaction between people and their environment. In addition to studying business, I have taken courses in industrial design and industrial psychology. I also have some personal experience in building furniture. My grandfather is a cabinetmaker and an antique restorer, and I have been his apprentice since I was 12 years old. I've paid for college by working as a carpenter during summer vacations."

b. "I'm an independent person with a lot of internal drive. I do my best work when I'm given a fairly free reign to use my creativity. From what I've read about your corporate culture, I think my working style would fit very well with your management philosophy. I'm also the sort of person who identifies very strongly with my job. For better or worse, I define myself through my affiliation with my employer. I get a great sense of pride from being part of a first-rate operation, and I think Herman Miller is first-rate. I've read about the design awards you've won and about your selection as one of America's most admired companies. The articles say that Herman Miller is a well-managed company. I think I would learn a lot working here, and I think my drive and creativity would be appreciated."

c. "There are several reasons why I'd like to work for Herman Miller. For one thing, I have family and friends in Zeeland, and I'd like to stay in the area. Also, I have friends who work for Herman Miller, and they both say it's terrific. I've also heard good things about your compensation and benefits."

d. "My ultimate goal is to start my own company, but first I need to learn more about managing a business. I read in *Fortune* that Herman Miller is one of America's most admired corporations. I think I could learn a lot by joining your management training program and observing your operations."

3. You are preparing questions for the professional staff to use when conducting follow-up interviews at Herman Miller's headquarters. You want a question that will reveal something about the candidates' probable loyalty to the organization. Which of the following questions is the best choice?

a. If you knew you could be one of the world's most successful people in a single occupation, such as music, politics, medicine, or business, what occupation would you choose? If you knew you had only a 10 percent chance of being so successful, would you still choose the same occupation?

b. We value loyalty among our employees. Tell me something about yourself that demonstrates your loyalty as a member of an organization.

c. What would you do if you discovered that a co-worker routinely made personal, unauthorized long-distance phone calls from work?

d. What other companies are you interviewing with?

4. In concluding an evaluation interview, you ask the candidate, "Do you have any questions?" Which of the following answers would you respond most favorably to?

a. "No. I can't think of anything. You've been very thorough in describing the job and the company. Thank you for taking the time to talk with me."

b. "Yes. I have an interview with one of your competitors, Steelcase, next week. How would you sum up the differences between your two firms?"

c. "Yes. If I were offered a position here, what would my chances be of getting promoted within the next 12 months?"

d. "Yes. Do you think Herman Miller will be a better or worse company 15 years from now?"

Critical Thinking Questions

1. How can you distinguish yourself from other candidates in a screening interview and still keep your responses short and to the point? Explain.

2. What can you do to make a favorable impression when you discover that an open-ended interview has turned into a stress interview? Briefly explain your answer.

3. Should applicants ask about preemployment testing during an interview? Explain your answer.

4. Why is it important to distinguish unethical or illegal interview questions from acceptable questions? Explain.

5. If you want to switch jobs because you can't work with your supervisor, how can you explain this reason to a prospective employer? Give an example.

6. If you think you've gotten off to a bad start during a preliminary screening, what can you do to try to save the interview? Explain your answer.

Documents for Analysis

Read the following documents; then (1) analyze the strengths or weaknesses of each sentence and (2) revise each document so that it follows this chapter's guidelines.

DOCUMENT 16.A: THANK-YOU LETTER

Thank you for the really marvelous opportunity to meet you and your colleagues at Starret Engine Company. I really enjoyed touring your facilities and talking with all the people there. You have

quite a crew! Some of the other companies I have visited have been so rigid and uptight that I can't imagine how I would fit in. It's a relief to run into a group of people who seem to enjoy their work as much as all of you do.

I know that you must be looking at many other candidates for this job, and I know that some of them will probably be more experienced than I am. But I do want to emphasize that my two-year hitch in the Navy involved a good deal of engineering work. I don't think I mentioned all my shipboard responsibilities during the interview.

Please give me a call within the next week to let me know your decision. You can usually find me at my dormitory in the evening after dinner (phone: 877-9080).

DOCUMENT 16.B: LETTER OF INQUIRY
I have recently received a very attractive job offer from the Warrington Company. But before I let them know one way or another, I would like to consider any offer that your firm may extend. I was quite impressed with your company during my recent interview, and I am still very interested in a career there.

I don't mean to pressure you, but Warrington has asked for my decision within ten days. Could you let me know by Tuesday whether you plan to offer me a position? That would give me enough time to compare the two offers.

DOCUMENT 16.C: LETTER DECLINING A JOB OFFER
I'm writing to say that I must decline your job offer. Another company has made me a more generous offer, and I have decided to accept. However, if things don't work out for me there, I will let you know. I sincerely appreciate your interest in me.

Cases

INTERVIEWING WITH POTENTIAL EMPLOYERS

1. Interviewers and interviewees: Classroom exercise in interviewing Interviewing is clearly an interactive process involving at least two people. So the best way to practice for interviews is to work with others.

Your Task: You and all other members of your class are to write letters of application for an entry-level or management-trainee position requiring a pleasant personality and intelligence but a minimum of specialized education or experience. Sign your letter with a fictitious name that conceals your identity. Next polish (or prepare) a résumé that accurately identifies you and your educational and professional accomplishments.

Three members of the class, who volunteer as interviewers, divide equally among themselves all the anonymously written application letters. Then each interviewer selects a candidate who seems the most pleasant and convincing in his or her letter. At this time the selected candidates identify themselves and give the interviewers their résumés.

Each interviewer then interviews his or her chosen candidate in front of the class, seeking to understand how the items on the résumé qualify the candidate for the job. At the end of the interviews, the class may decide who gets the job and discuss why this candidate was successful. Then retrieve your letter, sign it with the right name, and submit it to the instructor for credit.

2. Internet interview: Exercise in interviewing Using the Web 100 site at <http://www.w100.com>, locate the Web home page of a company you would like to work for. Then identify a position within the company you would like to apply for. Working with a partner, review each other's company home page.

Your Task: Interview your partner in person for his or her chosen position. Take notes during the interview. Now revisit your company's home page, and consider the information generated during your interview. Write a follow-up letter thanking your interviewer, and print it out along with your interview notes for submission to your instructor.

FOLLOWING UP AFTER THE INTERVIEW

3. A slight error in timing: Letter asking for delay of an employment decision You botched up your timing and applied for your third-choice job before going after what you really wanted. What you want to do is work in retail marketing with Neiman-Marcus in Dallas; what you have been offered is a similar job with Longhorn Leather and Lumber, 55 dry and dusty miles away in Commerce, just south of the Oklahoma panhandle.

You review your notes. Your Longhorn interview was three weeks ago with the human resources manager, R. P. Bronson, a congenial person who has just written to offer you the position. The store's address is 27 Sam Rayburn Dr., Commerce, TX 75428. Mr. Bronson notes that he can hold the position open for ten days. You have an interview scheduled with Neiman-Marcus next week, but it is unlikely that you will know the store's decision within this ten-day period.

Your Task: Write to R. P. Bronson, requesting a reasonable delay in your consideration of his job offer.

4. Job hunt: Set of employment-related letters to a single company Where would you like to work? Pick a real or an imagined company, and assume that a month ago you sent your résumé and application letter. Not long afterward, you were invited to come for an interview, which seemed to go very well.

Your Task: Use your imagination to write the following: (a) a thank-you letter for the interview, (b) a note of inquiry, (c) a request for more time to decide, (d) a letter of acceptance, and (e) a letter declining the job offer.

DEVELOPING YOUR INTERNET SKILLS

GOING ONLINE: BE PREPARED FOR CHALLENGING INTERVIEW QUESTIONS, P. 404

By now, you've probably read about and practiced many different approaches to job interviews, including what you've learned from this chapter and the *Career* magazine Web site. If you were going to write a "how-to" magazine article about job interviews and you didn't have space for everything, what interviewing advice would you include as the best and most important?

Communicating Orally · Conducting Interviews on the Job · Participating in Small Groups and Meetings

ORAL

Speaking and Presenting in a Business Environment · Preparing to Speak · Developing Your Speech

COMMUNICATION

Presentation · Mastering the Art of Delivery · Speaking and Presenting in a Business Environment ·

17

C h a p t e r

After studying this chapter, you will be able to

Apply the composition process to your spoken comments

Summarize the skills involved in being an effective listener

Explain how to resolve conflicts, overcome resistance, and handle negotiations

Identify nine common types of business interviews

Define four types of interview questions and clarify when to use each type

Describe how groups make decisions

Discuss the preparations and duties necessary for productive meetings

LISTENING, INTERVIEWING, AND CONDUCTING MEETINGS

O *n the Job*

FACING A COMMUNICATION DILEMMA
AT ROCKPORT

Convening an Unconventional Meeting

Calling a meeting isn't unusual; executives do it every day. Even so, few executives shut down entire companies to bring everyone to a meeting, but that's exactly what Rockport president John Thorbeck decided to do. Rockport is a footwear subsidiary of Reebok, and except for the handful of people left behind to answer telephones in the company's Marlboro, Massachusetts, headquarters, all 350 managers and employees were asked to gather in a huge room for a two-day meeting.

Many of Thorbeck's top managers questioned the need for halting the daily functions that had built Rockport's annual sales to $300 million. The chief financial officer complained that "a company as large as ours can't afford to lose two whole shipping days." He also doubted that the discussions would yield any concrete results. But Thorbeck believed this meeting was important enough to involve every employee at every level. His objective was nothing less than to increase the company's potential. "I felt that there was so much more we could do, given our profitability and resources," he said. "Our goals were far too modest."

If you were John Thorbeck, how would you use a two-day meeting to elicit input from your employees? What factors of oral communication would you use to get them talking? Would good listening skills be valuable? What would you do to be sure the meeting was productive?[1]

C OMMUNICATING ORALLY

Rockport's John Thorbeck knows that speaking and listening are the communication skills we use most. Given a choice, people would rather talk to each other than write to each other. Talking takes less time and needs no composing, keyboarding, rewriting, duplicating, or distributing.

Oral communication saves time and provides opportunities for feedback and social interaction.

More important, oral communication provides the opportunity for feedback. When people communicate orally, they can ask questions and test their understanding of the message; they can share ideas and work together to solve problems. They can also convey and absorb nonverbal information, which reveals far more than words alone. By communicating with facial expressions, eye contact, tone of voice, gestures, and postures, people can send subtle messages that add another dimension to spoken words. Oral communication satisfies our common need to be part of the human community and makes us feel good. Talking things over helps people in organizations build morale and establish a group identity.

Nonetheless, oral communication also has its dangers. Under most circumstances, oral communication occurs spontaneously. You have far less opportunity to revise your spoken words than to revise your written words. You can't cross out what you just said and start all over. Your dumbest comments will be etched in the other person's memory, regardless of how much you try to explain that you really meant something else entirely. Moreover, if you let your attention wander while someone else is speaking, you miss the point. You either have to muddle along without knowing what the other person said or admit you were daydreaming and ask the person to repeat the comment. One other problem is that oral communication is personal. People tend to confuse your message with you as an individual. They're likely to judge the content of what you say by your appearance and delivery style.

Intercultural barriers can also be as much a problem in oral communication as in written communication. Naturally, it's best to know your audience, including any cultural differences they may have. Then communicate your message in the tone, manner, and situation your audience will feel most comfortable with. (Chapter 3 has more information on intercultural barriers.)

Whether you're using the telephone, engaging in a quick conversation with a colleague, participating in a formal interview, or attending a meeting, oral communication is the vehicle you use to get your message across. When communicating orally, make it your goal to take advantage of the positive characteristics while minimizing the dangers. To achieve that goal, work on improving two key skills: speaking and listening.

To be successful at Rockport, employees must be skilled in oral communication. Their skills are constantly put to the test, whether they're engaging in one-on-one interviews, dealing with customers, or participating in meetings.

Speaking

Because speaking is such an ingrained activity, we tend to do it without much thought, but that casual approach can be a problem in business. Be more aware of using speech as a tool for accomplishing your objectives in a business context. To do this, break the habit of talking spontaneously, without planning *what* you're going to say or *how* you're going to say it. Learn to manage the impression you create by consciously tailoring your remarks and delivery style to suit the situation. Become as aware of the consequences of what you say as you are of the consequences of what you write.

The spontaneous quality of oral communication limits your ability to edit your thoughts.

With a little effort, you can learn to apply the composition process to oral communication. Before you speak, think about your purpose, your main idea, and your audience. Organize your thoughts in a logical way, decide on a style that suits the occasion (for example, formal or informal, lecture or conversation), and edit your remarks mentally. Try to predict how the other person will react, and organize the message accordingly. Your audience may not react the way you expect, so have alternative approaches ready. As you speak, watch the other person, judging from verbal and nonverbal feedback whether your message is making the desired impression. If it isn't, revise and try again.

Learn to think before you speak.

Just as various writing assignments call for different writing styles, various situations call for different speaking styles. Your speaking style depends on the level of intimacy between you and the other person and on the nature of your conversation. When you're talking with a friend, you naturally speak more frankly than when you're talking with your boss or a stranger. When you're talking about a serious subject, you use a serious tone. As you think about which speaking style is appropriate, also think about the nonverbal message you want to convey. People derive less meaning from your words than they do from your facial expressions, vocal characteristics, and body language. The nonverbal message

Adjust your speaking style to suit the situation.

Apply the "you" attitude to oral communication.

should reinforce your words. Perhaps the most important thing you can do to project yourself more effectively is to remember the "you" attitude, earning other people's attention and goodwill by focusing on them. For example, professionals like Rockport's John Thorbeck elicit opinions from others not only by asking them pointed questions but also by paying attention to their responses.

An important tool of oral communication, the telephone can extend your reach across town and around the world. However, if your telephone skills are lacking, you may waste valuable time and appear rude.[2] You can minimize your time on the phone while raising your phone productivity by delivering one-way information by fax or e-mail, jotting down an agenda before making a call, saving social chit-chat for the end of a call (in case your conversation is cut short), saving up all the short calls you need to make to one person during a given day, and making sure your assistant has a list of people whose calls you'll accept even if you're in a meeting.[3]

Much telephone communication now happens through voice mail rather than directly person to person. Organize your thoughts before you make the phone call so that your message will be concise and accurate. Be sure to take advantage of the system's review and editing features to make your message as effective as possible. And keep in mind that voice mail messages aren't necessarily private. Many systems make it easy to forward messages to other people, so be careful when recording sensitive or personal messages.

Listening

The ability to listen is a vital skill in business.

If you're typical, you spend over half your communication time listening.[4] Listening supports effective relationships within the organization, enhances the organization's delivery of products, alerts the organization to the innovation growing from both internal and external forces, and allows organizations to manage the growing diversity both in the work force and in the customers they serve.[5] An individual with good listening ability is likely to succeed; good listening enhances performance, leading to raises, promotions, status, and power.[6] However, no one is born with the ability to listen; the skill is learned and improved through practice.[7] Cultural barriers present a potential challenge with listening as well as with speaking. You might misinterpret what you hear if you fail to consider any cultural differences between you and the speaker. Even though most of us like to think of ourselves as being good listeners, the average person remembers only about half of what's said during a 10-minute conversation and forgets half of that within 48 hours.[8]

Most people need to improve their listening skills.

What Happens When You Listen

Listening involves five related activities, which most often occur in sequence:[9]

Listening involves five steps: sensing, interpreting, evaluating, remembering, and responding.

- *Sensing* is physically hearing the message and taking note of it. This reception can be blocked by interfering noises, impaired hearing, or inattention. Tune out distractions by focusing on the message.
- *Interpreting* is decoding and absorbing what you hear. As you listen, you assign meaning to the words according to your own values, beliefs, ideas, expectations, roles, needs, and personal history. The speaker's frame of reference may be quite different from yours, so you may need to determine what the speaker really means. Pay attention to nonverbal cues—things such as gestures, body language, and facial expressions—but be careful not to assign meanings that aren't there. For example, a speaker who nervously stumbles over his or her words might be hiding something or might simply be nervous.
- *Evaluating* is forming an opinion about the message. Sorting through the speaker's remarks, separating fact from opinion, and evaluating the quality of the evidence require a good deal of effort, particularly if the subject is complex or emotionally charged. Avoid the temptations to dismiss ideas offered by people who are unattractive or abrasive and to embrace ideas offered by people who are charismatic speakers.
- *Remembering* is storing a message for future reference. As you listen, retain what you hear by taking notes or by making a mental outline of the speaker's key points.

■ *Responding* is acknowledging the message by reacting to the speaker in some fashion. If you're communicating one on one or in a small group, the initial response generally takes the form of verbal feedback. If you're one of many in an audience, your initial response may take the form of applause, laughter, or silence. Later on, you may act on what you have heard. Actively provide feedback to help the speaker refine the message.

Listening requires a mix of physical and mental activities and is subject to a mix of physical and mental barriers.

The Three Types of Listening

Various situations call for different listening skills. When you attend a briefing on the company's new medical insurance, you listen mainly for content. You want to know what the policy is. As the speaker describes the prescription drug plan, you begin to listen more critically, assessing the benefits of the new plan relative to your own needs. Later, as a friend talks to you about his medical problems, you listen empathetically, trying to understand his feelings.

These three types of listening differ not only in purpose but also in the amount of feedback or interaction that occurs. The goal of **content listening** is to understand and retain information imparted by a speaker. You may ask questions, but basically information flows from the speaker to you. Your job is to identify the key points of the message, so be sure to listen for clues to its structure: previews, transitions, summaries, enumerated points. In your mind create an outline of the speaker's remarks; afterward silently review what you've learned. You may take notes, but you do this sparingly so that you can concentrate on the key points. It doesn't matter whether you agree or disagree, approve or disapprove—only that you understand.[10] When you listen to a regional sales manager's monthly report on how many of your products sold that month, you are listening for content.

The goal of **critical listening** is to evaluate the message at several levels: the logic of the argument, strength of the evidence, and validity of the conclusions; the implications of the message for you or your organization; the speaker's intentions and motives; the omission of any important or relevant points. Because it's hard to absorb information and evaluate it at the same time, reserve judgment until the speaker has finished. Critical listening generally involves interaction as you try to uncover the speaker's point of view. You are bound to evaluate the speaker's credibility as well. Nonverbal signals are often your best clue.[11] When the regional sales manager presents sales projections for the next few months, you listen critically, evaluating whether the estimates are valid and what the implications are for your manufacturing department.

The goal of **active,** or **empathic, listening** is to understand the speaker's feelings, needs, and wants so that you can appreciate his or her point of view, regardless of whether you share that perspective. By listening in an active or empathic way, you help the individual vent the emotions that prevent a dispassionate approach to the subject. Avoid the temptation to give advice. Try not to judge the individual's feelings. Just let the other person talk.[12] You listen empathically when your regional sales manager tells you about the problems he had with his recreational vehicle while vacationing with his family.

All three types of listening can be useful in work-related situations, so it pays to learn how to apply them.

How to Be a Better Listener

Regardless of whether the situation calls for content, critical, or active listening, you can improve your listening ability by becoming more aware of the habits that distinguish good listeners from bad (Table 17.1). In addition, use nonverbal skills to help you focus: maintain eye contact, react responsively with head nods or spoken signals, and pay attention to the speaker's body language. You might even test yourself from time to time: When someone else is talking, ask yourself whether you're actually listening to the speaker or mentally rehearsing how you'll respond. Above all, try to be open to the information that will lead to higher-quality decisions, and try to accept the feelings that will build understanding and mutual respect. If you do, you'll be well on the way to becoming a good listener—an important quality when conducting interviews on the job.

When Keith Dunn and his partners started McGuffey's Restaurants, their goals were people oriented—they wanted a restaurant that wouldn't mistreat employees. But it wasn't until Dunn truly began listening to employees that the approach began to work, resulting in increased profits and lowered turnover. Listening is hard, says Dunn, but you have to learn how to do it.

The three forms of listening:

■ Content listening enables you to understand and retain the message.
■ Critical listening enables you to evaluate the information.
■ Active listening is used to draw out the other person.

Effective listening involves being receptive to both information and feelings.

Table 17.1	DISTINGUISHING GOOD LISTENERS FROM BAD LISTENERS	
To Listen Effectively	*The Bad Listener*	*The Good Listener*
Find areas of interest.	Tunes out dry subjects	Opportunizes; asks "What's in it for me?"
Judge content, not delivery.	Tunes out the message if the delivery is poor	Judges content; skips over delivery errors
Hold your fire.	Tends to enter into argument	Doesn't judge until comprehension is complete; interrupts only to clarify
Listen for ideas.	Listens for facts	Listens for central themes
Be flexible.	Takes extensive notes using only one system	Takes fewer notes; uses four to five different systems, depending on speaker
Work at listening.	Shows no energy output; fakes attention	Works hard; exhibits active body state
Resist distractions.	Is distracted easily	Fights or avoids distractions; tolerates bad habits; knows how to concentrate
Exercise your mind.	Resists difficult expository material; seeks light, recreational material	Uses heavier material as exercise for the mind
Keep your mind open.	Reacts to emotional words	Interprets emotional words; does not get hung up on them
Capitalize on the fact that thought is faster than speech.	Tends to daydream with slow speakers	Challenges; anticipates; mentally summarizes; weighs the evidence; listens between the lines to tone of voice

CONDUCTING INTERVIEWS ON THE JOB

In addition to handling difficult interpersonal situations, planning what to say and developing good listening skills will also help you participate in on-the-job interviews. From the day you apply for your first job until the day you retire, you'll be involved in a wide variety of business **interviews**—planned conversations with a predetermined purpose that involve asking and answering questions. In a typical interview the action is controlled by the interviewer, the person who scheduled the session. This individual poses a series of questions designed to elicit information from the interviewee. Interviews sometimes involve several interviewers or several interviewees, but more often only two people participate. The conversation bounces back and forth from interviewer to interviewee. Although the interviewer guides the conversation, the interviewee may also seek to accomplish a purpose, perhaps to obtain or provide information, to solve a problem, to create goodwill, or to persuade the other person to take action. If the participants establish rapport and stick to the subject at hand, both parties have a chance of achieving their objectives.

An interview is any planned conversation with a specific purpose involving two or more people.

When both the interviewer and the interviewee achieve their purpose, the interview is a success.

Categorizing Interviews

The interviewer establishes the style and structure of the session, depending on the purpose of the interview and the relationship between the parties, much as a writer varies the style and structure of a written message to suit the situation. Each situation calls for a slightly different approach, as you can imagine when you try to picture yourself conducting some of these common business interviews:

The various types of interviews call for different communication skills.

■ *Job interviews.* The job candidate wants to learn about the position and the organization; the employer wants to learn about the applicant's abilities and experience. Both hope to make a good impression and to establish rapport. Initial job interviews are usually fairly formal and structured, but later interviews may be relatively spontaneous as the interviewer explores the candidate's responses.

- *Information interviews.* The interviewer seeks facts that bear on a decision or contribute to basic understanding. Information flows mainly in one direction: One person asks a list of questions that must be covered and listens to the answers supplied by the other person. This kind of interview is a valuable form of primary research. Of course, the person you interview must be credible and knowledgeable about the subject. It is also important to decide in advance what kind of information you want and how you will use it; this planning will save time and build goodwill.

- *Persuasive interviews.* One person tells another about a new idea, product, or service and explains why the other should act on the recommendations. Persuasive interviews are often associated with, but are certainly not limited to, selling. The persuader asks about the other person's needs and shows how the product or concept is able to meet those needs. Thus persuasive interviews require skill in drawing out and listening to others as well as the ability to impart information.

- *Exit interviews.* The interviewer tries to understand why the interviewee is leaving the organization or transferring to another department or division. A departing employee can often provide insight into whether the business is being handled efficiently or whether things could be improved. The interviewer tends to ask all the questions while the interviewee provides answers. Encouraging the employee to focus on events and processes rather than on personal gripes will elicit more useful information for the organization.

- *Evaluation interviews.* A supervisor periodically gives an employee feedback on his or her performance. The supervisor and the employee discuss progress toward predetermined standards or goals and evaluate areas that require improvement. They may also discuss goals for the coming year, as well as the employee's longer-term aspirations and general concerns.

- *Counseling interviews.* A supervisor talks with an employee about personal problems that are interfering with work performance. The interviewer is concerned with the welfare of both the employee and the organization. The goal is to establish the facts, convey the company's concern, and steer the person toward a source of help. (Only a trained professional should offer advice on such problems as substance abuse, marital tension, and financial trouble.)

- *Conflict-resolution interviews.* Two competing people or groups of people (such as Smith versus Jones, day shift versus night shift, General Motors versus the United Auto Workers) explore their problems and attitudes. The goal is to bring the two parties closer together, cause adjustments in perceptions and attitudes, and create a more productive climate.

- *Disciplinary interviews.* A supervisor tries to correct the behavior of an employee who has ignored the organization's rules and regulations. The interviewer tries to get the employee to see the reason for the rules and to agree to comply. The interviewer also reviews the facts and explores the person's attitude. Because of the emotional reaction that is likely, neutral observations are more effective than critical comments.

- *Termination interviews.* A supervisor informs an employee of the reasons for the termination. The interviewer tries to avoid involving the company in legal action and tries to maintain as positive a relationship as possible with the interviewee. To accomplish these goals, the interviewer gives reasons that are specific, accurate, and verifiable.

Planning Interviews

Planning an interview is similar to planning any other form of communication. You begin by stating your purpose, analyzing the other person, and formulating your main idea. Then you decide on the length, style, and organization of the interview.

Even as an interviewee, you have some control over the conversation by anticipating the interviewer's questions and then planning your answers so that the points you want to make will be covered. You can also introduce questions and topics of your own. In addi-

To accomplish their objectives, interviewees develop a communication strategy.

tion, by your comments and nonverbal cues, you can affect the relationship between you and the interviewer. Think about your respective roles. What does this person expect from you? Is it to your advantage to confirm those expectations? Will you be more likely to accomplish your objective by being friendly and open or by conveying an impression of professional detachment? Should you allow the interviewer to dominate the exchange, or should you try to take control?

The interviewer assumes the main responsibility for planning the interview.

If you're the interviewer, responsibility for planning the session falls on you. On the simplest level, your job is to schedule the interview and see that it's held in a comfortable and convenient location. Good interviewers are good at collecting information, listening, and probing.[13] So you'll also develop a set of interview questions and decide on their sequence. Having a plan will enable you to conduct the interview more efficiently, even if you find it advantageous to deviate from the plan during the interview. If your questions might require research or extensive thinking, or if you'd like to quote the interviewee in writing, consider providing a list of questions a day or two before the interview so that the person will have time to prepare more complete (and therefore more helpful) answers. You might also want to tape record the interview if the topic is complex or if you plan to quote or paraphrase the interviewee in a written document.

Interview Questions

The purpose of the interview and the nature of the participants determine the types of questions that are asked. When you plan the interview, bear in mind that you ask questions (1) to get information, (2) to motivate the interviewee to respond honestly and appropriately, and (3) to create a good working relationship with the other person. While you're drafting your questions, be aware of ethical implications. For example, asking someone to divulge personal information about a co-worker may be asking that person to make an unethical decision. Always be careful about issues of confidentiality, politics, and other sensitive issues.

Four basic types of interview questions:

- Open-ended questions
- Direct open-ended questions
- Closed-ended questions
- Restatement questions

To obtain both factual information and underlying feelings, you'll probably use various types of questions. **Open-ended questions** invite the interviewee to offer an opinion, not just a yes, no, or one-word answer: "What do you think your company wants most from its suppliers?" This kind of question is useful when you want to learn the reasons behind a decision rather than just the facts. You can learn some interesting and unexpected things from open-ended questions, but they diminish your control of the interview. The other person's idea of what's relevant may not coincide with yours, and you may waste some time getting the interview back on track. Use open-ended questions to warm up the interviewee and to look for information when you have plenty of time to conduct the conversation.

To suggest a response, use **direct open-ended questions.** For example, asking "What have you done about . . ." assumes that something has been done and calls for an explanation. With direct open-ended questions you have somewhat more control over the interview, but you still give the other person some freedom in framing a response. This form is good to use when you want to get a specific conclusion or recommendation from someone: for example, "What would you do to improve customer satisfaction in the southern region?" Take care to avoid biasing the response with the way you word the question, however. Asking "What should Roger Vanque do to improve customer satisfaction in his region?" implies that Vanque is doing something wrong, which may not be the case.

Closed-ended questions require yes or no answers or call for short responses: "Did you make a reservation for the flight?" "What is your grade-point average: 3.5 to 4.0, 3.0 to 3.5, 2.5 to 3.0, 2.0 to 2.5?" Questions like these produce specific information, save time, require little effort from the interviewee, and eliminate bias and prejudice in answers. The disadvantage is that they limit the respondent's initiative and may prevent important information from being revealed. They're better for gathering information than for prompting an exchange of feelings.

Questions that mirror a respondent's answer are called **restatement questions.** They invite the respondent to expand on an answer: "You said you dislike completing travel vouchers. Is that correct?" They also signal to the interviewee that you're paying attention.

Restatements provide opportunities to clarify points and to correct misunderstandings. Use them to pursue a subject further or to encourage the other person to explain a statement. You can also use restatement questions to soothe upset customers or co-workers. The simple act of acknowledging the other person's complaint provides a wealth of gains in information, rapport, and mutual trust and respect.

Interview Structure

Good interviews have an opening, a body, and a close. The opening establishes rapport and orients the interviewee to the remainder of the session. You might begin by introducing yourself, asking a few polite questions, and then explaining the purpose and ground rules of the interview.

Use the opening to set the tone and orient the interviewee.

The questions in the body of the interview reflect the nature of your relationship with the interviewee. For an informational session, such as a market research interview, you may want to structure the interview and prepare a detailed list of specific questions. This approach enables you to control the interview and use your time efficiently. It also facilitates repeating the interview with other participants. On the other hand, if the interview is designed to explore problems or to persuade the interviewee, you may prefer a less structured approach. You might simply prepare a checklist of general subjects and then let the interview evolve on the basis of the participant's responses.

In the body of the interview, use a mix of question types. One good technique is to use closed-ended questions to pin down specific facts that emerge during an open-ended response. You might follow up an open-ended response by asking, "How many people did you contact to get this information?" or "Can we get this product in stock before May 15?"

Use a mix of question types to give the body of the interview rhythm.

The close of the interview is when you summarize the outcome, preview what comes next, and underscore the rapport that has been established. To signal that the interview is coming to an end, you might lean back in your chair, smile, and use an open, palms-up gesture as you say, "Well, I guess that takes care of all my questions. Would you like to add anything?" If the interviewee has no comments, you might go on to say, "Thank you so much for your help. You've given me all the information I need to finish my report. I should have it completed within two weeks; I'll send you a copy." Then you might rise, shake hands, and approach the door. In parting, you could add a friendly comment to reaffirm your interest in the other person: "I hope you have a nice trip to Yellowstone. I was there when I was a kid, and I've never forgotten the experience."

Use the close to sum up the interview and leave the interviewee with a cordial feeling.

From a practical standpoint, you need to be certain that your interview outline is about the right length for the time you've scheduled. People can speak at the rate of about 125 to 150 words a minute. If you're using a mix of various types of questions, you can probably handle about 20 questions in half an hour (or about the same amount of information that you would cover in a 10- to 12-page single-spaced document). However, you may want to allow more or less time for each question and response, depending on the subject matter and the complexity of the questions. Bear in mind that open-ended questions take longer to answer than other types do.

Don't try to cover more questions than you have time for.

When you've concluded the interview, take a few moments to write down your thoughts. If it was an information-gathering session, go over your notes. Fill in any blanks while the interview is fresh in your mind. In addition, you might write a short letter or memo that thanks the interviewee for cooperating, confirms understandings between you, and if appropriate, outlines the next steps. As a reminder of the tasks involved in interviews, see this chapter's Checklist for Interviews on the Job.

PARTICIPATING IN SMALL GROUPS AND MEETINGS

As in interviews, your speaking and listening skills are put to the test during meetings. Moreover, the skills you develop to handle difficult interpersonal situations and interviews are just as helpful when operating in small groups. By being a good listener, relying on a win-win strategy, and using the appropriate types of questions for each situation, you can contribute positively to any small group or meeting.

Meetings are called to solve problems or to share information.

CHECKLIST FOR INTERVIEWS ON THE JOB

A. Preparation

1. Decide on the purpose and goals of the interview.
2. Outline your interview on the basis of your goals and the interview category.
   - a. Set the level of formality.
   - b. Choose a structured or an unstructured approach.
3. Determine the needs of your interviewee, and gather background information.
4. Formulate questions as clearly and concisely as possible, and plot their order.
5. Project the outcome of the interview, and develop a plan for accomplishing the goal.
6. Select a time and a site.
7. Inform the interviewee of the nature of the interview and the agenda to be covered.
8. Provide a list of questions in advance if the interviewee will need time to research and formulate quality answers.

B. Conduct

1. Be on time for the interview appointment.
2. Remind the interviewee of the purpose and format.
3. Clear the taking of notes or the use of a tape recorder with the interviewee.
4. Use ears and eyes to pick up verbal and nonverbal cues.
5. Follow the stated agenda, but be willing to explore relevant subtopics.
6. At the end of the interview, restate the interviewee's key ideas and review the actions, goals, and tasks each of you has agreed to.
7. Close the interview with a friendly comment to underscore the rapport that's been established.

C. Follow-Up

1. Write a thank-you memo or letter that provides the interviewee with a record of the meeting.
2. Provide the assistance that you agreed to during your meeting.
3. Monitor progress by keeping in touch with your interviewee.

"Today the drive is to go beyond competence to expertise," says Dr. Patricia Sachs, a senior research scientist at the Institute for Research on Learning. "But expertise takes place inside communities. Work communities—communities of practice—develop when people work together, when they coordinate their efforts, exchange information, and solve problems to get something done."

A meeting's success depends not only on what the goal is but also on how the group approaches the task.

As more and more corporations embrace the concept of **participative management** and involve employees in the company's decision making, the importance of teamwork has increased. Companies are looking for people who can interact successfully in small groups and make useful contributions during meetings. When Hewlett-Packard studied its most successful managers to identify the personality traits that contribute to their effectiveness, it found that all of them are good at team building. This finding prompted the company to emphasize team-building skills in its management development program.[14]

At their best, meetings can be an extremely useful forum for making key decisions and coordinating the activities of people and departments. Theoretically, the interaction of the participants should lead to good decisions based on the combined intelligence of the group. Whether the meeting is held to solve a problem or to share information, the participants gain a sense of involvement and importance from their attendance. Because they share in the decision, they accept it and are committed to seeing it succeed.

At their worst, meetings are unproductive and frustrating. They waste everyone's time and they're expensive. More important, poor meetings may actually be counterproductive, because they may result in bad decisions. When people are pressured to conform, they abandon their sense of personal responsibility and agree to ill-founded plans.

Understanding Group Dynamics

A meeting is called for some purpose, and this purpose gives form to the meeting. In addition, however, the interactions and processes that take place during a meeting, the **group dynamics,** affect the outcome. People are assembled to achieve a work-related task, but, at the same time, each person has a **hidden agenda,** private motives that affect the group's interaction. Sam might want to prove that he's more powerful than Sherry; Sherry might be trying to share the risk of making a decision; Don might be looking for a chance to postpone doing "real" work; and Rachel might be looking for approval from her peers. Each person's hidden agenda either contributes to or detracts from the group's ability to perform its task. Although it would be unethical for any group member to make decisions solely on the basis of his or her hidden agenda, a person's private motives cannot be left on a coat rack outside the conference room.

Role-Playing

We all have many-faceted personalities: Sometimes we're carefree and fun-loving; sometimes we're serious and hard working. We assume various roles to suit various occasions, playing the part that's expected of us in a particular context. The roles are all consistent with our self-concept, but we vary the image we project depending on the demands of the situation and the cues we receive from other people.

The roles people play in meetings fall into three categories (Table 17.2). Members who assume **self-oriented roles** are motivated mainly to fulfill personal needs, and they tend to be less productive than the other two types. Far more likely to contribute to group goals are those who assume **group maintenance roles** to help members work well together and those who assume **task-facilitating roles** to help members solve the problem or make the decision.

To a great extent, the role we assume in a group depends on our status in that group: High-status people play dominant roles; low-status people play passive roles. Status depends on many variables, such as personal attractiveness, competence in a particular field, past successes, education, age, social background, and position in the organization. It also varies from group to group: You may have a high status in one group (say, a college fraternity) and very low status in another (say, a Fortune 500 company).

In most groups a certain amount of "politics" occurs as people try to establish their status. One or two people typically emerge as the leaders, but often an undercurrent of tension remains as members of the group vie for better positions in the pecking order. These power struggles often get in the way of the real work. One person might refuse to go along with a decision simply because it was suggested by a rival. Until roles and status have stabilized, the group may have trouble accomplishing its goals.

Group Norms

A group that meets regularly develops unwritten rules governing the behavior of the members, and people are expected to conform to these norms. For example, there may be an unspoken agreement that it's okay to be 10 minutes late for meetings but not 15 minutes late. In the context of work, the most productive groups tend to develop norms that are conducive to business.

Some groups are more cohesive than others. When the group has a strong identity, the members all observe the norms religiously. They're upset by any deviation, and individuals feel a great deal of pressure to conform. This sense of group loyalty can be positive: Members generally have a strong commitment to one another, and they're highly moti-

Margin notes:

Each member of a group plays a role that affects the outcome of the group's activities.

Group members' personal motives may interfere with the group's efforts to accomplish its mission.

Because they feel pressured to conform, members of a group may agree to unwise decisions.

Table 17.2	ROLES PEOPLE PLAY IN GROUPS	
Self-Oriented Roles	**Group Maintenance Roles**	**Task-Facilitating Roles**
Controlling: dominating others by exhibiting superiority or authority	**Encouraging:** drawing out other members by showing verbal and nonverbal support, praise, or agreement	**Initiating:** getting the group started on a line of inquiry
Withdrawing: retiring from the group either by becoming silent or by refusing to deal with a particular aspect of the group's work	**Harmonizing:** reconciling differences among group members through mediation or by using humor to relieve tension	**Information giving or seeking:** offering (or seeking) information relevant to questions facing the group
Attention seeking: calling attention to oneself and demanding recognition from others	**Compromising:** offering to yield on a point in the interest of reaching a mutually acceptable decision	**Coordinating:** showing relationships among ideas, clarifying issues, summarizing what the group has done
Diverting: focusing group discussion on topics of interest to the individual rather than on topics relevant to the task		**Procedure setting:** suggesting decision-making procedures that will move the group toward a goal

BEHIND THE SCENES AT 3M
The Keys to Masterful Meetings

Virginia Johnson is the manager of 3M's recently established Meeting Management Institute. Among American companies, 3M is known for its role in promoting the importance of effective meetings (as well as for producing such brand names as Scotch cellophane tape and Post-it notes). The company also produces graphics and presentation equipment, which suggests a natural connection between 3M's products and its emphasis on effective meetings. The company finances research, sponsors seminars, and publishes articles and books on the subject.

"We define a meeting as three or more people gathering for an expected outcome," explains Johnson. But top executives spend 17 hours a week in such gatherings and another 6 hours preparing for them: a total of 38 percent of their typical 61-hour week. So why call meetings at all? Why not put what has to be said in writing and save everybody some time? Johnson says, "You can't accomplish some things without getting your people together—when you want to provide them direct access to an expert, for example, or show that avenues of communication in the company are open. Meetings here at 3M serve other needs too. They allow us to share information, build teams, brainstorm problems and solutions, reach decisions, and train people. Young companies, especially, and companies in trouble may find meetings indispensable."

To determine whether to hold a meeting, Johnson says she writes "one 25-word sentence stating what I expect people to know, do, and believe after attending. If I can't create that sentence, the need for a meeting isn't apparent." When a meeting is appropriate, she believes that preparation is what makes it successful. "I start by thinking in terms of the agenda. Once it's outlined, I create the visuals that will illustrate the points I want to make.

"Listening is an important skill. Traditionally you help yourself listen by taking notes. We've found that graphics also help people listen, enabling them to visualize and retain information. That's why I plan my graphics early." Johnson

At 3M, meetings help participants share information, solve problems, make decisions, and train employees. As manager of 3M's Meeting Management Institute, Virginia Johnson believes that successful meetings depend on preparation.

---

vated to see that the group succeeds. However, such group loyalty can also lead members into **groupthink,** the willingness of individual members to set aside their personal opinions and go along with everyone else, even if everyone else is wrong, simply because belonging to the group is important to them. Because decisions based on groupthink are more a result of group loyalty and conformity than of carefully considered opinion and fact finding, groupthink can lead to poor-quality decisions and ill-advised actions. Groupthink can even induce people to act against their own sense of ethics.

Group Decision Making

Group decision making passes through four phases: orientation, conflict, emergence, reinforcement.

Groups usually reach their decisions in a predictable pattern. The process can be viewed as passing through four phases. In the *orientation phase,* group members socialize, establish their roles, and agree on their reason for meeting. In the *conflict phase* members begin to discuss their positions on the problem. If group members have been carefully selected to represent a variety of viewpoints and expertise, disagreements are a natural part of this phase. The point is to air all the options and all the pros and cons fully. At the end of this phase, group members begin to settle on a single solution to the problem. In the *emergence phase* members reach a decision. Those who advocated different solutions put aside their objections, either because they're convinced that the majority solution is better or because they recognize that arguing is futile. Finally, in the *reinforcement phase* group feeling is rebuilt, and the solution is summarized. Members receive their assignments for carrying out the group's decision and make arrangements for following up on those assignments.[15]

These four phases almost always occur, regardless of what type of decision is being considered. Group members naturally employ this decision process, even when they lack experience or training in group communication. However, just as a natural athlete can im-

finishes by preparing notes containing her main ideas or key phrases. "I never write a speech," she explains. "Speeches are not meetings. My personal style is to be natural and extemporaneous. My agenda, visuals, and notes help me achieve that tone.

"For me, the toughest meeting to run is the creative session. Trying to bring out the child in adults, achieving fantasy and free thinking by breaking down management roles, is very demanding." A meeting to generate new ideas in sales training was Johnson's most recent challenge. "I used what I call a 'brain writing' sheet. I asked the eight managers to write down three things about sales training they'd like to see added or changed. They handed their ideas in and took the sheet of another participant. They read that person's suggestions and wrote down three more. After a few rounds of this, they'd forgotten their jobs and titles and were busy scribbling. Each round triggered new ideas."

Johnson is more alert than most to the conduct of meetings, and, as a participant, she has the greatest trouble when there is little or no leadership from the meeting facilitator. "My mind wanders," she admits. "If a leader speaks more than 15 or 20 percent of the time, for example, he or she is not being effective. The role of the facilitator is to help other people get their opinions or questions out and responded to." To get the most out of her attendance, Johnson adopts a listening behavior appropriate to the meeting. "If it's a formal meeting, I'll take notes to help me listen and for later recall. At creative sessions I may have to listen intently or shout out my responses. Either way, I want to be free of the technical aspects of meeting attendance." For Virginia Johnson and 3M, planning, conducting, or attending a well-run meeting rewards everyone involved. "If it produces that 'expected outcome,' it's a job well done."

Apply Your Knowledge

1. You followed Virginia Johnson's advice. For a meeting on the need to improve office telephone techniques, you created 30 visuals to guide you and eight managers through your agenda. On your way to the meeting, you lost the case with your visuals. What steps can you take to carry off a productive meeting anyway?

2. Determine the hourly cost of meetings. Create a grid of six vertical columns with these labels: Salary, 2 (executives), 4, 6, 8, and 10. Down the left side, under salary, label five lines with these annual salaries: $20,000, $40,000, $60,000, $80,000, and $100,000. Do the arithmetic and fill in the grid with how much a 1-hour meeting of each group would cost a company (assuming fifty 40-hour weeks to a year). For example, a 1-hour meeting of four executives earning $80,000 a year costs the company $160. Next, determine the cost of an all-morning (3-hour) meeting involving eight executives: one earning $20,000, three earning $40,000, one earning $60,000, two earning $80,000, and one earning $100,000.

prove by practicing, the group leader can make this natural decision process proceed more smoothly by preparing carefully.

Group decision-making software (also called electronic meeting systems) can save time and streamline the decision process. These systems can also make meetings more democratic by putting everyone on equal footing.

Arranging the Meeting

By being aware of how small groups of people interact, meeting leaders can take steps to ensure that their meetings are productive. The three most frequently reported problems with meetings are (1) getting off the subject, (2) not having an agenda, and (3) meeting for too long.[16] The key to productive meetings is careful planning of purpose, participants, agenda, and location. The trick is to bring the right people together in the right place for just enough time to accomplish your goals.

■ *Determining the purpose.* Rockport's John Thorbeck warns that the biggest mistake is having no specific goal. In general, the purpose of a meeting is either to get information or to make a decision, although many meetings comprise both purposes. An informational meeting is called so that the participants can share information and, possibly, coordinate actions. This type of meeting may involve individual briefings by each participant or a speech by the leader followed by questions from the attendees. Decision-making meetings are mainly concerned with persuasion, analysis, and problem solving. They often include a brainstorming session that is followed by a debate on the alternatives. These meetings tend to be somewhat less predictable than informational meetings.

Before calling a meeting, ask yourself whether it is really needed.

Limit the number of participants, but include all key people.

Prepare a detailed agenda well in advance of the meeting.

GOING ONLINE
MEET THE
HIGH-TECH WAY
Learn the pitfalls to avoid when setting up a desktop videoconferencing system. The site discusses what features to look for and how to evaluate the three types of systems. It evaluates specific brands and provides online resources for further information.

http://www.hyperstand.com/New
Media/95/11/td/vidconf/main.htm1

The meeting leader's duties:

- Pacing the meeting
- Appointing a note taker
- Following the agenda
- Stimulating participation and discussion
- Summarizing the debate
- Reviewing recommendations
- Circulating the minutes

Tom Chappell is co-founder and president of Tom's of Maine, a manufacturer of all-natural health and beauty products, and author of The Soul of Business. *He believes a good portion of that soul comes from his employees. "We flatten the hierarchy and create a circle of people who can offer diverse perspectives." A final decision often rests with one person of authority, "but that person always benefits from the dialogue," says Chappell.*

- *Selecting the participants.* Try to invite only those whose presence is essential. The number of participants should reflect the purpose of the meeting. If the session is purely informational and one person will be doing most of the talking, you can include a relatively large group. However, if you're trying to solve a problem, develop a plan, or reach a decision, try to limit participation to between 6 and 12 people.[17] Of course, be sure to include those who can make an important contribution and those who are key decision makers.
- *Setting the agenda.* Although the nature of a meeting may sometimes prevent you from developing a fixed agenda, at least prepare a list of matters to be discussed (see Appendix A). Distribute the agenda to the participants several days before the meeting. The more participants know ahead of time about the purpose of the meeting, the better prepared they'll be to respond to the issues at hand.
- *Preparing the location.* Decide where you'll hold the meeting, and reserve the location. For work sessions, morning meetings are usually more productive than afternoon sessions. If you work for an organization with technological capabilities, you may want to use teleconferencing or videoconferencing for your meeting. Also, consider the seating arrangements. Are rows of chairs suitable, or do you need a conference table? Give some attention to such details as room temperature, lighting, ventilation, acoustics, and refreshments. These things may seem trivial, but they can make or break a meeting.

Contributing to a Productive Meeting

Whether the meeting is conducted electronically or conventionally, its success depends largely on how effective the leader is. If the leader is prepared and has selected the participants carefully, the meeting will probably be productive. Moreover, according to Rockport's John Thorbeck, listening skills are especially important to meeting leaders. The leader's ability to listen well facilitates good meetings.

As meeting leader, you're responsible for keeping the ball rolling. Avoid being so domineering that you close off suggestions, but don't be so passive that you lose control of the group. If the discussion lags, call on people who haven't spoken. Pace the presentation and discussion so that you'll have time to complete the agenda. As time begins to run out, interrupt the discussion and summarize what has been accomplished. Another leadership task is either to arrange for someone to record the proceedings or to ask a participant to take notes during the meeting. (Appendix A includes an example of the format for minutes of meetings.)

As leader, you're expected to follow the agenda; participants have prepared for the meeting on the basis of the announced agenda. However, don't be rigid. Allow enough time for discussion, and give people a chance to raise related issues. If you cut off discussion too quickly or limit the subject too narrowly, no real consensus can emerge.

You can improve the productivity of a meeting by using **parliamentary procedure,** a time-tested method for planning and running effective meetings. Anyone belonging to an organization should understand the basic principles of parliamentary procedure. Used correctly, it can help groups in several important ways:[18]

- Transact business efficiently
- Protect individual rights
- Maintain order
- Preserve a spirit of harmony
- Help the organization accomplish its goals

The most common guide to parliamentary procedure is *Robert's Rules of Order,* available in various editions and revisions. Also available are less technical guides based on "Robert's Rules." You can determine how strictly you want to adhere to parliamentary procedure. For small groups you may be quite flexible, but for larger groups you'll want to use a more formal approach.

As the meeting gets under way, you'll discover that some participants are too quiet and others are too talkative. To draw out the shy types, ask for their input on issues that par-

CHECKLIST FOR MEETINGS

A. Preparation
1. Determine the meeting's objectives.
2. Work out an agenda that will achieve your objectives.
3. Select participants.
4. Determine the location, and reserve a room.
5. Arrange for light refreshments, if appropriate.
6. Determine whether the lighting, ventilation, acoustics, and temperature of the room are adequate.
7. Determine seating needs: chairs only or table and chairs.

B. Conduct
1. Begin and end the meeting on time.
2. Control the meeting by following the announced agenda.
3. Encourage full participation, and either confront or ignore those who seem to be working at cross-purposes with the group.
4. Sum up decisions, actions, and recommendations as you move through the agenda, and restate main points at the end.

C. Follow-Up
1. Distribute the meeting's notes or minutes on a timely basis.
2. Take the follow-up action agreed to.

ticularly pertain to them. You might say something like, "Roberto, you've done a lot of work in this area. What do you think?" For the overly talkative, simply say that time is limited and others need a chance to speak. The best meetings are those in which everyone participates, so don't let one or two people dominate your meeting while others doodle on their notepads. As you move through your agenda, stop at the end of each item, summarize what you understand to be the feelings of the group, and state the important points made during the discussion.

At the conclusion of the meeting, tie up the loose ends. Either summarize the general conclusion of the group or list the suggestions. Wrapping things up ensures that all participants agree on the outcome and gives people a chance to clear up any misunderstandings. Before the meeting breaks up, briefly review who has agreed to do what by what date.

As soon as possible after the meeting, the leader gives all participants a copy of the minutes or notes, showing recommended actions, schedules, and responsibilities. The minutes will remind everyone of what took place and will provide a reference for future actions.

Like leaders, participants have responsibilities during meetings. If you've been included in the group, try to contribute to both the subject of the meeting and the smooth interaction of the participants. Use your listening skills and powers of observation to size up the interpersonal dynamics of the people; then adapt your behavior to help the group achieve its goals. Speak up if you have something useful to say, but don't monopolize the discussion. To review the tasks that contribute to productive meetings, see this chapter's Checklist for Meetings.

Cuban immigrant Fernando Espinosa, CEO and founder of Andes Chemical of Miami, believes "you've got to work for a living; you might as well do it right." This Hispanic Business *magazine's Entrepreneur of the Year believes "empowerment and employee involvement are the bonds that keep morale high and employees motivated."*

On the Job
SOLVING A COMMUNICATION DILEMMA AT ROCKPORT

Many executives shook their heads over John Thorbeck's idea of shutting down the entire Rockport operation so that everyone could attend a two-day meeting. They were even more baffled when they arrived at the cavernous distribution center where the meeting was held. Instead of finding an agenda, a set of reading materials, or a keynote speaker, they were confronted by hundreds of chairs, loosely arranged in a circle. They also found large, empty sheets of paper; a pile of felt-tip markers; several rolls of masking tape; and 12 computers.

Nobody knew quite what to expect when Harrison Owen, a consultant hired by Thorbeck, stepped into the center of the circle and began to talk. Rockport was holding an "open-space meeting," he explained, and what happened during the next two days was up to the participants. The rules were simple: Anyone who felt "passionate" about a business-related topic should step forward, announce the topic, write it on one of the sheets of paper, and tack it on the wall. The company's 350 managers and employees would then sign up to discuss the topics that interested them. The employee who initiated a particular idea would be responsible for leading the discussion in his or her group and for recording the minutes of that meeting.

Before leaving the circle, Owen outlined one more rule: "The Law of Two Feet." All discussions were voluntary, he said, so anyone who was bored, not learning anything, or not able to contribute information should simply walk out. Allowing people to leave any group at any time would serve as a safeguard against discussion leaders who acted pompous or self-important.

After Owen made his way out of the circle, the room was silent for a time. In the words of Keith Mathis, director of distribution, "I thought the meeting had ended right there. With so much of the top brass around, I fully expected that no one would write anything down. But one person rose tentatively, then another, and soon it was like ants going to sugar." One employee introduced the topic of compensation policy; another proposed a discussion of office politics; a third wanted to talk about reducing paperwork.

What had begun as a leaderless, agendaless meeting soon turned into a series of smaller meetings, each with a real sense of purpose. More than 60 topics were tacked to the wall, and Rockport personnel eagerly signed up for the groups of their choice. The hottest topics drew 150 people, but even the smallest group had at least 5 participants. After each group met, its leader entered the results and recommendations into one of the 12 computers.

John Thorbeck knew that coming up with ideas was only the first step in releasing the company's potential. The next step was following through to see that the ideas were implemented. Rockport managers didn't have to worry about supervising this part of the process: The energized work force got busy right after the meeting. All the recorded suggestions were assembled into a book, and many people who had led discussion groups went on to establish committees that put the recommended changes into practice.

Both large and small changes came about as a result of the meeting. Thanks to ideas contributed by people from sales, production, purchasing, and merchandising, the company found a way to cut its purchasing cycle and save $4 million. A security guard suggested a new line of shoes that is expected to bring in $20 million in annual sales. In addition, Rockport installed an e-mail system, hired a training specialist, and published an employee directory.

As effective as it was for Rockport, the open-space meeting isn't appropriate for every situation or every company. For example, an open-space meeting isn't a good way to implement a new word-processing system. It's also unlikely to yield results when top management wants to control the process and the outcome. But it can help when an organization wants to examine such open-ended questions as "What should we be doing?" and "How can we feel more involved and alive at work?"[19]

Your Mission: As John Thorbeck's executive assistant, you handle a wide range of assignments that put you in daily contact with managers and employees at all levels of the company. Oral communication skills are vitally important to your success in this key role. Choose the best alternative for handling the following situations, and be prepared to explain why your choice is best.

1. One of the employees who works at the distribution center comes to you with the following complaint: "I told my supervisor that I could do my job better if he would arrange to adjust the lighting over my work area. It's so dark that I can hardly see what I'm doing. I know I could work faster if I could see without squinting and straining my eyes. Now you'd think that with everybody pushing to increase productivity, the supervisor would jump at the chance to boost my output, wouldn't you? But what does he do? He says, 'Hey, try bifocals.' It's a big joke to him. I don't think it's fair that people like me have to be held back by people like him, who are too lazy or too cheap to change the lighting." Which of the following remarks is the best way to begin your reply to the employee's complaint?
   a. "It sounds as though you and your supervisor don't see eye to eye on this issue."
   b. "I can see why you're provoked. I'd be annoyed too if somebody treated me that way."
   c. "Maybe your supervisor has a good point. I think you should have your eyes checked and see if that might be the problem."
   d. "I'd like to take a look at the situation. Let's go to your workstation right now so I can get a better idea of the lighting conditions there."

2. A benefits expert from the human resources department has asked you to attend a meeting and answer questions about using open-space meetings within departments that have fewer than 20 people. The benefits specialist launches the meeting by summarizing a variety of concerns about how small groups might react to open-space meetings. His comments last about 15 minutes. After responding to these points, you throw the meeting open to additional questions from the group. One employee stands up, crosses his arms in front of his chest, and says, "How do we know that management will allow us enough time to hold this kind of meeting when a department like ours sees the need to address important issues?" The question seems straightforward, but the employee's tone of voice strikes you as being belligerent. His posture is aggressive, and he has a sneer on his face. How would you interpret his question?
   a. The employee is implying that management will not allow departmental employees to take time from their regular duties to hold open-space meetings when important issues should be addressed.
   b. The employee is simply trying to learn about management's attitude toward future open-space meetings around the company.
   c. The employee is implying that Rockport should encourage employees to take time from their regular duties to hold open-space meetings every week or two.
   d. The employee wants to know whether future open-space meetings to address important issues will be long or short.

3. John Thorbeck has asked you to explain the electronic mail system to a new manager who will be running the company's accounting department. The manager is expected to exchange e-mail messages about accounting practices with people in other departments and other locations, so you want to be sure that he fully understands the system's details and will be able to use it. Which of the following versions would provide the best structure for this interview?
   a. Version One

      1. Overview of e-mail and Rockport's reasons for adopting it
      2. Feature-by-feature description of the e-mail system
      3. Description of accounting department's use of e-mail
      4. Problems the manager might encounter in learning the e-mail system
      5. Questions the manager might have about the system

b. Version Two

1. Do you have any experience with e-mail systems?
2. What advantages and disadvantages do you see in using e-mail to communicate internally?
3. If you were designing an e-mail system, what features would you include?
4. What steps will you take to ensure that the e-mail system is used throughout your department?
5. How will you deal with technical problems that might arise when you use the system?

c. Version Three

1. The problem: Employees waste a lot of time waiting for memos to arrive in the interoffice mail.
2. Background: Rockport implemented e-mail to eliminate paper memos.
3. Objectives: To boost productivity and slash the time needed to send and receive messages.
4. Alternatives: Various types of e-mail systems were evaluated (give a description and the pros and cons of each approach).
5. Solution: Give key features of selected system.
6. Next steps: Discuss manager's role in using e-mail in his department.
7. Answer manager's questions.

d. Version Four

1. Conclusions: Show how e-mail saves a lot of time and paper.
2. Supporting details: Discuss specific time-saving features of the system, and mention how much paper is saved in a typical week, month, or year.
3. External evidence: Introduce facts about how other companies have used e-mail systems to speed internal communication.
4. Concerns: Bring out specific fears others have expressed about e-mail systems.

4. Some Rockport employees have been pushing the company to adopt a corporate statement of goals. In response, John Thorbeck has decided to call a companywide meeting to discuss goals. Which purpose should Thorbeck focus on during the meeting?
   a. Purpose: To find out about competitors' goals and determine whether they are appropriate for Rockport
   b. Purpose: To inform employees of his intention to evaluate all employees on the basis of their contributions to corporate goals
   c. Purpose: To decide which employees should be asked to come to a meeting about corporate goals
   d. Purpose: To reach agreement about Rockport's primary corporate goals

Critical Thinking Questions

1. Do you believe that you're best at sending written, oral, or nonverbal messages? Why does this form of communication appeal to you? When receiving messages, are you best at reading, listening, or interpreting nonverbal cues? Why do you think this is true?
2. Have you ever made a comment you later regretted? Describe the circumstances of your verbal blunder, and explain the consequences.
3. When communicating across cultures, U.S. businesspeople tend to be impatient. What are the drawbacks of such impatience? How would you suggest dealing with this trait? Explain.
4. When was the last time you negotiated for something? Were you successful in achieving your aims? If you could repeat the experience, what would you do differently? Briefly explain.
5. Should meeting leaders always use a participatory style, or are there some circumstances when this might not be advisable? Explain your answer.
6. During your meeting with members of your project team, one member keeps raising objections to points of style in a rough draft of your group's report. At this rate, you'll be here for hours debating whether to use the word *criteria* or the word *parameter* on page 27. What should you do? Explain your answer.

Exercises

1. Visit the 3M home page on the Internet at <http://www.3m.com>. To gain more information from 3M, write an e-mail message in which you ask two open-ended and two closed-ended questions about products and markets. Print out your e-mail message for submission.
2. Read through the following situations, and think about them from the viewpoint of both participants.
   a. A high school debate coach has scheduled an appointment with the school principal in an attempt to obtain $250 to take her debate team to the state finals in Peoria, Illinois. The team is strong, and she feels that it has a good chance of winning some type of award. However, the school activities budget is limited.
   b. A counselor has scheduled an interview with a company employee who has a long, consistent record of excellent work. Recently, however, the employee has been coming to work late and often appears distracted on the job.
   c. As part of the job-evaluation process and in an attempt to have her civil service position upgraded, an employee has submitted a job description of her work. An evaluator from the civil service administration has scheduled an interview at the job location to discuss the candidate's requested upgrading.

For each participant, what is the general purpose of the interview? What sequence of conversation might best accomplish this purpose? What type of information should be sought or presented? Explain your answers.

3. Attend a campus meeting (preferably a preprofessional organization). Evaluate the meeting with regard to (a) the leader's ability to clearly articulate the meeting's goals, (b) the leader's ability to engage members in a meaningful discussion, (c) the group's dynamics, and (d) the group's listening skills. Prepare a memo summarizing your evaluations.

4. Two of your employees have personal differences that are beginning to interfere with their work. Suggest some ways that you might resolve the conflict. Put your suggestions and explanations into a memo to be submitted.

5. At your department staff meetings one person tends to dominate the discussion, presenting her ideas and ignoring the contributions of others. As department manager, you can see that the more forceful this person becomes, the more others in the group withdraw and the less they contribute to the discussion. How would you encourage more equitable participation? Please explain.

6. Your company is opening a new office in Japan, and you are unfamiliar with Japanese culture and business practices. Suggest some ways you and your co-workers could learn more about the cultural differences that might affect work relationships. Briefly explain your suggestions.

DEVELOPING YOUR INTERNET SKILLS

GOING ONLINE: MEET THE HIGH-TECH WAY, P. 436

Plow through the techno-talk and read the descriptions of various desktop videoconferencing systems. Familiarize yourself with their basic features so that if you encounter a business associate who starts talking about this kind of technology, you'll be able to participate intelligently in the conversation. If you had such a system available to you right now, and if you knew there was another system available to business students at a university across the country, how could you use it to your benefit? What information could you share that you can't share through regular e-mail, file transfers, or usenet or chat groups?

GIVING SPEECHES AND ORAL PRESENTATIONS

O*n the Job*

FACING A COMMUNICATION DILEMMA
AT THE KEYS GROUP

The Key to Giving Speeches

After studying this chapter, you will be able to

Categorize speeches and presentations according to their purpose

Identify the audience characteristics that govern decisions about the style and content of speeches and presentations

Discuss four steps required in planning a speech or presentation

Develop an introduction, a body, and a close for a long formal presentation

Select, design, and use visual aids that are appropriate for various types of speeches and presentations

Explain techniques you can use to improve your public-speaking skills

"Acceptance in the community is the key," says Brady Keys Jr. His company—the Keys Group—operates 11 KFC fast-food restaurants in Georgia. With annual sales of more than $7 million, the Keys Group ranks among the most respected African American–owned businesses in the country.

When Keys started out in the restaurant business nearly 30 years ago, he realized that good food was only half the battle. Consumers have hundreds of fast-food outlets to choose from, all with similar menus. If you want the public to eat at your restaurant instead of the one across the street, you have to do something extra.

For Brady Keys, the extra ingredient has been personal charisma. A former all-pro defensive halfback for the Pittsburgh Steelers, Keys has used his forceful personality along with expert speaking skills to inspire both investors and employees and to build a presence in the communities in which he does business. Today, he's a well known and highly respected member of the business community, but winning acceptance hasn't been a fast or an easy process.

Keys realized that if he wanted to succeed in business, he'd have to gain people's respect. He'd have to persuade bankers to lend him money and big companies to do business with him. He'd have to convince employees to work hard and customers to trust him. But how? If you were Keys, whether you were addressing a large crowd or an audience of one, what would you need to know about preparing, developing, and delivering speeches? Can improving your speaking skills really lead to the success that Keys has realized?[1]

S*PEAKING AND PRESENTING IN A BUSINESS ENVIRONMENT*

As Brady Keys will tell you, giving speeches and oral presentations can be an integral part of your business career. Chances are you'll have an opportunity to deliver a number of speeches and presentations throughout your career. You may not speak before large audi-

As president of the Keys Group, Brady Keys Jr. is responsible for addressing many different kinds of audiences. Whether he is explaining market trends to colleagues, motivating employees, or persuading investors, his speeches and presentations are successful because he focuses on his audiences and on making his ideas as clear and interesting as possible.

The amount of audience interaction varies from presentation to presentation, depending on your purpose.

ences of employees or the media, but you'll certainly be expected to present ideas to your colleagues, make sales presentations to potential customers, or engage in other kinds of spoken communication. For most speeches and formal presentations, you'll follow three general steps:

1. Prepare to speak (by defining your purpose, analyzing your audience, and planning your speech's content, length, and style)
2. Develop your speech or presentation (including the introduction, body, close, question-and-answer period, and visual aids)
3. Deliver your speech or presentation

PREPARING TO SPEAK

Preparing speeches and oral presentations is much like preparing any other message: You define your purpose, analyze your audience, and plan how to present your points. However, because speeches and presentations are delivered orally under relatively public circumstances, they require a few special communication techniques. A speech is a one-shot event; your audience cannot leaf back through pages to review something you said earlier. For this reason, you must make sure audience members will hear what you say and remember it.

Define Your Purpose

Speeches and presentations can be categorized according to their purpose, which helps you determine content, style, and audience participation. The four basic categories are to inform, to persuade, to motivate, and to entertain. Here are sample statements of purpose for business speeches:

- To inform the accounting department of the new remote data-access policy
- To explain to the executive committee the financial ramifications of OmniGroup's takeover offer
- To persuade potential customers that our bank offers the best commercial banking services for their needs
- To motivate the sales force to close 10 percent more business this quarter

Many of your business speeches and presentations will be informative, and if you're involved in a marketing or sales position, you'll need to do persuasive presentations as well. Motivational speeches tend to be more specialized. Many companies bring in outside speakers who specialize in motivational speaking. Entertainment speeches are perhaps the rarest in the business world, and they are usually limited to after-dinner speeches and speeches at conventions or retreats. But no matter which kind of speech you plan to make, it will always start with understanding your audience.

Analyze Your Audience

The nature of the audience affects your strategy for achieving your purpose.

Gear the content, organization, and style of your message to the audience's size, background, and attitude.

Once you have your purpose firmly in mind, you should think about another basic element of your speech or presentation: your audience. As Brady Keys points out, analyzing your audience is an important step because you'll be gearing the style and content of your speech to your audience's needs and interests. When you're preparing to speak, be sure to review the discussion of audience analysis in Chapter 5. Of course, for even more insight into audience evaluation (including emotional and cultural issues) consult a good public-speaking textbook.

If you're involved in selecting the audience, you'll certainly have information about their characteristics. However, you'll often be speaking to a group of people you know very little about. You'll have a much better chance of achieving your purpose if you investigate the au-

---

CHECKLIST FOR AUDIENCE ANALYSIS

A. Audience Size and Composition
1. Estimate how many people will attend.
2. Consider whether they have some political, religious, professional, or other affiliation in common.
3. Analyze the mix of men and women, age ranges, socioeconomic and ethnic groups, occupations, and geographical regions represented.

B. Probable Audience Reaction
1. Analyze why audience members are attending the speech or presentation.
2. Determine the audience's general attitude toward the topic.
   - a. Decide whether the audience is very interested, moderately interested, or unconcerned.
   - b. Review how the audience has reacted to similar issues in the past.
   - c. Determine which facets of the subject are most likely to appeal to the audience.
   - d. Decide whether portions of your message will create problems for any members of the audience.
3. Analyze the mood that people will be in when you speak to them: tired from listening to other presentations like yours or fresh because your presentation comes early in the agenda, interested in hearing a unique presentation, restless from sitting too long in one position and needing a minute to stretch.
4. Figure out which sort of backup information will most impress the audience: technical data, statistical comparisons, cost figures, historical information, generalizations, demonstrations, samples, and so on.
5. Predict audience response.
   - a. List ways that the audience will benefit from your message.
   - b. Formulate an idea of the most desirable audience reaction and the best possible result

(what you want the audience to believe or to do afterward).
   - c. Anticipate possible objections or questions.
   - d. Analyze the worst thing that might happen and how you might respond.

C. Level of Audience Understanding
1. Determine whether the audience already knows something about the subject.
   - a. Analyze whether everybody has about the same amount of knowledge.
   - b. Consider whether the audience is familiar with your vocabulary.
2. Estimate whether everybody is equally capable of understanding the message.
3. Decide what background information the audience will need to understand the subject.
4. Think about the mix of general concepts and specific details you will need to explain.
5. Consider whether the subject involves routine, recurring information or an unfamiliar topic.

D. Audience Relationship with the Speaker
1. Analyze how this audience usually reacts to speakers.
2. Determine whether the audience is likely to be friendly, open-minded, or hostile toward your purpose in making the speech or presentation.
3. Decide how the audience is likely to respond to you.
   - a. Analyze what the audience expects from you.
   - b. Think about your past interactions with the audience.
   - c. Consider your relative status.
   - d. Consider whether the audience has any biases that might work against you.
   - e. Take into account the audience's probable attitude toward the organization you represent.
4. Decide which aspects of your background are most likely to build credibility.

---

dience's characteristics before you show up to speak. Ask your host or some other contact person for help with audience analysis, and supplement that information with some informed estimates of your own. The Checklist for Audience Analysis summarizes these points.

Plan Your Speech or Presentation

Planning an oral message is similar to planning a written message: You establish the main idea, organize an outline, estimate the appropriate length, and decide on the most effective style.

Establishing the Main Idea

What is the main idea, or theme, that you want to convey to the audience? Look for a one-sentence generalization that links your subject and purpose to the audience's

The main idea points up how the audience can benefit from your message.

General H. Norman Schwarzkopf was the military commander of the allied liberation of Kuwait from Iraqi occupation. Now retired from the military, he's a consultant for NBC News and makes frequent speeches, highlighting his perspective on the Persian Gulf War. A direct and forceful speaker, Schwarzkopf advices you to catch the audience's interest by clearly spelling out your main idea.

Structure a short speech or presentation like a letter or a memo; organize long speeches and presentations like formal reports.

Use a clear, direct organization to accommodate your listeners' limitations.

Use an outline as your "script," but be prepared to deviate in response to audience feedback.

frame of reference, much as an advertising slogan points out how a product can benefit consumers:

- Demand for low-calorie, high-quality frozen foods will increase because of basic social and economic trends.
- Reorganizing the data-processing department will lead to better service at a lower cost.
- We should build a new plant in Texas to reduce operating costs and to capitalize on growing demand in the Southwest.
- The new health plan reduces our costs by 12 percent while maintaining quality coverage.

Each of these statements puts a particular slant on the subject, one that is positive and directly related to the audience's interests. This sort of "you" attitude helps keep the audience's attention and convinces people that your points are relevant.

Organizing an Outline

With a well-crafted main idea to guide you, you can begin to outline your speech or presentation. This outline will be affected by your subject, your purpose, and your audience, as well as by the time allotted for your presentation. If you have ten minutes or less to deliver your message, organize your thoughts much as you would for a letter or a brief memo. Use the direct approach if the subject involves routine information or good news; use the indirect approach if the subject involves bad news or persuasion. Plan your introduction to arouse interest and to give a preview of what's to come. For the body of the presentation, be prepared to explain the who, what, when, where, why, and how of your subject. In the final paragraph or two, review the points you've made, and close with a statement that will help your audience remember the subject of your speech (Figure 18.1).

Long speeches and presentations are organized like reports (see Chapter 13 for specific suggestions). If the purpose is to entertain, motivate, or inform, use direct order and a structure imposed naturally by the subject (importance, sequence, chronology, spatial orientation, geography, category—as discussed in Chapter 13). If the purpose is to analyze, persuade, or collaborate, organize your material around conclusions and recommendations or around a logical argument. Use direct order if the audience is receptive and indirect if you expect resistance. Regardless of the length of your speech or presentation, bear in mind that simplicity of organization is especially useful in oral communication.

A carefully prepared outline may be more than just the starting point for composing a speech or presentation. If you plan to deliver your presentation from notes rather than from a written text, your outline can also become your final "script." The headings on this type of outline should be complete sentences or lengthy phrases rather than one- or two-word topic headings. Many speakers also include notes that indicate where visual aids will be used. You might want to write out the transitional sentences you'll use to connect main points. Experienced speakers often use a two-column format, which separates the "stage directions" from the content (Figure 18.2, page 446).

Presentation software can help you organize your speech. Packages such as PowerPoint and Freelance Graphics include special outline tools that simplify organizing and formatting your outline. Both provide a variety of ways to print notes and handouts. For example, PowerPoint allows you to view all your overhead transparencies and slides in thumbnail to help you choose the items you want to discuss and display.

Of course, you may have to adjust your organization in response to feedback from your audience, especially if your purpose is to collaborate. You can plan ahead by thinking of several organizational possibilities (based on "what if" assumptions about your audience's reactions). Then if someone says something that undercuts your planned approach, you can switch smoothly to another one.

Estimating Length

Time for speeches and presentations is often strictly regulated, so you'll need to tailor your material to the available time. You can use your outline to estimate how much time your

A human resources manager used this outline for a brief speech he delivered to persuade a group of executives to invest in an on-site fitness center for employees.

Figure 18.1
In-Depth Critique: Sample Outline for a Brief Speech

PHYSICAL FITNESS IS GOOD FOR BUSINESS

Purpose: To convince company officers to approve an on-site fitness center.

I. Introduction

Mention the words *computer programmer*, and the picture that comes to mind is a person sitting in a cubicle and pounding away at a keyboard for 12 or more hours a day. This may be the stereotype, but it is outdated. Programmers and employees in general are more and more aware that physical activity makes them more healthy, happy and productive. Corporations have also learned the benefits of having healthy, fit employees.

II. The most obvious improvement is in lowered health costs. [slides]

A. People who are physically active generally are healthier and take fewer sick days.

B. Increased activity leads to better general health and fewer visits to the doctor, which means lower health insurance costs for the company and less absenteeism.

C. Better physical fitness results in a reduction in work-related injuries.

III. Improving employees' physical fitness increases company profitability.

A. Studies show that improved physical fitness increases employee productivity. [slide]

B. Physical activity also increases creativity.

IV. A survey of college seniors showed fringe benefits to be the second most important factor (after salary) **in choosing a company.**

V. Conclusion: Installing an on-site fitness center makes good business sense.

This introduction will arouse interest and preview what is coming in the presentation.

Items II, III, and IV support the main idea (that an on-site fitness center would be a good investment).

The conclusion will summarize all the evidence that makes the installation of the center such a good business decision.

---

speech or presentation will take. The average speaker can deliver about 125 to 150 words a minute (or roughly 7,500 to 9,000 words an hour), which corresponds to 20 to 25 double-spaced, typed pages of text an hour. The average paragraph is about 125 to 150 words in length, so most of us can speak at a rate of about one paragraph a minute.

Say you want to make three basic points. In a 10-minute speech, you could take about 2 minutes to explain each point, using roughly two paragraphs for each. If you devoted a minute each to the introduction and the conclusion, you would have 2 minutes left over to interact with the audience. If you had an hour, however, you could spend the first 5 minutes introducing the presentation, establishing rapport with the audience, providing background information, and giving an overview of your topic. In the next 30 to 40 minutes,

The average speaker can deliver about 125 to 150 words in a minute.

Figure 18.2
In-Depth Critique: Excerpt from Sample Outline with Delivery Notes

This excerpt is taken from a presentation that was made to persuade a company's marketing department to reassess its strategies.

The introduction is geared to arouse interest.

Outline items are in complete sentences.

Each slide noted here highlights a point being made and can even be used by the speaker as a prompt during delivery.

The transition leads listeners to the second main point: a review of marketing techniques currently being used.

Slide 1:
Text
Overview
Slide 2:
Web site screen
Highlight 1st point
Slide 3:
Bar chart
Internet usage, 1975 to present
Slide 4:
Bar chart
Internet advertising, 1985 to present
Slide 5:
Table
Current costs versus Internet marketing estimates
Slide 6:
Text
Preview second point

INTRO: Have our marketing techniques become stale?

I. The Internet and World Wide Web open up 24 B/B totally new marketing possibilities.

   A. Usage of the Internet has mushroomed since its introduction.

      1. The number of business advertising outlets on the Internet has increased significantly in the last few years.

      2. Selling products via the Internet is gaining popularity.

   B. Marketing via the Internet can increase profitability.

Transition: Compared with the excitement of the Internet, our marketing techniques seem dated.

you could explain each of the three points, spending about 10 to 13 minutes on each point (the equivalent of five or six printed pages). Your conclusion might take another 3 to 5 minutes. The remaining 10 to 20 minutes would then be available for responding to questions and comments from the audience.

Be sure that your subject, purpose, and organization are compatible with the time available.

Which is better, the 10-minute speech or the hour-long presentation? If your speech doesn't have to fit into a specified time slot, the answer depends on your subject, your audience's attitude and knowledge, and the relationship you have with your audience. For a simple, easily accepted message, 10 minutes may be enough. On the other hand, if your subject is complex or your audience is skeptical, you'll probably need more time. Don't squeeze a complex presentation into a period that is too brief, and don't draw out a simple talk any longer than necessary.

Deciding on Style
Another important element in your planning is the style you choose. Will you present a formal speech in an impressive setting, with professionally produced visual aids? Or will you lead a casual, roll-up-your-sleeves working session? Choose your style to fit the occasion. The size of the audience, the subject, your purpose, your budget, and the time available for preparation all determine the style.

Use a casual style for small groups; use a formal style for large groups and important events.

In general, if you're speaking to a relatively small group, you can use a casual style that encourages audience participation. A small conference room, with the audience seated around a table, may be appropriate. Use simple visual aids. Invite the audience to interject comments. Deliver your remarks in a conversational tone, using notes to jog your memory if necessary.

On the other hand, if you're addressing a large audience and the event is an important one, you'll want to establish a more formal atmosphere. A formal style is well suited to announcements about mergers or acquisitions, new products, financial results, and other business milestones. During these formal presentations, the speakers generally stand behind a lectern on a stage or platform and use a microphone so that their remarks can be heard throughout the room. These speeches are often accompanied by multimedia presentations showcasing major products, technological breakthroughs, and other information that the speakers want audience members to remember.

DEVELOPING YOUR SPEECH OR PRESENTATION

Developing a major speech or presentation is much like writing a formal report, with one important difference: You need to adjust your technique to an oral communication channel. This channel presents both an opportunity and a challenge.

The opportunity lies in the interaction that is possible between you and the audience. When you speak before a group, you can receive information as well as transmit it. So you can adjust both the content and the delivery of your message as you go along, editing your speech or presentation to make it clearer and more compelling. Instead of simply expressing your ideas, you can draw out the audience's ideas and use them to reach a mutually acceptable conclusion.

To realize the benefits of oral communication, though, you need to plan carefully. The challenge of this channel is controlling what happens. As you develop each part of your speech or presentation, stop and think about how you plan to deliver the information. The more you plan to interact with your audience, the less control you'll have. Halfway through your presentation a comment from someone in the audience might force you to shift topics. If you can anticipate such shifts, you'll have a chance to prepare for them.

How formal speeches and presentations differ from formal reports:
- *More interaction with the audience*
- *Use of nonverbal cues to express meaning*
- *Less control of content*
- *Greater need to help the audience stay on track*

The Introduction

You'll have a lot to accomplish during the first few minutes of your speech or presentation, including arousing your audience's interest in your topic, establishing your credibility, and preparing the audience for what will follow. That's why preparing the introduction often requires a disproportionate amount of your attention.

The introduction captures attention, inspires confidence, and previews the contents.

Arousing Interest

Some subjects are naturally more interesting than others. If you will be discussing a matter of profound significance that will personally affect the members of your audience, chances are they'll listen regardless of how you begin. All you really have to do is announce your topic ("Today I'd like to announce the reorganization of the company").

The best approach to dealing with an uninterested audience is to appeal to human nature. Encourage people to take the subject personally. Show them how they'll be affected as individuals. You might plan to begin your address to new clerical employees like this:

Connect the topic to the listeners' needs and interests.

If somebody offered to give you $200,000 in exchange for $5 per week, would you be interested? That's the amount you can expect to collect during your retirement years if you choose to contribute to the voluntary pension plan. During the next two weeks, you will have to decide whether you want to participate. Although for most of you retirement is many years away, this is an important financial decision. During the next 20 minutes, I hope to give you the information you need to make that decision intelligently.

Make sure your introduction matches the tone of your speech or presentation. If the occasion is supposed to be fun, you may begin with something light; but if you're talking business to a group of executives, don't waste their time with cute openings. Avoid jokes and personal anecdotes when you're discussing a serious problem. If you're giving a rou-

As founder of the consulting firm Success Strategies, Lynda R. Paulson addresses the "people needs" of companies of all sizes. A dynamic speaker, Paulson advises that you establish your credibility early on, including your listeners' acceptance of you and their respect for your opinion.

tine oral report, don't be overly dramatic. Most of all, be natural. Nothing turns off the average audience faster than a trite, staged beginning.

Building Credibility

One of the chief drawbacks of overblown openings is that they damage the speaker's credibility, and building credibility is probably even more important than arousing interest. A speaker with high credibility is more persuasive than a speaker with low credibility.[2] So it's important to establish your credentials—and quickly; people will decide within a few minutes whether you're worth listening to.[3] You want the audience to like you as a person and to respect your opinion, and you have to plan for this while you're developing your speech.

Establishing credibility is relatively easy if you're speaking to a familiar, open-minded audience. The difficulty comes when you try to earn the confidence of strangers, especially those predisposed to be skeptical or antagonistic.

One way to handle the problem is to let someone else introduce you. That person can present your credentials so that you won't appear boastful, but make sure the person introducing you doesn't exaggerate your qualifications. If Brady Keys were to address a group of fast-food franchisees on inner-city operations, some of them might bristle at his being billed as the world's only authority on the subject.

> **Without boasting, explain why you are qualified to speak on the subject.**

If you plan to introduce yourself, keep your comments simple. At the same time, don't be afraid to mention your accomplishments. Your listeners will be curious about your qualifications, so tell them briefly who you are and why you're there. Generally speaking, one or two aspects of your background are all you need to mention: your position in an organization, your profession, and the name of your company. You might plan to say something like this:

I'm Karen Whitney, a market research analyst with Information Resources Corporation. For the past five years, I've specialized in studying high-technology markets. Your director of engineering, John LaBarre, has asked me to brief you on recent trends in computer-aided design so that you'll have a better idea of how to direct your R&D efforts.

This speaker would establish credibility by tying her credentials to the purpose of her presentation. By mentioning her company's name, her position, and the name of the audience's boss, she will let her listeners know immediately that she's qualified to tell them something they need to know. She connects her background to their concerns.

Previewing the Presentation

> **Let the audience know what lies ahead.**

Brady Keys strongly believes that you need to "tell them what you're going to tell them." Giving your audience a preview of what's ahead adds to your authority and, more important, helps people understand your message. In an oral presentation, the speaker provides the framework. Your introduction will summarize your main idea, identify the supporting points, and indicate the order in which you'll develop those points. Once you've established the framework, you can move into the body of the presentation, confident that the audience will understand how the individual facts and figures relate to your main idea.

The Body

> **Limit the body to three or four main points.**

The bulk of your speech or presentation is devoted to a discussion of the three or four main points in your outline. Use the same organizational patterns you'd use in a letter, memo, or report, but keep things simple. Your goals are (1) to make sure the structure of your speech or presentation will be clear and (2) to make sure your speech will keep your audience's attention.

Emphasizing Structure

To show how ideas are related in an oral presentation, you rely more on words than you do in a written a report. For the small links between sentences and paragraphs, one or two transitional words are enough: *therefore, because, in addition, in contrast, moreover, for example, consequently, nevertheless, finally.* To link major sections of the speech or presentation, you need complete sentences or paragraphs, such as "Now that we've reviewed the problem, let's take a look at some solutions." Every time you shift topics, stress the connection between ideas. Summarize what's been said, and then preview what's to come.

The longer your presentation, the more important the transitions become. If you will be presenting many ideas, the audience will have trouble absorbing them and seeing the relationship among them. Listeners need clear transitions to guide them to the most important points. Furthermore, they need transitions to pick up any ideas they may have missed. If you plan to repeat key ideas in the transitions, you can compensate for lapses in the audience's attention. When you actually deliver your speech, you might also want to call attention to the transitions by using gestures, changing your tone of voice, or introducing a visual aid.

Help your audience follow your presentation

- By summarizing as you go along
- By emphasizing the transitions from one idea to the next

Holding the Audience's Attention

To communicate your points effectively, you have to maintain the audience's attention. Here are a few tips for developing memorable speeches:

Make a special effort to capture wandering attention.

- *Relate your subject to the audience's needs.* People are interested in things that affect them personally. Plan to present every point in light of the audience's needs and values.
- *Use clear, vivid language.* People become bored quickly when they don't understand the speaker. If your presentation will involve abstract ideas, plan to show how those abstractions are connected with everyday life. Use familiar words, short sentences, and concrete examples.
- *Explain the relationship between your subject and familiar ideas.* Plan to show how your subject relates to ideas the audience already understands so that you give people a way to categorize and remember your points.[4]

You can also hold the audience's interest by introducing variety into your presentation. One useful technique is to pause occasionally for questions or comments from the audience. This technique helps you determine whether the audience understands key points before you launch into another section; it also gives the audience a chance to switch for a time from listening to participating. Visual aids will also help clarify points and stimulate interest.

Children's book illustrator Chris K. Soentpiet (pronounced "soonpete"), illustrator of Peacebound Trains, The Last Dragon, *and other books, never dreamed he'd be traveling to schools to give inspirational talks, but now he enjoys it. He's learned to enliven speeches with anecdotes from his unique experiences as an adopted child, as a youthful success in a difficult career, as a Korean American, and as one-half of a successful husband-wife business team.*

The Close

The close of a speech or presentation is almost as important as the beginning because audience attention peaks at this point. Plan to devote about 10 percent of the total time to the ending. When developing your conclusion, begin by telling listeners that you're about to finish so that they'll make one final effort to listen intently. Don't be afraid to sound obvious. Consider saying something like "in conclusion" or "to sum it all up." You want people to know that this is the home stretch.

The close should leave a strong and lasting impression.

Restating the Main Points

Once you've planned how to get everyone's attention, you'll repeat your main idea. Be sure to emphasize what you want the audience to do or think. Then state the key motivating factor. Reinforce your theme by repeating the three or four main supporting points. A few sentences are generally enough to refresh people's memories. Here's how one speaker ended a presentation on the company's executive compensation program:

Summarize the main idea, and restate the main points.

We can all be proud of the way our company has grown. If we want to continue that growth, however, we will have to adjust our executive compensation program to reflect competitive practices. If we don't, our best people will look for opportunities elsewhere.

GOING ONLINE
SPEAK LIKE A PRO
The Speaker's Companion Reference Page offers leads to dozens of sites containing valuable help for business speakers and presenters. If you're stuck for a topic, need a good quote, want some speaking advice, need ideas and support for your ideas, want to link your topic to current events overseas, or just want to browse the latest tips or borrow some techniques from the "experts," click on a few of the links provided here. Your thoughts will soon be filled with new material and renewed enthusiasm for your speaking project.

http://www.lm.com/~chipp/spkrref.htm

Be certain that everyone agrees on the outcome and understands what should happen next.

Be sure your close is natural as well as positive.

In summary, our survey has shown that we need to do four things to improve executive compensation:

- Increase the overall level of compensation.

- Install a cash bonus program.

- Offer a variety of stock-based incentives.

- Improve our health insurance and pension benefits.

By making these improvements, we can help our company cross the threshold of growth into the major leagues.

The speaker repeats his recommendations and then concludes with a memorable statement that motivates the audience to take action.

Describing the Next Steps

Some speeches and presentations require the audience to reach a decision or agree to take specific action. In such cases the close provides a clear wrap-up. If the audience agrees on an issue covered in the presentation, plan to review the consensus in a sentence or two. If not, make the lack of consensus clear by saying something like "We seem to have some fundamental disagreement on this question." Then you'll be ready to suggest a method of resolving the differences.

If you expect any action to occur, you must explain who is responsible for doing what. One effective technique is to list the action items, with an estimated completion date and the name of the person responsible. Plan to present this list in a visual aid that can be seen by the entire audience, and ask each person on the list to agree to accomplish his or her assigned task by the target date. This public commitment to action is the best insurance that something will happen.

If the required action is likely to be difficult, make sure everyone understands the problems involved. You don't want people to leave the presentation thinking their tasks will be easy, only to discover later that the jobs are quite demanding. If that happens, they may become discouraged and fail to complete their assignments. You'll want everyone to have a realistic attitude and to be prepared to handle whatever arises. So when planning your presentation, use the close to alert people to potential difficulties.

Ending on a Positive Note

Make sure that your final remarks are enthusiastic and memorable. Even if parts of your speech are downbeat, plan to close on a positive note. You might stress the benefits of action or express confidence in the listeners' ability to accomplish the work ahead. An alternative is to end with a question or a statement that will leave your audience thinking.

Remember that your final words round out the presentation. You'll want to leave the audience with a satisfied feeling, a feeling of completeness. The close is not the place to introduce new ideas or to alter the mood of the presentation. Although you want to close on a positive note, avoid using a staged finale. Keep it natural.

The Question-and-Answer Period

Along with the introduction, body, and close, include in your speech or presentation an opportunity for questions and answers. Otherwise, you might just as well write a report. If you aren't planning to interact with the audience, you're wasting the chief advantage of an oral format.

Specifics about handling questions from the audience are discussed in this chapter under the heading "Handling Questions." In general, the important things to consider when you're developing your speech are the nature and timing of audience interaction. Responding to questions and comments during the presentation can interrupt the flow of your argument and reduce your control of the situation. If you'll be addressing a large group, particularly a hostile or an unknown group, questions can be dangerous. Your best bet in this case is to ask people to hold their questions until after you have concluded your remarks. On the other hand, if you're working with a small group and need to draw out ideas, encourage comments from the audience throughout the presentation.

Encourage questions throughout your speech if you are addressing a small group, but ask a large audience to defer questions until later.

The Visual Aids

Whether soliciting funds or outlining a company's strategy, Brady Keys uses visual aids to create interest and to clarify his ideas. From a purely practical standpoint, visuals are a convenience for the speaker, who can use them as a tool for remembering the details of the message (no small feat in a lengthy presentation); novice speakers also like visual aids because they draw audience attention away from the speaker. More important, visual aids dramatically increase the audience's ability to absorb and remember information.

Visual aids help both the speaker and the audience remember the important points.

Designing and Presenting Visual Aids

Two types of visual aids are used to supplement speeches and presentations. Text visuals consist of words and help the audience follow the flow of ideas. Because text visuals are simplified outlines of your presentation, you can use them to summarize and preview the message and to signal major shifts in thought. On the other hand, graphic visual aids illustrate the main points. They help the audience grasp numerical data and other information that would be hard to follow if presented orally.

Two kinds of visual aids:
- Text visuals help listeners follow the flow of ideas.
- Graphic visuals present and emphasize important facts.

Simplicity is the key to effectiveness when designing both types of visual aids. Because people can't read and listen at the same time, the visual aids have to be simple enough for the audience to understand within a moment or two. As a rule, text visuals are most effective when they consist of no more than six lines, with a maximum of six words on each line. Produce them in large, clear type, using uppercase and lowercase letters, with extra white space between lines of text. Make sure the type is large enough to be seen from any place in the room. Phrase list items in parallel grammatical form. Use telegraphic wording ("Compensation Soars," for example) without being cryptic ("Compensation"); including both a noun and a verb in each item is a good rule of thumb.

Visual aids are counterproductive if the audience can't clearly see or understand them within a few moments.

You can use any of the graphic visuals you might show in a formal report, including line, pie, and bar charts, as well as flowcharts, organization charts, diagrams, maps, drawings, and tables. However, graphic visuals used in oral presentations are simplified versions of those that appear in written documents. Eliminate anything that is not absolutely essential to the message. To help the audience focus immediately on the point of each graphic visual, use headings that state the message in one clear phrase or sentence: "Earnings have increased by 15 percent."

When you present visual aids, you want people to have the chance to read what's there, but you also want them to listen to your explanation:

- Be sure that all members of the audience can see the visual aids.
- Allow the audience time to read a visual aid before you begin your explanation.
- Limit each visual aid to one idea.
- Illustrate only the main points, not the entire presentation.
- Avoid visual aids that conflict with your verbal message.
- Paraphrase the text of your visual aid; don't read it word for word.
- When you've finished discussing the point illustrated by the visual aid, remove it from the audience's view.[5]

The visual aids are there to supplement your words—not the other way around.

Selecting the Right Medium

Visual aids for documents are usually limited to paper. For speeches and presentations, however, you can choose from a variety of media:

Visual aids may be presented in a variety of media.

■ *Handouts.* Even in a presentation, you may choose to distribute sheets of paper bearing an agenda, an outline of the program, an abstract, a written report, or supplementary material such as tables, charts, and graphs. Listeners can keep the handout to remind them of the subject and the main ideas of your presentation. In addition, they can refer to it while you're speaking. Handouts work especially well in informal situations in which the audience takes an active role; they often make their own notes on the handouts. However, handouts can be distracting because people are inclined to read the material rather than listen to you, so many speakers distribute handouts after the presentation.

■ *Chalkboards and whiteboards.* When you're addressing a small group of people and want to draw out their ideas, use a board to list points as they are mentioned. Because visual aids using this medium are produced on the spot, boards provide flexibility. However, they're too informal for some situations.

■ *Flip charts.* Large sheets of paper attached at the top like a tablet can be propped on an easel so that you can flip the pages as you speak. Each chart illustrates or clarifies a point. You might have a few lines from your outline on one, a graph or diagram on another, and so on. By using felt-tip markers of various colors, you can highlight ideas as you go along. Keep it simple: Try to limit each flip-chart page to three or four graphed lines or to five or six points in list format.

■ *Overheads.* One of the most common visual aids in business is the overhead transparency, which can be projected on a screen in full daylight. Because you don't have to dim the lights, you don't lose eye contact with your audience. Transparencies are easy to make using a typed original on regular paper, a copying machine, and a page-size sheet of plastic. Opaque projections are similar to transparencies but do not require as much preparation. You could use an opaque projector to show the audience a photograph or an excerpt from a report or manual.

■ *Slides.* The content of slides may be text, graphics, or pictures. If you're trying to create a polished, professional atmosphere, you might find this approach worthwhile, particularly if you'll be addressing a crowd and don't mind speaking in a darkened room. However, remember that you may need someone to operate the projector and that you'll need to coordinate the slides with your speech. Take a few minutes before your speech to verify that the equipment works correctly.

■ *Computers.* With special projection equipment, a personal computer can be turned into a large-screen "intelligent chalkboard" that allows you to create and modify your visual aids as the presentation unfolds. If you're discussing financial projections, you can type in a new number to show how a change in sales will affect profits. When the presentation is over, you can print out hard copies of the visual aids and distribute them to interested members of the audience. Using this technology, you can prepare a multimedia presentation incorporating photos, sound, video, and animation.[6]

■ *Other visual aids.* In technical or scientific presentations, a sample of a product or material allows the audience to experience your subject directly. Models built to scale are convenient representations of an object. Audiotapes are often used to supplement a slide show or to present a precisely worded and timed message. Filmstrips and movies can capture the audience's attention with color and movement. Television and videotapes are good for showing demonstrations, interviews, and other events. In addition, filmstrips, movies, television, and videotapes can be used as stand-alone vehicles (independent of a speaker) to communicate with dispersed audiences at various times. For example, PepsiCo's CEO, Wayne Calloway, videotapes many of his important presentations and sends them to all the company's operating divisions to keep employees updated on the business.[7]

Table 18.1 summarizes some of the factors to consider when selecting a visual medium.

With all visual aids, the crucial factor is how you use them. Properly integrated into an oral presentation, they can save time, create interest, add variety, make an impression, and illustrate points that are difficult to explain in words alone.

Use visual aids to highlight your spoken words, not as a substitute for them.

Table 18.1	GUIDELINES FOR SELECTING VISUALS					
Visual	**Optimal Audience Size**	**Degree of Formality**	**Design Complexity**	**Equipment and Room Requirements**	**Production Time**	**Cost**
Handouts	Fewer than 110	Informal	Simple	Typed text and photocopying machine	Typing or drawing time; photocopying time	Inexpensive
Boards and flip charts	Fewer than 20	Informal	Simple	Chalkboard or whiteboard or easel and chart, with writing implements	Drawing time only	Inexpensive
Overheads	About 100	Formal or informal	Simple	Text, copy machine, plastic sheets, and projector screen	Drawing or typing time; photocopying time	Inexpensive—unless designed or typeset professionally
Slides	Several hundred	Formal	Anything that can be photographed	Slides, projector, and screen; dim lighting	Design and photographing time; at least 24 hours' production time	More expensive

MASTERING THE ART OF DELIVERY

When you've planned all the parts of your presentation and have your visual aids in hand, you're ready to begin practicing your delivery. Of the four main delivery methods, some are easier to handle than others:

- *Memorizing.* Unless you're a trained actor, avoid memorizing an entire speech, particularly a long one. You're likely to forget your lines. Furthermore, a memorized speech often sounds stiff and stilted. And in many business speaking situations, you'll need to address questions and comments from the audience during your speech, so you have to be flexible and sometimes adjust your speech as you go. On the other hand, memorizing a quotation, an opening paragraph, or a few concluding remarks can bolster your confidence and strengthen your delivery.
- *Reading.* If you're delivering a technical or complex presentation, you may want to read it. Policy statements by government officials are sometimes read because the wording may be critical. If you choose to read your speech, practice enough so that you can still maintain eye contact with the audience. Triple-spaced copy, wide margins, and large type help too. You might even want to include stage cues for yourself, such as *pause, raise hands, lower voice.*
- *Speaking from notes.* Making a presentation with the help of an outline, note cards, or visual aids is probably the most effective and easiest delivery mode. It gives you something to refer to and still allows for eye contact and interaction with the audience. If your listeners look puzzled, you can expand on a point or put it another way. (Note cards are generally preferable to sheets of paper; nervousness is more evident in shaking sheets of paper.)
- *Impromptu speaking.* You might give an impromptu, or unrehearsed, speech in two situations: when you've agreed to speak but have neglected to prepare your remarks or when you're called on to speak unexpectedly. Avoid speaking unprepared unless you've spoken countless times on the same topic or are an extremely good public speaker. When you're asked to speak "off the cuff," take a moment or two to think through what you're going to say. Then avoid the temptation to ramble.

Speaking from notes is generally the best way to handle delivery.

Regardless of which delivery mode you use, be sure that you're thoroughly familiar with the subject. Knowing what you're talking about is the best way to build your self-confidence. It's also helpful to know how you'll approach preparing for successful speaking, delivering the speech, and handling questions.

Getting Ready to Give Your Presentation

Before you speak
- Practice
- Prepare the location

In addition to knowing your material, you can build self-confidence by practicing, especially if you haven't had much experience with public speaking. Even if you practice in front of a mirror, try to visualize the room filled with listeners. Put your talk on tape to check the sound of your voice and your timing, phrasing, and emphasis. If possible, rehearse on videotape to see yourself as your audience will. Go over your visual aids and coordinate them with the talk.

Whenever you can, check the location for your presentation in advance. Look at the seating arrangements, and make sure they're appropriate for your needs. If you want the audience to sit at tables, be sure tables are available. Check the room for outlets that may be needed for your projector or microphone. Locate the light switches and dimmers. If you need a flip-chart easel or a chalkboard, be sure it's on hand. Check for chalk, an eraser, extension cords, and any other small but crucial items you might need.

If you're addressing an audience that doesn't speak your language, consider using an interpreter. Of course, any time you make a speech or presentation to people from other cultures, take into account cultural differences in appearance, mannerisms, and other customs, in addition to adapting the content of your speech. If you are working with an interpreter, the interpreter will be able to suggest appropriate changes for the audience or occasion. When you're addressing a U.S. or Canadian audience with few cultural differences, follow the specific guidelines in this chapter.

Behind the Scenes with Leann Anderson
Improving Your Podium Power

When Leann Anderson prepares a speech, she doesn't worry about whether her audience is going to like her; instead she focuses on whether she will offer useful information to her audience. As the owner of Anderson Business Resources, Anderson helps businesspeople improve their business relationships by showing them how to enhance their image and become better public speakers. Anderson advises her clients to "know as much as possible about your audience." By understanding your audience, "you can create examples specifically for them, personalize your message, avoid sensitive topics, and appeal to the most important issues on their minds."

Anderson learns about her audience by being an active listener—something she believes is an essential skill for successful businesspeople. Whether she is speaking to an audience in Bangkok about how to do business in the United States, consulting with clients on how to project a favorable image, or lecturing to college students on how to survive after they graduate, Anderson always focuses on giving something of value to her audience. She anticipates her audience's needs, carefully selects her topic, does extensive research, organizes her thoughts, and prepares her speeches meticulously. "Too many people wait until the last minute to work on their speeches, and once they've finished writing their rough drafts, they have no time left to edit and revise them."

When Leann Anderson helps businesspeople improve their public-speaking skills, she emphasizes learning as much as possible about the audience they will be addressing.

Anderson advocates being a ruthless editor. "Most of us fall in love with our own words, and our presentations get too long and complicated. A good speech is built on an intriguing introduction, a substantive body, and a memorable conclusion. Eliminate anything that is not truly necessary to make your talk more interesting. Keep sentences simple,

Delivering the Speech

When it's time to deliver the speech, you may feel a bit of stage fright. Most people do, even professional actors. A good way to overcome your fears is to rehearse until you're thoroughly familiar with your material.[8] Communication professionals have suggested other tips:

A little stage fright is normal.

- Prepare more material than necessary. Extra knowledge, combined with a genuine interest in the topic, will boost your confidence.
- Think positively about your audience, yourself, and what you have to say. See yourself as polished and professional, and your audience will too.
- Be realistic about stage fright. After all, even experienced speakers admit that they feel butterflies before they address an audience. A little nervous excitement can actually provide the extra lift that will make your presentation sparkle.
- Use the few minutes while you're arranging your materials, before you actually begin speaking, to tell yourself you're on and you're ready.
- Before you begin speaking, take a few deep breaths.
- Have your first sentence memorized and on the tip of your tongue.
- If your throat is dry, drink some water.
- If you feel that you're losing your audience during the speech, don't panic. Try to pull them back by involving them in the action.
- Use your visual aids to maintain and revive audience interest.
- Keep going. Things usually get better, and your audience will silently be wishing you success.

---

work from an outline if possible, and highlight key points. If you use generalized statements, be sure to follow them with specific examples and facts. Support your points with evidence, anecdotes, and data to strengthen your message and reinforce your position as an expert."

However, being an expert is not enough. "Learn to be conversational. Cultivate the art of small talk—be an interesting person first; then be an expert in your field. When you talk to people, make them feel at ease with you—then they will be in a frame of mind to accept what you have to offer. When writing a speech, use *we* and *you* frequently to make your talk seem like more of a dialogue. Ask yourself, does that sound like something a person would say naturally—you have to sound conversational."

One way to increase your conversational ability is by reading magazines, books, journals, and newspapers. Anderson knows the value of being well-informed when preparing and delivering speeches, so she clips articles, collects meaningful quotes, jots down ideas, and collects words. "Words can distinguish you from others. By using visual words you catch people off guard, and they pay attention to what you have to say. . . . For example, consider the words *seamless* and *embroidered*; both are visual words and have a greater impact than the words *smooth* and *included*. Economy of language is the real key to good communication—that means choosing the best way of saying something to get the desired result."

In fact, getting results is one of the many reasons Anderson's clients seek her advice. "If entrepreneurs knew how much they could improve the health of their businesses by becoming effective public speakers, more of them would jump on the bandwagon. . . . When you are successful as a public speaker, most people will assume you are a successful businessperson too." So Anderson offers this advice: "Fine-tune your public-speaking skills. Be prepared and rehearse more than you think you need. The more you practice, the more confident and relaxed you will be." Anderson cautions speakers to "inject your personality into the speech. Have some fun with it. . . . Stop concentrating on 'will they like me?' and instead focus on 'what will they gain from hearing me?'"

Apply Your Knowledge

1. Using the information in this chapter and the recommendations by Leann Anderson, discuss the meaning of the following quotes:
a. "Speak clearly, if you speak at all; carve every word before you let it fall."—*Oliver Wendell Holmes*
b. "It usually takes more than three weeks to prepare a good impromptu speech."—*Mark Twain*
2. List some of the things you should know about your audience before preparing a speech.

Perhaps the best way to overcome stage fright is to concentrate on your message and your audience, not on yourself. When you're busy thinking about your subject and observing the audience's response, you tend to forget your fears. Even so, as you deliver your presentation, try to be aware of the nonverbal signals you're transmitting. To a great degree, your effectiveness will depend on how you look and sound.

Don't rush the opening.

As you approach the speaker's lectern, breathe deeply, stand up straight, and walk slowly. Face the audience. Adjust the microphone. Count to three slowly; then survey the room. When you find a friendly face, make eye contact and smile. Count to three again; then begin your presentation.[9] Even if you feel nervous inside, this slow, controlled beginning will help you establish rapport.

Use eye contact, posture, gestures, and voice to convey an aura of mastery and to keep your audience's attention.

Once your speech is under way, be particularly careful to maintain eye contact with the audience. Pick out several people positioned around the room, and shift your gaze from one to another. Doing this will make you appear to be sincere, confident, and trustworthy; moreover, it will help you perceive the impression you're creating.

Your posture is also important in projecting the right image. Stand tall, with your weight on both feet and your shoulders back. Avoid gripping the lectern. In fact, you might step out from behind the lectern to help the audience feel more comfortable with you and to express your own comfort and confidence in what you're saying. Use your hands to emphasize your remarks with appropriate gestures. At the same time, vary your facial expressions to make the message more dynamic.

Finally, think about the sound of your voice. Studies indicate that people who speak with low voice tones at a slightly faster than average rate are perceived as being most credible.[10] Speak in a normal, conversational tone but with enough volume so that everyone in the audience can hear you. Try to sound poised and confident, varying your pitch and speaking rate to add emphasis. Don't ramble or use meaningless filler words such as *um, you know, okay,* and *like.* Speak clearly and crisply, articulating all the syllables, and sound enthusiastic about what you're saying.

A. Barry Rand is executive vice president of operations for Xerox. Known as a persuasive and gifted speaker, Rand uses his talents to inspire employees and colleagues. The more familiar you are with your subject, the better, says Rand. Not only will you feel more comfortable during your speech, but your ease will come across as self-confidence.

Handling Questions

Brady Keys believes that preparation is the key to handling questions effectively. Spend time before your speech thinking about the questions that might arise—including abrasive or difficult questions. Then be ready with answers. In fact, some experts recommend that you hold back some dramatic statistics as ammunition for the question-and-answer session.[11] Bear in mind, however, that circumstances may require some changes in the answers you've prepared.

Keep your answers short and to the point.

When someone poses a question, focus your attention on that individual. Pay attention to body language and facial expression to help determine what the person really means. Nod your head to acknowledge the question; then repeat it aloud to confirm your understanding and to ensure that the entire audience has heard it. If the question is vague or confusing, ask for clarification. Then give a simple, direct answer. Don't say more than you need to if you want to have enough time to cover all the questions. If giving an adequate answer would take too long, simply say, "I'm sorry that we don't have time to get into that issue right now, but if you'll see me after the presentation, I'll be happy to discuss it with you." If you don't know the answer, don't pretend that you do. Instead, say something like "I don't have those figures. I'll get them for you as quickly as possible." Remember that you don't have to answer every question that is asked.

Don't let any member of the audience monopolize your attention or turn a question into a debate.

Don't allow one or two people to monopolize the question period. Try to give everyone a chance to participate; call on people from different parts of the room. If the same person keeps angling for attention, say something like "Several other people have questions; I'll get back to you if time permits." If audience members try to turn a question into an opportunity to mount their own soapboxes, it's up to you to maintain control. You might admit that you and the questioner have a difference of opinion and offer to get back to the questioner after you've done more research. Then call on someone else. Another approach is to respond with a brief answer, thus avoiding a lengthy debate or additional questions.[12]

CHECKLIST FOR SPEECHES AND ORAL PRESENTATIONS

A. Development of the Speech or Presentation
1. Analyze the audience.
2. Begin with an attention-getter.
3. Preview the main points.
4. Limit the discussion to no more than three or four points.
5. Explain who, what, when, where, why, and how.
6. In longer presentations, include previews and summaries of major points as you go along.
7. Close by reviewing your main points and making a memorable statement.

B. Visual Aids
1. Use visual aids to show how things look, work, or are related to one another.
2. Use visual aids to highlight important information and to create interest.
3. Select appropriate visual aids.
   ■ a. Use flip charts, boards, or transparencies for small, informal groups.
   ■ b. Use slides or films for major occasions and large groups.
4. Limit each visual aid to three or four graphed lines or five or six points.
5. Use short phrases.
6. Use large, readable type.
7. Make sure equipment works.

C. Delivery
1. Establish eye contact.
2. Speak clearly and distinctly.
3. Do not go too fast.
4. Be sure everyone can hear.
5. Speak in your natural style.
6. Stand up straight.
7. Use gestures in a natural, appropriate way.
8. Encourage questions.
   ■ a. Allow questions during the presentation if the group is small.
   ■ b. Ask the audience to hold their questions until the end if the group is large or hostile.
9. Respond to questions without getting sidetracked.
10. Maintain control of your feelings despite criticism.

Finally, you might thank the person for the question and then remind the questioner that you were looking for specific questions. Don't indulge in put-downs, which may backfire and make the audience more sympathetic to the questioner.

When the time allotted for your presentation is up, call a halt to the question-and-answer session, even if more people want to talk. Prepare the audience for the end by saying: "Our time is almost up. Let's have one more question." After you've made your reply, summarize the main idea of the presentation and thank people for their attention. Conclude the way you opened: by looking around the room and making eye contact. Then gather your notes and leave the podium, shoulders straight, head up. The Checklist for Speeches and Oral Presentations is a reminder of the tasks involved in these types of oral communication.

On the Job

SOLVING A COMMUNICATION DILEMMA AT THE KEYS GROUP

When Brady Keys retired from professional football in the late 1960s, he pursued his dream of owning his own business. After noticing how well a friend's restaurant was doing, he decided on a fried-chicken business.

His first hurdle was raising enough money to launch the restaurant. Ten banks said "No thanks," but he finally persuaded his former team to loan him $10,000—enough to open his first All-Pro Fried Chicken store. Within three years, he'd presented himself and his ideas to banks and to the government, convincing them to loan him enough capital to open 35 more outlets in Pittsburgh, New

York, and Cleveland. By that time, he was selling a million dollar's worth of fried chicken a year.

He decided it was time to try something new—hamburgers. Keys convinced Burger King to let him try turning around a struggling Burger King franchise in Detroit's inner city. Realizing that something had to spark sales, "we introduced a couple of themes that are now universal in the industry," says Keys. "We found that black people didn't want the Whopper fixed the usual way, so we made it to order." That concept eventually formed the basis for Burger King's successful "Have It Your Way" advertising campaign.

Then as lines began to form for the new customized Whopper, Keys stationed employees at the end of the lines to take orders and cut the waiting time—a practice that has become standard in many fast-food restaurants. These innovations transformed the struggling franchise into the top-selling U.S. Burger King outlet, which Keys eventually sold.

As Keys points out, "You don't get acceptance by going in and saying 'accept me.' You get it by doing worthy activities." For example, Keys has used his position to help other African Americans succeed in franchising: He founded both Burger King's and KFC's Minority Franchise associations; he talked Burger King's management into awarding the construction contract for the company's first inner-city outlet to an African American general contractor; and he convinced management to increase the number of minority people on Burger King's roster of franchisees, employees, and vendors.

After taking over the Burger King franchise, Keys sold his All-Pro Fried Chicken stores and became a KFC franchisee. Most of his new outlets were in Albany, Georgia, where worthy activities became even more important. Gaining acceptance in the predominantly white community was more of a challenge than it had been in either Detroit or Pittsburgh. So, says Keys, "I became a philanthropist, I stressed my athletic background, and we brought in the Harlem Globetrotters as a benefit to the Special Olympics." He also served as chairman of the board of the Albany Civic Center Commission, and he is one of the largest individual contributors to the city's March of Dimes fund.

Keys's abilities to speak, to win friends, and to influence people help him deal with employees too. He believes in giving people a chance to live up to their potential. He promotes from within, and he rewards long-term employees with a piece of the business. In return, his employees are loyal, and his low turnover keeps costs down and service up. His restaurants actually serve as a "business school" for many young people who eventually move on to more challenging careers. In fact, a recent ad campaign featured distinguished graduates of the Brady Keys "School of Practical Experience."

Keys's current projects include real estate development, a video game company, a mining and brokering business, and a movie production company. In the process of selling these ideas, he uses his speaking skills to present his ideas to potential investors, to build goodwill in the communities where he operates, and to motivate his employees.[13]

Your Mission: As a member of the Keys Group's public relations department, you help Brady Keys plan some of the speeches he delivers to employees and to business, professional, and civic groups. For the following assignments, choose the best solution and be prepared to explain your choice.

1. Keys has agreed to give a 20-minute talk in Albany, Georgia, to a group of approximately 35 businesspeople who meet for lunch and networking on a monthly basis. The president of the group has suggested that Keys deal with the topic of franchising. Which of the following purposes do you think he should try to accomplish?
   a. To inform the audience about the history of franchising in America
   b. To inspire members of the audience to buy a franchise
   c. To entertain the audience with stories about Keys's franchising experiences
   d. To analyze the impact of national franchises on small, independently owned local businesses
2. Keys has asked you to help plan a ten-minute speech that he can give to his KFC employees during the annual summer picnic.

He expects up to 1,000 employees to attend. His topic is "the state of the company." His purpose is to inspire employees to keep up the good work. His main idea is that the Keys Group is doing an excellent job in meeting the competition, thanks to the efforts of the workers. What general organizational scheme do you recommend for developing this idea?
   a. Chronological: Highlights of company performance over the past year and outlook for the future
   b. Geographical: Performance, problems, and opportunities in each of the 11 KFC outlets
   c. Topical: Achievements of various types of employees such as store managers, kitchen workers, order takers, maintenance workers, and so on
   d. Comparison and contrast: KFC versus Boston Chicken and other fast-food competitors
3. Keys is trying to persuade a group of investors to put some money into his new movie production company. He has prepared a presentation that describes the company's goals, activities, and financial prospects. He is currently wrestling with the introduction to the presentation. Which of the following introductions would you recommend?

   a. Years ago, when I opened my first restaurant, I knew I had to do something to attract business. So I said to myself, why not try some TV advertising? I was operating on a shoestring, so I decided to write, produce, direct, and star in the commercial myself. If I'd had more money and more sense, I probably wouldn't have taken on the job, but lacking both money and experience, I was willing to try anything. Anyway, once I got started, I discovered that making commercials isn't really all that tricky. All you need is a little money, a little equipment, a little imagination, and a little luck. And Bingo! You're in business. I've made a lot of my own commercials since then, and I've thoroughly enjoyed the process.

   That's one of the reasons I decided to get into the movie business. I said to myself, "Brady, if making commercials is fun, imagine what a ball you can have making movies." But fun is only one reason to start a movie production company. My principal motive is making money. And that's what I want to talk to you about today: how you can make money in the movie business.
   b. In the last ten years, the number of movie screens in the United States has increased by 50 percent, to nearly 25,000. Those screens are all designed to do one thing: show films. But the major studios cannot possibly provide enough films to fill all these new theaters. As a result, a new breed of independent filmmaker is springing up, many of whom are far more profitable than their larger rivals.

   I'd like to talk to you today about how you can participate in this exciting business opportunity. I think you will be intrigued by the potential payoff and the relatively limited risk involved. I'll begin by giving you a little background on the revolution currently under way in the movie industry. Then I'll describe the film production company that I'm forming in partnership with actor Leon Issac Kennedy. After you've heard our strategy and plans, I'll brief you on the returns that you could expect on your investment in my business.

c. When's the last time you went to the movies? And when did you last see a film on HBO or network TV? What about videocassettes? Have you rented any of them lately?

If you're like most people, you're hooked on movies, whether you see them in theaters or on TV. Somebody is making all those movies, and it isn't necessarily Paramount or Walt Disney. Many of the films you see are created by independent companies.

Starting an independent film production company requires relatively little capital, and the financial returns can be considerable. If you're careful, you can whip out a low-budget film for as little as $2 million. Even if you don't do well at the box office, you can still clear maybe $3 or $4 million from the TV rights and videocassette sales. Multiply that by, say, ten movies per year, and you have a $30 to $40 million business.

d. Who wouldn't jump at the chance to rub shoulders with Jennifer Jason Leigh, Spike Lee, Julia Roberts, Tom Cruise, Winona Ryder, Denzel Washington, Martin Lawrence, Michael Keaton, Marisa Tomei, and all the other box-office stars of the 1990s? Well, those are just some of the famous actors you'll meet when you visit the movie production company we're going to build together. Notice that I said "when" and not "if." After you've heard my speech today, you'll agree that there's no better place to invest your cash than in our movie production company.

Although you'll be happy you made this investment, we all know that money isn't everything. You'll also have the prestige of working on Hollywood's most exciting movies with the biggest names in the business. Give me your attention for a few minutes as I talk about the movies we're considering right now.

4. In his role as chairman of the board of the Albany Civic Center Commission, Keys must give a speech outlining the center's financial position. The audience will include other board members, the mayor and members of the city council, and a group of 15 to 20 influential business and professional people. How should he handle the quantitative financial details?
   a. He should prepare handouts that summarize the financial data in tabular and graphic form. As the audience arrives, he should give everyone a copy of the handout and refer to it during the speech.
   b. Keys should write the information on a blackboard while he delivers the speech.
   c. He should prepare simple overhead transparencies to use during the speech. As he concludes his remarks, he should tell the audience that detailed financial statements are available at the door for those who are interested.
   d. Given the size and importance of the audience, he should show full-color 35-mm slides that summarize the financial information in tabular and graphic format. The slides should be professionally prepared to ensure their quality.

Critical Thinking Questions

1. Would you rather (a) give a speech to an outside audience, (b) be interviewed for a news story, or (c) make a presentation to a departmental meeting? Why? How do the communication skills differ in each situation? Explain.
2. How might the audience's attitude affect the amount of audience interaction during or after a presentation? Explain your answer.
3. Have you ever attended a presentation or a speech in which the speaker's style seemed inappropriate? What effect did that style have on the audience? Briefly explain.
4. What similarities and differences would you expect to see in the introduction to a formal presentation and the introduction to a formal report? Explain.
5. What problems could result from using visual aids during your speech?
6. From the speaker's perspective, what are the advantages and disadvantages of responding to questions from the audience throughout a speech or presentation? From the listener's perspective, which approach would you prefer? Why?

Exercises

1. For many years, Toastmasters has been dedicated to helping its members give speeches. Instruction, good speakers as models, and practice sessions aim to teach members to convey information in lively and informative ways. Visit the Toastmasters Web site at <http://www.toastmasters.com> and carefully review the linked pages about listening, speaking, voice, and body. Evaluate the information and outline a three-minute presentation to your class telling why Toastmasters and its Web site would or would not help you and your classmates write and deliver an effective speech.

2. Attend a speech at your school or in your area, or watch a speech on television. Categorize the speech as one that motivates or entertains, one that informs or analyzes, or one that persuades or urges collaboration. Then compare the speaker's delivery and use of visual aids with the Checklist for Speeches and Oral Presentations. Write a two-page report analyzing the speaker's performance and suggesting improvements.

3. Analyze the speech given by someone introducing the main speaker at an awards ceremony, a graduation, or some other special occasion. Does the speech fit the occasion and grab

attention? Is it related to the audience's interests? How well does the speech motivate the audience to listen to the featured speaker? Does the speech provide the information necessary for the audience to understand, respect, and appreciate the speaker's background and viewpoint? Put yourself in the shoes of the person who made that introduction. Draft a brief (two-minute) speech that prepares the audience for the featured speaker.

4. Which media would you use for the visual aids that accompany each of the following speeches? Explain your answers.
   a. An informal ten-minute speech explaining the purpose of a new training program to 300 assembly-line employees
   b. An informal ten-minute speech explaining the purpose of a new training program to five vice presidents
   c. A formal five-minute presentation explaining the purpose of a new training program to the company's 12-member board of directors
   d. A formal five-minute speech explaining the purpose of a new company training program to 35 members of the press

5. With three classmates, practice audience analysis by analyzing the audience of a particular television program. Note the age, gender, race, marital status, relationships, and occupations of the characters. Also pay attention to the commercials that run during the program. On the basis of these clues, who do you think watches this program? Now choose a topic that this audi-ence is likely to feel strongly about. How would you prepare a speech on that topic if you thought the audience would probably be hostile? What would you do differently if you thought the audience would be sympathetic? Present your group's analysis to the class, and defend your answers.

6. Select one of the following main ideas and outline a brief (three- to five-minute) persuasive speech to your business communication class.
   a. As a requirement for graduation, every college student should demonstrate proficiency in basic writing skills by passing a standardized national test.
   b. College students should be allowed access to their confidential academic records at least once a year and, if they choose, to submit a written statement disputing or correcting information in the files.
   c. Rather than ask all students to pay an activities fee to support campus sports, require only those students who participate pay a special sports fee.
   d. The campus computer laboratory should remain open 24 hours a day throughout the week to give students the opportunity to complete their assignments at their own convenience.
   e. All college students should be required to complete a period of community service during their junior or senior year.

DEVELOPING YOUR INTERNET SKILLS

GOING ONLINE: SPEAK LIKE A PRO, P. 450

Take time to peruse some linked sites from the Speaker's Companion Reference Page. Try something familiar (*Bartlett's Familiar Quotations* or the *World History Compass*) and then try something foreign (*Asahi.com* for Japanese news and current events or the *St. Petersburg Press*). Explore new ideas and old ones. Take a look at some of the advice offered by the many experts found here. Look for material you can use in an upcoming speech. What did you find that you can incorporate into a classroom speaking project? How could you use what you learned from overseas news and events to bolster a premise or to refute an argument? Did your perusal of this site and its linked sites cause you to make any changes in your speaking plans? What new ideas did you glean from this wealth of material? (If you didn't find anything to spark your interest, explain why.)

APPENDIX A

Format and Layout of Business Documents

An effective letter, memo, or report does more than store words on paper. It communicates with the right person, makes an impression, and tells the recipient who wrote it and when it was written. It may even carry responses back to the sender, if only to relate how and by whom it was received and processed.

Over the centuries certain conventions have developed for the format and layout of business documents. Of course, conventions vary from country to country, and, even within the United States, few hard-and-fast rules exist. Many organizations develop variations of standard styles to suit their own needs, adopting the style that's best for the types of messages they send and for the kinds of audiences that receive them. The conventions described here are more common than others. Whether you handle all your own communication on your computer or rely on someone else to handle it for you, knowing the proper form for your documents and knowing how to make them attractive to your readers are crucial.

*F*IRST IMPRESSIONS

A letter or other written document is often the first (sometimes the only) contact you have with an external audience. Memos and other documents used within an organization represent you to supervisors, colleagues, and employees. So it's important that your documents look neat and professional and that they're easy to read. Your audience's first impressions come from the paper you use, the way you customize it, and the general appearance of your document. These elements tell readers a lot about you and about your company's professionalism.

Paper

From your own experience, you know that a flimsy, see-through piece of paper gives a much less favorable impression than a richly textured piece. Paper quality is measured in two ways: The first measure of quality is weight, specifically the weight of four reams (each a 500-sheet package) of letter-size paper. The quality most commonly used by U.S. business organizations is 20-pound paper, but 16- and 24-pound versions are also used. The second measure of quality is the percentage of cotton in the paper. Cotton doesn't yellow over time the way wood pulp does, and it's both strong and soft. In general, paper with a 25 percent cotton content is an appropriate quality for letters and outside reports. For memos and other internal documents, lighter-weight paper and paper with a lower cotton content may be used. Also, airmail-weight paper may be more cost effective for international correspondence, but make sure it isn't too flimsy.[1]

In the United States the standard size of paper for business documents is 8½ by 11 inches. Standard legal documents are 8½ by 14 inches. Executives sometimes have heavier 7-by-10-inch paper on hand (with matching envelopes) for such personal messages as congratulations and recommendations.[2] They may also have a box of correspondence note cards imprinted with their initials and a box of plain folded notes for condolences or for acknowledging formal invitations.

Stationery may vary in color. Of course, white is standard for business purposes, although neutral colors such as gray and ivory are sometimes used. Memos are sometimes produced on pastel-colored paper so that internal correspondence can be more easily distinguished from external, and memos are sometimes printed or typed on various colors of paper for routing to separate departments. Light-colored papers are distinctive and often appropriate; bright or dark colors make reading difficult and may appear too frivolous.

Customization

For letters to outsiders, U.S. businesses commonly use letterhead stationery printed with the company's name and address, usually at the top of the page but sometimes along the left side or even at the bottom of the page. Other information may be included in the letterhead as well: the company's telephone number, fax number, cable address, Web site address, product lines, date of establishment, officers and directors, slogan, and symbol (logo). The idea is to give the recipient pertinent reference data and a good idea not only of what the company does but also of the company's image.[3] Nevertheless, the letterhead should be as simple as possible; too much information gives the page a cluttered look, cuts into the space needed for the letter, and may become outdated before all the letterhead has been used. If you correspond frequently with people in foreign countries, your letterhead can be misleading. If you do a lot of business abroad, be sure your letterhead is intelligible to foreigners, and make sure it includes the name of your country as well as your cable, telex, e-mail address, or fax information.

In the United States, company letterhead is always used for the first page of a letter. Successive pages are plain sheets of paper that match the letterhead in color and quality, or some companies use a specially printed second-page letterhead bearing only the company's name. Other countries have other conventions. For example, Latin American companies use a cover page with their printed seal in the center.

Many companies also design and print standardized forms for memos and for reports that are written frequently and always require the same sort of information (such as sales reports and expense reports). These forms may be printed in sets for use with carbon paper or in carbonless copy sets that produce multiple copies automatically with the original. More and more, organizations are using computers to generate their standardized forms. These electronic forms can save money and time.[4]

Appearance

Most business documents are produced using either a letter-quality (not a dot matrix) printer or a typewriter. Some short informal memos are handwritten, and it's appropriate to handwrite a note of condolence to a close business associate. Of course, the envelope is handwritten, printed, or typed to match the document. However, even a letter on the best-quality paper with the best-designed letterhead may look unprofessional if it's poorly produced.

Companies in the United States make sure that documents (especially external ones) are centered on the page, with margins of at least an inch all around (unlike documents produced in Latin America, which use much wider margins and thus look much longer). Using word-processing or desktop publishing software, you can achieve this balanced appearance simply by defining the format parameters. If you are using a typewriter, such balance can be achieved either by establishing a standard line length or by establishing a "picture frame."

The most common line length is about 6 inches. Lines aren't usually right-hand justified because the resulting text can be hard to read, even with proportional spacing, and because the document generally looks too much like a form letter. Varying line length makes the document look more personal and interesting. If you're using a typewriter, the larger, pica type will give you 60 characters in a line; the smaller, elite type will give you 72 characters in a line. Sometimes a guide sheet, with the margins and the center point marked in dark ink, is used as a backing. The number of lines between elements of the document (such as between the date line and inside address in a letter) can be adjusted to ensure that a short document fills the page vertically or that a longer document extends to at least three lines of body on the last page.

Another important aspect of a professional-looking document is the proper spacing after punctuation. For example, U.S. conventions include (1) leaving one space after commas and semicolons and (2) leaving two spaces after periods at the ends of sentences and after colons (unless your typeface is proportional, requiring only one space). Each letter in a person's initials is followed by a period and a single space. Abbreviations for organizations, such as P.T.A., may or may not have periods, but they never have internal spaces. On computers and typewriters that have no special characters for dashes, use two hyphens with no space before, between, or

after. Other details of this sort are provided in your company's style book or in most secretarial handbooks.

Finally, messy corrections are dreadfully obvious and unacceptable in business documents. Be sure that any letter, report, or memo requiring a lot of corrections is reprinted or retyped. Word-processing software and self-correcting typewriters can produce correction-free documents at the push of a button.

LETTERS

For a long time, letters have begun with some kind of phrase in greeting and have ended with some sort of polite expression before the writer's signature. In fact, books printed in the sixteenth century prescribed letter formats for writers to follow. Styles have changed some since then, but all business letters still have certain elements in common. Several of these elements appear in every letter; others appear only when desirable or appropriate. In addition, these letter parts are usually arranged in one of three basic formats.

Standard Letter Parts

All business letters typically include seven elements, in the following order: (1) heading, (2) date, (3) inside address, (4) salutation, (5) body, (6) complimentary close, and (7) signature block. The letter in Figure A.1 shows the placement of these standard letter parts.

Heading

Letterhead (the usual heading) shows the organization's name, full address, and (almost always) telephone number. Executive letterhead also bears the name of an individual within the organization. Computers allow you to design your own letterhead (either one to use for all correspondence or a new one for each piece of correspondence). If letterhead stationery is not available, the heading consists of a return address (but not a name) starting 13 lines from the top of the page, which leaves 2 inches between the return address and the top of the page.

Date

If you're using letterhead, place the date at least one blank line beneath the lowest part of the letterhead. Without letterhead, place the date immediately below the return address. The standard method of writing the date in the United States uses the full name of the month (no abbreviations), followed by the day (in numerals, without *st, rd,* or *th*), a comma, and then the year: July 14, 1997 (7/14/97). The U.S. government and some U.S. industries place the day (in numerals) first, followed by the month (unabbreviated), followed by the year—with no comma: 14 July 1997 (14/7/97). This convention is similar to the one used in Europe, except that European convention replaces the U.S. solidus (diagonal line) with periods when the date appears all in numerals: 14 July 1997 (14.7.1997). The international standard places the year first, followed by the month and the day, using commas in the all-numeral form: 1997 July 14 (1997,7,14). To maintain the utmost clarity, always spell out the name of the month in dates for international correspondence.[5]

When communicating internationally, you may also experience some confusion over time. Some companies in the United States refer to morning (A.M.) and afternoon (P.M.), dividing a 24-hour day into 12-hour blocks so that they refer to four o'clock in the morning (4:00 A.M.) or four o'clock in the afternoon (4:00 P.M.).

The writer of this business letter had no letterhead available, but correctly included a heading.

6412 Belmont Drive
New Weston, OH 45348
June 22, 1997

Mr. Richard Garcia
Director of Franchises
Snack Shoppes
2344 Western Avenue
Seattle, WA 98123

Dear Mr. Garcia:

Last Monday, my wife and I were on our way home from a long weekend, and we stopped at a Snack Shoppe for a quick sandwich. A sign on the cash register gave your address in the event customers were interested in operating a franchise of their own somewhere else. We talked about the idea all evening and into the night.

Although we had talked about changing jobs—I'm an administrative analyst for a utility company and my wife sells real estate—the thought of operating a franchised business had never occurred to us. We'd always thought in terms of starting a business from scratch. However, owning a Snack Shoppe is an intriguing idea.

We would appreciate your sending us full details on owning our own outlet. Please include the names and telephone numbers of other Snack Shoppe owners so that we can talk to them before we make any decision to proceed further. We're excited about hearing from you.

Cordially,

Peter Simond

Peter Simond

Heading

Date

Inside Address

Salutation

Body

Complimentary Closing

Typewritten Name

□ *One blank space*
* *Variable spacing depending on length of letter*

The U.S. military and European companies refer to one 24-hour period so that 0400 hours (4:00 A.M.) is always in the morning and 1600 hours (4:00 P.M.) is always in the afternoon.[6] Make sure your references to time are as clear as possible, and be sure you clearly understand your audience's time references.

Inside Address

The inside address identifies the recipient of the letter. For U.S. correspondence, begin the inside address one or more lines below the date,

depending on how long the letter is. Precede the addressee's name with a courtesy title, such as *Dr., Mr.,* or *Ms.* The accepted courtesy title for women in business is Ms., although a woman known to prefer the title *Miss* or *Mrs.* is always accommodated. If you don't know whether a person is a man or a woman (and you have no way of finding out), do not use a courtesy title. For example, Terry Smith could be either a man or a woman. The first line of the inside address would be just Terry Smith, and the salutation would be Dear Terry Smith. The same is true if you know only a person's initials, as in S. J. Adams.

Table A.1	FORMS OF ADDRESS	
Person	**In Address**	**In Salutation**
Personal Titles		
Man	Mr. [first & last name]	Dear Mr. [last name]:
Woman (marital status unknown)	Ms. [first & last name]	Dear Ms. [last name]:
Woman (single)	Ms. *or* Miss [first & last name]	Dear Ms. *or* Miss [last name]:
Woman (married)	Ms. *or* Mrs. [wife's first & last name] *or* Mrs. [husband's first & last name]	Dear Ms. *or* Mrs. [last name]:
Woman (widowed)	Ms. *or* Mrs. [wife's first name & last name] *or* Mrs. [husband's first & last name]	Dear Ms. *or* Mrs. [last name]:
Woman (separated or divorced)	Ms. *or* Mrs. [first & last name]	Dear Ms. *or* Mrs. [last name]:
Two men (or more)	Mr. [first & last name] and Mr. [first & last name]	Dear Mr. [last name] and Mr. [last name] *or* Messrs. [last name] and [last name]:
Two women (or more)	Ms. [first & last name] and Ms. [first & last name]	Dear Ms. [last name] and Ms. [last name] *or* Mses. [last name] and [last name]:
	or Mrs. [first & last name] and Mrs. [first & last name]	Dear Mrs. [last name] and Mrs. [last name]: *or* Dear Mesdames [last name] and [last name] *or* Mesdames:
	or Miss [first & last name] and Mrs. [first & last name]	Dear Miss [last name] and Mrs. [last name]:
One woman and one man	Ms. [first & last name] and Mr. [first & last name]	Dear Ms. [last name] and Mr. [last name]:
Couple (married)	Mr. and Mrs. [husband's first & last name]	Dear Mr. and Mrs. [last name]:
Couple (married with different last names)	[title] [first & last name of husband] [title] [first & last name of wife]	Dear [title] [husband's last name] and [title] [wife's last name]:
Couple (married professionals with same title & same last name)	[title in plural form] [husband's first name] and [wife's first name] [last name]	Dear [title in plural form] [last name]:
Couple (married professionals with different titles & same last name)	[title] [first & last name of husband] [title] [first & last name of wife]	Dear [title] and [title] [last name]:

Spell out and capitalize titles that precede a person's name, such as *Professor* or *General* (see Table A.1 for the proper forms of address). The person's organizational title, such as *Director*, may be included on this first line (if it is short) or on the line below; the name of a department may follow. In addresses and signature lines, don't forget to capitalize any professional title that follows a person's name:

Mr. Ray Johnson, Dean

Ms. Patricia T. Higgins
Assistant Vice President

However, professional titles not appearing in an address or signature line are capitalized only when they directly precede the name.

President Kenneth Johanson will deliver the speech.

Maria Morales, president of ABC Enterprises, will deliver the speech.

The Honorable Helen Masters, senator from Arizona, will deliver the speech.

If the name of a specific person is unavailable, you may address the letter to the department or to a specific position within the department. Also, be sure to spell out company names in full, unless the company itself uses abbreviations in its official name.

Other address information includes the treatment of buildings, house numbers, and compass directions. Capitalize the names of

Person	In Address	In Salutation
Professional Titles		
President of a college or university (doctor)	Dr. [first & last name], President	Dear Dr. [last name]:
Dean of a school or college	Dean [first & last name] *or* Dr., Mr., Ms., Mrs., or Miss [first & last name] Dean of (title)	Dear Dean [last name]: Dear Dr., Mr., Ms., Mrs., *or* Miss [last name]:
Professor	Professor [first & last name]	Dear Professor [last name]:
Physician	[first & last name], M.D.	Dear Dr. [last name]:
Lawyer	Mr., Ms., Mrs., *or* Miss [first & last name]	Dear Mr., Ms., Mrs., *or* Miss [last name]:
Service personnel	[full rank, first & last name, abbreviation of service designation] (add *Retired* if applicable)	Dear [rank] [last name]:
Company or corporation	[name of organization]	Ladies and Gentlemen *or* Gentlemen and Ladies
Governmental Titles		
President of the United States	The President	Dear Mr. *or* Madam President:
Senator of the United States	Honorable [first & last name]	Dear Senator [last name]:
Cabinet member	Honorable [first & last name]	Dear Mr. *or* Madam Secretary:
Postmaster General		Dear Mr. *or* Madam Postmaster General:
Attorney General		Dear Mr. *or* Madam Attorney General:
Mayor	Honorable [first & last name] Mayor of [name of city]	Dear Mayor [last name]:
Judge	The Honorable [first and last name]	Dear Judge [last name]:
Religious Titles		
Priest	The Reverend [first & last name], [initials of order, if any]	Reverend Sir: (formal) *or* Dear Father [last name]: (informal)
Rabbi	Rabbi [first & last name]	Dear Rabbi [last name]:
Minister	The Reverend [first & last name] [title, if any]	Dear Reverend [last name]:

buildings, and if you specify a location within a building (suite, room, and so on), capitalize it and use a comma to separate it from the building name.

Empire State Building, Suite 1073

Use figures for all house or building numbers, except the number *one.*

One Trinity Lane
637 Adams Avenue, Apt. 7

Spell out compass directions that fall within a street address, but abbreviate compass directions that follow the street address:

1074 West Connover Street
783 Main Street, N.E., Apt. 27

Also remember that apartment, suite, and room numbers always appear in numerals (as in the examples already listed in this paragraph). The following example shows all the information that may be included in the inside address and its proper order for U.S. correspondence:

Ms. Linda Coolidge, Vice President
Corporate Planning Department
Midwest Airlines
Kowalski Building, Suite 21-A
7279 Bristol Avenue
Toledo, OH 43617

Canadian addresses are similar, except that the name of the province is usually spelled out:

Dr. H. C. Armstrong
Research and Development
Commonwealth Mining Consortium
The Chelton Building, Suite 301
585 Second Street SW
Calgary, Alberta T2P 2P5

When addressing correspondence for other countries, follow the format and information that appear in the company's letterhead.[7] You want to be especially careful about the format of international correspondence because you want everything to be as clear as possible.[8] The order and layout of address information vary from country to country, so follow the conventions of the country of the recipient. When you're sending mail from the United States, however, be sure that the name of the destination country appears on the last line of the address in capital letters. Also, use the English version of the country name so that your mail is routed from the United States to the right country. Then, to be sure your mail is routed correctly within the destination country, use the foreign spelling of the city name (using the characters and diacritical marks that would be commonly used in the region). For example, the following address uses Köln, instead of Cologne:

H. R. Veith, Director	Addressee
Eisfieren Glaswerk	Company Name
Blaubachstraße 13	Street address
Postfach 10 80 07	Post office box
D-5000 Köln I	District, city
GERMANY	Country

Additional addresses might look similar to the following:

Mr. Toru Hasegawa
7-35 Kitashinagawa
6 Chome—141 Shinagawa-ku
Tokyo
JAPAN

Cairo
Cleopatra
165 El Corniche Road
Mrs. Ahmed Abbas Zaki
EGYPT

Crédit Lyonnais
c/o Claude Rubinowicz
19, Boulevard des Italiens
75002 Paris
FRANCE

Sr. Ari Matos Cardoso
Superintendent of Human Resources and Personnel
Av. República do Chile, 65
Centro-Rio de Janeiro, RJ
CEP 20035
BRAZIL

Be sure to get organizational titles right when addressing international correspondence. Unfortunately, job designations vary around the world. In England, for example, a managing director is often what a U.S. company would call its chief executive officer or president, and a British deputy is the equivalent of a vice president. In France, responsibilities are assigned to individuals without regard to title or organizational structure, and in China the title *project manager* has meaning, but the title *sales manager* may not. To make matters worse, businesspeople in some countries sign correspondence without their names typed below. In Germany, for example, the belief is that employees represent the company, so it's inappropriate to emphasize personal names.[9]

Salutation

In the salutation of your letter, follow the first line of the inside address. That is, if the first line is a person's name, the salutation is *Dear Mr.* or *Ms. Name.* Base the formality of the salutation on your relationship with the addressee. If in conversation you would say "Mary," your letter's salutation should be *Dear Mary,* followed by a colon. In letters to people you don't know well enough to address personally, include the courtesy title and last name, followed by a colon. Presuming to write *Dear Lewis* instead of *Dear Professor Chang* demonstrates a disrespectful familiarity that a stranger will probably resent. If the first line is a position title such as Director of Personnel, then use *Dear Director;* if the addressee is unknown, use a polite description, such as *Dear Alumnus, Dear SPCA Supporter,* or *Dear Voter.* If the first line is plural (a department or company), then use *Ladies and Gentlemen* (look again at Table A.1). When you do not know whether you're writing to an individual or a group (for example, when writing a reference or a letter of recommendation), use *To whom it may concern.*

In the United States some letter writers use a salutopening on the salutation line. A salutopening omits *Dear* but includes the first few words of the opening paragraph along with the recipient's name. After this line, the sentence continues a double space below as part of the body of the letter, as in these examples:

Thank you, Mr. Brown,	Salutopening
for your prompt payment of your bill.	Body
Congratulations, Ms. Lake!	Salutopening
Your promotion is well deserved.	Body

Don't overlook an especially important point with personalized salutations: Whether they're informal or formal, make sure names are spelled right. A misspelled name is glaring evidence of carelessness, and it belies the personal interest you're trying to express.

Body

The body of the letter is your message. Almost all letters are single-spaced, with double spacing (one blank line) before and after the salutation or salutopening, between paragraphs, and before the complimentary close. The body may include indented lists, entire paragraphs indented for emphasis, and even subheadings. If it does, all similar elements should be treated in the same way. Your department or company may select a format to use for all letters.

Complimentary Close

The complimentary close begins on the second line below the body of the letter. Alternatives for wording are available, but currently the trend seems to be toward using one-word closes, such as *Sincerely* and *Cordially*. In any case, the complimentary close reflects the relationship between you and the person you're writing to. Avoid cute closes, such as *Yours for bigger profits*. If your audience doesn't know you well, your sense of humor may be misunderstood.

Signature Block

Leave three blank lines for a written signature below the complimentary close, and then include the sender's name (unless it appears in the letterhead). The person's title may appear on the same line as the name or on the line below:

Cordially,

Raymond Dunnigan
Director of Personnel

Your letterhead indicates that you're representing your company. However, if your letter is on plain paper or runs to a second page, you may want to emphasize that you're speaking legally for the company. The accepted way of doing that is to place the company's name in capital letters a double space below the complimentary close and then include the sender's name and title four lines below that:

Sincerely,

WENTWORTH INDUSTRIES

(Mrs.) Helen B. Taylor
President

If your name could be taken for either a man's or a woman's, a courtesy title indicating gender should be included, with or without parentheses. Also, women who prefer a particular courtesy title should include it:

Mrs. Nancy Winters
(Miss) Juana Flores
Ms. Pat Li
(Mr.) Jamie Saunders

Additional Letter Parts

Letters vary greatly in subject matter and thus in the identifying information they need and the format they adopt. The following elements may be used in any combination, depending on the requirements of the particular letter, but generally in this order:

1. Addressee notation
2. Attention line
3. Subject line
4. Second-page heading
5. Company name
6. Reference initials
7. Enclosure notation
8. Copy notation
9. Mailing notation
10. Postscript

The letter in Figure A.2 shows how these additional parts should be arranged.

Addressee Notation

Letters that have a restricted readership or that must be handled in a special way should include such addressee notations as *Personal, Confidential,* or *Please Forward*. This sort of notation appears a double space above the inside address, in all capital letters.

Attention Line

Although an attention line is not commonly used today, you may find it useful if you know only the last name of the person you're writing to. An attention line can also be used to direct a letter to a position title or department. An attention line may take any of the following forms or variants of them: *Attention Dr. McHenry, Attention Director of Marketing,* or *Attention Marketing Department*. You may place the attention line on the first line and use the company name as the second line of the inside address.[10] With either approach, the address on the envelope should always match the style of the inside address shown in Figure A.2, to conform to postal specifications.

Subject Line

The subject line lets the recipient know at a glance what the letter is about; it also indicates where to file the letter for future reference. It usually appears below the salutation—against the left margin, indented as the paragraphs in the body of the letter, or centered on the line. Sometimes the subject line is placed above the salutation or at the very top of the page. The subject line may take a variety of forms, including the following:

Subject: RainMaster Sprinklers
About your February 2, 1998, order
FALL 1998 SALES MEETING
Reference Order No. 27920

Sometimes the subject line (or the last line of a long subject "line") is underscored. Some writers omit the word *Subject* and put the other information all in capitals to distinguish it from the other letter parts. Organizations such as insurance and financial institutions, attorneys, and government offices may use the words *Re:* or *In re:* (meaning "concerning" or "in the matter of") rather than using the word *Subject*.

Second-Page Heading

If the letter is long and an additional page is required, use a second-page heading. Some companies have second-page letterhead, with the company name and address on one line and in a smaller typeface than on the regular letterhead. In any case, the second-page heading bears the name that appears in the first line of the inside address (the person or organization receiving the letter), the page number, and the date of the letter; you can also include a reference number. All the following are acceptable:

Ms. Melissa Baker
May 10, 1998
Page 2

Ms. Melissa Baker, May 10, 1998, Page 2

Ms. Melissa Baker   -2-   May 10, 1998

Figure A.2
In-Depth Critique: Additional Letter Parts

This excerpt from a letter written by J. Elizabeth Spencer of the Worldwide Talent Agency includes many of the elements often appearing in business letters.

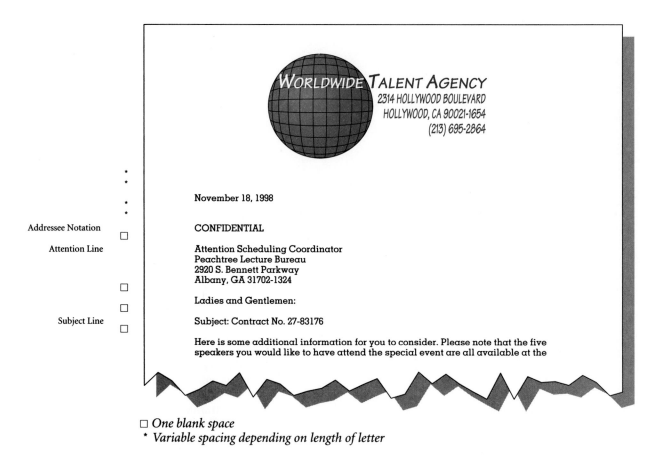

Addressee Notation

Attention Line

Subject Line

□ *One blank space*
* *Variable spacing depending on length of letter*

Triple-space (leave two blank lines) between the second-page heading and the body. If a paragraph must be continued on a second page, make sure at least two lines of that paragraph appear on the first page and on the second page. Also, the closing lines of a business letter must never appear alone on a continued page. At least two lines of the body must precede the complimentary close or signature lines. And finally, don't hyphenate the last word on a page.

Company Name

If you include the company's name in the signature block, put it all in capital letters a double space below the complimentary close. You usually include the company's name in the signature block only when the writer is serving as the company's official spokesperson or when letterhead has not been used.

Reference Initials

Because it can happen in business that one person may dictate or write a letter and another person may produce it, reference initials are used to show who helped prepare the letter. Reference initials appear at the left margin, a double space below the last line of the signature block. When the writer's name has been in-

cluded in the signature block, only the preparer's initials are necessary. If only the department name appears in the signature block, both sets of initials should appear, usually in one of the following forms:

RSR/sm

RSR:sm

RSR:SM

The first set of initials is the writer's; the second set is the preparer's.

Sometimes the writer and the signer of a letter are different people. In that case, at least the file copy of a letter should bear both their initials as well as those of the typist: JFS/RSR/sm (signer, writer, preparer). When businesspeople keyboard their own letters, reference initials are not included, so such initials are becoming more and more rare.

Enclosure Notation

Enclosure notations also appear at the bottom of a letter, one or two lines below the reference initials. Some common forms:

Figure A.2 (continued)

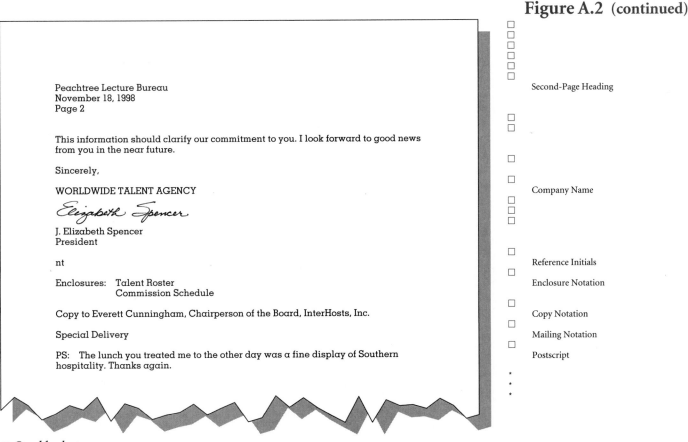

Peachtree Lecture Bureau
November 18, 1998
Page 2

This information should clarify our commitment to you. I look forward to good news from you in the near future.

Sincerely,

WORLDWIDE TALENT AGENCY

Elizabeth Spencer

J. Elizabeth Spencer
President

nt

Enclosures: Talent Roster
              Commission Schedule

Copy to Everett Cunningham, Chairperson of the Board, InterHosts, Inc.

Special Delivery

PS: The lunch you treated me to the other day was a fine display of Southern hospitality. Thanks again.

□	Second-Page Heading
□	Company Name
□	Reference Initials
□	Enclosure Notation
□	Copy Notation
□	Mailing Notation
□	Postscript

□ *One blank space*
* *Variable spacing depending on length of letter*

Enclosure

Enclosures (2)

Enclosures: Résumé
            Photograph

Attachment

Copy Notation

Copy notations may follow reference initials or enclosure notations. They indicate who's receiving a *courtesy copy* (cc). Some companies indicate copies made on a photocopier (*pc*), or they simply use *copy* (*c*). Recipients are listed in order of rank or (rank being equal) in alphabetical order. Among the forms used:

cc: David Wentworth

pc: Martha Littlefield

Copy to Hans Vogel

c: Joseph Martinez

In addition to the name of an individual, copy notations may include any combination of that person's courtesy title, position, department, company, and complete address, along with notations about any enclosures being sent with the copies.

On occasion, copies are sent to benefit readers other than the person who receives the original letter. In that case, place the notation *bc*, *bcc*, or *bpc* (for blind copy, blind courtesy copy, or blind photocopy) with the name, where the copy notation would normally appear—but only on the copy, not on the original.

Mailing Notation

You may place a mailing notation (such as *Special Delivery* or *Registered Mail*) at the bottom of the letter, after reference initials or enclosure notations (whichever one is last) and before copy notations. Or you may place it at the top of the letter, either above the inside address on the left-hand side or just below the date on the right-hand side. For greater visibility, mailing notations may appear in capital letters.

Postscript

Letters may also bear postscripts: afterthoughts to the letter, messages that require emphasis, or personal notes. The postscript is usually the last thing on any letter and may be preceded by *P.S.*, *PS*, *PS:*, or nothing at all. A second afterthought would be designated *P.P.S.*, meaning "post postscript."

Postscripts usually indicate poor planning, so generally avoid them. However, they're commonly used in sales letters, not as an afterthought but as a punch line to remind the reader of a benefit for taking advantage of the offer.

Figure A.3
In-Depth Critique: Block Letter Format

Rogers can be sure that her company's letterhead and the block format give her letter a crisp, businesslike appearance.

Beverly Hills Toys
3460 Rodeo Drive
Beverly Hills, California 90213
(310) 276-4839

September 5, 1998

Mr. Clifford Hanson
General Manager
The Toy Trunk
356 Emerald Drive
Lexington, KY 40501

Dear Mr. Hanson:

You should receive your shipment of Barbie dolls and accessories within two weeks, just in time for the holiday shopping season. The merchandise is being shipped by United Parcel Service. As the enclosed invoice indicates, the amount due is $352.32.

When preparing to ship your order, I noticed that this is your fifteenth year as a Mattel customer. During that period, you have sold over 3,750 Barbie dolls! We sincerely appreciate the part you have played in marketing our toys to the public.

Your customers should be particularly excited about the new Barbie vacation outfits that you have ordered. Our winter advertising campaign will portray Barbie trekking through the jungle in her safari suit, climbing mountains in her down parka, and snorkeling off a coral reef in her diving gear.

Next month, you'll be receiving our spring catalog. Notice the new series of action figures that will tie in with a TV cartoon featuring King Arthur and the Knights of the Round Table. As a special introductory incentive, you can receive a 15 percent discount on all items in this line until the end of January. Please send your order soon.

Sincerely,

Rhonda Rogers

Ms. Rhonda Rogers
Customer Service Representative

jhb

Enclosure

☐ *One blank space*
 * *Variable spacing depending on length of letter*

Letter Formats

Although the basic letter parts have remained the same for centuries, ways of arranging them do change. Sometimes a company adopts a certain format as its policy; sometimes the individual letter writer or preparer is allowed to choose the format most appropriate for a given letter or to settle on a personal preference. In the United States, three major letter formats are commonly used:

- ■ *Block format.* Each letter part begins at the left margin. The main advantage is quick and efficient preparation (Figure A.3).
- ■ *Modified block format.* Same as block format, except the date, complimentary close, and signature block start near the center of the page (Figure A.4). The modified block format does permit indentions as an option. This format mixes preparation speed with traditional placement of some letter parts. It also looks more balanced on the page than the block format does.

O'Donnell's choice of a modified block format appears no less crisp or businesslike than the previous figure, but indenting the date and the signature block can make the letter appear somewhat more balanced.

JCPenney

June 3, 1998

Ms. Clara Simpson, President
League of Women Voters of Miami
P.O. Box 112
Miami, FL 33152

Dear Ms. Simpson:

Thank you for inviting us to participate in the League of Women Voters' Spring Fashion Show. We will be delighted to provide some clothing samples for the May 15 event.

You indicated that you would like us to supply about 12 outfits from our designer collection, all in size 6. We can certainly accommodate your request. To give your audience a representative overview of our merchandise, I suggest we provide the following: three tailored daytime dresses or suits, two dressy dresses, one formal ball gown, four casual weekend outfits, and two active sports outfits.

Please give me a call to schedule a "shopping" trip for you and your committee members. Together, I'm sure we can find exactly what you need to stage a well-rounded show. In the meantime, you might enjoy looking through the enclosed catalog. It will introduce you to some of the options.

Sincerely,

Vera O'Donnell

(Mrs.) Vera O'Donnell
Special Events Manager

bcg

Enclosure

J.C. Penney Company, Inc. 6501 Legacy Drive, Plano, Texas 75024

☐ *One blank space*
* *Variable spacing depending on length of letter*

■ *Simplified format.* Instead of using a salutation, this format often works the audience's name into the first line or two of the body and often includes a subject line in capital letters (Figure A.5). It also omits the complimentary close, so you sign your name after the body of the letter, followed by the printed (or typewritten) name (customarily in all capital letters). The advantages include convenience when you don't know your audience's name. However, some people object to this format because it seems mechanical and impersonal (a drawback that may be overcome with a warm writing style). In this format, the elimination of certain letter parts changes some of the spacing between lines.

These formats differ in the way paragraphs are indented, in the way letter parts are placed, and in some punctuation. However, the elements are always separated by at least one blank line, and the

Figure A.5
In-Depth Critique: Simplified Letter Format

Davis's use of the simplified format seems less personal than either the block or the modified block format.

PERFORMANCE TOOLS INTERNATIONAL
800 Superior Avenue • Cleveland Ohio 44114 • (216) 846-3286

May 5, 1998

Mr. Michael Ferraro
Pacific Coast Appliances
5748 Catalina Avenue
Laguna Beach, CA 92677

NEW PRODUCT INFORMATION

Thank you, Mr. Ferraro, for your recent inquiry about our product line. We appreciate your enthusiasm for our products, and we are confident that your customers will enjoy the improved performance of the new product line.

I have enclosed a package of information for your review, including product specifications, dealer prices, and an order form. The package also contains reprints of Performance Tools reviews and a comparison sheet showing how our products measure up against competing brands.

Please call with any questions you may have about shipping or payment arrangements.

Joanna Davis

JOANNA DAVIS
PRODUCT SPECIALIST

ek

Enclosures

---

printed (or typewritten) name is always separated from the line above by at least three blank lines to allow space for a signature. If paragraphs are indented, the indention is normally five spaces.

The most common formats for intercultural business letters are the block style and the modified block style. Use either the U.S. or the European format for dates. For the salutation, use *Dear (Title/Last name)*. Close the letter with *Sincerely* or *Cordially,* and sign it.

In addition to these three letter formats, letters may also be classified according to the style of punctuation they use. *Standard, or mixed, punctuation* uses a colon after the salutation (a comma if the letter is social or personal) and a comma after the complimentary close. *Open punctuation* uses no colon or comma after the salutation or the complimentary close. Although the most popular style in business communication is mixed punctuation, either style of punctuation may be used with block or modified block letter formats. Because the simplified letter format has no salutation or complimentary close, the style of punctuation is irrelevant.

Figure A.6
Prescribed Envelope Format

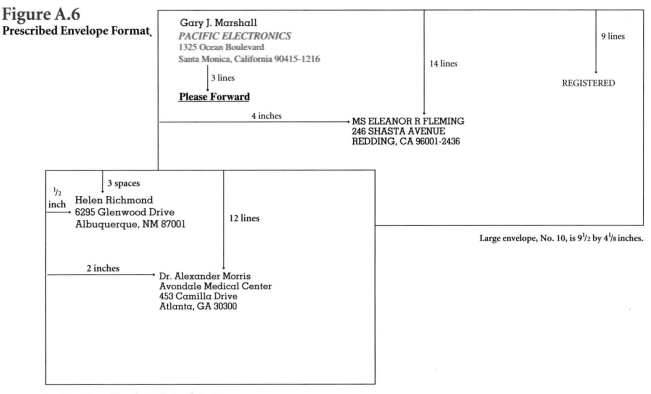

Large envelope, No. 10, is 9½ by 4⅛ inches.

Small envelope, No. 6¾, is 6½ by 3⅝ inches.

NVELOPES

The quality of the envelope is just as important for first impressions as the quality of the stationery. In fact, letterhead and envelopes should be of the same paper stock, have the same color ink, and be imprinted with the same address and logo. Most envelopes used by U.S. businesses are No. 10 envelopes (9½ inches long), which are sized to contain an 8½-by-11-inch piece of paper folded in thirds. Some occasions call for a smaller, No. 6¾, envelope or for envelopes proportioned to fit special stationery. Figure A.6 shows the two most common sizes.

Addressing the Envelope

No matter what size the envelope, the address is always single-spaced and in block form—that is, with all lines aligned on the left. The address on the envelope is in the same style as the inside address and presents the same information. The order to follow is from the smallest division to the largest:

1. Name and title of recipient
2. Name of department or subgroup
3. Name of organization
4. Name of building
5. Street address and suite number, or post office box number
6. City, state or province, and ZIP code or Postal Code
7. Name of country (if the letter is being sent abroad)

Because the U.S. Postal Service uses optical scanners to sort mail, envelopes for quantity mailings, in particular, should be addressed in the prescribed format. As in the mailing address on the No. 10 envelope in Figure A.6, everything is in capital letters, no punctuation is included, and all mailing instructions of interest to the post office are placed above the address area. Canada Post requires a similar format, except that only the city is all in capitals and the Postal Code is placed on the line below the name of the city. The post office scanners read addresses from the bottom up, so if a letter is to be sent to a post office box rather than to a street address, the street address should appear on the line above the box number. Figure A.6 also shows the proper spacing for addresses and return addresses.

The U.S. Postal Service and the Canada Post Corporation have published lists of two-letter mailing abbreviations for states, provinces, and territories (see Table A.2), to be used without periods or commas. Nevertheless, some executives prefer that state and province names be spelled out in full and that a comma be used to separate the city and state or province names. Thus the use of a comma between the name of the city and the state or province name is an unresolved issue. Most commonly, the comma is included; sometimes, however, the comma is eliminated to conform with post office standards.

Quantity mailings follow post office requirements. For letters that aren't mailed in quantity, a reasonable compromise is to use traditional punctuation and uppercase and lowercase letters for names and street addresses but two-letter state or province abbreviations, as shown here:

Table A.2	TWO-LETTER MAILING ABBREVATIONS FOR THE UNITED STATES AND CANADA				

State/Territory/Province	Abbreviation	State/Territory/Province	Abbreviation	State/Territory/Province	Abbreviation
UNITED STATES					
Alabama	AL	Michigan	MI	Utah	UT
Alaska	AK	Minnesota	MN	Vermont	VT
Arizona	AZ	Mississippi	MS	Virginia	VA
Arkansas	AR	Missouri	MO	Virgin Islands	VI
American Samoa	AS	Montana	MT	Washington	WA
California	CA	Nebraska	NE	West Virginia	WV
Canal Zone	CZ	Nevada	NV	Wisconsin	WI
Colorado	CO	New Hampshire	NH	Wyoming	WY
Connecticut	CT	New Jersey	NJ		
Delaware	DE	New Mexico	NM	**CANADA**	
District of Columbia	DC	New York	NY	Alberta	AB
Florida	FL	North Carolina	NC	British Columbia	BC
Georgia	GA	North Dakota	ND	Labrador	LB
Guam	GU	Northern Mariana Is.	CM	Manitoba	MB
Hawaii	HI	Ohio	OH	New Brunswick	NB
Idaho	ID	Oklahoma	OK	Newfoundland	NF
Illinois	IL	Oregon	OR	Northwest Territories	NT
Indiana	IN	Pennsylvania	PA	Nova Scotia	NS
Iowa	IA	Puerto Rico	PR	Ontario	ON
Kansas	KS	Rhode Island	RI	Prince Edward Island	PE
Kentucky	KY	South Carolina	SC	Quebec	PQ
Louisiana	LA	South Dakota	SD	Saskatchewan	SK
Maine	ME	Tennessee	TN	Yukon Territory	YT
Maryland	MD	Trust Territories	TT		
Massachusetts	MA	Texas	TX		

Mr. Kevin Kennedy
2107 E. Packer Drive
Amarillo, TX 79108

For all out-of-office correspondence use ZIP codes and Postal Codes, assigned to speed mail delivery. The U.S. Postal Service has divided the United States and its territories into ten zones, each represented by a digit from 0 to 9; this digit comes first in the ZIP code. The second and third digits represent smaller geographical areas within a state, and the last two digits identify a "local delivery area." Canadian Postal Codes are alphanumeric, with a three-character "area code" and a three-character "local code" separated by a single space (K2P 5A5). ZIP codes and Postal Codes should be separated from state and province names by one space. As an alternative, a Canadian Postal Code may be put on the bottom line of the address all by itself.

The U.S. Postal Service has introduced ZIP + 4 codes, which add a hyphen and four more numbers to the standard ZIP codes.

The first two of the new numbers may identify an area as small as a single large building, and the last two digits may identify one floor in a large building or even a specific department of an organization. The ZIP + 4 codes are especially useful for business correspondence. The Canada Post Corporation achieves the same result with special postal codes assigned to buildings and organizations that receive a large volume of mail.

Folding to Fit

Trivial as it may seem, the way a letter is folded also contributes to the recipient's overall impression of your organization's professionalism. When sending a standard-size piece of paper in a No. 10 envelope, fold it in thirds, with the bottom folded up first and the top folded down over it (Figure A.7); the open end should be at the top of the envelope and facing out. Fit smaller stationery neatly into the appropriate envelope simply by folding it in half or in thirds. When sending a

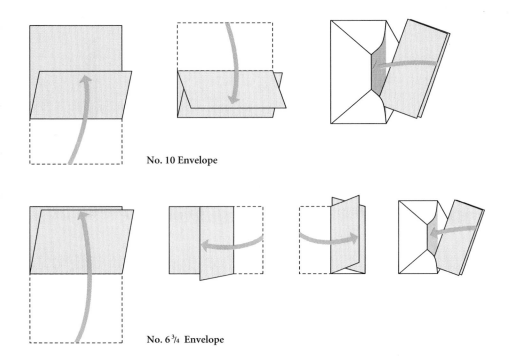

Figure A.7
Letter Folds for Standard-Size Letterhead

No. 10 Envelope

No. 6 ¾ Envelope

standard-size letterhead in a No. 6 ¾ envelope, fold it in half from top to bottom and then in thirds from side to side.

International Mail

When sending mail internationally, remember that postal service differs from country to country. For example, street addresses are uncommon in India, and the mail there is unreliable.[11] It's usually a good idea to send international correspondence by air mail and to ask that responses be sent that way as well. Also, remember to check the postage; rates for sending mail to most other countries aren't the same as the rates for sending mail within your own country.

Three main categories of international mail are the following:

- *LC mail.* An abbreviation of the French *Lettres et Cartes* ("letters and cards"), this category consists of letters, letter packages, aerograms, and postcards.
- *AO mail.* An abbreviation of the French *Autres Objets* ("other articles"), this category includes regular printed matter, books and sheet music, matter for the blind, small packets, and publishers' periodicals (second class).
- *CP mail.* An abbreviation of the French *Colis Postaux* ("parcel post"), this category resembles fourth-class mail, including packages of merchandise or any other articles not required to be mailed at letter postage rates.

The U.S. Postal Service also offers Express Mail International Service (EMS), a high-speed mail service to many countries; International Priority Airmail (IPA), an international service that's as fast as or faster than regular airmail service; International Surface Air Lift (ISAL), a service providing quicker delivery and lower cost for all kinds of printed matter; Bulk Letter Service to Canada, an economical airmail service for letters weighing 1 ounce or less; VALUEPOST/CANADA, a reduced postage rate for bulk mailings; In-

ternational Electronic Post (INTELPOST), a service offering same- or next-day delivery of fax documents; International Postal Money Orders, a service for transferring funds to other countries; and several optional special services.

To prepare your mail for international delivery, follow the instructions in the U.S. Postal Service Publication 51, *International Postal Rates and Fees.* Be sure to note instructions for the address, return address, and size limits. Envelopes and wrappers must be clearly marked to show their classification (letter, small packet, printed matter, air mail). All registered letters, letter packages, and parcel post packages must be securely sealed. Printed matter may be sealed only if postage is paid by permit imprint, postage meter, precanceled stamps, or second-class imprint. Otherwise, prepare contents so that they're protected but in such a way that they won't hinder inspection. Finally, because international mail is subject to customs examination in the country of destination, the contents and value must be declared on special forms.

 EMOS

Interoffice memos aren't distributed outside the organization, so they may not need the best-quality paper. However, they still convey important information, so clarity, careful arrangement, and neatness are important. As do those for letters, the guidelines for formatting memos help recipients understand at a glance what they've received and from whom.

Many organizations have memo forms printed, with labeled spaces for the recipient's name (or sometimes a checklist of all departments in an organization or all persons in a department), the sender's name, the date, and the subject (Figure A.8). If such forms don't exist, you can use plain paper or sometimes letterhead.

When using plain paper or letterhead, include a title such as *Memo* or *Interoffice Correspondence* (all in capitals) centered at the top of the page or aligned with the left margin. Also include the

Figure A.8
Preprinted Memo Form

MEMO

TO: _____

DEPT: _____   FROM: _____

DATE: _____   TELEPHONE: _____

SUBJECT: _____   *For your*
           ☐ APPROVAL ☐ INFORMATION ☐ COMMENT

words *To, From, Date,* and *Subject*—followed by the appropriate information—at the top with a blank line between, as shown here:

MEMO

TO:

FROM:

DATE:

SUBJECT:

Sometimes the heading is organized like this:

MEMO

TO: DATE:

FROM: SUBJECT:

You can arrange these four pieces of information in almost any order. The date sometimes appears without the heading *Date.* The subject may be presented with the letters *Re:* (in place of *SUBJECT:*) or may even be presented without any heading (but put it in capital letters so that it stands out clearly). You may want to include a file or reference number, introduced by the word *File.*

If you send a memo to a long list of people, include the notation *See distribution list* or *See below* in the *To* position at the top; then list the names at the end of the memo. Arranging such a list alphabetically is usually the most diplomatic course, although high-ranking officials may deserve more prominent placement. You can also address memos to groups of people—*All Sales Representatives, Production Group, Assistant Vice Presidents.*

You don't need to use courtesy titles anywhere in a memo; in fact, first initials and last names, first names, or even initials alone are often sufficient. As a general rule, however, use a courtesy title if you would use one in face-to-face encounters with the person.

The subject line of a memo helps busy colleagues find out quickly what your memo is about. Although the subject "line" may overflow onto a second line, it's most helpful when it's short (but still informative).

Start the body of the memo on the second or third line below the heading. Like the body of a letter, it's usually single-spaced. Separate paragraphs with blank lines. Indenting them is optional. Handle lists, important passages, and subheadings as you do in letters. If the memo is very short, you may double-space it.

If the memo carries over to a second page, head the second page just as you head the second page of a letter.

Unlike a letter, a memo doesn't require a complimentary close or a signature, because your name is already prominent at the top. However, you may initial the memo—either beside the name appearing at the top of the memo or at the bottom of the memo—or you may even sign your name at the bottom, particularly if the memo deals with money or confidential matters. Treat all other elements—reference initials, enclosure notations, and copy notations—as you would in a letter.

Memos may be delivered by hand, by the post office (when the recipient doesn't work at the same location as the memo writer), or through interoffice mail. Interoffice mail may require the use of special reusable envelopes that have spaces for the recipient's name and department or room number; the name of the previous recipient is simply crossed out. If a regular envelope is used, the words *Interoffice Mail* appear where the stamp normally goes so that it won't accidentally be stamped and mailed with the rest of the office correspondence.

Informal, routine, or brief reports for distribution within a company are often presented in memo form (see Chapter 12). Don't include such report parts as a table of contents and appendixes, but write the body of the memo report just as carefully as you'd write a formal report.

 -MAIL

Because e-mail messages can act both as memos (carrying information within your company) and as letters (carrying information outside your company and around the world), their format depends on your audience and purpose. You may choose to have your e-mail resemble a formal letter or a detailed report, or you may decide to keep things as simple as an interoffice memo. In fact, a modified memo format is probably appropriate for most e-mail messages.[12] All e-mail programs include two major elements: the header and the body (Figure A.9).

```
┌────────────────────────────────────────────────────────┐
│ ▣ ▤▤▤▤▤▤▤▤▤▤▤▤ E-Mail ▤▤▤▤▤▤▤▤▤▤▤▤ ▣            │
├────────────────────────────────────────────────────────┤
│                                                    ⬆    │
│  Date: Tuesday, 17 May 1997, 9:34:27, PDT               │
│  X-Sender: KeithW@Bluecrane.com                         │
│  To: bookco@artech.demon.co.uk                          │
│  From: "Keith D. Wells" <keithw@bluecrane.com>          │
│  Subject: Please confirm shipping date                  │
│  X-info: Demon.co.uk                                    │
│                                                         │
│  To:    Jeffrey Coombs, International Sales Desk         │
│         Artech House, London                            │
│                                                         │
│  From:  Keith Wells, Proprietor                         │
│         Blue Crane Books, Laguna Beach                  │
│                                                         │
│  Re:    Order # 1-SD-95466                              │
│         Dated: 7 April 1997                             │
│                                                         │
│  Dear Jeffrey:                                          │
│                                                         │
│  On 7 April 1996, we ordered the following books:       │
│    1 copy   _Electronic Mail_                           │
│             by Jacob Palme                              │
│             (ISBN# 0-89006-802-X)                       │
│                                                         │
│    2 copies _Distance Learning Technology and           │
│             Applications_                               │
│             by Daniel Minoli                           │
│             (ISBN# 0-89006-739-2)                       │
│                                                         │
│  Please confirm the date you shipped this order. My     │
│  customers are eager to receive their copies and have   │
│  been calling me almost daily.                          │
│                                                         │
│  You said in your last message that you would be        │
│  shipping them UPS on 10 April, so I would have         │
│  expected to receive them by now. Of course, I am       │
│  used to ordering through your Boston office, so I may   │
│  have misjudged the time it takes from London.          │
│                                                         │
│  Anything you can tell me about when they were shipped  │
│  will be most helpful.                                  │
│                                                         │
│  Thank you,                                             │
│                                                         │
│  Keith                                                  │
│                                                    ⬇    │
└────────────────────────────────────────────────────────┘
```

Figure A.9
In-Depth Critique: A Typical E-Mail Message

HEADER (May vary from program to program)

> *Date: Includes the day, date, time, and time zone*
>
> *To: Includes the recipient's address (perhaps addressee's proper name)*
>
> *From: Includes your address (perhaps your proper name)*
>
> *Subject (Re): Describes what your message concerns (an opportunity to gain interest)*
>
> *Cc: Includes the address of anyone you want to receive a copy of the message*
>
> *Bcc: Includes the address of anyone you want to receive a copy of the message but don't want listed as a receiver*
>
> *Attachments: Includes the name of any files you have attached to your message*

BODY (Format depends on your audience and purpose)

> *Your own header (optional): Used only if this information isn't easily obtained from program's header*
>
> *Greeting: Makes the message more personal*
>
> *Message: Includes line space between paragraphs, and can include headings, lists, and other common devices used in letters and memos*
>
> *Closing: Personalizes your message and resembles simple closings in letters*
>
> *Signature: Can be simply your name typed or can be a signature file*

Header

The e-mail header depends on the particular program you use. Some programs even allow you to choose between a shorter and a longer version. However, most headers contain similar information.

The *To:* line contains your audience's e-mail address. The most common e-mail addresses are Internet addresses, like the following:

- NMAA.BETSY@C.SI.EDU   Smithsonian Institute's National Museum of American Art
- webwsj@dowjones.com   *Wall Street Journal's* home page
- mailto:cci31@iway.fr   Chamber of Commerce and Industry in Toulouse, France

On the Internet, everything on the left side of the @ symbol is the user name; everything on the right side describes the computer where that user has an account. This machine name usually ends with a country code (such as fr for France, dk for Denmark, hk for Hong Kong, ca for Canada). But within the United States, the country code is replaced with the type of organization that operates that particular computer.[13]

- .com   business and commercial users
- .edu   educational institutions
- .gov   nonmilitary government and related groups
- .mil   military-related groups
- .net   network providers
- .org   organizations and nonprofit groups

Most e-mail programs will also allow you to send mail to an entire group of people all at once. First, you create a distribution list. Then you type the name of the list in the *To:* line instead of typing the addresses of every person in the group.[14]

The *From:* line contains your e-mail address. The *Date:* line contains the day of the week, date (day, month, year), time, and time zone. The *Subject:* line describes the content of the message and presents an opportunity for you to build interest in your message. The *cc:* line allows you to send copies of a message to more than one person at a time. It also allows everyone on the list to see who else received the same message. The *Bcc:* line lets you send copies to people without the other recipients knowing—a practice considered unethical by some.[15] The *Attachments:* line contains the name(s) of the file(s) you attach to your e-mail message. The file can be a word-processing document, a digital image, an audio or video message, a spreadsheet, or a software program.[16]

Other lines containing more detailed information can be listed in your e-mail's header, including *Message-Id* (the exact location of this e-mail message on the sender's system), *X-mailer:* (the version of the e-mail program being used), and *Content type:* (a description of what kind of text and character set is contained in the message). Also, the *Received:* lines include information about each of the systems your e-mail passed through en route to your mailbox.[17] Most e-mail programs now allow you the choice of hiding or revealing this sort of detailed information.

Body

You might consider your mail program's header to be something like letterhead, because the rest of the space below the header is for the body of your message. In the *To:* and *From:* lines, some headers actually print out the names of the sender and the receiver (in addition to the e-mail addresses). Other headers do not. If your mail program includes only the e-mail addresses, you might consider including your own memo-type header, as was done in Figure A.9. The writer even included a subject line in his memo-type header that is more specific than the one in the mail program header. Although some may applaud the clarity such a second header provides, others may criticize the space it takes. Your decision depends on how formal you want to be.

Do include a greeting in your e-mail. As pointed out in Chapter 6, greetings personalize your message. Leave one line space above and below your greeting to set it off from the rest of your message. Again, depending on the level of formality you want, you may choose to end your greeting with a colon (most formal), a comma (conversational), or even two hyphens (informal).

Your message begins one blank line space below your greeting. Just as in memos and letters, skip one line space between paragraphs and include headings, numbered lists, bulleted lists, and embedded

lists when appropriate. Limit your line lengths to a maximum of 80 characters by inserting a hard return at the end of each line.

One blank line space below your message, include a simple closing, often just one word. A blank line space below that, include your signature. Whether you type your name or use a signature file, including your signature personalizes your message.

TIME-SAVING MESSAGES

If there's a way to speed up the communication process, the organization stands to gain. Telephones and electronic mail systems are quick, as are mailgrams, telegrams, faxes, and the like. In addition, organizations have developed special formats to reduce the amount of time spent writing and typing short messages:

- *Fax cover sheets.* When faxing messages, you may use a fax cover sheet, which includes the recipient's name, company, fax number, and city; the sender's name, complete address, fax number, and telephone number; the number of pages being sent; a phone number to call if the faxed transmission isn't successful; and enough space for any brief message.[18] The format for this information varies widely. When a document is self-explanatory, a cover sheet may be unnecessary, so be sure not to waste paper or transmission time.
- *Memo-letters.* Printed with a heading somewhat like a memo's, memo-letters provide a space for an inside address so that the message may be sent outside the company (see Figure A.10). When the memo is folded properly, the address shows through a window in the envelope, thereby eliminating the need to address the envelope separately. Memo-letters often include a space for a reply message so that the recipient doesn't have to print out or type a whole new letter in response; carbonless copy sets allow sender and recipient to keep on file a copy of the entire correspondence.
- *Short-note reply technique.* Popular in many organizations, this technique can be used even without a special form. The recipient of a memo (or sometimes a letter) simply handwrites a response on the original document, makes a copy for the files, and sends the annotated original back to the person who wrote it.
- *Letterhead postcards.* Ideal for short, impersonal messages, letterhead postcards are preprinted with a list of responses so that the "writer" merely checks the appropriate response(s) and slips the postcard into the mail. Organizations such as mail-order companies and government agencies use these time-saving devices to communicate frequently with individuals by mail.

The important thing to realize about these and all other message formats is that they've developed over time to meet the need for clear communication and to speed responses to the needs of customers, suppliers, and associates.

REPORTS

You can enhance your report's effectiveness by paying careful attention to its appearance and layout. Follow whatever guidelines your organization prefers, but remember to be neat and consistent throughout. If it's up to you to decide formatting questions, the following conventions may help you decide how to handle margins, headings, spacing and indention, and page numbers.

Memo-letters such as this one are convenient for the writer, and, with the space for a reply message, they can be convenient for the recipient. However, they are much less formal than a business letter for outside correspondence.

MEMO

TO: Green Ridge Gifts
          1786 Century Road
          Nashua, NH 03060
          USA

FROM: Whiteside Import/Export, Ltd.
          1601 Ronson Drive
          Toronto, Ontario M9W 3E3
          CANADA

SUBJECT: Order for Royal Dorchester china
          completer sets

DATE: October 11, 1997

MESSAGE:

The six Wellington pattern completer sets that you ordered by telephone October 9 are on their way and should reach your shop by October 18.

The three Mayfield pattern completer sets are coming from the factory, however, and will not arrive here until October 26 or 27. That means you will get them around November 2 or 3.

Do you still want the Mayfield sets? Would you like us to bill you for the Wellington sets only so that you can pay for the Mayfield order separately? Please add your reply below, retain the yellow copy for your records, and send us the white and pink copies.

SIGNED: *Barbara Hutchins*

REPLY: PLEASE SEND THE MAYFIELD SETS AS SOON AS POSSIBLE. YOU MAY BILL FOR BOTH MAYFIELD AND WELLINGTON SETS.

DATE: OCT. 15, 1997

SIGNED: *William L. Smith*

☐ One blank space
 * Variable spacing depending on length of letter

Margins

All margins on a report page are at least 1 inch wide. Margins of 1 inch are customary for double-spaced pages, and margins of between 1¼ and 1½ inches are customary for single-spaced pages. The top, left, and right margins are usually the same, but the bottom margins can be 1½ times as deep as the others. Some special pages also have deeper top margins. Set top margins as deep as 2 inches for pages that contain major titles: prefatory parts such as the table of contents or the executive summary, supplementary parts such as the reference notes or bibliography, and textual parts such as the first page of the text or the first page of each chapter.

If you're going to bind your report at the left or at the top, add half an inch to the margin on the bound edge (Figure A.11). Because of the space taken by the binding on left-bound reports,

Figure A.11
Margins for Formal Reports

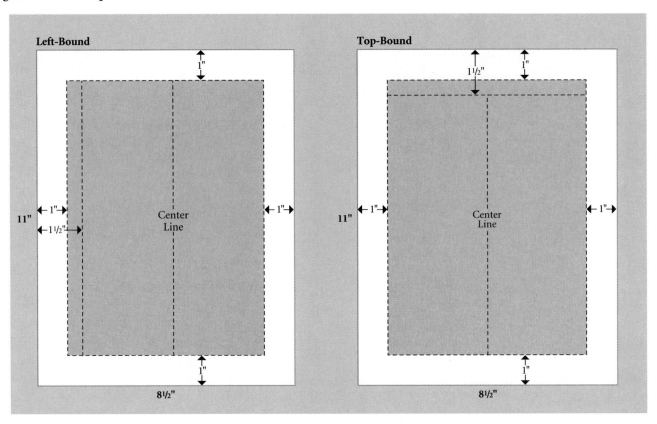

make the center point of the page a quarter inch to the right of the center of the paper. Be sure that centered headings are centered between the margins, not centered on the paper. Of course, computers can do this for you automatically. Other guidelines for formatting a report can be found in the sample in Chapter 14.

Headings

Headings of various levels provide visual clues to a report's organization. Figure 12.7, on page 284, illustrates one good system for showing these levels, but many variations exist. No matter which system you use, be sure to be consistent.

Spacing and Indentions

The spacing and indention of most elements of a report are relatively easy. If your report is double-spaced (perhaps to ease comprehension of technical material), indent all paragraphs five character spaces (or about ½ inch). In single-spaced reports, you can block the paragraphs (no indentions), leaving one blank line between them.

When using a typewriter, properly spacing the material on the title page is more complicated. For reports that will be bound on the left, start a quarter inch to the right of center. From that point, backspace once for each two letters in the line so that the line will appear centered once the report is bound.

To correctly place lines of type on the title page, first count the number of lines in each block of copy, including blank lines. Subtract the total from 66 (the total number of lines on an 11-inch page) to get the number of unused lines. To allocate these unused lines equally among the spaces between the blocks of copy, divide the number of unused lines by the number of blank areas (always one more than the number of blocks of copy). The result is the number of blank lines to devote to each section. Of course, a computer with a good word-processing program will do these calculations for you at the click of a mouse. As the title page of the sample report in Chapter 14 shows, the title page should look well balanced.

Page Numbers

Remember that every page in the report is counted but that not all pages have numbers shown on them. The first page of the report, normally the title page, is not numbered. All other pages in the prefatory section are numbered with a lowercase roman numeral, beginning with ii and continuing with iii, iv, v, and so on. The unadorned (no dashes, no period) page number is centered at the bottom margin.

Number the first page of the text of the report with the unadorned arabic numeral 1, centered at the bottom margin (double- or triple-spaced below the text). In left-bound reports, number the following pages (including the supplementary parts) consecutively with unadorned arabic numerals (2, 3, and so on), placed at the top right-hand margin (double- or triple-spaced above the text). For top-bound reports and for special pages having 2-inch top margins, center these page numbers at the bottom margin.

MEETING DOCUMENTS

The success of any meeting depends on the preparation of the participants and on the follow-up measures they take to implement decisions or to seek information after the meeting. Meeting documents—agendas and minutes—aid this process by putting the meeting plan and results into permanent, written form. Although small informal meetings may not require a written agenda, any meeting involving a relatively large number of people or covering a lot of ground will run more smoothly if an agenda is distributed in advance. A written agenda helps participants prepare by telling them what will be discussed, and it helps keep them on track once the meeting begins. The typical agenda format (shown in Figure A.12) may seem stiff and formal, but it helps structure a meeting so that as little time as possible is wasted. It also provides opportunities for discussion, if that's what is called for.

The presentation, a special form of meeting that allows for relatively little group interaction, may also require an agenda or a detailed outline. Special visual aids such as flip charts help attendees grasp the message, and copies of the charts are often provided for future reference.

After a meeting the secretary who attended prepares a set of minutes for distribution to all attendees and to any other interested parties. The minutes are prepared in much the same format as a memo or letter, except for the heading, which takes this form:

MINUTES
PLANNING COMMITTEE MEETING
MONDAY, AUGUST 21, 1998

Present: [All invited attendees who were present are listed here, generally by rank, in alphabetical order, or in some combination.]

Absent: [All invited attendees who were not present are listed here, in similar order.]

Figure A.12
Agenda Format

AGENDA

PLANNING COMMITTEE MEETING

Tuesday, August 21, 1998
10:00 A.M.

Executive Conference Room

   I. Call to Order

  II. Roll Call

 III. Approval of Agenda

 IV. Approval of Minutes from Previous Meeting

  V. Chairperson's Report

 VI. Subcommittee Reports
     A. New Markets
     B. New Products
     C. Finance

 VII. Unfinished Business

VIII. New Business
     A. Carson and Canfield Data
     B. Reassignments

 IX. Announcements

  X. Adjournment

The body of the minutes follows the heading, and it notes the times the meeting started and ended, all major decisions reached at the meeting, all assignments of tasks to meeting participants, and all subjects that were deferred to a later meeting. In addition, the minutes objectively summarize important discussions, noting the names of those who contributed major points. Outlines, subheadings, and lists help organize the minutes, and additional documentation (such as tables or charts submitted by meeting participants) are noted in the minutes and attached.

At the end of the minutes, the words *Submitted by* should be added, followed by a couple of blank lines for a signature and then the signer's printed (or typed) name and title (if appropriate). If the minutes have been written by one person and prepared by another, the preparer's initials should be added, as in the reference initials on a letter or memo.

An informal meeting may not require minutes. Attendees simply pencil their own notes onto their copies of the agenda. Follow-up is then their responsibility, although the meeting leader may need to remind them through a memo, phone call, or face-to-face talk.

APPENDIX B

Documentation of Report Sources

Documenting a report is too important a task to undertake haphazardly. By providing information about your sources, you improve your own credibility—as well as the credibility of the facts and opinions you present. By documenting your work, you give readers the means for checking your findings and pursuing the subject further. Also, documenting your report is the accepted way to give credit to the people from whose work you have drawn.

The specific style you use to document your report may vary from the styles recommended here. Experts recommend various forms, depending on your field or discipline. Moreover, your employer or client may use a form different from any the experts suggest. Don't let this discrepancy confuse you. If your employer specifies a form, use it; the standardized form is easier for colleagues to understand. However, if the choice of form is left to you, adopt a style like one of those described here. Just be consistent within any given report, using the same order, punctuation, and format from one reference citation or bibliography entry to the next. Of course, to document report sources, you have to find the information you need.

*F*INDING SOURCES

Chapter 13 describes the difference between primary data and secondary data and tells how to gather both kinds of research. Primary research (such as conducting studies and surveys yourself) is documented within the text of your report through descriptions of your methods and findings. This appendix describes how to present the results of secondary research in your report. Secondary sources for business research can be obtained from libraries and computerized databases.

Libraries

Today the first hurdle in getting information is to figure out which library to visit or to phone with your query. The *American Library Directory* lists more than 30,000 public, college, university, and special libraries in the United States and 3,000 in Canada. In addition, many companies have their own libraries. The Internet can help you get a better idea of what a library has to offer. Many libraries can be reached online for general information, access to the

computerized catalog, and even information about which books are out on loan and thus unavailable.

Basic References

Once you've decided which library to use, head for the reference section. A librarian with specialized knowledge of general sources of information can direct you to the appropriate dictionaries, encyclopedias, almanacs, atlases, biographical reference books, handbooks, manuals, directories of companies and associations, and perhaps even a collection of corporations' annual reports. In the absence of a knowledgeable reference librarian, consult *Reference Books: A Brief Guide* or *Business Information Sources,* or you can refer to Figure B.1, which lists the major reference books used by business researchers.

Books and Articles

Both books and articles provide in-depth coverage of specific topics. Although articles are more timely than books, books have a broader focus. A combination of the two often provides the best background for your report.

Numerous books and articles are published every year, and libraries must be selective when choosing works to put on their shelves. So when you need specialized information, a public library may not be very useful. You'll have better luck finding books and articles on technical subjects at college libraries (assuming the college offers courses in those subjects) and in company libraries.

All libraries provide bibliographies of the books and back issues of the publications they stock. The traditional card catalog contains vast numbers of index cards organized by subject, title, and author; a code on each card directs you to the shelf where the book or publication is located. However, some libraries have converted their card catalogs to microfilm or microfiche, which takes up far less space. Many other libraries have computerized the information about their holdings.

Abstracts

One way to find out a lot relatively quickly is to consult abstracts. Instead of just supplying a categorized list of article titles, as indexes do, abstracts summarize each article's contents as well. Many fields are served by abstracts that regularly review articles in the most useful periodicals. Here are the names of a few abstracts that may prove useful:

Figure B.1
Major Reference Works

- *Biography Index:* Indexes biographical data from more than 2,400 periodicals as well as from English-language books.

- *Books in Print:* Lists more than 425,000 books in 62,000 subject categories currently available from over 6,000 U.S. publishers. Also indexes books by author and by title.

- *Business Periodicals Index:* Lists articles from about 280 business-related periodicals; companion is *Canadian Business Index.*

- *Current Biography:* Features biographical data about individuals who have achieved fame during the period covered.

- *Directory of Directories:* Indexes several thousand business, industrial, and professional directories.

- *Dun & Bradstreet, Inc., Million Dollar Directory:* Lists more than 120,000 U.S. companies by net worth. Includes names of officers and directors, goods and services, approximate sales, and number of employees.

- *Encyclopedia of Associations:* Indexes thousands of associations by broad subject category, by specific subject, by name of association, and by geographical location.

- *Moody's Manuals:* In a series of publications for specific industries—such as banks and financial institutions, public utilities, and international companies—lists financial data of the sort found in corporate annual reports.

- *Reader's Guide to Periodical Literature:* Indexes articles in some 190 popular periodicals by subject and author.

- *Standard Periodical Directory:* Describes more than 66,000 U.S. and Canadian periodicals.

- *Standard & Poor's Register of Corporations:* Indexes more than 37,000 U.S., Canadian, and major international corporations. Lists officers, products, sales volume, and number of employees.

- *Statistical Abstract of the United States:* Presents U.S. economic, social, political, and industrial statistics.

- *Survey of Current Business:* Features national business statistics on construction, real estate, employment and earnings, finance, foreign trade, transportation, communication, and other key topics.

- *Thomas Register of American Manufacturers:* Presents information on thousands of U.S. manufacturers, indexed by company name and product.

- *U.S. Government Publications:* Monthly Catalog: Lists titles of more than 1,000 U.S. government publications in each issue.

- *Who's Who in America:* Summarizes the achievements of living U.S. citizens who have gained prominence in their fields; *Canadian Who's Who* and *Who's Who in Business and Finance* are similar.

- *World Almanac and Book of Facts:* Presents statistical information about many events, people, and places. Index contains both general subject headings and specific names. Similar information is available in the *Canadian Yearbook* and the *Corpus Almanac of Canada.*

- Other indexes of articles in newspapers, magazines, and journals:

  Accountants' Index
  Applied Science and Technology Index
  Art Index
  Biological and Agricultural Index
  Computer Literature Index
  Education Index
  Engineering Index
  General Science Index
  Humanities Index
  Index to Legal Periodicals
  Index Medicus
  The New York Times Index
  Predicasts (U.S. and international editions)
  Public Affairs Information Bulletin
  Social Sciences Index
  The Wall Street Journal Index

ABS Guide to Recent Publications
in the Social and Behavioral Sciences
Book Review Digest
Business Publications Index and Abstracts
Computer Abstracts
Dissertation Abstracts International
Educational Research Information Center (ERIC)
Personnel Management Abstracts
Psychological Abstracts
Sociological Abstracts

Government Documents

When you want to know the exact provisions of a law, the background of a court decision, or the current population patterns and business trends, you can consult the government documents section of a library. This sort of research can be rather complicated, but a librarian will direct you to the information you need. All you have to know is the government body you're interested in (U.S.

Congress, Ninth Court of Appeals, or Department of Labor) and some sort of identification for the specific information you need (such as the Safe Drinking Water Act of 1974, *Price v. Shell Oil,* or 1990 Census). If you have a date and the name of a publication containing the document, so much the better.

Computerized Databases

Many companies maintain their own computerized databases containing company-generated statistics on sales and expenses, product specifications, inventory status, market research data, and perhaps reports and correspondence as well. Your access to information expands greatly when you use Internet sources, on-line services such as CompuServe or America Online, or commercial databases such as Knowledge Index, Management Contents, National Newspaper Index, and Trade and Industry Index. A lot of this information can be downloaded directly, but some magazine articles will need to be ordered by e-mail, phone, or regular mail.

II-B-2a

Emily Card and Adam Miller, Business Capital for Women. An Essential Handbook for Entrepreneurs (New York: Macmillan, 1996), 4.

One of today's fastest-growing corporate categories is composed of female owned companies—especially in the small business sector, which is expanding rapidly.

(Great graph showing statistics!)

USING SOURCE INFORMATION

Locating all this information is just the first step, of course. Once you have the necessary information, you'll want to use what you've found. You begin by recording information effectively. By taking down information that's complete and well organized, you'll capture the information you need and avoid backtracking to look up something you forgot. Moreover, to maintain your credibility and ethics, you'll want to keep current with the issues of copyright and fair use.

Recording Information

The recording system that most students use (and many instructors recommend) is taking notes on 3-by-5-inch index cards, noting only one thought, quote, or other piece of information on each card. Try to summarize information in your own words, unless you think specific data or quotations may be useful. Using note cards has several advantages: Cards are easy to use, easy to carry around, and easy to sort and rearrange.

You're using these note cards to help you remember and retrieve useful information for your report, so be sure to record all bibliographical information carefully. Write the author's name, the title of the book or article, the publication information, and page numbers at the top of each card. (As an alternative, when you're collecting several pieces of information from each source, you might prepare a bibliography card for each one, number the cards, and then use these numbers to cross-reference your note cards.) It's helpful to note at the top of the card the general subject of the material (either in a simple phrase or with identifying numbers from your preliminary outline) so that you can sort your notes more easily when it comes time to write your report. Also indicate whether the information is a direct quote, a paraphrase of someone else's idea, or an idea of your own.[1] Figure B.2 shows a sample note card.

The card system works, without question. You won't go wrong with it. Until recently, people generally agreed that taking notes on computer was slower and more cumbersome than using index cards. Computers simply didn't have the tools to make this task easy, and they tended to get in the way more than they helped. However, advances in software are changing the picture. Here are several ways that computers can help you capture and organize research information:[2]

- *Organizing and outlining.* If you've used the outlining capability in a good word processor, you already know how helpful it can be. You can quickly move headings and blocks of information—about as easily as you can shuffle a deck of index cards. And outliners have a major advantage over index cards in that they let you select the amount of information you want to see at any given time. Sometimes it's hard to see the big picture if you have 30 or 40 pieces of detailed information strewn across the table. Outliners let you collapse or expand your outline, showing as many levels as you want. This feature can be a great help when you're trying to organize the flow of your speech.
- *Searching.* Now where was that quote about water pollution? If you have more than a few dozen cards, which is easy to do, finding a specific piece of information can be time consuming. With the notes in your computer, you simply use the "find" function to locate the information. It's faster, and you have much less chance of missing whatever information you're looking for.
- *Linking.* This is not a feature found in the typical word processor, but software packages such as Info Select make it easy to weave "threads" through your research materials. For instance, for some research on water pollution, information-management software could highlight for you all the research notes that involve government regulation. If you had organized your notes by problems and solutions, in chronological order, or from general concepts to specific details, these bits of information about regulation would probably be spread throughout your outline. By reminding you of such links, the software helps you handle all the themes and subthemes of your report clearly and consistently.

You may find that using a combination of index cards (to capture information while you're reading it) and computer software (to manage the information once you've captured it) is the best solution.

Whichever method you choose, be sure to record all the facts you need to responsibly credit your sources. Being thorough not only saves you time if you need to go back and check facts or quotes, but it is also your ethical responsibility.[3]

Understanding Copyright and Fair Use

You have an important reason for carefully documenting the sources you consult during secondary research: Although ideas belong to no one person, the way they're expressed provides the livelihood for many scholars, consultants, and writers. To protect the interests of these people, most countries have established copyright laws. If you transgress those laws, you or your company could be sued, not to mention embarrassed.

In addition to covering printed materials such as books and magazines, copyright law covers audiovisual materials, many forms of artistic expression, computer programs, maps, mailing lists, even answering machine messages. However, copyright law does not protect

- Titles, names, short phrases, and slogans
- Familiar symbols or designs
- Lists of ingredients or contents
- Ideas, procedures, methods, systems, processes, concepts, principles, discoveries, or devices (although it does cover their description, explanation, or illustration)

A work is considered copyrighted as soon as it's put into fixed form, even if it hasn't been registered.[4]

As discussed in Chapter 13, you can avoid plagiarism whenever you quote another person's work by telling where you found the statement. This documentation applies to books, articles, tables, charts, diagrams, song lyrics, scripted dialogue, letters, speeches—anything that you take verbatim (word for word) from someone else. Even if you paraphrase the material (change the wording somewhat), it's best to give credit to the person who has found an effective way of expressing an idea.

However, for general knowledge or for specialized knowledge that's generally known among your readers, you do not have to cite a source. For example, everyone knows that Franklin Roosevelt was elected to the presidency of the United States four times. You can say so on your own authority, even if you've read an article in which the author says the same thing.

Of course, merely crediting the source is not always enough. The fair use doctrine says that you can use other people's work only as long as you don't unfairly prevent them from benefiting as a result. For example, if you reproduce someone else's copyrighted questionnaire in a report you're writing (and identify the source thoroughly), you're preventing the author from selling a copy of that questionnaire to your readers.

In general, you do best to avoid relying to such a great extent on someone else's work. However, when you can't avoid it, contact the copyright holder (usually the author or publisher) for permission to reprint. You'll usually be asked to pay a fee.

Fair use is decided in the courts on a case-by-case basis. So you won't find any hard-and-fast rules about when to get permission. In general, however, you would probably request permission to use

- More than 250 words quoted from a book
- Any reproduction of a piece of artwork (including fully reproduced charts and tables) or excerpt from commercially produced audiovisual material
- Any dialogue from a play or line from a poem or song

- Any portion of consumable materials, such as workbooks
- Multiple copies of copyrighted works that you intend to distribute widely or repeatedly, especially for noneducational purposes

You do not need permission to use materials published before 1907, news articles more than three months old, or materials originally published by the government. Nor do you need permission to use copies as the basis for "criticism, comment, news reporting, teaching, scholarship, or research."[5]

When deciding whether you may use someone else's work without permission, remember that the courts (if they get involved) will consider the length of your quotation in relation to the total length of the work from which it is taken, the type of work you are taking it from, your purpose, and the effect your action has on the original author's efforts to distribute the work. If you think you may be infringing on the author's rights, write for permission and provide a credit line. In any case, be sure to acknowledge the original author's work with a source note.

P REPARING REFERENCE LISTS

In every report you write, you'll need to give your readers a complete list of the sources you used. You can assign a title to this list, such as Sources, Bibliography, Reference List, Works Cited (if you include only those sources you actually cited in your report), or Works Consulted (if you include uncited sources as well). Your reference list also serves as a reading list for readers who want to pursue the subject of your report further, so you may want to annotate each entry—that is, comment on the subject matter and viewpoint of the source, as well as on its usefulness. Annotations may be written in either complete or incomplete sentences:

Helgeson, Donald V. *Engineer's and Manager's Guide to Winning Proposals*. Boston: Artech House, 1994. Makes proposal writing almost as easy as filling-in-the-blanks pages; contains a step-by-step process for analyzing a request for proposal; 283 pages.

Depending on the length of your report and the complexity and number of your sources, you may either place the entire bibliography at the end of the report (after the endnotes) or place relevant sections at the end of each chapter. Another way to make a long bibliography more manageable is to subdivide it into categories (a classified bibliography), either by type of reference (such as books, articles, and unpublished material) or by subject matter (such as government regulation, market forces, and so on).

Reference List Construction

When preparing the reference list, start each entry at the left margin, with the author's last name first. Entries are alphabetized and single-spaced (with a double space between entries). After the first line, these entries are usually indented (customarily five spaces or as few as two). See Figure B.3 and the Electrovision report that appears in Chapter 14.

Many schemes have been proposed for organizing the information in source notes, but all of them break the information into three main parts: (1) information about the author, (2) information about the work, and (3) information about the publication.

Reference List

"Acquired Immunodeficiency Syndrome." In Mesh vocabulary file [database online]. Bethesda, Md.: National Library of Medicine, 1990 [cited 3 October 1990] Identifier no. D000163. [49 lines.]

Asakawa, Frances. "Recommendations for Replacing the Sales Fleet Based on a Comparison of Three Midsize Automobiles." Report to Daniel Standish, Director of Sales, Midwest Marketing, Inc., 17 November 1994.

Baron, Robert A. <rabaron@pipeline.com> "Copyright and Fair Use of Images." 9 February 1997. <fj.soc.copyright> (3 March 1997).

Choon, Tang Meng. <tanmeng@biomed.nus.sg> "Broadcasting Standards." 29 January 1997. Personal e-mail (30 January 1997).

Conrad, Charles. *Strategic Organizational Communication: An Integrated Perspective.* 2d ed. Fort Worth, Tx.: Holt, Rinehart and Winston, 1990.

Donaldson, John, ed. *Business Ethics.* San Diego: Academic Press, 1992.

Fenwick, Rose, et al. *Guidelines for Teaching Persuasive Writing.* Chicago: Illinois State Department of Education, Chicago Division of Education Services, July 1990. 87, DIALOG, ERIC, ED 179423.

"Forecasters Predict Economy Won't Change Much." *Wall Street Journal,* 12 October 1993, sec. A, 16.

Gabbei, Dorothy. Interview with the author. Emporia, Kans., 14 July 1992.

Group Productivity. Del Mar, Calif.: CRM/McGraw-Hill Films, 1995. Videotape, 22 min.

Hawkins, Katherine W. "Effects of Gender and Communication Content on Leadership Emergence in Small Task-Oriented Groups." Paper presented at the 78th annual meeting of the Speech Communication Association, Chicago, 1992.

Ivey, Keith C. "Joining a Usenet Community," *The Editorial Eye,* n.d.,<http://www.eeicom.com/eye/utw/96dec.html> (10 February 1997).

"Jericho's Walls." In History Log9008 [electronic bulletin board]. S.1. 27 August 1990—[cited 15 December 1990]. Available from <listserv@FINHUTC.BITNET>.

Lamude, Kevin G., and Joseph Scudder. "Compliance-Gaining Techniques of Type-A Managers." *Journal of Business Communication* 30, no. 1 (1993): 63–79.

Landes, Les L. "Down with Quality Programitis." *IABC Communication World,* February 1992, 31.

Lotus 1-2-3 Rel. 2 Lotus Development Corporation, Cambridge, Mass.

Presner, Lewis A. *The International Business Dictionary and Reference.* New York: Wiley, 1991.

Steele, Peter A. "Implementation of Cyber Appliances Through Cable Television." Master's thesis, San Diego State University, 1996.

"Time to Call in the Boss." *Brandweek,* 27 July 1992, 32–36, 60.

U.S. Bureau of the Census. *Statistical Abstract of the United States: 1996.* 116th ed. Washington, D.C.: GPO, 1996.

U.S. Congress. Senate Committee on Foreign Relations. *Famine in Africa: Hearing Before the Committee on Foreign Relations.* 99th Cong., 1st sess., 17 January 1985. [pp. 53–57 for footnote.]

U.S. Department of Commerce. *Falling Through the Net: A Survey of the "Have Nots" in Rural and Urban America.* July 1995. <http://www.ntia.doc.gov/ntiahome/fallingthru.html>. [accessed online 5 December 1996.]

Wallace, Mike. *60 Minutes.* CBS-TV, 22 August 1993.

Figure B.3
Sample Reference List

The first part includes the author's name, last name first. The second part includes the title of the work, and such other identifying information as the edition and volume number. The third part includes the place of publication, the publisher, and the date of publication, followed by relevant page numbers. A few details about these elements are described in the sections that follow.

Author's Name
If the author of the work is only one person, spell out the name (last name first) and follow it with a period. For multiple authors, only the first author's name appears in reversed order. Two authors' names are separated with *and.* For three or more authors, separate the names with commas and insert *and* before the last author's name. For more than three authors, you usually list all the authors; however, it's also acceptable simply to insert *et al.* or *and others* after the first author's name, with no preceding comma.

Title of the Work
Titles commonly appear uppercase and lowercase, which means that the first and last words start with a capital letter, as do all nouns, pronouns, verbs, adverbs, and adjectives. However, prepositions, conjunctions, and articles start with a lowercase letter; exceptions include prepositions that are an inseparable part of an expression (as in "Looking Up New Words") and often prepositions

and conjunctions with more than four letters. For works that have a two-part title, use a colon to separate the two parts, and capitalize the letter that comes right after the colon.

Managerial Communications: A Strategic Approach

Titles of books, periodicals (journals and magazines published at regular intervals), and other major works are usually italicized on computer (or underlined on a typewriter). Sometimes they appear in all capitals (with no italics or underlining) to make the keyboarding task easier and to make the title stand out more. Titles of articles, pamphlets, chapters in books, and the like are most often placed in quotation marks.

Publication Information

Bibliographic entries referring to periodicals don't usually include the publisher's name and place of business, but entries for books, pamphlets, and other hard-to-find works do include such publication information. In a book entry, the first item of publication data is the city where the publisher is located. If the city is large and well known and if there are no other well-known cities by the same name, its name can appear alone. However, if necessary for proper identification, the state, province, or country should also be indicated. Abbreviations are used for states and provinces. A colon follows the name of the place.

The publisher's name comes after the colon, often in a shortened form. For example, Prentice Hall, Inc., can easily be identified when shortened to Prentice Hall. If you begin with shortened publishers' names, be sure to carry through with the same short forms throughout. Use a publisher's full name if it's not well known or if it might be confused with some other organization. The publisher's name is followed by a comma.

The publication date is the most recent year on the copyright notice. Ignore the dates of printing.

Manuals of Style

For more specific format guidelines about capitalization, punctuation, abbreviation, and order of the elements within these three main parts, follow the style established by your employer or consult a style manual. A wide variety of style manuals provide information on constructing reference lists (and on documentation in general):

Achtert, Walter S., and Joseph Gibaldi. *The MLA Style Manual.* New York: Modern Language Association, 1985. Basis for the note and bibliography style used in much academic writing and recommended in many college textbooks on writing term papers; provides a lot of examples in the humanities.

American Psychological Association. *Publication Manual of the American Psychological Association.* 4th ed. Washington, D.C.: American Psychological Association, 1994. Details the author-date system, which is preferred in the social sciences and often in the natural sciences as well.

The Chicago Manual of Style. 14th ed. Chicago: University of Chicago Press, 1993. Known as the *Chicago Manual* and widely used in the publishing industry; detailed treatment of documentation in Chapters 15 and 16.

Gibaldi, Joseph. *MLA Handbook for Writers of Research Papers.* 4th ed. New York: Modern Language Association, 1995. One of the standard style manuals for footnote and bibliography form.

Gibaldi, Joseph. *MLA Style Manual and Guide to Scholarly Publishing.* 2d ed. New York: Modern Language Association, 1998. Full treatment of documentation and a discussion of scholarly publishing.

Harnack, Andrew, and Eugene Kleppinger. *Online! A Reference Guide to Using Internet Sources.* New York: St. Martin's Press, 1997. A comprehensive review of style for citing online references.

Slade, Carol. *Form and Style: Research Papers, Reports, Theses.* 10th ed. Boston: Houghton Mifflin, 1997. A comprehensive review of the *Chicago* style, MLA style, and APA style.

Turabian, Kate L. *A Manual for Writers of Term Papers, Theses, and Dissertations.* Revised and expanded by Bonnie Birtwhistle Honigsblum. 6th ed. Chicago: University of Chicago Press, 1995. Based on the *Chicago Manual,* but smaller and limited to matters of concern to report writers; many examples of documenting nonstandard references.

Warren, Thomas L. *Words into Type.* 3d ed. Englewood Cliffs, N.J.: Prentice Hall, 1992. Useful information on the classic use of scholarly notes and bibliographies.

Reference List Entries

Because you're referring your reader to a work as a whole, bibliographic entries do not usually include page numbers (unless you're citing a chapter in a book or an article). To be sure you have all the information you need when it's time to construct a reference list, use the same format during your research that you'll be using in your report. Figure B.3 contains some sample bibliographic entries, based on guidelines recommended in the *Chicago Manual of Style.*

Books

In their simplest form, references to books look like the Presner entry in Figure B.3. Sometimes, however, you'll want to include additional information:

- For the edition of a book, place the information after the title (using abbreviations such as 1st, 2d, 3d, 4th, and so on—as in the Conrad entry in Figure B.3).
- For more than one work by the same author, use three em dashes (or six hyphens) in place of the author's name. (However, repeat the name if one of the books is by a single author and another is by that author with others.)
- To cite a volume number, place *vol. 3* (or the correct number) after the title or edition number and before the publication data.
- To use the name of an editor instead of an author, simply place *ed.* after the editor's name (as in the Donaldson entry).

Periodicals

The typical periodical reference looks like the Landes entry in Figure B.3. The article author's name (if there is one) is handled as a book author's is, but the title of the article appears in quotation marks. Like the title of a book, the title of the magazine or journal appears either in italics (underlined) or in all capital letters. The page numbers are always inclusive (that is, they show the page numbers for the entire article). Entries that have no author are listed alphabetically by title.

The rest of the periodical entry can be tricky, however. For popular and business magazines, you need include only the date and page number(s) after the title (as in the "Time to Call in the Boss" entry in Figure B.3). Be sure the date is inverted (14 June 1997)—unlike the dates you use in text. For scientific or academic journals, include the volume number and treat the page number(s) as shown in the Lamude and Scudder entry in Figure B.3.

As a rule of thumb, use the more scholarly style if your report is weighted heavily toward serious research in professional journals; however, if popular and trade magazines dominate your references, you may stick with the simpler style that leaves out the volume number. Another option is to use both styles, depending on the type of periodical being referenced. Your guiding principle in choosing a style is to provide the information that your readers need to find your source easily.

Newspapers

When a newspaper article doesn't have an author, the citation begins with the name of the article (and the entry is alphabetized by the first word of that title). The name of the newspaper is treated like the title of a book or periodical. Many of the best-known newspapers—such as the *New York Times,* the *Wall Street Journal,* and the *Christian Science Monitor*—are not easily mistaken for other newspapers, but many smaller newspapers are less easily identified. If the name of the city (plus the state or province for obscure or small cities) doesn't appear in the title of these newspapers, put the place name in brackets after the title. Finally, a newspaper reference specifies the date of publication in the same way a magazine does, and it ends with a section name or number (if appropriate) and a page number (see the entry in Figure B.3 that begins "Forecasters Predict Economy . . . ").

Public Documents

Government documents and court cases are often useful in business reports, but bibliographic entries referring to them can be difficult to construct. As you struggle with a complex set of "authors" and publication data, remember that the goal is to provide just enough information to identify the work and to distinguish it from others. In Figure B.3, the entries for the U.S. Bureau of the Census and for the U.S. Congress are examples of how to format government documents.

Unpublished Material

Theses, dissertations, and company reports—which are usually prepared for a limited audience of insiders—are handled similarly. The title, like an article title, is in quotation marks, and "publication" data are included to help the reader find the work (see Figure B.3 entries for Asakawa and for Steele). This format can be used for any written source that doesn't fall into one of the other categories, such as a sales brochure or a presentation handout. Identify the author, title, and place and date of publication as completely as you can so that your readers have a way to refer to the source.

Formal letters, speeches, interviews, and other types of unpublished references are also identified as completely as possible to give readers some means of checking your sources. Begin with the name, title, and affiliation of the "author"; then describe the nature of the communication, the date and possibly the place, and if appropriate, the location of the files containing the document (as in Figure B.3, entries for Gabbei and Hawkins). Casual letters, interviews, and telephone conversations are rarely included in bibliographies; however, in notes you can identify the communication as personal (see Figure B.3 entry for Choon).

Electronic Media

Television and radio programs, films, computer programs, Internet sources, electronic databases, and the like are also documented. It may be more difficult for a reader to refer to some of these media (especially television and radio programs), but you still want to acknowledge ideas and facts borrowed from someone else. Figure B.3 lists ten electronic entries. The information provided in these entries is sufficient to give readers a clear idea of the works you consulted. For more details on the formatting of electronic sources, consult style manuals such as the *Chicago Manual of Style* and the *MLA Style Manual.*

CHOOSING A METHOD OF IN-TEXT CITATION

Once you have constructed a complete and well-organized reference list, you can choose from several methods of documenting report sources in text. Three popular ways of handling citations are the author-date system, the key-number system, and the superscript system. Although the author-date system is preferred by many style manuals, the classic superscript system is still often used in scholarly works. The key-number system is least preferred by most authorities.

Author-Date System

When using the author-date system to make a reference citation in text, simply insert the author's last name and the year of the publication within parentheses. You can add a page number when necessary:

. . . a basic understanding of the problem (Landes 1992, 31).

An alternative is to weave the name of the author into the sentence:

According to Landes (1992), no solution is likely to come . . .

When no author is named, use a short form of the title of the work. If the "author" is an organization, then shorten the name of the organization. In either case, make sure a reader can easily find this entry in the reference list:

. . . with an emphasis on environmental matters (U.S. Department of Commerce 1995).

If this entry were identified as "Department of Commerce," your reader would be searching the *D*s instead of the *U*s for the correct reference.

When listing more than one work by the same author, rely on the year of publication to distinguish between them. A lowercase letter (*a, b,* and so on) after the year differentiates two works by the same author published in the same year.

The author-date system requires a reference list containing all your sources with all the pertinent publication information. The only variable is the placement of the year of publication; for the convenience of readers, the year of publication is placed just after the author's name:

Presner, Lewis A. 1991. *The International Business Dictionary and Reference.* New York, Wiley.

Landes, Les L. 1992. "Down with Quality Programitis." *IABC Communication World,* February, 31.

A modification of the author-date system uses author-page information. Like the author-date system, the author-page system lets you weave references into the text. However, instead of using the author's name with the year of publication, this system uses the author's name and a page reference:

. . . giving retailers some additional options (Landes, 31).

Parenthetical references can often be reduced to just the page number:

In their article on management cooperation, Lamude and Scudder emphasize type-A managers (63–79).

Conrad offers specific guidelines for handling problems with organizational communication (127).

Key-Number System

To use the least preferred method of documenting sources, you number each reference-list entry in sequence, with an arabic numeral followed by a period. A key-number reference list is sometimes arranged in order of the appearance of each source in the text (rather than in alphabetical order).

In the text, references are documented with numbers. The first is the number assigned to the source, the second is the page number:

. . . a basic understanding of the problem (12:7).

This reference cites page 7 of item 12 in the reference list. The goal of using the author-date, author-page, and key-number systems is to simplify the traditional method of documentation using superscripts.

Superscript System

Source information has been traditionally handled using superscripts, which are arabic numerals placed just above the line of type. Scholarly works in the humanities are still documented using this method. The superscript lets the reader know to look for source information either in a **footnote** (at the bottom of report pages) or in an **endnote** (at the end of each chapter or at the end of the report). Footnotes can be handier for readers, but some readers find them distracting. Endnotes are less intrusive, but readers may become annoyed with flipping to the end of the report to find them.

For the reader's convenience, you can use footnotes for **content notes** (which may supplement your main text with asides about a particular issue or event, provide a cross-reference to another section of your report, or direct the reader to a related source). Then you can use endnotes for **source notes** (which document direct quotations, paraphrased passages, and visual aids). Consider which type of note is most common in your report, and then choose whether to present them all as endnotes or all as footnotes. If all your sources are listed as endnotes, you may find that a bibliography is unnecessary. However, the larger and more formal the report, the greater the need for a separate reference list. Regardless of the method you choose for referencing textual information in your report, both content notes and source notes pertaining to visual aids are placed on the same page as the visual aid.

Superscripts usually come at the end of the sentence containing the referenced statement, but a superscript may be placed right after the referenced statement to avoid confusion:

Rising interest rates put a damper on third-quarter profits in all industries,[1] and profits did not pick up again until the Federal Reserve loosened the money supply.[2]

The first superscript in this example comes after the comma. Superscripts follow all punctuation marks except the dash (which follows the superscript).

Superscripts are numbered consecutively throughout the report. (In very long reports, they may be numbered consecutively throughout each chapter instead, as in this textbook.) If a note is added or deleted, all the reference marks that follow must be changed to maintain an unbroken sequence. If you change the superscript, be sure to renumber the corresponding notes as well. (Of course, word-processing software contains a note feature that will automatically renumber for you.) Content notes appearing in visual aids are marked with asterisks and other symbols (or italicized lowercase letters if the visual aids contain many numbers).

Source Note Mechanics

Source notes generally follow the same order as bibliographic entries; however, commas are often substituted for periods, and the publication information appears in parentheses. A source note often refers to a specific page number. If it does, the closing parenthesis is followed by a comma, which in turn is followed by the page number(s):

4. Lewis A. Presner, *The International Business Dictionary and Reference* (New York: Wiley, 1991), 62–63.

Notes of all varieties are single-spaced and separated from one another by a double space. In footnotes to textual information, the identifying number is indented five spaces and followed by a period (as in the Presner note just cited). However, endnotes begin at the left margin (see the "References" section at the end of this book). Notes referring to visual aids are handled differently too: A source note, preceded by the underlined (italicized) word *Source* and a colon, is placed at the bottom of the visual aid; content notes, if any, are listed below the source note. Figure 14.2, on page 330, shows the placement of these notes on visual aids.

When using footnotes, plan carefully to leave enough space for the footnote at the bottom of the page and still maintain the standard margin. Word-processing software handles the layout and numbering of notes for you, whether footnotes or endnotes. When using a typewriter, separate the footnotes from the text with a line (made using the underscore key) about 1½ inches long (15 spaces in pica type, 20 in elite).

Quotations   Quotations from secondary sources must always be followed by a reference mark. However, quotations may appear in one of two forms, depending on their length. A brief quotation (three lines or less) can be typed right into the main body of the text. Quotation marks at the beginning and end of the quotation separate the other person's words from your own.

Longer quotations must be set off as extracts. An extract begins on a new line, and both right and left margins are indented five to seven spaces. No quotation marks are needed. Although the main text may be single- or double-spaced, an extract is always single-spaced.

You'll often want to leave out some part of a quotation. Ellipsis points (or dots) are the three periodlike punctuation marks that show something is missing.

Brant has demonstrated . . . a wanton disregard for the realities of the marketplace. His days at the helm are numbered. . . . Already several lower-level executives are jockeying for position.[3]

The second sentence in this example shows you how ellipsis points are handled between sentences: A period is followed by the three dots. Also, make sure ellipsis points appear with spaces before, after, and between them.

Repeated Notes   When you cite the same reference more than once in the course of your report, you can save time and effort by using a full citation for the first source note and a shortened form for later references. The information in repeated source notes can be handled in two ways: in a formal, traditional style or in an informal style. The formal style uses Latin abbreviations to indicate certain information; the informal style uses shortened versions of the source information instead. Here are some repeated source notes using the formal style:

4. Lewis A. Presner, *The International Business Dictionary and Reference* (New York: Wiley, 1991), 62–63.

5. Ibid., 130. [refers to page 130 in the Presner book]

6. Charles Conrad, *Strategic Organizational Communication: An Integrated Perspective*, 2d ed. (Fort Worth, Tx.: Holt, Rinehart and Winston, 1990), 107.

7. Les L. Landes, "Down with Quality Programitis," *IABC Communication World*, February 1992, 31.

8. Conrad, op. cit., 28. [refers to a new page in the book cited in note 6]

9. Landes, loc. cit. [refers to page 31 of the book cited in note 7]

Ibid. means "in the same place"—that is, the same reference mentioned in the immediately preceding entry but perhaps a different page (indicated by giving the page number). *Op. cit.* means "in the work cited"; because it's used when at least one other reference has come between it and the original citation, you must include the last name of the author. You must also use a new page number; otherwise, you would use *loc. cit.* ("in the place cited") and omit the page number.

The informal style, which is commonly used today, avoids Latin abbreviations by adopting a shortened form for the title of a reference that is repeated. In this style, the previous list of source notes would appear as follows:

4. Lewis A. Presner, *The International Business Dictionary and Reference* (New York: Wiley, 1991), 62–63.

5. Presner, *The International Business Dictionary and Reference*, 130.

6. Charles Conrad, *Strategic Organizational Communication: An Integrated Perspective*, 2d ed. (Fort Worth, Tx.: Holt, Rinehart and Winston, 1990), 107.

7. Les L. Landes, "Down with Quality Programitis," *IABC Communication World*, February 1992, 31.

8. Conrad, *Strategic Organizational Communication*, 28.

9. Landes, "Down with Quality Programitis," 31.

Only the author's last name, a short form of the title, and the page number are used in this style of repeated source note. If your report has a comprehensive alphabetical bibliography, you may opt to use the short form for all your source notes, not just for first citations.

Source Note Format

Source notes present the same information as bibliographic entries, in some cases with the addition of page numbers. Source note punctuation differs from bibliographic style, and parentheses are placed around the publication data. To emphasize the differences between source notes and bibliographic entries, the examples in Figure B.4 use the same sources as the references appearing in Figure B.3.

Remember, even though legal cases such as reference note 19 are often not listed in bibliographies, they may be mentioned in the text or cited in source notes. Be sure to provide the name of the case, the volume and page numbers of the law report, the name of the court that decided the case (the U.S. Supreme Court here), and the year of the decision. References to unpublished sources such as notes 20–23 may also be woven into the text of your report and thus require no source note.

The exact information you provide for electronic references such as notes 24–33 depends on your subject and audience and on the context of the reference. For example, when you are citing a film, it may be appropriate to note the scriptwriter or director. When constructing source notes for electronic media, consult a good style manual and use good judgment about how much information is needed.

Figure B.4
Sample Source Notes

BOOKS

10. Lewis A. Presner, *The International Business Dictionary and Reference* (New York: Wiley, 1991), 62–63.

11. Charles Conrad, *Strategic Organizational Communication: An Integrated Perspective,* 2d ed. (Fort Worth, Tx.: Holt, Rinehart and Winston, 1990), 107.

12. John Donaldson, ed., *Business Ethics* (San Diego: Academic Press, 1992), 74.

PERIODICALS AND NEWSPAPERS

13. Les L. Landes, "Down with Quality Programitis," *IABC Communication World,* February 1992, 31.

14. "Time to Call in the Boss," *Brandweek,* 27 July 1992, 32–36, 60.

15. Kevin G. Lamude and Joseph Scudder, "Compliance-Gaining Techniques of Type-A Managers," *Journal of Business Communication* 30, no. 1 (1993): 63–79.

16. "Forecasters Predict Economy Won't Change Much," *Wall Street Journal,* 12 October 1993, sec. A, 16.

PUBLIC DOCUMENTS

17. U.S. Bureau of the Census, *Statistical Abstract of the United States: 1996,* 116th ed. (Washington, D.C.: GPO, 1996), 337.

18. U.S. Congress, Senate Committee on Foreign Relations, *Famine in Africa: Hearing Before the Committee on Foreign Relations,* 99th Cong., 1st sess., 17 January 1985, 53–57.

19. *Simpson v. Union Oil Co. of California,* 377 U.S. 13 (U.S. Sup. Ct. 1964).

UNPUBLISHED MATERIALS

20. Katherine W. Hawkins, "Effects of Gender and Communication Content on Leadership Emergence in Small Task-Oriented Groups" (paper presented at the 78th annual meeting of the Speech Communication Association, Chicago), 1992.

21. Peter A. Steele, "Implementation of Cyber Appliances Through Cable Television" (Master's thesis, San Diego State University, 1996), 56–61.

22. Frances Asakawa, "Recommendations for Replacing the Sales Fleet Based on a Comparison of Three Midsize Automobiles." Report to Daniel Standish, Director of Sales, Midwest Marketing, 17 November 1994, 12.

23. Dorothy Gabbei, interview with the author, Emporia, Kans., 14 July 1992.

ELECTRONIC MEDIA

24. Mike Wallace, *60 Minutes,* CBS-TV, 22 August 1993.

25. *Group Productivity* (Del Mar, Calif.: CRM/McGraw-Hill Films, 1995), videotape, 22 min.

26. Lotus 1-2-3 Rel. 2, Lotus Development Corporation, Cambridge, Mass.

27. "Acquired Immunodeficiency Syndrome," in Mesh vocabulary file [database online] (Bethesda, Md.: National Library of Medicine, 1990 [cited 3 October 1990]) identifier no. D000163 [49 lines].

28. U.S. Department of Commerce, *Falling Through the Net: A Survey of the "Have Nots" in Rural and Urban America,* July 1995 <http://www.ntia.doc.gov/ntiahome/fallingthru. html> [accessed online 5 December 1996].

29. Rose Fenwick et al., *Guidelines for Teaching Persuasive Writing* (Chicago: Illinois State Department of Education, Chicago Division of Education Services, July 1990), 87, DIALOG, ERIC, ED 179423.

30. "Jericho's Walls," in History Log 9008 [electronic bulletin board], S.1. 27 August 1990—[cited 15 December 1990]; available from <listserv@FIN-HUTC.BITNET>.

31. Keith C. Ivey, "Joining a Usenet Community," *The Editorial Eye,* n.d., <http://www.eeicom.com/eye/utw/96dec.html> (10 February 1997).

32. Tang Meng Choon, <tanmeng@biomed.nus.sg> "Broadcasting Standards," 29 January 1997, personal e-mail (30 January 1997).

33. Robert A. Baron, <rabaron@pipeline.com> "Copyright and Fair Use of Images," 9 February 1997 <fj.soc.copyright> (3 March 1997).

APPENDIX C

Fundamentals of Grammar and Usage

Grammar is nothing more than the way words are combined into sentences, and usage is the way words are used by a network of people—in this case, the community of businesspeople who use English. You'll find it easier to get along in this community if you know the accepted standards of grammar and usage. What follows is a review of the basics of grammar and usage, things you've probably learned but may have forgotten. Without a firm grasp of these basics, you risk not only being misunderstood but also damaging your company's image, losing money for your company, and possibly even losing your job.

 **GRAMMAR**

The sentence below looks innocent, but is it really?

We sell tuxedos as well as rent.

You might sell rent, but it's highly unlikely. Whatever you're selling, some people will ignore your message because of a blunder like this. The following sentence has a similar problem:

Vice President Eldon Neale told his chief engineer that he would no longer be with Avix, Inc., as of June 30.

Is Eldon or the engineer leaving? No matter which side the facts are on, the sentence can be read the other way. You may have a hard time convincing either person that your simple mistake was not a move in a game of office politics. Now look at this sentence:

The year before we budgeted more for advertising sales were up.

Confused? Perhaps this is what you meant:

The year before, we budgeted more for advertising. Sales were up.

Maybe you meant this:

The year before we budgeted more for advertising, sales were up.

The meaning of language falls into bundles called sentences. A listener or reader can take only so much meaning before filing a sentence away and getting ready for the next one. So, as a writer, you have to know what a sentence is. You need to know where one ends and the next one begins.

If you want to know what a thing is, you have to find out what goes into it, what its ingredients are. Luckily, the basic ingredients of an English sentence are simple. They're called the parts of speech, and the content-bearing ones are nouns, pronouns, verbs, adjectives, and adverbs. They combine with a few functional parts of speech to convey meaning. Meaning is also transmitted by punctuation, mechanics, and vocabulary.

1.1 Nouns

A noun names a person, place, or thing. Anything you can see or detect with one of your other senses has a noun to name it. Some things you can't see or sense are also nouns—ions, for example, or space. So are things that exist as ideas, such as accuracy and height. (You can see that something is accurate or that a building is tall, but you can't see the idea of accuracy or the idea of height.) These names for ideas are known as abstract nouns. The simplest nouns are the names of things you can see or touch: car, building, cloud, brick.

1.1.1 Proper Nouns and Common Nouns
So far, all the examples of nouns have been common nouns, referring to general classes of things. The word *building* refers to a whole class of structures. Common nouns such as *building* are not capitalized.

If you want to talk about one particular building, however, you might refer to the Glazier Building. The name is capitalized, indicating that *Glazier Building* is a proper noun.

Here are three sets of common and proper nouns for comparison:

COMMON	PROPER
city	Kansas City
company	Blaisden Company
store	Books Galore

493

1.1.2 Plural Nouns

Nouns can be either singular or plural. The usual way to make a plural noun is to add *s* to the singular form of the word:

SINGULAR	PLURAL
rock	rocks
picture	pictures
song	songs

Many nouns have other ways of forming the plural. Letters, numbers, and words used as words are sometimes made plural by adding an apostrophe and an *s*. Very often, *'s* is used with abbreviations that have periods, lowercase letters that stand alone, and capital letters that might be confused with words when made into plurals:'

Spell out all *St.'s* and *Ave.'s*.

He divided the page with a row of *x's*.

Sarah will register the *A's* through the *I's* at the convention.

In other cases, however, the apostrophe may be left out:

They'll review their *ABCs*.

The stock market climbed through most of the 1980s.

Circle all *thes* in the paragraph.

In these examples, the letters used as letters and words used as words *are italicized* (discussed later in the chapter).

Other nouns, such as those below, are so-called irregular nouns; they form the plural in some way other than simply adding *s*:

SINGULAR	PLURAL
tax	taxes
specialty	specialties
cargo	cargoes
shelf	shelves
child	children
woman	women
tooth	teeth
mouse	mice
parenthesis	parentheses
son-in-law	sons-in-law
editor-in-chief	editors-in-chief

Rather than memorize a lot of rules about forming plurals, use a dictionary. If the dictionary says nothing about the plural of a word, it's formed the usual way: by adding *s*. If the plural is formed in some irregular way, the dictionary shows the plural or has a note something like this: *ples*.

1.1.3 Possessive Nouns

A noun becomes possessive when it's used to show the ownership of something. Then you add *'s* to the word:

the man's car   the woman's apartment

However, ownership does not need to be legal:

the secretary's desk   the company's assets

Also, ownership may be nothing more than an automatic association:

a day's work   a job's prestige

An exception to the rule about adding *'s* to make a noun possessive occurs when the word is singular and already has two *s* sounds at the end. In cases like the following, an apostrophe is all that's needed:

crisis' dimensions   Mr. Moses' application

When the noun has only one *s* sound at the end, however, retain the *'s*:

Chris's book   Carolyn Nuss's office

With hyphenated nouns (compound nouns), add *'s* to the last word:

HYPHENATED NOUN	POSSESSIVE NOUN
mother-in-law	mother-in-law's
mayor-elect	mayor-elect's

To form the possessive of plural nouns, just begin by following the same rule as with singular nouns: add *'s*. However, if the plural noun already ends in an *s* (as most do), drop the one you've added, leaving only the apostrophe:

the clients' complaints   employees' benefits

1.2 Pronouns

A pronoun is a word that stands for a noun; it saves repeating the noun:

Drivers have some choice of weeks for vacation, but *they* must notify this office of *their* preference by March 1.

The pronouns *they* and *their* stand in for the noun *drivers*. The noun that a pronoun stands for is called the antecedent of the pronoun; *drivers* is the antecedent of *they* and *their*.

When the antecedent is plural, the pronoun that stands in for it has to be plural; *they* and *their* are plural pronouns because *drivers* is plural. Likewise, when the antecedent is singular, the pronoun has to be singular:

We thought the *contract* had been signed, but we soon learned that *it* had not been.

1.2.1 Multiple Antecedents

Sometimes a pronoun has a double (or even a triple) antecedent:

Kathryn Boettcher and Luis Gutierrez went beyond *their* sales quotas for January.

Kathryn Boettcher, if taken alone, is a singular antecedent. So is *Luis Gutierrez*. However, when together they are the antecedent of a pronoun, they're plural and the pronoun has to be plural. Thus the pronoun is *their* instead of *her* or *his*.

1.2.2 Unclear Antecedents

In some sentences the pronoun's antecedent is unclear:

Sandy Wright sent Jane Brougham *her* production figures for the previous year. *She* thought they were too low.

To which person does the pronoun *her* refer? Someone who knew Sandy and Jane and knew their business relationship might be able to figure out the antecedent for *her*. Even with such an advantage, however, a reader might receive the wrong meaning. Also, it would be nearly impossible for any reader to know which name is the antecedent of *she*.

The best way to clarify an ambiguous pronoun is usually to rewrite the sentence, repeating nouns when needed for clarity:

Sandy Wright sent her production figures for the previous year to Jane Brougham. *Jane* thought they were too low.

The noun needs to be repeated only when the antecedent is unclear.

1.2.3 Gender-Neutral Pronouns

The pronouns that stand for males are *he*, *his*, and *him*. The pronouns that stand for females are *she*, *hers*, and *her*. However, you'll often be faced with the problem of choosing a pronoun for a noun that refers to both females and males:

Each manager must make up (his, her, his or her, its, their) own mind about stocking this item and about the quantity that (he, she, he or she, it, they) can sell.

This sentence calls for a pronoun that's neither masculine nor feminine. The issue of gender-neutral pronouns responds to efforts to treat females and males evenhandedly. Here are some possible ways to deal with this issue:

Each manager must make up *his* . . .

(Not all managers are men.)

Each manager must make up *her* . . .

(Not all managers are women.)

Each manager must make up *his or her* . . .

(This solution is acceptable but becomes awkward when repeated more than once or twice in a document.)

Each manager must make up *her* . . . Every manager will receive *his* . . . A manager may send *her* . . .

(A manager's gender does not alternate like a windshield wiper!)

Each manager must make up *their* . . .

(The pronoun can't be plural when the antecedent is singular.)

Each manager must make up *its* . . .

(*It* never refers to people.)

The best solution is to make the noun plural or to revise the passage altogether:

Managers must make up *their* minds . . .

Each manager must decide whether . . .

Be careful not to change the original meaning.

1.2.4 Case of Pronouns

The case of a pronoun tells whether it's acting or acted upon:

She sells an average of five packages each week.

In this sentence *she* is doing the selling. Because *she* is acting, *she* is said to be in the nominative case. Now consider what happens when the pronoun is acted upon:

After six months Ms. Browning promoted *her*.

In this sentence the pronoun *her* is acted upon. The pronoun *her* is thus said to be in the objective case.

Contrast the nominative and objective pronouns in this list:

NOMINATIVE	OBJECTIVE
I	me
we	us
he	him
she	her
they	them
who	whom
whoever	whomever

Objective pronouns may be used as either the object of a verb (such as *promoted*) or the object of a preposition (such as *with*):

Rob worked with *them* until the order was filled.

In this example *them* is the object of the preposition *with* because Rob acted upon—worked with—them.

Here's a sample sentence with three pronouns, the first one nominative, the second the object of a verb, and the third the object of a preposition:

He paid *us* as soon as the check came from *them*.

He is nominative; *us* is objective because it's the object of the verb *paid; them* is objective because it's the object of the preposition *from*.

Every writer sometimes wonders whether to use *who* or *whom*:

(Who, Whom) will you hire?

Because this sentence is a question, it's difficult to see that *whom* is the object of the verb *hire*. You can figure out which pronoun to use if you rearrange the question and temporarily try *she* and *her* in place of *who* and *whom*: "Will you hire *she*?" or "Will you hire *her*?" *Her* and *whom* are both objective, so the correct choice is "*Whom* will you hire?" Here's a different example:

(Who, Whom) logged so much travel time?

Turning the question into a statement, you get:

He logged so much travel time.

Therefore, the correct statement is:

Who logged so much travel time?

1.2.5 Possessive Pronouns

Possessive pronouns are like possessive nouns in the way they work: They show ownership or automatic association.

her job	their preferences
his account	its equipment

However, possessive pronouns are different from possessive nouns in the way they are written. That is, possessive pronouns never have an apostrophe.

POSSESSIVE NOUN	POSSESSIVE PRONOUN
the woman's estate	her estate
Roger Franklin's plans	his plans
the shareholders' feelings	their feelings
the vacuum cleaner's attachments	its attachments

The word *its* is the possessive of *it*. Like all other possessive pronouns, *its* doesn't have an apostrophe. Some people confuse *its* with *it's*, the contraction of *it is*. Contractions are discussed later.

1.3 Verbs

A verb describes an action:

They all *quit* in disgust.

It may also describe a state of being:

Working conditions *were* substandard.

The English language is full of action verbs. Here are a few you'll often run across in the business world:

verify	perform	fulfill
hire	succeed	send
leave	improve	receive
accept	develop	pay

You could undoubtedly list many more.

The most common verb describing a state of being instead of an action is *to be* and all its forms:

I *am*, *was*, or *will be*; you *are*, *were*, or *will be*

Other verbs also describe a state of being:

It *seemed* a good plan at the time.

She *sounds* impressive at a meeting.

These verbs link what comes before them in the sentence with what comes after; no action is involved. (See Section 1.7.5 for a fuller discussion of linking verbs.)

1.3.1 Verb Tenses

English has three simple verb tenses: present, past, and future.

PRESENT: Our branches in Hawaii *stock* other items.
PAST: When we *stocked* Purquil pens, we received a great many complaints.
FUTURE: Rotex Tire Stores *will stock* your line of tires when you begin a program of effective national advertising.

With most verbs (the regular ones), the past tense ends in *ed;* the future tense always has *will* or *shall* in front of it. But the present tense is more complex:

SINGULAR	PLURAL
I stock	we stock
you stock	you stock
he, she, it stocks	they stock

The basic form, *stock,* takes an additional *s* when *he, she,* or *it* precedes it.

In addition to the three simple tenses, there are three perfect tenses using forms of the helping verb *have.* The present perfect tense uses the past participle (regularly the past tense) of the main verb, *stocked,* and adds the present-tense *have* or *has* to the front of it:

(I, we, you, they) *have stocked.*

(He, she, it) *has stocked.*

The past perfect tense uses the past participle of the main verb, *stocked,* and adds the past-tense *had* to the front of it:

(I, you, he, she, it, we, they) *had stocked.*

The future perfect tense also uses the past participle of the main verb, *stocked,* but adds the future-tense *will have:*

(I, you, he, she, it, we, they) *will have stocked.*

Keep verbs in the same tense when the actions occur at the same time:

When the payroll checks *came* in, everyone *showed* up for work.

We *have found* that everyone *has pitched* in to help.

Of course, when the actions occur at different times, you may change tense accordingly:

A shipment *came* last Wednesday, so when another one *comes* in today, please return it.

The new employee *had been* ill at ease, but now she *has become* a full-fledged member of the team.

1.3.2 Irregular Verbs

Many verbs don't follow in every detail the patterns already described. The most irregular of these verbs is *to be*:

TENSE	SINGULAR	PLURAL
PRESENT:	I *am*	we *are*
	you *are*	you *are*
	he, she, it *is*	they *are*
PAST:	I *was*	we *were*
	you *were*	you *were*
	he, she, it *was*	they *were*

The future tense of *to be* is formed in the same way that the future tense of a regular verb is formed.

The perfect tenses of *to be* are also formed as they would be for a regular verb, except that the past participle is a special form, *been*, instead of just the past tense:

PRESENT PERFECT:	you *have been*
PAST PERFECT:	you *had been*
FUTURE PERFECT:	you *will have been*

Here's a sampling of other irregular verbs:

PRESENT	PAST	PAST PARTICIPLE
begin	began	begun
shrink	shrank	shrunk
know	knew	known
rise	rose	risen
become	became	become
go	went	gone
do	did	done

Dictionaries list the various forms of other irregular verbs.

1.3.3 Transitive and Intransitive Verbs

Many people are confused by three particular sets of verbs:

lie/lay	sit/set	rise/raise

Using these verbs correctly is much easier when you learn the difference between transitive and intransitive verbs.

Transitive verbs convey their action to an object; they "transfer" their action to an object. Intransitive verbs do not. Here are some sample uses of transitive and intransitive verbs:

INTRANSITIVE	TRANSITIVE
We should include in our new offices a place to *lie* down for a nap.	The workers will be here on Monday to *lay* new carpeting.
Even the way an interviewee *sits* is important.	That crate is full of stemware, so *set* it down carefully.
Salaries at Compu-Link, Inc., *rise* swiftly.	They *raise* their level of production every year.

The workers *lay* carpeting, you *set* down the crate, they *raise* production; each action is transferred to something. In the intransitive sentences, one *lies* down, an interviewee *sits*, and salaries *rise* without (at least grammatically) affecting anything else. Intransitive sentences are complete with only a subject and a verb; transitive sentences are not complete unless they also include an object, or something to transfer the action to.

Tenses are a confusing element of the *lie/lay* problem:

PRESENT	PAST	PAST PARTICIPLE
I *lie*	I *lay*	I have *lain*
I *lay* (something down)	I *laid* (something down)	I have *laid* (something down)

The past tense of *lie* and the present tense of *lay* look and sound alike, even though they're different verbs.

1.3.4 Voice of Verbs

Verbs have two voices, active and passive:

ACTIVE:	The buyer paid a large amount.
PASSIVE:	A large amount was paid by the buyer.

The passive voice uses a form of the verb *to be*.

Also, the passive-voice sentence uses eight words, whereas the active-voice sentence uses only six words to say the same thing. The words *was* and *by* are unnecessary to convey the meaning of the sentence. In fact, extra words usually clog meaning. So be sure to opt for the active voice when you have a choice.

At times, however, you have no choice:

Several items *have been taken*, but so far we don't know who took them.

The passive voice becomes necessary when you don't know (or don't want to say) who performed the action; the active voice is bolder and more direct.

1.3.5 Mood of Verbs

You have three moods to choose from, depending on your intentions. Most of the time you use the indicative mood to make a statement or to ask a question:

The secretary *mailed* a letter to each supplier.

Did the secretary *mail* a letter to each supplier?

When you wish to command or request, use the imperative mood:

Please *mail* a letter to each supplier.

Sometimes, especially in business, a courteous request is stated like a question; in that case, however, no question mark is required.

Would you *mail* a letter to each supplier.

The subjunctive mood, most often used in formal writing or in presenting bad news, expresses a possibility or a recommendation. The subjunctive is usually signaled by a word such as *if* or *that*. In these examples, the subjunctive mood uses special verb forms:

If the secretary *were to mail* a letter to each supplier, we might save some money.

I suggested that the secretary *mail* a letter to each supplier.

Although the subjunctive mood is not used as often as it once was, it's still found in such expressions as *Come what may* and *If I were you*. In general, it is used to convey an idea that is contrary to fact: If iron *were* lighter than air.

1.4 Adjectives

An adjective modifies (tells something about) a noun or pronoun:

an *efficient* staff	a *heavy* price
brisk trade	*poor* you

Each of these phrases says more about the noun or pronoun than the noun or pronoun would say alone.

Adjectives always tell us something we wouldn't know without them. So you don't need to use adjectives when the noun alone, or a different noun, will give the meaning:

a *company* employee

(An employee ordinarily works for a company.)

a *crate-type* container

(*Crate* gives the entire meaning.)

At times, adjectives pile up in a series:

It was a *long, hot,* and *active* workday.

Such strings of adjectives are acceptable as long as they all convey a different part of the phrase's meaning.

Verbs in the *ing* (present participle) form can be used as adjectives:

A *boring* job can sometimes turn into a *fascinating* career.

So can the past participle of verbs:

A freshly *painted* house is a *sold* house.

Adjectives modify nouns more often than they modify pronouns. When adjectives do modify pronouns, however, the sentence usually has a linking verb:

They were *attentive*.	It looked *appropriate*.
He seems *interested*.	You are *skillful*.

Most adjectives can take three forms: simple, comparative, and superlative. The simple form modifies a single noun or pronoun. Use the comparative form when comparing two items. When comparing three or more items, use the superlative form.

SIMPLE	COMPARATIVE	SUPERLATIVE
hard	harder	hardest
safe	safer	safest
dry	drier	driest

The comparative form adds er to the simple form, and the superlative form adds *est*. (The *y* at the end of a word changes to *i* before the *er* or *est* is added.)

A small number of adjectives are irregular, including these:

SIMPLE	COMPARATIVE	SUPERLATIVE
good	better	best
bad	worse	worst
little	less	least

When the simple form of an adjective is two or more syllables, you usually add *more* to form the comparative and *most* to form the superlative:

SIMPLE	COMPARATIVE	SUPERLATIVE
useful	more useful	most useful
exhausting	more exhausting	most exhausting
expensive	more expensive	most expensive

The most common exceptions are two-syllable adjectives that end in *y*:

SIMPLE	COMPARATIVE	SUPERLATIVE
happy	happier	happiest
costly	costlier	costliest

If you choose this option, change the *y* to *i*, and tack *er* or *est* onto the end.

1.5 Adverbs

An adverb modifies a verb, an adjective, or another adverb:

MODIFYING A VERB:	Our marketing department works *efficiently*.
MODIFYING AN ADJECTIVE:	She was not dependable, although she was *highly* intelligent.
MODIFYING ANOTHER ADVERB:	His territory was *too* broadly diversified, so he moved *extremely* cautiously.

Most of the adverbs mentioned are adjectives turned into adverbs by adding *ly,* which is how many adverbs are formed:

ADJECTIVE	ADVERB
efficient	efficiently
high	highly
extreme	extremely
special	specially
official	officially
separate	separately

Some adverbs are made by dropping or changing the final letter of the adjective and then adding *ly:*

ADJECTIVE	ADVERB
due	duly
busy	busily

Other adverbs don't end in *ly* at all. Here are a few examples of this type:

often	fast	too
soon	very	so

1.6 Other Parts of Speech

Nouns, pronouns, verbs, adjectives, and adverbs carry most of the meaning in a sentence. Four other parts of speech link them together in sentences: prepositions, conjunctions, articles, and interjections.

1.6.1 Prepositions
Prepositions are words like these:

of	to	for	with
at	by	from	about

They most often begin prepositional phrases, which function like adjectives and adverbs by telling more about a pronoun, noun, or verb:

of a type	*by* Friday
to the point	*with* characteristic flair

1.6.2 Conjunctions, Articles, and Interjections
Conjunctions are words that usually join parts of a sentence. Here are a few:

and	but	because
yet	although	if

Using conjunctions is discussed in sections 1.7.3 and 1.7.4.

Only three articles exist in English: *the, a,* and *an.* These words are used, like adjectives, to specify which item you are talking about.

Interjections are words that express no solid information, only emotion:

Wow!	Well, well!
Oh no!	Good!

Such purely emotional language has its place in private life and advertising copy, but it only weakens the effect of most business writing.

1.7 Sentences

Sentences are constructed with the major building blocks, the parts of speech.

Money talks.

This two-word sentence consists of a noun (*money*) and a verb (*talks*). When used in this way, the noun works as the first requirement for a sentence, the subject, and the verb works as the second requirement, the predicate. Now look at this sentence:

They merged.

The subject in this case is a pronoun (*they*), and the predicate is a verb (*merged*). This is a sentence because it has a subject and a predicate. Here is yet another kind of sentence:

The plans are ready.

This sentence has a more complicated subject, the noun *plans* and the article *the;* the complete predicate is a state-of-being verb (*are*) and an adjective (*ready*).

Without these two parts, the subject (who or what does something) and the predicate (the doing of it), no collection of words is a sentence.

1.7.1 Commands
In commands, the subject (always *you*) is only understood, not stated:

(You) Move your desk to the better office.
(You) Please try to finish by six o'clock.

1.7.2 Longer Sentences
More complicated sentences have more complicated subjects and predicates, but they still have a simple subject and a predicate verb. In the following examples, the simple subject is underlined once, the predicate verb twice:

Marex and Contron enjoy higher earnings each quarter.

(Marex [and] Contron did something; enjoy is what they did.)

My interview, coming minutes after my freeway accident, did not impress or move anyone.

(Interview is what did something. What did it do? It did [not] impress [or] move .)

In terms of usable space, a steel warehouse, with its extremely long span of roof unsupported by pillars, makes more sense.

(Warehouse is what makes.)

These three sentences demonstrate several things. First, in all three sentences the simple subject and predicate verb are the "bare bones" of the sentence, the parts that carry the core idea of the sentence. When trying to find the simple subject and predicate verb, disregard all prepositional phrases, modifiers, conjunctions, and articles.

Second, in the third sentence the verb is singular (*makes*) because the subject is singular (*warehouse*). Even though the plural noun *pillars* is closer to the verb, *warehouse* is the subject. So *warehouse* determines whether the verb is singular or plural. Subject and predicate must agree.

Third, the subject in the first sentence is compound (*Marex* [and] *Contron*). A compound subject, when connected by *and,* requires a plural verb (*enjoy*). Also in the second sentence, compound predicates are possible (*did* [not] *impress* [or] *move*).

Fourth, the second sentence incorporates a group of words—*coming minutes after my freeway accident*—containing a form of a verb (*coming*) and a noun (*accident*). Yet this group of words is not a complete sentence for two reasons:

- Accident is not the subject of coming. Not all nouns are subjects.
- A verb that ends in *ing* can never be the predicate of a sentence (unless preceded by a form of *to be,* as in *was coming*). Not all verbs are predicates.

Because they don't contain a subject and a predicate, the words *coming minutes after my freeway accident* (called a phrase) can't be written as a sentence. That is, the phrase can't stand alone; it can't begin with a capital letter and end with a period. So a phrase must always be just one part of a sentence.

Sometimes a sentence incorporates two or more groups of words that do contain a subject and a predicate; these word groups are called clauses.

My <u>interview</u>, because it <u>came</u> minutes after my freeway accident, <u>did</u> not <u>impress</u> or <u>move</u> anyone.

The independent clause is the portion of the sentence that could stand alone without revision:

My <u>interview</u> <u>did</u> not <u>impress</u> or <u>move</u> anyone.

The other part of the sentence could stand alone only by removing *because:*

(because) <u>It</u> <u>came</u> minutes after my freeway accident.

This part of the sentence is known as a dependent clause; although it has a subject and a predicate (just as an independent clause does), it's linked to the main part of the sentence by a word (*because*) showing its dependence.

In summary, the two types of clauses—dependent and independent—both have a subject and a predicate. Dependent clauses, however, do not bear the main meaning of the sentence and are therefore linked to an independent clause. Nor can phrases stand alone, because they lack both a subject and a predicate. Only independent clauses can be written as sentences without revision.

1.7.3 Sentence Fragments

An incomplete sentence (a phrase or a dependent clause) that is written as though it were a complete sentence is called a fragment. Consider the following sentence fragments:

Marilyn Sanders, having had pilferage problems in her store for the past year. Refuses to accept the results of our investigation.

This serious error can easily be corrected by putting the two fragments together:

Marilyn Sanders, having had pilferage problems in her store for the past year, refuses to accept the results of our investigation.

Not all fragments can be corrected so easily. Here's more information on Sanders's pilferage problem.

Employees a part of it. No authority or discipline.

Only the writer knows the intended meaning of these two phrases. Perhaps the employees are taking part in the pilferage. If so, the sentence should read:

Some employees are part of the pilferage problem.

On the other hand, it's possible that some employees are helping with the investigation. Then the sentence would read:

Some employees are taking part in our investigation.

It's just as likely, however, that the employees are not only taking part in the pilferage but are also being analyzed:

Those employees who are part of the pilferage problem will accept no authority or discipline.

In fact, even more meanings could be read into these fragments. Because fragments can mean so many things, they mean nothing. No well-written memo, letter, or report ever demands the reader to be an imaginative genius.

One more type of fragment exists, the kind represented by a dependent clause. Note what *because* does to change what was once a unified sentence:

Our stock of sprinklers is depleted.

Because our stock of sprinklers is depleted.

Although the second version contains a subject and a predicate, adding *because* makes it a fragment. Words such as *because* form a special group of words called subordinating conjunctions. Here's a partial list:

since	though	whenever
although	if	unless
while	even if	after

When a word of this type begins a clause, the clause is dependent and cannot stand alone as a sentence. However, if a dependent clause is combined with an independent clause, it can convey a complete meaning. The independent clause may come before or after the dependent clause:

We are unable to fill your order because our stock of sprinklers is depleted.

Because our stock of sprinklers is depleted, we are unable to fill your order.

Another remedy for a fragment that is a dependent clause is to remove the subordinating conjunction. That solution leaves a simple but complete sentence:

Our stock of sprinklers is depleted.

The actual details of a transaction will determine the best way to remedy a fragment problem.

The ban on fragments has one exception. Some advertising copy contains sentence fragments, written knowingly to convey a certain rhythm. However, advertising is the only area of business in which fragments are acceptable.

1.7.4 Fused Sentences and Comma Splices

Just as there can be too little in a group of words to make it a sentence, there can also be too much:

All our mail is run through a postage meter every afternoon someone picks it up.

This example contains two sentences, not one, but the two have been blended so that it's hard to tell where one ends and the next begins. Is the mail run through a meter every afternoon? If so, the sentences should read:

All our mail is run through a postage meter every afternoon. Someone picks it up.

Perhaps the mail is run through a meter at some other time (morning, for example) and is picked up every afternoon:

All our mail is run through a postage meter. Every afternoon someone picks it up.

The order of words is the same in all three cases; sentence division makes all the difference. Either of the last two cases is grammatically correct. The choice depends on the facts of the situation.

Sometimes these so-called fused sentences have a more obvious point of separation:

Several large orders arrived within a few days of one another, too many came in for us to process by the end of the month.

Here the comma has been put between two independent clauses in an attempt to link them. When a lowly comma separates two com-plete sentences, the result is called a comma splice. A comma splice can be remedied in one of three ways:

- Replace the comma with a period and capitalize the next word: " . . . one another. Too many . . . "
- Replace the comma with a semicolon and do not capitalize the next word: " . . . one another; too many . . . " This remedy works only when the two sentences have closely related meanings.
- Change one of the sentences so that it becomes a phrase or a dependent clause. This remedy often produces the best writing, but it takes more work.

The third alternative can be carried out in several ways. One is to begin the blended sentence with a subordinating conjunction:

Whenever several large orders arrived within a few days of one another, too many came in for us to process by the end of the month.

Another way is to remove part of the subject or the predicate verb from one of the independent clauses, thereby creating a phrase:

Several large orders arrived within a few days of one another, too many for us to process by the end of the month.

Finally, you can change one of the predicate verbs to its *ing* form:

Several large orders arrived within a few days of one another, too many coming in for us to process by the end of the month.

At other times a simple coordinating conjunction (such as *or, and,* or *but*) can separate fused sentences:

You can fire them, or you can make better use of their abilities.

Margaret drew up the designs, *and* Matt carried them out.

We will have three strong months, *but* after that sales will taper off.

Be careful using coordinating conjunctions: Use them only to join simple sentences that express similar ideas.

Also, because they say relatively little about the relationship between the two clauses they join, avoid using coordinating conjunctions too often: *and* is merely an addition sign; *but* is just a turn signal; *or* only points to an alternative. Subordinating conjunctions such as *because* and *whenever* tell the reader a lot more.

1.7.5 Sentences with Linking Verbs

Linking verbs were discussed briefly in the section on verbs (Section 1.3). Here you can see more fully the way they function in a sentence. The following is a model of any sentence with a linking verb:

A (verb) B.

Although words such as *seems* and *feels* can also be linking verbs, let's assume that the verb is a form of *to be:*

A *is* B.

In such a sentence, A and B are always nouns, pronouns, or adjectives. When one is a noun and the other is a pronoun, or when both are nouns, the sentence says that one is the same as the other:

She is president.

Rachel is president.

When one is an adjective, it modifies or describes the other:

She is forceful.

Remember that when one is an adjective, it modifies the other as any adjective modifies a noun or pronoun, except that a linking verb stands between the adjective and the word it modifies.

1.7.6 Misplaced Modifiers

The position of a modifier in a sentence is important. The movement of *only* changes the meaning in the following sentences:

Only we are obliged to supply those items specified in your contract.

We are obliged *only* to supply those items specified in your contract.

We are obliged to supply *only* those items specified in your contract.

We are obliged to supply those items specified *only* in your contract.

In any particular set of circumstances, only one of these sentences would be accurate. The others would very likely cause problems. To prevent misunderstanding, place modifiers such as *only* as close as possible to the noun or verb they modify.

For similar reasons, whole phrases that are modifiers must be placed near the right noun or verb. Mistakes in placement create ludicrous meanings:

Antia Information Systems has bought new computer chairs for the programmers *with more comfortable seats.*

The anatomy of programmers is not normally a concern of business writers. Obviously, the comfort of the chairs was the issue:

Antia Information Systems has bought new computer chairs *with more comfortable seats* for the programmers.

Here is another example:

I asked him to file all the letters in the cabinet *that had been answered.*

In this ridiculous sentence the cabinet has been answered, even though no cabinet in history is known to have asked a question.

That had been answered is too far from *letters* and too close to *cabinet.* Here's an improvement:

I asked him to file in the cabinet all the letters *that had been answered.*

In some cases, instead of moving the modifying phrase closer to the word it modifies, the best solution is to move the word closer to the modifying phrase.

2.0 PUNCTUATION

On the highway, signs tell you when to slow down or stop, where to turn, when to merge. In similar fashion, punctuation helps readers negotiate your prose. The proper use of punctuation keeps readers from losing track of your meaning.

2.1 Periods

Use a period (1) to end any sentence that is not a question, (2) with certain abbreviations, and (3) between dollars and cents in an amount of money.

2.2 Question Marks

Use a question mark after any direct question that requests an answer:

Are you planning to enclose a check, or shall we bill you?

Don't use a question mark with commands phrased as questions for the sake of politeness:

Will you send us a check today.

2.3 Exclamation Points

Use exclamation points after highly emotional language. Because business writing almost never calls for emotional language, you will seldom use exclamation points.

2.4 Semicolons

Semicolons have three main uses. One is to separate two closely related independent clauses:

The outline for the report is due within a week; the report itself is due at the end of the month.

A semicolon should also be used instead of a comma when the items in a series have commas within them:

Our previous meetings were on November 11, 1994; February 20, 1989; and April 28, 1995.

Finally, a semicolon should be used to separate independent clauses when the second one begins with a word such as *however, therefore,* or *nevertheless* or a phrase such as *for example* or *in that case:*

Our supplier has been out of part D712 for 10 weeks; however, we have found another source that can ship the part right away.

His test scores were quite low; on the other hand, he has a lot of relevant experience.

Section 4.4 has more information on using transitional words and phrases.

2.5 Colons

Use a colon (1) after the salutation in a business letter, (2) at the end of a sentence or phrase introducing a list or (sometimes) a quotation, and (3) to separate two closely related independent clauses not joined by *and, but,* or *or.*

Our study included the three most critical problems: insufficient capital, incompetent management, and inappropriate location.

In some introductory sentences, phrases such as *the following* or *that is* are implied by using a colon.

A colon should not be used when the list, quotation, or idea is a direct object or part of the introductory sentence:

We are able to supply

    staples
    wood screws
    nails
    toggle bolts

This shipment includes 9 videotapes, 12 CDs, and 14 cassette tapes.

2.6 Commas

Commas have many uses; the most common is to separate items in a series:

He took the job, learned it well, worked hard, and succeeded.

Put paper, pencils, and paper clips on the requisition list.

Company style often dictates omitting the final comma in a series. However, if you have a choice, use the final comma; it's often necessary to prevent misunderstanding.

A second place to use a comma is between independent clauses that are joined by a coordinating conjunction (*and, but,* or *or*) unless one or both are very short:

She spoke to the sales staff, and he spoke to the production staff.

I was advised to proceed and I did.

A third use for the comma is to separate a dependent clause at the beginning of a sentence from an independent clause:

Because of our lead in the market, we may be able to risk introducing a new product.

However, a dependent clause at the end of a sentence is separated from the independent clause by a comma only when the dependent clause is unnecessary to the main meaning of the sentence:

We may be able to introduce a new product, although it may involve some risk.

A fourth use for the comma is after an introductory phrase or word:

Starting with this amount of capital, we can survive in the red for one year.

Through more careful planning, we may be able to serve more people.

Yes, you may proceed as originally planned.

However, with short introductory prepositional phrases and some one-syllable words (such as *hence* and *thus*), the comma is often omitted:

Before January 1 we must complete the inventory.

Thus we may not need to hire anyone.

In short the move to Tulsa was a good idea.

Fifth, commas are used to surround nonrestrictive phrases or words (expressions that can be removed from the sentence without changing the meaning):

The new owners, the Kowacks, are pleased with their purchase.

Sixth, commas are used between adjectives modifying the same noun (coordinate adjectives):

She left Monday for a long, difficult recruiting trip.

To test the appropriateness of such a comma, try reversing the order of the adjectives: *a difficult, long recruiting trip.* If the order cannot be reversed, leave out the comma (*a good old friend* isn't the same as *an old good friend*). A comma is also not used when one of the adjectives is part of the noun. Compare these two phrases:

a distinguished, well-known figure

a distinguished public figure

The adjective-noun combination of *public* and *figure* has been used together so often that it has come to be considered a single thing: *public figure.* So no comma is required.

Seventh, commas should precede *Inc., Ltd.,* and the like:

Cloverdell, Inc.   Beamer, Ltd.

In a sentence, a comma also follows such abbreviations:

Belle Brown, Ph.D., is the new tenant.

Eighth, commas are used both before and after the year in sentences that include month, day, and year:

It will be sent by December 15, 1999, from our Cincinnati plant.

Some companies write dates in another form: 15 December 1999. No commas should be used in that case. Nor is a comma needed when only the month and year are present (December 1999).

Ninth, a comma may be used after an informal salutation in a letter to a personal friend. (In business letters, however, the salutation is followed by a colon.)

Tenth, a comma is used to separate a quotation from the rest of the sentence:

Your warranty reads, "These conditions remain in effect for one year from date of purchase."

However, the comma is left out when the quotation as a whole is built into the structure of the sentence:

He hurried off with an angry "Look where you're going."

Finally, a comma should be used whenever it's needed to avoid confusion or an unintended meaning. Compare the following:

Ever since they have planned new ventures more carefully.

Ever since, they have planned new ventures more carefully.

2.7 Dashes

Use a dash to surround a comment that is a sudden turn in thought:

Membership in the IBSA—it's expensive but worth it—may be obtained by applying to our New York office.

A dash can also be used to emphasize a parenthetical word or phrase:

Third-quarter profits—in excess of $2 million—are up sharply.

Finally, use dashes to set off a phrase that contains commas:

All our offices—Milwaukee, New Orleans, and Phoenix—have sent representatives.

Don't confuse a dash with a hyphen. A dash separates and emphasizes words, phrases, and clauses more strongly than a comma or parentheses can; a hyphen ties two words so tightly that they almost become one word.

When typing a dash, type two hyphens with no space before, between, or after.

2.8 Hyphens

Hyphens are mainly used in three ways. The first is to separate the parts of compound words beginning with such prefixes as self-, ex-, quasi-, and all:

self-assured	quasi-official
ex-wife	all-important

However, hyphens are usually left out and the words closed up in words that have such prefixes as *pro, anti, non, un, inter,* and *extra*:

prolabor	nonunion
antifascist	interdepartmental

Exceptions occur when (1) the prefix occurs before a proper noun or (2) the vowel at the end of the prefix is the same as the first letter of the root word:

pro-Republican	anti-American
anti-inflammatory	extra-atmospheric

When in doubt, consult your dictionary.

Hyphens are also used in some compound adjectives, which are adjectives made up of two or more words. Specifically, you should use hyphens in compound adjectives that come before the noun:

an interest-bearing account	well-informed executives

However, you need not hyphenate when the adjective follows a linking verb:

This account is interest bearing.
Their executives are well informed.

You can shorten sentences that list similar hyphenated words by dropping the common part from all but the last word:

Check the costs of first-, second-, and third-class postage.

Finally, hyphens may be used to divide words at the end of a typed line. Such hyphenation is best avoided, but when you have to divide words at the end of a line, do so correctly (see Section 3.4). A dictionary will show how words are divided into syllables.

2.9 Apostrophes

Use an apostrophe in the possessive form of a noun (but not in a pronoun):

On *his* desk was a reply to *Bette Ainsley's* application for the *manager's* position.

Apostrophes are also used in place of the missing letter(s) of a contraction:

WHOLE WORDS	CONTRACTION
we will	we'll
do not	don't
they are	they're

2.10 Quotation Marks

Use quotation marks to surround words that are repeated exactly as they were said or written:

The collection letter ended by saying, "This is your third and final notice."

Remember: (1) When the quoted material is a complete sentence, the first word is capitalized. (2) The final comma or period goes inside the closing quotation marks.

Quotation marks are also used to set off the title of a newspaper story, magazine article, or book chapter:

You should read "Legal Aspects of the Collection Letter" in *Today's Credit.*

The book title is shown here in italics. When typewritten, the title is underlined. The same treatment is proper for newspaper and magazine titles. (Appendix B explains documentation style in more detail.)

Quotation marks may also be used to indicate special treatment for words or phrases, such as terms that you're using in an unusual or ironic way:

Our management "team" spends more time squabbling than working to solve company problems.

When using quotation marks, take care to put in both sets, the closing marks as well as the opening ones.

Although periods and commas go inside any quotation marks, colons and semicolons go outside them. A question mark goes inside the quotation marks only if the quotation is a question:

All that day we wondered, "Is he with us?"

If the quotation is not a question but the entire sentence is, the question mark goes outside:

What did she mean by "You will hear from me"?

2.11 Parentheses

Use parentheses to surround comments that are entirely incidental:

Our figures do not match yours, although (if my calculations are correct) they are closer than we thought.

Parentheses are also used in legal documents to surround figures in arabic numerals that follow the same amount in words:

Remittance will be One Thousand Two Hundred Dollars ($1,200).

Be careful to put punctuation (period, comma, and so on) outside the parentheses unless it is part of the statement in parentheses.

2.12 Ellipses

Use ellipsis points, or dots, to indicate that material has been left out of a direct quotation. Use them only in direct quotations and only at the point where material was left out. In the following example, the first sentence is quoted in the second:

The Dow Jones Industrial Average, which skidded 38.17 points in the previous five sessions, gained 4.61 to end at 2213.84.

According to the Honolulu *Star Bulletin,* "The Dow Jones Industrial Average . . . gained 4.61" on June 10.

The number of dots in ellipses is not optional; always use three. Occasionally, the points of ellipsis come at the end of a sentence, where they seem to grow a fourth dot. Don't be fooled: One of the dots is a period.

2.13 Underscores and Italics

Usually a line typed underneath a word or phrase either provides emphasis or indicates the title of a book, magazine, or newspaper. If possible, use italics instead of an underscore. Italics (or underlining) should also be used for defining terms and for discussing words as words:

In this report *net sales* refers to after-tax sales dollars.

The word *building* is a common noun and should not be capitalized.

3.0 MECHANICS

The most obvious and least tolerable mistakes that a business writer makes are probably those related to grammar and punctuation. However, a number of small details, known as writing mechanics, demonstrate the writer's polish and reflect on the company's professionalism.

3.1 Capitals

You should, of course, capitalize words that begin sentences:

Before hanging up, he said, "*We'll* meet here on Wednesday at noon."

A quotation that is a complete sentence should also begin with a capitalized word.

Capitalize the names of particular persons, places, and things (proper nouns):

We sent *Ms. Larson* an application form, informing her that not all *applicants* are interviewed.

Let's consider opening a branch in the *West,* perhaps at the *west* end of *Tucson, Arizona.*

As office *buildings* go, the *Kinney Building* is a pleasant setting for *TDG Office Equipment.*

Ms. Larson's name is capitalized because she is a particular applicant, whereas the general term *applicant* is left uncapitalized. Likewise,

West is capitalized when it refers to a particular place but not when it means a direction. In the same way, *office* and *building* are not capitalized when they are general terms (common nouns), but they are capitalized when they are part of the title of a particular office or building (proper nouns).

Titles within families, governments, or companies may also be capitalized:

My *Uncle David* offered me a job, but I wouldn't be comfortable working for one of my *uncles*.

We've never had a *president* quite like *President Sweeney*.

In addition, always capitalize the first word of the salutation and complimentary close of a letter:

Dear Mr. Andrews: *Yours* very truly,

Finally, capitalize the first word after a colon when it begins a complete sentence:

Follow this rule: *When* in doubt, leave it out.

Otherwise, the first word after a colon should not be capitalized (see Section 2.5).

3.2 Abbreviations

Abbreviations are used heavily in tables, charts, lists, and forms. They're used sparingly in prose paragraphs, however. Here are some abbreviations often used in business writing:

ABBREVIATION	FULL TERM
b/l	bill of lading
ca.	circa (about)
dol., dols.	dollar, dollars
etc.	et cetera (and so on)
FDIC	Federal Deposit Insurance Corporation
Inc.	Incorporated
L.f.	Ledger folio
Ltd.	Limited
mgr.	manager
NSF or N/S	not sufficient funds
P&L or P/L	profit and loss
reg.	regular
whsle.	wholesale

Because *etc.* contains a word meaning *and*, never write *and etc.*

3.3 Numbers

Numbers may correctly be handled many ways in business writing, so follow company style. In the absence of a set style, however, generally spell out all numbers from one to ten and use arabic numerals for the rest.

There are some exceptions to this general rule. First, never begin a sentence with a numeral:

Twenty of us produced *641* units per week in the first *12* weeks of the year.

Second, use numerals for the numbers one through ten if they're in the same list as larger numbers:

Our weekly quota rose from *9* to *15* to *27*.

Third, use numerals for percentages, time of day (except with *o'clock*), dates, and (in general) dollar amounts.

Our division is responsible for *7* percent of total sales.

The meeting is scheduled for *8:30* A.M. on August *2*.

Add *$3* for postage and handling.

Use a comma in numbers with four digits (*1,257*) unless the company specifies another style.

When writing dollar amounts, use a decimal point only if cents are included. In lists of two or more dollar amounts, use the decimal point either for all or for none:

He sent two checks, one for *$67.92* and one for *$90.00*.

3.4 Word Division

In general, avoid dividing words at the ends of lines. When you must, follow these rules:

- Don't divide one-syllable words (such as *since, walked,* and *thought*); abbreviations (*mgr.*); contractions (*isn't*); or numbers expressed in numerals (*117,500*).
- Divide words between syllables, as specified in a dictionary or word-division manual.
- Make sure that at least three letters of the divided word are moved to the second line: *sin-cerely* instead of *sincere-ly*.
- Do not end a page or more than three consecutive lines with hyphens.
- Leave syllables consisting of a single vowel at the end of the first line (*impedi-ment* instead of *imped-iment*), except when the single vowel is part of a suffix such as *-able, -ible, -ical,* or *-ity* (*respons-ible* instead of *responsi-ble*).
- Divide between double letters (*tomor-row*), except when the root word ends in double letters (*call-ing* instead of *cal-ling*).
- Divide hyphenated words after the hyphen only: *anti-independence* instead of *anti-inde-pendence*.

4.0 VOCABULARY

Using the right word in the right place is a crucial skill in business communication. However, many pitfalls await the unwary.

4.1 Frequently Confused Words

Because the following sets of words sound similar, be careful not to use one when you mean to use the other:

Word	Meaning
accede	to comply with
exceed	to go beyond
accept	to take
except	to exclude
access	admittance
excess	too much
advice	suggestion
advise	to suggest
affect	to influence
effect	the result
allot	to distribute
a lot	much or many
all ready	completely prepared
already	completed earlier
born	given birth to
borne	carried
capital	money; chief city
capitol	a government building
cite	to quote
sight	a view
site	a location
complement	complete amount; to go well with
compliment	to flatter
corespondent	party in a divorce suit
correspondent	letter writer
council	a panel of people
counsel	advice; a lawyer
defer	to put off until later
differ	to be different
device	a mechanism
devise	to plan
die	to stop living; a tool
dye	to color
discreet	careful
discrete	separate

envelop	to surround
envelope	a covering for a letter
forth	forward
fourth	number four
holey	full of holes
holy	sacred
wholly	completely
human	of people
humane	kindly
incidence	frequency
incidents	events
instance	example
instants	moments
interstate	between states
intrastate	within a state
later	afterward
latter	the second of two
lead	a metal
led	guided
lean	to rest at an angle
lien	a claim
levee	embankment
levy	tax
loath	reluctant
loathe	to hate
loose	free; not tight
lose	to mislay
material	substance
materiel	equipment
miner	mineworker
minor	underage person
moral	virtuous; a lesson
morale	sense of well-being
ordinance	law
ordnance	weapons
overdo	to do in excess
overdue	past due

peace	lack of conflict
piece	a fragment
pedal	a foot lever
peddle	to sell
persecute	to torment
prosecute	to sue
personal	private
personnel	employees
precedence	priority
precedents	previous events
principal	sum of money; chief; main
principle	general rule
rap	to knock
wrap	to cover
residence	home
residents	inhabitants
right	correct
rite	ceremony
write	to form words on a surface
role	a part to play
roll	to tumble; a list
root	part of a plant
rout	to defeat
route	a traveler's way
shear	to cut
sheer	thin, steep
stationary	immovable
stationery	paper
than	as compared with
then	at that time
their	belonging to them
there	in that place
they're	they are
to	a preposition
too	excessively; also
two	the number
waive	to set aside
wave	a swell of water; a gesture
weather	atmospheric conditions
whether	if

In the preceding list only enough of each word's meaning is given to help you distinguish between the words in each group. Several meanings are left out entirely. For more complete definitions, consult a dictionary.

4.2 Frequently Misused Words

The following words tend to be misused for reasons other than their sound. Reference books (including the *Random House College Dictionary,* revised edition; Follett's *Modern American Usage;* and Fowler's *Modern English Usage*) can help you with similar questions of usage.

a lot: When the writer means "many," *a lot* is always two separate words, never one.

correspond with: Use this phrase when you are talking about exchanging letters. Use *correspond to* when you mean "similar to." Use either *correspond with* or *correspond to* when you mean "relate to."

disinterested: This word means "fair, unbiased, having no favorites, impartial." If you mean "bored" or "not interested," use *uninterested.*

etc.: This is the abbreviated form of a Latin phrase, *et cetera.* It means "and so on" or "and so forth." The current tendency among business writers is to use English rather than Latin.

imply/infer: Both refer to hints. Their great difference lies in who is acting. The writer *implies;* the reader *infers,* sees between the lines.

lay: This is a transitive verb. Never use it for the intransitive *lie.* (See Section 1.3.3.)

less: Use *less* for uncountable quantities (such as amounts of water, air, sugar, and oil). Use *fewer* for countable quantities (such as numbers of jars, saws, words, pages, and humans). The same distinction applies to *much* and *little* (uncountable) versus *many* and *few* (countable).

like: Use *like* only when the word that follows is just a noun or a pronoun. Use *as* or *as if* when a phrase or clause follows:
She looks *like* him.
She did just *as* he had expected.
It seems *as if* she had plenty of time.

many/much: See *less.*

regardless: The *less* ending is the negative part. No word needs two negative parts, so it is illiterate to add *ir* (a negative prefix) at the beginning.

to me/personally: Use these phrases only when personal reactions, apart from company policy, are being stated (not often the case in business writing).

try: Always follow with *to,* never *and.*

verbal: People in the business community who are careful with language frown on those who use *verbal* to mean "spoken" or "oral." Many others do say "verbal agreement." Strictly speaking, *verbal* means "of words" and therefore includes both spoken and written words. Be guided in this matter by company usage.

4.3 Frequently Misspelled Words

All of us, even the world's best spellers, sometimes have to check a dictionary for the spelling of some words. People who have never memorized the spelling of commonly used words must look up so many that they grow exasperated and give up on spelling words correctly.

Don't expect perfection, and don't surrender. If you can memorize the spelling of just the words listed here, you'll need the dictionary far less often and you'll write with more confidence.

absence	endorsement
absorption	exaggerate
accessible	exceed
accommodate	exhaust
accumulate	existence
achieve	extraordinary
advantageous	
affiliated	fallacy
aggressive	familiar
alignment	flexible
aluminum	fluctuation
ambience	forty
analyze	
apparent	gesture
appropriate	grievous
argument	
asphalt	haphazard
assistant	harassment
asterisk	holiday
auditor	
	illegible
bankruptcy	immigrant
believable	incidentally
brilliant	indelible
bulletin	independent
	indispensable
calendar	insistent
campaign	intermediary
category	irresistible
ceiling	
changeable	jewelry
clientele	judgment
collateral	judicial
committee	
comparative	labeling
competitor	legitimate
concede	leisure
congratulations	license
connoisseur	litigation
consensus	
convenient	maintenance
convertible	mathematics
corroborate	mediocre
criticism	minimum
definitely	necessary
description	negligence
desirable	negotiable
dilemma	newsstand
disappear	noticeable
disappoint	
disbursement	occurrence
discrepancy	omission
dissatisfied	
dissipate	parallel
	pastime
eligible	peaceable
embarrassing	permanent

perseverance	salable
persistent	secretary
personnel	seize
persuade	separate
possesses	sincerely
precede	succeed
predictable	suddenness
preferred	superintendent
privilege	supersede
procedure	surprise
proceed	
pronunciation	tangible
psychology	tariff
pursue	technique
	tenant
questionnaire	truly
receive	unanimous
recommend	until
repetition	
rescind	vacillate
rhythmical	vacuum
ridiculous	vicious

4.4 Transitional Words and Phrases

The following two sentences don't communicate as well as they might because they lack a transitional word or phrase:

Production delays are inevitable. Our current lag time in filling orders is one month.

A semicolon between the two sentences would signal a close relationship between their meanings, but it wouldn't even hint at what that relationship is. Here are the sentences, now linked by means of a semicolon, with a space for a transitional word or phrase:

Production delays are inevitable; _____ , our current lag time in filling orders is one month.

Now read the sentence with *nevertheless* in the blank space. Now try *therefore, incidentally, in fact,* and *at any rate* in the blank. Each substitution changes the meaning of the sentence.

Here are some transitional words (called conjunctive adverbs) that will help you write more clearly:

accordingly	furthermore	moreover
anyway	however	otherwise
besides	incidentally	still
consequently	likewise	therefore
finally	meanwhile	

The following transitional phrases are used in the same way:

as a result

at any rate

for example

in fact

in other words

in the second place

on the other hand

to the contrary

When one of these words or phrases joins two independent clauses, it should be preceded by a semicolon and followed by a comma, as shown here:

The consultant recommended a complete reorganization; moreover, she suggested that we drop several products.

APPENDIX D

Correction Symbols

Instructors often use these short, easy-to-remember correction symbols and abbreviations when evaluating students' writing. You can use them too, to understand your instructor's suggestions and to revise and proofread your own letters, memos, and reports. Refer to Appendix C for information on grammar and usage.

CONTENT AND STYLE

Acc	Accuracy. Check to be sure information is correct.	GNF	Good news first. Use direct order.
ACE	Avoid copying examples.	GRF	Give reasons first. Use indirect order.
ACP	Avoid copying problems.	GW	Goodwill. Put more emphasis on expressions of goodwill.
Adp	Adapt. Tailor message to reader.	H/E	Honesty/ethics. Revise statement to reflect good business practices.
Assign	Assignment. Review instructions for assignment.		
AV	Active verb. Substitute active for passive.	Imp	Imply. Avoid being direct.
Awk	Awkward phrasing. Rewrite.	Inc	Incomplete. Develop further.
BC	Be consistent.	Jar	Jargon. Use less specialized language.
BMS	Be more sincere.	Log	Logic. Check development of argument.
Chop	Choppy sentences. Use longer sentences and more transitional phrases.	Neg	Negative. Use more positive approach or expression.
Con	Condense. Use fewer words.	Obv	Obvious. Do not state point in such detail.
CT	Conversational tone. Avoid using overly formal language.	OC	Overconfident. Adopt humbler language.
Depers	Depersonalize. Avoid attributing credit or blame to any individual or group.	OM	Omission.
		Org	Organization. Strengthen outline.
Dev	Develop. Provide greater detail.	OS	Off the subject. Close with point on main subject.
Dir	Direct. Use direct approach; get to the point.	Par	Parallel. Use same structure.
Emph	Emphasize. Develop this point more fully.	Plan	Follow proper organizational plan. (Refer to Chapter 4.)
EW	Explanation weak. Check logic; provide more proof.	Pom	Pompous. Rephrase in down-to-earth terms.
Fl	Flattery. Avoid compliments that are insincere.	PV	Point of view. Make statement from reader's perspective rather than your own.
FS	Figure of speech. Find a more accurate expression.	RB	Reader benefit. Explain what reader stands to gain.

Red	Redundant. Reduce number of times this point is made.	Tone	Tone needs improvement.
Ref	Reference. Cite source of information.	Trans	Transition. Show connection between points.
Rep	Repetitive. Provide different expression.	UAE	Use action ending. Close by stating what reader should do next.
RS	Resale. Reassure reader that he or she has made a good choice.	UAS	Use appropriate salutation.
SA	Service attitude. Put more emphasis on helping reader.	UAV	Use active voice.
Sin	Sincerity. Avoid sounding glib or uncaring.	Unc	Unclear. Rewrite to clarify meaning.
SL	Stereotyped language. Focus on individual's characteristics instead of on false generalizations.	UPV	Use passive voice.
		USS	Use shorter sentences.
Spec	Specific. Provide more specific statement.	V	Variety. Use different expression or sentence pattern.
SPM	Sales promotion material. Tell reader about related goods or services.	W	Wordy. Eliminate unnecessary words.
Stet	Let stand in original form.	WC	Word choice. Find a more appropriate word.
Sub	Subordinate. Make this point less important.	YA	"You" attitude. Rewrite to emphasize reader's needs.
SX	Sexist. Avoid language that contributes to gender stereotypes.		

GRAMMAR, USAGE, AND MECHANICS

Ab	Abbreviation. Avoid abbreviations in most cases; use correct abbreviation.	lc	Lowercase. Do not use capital letter.
Adj	Adjective. Use adjective instead.	M	Margins. Improve frame around document.
Adv	Adverb. Use adverb instead.	MM	Misplaced modifier. Place modifier close to word it modifies.
Agr	Agreement. Make subject and verb or noun and pronoun agree.	NRC	Nonrestrictive clause (or phrase). Separate from rest of sentence with commas.
Ap	Appearance. Improve appearance.	P	Punctuation. Use correct punctuation.
Apos	Apostrophe. Check use of apostrophe.	Par	Parallel. Use same structure.
Art	Article. Use correct article.	PH	Place higher. Move document up on page.
BC	Be consistent.	PL	Place lower. Move document down on page.
Cap	Capitalize.	Prep	Preposition. Use correct preposition.
Case	Use cases correctly.	RC	Restrictive clause (or phrase). Remove commas that separate clause from rest of sentence.
CoAdj	Coordinate adjective. Insert comma between coordinate adjectives; delete comma between adjective and compound noun.	RO	Run-on sentence. Separate two sentences with comma and coordinating conjunction or with semicolon.
CS	Comma splice. Use period or semicolon to separate clauses.	SC	Series comma. Add comma before and.
DM	Dangling modifier. Rewrite so that modifier clearly relates to subject of sentence.	SI	Split infinitive. Do not separate to from rest of verb.
		Sp	Spelling error. Consult dictionary.
Exp	Expletive. Avoid expletive beginnings, such as it is, there are, there is, this is, and these are.	Stet	Let stand in original form.
		S-V	Subject-verb pair. Do not separate with comma.
F	Format. Improve layout of document.	Syl	Syllabification. Divide word between syllables.
Frag	Fragment. Rewrite as complete sentence.	WD	Word division. Check dictionary for proper end-of-line hyphenation.
Gram	Grammar. Correct grammatical error.		
HCA	Hyphenate compound adjective.	WW	Wrong word. Replace with another word.

${P}$ROOFREADING MARKS

Symbol	Meaning	Symbol Used in Context	Corrected Copy
═	Align horizontally	meaningful result	meaningful result
‖	Align vertically	1. Power cable 2. Keyboard	1. Power cable 2. Keyboard
ⓐⓒ	Capitalize	Do not immerse.	DO NOT IMMERSE.
≡	Capitalize	Pepsico, Inc.	PepsiCo, Inc.
⌒	Close up	self- confidence	self-confidence
℘	Delete	harrassment and abuse	harassment
ⓈⓉⒺⓉ	Restore to original	none of the ⓈⓉⒺⓉ	none of the
∧	Insert	and white tirquoise shirts	turquoise and white shirts
⟨	Insert comma	a, b and c	a, b, and c
⊙	Insert period	Harrigan et al	Harrigan et al.
/	Lowercase	TULSA, South of here	Tulsa, south of here
⊏	Move left	Attention: ⊏ Security	Attention: Security
⊐	Move right	February 2, 1996 ═══	February 2, 1996
⊔	Move down	Sincerely,	Sincerely,
⊓	Move up	THIRD-QUARTER SALES	THIRD-QUARTER SALES
⊐⊏	Center	⊐Awards Banquet⊏	Awards Banquet
⌐	Start new line	Marla Fenton, Manager, Distri- bution	Marla Fenton Manager, Distribution
⌐	Run lines together	Manager, Distribution	Manager, Distribution
¶	Start paragraph	¶ The solution is easy to determine but difficult to implement in a competitive environment like the one we now face.	The solution is easy to determine but difficult to implement in a competitive environment like the one we now face.
#	Leave space	# # real estate testcase	real estate test case
⏝	Spell out	ⓒⓞⓓ	cash on delivery
ⓈⓅ	Spell out	ⓈⓅ Assn. of Biochem. Engrs.	Association of Biochemical Engineers
∿	Transpose	airy, light, casaul tone	light, airy, casual tone

REFERENCES

Chapter 1

1. Adapted from Doug Glass, "Escaping the Rut Is Good Idea for Hallmark Artists, Writers; Creativity: Greeting Card Company Sends Its Employees on Retreats or to the Movies to Spark New Inspiration," Orange County Edition, *Los Angeles Times*, 6 June 1996, D-7; Gillian Flynn, "Sending a Quality of Life Message: Hallmark Cares," *Personnel Journal*, March 1996, 56; Karen Matthes, "Greetings from Hallmark," *HR Focus* 70 (August 1, 1993): 12.

2. Joseph N. Scudder and Patricia J. Guinan, "Communication Competencies as Discriminators of Superiors' Ratings of Employee Performance," *Journal of Business Communication* 26, no. 3 (Summer 1989): 217–29; Joseph F. Coates, "Today's Events Produce Tomorrow's Communication Issues," *IABC Communication World*, June–July 1991, 20–25.

3. J. Michael Sproule, *Communication Today* (Glenview, Ill.: Scott Foresman, 1981), 329.

4. Jaesub Lee and Fredric Jablan, "A Cross-Cultural Investigation of Exit, Voice, Loyalty and Neglect as Responses to Dissatisfying Job Conditions," *Journal of Business Communication* 23, no. 3 (1992): 203–28; Barron Wells and Nelda Spinks, "What Do You Mean People Communicate with Audiences?" *The Bulletin of the Association for Business Communication* 54, no. 3 (September 1991): 100–102.

5. Jim Braham, "A Rewarding Place to Work," *Industry Week*, 18 September 1989, 18.

6. Donald O. Wilson, "Diagonal Communication Links with Organizations," *Journal of Business Communication* 29, no. 2 (Spring 1992): 129–43.

7. Valorie A. McClelland and Richard E. Wilmot, "Communication: Improve Lateral Communication," *Personnel Journal*, August 1990, 32–38; Valorie A. McClelland and Dick Wilmot, "Lateral Communication: As Seen Through the Eyes of Employees," *IABC Communication World*, December 1990, 32–35.

8. Carol Hymowitz, "Spread the Word: Gossip Is Good," *Wall Street Journal*, 4 November 1988, B1; Donald B. Simmons, "The Nature of the Organizational Grapevine," *Supervisory Management*, November 1985, 40.

9. J. David Johnson, William A. Donohoe, Charles K. Atkin, and Sally Johnson, "Differences Between Formal and Informal Communication Channels," *Journal of Business Communication* 31, no. 2 (1994): 111–22.

10. Maureen Weiss, "Manager's Tool Kit: Tapping the Grapevine," *Across the Board*, April 1992, 62–63.

11. "Walk More, Talk More," *Across the Board*, December 1992, 57; Jonathan H. Amsbary and Patricia J. Staples, "Improving Administrator/Nurse Communication: A Case Study of 'Management by Wandering Around'" *Journal of Business Communication* 28, no. 2 (Spring 1991): 101–12; Christopher Knowlton, "How Disney Keeps the Magic Going," *Fortune*, 4 December 1989, 112.

12. "2 Major PR Problems, 2 Approaches," *San Diego Union*, 21 January 1990, I-1.

13. "Presumed Guilty: Managing When Your Company's Name Is Mud," *Working Woman*, November 1991, 31.

14. John Huey, "Wal-Mart: Will It Take Over the World?" *Fortune*, 30 January 1989, 56; Patricia Sellers, "Getting Customers to Love You," *Fortune*, 13 March 1989, 39; Stephen Phillips and Amy Dunkin, "King Customer," *Business Week*, 12 March 1990, 91; Charles Leerhsen, "How Disney Does It," *Newsweek*, 3 April 1989, 52.

15. Phillip G. Clampitt and Cal W. Downs, "Employee Perceptions of the Relationship Between Communication and Productivity: A Field Study," *Journal of Business Communication* 30, no. 1 (1993): 5–28.

16. Douglas McGregor, *The Human Side of Enterprise* (New York: McGraw-Hill, 1960), 33–34, 47–48.

17. William G. Ouchi, *Theory Z: How American Business Can Meet the Japanese Challenge* (Reading, Mass.: Addison-Wesley, 1981), 17.

18. Shlomo Maital, "Zen and the Art of Total Quality," *Across the Board*, March 1992, 50–51; James C. Shaffer, "Seven Emerging Trends in Organizational Communication," *IABC Communication World*, February 1986, 18.

19. A. Thomas Young, "Ethics in Business: Business of Ethics," *Vital Speeches*, 15 September 1992, 725–30.

20. Bruce W. Speck, "Writing Professional Codes of Ethics to Introduce Ethics in Business Writing," *The Bulletin of the Association for Business Communication* 53, no. 3 (September 1990): 21–26; H. W. Love, "Communication, Accountability and Professional Discourse: The Interaction of Language Values and Ethical Values," *Journal of Business Ethics* 11 (1992): 883–92; Kathryn C. Rentz and Mary Beth Debs, "Language and Corporate Values: Teaching Ethics in Business Writing Courses," *Journal of Business Communication* 24, no. 3 (Summer 1987): 37–48.

21. Joseph L. Badaracco Jr., "Business Ethics: Four Spheres of Executive Responsibility," *California Management Review*, Spring 1992, 64–79; Kenneth Blanchard and Norman Vincent Peale, *The Power of Ethical Management* (Reprint, 1989; New York: Fawcett Crest, 1991), 7–17.

22. John D. Pettit, Bobby Vaught, and Kathy J. Pulley, "The Role of Communication in Organizations," *Journal of Business Communication* 27, no. 3 (Summer 1990): 233–49; Kenneth Labich, "The New Crisis in Business Ethics," *Fortune*, 20 April 1992, 167, 168, 172, 176; Kenneth R. Andrews, "Ethics in Practice," *Harvard Business Review*, September–October 1989, 99–104; Priscilla S. Rogers and John M. Swales, "We the People? An Analysis of the Dana Corporation Policies Document," *Journal of Business Communication* 27, no. 3 (Summer 1990): 293–313; Larry Reynolds, "The Ethics Audit," *Business Ethics*, July–August 1991, 120–22.

23. Susan L. Fry, "How to Succeed in the New Europe," *Public Relations Journal*, January 1991, 17–21.

24. U.S. Bureau of Labor Statistics, *Occupational Outlook Quarterly, 1994* (Washington, D.C.: GPO, 1994).

25. Rick Tetzeli, "Surviving Information Overload, *Fortune*, July 1994, 60–65.

26. "1995 Cost of a Business Letter," Dartnell Study (Chicago: The Dartnell Corporation, 1995).

27. Selwyn Feinstein, "Remedial Training," *Wall Street Journal*, 20 February 1990, A1.

28. Based on Glass, "Escaping the Rut"; Flynn, "Sending a Quality of Life Message"; Matthes, "Greetings from Hallmark."

29. Based on Keith Denton, "Improving Community Relations," *Small Business Reports*, August 1990, 33–34, 35–41.

Chapter 2

1. Adapted from Ben & Jerry's Web site, <http://www.benjerry.com>, accessed 8 October 1997; Maureen Martin, coordinator, employee communications, Ben & Jerry's Homemade, personal communication, 22 January 1990; Gusting Burke, "Russia Gets a Triple Dip of 'Caring Capitalism,'" *Christian Science Monitor*, 5 March 1993, 8; Carolyn Friday, "Cookies, Cream 'n' Controversy," *Newsweek*, 5 July 1993, 40; Leonard L. Drey, "Making a Difference: Ice Cream Meets Charity in Harlem," *New York Times*, 21 February 1993, sec. 3, 13; Suein L. Hwang, "While Many Competitors See Sales Melt, Ben & Jerry's Scoops Out Solid Growth," *Wall Street Journal*, 25 May 1993, B1, B5; Joanie M. Wexler, "Videoconferences Give Life to Team Approach," *Computerworld*, 14 September 1992, 67–68; Jennifer J. Laabs, "Ben & Jerry's Caring Capitalism," *Personnel Journal*, November 1992, 50–57; Eric J. Wieffering, "Trouble in Camelot," *Business Ethics*, January–February 1991, 16–19; N. R. Keinfield, "Wanted: C.F.O. with 'Flair for Funk,'" *New York Times*, 26 March 1989, sec. 3, 4; Paul Cissel,

"Ben & Jerry's Adds to Its Recipe for Success," *P&MI Review,* February 1989, 37–40; Joe Queenan, "Purveying Yuppie Porn," *Forbes,* 13 December 1989, 60–64.

2. David Givens, "You Animal? How to Win Friends and Influence Homosapiens," *The Toastmaster,* August 1986, 9.

3. Mark L. Hickson III and Don W. Stacks, *Nonverbal Communication: Studies and Applications* (Dubuque, Iowa: Brown, 1985), 4.

4. Gerald H. Graham, Jeanne Unrue, and Paul Jennings, "The Impact of Nonverbal Communication in Organizations: A Survey of Perceptions," *Journal of Business Communication* 28, no. 1 (Winter 1991): 45–62.

5. David Lewis, *The Secret Language of Success* (New York: Carroll & Graf, 1989), 67, 170.

6. Nido Qubein, *Communicate Like a Pro* (New York: Berkley Books, 1986), 97.

7. Dale G. Leathers, *Successful Nonverbal Communication: Principles and Applications* (New York: Macmillan, 1986), 19.

8. Margaret Ann Baker, "Reciprocal Accommodation: A Model for Reducing Gender Bias in Managerial Communication," *Journal of Business Communication* 28, no. 2 (Spring 1991): 113–27; Graham, Unrue, and Jennings, "The Impact of Nonverbal Communication in Organizations," 45–62.

9. Graham, Unrue, and Jennings, "The Impact of Nonverbal Communication in Organizations," 45–62.

10. Stuart Berg Flexner, "From 'Gadzooks' to 'Nice,' the Language Keeps Changing," *U.S. News & World Report,* 18 February 1985, 59.

11. Erik Larson, "Forever Young," *Inc.,* July 1988, 56.

12. Phillip Morgan and H. Kent Baker, "Building a Professional Image: Improving Listening Behavior," *Supervisory Management,* November 1985, 35, 36.

13. Augusta M. Simon, "Effective Listening: Barriers to Listening in a Diverse Business Environment," *The Bulletin of the Association for Business Communication* 54, no. 3 (September 1991): 73–74.

14. Irwin Ross, "Corporations Take Aim at Illiteracy," *Fortune,* 29 September 1986, 49.

15. Some material adapted from Courtland L. Bovée, John V. Thill, Marian Burk Wood, and George P. Dovel, *Management* (New York: McGraw-Hill, 1993), 537–38.

16. Much of the material contained in the entire section on communication barriers has been adapted from Bovée, Thill, Wood, and Dovel, *Management,* 549–57.

17. Adapted from C. Glenn Pearce, Ross Figgins, and Steve F. Golen, *Principles of Business Communication: Theory, Application, and Technology* (New York: Wiley, 1984), 520–38.

18. Linlin Ku, "Social and Nonsocial Uses of Electronic Messaging Systems in Organizations," *Journal of Business Communication* 33, no. 3 (July 1996): 297–325.

19. Bovée, Thill, Wood, and Dovel, *Management,* 555.

20. Based on Ben & Jerry's Web site; Martin, personal communication, 22 January 1990; Burke, "Russia Gets a Triple Dip of 'Caring Capitalism'"; Friday, "Cookies, Cream 'n' Controversy"; Drey, "Making a Difference"; Hwang, "While Many Companies See Sales Melt"; Wexler, "Videoconferences Give Life to Team Approach"; Laabs, "Ben & Jerry's Caring Capitalism"; Wieffering, "Trouble in Camelot"; Keinfield, "Wanted"; Cissel, "Ben & Jerry's Adds to Its Recipe for Success"; Queenan, "Purveying Yuppie Porn."

Chapter 3

1. Adapted from Target stores Web site, <http://www.targetstores.com/TargetWWW/html/about01.htm>, accessed 21 March 1997; D.R. Barnes, "Company Plans to Establish Community Partnerships," *Washington Informer,* 13 December 1995, PG; Susan Moffat, "Workforce Diversity; The Young and the Diverse; The Next Generation May Be Better Equipped to Deal with Cultural Complexities at Work," Home Edition, *Los Angeles Times,* 16 May 1994, 2–15.

2. Paul Magnusson, "Grabbing New World Orders," *Business Week: Reinventing America* 1992, 110–12, 114, 116; Jeffrey Hawkins, "Canada: Appetite Remains Strong for U.S. Goods and Services Despite Sluggish Domestic Demand; Recovery Under Way," *Business America,* 19 April 1993, 6–7.

3. Elizabeth Howard, "Going Global: What It Really Means to Communicators," *IABC Communication World,* April 1995, 12–15.

4. Paul Magnusson, "Free Trade? They Can Hardly Wait," *Business Week,* 14 September 1992, 24–25; Bill Javetski, "Continental Drift," *Business Week,* 5 October 1992, 34–36.

5. John P. Fernandez, *Managing a Diverse Workforce* (Lexington, Mass: Lexington Books, 1991), 5; David A. Victor, *International Business Communication* (New York: HarperCollins, 1992), 7–8; Michael Mandel and Christopher Farrell, "The Immigrants," *Business Week,* 13 July 1992, 114–120, 122; David Jamieson and Julie O'Mara, *Managing Workforce 2000: Gaining the Diversity Advantage* (San Francisco: Jossey-Bass, 1991), 21.

6. "Less Yiddish, More Tagalog," *U.S. News & World Report,* 10 May 1993, 16; Gary Levin, "Marketers Learning New Languages for Ads," *Advertising Age,* 10 May 1993, 33.

7. Marilyn Kern-Foxworth, "Colorizing Advertising: What Ad Clubs Can Do to Make the Business More Inclusive," *American Advertising,* Winter 1991–1992, 26–28; Margaret Ambry and Cheryl Russell, *The Official Guide to the American Marketplace* (Ithaca, N.Y.: New Strategist Publications, 1992), 271.

8. Gus Tyler, "Tokyo Signs the Paychecks," *New York Times Book Review,* 12 August 1990, 7.

9. Tzöl Zae Chung, "Culture: A Key to Management Communication Between the Asian-Pacific Area and Europe," *European Management Journal* 9, no. 4 (December 1991): 419–24.

10. James S. O'Rourke IV, "International Business Communication: Building a Course from the Ground Up," *Bulletin of the Association for Business Communication* 56, no. 4 (1993): 22–27.

11. Larry A. Samovar and Richard E. Porter, "Basic Principles of Intercultural Communication," in *Intercultural Communication: A Reader,* 6th ed., edited by Larry A. Samovar and Richard E. Porter (Belmont, Calif.: Wadsworth, 1991), 12.

12. Tim Jones, "Shrinking World Reshapes Auto Industry," *Chicago Tribune,* 10 May 1998, sec. 5, 1, 14.

13. Edmund L. Andrews and Laura M. Holson, "Significant Risks—The Largest Acquistion of a Company in U.S. by a Foreign Buyer," *New York Times,* 7 May 1998, A-1, C-4,: Robyn Meredith, "Two Auto Makers With Long Histories Attempt a Trans-Atlantic Marriage," *New York Times,* 7 May 1998, C-4.

14. James Calvert Scott, "Using an International Business-Meal Function to Develop Sociocultural Skills," *Business Communication Quarterly* 58, no. 3 (1995): 55–57.

15. Mary A. DeVries, *Internationally Yours* (New York: Houghton Mifflin, 1994), 194.

16. "Pakistan: A Congenial Business Climate," *Nation's Business,* July 1986, 50.

17. Victor, *International Business Communication,* 234–39; Mohan R. Limaye and David A. Victor, "Cross Cultural Business Communication Research: State of the Art and Hypotheses for the 1990s," *Journal of Business Communication,* 28, no. 3 (Summer 1991): 277–99.

18. Carley H. Dodd, *Dynamics of Intercultural Communication,* 3d ed. (Dubuque, Iowa: Brown, 1991), 215.

19. Edward T. Hall, "Context and Meaning," in *Intercultural Communication,* Samovar and Porter, 46–55.

20. Dodd, *Dynamics of Intercultural Communication,* 69–70.

21. Porter and Samovar, "Basic Principles of Intercultural Communication," 5–22; David A. Victor, personal communication, 1993.

22. Laray M. Barna, "Stumbling Blocks in Intercultural Communication," in *Intercultural Communication,* Samovar and Porter, 345–52.

23. Jean A. Mausehund, Susan A. Timm, and Albert S. King, "Diversity Training: Effects of an Intervention Treatment on Nonverbal Awareness," *Business Communication Quarterly* 38, no. 1 (1995): 27–30.

24. Sharon Ruhly, *Intercultural Communication,* 2d ed. MODCOM (Modules in Speech Communication) (Chicago: Science Research Associates, 1982), 14.

25. Karen P. H. Lane, "Greasing the Bureaucratic Wheel," *North American International Business*, August 1990, 35–37; Arthur Aronoff, "Complying with the Foreign Corrupt Practices Act," *Business America*, 11 February 1991, 10–11; Bill Shaw, "Foreign Corrupt Practices Act: A Legal and Moral Analysis," *Journal of Business Ethics* 7 (1988): 789–95.

26. Philip R. Harris and Robert T. Moran, *Managing Cultural Differences*, 3d ed. (Houston: Gulf, 1991), 260.

27. David J. McIntyre, "When Your National Language Is Just *Another* Language," *IABC Communication World*, May 1991, 18–21.

28. Linda Beamer, "Teaching English Business Writing to Chinese-Speaking Business Students," *Bulletin of the Association for Business Communication* 57, no. 1 (1994): 12–18.

29. David A. Ricks, "International Business Blunders: An Update," *B&E Review*, January–March 1988, 12.

30. Vern Terpstra, *The Cultural Environment of International Business* (Cincinnati: South-Western, 1979), 19.

31. Victor, *International Business Communication*, 36.

32. Doreen Mangan, "What's New in Language Translation: A Tool for Examining Foreign Patents and Research," *New York Times*, 19 November 1989, sec. 3, 15.

33. Victor, *International Business Communication*, 39; Harris and Moran, *Managing Cultural Differences*, 64.

34. Mona Casady and Lynn Wasson, "Written Communication Skills of International Business Persons," *The Bulletin of the Association for Business Communication* 57, no. 4 (1994): 36–40.

35. Geert Hofstede, *Cultures and Organizations* (London: McGraw-Hill, 1991), 211.

36. Richard W. Brislin, "Prejudice in Intercultural Communication," in *Intercultural Communication*, Samovar and Porter, 366–70.

37. Jensen J. Zhao and Calvin Parks, "Self-Assessment of Communication Behavior: An Experiential Learning Exercise for Intercultural Business Success," *Business Communication Quarterly* 58, no. 1 (1995): 20–26; Dodd, *Dynamics of Intercultural Communication*, 142–43, 297–99.

38. Marita van Oldenborgh, "Court with Care," *International Business*, April 1995, 20–22.

39. Susan A. Hellweg, Larry A. Samovar, and Lisa Skow, "Cultural Variations in Negotiation Styles," in *Intercultural Communication*, Samovar and Porter, 185–92.

40. Brian Dumaine, "P&G Rewrites the Marketing Rules," *Fortune*, 6 November 1989, 38.

41. Based on Target Stores Web site; Barnes, "Company Plans to Establish Community Partnerships"; Moffat, "Workforce Diversity."

42. Michael Copeland, specialist, international training, personal communication, 24 January 1990; Dumaine, "P&G Rewrites the Maketing Rules," 34–48; Procter & Gamble Company 1992 Annual Report, 24.

Chapter 4

1. Mike Stevens, systems technology specialist, Hewlett-Packard, Colorado Springs, Colorado, personal communication, April 1996.

2. Eric J. Adams, "A Real Global Office," *World Trade*, October 1992, 97–98.

3. *Dialog Database Catalog 1993*, 62–63, 130.

4. Microsoft Corporation, *Encarta*, CD-ROM, 1992–1994.

5. Inspiration demonstration, Disk (Inspiration Software, 1994).

6. Jack Nimersheim, "Grammar Checker Face-Off," *Home-Office Computing*, July 1992, 49–53.

7. Eric J. Adams, "The Fax of Global Business," *World Trade*, August–September 1991, 34–39.

8. Bill Eager, *Using the Internet* (Indianapolis: Que, 1994), 13.

9. Don Clark and Joan E. Rigdon, "Stripped Down PCs Will Be Talk of Comdex," *Wall Street Journal*, 10 November 1995, B1.

10. "All About E-Mail: Use E-Mail to Communicate with Anyone, Anywhere," *Microsoft Magazine*, April–May 1996, 14–26.

11. William Eager, Larry Donahue, David Forsyth, Kenneth Mitton, and Martin Waterhouse, *Net.search* (Indianapolis: Que, 1995), 226.

12. Sheri Rosen, "Who Says E-Mail Is Mundane?" *IABC Communication World*, September 1995, 42.

13. Jolie Solomon, "As Electronic Mail Loosens Inhibitions, Impetuous Senders Feel Anything Goes," *Wall Street Journal*, 10 December 1990, B1–B2.

14. Mike Snyder, "E-Mail Isn't as Private as You May Think," *USA Today*, 10 October 1995, 6D.

15. Karen Kaplan, "Your Voicemail Box May Have Ears," *Los Angeles Times*, 15 July 1996, D8.

16. Wayne Rash Jr., "Before You Press That Send Button, Keep in Mind That E-Mail Is Forever," *Communications Week*, 16 October 1995, 72.

17. Michael Mathiesen, *Marketing on the Internet* (Gulf Breeze, Fla.: Maximum Press, 1995), 11–12.

18. Mathiesen, *Marketing on the Internet*, 12–14.

19. Amy Cortese, "Here Comes the Intranet," *BusinessWeek*, 26 February 1996, *BusinessWeek Online*, Online, 15 May 1996 <www.businessweek.com/1996/09/b34641.htm>.

20. "HP and Netscape Outline Strategic Alliance to Deliver Enterprise Intranet Solutions Across UNIX and NT System Platforms," press release, *Netscape*, Online, 14 May 1996.

21. "Internal Webs as Corporate Information Systems," White paper, *Netscape Communications*, Online, 25 April 1996.

22. Mike Bransby, "Voice Mail Makes a Difference," *Journal of Business Strategy*, January–February 1990, 7–10.

23. Harris Collingswood, "Voice Mail Hangups," *Business Week*, 17 February 1992, 46.

24. Andrew Kupfer, "Prime Time for Videoconferences," *Fortune*, 28 December 1992, 90–95.

25. Michael Finley, "The New Meaning of Meetings," *IABC Communication World*, March 1991, 25–27.

26. Mark Mabrito, "Computer-Mediated Communication and High-Apprehensive Writers: Rethinking the Collaborative Process," *The Bulletin of the Association for Business Communication*, December 1992, 26–29; Susan M. Gelfond, "It's Fax, Fax, Fax, Fax World," *Business Week*, 21 March 1988, 138.

27. Chris Campbell, "Outerstreaming: The Fourth Communication Paradigm," *IABC Communication World*, December 1990, 18–22.

28. Based on Mike Stevens, personal communication, April 1996.

Chapter 5

1. Adapted from Mattel Barbie Web site, <http://www.barbie.com>, accessed 9 October 1997; Mattel 1993 Annual Report, 2–6; Michelle Greene and Denise Gellene, "As a Tiny Plastic Star Turns 30, the Real Barbie and Ken Reflect on Life in the Shadow of the Dolls," *People*, 6 March 1989, 186–89; Denise Gellene, "Forever Young," *Los Angeles Times*, 29 January 1989, D1, D4; Ann Hornaday, "Top Guns: The Most Powerful Women in Corporate America," *Savvy*, May 1989, 57, 60; Jennifer Roethe, "Dolls and Dollars Go Together Like Ken and Barbie," *Cincinnati Business Courier*, 10 July 1989, 1.

2. Mary K. Kirtz and Diana C. Reep, "A Survey of the Frequency, Types, and Importance of Writing Tasks in Four Career Areas," *The Bulletin of the Association for Business Communication* 53, no. 4 (December 1990): 3–4.

3. Mary Cullinan and Ce Ce Iandoli, "What Activities Help to Improve Your Writing? Some Unsettling Student Responses," *The Bulletin of the Association for Business Communication* 54, no. 4 (December 1991): 8–10; Ruth Yontz, "Providing a Rationale for the Process Approach," *Journal of Business Communication* 24, no. 1 (Winter 1987): 17–19; Annette Shelby, "Note on Process," *Journal of Business Communication* 24, no. 1 (Winter 1987): 21.

4. Peter Bracher, "Process, Pedagogy, and Business Writing," *Journal of Business Communication* 24, no. 1 (Winter 1987): 43–50.

5. John J. Stallard, Sandra F. Price, and E. Ray Smith, "A Strategy for Teaching Critical-Thinking Skills in Business Communication," *The Bulletin of the Association for Business Communication* 55, no. 3 (September 1992): 20–22.

6. Rodney P. Rice and John T. Huguley Jr., "Describing Collaborative Forms: A Profile of the Team-Writing Process," *IEEE Transactions on*

Professional Communication 37, no. 3 (1994), 163–70; Mary Beth Debs, "Recent Research on Collaborative Writing in Industry," *Technical Communication* (November 1991): 476–84.

7. William P. Galle Jr., Beverly H. Nelson, Donna W. Luse, and Maurice F. Villere, *Business Communication: A Technology-Based Approach* (Chicago: Irwin, 1996), 256.

8. Galle, Nelson, Luse, and Villere, *Business Communication*, 260.

9. Charles R. Stratton, "Collaborative Writing in the Workplace," *IEEE Transactions on Professional Communication* 32, no. 3(1989): 178–82.

10. Debs, "Recent Research on Collaborative Writing in Industry," 476–84.

11. Sanford Kaye, "Writing Under Pressure," *Soundview Executive Book Summaries* 10, no. 12, part 2 (December 1988): 1–8.

12. Al Schlachtmeyer and Max Caldwell, "Communicating Creatively," *IABC Communication World,* June–July 1991, 28.

13. Morgan W. McCall Jr. and Robert L. Hannon, *Studies of Managerial Work: Results and Methods,* Technical Report no. 9 (Greensboro, N.C.: Center for Creative Leadership, 1978), 6–10.

14. Ernest Thompson, "Some Effects of Message Structure on Listener's Comprehension," *Speech Monographs* 34 (March 1967): 51–57.

15. Laurey Berk and Phillip G. Clampitt, "Finding the Right Path in the Communication Maze," *IABC Communication World,* October 1991, 28–32.

16. Schlachtmeyer and Caldwell, "Communicating Creatively," 26–29.

17. Adapted from Berk and Clampitt, "Finding the Right Path in the Communication Maze," 28–32.

18. Mohan R. Limaye and David A. Victor, "Cross-Cultural Business Communication Research: State of the Art and Hypotheses for the 1990s," *Journal of Business Communication* 28, no. 3 (Summer 1991): 277–99.

19. Berk and Clampitt, "Finding the Right Path in the Communication Maze," 28–32.

20. Berk and Clampitt, "Finding the Right Path in the Communication Maze," 28–32.

21. Based on Mattel Barbie Web site; Mattel 1993 Annual Report; Green and Gellene, "As a Tiny Plastic Star Turns 30"; Gellene, "Forever Young"; Hornaday, "Top Guns"; Roethe, "Dolls and Dollars Go Together Like Ken and Barbie."

Chapter 6

1. Hoover's Online, "Club Mediterranee S.A.," <http:/www.hoovers.com>, accessed 22 January 1997; Elaine Underwood, "Club Med Continues to Broaden, Soften Image," *Brandweek,* 30 October 1995, 12; Jorge Sidron, "Club Med Finds Success Sticking to Key Formula: Fun, Relaxation," *Travel Weekly,* 25 November 1996, 100; Patrick Flanagan, "Don't Call 'Em Old, Call 'Em Customers," *Management Review,* October 1994, 18; Stewart Troy, "Storms, Terrorists—Why Is Club Med Smiling?" *Business Week,* 6 November 1995, 160C.

2. Carol S. Mull, "Orchestrate Your Ideas," *The Toastmaster,* February 1987, 19.

3. Susan Hall and Theresa Tiggeman, "Getting the Big Picture: Writing to Learn in a Finance Class," *Business Communication Quarterly* 58, no. 1 (1995): 12–15.

4. Based on the Pyramid Model developed by Barbara Minto of McKinsey & Company, management consultants.

5. Philip Subanks, "Messages, Models, and the Messy World of Memos," *The Bulletin of the Association for Business Communication* 57, no. 1 (1994): 33–34.

6. Iris I. Varner, "Internationalizing Business Communication Courses," *The Bulletin of the Association for Business Communication* 50, no. 4 (December 1987): 7–11.

7. Mary A. DeVries, *Internationally Yours* (New York: Houghton Mifflin, 1994), 61.

8. Elizabeth Blackburn and Kelly Belanger, "You-Attitude and Positive Emphasis: Testing Received Wisdom in Business Communication," *The Bulletin of the Association for Business Communication* 56, no. 2 (June 1993): 1–9.

9. Blackburn and Belanger, "You-Attitude and Positive Emphasis," 1–9.

10. DeVries, *Internationally Yours,* 61.

11. Annette N. Shelby and N. Lamar Reinsch Jr., "Positive Emphasis and You Attitude: An Empirical Study," *Journal of Business Communication* 32, no. 4 (1995): 303–22.

12. John S. Fielden, Jean D. Fielden, and Ronald E. Dulek, *The Business Writing Style Book* (Englewood Cliffs, N.J.: Prentice Hall, 1984), 7.

13. Renee B. Horowitz and Marian G. Barchilon, "Stylistic Guidelines for E-Mail," *IEEE Transactions on Professional Communications* 37, no. 4 (December 1994): 207–12.

14. David Angell and Brent Heslop, *The Elements of E-Mail Style* (Reading, Mass.: Addison-Wesley, 1994), 10.

15. Jill H. Ellsworth and Matthew V. Ellsworth, *The Internet Business Book* (New York: Wiley, 1994), 91.

16. Lance Cohen, "How to Improve Your E-Mail Messages," <http://galaxy.einet/galaxy/Business-and-Commerce/Management/Communications/How_to_Improve_Your_E_Mail.html>.

17. Angell and Heslop, *The Elements of E-Mail Style,* 10.

18. Angell and Heslop, *The Elements of E-Mail Style,* 20.

19. Angell and Heslop, *The Elements of E-Mail Style,* 24.

20. Angell and Heslop, *The Elements of E-Mail Style,* 22.

21. Cohen, "How to Improve Your E-Mail Messages"; Angell and Heslop, *The Elements of E-Mail Style,* 20; Horowitz and Barchilon, "Stylistic Guidelines for E-Mail."

22. Angell and Heslop, *The Elements of E-Mail Style,* 18–19.

23. Angell and Heslop, *The Elements of E-Mail Style,* 21.

24. Angell and Heslop, *The Elements of E-Mail Style,* 20; Cohen, "How to Improve Your E-Mail Messages"; Ellsworth and Ellsworth, *The Internet Business Book,* 101.

25. Cohen, "How to Improve Your E-Mail Messages"; William Eager, *Using the Internet* (Indianapolis: Que, 1994), 99.

26 Angell and Heslop, *The Elements of E-Mail Style,* 30, 117; Ellsworth and Ellsworth, *The Internet Business Book,* 99; Eager, *Using the Internet,* 99; Cohen, "How to Improve Your E-Mail Messages"; William Eager, Larry Donahue, David Forsyth, Kenneth Mitton, and Martin Waterhouse, *Net.Search* (Indianapolis: Que, 1995), 225.

27. Based on Hoover's Online, "Club Mediterranee S.A."; Underwood, "Club Med Continues to Broaden, Soften Image"; Sidron, "Club Med Finds Success Sticking to Key Formula"; Flanagan, "Don't Call 'Em Old, Call 'Em Customers"; Troy, "Storms, Terrorists."

Chapter 7

1. Adapted from Brian Bremmer, "The Burger Wars Were Just a Warmup for McDonald's," *Business Week,* 8 May 1989, 67, 70; Richard Gibson and Robert Johnson, "Big Mac Plots Strategy to Regain Sizzle; Besides Pizza, It Ponders Music and Low Lights," *Wall Street Journal,* 29 September 1989, B1; Dyan Machan, "Great Hash Browns, But Watch Those Biscuits," *Forbes,* 19 September 1988, 192–96; Penny Moser, "The McDonald's Mystique," *Fortune,* 4 July 1988, 112–16; Thomas N. Cochran, "McDonald's Corporation," *Barron's,* 16 November 1987, 53–55; Lenore Skenazy, "McDonald's Colors Its World," *Advertising Age,* 9 February 1987, 37.

2. Iris I. Varner, "Internationalizing Business Communication Courses," *The Bulletin of the Association for Business Communication* 50, no. 4 (December 1987): 7–11.

3. Kevin T. Stevens, Kathleen C. Stevens, and William P. Stevens, "Measuring the Readability of Business Writing: The Cloze Procedure versus Readability Formulas," *Journal of Business Communication* 29, no. 4 (1992): 367–82; Alinda Drury, "Evaluating Readability," *IEEE Transactions of Professional Communication* PC-28 (December 1985): 11.

4. Portions of this section are adapted from Courtland L. Bovée, *Techniques of Writing Business Letters, Memos, and Reports* (Sherman Oaks, Calif.: Banner Books International, 1978), 13–90.

5. Randolph H. Hudson, Gertrude M. McGuire, and Bernard J. Selzler, *Business Writing: Concepts and Applications* (Los Angeles: Roxbury, 1983), 79–82.

6. Peter Crow, "Plain English: What Counts Besides Readability?" *Journal of Business Communication* 25, no. 1 (Winter 1988): 87–95.

7. Judy E. Pickens, "Terms of Equality: A Guide to Bias-Free Language," *Personnel Journal*, August 1985, 24.

8. Rose Knotts and Mary S. Thibodeaux, "Verbal Skills in Cross-Culture Managerial Communication," *European Business Review* 92, no. 2 (1992): 5–7.

9. Lisa Taylor, "Communicating About People with Disabilities: Does the Language We Use Make a Difference?" *The Bulletin of the Association for Business Communication* 53, no. 3 (September 1990): 65–67.

10. Taylor, "Communicating About People with Disabilities," 65–67.

11. Charles E. Risch, "Critiquing Written Material," *Manage* 35, no. 4 (1983): 4–6.

12. Risch, "Critiquing Written Material."

13. Risch, "Critiquing Written Material."

14. Varner, "Internationalizing Business Communication Courses."

15. Drury, "Evaluating Readability," 12.

16. Portions of the following sections are adapted from Roger C. Parker, *Looking Good in Print*, 2d ed. (Chapel Hill, N.C.: Ventana Press, 1990).

17. Raymond W. Beswick, "Designing Documents for Legibility," *The Bulletin of the Association for Business Communication* 50, no. 4 (December 1987): 34–35.

18. Beswick, "Designing Documents for Legibility."

19. "The Process Model of Document Design," *IEEE Transactions on Professional Communication* PC-24, no. 4 (December 1981): 176–78.

20. Based on Bremmer, "The Burger Wars Were Just a Warmup for McDonald's"; Gibson and Johnson, "Big Mac Plots Strategy to Regain Sizzle"; Machan, "Great Hash Browns"; Moser, "The McDonald's Mystique"; Cochran, "McDonald's Corporation"; Skenazy, "McDonald's Colors Its World."

Chapter 8

1. Adapted from Barnes & Noble Web sites, <http://www.barnesandnoble.com> and <http://www.shareholder.com/bks>, accessed 21 October 1997; "Barnes & Noble, Inc.," Hoover's Online, <http://www.hoovers.com>, accessed 23 January 1997; Michael Hartnett, "Barnes & Noble Reshapes Book Market with Superstore Success," *Stores*, April 1996, 40–41; Patrick M. Reilly, "Booksellers Prepare to Do Battle in Cyberspace," *Wall Street Journal*, 28 January 1997, B1, B8; Jim Milliot, "Chains' Market Share Nears 50% of Book Sales," *Publishers Weekly*, 21 October 1996, 11; Meryl Davids, "Leonard Riggio: Coffee and Camus," *Journal of Business Strategy*, September–October 1995, 44–45; Bridget Kinsella, "Kroch's & Brentano's: What Went Wrong," *Publishers Weekly*, 4 September 1995, 21–22; Jim Milliot, "Superstore Strength Results in 21% Sales Increase at B&N," *Publishers Weekly*, 20 February 1995, 107; Myron Magnet, "Let's Go for Growth," *Fortune*, 7 March 1994, 60, 62, 64, 68, 70, 72; Richard Phalon, "A Bold Gamble," *Forbes*, 28 February 1994, 90–91; Barnes & Noble 1993 Annual Report; Kate Fitzgerald, "Bookstores in Competitive Thriller," *Advertising Age*, 12 April 1993, 12; John Mutter, "The Fine Print: Walden Edges Toward Borders," *Publishers Weekly*, 23 May 1994, 38–39; John Mutter, "A Chat with Bookseller Len Riggio," *Publishers Weekly*, 3 May 1992, 33–34, 36, 38.

2. Lennie Copeland and Lewis Griggs, *Going International: How to Make Friends and Deal Effectively in the Global Marketplace*, 2d ed. (New York: Random House, 1985), 24–27.

3. Linda Beamer, "Learning Intercultural Communication Competence," *Journal of Business Communication* 29, no. 3 (1992): 285–303.

4. Owen Edwards, "Send Me a Memo or Better Yet, Don't," *Across the Board*, November 1992, 12–13.

5. Based on Barnes & Noble Web sites; "Barnes & Noble Inc.," Hoover's Online; Hartnett, "Barnes & Noble Reshapes Bookmarket with Superstore Success"; Reilly, "Booksellers Prepare to Do Battle in Cyberspace"; Milliot, "Chains' Market Share Nears 50% of Book Sales"; Davids, "Leonard Riggio"; Kinsella, "Kroch's & Brentano's"; Milliot, "Superstore Strength Results in 21% Sales Increase at B&N"; Magnet, "Let's Go for Growth"; Phalon, "A Bold Gamble"; Barnes & Noble 1993 Annual Report; Fitzgerald, "Bookstores in Competitive Thriller"; Mutter, "The Fine Print"; Mutter, "A Chat with Bookseller Len Riggio."

6. Adapted from Reliable Office Supplies Private Customer Sale Catalog, August 1996.

7. Adapted from Kendall Hamilton, "Getting Up, Getting Air," *Newsweek*, 13 May 1996, 68.

8. Trinidad & Tobago advertisement, *Saveur*, March–April 1996, 79.

9. Adapted from Joanne Cleaver, "Back from the Brink," *Home Office Computing*, April 1995, 58, 60; Webs Are Us classified advertisement, *Computer Edge*, 26 July 1996, 81.

10. "Shop Talk: Unauthorized Tardies Can Cut into Your Vacation Time," *Los Angeles Times*, 30 March 1997, D5.

11. Frederick Rose, "Need an Electrician? Here's One Who Works Both Fast and Cheap," *Wall Street Journal*, 6 May 1997, B1; Laurie Becklund, "A Rodent That Wires Schools?" *NetDay Wire*, <www.judyrat.com>, accessed on 10 June 1997.

12. Eben Shapiro, "Blockbuster Rescue Bid Stars Viacom Top Guns," *Wall Street Journal*, 7 May 1997, B1, B10.

13. Adapted from Michael M. Phillips, "Carving Out an Export Industry, and Hope, in Africa," *Wall Street Journal*, 18 July 1996, A8.

14. Adapted from Alexandra Peers, " Ruling Britannia, or a Little Portion of It," *Wall Street Journal*, 19 July 1996, B6.

15. Adapted from "Periscope: Beanie Mania," *Newsweek*, 3 June 1996, 8.

16. "Starters: Spearing the Best," *Bon Appétit*, March 1997, 20; Mary Alice Kellogg, "The Reel Dish," *Bon Appétit*, March 1997, 38.

Chapter 9

1. Adapted from Campbell Soup Web site, <http://www.campbellsoup.com> (various pages), accessed 13 October 1997; "Campbell Soup Company," Hoover's Online, <http://www.hoovers.com>, acessed 23 January 1997; Campbell Soup 1993 Annual Report; Joseph Weber, "Campbell: Now It's M-M-Global," *Business Week*, 15 March 1993, 52–54; Pete Engardio, "Hmm. Could Use a Little More Snake," *Business Week*, 15 March 1993, 53; Joseph Weber, "Campbell Is Bubbling, But for How Long?" *Business Week*, 17 June 1991, 56–57; Joseph Weber, "From Soup to Nuts and Back to Soup," *Business Week*, 5 November 1990, 114, 116; Alix Freedman and Frank Allen, "John Dorrance's Death Leaves Campbell Soup with Cloudy Future," *Wall Street Journal*, 19 April 1989, A1, A14; Claudia H. Deutsch," Stirring Up Profits at Campbell," *New York Times*, 20 November 1988, sec. 3, 1, 22; Bill Saporito, "The Fly in Campbell's Soup," *Fortune*, 9 May 1988, 67–70.

2. Daniel P. Finkelman and Anthony R. Goland, "Customers Once Can Be Customers for Life," *Information Strategy: The Executive's Journal*, Summer 1990, 5–9.

3. Cathy Goodwin and Ivan Ross, "Consumer Evaluations of Responses to Complaints: What's Fair and Why," *Journal of Consumer Marketing* 7, no. 2 (Spring 1990): 39–46.

4. Maura Dolan and Stuart Silverstein, " Court Broadens Liability for Job References," *Los Angeles Times*, 28 January 1997, A1, A11.

5. Susan Stobaugh, "Watch Your Language," *Inc.*, May 1985, 156.

6. Claudia Mon Pere McIsaac, "Improving Student Summaries Through Sequencing," *The Bulletin of the Association for Business Communication*, September 1987, 17–20.

7. David A. Hayes, "Helping Students GRASP the Knack of Writing Summaries," *Journal of Reading*, November 1989, 96–101.

8. *Techniques for Communicators* (Chicago: Lawrence Ragan Communication, 1995), 34, 36.

9. Adapted from Donna Larcen, "Authors Share the Words of Condolence," *Los Angeles Times*, December 20, 1991, E11.

10. Based on Campbell Soup Web site; "Campbell Soup Company," Hoover's Online; Campbell Soup 1993 Annual Report; Weber, "Campbell"; Engardio, "Hmm"; Weber, "Campbell Is Bubbling, But for How Long"; Weber, "From Soup to Nuts and Back to Soup"; Freedman and Allen, "John Dorrance's Death Leave's Campbell Soup with Cloudy Future"; Deutsch, "Stirring Up Profits at Campbell"; Saporito, "The Fly in Campbell's Soup."

11. Adapted from Paul Dean, "Auto Makers Shift into New Gear," *Los Angeles Times,* 15 January 1997, E1, E6.
12. Adapted from "Entrepreneurs Across America," *Entrepreneur Magazine Online,* <http://www.entrepreneurmag.com/entmag/50states5.hts>, accessed 12 June 1997.
13. Adapted from Barbara Carton, "Farmers Begin Harvesting Satellite Data to Boost Yields," *Wall Street Journal,* 11 July 1996, B4.
14. Adapted from Campbell Soup Web site; "Campbell Soup Company," Hoover's Online; Campbell Soup 1993 Annual Report; Weber, "Campbell"; Engardio, "Hmm"; Weber, "Campbell Is Bubbling, But for How Long"; Weber, "From Soup to Nuts and Back to Soup"; Freedman and Allen, "John Dorrance's Death Leaves Campbell Soup with Cloudy Future"; Deutsch, "Stirring Up Profits at Campbell"; Saporito, "The Fly in Campbell's Soup."
15. Adapted from "Entrepreneurs Across America," *Entrepreneur Magazine Online,* <http://www.entrepreneurmag.com/entmag/50states5.hts#top>, accessed 12 June 1997.
16. Adapted from Larry Reibstein (with Martha Brant and Nina Archer Biddle), "The Battle of the TV News Magazine Shows," *Newsweek,* 11 April 1994, 60–66.
17. Adapted from Rodale's home page at <http://www.rodalepress.com/mssn2.html>, accessed 17 July 1997; Kim Komando, "Computer Basics: The Perfect Garden Is a Mouse Click Away," *Los Angeles Times,* 31 March 1997, D5.
18. Adapted from "Group Accuses Nike of Vietnam Abuses," *Los Angeles Times,* 28 March 1997, D3; Greg Rushford, "Manager's Journal: Nike Lets Critics Kick It Around," *Wall Street Journal,* 12 May 1997; "Nike vs. Doonesbury," *People Online Daily,* <http://pathfinder.com/@SX8oXwUA238MYHni/people/daily/pages/peephole.html>, accessed 6 June 1997.
19. Adapted from "AT&T, 9 Others to Build Transpacific Cable," *Los Angeles Times,* 31 March 1997, D2.
20. Adapted from Karen Kaplan, "Heard on the Beat: M-I-C, K-E-Y—Why? Because It's Disney," *Los Angeles Times,* 31 March 1997, D1, D6; <http://www.disneyblast.com>, accessed 23 July 1997.
21. Adapted from Leon E. Wynter, "Group Finds Right Recipe for Milk Ads in Spanish," *Wall Street Journal,* 6 March 1996, B1.
22. Adapted from Denise Hamilton, "Speaking Volumes," *Los Angeles Times,* 5 February 1997, E1, E6.

Chapter 10
1. "Purchasing: Professional Profile, American Airlines," *Purchasing,* 17 October 1996, 32; "AMR Corporation," Hoover's Online, <http://www.hoovers.com>, accessed 22 January 1997; Carole A. Shifrin, "American Commits to All-Boeing Jet Fleet," *Aviation Week & Space Technology,* 25 November 1996, 34.
2. James Calvert Scott and Diana J. Green, "British Perspectives on Organizing Bad-News Letters: Organizational Patterns Used by Major U.K. Companies," *The Bulletin of the Association for Business Communication* 55, no. 1 (March 1992): 17–19.
3. Iris I. Varner, "Internationalizing Business Communication Courses," *The Bulletin of the Association for Business Communication* 50, no. 4 (December 1987): 7–11.
4. Ram Subramanian, Robert G. Insley, and Rodney D. Blackwell, "Performance and Readability: A Comparison of Annual Reports of Profitable and Unprofitable Corporations," *Journal of Business Communication* 30, no. 2 (1993): 49–61.
5. *Techniques for Communicators* (Chicago: Lawrence Ragan Communication, 1995), 18.
6. Maura Dolan and Stuart Silverstein, "Court Broadens Liability for Job References," *Los Angeles Times,* 28 January 1997, A1, A11; Frances A. McMorris, "Ex-Bosses Face Less Peril Giving Honest Job References," *Wall Street Journal,* 8 July 1996, B1, B8.
7. Thomas S. Brice and Marie Waung, "Applicant Rejection Letters: Are Businesses Sending the Wrong Message?" Business Horizons, March–April 1995, 59–62.
8. Gwendolyn N. Smith, Rebecca F. Nolan, and Yong Dai, "Job-Refusal Letters: Readers' Affective Responses to Direct and Indirect Organizational Plans," Business Communication Quarterly 59, no. 1 (1996): 67–73; Brice and Waung, "Applicant Rejection Letters."
9. Judi Brownell, "The Performance Appraisal Interviews: A Multipurpose Communication Assignment," The Bulletin of the Association for Business Communication 57, no. 2 (May 1994): 11–21.
10. Brownell, "The Performance Appraisal Interviews."
11. Judith A. Kolb, "Leader Behaviors Affecting Team Performance: Similarities and Differences Between Leader/Member Assessments," Journal of Business Communication 32, no. 3 (1995): 233–48.
12. Howard M. Bloom, "Performance Evaluations," New England Business, December 1991, 14.
13. David I. Rosen, "Appraisals Can Make—or Break—Your Court Case," Personnel Journal, November 1992, 113.
14. Patricia A. McLagan, "Advice for Bad-News Bearers: How to Tell Employees They're Not Hacking It and Get Results," Industry Week, 15 February 1993, 42; Michael Lee Smith, "Give Feedback, Not Criticism," Supervisory Management, March 1993, 4; "A Checklist for Conducting Problem Performer Appraisals," Supervisory Management, December 1993, 7–9.
15. Jane R. Goodson, Gail W. McGee, and Anson Seers, "Giving Appropriate Performance Feedback to Managers: An Empirical Test of Content and Outcomes," Journal of Business Communication 29, no. 4 (1992): 329–42.
16. Craig Cox, "On the Firing Line," Business Ethics, May–June 1992, 33–34.
17. Cox, "On the Firing Line."
18. Based on "Purchasing," *Purchasing;* "AMR Corporation," Hoover's Online; Shifrin, "American Commits to All-Boeing Jet Fleet," 1998.
19. Adapted from International Tesla Society Museum Bookstore Catalog, Fall 1993.
20. Adapted from Sewell Chan, "A Seattle Blend Is Praised as Rich, Smooth, and Better Than Worms," *Wall Street Journal,* 16 July 1996, B1.
21. Adapted from Michael A. Champ and Michael W. Willinsky, "Farming the Oceans," The World and I, April 1994, 200–207.
22. Adapted from Leo W. Banks, "Not Your Average Joe," Los Angeles Times, 7 January 1997, E1, E6.
23. Adapted from Robert Johnson, "Your Little Monkey Is So Cuddly. Here, Let Me—OUCH!" Wall Street Journal, 2 December 1991, A1, A14.
24. Adapted from Matt Murray, "Hey Kids! Marketers Want Your Help!" Wall Street Journal, 6 May 1997, B1, B8.
25. Adapted from Associated Press, "Is the Boss Watching? Surveillance Common at Work," *CNN Interactive,* <http://cnn.com/US/9705/23/watching.workers.ap/index/html>, accessed 30 May 1997.
26. Adapted from David Colker, "Rest in Space," *Los Angeles Times,* 25 July 1996, B2.
27. Adapted from Wendy Bounds, "Here, Haute Couture Takes a Back Seat to the Front Row," *Wall Street Journal,* 9 May 1997, A1, A6.
28. Adapted from Carla Koehl and Sarah Van Boven, "The Geek Squad Gets a Taste of Hollywood," Newsweek, 23 December 1996; Geek Squad Web site <http://www.geeksquad.com>, accessed 30 May 1997.
29. Adapted from "Entrepreneurs Across America," *Entrepreneur Magazine Online,* <http://www.entrepreneurmag.com/entmag/50states2.hts>, accessed on 25 June 1997.

Chapter 11
1. Adapted from UNCF Web site, <http://www.uncf.org>, accessed 21 October 1997; "BDM Makes $50,000 Grant to United Negro College Fund's Campaign 2000; Establishes Scholarship and Internship Program with Four Schools," press release issued by BDM International, 11 January 1996; United Negro College Fund 1994 Annual Report; Margie Markarian, "Fundraising in Tough Times," *Black Enterprise,* December 1993, 77–78, 81–82; "Fundraising: The Bottom Line," *Black Enterprise,* December 1993, 82; Caroline V. Clarke, "Redefining Beautiful," *Black Enterprise,* June 1993, 243–44, 246, 248; Matthew S. Scott, "A Higher Calling," *Black Enterprise,* February 1992, 227–28, 230.

2. Jeanette W. Gilsdorf, "Write Me Your Best Case for . . . ," *The Bulletin of the Association for Business Communication* 54, no. 1 (March 1991): 7–12.

3. Gilsdorf, "Write Me Your Best Case for . . ."

4. Mary Cross, "Aristotle and Business Writing: Why We Need to Teach Persuasion," *The Bulletin of the Association for Business Communication* 54, no. 1 (March 1991): 3–6.

5. Abraham H. Maslow, *Motivation and Personality* (New York: Harper & Row, 1954), 12, 19.

6. Robert T. Moran, "Tips on Making Speeches to International Audiences," *International Management*, April 1980, 58–59.

7. Tamra B. Orr, "Persuasion Without Pressure," The Toastmaster, January 1994, 19–22; William Friend, "Winning Techniques of Great Persuaders," *Association Management*, February 1985, 82–86; Patricia Buhler, "How to Ask For—and Get—What You Want!" Supervision, February 1990, 11–13.

8. Gilsdorf, "Write Me Your Best Case for . . ."

9. John D. Ramage and John C. Bean, *Writing Arguments: A Rhetoric with Readings*, 3d ed. (Boston: Allyn and Bacon, 1995), 430–42.

10. Ramage and Bean, *Writing Arguments*, 102–17.

11. James Suchan and Ron Dulek, "Toward a Better Understanding of Reader Analysis," *Journal of Business Communication* 25, no. 2 (1988): 29–45.

12. Jeanette W. Gilsdorf, "Executives' and Academics' Perceptions on the Need for Instruction in Written Persuasion," *Journal of Business Communication* 23 (Fall 1986): 67.

13. Robert L. Hemmings, "Think Before You Write," *Fund Raising Management*, February 1990, 23–24.

14. Teri Lammers, "The Elements of Perfect Pitch," *Inc.*, March 1992, 53–55.

15. William North Jayme, quoted in Albert Haas Jr., "How to Sell Almost Anything by Direct Mail," *Across the Board*, November 1986, 50.

16. Hemmings, "Think Before You Write."

17. Hemmings, "Think Before You Write."

18. Conrad Squires, "How to Write a Strong Letter, Part Two: Choosing a Theme," *Fund Raising Management*, November 1991, 65–66.

19. Conrad Squires, "Getting the Compassion Out of the Box," *Fund Raising Management*, September 1992, 55, 60.

20. Squires, "How to Write a Strong Letter, Part Two."

21. Constance L. Clark, "25 Steps to Better Direct Mail Fundraising," *Nonprofit World*, July–August 1989, 11–13; Squires, "How to Write a Strong Letter, Part Two."

22. Squires, "How to Write a Strong Letter, Part Two."

23. Clark, "25 Steps to Better Direct Mail Fundraising."

24. Conrad Squires, "Why Some Letters Outpull Others," *Fund Raising Management*, January 1991, 67, 72.

25. Squires, "Why Some Letters Outpull Others"; Clark, "25 Steps to Better Direct Mail Fundraising"; Jerry Huntsinger, "My First 29½ Years in Direct-Mail Fund Raising: What I've Learned," *Fund Raising Management*, January 1992, 40–43.

26. "The Ideal Collection Letter," *Inc.*, February 1991, 59–61.

27. Based on UNCF Web site; "BDM Makes $50,000 Grant to United Negro College Fund's Campaign 2000," BDM International; United Negro College Fund 1994 Annual Report; Markarian, "Fundraising in Tough Times"; "Fundraising," *Black Enterprise*; Clarke, "Redefining Beautiful"; Scott, "A Higher Calling."

28. Adapted from Jane Bryant Quinn, "A Primer on Downsizing," *Newsweek*, 13 May 1996, 50; Marshall Loeb, "What to Do If You Get Fired," *Fortune*, 15 January 1996, p. 43; and "Urohealth Sets Sights on Eighth Acquisition," Los Angeles Times, 5 May 1996, p. B1.

29. Adapted from Andrew Ferguson, "Supermarket of the Vanities," *Fortune*, 10 June 1996, 30, 32.

30. Adapted from Peter Coy, "Peddling Better Bike Designs," *Business Week*, 1 July 1996, 103.

31. Albert R. Karr, "Work Week: Wake Up and Read This," *Wall Street Journal*, 6 May 1997, A1.

32. Adapted from Cathy Werblin, "Korean Business Owners Want Signs to Mark Area," *Los Angeles Times*, 29 March 1997, B3.

33. Adapted from Steve Bass, "ISDN Not; The Agony, the Ecstasy, the Migraines," *Computer Currents*, 7 May 1996, p. 9.

34. Adapted from Marcia Joseph, Deodorant Stones of America (DSA), personal communication, 14 July 1994; DSA product literature.

35. Adapted from Karen E. Klein and Steve Scauzillo, "The Fuel Cell Future," *The World & I*, April 1994, 192–99.

36. Adapted from "Down These Aisles Is Matrimonial Bliss," *Los Angeles Times*, 22 March 1996, D3.

37. Adapted from Chris Pasles, "Long Beach Opera Cancels Rest of Season as Deal Nears," *Los Angeles Times*, 16 May 1996, F4, F9.

38. Adapted from Tom Morganthau and Seema Nayyar, "Those Scary College Costs," *Newsweek*, 29 April 1996, 52–56; Jane Bryant Quinn, "Save First, Then Borrow," Newsweek, 29 April 1996, 67–68.

39. Adapted from Edmund Sanders, "Subcontractors Still Waiting for Payoff from Giant Irvine Theater," *The Orange County Register*, 9 May 1996, 2.

Chapter 12

1. Adapted from Federal Express Web site, <http://www.fedex.com>, accessed 27 October 1997; UPS Web site, <http://www.ups.com>, accessed 27 October 1997; DHL Web site, <http://www.dhl.com>, accessed 27 October 1997; Airborne Express Web site, <http://www.airborne.com>, accessed 27 October 1997; Hoover's Online, <http://www.hoovers.com>, accessed 27 October 1997; "All Strung Up," *The Economist*, 17 April 1993, 70; Gary M. Stern, "Improving Verbal Communications," *Internal Auditor*, August 1993, 49–54; Gary Hoover, Alta Campbell, and Patrick J. Spain, *Hoover's Handbook of American Business 1994* (Austin, Tex.: Reference Press, 1993), 488–89; "Pass the Parcel," The Economist, 21 March 1992, 73–74; "Federal Express," *Personnel Journal*, January 1992, 52.

2. Susan L. Leach, "SEC Takes Next Leap into Computer Age," *Christian Science Monitor*, 7 June 1994, 8.

3. John Taschek, "New Report Writers Provide Improved Access to Data," *PC Week*, 6 February 1995, 81–85.

4. Stephan Manes, "E-Mail Troubles? You Have No Idea!" *PC World*, July 1996, 39.

5. Dan Steinhoff and John F. Burgess, *Small Business Management Fundamentals*, 5th ed. (New York: McGraw-Hill, 1989), 37.

6. Joan F. Vesper and Karl H. Vesper, "Writing a Business Plan: The Total Term Assignment," *The Bulletin of the Association for Business Communication* 56, no. 2 (June 1993): 29–32.

7. Eleanor Rizzo, "Document Design Basics," *Technical Communication*, Fourth Quarter 1992, 645.

8. A. S. C. Ehrenberg, "Report Writing—Six Simple Rules for Better Business Documents," *Admap*, June 1992, 39–42.

9. Based on Federal Express Web site; UPS Web site; DHL Web site; Airborne Express Web site; Hoover's Online; "All Strung Up," *The Economist*; Stern, "Improving Verbal Communications"; Hoover, Campbell, and Spain, *Hoover's Handbook of American Business*; "Pass the Parcel," The Economist; "Federal Express," Personnel Journal.

10. Adapted from J. Roberto Whitaker-Penteado, "Oil Cos. Pump Up Advertising in Brazil," *Adweek*, 6 September 1993, 14.

11. Adapted from Nancy Jeffrey, "Preparing for the Worst: Firms Set Up Plans to Help Deal with Corporate Crises," *Wall Street Journal*, 7 December 1987, 23.

Chapter 13

1. Adapted from On Call Plus, Company News, PRNewswire, <http://www.prnewswire.com/gh/cnoc/comp/106632.html>, accessed 7 November 1997; Harley-Davidson 1993 Annual Report; Brian S. Moskal, "Born to Be Real," *Industry Week*, 2 August 1993, 14–18; Martha H. Peak, "Harley-Davidson: Going Whole Hog to Provide Stakeholder Satisfaction," *Management Review*, June 1993, 53–55; Gary Slutsker, "Hog Wild," *Forbes*, 24 May 1993, 45–46; Kevin Kelly and Karen Lowry Miller, "The Rumble Heard Round the World: Harleys," *Business Week*, 24 May 1993, 58, 60; James B. Shuman, "Easy

Rider Rides Again," *Business Tokyo*, July 1991, 26–30; Holt Hackney, "Easy Rider," *Financial World*, 4 September 1990, 48–49; Roy L. Harmon and Leroy D. Peterson, "Reinventing the Factory," *Across the Board*, March 1990, 30–38; John Holusha," How Harley Outfoxed Japan with Exports," *New York Times*, 12 August 1990, F5; Peter C. Reid, "How Harley Beat Back the Japanese," *Fortune*, 25 September 1989, 155–64.

2. Bruce McComiskey, "Defining Institutional Problems: A Heuristic Procedure," *Business Communication Quarterly* 58, no. 4 (1995): 21–24.

3. Iris I. Varner, *Contemporary Business Report Writing*, 2d ed. (Chicago: Dryden Press, 1991), 135.

4. F. Stanford Wayne and Jolene D. Scriven, "Problem and Purpose Statements: Are They Synonymous Terms in Writing Reports for Business?" *The Bulletin of the Association for Business Communication* 54, no. 1 (1991): 30–37.

5. Maridell Fryar and David A. Thomas, *Successful Problem Solving* (Lincolnwood, Ill.: NTC, 1989), 20.

6. David A. Aaker and George S. Day, *Marketing Research*, 2d ed. (New York: Wiley, 1983), 79, 111.

7. Aaker and Day, *Marketing Research*, 88–89.

8. Lisa Gubernick, "Making History Pay," *Forbes*, 13 May 1991, 132.

9. Aaker and Day, *Marketing Research*, 124.

10. Paul L. Riedesel, "Understanding Validity Is Easy; Doing Right Research Is Hard," *Marketing News*, 12 September 1986, 24.

11. "How to Design and Conduct a Study," *Credit Union Magazine*, October 1983, 36–46.

12. TK Associates International, Internet Web site, <http://www.diyer.com>, accessed 29 July 1996.

13. Charles L. Olson and Mario J. Picconi, *Statistics for Business Decision Making* (Glenview, Ill.: Scott, Foresman, 1983), 105.

14. Olson and Picconi, *Statistics for Business Decision Making*, 105.

15. Based on On Call Plus, Company News, PRNewswire; Harley-Davidson 1993 Annual Report; Moskal, "Born to Be Real"; Peak, "Harley-Davidson"; Slutsker, "Hog Wild"; Kelly and Miller, "The Rumble Heard Round the World"; Shuman, "Easy Rider Rides Again"; Hackney, "Easy Rider"; Harmon and Peterson, "Reinventing the Factory"; Holusha,"How Harley Outfoxed Japan with Exports"; Reid, "How Harley Beat Back the Japanese."

Chapter 14

1. "Responsible Commercial Success," "A Unique Company Culture at Levi Strauss & Co.," "Levi Strauss & Co. Global Sourcing & Operating Guidelines," "Levi Strauss & Co. General Information," Levi Strauss & Co. Web site, <http://www.levistrauss.com>, accessed 29 September 1997; Charlene Marmer Solomon, "Put Your Ethics to the Test," *Personnel Journal* 75, no. 1 (January 1996): 66–74; Russell Mitchell and Michael Oneal, "Managing by Values," *Business Week*, 1 August 1994, 46–52.

2. Oswald M. T. Ratteray, "Hit the Mark with Better Summaries," *Supervisory Management*, September 1989, 43–45.

3. Sheri Rosen, "What Is Truth?" *IABC Communication World*, March 1995, 40.

4. Based on "Responsible Commercial Success," "A Unique Company Culture at Levi Strauss & Company," "Levi Strauss & Co. Global Sourcing & Operating Guidelines," "Levi Strauss & Co. General Information," Levi Strauss & Co. Web site; Solomon, "Put Your Ethics to the Test"; Mitchell and Oneal, "Managing by Values."

5. Adapted from Nicholas E. Lefferts, "What's New in the Pet Business," *New York Times*, 3 August 1985, sec. 3, 15.

6. Adapted from David J. Jefferson and Thomas R. King, "'Infomercials' Fill Up Prime Time on Cable, Aim for Prime Time," *Wall Street Journal*, 22 October 1992, A1.

Chapter 15

1. Adapted from U.S. Securities and Exchange Commission EDGAR database, <http://www.sec.gov/Archives/edgar/data/78666/0000898430-

97-001002.txt>, accessed 7 November 1997; Pinkerton Web site, <http://www.pinkertons.com>, accessed 7 November 1997; Seth Lubove, "High-Tech Cops," *Forbes*, 25 September 1995, 44–45; Hoover's Online, <http://www.hoovers.com>, accessed 23 January 1997; Bob Smith, "The Evolution of Pinkerton," *Management Review*, September 1993, 54–58; Smith, "Pinkerton Keeps Its Eye on Recruitment," *HR Focus*, 6 September 1993, 1, 6; "Oscar's News," *Security Management*, 14 June 1993, 14; Pinkerton 1993 Annual Report.

2. Adapted from Richard Nelson Bolles, *The 1997 What Color Is Your Parachute?* (Berkeley, Calif.: Ten Speed Press, 1996), 129–66; Karen W. Arenson, "Placement Offices Leave Old Niches to Become Computerized Job Bazaars,"*New York Times*, 17 July 1996, B12; Lawrence J. Magid, "Job Hunters Cast Wide Net Online," *Los Angeles Times*, 26 February 1996, 20; Richard Van Doren, "On-Line Career Advice Speeds Search for Jobs," *Network World*, 4 March 1996, 54; Alex Markels, "Job Hunting Takes Off in Cyberspace," *Wall Street Journal*, 20 September 1996, B1, B2; Michael Chorost, "Jobs on the Web," *Hispanic*, October 1995, 50–53; Zane K. Quible, "Electronic Résumés: Their Time Is Coming," *Business Communication Quarterly* 58, no. 3 (1995): 5–9; Margaret Mannix, "The Home-Page Help Wanteds," *U.S. News & World Report*, 30 October 1995, 88, 90; Pam Dixon and Silvia Tiersten, *Be Your Own Headhunter Online* (New York: Random House, 1995), 53–69.

3. Amanda Bennett, "GE Redesigns Rungs of Career Ladder," *Wall Street Journal*, 15 March 1993, B1, B3.

4. Robin White Goode, "International and Foreign Language Skills Have an Edge," *Black Enterprise*, May 1995, 53.

5. Nancy M. Somerick, "Managing a Communication Internship Program," *The Bulletin of the Association for Business Communication* 56, no. 3 (1993): 10–20.

6. Cheryl L. Noll, "Collaborating with the Career Planning and Placement Center in the Job-Search Project," *Business Communication Quarterly* 58, no. 3 (1995): 53–55.

7. Pam Stanley-Weigand, "Organizing the Writing of Your Resume," *The Bulletin of the Association for Business Communication* 54, no. 3 (1991): 11–12.

8. Beverly Culwell-Block and Jean Anna Sellers, "Résumé Content and Format—Do the Authorities Agree?" *The Bulletin of the Association for Business Communication* 57, no. 4 (1994): 27–30.

9. Janice Tovey, "Using Visual Theory in the Creation of Resumes: A Bibliography," *The Bulletin of the Association for Business Communication* 54, no. 3 (1991): 97–99.

10. Myra Fournier, "Looking Good on Paper," *Managing Your Career*, Spring 1990, 34–35.

11. Adapted from Burdette E. Bostwick, *How to Find the Job You've Always Wanted* (New York: Wiley, 1982), 69–70.

12. Jennifer J. Laabs, "For Your Information," *Personnel Journal*, August 1993, 16.

13. Dixon and Tiersten, *Be Your Own Headhunter Online*, 75.

14. Bronwyn Fryer, "Job Hunting the Electronic Way," *Working Woman*, March 1995, 59–60, 78; Joyce Lane Kennedy and Thomas J. Morrow, *Electronic Resume Revolution*, 2d ed. (New York: Wiley, 1995), 30–33; Mary Goodwin, Deborah Cohn, and Donna Spivey, *Netjobs: Use the Internet to Land Your Dream Job* (New York: Michael Wolff, 1996), 149–50; Zane K. Quible, "Electronic Résumés: Their Time Is Coming," *Business Communication Quarterly* 58, no. 3 (1995): 5–9; Alfred Glossbrenner and Emily Glossbrenner, *Finding a Job on the Internet* (New York: McGraw-Hill, 1995), 194–97; Dixon and Tiersten, *Be Your Own Headhunter Online*, 80–83.

15. Quible, "Electronic Résumés"; Goodwin, Cohn, and Spivey, *Netjobs*.

16. Louis S. Richman, "How to Get Ahead," *Fortune*, 16 May 1994, 46–51; Bruce Nussbaum, "I'm Worried About My Job," *Business Week*, 7 October 1991, 94–97.

17. William J. Banis, "The Art of Writing Job-Search Letters," *CPC Annual*, 36th Edition 2 (1992): 42–50.

18. Based on U.S. Securities and Exchange Commission EDGAR database; Pinkerton Web site; Lubove, "High-Tech Cops"; Hoover's Online;

Smith, "The Evolution of Pinkerton"; Smith, "Pinkerton Keeps Its Eye on Recruitment"; "Oscar's News"; Pinkerton 1993 Annual Report.

Chapter 16

1. Adapted from On Call Plus Company News, PRNewswire, <http://www.prnewswire.com/cgibin/liststory?406325^1>, accessed 9 November 1997; Herman Miller Web site, <http://www.hermanmiller.com>, accessed 9 November 1997; Hoover's Online, <http://www.hoovers.com>, accessed 23 January 1997; A. J. Vogl, "Risky Work," *Across the Board*, July–August 1993, 27–31; Kenneth Labich, "Hot Company, Warm Culture," *Fortune*, 27 February 1989, 74–78; George Melloan, "Herman Miller's Secrets of Corporate Creativity," *Wall Street Journal*, 3 May 1988, A31; Beverly Geber, "Herman Miller: Where Profits and Participation Meet," *Training*, November 1987, 62–66; Robert J. McClory, "The Creative Process at Herman Miller," Across the Board, May 1985, 8–22; Tom Peters and Nancy Austin, *A Passion for Excellence* (New York: Random House, 1985), 204–05.

2. Charlene Marmer Solomon, "How Does Disney Do It?" *Personnel Journal*, December 1989, 53.

3. Peter Rea, Julie Rea, and Charles Moonmaw, "Training: Use Assessment Centers in Skill Development," *Personnel Journal*, April 1990, 126–31.

4. Barron Wells and Nelda Spinks, "Interviewing: What Small Companies Say," *The Bulletin of the Association for Business Communication* 55, no. 2 (1992): 18–22; Clive Fletcher, "Ethics and the Job Interview," *Personnel Management*, March 1992, 36–39.

5. Eric R. Chabrow, "High-Tech Hiring: CD-ROM and Video Aid Recruiters' Efforts," *Informationweek*, 23 January 1995, 44.

6. Joyce Lain Kennedy and Thomas J. Morrow, *Electronic Resume Revolution* (New York: Wiley, 1995), 208–10.

7. "Read Between the Lines," *Inc.*, June 1995, 90.

8. Joel Russell, "Finding Solid Ground," *Hispanic Business*, February 1922, 42–44, 46.

9. Microsoft 1996 Annual Report, accessed online 1 July 1997.

10. Robert Gifford, Cheuk Fan Ng, and Margaret Wilkinson, "Nonverbal Cues in the Employment Interview: Links Between Applicant Qualities and Interviewer Judgments," *Journal of Applied Psychology* 70, no. 4 (1985): 729.

11. Dale G. Leathers, *Successful Nonverbal Communication* (New York: Macmillan, 1986), 225.

12. Mary Goodwin, Deborah Cohn, and Donna Spivey, *Netjobs: Use the Internet to Land Your Dream Job* (New York: Michael Wolff, 1996), 170.

13. Shirley J. Shepherd, "How to Get That Job in 60 Minutes or Less," *Working Woman*, March 1986, 119.

14. Shepherd, "How to Get That Job in 60 Minutes or Less," 118.

15. H. Anthony Medley, *Sweaty Palms: The Neglected Art of Being Interviewed* (Berkeley, Calif.: Ten Speed Press, 1993), 179.

16. Gerald L. Wilson, "Preparing Students for Responding to Illegal Selection Interview Questions," *The Bulletin of the Association for Business Communication* 54, no. 2 (1991): 44–49.

17. Jeff Springston and Joann Keyton, "Interview Response Training," *The Bulletin of the Association for Business Communication* 54, no. 3 (1991): 28–30; Gerald L. Wilson, "An Analysis of Instructional Strategies for Responding to Illegal Selection Interview Questions," *The Bulletin of the Association for Business Communication* 54, no. 3 (1991): 31–35.

18. Stephen J. Pullum, "Illegal Questions in the Selection Process: Going Beyond Contemporary Business and Professional Communication Textbooks," *The Bulletin of the Association for Business Communication* 54, no. 3 (1991): 36–43; Alicia Kitsuse, "'Have You Ever Been Arrested?'" *Across the Board*, November 1992, 46–49; Christina L. Greathouse, "10 Common Hiring Mistakes," *Industry Week*, 20 January 1992, 22–23, 26.

19. Marilyn Moats Kennedy, "Are You Getting Paid What You're Worth?" *New Woman*, November 1984, 110.

20. Harold H. Hellwig, "Job Interviewing: Process and Practice," *The Bulletin of the Association for Business Communication* 55, no. 2 (1992): 8–14.

21. Based on On Call Plus Company News, PRNewswire; Herman Miller Web site; Hoover's Online; Vogl, "Risky Work"; Labich, "Hot Company, Warm Culture"; Melloan, "Herman Miller's Secrets of Corporate Creativity"; Geber, "Herman Miller"; McClory, "The Creative Process at Herman Miller"; Peters and Austin, *A Passion for Excellence*.

Chapter 17

1. Adapted from Srikumar S. Rao, "Welcome to Open Space," Training, April 1994, 52–56; Claudia H. Deutsch, "Round-Table Meetings with No Agendas, No Tables," *New York Times*, 5 June 1994, sec. 3, 5; Charles D. Bader, "These Shoes Are Made for Walkin'," *Bobbin*, November 1991, 118–21.

2. Edward F. Walsh, "Telephone Tyranny," *Industry Week*, 1 April 1991, 24–26.

3. Madeline Bodin, "Making the Most of Your Telephone," *Nation's Business*, April 1992, 62.

4. Beverly Davenport Sypher, Robert N. Bastrom, and Joy Hart Seibert, "Listening, Communication Abilities, and Success at Work," *Journal of Business Communication* 26, no. 4 (Fall 1989): 293–301.

5. Augusta M. Simon, "Effective Listening: Barriers to Listening in a Diverse Business Environment," *The Bulletin of the Association for Business Communication* 54, no. 3 (September 1991): 73–74.

6. Sypher, Bastrom, and Seibert, "Listening, Communication Abilities, and Success at Work."

7. Thomas L. Means, "A Unit to Develop Listening Skill," *The Bulletin of the Association for Business Communication* 54, no. 3 (September 1991): 70–72.

8. Phillip Morgan and H. Kent Baker, "Building a Professional Image: Improving Listening Behavior," *Supervisory Management*, November 1985, 35–36.

9. Lyman K. Steil, Larry L. Barker, and Kittie W. Watson, *Effective Listening: Key to Your Success* (Reading, Mass.: Addison-Wesley, 1983), 21–22.

10. J. Michael Sproule, *Communication Today* (Glenview, Ill.: Scott, Foresman, 1981), 69.

11. Sproule, *Communication Today*, 69.

12. Sproule, *Communication Today*, 69.

13. Thomas L. Brown, "The Art of the Interview," *Industry Week*, 1 March 1993, 19.

14. Claudia H. Deutsch, "Teamwork or Tug of War?" *New York Times*, 26 August 1990, sec. 3, 27.

15. B. Aubrey Fisher, *Small Group Decision Making: Communication and the Group Process*, 2d ed. (New York: McGraw-Hill, 1980), 145–49.

16. Ken Blanchard, "Meetings Can Be Effective," *Supervisory Management*, October 1992, 5.

17. William C. Waddell and Thomas A. Rosko, "Conducting an Effective Off-Site Meeting," *Management Review*, February 1993, 40–44.

18. Kathy E. Gill, "Board Primer: Parliamentary Procedure," *Association Management*, 1993, L-39.

19. Based on Rao, "Welcome to Open Space"; Deutsch, "Round-Table Meetings with No Agendas, No Table"; Bader, "These Shoes Are Made for Walkin.'"

Chapter 18

1. Adapted from Trudy Gallant-Stokes, "Brady Keys Does Franchising Right," *Black Enterprise*, September 1988, 56–62; Cynthia Legette, "The New Entrepreneur: Nobody Does It Better," *Black Enterprise*, December 1988, 56–60; Bill Carlino, "Keys Opens Doors for Minorities," *Nation's Restaurant News*, 10 October 1988, 1; Marsha Westbrook, "Burger King Honors a Pioneering Food Franchisee," *Black Enterprise*, February 1988, 40.

2. Sherron B. Kenton, "Speaker Credibility in Persuasive Business Communication: A Model Which Explains Gender Differences," *Journal of Business Communication* 26, no. 2 (Spring 1989): 143–57.

3. Walter Kiechel III, "How to Give a Speech," *Fortune*, 8 June 1987, 180.

4. *Communication and Leadership Program* (Santa Ana, Calif.: Toastmasters International, 1980), 44, 45.

5. *How to Prepare and Use Effective Visual Aids,* Info-Line series, Elizabeth Lean, managing ed. (Washington, D.C.: American Society for Training and Development, October 1984), 2.

6. Kathleen K. Weigner, "Visual Persuasion," *Forbes,* 16 September 1991, 176; Kathleen K. Weigner, " Showtime!" *Forbes,* 13 May 1991, 118.

7. Eric Arndt, "Nobody Does It Better," *IABC Communication World,* May 1988, 28.

8. Daniel Goleman, "For Victims of Stage Fright, Rehearsal Is the Therapy," *New York Times,* 12 June 1991, sec. B1.

9. Judy Linscott, "Getting On and Off the Podium," *Savvy,* October 1985, 44.

10. Iris R. Johnson, "Before You Approach the Podium," *MW,* January–February 1989, 7.

11. Sandra Moyer, "Braving No Woman's Land," *The Toastmaster,* August 1986, 13.

12. Teresa Brady, "Fielding Abrasive Questions During Presentations," *Supervisory Management,* February 1993, 6.

13. Based on Gallant-Stokes, "Brady Keys Does Franchising Right"; Legette, "The New Entrepreneur"; Carlino, "Keys Opens Doors for Minorities"; Westbrook, "Burger King Honors a Pioneering Food Franchisee."

Appendix A

1. Mary A. DeVries, Internationally Yours (Boston: Houghton Mifflin, 1994), 9.

2. Patricia A. Dreyfus, "Paper That's Letter Perfect," Money, May 1985, 184.

3. "When Image Counts, Letterhead Says It All," The Advocate and Greenwich Time, 10 January 1993, F4.

4. Mel Mandell, "Electronic Forms Are Cheap and Speedy," D&B Reports, July–August 1993, 44–45.

5. Linda Driskill, Business & Managerial Communication: New Perspectives (Orlando, Fla.: Harcourt Brace Jovanovich, 1992), 470.

6. Driskill, Business & Managerial Communication, 470.

7. Lennie Copeland and Lewis Griggs, Going International: How to Make Friends and Deal Effectively in the Global Marketplace, 2d ed. (New York: Random House, 1985), 24–27.

8. DeVries, Internationally Yours, 8.

9. Copeland and Griggs, Going International, 24–27.

10. U.S. Postal Service, Postal Addressing Standards (Washington, D.C.: GPO, 1992).

11. Copeland and Griggs, Going International, 24–27.

12. Renee B. Horowitz and Marian G. Barchilon, "Stylistic Guidelines for E-Mail," IEEE Transactions on Professional Communications 37, no. 4 (1994): 207–12.

13. Jill H. Ellsworth and Matthew V. Ellsworth, The Internet Business Book(New York: Wiley, 1994), 93.

14. Bill Eager, Using the Internet(Indianapolis, Ind.: Que, 1994), 11.

15. Eager, Using the Internet, 10.

16. William Eager, Larry Donahue, David Forsyth, Kenneth Mitton, and Martin Waterhouse, net.Search(Indianapolis, Ind.: Que, 1995), 221.

17. Rosalind Resnick and Dave Taylor, Internet Business Guide (Indianapolis, Ind.: Sams.net Publishing, 1995), 117.

18. James L. Clark and Lyn R. Clark, How 7: A Handbook for Office Workers, 7th ed. (Cincinnati: South-Western, 1995), 431–32.

Appendix B

1. Sherwyn Morreale and Courtland Bovée, *Excellence in Public Speaking* (Fort Worth, Tx.: Harcourt Brace, 1997), 173.

2. Morreale and Bovée, *Excellence in Public Speaking,* 174.

3. Morreale and Bovée, *Excellence in Public Speaking,* 174–175.

4. Dorothy Geisler, "How to Avoid Copyright Lawsuits, *"IABC Communication World,* June 1984, 34–37.

5. Robert W. Goddard, "The Crime of Copying," *Management World,* July–August 1986, 20–22.

ACKNOWLEDGMENTS

Text, Figures, and Tables

5 (Figure 1.2): From David J. Rachman and Michael Mescon, *Business Today*, 5th edition, p. 27, 1987. McGraw Hill.   7 (Figure 1.4): From David J. Rachman and Michael Mescon, *Business Today*, 5th edition, p. 127, 1987. McGraw Hill.   14–15 (Behind the Scenes at Molex): Louis Hecht, personal interview, May 1997; Matt Krantz, "Molex Inc.'s Fred Krehbiel," *Investor's Business Daily*, 7 January 1997, 1; Paul Conley, "Molex Sets Record-Breaking Global Pace," *Chicago Tribune*, 2 August 1996, 12; Dave Savona, "The Billion-Dollar Globetrotter," *International Business*, November 1995, 52–56; Robert Knight, "How Molex Inc. Connected in World Markets," *Chicago Enterprise*, July–August 1994, 24–27; Ronald Yates, "Firm's Growth Tied to Global Connections," *Chicago Tribune*, 6 February 1994, 8.   23 (Figure 2.1): Reprinted by permission of publisher, from *Supervisory Management*, November 1985 © 1985. American Management Association, New York. http:wwww.amanet.org. All rights reserved.   30 (Behind the Scenes at J·A·M·S/Endispute): Jack Unroe, president and CEO of J·A·M·S/Endispute, personal interview, May 1997; Dwight Golann, senior mediator, personal interview, May 1997.   44–45 (Behind the Scenes at Parker Pens): Roger Axtel, personal communication, June 1989. Used with permission.   77–73 (Behind the Scenes at Best Domestic Service Agency): Maurice Wingate, personal interview, May 1997.   68 (Figure 4.3): Copyright © Hewlett-Packard Company. Reproduced with permission.   90 (Figure 5.2): General Mills Consumer Services.   108–109 (Behind the Scenes at Ran Decisions): Adapted from Randy Petersen, "AirMail," *InsideFlyer*, April 1997, 4; Randy Petersen, editor/publisher, *InsideFlyer*, personal interview, April 1997.   125 (Figure 7.3): Adapted from Robert Gunning, *The Technique of Clear Writing* (New York: McGraw-Hill, rev. ed., 1973). Used with permission of copyright owners, Gunning-Mueller Clear Writing Institute, Inc.   142–143 (Behind the Scenes at the La Jolla Playhouse): Constance Harvey, publicist, La Jolla Playhouse, personal communication, May 1992.   160–161 (Behind the Scenes at Numa Financial Systems): Stephen Eckett, managing director of Numa Financial Systems, personal communication, July 1997.   176–177 (Behind the Scenes at Citibank): Jane Wolchonok, personal interview, June 1989. Used with permission.   179 (Figure 9.1): Letterhead courtesy of Woolworth.   189–190 (Figure 9.3): Letterhead courtesy of Blockbuster.   192 (Figure 9.4): Letterhead courtesy of Office Depot.   208–209 (Behind the Scenes at Adlai Stevenson High School): Richard DuFour, superintendent of Adlai Stevensen High School, personal interview, May 1997.   212 (Figure 10.1): Letterhead courtesy of La-Z-Boy.   234–235 (Behind the Scenes at Norton's Florist and Gifts): Dennis Norton, personal interview, April 1997.   238 (Figure 11.1): Letterhead courtesy of Host Marriot.   268–269 (Behind the Scenes at the San Diego Zoo): Rick Barongi, San Diego Zoo, personal interview, June 1989.   278–279 (Figure 12.5): Letterhead courtesy of Business Plan Excerpt.   304–305 (Figure 13.4): Yahoo Website Home Page (www.yahoo.com). Yahoo, Inc. Infoseek Website Home Page (www.infoseek.com). Infoseek Corporation. Reprinted by permission. Infoseek, Infoseek Ultra, Ultrasmart, Ultraseek, Ultraseek Server, Infoseek Desktop, iSeek, Quickseek, Imageseek, Ultrashop, the Infoseek logos, and the tagline "Once you know, you know" are trademarks of Infoseek Corporation which may be registered in certain jurisdictions. Other trademarks shown are trademarks of their respective owners. Copyright © 1994–1998 Infoseek Corporation. All rights reserved. AltaVista Website Home Page (www.altavista.digital.com). Digital Equipment Corporation. Digital, AltaVista, and the Alta Vista logo are trademarks or service marks of Digital Equipment Corporation. Used with permission. Excite Website Home Page. Excite, Excite Search, and the Excite Logo are trademarks of Excite, Inc., and may be registered in various jurisdictions. Excite screen display copyright 1995–1998 Excite, Inc. Hotbot Website Home Page. Copyright © 1994–97 Wired Digital, Inc. All rights reserved. Cyber 411 Website Home Page (http://cyber411.com/index.html). © 1998 Cyber 411 & C4 are registered trademarks of Cyber Network, Inc.   329 (Table 14.1): Adapted from Robert Lefferts, *Elements of Graphics*, pp. 18–35. Copyright 1981 by Robert Lefferts, Harper & Rowe.   330 (Unnumbered Table 14.1): *Food Processing News*, January 1995, 113.   333 (Figure 14.6): Nation's Restaurant News.   334 (Figure 14.7): Balkin Agency.   334 (Figure 14.8): From John M. Lannon, *Technical Writing*, 3rd edition. Copyright © 1985 by John M. Lannon. Reprinted by permission of Addison Wesley Educational Publishers, Inc.   335 (Figure 14.9): Copyright 1993, *USA Today*. Reprinted with permission.   374 (Figure 15.1): Richard Nelson Bolles, *What Color Is Your Parachute*, Ten Speed Press 1997, p. 67.   384–385 (Behind the Scenes at Mobil Corporation): Henry Halaiko, personal interview, June 1989.   410–411 (Behind the Scenes at IBM): Jim Greenwood, personal interview, June 1989.   428 (Table 17.1): Copyright Dr. Lyman K. Steil, President, Communication Development, Inc., St. Paul, MN. Prepared for Sperry Corporation, reprinted with permission of Dr. Steil & Unisys Corporation.   433 (Table 18.2): J. Michael Sproule, *Communication Today*, 1981.   434–435 (Behind the Scenes at 3M): Virginia Johnson, director of human relations, 3M, personal communication, June 1989. Used with permission.   454–455 (Behind the Scenes with Leann Anderson): Adapted from Leann Anderson, personal interview, April 1997; Leann Anderson, "Speak Up," *Entrepreneur*, March 1997, pp. 94–95.   463 (Table A.1): From *How 7: A Handbook for Office Workers*,

7/e, by James L. Clark and Lyn R. Clark. Copyright © 1995. Used with permission of South-Western College Publishing, a division of International Thomson Publishing, Inc. Cincinatti, Ohio 45227. **470** (Figure A.3): Letterhead courtesy of Mattel Toys. **471** (Figure A.4): Letterhead courtesy of J.C. Penney. **472** (Figure A.5): Letterhead courtesy of Black & Decker.

Photos
3 Churchill & Klehr Photography 8 Louis Psihoyos/Matrix International 11 Theo Westenberger/Gamma-Liaison, Inc. 14 Debbie Fields/Outline Press Syndicate, Inc. 14 IBM Corporation. 21 AP/Wide World Photos. 25 UPI/Bettmann. 26 NBC, Inc. 28 Avon Products, Inc. 30 Charley Shin. 30 Nawrocki Stock Photo, Inc. 38 James Leynse/SABA Press Photos, Inc. 41 Tom Sobolik/Black Star. 43 William Coupon/Gamma-Liaison, Inc. 45 AP/World Wide Photos. 47 Eddie Adams/ Outline/Outline Press Syndicate, Inc. 50 Wilma Mankiller. 59 John Coletti/Stock Boston. 59 George Bennett. 65 Weyerhaeuser Company. 69 Digital Equipment Corporation. 70 Eastman Kodak Company. 72 SuperStock, Inc. 79 John Coletti/Stock Boston. 80 Cynthia Johnson/ Gamma-Liaison, Inc. 81 General Motors Corporation. 83 George Lange/Outline Press Syndicate, Inc. 84 Lynn Goldsmith/Yanni Management Company. 86 AllState Insurance Company. 97 SUNSTAR/Photo Researchers, Inc. 98 Courtesy of Ford Plastic Products Division. 102 Deborah Feingold/Outline Press Syndicate, Inc. 108 *Inside-Flyer* Magazine. 112 Christopher Pillitz/Matrix International. 113 Microsoft Corporation. 122 AP/World Wide Photos. 124 I. Uimonen/Sygma. 126 CBS Photo Archive. 131 James Schnepf/Gamma-Liaison, Inc. 136 Morry Gash/AP/World Wide Photos. 152 AP/World Wide Photos. 153 Sygma. 154 Essence Communications, Inc. 155 Kim Kullish/SABA Press Photos, Inc. 159 SBA, U.S. Small Business Administration. 170 Gamma-Liaison, Inc. 171 D. Young Wolff/PhotoEdit. 173 AP/World Wide Photos. 175 McGraw-Hill Companies. 176 Lance Staedler/Outline Press Syndicate, Inc. 177 Stock Boston. 185 Cambridge Technology Partners. 186 Martin Simon/SABA Press Photos, Inc. 193 Steinway & Sons. 198 Cindy Lewis/ Cindy Lewis Photography. 199 John Deere & Company. 201 Tom Mareschal/The Image Bank. 205 David Weintraub/ Stock Boston. 206 Jemison Group. 208 Picture Perfect USA, Inc. 210 Newsweek. 211 Courtesy of Metropolitan Life Insurance Company. 215 George Merillon/Gamma-Liaison, Inc. 226 Joel Grimes/Joel Grimes Photography. 228 Celestis. 229 Ron Watts/Westlight 232 Haviv/SABA Press Photos, Inc. 233 Greg Watermann/ Outline Press Syndicate, Inc. 234 Daniel Bosler/Tony Stone Images. 239 Black & Decker. 240 Kermani/ Gamma Liaison, Inc. 245 National Easter Society. 258 Ed Quinn/SABA Press Photos, Inc. 260 Deodorant Stones of America. 261 Keith Polakoff/Long Beach Opera. 265 Geoge Disario/The Stock Market. 269 The Zooilogical Society of San Diego. 269 Chris Carroll/Outline Press Syndicate, Inc. 273 Urban City Foods. 277 Liz Claiborne, Special Markets. 285 Starbucks Coffee Company. 291 Churchill & Klehr Photography 291 Susan Lapides/ Lapides Photography. 294 James Schnepf/ Gamma-Liaison, Inc. 295 Bob D'Amico/ ABC, Inc. 301 Exley/Gamma-Liaison. 307 Kim Kullish/ SABA Press Photos, Inc. 311 Rob Crandall/Stock Boston. 313 Kirk Griswold. 319 Najlah Feanny/SABA Press Photos, Inc. 321 Merix Corporation. 324 Reglain Frederic/Gamma Liaison, Inc. 327 Rocky Mountain Intstitute. 328 Larry Ford Foto. 338 SuperStock, Inc. 357 Computer Associates International, Inc. 365 Tom McCarthy/PhotoEdit. 367 Picture Perfect USA, Inc. 370 Pinkerton Security and Investigation Services. 372 AT&T Photo Center. 373 FBI Phoenix Division. 384 Michael Newman/PhotoEdit. 388 Godfathers Pizza. 389 Thomas Lau/Outline Press Syndicate, Inc. 398 America's Job Bank Website Home Page (www.ajb.dni.us). America's Job Bank. 399 Jim Zuckerman/Westlight. 401 Courtesy of Herman Miller, Inc. 407 Outline Press Syndicate, Inc. 409 Frank DiMeo/Johnson Graduate School of Management. 410 Monkmeyer Press. 412 FireKing International, Inc. 414 Levi Strauss & Co. 421 Web100 Website Home Page (www.w100.com). The Web100. 425 RW Jones/Westlight. 427 McGuffy's Restaurant. 432 Institute for Research on Learning. 434 3M Corporation. 436 Tom's of Maine. 437 Andes Chemical Corporation. 442 Courtesy of Keys Group. 444 C. Bankenhorn/Black Star. 448 Success Strategy, Inc. 449 Chris K. Soentpiet. 454 Shadowfax/ Leann Anderson. 456 Xerox Corporation.

ORGANIZATION/COMPANY/BRAND INDEX

SUBJECT INDEX